Who's W[...]ica

JUNIOR &

Biographical Titles Currently Published by Marquis Who's Who

Who's Who in America
Who's Who in America derivatives:
  Who's Who in America Junior & Senior High School Version
  Geographic/Professional Index
  Supplement to Who's Who in America
  Who's Who in America Classroom Project Book
Who Was Who in America
  Historical Volume (1607-1896)
  Volume I (1897-1942)
  Volume II (1943-1950)
  Volume III (1951-1960)
  Volume IV (1961-1968)
  Volume V (1969-1973)
  Volume VI (1974-1976)
  Volume VII (1977-1981)
  Volume VIII (1982-1985)
  Volume IX (1985-1989)
  Index Volume (1607-1989)
Who's Who in the World
Who's Who in the East
Who's Who in the Midwest
Who's Who in the South and Southwest
Who's Who in the West
Who's Who in Advertising
Who's Who in American Law
Who's Who of American Women
Who's Who of Emerging Leaders in America
Who's Who in Entertainment
Who's Who in Finance and Industry
Who's Who in Religion
Who's Who in Science and Engineering
Index to Who's Who Books
Directory of Medical Specialists
Supplement to Directory of Medical Specialists

Who's Who in America®

JUNIOR & SENIOR HIGH SCHOOL VERSION

VOLUME 5: BUSINESS & INDUSTRY
1991-1993

Macmillan Directory Division
3002 Glenview Road
Wilmette, Illinois 60091 U.S.A.

Sandra S. Barnes—President
Sallie A. Lambert—Senior Product Manager
William H. Hamblin—Director of Production
John L. Daniels—Product Manager
Frederick M. Marks—Manager, Biographical Research
Jean S. Donnelly—Researcher/Librarian
Sharon S. Hoffman—Researcher/Special Projects Editor
Lawrence J. Hartmann—Researcher
Samuel C. Moore—Publication Manager

Paul E. Rose—Executive Vice President, Macmillan Information Services Group
Dean A. Davis—Chief Financial Officer, Macmillan Information Services Group

Library of Congress Catalog Card Number 04–16934
International Standard Book Number 0–8379–1251–2
Product Code Number 030645

Manufactured in the United States of America

Table of Contents

Preface

The editors of Marquis Who's Who are pleased to present additional volumes of the *Who's Who in America Junior & Senior High School Version.* This series is specifically designed for junior and senior high school students and focuses on subjects and individuals of great interest to young people. Entries in the *Junior & Senior High School Version*, originally published in *Who's Who in America* or other Marquis books, differ from our usual format in two ways. First, the type size is more than twice as large. Second, each biographical profile appears in an unabbreviated, full-text format. These two features enhance the book's overall readability. Volumes five through eight of the Junior and Senior High School Version have approximately 5,000 entries and highlight leaders from four areas of influence: Business and Industry, Literary Arts, Visual Arts, and World Leaders. In addition, a names index listing biographees from Volumes 1- 8 appears at the end of Volume 8.

In the Business and Industry volume, the backgrounds of leaders from the most notable corporations in the United States are highlighted. From the place of birth, to names of colleges attended, to employment history, each biographical sketch offers invaluable information about the movers and shakers of American business.

The *Who's Who in America Junior & Senior High School Version* will help junior and senior high school students with social studies research projects and assignments. Its large type size, full-text format, and subject organization will make information more accessible.

The standards of admission are exactly the same as those used in *Who's Who in America.* The research staff provided important information on high profile individuals who failed to submit addenda to their biographies on their own. As always, ultimate selection for the *Junior & Senior High School Version* was based on reference value. Individuals became eligible for listing by virtue of their positions and/or noteworthy achievements that have proved to be of significant value to society.

The editors exercise the utmost care in preparing each sketch for publication. Occasionally, however, errors do appear. Students and school librarians who use the directory are encouraged to draw to the attention of the publisher any errors found so that corrections can be made in a subsequent edition.

Key to Information

[1] **Reynolds, Frank Alan,** [2] toy company executive; [3] born Highland Park, Illinois, March 23, 1926; [4] son of Miles Benjamin and Thelma Ruth (Williams) R.; [5] married Leota Gruber, January 28, 1946; [6] children: Evangeline Marie, Joseph Paul. [7] Bachelor of Science, University of Illinois, 1948, Master of Science, 1951. [8] Registered professional engineer. [9] With Toys International Corporation, Providence, Rhode Island, 1954—, member technical staff, 1956-60, design engineer, 1960-65, senior research engineer, 1965-72, senior vice president, 1972-80, executive vice president, 1980-85, president, 1985—; [10] consultant Toys of the World Corporation, Chicago, London. [11] Contributor articles to professional journals. [12] Active Boy Scouts of America; secretary Rhode Island Governor's Commission on Public Safety, 1982—. [13] Served United States Navy, 1944-1946, Pacific Theater of Operations. [14] Decorated Purple Heart; recipient Silver Beaver Award Boy Scouts of America, 1979. [15] Fellow American Society for Testing and Materials, National Society of Professional Engineers, Masons, Shriners, Sigma XI. [16] Republican. [17] Presbyterian. [18] Avocations: stamp collecting, boating. [19] Home: 903 Deering Road Providence Rhode Island 02912 [20] Office: Toys International Corporation 1912 Main Street Providence Rhode Island 02913

KEY

[1] Name
[2] Occupation
[3] Vital Statistics
[4] Parents
[5] Marriage
[6] Children
[7] Education
[8] Professional certifications
[9] Career
[10] Career Related
[11] Writings and creative works
[12] Civic and political activities
[13] Military
[14] Awards and fellowships
[15] Professional and association memberships, Clubs and Lodges
[16] Political affiliation
[17] Religion
[18] Avocations
[19] Home address
[20] Office address

Table of Abbreviations

The following abbreviations were not expanded into full text because they have more than one meaning.

acad.–academy, academic
adj.–adjunct, adjutant
adv.–advocate, advisory
Am.–America, American
Brit.–British, Brittanica
Can.–Canada, Canadian
cert.–certificate, certification, certified
cons.–consultant, consultants
corp.–corporation, corporate
Corp.–Corporation, Corporate
corr.–correspondent, corresponding, correspondence
del.–delegate, delegation
Del.–Delaware, Delegate, Delegation
Dem.–Democrat, Democratic
denom.–denomination, denominational
devel.–development, developmental
div.–division, divinity, divorce
exam.–examination, examining
fin.–financial, finance
geog.–geographic, geographical
grad.–graduate, graduated
hon.–honorary, honorable
Ind.–Indiana, Independent
legis.–legislation, legislative
libr.–librarian, library
lic.–licensed, license
lit.–literary, literature
math.–mathematics, mathematical
micros.–microscopic, microscopical
mus.–museum, musical
NAE–National Academy of Engineering National Association of Educators
NE–Nebraska, Northeast
PTO–Pacific Theatre of Operations, Parent Teacher Organization
pub.–publisher, publishing, published, public
rev.–review, revised
sci.–science, scientific
tech.–technical, technology
trans.–transaction, transferred
U–University ("U" does not expand in the address section)
VA–Virginia, Veterans' Administration
vet.–veteran, veterinary
vol.–volunteer, volume

Alphabetical Practices

Names are arranged alphabetically according to the surnames, and under identical surnames according to the first given name. If both surname and first given name are identical, names are arranged alphabetically according to the second given name. Where full names are identical, they are arranged in order of age—with the elder listed first.

Surnames beginning with De, Des, Du, however capitalized or spaced, are recorded with the prefix preceding the surname and arranged alphabetically under the letter D.

Surnames beginning with Mac and Mc are arranged alphabetically under M.

Surnames beginning with Saint or St. appear after names that begin Sains, and are arranged according to the second part of the name, e.g. St. Clair before Saint Dennis.

Surnames beginning with Van, Von or von are arranged alphabetically under letter V.

Compound hyphenated surnames are arranged according to the first member of the compound. Compound unhyphenated surnames are treated as hyphenated names.

Parentheses used in connection with a name indicate which part of the full name is usually deleted in common usage. Hence Abbott, W(illiam) Lewis indicates that the usual form of the given name is W. Lewis. In such a case, the parentheses are ignored in alphabetizing. However, if the name is recorded Abbott, (William) Lewis, signifying that the entire name William is not commonly used, the alphabetizing would be arranged as though the name were Abbott, Lewis.

Who's Who in America

JUNIOR & SENIOR HIGH SCHOOL VERSION

ABLON, RALPH E., manufacturing company executive; born 1916. Student, Ohio State University, 1939. With Luria Brothers & Company, 1939—, executive vice president, 1948-55, president, 1955-62, now board of directors; chairman, chief executive officer Ogden Corp., New York City, 1962—, president, director, 1972-86. With United States Naval Reserve, World War II. Office: Ogden Corp 2 Pennsylvania Plaza New York New York 10121

ADAMS, HALL, JR. (CAP ADAMS), advertising agency executive; born Chicago, July 28, 1933. Bachelor of Arts, Williams College, 1954. Assistant account executive Leo Burnett Company Incorporated, Chicago, 1960-62, account executive, 1962-66, brand supervisor, 1966-68, vice president, account supervisor, 1968-69, senior vice president, from 1969, now chairman, chief executive officer. Served with United States Army, 1954-56. Office: Leo Burnett Company Incorporated 35 W Wacker Dr Chicago Illinois 60601

ADAMS, WILLIAM WHITE, manufacturing company executive; born Dubuque, Iowa, May 14, 1934; son of Waldo and Therese (White) A.; married Susan Joanne Cole, December 29, 1956; children: Nancy, Sara, Mark, Catherine. Bachelor of Science in Industrial Administration, Iowa State University, 1956. With Armstrong World Industries, Incorporated, Lancaster, Pennsylvania, 1956—, general sales manager residential ceiling systems div., 1975-80, group vice president building products operations, 1981, executive vice president, 1982-88, chairman, president, chief executive officer, 1988—; director Bell Telephone Company of Pennsylvania, 1986—. Chairman adv. board Lancaster-Lebanon council Boy Scouts Am., 1970—; board of directors United Way Lancaster County, (Pennsylvania), 1977-82, WITF Pub. Broadcasting, 1986-88; board of directors Lancaster Symphony Association, 1978-87, president, 1983-84. Recipient Silver Beaver award Boy Scouts Am., 1979. Member Pennsylvania Chamber of Commerce (director), Pennsylvania Business Roundtable (director), National Association Mfgrs. (director), Business Roundtable. Club: Lancaster Country (director 1978-84). Office: Armstrong World Industries Incorporated 333 W Liberty St Post Office Box 3001 Lancaster Pennsylvania 17604

ADDERLEY, TERENCE E., corporate executive; born 1933; married. Bachelor of Business Administration, University Michigan, 1951, BMA, 1956. Former fin. analyst Standard Oil Company of New Jersey, 1956-57; with Kelly Services, Incorporated, Troy, Michigan, 1957—, vice president, 1961-65, executive vice president, 1965-67, president, chief operating officer, 1967—, also director. Office: Kelly Services Incorporated 999 W Big Beaver Road Troy Michigan 48084

ADDISON, EDWARD L., utility holding company executive; born 1930; married. Bachelor of Electrical Engineering, University South Carolina, 1950. President, chief executive officer The Southern Company, Atlanta, 1983—, also board of directors; director, chairman executive committee Southern Company Services Incorporated (subsidiary The Southern Company), Birmingham, Alabama; with Alabama Power Company, Georgia Power Company, Gulf Power Company, Mississippi Power Company, Savannah Electric, Southern Electric International Incorporated; board of directors CSX Corp., First Atlanta Corp., Forst National Bank Atlanta, Phelps Dodge Corp., Protective Life Corp., Southern Investment Group, Southern Electric Generating Company. Served with United States Army, 1951-53. Office: Southern Company Services Incorporated 64 Perimeter Center E care Steve Higginbottom Atlanta Georgia 30346

ADELSON, MERVYN LEE, entertainment and communication industry executive; born Los Angeles, October 23, 1929; son of Nathan and Pearl (Schwarzman) A.; married Barbara Walters, May 10, 1986; children from previous marriage: Ellen, Gary, Andrew. Student, Menlo Park Junior College. President Markettown Supermarket and Builders Emporium, Las Vegas, 1953-63; managing partner Paradise Devel., Las Vegas, 1958—; president Realty Holdings, 1962—, La Costa, Incorporated, 1963-87; chairman board of directors Lorimar Incorporated, Culver City, California, 1969-86; chairman board of directors, chief executive officer Lorimar Telepictures Corp., Culver City, 1986-89; vice chairman Warner Communications, 1989—; chairman East-West Capital Associates, Incorporated, 1989—; board of directors Time-Warner Incorporated. Co-founder Nathan Adelson Hospice Foundation. Recipient Sherill Corwin Human Relations award Am. Jewish Committee, 1987. Member Am. Film Institute (trustee), Am. Mus. of Moving Images (trustee), Entertainment Industries Council (trustee), Acad. Motion Pictures Arts and Sciences, Acad. TV Arts and Sciences, National Acad. Cable Programming, Alliance for Capital Access (board directors), Committee Publicly Owned Companies (board directors).

AGEE, WILLIAM M., construction company executive; born Boise, Idaho, January 5, 1938; son of Harold J. and Suzanne (McReynolds) A.; married Mary Cunningham, June 5, 1982; children: Mary Alana, William N. Associate of Arts, Boise Junior College, 1958; Bachelor of Science with high honors, University Idaho, 1960; Master of Business Administration with distinction, Harvard University, 1963; Doctor of Science in Industrial Management (honorary), Lawrence Institute Tech., 1977, Nathaniel Hawthorne College, 1977; Doctor of Commercial Science, Eastern Michigan University, 1978; Doctor of Laws (honorary), University Detroit, 1980; DBA (honorary), Bryant College, 1980, Cleary College, 1980. Various positions Boise Cascade Corp., 1963-69, senior vice president, chief fin. officer, 1969-72; executive vice president, chief fin. officer

Bendix Corp., Southfield, Michigan, 1972-76, president, 1976-79, chief operating officer, 1976-77, chairman board, 1977-83; chairman, chief executive officer Semper Enterprises, Incorporated, Osterville, Massachusetts, from 1983; chairman board, president, chief executive officer Morrison Knudsen Corp., Boise, 1988—; board of directors Dow Jones & Company; chairman data processing and office automation Grace Commission, 1981-82; presidential appointee United States Quadrennial Commission, 1988. Chairman Governor's Higher Education Capital Investment Adv. Committee, 1979; member adv. council Japan-U.S. Economic Relations, 1982-84. Named Distinguished Alumnus Boise State University (formerly Boise Junior College), 1972; recipient Alumni Achievement Award Harvard University Business School, 1977; named to University Idaho Hall of Fame, 1978. Member American Institute of Certified Public Accountants, Idaho Society Certified Public Accountants, Michigan Association Certified Public Accountants, Council on Foreign Relations, Brit-N.Am. Committee, Conference Board, Business Roundtable, Harvard Business School Assocs., Phi Kappa Phi, Arid Club Boise, Economic Club, Hillcrest Country Club, Boise Oyster Harbors. Republican. Roman Catholic. Office: Morrison Knudsen Corp Morrison-Knudsen Plaza Post Office Box 73 Boise Idaho 83707

AGNEW, JAMES KEMPER, advertising agency executive; born Parkersburg, West Virginia, May 10, 1939; son of James Pugh and Elinor Mary (Kemper) A.; married Ann Haughey, September 15, 1962; children: Scott Kemper, Steven James, Derek John. Bachelor of Business Administration, University Michigan, 1961; Master of Business Administration, University California, Berkeley, 1962; postgraduate special business studies, University Oslo. With J. Walter Thompson, New York City and Paris, 1962-73; account executive J. Walter Thompson, 1962-67; chairman management committee J. Walter Thompson, Paris, 1967-70; vice president, management supr J. Walter Thompson, New York City, 1970-73; executive vice president J. Walter Thompson Company, Los Angeles, 1982—; head JWT/West, Los Angeles and San Francisco, 1982—; senior vice president, group account director McCann Erickson, Incorporated, New York City, 1973-76; executive vice president, general manager McCann Erickson, Incorporated, Los Angeles, 1976-79; president, chief executive officer McCann Erickson, Incorporated, New York City, 1979-81. Board advisors Pacific Crest Outward Bound School. Member Am. Association Advertising Agys. (secretary, treasurer, board govs. we. council, chairman western region 1989), Los Angeles Natural History Mus. (board directors), University Michigan Alumnae Club New York, University California Berkeley Alumnae Club. Office: J Walter Thompson Company 10100 Santa Monica Boulevard Los Angeles California 90067

AKERS, JOHN FELLOWS, information processing company executive; born Boston, December 28, 1934; son of Kenneth Fellows and Mary Joan (Reed) A.; married Susan Davis, April 16, 1960; children: Scott, Pamela, Anne. Bachelor of Science,

Yale University, 1956. With International Business Machines Corporation Corp., Armonk, New York, 1960—, vice president, assistant group executive, 1976-78, vice president, group executive, 1978-82, senior vice president, group executive, 1982-83, president, director, from 1983, chief executive officer, 1985—, chairman board, 1986—; director New York Times Company, PepsiCo, Incorporated. Member President Bush's Education Policy Adv. Commission, President's Committee on the Points of Light Initiative Foundation; trustee Metropolitan Mus. Art, California Institute Tech.; chairman, board governors United Way Am. Served to lieutenant United States Naval Reserve, 1956-60. Office: International Business Machines Corporation Corp Old Orchard Road Armonk New York 10504

ALBRIGHT, HARRY WESLEY, JR., banker; born Albany, New York, March 19, 1925; son of Harry Wesley and Ruth Agnes (Kerwin) A.; married Joan Diekman, June 27, 1953; children: Mary Kimberly, Deborah V., Harry Wesley, III, Peter D., Joan Kerwin, John D. Bachelor of Arts, Yale University, 1949; Bachelor of Laws, Cornell University, 1952. Bar: New York State bar 1954. With firm DeGraff, Foy, Conway & Holt-Harris, Albany, 1964-67; deputy secretary to governor New York State, 1967-68, deputy secretary, appointments officer, 1968-70, executive assistant to governor, 1970-72, superintendent banks, 1972-74; special counsel to Vice President Nelson A. Rockefeller, 1974-75; president; chief operating officer, trustee Dime Savings Bank New York, Brooklyn, 1975-81, chairman, chief executive officer, 1981—; president Thrift Institutions Adv. Council Federal Reserve Board, 1983—. Board editors: New York Law Jour, 1974. Board trustees Achiles & Bodman Foundation; board of directors Pratt Institute, Brooklyn; member regional panel selection White House Fellows; chairman board Marymount College; greater New York adv. board Salvation Army. With Army of the United States, 1943-46. Member American Bar Association, New York State Bar Association, Association of Bar of City of New York. Clubs: University (New York City); Sleepy Hollow Country (Scarborough-on-Hudson, New York); Stockbridge (Massachusetts) Golf. Home: 567 Bedford Road North Tarrytown New York 10591 Office: Dime Savings Bank 1225 Franklin Avenue Garden City New York 11530

ALEXANDER, NORMAN E., diversified manufacturing company executive; born New York City, 1914; married Marjorie Wulf; four children. Bachelor of Arts, Columbia University, 1934, Bachelor of Laws, 1936. Chairman board, chief executive officer Sequa Corp., New York City, 1957—; chairman board Ampacet Corp., Mount Vernon, New York, Chromalloy Am. Corp., St. Louis, 1980-86, Ampacet Corp., Tarrytown, New York; board of directors Chock Full o' Nuts, New York City, 1982—, Interim Systems Corp., New York City, 1987. Past chairman board trustees New York Medical Coll./ Flower-Fifth Avenue Hosps.; trustee Rockefeller U. Council. Member National Association of Manufacturers (trustee), Conference Board, Chief Executives Forum (board director). Office: Sequa Corp 200 Park Avenue New York New York 10106 also:

Ampacet Corp 660 White Plains Road Tarrytown New York 10591

ALFIERO, SALVATORE HARRY, manufacturing company executive; born Westerly, Rhode Island, November 11, 1937; son of Charles and Ann Rose (Augeri) A.; married Victoria Margarita Blanco, October 17, 1959 (divorced 1986); children: Victor S., Charles C., James J. Bachelor of Science in Engineering, Rensselaer Polytechnic Institute, 1964; Master of Business Administration, Harvard University, 1966. Founder, chairman, chief executive officer Mark IV Industries, Incorporated, Williamsville, New York, 1969—; board of directors Phoenix Mutual Insurance Company, Hartford, Connecticut, Marine Midland Bank-Western, Buffalo. Trustee Children's Hospital Buffalo, 1987—; board of directors Greater Buffalo Devel. Foundation, 1988—; advisor School Mgmt. SUNY Buffalo, 1989. Captain United States Marine Corps Reserve, 1958-67. Named Entrepreneur of Year Medaille College, Buffalo, 1988. Member Marine Corps Reserve Officers Association, Beta Gamma Sigma. Republican. Avocations: tennis, skiing, flying (rated airline transport pilot). Office: Mark IV Industries Incorporated 501 John James Audubon Parkway Box 450 Amherst New York 14228

ALLAIRE, PAUL ARTHUR, office equipment company executive; born Worcester, Massachusetts, July 21, 1938; son of Arthur E. Allaire and Elodie (LePrade) Murphy; married Kathleen Buckley, January 26, 1963; children: Brian, Christiana. Bachelor of Science in Electrical Engineering, Worcester Polytechnic Institute, 60; IMA, Carnegie-Mellon University, 1966. Fin. analyst Xerox Corp., Rochester, New York, 1966-70; chief staff officer Xerox Corp., Stamford, Connecticut, 1973-75; director fin. analysis Rank Xerox Limited, London, New York, 1970-73; chief staff officer Rank Xerox Limited, London, Connecticut, 1975-79, managing director, 1979-83, senior vice president, chief staff officer Xerox Corp., Stamford, 1983-86, president, 1986-91, chief executive officer, 1990—, chairman board of directors, 1991—; member investment policy adv. committee United States Trade Republican; board of directors Rank Xerox Limited, Fuji Xerox Company Limited, Sara Lee Corp., Crum & Forster, Morristown, New Jersey National Planning Association, Washington, 1986SCIVbd. directors, member business adv. council, trustee Grad. School Industrial Administration Carnegie Mellon University; trustee Worchester Polytechnic Institute. Member Tau Beta Pi, Eta Kappa Nu. Democrat. Office: Xerox Corp Post Office Box 1600 Stamford Connecticut 06904

ALLAIS, MAURICE, economist; born Paris, May 31, 1911; son of Maurice and Louise (Caubet) A.; married Jacqueline Bouteloup, September 6, 1960; 1 child, Christine. Graduate, Polytechnic School, Paris, 1933, National Higher School Mines, Paris, 1936; Doctor of Engineering, Faculty of Sciences, Paris, 1949; Doctor honoris causa, University Groningen, The Netherlands, 1964. Engineer Department Mines and Quarries, 1937-43; director Bureau Documentation and Statistics, 1943-48, Economic and Social Research Group, Paris, 1944-53; professor economic analysis National Higher School Mines, Paris, 1944-88; director Economic Analysis Center,

Paris, 1944—; professor economic theory Institute Statistics University Paris, 1947-58, director Center Clement Juglar for Monetary Analysis, 1970-85; director research National Center Sci. Research, Paris, 1954-79; professor Grad. Institute International Studies, Geneva, 1967-70; distinguished visiting scholar Thomas Jefferson, University Virginia, Charlottesville, 1958-59; member energy commission Economic Council, Paris, 1960-61; chairman committee of experts for study of options in transport tariff policy EEC, Brussels, 1963-64. Author: A la Recherche d'une Discipline Economique, 1943, 2d edition, 1952, 3d edition, 1990, Abondance ou Misère, 1946, 2d edition, 1990, Economie et Intérêt, 1947, 2d edition, 1990, La Gestion des Houillères Nationalisées et la Thérie Economique, 1949, Les Fondements Comptables de la Macroéconomique, 1954, 2d edition, 1990, Fondements d'une Théorie positive des choix comportant un risque, 1955, Notes to French Academy of Science on the Anomolies in the Movements of the Paraconic Pendulum, 1957-58, Should the Law of Gravitation Be Reconsidered?, 1959, L'Europe Unie, Route de la Prospérité, 1959, 2d edition, 1990, L'Algérie d'Evian, 1962, The Role of Capital in Economic Development, 1963, Reformulation de la Théorie Quantitative de la Monnaie, 1965, L'Impôt sur le Capital, 1966, Les Conditions de l'Efficacité dans l'Economie, 1967, Growth Without Inflation, 1968, Growth and Inflation, 1969, La Libéralisation des Relations Economiques Internationales, 1970, 2d edition, 1990, Les Théories de l'Equilibre Economique Général et de l'Efficacité Maximale, 1971, Inégalité et Civilisations, 1971, Inequality and Civilizations, 1973, L'Inflation Française et la Croissance, 1974, Inflation, Income Distribution and Indexation, 1976, L'Impôt sur le Capital et la Réforme Monétaire, 1976, 2d edition, 1988, Expected Utility Hypothesis and the Allais' Paradox, 1979, La Théorie Générale des Surplus, 1980, 2d edition, 1989, Frequency, Probability and Chance, 1982, Foundations of Utility and Risk Theory, 1983, Détermination de l'Utilité Cardinale suivant un modèle intrinsèque invariant, 1984, Credit Mechanism, 1984, The Empirical Approaches of the Hereditary and Relativistic Theory of the Demand for Money, 1986, The Concepts of Surplus and Loss and the Reformulation of the General Theory of Economic Equilibrium and Maximum Efficiency, 1986, The General Theory of Random Choices in Relation to the Invariant Cardinal Utility Function and the Specific Probability Function, 1986, The Equimarginal Principle: Meaning, Limits and Generalization, 1987, Les Conditions Monétaires d'une Economie de Marchés, 1987, My Life Philosophy, 1988, Autoportraits, 1989, also sci. papers on risk and utility theory; editorial board Political Econ. Rev., 1952—. Lieutenant artillery, French Army, 1939-40. Recipient Lancaster prize Johns Hopkins University and Operational Rsch. Society Am., 1958, award Gravity Rsch. Foundation, 1959, French Association for Atlantic Community, 1959, Galabert prize French Astronautical Society, 1959, French, Grand Prix André Arnoux, 1968, Zerilli Marimo, 1984, Gold medal Society for Promotion of National Industry, 1971, City of Paris, 1989, Prix Special Jury Dupuit-de Lesseps, 1987, Nobel prize in econ.

scis., 1988, medal University Paris, 1989, Great Gold medal City of Nice, France, 1989; named Laureate French Acad. Sciences, 1933, French Acad. Moral and Political Sciences, 1954, 59, 83, 84, Officer of Palmes Académiques, 1949, Chevalier National Economy Order, 1962, Commander Legion of Honor, 1977. Fellow Ops. Research Society Am., International Econometric Society (editorial board 1959-69); member French Association Econ. Sci. (chairman 1972), Am. Econ. Association (hon.), International Statistical Institute, Statistical Society Paris, Racing Club. Avocations: history, theoretical and experimental physics. Home: 15 rue Des Gate-Ceps, 92210 Saint Cloud France Office: Econ Analysis Center, 62 Boulevard Saint-Michel, 75006 Paris France

ALLBRITTON, JOE LEWIS, business executive; born D'Lo, Mississippi, December 29, 1924; son of Lewis A. and Ada (Carpenter) A.; married Barbara Jean Balfanz, February 23, 1967; 1 son, Robert Lewis. Bachelor of Laws, Baylor University, 1949, Doctor of Laws (honorary), 1964, Juris Doctor, 1969; Doctor of Humane Letters, California Baptist College, 1973. Bar: Texas 1949. Director Perpetual Corp., Houston, 1958—; president Perpetual Corp., 1965-76, 78-81, chairman board, 1973—; chairman board Pierce National Life Insurance Company, Los Angeles, 1958-72, 75—, also board of directors; chairman board University Bancshares, Incorporated, Houston, 1975—, Allbritton Communications Company, 1974—, Houston Fin. Services, Limited, London, 1977—, Riggs National Corp., Washington, 1981—; chairman Riggs National Bank, Washington, 1983—, also board of directors; deputy chairman Riggs Associated Press Bank, Limited, London, 1986—, also board of directors; member Greater Washington Board Trade, 1983-88; trustee The Mitre Corp., Bedford, Massachusetts, 1987—; director Georgetown University, Washington, 1990—. Trustee Federal City Council, Washington, 1975—, John F. Kennedy Center for Performing Arts, Washington, 1985-90, National Geog. Society, 1986—, The Ronald Reagan Presidential Foundation, Washington, 1990—; board of directors The Lyndon Baines Johnson Foundation, 1989—, Georgetown U., Washington, 1990—. With United States Navy, 1943-46. Member State Bar Texas, Association Reserve City Bankers. Office: Perpetual Corp 800 17th St Northwest Washington District of Columbia 20006

ALLEN, DARRYL FRANK, industrial company executive; born Detroit, September 7, 1943; son of Hairston Ulysses and Frances (Akers) A.; married Sharon Mae Baines, August 27, 1966; children: Richard Baines, James Bretten, Michael Jeffery. Bachelor of Arts, Michigan State University, 1965; Master of Business Administration, University Michigan, 1966. Manager Arthur Andersen & Company, Detroit, 1965-72; corporate controller Aeroquip Corp., Jackson, Michigan, 1972-76, vice president finance, 1976-78, vice president fin. and administration, 1978-79; vice president fin. services Libbey-Owens-Ford Company, Toledo, 1980-81, chief fin. officer, 1981-83, group vice president, 1983-84, president, 1984-86, chief operating officer; president, chief executive officer Trinova Corp. (formerly Libbey-Owens-Ford Company), Toledo, 1986—; board of directors First Ohio Bancshares. Member American Institute of Certified Public Accountants, Michigan Association Certified Public Accountants. Home: 2808 Westchester Toledo Ohio 43615 Office: Trinova Corp 3000 Strayer Post Office Box 50 Maumee Ohio 43537

ALLEN, KENNETH J., diversified agricultural products company executive. Formerly general manager Perryton Equity Exchange, Perryton, Texas; now, chairman Farmland Industries Incorporated, Kansas City, Missouri. Office: Farmland Industries Incorporated 3315 N Oak Trafficway Kansas City Missouri 64116

ALLEN, ROBERT EUGENE, communications company executive; born Joplin, Missouri, January 25, 1935; son of Walter Clark and Frances (Patton) A.; married Elizabeth Terese Pfeffer, August 4, 1956; children: Jay Robert, Daniel Scott, Katherine Louise, Ann Elizabeth, Amy Susan. Bachelor of Arts, Wabash College, 1957, LL.Doctor (honorary), 1984; postgraduate, Harvard Business School, 1965. With Ind. Bell Telephone Company Incorporated, Indianapolis, 1957-74, traffic student, 1957-61; district traffic supervisor Ind. Bell Telephone Company Incorporated, Bloomington, 1961-62, district commercial manager, 1962-66; div. commercial manager Ind. Bell Telephone Company Incorporated, Bloomington, Indianapolis, 1966-68, assistant to operations vice president, 1968, general commercial manager, 1968-72, vice president, secretary, treasurer, 1972-74; vice president, general manager Bell Telephone Company of Pennsylvania, Philadelphia, 1974-76; vice president, chief operating officer, director Illinois Bell Telephone Company, Philadelphia, 1976-78; vice president American Telephone and Telegraph Company, Basking Ridge, New Jersey, 1978-81; president, chairman board C&P Telephone Companies, Washington, 1981-83, executive vice president corp. administration and fin., 1983-84; chairman, chief executive officer American Telephone and Telegraph Company Information Systems, Morristown, New Jersey, 1985; president, chief operating officer American Telephone and Telegraph Company, New York City, 1986-88, chairman, chief executive officer, 1988—, also board of directors; board of directors Bristol Myers Squibb Company, Business Council New York State Incorporated, Japan Society. Trustee Wabash College; member leadership committee for Lincoln Center Consol. Corp. Fund, United Way of Am. Member National Association Wabash Men, Conference Board, Business Roundtable (policy committee), Business Council. Presbyterian. Clubs: Short Hills, Baltusrol Golf, Burning Tree, Congressional Country; Bay Head Yacht; Country of Florida. Home: 60 Stewart Road Short Hills New Jersey 07078 Office: AT&T 550 Madison Avenue New York New York 10022

ALLEN, RONALD W., airline company executive; born 1941; married. Bachelor in Industrial Engineering, Georgia Institute Tech. With Delta Air Lines, Incorporated, Atlanta, 1963—, assistant vice president administration, 1967-69, vice president administration, 1969-70, senior vice president personnel, 1970-79, senior vice president administration and personnel, 1979-83, president, chief operating officer, 1983-87, chairman, chief executive officer, 1987—, also director. Office: Delta Air Lines Incorporated Hartsfield Atlanta International Airport Atlanta Georgia 30320

ALLEY, WILLIAM JACK, holding company executive; born Vernon, Texas, December 27, 1929; son of W. H. and Opal M. (Cater) A.; married Deborah Bunn, December 28, 1979; children: Susan Jane, Pamela Jean, Patricia Ann, Sarah Elizabeth, Brayton. Associate of Arts, Northeastern A. and Master College, 1949; Bachelor of Business Administration, University Oklahoma, 1951, Juris Doctor, 1954. Bar: Oklahoma 1954; Chartered Life Underwriter. Attorney State Insurance Board Oklahoma, 1956-57; assistant vice president Pioneer Am. Insurance Company, 1957-59, vice president, 1959-60, vice president, agency director, 1960-66, director, 1961, senior vice president marketing, 1966; vice president Franklin Life Insurance Company, 1967-69, senior vice president agency, 1969-74, executive vice president, 1974-75, president, chief executive officer, 1976-85, chairman board, 1977-87; director Am. Brands Incorporated, 1979, senior vice president strategic planning, 1983-85; senior vice president, chief fin. officer Am. Brands, Incorporated, Old Greenwich, Connecticut, 1985-86, vice chairman, 1986-87, chairman, chief executive officer, 1987—; board of directors subsidiary companies; board of directors Central Illinois Pub. Service Company, Bunn-o-matic Corp., Southwestern Area Commerce and Industry Association Connecticut; board governors International Insurance Society Incorporated; emeritus elector Insurance Hall of Fame; trustee National Sales Hall of Fame. board of directors Cooperation Ireland, United Way Tri-State, The Silvermine Guild Arts Center, Connecticut Business for Education Coalition; board overseers Executive Council Foreign Diplomats; member The Business Roundtable, The Conference Board and The Ambassadors' Roundtable adv. council Captain United States Air Force, 1954-56. Member Oklahoma Bar Association, National Sales Hall of Fame (board trustees), Delta Sigma Pi, Phi Kappa Sigma, Phi Alpha Delta. Clubs: Illini Country, Sangamo, Tavern (Chicago), Northport Point, New Canaan Country; Economic (New York City) (board governors). Lodges: Masons, Shriners. Office: Am Brands Incorporated 1700 E Putnam Avenue Post Office Box 819 Old Greenwich Connecticut 06870-0819

AMELIO, GILBERT FRANK, electronics company executive; born New York City, March 1, 1943; son of Anthony and Elizabeth (DeAngelis) A.; married Glenda Charlene Amelio; children: Anthony Todd, Tracy Elizabeth, Andrew Ryan; stepchildren: Brent Paul Chappell, Tina Larae Chappell. Bachelor of Science in Physics, Georgia Institute Tech., 1965, Master of Science in Physics, 1967, Doctor of Philosophy in Physics, 1968. Tech. director, cofounder Information Sci., Atlanta, 1962-65; member tech. staff Bell Telephone Laboratories, Murray Hill, New Jersey, 1968-71; div. vice president, general manager Fairchild, Mountain View, California, 1971-83;

president semiconductor products div. Rockwell International, Newport Beach, California, 1983-88; president communication systems Rockwell International, Dallas, 1988-91; president, chief executive officer National Semicondr. Corp., Santa Clara, California, 1991; director Georgia Institute Tech. National Adv. Board, Atlanta, 1981-87, Georgia Institute Tech. Research Institute, Atlanta, 1982-89, Sematech; director, chairman Recticon, Pottstown, Pennsylvania, 1983-87. Patentee in field. Member chief executive roundtable University California, Irvine, 1985-89. Fellow Institute of Electrical and Electronics Engineers (chairman subcommittee 1974-81, recipient consumer electronics award 1991); member Semicondr. Industry Association (board directors 1983—). Republican. Roman Catholic. Home: 13416 Middle Fork Lane Los Altos Hills California 94022

AMERMAN, JOHN W., toy company executive; born 1932; married. Bachelor of Arts, Dartmouth College, 1953, Master of Business Administration, 1954. With Colgate-Palmolive Company, 1958-64, Warner-Lambert Company, 1965-80; vice president Du Barry Cosmetics, 1971-72, vice president international group, 1972-77, vice president Am. Chicle div., 1977-79, president Am. Chicle div., 1979-80; president Mattel International, from 1980; chairman, chief executive officer Mattel Incorporated, Hawthorne, California, 1987—, also board of directors. Served with United States Army, 1954-57. Office: Mattel Incorporated 333 Continental Boulevard El Segundo California 90245

AMOS, DANIEL PAUL, insurance executive; born Pensacola, Florida, August 13, 1951; son of Paul Shelby and Mary Jean (Roberts) A.; married Mary Shannon Landing, September 12, 1972; children—Paul Shelby, Lauren Alyse. Bachelor of Science in Risk and Insurance Management, University Georgia, 1973. Co-state manager Am. Family Life Assurance Company, Columbus, Georgia, 1973-78, state manager, 1978-83, president, 1983—; now also deputy chief executive officer Am. Family Corp., Columbus, Georgia; director Columbus Bank & Trust Company. Trustee LaGrange College, Georgia, 1983—, Brookstone School, Columbus, 1983—. Methodist. Avocations: tennis; bridge. Office: Am Family Life Assurance 1932 Wynnton Road Columbus Georgia 31999

AMOS, JOHN BEVERLY, insurance company executive; born Enterprise, Alabama, June 5, 1924; son of John Shelby and Mary Helen (Mullins) A.; married Elena Diaz-Verson, September 23, 1945; children: John Shelby, II, Maria Teresa. Educated, University Miami, Florida, 1947, Doctor of Laws, 1979; Juris Doctor, University Florida, 1949; Doctor of Laws (honorary), University West Florida, Mercer University. Bar: Florida 1949. Private practice Fort Walton Beach, Florida, 1949-55; founder 1955, Am. Family Life Assurance Company, Columbus, Georgia, 1955; former president, now chairman board, chief executive officer Am. Family Corp. Past president Goodwill Industries, Columbus; past chairman 3d District Georgia Democratic Committee; trustee Morris Brown College, Atlanta, Roosevelt Warm Springs (Georgia) Foundation, Hughston Sports Medicine Foundation, Incorporated,

Columbus; member national committee National Mus. Jewish History, Philadelphia; vice chairman National Bipartisan Political Action Committee; board of directors Metropolitan Columbus Urban League; member board visitors Boston U. School Medicine, Walter F. Gerge College Law, Mercer. U., Macon, Georgia; member president adv. board Duke U., Durham, North Carolina, member board overseers Duke Comprehensive Cancer Center; chairman School of Ams. Columbus Support Group, Fort Benning, Georgia; member numerous civic bds. and organizations. Named Man of Year, Georgia Conference African Methodist Episcopal Church, 1984, National Association for the Advancement of Colored People, 1985, Georgian of Year Georgia Association Broadcasters, 1986; recipient Distinguished Service award Small Business Council Am., 1985, Distinguished Citizen award Chattahoochee council Boy Scouts Am., 1985. Member Member National Association Manufacturers (board directors), National Association Life Companies (vice president), Florida Bar Association. Roman Catholic. Clubs: Metropolitan (New York City); Big Eddy (Columbus), Harmony (Columbus). Office: Am Family Life Assurance 1932 Wynnton Road Columbus Georgia 31999

ANDERS, WILLIAM ALISON, aerospace and diversified manufacturing company executive, former astronaut, former ambassador; born Hong Kong, October 17, 1933; son of Arthur Ferdinand and Muriel Florence (Adams) A.; married Valerie Elizabeth Hoard, June 26, 1955; children: Alan Frank, Glen Thomas, Gayle Alison, Gregory Michael, Eric William, Diana Elizabeth. Bachelor of Science, United States Naval Academy, Annapolis, 1955; Master of Science in Naval Engineering, United States Institute Tech., Wright-Patterson AFB, 1962; vice chmn., General Dynamics, St. Louis, 1990-91, chmn., chief exec. officer, 1991—. Commnd. 2d lieutenant United States Air Force, 1955, pilot, engineer, 1955-69; astronaut NASA-Johnson Space Center, Houston, 1963-69, Apollo 8, 1st lunar flight, 1968; executive secretary National Aeronautical and Space Council, Washington, 1963-72; commissioner Atomic Energy Commission, Washington, 1973-74; chairman Nuclear Regulatory Commission, Washington, 1975-76; United States Ambassador to Norway 1976-77; vice president, general manager nuclear energy products div. General Electric Company, 1977-80; vice president, general manager aircraft equipment div. General Electric Company, DeWitt, New York, 1980-84; senior executive, vice president operations Textron Incorporated, Providence, Rhode Island, 1984-89; chairman, chief executive officer General Dynamics, St. Louis, 1990—; board of directors Enron Corp. Trustee Battell Memorial Institute Maj.-gen. United States Air Force Reserve, 1983-88. Decorated various mil. awards; recipient Wright, Collier, Goddard and Arnold flight awards; co-holder several world flight records. Member Society Experimental Test Pilots (holder several world speed and altitude records), National Acad. Engineering, Defense Sci. Board, Tau Beta Pi. Office: General Dynamics Corp Pierre Laclede Center Saint Louis Missouri 63105

ANDERSEN, ELMER LEE, manufacturing executive, former governor of Minnesota; born Chicago, June 17, 1909; son of Arne and Jennie (Johnson) A.; married Eleanor Johnson, 1932; children: Anthony L., Julian L., Emily E. Bachelor of Business Administration, University Minnesota, 1931; Doctor of Laws (honorary), Macalester College, St. Paul, 1965; Doctor of Humane Letters, Carleton College, 1972; Doctor of Management (honorary), University Minnesota, 1984. With H.B. Fuller Company (manufacturers industrial adhesives), 1934—, sales manager, 1937-41, president, 1941-61, 63-71, chairman, 1961-63, 71—, chief executive officer, 1971-74, chairman board, 1974—; director Davis Consolidated Industries, Sydney, Australia, Prenor Group Limited, Montreal, Quebec, 1972-76, Geo. A. Hormel & Company, Austin, 1971-75, First Trust Company, St. Paul, 1969-74; member Minnesota Senate, 1949-58; governor of Minnesota 1961-63; pub. Princeton (Minnesota) Union Eagle, 1976—, Sun Newspapers, 1978-84; chairman board ECM Publishers, Princeton, Minnesota, 1987—. Campaign chairman St. Paul Community Chest, 1959—; executive committee Boy Scouts Am.; member National Parks Centennial Commission, 1971, Governor's Voyageurs National Park Adv. Commission, Select Committee on Minnesota Judicial System; chairman Minnesota Constitutional Study Commission; Board of directors, president Child Welfare League Am., 1965-67; past president St. Paul Gallery and School of Art; past trustee Augsburg College, Minneapolis; president Charles A. Lindbergh Memorial Fund, 1978-88, chairman 1986-88; regent U. Minnesota, 1967-75; chairman board, 1971-75; chairman Bush Foundation, St. Paul; board of directors Council on Founds., N.Y.C; chairman U. Minnesota Foundation; chairman board Alliss Foundation, 1982-88; member executive council Minnesota Historical Society. Decorated Order of Lion Finland; recipient Outstanding Achievement award University Minnesota, 1959; award of merit Izaak Walton League; Silver Beaver award; Silver Antelope award Boy Scouts Am.; Conservation award Minneapolis Chamber of Commerce; Taconite award Minnesota chapter Am. Institute Mining Engineers, 1976; National Phi Kappa Phi award University Minnesota, 1977; Minnesota Business Hall Fame award, 1977; Greatest Living St. Paulite award St. Paul Chamber of Commerce, 1980; award Adhesive and Sealant Council, 1980; others. Fellow Morgan Library (N.Y.C); Member Adhesive Manufacturers Association Am. (past president), Voyageurs National Park Association (past president), Minnesota Historical Society (executive committee, president 1966-70), Am. Antiquarian Society. Republican. Lutheran. Clubs: Rotary (St. Paul) (past president St. Paul, past dist. gov.), Grolier, University (New York City); St. Paul Gavel (past president). Home and Office: 1483 Bussard Court Arden Hills Minnesota 55112

ANDERSON, THOMAS RALPH, financial services company executive; born Aurora, Illinois, February 12, 1938; son of Ralph A. and Jeannette C. (Malmer) A.; married Carol Tremaine, October 6, 1962; children: Brian, Rodney, Nicole. Bachelor of Science, University Illinois, 1961. Certified Public Accountant, Illinois.

Auditor Arthur Young & Company, Chicago, 1961-66; comptroller Kemper Fin. Services, Incorporated, Chicago, 1966-71, vice president, comptroller, 1971-75, executive vice president, 1975-77, president, chief executive officer, board of directors, 1977-83, chairman, chief executive officer, board of directors, 1983—; chairman, treasurer Kemper Investors Life Insurance Company, Chicago, 1976-78, chairman, chief executive officer, treasurer, 1978-79, chairman, chief executive officer, 1979—, manager, director separate accounts, 1983-90; senior vice president, board of directors Kemper Corp., Long Grove, Illinois, 1983-86, executive vice president, board of directors, 1986—; senior vice president, board of directors Lumbermens Mutual Casualty Company, Chicago, 1983-86, executive vice president, board of directors, 1986-90; senior vice president, board of directors Am. Motorists Insurance Company, Long Grove, 1983-86, executive vice president, board of directors, 1986-90; senior vice president, board of directors Am. Manufacturers Mutual Insurance Company, Long Grove, 1983-86, now executive vice president, board of directors, 1986-90; chairman board of directors Kemper/Cymrot, Incorporated, Chicago, 1983—; chairman board of directors, president and chief executive officer Kemper Fin. Companies, Incorporated, Chicago, 1986-91; vice president, trustees Kemper Multi-Market Income Trust, Kemper Strategic Municipal Income Trust, Kemper Tech. Fund, Kemper Growth Fund, Kemper Summit Fund, Kemper Total Return Fund, Kemper Income & Capital Preservation Fund, Kemper Money Market Fund, Kemper Municipal Bond Fund, Kemper Option Income Fund, Kemper United States Government Securities Fund, Kemper High Yield Fund, Cash Equivalent Fund, Kemper International Fund, Kemper Government Money Market Fund, Kemper Tax-Exempt Money Market Fund, Economy Fire & Casualty Company, Economy Preferred Insurance Company, Economy Premier Assurance Company, Federal Kemper Insurance Company, Federal Kemper Life Assurance Company, Fidelity Life Association, Kemper Reins. Company, Kemper Reins. Company Bermuda, Limited, Kemper Europe Reassurances, S.A., Kemper High Income Trust, Kemper Intermediate Government Trust, Kemper Municipal Income Trust, Kemper Blue Chip Fund, Kemper Enhanced Government Fund, Kemper Gold Fund, Kemper Investment Portfolios, Incorporated, Kemper Clearing Corp., Kemper High Income Trust, Kemper Intermediate Government Trust, Kemper Municipal Income Trust, Growth Fund of Spain, Incorporated, Kemper Short-term Global Income Fund, Kemper Retirement Fund, Kemper State Tax-free Income Series, Kemper Investors Fund, Cash Account Trust, Tax-exempt New York Money Market Fund, Tax-exempt California Money Market Fund, Kemper Securities Group, Incorporated, Kemper Securities Group Holding, Incorporated. Trustee, chairman fin. committee Illinois chapter Leukemia Society Am., 1980-86; trustee James S. Kemper Foundation, 1983—; board of directors Robert Crown Center Health Education, 1986-90, Plymouth Pl., Incorporated, 1986—, Illinois Cancer Council foun., 1990—, National Conference of Christians and

Jews, 1990—, Lyric Opera Chicago, 1991—, Chicago Symphony Orchestra, special events committee, 1991—. Member Am. Institute Certified Public Accountants, Illinois Society Certified Public Accountants, Am. Institute Corp. Contrs., Alpha Tau Omega. Congregationalist. Clubs: Economics, LaGrange (Illinois) Country; University, Attic, Whitehall (Chicago); Chicago Golf (Wheaton, Illinois); Wynstone Golf Club (North Barrington, Illinois). Lodge: Masons. Home: 209 S Blackstone Avenue LaGrange Illinois 60525 Office: Kemper Fin Services 120 S LaSalle St Chicago Illinois 6060

ANDREAS, DWAYNE ORVILLE, corporation executive; born Worthington, Minnesota, March 4, 1918; son of Reuben P. and Lydia (Stoltz) A.; married Bertha Benedict, 1938 (divorced); 1 daughter, Sandra Ann Andreas McMurtie; married Dorothy Inez Snyder, December 21, 1947; children: TerryLynn, Michael D. Student, Wheaton (Illinois) College, 1935-36; honorary degree, Barry University. Vice president, director Honeymead Products Company, Cedar Rapids, Iowa, 1936-46; chairman board, chief executive officer Honeymead Products Company (now National City Bancorp.), Mankato, Minnesota, 1952-72; vice president Cargill, Incorporated, Minneapolis, 1946-52; executive vice president Farmers Union Grain Terminal Association, St. Paul, 1960-66; chairman board, chief executive officer Archer-Daniels-Midland Company, Decatur, Illinois, 1970—, also member executive committee, director; president Seaview Hotel Corp., 1958—; board of directors Salomon, Incorporated, Lone Star Industries, Incorporated, Greenwich, Connecticut; member President's General Adv. Commission on Foreign Assistance Programs, 1965-68, President's Adv. Council on Management Improvement, 1969-73; chairman President's Task Force on International Private Enterprise. President Andreas Foundation; trustee United States Naval Acad. Foundation, Freedom from Hunger Foundation; national board of directors Boys' Club Am.; former chairman U.S.-USSR Trade and Economic Council; former chairman Executive Council on Foreign Diplomats; trustee Hoover Institute on War, Revolution and Peace, Woodrow Wilson International Center for Scholars; member Trilateral Commission; chairman Foundation for Commemoration of the United States Constitution, 1986. Member Foreign Policy Association New York (director). Clubs: Union League (Chicago); Indian Creek Country (Miami Beach, Florida); Minneapolis, Minikahda (Minneapolis); Blind Brook Country (Purchase, New York); Economic of New York (chmn.), Links, Knickerbocker, Friars (New York City).

ANGERMUELLER, HANS H., banker; born 1924; married. Bachelor of Arts, Harvard University, 1946, Master of Science in Engineering, 1947, Bachelor of Laws, 1950. Partner Shearman & Sterling, New York City, 1950-72; with Citicorp, New York City, 1972—, senior vice president, general counsel, then senior executive vice president, then vice chairman, 1982—, board of directors; also vice chairman, board of directors Citibank N.A., New York City. Served with United States Navy. Office: Citibank 399 Park Avenue New York New York 10043

ANSCHUTZ, PHILLIP F., diversified company executive; born 1939. Bachelor of Science, University Kansas, 1961. Chairman, president Anschutz Corp., 1965—, also director, 1965—. Office: Anschutz Corp 2400 Anaconda Tower Denver Colorado 80202

ANTONINI, JOSEPH E., apparel company executive; born Morgantown, West Virginia, July 13, 1941. Graduate, West Virginia University. With K Mart Corp., Troy, Michigan, 1964—, president, director, K Mart Apparel Corp., North Bergen, New Jersey, 1984-86, chief operating officer, 1986-87, president, 1986—, chairman, chief executive officer, 1987—, president, 1988—; board of directors Michigan Bell Telephone Company. Office: K Mart Corp 3100 W Big Beaver Road Troy Michigan 48084 also: K Mart Apparel Corp 7373 Westside Avenue N North Bergen New Jersey 07047

ARASKOG, RAND VINCENT, diversified multinational company executive; born Fergus Falls, Minnesota, October 30, 1931; son of Randolph Victor and Hilfred Mathilda A.; married Jessie Marie Gustafson, July 29, 1956; children: William Roy, Julie Kay, Kathleen Melinda. Bachelor of Science in Mechanical Engineering, United States Military Academy, 1953; postgraduate, Harvard University, 1953-54; Doctor of Humane Letters (honorary), Hofstra University, 1990. With Defense Department, Washington, 1954-59, Special assistant to director, 1958-59; director marketing aeronautical div. Honeywell, Incorporated, Minneapolis, 1960-66; vice president International Telephone & Telegraph Corporation Corp., 1971-76; executive vice president International Telephone & Telegraph Corporation Aerospace, Electronics, Components and Energy Group, Nutley, New Jersey, 1976-79; president, chief executive officer International Telephone & Telegraph Corporation Corp., New York City, 1979—, chairman board, chairman executive and policy committees, 1980—; director International Telephone & Telegraph Corporation Corp., Hartford Insurance, Dayton-Hudson Corp., Shell Oil Corp., Dow Jones and Company, New York Stock Exchange; member National Security Telecommunications Adv. Committee, 1983—. Author: ITT Wars, 1989; contributor articles to journals including Reader's Digest, The New York Times. Member Business Council; board trustees Institute for Advanced Study; trustee, board advisors New York Zool. Society, National Aeronautics and Space Administration Comml. Space Committee; member Rockefeller U. Council Served with United States Army, 1954-56. Decorated Officer of National Order of Legion of Honor (France). Member The Business Council, Aerospace Industries Association (board govs.), Air Force Association (member executive council), Econ. Club (chairman), Business Roundtable, Council Foreign Relations, West Point Society New York, New York City Partnership (board directors), Links Club, River Club, Meadow Club, Knickerbocker Club, Council U.S.-Italy (co-chmn.). Episcopalian. Office: International Telephone and Telegraph Corporation Corp 320 Park Avenue New York New York 10022

ARCHIBALD, NOLAN D., power tools and home improvement, household and industrial products company executive; born Ogden, Utah, June 22, 1943; married Margaret Hafen, June 8, 1967. Associate of Arts, Dixie College, 1966; Bachelor of Science, Weber State College, 1968; Master of Business Administration, Harvard University, 1970. Executive vice president, general manager Sno Jet, Incorporated div. Conroy, Incorporated, Burlington, Vermont, 1970-77; senior vice president, and president non-foods companies Beatrice Foods, Chicago, 1977-85; chairman, president, chief executive officer The Black & Decker Corp., Towson, Maryland, 1985—; former All Am. basketball player. Named One of 10 Most Wanted Execs in United States, Fortune Magazine, Six Best Managers in United States, Business Week Magazine. Avocation: theater.

ARDIA, STEPHEN VINCENT, pump manufacturing company executive; born Hackensack, New Jersey, August 3, 1941; son of Vincent Henry and Anita Deborah A.; married Virginia Ellis, July 11, 1964; children: David, Daniel, Deborah. Bachelor of Science, United States Merchant Marine Academy, 1963; Master of Business Administration, Rutgers University, 1969. General manager Standard Pump Div., Worthington Pump Company, East Orange, New Jersey, 1976-79; vice president international operations Goulds Pumps Incorporated, Seneca Falls, New York, 1979-82, vice president sales, 1982-84, president, 1984-85, president, chief executive officer, 1985—; board of directors Chase Lincoln Bank, Rochester, New York, Business Council New York State. Board of directors Women's Hall of Fame, Seneca Falls, New York, Pub. TV. Sta. WCNY, Cayuga Community College; member adv. council Clarkson U. School Mgmt.; president Hydraulic Institute. Member Skaneateles Country Club (board directors). Home: 3 W Lake St Skaneateles New York 13152 Office: Goulds Pumps Incorporated 240 Fall St Seneca Falls New York 13148

ARISON, MICKY, cruise line company executive; born Tel Aviv, June 29, 1949. Student, University Miami. President, chief executive officer Carnival Cruise Lines Incorporated. Office: Carnival Cruise Lines Incorporated 5225 Northwest 87th Avenue Miami Florida 33178

ARPEL, ADRIEN, cosmetic company executive; born New Jersey, July 15, 1941; daughter of Samuel and Ada (Stark) Joachim; married Ronald Monroe Newman, October 30, 1960; 1 daughter, Lauren Nicole Arpel Greenwald. Student, Pace College, 1960-62. President Adrienne Cosmetics, Englewood, New Jersey, 1959-60, Lisa Lauren Cosmetics, New York City, 1962-65; president Adrien Arpel, Incorporated, New York City, from 1965, now chairman; director Seligman and Latz, Incorporated, 1975-77. Author: Adrien Arepl 21 Day Make Over Shape Over, 1978, Adrien Arpel How to Look 10 Years Younger, 1980; 851 Fast Beauty Facts, 1985. Board of directors Cradle Adoption Agency, Chicago, Kings Point (New York) Civic Association, Children's Aid Society, New York City. Member Cosmetic Career Women. Office: 521-5th Avenue New York New York 10175

ARRISON, CLEMENT R., manufacturing company executive; born 1930; married. Bachelor of Science, University Michigan, 1953. Engineer

Bell Aircraft Corp., 1953-59, Am. Machine and Foundry; mfrs.' representative 1959-62; vice president Radatron Corp., Buffalo, 1962-69; president, director Mark IV Industries Incorporated, Amherst, New York, 1970—. Office: Mark IV Industries Incorporated 501 John James Audobon Parkway Box 450 Amherst New York 14228

ARROW, KENNETH JOSEPH, economist, educator; born New York City, August 23, 1921; son of Harry I. and Lillian (Greenberg) A.; married Selma Schweitzer, August 31, 1947; children: David Michael, Andrew. Bachelor of Science in Social Science, City College of New York, 1940; Master of Arts, Columbia University, 1941, Doctor of Philosophy, 1951, Doctor of Science, 1973; Doctor of Laws (honorary), University Chicago, 1967, City University New York, 1972, Hebrew University Jerusalem, 1975, University Pennsylvania, 1976, Washington University, St. Louis, 1989; Doctor.Social and Economic Sciences (honorary), University Vienna, Austria, 1971; Doctor.Social Sciences (honorary), Yale, 1974; Doctor (honorary), Université René Descartes, Paris, 1974, University Aix-Marseille III, 1985; Dr.Pol., University Helsinki, 1976; Master of Arts (honorary), Harvard University, 1968; Doctor of Literature, Cambridge University, 1985. Research associate Cowles Commission for Research in Economics, 1947-49; assistant professor economics University Chicago, 1948-49; acting assistant professor economics and statistics Stanford, 1949-50, associate professor, 1950-53, professor economics, statistics and operations research, 1953-68; professor economics Harvard, 1968-74, James Bryant Conant university professor, 1974-79; executive head department economics Stanford University, 1954-56, acting executive head department, 1962-63, Joan Kenney professor economics and professor operations research, 1979—; economist Council Economic Advisers, United States Government, 1962; consultant RAND Corp. Author: Social Choice and Individual Values, 1951, Essays in the Theory of Risk Bearing, 1971, The Limits of Organization, 1974, Collected Papers, Volumes I-VI, 1983-85; co-author: Mathematical Studies in Inventory and Production, 1958, Studies in Linear and Nonlinear Programming, 1958, Time Series Analysis of Interindustry Demands, 1959, Public Investment, The Rate of Return and Optimal Fiscal Policy, 1971, General Competitive Analysis, 1971, Studies in Resource Allocation Processes, 1977, Social Choice and Multicriterion Decision Making, 1985. Served as captain Army of the United States, 1942-46. Social Sci. Research fellow, 1952; fellow Center for Advanced Study in the Behavioral Sciences, 1956-57; fellow Churchill College, Cambridge, England, 1963-64, 70, 73, 86; Guggenheim fellow, 1972-73; Recipient John Bates Clark medal Am. Economic Association, 1957; Alfred Nobel Memorial prize in econ. scis., 1972, von Neumann prize, 1986. Fellow American Association for the Advancement of Science (chairman section K 1983), Am. Acad. Arts and Sciences (vice president 1979-81, 1991—), Econometric Society (vice president 1955, president 1956), Am. Statistical Association, Institute Math. Statistical, Am. Econ. Association (executive committee 1967-69, president

1973), International Society for Inventory Research (president 1983-90); member National Academy of Sciences (member council 1990—), International Economics Association (president 1983-86), Am. Philosophical Society, Institute Management Sciences (president 1963, chairman council 1964), Finnish Acad. Sciences (foreign hon.), Brit. Acad. (corr.), Western Econ. Association (president 1980-81). Office: Stanford U Department Econs Stanford California 94305

ARTHUR, LLOYD, agricultural products company executive; born 1930; married. President Ind. Farm Bureau Cooperative, 1983—. Office: Indiana Farm Bur Coop Association Incorporated 120 E Market St Indianapolis Indiana 46204 also: 950 N Meridian St Indianapolis Indiana 46204

ARTZT, EDWIN LEWIS, consumer products company executive; born New York City, April 15, 1930; son of William and Ida A.; married Ruth Nadine Martin, May 12, 1950; children—Wendy Anne, Karen Susan, William M., Laura Grace, Elizabeth Louise. Bachelor of Journalism, University Oregon, 1951. Account executive Glasser Gailey Advertising Agency, Los Angeles, 1952-53; with Procter & Gamble Company, Cincinnati, 1953—, brand manager advertising department, 1956-58, associate brand promotion manager, 1958-60, brand promotion manager, 1960, 62-65, copy manager, 1960-62, advertising manager paper products div., 1965-68, manager products food div., 1968-69, vice president, 1969, vice president, acting manager coffee div., 1970, vice president, group executive, 1970-75, director, 1972-75, 80—, vice chairman, 1980—; group vice president Procter & Gamble Company, Europe, Belgium, 1975-80; president Procter & Gamble International, 1980—. Past chairman residential div. United Appeal; past chairman Public Library Capital Funds campaign; past district chairman Capital Fund Raising dr. Boy Scouts Am., past leadership training chairman; past chairman advt. committee School Tax Levy, County Government Issue; past trustee Kansas City Philharmonic, Nutrition Foundation, Boys' Clubs Greater Cincinnati; past board of directors Kansas City Lyric Theater; past board governors Kansas City Art Institute. Member Am. Chamber of Commerce Belgium (vice president), Conference Board Europe (adv. council), International Chamber of Commerce (executive committee United States council), National Foreign Trade Council. Clubs: Queen City (Cincinnati), Cincinnati Country (Cincinnati), Comml. (Cincinnati). Home: 9005 Cunningham Road Cincinnati Ohio 45243 Office: Procter & Gamble Company 1 Procter & Gamble Plaza Cincinnati Ohio 45202

ATTALI, JACQUES, educator, French government official; born Algiers, Algiers, November 1, 1943; son of Simon and Fernande Ataali; married Elisbaeth Allain, 1981; 2 children. Educated, École Polytechnic Institute d'Etudes Politiques de Paris, Écoles des mines de Paris, École National d'Adminstrn. Lecturer economics École Polytechnic Institute d'Etudes Politiques de Paris, 1970—, École des mines de Ponts et Chaussées, 1971; advisor to president of France, ofcl. to Council of State, Paris, 1981-89, state councillor, 1989-91; president European Bank Reconstrn. & Devel.,

London, 1991—. Author: Analyse économique de la vie politique, 1972, Modèles poliques, 1973, La parole et l'outil, 1975, Bruits, Essai sur l'economie politique de la musique, 1976, La nouvelle économique politique de la musique, 1976, La nouvelle économie française, 1977, L'ordre cannibale, 1979, Les Trois mondes, 1981, Histoires du temp, 1982, La figure de Fraser, 1984, Un Homme d'influence, 1985, Au propre et au Figuré, 1988, La vie éternelle, 1989; (with Marc Guillaume) Antiéconomique, 1974. Address: European Bank Reconstrn & Devel, Broadgate 6 Level 7, London EC 2M 205, England

ATWATER, HORACE BREWSTER, JR., food company executive; born Minneapolis, April 19, 1931; son of Horace Brewster and Eleanor (Cook) A.; married Martha Joan Clark, May 8, 1955; children—Elizabeth C., Mary M., John C., Joan P. Bachelor of Arts, Princeton University, 1952; Master of Business Administration, Stanford University, 1954. Divisional vice president, director marketing General Mills. Incorporated, Minneapolis, 1958-65, marketing vice president, 1965-70, executive vice president, 1970-76, chief operating officer, 1976-81, president, 1977-82, chief executive officer, 1981—, chairman board, 1982—, also director; board of directors Merck & Company Incorporated, General Electric Company. Member adv. council Stanford U. Grad. School Business; president board of directors Walker Art Center Served to lieutenant United States Naval Reserve, 1955-58. Club: Woodhill Country (Wayzata, Minnesota). Office: General Mills Incorporated 1 General Mills Boulevard Minneapolis Minnesota 55426

AUCOTT, GEORGE W., rubber products and automotive services company executive; born 1934; married. Bachelor of Science, Ursinus College, 1956. With Firestone Tire and Rubber Company, Akron, Ohio, 1956—, executive vice president, 1980; corp. vice president, div. executive, vice president operations NA Tire, 1981; corp. executive vice president, group president Firestone International, from 1982, World Tire; executive vice president World Tire group, 1986-88, president, chief operating officer, 1988—, also board of directors; chairman, president, chief executive offficer Bridgestone/Firestone, Incorporated, Chicago, 1990—. Office: Bridgeston/Firestone Incorporated 1200 Firestone Parkway Akron Ohio 44317

AUGUSTINE, NORMAN RALPH, industrial executive; born Denver, July 27, 1935; son of Ralph Harvey and Freda Irene (Immenga) A.; married Margareta Engman, January 20, 1962; children: Gregory Eugen, René Irene. Bachelor of Science in Engineering magna cum laude, Princeton University, 1957, Master.Southeast, 1959; Doctor of Engineering (honorary), Rennsselaer Polytechnic Institute, 1988; Doctor of Science (honorary), University Colorado, 1989; Doctor of Engineering(honorary), W. Maryland College, 1990. Research assistant Princeton University, 1957-58; program manager, chief engineer Douglas Aircraft Company, Incorporated, Santa Monica, California, 1958-65; assistant director defense research and engineering United States Government, Office of Secretary Defense, Washington, 1965-70; vice president advanced systems Missiles and Space Company, LTV Aerospace Corp., Dallas, 1970-73; assistant secretary army The Pentagon, Washington, 1973-75; undersecretary army The Pentagon, 1975-77; vice president operations Martin Marietta Aerospace Corp., Bethesda, Maryland, 1977-82; president Martin Marietta Denver Aerospace Company, 1982-85, senior vice president, information systems, 1985, president, chief operating officer, 1986-87, vice chairman, chief executive officer, 1987-88, chairman, chief executive officer, 1988—, also board of directors; board of directors Phillips Petroleum Company, Procter & Gamble Corp., Riggs National Bank Corp. ; consultant office Secretary of Def., 1971—, Executive Office President, 1971-73, Department Army, Department Air Force, Department Navy, Department Energy, Department Transportation; member United States Air Force Sci. Adv. Board; chairman Def. Sci. Board; member North Atlantic Treaty Organization Group Experts on Air Def., 1966-70, National Aeronautics and Space Administration Research and Tech. Adv. Council, 1973-75; chairman National Aeronautics and Space Administration Space Sytems and Tech. Adv. Board, 1985—; member Chief of Naval Operations Executive Board, 1989—; chairman defense policy adv. committee on trade, 1988—. Author: Augustine's Laws; co-author: The Defense Revolution, 1990; member adv. board: Journal of Def. Research, 1970—; associate editor: Def. System Management Rev, 1977-82; editorial board: Astronautics & Aeros; contributor articles to professional journals. Trustee Johns Hopkins U.; chairman national program evaluation committee, council vice president, national vice president Boy Scouts Am., 1990—; member Immanuel Presbyterian Church, McLean, Virginia, Policy Council Business Roundtable, 1988—, Business Council, 1989—. Recipient Meritorious Service medal Department Defense, 1970, 4 Distinguished Civilian Service medals Department Defense, James Forrestal medal National Security Industrial Association, 1988. Fellow Institute of Electrical and Electronics Engineers, Am. Astronomical Society, American Institute of Aeronautics and Astronautics (director 1978-85, president 1983-84, Goddard medal 1988), Am. Helicopter Society (director 1974-75); member National Acad. Engineering, International Acad. Astronautics, Association United States Army (president 1980-84, chairman 1990—), National Security Industrial Association (Forrestal medal 1988), Industrial College Armed Forces (Eisenhower award 1990), Armed Forces Communications and Electronics Association (Sarnoff medal 1990), National Space Club (Goddard Trophy 1991) Phi Beta Kappa, Sigma Xi, Tau Beta Pi. Office: Martin Marietta Corp 6801 Rockledge Dr Bethesda Maryland 20817

AUTRY, GENE (ORVON GENE AUTRY), actor, radio entertainer, broadcasting executive, baseball team executive; born Tioga, Texas, September 29, 1907; son of Delbert and Elnora (Ozmont) A.; married Ina Mae Spivey, April 1, 1932; married Jacqueline Ellam, 1981. Graduate, Tioga (Texas) High School, 1925. Railroad telegraph operator Sapulpa, Oklahoma, 1925; owner, chairman board California Angels; president Flying A Productions; owner Station

KMPC AM & KLITE FM, Hollywood, California, Stations KVI & KPLZ Radio, Seattle, Golden West Broadcasters; president several music and publication companies. Made first phonograph record of cowboy songs, 1929; radio artist Station WLS, Chicago, 1930-34; motion picture actor, 1934-53, including In Old Santa Fe; starred in 88 musical Western feature pictures, 91 half-hour TV pictures 1950-55; has written or co-written over 200 songs including That Silver-Haired Daddy of Mine, 1931, You're the Only Star in My Blue Heaven, 1938, Dust, 1938, Tears On My Pillow, 1941, Be Honest With Me, 1941, Tweedle O'Twill, 1942, Here Comes Santa Claus, 1948; host Melody Ranch Theater Nashville Network, 1987, 88. Served with United States Army Air Force, 1942-45. Member International Footprinters. Clubs: Masons (33 degree), Shriners, Elks. Address: Post Office Box 710 Los Angeles California 90078 Office: care California Angels Post Office Box 2000 Anaheim California 92803

AVERY, WILLIAM JOSEPH, packaging manufacturing company executive; born Chicago, June 20, 1940; son of Floyd Joseph and Margaret Mildred (Musard) A.; married Sharon Bajorek, September 5, 1959; children: Michelle, Martin, Sheryl. Graduate in industrial management, University Chicago, 1968. With Crown Cork & Seal Company Incorporated, Philadelphia, 1959—, vice president sales, 1974-79, senior vice president manufacturing and sales, 1979-80, executive vice president, 1980-81, president, 1981—, also chief executive officer and director. Roman Catholic. Office: Crown Cork & Seal Company Incorporated 9300 Ashton Road Philadelphia Pennsylvania 19136

AYCOCK, HUGH DAVID, steel manufacturing company executive; born Lilesville, North Carolina, 1930; married. With Nucor Corp., Charlotte, North Carolina, 1954—, div. shop superintendent, 1955-57, div. sales manager, 1957-63, div. general manager, 1963-84, vice president, 1965-84, president, 1984—, also board of directors; vice president Nucor Steel SC div. Nucor Corp., 1965-84; board of directors Bowater Incorporated. Served with United States Navy, 1950-54. Office: Nucor Corp 4425 Randolph Road Charlotte North Carolina 28270

AYERS, RICHARD H., manufacturing company executive; born Newton, Massachusetts, October 12, 1942; son of J. Robert and Virginia (Hixon) A.; married Gay Boas, August 12, 1964 (divorced June 1973); children—Ashley C., Jennifer B., Bradford M.; married Suzanne M. Lefebvre, October 13, 1973; children—Kelly V., David R. Bachelor of Science in Industrial Management, Massachusetts Institute of Technology, 1965, Master of Science in Industrial Management, 1965. General foreman Wyman-Gordon Company, North Grafton, Massachusetts, 1965-69; vice president manufacturing Britton Corp., Newington, Connecticut, 1969-72; line manufacturing positions The Stanley Works, New Britain, Connecticut, 1972-85, president, 1985—, chief operating officer, 1985-87, president, chief executive officer, 1987—, also director; director Connecticut Mutual Funds, Hartford, Connecticut, Southern New England Telecommunications Company; associate director Perkin Elmer. Board of directors New Britain General Hospital, 1984—; trustee Hartford Grad. Center, 1986—. Am. Leadership Forum fellow, Hartford, 1985. Member Econ. Club New York, Hand Tools Institute (board directors 1982-84), National Association Manufacturers. Republican. Club: Farmington Country (Connecticut). Avocations: jogging; golf; tennis. Office: Stanley Works 1000 Stanley Dr New Britain Connecticut 06053

AZZATO, LOUIS ENRICO, manufacturing company executive; born New York City, October 8, 1930; son of John A. and Margaret (Ronca) A.; married Margaret Jean McCarthy, June 25, 1955; children—Jean Bernadette and Patricia Bernadette Stephens (twins), John Kevin, Maureen Ann. Bachelor of Science in Chemical Engineering cum laude, City College of New York, 1952. Process, project engineer Foster Wheeler Corp., Clinton, New Jersey, 1952-63; project manager Foster Wheeler Energy Corp., Clinton, New Jersey, 1963-67, senior vice president, group executive, 1978-80, also board of directors; vice president, manager process plants and fired hired heater activities Foster Wheeler Italiana, Milan, 1967-74; executive vice president equipment div. operations Foster Wheeler Corp., 1980-81, president, chief executive officer, 1981-88; chairman, president, chief executive officer Foster Wheeler Corp., Clinton, New Jersey, 1988—; chairman chief executive officer Glitsch, Incorporated, Dallas, 1974-78; board of directors various subsidiary companies of Foster Wheeler Corp, First Fidelity Bank, N.A., New Jersey, First Fidelity Bancorp. New Jersey; board regents Seton Hall University, South Orange, New Jersey. Patentee catalytic cracking. Member Am. Institute Chemical Engineers, American Society of Mechanical Engineers (industry adv. board), New Jersey State Chamber of Commerce (board director). Roman Catholic. Avocations: golfing, swimming, jogging. Home: 22 Lord William Penn Dr Morristown New Jersey 07960

BACOT, JOHN CARTER, banker; born Utica, New York, February 7, 1933; son of John Vacher and Edna (Gunn) B.; married Shirley Schou, November 26, 1960; children: Elizabeth, Susan. Bachelor of Arts, Hamilton College, Clinton, New York, 1955; Bachelor of Laws, Cornell University, 1958. Bar: New York 1959. With firm Utica, 1959-60; with Bank of New York, New York City, 1960—, president, 1974-84, chief executive officer, chairman, 1982—; also board director Bank of New York; board of directors Home Life Insurance Company, Atlantic Reins. Company, Centennial Insurance Company, Bank of New York International Corp., Bank of New York Company, Incorporated; trustee Atlantic Mutual Insurance Company; chairman board trustees Hamilton College. Member Econ. Club New York, Pilgrims of United States, Association Reserve City Bankers, New York State Bar Association, Council on Foreign Relations, Montclair Golf Club, Link Club, Union Club. Episcopalian. Home: 48 Porter Place Montclair New Jersey 07042 Office: Bank New York Company Incorporated 48 Wall St New York New York 10286

BAILEY, IRVING WIDMER, II, insurance holding company executive; born Cambridge, Massachusetts, June 8, 1941; son of

Harwood and Esther (Hill) B.; married Nancy Lawrence, September 21, 1963; children: Christopher L., Michele. Graduate, Phillips-Exeter Academy, 1959; student, University Paris, 1961-62; Bachelor of Arts in French, University Colorado, 1963; Master of Business Administration, New York University, 1968. Investment officer, assistant vice president Mutual Life Insurance Company, New York City, 1963-71; vice president bond investment Phoenix Mutual Life Insurance Company, Hartford, Connecticut, 1971-76, senior vice president investments, 1976-81; executive vice president, chief investment officer Capital Holding Corp., Louisville, 1981-87, president, chief operating officer, 1987-88, chairman, president, chief. executive officer, 1988—; also board of directors 1987—; board of directors Southern Bell Telephone Company, South Central Bell Telephone Company. Board of directors U. Kentucky Business Partnership Foundation, Lexington, 1981—, Leadership Louisville Foundation, 1989—; member executive committee Downtown Devel. Corp., 1988, Kentucky Economic Devel. Corp., 1988; board of directors, member executive committee Greater Louisville Economic Devel. Partnership, 1988—; board governors J.B. Speed Art Mus., 1988—, Life Span, 1989—, Metro United Way, 1989—; member trust investment committee U. Louisville, 1982—. Member Am. Council Life Insurance (audit, annual mtg., executive, fin. committees), New York Society Security Analysts, River Valley Club, Jefferson Club. Republican. Presbyterian. Avocation: skiing. Office: Capital Holding Corp 680 4th Avenue Post Office Box 32830 Louisville Kentucky 40232

BAKER, DEXTER FARRINGTON, manufacturing company executive; born Worcester, Massachusetts, April 16, 1927; son of Leland Dyer and Edith (Quimby) B.; married Dorothy Ellen Hess, June 23, 1951; children: Ellen L., Susan A., Leslie A., Carolyn J. Bachelor of Science, Lehigh University, 1950, Master of Business Administration, 1957. Sales engineer Air Products & Chemicals, Incorporated, Allentown, Pennsylvania, 1952-56, general sales manager, 1956-57, director, 1964—, group vice president, 1967-68, executive vice president, 1968-78, president, 1978-88, 90—, chairman, chief executive officer, 1986—; managing director Air Products, Limited, 1957-67, director, 1964-80; board of directors AMP Incorporated. Board assocs. Muhlenberg College; trustee Lehigh U., Harry C. and Mary M. Trexler Foundation Served with United States Naval Reserve, 1945-46; with United States Army, 1950-52. Member Am. Management Association, Am. Institute Chemical Engineers, Society Chemical Industry, Asa Packer Society Lehigh University, Theta Chi. Presbyterian (elder). Office: Air Products & Chems Incorporated 7201 Hamilton Boulevard Allentown Pennsylvania 18195

BAKER, JAMES KENDRICK, specialty metals manufacturing company executive; born Wabash, Indiana, December 21, 1931; son of Donald Dale and Edith (Swain) B.; married Beverly Baker, April 11, 1959; children—Betsy Ann, Dirk Emerson, Hugh Kendrick (deceased). Bachelor of Arts, DePauw University, 1953; Master of Business Administration, Harvard University, 1958. Regional sales manager Arvinyl div. Arvin Industries, Incorporated,

Columbus, Ind., 1958-60; general manager div. Arvinyl div. Arvin Industries, Incorporated, 1960-68, vice president, 1966-68, executive vice president, 1968-81, president, chief executive officer, 1981-86, chairman, chief executive officer, 1986—, board of directors; board of directors INB Fin. Corp., Pub. Service Ind., Plainfield. Board of directors Associated Colleges Ind., De Pauw U., vice chairman; president Columbus Foundation for Youth, 1965, United Way of Bartholomew County, 1979; board of directors Vinyl-Metal Laminators Institute div. Society for Plastics Industry, 1960—, president, 1963-64; vice chairman Ind. Republican Convention, 1966; chairman United States Chamber of Commerce, 1990-91; trustee Institute for Global Ethics; adv. board Kellogg Sch./Northwestern U.; founding chairman Ind. Center on Philanthropy; founding trustee New Am. Schools Devel. Corp. Named Outstanding Boss Chamber of Commerce, 1965; recipient Distinguished Service award Ind. Junior Chamber of Commerce, 1966, Distinguished Community Service award Columbus Area Chamber of Commerce, 1983, Significant Sigma Chi award; named One of 5 Outstanding Young Men of Ind., 1966. Member Columbus Chamber of Commerce (board directors), Ind. Chamber of Commerce (board directors). Clubs: Rotary, DePauw University Alumni (president 1974), Harrison Lake Country. Home: 12044 W State Road 46 Deer Crossing Columbus Indiana 47201 Office: Arvin Industries Incorporated 1 Noblitt Plaza Columbus Indiana 47201

BALDWIN, HENRY FURLONG, banker; born Baltimore, January 15, 1932; son of Henry du Pont and Margaret (Taylor) B.; divorced; children: Mary Stevenson, Severn Eyre. Bachelor of Arts, Princeton University, 1954. With Merc.-Safe Deposit & Trust Company, Baltimore, 1956; vice president Merc.-Safe Deposit & Trust Company, 1963-65, senior vice president, 1965, executive vice president, 1965-70, president, 1970-76, chairman board, 1976—; president, director Mercantile Bankshares Corp., 1970-84, chairman board, 1984—; board of directors Baltimore Gas and Electric Company, Mercantile Safe Deposit & Trust Company, USF&G Corp., GRC International, Consolidated Rail Corp., Offitbank, Baltimore Orioles, Incorporated, Wills Group, Incorporated, Constellation Holdings, Incorporated. Trustee Johns Hopkins U., Johns Hopkins Hospital With United States Marine Corps Reserve, 1954-56. Office: Merc Bankshares Corp 2 Hopkins Plaza Post Office Box 1477 Baltimore Maryland 21203

BANKS, DAVID RUSSELL, health care executive; born Arcadia, Wisconsin, February 15, 1937; son of J.R. and Cleone B.; married; children: Melissa, Michael. Bachelor of Arts, University Arkansas, 1959. Vice president Dabbs, Sullivan, Trulock, Arkansas, 1963-74; chairman, chief executive officer Leisure Lodges, Fort Smith, Arkansas, 1974-77; registered representative Stephens Incorporated, Little Rock, 1974-79; president, chief operating officer Beverly Enterprises, Pasadena, California, 1979—; director National Council Health Centers, Pulaski Bank, Little Rock. Served with United States Army. Office: Beverly Enterprises Incorporated 99 S Oakland Avenue Pasadena California 91101

BANTA, MERLE HENRY, graphics equipment and service company executive; born East St. Louis, Illinois, December 11, 1932; son of Albert Merle and Vivian Mae (Brown) B.; married June M. Mueller, June 17, 1955; children—Brenda J. Williams, Berton M., Bradford C. Bachelor of Science, Washington University, St. Louis, 1954; Master of Science, Iowa State University, 1955; Master of Business Administration, Harvard University, 1961. Registered professional engineer. Cons. McKinsey & Company, Los Angeles, 1961-64; chairman, president, chief executive officer Leisure Group, Los Angeles, 1964-84, Pacific Homes, Los Angeles, 1981-84; chairman, chief executive officer AM International, Incorporated, Chicago, 1984—, president, 1984-85, 88—; director Mark Controls Corp., Evanston, Illinois, Leisure Group, Los Angeles, Pacific Homes, Los Angeles. Trustee Pasadena Polytechnical School, California, 1977—; board overseers Huntington Library, San Marino, California, 1972—. Served to lieutenant United States Navy, 1955-59; North Africa. Recipient Daniel Mead award American Society of Civil Engineers, 1955. Named Baker scholar Harvard University Business School, Boston, 1961. Republican. Presbyterian. Clubs: California, Jonathon (Los Angeles); Economic, Chicago (Chicago). Home: 180 E Pearson Apartment 5006 Chicago Illinois 60611 Office: A M International Incorporated 333 W Wacker Dr Suite 900 Chicago Illinois 60606

BANTLE, LOUIS FRANCIS, tobacco company executive; born Bridgeport, Connecticut, November 22, 1928; son of Louis A. and Marie E. (Daisenberger) B.; married Virginia Clark, January 20, 1961; children: Robert C., Terri Ann. Bachelor of Science, Syracuse (New York) University, 1951. Vice president United States Tobacco Company, Greenwich, Connecticut, 1966-73; director United States Tobacco Company, 1967—, chairman board, president, 1973-85, chairman, chief executive officer, 1985-89, chairman, chief executive officer, president, 1989—; board of directors Americares, Incorporated. Member Statue of Liberty-Ellis Island Committee; trustee Syracuse U., Fairfield U. Served to captain United States Marine Corps, 1951-53. Decorated knight of the North Star Sweden, 1976; recipient Lettermen of Distinction award University Syracuse, 1986, Regional Plan Association award, 1986; named to Hall of Fame, National Association Tobacco Distbrs., 1980; recipient Good Scout award Greater New York Couns. Boy Scouts Am., 1988. Republican. Roman Catholic. Clubs: Winged Foot Country, Wee Burn Country, Blind Brook. Office: UST 100 W Putnam Avenue Greenwich Connecticut 06830

BARACH, PHILIP G., shoe company executive; born Boston, 1930; married; 3 children. Educated, Boston University, 1951, Harvard Graduate School Business Administration, 1955. With United States Shoe Corp. Cincinnati, 1960—; division head, Vaisey-Bristol div. 1961-65, Corp. vice president (United States Shoe Corp.), president Vaisey-Bristol div.; president, chief executive officer United States Shoe Corp., Cincinnati, 1968—, President, chairman board, 1972—; director Fifth Third Union Trust Company. Home: 7600 Willow Brook Lane Cincinnati Ohio 45237

Office: United States Shoe Corp 1 Eastwood Dr Cincinnati Ohio 45227

BARAD, JILL ELIKANN, toy company executive; born New York City, May 23, 1951; daughter of Lawrence Stanley and Corinne (Schuman) Elikann; married Thomas Kenneth Barad, January, 28, 1979; children: Alexander David, Justin Harris. Bachelor of Arts English and Psychology, Queens College, 1973. Assistant produced manager marketing Coty Cosmetics, New York City, 1976-77, produced manager marketing, 1977; account executive Wells Rich Greene Advertising Agency, Los Angeles, 1978-79; product manager marketing Mattel Toys, Incorporated, Los Angeles, 1981-82, director marketing, 1982-83, vice president marketing, 1983-85, senior vice president marketing, 1985-86, senior vice president product devel., from 1986, executive vice president product design and devel., executive vice president marketing and worldwide product devel., 1988-89; president girls and activity toys div. Mattel Toys, Incorporated, Los Angeles, 1989-; board of directors Arco Toys. Charter member Rainbow Guild/Amie Karen Cancer Fund, Los Angeles, 1983, Los Angeles County Mus., 1985; trustee Queens College. Member Am. Film Institute (charter). Avocations: film, weight lifting. Office: Mattel Incorporated 5150 Rosecrans Avenue Hawthorne California 90250

BARCELONA, CHARLES B., wholesale food company executive. President, director Peter J. Schmitt Company, Incorporated, Buffalo, chief executive offficer. Office: Peter J Schmitt Company Incorporated 355 Harlem Road Buffalo New York 14240

BARES, WILLIAM G., chemical company executive; born 1941; married. Bachelor of Science in Chemical Engineering, Purdue University, 1963; Master of Business Administration, Case Western Reserve University, 1969. Process devel. engineer Lubrizol Corp., Wickliffe, Ohio, 1963-67; group leader, pilot plant Lubrizol Corop., Wickliffe, Ohio, 1967-71; assistant department head Lubrizol Corp., Wickliffe, Ohio, 1971-72, department head., 1972-78, assistant to president, 1978, vice president, 1978-80, executive vice president, 1980-82, president, director, 1982—, chief operating officer, 1987—. Office: Lubrizol Corp 29400 Lakeland Boulevard Wickliffe Ohio 44092

BARNES, JAMES E., energy company executive; born Ponca City, Oklahoma, 1934; married. Graduate, Oklahoma State University; graduate advanced management program, Harvard University. With Continental Pipe Line Company, 1956-62, Cherokee Pipe Line Company, 1962-64; with Conoco, Incorporated, Stamford, Connecticut, 1964-83, manager gas products div., 1964-65, general manager natural gas and gas products department, 1965-70, vice president purchasing, 1970-75, vice president supply and trading, 1975-78, executive vice president supply and transportation, 1978-83; senior executive vice president, chief operating officer Mapco, Incorporated, Tulsa, 1983-84, president, chief executive officer, board of directors, 1984—, chairman board, 1986—. Office: Mapco Incorporated 1800 S Baltimore Avenue Tulsa Oklahoma 74119

BARNES, ROBERT E., banking executive; born 1933; married. Bachelor of Arts, Princeton University, 1955;

postgraduate, Am. University Graduate School International Management, 1959. Vice president div. executives Western Hemisphere branch Chase Manhattan Bank, New York City, 1961-73; president, board of directors Alaska State Bank, Anchorage, 1973-77; chief operating officer Bank of the West, 1977-84; president, chief executive officer Bay View Federal Savings and Loan Association, San Mateo, California, 1984—, also board of directors. Captain United States Air Force, 1956-58. Office: Bay View Federal Savings & Loan Association 2121 S El Camino Real San Mateo California 94403

BARNES, THEODORE W., bank holding company executive; born 1931. With Old Stone Corp., Providence, 1948—, president, chief executive officer, 1975—, also board of directors. Office: Old Stone Corp 150 S Main St Providence Rhode Island 02903

BARNES, WALLACE, manufacturing executive; born Bristol, Connecticut, March 22, 1926; son of Harry Clarke and Lillian (Houbertz) B.; married Audrey Kent, June 14, 1947 (divorced August 1962); children: Thomas Oliver, Jarre Ann; married Mrs. Frederick B. Hollister, Jr. (divorced February 1973); 1 adopted son, Frederick Hollister; married Joan C. Fierri, March 3, 1973 (divorced May 1985); married Barbara Hackman Franklin, November 29, 1986. Bachelor of Arts, Williams College, 1949; Bachelor of Laws, Yale University, 1952; graduate, Advanced Management Program, Harvard, 1973; Bachelor of Laws (honorary), University Hartford, 1988. Bar: Connecticut 1952. Associate firm Beach, Calder & Barnes (and predecessor), Bristol, 1952-55; partner Beach, Calder & Barnes (and predecessor), 1956-62; executive vice president Associate Spring Corp. (name changed to Barnes Group Incorporated), 1962-64, president, 1964-77, chairman, chief executive officer, 1977—; president Nutmeg Air Transport, Incorporated, 1949-55; assistant to treasurer Northeast Airlines, Incorporated, Boston, 1951; director, member executive committee Aetna Life and Casualty Company,; director Motalink Limited, Wiltshire, England, Autoliaisons France S.A.; president Barnes Group Can.; director, president Resortes Mecanicos S.A., Mexico City, Resortes Industriales del Norte S.A., Monterrey; president Associate Spring-Asia; chairman, director Barnes Group Foundation, Incorporated; director Connecticut Innovations, Incorporated, Rogers Corp., Rohr Industries, Incorporated, Loctite Corp., and others. President Bristol Community Chest, 1956; board of directors, member executive committee Bristol Boys Club, president, 1965-68; member board regents, U. Hartford, 1981-87, chairman, 1988—; trustee Bristol Girls' Club Association; board of directors New England Legal Foundation, 1986-90, New England Council, 1980-83, Junior Achievement N. Central Connecticut, 1980-90; Nominee for Congress, 1st Congl. District Connecticut, 1954; town chairman, Bristol, 1953-55; member Connecticut Senate from 5th District, 1958-62, from 8th District, 1966-70, minority leader, 1969; Board of directors Community Council of Capital Region, 1975-77, Hartford Symphony Society, 1971-78, Council on Employment and Fair Taxation, 1978-80, Business Coalition on Health, 1983-88, Connecticut Pub. Expenditure Council, 1979-85; trustee Am. Clock and Watch Mus., Bristol Regional Environmental Center; board trustees New England Air Mus.; corporator Institute of Living, Hartford; board of directors Connecticut Economic Devel. Corp. Served as aviation cadet United States Army Air Force, 1944-45. Recipient Distinguished Service award Bristol Jaycees, Keystone award Boys Clubs Am., 1967, Humanitarian award Bristol Boys Club Association, 1989, Hon. Alumnus award University Hartford, 1985. Member American Bar Association, Connecticut Bar Association, Am. Judicature Society, National Association Manufacturers (board directors), Am. Arbitration Association, Bristol Historical Society, Newcomen Society, Connecticut Business and Industry Association (past chairman, director), Bus.-Industry Political Action Committee (board directors), Am. Legion, Elks, Econ. Club, Yale Club, Williams Club, Hundred of Connecticut Club. Home: 1875 Perkins St Bristol Connecticut 06010 Office: Barnes Group Incorporated 123 Main St Bristol Connecticut 06011-0489

BARRETT, TOM HANS, rubber company executive; born Topeka, August 13, 1930; son of William V. and Myrtle B.; married Marilyn Dunn, July 22, 1956; children: Susan and Sara (twins), Jennifer. Graduate Chemical Engineer, Kansas State University, 1953; graduate, Sloan School Management Massachusetts Institute of Technology, 1969. With Goodyear Tire & Rubber Company, various locations, 1953—; president Goodyear Tire and Rubber Company, Akron, OH, 1982-89, chief operating officer, 1982-89; chairman, president, chief executive officer Goodyear Tire & Rubber Company, Akron, Ohio, 1989—, also director; board of directors A.O. Smith Corp., Rubbermaid Corp.; board trustees Ec Devel.; board of directors Highway Users Federation. Served with United States Army, 1953-55. Decorated officer with crown Order Merite Civil et Militaire, Luxembourg, 1976; recipient Sigma Phi Epsilon citation, 1979. Member National Association Manufacturers (executive committee, board directors), Rubber Manufacturers Association (executive committee, board directors), Business Roundtable (policy committee). Home: 2135 Stockbridge Road Akron Ohio 44313 Office: Goodyear Tire & Rubber Company 1144 E Market St Akron Ohio 44316

BARRONE, GERALD DORAN, savings and loan association executive; born Tujunga, California, 1931; married. Bachelor of Science, University of California at Los Angeles, 1955. President, chief executive officer Fidelity Federal Savs and Loan Association, Glendale, California, from 1955, also board of directors; now, president, chief operating officer Coast Federal Bank, Los Angeles; board of directors Citadel Holding Corp., Glendale. Served with United States Navy, 1951-53. Office: Coast Federal Bank 1000 Wilshire Boulevard 22d Floor Los Angeles California 90017

BARTON, GERALD GAYLORD, land development company executive; born Oklahoma City, 1931. Student, University Oklahoma. President, chief executive officer, director Landmark Land Company, Carmel, California; also president, director Barton Theatre Company; board of directors

LSB Industries, Incorporated. Office: Landmark Land Company Incorporated 100 Clock Tower Place Suite 200 Carmel California 93923

BASS, ROBERT MUSE, entrepreneur; born Fort Worth, 1948; son of Perry Richardson and Nancy Lee (Muse) B.; married Anne Bass, 1970; 3 children. Bachelor of Arts, Yale University, 1970; Master of Business Administration, Stanford University. Vice president, board of directors Bass Brothers Enterprises Incorporated, Fort Worth, until 1985; principal Robert M. Bass Group Incorporated, Fort Worth, 1985—. Member Texas State Hwy. and Pub. Transportation Commission, 1986-87; trustee National Trust for Historical Preservation; member collector's committee National Gallery, Washington. Office: Robert M Bass Group Incorporated 201 Main St Fort Worth Texas 76102

BATTEN, JAMES KNOX, newspaper executive; born Suffolk, Virginia, January 11, 1936; son of Eugene Taylor and Josephine (Winslow) B.; married Jean Elaine Trueworthy, February 22, 1958; children: Mark Winslow, Laura Taylor, Taylor Edison. Bachelor of Science, Davidson College, 1957; Master Pub. Affairs, Princeton, 1962. Reporter Charlotte (North Carolina) Observer, 1957-58, 62-65; corr. Washington bureau Knight Newspapers, 1965-70; editorial staff Detroit Free Press, 1970-72; executive editor Charlotte (North Carolina) Observer, 1972-75; vice president Knight-Ridder Newspapers, Incorporated, Miami, Florida, 1975-80, senior vice president, 1980-82, president, 1982-88, president, chief executive officer, 1988-89, chairman, chief executive officer, 1989—; director Associated Press. Trustee Davidson College (North Carolina), U. Miami. Served with Army of the United States, 1958-60. Recipient George Polk Memorial award for regional reporting, 1968; Sidney Hillman Foundation award, 1968. Member Greater Miami C. of C. Methodist. Office: Knight-Ridder Incorporated 1 Herald Plaza Miami Florida 33132-1693

BATTS, WARREN LEIGHTON, diversified industry executive; born Norfolk, Virginia, September 4, 1932; son of John Leighton and Allie Belle (Johnson) B.; married Eloise Pitts, December 24, 1957; 1 daughter, Terri Allison. Bachelor of Electrical Engineering, Georgia Institute Tech., 1961; Master of Business Administration, Harvard University, 1963. With Kendall Company, Charlotte, North Carolina, 1963-64; executive vice president Fashion Devel. Company, Santa Paula, California, 1964-66; director manufacturing Olga Company, Van Nuys, California, 1964-66; vice president Douglas Williams Associates, New York City, 1966-67; co-founder Triangle Corp., Orangeburg, South Carolina, 1967; president, chief executive officer Triangle Corp., 1967-71; vice president Mead Corp., Dayton, Ohio, 1971-73; president Mead Corp., Dayton, 1973-80, chief executive officer, 1978-80; president, chief operating officer Dart Industries, Incorporated, Los Angeles, 1980-81, Dart & Kraft, Incorporated, Northbrook, Illinois, 1981-86; chairman, chief executive officer Premark International Incorporated, Deerfield, 1986—. Trustee Art Institute Chicago, 1983-90, Children's Memorial Hospital, Cgo., 1984—, Chicago Symphony Orchestra, 1986-90, Northwestern U., 1989—. Member The Chicago Club,

Commercial Club Chicago, Econ. Club Chicago, Glen View Club, Indian Hill Club, Los Angeles country Club, Moraine country Club, Citrus Club. Office: Premark International Incorporated 1717 Deerfield Avenue Deerfield Illinois 60015

BEALL, DONALD RAY, manufacturing company executive; born Beaumont, California, November 29, 1938; son of Ray C. and Margaret (Murray) B. Bachelor of Science, San Jose State College, 1960; Master of Business Administration, University Pittsburgh, 1961; postgraduate, University of California at Los Angeles. With Ford Motor Company, 1961-68; fin. management positions Newport Beach, California, 1961-66; manager corp. fin. planning and contracts Philadelphia, 1966-67; controller Palo Alto, California, 1967-68; executive director corp. fin. planning North America Rockwell, El Segundo, California, 1968-69, executive vice president electronics group, 1969-71; executive vice president Collins Radio Company, Dallas, 1971-74; president Collins Radio Group, Rockwell International Corp., Dallas, 1974-76; corp. vice president, president Electronic Operations, Dallas, 1976-77; executive vice president Rockwell International Corp., Dallas, 1977-79; president, chief operating officer Rockwell International Corp., Pittsburgh, 1979-88; chairman board, chief executive officer Rockwell International Corp., El Segundo, California, 1988—; board overseers University California, Irvine, 1988—. Member Bus.-Higher Education Forum. Recipient award of distinction San Jose State University School Engineering, 1980. Member Armed Forces Communications and Electronics Association (national director), Electronic Industries Association, Aerospace Industries Association (chairman board govs. 1987), Society Automotive Engineers, Society Manufacturing Engineers (hon.), Am. Defense Preparedness Association, Young Pres.'s Organization, Navy League of United States, Sigma Alpha Epsilon, Beta Gamma Sigma. Office: Rockwell International Corp 2230 E Imperial Highway El Segundo California 90245

BEALS, VAUGHN LEROY, JR., vehicle manufacturing company executive; born Cambridge, Massachusetts, January 2, 1928; son of Vaughn LeRoy and Pearl Uela (Wilmarth) B.; married Eleanore May Woods, July 15, 1951; children: Susan Lynn, Laurie Jean. Bachelor of Science, Massachusetts Institute of Technology, 1948, Master of Science, 1954. Research engineer Cornell Aeronautical Laboratory, Buffalo, 1948-52, Massachusetts Institute of Technology Aero Elastic and Structures Research Laboratory, 1952-55; director research and tech. North America Aviation, Incorporated, Columbus, Ohio, 1955-65; executive vice president Cummins Engine Company, Columbus, Ind., 1965-70, also director; chairman board, chief executive officer Formac International, Incorporated, Seattle, 1970-75; deputy group executive Motorcycle Products Group, AMF Incorporated, Milwaukee, 1975-77; vice president and group executive Motorcycle Products Group, AMF Incorporated, Stamford, Connecticut, 1977-81; chief executive officer Harley-Davidson, Incorporated, Milwaukee, 1981-89, chairman, 1981—; member adv. board, chairman executive committee Traffic Institute Northwestern University; board of directors Simplicity Manufacturing, Incorporated, R.F. Richard Corp., First Wisconsin National Bank, Milwaukee. Board of directors Greater Milwaukee Committee, Metropolitan Milwaukee Association Commerce, Business Against Drunk Drivers Incorporated. Member University Club, Milwaukee Country Club. Home: 1707 E Fox Lane Milwaukee Wisconsin 53217 Office: Harley-Davidson Incorporated 3700 W Juneau Avenue Box 653 Milwaukee Wisconsin 53201

BEAUVAIS, EDWARD R., airline executive; born 1936. Bachelor of Science, Regis College, 1958. With Frontier Airlines, 1960-63; assistant vice president Airwest Incorporated, Phoenix, 1963-70; chief executive officer, principal Beauvais Roberts and Kurth, 1970-81; with Am. West Airlines, Incorporated, 1981—; now chairman, chief executive officer. Office: Am W Airlines Incorporated 4000 E Sky Harbor Boulevard Phoenix Arizona 85034

BECHERER, HANS WALTER, agricultural equipment manufacturing executive; born Detroit, April 19, 1935; son of Max and Mariele (Specht) B.; married Michele Beigbeder, November 28, 1959; children: Maxime, Vanessa. Bachelor of Arts, Trinity College, Hartford, Connecticut, 1957; student, Munich University, Germany, 1958; Master of Business Administration, Harvard University, 1962. Executive assistant office of chairman Deere & Company, Moline, Illinois, 1966-69; general manager John Deere Export, Mannheim, Germany, 1969-73; director export marketing Deere & Company, Moline, 1973-77, vice president, 1977-83, senior vice president, 1983-86, executive vice president, 1986-87, president, 1987-90, chief operating officer, 1987-89, chief executive officer, 1989—, chairman, 1990—, also board of directors; director Deere & Company; member industry sector adv. committee United States Department Commerce, 1975-81; board of directors Schering/Plough Corp., 1989; member The Business Roundtable, 1989—; member adv. committee Chase Manhattan Bank International, 1990—; trustee Committee for Economic Devel., 1990—; member Industry Policy Adv. Committee for Trade Policy Matters. Trustee St. Katherine's/St. Mark's School, Bettendorf, Iowa, 1983—. 1st lieutenant United States Air Force, 1958-60. Member Council on Foreign Relations, Illinois Business Roundtable, The Conference Board, Equipment Mfgs. Institute (board directors 1987-90), Chicago Club, Rock Island (Illinois) Arsenal Golf Club. Republican. Roman Catholic. Home: 788 25th Avenue Court Moline Illinois 61265 Office: Deere & Company John Deere Road Moline Illinois 61265

BECHTEL, RILEY, engineering company executive. son of Stephen Davison Bechtel, Jr. Formerly executive vice president Bechtel Group Incorporated, San Francisco, president, 1989—. Office: Bechtel Group Incorporated Post Office Box 3965 San Francisco California 94119

BECKER, GARY STANLEY, economist, educator; born Pottsville, Pennsylvania, December 2, 1930; son of Louis William and Anna (Siskind) B.; married Doria Slote, September 19, 1954 (deceased); children: Judith Sarah, Catherine Jean; married Guity Nashat, October

31, 1979; children: Michael Claffey, Cyrus Claffey. Bachelor of Arts summa cum laude, Princeton (New Jersey) University, 1951; Master of Arts, University Chicago, 1953, Doctor of Philosophy, 1955; Doctor of Philosophy (honorary), Hebrew University, Jerusalem, 1985, Knox College, 1985, University Illinois, Chicago, 1988, State University of New York, 1990, Princeton University, 1991. Assistant professor University Chicago, 1954-57; from assistant professor to associate professor Columbia University, New York City, 1957-60, professor economics, 1960-68, Arthur Lehman professor economics, 1968-70; University professor University Chicago, 1970-83, University professor economics and sociology, 1983—, chairman department economics, 1984-85; Ford Foundation visiting professor economics University Chicago, 1969-70; associate Economics Research Center National Opinion Research Center, Chicago, 1980—; member domestic adv. board Hoover Institution, Stanford, California, 1973-90, senior fellow, 1990—; member acad. adv. board Am. Enterprise Institute, 1987-90; research policy advisor Center for Economic Analysis Human Behavior National Bureau Economic Research, 1972-78, member and senior research associate, 1957-79; associate member Institute Fiscal and Monetary Policy, Ministry of Japan, 1988—. Author: The Economics of Discrimination, 1957, 2d edition, 1971, Human Capital, 1964, 2d edition, 1975 (W.S. Woytinsky award University Michigan 1967), Human Capital and the Personal Distribution of Income: An Analytical Approach, 1967, Economic Theory, 1971, (with Gilbert Ghez) The Allocation of Time and Goods Over the Life Cycle, 1975, The Economic Approach to Human Behavior, 1976, A Treatise on the Family, 1981, expanded edition, 1991; editor: Essays in Labor Economics in Honor of H. Gregg Lewis, 1976; co-editor: (with William M. Landes) Essays in the Economics of Crime and Punishment, 1974; columnist, Bus. Week, 1985—; contributor articles to professional journals. Recipient Professional Achievement award University Chicago Alumni Association, 1968, Frank E. Seidman Distinguished award in Political Economy, 1985, MERIT award National Institutes of Health, 1986, John R. Commons award Omicron Delta Epsilon, 1987. Fellow Am. Statistical Association, Econometric Society, Am. Acad. Arts and Sciences, Am. Econ. Association (Distinguished; vice president 1974, president 1987, John Bates Clark medal 1967); member National Academy of Sciences, National Academy of Engineering (founding, vice president 1965-67), Am. Philosophical Society, International Union for Scientific Study Population, Mont Pelerin Society (executive board directors 1985—. vice president 1989-90, president 1990—), Phi Beta Kappa. Office: U Chicago Department of Econs 1126 E 59th St Chicago Illinois 60637

BECKER, JOHN ALPHONSIS, banker; born Kenosha, Wisconsin, January 26, 1942; son of Paul Joseph and Hedwig (Hammacke) B.; married Bonny J. Anderson, July 4, 1963; children: Danial, Todd, Kathryn, Erik. Bachelor of Science, Marquette University, 1963, Master of Business Administration, 1965. Assistant vice president 1st Wisconsin National Bank of Milwaukee,

1970-73, vice president, 1973-76, 1st vice president, 1976-79; president 1st Wisconsin National Bank of Madison, 1979-86; executive vice president 1st Wisconsin National Bank of Milwaukee, 1986—. Div. chairman United Way, Madison, 1984; trustee Edgewood College, Madison, 1980—; member fin. committee Madison Republican Committee Served to 1st lieutenant United States Army, 1965-67. Member Wisconsin Bankers Association (executive committee), Greater madison Chamber of Commerce (chairman board 1983). Roman Catholic. Clubs: Madison, Maple Bluff Country. Office: First Wisconsin National Bank 777 E Wisconsin Avenue Milwaukee Wisconsin 53202

BELIN, JACOB CHAPMAN, paper company executive; born DeFuniak Springs, Florida, October 28, 1914; son of William Jacob and Addie (Leonard) B.; married Myrle Fillingim, November 28, 1940; children: Jacob Chapman, Stephen Andrew. Student, George Washington University, 1935-38. Director sales St. St. Joe Paper Company, Florida, 1949-56; vice president St. Joe Paper Company, 1956-68, president, director, 1968—, chairman board, chief executive officer, 1982—; president, director St. Joseph Land & Devel. Company, Jacksonville Properties, Incorporated; chairman, chief executive officer St. Joe Container Company; chairman Florala Telephone Company, Gulf Telephone Company; chairman, president St. Joseph Telephone & Telegraph Company; director Talisman Sugar Corp. Board of directors Nemours Foundation, Alfred I. duPont Foundation; trustee Estate of Alfred I. DuPont. Member Elks, Rotary, Kappa Alpha. Baptist. Office: St Joe Paper Company 1650 Prudential Dr Jacksonville Florida 32207

BELK, THOMAS MILBURN, corporate executive; born Charlotte, North Carolina, February 6, 1925; son of William Henry and Mary Leonora (Irwin) B.; married Katherine McKay, May 19, 1953; children: Katherine Belk Morris, Thomas Milburn, Jr., Hamilton McKay, John Robert. Bachelor of Science in Marketing, University North Carolina, 1948; Doctor of Hebrew Literature, St. Andrews Presbyterian College, 1978; Doctor of Pub. Service, University North Carolina, 1987. With Belk Stores Services, Incorporated, 1948—, president, 1980—; also president of most Belk Stores throughout Southeast; board of directors executive committee NCNB Corp.; board of directors Business Devel. Corp. of North Carolina, Jefferson-Pilot Corp., Ruddick Corp. (group of supermarkets textile and paper companies). Board of directors Mecklenburg County council Boy Scouts Am., U. North Carolina at Chalotte Foundation, Incorporated; board of directors Young Men's Christian Association, president, 1978-79; general chairman Shrine Bowl of Carolinas, 1963-64, United Appeal, 1959; past president United Community Service ; past chairman, trustee Montreat-Anderson College, 1964-68, St. Andrews Presbyterian College, Laurinburg, North Carolina, 1967-71; trustee Crossnore (North Carolina) School, Incorporated, Davidson (North Carolina) College, 1974—, Endowment Fund, 1975-78, Presbyterian Hospital, Charlotte; trustee U. North Carolina, Charlotte, 1975—, chairman 1982—; member board visitors Wake Forest U.

Lieutenant (junior grade), United States Navy, 1943-46. Recipient Green Thumb award Apparel Foundation of Am. Apparel Mfrs. Association, 1989; named Young Man of Year, Junior Chamber of Commerce, 1960, Man of Year, Charlotte News, 1962, Tarheel of Week, Raleigh News & Observer, 1964, Man of Year, Delta Sigma Pi, 1962. Member Charlotte Chamber of Commerce (chairman 1977), North Carolina Citizens for Business and Industry (past president), Central Charlotte Association (president 1965-66), Mountain Retreat Association (past chairman board trustees). Democrat. Clubs: Charlotte Country, Quail Hollow Country, Country of North Carolina, Biltmore Forest, Grandfather Golf and Country (Linville, North Carolina). Lodges: Rotary, Masons, Shriners (Charlotte board dirs.). Home: 2441 Lemon Tree Lane Charlotte North Carolina 28211 Office: Belk Stores Services 2801 W Tyvola Road Charlotte North Carolina 28217-4500

BELL, RICHARD EUGENE, grain company executive; born Clinton, Illinois, January 7, 1934; son of Lloyd Richard and Ina (Oglesby) B.; married Maria Christina Mendoza, October 22, 1960; children—David Lloyd, Stephen Richard. Bachelor of Science with honors, University Illinois, 1957, Master of Science, 1958. International economist Department Agriculture, Washington, 1959-60; director grain div. Department Agriculture, 1969-72; agricultural attache Am. embassies in Ottawa, Can., Brussels, and Dublin, Ireland, 1961-68; assistant secretary agriculture international affairs and commodity programs 1973-77; president Riceland Foods Incorporated, Stuttgart, Arkansas, 1977—; now also chief executive officer Riceland Foods Incorporated; president, director Commodity Credit Corp., also Federal Crop Insurance Corp., 1975-77; executive secretary President's Agricultural Policy Committee, 1976-77; representative International Wheat Council, London, 1970-77; adv. World Food Conference, Rome, 1974. Recipient Distinguished Service award Department Agr., 1975. Member Alpha Gamma Rho, Alpha Zeta. Republican. Member Christian Church (Disciples of Christ). Office: Riceland Foods Incorporated 2120 Park Avenue Post Office Box 927 Stuttgart Arkansas 72160

BELZER, ALAN, diversified manufacturing company executive; born Brooklyn, November 27, 1932; son of Morris and Vera B.; children: Debra, Frances. Bachelor of Science, New York University, 1953. With Allied Corp., New York City, 1955—; general manager plastic film business Allied Corp., 1970-71; president Allied Corp. (Fabricated Products div.), 1971-72; vice president operations Allied Corp. (Fibers div.), 1972-73, executive vice president, president, 1973-75; group vice president corp. office Allied Corp. (name changed to Allied-Signal Incorporated), 1975-79, group vice president, president fibers and plastics company, 1979-83, corp. executive vice president, president engineered materials sector, 1983-88, corp. president, chief operating officer fibers and plastics company, 1988—; board trustees Manhattan Bowery Corp., New York, 1987—. Served with United States Coast Guard Reserve, 1953-55. Member North America Society for Corp. Planning (board directors 1968),

Opportunity Resources for the Arts (board directors 1981), Chemical Manufacturers Association (board directors 1983-88). Office: Allied-Signal Incorporated Columbia Road & Park Avenue Morristown New Jersey 07960

BENNACK, FRANK ANTHONY, JR., publishing company executive; born San Antonio, February 12, 1933; son of Frank Anthony and Lula W. (Connally) B.; married Luella M. Smith, September 1, 1951; children: Shelley, Laura, Diane, Cynthia, Julie. Student, University Maryland, 1954-56, St. Mary's University, 1956-58. Advertising account executive San Antonio Light, 1950-53, 56-58, adv. manager, 1961-65, assistant pub., 1965-67, pub., 1967-74; general manager newspapers Hearst Corp., New York City, 1974-76, executive vice president, chief operating officer, 1975-78, president, chief executive officer, 1978—; chairman Museum of Broadcasting, New York City, 1991—; director Manufacturers Hanover Trust Company, New York City. Chairman board San Antonio Symphony, 1973-74; Trustee Our Lady of Lake College; hon. trustee Witte Memorial Mus.; board governors New York Hospital, New York City Served with Army of the United States, 1954-56. Member Texas Daily Newspaper Association (president 1973—), Am. Newspaper Pubs. Association (director), Greater San Antonio Chamber of Commerce (president 1971—). Club: Rotarian (president 1974-75). Office: The Mus of TV and Radio 1 E 53rd St New York New York 10022

BENTON, PHILIP EGLIN, JR., automobile company executive; born Charlottesville, Virginia, December 31, 1928; son of Philip Eglin and Orient (Nichols) B.; married Mary Ann Zadosko, May 23, 1974; children: Katharine Benton Harris, Deborah A., Cynthia Benton Nelson, Philip Eglin, III, Paula R. Bachelor of Arts in Economics and Math. magna cum laude, Dartmouth College, 1952; Master of Business Administration in Fin. with highest distinction, Amos Tuck School, 1953. With Ford Motor Company, 1953—; vice president truck operations Ford of Europe 1977-79; vice president Ford Div., Detroit, 1979-81; vice president sales operations North America Auto Operations, Detroit, 1981-85; executive vice president diversified products Dearborn, Michigan, 1985-86; executive vice president Ford International Automotive Operations Ford Motor Company, Dearborn, Michigan, 1986-87; president Ford Automotive Group, Dearborn, 1987-90; president and chief operating officer Ford Motor Company, 1990—; board of directors Automotive Hall of Fame. Trustee Michigan Opera Theatre; board of directors United Foundation; member President's Society, The Edison Institute, Founders Society, Detroit Institute Arts; board overseers Amos Tuck School Business Administration; executive committee Meadow Brook. Served with United States Marine Corps Reserve, 1946-48. Member Society Automotive Engineers, Motor Vehicle Manufacturers Association, Engineering Society Detroit, Econ. Forum, Am. Institute for Contemporary German Studies (board directors), Traffic Improvement Association Oakland (board directors), Overseas Devel. (council member), Econ. Club (board directors), The Old Club, Bloomfield Hills Country Club, Grosse Pointe Club, Dartmouth Club Detroit, Phi Beta Kappa. Office: Ford

Motor Company The American Road Dearborn Michigan 48121

BERE, JAMES FREDERICK, diversified manufacturing company executive; born Chicago, July 25, 1922; son of Lambert Sr. and Madeline (Van Tatenhove) B.; married Barbara Van Dellen, June 27, 1947; children—Robert Paul, James Frederick, David Lambert, Lynn Barbara, Becky Ann. Student, Calvin College, 1940-42; Bachelor of Science, Northwestern University, 1946, Master of Business Administration, 1950. With Clearing Machine Corp. div. United States Industries, Incorporated, 1946-53, general manager, 1953-56; general manager Axelson Manufacturing Company div., 1956, president, 1957-61; president, general manager Borg & Beck div. Borg-Warner Corp., Chicago, 1961-64, group vice president, 1964-66, executive vice president automotive, 1966-68, corp. president, 1968-84, chief executive officer, 1972-86, chief executive officer, chairman board, 1987—; board of directors Abbott Laboratories, North Chicago, Time, Incorporated, Ameritech, Tribune Company, Temple-Inland Incorporated, K-mart Corp. Trustee U. Chicago Served as lieutenant Army of the United States, 1943-45. Member Am. Management Association, Business Roundtable, Business Council, Alpha Tau Omega. Office: Borg-Warner Corp 200 S Michigan Avenue Chicago Illinois 60604

BERNARD, JAMES WILLIAM, industry executive; born Brainerd, Minnesota, June 25, 1937; son of Paul Raymond and Maybelle Gertrude (Fynskov) B.; married Maureen Day, September 6, 1958; children: David, Kenneth, Kathleen. Bachelor of Science, University Oregon, 1960. Trainee Univar Corp., San Francisco, 1960-61; resident manager Univar Corp., Honolulu, 1961-65; sales manager Univar Corp., San Francisco, 1965-67; vice president Univar Corp., Phoenix, 1967-71; vice president Univar Corp., San Francisco, 1971-74, corp. vice president, 1974-82; senior vice president Univar Corp., Seattle, 1982-83, executive vice president, 1983-86, president, chief executive officer, 1986—, also board of directors; board of directors University Washington Executive MBA Program, Seattle, 1984—, VMR Corp., Bellevue, Washington. Member Am. Chemical Society, Seattle Chamber of Commerce, Columbia Tower Club, Rainier (Seattle) Club. Republican. Avocations: fishing, skiing. Office: Univar Corp 801 2nd Avenue Suite 1600 Seattle Washington 98104

BERNICK, HOWARD BARRY, manufacturing company executive; born Midland, Ontario, Canada, April 10, 1952; came to United States, 1974, naturalized, 1976; son of Henry and Esther (Starkman) B.; married Carol Lavin, May 30, 1976; children: Craig, Peter, Elizabeth. Bachelor of Arts, University Toronto, Ontario, 1973. Investment banker Wood Gundy Limited, Toronto, 1973-74, First Boston Corp., Chicago, 1974-77; director of profit planning Alberto Culver Company, Melrose Park, Illinois, 1977-79, vice president corp. devel., 1979-81, group vice president, chief fin. officer, 1981-85, executive vice president, 1985-88, president, chief operating officer, 1988—, also board of directors. Office: Alberto-Culver Company 2525 Armitage Avenue Melrose Park Illinois 60160

BERRY, WILLIAM WILLIS, utility executive; born Norfolk, Virginia, May 18, 1932; son of Joel Halbert and Julia Lee (Godwin) B.; married Elizabeth Mangum, August 23, 1958; children: E. Preston, John Willis, William Godwin. Bachelor of Science in Electrical Engineering, Virginia Military Institute, 1954; Master of Science in Commerce, University Richmond, 1964. Registered professional engineer, Virginia. Engineer General Electric Company, 1954-55; with Virginia Power, Richmond, 1957—, vice president div. operations, then senior vice president commercial operations, 1976-78, executive vice president, 1978-80, president, chief operating officer, 1980-83, president chief executive officer, 1983-85, chairman, chief executive officer, 1985-86; chairman, chief executive officer Dominion Resources Incorporated, 1986-90; chairman Dominion Resources Incorporated, Richmond, 1990—; board of directors C&S/Sovran, Norfolk, Ethyl Corp., Richmond, Universal Corp., Richmond. Trustee Union Theol. Sem., Richmond, Hollins College, Roanoke Virginia Mil. Institute, Lexington. 1st lieutenant Army of the United States, 1955-57. Republican. Clubs: Richmond Kiwanis (past president), Commonwealth, Country of Va, Downtown, Norfolk Yacht and Country. Office: Dominion Resources Incorporated 701 E Byrd St Richmond Virginia 23219

BERSTICKER, ALBERT CHARLES, chemical company executive; born Toledo, March 22, 1934; son of Albert Charles and Lillian (Schorling) B.; married Frances Ploeger, September 15, 1956; children: Steven, Susan, Karen, Cristina. Master of Science in Geo-Chemistry, Miami University, Oxford, Ohio, 1958. Chemist Interlake Iron Corp., Toledo, 1956; engineer Mobile Producing Corp., Billings, Montana, 1957-58; with Ferro Corp., Cleveland, 1958—; assistant to group vice president international Ferro Corp., 1973-74, group vice president international, 1974-76, executive vice president operations, chief operating officer, 1976-86, president, chief operating officer, 1988-91, president, chief executive officer, 1991—, also board of directors; board of directors Ferro Enamel Espanola, S.A., Castellon, Spain, Ferro Holland B.V., Rotterdam, Metal Portuguesa, S.A.R.L., Lisbon, Duramax, Incorporated, Nissan Ferro Organic Chemical Company Limited, Tokyo, Ferro Far East, Limited, Hong Kong, Ferro Industrial Products, Limited, Oakville, Ontario, Can., Queen City Distributors, Limited, Downsview, Ontario, Ferro South East Asia Pte., Limited, Singapore, Centerior Energy Corp., Employers Resource Council, Cleveland, Society National Bank., Society Corp. Editor: Symposium on Salt, 1963. Board of directors Cleve State U. Foundation. Member Chemical Manufacturing Association, Leadership Cleveland. Episcopalian. Office: Ferro Corp 1000 Lakeside Avenue Cleveland Ohio 44114

BEYSTER, JOHN ROBERT, engineering company executive; born Detroit, July 26, 1924; son of John Frederick and Lillian Edith (Jondro) B.; married Betty Jean Brock, September 8, 1955; children: James Frederick, Mark Daneil, Mary Ann. Bachelor of Science in Engineering, University Michigan, 1945, Master of Science, 1948, Doctor of Philosophy, 1950. Registered professional engineer, California. Member staff Los Alamos Sci. Laboratory, 1951-56; chairman department accel. physics Gulf General Atomic Company, San Diego, 1957-69; president Sci. Applications, Incorporated, La Jolla, California, from 1969; chairman board Sci. Applications, Incorporated, La Jolla, California, 1969—; member Joint Strategic Target Planning Staff, Sci. Adv. Group, Omaha, 1978—; panel member National Measurement Laboratory Evaluation panel for Radiation Research, Washington, 1983—; director Scripps Bancorp, La Jolla, 1983. Co-author: Slow Neutron Scattering and Thermalization, 1970. Served to lieutenant commander United States Navy, 1943-46. Fellow Am. Nuclear Society, Am. Physical Society. Republican. Roman Catholic. Home: 9321 La Jolla Farms Road La Jolla California 92037 Office: Sci Applications International Corp 10260 Campus Point Dr San Diego California 92121

BIAFORA, JOSEPH R., lawyer, banker executive. Chairman Valley Federal Savings and Loan Association, Van Nuys, California. Office: Valley Federal Savings & Loan Association 6842 Van Nuts Boulevard Van Nuys California 91405

BICKEL, STEPHEN DOUGLAS, insurance company executive; born Lincoln, Nebraska, December 20, 1939; son of Myron Overton and Jane (Sawyer) B.; married Linda Wall, April 18, 1970; children: Stephanie, Loretta, Valerie. Bachelor of Arts, Dartmouth College, 1962; Bachelor of Laws, University Texas, 1965. Vice president, actuary Am. General Life Insurance Company, Houston, 1965-80; vice president, actuary Am. General Corp., Houston, 1980-83, senior vice president, actuary, 1983-87, executive vice president, 1987-88; president, chief executive officer Variable Annuity Life Insurance Company, Houston, 1988—. Trustee Houston Mus. Natural Sci., 1989. Fellow Society Actuaries; member Acad. Actuaries, Texas Life Insurance Association (board directors 1990), Texas Life, Accident, Health and Hospital Service Insurance Guaranty Association (board directors 1990—). Home: 55 Saddlebrook Houston Texas 77024 Office: Variable Annuity Life Ins Company 2929 Allen Parkway Houston Texas 77019

BIES, SUSAN SCHMIDT, finance company executive; born Buffalo, May 5, 1947; daughter of Louis Howard and Gladys May (Metke) Schmidt; married John David Bies, August 29, 1970; children: John Matthew, Scott Louis. Bachelor of Science, State University Coll.-Buffalo, 1967; Master of Arts, Northwestern University, 1968, Doctor of Philosophy, 1972. Banking structure economist Federal Reserve System, St. Louis, 1970-72; assistant professor economics Wayne State University, Detroit, 1972-77; associate professor Rhodes College, Memphis, 1977-80; tactical planning manager First Tennessee National Corp., Memphis, 1980-81, director corp. devel., 1982-83, treasurer, 1983-84, senior vice president, chief fin. officer, 1984-85, executive vice president, chief fin. officer, 1985—; member fin. adv. committee City of Germantown, Tennessee, 1978—, also budget committee; member investment adv. committee Tennessee Consolidated Retirement System, Nashville, 1981-86; instructor Mid-South School Banking, 1985-86;

board of directors Memphis Ptnrs. President, board of directors North Germantown Homewoners Association, 1978-83; treasurer Germantown Area Soccer Association, 1985-86; treasurer Fury Soccer Club, 1988—; vice chairman task force Committee on 21st Century, Rhodes College, Memphis, 1986-87; member executive adv. board School Accountancy Memphis State U.; board of directors Memphis Youth Initiative, 1988; member BAI Acctg. and Fin. Commission, 1988—. Fellow Center for Urban Affairs, 1968-69, Federal Res. Bank Chicago, 1970. Member Am. Bankers Association (executive committee 1986-88), National Association Business Economists, Am. Econ. Association, Planning Executives Institute, Fin. Executives Institute, (board directors Memphis chapter 1988—), Planning Forum (Managerial Excellence award Memphis chapter 1986), Memphis Area Chamber of Commerce (board directors 1988—, tax committee 1988—, chair 1989—), Econ. Club Memphis (board directors 1986—, vice chairman 1987-88, chairman 1988-89), Omicron Delta Epsilon, Lambda Alpha. Episcopalian. Avocations: gardening, golf, soccer. Office: 1st Tennessee National Corp 165 Madison Avenue Memphis Tennessee 38103

BILLIG, ERWIN H., manufacturing company executive; born 1927. Graduate, Loughborough University, 1955. With Wilmot Breeden Tru flo Limited, 1960-72; vice president, group executive Chicago Pneumatic Tool Company, 1972-76; group vice president Masco Corp., Taylor, Michigan, 1976-84; executive vice president Masco Industries, Taylor, 1984-87, president, chief operating officer, 1987—. Office: Masco Industries Incorporated 21001 Van Born Road Taylor Michigan 48180

BINDLEY, WILLIAM EDWARD, pharmaceutical executive; born Terre Haute, Indiana, October 6, 1940; son of William F. and Gertrude (Lynch) B.; married Martha Leinenbach, June 10, 1961; children: William Franklin, Blair Scott, Sally Ann. Bachelor of Science, Purdue University, 1961; graduate wholesale management program, Stanford University, 1966. Assistant treasurer Controls Company Am., Melrose Park, Illinois, 1962-65; vice-chairman E.H. Bindley & Company, Terre Haute, 1965-68; chairman board, chief executive officer Bindley Western Industries, Incorporated, Indianapolis, 1968—; Scholl Scholarship guest lecturer Loyola University, Chicago, 1982; guest lecturer Young President Organization, Palm Springs, California and Dallas, 1981, 82, 84; guest instructor Center for Entrepreneurs, Indianapolis, 1983; board of directors AmeriTrust Ind. Corp.; distinguished lecturer, member adv. board Georgetown University, 1989—. State director Business for Reagan-Bush, Washington and Indianapolis, 1980; trustee Indianapolis Civic Theatre, St. Vincent Hospital, Indianapolis, United States Ski Team; board of directors National Entrepreneurship Foundation; member president's council Purdue U., West Lafayette, Ind.; hon. secretary of state State of Ind.; trustee Marian coll., Indianapolis. Named hon. Kentucky Colonel, 1980, "Sagamore of the Wabash" Gov. Orr., State of Ind. Member Young President Organization (area director, chairman 1982, award 1983), National Wholesale Druggists Association (director 1981-

84, Service award 1984), Purdue University Alumni Association (life), Woodstock Club, Meridian Hills Countryn Club. Republican. Roman Catholic. Avocations: skiing; tennis; golf; boating. Office: Bindley Western Industries Incorporated 4212 W 71st St Indianapolis Indiana 46268

BIONDI, FRANK J., JR., entertainment company executive; born New York City, January 9, 1945; son of Frank J. and Virginia (Willis) B.; married Carol Oughton, March 16, 1974; children: Anne, Jane. Bachelor of Arts, Princeton University, 1966; Master of Business Administration, Harvard University, 1968. Assoc.-corp. fin. Shearson Lehman, Incorporated, New York City, 1970-71, Prudential Securities, New York City, 1969; principal Frank J. Biondi Junior & Associates, New York City, 1972; director business analysis Teleprompter Corp., New York City, 1972-73; assistant treasurer, associate director business affairs Children's TV Workshop, New York City, 1974-78; director entertainment program planning Home Box Office, New York City, 1978, vice president programming operations, 1979-82, executive vice president planning and administration, 1982-83, president, chief executive officer, 1983, chairman, chief executive officer, 1984; executive vice president entertainment business sector The Coca-Cola Company, 1985; chairman, chief executive officer Coca-Cola TV, 1986; president, chief executive officer Viacom International Incorporated, New York City, 1987—, also board of directors; board of directors Viacom Incorporated, New York City. Trustee Citizens Budget Commission, New York City; board of directors Leake-Watts Child Care Agency, Yonkers, New York, 1975, Morningside Nursing Home, Bronx, New York, 1977, Mus. Broadcasting, New York City, Am. Mus. of Moving Image, New York City. Recipient Best of a New Generation award Esquire magazine, 1984. Member Am. Film Institute. Am. Mus. Moving Image, International Radio and TV Society (former treasurer and vice president), Center for Communications, Mus. of TV and Radio, Riverdale Yacht Club, Princeton of New York Club, Edgartown Yacht Club. Office: Viacom International Incorporated 1515 Broadway New York New York 10036 also: Viacom Incorporated 200 Elm St Dedham Massachusetts 02026

BIRK, ROGER EMIL, federal mortgage association executive; born St. Cloud, Minnesota, July 14, 1930; son of Emil S. and Barbara E. (Zimmer) B.; married Mary Lou Schrank, June 25, 1955; children: Kathleen, Steven, Mary Beth, Barbara. Bachelor of Arts, St. John's University, 1952. Manager Merrill Lynch, Pierce, Fenner and Smith, Incorporated, Fort Wayne, Ind., 1964-66, Kansas City, Missouri, 1966-68; assistant div. director Merrill Lynch, Pierce, Fenner and Smith, Incorporated, New York City, 1968-70, div. director, 1971-74, president, 1974-76, chairman, 1980-85; president Merrill Lynch & Company, New York City, 1976-81, chairman, chief executive officer, 1981-85, chairman emeritus, 1985—; chairman board International Securities Clearing Corp., New York City, 1986-87; president, chief operating officer Federal National Mortgage Association, Washington, 1987—; director New York Stock Exchange, 1981-85, vice chairman, 1983-85; member Business Roundtable, 1981-85, President's Commission on Executive Exchange, 1981-85, President's Private Sector Survey on Cost Control, 1982-85. Chairman national adv. council St. John's U., 1975-76, board regents, 1975-78; trustee U. Notre Dame, 1981—. Served with Army of the United States, 1952-54. Member National Association Securities Dealers (member long-range planning committee 1975-78), Council on Foreign Relations. Club: Navesink Country (Middletown, New Jersey). Office: Federal National Mortgage Association 3900 Wisconsin Avenue Northwest Washington District of Columbia 20016

BLACK, THEODORE HALSEY, manufacturing company executive; born Jersey City, October 22, 1928; son of Theodore Charles and Mary (Carroll) B.; married Marilyn Rigsby, 1979; children: Deborah, Theodore Jr., Susan, Zelda, Carol, Brian. Bachelor of Science in Electrical Engineering, United States Naval Academy, Annapolis, 1953; Advanced Mgt. Program, Harvard University, 1974. Salesman, sales manager Ingersoll-Rand Company, New York City, 1957-67, general manager turbo products div., 1967-72, vice president, 1972-87; president, chief operating officer Ingersoll-Rand Company, Woodcliff Lake, New Jersey, 1988, chairman, president, chief executive officer, 1988—; president, chief executive officer Dresser-Rand Company, Corning, New York, 1987-88; president, chief executive officer Dresser-Rand Company, Corning, New York, 1987-88; board of directors General Pub. Utilities, Parsippany, New Jersey, CPC International, Englewood Cliffs, New Jersey, Zeigler Coal Holdings Company, St. Louis. Trustee Business Council for United Nations, Boys Clubs Am. Captain United States Marine Corps, 1946-49, 53-59. Recipient Naval Aviator award USN, Corpus Christi, Texas, 1955. Member Machinery and Allied Products Insustry Association (executive committee). Roman Catholic. Avocations: hunting, fishing, tennis, golf. Office: Ingersoll-Rand Company 200 Chestnut Ridge Road Woodcliff Lake New Jersey 07675

BLACKBURN, CHARLES LEE, oil company executive; born Cushing, Oklahoma, January 9, 1928; son of Samuel and Lillian (Beall) B.; married Mary Ann Bullock Colburn, July 14, 1984; children: Kern A., Alan J., Charles L., Derek R. Bachelor of Science in Engineering Physics, University Oklahoma, 1952. With Shell Oil Company, 1952-86, executive vice president exploration and production, 1976-86; president, chief executive officer Diamond Shamrock Corp. (name changed to Maxus Energy Corp., 1987), Dallas, 1987—; chairman, president, chief executive officer Maxus Energy Corp., 1987—. Served with United States Army, 1946-48. Member Am. Petroleum Institute (director), Society Petroleum Engineers, Mid-Continent Oil and Gas Association, Tau Beta Pi, Sigma Tau. Methodist. Clubs: Houston Country, Coronado; Dallas Country, Dallas Petroleum. Office: Maxus Energy Corp 717 N Harwood St Dallas Texas 75201

BLANKLEY, WALTER ELWOOD, manufacturing company executive; born Philadelphia, September 23, 1935; son of George William and Martha Emily (McCord) B.; married Rosemary Deniken, August 16, 1958; children: Stephen Michael, Laura

Ann. Bachelor of Science in Mechanical Engineering, Princeton University, 1957. Manager planning Ametek Hunter Spring, Hatfield, Pennsylvania, 1965-66, general manager, 1966-69; assistant to president Ametek, Incorporated, San Francisco, 1969-71; vice president Ametek, Incorporated, Watsonville, California, 1971-78, group vice president, 1978-82, senior vice president, 1982-90; president, chief executive officer Ametek, Incorporated, Paoli, Pennsylvania, 1990—; director Kinark Corp., Tulsa, 1988-90. Member Aluminum Extruders Council (president 1974-76, director 1971-78). Office: Ametek Incorporated Station Square Paoli Pennsylvania 19301

BLOCH, HENRY WOLLMAN, tax preparation company executive; born Kansas City, Missouri, July 30, 1922; son of Leon Edwin and Hortense Bienenstok; married Marion Ruth Helzberg, June 16, 1951; children: Robert, Thomas M., Mary Jo, Elizabeth Ann. Bachelor of Science, University Michigan, 1943; Doctor of Business Administration (honorary), Avila College, Kansas City, Missouri, 1977, University Missouri, Kansas City, 1989; Doctor of Laws (honorary), New Hampshire College, 1983. Partner United Business Company, 1946-55; president, chief executive officer H & R Block, Incorporated, Kansas City, 1955—, also director; director Commerce Bancshares, Incorporated, Kansas City, CompuServe, Incorporated; past director Southwestern Bell Corp., Jason Empire, Incorporated, The Vendo Company, Employers Reinsurance Corp., Commerce Bank Kansas City. Past trustee Clearinghouse for Midcontinent Founds.; past board of directors Menorah Medical Center; board of directors, past president Menorah Medical Center Foundation; former member president's adv. council Kansas City Philharmonic Association; chairman, director H & R Block Foundation; president of trustees U. Kansas City, Nelson-Atkins Mus. Art, chairman business council; former trustee Am. Mus. Association; board of directors Jewish Federation and Council Greater Kansas City; director, past president Civic Council Greater Kansas City; general chairman United Negro Colleges Fund, 1986; board of directors St. Luke's Hospital; former member board of directors Council of Fellows of Nelson Gallery Foundation, Am. Jewish Committee; former member board governors Kansas City Mus. History and Sci.; board of directors Midwest Research Institute, vice chairman; board of directors Kansas City Symphony, past director; board of directors Greater Kansas City Community Foundation; general chairman Heart of Am. United Way Executive Committee, 1978; past metropolitan chairman National Alliance Businessmen; former member board regents Rockhurst College; former member board chancellor's assocs. U. Kansas at Lawrence; former member board of directors Harry S. Truman Good Neighbor Award Foundation; board of directors International Rels. Council; board of directors, vice president Kansas City Area Health Planning Council; past president Foundation for a Greater Kansas City; director Mid-Am. Coalition on Health Care, St; Luke's Foundation; trustee Junior Achievement of Mid-Am.; vice chairman corp. fund Kennedy Center 1st lieutenant United States Army Air

Force, 1943-45. Decorated Air medal with 3 oak leaf clusters; named Marketing Man of Year Sales and Marketing Executives Club, 1971, Chief Executive Officer of Year for svc. industry Fin. World, 1976, Mainstreeter of Decade, 1988, Entrepreneur of Year, 1986; recipient Distinguished Executive award Boy Scouts Am., 1977, Salesman of Year Kansas City Advertising Club, 1978, Civic Service award Hyman Brand Hebrew Acad., 1980, Golden Plate award Am. Acad. Achievement, 1980, Chancellor's medal University Mo.-Kansas City, 1980, President's trophy Kansas City Jaycees, 1980, W.F. Yates medal for distinguished svc. in civic affairs William Jewell College, 1981, bronze award for svc. industry Wall Street Transcript, 1981, Distinguished Missourian award National Conference of Christians and Jews, 1982, Lester A. Milgram Humanitarian award, 1983, Hall of Fame award International Franchise Association, 1983; named to Business Leader Hall of Fame Junior Achievement, 1980. Member Greater Kansas City Chamber of Commerce (past president), Chamber of Commerce Greater Kansas City (Mr. Kansas City award 1978), Acad. Squires, Golden Key National Honor Society (hon.), Oakwood Country Club, River Club, Carriage Club, Kansas City Racquet Club. Jewish. Office: H&R Block Incorporated 4410 Main St Kansas City Missouri 64111

BLOOMFIELD, COLEMAN, insurance company executive; born Winnipeg, Manitoba, Canada, July 2, 1926; came to United States, 1952, naturalized, 1958; son of Samuel and Bessie (Staniloff) B.; married Shirley Rosenbaum, November 4, 1948; children: Catherine, Laura, Leon, Diane, Richard. Bachelor.Commerce, University Manitoba, 1948. With Commonwealth Life Insurance Company, Louisville, 1948-51; actuary, senior vice president Minnesota Mutual Life Insurance Company, St. Paul, 1952-70, executive vice president, 1970-71, president, chief executive officer, 1971—, chairman board, 1977—; director First Bank System, Incorporated. Board of directors Minnesota Orchestra Association; board of directors St. Paul United Way, Ordway Music Theatre. Fellow Society Actuaries. Office: The Minnesota Mut Life Ins Company 400 N Robert St Saint Paul Minnesota 55101

BLUHM, NEIL G., real estate company executive; born 1938; married. Bachelor of Science, University Illinois; Juris Doctor, Northwestern University. Bar: Illinois. Partner firm Mayer, Brown & Platt, Chicago, 1962-70; president JMB Realty Corp., Chicago, from 1970; president, trustee JMB Realty Trust, Chicago, 1972—. Office: JMB Realty Corp 900 N Michigan Avenue Chicago Illinois 60611

BLUMENTHAL, W. MICHAEL, manufacturing company executive, former secretary of treasury, investment banker; born 1926. Bachelor of Science, University California, Berkeley, 1951; Master of Arts, Master of Public Adminstration, Princeton University, 1953, Doctor of Philosophy, 1956. Research associate Princeton University, 1954-57; vice president, board of directors Crown Cork International Corp., 1957-61; deputy assistant secretary for economic affairs State Department, 1961; appointed Pres.'s deputy special representative for trade negotiations with rank of ambassador 1963-67; president Bendix International, 1967-70; also board of directors Bendix Corp., 1967-77, vice-chairman, 1970-71, president, chief operating officer, 1971-72, chairman, president, chief executive officer, 1972-77; secretary of Treasury Washington, 1977-79; also board of directors UNISYS Corp. (formerly Burroughs Corp.), Detroit, 1979—; vice-chairman, chief executive officer Unisys Corp. (formerly Burroughs Corp.), Detroit, 1980-81, chairman, chief executive officer, 1981-1990, chairman, 1990—; limited partner Lazard Fieres & Company; board of directors Tenneco, Incorporated. Board of directors Greater Philadelphia First Corp., The Philadelphia Orchestra, Detroit Renaissance, New Detroit, Detroit Symphony Orchestra; vice president, board of directors, member executive committee United Foundation Detroit. Member Business Council, Am. Econ. Association, U.S.-Japan Business Council (steering committee), Am.-China Society (board directors), Econ. Club Detroit (board directors). Office: Lazard Fieres & Company 1 Rockefeller Plaza New York New York 10020

BODMAN, SAMUEL W., III, specialty chemicals and materials company executive; born Chicago, November 26, 1938; son of Samuel W. Jr. and Lina (Lindsay) B.; children: Elizabeth L., Andrew M., Sarah H. Bachelor of Science in Chemical Engineering, Cornell University, 1961; Doctor of Science, Massachusetts Institute of Technology, 1964. Tech. director Am. Research and Devel., Boston, 1964-70; professor and lecturer Massachusetts Institute of Technology, Cambridge, Massachusetts, 1964-70; vice president Fidelity Venture Association, Boston, 1970-74; president Fidelity Venture Associates, 1974-77; chairman Fidelity Venture Association, 1977; president Fidelity Management & Research Company, Boston, 1976-86; president, chief operating officer FMR Corp., 1982-86; executive vice president, director Fidelity Group Mutual Funds, 1980-86; president, chief operating officer Cabot Corp., Waltham, Massachusetts, 1987-88, chairman, chief executive officer, 1988—; board of directors Cabot Corp., Bank of Boston Corp., Boston, Westvaco, Incorporated, New York, Am. Oil and Gas Corp., Cabot Oil & Gas Corp. Trustee, member executive committee Massachusetts Institute of Technology, Cambridge, Massachusetts; trustee MITRE Corp., Bedford, Massachusetts, Isabella Stewart Gardner Mus., Boston, New England Aquarium, Boston. Episcopalian. Home: 24 Chestnut St Boston Massachusetts 02108 Office: Cabot Corp 950 Winter St Waltham Massachusetts 02254-9073

BOESCHENSTEIN, WILLIAM WADE, glass products manufacturing executive; born Chicago, September 7, 1925; son of Harold and Elizabeth (Wade) B.; married Josephine H. Moll, November 28, 1953; children: William Wade, Michael M., Peter H., Stephen S. Student, Phillips Academy, 1944; Bachelor of Science, Yale, 1950. With Owens-Corning Fiberglas Corp., 1950-90, vice president central region, 1959-61, vice president sales branch operations, Toledo, 1961-63, vice president marketing, 1963-67, executive vice president, 1967-71, president, 1971-88, chief executive officer, from 1972, chairman, 1981-90, also board of directors; board of directors Prudential Insurance Company Am., Federal Maritime Commission Corp., Chicago. Trustee Toledo Mus. Art, Edison Institute. Member Business Council, Links Club, Toledo Club, Inverness Club, Belmont Country Club, Augusta National Golf Club. Home: 3 Locust St Perrysburg Ohio 43551 Office: Owens-Corning Fiberglas Corp Fiberglas Tower Toledo Ohio 43659

BOLDUC, J. P., energy products company executive; born 1940. Bachelor of Arts, St. Cloud State University. Assistant secretary United States Department Agriculture, Washington, until 1977; vice president Booz, Allen & Hamilton, New York City, 1977-83; senior vice president W.R. Grace & Company, New York City, 1983-86, executive vice president, chief fin. officer, 1986—. Office: W R Grace & Company 1114 Avenue of the Americas New York New York 10036

BOLINGBROKE, ROBERT A., consumer products company executive; born Rexburg, Idaho, May 2, 1938; son of Delbert Thomas and Ina Leota (Anderson) B.; married Marilyn Joan Wolfe, September 19, 1961; children: Debbie, Cindy, Tami. Bachelor of Arts, Washington State University, 1960; Master of Business Administration, Stanford University, 1962. With marketing department Clorox Company, Oakland, California, 1962-64, 68-72, vice president business devel., 1983-84, group vice president staff services, 1984-89, group vice president operations, 1989-90; with marketing department Procter & Gamble International, Rome, 1964-68; president, chief operating officer Clorox Company, Oakland, California, 1990—; general manager Grocery Stone Products div., West Chester, Pennsylvania, 1972-75, Household Products div., Oakland, 1975-76; vice president Kingsford div., Oakland, 1976-83. Treasurer Golden Gate Scouting, San Francisco, 1985-89, vice president, 1989-90, president, 1991—; member executive board of directors Mount Diablo council Boy Scouts Am., Walnut Creek, California, 1983—, president, 1981-83. Member Association for Corp. Growth, Round Hill Club (Alamo, California), Lakeview Club (Oakland). Member Church of Jesus Christ of Latter Day Saints. Office: The Clorox Company 1221 Broadway Oakland California 94612

BONI, ROBERT EUGENE, industrial company executive; born Canton, Ohio, February 18, 1928; son of Frank and Sara B.; married Janet Virginia Klotz, August 16, 1952; children: Susan, Leslie. Bachelor of Science in Metallurgical Engineering, University Cincinnati, 1951; Master of Science, Carnegie Institute Tech., 1954, Doctor of Philosophy, 1954. Research engineer Armco Incorporated, Middletown, Ohio, 1956-61, senior research engineer, 1961-68, manager applied sci., 1968-70, director metallurgical research, 1970-75, assistant vice president research and tech., 1976, vice president research and tech., 1976-78, group vice president material resources and strata energy, 1978-80, group vice president steel group, 1980-82, executive vice president, chief operating officer, 1982-83, president, chief executive officer, 1985-86; chairman, chief executive officer Armco Incorporated, Parsippany, New Jersey, 1986-90, chairman, 1990; board of directors Armco Incorporated, Maritrans GP Incorporated, Nova Pharmaceutical Corp., Alexander & Alexander Service. With United States Army, 1954-56. Recipient Distinguished Engineering Alumnus award University Cincinnati, 1970, ASM International medal for the advancement of rsch., 1990. Member American Institute of Mining, Metallurgy and Petroleum Engineers (Fairless award Iron & Steel Society of American Institute of Mining, Metallurgy and Petroleum Engineers 1987), Industrial Research Institute, Am. Iron and Steel Institute, Am. Iron and Steel Engineers, American Society for Testing and Materials, Welding Research Council. Office: care Personal Lines Ins 177 Madison Avenue Box 1277 Morristown New Jersey 07962-1277

BONNEY, WESTON LEONARD, bank executive; born Lewiston, Maine, September 9, 1925; son of Leonard W. and Olive (Jones) B.; married Elaine Gilbert, June 29, 1946; children—Melody Elaine, Merrilee, Michael, Melissa Jane. Bachelor of Arts in Economics, Bates College, Lewiston, 195O. With Union Mutual Life Insurance Company, 1950-52, Federal Reserve Bank Boston, 1952-63; corp. services officer First National Bank Boston, 1963-65; with Depositors Corp., Augusta, Maine, 1966-74; president Depositors Corp., 1970-74; also director; with Depositors Trust Company, Augusta, 1965-74; president, senior administrative officer Depositors Trust Company, 1967-71, president, chief executive officer, 1971-74, also director; president, director Cape Ann Bank & Trust Company, Gloucester, Massachusetts, 1975-78, Yankee Bancorp., Gloucester, 1975-76, Massachusetts Bay Bancorp, 1976-80, Bank of New England Bay State, Lawrence, Massachusetts, 1978-84; senior vice president, director Bank New England Corp., Boston, 1980-84; chief executive officer People's Heritage Savings Bank, Portland, Maine, 1985—, also chairman board of directors; president, chief executive officer Peoples Heritage Fin. Group Incorporated, Portland, Maine, 1985—; chairman board of directors Am. Management Group, Portland Glass Company; board of directors Drayton Company, Limited, Drayton Insurance Risk Retention Group, Limited. Trustee Bates College, Lewiston, Maine, 1969—, Portland Symphony Orchestra, 1985—; board of directors United Way, Portland, Maine, 1987; member president's adv. council U. Southern Maine, 1986—; board of directors Maine Devel. Foundation, 1987—; member chief executive officers adv. board Maine Council on Economic Education, 1986—; member U. Maine Commission on Pluralism; director National Council Savs. Instns.; member Special Commission Restructuring State Gout, Maine. Served with United States Naval Reserve, 1943-46. Member Savings Bank Association Maine (executive committee 1985—, vice chairman 1986-87, chairman 1987-88), Greater Portland Chamber of Commerce (board directors 1988—). Home: 11 Wildwood Circle Alden's Walk Portland Maine 04103 Office: Peoples Heritage Savings Bank 1 Portland Square Portland Maine 04112

BOOTH, I(SRAEL) MACALLISTER, photographic products company executive; born Atlanta, December 7, 1931; son of Charles Victor and Charlotte Ann (Beattie) B.; married

Frances Marie Henry, September 22, 1956; children—David M., Thomas H., Mary E., Charlotte M. Bachelor of Mechanical Engineering, Cornell University, 1955, Master of Business Administration, 1958. With Polaroid Corp., Cambridge, Massachusetts, 1958—, vice president, 1976-78, executive vice president, 1980-84, chief operating officer, 1982-86, president, 1984—, chief executive officer, 1986—, also board of directors. Served to captain United States Air Force, 1955-57. Episcopalian. Office: Polaroid Corp 549 Technology Square Cambridge Massachusetts 02139

BOOTH, RICHARD H., insurance company executive. Vice chairman, chief investment officer The Travelers Corp, Hartford, Connecticut, until 1991; president, chief operating officer The Travelers Corp, Hartford, 1991—. Office: The Travelers Corp 1 Tower Square Hartford Connecticut 06183

BORCHELT, MERLE LLOYD, electric utility company executive; born Mercedes, Texas, January 4, 1926; son of George Cornelius and Pauline Caroline (Lange) B.; married Virginia Mae Gullatt, August 3, 1947; children: Lawrence Frederick, Linda Diane, Mark Randall. Bachelor of Science in Electrical Engineering, Louisiana Tech. University, 1949; postgraduate, Westinghouse Advanced Electric Utility Program, 1958, Harvard University Advanced Management Program, 1983. Registered professional engineer, Texas. With Central Power & Light Company, Corpus Christi, Texas, from 1949, general manager fuels-systems planning, 1975-77, vice president, 1977-79, executive vice president, chief engineer, 1979-81, president, chief executive officer, from 1981, also board of directors; vice chairman, director Central & Southwest Corp., Dallas, 1986-88, chairman, chief executive officer, 1988—; president Central & Southwest Corp., 1988-90; also chairman Central & Southwest Services Incorporated (subsidiary Central & Southwest Corp.), Dallas. Chairman United Way of Coastal Bend, 1982, 84, United Way of Metropolitan Dallas (director 1988), Boy Scouts Am., Circle 10 Council (executive board); member adv. council College Natural Scis. Foundation, U. Texas, Austin; board of directors, past president Texas Association Taxpayers. Served with United States Navy, 1943-45. Member Institute of Electrical and Electronics Engineers (president Corpus Christi chapter), Edison Electric Institute (director), Texas Atomic Energy Research Foundation (director), Electric Power Research Institute (director), South Texas Foundation Econ. Education, Association Electric Companies Texas (director 1980—). Office: Central & Southwest Corp Post Office Box 660164 Dallas Texas 75266-0164

BORMAN, FRANK, former astronaut, laser patent company executive; born Gary, Indiana, March 14, 1928; son of Edwin Borman; married Susan Bugbee; children: Fredrick, Edwin. Bachelor of Science, United States Military Academy, 1950; Master Aeronautical Engineering, California Institute Tech., 1957; graduate, United States Air Force Aerospace Research Pilots School, 1960, Advanced Management Program, Harvard Business School, 1970. Commissioned 2d lieutenant United States Air Force, advanced through grades to colonel, 1965, retired, 1970; assigned various fighter squadrons United States and Philippines, 1951-56; instructor thermodynamics and fluid mechanics United States Military Acad., 1957-60; instructor United States Air Force Aerospace Research Pilots School, 1960-62; astronaut Manned Spacecraft Center, National Aeronautics and Space Administration, until 1970; command pilot on 14 day orbital Gemini 7 flight December 1965, including rendezvous with Gemini 6; command pilot Apollo 8, 1st lunar orbital mission, December 1968; senior vice president for operations Eastern Air Lines, Incorporated, Miami, Florida, 1970-74, executive vice president, general operations manager, 1974-75, president, chief executive officer, 1975-85, chief executive officer, 1975-86, chairman board, 1976-86; vice chairman, director Texas Air Corp., Houston, from 1986; now chairman, chief executive officer, director Patlex Corp., Las Cruces, New Mexico. Recipient Distinguished Service award National Aeronautics and Space Administration, 1965; Collier Trophy. National Aeros. Association, 1968. Office: Patlex Corp 250 Cotorro Court Las Cruces New Mexico 88005

BORN, ALLEN, mining executive; born Durango, Colorado, July 4, 1933; son of C. S. and Bertha G. (Tausch) B.; married Patricia Beaubien, March 23, 1953; children—Michael, Scott, Brett. Bachelor of Science in Metallurgy and Geology, University Tex.-El Paso, 1958. Exploration geologist El Paso Natural Gas, Texas, 1958-60; metallurgist Vanadium Corp. Am., 1960-62; general foreman Pima Mining, 1962-64; assistant superintendent MolyCorp, 1964-67; chief metallurgist and superintendent, manager AMAX Incorporated, Greenwich, Connecticut, 1967-76, president, chief operating officer, 1985—, chief executive officer, 1986—, chairman, 1988—; president, chief executive officer Can. Tungsten Mining Corp. Limited, 1976-81; president AMAX of Can. Limited, 1977-81; president, chairman, chief executive officer Placer Devel. Limited, Vancouver, British Columbia, Can., 1981-85; chairman board Alumax, Incorporated, Amax Gold, Incorporated; board of directors Can. Tungsten Mining Corp., Aztec Mining Company Limited, Australia, Aztec Resources. Contributor numerous articles to mining journals. Served with United States Army, 1952-55. Named Chief Executive Officer of Year in mining industry, silver award winner all industry Financial World magazine, 1987; recipient Golden Nugget award College Sci. University Texas at El Paso, Daniel C. Jackling award Society Mining Engineers, Business Leader award Citizens Union of New York City, 1990. Member American Institute of Mining, Metallurgy and Petroleum Engineers, Am. Mining Congress (chmn.-elect, chairman fin. committee, board directors), Sky Club (New York City), Indian Harbor Yacht Club, Vancouver Club. Republican. Office: Amax Incorporated 200 Park Avenue Post Office Box 1700 New York New York 10166 also: Alumax Incorporated 400 S El Camino Real San Mateo California 94402

BOSKIN, MICHAEL JAY, economist, government official, university educator, consultant; born New York City, September 23, 1945; son of

Irving and Jean B.; married Chris Dornin, October 20, 1981. Bachelor of Arts with highest honors, University California, Berkeley, 1967, Master of Arts in Economics, 1968, Doctor of Philosophy in Economics, 1971. Assistant professor Stanford (California) University, 1970-75, associate professor, 1976-78, professor, 1978—, director Center for Economic Policy Research, 1986-89, Wohlford professor economics, 1987-89; chairman Pres.'s Council Economic Advisors, The White House, Washington, 1989—; visiting professor Harvard University, Cambridge, Massachusetts, 1977-78; consultant in field. Author: Too Many Promises: The Uncertain Future of Social Secruity, 1986, Reagan and the Economy: Successes, Failures Unfinished Agenda, 1987; contributor articles to professional journals. Faculty Rsch. fellow Mellon Foundation, 1973; recipient Outstanding Rsch. award National Association Business Economists, 1987. Avocations: tennis, skiing, reading, theater. Office: The White House Coun Econ Advisers 1600 Pennsylvania Avenue Washington District of Columbia 20500

BOSSIDY, LAWRENCE ARTHUR, utility company executive; born Pittsfield, Massachusetts, March 5, 1935; married Nancy, 1956; children: Lynn, Larry, Paul, Pam, Nancy, Mary Jane, Lucy, Michael, Kathleen. Bachelor of Arts in Economics, Colgate University. With General Electric Company 1957—; former executive vice president, sector executive services and materials General Electric Company, Fairfield, Connecticut, 1981-84, vice chairman, director, New York City, 1984—; now vice chairman, director General Electric Company Investment Corp., General Electric Company Industrial and Power systems, General Electric Company Lighting, General Electric Company Motors, General Electric Company Electrical Distribution and Control, General Electric Company Can. Incorporated, General Electric Company Communications and Services, Ladd Petroleum Corp., General Electric Company Fin. Services Incorporated, General Electric Company Capital Corp., Employers Reinsurance Corp., Kidder Peabody; member adv. committee on Trade policy and Negotiations, 1987 (chairman Europe 1992 task force); member Elfun. Roman Catholic. Office: General Electric Company Capital Corp 3135 Easton Turnpike Fairfield Connecticut 06431

BOTTORFF, DENNIS C., banker; born Clarksville, Indiana, September 19, 1944; son of Irvin H. and Lucille H. B.; married Jean Brewington, August 21, 1964; children: Todd, Chad. Bachelor of Education, Vanderbilt University, 1966; Master of Business Administration, Northwestern University, Evanston, Illinois, 1968. President Commerce Union Bank, Nashville; also executive vice president Commerce Union Corp., Nashville; chairman, chief executive officer Commerce Union Bank and Commerce Union Corp., Nashville, 1984-87; vice chairman, chief operating officer Sovran Fin. Corp., Norfolk, Virginia, 1988-89, president, chief operating officer, 1989-90; president, chief operating officer C&S/Sovran Corp., Norfolk, Virginia, 1990—, C&S/Sovran Corp. (merger Citizens & Southern Corp. and Sovran Fin. Corp. 1990), 1990—; board advisors The Jack C. Massey Grad. School of Business (Belmont

College, Nashville); trustee Committee for Economic Devel.; member Association of Reserve City Bankers, Young Presidents' Organization; board of directors Shoney's Incorporated. Board of directors Virginia Symphony; member board of trust Vanderbilt U., Nashville. Member Hampton Roads Chamber of Commerce, Farmington (Virginia) Country Club, The Harbor Club, Town Point Club (Norfolk), Princess Anne Country Club (Virginia Beach, Virginia), Belle Meade Country Club, Cumberland Club, Commerce Club (Atlanta). Presbyterian. Home: 600 55th St Virginia Beach Virginia 23451 Office: C&S/Sovran Corp Sovran Center 1 Commercial Place Norfolk Virginia 23510

BOULDING, KENNETH EWART, economist, educator; born Liverpool, England, January 18, 1910; came to United States, 1937, naturalized, 1948; son of William Couchman and Elizabeth Ann (Rowe) B.; married Elise Bjorn-Hansen, August 31, 1941; children: Russell, Mark, Christine, Philip, William. Student, Oxford University, 1928-32, Bachelor of Arts with 1st class honors, 1931, Master of Arts, 1939; postgraduate, University Chicago, 1932-34; over 30 honorary degrees. Assistant University Edinburgh, Scotland, 1934-37; instructor Colgate University, 1937-41; economist League of Nations Economic and Fin. Section, 1941-42; professor Fisk University, 1942-43; associate professor Iowa State College, 1943-46, professor, 1947-49; Angus professor political economy McGill University, 1946-47; professor economics University Michigan, 1949-68, research director Center for Research in Conflict Resolution, 1964-66; visiting professor University Colorado, Boulder, 1967-68, professor, 1968-77, distinguished professor, 1977-80, distinguished professor emeritus, 1980—, director program on general social and economic dynamics Institute Behavioral Sci., 1967-81, research associate, project director program on political and economic change, 1981—; visiting professor University College West Indies, Kingston, Jamaica, 1959-60, University Natal, 1970, University Edinburgh, fall 1972, Joseph H. Lauder Institute, University Pennsylvania, June 1984, Butler University, fall 1984, University Colorado, fall 1986, Adlai East Stevenson College, University California, Santa Cruz, spring 1987, Fort Lewis College, Durango, Colorado, spring 1987; Danforth visiting professor International Christian University, Tokyo, 1963-64; visiting lecturer Japanese Broadcasting Company, Tokyo, 1970, Patten lecturer Ind. University, Bloomington, fall 1973; Andrew D. White prof.-at-large Cornell University, 1974-79; Barnette Miller visiting professor Wellesley College, fall 1975; Distinguished Visiting Tom Slick professor world peace L.B. Johnson School, University Texas, Austin, 1976-77; Montgomery visiting professor Dartmouth College, fall 1978; distinguished visiting professor School Pub. Administration, Ohio State University, spring 1981; Winegard visiting professor University Guelph, Ontario, Can., fall 1981; Downing fellow Melbourne (Australia) University, spring 1982; Eugene M. Lang visiting professor social change Swarthmore College, 1982-83; A. Lindsay O'Connor visiting professor Am. institutions Colgate University, fall 1983; 1st visiting scholar United Nations University, Tokyo, spring

1984; Aspinall visiting professor Mesa College, Apr. 1984; Mitchell distinguished visiting professor Trinity University, spring 1985; distinguished visiting professor, George Mason University, fall 1985; visiting scholar Russell Sage Foundation, New York, spring 1986; friend in residence Pendle Hill, Wallingford, Pennsylvania, fall 1988; Hitchcock visiting professor University California, 1989; Robinson visiting professor George Mason University, Fall 1989. Author: Economic Analysis, 1941, 4th rev. edition, 1966, Economics of Peace, 1945, reissued, 1972, There is a Spirit (The Naylor Sonnets), 1945, A Reconstruction of Economics, 1950, The Organizational Revolution, 1953, reissued, 1984, The Image, 1956, Principles of Economic Policy, 1958, The Skills of the Economist, 1958, Conflict and Defense, 1962, reissued, 1988, The Meaning of the Twentieth Century, 1964, reissued, 1988, The Impact of the Social Sciences, 1966, Beyond Economics, 1968, Economics as a Science, 1970, reissued, 1988, A Primer on Social Dynamics, 1970, The Prospering of Truth (Swarthmore Lecture), 1970, Collected Papers, Volumes 1-5, 1971-75, Volume 6, 1985, The Appraisal of Change (in Japanese), 1972, The Economy of Love and Fear, 1973, Sonnets from the Interior Life and Other Autobiographical Verse, 1975, Stable Peace, 1978, Ecodynamics, 1978, Beasts, Ballads and Bouldingisms, 1980, Evolutionary Economics, 1981, A Preface to Grants Economics, 19, Human Betterment, 1985, The World as a Total System, 1985, Three Faces of Power, 1989; author: (with Elise Boulding and Guy M. Burgess) The Social System of Planet Earth, 1977, 80; editor: (with George J. Stigler) Readings in Price Theory, 1952; (with W.A. Spivey) Linear Programming and the Theory of the Firm, 1960; (with Emile Benoit) Disarmament and the Economy, 1963; Peace and the War Industry, 1970, 73; (with Tapan Mukerjee) Economic Imperialism, 1972; (with Martin Pfaff) Redistribution to the Rich and the Poor, 1972; (with Martin and Anita Pfaff) Transfers in an Urbanized Economy, 1973; (with Thomas F. Wilson) Redistribution through the Financial System, 1978; (with H.R. Porter) General Systems Yearbook, volume 23, 1979; (with Lawrence Senesh) The Optimum Utilization of Knowledge: Making Knowledge Serve Human Betterment, 1983; edited The Economics of Human Betterment, 1984; Bibliography of Published Works by Kenneth E. Boulding (1932-84) compiled by Vivian L. Wilson, 1985. Recipient prize for distinguished scholarship in humanities Am. Council Learned Socs., 1962, Frank E. Seidman Distinguished award in political economy, 1976, Rufus Jones award World Acad. Art and Sci., 1979, John R. Commons award Omicron Delta Epsilon, 1985, (with Elise Boulding) 18th Boise Peace Quilt, 1988, co-recipient Lentz International Peace Rsch. award, 1976; Commonwealth fellow University Chicago, 1932-34; fellow Center Advanced Study Behvior Sciences, Palo Alto, California, 1954-55. Fellow Am. Acad. Arts and Sciences, Am. Philosophical Society, Brit Acad. (corr.); member Am. Econ. Association (John B. Clark medal 1949, president 1968), National Academy of Sciences (senior member Institute Medicine), Society General Systems Research (president 1957-59, Leadership award 1984), International Studies Association (vice president 1969-70, president 1974-75), American Association for the Advancement of Science (vice president, chairman section K 1966-67, president 1979, chairman board directors 1980), Peace Research Society International (president 1969-70), Association Study Grants Economy (president 1969-89), Brit. Association Advancement of Sci. (president section on econs. 1982-83). Democrat. Member Society of Friends. Avocations: poetry, sketching, water-colors. Home: 624 Pearl St #206 Boulder Colorado 80302 Office: U Colorado Institute Behavioral Sci Campus Box 483 Boulder Colorado 80309

BOURKE, WILLIAM OLIVER, metals company executive; born Chicago, April 12, 1927; son of Robert Emmett and Mable Elizabeth (D'Arcy) B.; married Elizabeth Philbey, September 4, 1970; children: William Oliver, Judith A., Andrew E., Edward A. Student, University Illinois, 1944-45; Bachelor of Science in Commerce, DePaul University, 1951. With Ford Motor Company, Dearborn, Michigan, 1956-60, national distribution manager, 1960-64; general sales manager Ford Can., Toronto, Ontario, 1964-67; assistant managing director Ford Australia, Melbourne, 1967-70, manager director, 1970-71; president Ford Asia-Pacific and South Africa, Incorporated, Melbourne, 1971-72, Ford Asia-Pacific, Incorporated, Melbourne, 1972-73; president Europe, Incorporated, 1973-75, chairman board, 1975-80; executive vice president Ford North America Automotive Operations, Dearborn, 1980-81, also board of directors; executive vice president Reynolds Metals Company, Richmond, Virginia, 1981-83, president, chief operating officer, 1983-86, president, chief executive officer, 1986-88, chairman board, chief executive officer, 1988—, also chairman board of directors, also board of directors; board of directors Premark International, Incorporated, Merrill Lynch, Sonat, Incorporated. 1st lieutenant Military Intelligence United States Army, 1944-48. Member United States Chamber of Commerce (board directors). Office: Reynolds Metals Company 6601 Broad Street Road Richmond Virginia 23261 also: Can Reynolds Metals Company Limited, 420 Sherbrooke St W, Montreal, Province of Quebec Canada H3G 1K9

BOWER, MARVIN D., insurance company executive; born Stanford, Illinois, July 20, 1924; son of Charles Howard and Marjorie Dale (Garst) B.; married Mari Morrissey, June 1, 1946 (deceased 1981); children: Stacie Bower Killian, Jim Pete, Molly, Tom, John; married Carolyn Paine Newland, April 24, 1983; stepchildren: Linda Gleason, Lori Lorenz, Leslie Harris, William David. Bachelor of Philosophy, Illinois Wesleyan University, 1948. C.L.U. Agent Northwestern Mutual Life, Bloomington, Illinois, 1949-52; with State Farm Life Insurance Company, 1952—; secretary for Can. State Farm Life Insurance Company, Toronto, 1955-58; executive vice president, secretary State Farm Life and Accident Assurance Company, 1961-91, also board of directors; vice president health State Farm Mutual Auto Insurance Company, 1968-91; executive vice president State Farm Life Insurance Company, Bloomington, Illinois, 1973-91, chairman board, 1985—, also director. Served to captain Army of the United States,

1943-46. Fellow Life Office Management Institute; member Phi Gamma Delta. Home: Rural Route 2 Box 56 Hudson Illinois 61748 Office: State Farm Life Ins Company 1 State Farm Plaza Bloomington Illinois 61710

BOWLEN, PATRICK DENNIS, holding company executive, lawyer; born Prairie du Chien, Wisconsin, February 18, 1944; son of Paul Dennis and Arvella (Woods) B. Bachelor of Business Administration, University Oklahoma, 1966, Juris Doctor, 1968. Bar: Alberta 1969. Read law Saucier, Jones, Calgary, Alberta, Can., associate, 1969-70; assistant to president Regent Drilling Limited, 1970-71; president Batoni-Bowlen Enterprises Limited, 1971-79, Bowlen Holdings Limited, Edmonton, Alberta, Can., 1979—; president, chief executive officer, owner Denver Broncos, 1984—. Member Law Society Alberta, Can. Bar Association, Young Presidents Organization. Roman Catholic. Clubs: Mayfair Golf and Country; Edmonton Petroleum; Outrigger Canoe (Honolulu). Avocations: golf, skiing, surfing. Office: Denver Broncos 5700 Logan St Denver Colorado 80216 also: Denver Broncos 13665 E Dove Valley Parkway Englewood Colorado 80112

BOZZONE, ROBERT P., steel company executive; born 1933; married; 3 children. Bachelor of Science, Rensselaer Poly Tech. Institute, 1955. With Allegheny Ludlum Steel Corp., Pittsburgh, 1955—, former vice president, general manager, former executive vice president, general manager, now president, chief operating officer, from 1985, also board of directors. Office: Allegheny Ludlum Steel Corp 1000 6th PPG Place Pittsburgh Pennsylvania 15222

BRADDOCK, RICHARD S., banker; born Oklahoma City, November 30, 1941; son of Robert L. and Mary Alice (Krueger) B.; married Susan Schulte, February 14, 1978; 1 child, Christina; children by previous marriage: Jennifer, Richard, Derek. Bachelor of Arts, Dartmouth College, 1963; Master of Business Administration, Harvard Business School, 1965. Member marketing staff General Foods, White Plains, New York, 1965-73; member staff Citicorp, New York City, 1973—, sector executive in charge of worldwide consumer fin. services, information business, investor relations, corp. pub. affairs, customer affairs, corp. advertising, 1985-90, also board of directors; president Citibank/Citicorp, New York City, 1990—; board of directors Eastman Kodak. Board of directors Cancer Research Institute, New York City, Lincoln Center, New York City Partnership; member Council on Fgn Rels. Member New York Chamber of Commerce (board directors). Office: Citicorp 399 Park Avenue New York New York 10043

BRADFORD, WILLIAM EDWARD, oilfield equipment manufacturing company executive; born Dallas, January 8, 1935; married JoDeane Browning, August 18, 1955; children: William B., A. Kathleen, Jon E. Bachelor of Science in Geology, Centenary College, 1958; graduate exec. devel. course, Texas Agricultural and Mechanical University, 1975. Salesman Hycalog, Incorporated, 1958-61; vice president, general partner Analytical Logging, Incorporated, 1961-70; with Dresser Industries, Incorporated, 1970—, director, president, 1979-80, group president, 1980-83, vice president operations, 1983-84, senior vice president, 1984—; president, chief executive officer Dresser Rand, Corning, New York. Member Society Petroleum Engineers, Am. Association Petroleum Geologists, Petroleum Equipment Suppliers Association, American Association for the Advancement of Science, Association Oilwell Drilling Contractors, International Petroleum Association, National Ocean Industries Association, Texas Mid-Continentant Oil and Gas Association. Republican. Presbyterian. Clubs: Petroleum, Raveneaux Country, Houston, University (Houston); Champions Golf, Heritage. Office: Dresser Rand Baron Steuben Place Suite 500 Corning New York 14830

BRADY, NICHOLAS FREDERICK, secretary of the treasury; born New York City, April 11, 1930; son of James C. and Eliot (Chace) B.; married Katherine Douglas, September 5, 1952; children: Nicholas Frederick, Christopher D., Anthony N., Katherine C. Bachelor of Arts, Yale University, 1952; Master of Business Administration, Harvard University, 1954. With Dillon Read & Company Incorporated, New York City, 1954-82, former chairman, chief executive officer, from 1982; former director, chairman executive committee Purolator Courier Corp. Incorporated, Basking Ridge, New Jersey, from 1983; appointee to United States Senate from New Jersey to fill unexpired term of Harrison Williams 1982, resigned, December 1982; secretary Department of the Treasury, Washington, 1988—; director Bessemer Securities Corp., Doubleday & Company, Georgia International Corp., Wolverne World Wide Incorporated, ASA Limited, Media General Incorporated, NCR Corp. Trustee associate Boys' Club Newark.; Reagan appointee MX missile devel. options panel, Central Am. Study Commission, 1983. Clubs: Bond (New York City), Lunch (New York City) (board governors), Links (New York City). Office: Treasury Department 15th & Pennsylvania Aves Northwest Washington District of Columbia 20220

BRANDON, EDWARD BERMETZ, banker; born Davenport, Iowa, September 15, 1931; son of William McKinley and Mary Elizabeth (Bermetz) B.; married Phyllis Anne Probeck, August 7, 1954; children: William M., Robert P., Beverly A., Beth A., E. Matthew. Bachelor of Science, Northwestern University, 1953; Master of Business Administration, Wharton School Banking & Fin., 1956. Management trainee National City Bank, Cleveland, 1956-61, senior vice president, corp. banking head, 1978-79, executive vice president corp. banking group, 1979-82, vice chairman, 1982-83, president, 1984-87, chief executive officer, 1985-89; executive vice president National City Corp., 1982-83, president, director, 1986-88, chairman, chief executive officer, 1987—, director, 1986—; board of directors Standard Products Company, RPM, Incorporated, Premier Industrial Corp. Trustee Notre Dame College of Ohio; trustee St. Vincent Charity Hospital, John Carroll U., North Coast Harbor, Incorporated, National Conference of Christians and Jews, Greater Cleveland Growth Association, Leadership Cleveland, Playhouse Square Foundation, Cleveland Tomorrow, United Way Svcs., Cleveland Orchestra Lieutenant United States

Navy, 1953-55; chairman board trustees Cleveland Devel. Part. Member Am. Bankers Association (board directors), Association Reserve City Bankers (board directors), Association Bank Holding Companies (board directors), International Monetary Conference, Union Club, Shaker Heights Country Club, Firestone Country Club, Pepper Pike Club, 50 Club, Tavern Club, Kirtland Country Club. Republican. Methodist. Office: National City Corp 1900 E 9th St Cleveland Ohio 44114-3484

BRANNON, TERENCE C., bank executive; born Mobile, Alabama, January 1, 1938; married Sybil Jean Brown, June 7, 1958; 1 child, J. Michael Brannon. Bachelor of Arts in Economics and Business Administration, Birmingham Southern College, 1960. Vice president Central Bank of South, Birmingham, Alabama, 1970-74, senior vice president, 1974-75; president Central Bank of South, Birmingham, 1977-88, also board of directors, vice chairman, 1989—; executive vice president Central Bancshares of South, Incorporated, Birmingham, 1975-77, president, 1977-88. Board of directors Salvation Army, Birmingham, 1984—; former director Birmingham Association of Home Builders; former director American Red Cross. Republican. Methodist. Avocations: travel, fishing, reading. Home: 3553 Hampshire Dr Birmingham Alabama 35223 Office: Central Bank of the South 701 S 20th St Birmingham Alabama 35233

BRAZIER, ROBERT G., transportation executive. Student, Stanford University. With Airbone Aircraft Service Incorporated, 1953-63; vice president operations Pacific Air Freight Incorporated, 1963-68; senior vice president operations Airbone Freight Corp., Seattle, 1968-73, executive vice president, chief operating officer, 1973-78, president, chief operating officer, director, 1978—. Office: Airborne Freight Corp Post Office Box 662 Seattle Washington 98111

BREEDEN, RICHARD C., federal agency administrator. Chairman Securities and Exchange Commission, Washington. Office: Securities and Exchange Commission Office of the Chairman 450 5th St Northwest Washington District of Columbia 20549

BREEN, JOHN GERALD, manufacturing company executive; born Cleveland, July 21, 1934; son of Hugh Gerald and Margaret Cecelia (Bonner) B.; married Mary Jane Brubach, April 12, 1958; children: Kathleen Anne, John Patrick, James Phillip, David Hugh, Anne Margaret. Bachelor of Science, John Carroll University, 1956; Master of Business Administration, Case Western Reserve University, 1961. With Clevite Corp., Cleveland, 1957-73, general manager foil div., 1969-73, general manager engine parts div., 1973-74; group vice president industrial group Gould Incorporated, Rolling Meadows, Illinois, 1974-77, executive vice president, 1977-79; president Sherwin Williams Company, Cleveland, 1979-86, chief executive officer, 1979—, chairman, 1980—, also director; director Parker Hannifin Corp., Cleveland, National City Bank, Cleveland, Mead Corp., Dayton, Ohio. Served with United States Army, 1956-57. Clubs: Pepper Pike, Union, Cleveland Skating. Home: 2727 Cranlyn Road Shaker Heights Ohio 44122 Office: Sherwin-Williams

Company 101 Prospect Avenue Northwest Cleveland Ohio 44115

BREEZLEY, ROGER LEE, banker; born Williston, North Dakota, April 1, 1938. Bachelor of Business Administration, University North Dakota. C.P.A., Oregon. Accountant Haskins & Sells, 1960-68; president Moduline International Incorporated, 1968-77; with United States Bancorp, Portland, Oregon, 1977—, with corp. devel. and fin. analysis departments, 1977-79, senior vice president fin. analysis planning, 1979-80, executive vice president, 1980-82, treasurer, 1980-87, vice chairman, 1982-87, chief operating officer, 1983-87, director, chairman, chief executive officer, 1987—. Office: United States Bancorp United States Bancorp Tower 111 Southwest 5th Avenue Post Office Box 8837 Portland Oregon 97208

BRENDSEL, LELAND C., federal mortgage company executive. married. Doctor in Fin., Northwestern University; prof., University Utah. Professor University Utah; economist Farm Credit Banks, Federal Home Loan Bank, Des Moines; executive vice president, chief fin. officer Federal Home Loan Mortgage Corp., Washington, 1982, president, chief executive officer. Office: Federal Home Loan Mortgage Corp 1759 Business Center Dr Post Office Box 4112 Reston Virginia 22090

BRENGEL, FRED LENHARDT, manufacturing company executive; born Hicksville, New York, March 31, 1923; son of Henry C. and Anna (Jones) B.; married Joan E. Brengel, December 4, 1948; children: Douglas, Edith, Kenneth. Bachelor of Science in Mechanical Engineering, Stevens Institute Tech., 1944, Doctor Engineering (honorary), 1982. With Johnson Controls Incorporated (formerly Johnson Service Company), Milwaukee, 1948—, vice president sales, 1965-67, president, 1967-86, chief executive officer, 1967-88, chairman, 1985—, also director; board of directors Firststar, Heil Company, Harley-Davidson. Chairman Junior Achievement Southeast Wisconsin, Milwaukee, 1987, NEMA, Washington, 1970-88, NAM, Washington, 1985-88. Served to lieutenant United States Navy, 1943-46. Member Milwaukee Association Commerce (chairman 1985), Town Club, Milwaukee Country Club, Milwaukee Club, Jupiter Hills Club. Republican. Avocations: golf, tennis, skiing.

BRENNAN, BERNARD FRANCIS, retail chain store executive; born Chicago, 1938; married. Bachelor of Arts, College St. Thomas, 1964. With Sears, Roebuck & Company, Chicago, 1964-76; with Sav-A-Stop, Incorporated, 1976-82, group v.p.-service merchandise group, 1976-78, president, chief operating officer, 1978-79, president, chief executive officer, 1979-82, chairman, 1982; executive vice president Montgomery Ward & Company, Incorporated, Chicago, 1982-83, president, chief executive officer, 1985—; president Household Merchandising Incorporated, Des Plaines, Illinois, 1983-85. Served with United States Army, 1958-60, 62. Office: Montgomery Ward & Company Incorporated 1 Montgomery Ward Plaza Chicago Illinois 60671

BRENNAN, DONALD P., investment company executive; born New York City, December 31, 1940; son of Patrick James and Mary B.; married Patricia A. Callahan, September 22,

1962; children: Eileen, Donald, Maureen, Patrick, Jonathan, Erin. Bachelor of Science in Marine Sci, Maritime College, 1961; Master of Business Administration in Management Sci, City University of New York, 1966; postgraduate in operations research, Baruch School, 1967-70. Senior planning analyst Corning Glass Work, New York, 1966-67; with International Paper Company, 1967-82; executive vice president planning and administration International Paper Company, New York City, 1977; executive vice president paper and packaging business International Paper Company, 1977-82, vice-chairman, 1980-82; vice-chairman, director Can. International Paper Company, 1980-82; adviser, then managing director Morgan Stanley & Company, 1982—; chairman, director Bodcaw Company; Trustee Mary Baldwin College; member President's Commission on Executive Exchange, 1977—, Ireland-U.South Council Commerce and Industry; member dean's adv. council Purdue University. Served with United States Navy, 1961-66. Member Beta Gamma Sigma (dir.'s table). Home: Foxmount Hoagland's Lane Old Brookville New York 11545 Office: Morgan Stanley & Company 1251 Avenue of the Americas New York New York 10020

BRENNAN, EDWARD A., retail and financial services executive; born Chicago, January 16, 1934; son of Edward and Margaret (Bourget) B.; married Lois Lyon, June 11, 1955; children: Edward J., Cynthia Walls, Sharon Lisnow, Donald A., John L., Linda. Bachelor of Arts, Marquette University, Milwaukee, 1955. With Sears, Roebuck and Company, 1956—; executive vice president Southern terr. Sears, Roebuck and Company, Atlanta, 1978-80; president, chief operating officer for merchandising Sears, Roebuck and Company, Chicago, 1980-81, chairman board, chief executive officer merchandise group, 1981-84, president, chief operating officer, 1984-86, chairman, president, chief executive officer, 1986—; board of directors Minnesota Mining & Manufacturing Company. Trustee, Marquette U., De Paul U., Rush-Presbyn.-St. Luke's Medical Center, Chicago Mus. Sci. and Industry; member Chicago Urban League, 1980—, The Sears Roebuck Foundation; chairman board governors United Way Am. Member Business Roundtable, Conference Board, Business Council, Commercial Club. Office: Sears Roebuck & Company Sears Tower Chicago Illinois 60684

BRENNAN, PATRICK FRANCIS, printing paper manufacturing executive; born New York City, August 1, 1931; son of Patrick F. and Mary Ellen (Costello) B.; married Barbara Fleischman; children: Sean, Peter, Gerald. Graduate, Fordham University, 1957; Advanced Management Cert., Harvard University, 1983. District manager Consolidated Papers, Incorporated, New York City, 1963-67; regional manager Consolidated Papers, Incorporated, Chicago, 1967-71, national sales manager, 1971-76, vice president sales, 1976-84; executive vice president Consolidated Papers, Incorporated, Wisconsin Rapids, Wisconsin, 1984-88, president, 1988—; board of directors Consolidated Water Power Company, Wisconsin Rapids, Mead Realty, Wisconsin Rapids, Northland Cranberries, Incorporated; board of directors paper sci. and engineering University Minnesota College Natural Resources. Member Am. Paper Institute (vice chairman printing and writing division 1991—), Rotary, Bulls Eye Country Club (Wisconsin Rapids) (board directors 1988—). Office: Consol Papers Incorporated 231 1st Avenue N Post Office Box 8050 Wisconsin Rapids Wisconsin 54494

BRESSLER, RICHARD MAIN, railroad executive; born Wayne, Nebraska, October 8, 1930; son of John T. and Helen (Main) B.; married Dianne G. Pearson, April 17, 1981; children: Kristin M., Alan L. Bachelor of Arts, Dartmouth College, 1952. With General Electric Company, 1952-68; vice president, treasurer Am. Airlines Incorporated, 1968-72, senior vice president, 1972-73; vice president finance Atlantic Richfield Company, Los Angeles, 1973-75, senior vice president fin., 1975-77; president Arco Chemical Company, 1977-78, executive vice president, 1978-80; president, director Burlington Northern, Incorporated, St. Paul, 1980—, chief executive officer, 1980-88; chairman Burlington Northern, Incorporated, Seattle, 1982—; director Baker International, El Paso Company, Seafirst Corp., Honeywell Incorporated, General Mills, Incorporated; trustee Penn Mutual Life Insurance Company. Office: Burlington Resources Incorporated 999 Third Avenue Seattle Washington 98104-4097

BRINCKMAN, DONALD WESLEY, industrial company executive; born Chicago, March 17, 1931; married Beverly Washo; children: Scott, Bonny, Barbara, Donna, Dawn. Bachelor of Science, Northwestern University, 1954, Master of Business Administration, 1959; Doctor Business Management (honorary), Judson College, 1987. Marketing researcher Elgin (Illinois) Watch Company, 1954; market research manager Crane Corp., Evanston, Illinois, 1955-59, Johnson Motors, Waukegan, Illinois, 1959-60; vice president, general manager replacement C/R Industries, Elgin, 1960-74; president, chief executive officer Safety-Kleen Corp., Elgin, 1968-90; chairman board, chief executive officer Safety-Kleen Corp., Elgin, Illinois, 1990—; board of directors Johnson Worldwide Associates, Paychex, Incorporated. Chairman industrial div. Elgin United Way, 1985; member adv. Elgin Community College, 1987-88; trustee Coe College, Cedar Rapids, Iowa, 1987—; board mgrs. Sherman Hospital, Elgin, 1982—. Named fellow Illinois Business Hall of Fame, 1986. Member Am. Business Conference (founding), Illinois Chamber of Commerce, Motor Equipment Manufacturers Association. Republican. Roman Catholic. Avocation: golf. Office: Safety-Kleen Corp 777 Big Timber Road Elgin Illinois 60123

BROAD, ELI, financial services and home construction company executive; born New York City, June 6, 1933; son of Leon and Rebecca (Jacobson) B.; married Edythe Lois Lawson, December 19, 1954; children: Jeffrey Alan, Gary Steven. Bachelor of Arts cum laude in Business Administration, Michigan State University, 1954. Accountant 1954-56; assistant professor Detroit Institute Tech., 1956-57; co-founder Broad Incorporated, (formerly Kaufman and Broad, Incorporated), Los Angeles, 1957; president, chairman Broad, Incorporated (formerly Kaufman & Broad, Incorporated), Los Angeles, 1957-72, part-time chairman, 1973-75, chairman, chief executive officer, 1976—, president, 1990—; chairman, chief executive officer Sun Life Insurance Company Am., Baltimore, 1976-79, Sun Life United States of America (merged into SunAmerica Corp.), 1986-89; chief executive officer SunAmerica Corp., Atlanta, 1978—; chairman Kaufman and Broad Home Corp., 1986—; board director Federal National Mortgage Association, Anchor National Life Insurance Company; past director The Advest Group, Verex Corp.; member real estate adv. board Citibank, New York City. Director devel. board Michigan State U., 1969-72; member National Industrial Pollution Control Council, 1970-73; co-founder Council Housing Producers; chairman Los Angeles Mayor's Housing Policy Committee, 1974-75; del. Dem. National Convention, 1968; president California Non-Partisan Voter Registration Foundation, 1971; board of directors National Energy Foundation, 1979—, National Conference of Christians and Jews, Young Men's Christian Association, Los Angeles United Way, Haifa U.; board of directors, trustee Windward School; member acquisition committee Los Angeles County Mus. Art, 1979-81; executive committee International Forum for Los Angeles World Affairs Council; executive committee, board fellows Claremont Colleges; adv. board Institute International Education; founding chairman Mus. Contemporary Art, Los Angeles, 1980-83, trustee, 1980—; visiting committee Grad. School Mgmt., University of California at Los Angeles, 1972-90; trustee City of Hope, California State Univs. and Colleges; trustee Pitzer College, 1979—, chairman board trustees, 1972-79. Recipient Man of Year award City of Hope, 1965; Golden Plate award Am. Acad. Achievement, 1971; Humanitarian award National Conference of Christians and Jews, 1977; Housing Man of Year National Housing Conference, 1979; Am. Heritage award Anti-Defamation League, 1984, Pub. Affairs award Coro Foundation, 1987, Honors award visual arts Los Angeles Arts Council, 1989. Member Beta Alpha Psi. Clubs: Regency, Hillcrest Country (Los Angeles). Home: 1 Oakmont Dr Los Angeles California 90049 Office: Railway Exchange Building Suite 20F 611 Olive St Saint Louis Missouri 63101

BROADHEAD, JAMES LOWELL, business executive; born New Rochelle, New York, November 28, 1935; son of Clarence James and Mabel Roseader (Bowser) B.; married Sharon Ann Rulon, May 6, 1967; children: Jeffrey Thorton, Kristen Ann, Carolyn Mary, Catherine Lee. Bachelor.Mechanical Engineer, Cornell University, 1958; Bachelor of Laws, Columbia University, 1963. Bar: New York 1963. Mechanical engineer sales department Ingersoll-Rand Company, 1958-59; associate Debevoise, Plimpton, Lyons & Gates, New York City, 1963-68; assistant secretary St. Joe Minerals Corp., New York City, 1968-70, secretary, 1970-77, general counsel, 1973-74, vice president devel., 1976-77, executive vice president, 1980-81, president, 1981-82, also director; senior vp. General Telephone and Telegraph Corp., Stamford, Connecticut, 1984-88; also president General Telephone and Telegraph Corp. telephone operations,

Stamford, Connecticut, 1984-88; chairman, chief executive officer Energy Research Corp., Danbury, Connecticut, 1973-74, FPL Group Incorporated, 1989—; vice president St. Joe Petroleum Company, New York City, 1974-76; president St. Joe Zinc Company, Pittsburgh, 1977-80; executive vice president, director United States Industries, 1983; senior vice president General Telephone and Telegraph Corp., New York City, 1984-88; director Pittston Company, Barnett Banks, Incorporated, Delta Air Lines, Incorporated. Editor: Columbia Law Rev., 1963. Served with United States Army, 1960-61. Club:; Union League, Middlesex. Office: FPL Group Incorporated Post Office Box 14000 Juno Beach Florida 33408

BROCK, HARRY BLACKWELL, JR., banker; born Fort Payne, Alabama, March 31, 1926; son of Harry B. and Cornelia (Macfarlane) B.; married Jane Hollock, October 22, 1949; children—Stanley M., Barrett, Harry B. III. Bachelor of Science, University Alabama, 1949; graduate, School Financial Pub. Relations, Northwestern University, 1957; graduate certificate, Am. Institute Banking, 1964. Executive vice president Exchange Security Bank, Birmingham, Alabama, 1955-64; president Central Bank & Trust Company, Birmingham, 1964-72; chairman, treasurer, chief executive officer, director Central Bancshares of the South, Incorporated, Birmingham, Central Bank of South, 1964-91; founder, chairman Central Bancshares of the South, Incorporated, 1991—; director Daniel Foundation of Alabama; board of directors, president Daniel Ind. of Alabama. Chairman board, past president Junior Achievement Jefferson County; member president's council U. Alabama; member executive board Birmingham Area council Boy Scouts Am.; trustee Gorgas Scholarship Foundation; trustee Samford U.; member executive committee Southern Research Institute With United States Naval Reserve, 1944-46. Named Ala.'s Outstanding Young Banker, 1957. Member Young President's Organization, Chief Executives Forum, Alabama Acad. of Honor. Baptist. Clubs: Birmingham Country, Birmingham, Shoal Creek Country. Home: Yamasee Shoal Creek Alabama 35094 Office: Central Bancshares South Incorporated 701 S 20th St Birmingham Alabama 35233

BRONFMAN, CHARLES ROSNER, distillery executive; born Montreal, Quebec, Canada, June 27, 1931; son of Samuel and Saidye (Rosner) B.; married Andrea Morrison, 1982; children: Stephen Rosner, Ellen Jane. Student, McGill University, 1948-51. With Seagram Company, Limited, 1951—, vice president, director, 1958-71, executive vice president, 1971-75, president, 1975-79, department chairman, 1979-86, chairman executive committee, 1975—, co-chairman, 1986—; chairman board Montreal Baseball Club Limited, CRB Foundation; director E.I. duPont de Nemours & Company, Power Corp. Can. past president Allied Jewish Community Services, Montreal; life governor Jewish General Hospital; 23 for hon. chairman Can.-Israel Securities Limited (State of Israel Bonds Can.); board of directors Can. Council Christians and Jews. Clubs: Montefiore (Montreal), Mt. Royal (Montreal), Saint-Denis (Montreal), Elm Ridge Golf and Country (Montreal); Palm Beach Country. Office: Seagram Company Limited, 1430 Peel St, Montreal, Province of Quebec Canada H3A 1S9

BRONFMAN, EDGAR MILES, distillery executive; born Montreal, Quebec, Canada, June 20, 1929; son of Samuel and Saidye (Rosner) B. Student, Williams College, 1946-49; Bachelor of Arts, McGill University, 1951; Doctor of Humane Letters (honorary), Pace University, 1982; Doctor of Laws (honorary), Williams College, 1986. Chairman administrative committee Joseph East Seagram & Sons, Incorporated, 1955-57, president, 1957-71; chairman, chief executive officer, president Distillers Corp.-Seagram Limited, Montreal, 1971-75; now chairman, chief executive officer Seagram Company Limited and Joseph East Seagram & Sons Incorporated; board of directors Am. Technion Society, International Executive Service Corps, E.I. duPont de Nemours & Company. Member citizens committee for New York City, U.S.-USSR Trade and Economic Council; chairman Samuel Bronfman Foundation, World Jewish Congress; member executive committee Am. Jewish Congress, Am. Jewish Committee; chairman Anti-Defamation League New York; board of directors Am. committee Weizmann Institute Sci., Israel; chairman planning committee, member adv. council School of International and Pub. Affairs, Columbia U. Named Chevalier de la Légion d'Honneur French Government. Member Center for Intern-Am. Relations, Council Foreign Relations, Hundred Year Association New York, United Jewish Appeal, Federation Jewish Philanthropies (hon. chairman), Committee for Econ. Devel., Foreign Policy Association, Business Committee for Arts, Incorporated, Union Am. Hebrew Congregation (board dels.), School International Pub. Affairs International, B'nai B'rith International (board overseers). Office: Joseph E Seagram & Ss Incorporated 375 Park Avenue New York New York 10152

BROPHY, JOSEPH THOMAS, insurance company executive; born New York City, October 25, 1933; son of Joseph R. and Mary (Mitchell) B.; married Carole A. Johnson, June 8, 1957; children: Thomas J., David W., Patricia J., Maureen A., Kathleen M. Bachelor of Science cum laude, Fordham University, 1957; graduate senior exec. program, Massachusetts Institute of Technology, 1987. Mathematician Vitro Laboratories, West Orange, New Jersey, 1957; director management information systems Prudential Insurance Company, Newark, 1957-67; vice president Huggins & Company (consultant actuaries and management consultant), Philadelphia, 1967-68; vice president, chief actuary Bankers National Life Insurance Company, 1968-72; president Travelers Insurance Company, Hartford, Connecticut, 1972—; board of directors Engineered Business Systems, Travtech, Incorporated, Travelers TPA, Incorporated ; consultant in field, 1967—; enrolled actuary Employee Retirement Income Security Act (ERISA). Author: A User's Guide to Project Management. Tech. editor: Actuarial Digest. President St. Patrick's Pipe Band, Incorporated; board of directors Catholic Family Services; corporator St. Francis Hospital; chairman adv. board information scis. Grad. Business School, Fordham U., Bronx, New

York With United States Marine Corps Reserve, 1949-50, Army of the United States, 1952-54. Recipient Distinguished Info. Sci. award Data Processing Mgmt. Association, 1986. Fellow Society Actuaries; member Am. Acad. Actuaries, Acoustical Society Am., Hartford Actuaries Club, New York Actuaries Club, Am. Arbitration Society (arbitrator), Greater Hartford Chamber of Commerce (board directors). Club: Hartford. Home: 33 Rushleigh Road West Hartford Connecticut 06117 Office: Travelers Corp 1 Tower Square Hartford Connecticut 06183

BROWN, BENNETT ALEXANDER, banker; born Kingstree, South Carolina, June 1, 1929; married Mary Alice Rustin, November 30, 1957; children—Charlotte, Bennett, Leila, Katherine. Bachelor of Science, Presbyterian College, Clinton, South Carolina, 1950, Louisiana State University School Banking, 1960; graduate, Advanced Management Program, Harvard University, 1965. With Chemical Bank, New York City, 1950, Federal Reserve Bank Atlanta, 1953-55; with Citizens and Southern Corp. (name formerly C&S National Bank now Avantor Fin. Corp.), Atlanta, 1955—, chairman, chief executive officer, 1979—, director, 1986—; board of directors Citizens and Southern National Bank, Georgia Power Company, Confedn. Life Insurance Company, Toronto, Can. Board of directors national adv. board and Metro Atlanta adv. board Salvation Army; trustee Agnes Scott College, Pace Acad., Brookgreen Gardens, Murrells Inlet, South Carolina; member chmn.'s council Central Atlanta Progress; elder Peachtree Presbyterian Church With United States Army, 1951-53. Recipient William Booth award Salvation Army. Member International Monetary Conference (board directors), Association Bank Holding Companies, Association Reserve City Bankers (president), Atlanta Chamber of Commerce (board directors), Commerce Club of Atlanta (board directors), Buckhead Club, Piedmont Driving Club, Capital City Club. Office: Citizens & Southern Corp 35 Broad St Northwest Post Office Box 4899 Atlanta Georgia 30303

BROWN, NORMAN WESLEY, advertising agency executive; born Columbus, Ohio, January 27, 1931; son of Leonard and Alvena (Folker) B.; married Blanche; children—Pamela, Kendall; married Lynn Godfrey, January 3, 1980; children—Justin Godfrey, Brendan Godfrey. Bachelor of Arts, Ohio State University, 1953; Master of Business Administration, Harvard University, 1958. Account executive Foote, Cone & Belding, Los Angeles, 1959-63, account superintendent, 1963-73, general manager, 1973-79; general manager Foote, Cone & Belding, Chicago, 1979-81, president, from 1981, chief executive officer, 1982—, chairman; chairman board, chief executive officer, director Foote, Cone & Belding Communications Incorporated, Chicago. Member business adv. council Chicago Urban League, 1983—; board governors School Art Institute Chicago, 1983—; director Chicago Council on Foreign Relations. Served to 1st lieutenant United States Air Force, 1954-56. Member Am. Association Advertising Agys. (governor at large 1983—). Republican. Clubs: Tavern, East Bank (Chicago), Saddle and Cycle. Avocation: mountainclimbing. Home:

209 E Lake Shore Dr Chicago Illinois 60611 Office: Foote Cone & Belding Communications Incorporated 101 E Erie St Chicago Illinois 60611

BROWN, OWSLEY, II, diversified consumer products company executive; born Louisville, September 10, 1942; son of William Lee Lyons and Sara (Shallenberger) B.; married Christina Lee, October 26, 1968; children—Owsley, Brooke Lee, Augusta Wilson. Bachelor of Arts, Yale University, 1964; Master of Business Administration, Stanford University, 1966. With Brown Forman Corp., Louisville, 1961-83, president, 1983—; chairman, chief executive officer Brown-Forman Beverage Company Div. Brown-Forman Corp., Louisville, 1986—. President Actors Theatre, 1985, 89-90; board of directors Greater Louisville Fund for Arts. 1st lieutenant United States Army, 1966-68. Member Pendennis Club, Louisville Country Club, Wynn Stay Club, Filson Club. Republican. Episcopalian. Office: Brown Forman Corp 850 Dixie Highway Louisville Kentucky 40210

BROWN, STEPHEN LEE, insurance company executive; born Providence, July 6, 1937; son of Eugene R. and Florence M. (Zetlin) B.; married Arleen Claire Elliott, June 12, 1960; children: Beverly, William. Bachelor of Arts, Middlebury College, 1958. With John Hancock Mutual Life Insurance Company, Boston, 1958—, assistant actuary, 1963-67, associate actuary, 1967-70, 2d vice president, 1970-73, vice president, actuary, 1973-77, senior vice president, treasurer, 1977-81, executive vice president, 1981-87, president, chief operations officer, vice chairman board, 1987—, also board of directors; trustee Alfred P. Sloan Foundation, New York City, 1986—; board of directors John Hancock Subs. Incorporated, Boston. Board of directors Boston Housing Partnership, Incorporated, Boston, 1984—, United Way Massachusetts Bay, 1990, Million Dollar Round Table Foundation, 1989, Boston Police Athletic League, 1987—; trustee Mus. of Sci., Boston, The Wang Center for Performing Arts, 1990. 1st lieutenant United States Army, 1958-59. Fellow Society Actuaries; member Am. Acad. Acad. Actuaries, Actuaries Club Boston. Clubs: Algonquin, Commercial, Economic (Boston). Office: John Hancock Mut Life Ins Post Office Box 111 Boston Massachusetts 02117

BROWN, WILLIAM LEE LYONS, JR., consumer products company executive; born Louisville, August 22, 1936; son of William Lee Lyons and Sara (Shallenberger) B.; married Alice Cary Farmer, June 13, 1959; children—William Lee Lyons III, Alice Cary, Stuart Randolph. Bachelor of Arts, University Virginia, 1958; Bachelor of Science, Am. Graduate School International Management, 1960. Sales representative Brown-Forman Corp., Phoenix, 1960-61; vice president Louisville, 1965-68; senior vice president Arizona, 1968-72, executive vice president, 1972-76, president, chief executive officer, 1976-83, chairman, chief executive officer, 1983—; assistant vice president Jos. Garneau Company import div. Brown-Forman, New York City, 1961-62, director, Paris, France, 1962-65; board director Brown-Forman Corp.; member Pres's. Adv. Committee for Trade Negotiations. Member Business Committee Metropolitan Mus. of Art; board of directors Am. Business Conference,

Washington, past chairman; board visitors U. Virginia 1st lieutenant United States Army, 1958-59. Decorated chevalier de L'Ordre du Merite Agricole France; former hon. consul France. Member University Virginia Alumni Association (past president), Travellers Club, Fishers Island Club, River Valley Club, Pendennis Club, Louisville Country Club, University Club. Episcopalian. Home: Fincastle Prospect Kentucky 40059 also: Fishers Island New York 06390 Office: Brown Forman Corp 850 Dixie Highway Louisville Kentucky 40210

BRUCE, HARRY JAMES, transportation company executive; born Newark, July 2, 1931; son of John William and Anna Margaret (Ackerman) B.; married Vivienne Ruth Jennings, September 10, 1955; children: Robert, Stacy, Bethann. Bachelor of Science, Kent State University, 1957; Master of Science, University Tennessee, 1959; certificate Advanced Management Program, Harvard University, 1979. Diplomate: certified Am. Society Transp. and Logistics; 1960. Transportation research assistant United States Steel Company, Pittsburgh, 1959-64; director market devel. Spector Freight Company, Chicago, 1964-67, vice president marketing, 1967-69; director distribution Joseph Schlitz Brewing Company, Milwaukee, 1969-71, assistant vice president plant operations, 1971-72; vice president marketing Western Pacific Railroad, San Francisco, 1972-75; senior vice president marketing Illinois Central Railroad, Chicago, 1975-83, chairman, chief executive officer, 1983—; also director Illinois Central Gulf Railroad, Chicago; board of directors LaSalle Bank Lake View, Chicago, A.P. Green Industries Incorporated, Mexico, Missouri. Author: How to Apply Statistics to Physical Distribution, 1967, Distribution and Transportation Handbook, 1971; inventor vari-deck, 1970. Board of directors Glenwood School for Boys, Illinois; member adv. board U. Tennessee; business adv. committee Northwestern U. Served to 1st lieutenant United States Army, 952-55, European Theatre of Operations. Member Newcomen Society, National Council Physical Distbn., National Freight Transportation Association, National Defense Transportation Association, Northwestern University Assocs. Republican. Presbyterian. Clubs: Glenview (Illinois); Chicago, Mid-Am. (director) (Chicago); Metropolitan (New York City). Home: 88 Woodley Road Winnetka Illinois 60093 Office: Illinois Central Rural Route Company 233 N Michigan Avenue Chicago Illinois 60601

BRUMBACK, CHARLES TIEDTKE, communications executive; born Toledo, September 27, 1928; son of John Sanford and Frances Hannah (Tiedtke) B.; married Mary Louise Howe, July 7, 1951; children: Charles Tiedtke Jr., Anne Meyer, Wesley W., Ellen Allen. Bachelor of Arts in Economics, Princeton University, 1950; postgraduate, University Toledo, 1953-54. Certified Public Accountant, Ohio, Florida. With Arthur Young & Company, CPAs, 1950-57; business manager, vice president, treasurer, president, chief executive officer, director Sentinel Star Company subsidiary Tribune Company, Orlando, Florida, 1957-81; president, chief executive officer Chicago Tribune subsidiary Tribune

Company, 1981-88, president, chief operating officer, 1988-90, chief executive officer, 1990—; also board of directors Tribune Company, Chicago; board of directors Robert R. McCormick Tribune Foundation, Chicago Cubs, Chicago National League Ball Club, Incorporated. Trustee Northwestern U., Culver Educational Foundation, Chicago Symphony Orchestra, Chicago Historical Society, Northwestern Memorial Hospital, chairman, 1987-90. Decorated Bronze star. Member American Institute of Certified Public Accountants, Ohio, Florida Socs., Certified Public Accountants, Florida Press Association (treasurer 1969-76, president 1980, board directors), Am. Newspaper Pubs. Association (board directors), Commercial Club of Chicago, Chicago Club, Tavern Club. Home: 1500 N Lake Shore Dr Chicago Illinois 60610 Office: Tribune Company 435 N Michigan Avenue Chicago Illinois 60611

BRYAN, JOHN HENRY, food and consumer products company executive; born West Point, Mississippi, 1936. Bachelor of Arts in Economics and Business Adminstrn, Rhodes College, Memphis, 1958. Joined Bryan Foods, 1960; with Sara Lee Corp. (formerly known as Consol Food Corp.), Chicago, 1960—, from executive vice president to president, 1974, chief executive officer, 1975—, chairman board, 1976—, also board of directors; board director Amoco Corp., First Chicago. Member national corps. committee United Negro College Fund; member business adv. council Chicago Urban League; member fine arts committee United States Department State; board of directors Catalyst, National Women's Economic Alliance, Chicago United Way/Crusade of Mercy; trustee U. Chicago, Rush-Presbyn. Medical Center, Art. Institute Chicago, Committee Economic Devel. Recipient National Humanitarian award National Conference of Christians and Jews, William H. Albers award Food Marketing Ins. Member Grocery Manufacturers Association (senior, past. chairman board), Business Council, Business Roundtable. Office: Sara Lee Corp 3 First National Plaza Chicago Illinois 60602-4260

BRYAN, JOHN STEWART, III, newspaper publisher; born Richmond, Virginia, May 4, 1938; son of David Tennant and Mary Harkness (Davidson) B.; married Alice Pyle Zimmer, 1963 (divorced 1985); children: Elizabeth Talbott, Anna Saulsbury. Bachelor of Arts, University Virginia, 1960. Former advertising salesman Burlington (Vermont) Free Press; former reporter, vice president The Tampa (Florida) Times; pub. The Tampa Tribune and Times, Florida, 1976-77, Richmond Times-Dispatch, Richmond News Leader, Virginia, 1978-89; board of directors Media General, Incorporated, Richmond, 1974—, vice chairman, executive vice president, 1985—, chairman, president, chief executive officer, 1990—; board of directors Associated Press, 1984—, Newspaper Advertising Bureau, 1977—, vice chairman, 1990—; vice chairman Mutual Insurance Companies, Bermuda., 1990. Former president Tampa Bay Art Center, Tampa Citizens Safety Council, Tampa United Way, Florida Gulf Coast Symphony, Junior Achievement of Richmond, Goodwill Industries of Richmond; trustee U. Tampa, St. Catherine's School, Episcopal High School,

Alexandria, Virginia, chairman United Way Greater Richmond, 1984; trustee Virginia Foundation Ind. Colleges, Virginia Council Economic Education, Institute Bill of Rights Law, College William and Mary. With United States Marine Corps, 1960-62. Recipient medal of Honor, Daughters of the American Revolution, 1983. Member Sons of the American Revolution, Florida Society Newspaper Editors (life), Southern Newspapers Pub. Association (foundation chairman 1978-79, president 1981-82), Florida Press Association (life, president 1971-72, Distinguished Service award 1976), Virginia Press Association (board directors 1980-86), Am. Newspaper Pubs. Association (premium fund committee 1977—, chairman newspaper ins. adv. group 1987—), World Business Council, Florida Council of 100, Society Cincinnati, Bohemian Club (San Francisco), Alfalfa Club, Country Club of Virginia, Commonwealth Club, Tampa Yacht and Country Club, Sigma Delta Chi. Home: 4608 Sulgrave Road Richmond Virginia 23221 Office: Media General Incorporated 333 E Grace St Richmond Virginia 23219

BRYSON, JOHN E., utilities company executive; born New York City, July 24, 1943; married Louise Henry. Bachelor of Arts with great distinction, Stanford University, 1965; student, Freie University Berlin, Federal Republic Germany, 1965-66; Juris Doctor, Yale University, 1969. Bar: California, Oregon, District of Columbia. Assistant in instruction Law School, Yale University, New Haven, Connecticut, 1968-69; law clerk United States District Court, San Francisco, 1969-70; co-founder, attorney Natural Resources Defense Council, 1970-74; vice chairman Oregon Energy Facility Siting Council, 1975-76; associate Davies, Biggs, Strayer, Stoel & Boley, Portland, Oregon, 1975-76; chairman California State Water Resources Control Board, 1976-79; visiting faculty Stanford University Law School, California, 1977-79; president California Pub. Utilities Commission, 1979-82; partner Morrison & Foerster, San Francisco, 1983-84; senior vice president law and fin. Southern California Edison Company, Rosemead, 1984; executive vice president, chief fin. officer SCEcorp. and Southern California Edison Company, 1985-90; chairman of board, CEO SCE Corp. and Southern California Edison Company, Rosemead, 1990—; lecturer on pub. utility, energy, communications law.; former member executive committee National Association Regulatory Utility Commissioners, California Water Rights Law Rev. Commission, California Pollution Control Financing Authority; former member adv. board Solar Energy Research Institute, Electric Power Research Institute, Stanford Law School; board of directors Pacific Am. Income Shares Incorporated. Member board editors, associate editor: Yale University Law Journal. Board of directors World Resources Institute, Washington, California Environmental Trust, Claremont U. Center, Grad. School, Stanford U. Alumni Association; trustee Stanford U., 1991. Woodrow Wilson fellow. Member California Bar Association, Oregon Bar Association, District of Columbia Bar Association, National Association Regulatory Utility Commissioners (executive committee 1980-82), Stanford University Alumni Association (board directors 1983-86), Phi Beta Kappa.

Office: Southern California Edison Company 2244 Walnut Grove Avenue Rosemead California 91770

BUCHANAN, JAMES MCGILL, economist, educator; born Murfreesboro, Tennessee, October 2, 1919; son of James McGill and Lila (Scott) B.; married Anne Bakke, October 5, 1945. Bachelor of Science, Middle Tennessee State College, 1940; Master of Arts, University Tennessee, 1941; Doctor of Philosophy, University Chicago, 1948; Doctor honoris causa, University Giessen, 1982, University Zurich, 1984, George Mason University, University Valencia, New University Lisbon, 1987, Ball State University, 1988, City University, London, 1988. Professor economics University Tennessee, 1950-51; professor economics Florida State University, 1951-56; professor economics University Virginia, 1956-62, Paul G. McIntyre professor economics, 1962-68, chairman department, 1956-62; professor economics University California, Los Angeles, 1968-69; university distinguished professor economics Virginia Polytechnic Institute, 1969-83, George Mason University, 1983—; director Center for Pub. Choice, 1969—; Fulbright research scholar, Italy, 1955-56, Ford Faculty research fellow, 1959-60; Fulbright visiting professor Cambridge University, 1961-62. Author: (with C.L. Allen and M.R. Colberg) Prices, Income and Public Policy, 954, Public Principles of Public Debt, 1958, The Public Finances, 1960, Fiscal Theory and Political Economy, 1960, (with G. Tullock) The Calculus of Consent, 1962, Public Finance in Democratic Process, 1966, The Demand and Supply of Public Goods, 1968, Cost and Choice, 1969, (with N. Devletoglou) Academia in Anarchy, 1970; Editor: (with R. Tollison) Theory of Public Choice, 1972, (with G.F. Thirlby) LSE Essays on Cost, 1973, The Limits of Liberty, 1975, (with R. Wagner) Democracy in Deficit, 1977, Freedom in Constitutional Contract, 1978, What Should Economists Do?, 1979, (with G. Brennan) The Power to Tax, 1980; (with G. Brennan) The Reason of Rules, 1985; Liberty Market and State, 1985, Economics: Between Predictive Science and Moral Philosophy, 1987, Explorations in Constitutional Economics, 1989, Economics and Ethics of Constitutional Order, 1991; contributor articles to professional journals. Served as lieutenant United States Naval Reserve, 1941-46. Decorated Bronze Star medal. Recipient Nobel Prize in Economics, 1986. Fellow Am. Acad. Arts and Sciences; member Am. Econ. Association (executive committee 1966-69, vice president 1971, district fellow 1983—, Seidman award 1984), Southern Econ. Association (president 1963), Western Econ. Association (president 1983), Mount Pelerin Society (president 1984-86). Home: Post Office Box G Blacksburg Virginia 24063 Office: George Mason U Center for Pub Choice George's Hall Fairfax Virginia 22030 Office: George Mason U Department Econs 4400 University Dr Fairfax Virginia 22030

BUCKNER, FRED LYNN, chemical company executive; born Salt Lake City, February 29, 1932; son of Faye Wanita (MacDaniel) B.; married Faye Robinson; children: Cole, Dallas, Troy. Bachelor of Science in Mechanical Engineering, University Utah, 1958. Devel. engineer Bacchus works Hercules Incorporated, Salt

Lake City, 1961-63, senior devel. engineer, 1963-64; tech. sales representative polymers department Hercules Incorporated, Wilmington, Del., 1964-66, market supervisor polymers department, 1966-69, sales manager film, 1969-73, director sales film packaging div., 1973-78, director film worldwide business center, 1978-81, director organics business group, 1981-83, group vice president organics, 1983-84; president Hercules Engineered Polymers Company, Wilmington, 1984-86; president Hercules Specialty Chemicals Company, Wilmington, 1986-87, also board of directors, president, chief operating officer, 1987—. Trustee Medical Center Del.; Served with United States Army Reserve, 1951-54. Office: Hercules Incorporated 1313 N Market St Wilmington Delaware 19894

BUDD, EDWARD HEY, insurance company executive; born Zanesville, Ohio, April 30, 1933; son of Curtis Eugene and Mary (Hey) B.; married Mary Goodrich, August 24, 1957; children: Elizabeth, David, Susan. Bachelor of Science in Physics, Tufts University, 1955. With The Travelers Corp., Hartford, Connecticut, 1955—, vice president, then senior vice president, 1967-76, president, chief operating officer, 1976-82, chief executive officer, 1982—, chairman board, 1982—, also director, president, 1985-90; board of directors Delta Air Lines, General Telephone and Telegraph Corp., The Institute of Living. Chairman business committee National Center State Courts. Fellow Casualty Actuarial Society; member Business Roundtable, Am. Acad. Actuaries, Am. Insurance Association (board directors), Am. Council Life Insurance (board directors). Episcopalian. Office: Travelers Corp 1 Tower Square Hartford Connecticut 06183

BUENGER, CLEMENT LAWRENCE, banker; born Cincinnati, April 27, 1926; son of Clement Lawrence and Estelle (Pelzer) B.; married Ann McCabe, April 22, 1950. Student, University Wisconsin, 1943-44; Bachelor of Science in Business Administration, Xavier University, Cincinnati, 1950. Accountant Kroger Company, Cincinnati, 1950; executive vice president Selective Insurance Company, Cincinnati, 1952-67, Life Insurance Company Kentucky, Louisville, 1967-69; vice president Fifth Third Bank, Cincinnati, 1969-79, president, 1979-81, president, chief executive officer, 1988-89, chairman, chief executive officer, 1989-91; president, chief executive officer Fifth Third Bancorp, 1988-89, chairman, chief executive officer, 1989-91; chairman board Fifth Third Bank, Fifth Third Bancorp, 1991—, also board of directors; director, president Fifth Third Bancorp., parent company Fifth Third Bank; board of directors Cincinnati Gas and Electric Company. President Fund for Ind. Schools Cincinnati; trustee Xavier U.; board of directors Greater Cincinnati Airport, INROADS; member Cincinnati Business Committee; member adv. board Cincinnati Council World Affairs. With United States Navy, 1943-45. Member Association Reserve City Bankers, Greater Cincinnati Chamber of Commerce (trustee). Republican. Roman Catholic. Clubs: Cincinnati Country, Bankers, Comml, Queen City. Office: Fifth Third Bancorp 38 Fountain Square Plaza Cincinnati Ohio 45263

BUFFETT, WARREN EDWARD, corporate executive; born Omaha,

August 30, 1930; son of Howard Homan and Leila (Stahl) B.; married Susan Thompson, April 19, 1952; children: Susan, Howard, Peter. Student, University Pennsylvania, 1947-49; Bachelor of Science, University Nebraska, 1950; Master of Science, Columbia, 1951. Investment salesman Buffett-Falk & Company, Omaha, 1951-54; security analyst Graham-Newman Corp., New York City, 1954-56; general partner Buffett Partnership, Limited, Omaha, 1956-69; chairman board Berkshire Hathaway, Incorporated, National Indemnity Company, National Fire & Marine Insurance Company, See's Candy Shops, Incorporated, Columbia Insurance Company, Buffalo Evening News; board of directors Capital Cities/ABC, Solomon, Incorporated, Coca-Cola Company, Gillette Company. Board governors Boys Clubs Omaha, 1962—; life trustee Grinnell College, 1968—; trustee Urban Institute. Office: Berkshire Hathaway Incorporated 1440 Kiewit Plaza Omaha NE 68131

BUNDSCHUH, GEORGE AUGUST WILLIAM, insurance company executive; born Yonkers, New York, September 24, 1933; son of George and Anna B.; married Joanne Detjen; children: Russell, Erica. Bachelor of Business Administration, Pace University, 1955; Master of Science, Columbia University, 1959. Chartered fin. analyst. With New York Life Insurance Company, New York City, 1959—; senior vice president New York Life Insurance Company, 1979-80, executive vice president, 1980-84, vice chairman, 1984-90, president, 1990—. Trustee Pace U. Served with Army of the United States, 1956-58. Member Institute Chartered Fin. Analysts. Office: New York Life Ins Company 51 Madison Avenue New York New York 10010

BUNTROCK, DEAN LEWIS, waste management company executive. With Waste Management Incorporated, Oak Brook, Illinois, 1968—, chairman, chief executive officer, director, 1968—. member board trustees Chicago Symphony Orchestra. Office: Waste Management Incorporated 3003 Butterfield Road Oak Brook Illinois 60521

BURDGE, JEFFREY J., metal products executive. Student, Youngstown State University. C.P.A., Ohio. Accountant Clark & Collins, C.P.A.s, 1947-53; with Harsco Corp., 1953—, president Heckett Engineering Company div., 1969, executive vice president, chief operating officer, 1975, president, chief operating officer, 1976-77, president, chief executive officer, 1977-83, chairman board, chief executive officer, 1983-87, chairman board of directors, 1987—; board of directors Dauphin Deposit Corp., Dauphin Deposit Bank & Trust Company, AMP Incorporated, Pamcor Incorporated, Penn Blue Shield, Millers Mutual Insurance Company, Harrisburg, Pennsylvania, Pennsylvania Power & Light Company, Allentown, Pennsylvania. Board of directors Polyclinic Medical Center of Harrisburg. Served with Brit. Army, 1939-45. Member Am. Iron and Steel Institute (board directors). Office: Harsco Corp 350 Poplar Church Road Post Office Box 8888 Camp Hill Pennsylvania 17011

BURGESS, ROBERT K., construction company executive; born 1944. Bachelor of Science, Michigan State University, 1966. With Pulte Home Corp., West Bloomfield, Michigan,

1983—, vice president corp. devel., 1983-84, senior vice president, 1984-85, chief operating officer, executive vice president, 1985-86, president, chief operating officer, 1987—, also board of directors. Office: Pulte Home Corp 33 Bloomfield Hills Parkway Suite 300 Bloomfield Hills Michigan 48013

BURGUIERES, PHILIP JOSEPH, energy service and manufacturing company executive; born Franklin, Louisiana, September 3, 1943; son of Denis P.J. and Emma L. (LeBlanc) B.; married Cheryl A. Courrege, August 21, 1965; children: Emily Louise, Philip Martial. Bachelor of Science in Mechanical Engineering, University Southwestern Louisiana, 1965; Master of Business Administration, University Pennsylvania, 1970. Administrative assistant Cameron Iron Works, Incorporated, Houston, 1971, fin. manager European operations, 1972-75, vice president corp. services, 1975-77, vice president and general manager forged products div., 1977-79, executive vice president operations, 1979-81, president, chief operating officer, 1981-85, president, chief executive officer, 1986-89, chairman board, 1987-89; chairman, president, chief executive officer Panhandle Eastern Corp., Houston, 1990; president, chief executive officer Weatherford International Incorporated, Houston, 1991—; chairman board of directors J.M. Burguieres Company, Limited, Franklin; board of directors Texas Commerce Bancshares, McDermott International. President Duchesne Acad. Sacred Heart, Houston, 1987-90. With United States Navy, 1966-69. Member Petroleum Equipment Suppliers Association (president 1986-87), Petroleum Club Houston (president 1988-89), Tau Beta Pi, Pi Tau Sigma. Roman Catholic. Avocation: golf. Office: Post Office Box 27608 Houston Texas 77227

BURKE, DANIEL BARNETT, communications corporation executive; born Albany, New York, February 4, 1929; son of J. Frank and Mary (Barnett) B.; married Harriet Shore, August 31, 1957; children: Stephen, J.Frank, Sarah, William. Bachelor of Arts, University Vermont, 1950; Master of Business Administration, Harvard, 1955. Various positions product management and devel. Jell-O div. General Foods Corp., 1955-61; general manager WTEN-TV, Albany, 1961-64; corp. vice president WTEN-TV, 1962; general manager WJR AM/FM, Detroit, 1964-69; corporate executive vice president, director WJR AM/FM, 1967; president pub. div. Capital Cities Broadcasting Corp., New York City, 1969-72; president, chief operating officer Capital Cities Broadcasting Corp., 1972-85; president, chief operating officer Capital Cities ABC Incorporated, 1986-90, president, chief executive officer, 1990—; board of directors Rohm & Haas Company, Avon Products, Incorporated, Conrail. Bd directors Cities in Schools Incorporated, National Urban League, Am. women's Economic Devel. Corp., Am. Film Institute; past chairman board trustees U. Vermont; past chairman board trustees Medical Mission Sisters, Philadelphia Served to 1st lieutenant, infantry Army of the United States, 1951-53, Korea. Member Phi Delta Theta. Office: Capital Cities/ABC Incorporated 77 W 66th St New York New York 10023

BURNETT, ROBERT A., publisher; born Joplin, Missouri, June 4, 1927; son of Lee Worth and Gladys (Plummer) B.; married Gloria M. Cowden, December 25, 1948; children: Robert A., Stephen, Gregory, Douglas, David, Penelope. Bachelor of Arts, University Missouri, 1948. Salesman Cowden Motor Company, Guthrie Center, Iowa; then Equitable Life Assurance Society, Joplin, Missouri; now chairman Meredith Corp.; board of directors Whirlpool Corp., Norwest Bank Des Moines, International Telephone & Telegraph Corporation, Iowa Resources, Dayton Hudson Corp. Past chairman Travel Industry of Am.; board of directors Grinnell College Served with Army of the United States, 1945-46. Member National Association of Manufacturers (board directors), Phi Delta Theta. Congregationalist. Home: 2942 Sioux Court Des Moines Iowa 50321 Office: Meredith Corp 1716 Locust St Des Moines Iowa 50336

BURNHAM, DUANE LEE, pharmaceutical company executive; born Excelsior, Minnesota, January 22, 1942; son of Harold Lee and Hazel Evelyn (Johnson) B.; married Susan Elizabeth Klinner, June 22, 1963; children—David Lee, Matthew Beckwith. Bachelor of Science, University Minnesota, 1963, Master of Business Administration, 1972. C.P.A., Wisconsin. Fin. and management Maremont Corp., Chicago, 1969-75; vice president fin., chief fin. officer Bunker-Ramo Corp., Oak Brook, Illinois, 1975-79, executive vice president, director, 1979-80, president, chief executive officer, director, 1980-82; senior vice president fin., chief financial officer Abbott Laboratories, North Chicago, 1982-84, executive vice president, chief financial officer, director, 1985-87, vice chairman, chief fin. officer, 1987-89, chairman, chief executive officer, 1990—; board of directors Evanston Hospital Corp. Member council Grad. School Business, U. Chicago. Member Wisconsin Society Certified Public Accountants, Pharmaceutical Manufacturers Association (board directors 1990), Illinois State Chamber of Commerce (board directors), Beta Alpha Psi. Office: Abbott Labs 1 Abbott Park Road Abbott Park Illinois 60064

BURNS, JOHN DUDLEY, chemical company executive; born Houston, May 18, 1933; son of John Heard Burns and Annie (Lee) Peeples B.; married Margaret Alice Garrett, May 19, 1962; children: John Arthur, Dan Garrett, Kevin Norman, William Dudley. Bachelor of Arts in Chemical Engineering, Rice University, 1955, Bachelor of Science in Chemical Engineering, 1956; graduate Program for Management Devel., Harvard University, 1973. Assistant general manager Conoco Chemicals div., Saddle Brook, New Jersey, 1973-75; vice president commercial Conoco Chemicals div., Houston, 1975-78; vice president, general manager operations Conoco Chemicals div., 1978-79, senior vice president, 1979-80; executive vice president chemicals Conoco, Incorporated, 1980-84; chairman, president, chief executive officer Vista Chemical Company, 1984—, also chairman. Member adv. council Zool. Society Houston, 1983—, Rice U. Fund Council. Member Soap and Detergent Association (director), Society Chemical Industry. Clubs: River Oaks, Lochinvar Golf, Westlake (board governors 1982—). Home: 10 Stillforest Houston Texas 77024 Office: Vista Chem Company 900 Threadneedle Houston Texas 77079

BURNS, JOHN JOSEPH, JR., business executive; born Cambridge, Massachusetts, June 27, 1931; son of John Joseph and Alice (Blake) B.; married Barbara Ann Miller, October 18, 1958; children: John J. III, Christine, Gregory, Timothy, Jennifer. Bachelor of Science in Fin., Boston College, 1953; Master of Business Administration, Harvard University, 1955. Associate buying department and arbitrage department Goldman Sachs & Company, New York City, 1957-63; associate New York Securities, New York City, 1963-67, general partner, 1968; vice president fin., director Alleghany Corp., New York City, 1968-77, president, director, 1977—, member executive committee, 1977—; board of directors Chicago Title & Trust Company; board of directors Shelby (Ohio) Insurance Company, Cyclops Industries Incorporated, Pittsburgh. Served with United States Navy, 1955-57. Roman Catholic. Club: Oyster Harbors. Office: Alleghany Corp 55 E 52nd St New York New York 10055

BURNS, MITCHEL ANTHONY, transportation services company executive; born Las Vegas, Nevada, November 1, 1942; son of Mitchel and Zella (Pulsipher) B.; married Joyce Jordan, November 14, 1962; children: Jill, Mike, Shauna. Bachelor of Science in Business Mgmt, Brigham Young University, 1964; Master of Business Administration in Fin., University California, Berkeley, 1965; honorary doctorate, Florida International University, 1989. With Mobil Oil Corp., New York City, 1965-74, controller, 1970-72, cost-of-living coordinator, 1973, fin. analysis manager, 1973-74; with Ryder System, Incorporated, Miami, Florida, 1974—, executive vice president, chief fin. officer, 1978-79, president, chief operations officer, 1979-83, president, chief executive officer, 1983-85, chairman, president, chief executive officer, 1985—, also board of directors; executive vice president, chief fin. officer, president Ryder Truck Rental, Incorporated, 1980-81; board of directors J.C. Penney Company, Incorporated, Pfizer Incorporated, The Chase Manhattan Corp.; member national adv. council school management Brigham Young University, 1981—. Trustee U. Miami, 1984—; member board visitors Grad. School Business Administration, U. North Carolina, Chapel Hill, 1988—; board overseers Wharton School, 1989—; associate trustee U. Pennsylvania, 1989—; board of directors, trustee United Way Dade County, Florida, 1981—, chairman, 1991—, Dade County campaign, 1988; board governors, chairman Southeast region United Way of Am.; trustee, past chairman National Urban League. Named Marketer of Year Acad. Marketing Sci., 1983, Americanism award Anti-Defamation League, 1984, Business Leader of Year The Miami News, 1985, Ricks College Business Leader of the Century, 1989, Fin. World Chief Executive Officer of Decade in Transp., Freight & Leasing, 1989, Chief Executive Officer of Year, 1984, 85, 87; recipient Boneh Yisroel award Greater Miami Jewish Federation, 1989, Silver medallion award National Conference Christians & Jews, 1988, Community Service award Advertising Federation Great Miami, 1987. Member United States Chamber of Commerce (board directors 1985-91). Office: Ryder System Incorporated 3600 Northwest 82nd Avenue Miami Florida 33166

BURNSIDE, WALDO HOWARD, department store executive; born Washington, November 5, 1928; son of Waldo and Eleanor B.; married Jean Mae Culbert, June 24, 1950; children: Diane Louise, Leslie Ann, Arlene Kay, William Howard. Bachelor of Science, University Maryland, 1949. With Woodward & Lothrop, Washington, 1949-80; divisional merchandise manager Woodward & Lothrop, 1957-65, vice president, general merchandise manager, 1965-74, executive vice president, 1974-78, president, 1978-80; also director; vice chairman, chief operating officer Carter Hawley Hale Stores, Incorporated, Los Angeles, 1980-83, president, chief operating officer, 1983—; director Security Pacific Corp. Trustee Maryland Educational Foundation; trustee St. John's Hospital and Health Center Foundation; trustee, past chairman U. Maryland Alumni International. Member Ind. Colls. Southern California (board directors), Los Angeles Area Chamber of Commerce (board directors), Automobile Club Southern California (board directors), Phi Kappa Phi, Sigma Chi. Episcopalian. Clubs: California, Los Angeles Country, New York Athletic. Office: Carter Hawley Hale Stores Incorporated 444 S Flower St Los Angeles California 90071

BURT, ROBERT NORCROSS, diversified manufacturing company executive; born Lakewood, Ohio, May 24, 1937; son of Vernon Robert and Mary (Norcross) B.; married Lynn Chilton, April 19, 1969; children: Tracy, Randy, Charlie. Bachelor of Science in Chemical Engineering, Princeton University, 1959; Master of Business Administration, Harvard University, 1964. With Mobil Oil Corp., New York City and Tokyo, 1964-68; director corp. planning and acquisitions Chemetron Corp., Chicago, 1968-70, manager international div., 1970-73; director corp. planning Federal Maritime Commission Corp., Chicago, 1973-76; vice president agricultural chemicals group Federal Maritime Commission Corp., Philadelphia, 1976-83; vice president defense group Federal Maritime Commission Corp., San Jose, California, 1983-88; executive vice president Federal Maritime Commission Corp., Chicago, 1988-90, president, 1990—; chairman, chief executive officer Federal Maritime Commission Gold Company, 1989—. Member visiting committee College Arts and Scis., Northwestern U., 1990—. Lieutenant United States Marine Corps, 1959-62. Member MAPI (board trustees 1990—), World Gold Council (board directors 1990—), Econ. Club Chicago, Mid-Am. Club, Glen View Club (Golf, Illinois), Chicago Club. Avocations: reading, golfing, spectator sports. Home: 1171 Oakley Road Winnetka Illinois 60093 Office: FMC Corp 200 E Randolph Dr Chicago Illinois 60601

BUSBY, JHERYL, record company executive. With MCA Records; now president Motown Records. Office: Motown Records 6255 Sunset Boulevard 17th Floor Los Angeles California 90028

BUSCH, ALLAN JULIUS, JR., academic administrator, history educator; born Quincy, Illinois, November 24, 1942; son of Allan Julius Sr. and Etta May (Harwood) B.; married Connie Lea Hutchinson, July 4, 1974; 1 child, Roberto. Bachelor of Arts in History, Southern Illinois University,

1964; Master of Arts in History, University Nebraska, 1966; Doctor of Philosophy in History, University Kansas, 1971. Research fellow Am. Bar Foundation, Chicago, 1971-72; assistant professor history Fort Hays State University, Hays, Kansas, 1972-76, associate professor history, 1976-82, professor history, 1982—, chairman department history, 1986—; president faculty senate Fort Hays State University, 1978-79. Contributor articles to professional journals. Commissioner Coronado council Boy Scouts Am., Salina, Kansas, 1979-84; president Hays Lions, 1982. Member Am. Historical Association, Am. Society for Legal History, Kansas History Association (executive board 1982-89, vice president 1987-88, president 1988-89), Conference on Brit. Studies, Selden Society. Office: Fort Hays State U 600 Park St Hays Kansas 67601

BUSCH, AUGUST ADOLPHUS, III, brewery executive; born St. Louis, June 16, 1937; son of August Anheuser and Elizabeth (Overton) B.; married Susan Marie Hornibrook, August 17, 1963 (divorced 1969); children: August Adolphus IV, Susan Marie II; married Virginia L. Wiley, December 28, 1974; children: Steven August, Virginia Marie. Student, University Arizona, 1957-58, Siebel Institute Tech., 1960-61. With Anheuser-Busch, Incorporated, St. Louis, 1957—, sales manager, 1962-64, vice president marketing operations, 1964-65, vice president, general manager, 1965-74, president, 1975-79, chief executive officer, 1975—, chairman board, 1977—; chairman, president Anheuser Busch Companies, Incorporated, St. Louis, 1979—, also board of directors; board of directors St. Louis National Baseball Club, Manufacturers Railway Company, Southwestern Bell Corp., General Am. Life Insurance Company, Emerson Electric Company; trustee St. Louis Refrigerator Car Company. Chairman board St. Louis Boy Scouts Am.; chairman adv. board St. John's Mercy Medical Center; board of directors United Way Greater St. Louis; board overseers Wharton School, U. Pennsylvania. Clubs: St. Louis, Frontenac Racquet, St. Louis Country, Racquet (St. Louis); Noonday, Log Cabin, Stadium. Office: Anheuser-Busch Cos Incorporated 1 Busch Place Saint Louis Missouri 63118

BUSH, GEORGE HERBERT WALKER, President of the United States; born Milton, Massachusetts, June 12, 1924; son of Prescott Sheldon and Dorothy (Walker) B.; married Barbara Pierce, January 6, 1945; children: George W., John E., Neil M., Marvin P., Dorothy W. Bachelor of Arts in Economics, Yale University, 1948; Doctor of Laws (honorary), University Texas, 1990; numerous other honorary degrees. Co-founder, director Zapata Petroleum Corp., 1953-59; president Zapata Off Shore Company, Houston, 1956-64; chairman board Zapata Off Shore Company, 1964-66; member 90th-91st Congresses from 7th District Texas, 1967-71, Ways and Means committee; United States ambassdor to United Nations 1971-72; chairman Rep. National Committee, 1973-74; chief United States Liaison Office Peking, People's Republic China, 1974-75; director Central Intelligence Agency, 1976-77; adj. professor administrative sci. Rice University, Houston, 1978; Vice President of United States 1981-89, President of United States,

1989—. Chairman Republican Party Harris County, Texas, 1963-64; del. Republican National Convention, 1964, 68; Republican candidate United States senator from Texas, 1964, 70. Served to lieutenant (junior grade), pilot United States Navy, World War II. Decorated Distinguished Flying Cross, Air medals (3). Home and Office: The White House 1600 Pennsylvania Avenue Washington District of Columbia 20500

BUSS, JERRY HATTEN, real estate executive, sports team owner. Children: John, Jim, Jeanie, Jane. Bachelor of Science in Chemistry, University Wyoming; Master of Science, Doctor of Philosophy in Chemistry, University Southern California, 1957. Chemist Bureau Mines; past member faculty department chemistry University Southern California; member missile div. McDonnell Douglas, Los Angeles; partner Mariani-Buss Associates; former owner Los Angeles Strings; chairman board, owner Los Angeles Lakers (National Basketball Association); until 1988 owner Los Angeles Kings (National Hockey League). Office: care Los Angeles Lakers 3900 W Manchester Boulevard Post Office Box 10 Inglewood California 90306

BUTTERWORTH, KENNETH W., manufacturing company executive; born 1925. Graduate, Sydney Tech. College, 1955; A.Master.P., Harvard Business School. Director sales The Timken Company, 1957-68; managing director Bearings, Incorporated, 1968-76; corp. vice president and president European region Loctite Corp., Newington, Connecticut, 1976-83, president, chief operating officer, 1983-85, president, chief executive officer, 1985—. Office: Loctite Corp 10 Columbus Boulevard Hartford Connecticut 06106

BYNOE, PETER CHARLES BERNARD, real estate developer, legal consultant; born Boston, March 20, 1951; son of Victor Cameron Sr. and Ethel May (Stewart) B.; married Linda Jean Walker, November 20, 1987. Bachelor of Arts, Harvard University, 1972, Juris Doctor, 1976, Master of Business Administration, 1976. Bar: Illinois 1982; certified real estate broker, Illinois. Executive vice president James H. Lowry & Associates, Chicago, 1977-82; president Telemat Limited, Chicago, 1982—; managing director Howard Ecker & Company Real Estate, Chicago, 1986-87; of counsel Davis, Barnhill & Galland, Chicago, 1987-88; executive director Illinois Sports Facilities Authority, Chicago, 1988—; managing general partner Denver Nuggets, 1989—; board of directors Chicago Architecture Foundation. Chairman Chicago Landmarks Commission, 1985; board of directors Goodman Theatre, Chicago, 1986, Boys and Girls Clubs of Chicago, 1987, Cinema Chgo, 1988. Member Chicago Architecture Foundation, Chicago Bar Association, Chicago Board Realtors, Illinois Bar Association, Illinois Preservation Council, Urban Land Institute, Harvard Business School Alumni Council (board directors 1987). Democrat. Clubs: International (Chicago), East Bank. Avocations: squash, tennis, racquetball, skiing, travel. Office: 1 First National Plaza #2785 Chicago Illinois 60603 also: care Denver Nuggets McNichols Sports Arena 1635 Clay St Post Office Box 4658 Denver Colorado 80204

BYRNE, JOHN JOSEPH, JR., insurance executive; born Passaic, New Jersey, July 11, 1932; son of John Joseph and Winifred (Mohr) B.; married Dorothy M. Cain, July 22, 1958; children: John Joseph III, Mark James, Patrick Michael. Bs in Math., Rutgers University, 1954; postgraduate, Harvard Law School, 1957; Master of Science in Math., University Michigan, 1959; honorary degrees, University Maryland, St. Anselm College, Rutgers University, Mount St. Mary's College. C.L.U. With Lincoln National Life Insurance Company, Fort Wayne, Ind., 1959-63; executive vice president Massachusetts Life Insurance Company, Boston, 1963-67, Travelers Insurance Companies, Hartford, Connecticut, 1967-76; chairman board, chief executive officer Government Employees Insurance Company, 1976-85; chairman board, chief executive officer Fund Am. Companies (formerly Fireman's Fund Corp.), 1985—, also board of directors; board of directors Firemans Fund Mortgage Corp., Martin Marietta, Potomac Electric Power Company. Chairman National Symphony Orchestra Annual Fund; board overseers Amos Tuck School Business Administration, Stanford Urban Institute, Dartmouth College Major United States Air Force, 1954-57. Recipient Boss of Year award Junior Chamber of Commerce; Community Service award United Way. Member Society Actuaries (associate), Insurance Institute Am. (trustee), Am. Institute Property and Liability Underwriters (trustee), Knights of Malta, Cap and Skull, Zeta Psi. Republican. Roman Catholic. Clubs: University (Boston); University (Washington); Burning Tree, Mid Ocean. Office: Fund American Cos Post Office Box 2604 Greenwich Connecticut 06836-2604

CAGGIANO, JOSEPH, advertising executive; born New York City, October 22, 1925; son of Daniel Joseph and Lucia (Gaudiosi) C.; married Catherine Marie Gilmore, August 28, 1948; children—Cathleen, Mary Yvonne. Bachelor of Business Administration, Pace College, 1953. Chief accountant Criterion Advertising Company, New York City, 1947-57; treasurer Emerson Foote, Incorporated, New York City, 1957-67; became senior vice president Bozell & Jacobs, Incorporated (now Bozell, Jacobs, Kenyon & Eckhardt Incorporated), New York City, 1967; executive vice president finance and administration Bozell & Jacobs, Incorporated (now Bozell, Jacobs, Kenyon & Eckhardt Incorporated), Omaha, 1971-74; vice chairman board, chief financial officer Bozell & Jacobs, Incorporated (now Bozell, Jacobs, Kenyon & Eckhardt Incorporated), 1974—, also director, member executive committee; director Emerson Foote, Incorporated. Board of directors St. Mary's College, Omaha Zool. Society Served with United States Naval Reserve, 1943-46, European Theatre of Operations, PTO. Member New York Credit and Financial Management Association, Omaha Zool. Society (director). Home: 9731 Fieldcrest Dr Omaha NE 68114 Office: Bozell Jacobs Kenyon & Eckhardt Incorporated 40 W 23rd St New York New York 10010

CAHOUET, FRANK VONDELL, banker; born Cohasset, Massachusetts, May 25, 1932; son of Ralph Hubert and Mary Claire (Jordan) C.; married Ann Pleasonton Walsh, July 14, 1956; children: Ann

P., Mary G., Frank V., David R. Bachelor of Arts, Harvard University, 1954; Master of Business Administration, University Pennsylvania, 1959. Corp. loan assistant Security Pacific National Bank, Los Angeles, 1960-66, vice president, 1966-69; senior loan administrator Security Pacific National Bank, Europe/Middle East/Africa, 1969-73; executive vice president Security Pacific National Bank, 1978-80, vice chairman, 1980-84; executive vice president Security Pacific Corp., Los Angeles, 1973-80, vice chairman, 1980-84; chairman, president and chief executive officer Crocker National Bank, San Francisco, 1984-86; president, chief operating officer Federal National Mortgage Association, 1986-87; chairman, chief executive officer Mellon Bank, N.A., Pittsburgh, 1987—; board of directors Avery International Corp., Los Angeles. Trustee Carnegie-Mellon U., Pittsburgh, U. Pittsburgh, Pa's. S.W.Association, Pittsburgh; member board overseers Wharton School, U. Pennsylvania. Member Newcomen Society. Clubs: Duquesne, Edgeworth, Laurel Valley Golf (Pittsburgh); California (Los Angeles); Pacific Union (San Francisco). Office: Mellon Bank NA 1 Mellon Bank Center Room 411 Pittsburgh Pennsylvania 15258-0001

CALLENDER, WILLIAM LACEY, savings and loan executive, lawyer; born Oakland, California, February 1, 1933; son of William Clarence and Doris (Lacey) C.; married Joan Ingram, December 14, 1968; 1 child, William Ingram; 1 child from previous marriage, Suzanne. Associate of Arts, Hartnell Junior College, Salinas, California, 1952-53; student, University California, Berkeley, 1953-54; Bachelor of Arts in Economics, Fresno State College, 1955; Juris Doctor, University Southern California, 1960. Bar: California 1960, United States District Court (southern district) California 1960. Vice president, senior attorney California Federal Savings & Loan Association, Los Angeles, 1975-81, vice president, assistant general counsel, 1981-82, senior vice president, general counsel, secretary, 1982-83, executive vice president administration, secretary, 1985-87; president, chief executive officer California Federal Bank (formerly California Federal Savings and Loan Association), Los Angeles, 1987—; also board of directors California Federal Savings and Loan Association, Los Angeles; executive vice president , general counsel, secretary CalFed Incorporated, Los Angeles, 1983-87, also board of directors. Member California League Savings Institutions (legis. and regulation committee 1987—), Los Angeles Chamber of Commerce (executive committee, governor adminstrn. committee, chairman), Florida Council 100 Tampa, Order of Coif. Republican. Episcopalian. Avocations: boating, gardening, reading, spectator sports. Office: California Federal Bank 5700 Wilshire Boulevard Los Angeles California 90036

CALLOWAY, D. WAYNE, food and beverage products company executive; born 1935. Bachelor of Business Administration, Wake Forest University, 1959. Executive vice president, chief fin. officer Pepsico Incorporated, Purchase, New York, 1983-85, president, chief operating officer, 1985-86, chairman, chief executive officer, 1986—; former chairman, president, chief executive and operating officer Frito-Lay Incorporated (subsidiary Pepsico Incorporated), Dallas. Office: PepsiCo Incorporated Anderson Hill Road Purchase New York 10577

CAMPANELLA, ANTON J., telephone company executive; born 1932; (married). Bachelor of Arts, Upsala College, 1956. Salesman Englishtown Crafts, New York City, 1949-51; assistant traffic manager Riedl & Freede Advertising, 1955; with New Jersey Bell Telephone Company, 1956-81, div. traffic manager, 1963-66, director marketing, 1966-68, assistant vice president, 1968-70, general manager, 1970-72, vice president downstate, 1972-74, v.p, marketing, 1974-78, vice president business services, 1978-79, executive vice president business services, 1979-81, president, 1983-89; assistant vice president marketing operations American Telephone and Telegraph Company Communications, 1981-82, vice president marketing, 1982-83; president Bell Atlantic, 1989—. Office: Bell Atlantic Corp 1310 N Court House Road Arlington Virginia 22201

CAMPBELL, ROBERT H., oil company executive; born Pittsburgh, June 11, 1937; children--R. Douglas, Heather; married Nancy Wertz, February 27, 1976. Bachelor in ChemE, Princeton University, 1959; Master in ChemE, Carnegie Mellon University, 1961; Master in Management, Massachusetts Institute of Technology, 1978. Various engineering positions Sun Company, Philadelphia, 1960-75; manager refinery operations Sun Company, Corpus Christi, Texas, 1975-77; vice president human resources Sun Ship, Incorporated, Chester, Pennsylvania, 1978-80, president, 1980; president Sun Refining and Marketing Company, Philadelphia, 1983—; executive vice president Sun Company Incorporated, Radnor, Pennsylvania, 1988-91, president, chief operating officer, 1991—; director Suncor, Incorporated, Toronto, Ontario, Can.; board of directors The Philadelphia National Bank, Elwyn Institutes, National Annual Manufacturers. Appointed member by Deputy Secretary of Energy W. Henson Moore to Alternative Fuels Council, 1990. Member Am. Petroleum Institute (board directors 1988). Republican. Office: Sun Company Incorporated 100 Matsonford Road Radnor Pennsylvania 19087

CANAVAN, BERNARD, pharmaceutical company executive, physician; born Valleyfield, Fife, Scotland, 1936; son of Thomas and Helen (Toner) C.; married Margaret Reid, December 26, 1957; 1 child, Helen. Bachelor in Medicine, Bachelor of Surgery, University Edinburgh, Scotland, 1960. Licentiate Medical Council Can. Intern St. Joseph's Hospital, London, Ontario, Can., 1960-61; general practice medicine Toronto, Ontario, Can., 1961-69; medical director Wyeth Limited Can., Toronto, 1969-70, president, 1970-75; executive assistant to president Wyeth International Limited, Philadelphia, 1975, group vice president, 1975-78, executive vice president, 1978-80, president, 1980-84; president Wyeth Laboratories, Philadelphia, 1984-87; chairman Wyeth-Ayerst Laboratories, Philadelphia, 1987—; executive vice president Am. Home Products Corp., New York City, 1987—. Trustee School Nursing U. Pennsylvania; board of directors Bryn Mawr Hospital. Roman Catholic. Club: Philadelphia Country. Avocations: art collecting, golf, music. Office: Wyeth-Ayerst Labs Post Office Box 8299 Philadelphia Pennsylvania 19101 also: Am Home Products Corp 685 3rd Avenue New York New York 10017

CANEPA, JOHN CHARLES, banking executive; born Newburyport, Massachusetts, August 26, 1930; son of John Jere and Agnes R. (Barbour) C.; married Marie Olney, September 13, 1953; children: Claudia, John J., Peter C., Milissa L. Bachelor of Arts, Harvard University, 1953; Master of Business Administration, New York University, 1960. With Chase Manhattan Bank, New York City, 1957-63; senior vice president Provident Bank, Cincinnati, 1963-70; president Old Kent Fin. Corp., Grand Rapids, Michigan, 1970—; president, chief executive officer Old Kent Bank & Trust Company, Grand Rapids, 1970—. Served with United States Navy, 1953-57. Office: Old Kent Bank & Trust Company 1 Vandenberg Center Grand Rapids Michigan 49503

CANION, JOSEPH ROD, computer company executive; born Houston, January 19, 1945. Master of Science in Electrical Engineering, University Houston, 1967. With Texas Instruments, Incorporated, Houston, 1968-81; president, chief executive officer Compaq Computer Corp., Houston, 1982—, also board of directors. Office: COMPAQ Computer Corp 20555 SH 249 Post Office Box 69-2000 Houston Texas 77269

CANNON, JAMES W., insurance company executive; born 1927. With Safeco Corp., Seattle, 1948—, statistical supervisor, 1948-55, assistant controller, 1955-56, director operations, 1956-67, vice president operations, data processing, 1967-75, senior vice president administration, 1975-82, senior vice president, 1982-85, executive vice president, 1985—; also president General Insurance Company of Am. (subsidiary), Seattle, Safeco Insurance Company of Am. (subsidiary), Seattle, Safeco Lloyd's Insurance Company (subsidiary), Seattle, Safeco National Insurance Company (subsidiary), Seattle, Safeco Surplus Lines Insurance Company (subsidiary), Seattle. Served with United States Navy, 1945-47. Office: Safeco Ins Company of Am Safeco Plaza T-22 Seattle Washington 98185

CARLEY, JOHN BLYTHE, retail grocery executive; born Spokane, Washington, January 4, 1934; son of John Lewis and Freida June (Stiles) C.; married Joan Marie Hohenleitner, August 6, 1960; children: Christopher, Kathryn, Peter, Scott. Associate of Arts, Boise Junior College, 1955; student, University Washington, 1956-57, Stanford University Exec. Program, 1973. Store director Albertson's Incorporated, Boise, Idaho, 1961-65, grocery merchandiser, 1965-70, district manager, 1970-73, vice president general merchandise, 1973, vice president corp. merchandising, 1973-75, vice president retail operations, 1975-76, senior vice president retail operations, 1976-77, executive vice president retail operations, 1977-84, president, 1984—, also director. Active fund-raising drives United Way. Served with United States Army, 1957-59. Member Am. Management Association, Food Marketing Institute. Republican. Roman Catholic. Clubs: Arid, Hillcrest Country (Boise). Office: Albertson's

Incorporated 250 Parkcenter Boulevard Boise Idaho 83706

CARLISLE, DWIGHT L., JR., clothing manufacturing executive; born Alexander City, Alabama, November 7, 1935; son of Dwight L. Carlisle; married Sarah Wilbanks; children: Danice, Rebecca, Meredith. Bachelor of Science in Textile Engineering, Auburn University, 1958. Assistant general superintendent Russell Corp., Alexander City, Alabama, 968-70, superintendent, 1970-71, vice president manufacturing, 1971-80, executive vice president, 1980-82, president, chief operating officer, 1982—, president, chief executive officer, 1988—, also director, 1988—; board of directors First National Bank, Alexander City. Board of directors Russell Hospital, Alexander City, 1984—. Member National Knitwear Manufacturers Association (chairman 1988), Alabama Chamber of Commerce (board directors). Office: Russell Corp Lee St Post Office Box 272 Alexander City Alabama 35010

CARLSON, CURTIS LEROY, business executive; born Minneapolis, July 9, 1914; son of Charles A. and Letha (Peterson) C.; married Arleen Martin, June 30, 1938; children: Marilyn Carlson Nelson, Barbara Carlson Gage. Bachelor of Arts in Economics, University Minnesota, 1937. Salesman, Procter & Gamble Company, Minneapolis, 1937-39; founder, president Gold Bond Stamp Company, Minneapolis, 1938-84, president, chairman board of directors, 1938—; chairman board of directors Carlson Companies, Incorporated (formerly Premium Service Corp.), 1972-84; president MIP Agency, Incorporated; chairman board Radisson Hotel Corp., Radisson Group Incorporated, Radisson Missouri Corp., Colony Hotels and Resorts, Incorporated, Carlson Real Estate, Incorporated, Carlson Holdings, Incorporated, Carlson Leasing, Incorporated, Carlson Tours, Incorporated, TGI Friday's Incorporated, Dallas, Nordic-Am. Travel, Incorporated, K-Promotions, Incorporated; director Premiums International Limited, Can., Carlson Hospitality Group, Jason Empire Incorporated, Marquette Bank of Minneapolis, Bank Shares, Incorporated, Radisson Wilmington. Sr. vice president U. Minnesota Foundation; chairman emeritus Swedish Council Am.; board of directors, founder Boys Club Minneapolis; board of directors Minnesota Meetings; member adv. board U. Minnesota Curtis L. Carlson School of Mgmt., U. Minnesota; adv. council United States Swedish Foundation; member Hennepin Avenue Methodist Church. Member Trading Stamp Institute Am. (director, founder, president 1959-60), Swedish-Am. Chamber of Commerce (director), University Minnesota Alumni Association (honors committee), Sigma Phi Epsilon. (vice chairman board trustees). Clubs: Minneapolis, Minneapolis Athletic; Northland Country (Duluth); Minikahda, Woodhill Country; Ocean Reef Yacht (Key Largo); Palm Bay (Miami). Lodges: Masons, Shriners, Jesters. Office: Carlson Cos Incorporated Carlson Parkway Post Office Box 59159 Minneapolis Minnesota 55459-8215

CARPENTER, DAVID ROLAND, life insurance executive; born Fort Wayne, Indiana, March 24, 1939; son of Geary W. and Rita (Ueber) C.; married Karen Woodard, October 20,

1963 (divorced April 1975); children: Kimberly, Clayton; married Leila E.M. Sjogren, September 20, 1980; 1 daughter, Michelle. Bachelor of Business Administration, University Michigan, 1961, Master of Science, 1962. Senior vice president Booz, Allen Cons., Newport Beach, California, 1976-77; vice president Tillinghast, Nelson & Warren, Newport Beach, California, 1977-80; chief marketing officer Transam. Occidental Life Insurance Company, Los Angeles, 1980-81, executive vice president, chief marketing officer, 1981-82, president, 1982—, chief operating officer, 1982-83, president, director, chief executive officer, 1983—, also chairman; group vice president Transam. Corp.; director Transam. Life & Annuity Company, Transam. Assurance Company, Transam. Insurance Corp., Transam. International Insurance Services. Trustee, founding chairman Alliance for Aging Research, 1986—; chairman board of directors California Medical Center Foundation, 1985—; board of directors Central City Association, 1985—, chairman, 1987-88; board of directors Am. Women's Economic Devel. Corp., 1990—, Ind. Colleges Southern California, 1988—; vice-chmn. Uni-Health Am., 1988—, chairman, 1985-88; governor Ford's Theatre, 1985—; vice-chmn., trustee Mus. Contemporary Art, 1986—. Fellow Society Actuaries (board directors 1978-81); member Am. Acad. Actuaries (vice president 1981-83), International Insurance Society (governor 1987—), Association California Life Insurance Companies (chairman 1991), Los Angeles Chamber of Commerce (board directors 1984—). Presbyterian. Office: Transam Occidental Life Ins Company 1150 S Olive St Los Angeles California 90015

CARPENTER, EDMUND MOGFORD, manufacturing executive; born Toledo, December 28, 1941; son of Charles N. and Vivian (Mogford) C.; married Mary Winterhoff, May 20, 1962; children: Susan, Edmund Mogford, Molly. Bachelor of Science in Industrial Engineering, University Michigan, 1963, Master of Business Administration, 1964. District plant manager Michigan Bell Tel. Company, Detroit, 1964-68; partner Touche Ross & Company, CPA's, Detroit, 1968-74; president Fruehauf do Brasil, Sao Paulo, 1974-76; president auto truck group Kelsey-Hayes Company, Romulus, Michigan, 1976-81; group general manager world wide automotive operations International Telephone & Telegraph Corporation Corp., Southfield, Michigan, 1981-83; vice president International Telephone & Telegraph Corporation Corp., New York City, 1983-85, president, director, 1985-88; chief operating officer International Telephone & Telegraph Corporation Industrial Products, New York City, 1987-88; chairman, chief executive officer General Signal Corp., High Ridge Park, Stamford, Connecticut, 1988—; board of directors General Signal Corp., High Ridge Park, Stamford; board of directors Campbell Soup Company, Camden, New Jersey. Board of directors Junior Achievement. Member Machinery and Allied Products Institute (executive committee). Office: General Signal Corp High Ridge Park Post Office Box 10010 Stamford Connecticut 06904

CARPENTER, RICHARD M., chemical company executive; born 1927; married. Bachelor of Science,

University Wisconsin, 1949, Juris Doctor, 1952. With South Carolina Johnson & Son Incorporated, Racine, Wisconsin, 1952—, general attorney, 1960-65, assistant to president, 1965-67, regulations director, 1967-71, group product manager, 1971-76, vice president consumer products for East, 1976-80, executive vice president United States consumer products, 1980-83, executive vice president, 1983—. Served with Army of the United States, 1945-46. Office: S C Johnson & Son Incorporated 1525 Howe St Racine Wisconsin 53403

CARR, FRED, insurance company executive; born 1931; married. Student, University of California at Los Angeles. Former president Shareholders Management Corp., Los Angeles; fin. advisor Cons. Associates Incorporated, Los Angeles, 1970-71; president Carr Management & Research Corp., Los Angeles, 1971-74; with First Executive Corp., Los Angeles, 1974—, chairman, 1974—; president, chairman Executive Life Insurance Company (subsidiary First Executive Corp.), Los Angeles. Office: Exec Life Ins Company 11444 W Olympic Boulevard Los Angeles California 90064

CARRIGG, JAMES A., utility company executive; born 1933. Student, Union College, 1951-53; AAS in Electrical Engineering Tech., Broome Community College. Safety cadet New York State Electric & Gas Corp., Ithaca, 1958, safety director, 1958-61, personnel director, 1961-63, supervisor training, 1963-64, local manager, 1964-69, assistant to vice president, 1969-72, area manager, 1972-73, general manager, 1973-82; vice president New York State Electric & Gas Corp., Binghamton, 1982-83, president, director, 1983-86, president, chief operating officer, 1986-88, chairman, chief executive officer, 1988-90, chairman, president, chief executive officer, 1991—; board of directors Security Mutual Life Insurance Company New York, Endicott Trust Company, Home Mutual Insurance, Company, Utilities Mutual Insurance Company, Security Equity Life Insurance Company; board of directors, past president Empire State Electric Energy Research Corp. Board of directors Foundation of SUNY-Binghamton, Broome County Community Charities, Incorporated, United Health Svcs. Hosps. Incorporated, New York Business Devel. Corp.; member adv. council Clarkson U. School Mgmt.; trustee Pub. Policy Institute (Business Council New York State, Incorporated), Broome Community College With United States Army, 1954-55. Member Broome County Chamber of Commerce (former chairman). Office: New York State Electric & Gas Corp 4500 Vestal Parkway E Post Office Box 3607 Binghamton New York 13902-3607

CARROLL, RAOUL LORD, lawyer; born Washington, March 16, 1950; son of John Thomas and Gertrude Barbara (Jenkins) C.; married Elizabeth Jane Coleman, March 22, 1980; children: Alexandria Nicole, Christina Elizabeth. Bachelor of Science, Morgan State University, 1972; Juris Doctor, St. Johns University, Jamaica, New York, 1975; postgraduate, Georgetown University, 1980-81. Bar: New York 1976, District of Columbia 1979, United States District Court District of Columbia 1979, United States Supreme Court 1979, United States District Court (southern and eastern district) New York 1982. Assistant United States attorney Office United States Attorney, Department Justice, Washington, 1979-80; associate member United States Board Vets. Appeals, Washington, 1980-81; partner Hart, Carroll & Chavers, Washington, 1981-86, Bishop, Cook, Purcell & Reynolds, Washington, 1986-89; general counsel United States Department Vets. Affairs, 1989-91; president Government National Mortgage Association, Department of Housing and Urban Development, 1991—; director, treasurer Conwest-USA, Washington; chairman Am. Center for International Leadership, Baltimore. President Black Assistant United States Attys. Association, Washington, 1980-83; general counsel Md./D.C. Minority Supplier Devel. Council, Columbia, Maryland, 1984-86. Captain United States Army, 1975-79. Decorated Joint Service Commendation medal, Army Commendation medal; named Outstanding Young Man Am., United States Jaycees, 1979. Member New York State Bar, District of Columbia Bar Association, Washington Bar Association, National Association Bond Lawyers, Omega Psi Phi. Baptist. Home: 7821 Morningside Dr Northwest Washington District of Columbia 20012 also: Department of Housing and Urban Development Govt National Mortgage Association 451 7th St Southwest Room 6100 Washington District of Columbia 20410

CARSON, DAVID ELLIS ADAMS, banker; born Birkenhead, England, August 2, 1934; came to United States, 1938; son of Ellis and Hilda (Adams) C.; married Sara F. Samotus, July 1959; children—Rebecca, Elizabeth, Peter. Bachelor of Business Administration, University Mich, 1955; Doctor of Laws (honorary), University New Haven, 1988. Senior vice president Hartford Insurance, Hartford, Connecticut, 1969-74; president, chief executive officer Middlesex Mutual Assurance Company, Middletown, 1974-82; president People's Bank, Bridgeport, Connecticut, 1983—, chief executive officer, 1985—, also treasurer, trustee, from 1983; board of directors SACIA, Stamford, Connecticut. Director Private Industry Council Southwestern Connecticut; former chairman Connecticut Business and Industry Association, Hartford, United Way of Eastern Fairfield County, Bridgeport, Bridgeport Hospital; trustee Connecticut Trust for Historic Preservation, Sacred Heart U., General Theol. Sem., New York City; trustee Connecticut Pub. Broadcasting, former chairman board. Office: People's Bank 850 Main St Bridgeport Connecticut 06601

CARSON, EDWARD MANSFIELD, banker; born Tucson, November 6, 1929; son of Ernest Lee and Earline M. (Mansfield) C.; married Nadine Anne Severns, December 13, 1952; children: Dawn, Tod. Bachelor of Science in Business Administration, Arizona State University, 1951; graduate in banking, Rutgers University, 1963. With First Interstate Bank of Arizona, Phoenix, 1951-85, executive vice president, 1969-72, chief administrative officer, 1972-75, vice chairman board, 1975-77, president, chief executive officer, 1977-85, also board of directors; president First Interstate Bancorp, Los Angeles, 1985—, also board of directors; board of directors Inspiration Resources Corp., Ramada Inns, Incorporated, First Interstate Bank of Oregon. Board fellows Am. Grad. School International Mgmt. Recipient Service award Arizona State University Alumni Association, 1968; named to Arizona State University Alumni Association Hall of Fame, 1977. Member Association Reserve City Bankers, Association Bank Holding Companies (board directors). Clubs: Paradise Valley Country, Thunderbirds, Los Angeles Country, California; Phoenix Country. Office: 1st Interstate Bancorp 707 Wilshire Boulevard Los Angeles California 90017

CARTLEDGE, RAYMOND EUGENE, paper company executive; born Pensacola, Florida, June 12, 1929; son of Raymond H. and Meddie (Brookins) C.; married Gale Perry, June 30, 1962; children: John R., Perri Ann, Susan R. Bachelor of Science, University Alabama, 1952; postgraduate, Harvard Business School, 1970. With Procter & Gamble Company, 1955-56; with Union Camp Corp., Wayne, New Jersey, 1956-71, 81—, vice president, general manager container div., 1981-82, executive vice president, 1982-84, president, chief operating officer, 1983-86, chairman, president, chief executive officer, 1986-89, chairman, chief executive officer, 1989—, also board of directors; president, chief executive officer Clevepak Corp., White Plains, New York, 1971-80. Served with United States Army, 1952-55. Office: Union Camp Corp 1600 Valley Road Wayne New Jersey 07470

CARVER, MARTIN GREGORY, tire manufacturing company executive; born Davenport, Iowa, May 10, 1948; son of Roy James and Lucille Avis (Young) C. Bachelor of Arts in Math, University Iowa, 1970; Master of Business Administration, University Ind., 1972. Assistant treasurer Consolidated Foods Corp. now Sara Lee, 1975-79; regional vice president heavy duty parts, then vice chairman Bandag, Incorporated, Muscatine, 1979-81; chief executive officer Bandag, Incorporated (retreaded tires manufacturers), 1982—, chairman board, 1981. Board of directors Augustana College, 1986—; board visitors U. Iowa School Business. Named Chief Executive Officer of Year, rubber and plastics industry, Fin. World, 1986, Chief Executive Officer of Decade, 1989. Member National Association Manufacturers (director 1987—). Clubs: 33, Chicago. Lodge: Rotary. Office: Bandag Incorporated Bandag Center Muscatine Iowa 52761

CASPERSEN, FINN MICHAEL WESTBY, diversified financial services company executive; born New York City, October 27, 1941; son of Olaus Westby and Freda Caspersen; married Barbara Caspersen, June 17, 1967. Bachelor of Arts With honors in Economics, Brown University, 1963; Bachelor of Laws cum laude, Harvard University, 1966; Doctor of Laws, Hood College; Doctor of Humanities, Washington College, Chestertown, Maryland; Alderson-Broaddus College. Bar: Florida 1966, New York 1967. Associate Dewey, Ballantine, Bushby, Palmer & Wood, New York City, 1969-72; chairman board, chief executive officer, member executive committee Beneficial Corp., 1976—; board of directors, member executive committee Beneficial National Bank; chairman board of directors Beneficial Bank, P.L.C.; board advisors Institute Law and Economics, University Pennsylvania, John M. Olin speaker; president United States Equestrian Team. Former trustee New Jersey College Fund Association; emeritus trustee Brown U.; trustee emeritus Camp Nejeda Foundation for Diabetic Children; board of directors Shelter Harbor Fire District; board of directors, O.W. Caspersen Foundation; chairman board trustees Peddie School, Hightstown, New Jersey; past chairman board Drumthwacket Foundation; chairman Waterloo Foundation for Arts. Incorporated; charter member Partnership for New Jersey, New Brunswick; president Coalition of Service Industries,Incorporated, Washington; chairman board trustees Gladstone Equestrian Association Incorporated; member adv. committee to executive board Morris-Sussex Area Council Boy Scouts Am.; director driving committee Am. Horse Shows Incorporated; member corp. Cardigan Mountain School; member Harvard Resources Committee Lieutenant United States Coast Guard, 1966-69. Recipient President's medal Johns Hopkins University; named Civic Leader of Year Young Men's Christian Association, 1982. Member Am. Fin. Svcs. Association (board directors, chairman government affairs committee, chairman membership committee, adminstrn. committee, past chairman), Florida Bar Association, New York Bar Association, Harvard Club, Knickerbocker Club, University Club. Address: Post Office Box 911 Wilmington Delaware 19899

CATACOSINOS, WILLIAM JAMES, utility company executive; born New York City, April 12, 1930; son of James and Penelope (Paleologos) C.; married Florence Maken, October 16, 1955; children: William, James. Bachelor of Science, New York University, 1951, Master of Business Administration, 1952, Doctor of Philosophy, 1962. Assistant editor 20th Century-Fox, New York City, 1951-52; assistant director business management and administration Brookhaven National Laboratory, Upton, New York, 1956-69; president Applied Digital Data Systems, Incorporated, Hauppauge, New York, 1969-77; chairman and chief executive officer Applied Digital Data Systems, Incorporated, 1977-82; chairman, chief executive officer Long Island Lighting Company, Hicksville, New York, 1984—, also board of directors, 1978—; adj. assistant professor New York University, 1962-64; management counselor, 1962-69; chairman board Corometrics Medical, 1968-74; board of directors Utilities Mutual Insurance Company, 1985—; board of directors Ketema Incorporated, 1988—; member adv. committee, policy committee on strategic planning Edison Electric Institute, 1990—. Board of directors Brookhaven Town Industrial Commission, 1956-77, Suffolk County chapter Am. Cancer Society, 1969-77, Stony Brook Foundation, 1978-85; trustee Polytechnical Institute New York, 1981-85; national chairman Am. Society Prevention of Cruelty to Children, 1981-83; With United States Navy, 1952-56.

CATSIMATIDIS, JOHN ANDREAS, retail chain executive, airline executive; born Nissiros, Greece, September 7, 1948; came to United States, 1949, naturalized, 1950; son of Andreas John and Despina (Emmanulides) C. Bachelor of Science in Engineering, New York University,

1970. Chairman, chief executive officer Red Apple Companies (Gristedes, Red Apple, Pantry Pride supermarkets), New York City and Fort Lauderdale, Florida, 1970—, United Refining Incorporated, Warren, Pennsylvania, 1986—; chairman, chief executive officer Designcraft, New York City. Recipient Humanitarian award National Conference of Christians and Jews, 1978, Am. Jewish Committee, 1982, National Kidney Association, 1986; Entrepreneurship award New York University Business School, 1987. Member Westside Chamber of Commerce (vice chairman 1975—). Clubs: New York University, Wings, Young Men Philanthrapic League, New York Athletic. Office: Red Apple Group 823 11th Avenue New York New York 10019

CAWTHORN, ROBERT ELSTON, health care executive; born Masham, England, September 28, 1935; came to United States, 1982; son of Gerald P. and Gertrude E. (Longster) C.; married H. Susan Marshall, January 15, 1960; children: Amanda, Liza. Bachelor of Arts in Agriculture, Cambridge University, 1959. Various executive positions Pfizer, Incorporated, Can., Africa, Middle East and Europe, 1961-79; president Biogen S.A., Geneva, 1979-82, Rorer International Group, Fort Washington, Pennsylvania, 1982-83; executive vice president Rorer Group, Incorporated, 1982-84, president, 1985-85, president, chief executive officer, 1985-86, chairman, chief executive officer, 1986-88; chairman, president, chief executive officer Rorer Group, Incorporated, Fort Washington, Pennsylvania, 1988—; board of directors Universal Health Realty Income Trust, trustee, 1986—, Immune Response Corp., director, 1987—, Sun Company Incorporated, director, 1988—. Board of directors Pharm. Mfgs. Association, directors, 1985—, United Way Southeastern Pennsylvania, trustee, 1985—, Greater Philadelphia 1st Corp., director, 1986—, Greater Philadelphia Chamber of Commerce, director, 1987—, World Affairs Council Pennsylvania, director, 1986-90, International Business Forum, chairman, 1987-89, The Baldwin School, trustee, 1984-86. Member Pharmaceutical Manufacturers Association (board directors 1985—), Greater Philadelphia Chamber of Commerce (board directors 1987—), International Business Forum (chairman 1987-89), Baldwin School (trustee 1984-86). Home: 50 Crosby Brown Road Gladwyne Pennsylvania 19035 Office: Rorer Group Incorporated 500 Virginia Dr Fort Washington Pennsylvania 19034

CAYNE, JAMES E., investment banker; born 1934. With Bonn Bush Mach, 1954-66, Lebenthal and Company, 1966-69; now president, senior managing director Bear Stearns and Company Incorporated, also board of directors. Office: Bear Stearns Company Incorporated 245 Park Avenue 9th Floor New York New York 10167

CHAPMAN, JAMES CLAUDE, marine equipment manufacturing executive; born Detroit, March 16, 1931; son of Claude Byrand and Madolin C. (Werstine) C.; married Elizabeth Jane Quinley, May 1, 1954; children: Diane, Donna. BME cum laude, University Detroit, 1956, Master of Business Administration, 1966. Registered professional engineer, Michigan. Plant manager Rockwell International Corp., Marysville, Ohio, 1971-74; director facilities Rockwell International Corp., Troy, Michigan, 1974-78; director manufacturing Outboard Marine Corp., Waukegan, Illinois, 1978, vice president manufacturing, 1978-85, president, chief operating officer, 1985-90, president, chief executive officer, 1990—; director Advance Machine Company. President Northeast Illinois council Boy Scouts Am.; board of directors Lake Forest School of Mgmt., Illinois, 1984. Served with United States Naval Reserve, 1950-58. Member Society Manufacturing Engineers, Society Automotive Engineers, Waukegan-Lake County Chamber of Commerce (vice chairman 1985), Glen Flora Country Club. Republican. Roman Catholic. Avocations: boating; fishing; golfing; rock hounding; skiing. Home: 25310 W Hickory Antioch Illinois 60002 Office: Outboard Marine Corp 100 Sea Horse Dr Waukegan Illinois 60085

CHAZEN, JEROME A., apparel company executive; born New York City, March 21, 1927; son of David and Rose (Mark) C.; married Simona Chivian, June 26, 1949; children: Kathy Ann, Louise Sharon Chazen Banon, David Franklin. Bachelor of Arts, University Wisconsin, Madison, 948; Master of Business Administration, Columbia University, Madison, 1950. Security analyst Sutro Brothers, New York City, 1950-51; salesman/mgr. Rhea Manufacturing Company, Milwaukee, 1951-52, buyer Milwaukee Boston Stores, 1952-54; buyer Milwaukee Boston Stores Lit Brothers, Philadelphia, 1954-57; vice president Winkelman Stores, Detroit, 957-68; vice president sales Westwood Textiles, New York City, 1968-73, Eccobay Sports Wear, New York City, 1973-77; chairman board of directors Liz Claiborne, Incorporated, New York City, 1977—; board of directors Fashion Institute Tech., Shenkar College. Vice chairman International Peace Park/ Jewish National Fund, Israel, 1987; board of directors Greater New York council Boy Scouts Am., 1983-84, Rockland Center for Arts, Nyack, New York, 1983—, Lupus Foundation, New York City, 1984, Educational Foundation, Am. Craft Mus., 1989; board of directors, chairman, div. leader Federation United Jewish Appeal, New York City, 1983-86. Served with United States Navy, 1945-46. Jewish. Avocations: jazz music, travel, boating, glass art collecting. Office: Liz Claiborne Incorporated 1441 Broadway New York New York 10018

CHECCHI, ALFRED A., airline company executive; born 1948; married. Bachelor of Arts, Amherst College, 1970; Master of Business Administration, Harvard University, 1974. Vice president Marriott Corp., 1975-82; with Bass Brothers, 1982-86; president Alfred Checchi Associates, Incorporated, 1986—; with Northwest Industries Incorporated, 1989—; chairman, chief executive officer NWA Incorporated; chairman, director Northwest Airlines Incorporated; chairman, president Wings Holdings Incorporated. Office: Northwest Airlines Incorporated Mpls-St Paul International Airport Saint Paul Minnesota 55111

CHENEY, RICHARD EUGENE, public relations executive; born Pana, Illinois, August 30, 1921; son of Royal F. and Nelle E. (Henke) C.; married Betty L. McCray, October 17, 1943; children: R. Christopher, Elyn G. Cheney McInnis; married 2d,

Virginia B. Burns, January 23, 1966; children: Benjamin, Anne. Bachelor of Arts, Knox College, Galesburg, Illinois, 1943; Master of Arts, Columbia University, 1960. Associate editor Tide Magazine, 1953; director pub. relations Tri Continental Corp., 1953-55; assistant manager pub. relations department Mobil Corp., 1955-60; vice chairman board Hill & Knowlton, Incorporated, New York City, 1960-86, chairman board, 1987—; board of directors Chattem Incorporated, Chattanooga, C.R. Gibson Company, Norwalk, Connecticut, Alphabet Incorporated, Warren, Ohio, Rowe Furniture. Served to lieutenant (junior grade) United States Naval Reserve, 1943-47, PTO. Clubs: University, Dutch Treat (New York City); Edgewood (Tivoli, New York); Castalia (Ohio); Century Club (New York City). Home: 25 W 81st St Apartment 5A New York New York 10024 Office: Hill & Knowlton Incorporated 420 Lexington Avenue New York New York 10706

CHERRY, WENDELL, health care company executive; born Riverside, Kentucky Bachelor of Science, University Kentucky, 1957, Bachelor of Laws, 1959. Bar: Kentucky, 1959. Founder Humana Incorporated, Louisville, Kentucky; president, chief operating officer, director Humana Incorporated, Louisville, 1969—; chief operating officer Edison Homes-S.East, Louisville, Community Hospitals Humana, Incorporated Louisville, Gwinnett Community Hospital, Incorporated, Snellville, Georgia, Medical Specialties Incorporated, Humhosco Incorporated, Brandon, Florida, Humedicenters, Incorporated, Richlands, Virginia, Beaumont Hospitals Incorporated, Texas, numerous others. Named one of Outstanding Young Men Am. United States Jaycees, 1970. Office: Humana Incorporated 500 W Main St Post Office Box 1438 Louisville Kentucky 40201

CHEVALIER, SAMUEL FLETCHER, banker; born Islip, New York, March 9, 1934; married Elinor Louise Towell; children: David, Peter, Valerie. Bachelor of Arts, Northeastern University, 1957. Assistant secretary Irving Trust Company, New York City, 1965-67, assistant vice president, 1967-70, vice president, 1970-77, senior vice president, manager domestic/corp. bank corp, 1982-84; vice president Irving Bank Corp., New York City, 1975-77, senior vice president, 1977-80, executive vice president, 1980-84, president, 1984—; vice chairman The Bank of New York, 1989—. Board of directors Greater New York chapter March of Dimes, 1984—. Served to 1st lieutenant United States Army, 1957-59. Office: Bank of New York 1 Wall St New York New York 10286

CHIARUCCI, VINCENT A., machinery equipment company executive; born Canton, Ohio, 1929. Bachelor of Science, Kent State University, 1951. With Ernst & Ernst, 1951-60; controller Hupp Incorporated, 1960-67; vice president, fin. Gibson Products Corp., 1967-68; with White Consolidated Industries, Cleveland, 1968—, executive vice president, 1976—, group president; consultant Figgie International Incorporated, Willoughby, Ohio, now president. Office: White Consol Industries Incorporated 11770 Berea Road Cleveland Ohio 44111 also: 4420 Sherwin Road Willoughby Ohio 44094

CHIAT, JAY, advertising agency executive; born New York City, October 26, 1931; son of Sam and Min (Kretchmer) C.; children: Debra, Marc, Elyse. Bachelor of Science, Rutgers University. Formerly vice president Leland Oliver Company, Los Angeles; president, chief executive officer Jay Chiat & Associates; now chairman Chiat/Day Incorporated, New York City. Served with United States Air Force. Office: Chiat/Day/Mojo 79 Fifth Avenue New York New York 10003 also: Chiat/Day/Mojo Advt 320 Hampton Dr Venice California 90291 also: 77 Maiden Lane San Francisco California 94108 also: 10 Lower Spadina, Toronto, Ontario Canada M5V 2Z1

CHLEBOWSKI, JOHN FRANCIS, JR., financial executive; born Wilmington, Delaware, August 19, 1945; son of John Francis and Helen Ann (Cholewa) C.; married Roxanne J. Decyk, June 27, 1987; children: J. Christopher, Lauren R. Bachelor of Science, University Delaware, Newark, 1967; Master of Business Administration, Pennsylvania State University, State College, 1971. Fin. analyst Jones & Laughlin Steel, Pittsburgh, 1971-74; manager, fin. analyst W.R. Grace & Company, New York City, 1974-75; manager, fin. planner W.R. Grace & Company, Dallas, 1975-77; assistant treasurer W.R. Grace & Company, New York City, 1978-83; Vice president planning Polumbus Company, Denver, 1977-78; vice president fin. planning GATX Corp., Chicago, 1983-85, vice president fin., chief fin. officer, 1985—. Board of directors Chicago Heart Association, 1985—; board of directors Travelers & Immigrants Aid Association, 1987—; chief crusader United Way Crusade Mercy, Chicago. Leadership Greater Chicago fellow, 1984-85. Member Fin. Executives Institute, Econ. Club, Executive Club, River Club, McGraw Wildlife Club, Chicago Society Clubs, Beta Gamma Sigma. Roman Catholic. Office: GATX Corp 120 S Riverside Plaza Chicago Illinois 60606

CHRISTOPHERSON, WESTON ROBERT, banker; born Walum, North Dakota, May 5, 1925; son of Carl and Ermie (Larsen) C.; married Myrna Christensen, June 8, 1951; children: Mia Karen Kammerer, Mari Louisa Armour, Kari Marie. Bachelor of Science, University North Dakota, 1949, Juris Doctor, 1951. Bar: North Dakota 1951, Illinois 1952. With Jewel Companies, Incorporated, Chicago, 1951-84, president, 1970-80, chief executive officer, 1979-84, also director; chairman board, chief executive officer Northern Trust Company, 1984-89; chairman board Northern Trust Corp., 1989-90; also director; director Ameritech, GATX Corp., Quaker Oats Company. trustee U. Chicago, member Business Council. Presbyterian Clubs: Economic, Chicago, Onwentsia, Old Elm, Commercial, Commonwealth. Home: 200 N Green Bay Road Lake Forest Illinois 60045 Office: One First National Plaza #2530 Chicago Illinois 60603

CIECHANOVER, JOSEPH, banker, lawyer; born Haifa, Israel, October 1, 1933; married Atara Pchor; children: Tamar, Dafna, Isaac. Magister juris, Hebrew University, Jerusalem, 1958, postgraduate, 1961-62; Master of Laws, University California, Berkeley, 1967; Doctor of Philosophy, Boston University, 1991. Bar: Israel 1958, New York 1982. Head administration Ministry Agriculture, Israel, 1957-60, general counsel, 1960-68; head Israel Defense Mission to United States and Can., 1974-78; director general Ministry Foreign Affairs, Israel, 1979-80; vice chairman Israel Discount Bank, New York City, 1981-86; president PEC Israel Economic Corp., New York City, 1981—; chairman Israel Discount Bank Limited, 1986—; with Ministry of Defense; lecturer on administrative and agricultural law Hebrew University, 1962-74. Recipient Distinguished Pub. Service Medal award United States Department Defense, 1980. Office: Israel Discount Bank Limited 511 Fifth Avenue New York New York 10017

CIZIK, ROBERT, manufacturing company executive; born Scranton, Pennsylvania, April 4, 1931; son of John and Anna (Paraska) C.; married Jane Morin, October 3, 1953; children: Robert Morin, Jan Catherine, Paula Jane, Gregory Alan, Peter Nicholas. Bachelor of Science, University Connecticut, 1953; Master of Business Administration, Harvard University, 1958; Doctor of Laws (honorary), Kenyon College, 1983. Accountant Price Waterhouse & Company (C.P.A.s), New York City, 1953-54, 56; fin. analyst Exxon United States of America, New Jersey, 1958-61; executive assistant Cooper Industries, Incorporated, Houston, 1961-63, treasurer, 1963-64, controller, 1964-67, vice president planning, 1967-69, executive vice president, 1969-73, president, chief operating officer, 1973-75, president, chief executive officer, 1975-83, president, chief executive officer, chairman, 1983—, also director; board of directors Harris Corp., Temple Inland, Panhandle Eastern Corp.; member Business Roundtable; member host committee Houston Economic Summit Meeting, 1990; member nominationg committee New York Stock Exchange, 1990. Co-chairman Wortham Theater Foundation, 1981—; member Houston Business Committee for Arts; trustee Houston Grand Opera, Committee for Economic Devel.; board of directors Associate Harvard Business School, Boston, 1984—; campaign chairman flagship div. United Way, 1990-91. Recipient General Maurice Hirsch award Business Committee for Arts, 1984, Chief Executive Officer of Year bronze award Fin. World magazine, 1987; named Best Chief Executive Officer in Machinery Industry, Wall Street Transcript, 80, 81, 83, 86, 87, 88, 89 Chief Executive Officer of Decade bronze award in Industrial Equipment Cos., 1988; named International Executive of Year Greater Houston Partnership and Houston World Trade Association, 1990. Member Electrical Manufacturers Club (president 1990—, board govs. 1984—), Coronado Club, Houston Petroleum Club, River Oaks Country Club, Ramada Club, Forum Club Houston (founding), Houston Center. Office: Cooper Industries Incorporated 1001 Fannin Suite 4000 Houston Texas 77002

CLAPP, JOSEPH MARK, motor carrier company executive; born Greensboro, North Carolina, July 29, 1936; son of Frederick Lawrence and Mary Beatrice (Flaherty) C.; married Helen Grey Roberts, June 8, 1963; children: Kathryn Grey, Amy Elizabeth. Bachelor of Science in Business Administration, University North Carolina, 1958. Practitioner ICC. From management trainee to director safety, personnel Ryder

Tank Line, Incorporated, Greensboro, North Carolina, 1959-66; assistant to president T.I. McCormack Trucking, Incorporated, Woodbridge, New Jersey, 1966-67; div. employee relations manager to senior vice president Roadway Express, Incorporated, Akron, Ohio, 1967-74; vice chairman corp. services Roadway Services, Incorporated, Akron, 1985, president, chief executive officer, 1986—, chairman, 1987—; past chairman Transportation Research Board of National Research Council. Member National Motor Carrier Adv. Council, Washington, 1985; board trustees Akron City Hospital, 1985—; board of directors St. Edwards Home, Fairlawn, Ohio, 1985. Served to staff sergeant United States Air Force Reserve, 1959-65. Member Am. Trucking Association (vice president at large), Transportation Practitioners Association, Regular Commission Carrier Conference (chairman 1984). Roman Catholic. Clubs: Congl. Country (Bethesda, Maryland); Fairlawn Country (Akron). Office: Roadway Services Incorporated care Gayle Frank 1077 Gorge Boulevard Post Office Box 88 Akron Ohio 44309

CLARK, DONALD CAMERON, financial services company executive; born Brooklyn, August 9, 1931; son of Alexander and Sarah (Cameron) C.; married Jean Ann Williams, February 6, 1954; children: Donald, Barbara, Thomas. Bachelor of Business Administration, Clarkson University, 1953; Master of Business Administration, Northwestern University, 1961. With Household Fin. Corp., Chicago, 1955—, secretary, assistant treasurer, 1965-72, treasurer, 1972-74, director, 1974, senior vice president, office of chief executive officer, 1974-76, executive vice president, chief fin. officer, 1976-77, president, 1977-81, also board of directors; president holding company Household International, Incorporated, Prospect Heights, Illinois, 1981-88, director, 1981, chief operating officer, 1982-88, chief executive officer, 1982—, chairman, 1984—, also board of directors; chairman board dirs Schwitzer, Incorporated; director Scotsman Industries, Incorporated, Warner-Lambert Company, Ameritech, Eljer Industries, Incorporated. Board of directors Lyric Opera of Chicago; trustee Clarkson U., Evanston Hospital, Committee Economic Devel., Northwestern U. Lieutenant United States Army, 1953-55. Member Econ. Club Chicago (director, president 1985-87), Chicago Council Foreign Relations (director), Conference Board. Clubs: Chicago, Westmoreland Country, Mid-Am., Commercial (Chicago). Office: Household International Incorporated 2700 Sanders Road Prospect Heights Illinois 60070-2799

CLARK, WORLEY H., JR., specialty chemical company executive; born Big Stone Gap, Virginia, June 18, 1932; son of Worley H. and Grace Ethel (Bledsoe) C.; married Callie Anne Coughlin, August 20, 1955; children: Caryl Smith, Cindy Clark. Bachelor of Science in Industrial Engineering, North Carolina State University, 1956; student, Northwestern University; postgraduate, Cleve.-Marshall Law School; graduate exec. program, Stanford University. Sales engineer Standard Oil Ohio, 1956-60; district representative industrial div. Nalco Chemical Company, Houston, 1960-64, area manager, 1964-67;

district manager Wisconsin district Nalco Chemical Company, Naperville, Illinois, 1967-68, district manager Michigan district, 1968-71, sales manager water treatment chemicals group, 1971-74, general manager water treatment chemicals group, 1974-78, group vice president, president industrial div., 1978-82, executive vice president domestic operations, from 1982, now chairman, chief executive officer; board of directors Northern Trust Corp., USG Corp. Governing board Illinois Council Economic Education; member Northwestern U. Associates; trustee Rush-Presbyn. St. Lukes Medical Center, Field Mus., Mus. Sci. and Industry. Member Technical Association of the Pulp and Paper Industry, Paper Industry Management Association, Association Iron and Steel Engineers, Am. Petroleum Institute, Am. Institute Chemical Engineers, Chemical Manufacturers Association (chairman 1986-87), Society Chemical Industry (executive committee), Conference Board. Clubs: Commercial; Hinsdale Golf; Butler National Golf. Republican. Episcopalian. Avocations: golf; hunting; fishing. Office: Nalco Chem Company 1 Nalco Center Naperville Illinois 60563-1198

CLARKE, DAVID H., industrial products executive; born 1941; married. Vice chairman board Hanson Trust Pub. Limited Company, 1965-83; president, chief executive officer Hanson Industries North America (subsidiary Hanson Trust PLC, London), 1978—, also board of directors. Office: Hanson Industries N Am 100 Wood Avenue S Iselin New Jersey 08830

CLARKE, RICHARD ALAN, electric and gas utility company executive, lawyer; born San Francisco, May 18, 1930; son of Chauncey Frederick and Carolyn (Shannon) C.; married Mary Dell Fisher, February 5, 1955; children: Suzanne, Nancy C. Stephen, Douglas Alan. Bachelor of Arts Political Science cum laude, University California, Berkeley, 1952, Juris Doctor, 1955. Bar: California 1955. Attorney Pacific Gas and Electric Company, San Francisco, 1955-60, senior counsel, 1970-74, assistant general counsel, 1974-79, vice president, assistant to chairman, 1979-82, executive vice president, general manager utility operations, 1982-85, president, 1985-86, chairman board, chief executive officer, 1986—; partner Rockwell, Fulkerson and Clarke, San Rafael, California, 1960-69; board of directors Potlach Corp., Bank Am. Corp., Bank of Am.; member executive committee Edison Electric Institute; member The Business Council, Association Edison Illuminating Companies. Director, member executive committee Bay Area Council; member Bay Area Economic Forum, The Business Roundtable, The California Business Roundtable; trustee Committee for Economic Devel.; trustee Boalt Hall Trust, School Law U. Calif.-Berkeley; board governors San Francisco Symphony; member adv. board Walter A. Haas School Business U. California, Berkeley. Member State Bar California, Pacific Coast Electrical Association, Pacific Coast Gas Association, California Chamber of Commerce (past director), San Francisco Chamber of Commerce (past. director, vice president econ. devel.), Marin Tennis Club. Office: Pacific Gas & Electric Company 77 Beale St San Francisco California 94106

CLAUSEN, ALDEN WINSHIP, banker; born Hamilton, Illinois, February 17, 1923; son of Morton and Elsie (Kroll) C.; married Mary Margaret Crassweller, February 11, 1950; children: Eric David, Mark Winship. Bachelor of Arts, Carthage College, 1944, Doctor of Laws, 1970; Bachelor of Laws, University Minnesota, 1949; graduate, Advanced Management Program, Harvard University, 1966. Bar: Minnesota 1949, California 1950. With Bank Am. (NT & SA), San Francisco, 1949-81, 1986—; vice president Bank Am. (NT & SA), 1961-65, senior vice president, 1965-68, executive vice president, 1968-69, vice chairman board, 1969, president, chief executive officer, 1970-81, chairman, chief executive officer, 1986—; president World Bank, 1981-86; chairman, president, chief executive officer BankAmerica Corp., 1986-90, director; past president International Monetary Conference, San Francisco; Clearing House Association. Past president Federal Adv. Council, 1972; past chairman Bay Area Council; past board governors United Way of Am.; past chairman United Way of Bay Area; past member Business Roundtable; member Business Council; past member Japan-U.S. Adv. Council; past board of directors Conference Board, San Francisco Opera; past board of directors, member adv. council SRI International; member adv. council Stanford U. Grad. School Business; board of directors Harvard Business School; trustee Carthage College, Brookings Institution. Member Reserve City Bankers Association (hon.), California Bar Association. Clubs: Bankers of San Francisco, Pacific Union, Burlingame Country; Bohemian, Links (New York City); Metropolitan (Washington); Chevy Chase (Maryland). Office: BankAm Corp 555 California St San Francisco California 94104 also: Bank Am National Trust & Savings Association Bank of America Center San Francisco California 94104

CLAYTOR, WILLIAM GRAHAM, JR., railroad executive; born Roanoke, Virginia, March 14, 1912; son of William Graham and Gertrude Harris (Boatwright) C.; married Frances Murray Hammond, August 14, 1948; children: Frances Murray, William Graham III. Bachelor of Arts, University Virginia, 1933; Juris Doctor summa cum laude, Harvard University, 1936; Doctor of Laws, University Miami, 1985. Bar: New York 1937, District of Columbia 1938. Law clerk United States Judge Learned Hand, 1936-37, Mr. Justice Brandeis, 1937-38; associate firm Covington & Burling, Washington, 1938-47; partner Covington & Burling, 1947-67, counsel, 1981-82; vice president law Southern Railway Company, 1963-67, chief executive officer, 1967-77, president, 1967-76, chairman board, 1976-77; chairman board, president National Railroad Passenger Corp., Washington, 1982—; former chief executive officer, director various companies comprising Southern Railway System; secretary Navy, Washington, 1977-79, acting secretary Transportation, 1979, deputy secretary Def., 1979-81; board of directors Association Am. R.R.s, 1967-77, 82—. President Harvard Law Rev, 1935-36. Trustee Episcopal Home Children, Washington, 1960-65, vice president, 1960-63; trustee Center for Strategic and International Studies, 1987—; governors Beauvoir School, Washington, 1958-61, St.

Albans School, 1961-67; member adv. board Center for Advanced Studies, U. Virginia, 1974-80; trustee Eisenhower Fellowships, Incorporated, 1981—; member adv. committee Mount Vernon (Virginia) Ladies Association of the Union, 1980-86. Served to lieutenant commander United States Naval Reserve, 1941-46. Member American Bar Association, Am. Law Institute Am. Judicature Society, Harvard Law School Association, Am. Society Corp. Executives (associate member), Metropolitan Club, City Tavern Association (board govs. 1961-64), Chevy Chase Club, Shenandoah Club. Democrat. Episcopalian. Home: 2912 N St Northwest Washington District of Columbia 20007 Office: National Rural Route Passenger Corp 60 Massachusetts Avenue NE Washington District of Columbia 20002

CLIFFORD, CLARK MCADAMS, lawyer; born Fort Scott, Kansas, December 25, 1906; son of Frank Andrew and Georgia (McAdams) C.; married Margery Pepperell Kimball, October 3, 1931; children: Margery Pepperell Clifford Lanagan, Joyce Carter Clifford Burland, Randall Clifford Wight. Bachelor of Laws, Washington University, St. Louis, 1928. Associate Holland, Lashly & Donnell, St. Louis, 1928-33; associate Holland, Lashly & Lashly, 1933-37; partner Lashly, Lashly, Miller & Clifford, 1938-43; senior partner Clifford & Miller, Washington, 1950-68; secretary Department Defense, Washington, 1968-69; senior partner Clifford & Warnke, Washington, 1969—; Chairman board First Am. Bankshares, Incorporated, Washington, 1982—; director Knight-Ridder Newspapers; special counsel to President United States, 1946-50. Served to captain United States Naval Reserve, 1944-46; naval aide to President United States 1946. Recipient Medal of Freedom from President United States. Member American Bar Association, Missouri Bar Association , District of Columbia Bar Association, St. Louis Bar Association, Kappa Alpha. Clubs: Burning Tree (Washington), Metropolitan (Washington), Chevy Chase (Washington). Home: 9421 Rockville Pike Bethesda Maryland 20814 Office: Clifford & Warnke 815 Connecticut Avenue Northwest Washington District of Columbia 20006 also: 1st Am Bankshares Incorporated 15th & H Sts Northwest Washington District of Columbia 20005

CLINE, ROBERT STANLEY, air freight company executive; born Urbana, Illinois, July 17, 1937; son of Lyle Stanley and Mary Elizabeth (Prettyman) C.; married Judith Lee Stucker, July 7, 1979; children: Lisa Andre, Nicole Lesley, Christina Elaine, Leslie Jane. Bachelor of Arts, Dartmouth College, 1959. Assistant treasurer Chase Manhattan Bank, New York City, 1960-65; vice president fin. Pacific Air Freight Company, Seattle, 1965-68; executive vice president fin. Airborne Freight Corp., Seattle, 1968-78, vice chairman, chief fin. officer, director, 1978-84, chairman, chief executive officer, director, 1984—; board of directors Security Pacific Bancorp Northwest, Security Pacific Bank Washington, North Carolina Machinery Company, 1988—. Trustee Seattle Repertory Theatre, 1974-90, chairman board, 1979-83; trustee Children's Orthopedic Hospital Foundation, 1983—, Corp. Council of Arts, 1983—; board of directors Washington Roundtable, 1985—; chairman board of directors Children's Hospital Foundation, 1987-89. With United States Army, 1959-60. Home: 1209 39th Avenue E Seattle Washington 98112 Office: Airborne Freight Corp 3101 Western Avenue Post Office Box 662 Seattle Washington 98121

CLOUGH, CHARLES ELMER, corporation executive; born Concord, New Hampshire, August 7, 1930; son of Harold Roland and Roelene (Sawyer) C.; married Nancy Carter, July 18, 1985; children: Martha, John, David, Benjamin, Thomas. Bachelor of Arts, Dartmouth College, 1952, Master of Business Administration, 1953. Member rectifier department General Electric Company, Lynn, Massachusetts, 1956-57; with Nashua (New Hampshire) Corp., 1957—, budget director, then assistant treasurer, then treasurer, then vice president, then executive vice president, now president, chairman. Served to lieutenant United States Navy, 1953-56. Republican. Club: Dartmouth (New York City). Office: Nashua Corp 44 Franklin St Nashua New Hampshire 03061

COFFIN, DAVID LINWOOD, specialty chemicals and nonwoven materials manufacturing company executive; born Windsor Locks, Connecticut, December 15, 1925; son of Dexter Drake and Elizabeth (Dorr) C.; married Marie Jeanne Cosnard des Closets, September 15, 1973; children by previous marriage: Deborah Lee, David Linwood, Robert George. Student, Trinity College, Hartford, Connecticut, New England College. With Dexter Corp., Windsor Locks, Connecticut, 1947—, assistant secretary, assistant treasurer, assistant sales manager, 1949-51, vice president, assistant treasurer, assistant sales manager, assistant general manager, 1951-52, vice president, assistant general manager, sales manager, 1952-55, vice president, general manager, 1955-58, president, chief executive officer, from 1958, former chief executive officer, now chairman, director; board of directors Bank of New England Corp., Boston, Connecticut Health Systems Agency, Hartford, Connecticut, Connecticut Mutual Life Insurance, Hartford, Life Technologies Incorporated, Gaithersburg, Maryland. Board of directors Horace Bushnell Memorial Hall, Hartford, Connecticut Historical Society, Hartford, Connecticut Trust for Historical Preservation, Hartford, The Institute of Living, Hartford, Mystic Seaport Mus. and Stores, Mystic Connecticut Served with United States Naval Reserve, World War II. Clubs: Hartford Golf (West Hartford, Connecticut); Hartford; Lake Sunapee Yacht (New Hampshire); Links (New York City). Office: Dexter Corp 1 Elm St Windsor Locks Connecticut 06096

COGAN, MARSHALL S., entrepreneur; born Boston, 1937. Graduate, Harvard University, 1959, Master of Business Administration, 1962. With Carter Berlind Weill, 1962-67; vice chairman Cogan Weill & Levitt, 1968-71, CBWL Hayden-Stone, 1973; chairman, chief executive officer Knoll International Holdings Incorporated, New York City, 1989, 21 International Holdings, Incorporated, New York City, 1989—. Office: 21 International Holdings Incorporated 153 E 53rd St Suite 5901 New York New York 10022

COGHILL, MARVIN W., tobacco company executive; born 1933; married. With Standard Commercial Tobacco Company, Wilson, North Carolina, 1955—, president, 1981—, now also chief operating officer. Office: Standard Commercial Corp 2201 Miller Road Wilson North Carolina 27893

COHEN, ISRAEL, chain store executive; born 1912; married. With Giant Food Incorporated, Landover, Maryland, 1935—, executive vice president, 1974-75, executive vice president, chief operating officer, from 1975, now president, chief executive officer, chairman board, director. Office: Giant Food Incorporated Post Office Box 1804 Washington District of Columbia 20013 also: Giant Food Incorporated 6300 Sheriff Road Landover Maryland 20785

COLE, CHARLES W., JR., bank holding company executive. President First Maryland Bancorp., Baltimore. Office: 1st Maryland Bancorp 1st Maryland Building 25 S Charles St Baltimore Maryland 21201 also: First Omni Bank NA Mitchell St Millsboro Delaware 19966

COLEMAN, LESTER EARL, chemical company executive; born Akron, Ohio, November 6, 1930; son of Lester Earl and Ethel Angeline (Miller) C.; married Kathleen A. Liptak, September 9, 1988; children by previous marriage: Robert Scott, Kenneth John. Bachelor of Science, University Akron, 1952; Master of Science, University Illinois, 1953, Doctor of Philosophy, 1955. With Goodyear Tire & Rubber Company, Akron, 1951-52; with Lubrizol Corp., Cleveland, 1955—; assistant to president Lubrizol Corp., 1972, vice president international operations, 1973, executive vice president, 1974-76, president, 1976-83, chief executive officer, 1978—, chairman board, 1983—, also director; board of directors Norfolk (Virginia) Southern Corp., Harris Corp., Melbourne, Florida South Carolina Johnson & Son, Incorporated, Racine, Wisconsin. Contributor articles to professional journals; patentee in field. Member national executive board Boy Scouts Am.; chairman board trustees The Lubrizol Foundation Captain United States Air Force, 1955-57. Member Am. Chemical Society (local chairman 1973), Chemical Manufacturers Association, Sigma Xi, Alpha Chi Sigma, Phi Lambda Upsilon, Phi Delta Theta, Omicron Delta Kappa. Methodist. Office: Lubrizol Corp 29400 Lakeland Boulevard Wickliffe Ohio 44092-2298

COLEMAN, ROGER W., institutional food distribution company executive; born Newark, March 30, 1929; son of Bernard Simpson and Evelyn (Bornstein) C.; married Ruth Rykoff (divorced April 1982); children—William, Wendy, Paul, Eric; married Francesca Marie Wessilius, September 1983. Bachelor of Science, University of California at Los Angeles, 1950. General management positions Rogay Food Supply div. South East Rykoff & Company, Los Angeles, 1951-58; purchasing and general management positions Southeast Rykoff & Company, Los Angeles, 1958-63, general manager, 1963-67, president, chief executive officer, 1967-86; president, chief executive officer John Sexton Incorporated, 1983-86, Rykoff-Sexton, Incorporated, 1986—. Board of directors Los Angeles Convention Center, Reiss-Dis Child Study Center, Los Angeles chapter American Red Cross. Member National Institute

Food Service (board directors), California Chamber of Commerce (bd.directors), Los Angeles Chamber of Commerce (board of directors). Clubs: Los Angeles Athletic, Hillcrest Country, Regency, Metropolitan, Carlton, World Trade and Stock Exchange, Pebble Beach, Beach and Tennis of Pebble Beach, La Costa Country. Avocation: golf. Home: 515 Homewood Road Los Angeles California 90049 Office: Rykoff-Sexton Incorporated 761 Terminal St Los Angeles California 90021

COLLOMB, BERTRAND PIERRE, cement company executive; born Lyon, France, August 14, 1942; came to United States, 1985; son of Charles and Helene (Traon) C.; married Marie Caroline Wirth, June 31, 1967; children: Cedric, Alex, Stephanie. Engineering student, Ecole Polytechnic, Paris, 1960-62; engineering degree, Ecole des Mines, Paris, 1963-66; law degree, University Nancy, France, 1968; Doctor of Philosophy in Management, University Texas, 1971. Mining engineer Ministry of Industry, France, 1966-73; special assistant to Minister of Education Paris, 1974-75; vice president, then principal Ciments Lafarge, Paris, 1975-82; executive vice president Lafarge-Coppee, Paris, 1983-88, vice-chairman, chief operations officer, 1989, chairman, chief executive officer, Aug., 1989; chairman Orsan, Paris, 1983-86; president and chief executive officer General Portland, Incorporated, Dallas, 1985-87; vice chairman, chief executive officer LaFarge Corp., Dallas, 1987-88; chairman board of directors LaFarge Corp., 1989—; research director Ecole Polytechnic, 1972-74; board of directors Ciments Lafarge. Served as lieutenant French Cavalry, 1962-63. Home: Lyme Kiln Farm Leesburg Virginia 22075 Office: Lafarge Corp 11130 Sunrise Valley Dr Suite 300 Reston Virginia 22091

COLODNY, EDWIN IRVING, airline executive; born Burlington, Vermont, June 7, 1926; son of Myer and Lena (Yett) C.; married Nancy Dessoff, December 11, 1965; children: Elizabeth, Mark, David. Bachelor of Arts, University Rochester, 1948; Bachelor of Laws, Harvard, 1951. Bar: New York 1951, District of Columbia 1958. With Office General Counsel, General Services Administration, 1951-52, Civil Aeronautics Board, 1954-57; with USAir Incorporated (formerly Allegheny Airlines Incorporated), 1957—, executive vice president marketing and legal affairs, 1969-75, president, 1975-90, chief executive officer, 1975—, chairman board of directors, 1978—; also chairman, president USAIR Group Incorporated; board of directors PNC Fin. Corp., Martin Marietta Corp., Pittsburgh National Bank. director Martin Marietta Corp; member board trustees U. Rochester. Served to 1st lieutenant Army of the United States, 1952-54. Recipient James D. McGill Memorial award University Rochester. Member American Bar Association, United States Chamber of Commerce (board directors), University Rochester (board trustees).

COMER, CLARENCE C., oil, gas and cement company executive; born 1948; married. Bachelor of Business Administration, Lamar U, 1971. Auditor Arthur Andersen & Company, 1971-75; controller Stratford of Texas, Incorporated, 1975-77; vice president fin. Southdown Sugars Incorporated, 1977-79; treasurer Southdown Incorporated, Houston,

1979-80, controller, then vice president, 1980-85, executive vice president, 1985-86, president, 1986—, chief operating officer, from 1986, chief executive officer, 1987—. Office: Southdown Incorporated 1200 Smith St Suite 2200 Houston Texas 77002

COMMES, THOMAS A., manufacturing company executive; born 1942; married. Bachelor of Arts, College of St. Thomas, 1964. With Gould Incorporated, 1968-75; controller, treasurer, vice president, chief fin. officer W.T. Grant Company, 1975-76; vice president, controller Saks Fifth Avenue, 1976-79; chief fin. officer, senior vice president Sherwin-Williams Company, 1979-86, president, chief operating officer, 1986—, also board of directors; board of directors Society National Bank, Centerior Energy Corp. Office: Sherwin-Williams Company 101 Prospect Avenue Northwest Cleveland Ohio 44115

COMPTON, RONALD E., insurance and financial services executive; born 1933; married. Bachelor of Science, Northwestern University, 1954. With Aetna Life & Casualty Company, 1954—; senior vice president Am. Re-Ins. Company, New York City, 1980-81, executive vice president, 1981-83; president, director Am. Re-Ins. Company unit Aetna Life and Casualty Company, New York City, from 1983; corp. senior vice president Aetna Life and Casualty Company, 1987-88, executive vice president, 1988—, now president, chief operating officer; senior vice president, executive assistant to chairman Aetna Life Insurance Company, 1986-87, executive vice president, 1987; with Aetna Casualty and Surety Company, 1954-80, 1987—, senior vice president, 1987-88, executive vice president, office of chairman, from 1988, now president. Office: Aetna Life & Casualty Company Corp Hdqrs 151 Farmington Avenue Hartford Connecticut 06156

CONABLE, BARBER B., JR., international agency administrator; born Warsaw, New York, November 2, 1922; son of Barber B. and Agnes G. (Gouinlock) C.; married Charlotte Williams, September 13, 1952; 4 children. Bachelor of Arts, Cornell University, 1942, Bachelor of Laws, 1948. Bar: New York 1948. Private practice law Buffalo, 1948-50, Batavia, New York, 1952-64; United States senator from New York 1963-64; member 89th-98th congresses from 30th New York district, 1965-85, President Reagan's Commission on Defense Management, from 1985; professor University Rochester, New York, 1985-86; president International Bank for Reconstrn. and Devel. (World Bank), Washington, 1986—; senior fellow, Am. Enterprise Institute, 1985. Editor: Cornell University Law Quar., 1947-48. Member senior adv. committee Kennedy Institute Politics; trustee United States Capitol Historical Society, Mus. Am. Indian. Served with United States Marine Corps Reserve, 1942-46, 50-51. Republican. Lodge: Rotary (president Batavia chpt.). Office: International Bank Reconstrn & Devel 1818 H St Northwest Washington District of Columbia 20433

CONNELL, GROVER, food company executive; born New York City, April 12, 1918; son of Grover Clevel and Violet Regina (Connell) C.; married Patricia Day, July 31, 1940; children—Ted, Terry, Toni. Bachelor of Science in Business Adminstrn,

Columbia, 1939. With The Connell Company (formerly Connell Rice & Sugar Company, Incorporated), Westfield, New Jersey, 1939—, president, 1950—. Lieutenant United States Naval Reserve, 1942-46. Democrat. Presbyterian. Home: 207 Watchung Fork Westfield New Jersey 07090 Office: Connell Company 45 Cardinal Dr Westfield New Jersey 07092

CONNELL, WILLIAM FRANCIS, diversified company executive; born Lynn, Massachusetts, May 12, 1938; son of William J. and Theresa (Keaney) C.; married Margot C. Gensler, May 29, 1965; children: Monica Cameron, Lisa Terese, Courtenay Erin, William Christopher, Terence Alexander, Timothy Patrick. Bachelor of Science magna cum laude, Boston College, 1959; Master of Business Administration, Harvard University, 1963. Controller Olga Company, Incorporated, Van Nuys, California, 1963-65; assistant treasurer Litton Industries, Incorporated, 1965-68; president div. Marine Tech., Incorporated, 1965-68; treasurer Ogden Corp., New York City, 1968-69; vice president, treasurer Ogden Corp., 1969-71, senior vice president, 1971-72, executive vice president, 1980-85; chief executive officer, chairman board Ogden Leisure, Incorporated; chairman board, chief executive officer Ogden Food Service, Incorporated, Ogden Recreation, Incorporated, Ogden Security, Incorporated, Ogden Services Incorporated; board director Ogden Corp., various Ogden subsidiary, 1969-85; chairman, chief executive officer, president Avondale Industries, Incorporated 1985-87; chairman, chief executive officer Connell Limited Partnership, 1987—. Active fund raising Boston College, trustee, 1974-86, 88—, chairman board trustees, 1981-84; trustee St. Elizabeth Hospital, Boston, Boston 200 Corp. 1st lieutenant Army of the United States, 1959-61. Member Greater Boston Chamber of Commerce (chairman board directors 1988-90), Algonquin Club, University Club (Boston), Tedesco Country Club, Knights of Malta Club, Beta Gamma Sigma, Alpha Sigma Nu, Alpha Kappa Psi. Roman Catholic. Home: 111 Ocean Avenue Swampscott Massachusetts 01907 Office: Connell Limited Partnership One International Place 31st Floor Boston Massachusetts 02110

CONNER, FINIS, manufacturing company executive; born Gadsden, Alabama, July 28, 1943; son of William Otis and Vera Belle (Beasley) C.; married Julie Manchura, July 15, 1972. Bachelor of Science in Industrial Management, San Jose State University, 1969; graduate, University Santa Clara, 1971. President Mastec Corp., Cupertino, California, 1969-71; original equipment manufacturer market manager Memorex, Santa Clara, California, 1971-79 founder, western regional manager; original equipment manufacturer market manager Shugart Associates, Sunnyvale, California, 1971-79, founder, western regional manager, original equipment manufacturer market manager, 1973—; original equipment manufacturer market manager Seagate Tech., Scotts Valley, California, 1979-85, also director, 1979-85. With United States Navy Air Reserves. Member Eldorado Chamber of Commerce, Monterey Peninsula C of C., Preston Trails Chamber of Commerce, The Vintage Club, Castle Pines Country

Club (Denver). Democrat. Office: Conner Peripherals 3081 Zanker Road San Jose California 95134-2128

CONNOLLY, EUGENE B., JR., building materials company executive; born New York City, March 31, 1932; son of Eugene B. and Charlotte (Boquet) C.; married Dorothy E. O'Brien, June 5, 1954; children—Kathleen, Jennifer, Patrick, Michael, Amy, Daniel. Bachelor of Science in Management, Hofstra University, Hempstead, New York, 1954, Master of Business Administration in Marketing, 1964. With USG Corp. (formerly United States Gypsum Company), Chicago, 1958—; group vice president United States Gypsum Company, Chicago, 1983-85, president, chief operating officer, 1985-87, also board of directors; executive vice president USG Corp., 1987-89, president, chief executive officer, 1990—, also board of directors; president, chief executive officer, director DAP, Incorporated, Chicago, 1988-89; board of directors CGC Incorporated, USG International Limited, BPB Industries plc, USG Interiors; member Mid-Am. Committee. Member National Association Manufacturers, Chicago Club, Knollwood Country Club, Metropolitan Club, Can. Club Chicago. Office: USG Corp 101 S Wacker Dr Chicago Illinois 60606

CONNOLLY, WALTER JUSTIN, JR., banker; born Boston, August 3, 1928; son of Walter Justin and Helen Agnes (Cavanagh) C.; married Paulina Quilty, April 14, 1951; children: Timothy J., Kevin A., Mary-Elise, Walter Justin III, Paulina, Sarah D. Bachelor of Arts in History, Yale University, 1950. With Hartford Insurance Group, 1955-58; with Hornblower & Weeks, Hartford, Connecticut, 1958-61; with Connecticut Bank & Trust Company, Hartford, 1961-85, director investment operations, 1961-65, director marketing, 1965-66, senior vice president, 1966-68, executive vice president, director administrative staff, 1968-70, president, 1970-77, chief executive officer, 1977-80, chairman board, chief executive officer, 1980-85; chairman Bank of New England Corp., Boston, 1985-90; director Connecticut Mutual Life Insurance Company, Dexter Corp. Board of directors Greater Hartford Arts Council, St. Francis Hospital, Kingswood/Oxford School Served with United States Marine Corps, 1952-55. Member Am. Bankers Association, Association Reserve City Bankers, Connecticut Bankers Association, Greater Hartford Chamber of Commerce (director). Clubs: Hartford, Hartford Golf, Hyannis Port Yacht. Office: Bank New England Corp 28 State St Boston Massachusetts 02109

CONRAD, CONRAD A., oil company executive; born Pineville, Kentucky, February 27, 1946; son of Boyd J. and Jeanette A. (Hill) C.; married Patricia A. Chausse, June 24, 1947; children: Alison, Laura. Bachelor of Arts in Accounting, College of William & Mary, 1968. Certified Public Accountant. Senior accountant Price Waterhouse & Company, Washington, 1968-73; assistant manager internal audit Quaker State Corp., Oil City, Pennsylvania, 1974-77, assistant controller, 1977-82, controller, 1982-85, vice president fin., chief fin. officer, 1985—. Served with United States Army, 1969-71. Republican. Presbyterian. Clubs: Wanango Country, Oil City. Home: 6 Glenwood Dr Oil City Pennsylvania

16701 Office: Quaker State Corp Post Office Box 989 Oil City Pennsylvania 16301

COOK, JAY MICHAEL, accounting company executive; born New York City, September 16, 1942; son of Gerald Cook and Mary Elizabeth (McGill) Totten; married Mary Anne Griffith, July 11, 1964; children—Jennifer Lynn, Angela Marie, Jeffrey Thomas. Bachelor of Science in Business Administration cum laude, University Florida, 1964. C.P.A., New York, Florida. Staff accountant Deloitte, Haskins & Sells, Fort Lauderdale, Florida, 1964-70; manager Deloitte, Haskins & Sells, Miami, Florida, 1970-74; partner Deloitte, Haskins & Sells, New York City, 1974-81; ptnr.-in-charge Deloitte, Haskins & Sells, Miami, 1981-83; managing partner Deloitte, Haskins & Sells, New York City, 1983-86, chairman, 1986-89; chairman Deloitte & Touche, 1989—; advisor Securities and Exchange Commission Reporting Institute, University Southern California, Los Angeles, 1982—; advisor School Business, University Florida, Gainesville, 1981—. Author: Retained Earnings and Dividends, 1975; contributor articles to professional journals. Trustee Pace U., New York City, 1984-85, U. Miami, parents council Georgetown U., Central Park Conservancy; pacesetter United Way of Tri-State; board of directors New York City Ballet, Associates Harvard Business School; member dean's adv. council Columbia Business School; member Republican Eagles. Member Am. Institute C.P.A.s (chairman SEC regulations 1980-83, member council 1983—, vice chairman 1985-86, chairman 1986-87), Am. Accounting Association, Conference Board, United States Chamber of Commerce (commerce services industries council), Advertising Council (industries adv. committee). Republican. Methodist. Clubs: Greenwich Country (Connecticut); Sky, Princeton (New York City); City (Miami), Links. Avocations: tennis; golf; skiing. Home: 980 Lake Avenue Greenwich Connecticut 06830 Office: Deloitte & Touche 10 Westport Road Wilton Connecticut 06897

COOK, LODWRICK MONROE, petroleum company executive; born Castor, Louisiana, June 17, 1928; married. Bachelor of Science, Louisiana State University, 1950, Bachelor of Science in Petroleum Engineering, 1955; Master of Business Administration, Southern Methodist University, 1965. Petroleum engineer Union Producing Company, 1955-56; with Atlantic Richfield Company, Los Angeles, 1956—; engineering trainee Atlantic Richfield Company, Incorporated, Los Angeles, 1956-61, administrative assistant, 1961-64, senior personnel department, then personnel manager, 1964-67, labor reins. con., 1967-69, manager labor reins. department, 1969-70, vice president, general manager product div. Western area, 1970-72, vice president marketing products div., 1972-73, vice president corp. planning div., 1973-74, vice president products div., 1974-75, vice president transportation div., 1975-77, senior vice president transportation div., 1977-80, executive vice president, director, 1980-85, president, chief executive officer, 1985, chairman, chief executive officer, 1986—. Board of directors Louisiana State U. Foundation; board governors Music Center

Los Angeles 1st Lieutenant United States Army, 1950-53. Member National Petroleum Council (chair), Am. Petroleum Institute (director). Office: Atlantic Richfield Company 515 S Flower St Los Angeles California 90071

COOK, PAUL M., chemical manufacturing company executive; born Ridgewood, New Jersey Bachelor of Science in Chemical Engineering, Massachusetts Institute of Technology, 1947. With Stanford Research Institute, Palo Alto, California, 1949-53, Sequoia Process Corp., 1953-56; with Raychem Corp., Menlo Park, California, 1957—, former president, chief executive officer, until 1990, now chairman, board of directors. Recipient National Medal Tech., 1988. Member National Academy of Engineering. Office: Raychem Corp 300 Constitution Dr Menlo Park California 94025

COOK, STANTON R., media company executive; born Chicago, July 3, 1925; son of Rufus Merrill and Thelma Marie (Borgerson) C.; married Barbara Wilson, September 23, 1950. Bachelor of Science in Mechanical Engineering, Northwestern University, 1949. With Shell Oil Company, 1949-51; with Chicago Tribune Company, 1951-81, vice president, 1967-70, executive vice president, general manager, 1970-72, president, 1972-74, pub., 1973-90, president, 1972-74, chief executive officer, 1974-76, chairman, 1974-81; director Tribune Company, 1972—, vice president, 1973-74, president, 1974-88, chairman, 1989—, chief executive officer, 1974-90; board of directors Associated Press, 1975-84, 2d vice chairman, 1979-84; board of directors Newspaper Adv. Bureau, 1987—; former deputy chairman, board of directors Federal Reserve Bank Chicago, 1980-83, chmnn., 1984-85; board of directors Robert R. McCormick Tribune Foundation. Trustee, U. Chicago, 1973-87, Mus. Sci. and Industry, Chicago, 1973—, Field Mus. Natural History, Chicago, 1973—, General Douglas MacArthur Foundation, 1979—, Northwestern U., 1987—, Shedd Aquarium Society, 1987—, Am. Newspaper Pubs. Association Foundation, 1973-82. Member Chicago Council Foreign Relations (director 1973—). Clubs: Commercial (past president), Economic (past president, life mem.) (Chicago).

COOKE, JACK KENT, diversified company executive; born Hamilton, Ontario, Canada, October 25, 1912; son of Ralph Ercil and Nancy (Jacobs) C.; married Barbara Jean Carnegie, May 5, 1934 (divorced); children: Ralph Kent, John Kent; married Jeanne Maxwell Williams, October 31, 1980 (divorced); married Marlena LVR Chalmers, May 5, 1990. Student, Malvern Collegiate. Joined Northern Broadcasting and Pub. Limited, Can., 1937; partner Thomson Cooke Newspapers, 1937-52; president Station CKEY, Toronto, Ontario, Can., 1944-61, Liberty of Can. Limited, 1947-61, Toronto Maple Leaf Baseball Club Limited, 1951-64, Micro Plastics, Limited, Acton, Ontario, Can., 1955-60, Robinson Industrial Crafts, Limited, London, Ontario, Can., 1957-63, Precision Die Casting Limited, Toronto, Ontario, 1955-60, Consolidated Frybook Industries, Limited, 1952-61; chairman board, president Consolidated Press Limited, 1952-61; president Aubyn Investments, Limited, 1961-68, Continental Cablevision Incorporated, 1965-68; chairman Jack Kent Cooke Incorporated, 1976—; chairman board Transamerica Microwave, Incorporated, 1965-69; chairman Pro-Football Incorporated, Washington Redskins, National Football League, 1960—; president California Sports, Incorporated (Los Angeles Lakers, National Basketball Association, Los Angeles Kings, National Hockey League), 1965-79, The Forum of Inglewood, Incorporated, 1966-79; director, chairman executive committee H&B Am. Corp, 1969-70; chairman, chief executive officer Teleprompter Corp., 1974-81; chairman Group W Cable Incorporated (formerly Teleprompter Corp.), 1981-85, Cooke Properties Incorporated, 1966—, Chrysler & Kent Buildings, New York City, 1966—, Kent Farms, 1979—, Byrnley Farms, 1979-88, Cooke Media Group, Incorporated (Daily News), Los Angeles, 1985—, Cooke CableVision Incorporated, Warner Center, California, 1986-89, Ercil Pub. Incorporated, 1976—, Kent Plaza, Phoenix, 1983-85, Elmendorf Farm, Incorporated, Lexington, Kentucky, 1985—, Video Tape Enterprises, 1976-85, Raljon Pub. Company, Incorporated, 1988—. Trustee Little League Foundation. Member National Athletic Institute (board directors). Office: Washington Redskins Dulles International Airport Post Office Box 17247 Washington District of Columbia 20041 also: Daily News 21221 Oxnard St Woodland California 91367

COOLEY, RICHARD PIERCE, banker; born Dallas, November 25, 1923; son of Victor E. and Helen (Pierce) C. Bachelor of Science, Yale, 1944. With Wells Fargo Bank, San Francisco, 1949-82; executive vice president Wells Fargo Bank, 1965-66, president, chief executive officer, 1966-79, chairman board, chief executive officer, 1979-82, also director; chairman, chief executive officer, president Seattle-1st National Bank (now Seafirst Corp.), 1983-86, chairman, chief executive officer, 1986—; chairman board, chief executive officer, director Wells Fargo & Company, 1968-83; director UAL, Incorporated, Howmett Turbine Components Corp., Pechiney Ugine Kuhlmann Corp. Trustee Children's Hospital, San Francisco, Rand Corp., California Institute Tech., Pasadena. Served to 1st lieutenant Armed Services. Decorated Air medal. Member Association Reserve City Bankers, Smithsonian Institution National Association (board directors), California Chamber of Commerce (board directors). Office: Seafirst Corp Post Office Box 3586 Seattle Washington 98124

COOPER, THEODORE, pharmaceutical company executive, physician; born Trenton, New Jersey, December 28, 1928; son of Victor and Dora (Popkin) C.; married Vivian Cecilia Evans, June 16, 1956; children: Michael Harris, Mary Katherine, Victoria Susan, Frank Victor. Bachelor of Science, Georgetown University, 1949; Doctor of Medicine, St. Louis University, 1954, Doctor of Philosophy, 1956. United States Public Health Service fellow St. Louis University Department Physiology, 1955-56; clinical associate surgery branch National Heart Institute, Bethesda, Maryland, 1956-58; faculty St. Louis University, 1960-66, professor surgery, 1964-66; professor, chairman department pharmacology University New

Mexico, Albuquerque, 1966-68, on leave, 1967-69; associate director artificial heart, myocardial infarction programs National Heart Institute, Bethesda, 1967-68; director National Heart and Lung Institute, 1968-74; deputy assistant secretary for health Department of Health, Education and Welfare, 1974-75, assistant secretary health, 1975-77; dean Medical College, Cornell University, New York City, 1977-80; provost for medical affairs Cornell University, 1977-80; executive vice president Upjohn Company, Kalamazoo, 1980-84, vice chairman board, 1984-87, chairman board, chief executive officer, 1987-89, chairman board, president, chief executive officer, 1990-91, chairman board, chief executive officer, 1991—; member United States Public Health Service Pharmacology and Experimental Therapeutics Study Section, 1964-67; Board overseers Memorial Sloan-Kettering Cancer Center. Author: (with others) Nervous Control of the Heart, 1965, Heart Substitutes, 1966, The Baboon in Medical Research, Volume II, 1967, Factors Influencing Myocardial Contractility, 1967, Acute Myocardial Infarction, 1968, Advance in Transplantation, Prosthetic Heart Valves, 1969, Depressed Metabolism, 1969; Editorial board: Journal Pharmacology and Experimental Therapeutics, 1965-68, 77—, Circulation Research, 1966-71; editor: Supplements to Circulation, 1966-71; sect. co-editor for: Journal Applied Physiology, 1967-73; contributor numerous articles medical journals; discoverer new techniques of denervating heart which have helped delineate role of nerves in heart, on its ability to function under a wide variety of circumstances, and on its ability to respond to drugs. Board governors American Red Cross, 1980. Recipient Borden award, 1954; Albert Lasker Special Public Service award, 1978; Ellen Browning Scripps medal, 1980; medal for Distinguished Pub. Service, Department Defense, 1985. Member American Association for the Advancement of Science, American Association of University Professors, Am. Society Pharmacology and Experimental Therapeutics, Am. Physiological Society, Society Experimental Biology and Medicine, Am. Society Clinical Investigation, Am. Federation Clinical Research, Am. Society Artificial Internal Organs, International Cardiovascular Society, Am. College Chest Physicians, Am. College Cardiology, Sigma Xi. Home: 3605 Woodcliff Dr Kalamazoo Michigan 49008 Office: Upjohn Company 7000 Portage Road Kalamazoo Michigan 49001

COOPER, WILLIAM ALLEN, banking executive; born Detroit, July 3, 1943. Bachelor of Science in Accounting, Wayne State University, 1967. Certified Public Accountant, Michigan. With Touche, Ross & Company, Detroit, 1967-71; senior vice president Michigan National Bank of Detroit, 1971-72; senior vice president Michigan National Corp., 1971-78; executive vice president Huntington National Bank, Columbus, Ohio, 1978-83, president, 1983-84; president, Am. Savings & Loan Association of Florida, Miami, 1984-85 , also director; chairman board, chief executive officer TCF Bank, FSB, Minneapolis, 1985—; chairman, TCF Fin. Corp., Minneapolis, from 1987, now chairman board, chief executive officer. Member American Institute of Certified Public Accountants. Office: TCF Bank Office of Chairman Bd 801

Marquette Avenue Minneapolis Minnesota 55402

COORS, WILLIAM K., brewery executive; born Golden, Colorado, August 11, 1916. Bachelor of Science in Chemical Engineering, Princeton University, 1938, Master of Science in Chemical Engineering, 1939. President Adolph Coors Company, Golden, Colorado, from 1956, Chairman board, now chairman board, also corp. president. Office: Adolph Coors Company BC350 Golden Colorado 80401

CORDELL, JOE B., diversified corporation executive; born Daytona Beach, Florida, August 4, 1927; son of Joe Wynne and Ada Ruth (Wood) C.; married Joyce Hinton, June 16, 1951; children: Joe B., Coleman Wynn, Lauren. Student, Yale University, 1945-46, Florida Southern College, 1946-47; Bachelor of Science in Business Adminstrn, University Florida, 1949. C.P.A. Intern Price Waterhouse Corp., New York City, 1948-49, staff accountant, 1949-50; audit manager Price Waterhouse Corp., Atlanta, 1950-58; vice president Jim Walter Corp., Tampa, Florida, 1958-70, senior vice president, treasurer, 1970-74, president, 1974—, chief operating officer, from 1974; president, chief executive officer Walter Industries Incorporated (formerly Jim Walter Corp.), Tampa, Florida, also board of directors; board of directors Barnett Banks of Florida, Incorporated, Jacksonville. Chairman adv. board Tampa/Hillsborough County Area command The Salvation Army; trustee Palma Ceia United Methodist Church; member business adv. council U. Florida; past president U. Florida Foundation, also ex-officio member board trustees, member devel. committee With United States Navy, 1945-46. Member Greater Tampa Chamber of Commerce, Committee of 100, Tampa Yacht and Country Club, Palma Ceia Golf and Cuntry Club, Wildcat Cliffs Country Club, Avila Golf and Country Club, University Club of Tampa, Ye Mystic Krewe of Gasparilla, Alpha Kappa Psi, Alpha Tau Omega. Methodist. Office: Walter Industries Incorporated Post Office Box 31601 Tampa Florida 33631-3601

CORN, JACK W., oil company executive; born Cobb County, Georgia, October 8, 1929; son of Ezra and Sarah (Pruitt) C.; married Ann McConnel; children: Dana Corn Crissey, William E., Beth Ann. Bachelor of Business Administration, University Georgia, 1953. President, chief executive officer Quaker State Corp., Oil City, Pennsylvania, 1974-86, vice chairman to president and chief executive officer, 1988—; member emeritus Smyra Bank and Trust Company. Active 1st Baptist Church, Marietta, Georgia With United States Air Force, 1953-56. Member Am. Petroleum Institute (board directors), Allegheny Mountain Health Systems, Marietta Country Club, Georgian Club, Oil City Club, Wanango Country Club. Home: 9 Shady Oak Lane Oil City Pennsylvania 16301 Office: Quaker State Corp 255 Elm St Oil City Pennsylvania 16301

CORNELISSEN, MICHAEL ADRIAAN, trust company executive; born Durban, Republic of South Africa, June 1, 1943; arrived in Canada, 1967; son of Marinus and Koos (Van der Hoeven) C.; married Catriona Butcher, January 1967; 2 children. CA, University Natal, 1965; Master of Business Administration,

University Capetown, 1970. Audit supervisor Touche Ross and Company, 1961-69; director, vice president fin. Rennies Consolidated Holdings Limited, 1971-75; vice president Edper Investments Limited, 1976; executive vice president, chief operating officer Trizec Corp. Limited, 1977-83, now director; president, chief executive officer, director Royal Trustco Limited, Toronto, Ontario, Can., 1983—; board director Trilon Fin. Corp., Hees International Corp. Incorporated, London Life Insurance Company, Trizec Corp. Limited. Chairman United Way Greater Toronto, 1984; board governors Appleby College, Oakville; chairman capital campaign National Ballet School; chairman Can.'s Challenge for Am.'s Cup; board of directors The Chamber Players of Toronto, The Toronto symphony. Conservative. Clubs: Toronto, York, Royal Can. Yacht, Oakville Yacht Squadron. Office: Royal Trustco Limited, Post Office Box 7500, Toronto, Ontario Canada M5W 1P9

CORNELIUS, WILLIAM EDWARD, utilities company executive; born Salt Lake City, September 6, 1931; son of Edward Vernon and Gladys (Bray) C.; married Mary Virginia Bunker, June 13, 1953; children: Mary Jean, Linda Anne. Bachelor of Science, University Missouri, 1953; Master Liberal Arts, Washington University, St. Louis, 1983. C.P.A., Missouri. Manager Price Waterhouse & Company, St. Louis, 1955-62; assistant comptroller Union Electric Company, St. Louis, 1962-64, director corporate planning, 1964-67, executive vice president, 1968-80, president, 1980-88, chief executive officer, chairman, 1988—, also board of directors; board of directors Boatmen's Bancshares, General Am. Life Insurance Company, McDonnell Douglas Corp., INTERCO, Incorporated. Board of directors St. Louis Children's Hospital, Municipal Theater Association; trustee Washington U. Served to 1st lieutenant Army of the United States, 1953-55. Member Municipal Theater Association (board directors), Beta Theta Pi. Home: 2 Dunlora Lane Saint Louis Missouri 63131 Office: Union Electric Company Post Office Box 149 Saint Louis Missouri 63166

CORNELL, HARRY M., JR., home furnishings company executive; born 1928; married. Graduate, University Missouri, 1950. With Leggett & Platt, Incorporated, 1950—, salesman, 1950-53, general manager, 1953-55, vice president, 1955-60, president, chief executive officer, from 1960; now chairman, chief executive officer Leggett & Platt, Incorporated, Carthage, Missouri. Office: Leggett & Platt Incorporated 1 Leggett Road Post Office Box 757 Carthage Missouri 64836

CORRY, CHARLES ALBERT, steel company executive; born Wyoming, Ohio, February 14, 1932; s.Charles Albert and Rella Marie (Ulrich) C.; married Margaret Anna Stuve, December 9, 1961; children: Lynne, Diane, Elizabeth. Bachelor of Science, University Cincinnati, 1955, Juris Doctor, 1959. Bar: Ohio 1959. Tax attorney United States Steel Corp. (now USX Corp.), Pittsburgh, Cleveland and New York City, 1959-70; assistant comptr. Am. Bridge div. United States Steel Corp. (now USX Corp.), Pittsburgh, 1970-71; manager acctg.-steel, parent company United States Steel Corp. (now USX Corp.), Homestead, Pennsylvania, 1972-73; comptr., treasurer Engineers & Cons. United States Ship Engineers and

Cons., Pittsburgh, 1974; general manager taxes United States Steel Corp. (now USX Corp.), Pittsburgh, 1975-78; assistant comptr. United States Steel Corp. (now USX Corp.), Pittsburgh, Pennsylvania, 1978; vice president corp. planning United States Steel Corp. (now USX Corp.), Pittsburgh, 1979-82; senior vice president corp. planning, comptr. United States Steel Corp. (now USX Corp.), Pittsburgh, Pennsylvania, 1982-86; president USX Diversified Group, Pittsburgh, 1987—, corp. president, director, 1987—, also chairman, chief executive officer, 1989—. Board of directors Junior Achievement SW Pennsylvania, Pittsburgh, 1983. Served to captain United States Air Force, 1955-57, Europe. Member American Bar Association, Ohio Bar Association, Fin. Executives Institute, Machinery and Allied Products Institute (fin. council), Am. Iron and Steel Institute, North America Society Corp. Planning, Pennsylvania Chamber of Commerce (board directors 1982—). Lutheran. Clubs: Duquesne, St. Clair Country (Pittsburgh). Office: USX Corp 600 Grant St Pittsburgh Pennsylvania 15230

COSTOFF, THEODORE, hardware company executive; born 1925. Student, Bryant & Stratton Business College. Partner Certified Grocers, 1949-55; with Ace Hardware Corp., Hinsdale, Illinois, 1957—, chairman board, 1983—. Office: Ace Hardware Corp 2200 Kensington Court Oak Brook Illinois 60521

COTTING, JAMES CHARLES, manufacturing company executive; born Winchester, Massachusetts, October 15, 1933; son of Edward L. and Mary Ellen (Worrell) C.; married Marjorie A. Kirsch, February 8, 1963; children: James Charles, Steven Robert, Brenda Ann-Marie. Bachelor of Arts cum laude, Ohio State University, 1955. Acctg. supervisor United States Steel Corp., Pittsburgh, 1959-61; manager profit analysis Ford Motor Company, Dearborn, Michigan, 1961-63; manager devel. planning A.O. Smith Corp., Milwaukee, 1963-66; assistant controller General Foods Corp., White Plains, New York, 1966-71; vice president planning International Paper Company, New York City, 1971-76, vice president, controller, 1976-79; senior vice president fin. and planning, chief fin. officer Navistar International Corp. (formerly International Harvester Company), Chicago, 1979-82, executive vice president fin., 1982-83, vice chairman, chief fin. officer, 1983-87, chairman, chief executive officer, 1987—, also board of directors; member The Mid-Am. Committee, Chicago Committee, Conference Board, President Reagan's Task Force on Market Mechanisms; board of directors ASARCO Incorporated, USG Corp., Interlake Corp., Navistar Fin. Corp., Harbour Assurance Company of Bermuda; member adv. committee board New York Stock Exchange. Chairman Junior Achievement of Chicago; trustee Adler Planetarium; member visiting committee grad. school of business Fordham U. Lieutenant United States Navy, 1955-58. Member Commercial Club Chicago, Econ. Club Chicago, Montclair Golf Club, Barrington Hills Country Club, Mid-Am. Club, Chicago Club, Phi Beta Kappa, Alpha Tau Omega. Office: Navistar International Corp 455 N Cityfront Plaza Dr Chicago Illinois 60611

COULSON, NORMAN M., savings and loan executive; born Hilt,

California; married Helen; children—Virginia Coulson Bullard, Maria, Edward, Michael. Bachelor of Science, Long Beach State College, 1957; Master of Business Administration, Pepperdine University, 1973; postgraduate exec. program, University of California at Los Angeles, 1973; postgraduate in exec. devel, University Washington, 1973. With 1st Federal Savings, San Pedro (California), 1957-59; with Glendale (California) Federal Savings and Loan Association, 1959—, successively vice president, group vice president, executive vice president, senior executive vice president and general manager California div., president, chief executive officer, chairman, director, 1984—; also vice-chairman, president, chief executive officer, Glenfed Incorporated; instructor Institute Fin. Education, Community College Accreditation. Member council communication div. Pepperdine U.; past chairman adv. board Kennedy High School, Granada Halls, California; board of directors Citizens for Law and Order, Glendale, Glendale Adventist Medical Center Foundation; board governors Institute Fin. Education, Los Angeles; board of directors, member executive committee, chairman communications committee Am. Heart Association, Los Angeles Served with United States Coast Guard. Member Downey-Studio City Chamber of Commerce (board directors), Stonewood Mchts. Association (president), California Savings and Loan League (committee member), United States League Savings Association (member savs. account adminstrn. committee), National Council Savings Institutions (state director 1984-85), Newcomen Society United States Clubs: Lakeside Country, Verdugo (Glendale); Rotary (Los Angeles). Office: GLENFED Incorporated 700 N Brand Boulevard Glendale California 91203

COWAN, GEORGE ARTHUR, chemist, bank executive, director; born Worcester, Massachusetts, February 15, 1920; son of Louis Abraham and Anna (Listic) C.; married Helen Dunham, September 9, 1946. Bachelor of Science, Worcester Polytechnic Institute, 1941; Doctor of Science, Carnegie-Mellon University, 1950. Research assistant Princeton University, 1941-42, University Chicago, 1942-45; member staff Columbia University, New York City, 1945; member staff Los Alamos (New Mexico) Sci. Laboratory, 1945-46, 49-88, senior fellow emeritus, 1988—; teaching fellow Carnegie Mellon University, Pittsburgh, 1946-49; chairman board of directors Los Alamos National Bank, Trinity Capital Corp., Los Alamos; president Santa Fe Institute, 1984-91; member White House Sci. Council, Washington, 1982-85, consultant, 1985-90, Air Force Tech. Applications Center, 1952-88. Contributor sci. articles to professional journals. Board of directors Santa Fe Opera, 1964-79; treasurer New Mexico Opera Foundation, Santa Fe, 1970-79; regent New Mexico Institute Tech., Socorro, 1972-75. Recipient E.O. Lawrence award, 1965, Distinguished Scientist award New Mexico Acad. Sci., 1975, Robert H. Goddard award Worcester Polytechnic Institute, 1984, Enrico Fermi award, Presidential Citation, Department Energy, 1990. Fellow American Association for the Advancement of Science, Am. Physical Society; member Am. Chemical Society, New Mexico Acad. Sci.,

Cosmos Club (Washington). Avocation: skiing. Home: 721 42nd St Los Alamos New Mexico 87544 Office: Santa Fe Institute 1120 Canyon Road Santa Fe New Mexico 87501

COX, GLENN ANDREW, JR., petroleum company executive; born Sedalia, Missouri, August 6, 1929; son of Glenn Andrew and Ruth Lonsdale (Atkinson) C.; married Veronica Cecelia Martin, January 3, 1953; children: Martin Stuart, Grant Andrew, Cecelia Ruth. Bachelor of Business Administration, Southern Methodist University, 1951. With Phillips Petroleum Company, Bartlesville, Oklahoma, 1956—; assistant to chairman operating committee Phillips Petroleum Company, Bartlesville, 1973-74, vice president management information and control, 1974-80, executive vice president, 1980-85, director, 1982—, president, chief operating officer, 1985—; board of directors Banc Oklahoma Corp., Tulsa. President Cherokee Area council Boy Scouts Am., 1977-82, South Central region, 1987-90, member national executive board, 1987—; board curators Central Methodist College, Fayette, Missouri, 1984-88; trustee Philbrook Mus. Art, 1987—, Southern Methodist U., Dallas, 1988—; board of directors Oklahoma United Methodist Foundation; member Oklahoma State Regents for Higher Education. Member Am. Petroleum Institute (board directors), National Association Manufacturers (board directors), Bartlesville Area Chamber of Commerce (president 1978), Hillcrest Country Club. Methodist. Office: Phillips Petroleum Company 4th & Keeler Bartlesville Oklahoma 74004

COZAD, JAMES W., oil company executive; born Huntington, Indiana, February 10, 1927; son of Emmett and Helen (Motz) C.; married Virginia E. Alley, November 25, 1948; children: J. Michael, Catherine L., W. Scott, Jeffrey A., Amy Jo. Bachelor of Science in Accounting, Ind. University, 1950, Doctor of Laws (honorary), 1982. With Peat, Marwick, Mitchell, Detroit, 1950-57; treasurer Hygrade Food Products, Detroit, 1957-67, Philip Morris, Incorporated, New York City, 1967-69; vice president, fin. Amoco Oil Company, Chicago, 1969-71; various executive positions Standard Oil Company Ind., Chicago, 1971-83; vice chairman Amoco Corp., Chicago, 1983-89; chairman, chief executive officer Whitman Corp., Chicago, 1990—; board of directors Continental Bank Corp., Continental Bank, Eli Lilly and Company, GATX Corp., Whitman Corp., USG Corp. Active United Way, Crusade of Mercy, Chicago; chairman adv. board INROADS, Chicago, Incorporated; board of directors Chicago Medical School, Ind. U. Foundation, Ind. U. Grad. School Business Dean's adv. council, U. Chicago Council on Grad. School of Business, Lyric Opera of Chicago, Northwestern Memorial Hospital, board of directors, trustee Chicago Zool. Society, Mus. Sci. and Industry. With United States Navy, 1944-46. Clubs: Chicago, Mid-Am., Comml., Glen View, Old Elm Club, Shoreacres. Avocations: golf, hunting, fishing, sports. Home: 1205 Central Road Glenview Illinois 60025 Office: Whitman Corp 111 E Wacker Dr Chicago Illinois 60601

CRAIG, ANDREW BILLINGS, III, bank holding company executive; born Buffalo, New York, March 20, 1931; son of Andrew B. and Helen P. (House) C.; married Virginia Jean

Coskery, November 9, 1957; children—Andrea J., Laura D. Student, Cornell University, 1950-54; Bachelor of Arts, University Buffalo, 1955; Doctor of Humane Letters (honorary), Canisius College, 1981. Director WNY Nuclear Research Center, Buffalo, Transelco, Incorporated, Dresden, New York, Standard Mirror Company, Buffalo, Mowbot, Incorporated, Buffalo, Loblaw, Incorporated, Buffalo, Kistler Instrument Corp., Buffalo, Indianapolis Morris Plan, Indianapolis, Firstmark Fin. Corp., Indianapolis, Calspan Corp, Buffalo, Andco, Incorporated, Buffalo, Manufacturers & Traders Trust Company, Buffalo, M & T Capital Corp., Buffalo, 1st Empire Overseas Corp., Buffalo, BancOhio Corp., Columbus; now president, director, chief executive officer Boatmen's Bancshares, Incorporated, St. Louis; past chairman Boatmen's National Bank, St. Louis; chairman, chief executive officer BancOhio National Bank, 1983-85. Trustee Riverside Methodist Hospital Foundation, Columbus; board trustees Center Sci. and Industry, Columbus, Columbus Foundation, Buffalo General Hospital, Canisius College, 1975-80; director Buffalo Foundation, chairman Hospital Trustees New York State, 1980; member Syracuse District Adv. Council Small Business Administration, board of directors U. Buffalo School Mgmt., president Cornell Club Buffalo, 1969; vice chairman Cornell University Council; member Erie County Industrial Devel. Agency; member adv. board Junior League Buffalo; director New York State Association for Retarded Children, Erie County chapter; director Niagara Frontier Housing Devel. Corp., director United Way of Buffalo and Erie County, 1976-81; board deacons, trustees Westminster Presbyterian Church Served to lieutenant United States Army Intelligence, 1955-57. Recipient Niagara Frontier Executive of Year award University Buffalo School Mgmt., 1979, Outstanding Citizen of 1980 award Buffalo Evening News, Man of Year award Greater Buffalo Advertising Club, 1981, Western New Yorker of Year award Chamber of Commerce, 1981; named honoree Multiple Sclerosis Society, 1979. Member Association Reserve City Bankers, Phi Kappa Sigma (past president), United States Chamber of Commerce (member banking, monetary and fiscal affairs committee). Club: Country of Buffalo (board governors, past president). Office: Boatmen's Bancshares Incorporated Post Office Box 236 Saint Louis Missouri 63166

CRAIN, RANCE, publishing company executive. President Crain Communications, Incorporated, Chicago, New York City; editor-in-chief Advertising Age, Chicago, Crain's New York Business, New York City, 1984—. Office: Crain Commmunications Incorporated 740 Rush St Chicago Illinois 60611 also: Crain Communications Incorporated 220 E 42nd St New York New York 10017

CRANDALL, ROBERT LLOYD, airline executive; born Westerly, Rhode Island, December 6, 1935; son of Lloyd Evans and Virginia (Beard) C.; married Margaret Jan Schmults, July 6, 1957; children: Mark William, Martha Conway, Stephen Michael. Student, College William and Mary, 1953-55; Bachelor of Science, University Rhode Island, 1957; Master of Business Administration, Wharton School, University Pennsylvania, 1960. With Eastman Kodak Company, Rochester, 1960-62, Hallmark Cards, Kansas City, Missouri, 1962-66; assistant treasurer Trans World Airlines Incorporated, New York City, 1966-70; vice president systems and data services Trans World Airlines Incorporated, 1970-71, vice president, controller, 1971-72; senior vice president, treasurer Bloomingdale Brothers, New York City, 1972-73; senior vice president fin. Am. Airlines, Incorporated, New York City, 1973-74, senior vice president marketing, 1974-80, president, 1980—, chairman, chief executive officer, 1985—, also director, 1976—; president, chairman, chief executive officer AMR Corp., 1985—; board of directors Halliburton Company. Board of directors Boy Scouts Am. Served with Infantry United States Army, 1957.

CRAWFORD, BRUCE EDGAR, advertising executive; born West Bridgewater, Massachusetts, March 16, 1929; son of Harry Ellsworth and Nancy (Morrison) C.; married Christine Ameling, February 1, 1958; 1 son, Robert Bosworth. Bachelor of Science in Economics, University Pennsylvania, 1952. With Benton & Bowles, Incorporated, New York City, 1954-58; vice president Ted Bates & Company, New York City, 1958-61; advertising director Chesebrough Ponds Incorporated, New York City, 1961-63; with Batten, Barton, Durstine & Osborn, Incorporated, New York City, 1963-85, president, from 1978; president BBDO International, New York City, 1975-83, chief executive officer, 1977-85, chairman, 1985; director Metropolitan Opera Association, from 1976, vice president, 1981, president, 1984-85, general manager, 1986-88; president, chief executive officer Omnicom Group, New York City, 1989—. Served with United States Army, 1947-48. Republican. Clubs: Racquet and Tennis (New York City); Turf and Field. Office: Omnicom Group Incorporated 437 Madison Avenue New York New York 10022

CREAN, JOHN C., housing and recreational vehicles manufacturing company executive; born Bowden, North Dakota, 1925; married. Founder Fleetwood Enterprises, Incorporated, Riverside, California, 1951, president, 1952-70, chairman, chief executive officer, 1970—, also director. Served with United States Navy, 1942; with United States Merchant Marines, 1944-45. Office: Fleetwood Enterprises Incorporated 3125 Myers St Box 7638 Riverside California 92523

CREIGHTON, JOHN W., JR., forest products company executive; born Pittsburgh, September 1, 1932; married; 3 children. Bachelor of Science, Ohio State University, 1954, Juris Doctor, 1957; Master of Business Administration, University Miami, 1965. With Arthur Andersen and Company, 1957-59, Arvida Corp., 1959-66; executive vice president Mortgage Cons. Incorporated, 1966-70; general manager Shelter Group Weyerhaeuser Company, 1970, corp. vice president, 1970-85, executive vice president, 1985-88, president, director, 1988—; president Weyerhaeuser Real Estate Company; chairman board of directors Federal Home Loan Bank Seattle; board of directors National Corp. Housing Partnership, Puget Sound Bancorp, Mortgage Investments Plus, Incorporated, Am. Paper Institute. Trustee U. Puget Sound; board of directors Chief Seattle Council Boy Scouts Am., King County United Way. With United States Army, 1954-56. Office: Weyerhaeuser Company 33663 Weyerhaeuser Way S Federal Way Washington 98003

CRENSHAW, GORDON LEE, retired tobacco company executive; born Richmond, Virginia, January 19, 1922; son of Walter and Hattie (Ready) C.; married Deubre Anne Roper, May 12, 1945; children: Clarke Hutchins, Gordon Lee. Bachelor of Arts in Economics, University Virginia, 1943. With Universal Leaf Tobacco Company, Incorporated, Richmond, 1946—, vice president, 1958-65, president, 1965-88, president, chief executive officer, 1965-82, chairman, chief executive officer, 1982-88, chairman, 1988, retired, 1988, also board of directors; chairman, chief executive officer Universal Corp. (holding. company formed with Universal Leaf Tobacco Company, Incorporated and subsidiary), Richmond, 1988, chairman, 1989—; board of directors Crestar Fin. Corp., Lawyers Title Insurance Corp. (sub. Universal Corp.); chairman Universal Corp., 1988—. Board of directors Virginia Foundation for Ind. Colleges, Virginia Port Authority, Virginia Inter-Gov. Institute; board governors Virginia Home for Boys; trustee Richmond Memorial Hospital Lieutenant United States Naval Reserve, 1943-46. Member Tobacco Association United States (governor, past president), Commonwealth Club, Country Club of Virginia. Episcopalian. Office: Universal Corp Hamilton St at Broad Post Office Box 25099 Richmond Virginia 23230

CROOM, JOHN HENRY, III, utility company executive; born Fayetteville, North Carolina, December 12, 1932; son of John Henry and Mary Dalice (Howard) C.; married Verna Arlene Willetts, June 21, 1953; children: Mary, Karen, Elizabeth, John. Bachelor of Science in Mechanical Engineering, North Carolina State College, 1954. Engineer United Fuel Gas Company, Charleston, West Virginia, 1954-69; industrial sales manager Charleston Group Companies, 1969-73; industrial utilization manager Columbia Distribution Companies, Columbus, Ohio, 1973-74; vice president engineering and planning Columbia Distribution Companies, Columbus, 1974-79; senior vice president Columbia Gas System, Wilmington, Del., 1979-80; executive vice president, director Columbia Gas System, Wilmington, 1981-82, president, board of directors, 1982-84, chairman, president, chief executive officer, 1984—; chairman, president, chief executive officer Columbia Gas System Incorporated, Wilmington, 1984—; director Associated Electric & Gas Insurance Services. Board of directors Medical Center Del.; director, vice president Opportunities Center Incorporated, Wilmington; director Young Men's Christian Association of Del.; board of directors, past president Del.-Md.-Va. council Boy Scouts Am.; director, past chairman board Gas Research Institute, Chicago; trustee Westminster Presbyterian With Army of the United States, 1954-56, Korea. Member NSPE, Del. Roundtable (board directors, past chairman), Wilmington Country Club (board directors, vice president), Am. Gas Association (vice chairman), National Eagle Scout Association (board regents). Home: 255 Pondview Chadds Ford Pennsylvania 19317

Office: Columbia Gas System Incorporated 20 Montchanin Road Wilmington Delaware 19807

CROZIER, WILLIAM MARSHALL, JR., bank holding company executive; born New York City, October 2, 1932; son of William Marshall and Alice (Parsons) C.; married Prudence van Zandt Slitor, June 20, 1964; children: Matthew Eaton, Abigail Parsons, Patience Wells. Bachelor of Arts in Economics, Yale University, 1954; Master of Business Administration with distinction, Harvard University, 1963. With Hanover Bank, New York City, 1954-61; assistant secretary Hanover Bank, 1959; with BayBanks, Incorporated, Boston, 1964—; assistant treasurer BayBanks, Incorporated, 1965, assistant vice president, 1968, vice president, secretary, 1969, senior vice president, secretary, 1973, chairman board, chief executive officer, 1974—, president, 1977—, director, 1974—; board of directors BayBank, Boston, 1978. Trustee Boston Symphony Orchestra, Commonwealth Energy System. Served with United States Army, 1955-57. Member Massachusetts Business Roundtable (board directors), Jobs for Massachusetts (board directors). Episcopalian. Clubs: Comml.-Mchts. (Boston), Union (Boston), Harvard (Boston); Yale (New York City). Office: BayBanks Incorporated 175 Federal St Boston Massachusetts 02110

CRUIKSHANK, THOMAS HENRY, corporation executive; born Lake Charles, Louisiana, November 3, 1931; son of Louis James and Helene L. (Little) C.; married Ann Coe, November 17, 1955; children: Thomas Henry, Kate Martin, Stuart Coe. Bachelor of Arts, Rice University, 1952; postgraduate, University Texas Law School, 1952-53, University Houston Law School, 1953-55. Bar: Texas; C.P.A., Texas. Accountant Arthur Andersen & Company, Houston, 1953-55, 58-60; member firm Vinson & Elkins, Houston, 1961-69; vice president Halliburton Company, Dallas, 1969-72, senior vice president, 1972-80, executive vice president, 1980, president, chief executive officer subsidiary Otis Engineering Corp., 1980-81, president, 1981-83, president, chief executive officer, 1983-89, chairman, chief executive officer, 1989—, director, 1977—; board of directors Goodyear Tire & Rubber Company, Williams Companies, Incorporated; member National Petroleum Council; member policy committee Business Roundtable. President Junior Achievement, Dallas, 1974-76, chairman, 1976-78, member national board, 1976—, chairman 1989-90; board of directors Up With People. Lieutenant (junior grade) United States Naval Reserve, 1955-58. Member American Bar Association, American Institute of Certified Public Accountants, Texas Society Certified Public Accountants, Texas Bar Association, Am. Petroleum Institute, Dallas Petroleum Club, Dallas Country Club (board govs. 1977-79, 86-88), River Oaks Country Club (Houston), Pine Valley Golf Club (New Jersey), Haig Point Country Club (South Carolina), Preston Trail Golf Club, Peninsula Club (North Carolina). Home: 3508 Marquette Dallas Texas 75205 Office: Halliburton Company 3600 Lincoln Plaza 500 N Akard St Dallas Texas 75201-3391

CRULL, TIMM F., food company executive; born 1931; married.

Bachelor of Arts, Michigan State University, 1955. Chief operating officer Norton Simon Incorporated, 1977-79; with Carnation Company, Los Angeles, 1955-77, 80—, executive vice president, 1980-83, president, 1983—, chief executive officer, 1985—, vice chairman, director. Office: Carnation Company 5045 Wilshire Boulevard Los Angeles California 90036

CRUTCHFIELD, EDWARD ELLIOTT, JR., banker; born Detroit, July 14, 1941; son of Edward Elliott and Katherine (Sikes) C.; married Nancy Glass Kizer, July 27, 1963; children: Edward Elliott, III, Sarah Palmer. Bachelor of Arts, Davidson College, 1963; Master of Business Administration, University Pennsylvania, 1965. With First Union National Bank, Charlotte, North Carolina, 1965—, head retail bank services group, 1970-72, executive vice president general administration, 1972-73, president, 1973-84, vice chairman, from 1984; president First Union Corp. (parent), Charlotte, 1983-86, chief executive officer, 1984—, now also chairman, board of directors; board of directors Bernhardt Industries, Incorporated, Charlotte, 1983—. Board deacons Myers Park Presbyterian Church; board of directors United Community Services, Salvation Army, Charlotte Board, Charlotte Latin School; trustee Mint Mus. Art, North Carolina Nature Conservancy; board mgrs. Charlotte Memorial Hospital; board visitors Davidson College. Member Charlotte Chamber of Commerce, Association Reserve City Bankers, Am., North Carolina bankers associations, Am. Textile Manufacturers Association, Young Pres.'s Organization. Clubs: Charlotte City, Charlotte Country, Linville (North Carolina) Golf. Office: 1st Union Corp 1 First Union Plaza Charlotte North Carolina 28288

CUMMING, IAN M., holding company executive; born 1940. Bachelor of Arts, University Kansas, 1964; Master of Business Administration, Harvard University, 1970. Chairman Leucodia National Corp., New York City, Leukodia Incorporated, New York City, Brae Corp., San Francisco. Office: Leucadia National Corp 315 Park Avenue S New York New York 10010

CURLER, HOWARD J., business executive; born Mosinee, Wisconsin, April 11, 1925; married. Bachelor of Science in Chemical Engineering, University Wisconsin, 1948. With research department Marathon Corp., 1948-58; president Curwood Incorporated, 1958-68; corp. vice president Bemis Company Incorporated, 1965-76, executive vice president, chief operating officer, 1976, president, chief operating officer, 1977, president, chief executive officer, 1978-87, chairman, chief executive officer, 1987—. Office: Bemis Company Incorporated 800 Northstar Center 625 Marquette Avenue Minneapolis Minnesota 55402

CURLEY, JOHN J., diversified media company executive; born December 31, 1938; married Ann Conser; two sons. Bachelor of Arts, Dickinson College, 1960; Master of Science, Columbia University, 1963. Reporter, editor Associated Press, 1961-66; with Gannett Company Incorporated, Arlington, Virginia, 1969—; former president Mid-Atlantic newspaper group, senior vice president Gannett Company Incorporated, Washington, 1982-84, president, 1984—, chief operating officer, 1984-86, chief executive officer, 1986—, chairman, 1989—, also board of directors. Lieutenant United States Army, 1960-62. Office: Gannett Company Incorporated 1100 Wilson Boulevard Arlington Virginia 22234

CURRIE, MALCOLM RODERICK, scientist, aerospace and automotive executive; born Spokane, Washington, March 13, 1927; son of Erwin Casper and Genevieve (Hauenstein) C.; married Sunya Lofsky, June 24, 1951; children: Deborah, David, Diana; married Barbara L. Dyer, March 5, 1977. Bachelor of Arts, University California at Berkeley, 1949, Master of Science, 1951, Doctor of Philosophy, 1954. Research engineer Microwave Laboratory, University California at Berkeley, 1949-52, electrical engineering faculty, 1953-54; lecturer University California at Los Angeles, 1955-57; research engineer Hughes Aircraft Company, 1954-57, vice president, 1965-66; head electron dynamics department Hughes Research Laboratories, Culver City, California, 1957-60; director physics laboratory Hughes Research Laboratories, Malibu, California, 1960-61, associate director, 1961-63, vice president, director research laboratories, 1963-65, vice president, manager research and devel. div., 1965-69; vice president research and devel. Beckman Instruments, Incorporated, 1969-73; undersecretary research and engineering department Office Secretary Defense, Washington, 1973-77; president missile systems group Hughes Aircraft Company, Canoga Park, California, 1977-83, executive vice president, 1983-88, chief executive officer, chairman board, 1988—, also board of directors; president, chief executive officer Delco Electronics Corp., 1986-88, also board of directors; board of directors General Motors Corporation Hughes Electronics Company, group executive defense operations, 1986; chairman, chief executive officer Hughes Aircraft Company, 1988—; board of directors Unocal Corp.; member Def. Sci. Board. Contributor articles to professional journals; patentee in field. Member adv. board U. California, Berkeley, University of California at Los Angeles.; trustee U. So California, 1989—, Howard U., 1989—, University of California at Los Angeles Foundation; board of directors western region United Way, 1987; coordinator, head United States Savs. Bond Drive, so. California, 1991. With United States Naval Reserve, 1944-47. Decorated commander Legion of Honor France; named Nation's Outstanding Young Electrical Engineer Eta Kappa Nu, 1958, one of 5 Outstanding Young Men of California by California Junior Chamber of Commerce, 1960. Fellow Institute of Electrical and Electronics Engineers, American Institute of Aeronautics and Astronautics; member National Acad. Engineering, Am. Physical Society, Phi Beta Kappa, Sigma Xi, Lambda Chi Alpha. Club: Cosmos. Home: 28780 Wagon Road Agoura California 91301 Office: Hughes Aircraft Company 7200 Hughes Terrace Los Angeles California 90045

CUTHBERT, WILLIAM R., consumer goods manufacturing company executive; born Ogdensburg, New York, 1919. Student, Kenyon College. With Newell Company, Freeport, Illinois, 1962—, chairman board of directors, 1976—. With United States Air Force, 1943-46. Office: Newell

Company 29 E Stephenson St Freeport Illinois 61032

DALHOUSE, WARNER NORRIS, banker; born Roanoke, Virginia, June 4, 1934; son of Jefferson William and Gay-Nell (Henley) D.; married Barbara Ann Dalhouse, December 27, 1984. Student, Roanoke College, 1952-54; Bachelor of Science in Commerce, University Virginia, 1956. Vice president 1st National Exchange Bank, Roanoke, Virginia, 1967-69, senior vice president, 1969-73, executive vice president, 1973-77, president, chief administrative officer, 1977-81; executive vice president, chief administrative officer Dominion Bankshares Corp., Roanoke, Virginia, 1977-81, president, chief executive officer, 1981-89; chairman board, chief executive officer Dominion Bankshares Corp., Roanoke, 1989—; director Shenandoah Life Insurance Company, Roanoke, International Fin. Conference. President Roanoke Pub. Libr. Foundation, Virginia; chairman Ctr.-in-the Square; board of directors Carilion Health System Roanoke; member Governor's Economic Adv. Council; board of directors Community Hospital Roanoke. Member Association Bank Holding Companies. Office: Dominion Bankshares Corp Post Office Box 13327 Roanoke Virginia 24040

DALY, ROBERT ANTHONY, film executive; born Brooklyn, December 8, 1936; son of James and Eleanor D.; married Nancy MacNeil, October 7, 1961; children: Linda Marie, Robert Anthony, Brian James. Student, Brooklyn College. From director business affairs to vice president business affairs, to executive vice president CBS TV Network, 1955-80; president CBS Entertainment Company, from 1977; chairman, chief executive officer Warner Brothers, Incorporated, Burbank, California, 1981—; Board directors Am. Film Institute. Trustee Am. Film Institute; board of directors National Conference Christians and Jews. Member Acad. Motion Picture Arts and Sciences, National Acad. TV Arts and Sciences, Hollywood Radio and TV Society, Motion Picture Pioneers. Roman Catholic. Club: Bel Air Country. Office: Warner Bros Incorporated 4000 Warner Boulevard Burbank California 91522

D'AMATO, ANTHONY S., chemical company executive; born Brooklyn, New York, 1930. Bachelor of Science in Chemical Engineering, Polytechnic Institute of Brooklyn, 1952. Executive vice president Borden Incorporated, New York, 1985—; president Borden Packaging and Indl. Products (formerly Borden Chemical Div.), Columbus, Ohio, 1985—; chairman, chief executive officer Borden Packaging and Indl. Products (formerly Borden Chemical Div.), Columbus. Office: Borden Packaging & Indsl Products 180 E Broad St Columbus Ohio 43215

DAMMEYER, RODNEY FOSTER, leasing company executive; born Cleveland, November 5, 1940; son of Frederick and Marion (Foster) D.; married Diane Newins, February 8, 1975; children: Paul, Scott, Tom, Kimberley, Alice. Bachelor of Science in Accounting, Kent State University, 1962. Managing partner Arthur Andersen & Company, Seattle, 1962-79; executive vice president fin. Northwest Industries, Incorporated, Chicago, 1979-83; senior vice president, chief fin. officer Household International, Prospect Heights, Illinois, 1983-85; president, chief operating officer Itel Corp., Chicago,

1985—, also board of directors. Member Am. Institute C.P.A.s, Fin. Executives Institute, National Association Accts. Presbyterian. Club: Econs. Chicago. Office: ITEL Corp 2 N Riverside Plaza Chicago Illinois 60606

DAMSEL, RICHARD A., transportation company executive; born 1942; married. Bachelor of Science in Business Administration, John Carroll University, 1964. Audit manager Deloitte Haskins and Sells, to 1974; with Leaseway Transportation Corp., Cleveland, 1974—, manager fin. analysis, then treasurer, 1975-80, vice president fin., treasurer, 1980-83, senior vice president fin. administration, 1983-88, chairman, chief executive officer, 1988—; board of directors Midwestern Distribution Incorporated, Fort Scott, Kansas, Leaseway Personnel Corp., Cleveland. Office: Leaseway Transp Corp 3700 Park E Dr Cleveland Ohio 44122

DANAHY, JAMES PATRICK, textile executive; born Roanoke, Virginia, February 24, 1944; son of Frank and Anne (Garth) D.; married Mary Carol Richard, December 16, 1967; children: James Patrick Jr., Catherine Anne. Bachelor in Engineering, Notre Dame University, 1966; Master of Business Administration, University Virginia, 1971. Various management positions Cone Mills Corp., Greensboro, North Carolina, 1971-75; administrative assistant to general manager Carlisle (South Carolina) plant Cone Mills Corp., 1975-76, superintendent Carlisle plant, 1976-78, general manager Carlisle plant, 1978-81; vice president textile products div. Cone Mills Corp., Greensboro, 1981-84, president Cone Finishing Company, 1984-90, vice president, 1986-89, president, chief operating officer, 1989-90, president, chief executive officer, 1990—, also board of directors; Board directors North Carolina National Bank, Greensboro, J.East Sirrine Foundation, Greenville, South Carolina; trustee Institute of Textile Tech., Charlottesville, Virginia. Lieutenant (junior grade) United States Navy, 1966-69. Member South Carolina Textile Manufacturers Association (board directors), Am. Textile Manufacturers Institute, Institute of Textile Tech. (trustee), Greensboro Country Club, Greensboro City Club. Roman Catholic. Avocation: golf. Office: Cone Mills Corp 1201 Maple St Greensboro North Carolina 27405

DANIEL, RICHARD NICHOLAS, fabricated metals manufacturing company executive; born Brooklyn, September 18, 1935; son of Louis V. and Jean (D'Andrea) D.; married Elaine E. Sherman, September 24, 1966; children: Matthew, Jeffrey. Bachelor of Business Administration, St. John's University, 1957; Master of Business Administration, University Pennsylvania, 1959. C.P.A., Texas. Planning associate Mobil Oil Corp., New York City, 1962-70; vice president fin. Laird Enterprises Incorporated, New York City, 1970-71; vice president operations Wheelabrator-Frye, New York City, 1971; vice president, controller Handy & Harman, New York City, 1971-76, v.p.-fin., 1977-78, group vice president, 1978-79, president, chief operating officer, 1979-83, president, chief executive officer, 1983-87, chairman, president, chief executive officer, 1988—, also director. Home: 91 Hawthorn Place Briarcliff Manor New York 10510 Office: Handy &

Harman 850 3rd Avenue New York New York 10022

DANIELL, ROBERT F., diversified manufacturing company executive; born Milton, Massachusetts, 1933; married. Graduate, Boston University College Industrial Tech., 1954; Doctor of Science (honorary), University Bridgeport; Doctor of Laws (honorary), Trinity College, Boston University. With Sikorsky Aircraft, Stratford, Connecticut, 1956-82, design engineer, from 1956, program manager, 1968-71, commercial marketing manager, 1971-74, vice president commercial marketing, 1974-76, senior vice president marketing, 1976-77, executive vice president, 1977-80, chief executive officer, 1980-82, president, 1981-82; with United Techs. (parent company), Hartford, Connecticut, 1982—; vice president United Technologies (parent company), Hartford, Connecticut, 1982-83, senior vice president defense systems, 1983-84, president, chief operating officer, director, 1984—, chief executive officer, 1986—, chairman board of directors, 1987—; board of directors The Travelers Corp., Hartford, Connecticut, Shell Oil Company, Houston. Board trustees Boston U., Naval Aviation Mus. Foundation, Incorporated, Falcon Foundation; corporator Institute of Living. Served with United States Army, 1954-56. Fellow University Bridgeport. Member Wings Club (board govs.). Office: United Techs Corp United Techs Building Hartford Connecticut 06101

DARNALL, ROBERT J., steel company executive. married. Bachelor of Arts in Math., DePauw University, 1960; Bachelor of Science in Civil Engineering, Columbia University, 1962; Master of Business Administration, University Chicago, 1973. With Inland Steel Company, Chicago, 1962—; general mill foreman Inland Steel Company, East Chicago, Ind., 1967-68, assistant superintendent, 1969-1970, superintendent, 1971-75, then assistant to vice president steel manufacturing, 1975-77, assistant general manager flat product mills, 1977-79, general manager, 1979, vice president engring and corp. planning, 1981; executive vice president Inland Steel Company, Chicago, 1982, president, 1984-86, chief operating officer integrated steel segment, 1984-86; president, chief operating officer Inland Steel Industries, Incorporated, Chicago, 1986—, also board of directors; board of directors Household International. Active Flossmoor (Illinois) Community Church ; associate Northwestern U.; board of directors, United Way, Crusade of Mercy, United Way Suburban Chicago; trustee DePauw U., Glenwood School for Boys. Member Am. Iron and Steel Institute, Association Iron and Steel Engineers, Illinois Manufacturers Association (board directors). Office: Inland Steel Industries Incorporated 30 W Monroe St Chicago Illinois 60603

DARRAGH, JOHN K., printing company executive; born Cincinnati, 1929. Bachelor of Science, Arizona State University, 1959. Account auditor Arthur Andersen and Company, 1959-64; vice president fin. Sorg Paper Company, Middletown, Ohio, 1964-74; with Standard Register Company, Dayton, Ohio, 1974—, treasurer, 1974-80, vice president fin., 1976-80, executive vice president, 1980-83, chief fin. officer, 1980-81, chief operating officer, 1981-83, president, chief executive officer, 1983—. Served to lieutenant

United States Air Force, 1950-56. Office: Standard Register Company Post Office Box 1167 Dayton Ohio 45401

DASBURG, JOHN HAROLD, airline executive; born New York City, January 7, 1944; son of Jean Henry and Alice Etta Dasburg; married Mary Lois Diaz, July 6, 1968; 1 child, John Peter. Associate of Arts, University Miami, 1963; Bachelor of Science in Industrial Engineering, University Florida, 1966, Master of Business Administration, 1971, Juris Doctor, 1973. Admitted to Florida bar, 1974. Certified Public Accountant, Florida, Maryland. Member staff Peat Marwick Mitchell & Company, Jacksonville, Florida, 1973-78, tax partner in charge, 1978-80; vice president tax Marriott Corp., Washington, 1980-82, vice president fin. 1982-84, senior vice president, 1984-85, executive vice president, chief fin. officer, chief real estate officer, 1985-88; president lodging group Marriott Lodging, 1988-89; president, chief executive officer Northwest Airlines, 1990—; board of directors Genesco. Author numerous published articles on tax law and tax acct. Board of directors U. Florida Foundation Lieutenant (junior grade) United States Navy, 1966-69; Vietnam. Member American Bar Association, Urban Land Institute, American Institute of Certified Public Accountants, Florida Bar Association. Republican. Roman Catholic.

DAVIDSON, GEORGE A., JR., utility company executive; born Pittsburgh, July 28, 1938. Bachelor of Science, University of Pittsburgh, 1960. Chairman, chief executive officer, director Consolidated Natural Gas Company, Pittsburgh. Office: Consol Natural Gas Company CNG Tower Pittsburgh Pennsylvania 15222

DAVIDSON, HARVEY JUSTIN, university dean; born Gentryville, Indiana, November 15, 1930; son of Harvey Harrison and Dorothy (Eberhardt) D.; married Shirlee Jean Ploeger, September 4, 1954; children: Charles Justin, John Clinton, James Christopher, Mary Jennifer. Bachelor of Science in Industrial Mgmt, Carnegie-Mellon University, 1952, Master of Science in Math. Econs, 1955; C.P.A. Staff assistant Operations Evaluation Group, United States Navy-Mass. Institute Tech., 1955-56; economist Arabian-Am. Oil. Company, 1956-58; management consultant Touche Ross & Company, 1957-64; partner 1964-69; dean Grad. School Business and Pub. Administration, Cornell University, 1969-79, College Business, Ohio State University, Columbus, 1979—; board of directors Lukens, Incorporated, UNC Incorporated, Hubbell Incorporated. Co-author: Statistical Sampling for Accounting Information, 1962, The Future of Accounting Education, 1961. Served to 1st lieutenant, Corps of Engineers Army of the United States, 1952-54. Decorated Bronze Star. Member Am., Pennsylvania insts. C.P.A.s, Illinois Society C.P.A.s, Michigan Association C.P.A.s, Institute Management Sci., Am. Statistical Association. Unitarian. Home: 306 E Sycamore St Columbus Ohio 43206 Office: Ohio State U School Business Columbus Ohio 43210

DAVILA, WILLIAM S., supermarket chain executive; born 1931; married. Associate of Arts, Los Angeles City College. Produce clerk Von's Grocery Company, El Monte, California, 1948-56; produce manager Von's Grocery Company, El Monte, 1956-59, with advertising department, 1959-65, assistant advertising manager, 1965-67, advertising manager, 1967-73, manager sales promotion, 1973-75, vice president sales, 1975-77, group vice president marketing sales, 1977-80, senior vice president supermarkets, 1980-84, executive vice president, from 1984, now president, chief operating officer, also board of directors. Served with United States Air Force, 1951-54. Office: Von's Company Incorporated Post Office Box 3338 Terminal Annex Los Angeles California 90051

DAVIS, A. DANO, grocery store chain executive; born 1945. Student, Stetson University. With Winn-Dixie Stores Incorporated, Jacksonville, Florida, 1968—, corp. vice president, manager Jacksonville div., 1978-80, senior vice president and regional director Jacksonville and Orlando (Florida) and Atlanta divs., 1980-82, president, 1982-88, chief executive officer, 1982—, chairman, 1988—, also board of directors. Office: Winn-Dixie Stores Incorporated 5050 Edgewood Court Jacksonville Florida 32205

DAVIS, ALLEN, professional football team executive; born Brockton, Massachusetts, July 4, 1929; son of Louis and Rose (Kirschenbaum) D.; married Carol Segall, July 11, 1954; 1 son, Mark. Student, Wittenberg College, 1947; Bachelor of Arts, Syracuse University, 1950. Assistant football coach Adelphi College, 1950-51; head football coach Fort Belvoir, Virginia, 1952-53; player-personnel scout Baltimore Colts, 1954; line coach The Citadel, 1955-56, University Southern California, 1957-59; assistant coach San Diego Chargers, 1960-62; general manager, head coach Oakland Raiders (now Los Angeles Raiders), 1963-66, owner, managing general partner, 1966—; former member management council and competition committee National Football League. Served with Army of the United States, 1952-53. Named Professional Coach of Year Associated Press, Professional Coach of Year United Press International, Professional Coach of Year Sporting News, Professional Coach of Year Pro-Football Illustrated, 1963; Young Man of Year Oakland, 1963; only individual in history to be an assistant coach, head coach, general manager, league commissioner and owner. Member Am. Football Coaches Association. Office: Los Angeles Raiders 332 Center St El Segundo California 90245

DAVIS, CLIVE JAY, record company executive; born Brooklyn, April 4, 1935; son of Herman and Florence (Brooks) D.; children: Fred, Lauren, Mitchell, Douglas. Bachelor of Arts magna cum laude, New York University, 1953; Bachelor of Laws cum laude, Harvard University, 1956. Bar: New York bar 1957. Associate firm Rosenman Colin Freund Lewis & Cohen, New York City, 1958-60; general attorney Columbia Records, 1960-65, president, 1966-73; president Arista Records, New York City, 1974—. Author: Clive: Inside the Record Business, 1975. Recipient humanitarian award Anti-Defamation League, 1970, Martell Leukemia Foundation, 1980; named Man of Year Am. Parkinson Disease, 1972, Record Company Executive of Year National Association TV and Radio Announcers, 1973, National Pop Music Survey, 1974, 78, 80, 81, 87, 90, Man of Year City of Hope, 1978,

Martin Luther King Humanitarian of Year award Congress Racial Equality, 1991, Humanitarian of Year Am. Cancer Society, 1985. Member Record Industry Association Am. (president, chairman board 1972-73, now director). Office: Arista Records Incorporated Arista Building 6 W 57th St New York New York 10019

DAVIS, DELMONT ALVIN, JR., manufacturing company executive; born Hillside, Colorado, June 11, 1935; son of Delmont A. and Zelma M. (Townsend) D.; married L. June Clift, June 9, 1957; children: Terry, Curtis, Thayer. Bachelor of Science in Civil Engineering, University Colorado, 1959; student, University Southern Mississippi, 1966-68. Registered professional engineer, Colorado, Mississippi, Louisiana, Wisconsin; registered land surveyor, Louisiana. Civil engineer Federal Aviation Administration, 1956-61; supervisor facilities Martin Marietta Corp., 1961-63; supervisor mnfg. engineering 1963-65; project engineer General Electric Company, Bay St. Louis, Mississippi, 1969; project manager aerospace div. Ball Corp., Westminster, Colorado, 1968-69, director engineering and devel. Metal Container Group, 1969-74, vice president operations, then group vice president Metal Container Group, 1974-87, executive vice president Packaging Products Group, 1987-89, president, chief operating officer, member executive committee, fin. committee, chmn.'s committee, 1989-91, president, chief executive officer, 1991—, 1991—; board of directors MCP-Ball International Limited, Hong Kong, Ball-Incon Glass Pkg. Corp., Kent Plastics United Kingdom, Ball Packaging Products Can., Incorporated 1988—, United Banks of Broomfield, Arvada, Westminster and Northglenn, Colorado, 1988—. Board of directors Pres's Leadership Class U. Colorado, 1987. Member American Society of Civil Engineers, NSPE, Can. Mfrs.'s Institute (chairman, director, member executive committee 1976—), Tau Kappa Epsilon (president Boulder chapter 1956-57, chairman board directors chapter 1957-58). Republican. Member First Baptist Church. Office: Ball Corp 9300 W 108th Circuit Westminster Colorado 80038-0589 also: Ball Corp 345 S High St Muncie Indiana 47305

DAVIS, MARTIN S., entertainment and publishing executive; born New York City, 1927. With Samuel Goldwyn Productions, New York City, 1947-55, Allied Artists Pictures Corp., New York City, 1955-58; with Paramount Pictures Corp., New York City, 1958-69, vice president, 1962-66, executive vice president, chief operating officer, member executive committee, director, 1966-69; senior vice president Paramount Communications, Incorporated (formerly Gulf & Western Incorporated), New York City, 1969-74, executive vice president, member executive committee, 1974—, chairman and chief executive officer, 1983—, also board of directors; board of directors New York City Partnership. Board of directors National Multiple Sclerosis Society; board trustees Carnegie Hall. With Army of the United States, 1943-46. Member Econ. Club. Office: Paramount Communications Incorporated 15 Columbus Circle New York New York 10023-7780

DAVIS, ROBERT EDWIN, industrial executive; born Madison, Illinois, July 15, 1931; son of Harry Earl and Bernice (Prusak) D.; married Shirley M.

Krumbholz, September 4, 1954; children: Tom, Barbara, Sue Ann. Bachelor of Science in Chemical Engineering, University Missouri, 1953. With Socony-Mobil Oil Company, St. Louis and Chicago, 1953-54, 56-57; with petrochem. sales Nalco Corp., Chicago and Cleveland, 1957-58; district sales engineer Thiokol Corp., Newtown, Pennsylvania, 1958-82, group vice president general products, 1968-70, president, 1970-82, chief executive officer, 1973-82, chairman board, 1977-82; tech. director Thiokol Corp., Dayton, 1958-60, Eastern district manager, Washington, 1960-64, vice president aerospace marketing, 1964-68; president, chief operating officer Morton Thiokol, Incorporated, Chicago, 1982-83; president, chief operating officer Sequa Corp., New York City, 1983-91, also board of directors; managing director Axess Corp., Palm Beach, Florida, 1991—; member President's Commission on Pers. Interchange, 1976-79; board director H&R Block, Incorporated, Erbamont N.V., USF&G Corp. With United States Air Force, 1954-56. Member Am. Management Association, St. Andrews Club (Boca Raton, Florida), Marriott Seaview Club. Office: Axess Corp 440 Royal Palm Way Palm Beach Florida 33480

DEAN, HOWARD M., JR., food company executive; born 1937; married. Bachelor of Business Administration, Southern Methodist University, 1960; Master of Business Administration, Northwestern University, 1961. With Dean Foods Company, Incorporated, Franklin Park, Illinois, 1955—, internal auditor, 1965-68, assistant to vice president fin., 1968-70, president, 1970-89, also director, chief executive officer, 1987—, chairman, 1989—. Served to lieutenant (junior grade) United States Navy, 1962-65. Office: Dean Foods Company 3600 N River Road Franklin Park Illinois 60131

DEARTH, ROBERT ALFRED, JR., food processing executive; born Birmingham, Alabama, July 15, 1944; son of Robert Alfred and Regina (Miller) D.; married Barbara Jane Nacci, June 22, 1968; children: Matthew Louis, Christopher Miller. Bachelor of Arts, Wesleyan University, Middletown, Connecticut, 1966; Master of Business Administration, University Virginia, 1968. Office assistant Adam Opel Ag. (div. of General Motors), Russelsheim, Federal Republic Germany, 1965; engineer, change control clerk Ford Motor Company, Dearborn, Michigan, 1966, market survey analyst, 1967, cost analyst, 1968-70, budget analyst fin. staff, 1970-71, treasury analyst, 1971-72, treasury supervisor, 1972-73, supervisor controllers department, 1973-75; manager fin. planning and analysis Getty Refining and Marketing, New York City, 1975-77; director fin. analysis United Brands Company, New York City, 1977-79, assistant treasurer, 1979-82; vice president, chief administrative officer United Brands Company, Cincinnati, 1988—; senior vice president, chief fin. officer John Morrell & Company, Northfield, Illinois, 1983-87; member regional adv. board Arkwright Mutual Insurance Company, Boston, 1987—. Trustee Chi Psi Educational Trust, Ann Arbor, Michigan, 1985—; treasurer Boy Scouts Am., Winnetka, Illinois, 1986-87. Avocations: tennis, boating, antique collecting, hunting. Home: 2900 Grandin Road Cincinnati Ohio 45208

DEBARTOLO, EDWARD J., SR., real estate developer; born Youngstown, Ohio, May 17, 1919; son of Michael and Rose (Villani) DeB.; married Maria Patricia Montani, December 18, 1944 (deceased); children: Edward J., Marie D. Graduate, University Notre Dame; Doctor of Science (honorary), Florida Institute Tech., 1981. Registered professional engineer, registered surveyor. Partner Michael DeBartolo Construction Company, Youngstown, 1936-41; president Michael DeBartolo Construction Company, 1946-48, Edward J. DeBartolo Corp., Youngstown, 1958-79; chairman board, chief executive officer Edward J. DeBartolo Corp., 1979—; owner Thistledown Racing Club, Cleveland, Louisiana Downs race tracks, Remington Park, Oklahoma City; owner, chairman, president Pittsburgh Penguins (National Hockey League). 2d lieutenant Corps of Engineers United States Army, 1941-46, Okinawa. Named Man of Year Mahoning Valley Economic Devel. Corp., 1983, Man of Year City of Pitts., 1983; recipient Ellis Island Medal of Honor, 1986, Ohio Governor's award, 1984, Distinguished Citizen award Youngstown State University, 1984. Member Urban Land Institute, National Realty Committee, Thoroughbred Racing Assns. (Eclipse award 1989), University Notre Dame Advisory Council, International Council Shopping Centers. Roman Catholic.

DEBARTOLO, EDWARD JOHN, JR., professional football team owner, real estate developer; born Youngstown, Ohio, November 6, 1946; son of Edward J. and Marie Patricia (Montani) DeB.; married Cynthia Ruth Papalia, November 27, 1968; children: Lisa Marie, Tiffanie Lynne, Nicole Anne. Student, University Notre Dame, 1964-68. With Edward J. DeBartolo Corp., Youngstown, Ohio, 1960—, vice president, 1972-75, executive vice president, 1975—, president, chief administrative officer, 1979; owner, managing partner San Francisco 49ers, 1977—. Trustee Youngstown State U., 1974-77; member national adv. council St. Jude Children's Research Hospital, 1978—, local chairman, 1979-80; local chairman fund drive Am. Cancer Society, 1975—, City of Hope, 1977; member National Cambodia Crisis Committee, 1980—; chairman 19th Annual Victor awards City of Hope, 1985; appointed adv. council College Business Administration U. Notre Dame, 1988; board of directors Cleveland Clinic Foundation, 1991. Served with United States Army, 1969. Recipient Man of Year award St. Jude Children's Hospital, 1979, Boy's Town of Italy in San Francisco, 1985, Sportsman of Year award National Italian Am. Sports Hall of Fame, 1991; Salvation Army Citation of Merit, 1982. Member International Council of Shopping Centers. Roman Catholic. Clubs: Tippecanoe Country, Fonderlac Country, Dapper Dan (director 1980—). Office: Edward J DeBartolo Corp 7620 Market St Youngstown Ohio 44153-6085 also: care San Francisco 49ers 4949 Centennial Boulevard Santa Clara California 95054 also: Pittsburgh Penguins Civic Arena Gate #7 Pittsburgh Pennsylvania 15219

DEBREU, GERARD, economics and mathematics educator; born Calais, France, July 4, 1921; came to United States, 1950, naturalized, 1975; son of Camille and Fernande (Decharne) D.; married Françoise Bled, June 14, 1945; children: Chantal, Florence.

Student, Ecole Normale Supérieure, Paris, 1941-44, Agrégé de l'Université, France, 1946; Doctor of Science, University Paris, 1956; Doctor Rerum Politicarum honoris causa, University Bonn, 1977; Doctor Sciences Economiques (honorary), University Lausanne, 1980; Doctor of Science (honorary), Northwestern University, 1981; Doctor honoris causa, University des Sciences Sociales de Toulouse, 1983, Yale University, 1987, University Bordeaux I, 1988. Research associate Centre National De La Recherche Sci., Paris, 1946-48; Rockefeller fellow United States, Sweden and Norway, 1948-50; research associate Cowles Commission, University Chicago, 1950-55; associate professor economics Cowles Foundation, Yale, 1955-61; fellow Center Advanced Study Behavioral Sciences, 1960-61; visiting professor economics Yale University, fall 1961; professor economics University California at Berkeley, 1962—, professor math., 1975—, University professor, 1985—; Guggenheim fellow, visiting professor Center Operations Research and Econometrics, University Louvain, 1968-69, visiting professor, 1971, 72, 88; Erskine fellow University Canterbury, Christchurch, New Zealand, 1969, 87, visiting professor, 1973; Overseas fellow Churchill College, Cambridge, England, 1972; visiting professor Cowles Foundation for Research in Economics, Yale University, 1976; visiting professor University Bonn, 1977; research associate CEPREMAP, Paris, 1980; faculty research lecturer University California Berkeley, 1984-85, university professor, 1985—; Class of 1958 chair University California, Berkeley, 1986—; visiting professor University Sydney, Australia, 1987. Author: Theory of Value, 1959, Mathematical Economics: Twenty Papers of Gerard Debreu, 1983; Associate editor: International Econ. Rev, 1959-69; member editorial board: Journal Econ. theory, 1972—, Games and Econ. Behavior, 1989—; member adv. board: Journal Math. Econs, 1974—. Served with French Army, 1944-45. Decorated chevalier Légion d'Honneur; recipient Nobel Prize in Economic Sciences, 1983, Commandeur de l'Ordre du Merite, 1984; senior United States Scientist awardee Alexander von Humboldt Foundation. Fellow American Association for the Advancement of Science, Econometric Society (president 1971), Am. Econ. Association (distinguished fellow 1982, pres.-elect 1989); member National Academy of Sciences (committee human rights 1984—, chair class V behavioral and social scis. 1989—), Am. Philosophical Society, French Acad. Sciences (foreign associate). Office: U California Department Econs Berkeley California 94720

DE CASTRO, EDSON D., computer manufacturing corporation executive; born September 14, 1938; married. Graduate, Lowell Technological Institute, 1960. Engineering positions Digital Equipment Corp., 1961-68; with Data General Corp., Westborough, Massachusetts, 1968, president, chief executive officer, director, 1968-89, chairman, 1989—, 1986—. Office: Data General Corp 4400 Computer Dr Westborough Massachusetts 01580

DECRANE, ALFRED CHARLES, JR., petroleum company executive; born Cleveland, June 11, 1931; son of Alfred Charles and Verona (Marquard) DeC.; married Joan Elizabeth Hoffman, July 3, 1954; children:

David, Lisa, Stacie, Stephanie, Sarah, Jennifer. Bachelor of Arts, University Notre Dame, 1953; Juris Doctor, Georgetown University, 1959; Doctor of Humane Letters (honorary), Manhattanville College, 1990. Bar: Virginia bar 1959, District of Columbia bar 1959, Texas bar 1961, New York bar 1966. Legal department Texaco, Incorporated, Houston, 1959-64, New York City, 1964-66; assistant to vice chairman board Texaco, Incorporated, 1965-67, assistant to chairman board, 1967-68, general manager producing department Eastern hemisphere, 1968-70, vice president, 1970-76, senior vice president, general counsel, 1976-77, senior vice president, director, 1977-78, executive vice president, 1978-83, president, 1983-86, chairman board of directors, 1987—; director CIGNA Corp. Trustee Council for Economic Devel. 1st lieutenant United States Marine Corps Reserve, 1954-55. Member American Bar Association (section secretary 1964-67, co-founder Natural Resources Law Jour. mineral law section). Home: 55 Valley Road Bronxville New York 10708 Office: Texaco Incorporated 2000 Westchester Avenue White Plains New York 10650

DEIHL, RICHARD HARRY, savings and loan association executive; born Whittier, California, September 8, 1928; son of Victor Francis and Wilma Aileen (Thomas) D.; married Billie Dantz Beane, March 24, 1952; children: Catherine Kent, Michael, Victoria, Christine. Bachelor of Arts, Whittier College, 1949; postgraduate, University of California at Los Angeles, 1949, University Calif.-Berkeley, 1949-50. With National Cash Register Company, Pomona, California, 1955-59; trainee Rio Hondo Savings & Loan, California, 1959-60; loan consultant Home Savings & Loan Association (now Home Savings Am., A Federal Savings & Loan Association), Los Angeles, 1960-63; loan agent, supervisor, vice president Home Savings & Loan Association (now Home Savings Am., A Federal Savings & Loan Association), 1964, loan service supervisor, 1964, vice president operations, vice president loans, 1965, executive vice president, 1966, president, 1967-84, chief executive officer, 1967—, chairman, 1984—, also director; chief executive officer, director H.F. Ahmanson Company, 1984—, chairman, 1986—; board of directors Atlantic Richfield. Contributor articles to professional journals. Board of directors Good Samaritan Hospital 1st lieutenant United States Air Force, 1951-55. Decorated Distinguished Flying Cross, Air medal with three clusters. Republican. Club: Fairbanks Ranch Country (Rancho Santa Fe). Office: H F Ahmanson & Company 660 S Figueroa St Los Angeles California 90017 also: Home Savings of Am 4900 Rivergrade Road Irwindale California 91706

DELLA FEMINA, JERRY, advertising agency executive; born Brooklyn, July 22, 1936; (married); three children. Former advertising copywriter; former president, now chairman board, chief executive officer Della Femina, Travisano, & Ptnrs. Incorporated (now Della Femina McNamee WCRS Incorporated), 1967—; joing chairman Eurocom WCRS Della Femina Ball Ltd, London. Author: (1970) From Those Wonderful Folks Who Gave You Pearl Harbor. Named Advertising Executive of Year, 1970. Office: Della

Femina McNamee WCRS Incorporated 350 Hudson St New York New York 10014

DEL SANTO, LAWRENCE A., retail merchandising company executive; born 1934; married. Bachelor of Science, University San Francisco, 1955. With Household Merchandising Incorporated, Des Plaines, Illinois, from 1957, with advertising department subsidiary Vons Grocery Company, 1957-58, assistant advertising manager, 1958-61, advertising manager, 1961-68, manager sales and merchandise, 1968-71, senior vice president, 1971-73, president, chief executive officer, 1973-75, corp. senior vice president, 1975-79, executive vice president, from 1979, also board of directors; executive vice president Lucky Stores Incorporated, Dublin, California, to 1986, president, 1986—, now also chairman, chief executive officer, also board of directors. Served with United States Army, 1955-57. Office: Lucky Stores Incorporated 6300 Clark Avenue Post Office Box BB Dublin California 94568

DE MEUSE, DONALD HOWARD, paper products manufacturing executive; born 1936. With Fort Howard Company, Green Bay, Wisconsin, 1967—, vice president operations, 1977-79, executive vice president, from 1979, now president, chief executive officer, also board of directors; chairman elect Wisconsin Paper Council Executive Committee; board of directors Sweetheart Holdings Incorporated. Board of directors Wisconsin Industry Saving Our Environment, member recycling adv. council. Member Am. Paper Institute (board directors). Office: Fort Howard Corp 1919 S Broadway Box 19130 Green Bay Wisconsin 54307

DE PREE, MAX O., furniture manufacturing company executive; born 1924. Bachelor of Arts, Hope College, 1947. With Herman Miller Incorporated, Zeeland, Michigan, 1947—, executive vice president, secretary, 1962-71, chairman board of directors, 1971-80, 82, 87, chief executive officer, 1980-87, president, 1982-87, chairman, 1987—, also board of directors. Office: Herman Miller Incorporated 8500 Byron Road Zeeland Michigan 49464

DERR, KENNETH T., oil company executive. married Donna Mettler, September 12, 1959; 3 children. BME, Cornell University, 1959, Master of Business Administration, 1960. With Chevron Corp. (formerly Standard Oil Company of California), San Francisco, 1960—, vice president, 1972-85; president Chevron United States of America, Incorporated subsidiary Chevron Corp., San Francisco, 1978-84; head merger program Chevron Corp. and Gulf Oil Corp., San Francisco, 1984-85; vice-chairman Chevron Corp., San Francisco, 1985-88, chairman, chief executive officer, 1989—; board of directors Citicorp. Trustee Cornell U., The Conference Board. Member The Business Council, California Business Roundtable, Business Higher Education Forum, Am. Petroleum Institute (director), Business Roundtable, National Petroleum Council, San Francisco Golf Club, Orinda Country Club, Pacific Union Club. Office: Chevron Corp 225 Bush St San Francisco California 94104

DE SIMONE, LIVIO DIEGO, diversified manufacturing company executive; born Montreal, Que., Canada, July 16, 1936; son of Joseph D. and Maria E. (Bergamin) De S.; married Lise Marguerite Wong, 1957, children: Daniel J., Livia D., Mark A., Cynthia A. Bachelor of Chemical Engineering, McGill University, Montreal, 957. With Minnesota Mining & Manufacturing Company, St. Paul; now executive vice president Minnesota Mining & Manufacturing Company. Office: Minnesota Mining & Mfg Company 3M Center St Saint Paul Minnesota 55144

DESMARESCAUX, PHILIPPE, chemical company executive, engineer; born Eecke, Nord, France, July 16, 1938; son of Jean and Fernande (Dieusaert) D.; married Anne-Marie Rambaud; children: Jean-Philippe, Laurence, Olivier. Degree in Chemical Engineering, Ècole Nat Supérieure de Chemie, Paris; Doctor of Philosophy in Physical Science, Faculté des Sciences, 1964. Research attache Center National Research Sci. (CNRS), 1961-63; research management engineer Progil, 1963-73; from research manager to industrial manager, agrochemical div. Rhone-Poulenc, Lyon, 1974-76, marketing and exports manager, 1977-79, general manager, 1979-82; chairman general manager Rhone-Poulenc Agro, Lyon, 1982—; general manager Rhone-Poulenc Specialites Chimiques, Lyon, 1980-83; chairman, chief executive officer Rhone-Poulenc Incorporated, 1986—; member Rhone Poulenc Executive Committee. Avocations: skiing, tennis. Home: 73-77 Chemin des Esses, 69370 Saint Didier au Montana d'Or France Office: Rhone-Poulenc Agro, 14/20 rue Pierre Baizet, 69009 Lyon France also: Rhone-Poulenc Incorporated Black Horse Lane Box 125 Monmouth Junction New Jersey 08852

DEVITO, FRANCIS JOSEPH, advertising agency executive; born New York City, July 13, 1938; son of Basil and Mary (Mincielli) DeV.; married Lynn R. Brauneiss; children: Christopher F., Anthony P. Bachelor of Fine Arts, Pratt Institute, 1961. Assistant art director Batton, Barton, Dursteen & Osborne, New York, 1965-67; art director Young & Rubicam, New York City, 1967-73, creative supervisor, 1973-76, vice president associate creative director, 1976-80, senior vice president group creative director, 1980-83; executive vice president, co-creative director Young and Rubicam, New York City, 1983-84; president, director creative services Lintas: New York, 1984—. Served to captain United States Army, 1961-65. Home: 20 Harbor Hill Road Huntington New York 11743 Office: Lintas Worldwide 1 Dag Hammarskjold Plaza New York New York 10017

DEVOS, RICHARD MARVIN, network marketing company executive; born Grand Rapids, Michigan, March 4, 1926; son of Simon C. and Ethel R. (Dekker) DeV.; married Helen J. Van Wesep, February 7, 1953. Student, Calvin College, 1946; Doctor of Laws (honorary), Oral Roberts University, 1976, Grove City (Pennsylvania) College, Northwood Institute, Midland, Michigan, 1977, Dickinson School Law, Carlisle, Pennsylvania, 1980, Pepperdine University, 1980, Lubbock Christian College, 1981; Doctor of Literature (honorary), Hope College, 1982. Partner Wolverine Air Service, 1945-48; co-founder, president Ja-Ri Corp., 1949, Amway Corp., 1959—, Amway Communications Corp.; president Amway Hotel Corp., Amway Global, Incorporated, Ada, Michigan, Amway International, Incorporated, Ja-Ri Corp.; co-chairman board Nutrilite

Products Incorporated, Buena Park, California; board of directors Old Kent Fin. Corp.; chairman board Reference Map International. Author: Believe!. Chairman Gospel Films, Muskegon, Michigan; board of directors, chairman Midwest region BIPAC; board of directors past president Grand Rapids Junior Achievement, 1966-67; past member board control Grand Valley State College; past board of directors United Way Kent County; board of directors Robert Schuller Ministries, National Legal Center for Public Interest, Butterworth Corp., Grand Rapids; trustee Gerald R. Ford Foundation; past chairman New Grand Rapids Committee; special advisor President Council on Physical Fitness and Sports; member Am.-Australian Bicentennial Foundation Board; member Close-Up Foundation Hon. State Board Adv.; member council trustees Freedoms Foundation Served with United States Army Air Force, 1944-46. Recipient Alexander Hamilton award Economic Education from Freedoms Foundation; Distinguished Salesman of Year award Grand Rapids Sales and Marketing Association; Business Leader of Year award Religious Heritage Am.; Industry Week Excellence in Mgmt. award; Thomas Jefferson Freedom of Speech award Kiwanis International; Michigan Week Vol. Leadership award; Marketing Man of Year award West Michigan chapter Am. Marketing Association; Am. Enterprise Executive award National Mgmt. Association; Golden Plate award Acad. of Achievement; George Washington Honor Medal award Freedoms Foundation; Free Enterprise award Americanism Educational League; Am. Enterpirse Executive award National Mgmt. Association, Patron award Michigan Foundation for the Arts, 1982. Member National Association of Manufacturers (past director), Direct Selling Association (past chairman, director, Champion of Free Enterprise and Knights of Royal Way awards, Hall of Fame award), Newcomen Society, Round Table, Omicron Delta Kappa (hon.). Member Christian Reformed Church (elder, chmn. fin. com.; past president missionary soc.). Clubs: Economic (Grand Rapids) (director), Rotary (Disting. Service award) (Grand Rapids); Pillars board dirs. Home: Grand Rapids Michigan Office: Amway Corp 7575 Fulton St E Ada Michigan 49355

DICKSON, JOHN R., food products company executive, dairy products company executive; born 1930. Bachelor of Arts, Ashland College, 1954. With Loblaw Company, Buffalo, 1954-63, Colonial Foods Incorporated, 1963-71, Shoprite Foods Incorporated, Arlington, Texas, 1971-76, Fox Grocery Company, Pittsburgh, 1976-81, Wetterau Incorporated, St. Louis, to 1986; president, chief executive officer Roundy's Incorporated, Pewaukee, Wisconsin, 1986—. Office: Roundys Incorporated 23000 Roundy Dr Pewaukee Wisconsin 53072

DIESEL, JOHN PHILLIP, multinational corporation executive; born St. Louis, June 10, 1926; son of John Henry and Elsa A. (Poetting) D.; married Rita Jan Meyer, June 12, 1949; children: Holly, Gretchen, John, Dana. Bachelor of Science, Washington University, St. Louis, 1951. Executive assistant div. manager McQuay-Norris Manufacturing Company, St. Louis, 1951-57; partner Booz, Allen & Hamilton, Incorporated, Chicago, 1957-61; vice president operations Operations Research, Incorporated, Santa Monica, California, 1961-62; vice president, treasurer, director Management Tech., Incorporated, Los Angeles, 1962-63; director marketing and planning A.O. Smith Corp., Milwaukee, 1963-65, director manufacturing and engineering, 1965-67, vice president manufacturing and planning, 1967-70, group vice president, 1970-72; chairman board Armor Elevator Can., Limited, 1970-72; chairman board, president Armor Elevator Company, Incorporated, 1970-72; president, chief executive officer Newport News (Virginia) Shipbldg. & Dry Dock Company, 1972-78, chairman board, 1976-78; executive vice president Tenneco Incorporated, Houston, 1976-79, president, 1979-89, also director; director Cooper Industries, Incorporated, Aluminum Company of Am. Served with United States Naval Reserve, 1944-47. Methodist. Clubs: Pine Valley Golf, Seminole Golf, Metropolitan. Office: Tenneco Incorporated Post Office Box 2511 Houston Texas 77002

DILLARD, WILLIAM, II, department store executive; born 1945; married. Graduate, University Arkansas; Master of Business Administration, Harvard University. With Dillard Department Stores, Little Rock, 1967—, executive vice president, 1973-77, president and chief operating officer, 1977—, also director. Office: Dillard Department Stores Incorporated 900 W Capitol Avenue Box 486 Little Rock Arkansas 72203

DILLARD, WILLIAM T., department stores company executive; born Mineral Springs, Arkansas, 1914; son of Thomas Dillard. Bachelor of Business Administration, University Arkansas, 1935; Master of Science, Columbia University, 1937. With Sears Roebuck & Company, Tulsa, 1937; opened own department store Nashville, 1938; then with Wooten's Department Store (later Wooten & Dillard, then Dillard's), Texarkana; president Dillard Department Stores Incorporated, Little Rock, until 1977, chairman board, chief executive officer, 1977—; chairman board Frederick Atkins, Incorporated, New York City; member national adv. board First Comml. Bank, Little Rock. Member National Retail Mchts. Association (director). Office: Dillard Department Stores Incorporated 900 W Capitol Avenue Box 486 Little Rock Arkansas 72203

DILLER, BARRY, entertainment company executive; born San Francisco, February 2, 1942; son of Michael and Reva (Addison) D. Vice president feature films and movies of week ABC, 1971-73, ABC (prime time TV), 1973-74; chairman board Paramount Pictures Corp., 1974-84; president Gulf & Western Entertainment Group, 1983-84; chairman, chief executive officer Twentieth Century Fox Film Corp., Los Angeles, 1984—, Fox, Incorporated, 1985—. Office: Twentieth Century Fox Film Corp Post Office Box 900 Beverly Hills California 90213

DINGMAN, MICHAEL DAVID, industrial company executive; born New Haven, September 29, 1931; son of James Everett and Amelia (Williamson) D.; married Jean Hazlewood, May 16, 1953 (divorced); children: Michael David, Linda Channing (Mrs. Michael S. Cady), James Clifford; married Elizabeth G. Tharp, April 13, 1984; children: James Tharp, David Ross. Student, University Maryland. Various management positions Sigma Instruments, Incorporated, Braintree, Massachusetts, 1954-64; general and limited partner Drexel Burnham Lambert, Incorporated (formerly Burnham & Company), New York City, 1964-70; president, chief executive officer, board of directors Wheelabrator-Frye, Incorporated, Hampton, New Hampshire, 1970-83; chairman board Wheelabrator-Frye Incorporated, Hampton, New Hampshire, 1977-83; president, board of directors The Signal Companies, Incorporated, La Jolla, California, 1983-85, Allied-Signal Incorporated, Morristown, New Jersey, 1985-86; chairman board, chief executive officer The Henley Group, Incorporated, La Jolla, 1986—; board of directors Ford Motor Company, Time Incorporated. Trustee John A. Hartford Foundation. Member Institute of Electrical and Electronics Engineers (member adv. board). Clubs: Links, Bd. Room, New York Yacht (New York City); Union (Boston); Cruising of Am. (Connecticut); Bohemian (San Francisco), Fairbanks Ranch Country; Lyford Cay (Nassau); La Jolla Country, San Diego Yacht. Office: Henley Group Incorporated Liberty Lane Hampton New Hampshire 03842

DIONNE, JOSEPH LEWIS, publishing company executive; born Montgomery, Alabama, June 29, 1933; son of Antonio Ernest Joseph and Myrtle Mae (Armstrong) D.; married Joan F. Durand, June 12, 1954; children: Marsha Joan Dionne Guerin, Gary Joseph, Darren Durand. Bachelor of Arts, Hofstra University, 1955, Master of Science, 1957; Doctor of Education, Columbia University, 1965. Guidance counselor Long Island Public Schools, 1956-61; assistant professor Hofstra University, Hempstead, New York, 1962-63; director instruction, project director Ford Foundation School Improvement grant Brentwood (New York) Pub. Schools, 1963-66; vice president research and devel. Educational Developmental Laboratories, Huntington, New York, 1966-68; vice president, general manager CTB/McGraw-Hill, Monterey, California, 1968-73; senior vice president corp. planning McGraw-Hill, Incorporated, New York City, 1973-77, executive vice president operations, 1979-81; president McGraw-Hill Information Systems Company, New York City, 1977-79; president McGraw Hill, Incorporated, New York City, 1981-88, chief executive officer, 1983-88, chairman, 1988—; board of directors Equitable Life Insurance Company Am., United Telecommunications Incorporated, Harris Corp. Elder Presbyterian Church New Canaan; past president Society To Advance Retarded; past chairman board trustees Hofstra U. 2d lieutenant United States Army, 1955-56. Member Phi Alpha Theta, Kappa Delta Pi, Phi Delta Kappa. Clubs: Woodway Country (Darien, Connecticut), Blind Brook Club, Inc. (Purchase, New York). Home: 198 N Wilton Road New Canaan Connecticut 06840 Office: McGraw-Hill Incorporated 1221 Avenue of the Americas New York New York 10020

DISBROW, RICHARD EDWIN, utility executive; born Newark, September 20, 1930; son of Milton A. and Madeline Catherine (Segal) D.; married Patricia Fair Warner, June 27, 1953 (divorced September 1972); children: John Scott, Lisa Karen; married Teresa Marie Moser, May 12, 1973. Bachelor of Science, Lehigh

University, 1952; Master of Science in Electrical Engineering, Newark College Engineering, 1959; Master of Science in Industrial Management, Massachusetts Institute of Technology, 1965. With Am. Electric Power Service Corp., New York City, 1954-80; with Am. Electric Power Service Corp., Columbus, Ohio, 1980—, transmission and distribution manager, 1967-70, controller, 1970-71, vice president, controller, 1971-74; executive vice president Am. Electric Power Service Corp., Columbus, Ohio, 1974-75, vice chairman board, 1975-79, president, chief administrative officer, 1979-84; president, chief operating officer Am. Electric Power Service Corp., Columbus, Ohio, 1985-91; president, chief executive officer Am. Electric Power Service Corp., Columbus, 1991—; director Am. Electric Power Service Corp., Columbus, Ohio, 1991—, also board of directors; president, chief executive officer, board of directors Am. Electric Power Company; board of directors Banc Ohio National Bank, 1986; instructor Newark College Engineering, 1959-64; member New Jersey Engineers Committee for Student Guidance, 1960-64; industrial commissioner, Piscataway, New Jersey, 1960-64; vice chairman board of directors, chief executive officer Columbus Southern Power Company, Ind. Michigan Power Company, Wheeling Electric Company, Windsor Coal Company. Board of directors Ohio Foundation Ind. Colleges; board visitors New Jersey Institute Tech. 1st lieutenant United States Air Force, 1952-54. Sloan fellow Massachusetts Institute of Technology. Member Edison Electric Institute (director), Columbus Athletic Club, Worthington Hills Country Club, Breakers West Country Club, Psi Upsilon, Eta Kappa Nu. Office: Am Electric Power Company Incorporated 1 Riverside Plaza Post Office Box 16631 Columbus Ohio 43215

DISNEY, ROY EDWARD, broadcasting company executive; born Los Angeles, January 10, 1930; son of Roy Oliver and Edna (Francis) D.; married Patricia Ann Dailey, September 17, 1955; children: Roy Patrick, Susan Margaret, Abigail Edna, Timothy John. Bachelor of Arts, Pomona College, 1951. Guest relations executive NBC, Hollywood, California, 1952; apprentice film editor Mark VII Productions, Hollywood, 1942; assistant film editor, cameraman production assistant, writer, producer Walt Disney Productions, Burbank, California, 1954-77, director, 1967—; president Roy East Disney Productions Incorporated, Burbank, 1978—; chairman board director Shamrock Broadcasting Company, Hollywood, 1979—; chairman board director, founder Shamrock Holdings Incorporated, Burbank, 1980—; trustee California Institute Arts, Valencia, 1967—; vice chairman Walt Disney Company, Burbank. Author: novelized adaptation of Perri; producer movie: Pacific High; writer, director, producer numerous TV productions. Board of directors Big Brothers of Greater Los Angeles; member adv. board of directors St. Joseph Medical Center, Burbank; member United States Naval Acad. Sailing Squadron, Annapolis, Maryland; fellow U. Kentucky. Recipient Acad. award nomination for Mysteries of the Deep. Member Directors Guild Am. West, Writers Guild Am. Republican. Clubs: 100, Confrerie des Chevaliers du Tastevin, St. Francis Yacht, California Yacht, San Diego Yacht, Transpacific Yacht, Los Angeles Yacht. Office: Walt Disney Company 500 S Buena Vista St Burbank California 91521

DODS, WALTER ARTHUR, JR., bank executive; born Honolulu, May 26, 1941; son of Walter Arthur Sr. and Mildred (Phillips) D.; married Diane Lauren Nosse, September 18, 1971; children: Walter A. III, Christopher L., Peter D., Lauren S. Bachelor of Business Administration, University Hawaii, 1967. Marketing officer 1st Hawaiian Bank, Honolulu, 1969, assistant vice president marketing div., 1969-71, vice president, chairman marketing and research group, 1971-73, senior vice president marketing and research group, 1973-76, executive vice president retail banking group, 1976-78, executive vice president general banking group, 1978-84, president, 1984-89, chairman, chief executive officer, 1989—; chairman, president, chief executive officer First Hawaiian, Incorporated, 1989-90; chairman, chief executive officer First Hawaiian, Incorporated, First Hawaiian Crediticorp, Incorporated, First Hawaiian Leasing, Incorporated, 1989—; board of directors 1st Hawaiian Incorporated, 1st Hawaiian Creditcorp Incorporated, 1st Hawaiian Leasing Incorporated, Alexander & Baldwin Incorporated, A&B Hawaii Incorporated, Matson Navigation Company Incorporated, 1st Insurance Company Hawaii Limited, General Telephone and Telegraph California, General Telephone and Telegraph Hawaiian Telephone Company, General Telephone and Telegraph Northwest, Grace Pacific Corp., Oceanic Cablevision Incorporated, Pacific Guardian Life Insurance Company, Suntory Resorts Incorporated. Board of directors Ahahui Koa Anuenue, East-West Center Foundation, The Rehabilitation Hospital of the Pacific; executive board member Aloha Council, Boy Scouts Am.; trustee, past chairman Blood Bank Hawaii; past chairman board Aloha United Way; past chairman Board Water Supply; board of directors, treasurer Coalition for Drug-Free Hawaii; trustee Contemporary Mus. co-chairman corp. campaign committee; member Duty Free Shoppers Adv. Board; past chairman Gubernatorial Inauguration, 1974, 82; board governors Hawaii Employers Council; trustee Hawaii Maritime Ctr; member Governor's Adv. Board Geothermal/Inter-Island Cable Project, Governor's Blue Ribbon Panel on the Future of Healthcare in Hawaii; director, past chairman Hawaii Visitors Bureau; executive committee Hawaiian Open; board governor Honolulu Country Club, Japan Cultural Center Hawaii, Pacific Peace Foundation; trustee Japan-Am. Institute Mgmt. Sci., The Nature Conservancy Hawaii, Punahou School; chairman Japan-Hawaii Economic Council; chairman, director Pacific International Center for Higher Tech. Research; chairman bldg. fund St. Louis High School; treasurer The 200 Club; director World Cup Honolulu 1994. Named Outstanding Jaycee in Nation, 1963, Outstanding Young Man Am. from Hawaii, 1972, Marketer of Year, Am. Marketing Association, 1987; recipient Riley Allen Individual Devel. award, 1964, Hawaii State Jaycees 3 Outstanding Young Men award, 1971, Am. Advertising Federation Silver medal, 1977, St. Louis High Sch.'s Outstanding Alumnus award,

1980. Member Am. Bankers Association, Bank Marketing Association, Hawaii Bankers Association, Hawaii Business Roundtable, Chamber of Commerce of Hawaii, Honolulu Press Club. Office: 1st Hawaiian Bank 165 S King St Honolulu Hawaii 96813

DOERR, RONALD H., steel company executive; born 1940; married. Bachelor of Science, Washington University, 1962. With National Steel Corp., Pittsburgh, 1966—, vice president fin., 1984, now vice president, chief fin. officer. Office: National Steel Corp 20 Stanwix St Pittsburgh Pennsylvania 15222

DOLAN, BEVERLY FRANKLIN, diversified company executive; born Augusta, Georgia, 1927; married. Graduate, University Georgia, 1952; graduate Advanced Management Program, Harvard University, 1969. President, co-founder E-Z Go Car Corp., 1954-60; with Textron Incorporated, Providence, 1960—, president Homelite div., 1976-79, corp. executive vice president operations, 1979-80, president, 1980—, chief operating officer, 1980-85, chief executive officer, 1985—, chairman, 1986—, also director; director First Union Corp., Allendale Mutual Insurance Company. Served with Army of the United States, 1952-54. Office: Textron Incorporated 40 Westminster St Providence Rhode Island 02903

DOLAN, THOMAS IRONSIDE, manufacturing company executive; born Hastings, Michigan, March 31, 1927; son of Clifford and Katherine (Ironside) D.; married Barbara Jane Sisson, June 11, 1948; children—Nancy, Sarah. Bachelor of Science in Indsl.-Mech. Engineering, University Michigan, 1949. President Kelvinator, Incorporated, Grand Rapids, Michigan, 1969-75; senior group vice president White Consolidated Industries, Incorporated, Cleveland, 1975-80; senior vice president A.O. Smith Corp., Milwaukee, 1980-82, president, director, 1982-84, chairman, chief executive officer, 1984-89, chairman, 1984—; trustee Northwestern Mutual Life Insurance Company. Corp. member Milwaukee School Engring. Member Metropolitan Milwaukee Association Commerce (board directors, chairman 1988-89), Hwy. Users Federation (trustee), International Executive Service Corps. (council), Business Council.

DOLE, ELIZABETH HANFORD, charitable organization administrator, former secretary of labor; born Salisbury, North Carolina, July 29, 1936; daughter of John Van and Mary Ella (Cathey) Hanford; married Robert Joseph Dole (U.S. Senator from Kans.), December 6, 1975. Bachelor of Arts with honors in Political Science, Duke, 1958; postgraduate, Oxford (England) University, summer 1959; Master of Arts in Education, Harvard University, 1960, Juris Doctor, 1965. Bar: District of Columbia 1966. Staff assistant to assistant secretary for education Department of Health, Education and Welfare, Washington, 1966-67; practiced law Washington, 1967-68; associate director legis. affairs, then executive director Pres.'s Committee for Consumer Interests, Washington, 1968-71; deputy director Office Consumer Affairs, The White House, Washington, 1971-73; commissioner Federal Trade Commission, Washington, 1973-79; chairman Voters for Reagan-Bush, 1980; director Human Services Group, Office of Executive Branch Management, Office of Pres.-Elect, 1980; assistant to President for pub. liaison 1981-83; secretary United States Department Transportation, 1983-87; with Robert Dole Presidential Campaign, 1987-88; participant 1988 Presidential and Congressional campaigns; secretary United States Department Labor, 1989-90; president Am. Red Cross, 1991—; member nominating committee Am. Stock Exchange, 1972, North Carolina Consumer Council, 1972. Trustee Duke U., 1974-88; member council Harvard Law School Associates; hon. chairman board overseers Duke U. Comprehensive Cancer Center, 1988—; member visiting committee John F. Kennedy School Government Harvard U., 1988—, board overseers, 1989. Recipient Arthur S. Flemming award United States Government, 1972, Humanitarian award National Commn. Against Drunk Driving, 1988, Distinguished Alumni award Duke University, 1988; named one of Am.'s 200 Young Leaders, Time magazine, 1974, one of World's 10 Most Admired Women, Gallup Poll, 1988. Member Phi Beta Kappa, Pi Lambda Theta, Pi Sigma Alpha. Office: Am Red Cross 17th & D Sts Northwest Washington District of Columbia 20006

DONAHUE, DONALD JORDAN, mining company executive; born Brooklyn, July 5, 1924; son of John F. and Florence (Jordan) D.; married Mary Meyer, January 20, 1951 (deceased June 1990); children: Mary G., Judith A., Donald Jordan, Thomas, Nicholas P. Bachelor of Arts, Georgetown University, 1947; Master of Business Administration, New York University, 1951. With Chemical Corn Exchange Bank, New York City, 1947-49, Am. Metal Climax Incorporated (name changed to AMAX, Incorporated), New York City, 1949-75; treasurer Am. Metal Climax Incorporated (name changed to AMAX, Incorporated), 1957-67, vice president, 1963-65, executive vice president, 1965-69, president, 1969-75, also director, 1964-75; vice chairman Continental Can Company, Incorporated (name changed to Continental Group, Incorporated), New York City, 1975-84; chairman KMI Continental Can Company, Incorporated (formerly Continental Group, Incorporated), 1987, Magma Copper Company, San Manuel, Arizona, 1987—; board of directors National Starch & Chemical Company, Northeast Utilities, Incorporated, Counsellors Cash Reserve Fund, Counsellors Tandem Securities Fund, Finevest Foods, Incorporated; vice chairman Greenwall Federation. With Army of the United States, 1943-46. Member Greenwich Country Club, Blind Brook Country Club, University (New York City), Jupiter Hills (Florida) Golf Club. Home: Meads Point Greenwich Connecticut 06830 Office: Magma Copper Company Incorporated 99 Indian Field Road Greenwich Connecticut 06830

DONLON, WILLIAM JAMES, JR., lawyer; born Denver, February 18, 1948; son of William J. and Jo (Sanssen) D. Bachelor of Arts, Morehead State University, 1971; Juris Doctor, St. Louis University, 1974. Assistant attorney general State of Colorado, Denver, 1974-76; sole practice Denver, 1976—. Member Colorado Bar Association, Adams Bar Association, Association Trial Lawyers Am. Democrat. Roman Catholic. Home: 1177 York Denver Colorado 80206

Office: 8933 N Washington Thornton Colorado 80229

DONLON, WILLIAM JOSEPH, utility company executive; born Albany, New York, January 28, 1930; son of Charles Joseph and Margaret Mary (Shanahan) D.; married Patricia Pommer, August 26, 1952; children: Deborah, William, Robert, Susan, James, Brian. Bachelor of Science in Economics, Siena College, 1962. With Niagara Mohawk Power Corp., Syracuse, New York, 1948—; supervisor sales and services training Niagara Mohawk Power Corp., Albany, New York, 1960-62; supervisor sales and services training Niagara Mohawk Power Corp., Buffalo, New York, 1962-64, sales manager, 1964-68, commercial vice president western div., 1968-70; vice president, general manager Eastern div. Niagara Mohawk Power Corp., Albany, New York, 1970-76; senior vice president Niagara Mohawk Power Corp., Syracuse, New York, 1976, president, 1976—; board of directors National Comml. Bank & Trust Company, Utilities Mutual Insurance Company. Board of directors Albany area United Fund, Albany area American Red Cross, Capital district Junior Achievement, Better Albany Living; trustee College St. Rose; board governors Albany Medical Center Hospital Served with United States Navy, 1952-54, European Theatre of Operations. Member Capital District Chamber of Commerce (president 1973-74). Member Capital District Chamber of Commerce (membership chairman 1973-74). Republican. Roman Catholic. Clubs: Fort Orange (Albany); Century (Syracuse, New York). Office: Niagara Mohawk Power Corp 300 Erie Boulevard W Syracuse New York 13202

DONOVAN, THOMAS ROY, futures exchange executive; born Chicago, September 13, 1937. Bachelor of Arts in Business and Economics, Illinois Institute Tech., 1972, Master of Public Adminstration, 1975. Administrative assistant to mayor City of Chicago, 1969-79; vice president, secretary Chicago Board of Trade, 1979-81, executive vice president, secretary, 1981-82, president, chief executive officer, 1982—. Board of directors Illinois Leadership Council for Agricultural Education; chairman agribusiness adv. committee The Chicago High School for Agricultural Sci. Member National Futures Association (board directors, fin. committee), Chicago Association Commerce and Industry (board directors, executive committee), Chicago Central Area Committee Illinois Institute Tech., Council on Grad. School of Business University Chicago, Commercial Club of Chicago. Office: Chicago Bd Trade 141 W Jackson Boulevard Chicago Illinois 60604

DOOLEY, THOMAS HOWARD, insurance company executive; born New York City, September 22, 1934; son of Lawrence James and Lauretta May (Mulford) D.; married Antoinette Rose Russo, October 6, 1956; children: Karen M., Lawrence P. Bachelor of Business Administration, Clarkson University, 1956; Juris Doctor, University Connecticut, 1964. Bar: Connecticut 1964, United States Supreme Court 1968. Second vice president Connecticut Life Insurance Company, Bloomfield, 1968-77, vice president, 1977-83; senior vice president CIGNA Corp., Philadelphia, 1983-85, executive vice president,

1985—; member Connecticut House of Representatives, 1970-74; deputy mayor Town of Vernon, Connecticut, 1976-80. Trustee Clarkson U., 1989—. With United States Army, 1957-59. Recipient Distinguished Alumni award Clarkson University, 1981. Member Rockville Exchange Club (president 1970-72), Insurance Association Connecticut (director). Democrat. Roman Catholic. Office: Cigna Corp 900 Cottage Grove Road Bloomfield Connecticut 06002

DORFMAN, HENRY S., meat products company executive; born 1922; married. With Sausage Manufacturing Business, 1944-49, General Machines Company, 1949-50, Hudson Motor Car Company, 1950-51, B.M. Shindler Meats Company, 1951-52; chairman board, chief executive officer Thorn Apple Valley, Incorporated, Southfield, Michigan, 1952—, president, from 1952, also board of directors. Office: Thorn Apple Valley Incorporated 18700 W 10 Mile Road Southfield Michigan 48075

DORFMAN, JOEL MARVIN, meat products company executive; born Detroit, November 8, 1951; son of Henry S. and Mala (Weintraub) D.; married Carol Ann Park, December 21, 1980; children: Noah Max, Jordan Alexander. Bachelor of Science, University Michigan, 1973; Juris Doctor, University Detroit, 1977. Bar: Michigan, Detroit. Operations manager Thorn Apple Valley, Incorporated, Southfield, Michigan, 1973-78, executive vice president, 1978-85, president, chief operating officer, 1985—, also board of directors. Board of directors Henry Ford Hospital, West Bloomfield, Michigan, 1986—, Holocaust Memorial Center, West Bloomfield, Detroit Music Hall, Weizmann Institute Sci., Jewish Vocational Service; patron Detroit Symphony Orchestra, Detroit Institute Arts. Member Am. Meat Institute (board directors 1989—), Am. Jewish Federation, Michigan Bar Association, Detroit Bar Association, Tam-O-Shanter Club, B'nai B'rith. Republican. Jewish. Avocations: golf, skiing, scuba diving. Office: Thorn Apple Valley Incorporated 18700 W 10 Mile Road Southfield Michigan 48075

DOSKOCIL, LARRY, food company executive; born 1932. Student, Bethany Nazarene College, 1953. President, chief executive officer Doskocil Sausage Company, Hutchinson, Kansas, 1961-85, chairman board, 1985—, president, 1988—; also chairman Wilson Foods Corp., Oklahoma City.

DOUBLEDAY, NELSON, baseball executive. Graduate, Princeton, 1954. With Doubleday & Company Incorporated, New York City, 1954-56, from 59, former president, chief executive officer, chairman board of directors; chairman board, majority owner New York Mets Baseball Team, 1980—. Served with United States Air Force, 1956-59. Office: New York Mets Shea Stadium Flushing New York 11368

DOUGLAS, KENNETH JAY, food company executive; born Harbor Beach, Michigan, September 4, 1922; son of Harry Douglas and Xenia (Williamson) D.; married Elizabeth Ann Schweizer, August 17, 1946; children: Connie Ann, Andrew Jay. Student, University Illinois, 1940-41, 46-47; Juris Doctor, Chicago Kent College Law, 1950; graduate, Advanced Management Program, Harvard, 1962. Bar: Illinois 1950, Ind.

1952. Special agent Federal Bureau of Investigation, 1950-54; director industrial relations Dean Foods Company, Franklin Park, Illinois, 1954-64, vice president fin. and administration, 1964-70, chairman board, chief executive officer, 1970-87, chairman board, 1987-89, vice-chairman, 1989—; board of directors Centel Corp., Am. National Bank & Trust Company, Am. National Corp., Milk Industry Foundation, Richardson Electronics, Limited, Andrew Corp. Chairman board trustees West Suburban Hospital Medical Center, Oak Park, Illinois; board overseers Illinois Institute Tech. Chgo.-Kent College Law. With United States Naval Reserve, 1944-46. Republican. Clubs: Chicago, Economic, Executives, Commercial (Chicago); Oak Park Country, River Forest Tennis (Illinois); Steamboat Springs Country (Colorado); Old Baldy (Wyoming). Office: Dean Foods Company 3600 N River Road Franklin Park Illinois 60131

DOUGLAS, PAUL WOLFF, mining executive; born Springfield, Massachusetts, September 12, 1926; son of Paul Howard and Dorothy (Wolff) D.; married Colette Smith, November 19, 1926; children: Philip LeBreton, Carolyn Jory Jacobs, Christine Sanders Tansey, Paul Harding. Bachelor of Arts, Princeton University, 1948; student, Leeds (England) University, 1948. Director internal finance section ECA Mission to France, 1948-52; with Freeport Minerals Company, 1952—, executive, vice president, director, 1970-75, president, chairman executive committee, 1975—; president, chief executive officer Freeport-McMoran Incorporated, 1981-83; chairman, chief executive officer Pittston Company, 1984—; board of directors Phelps Dodge Corp., United States Trust Company, Philip Morris Incorporated, New York Life Insurance; chairman Community Planning Board, New York City, New York Life Insurance Company. Served with United States Naval Reserve, 1944-46. Home: 25 Charlton St New York New York 10014 Office: Pittston Company 1 Pickwick Plaza Box 8900 Greenwich Connecticut 06836

DRAPER, E. LINN, JR., electric utility executive; born Houston, February 6, 1942; son of Ernest L. and Marcia L. (Saylor) D.; married Mary Deborah Doyle, June 9, 1962; children—Susan Elizabeth, Robert Linn, Barbara Ann, David Doyle. Student, Williams College, 1960-62; Bachelor of Arts in Chemical Engineering, Rice University, 1964, Bachelor of Science in Chemical Engineering, 1965; Doctor of Philosophy in Nuclear Engineering, Cornell University, 1970. Assistant professor nuclear engineering University Texas, Austin, 1969-72, associate professor, 1972-79; tech. assistant to chief executive officer Gulf States Utilities Company, Beaumont, Texas, 1979, vice president nuclear tech., 1980-81, senior vice president engring, tech. services, 1981-82, senior vice president external affairs, 1982-84, senior vice president external affairs and production, 1984-85, executive vice president external affairs and production, vice chairman, 1985-86, vice chairman, executive vice president, 1985-86, vice. chairman, president, chief operating officer, 1986, vice chairman, president, chief executive officer, 1986-87, chairman, president, chief executive officer, 1987—; member adv. panel on alternative means of financing and managing radioactive waste management, 1984-85; board of directors Pacific Nuclear Systems, Texas Commerce Bank, Beaumont, Texas Research League, Edison Electric Institute. Editor: Proceedings of Texas Symposium on Technology of Controlled Thermonuclear Fusion Experiments and Engineering Aspects of Fusion Reactors, 1974. Recipient Clyde A. Lilly award Atomic Industrial Forum, 1983; fellow National Science Foundation, 1965-66, Atomic Energy Commission, 1967-68. Member Utility Nuclear Waste Management Group (chairman), Am. Nuclear Society (president 1984-85). Office: Gulf States Utilities Company 350 Pine St Beaumont Texas 77701

DREW, ERNEST HAROLD, chemical company executive; born Springfield, Massachusetts, April 15, 1937; son of Ernest L. and Marjorie E. (Canney) D.; married Katy Coe, March 24, 1989. Bachelor of Science, University Georgia, 1958, Doctor of Philosophy, 1962; Master of Science, University Illinois, 1959. Sales manager resins Celanese Coatings Company, Louisville, 1971-74; vice president, general manager resins Celanese Specialty Company, Louisville, 1974-75; vice president sales Celanese Chemical Company, N.Y.C.-Dallas, 1975-78; vice president planning Dallas, 1979-81; director strategic planning Celanese Corp., New York City, 1981-82; president, chief executive officer Celanese Can. Incorporated, Montreal, Quebec, 1982-84; president Celanese Fibers Operations, New York City, 1984-85; group vice president Celanese Corp., New York City, 1985-87; president Hoechst Celanese Corp., Somerville, New Jersey, 1987—, chief operating officer, 1987, chief executive officer, 1987—; director Celanese Can., Incorporated, Bank Montreal Mortgage Corp., 1983-84, Manville Corp., Thomas and Betts Corp; member Can. adv. board Allendale Insurance Company, Montreal, 1983-84. Board trustee Hampton U. Served to captain United States Air Force, 1962-65. Woodrow Wilson fellow, 1958. Member Society Chemical Industry (board directors Can. section 1983), Am. Chemical Society, Chemical Institute Can., Chemical Manufacturers Association (executive committee, board directors), Fiddlers Elbow Country Club , Phi Beta Kappa. Home: Lee's Hill Road Far Hills New Jersey 06902 Office: Hoechst Celanese Corp Route 202-206 N Somerville New Jersey 08876

DRUMMOND, GERARD KASPER, resource development company executive, lawyer; born New York City, October 9, 1937; son of John Landells and Margaret Louise (Kasper) D.; married Donna J. Mason, September 14, 1957 (divorced 1976); children: Alexander, Jane, Edmund; married Sandra Hamilton, August 31, 1985. Bachelor of Science, Cornell University, 1959, Bachelor of Laws with distinction, 1963. Bar: Oregon 1963. Associate Davies, Biggs, Strayer, Stoel & Boley, Portland, Oregon, 1963-64; associate, partner Rives, Bonyhadi, Drummond & Smith, Portland, 1964-77; president Nerco, Incorporated, Portland, from 1977, chairman board of directors, 1987—; member corp. policy group PacifiCorp, 1979—, executive vice president, 1987—; board of directors Pacific Telecom. President Tri-County Metropolitan Transit District, Portland, 1974-86, board of directors, 1974-86; member Oreg.-Korea Economic Cooperative Committee,

Portland, 1981-85, Oregon Investment Council, 1987—, chairman, 1990—; trustee Reed College, 1982—; board of directors Oregon Contemporary Theatre, 1983-85, Oregon Symphony, 1987—, president, 1990—, United Way, 1990—, Oregon Ind. College Foundation, 1990—; community board of directors Providence Hospital, 1986—. 1st lieutenant United States Army Reserve, 1959-67. Member American Bar Association, Oregon Bar Association, Am. Mining Congress (board directors 1986—), Silver Institute (board directors 1987-89). Clubs: Arlington, University. Home: 28815 S Needy Road Canby Oregon 97013 Office: Nerco Incorporated 700 NE Multnomah Portland Oregon 97232

DULIN, JOHN P., banker; born 1938. With First Tennessee National Corp., Memphis, 1961—, president, director, 1978—. Office: 1st Tennessee National Corp Post Office Box 84 Memphis Tennessee 38101

DUNN, JOSEPH MCELROY, manufacturing company executive; born Toledo, August 9, 1926; son of Robert C. and Myrtle (Bridgeman) D.; married Martha Louise Nutt, December 29, 1950; children: Christopher, Kathryn, Barbara, David. Bachelor of Business Administration, Ohio State University, 1949. Junior accountant Arthur Young & Company, Toledo, 1949-50; partner Bob Dunn Automobile, Seattle, 1950-58; vice president, then president Moline (Illinois) Corp., 1958-64; sales trainee to president PACCAR Incorporated, Bellevue, Washington, 1964—, now president, also board of directors. Board dirs. Seattle First National Bank, Seafirst Corp. Served with Quartermaster Corps United States Navy, 1944-45, PTO. Member Western Hwy. Institute (vice president at large 1987-88). Republican. Presbyterian. Clubs: Seattle Golf; Desert Island Golf (Rancho Mirage, California). Lodge: Masons. Home: 1556 77th Place NE Bellevue Washington 98004 Office: PACCAR Incorporated 777 106th Avenue NE Bellevue Washington 98004

DUNNIGAN, T. KEVIN, electrical and electronics manufacturing company executive; born 1938; married. Bachelor of Arts in Commerce, Loyola University, 1971. With Can. Electrical Distributing Company, prior to 1962; with Thomas & Betts Corp., Bridgewater, New Jersey, 1962—, div. president, 1974-78, corp. executive vice president electronics, 1978-80, president, 1980—, chief operating officer, 1980-85, chief executive officer, 1985—, also board of directors; board of directors National Starch and Chemical Corp. Member Electronics Industry Association (board govs.). Office: Thomas & Betts Corp 1001 Frontier Road Bridgewater New Jersey 08807

DWYER, ANDREW T., utility and utility service company executive; born Morristown, New Jersey, 1948. Student, Yale University, 1971; Juris Doctor, New York University, 1974. Chairman Jamaica Water Supply company, Lake Success, New York; chairman, president JWP Incorporated, Purchase, New York; chairman Welsbach Electrical Corp., Astoria, New York; board of directors Welsbach Corp., Welsbach Electrical Corp., JWP Incorporated. Office: JWP Incorporated 2975 Westchester Avenue Purchase New York 10577

DYSON, BRIAN G., beverage company executive; born Buenos Aires,

September 7, 1935. Bachelor of Arts, Facultad de Ciencas Economicas, 1959. Executive vice president, president North America soft drink business sector Coca-Cola Company, Incorporated, 1957-75, senior vice president, manager South Latin Am. div., 1975-78, vice president, president Coca-Cola USA div., 1978-81; senior vice president, now president, chief executive officer Coca-Cola Company, Incorporated, Atlanta, 1986—. Office: Coca-Cola Company Incorporated Coca-Cola Plaza Northwest Atlanta Georgia 30313

EAMER, RICHARD KEITH, health care company executive, lawyer; born Long Beach, California, February 13, 1928; son of George Pierce and Lillian (Newell) E.; married Eileen Laughlin, September 1, 1951; children: Brian Keith, Erin Maureen. Bachelor of Science in Accounting, University Southern California, 1955, Bachelor of Laws, 1959. Bar: California 1960; C.P.A., California. Accountant L. H. Penney & Company (C.P.A.s), 1956-59; associate firm Ervin, Cohen & Jessup, Beverly Hills, California, 1959-63; partner firm Eamer, Bell and Bedrosian, Beverly Hills, 1963-69; chairman board, chief executive officer National Medical Enterprises, Incorporated, Los Angeles, 1969—; also director National Medical Enterprises, Incorporated; director Union Oil Company California, Imperial Bank. Member Am. Bar Association, Am. Institute C.P.A.s, California Bar Association, Los Angeles County Bar Association. Republican. Clubs: Bel Air Country, Bel Air Bay; California. Office: National Med Enterprises Incorporated 11620 Wilshire Boulevard Los Angeles California 90025

EARLEY, ANTHONY FRANCIS, JR., utilities company executive, lawyer; born Jamaica, New York, July 29, 1949; son of Anthony Francis and Jean Ann (Draffen) E.; married Sarah Margaret Belanger, October 14, 1972; children: Michael Patrick, Anthony Matthew, Daniel Cartwright, Matthew Sean. Bachelor of Science in Physics, University Notre Dame, 1971, Master of Science in Engineering, 1979, Juris Doctor, 1979. Bar: Virginia 1980, New York 1985, United States Court Appeals (6th circuit) 1981. Associate Hunton & Williams, Richmond, Virginia, 1979-85, partner, 1985; general counsel Long Island Lighting Company, Hicksville, New York, 1985-89, executive vice president, 1988-89, president, chief operating officer, 1989—, also board of directors. Contributor articles to professional journals. Board of directors, vice chairman United Way of Long Island, 1987—. Served to lieutenant United States Navy, 1971-76. Member American Bar Association, Nassau County Bar Association, Association of Bar of City of New York. Roman Catholic. Avocations: tennis, skiing, furniture restoration. Office: LI Lighting Company 175 E Old Country Road Hicksville New York 11801

ECCLES, SPENCER FOX, banker; born Ogden, Utah, August 24, 1934; son of Spencer Stoddard and Hope (Fox) E.; married Cleone Emily Peterson, July 21, 1958; children: Clista Hope, Lisa Ellen, Katherine Ann, Spencer Peterson. Bachelor of Science, University Utah, 1956; Master of Arts, Columbia University, 1959; degree in Business (honorary), Southern Utah State College, 1982; Bachelor of Laws (honorary), Westminster College, Salt Lake City,

1986. Trainee First National City Bank, New York City, 1959-60; with First Security Bank of Utah, Salt Lake City, 1960-61, First Security Bank of Idaho, Boise, 1961-70; executive vice president First Security Corp. Salt Lake City, 1970-75, president, 1975-86, chief operating officer, 1980-82, chairman board of directors, chief executive officer, 1982—; director Union Pacific Corp., Anderson Lumber Company, Zions Corp., Mercantile Institution; member adv. council University Utah Business College. Served to 1st lieutenant United States Army. Recipient President's Circle award Presidential Commn., 1984, Minuteman award Utah National Guard, 1988; Named Distinguished Alumni University Utah, 1988. Member Am. Bankers Association, Association Bank Holding Companies, Association Reserve City Bankers, Salt Lake Country Club, Alta Club. Office: 1st Security Corp 79 S Main St Post Office Box 30006 Salt Lake City Utah 84130

EDGERLY, WILLIAM SKELTON, banker; born Lewiston, Maine, February 18, 1927; son of Stuart and Florence (Skelton) E.; married Lois Stiles, June 12, 1948; children: Leonard Stuart, Stephanie Lois. Bachelor of Science in Economics and Engineering, Massachusetts Institute of Technology, 1949; Master of Business Administration, Harvard University, 1955. With Eastman Kodak Company, 1949-50; with Cabot Corp., Boston, 1952-75, treasurer, 1960-63, vice president, 1963-66, vice president, general manager Oxides div., 1967-68, fin. vice president, 1969-75, also director; chief executive officer State St. Boston Corp., 1975—, president, 1975, chairman and president, 1976-85, chairman, 1985-91, chairman, president, 1991—; chairman Boston Housing Partnership. Board of directors Jobs for Massachusetts, former president; director Boston Private Industry Council, former chairman; board of directors Massachusetts Business Roundtable, Institute for Foreign Policy Analysis and Pioneer Institute; trustee Committee Economic Devel.; former member federal adv. council Federal Reserves Board, Washington; board of directors Federal Reserves Bank Boston, Depository Trust Company, New York City, Arkwright-Boston Ins. Company, National Alliance Business With United States Naval Reserve, 1945-46, 50-52. Member Massachusetts Institute of Technology Alumni Association (president 1973-74), Harvard Business School Association, Boston Econ. Club. Clubs: Somerset, Cambridge Boat. Office: State St Boston Corp 225 Franklin St Boston Massachusetts 02110

EIGSTI, ROGER HARRY, insurance company executive; born Vancouver, Washington, April 17, 1942; son of Harry A. and Alice E. (Huber) E.; married Mary Lou Nelson, June 8, 1963; children: Gregory, Ann. Bachelor of Science, Linfield College, 1964. Certified Public Accountant, Oregon, Washington. Staff Certified Public Accountant Touche Ross and Company, Portland, Oregon, 1964-72; assistant to controller Safeco Corp., Seattle, 1972-78, controller, 1980; controller Safeco Life Insurance Company, Seattle, 1978-80; president Safeco Credit Company, Seattle, 1980-81, Safeco Life Insurance Company, Seattle, 1981-85; executive vice president, chief fin. officer Safeco Corp., Seattle, 1985—. board of directors Ind. Colleges of

Washington, Seattle, 1981-87, business director Seattle Repertory Theatre, 1981—, board of directors 1981—. Member Am. Institute Certified Public Accountants, Life Office Management Association (board directors 1983—), Seattle Chamber of Commerce (chairman metro budget rev. committee 1984—). Republican. Clubs: Mercer Island (Washington) Country (treasurer, board dirs. 1981-84); Central Park Tennis. Home: 11701 NE 36th Place Bellevue Washington 98005

EISNER, MICHAEL DAMMANN, motion picture company executive; born Mount Kisco, New York, March 7, 1942; son of Lester and Margaret (Dammann) E.; married Jane Breckenridge; children: Michael, Eric, Anders. Bachelor of Arts, Denison University, 1964. Began career in programming department CBS; assistant to national programming director ABC, 1966-68, manager spls. and talent, director program devel.-East Coast, 1968-71, vice president daytime programming, 1971-75, vice president program planning and devel., 1975-76, senior vice president prime time production and devel., 1976; president, chief operating officer Paramount Pictures, 1976-84; chairman, chief executive officer Walt Disney Company, Burbank, California, 1984—. Board of directors Denison U., California Institute Arts, Am. Film Institute, Performing Arts Council Los Angeles Music Center. Office: Walt Disney Company 500 S Buena Vista St Burbank California 91521

ELISHA, WALTER Y., textile manufacturing company executive; born 1932; married. Student, Wabash (Ind.) College, Harvard University School Business. Vice chairman board, director Jewel Companies, 1965-80; chairman, chief executive officer Springs Industries Incorporated, Fort Mill, South Carolina, 1980—, also board of directors. Office: Springs Industries Incorporated 205 N White St Post Office Box 70 Fort Mill South Carolina 29715

ELKIN, IRVIN, milk marketing cooperative executive. President, director Associated Milk Producers, Incorporated, San Antonio. Office: Associated Wholesale Grocers Incorporated Post Office Box 2428 Kansas City Kansas 66110§

ELLIS, WILLIAM BEN, utility executive; born Vicksburg, Mississippi, July 4, 1940; son of Conrad Ben and Viola Elizabeth (Stigall) E.; children: Bradford, Katherine, Emily, Ben, John. Bachelor of Science, Carnegie-Mellon University, 1962; Doctor of Philosophy (NSF fellow), University Maryland, 1966; postgraduate, Louisiana State University, 1966, Am. University, 1968. Research assistant Olin Mathieson Chemical Corp., West Monroe, Louisiana, 1958, Commercial Solvents Corp., Sterlington, Louisiana, 1959; engineer Procter & Gamble Company, Cincinnati, 1961; process engineer Standard Oil New Jersey, Baton Rouge, 1962-67; associate McKinsey & Company, Incorporated, Washington, 1969-75, principal, 1975-76, executive vice president, chief fin. officer, 1976-78, president, chief fin. officer, 1978-80, president, chief operating officer, 1980-83; chairman, chief executive officer Northeast Utilities and Subs., Hartford, Connecticut, 1983—; trustee Northeast Utilities, Hartford, Connecticut, 1977—, chairman, chief executive officer,; chairman, director Connecticut Yankee Atomic Power Company; director Nuclear Electric

Insurance Limited, Connecticut Economic Devel. Corp., Connecticut Mutual Life Insurance Company, Hartford Steam Boiler Inspection and Insurance Company. Board of directors United Way of Capital Area, 1979-84, Hartford Hospital, 1980-86, Edison Electric Institute; elector Wadsworth Atheneum, Hartford, 1977—; corporator St. Francis Hospital and Medical Center, 1977—, Institute of Living, 1978—; board regents U. Hartford. With United States Army, 1967-69. Member Atomic Industrial Forum, Connecticut Business and Industry Association (director 1978—, chairman 1990), Greater Hartford Chamber of Commerce (director 1978—, chairman 1985). Office: NE Utilities Post Office Box 270 Hartford Connecticut 06141 also: Connecticut Light & Power Company Selden St Berlin Connecticut 06037

ELY, JOSEPH BUELL, II, corporate executive; born Boston, November 5, 1938; son of Richard and Louise (Ludwick) E.; married Barbara Kurzina, August 5, 1967; children: Joseph Buell, III, Christina, Peter Douglas, Sarah Ann. Bachelor of Science, Boston University, 1965. Chief executive officer Amoskeag Company, Boston, 1978-90, chairman, 1987—, also board of directors, 1977—; chairman Fieldcrest Cannon, Incorporated, Eden, North Carolina, 1982-90, chief executive officer, 1985-90, also board of directors, 1976—; chairman Bangor (Me.) & Aroostook Railroad Company, 1982—, also board of directors; chairman, chief executive officer, board of directors Westville Homes Corp., Plaistow, New Hampshire, 1974-90; board of directors Communications Resource Associates, Incorporated, 1988, Logistics Management Systems, Incorporated. Trustee Boston U., 1987—. Recipient Collegium Distinguished Alumni College Liberal Arts award Boston University, 1981.

EMMETT, MARTIN FREDERICK CHEERE, investment banker; born Johannesburg, South Africa, August 30, 1934; son of Cecil Frederick Cheere and Thelma Marie (Ford) E.; married Alice Ellen Lavers, August 18, 1956; children: Karen Ann, Robert Martin Cheere, Susan Marie. Bachelor of Science in Mechanical Engineering, University Witwatersrand, Johannesburg, 1957; Master of Business Administration, Queens University, Kingston, Ontario, Can., 1962. Vice president consumer products Alcan Aluminum Company, Montreal, Quebec, Can., 1962-72; president, chief executive officer Standard Brands Limited, Montreal, 1972-76, New York City, 1980-81; president International Standard Brands Limited, New York City, 1976-79; senior executive vice president, board of directors Nabisco Brands, Incorporated, New York City, 1981-83; chairman, chief executive officer International Nabisco Brands, 1981-83; vice chairman Nabisco Brands, Limited, Toronto, Ontario, Can., 1985—; vice chairman Burns, Fry and Timmins, Incorporated, New York City, 1983-85, chairman, 1985—; board of directors Fry Limited, Toronto. Member Association Professional Engineers Ontario. Clubs: Econ.; Brook. Home: Frost Road Greenwich Connecticut 06830 Office: Burns Fry & Timmins Incorporated Wall Street Plaza New York New York 10005 also: Tambrands Incorporated 1 Marcus

Avenue Lake Success New York 11042

ERBURU, ROBERT F., newspaper publishing company executive; born Ventura, California, September 27, 1930. Bachelor of Arts, University Southern California, 1952; Bachelor of Laws, Harvard University Law School, 1955. Chairman board, chief executive officer Times-Mirror Company, Los Angeles, also board of directors; board of directors Tejon Ranch Company; board of directors, chairman Federal Reserve Bank San Francisco. Trustee Huntington Library, Art Collections and Botanical Gardens, 1981—, Flora and William Hewlett Foundation, 1980—, Brookings Institution, 1983—, Tomas Rivera Center, 1985—, Carrie Estelle Doheny Foundation, Fletcher Jones Foundation, 1982—, Pfaffinger Foundation, 1974—, J. Paul Getty Trust; member executive panel on future of welfare state Ford. Foundation, 1985—; board of directors, chairman Times Mirror Foundation, 1962—; board of directors Los Angeles Festival, 1985—, Ralph M. Parsons Foundation, 1985—; member National Gallery of Art Trustees Council. Member Am. Newspaper Pubs. Association (treasurer, board directors 1980—), Council on Foreign Relations (board directors), Business Roundtable, Business Council. Home: 1518 Blue Jay Way Los Angeles California 90069 Office: Times Mirror Company Times Mirror Square Los Angeles California 90053

ERTEGUN, AHMET MUNIR, record company executive; born Istanbul, Turkey, 1923; son of M. Munir and Hayrunisa Rustem (Temel) E.; married Ioana Maria Banu, April 6, 1961. Bachelor of Arts, St. John's College, Annapolis, Maryland, 1944; postgraduate, Georgetown University, 1944-46. Co-founder Atlantic Records, New York City, 1947, chairman board, chief executive officer, 1947—; co-founder Cosmos Soccer Club, New York City, 1971, president, 1971-83; chairman Am. Turkish Society, Rock and Roll Hall Fame Foundation, Am. branch Nordoff-Robbins Music Therapy Center; trustee Parrish Art Mus.; member adv. council Department Near Eastern Studies Princeton University. Producer various Grammy-Award-winning records; writer various award-winning songs. Recipient Humanitarian award Conference Personal Managers, 1977, Humanitarian of Year award T.J. Martell Foundation Leukemia Research, 1978, Humanitarian award National Conference Christians and Jews, 1987, TTV Turkish Presl. award, 1987, Golden Plate Am. Acad. award, 1988 Achievement; named Man of Year United Jewish Appeal, 1970, Turkish Am. Year, Am. by Choice, 1986; inductee Rock and Roll Hall Fame, 1987, Best Dressed Hall Fame, 1987. Member Recording Industry Association Am. (director), Black Music Association (director), National Association Record Merchandisers (Presidential award 1977), National Acad. Recording Arts and Sciences, American Society of Composers, Authors and Publishers, Broadcast Music Industry. Office: Atlantic Records 75 Rockefeller Plaza New York New York 10019

ESREY, WILLIAM TODD, telecommunications company executive; born Philadelphia, January 17, 1940; son of Alexander J. and Dorothy (B.) E.; married Julie L. Campbell, June 13, 1964; children: William Todd, John Campbell.

Bachelor of Arts, Denison University, Granville, Ohio, 1961; Master of Business Administration, Harvard University, 1964. With Am. Tel & Tel. Company, also New York Tel. Company, 1964-69; president Empire City Subway Limited, New York City, 1969-70; managing director Dillon, Read & Company Incorporated, New York City, 1970-80; executive vice president corp. planning United Telecommunications, Incorporated, Westwood, Kansas, 1980-81, executive vice president, chief fin. officer, 1981-82, 84-85; president, chief executive officer United Telecommunications, Incorporated, 1985—; president United Telecom Communications, Incorporated, Kansas City, Missouri, 1982-85; board of directors The Equitable Life Assurance Society United States, Panhandle Eastern Corp., General Mills, Incorporated; president, chief executive officer United States Sprint, 1987—. Board of directors U. Kansas City, Greater Kansas City Community Foundation; trustee Denison U., Midwest Research Committee for Economic Devel. Member Mission Hills Country Club, River Club, Links Club, Kansas City Country Club, Phi Beta Kappa. Home: 2624 Verona Road Shawnee Mission Kansas 66208 Office: United Telecommunications Incorporated Post Office Box 11315 Kansas City Missouri 64112

EVANS, LOREN KENNETH, manufacturing company executive; born Aurora, Indiana, May 8, 1928; son of Fred W. and Wilma E. (Walser) E.; married Margaret Ann Ingels; children: Michael, Elaine, Scott. Bachelor of Science, Ind. University, 1950. Various manufacturing management positions Arvin Industries, Incorporated, Columbus, Ind., 1953-68, vice president, general manager, 1968-73, div. president, 1973-77, group vice president, 1977-84, executive vice president, 1985-87, president, chief operating officer, 1987-91, vice chairman, 1991—, also board of directors; board of directors Ind. Energy, Incorporated, Irwin Fin. Corp. Member dean's adv. council Ind. U. School Business, Bloomington, 1986. Served to 1st lieutenant United States Army, 1951-53. Decorated Bronze Star; named Alumni fellow Ind. University School Business, 1986. Member Harrison Lake Country Club (Columbus), Mission Valley Country Club (Venice, Florida). Republican. Methodist. Avocations: golf, reading, travel. Office: Arvin Industries Incorporated 1 Noblitt Plaza Box 3000 Columbus Indiana 47202-3000

EVANS, MORGAN J., service, management company executive. President, chief executive officer 1st Security Service Company, Salt Lake City. Office: 1st Security Service Company Post Office Box 30006 Salt Lake City Utah 84130§

EVANS, ROBERT SHELDON, corporate executive; born Pittsburgh, 1944. Bachelor of Arts in History, University Pennsylvania, 1966; Master of Business Administration in Fin., Columbia University, 1968. Vice president Evans & Company Incorporated, 1971-74; vice president international operations Crane Company, New York City, 1974-78, senior vice president, 1978-79, executive vice president, director, 1979-84, chairman, chief executive officer, 1984-85, also board of directors, chairman, chief executive officer, president, 1985—; chairman, chief executive officer, board of directors Medusa Corp.; board of directors

HBD Industries Incorporated. Member dean's adv. council Columbia Grad. School Business; trustee Allen Stevenson School. Office: Crane Company 757 3rd Avenue New York New York 10017

EXLEY, CHARLES ERROL, JR., manufacturing company executive; born Detroit, December 14, 1929; son of Charles Errol and Helen Margaret (Greenizen) E.; married Sara Elizabeth Yates, February 1, 1952; children: Sarah Helen, Evelyn Victoria, Thomas Yates. Bachelor of Arts, Wesleyan University, Middletown, Connecticut, 1952; Master of Business Administration, Columbia University, 1954. With Burroughs Corp., Detroit, 1954-76; controller Burroughs Corp. (Todd div.), 1960-63, corp. controller, 1963-66, vice president, group executive office products group, 1966-71, vice president fin., 1971-73, executive vice president fin., director, 1973-76; president NCR Corp., Dayton, Ohio, 1976-88; chief executive officer NCR Corp., Dayton, 1983—, chairman board, 1984—, board director, member executive committee; board of directors Merck and Company, Owens-Corning Fiberglass Corp.; trustee Andrew W. Mellon Foundation. Recipient Gold award Wall St. Transcript, 1986, 87, 89, 90, Bronze award, 1988, Leadership in Business award Columbia Business School, 1889. Clubs: Grosse Pointe (Grosse Pointe Farms, Michigan); Miami Valley Hunt and Polo, Moraine Country, Dayton Racquet; The Brook (New York City); The Question (Palm Beach, Florida); Elec. Mfrs. (The Homestead, West Virginia); Ocean Reef (Key Largo, Florida).

FALVO, ANTHONY J., JR., wood products manufacturing executive. With L&W Supply Corp., 1974-80; regional operations manager East 1974-75, director planning and devel., 1975-76, president, 1976-80; with USG Corp., Chicago, 1955-74, 1980-85; sales corr. 1955-56, sales representative, 1956-62, manager large jobs, 1962-64, district manager Hudson Valley, 1964-67, district manager Washington, 1967-70, area sales manager, 1970-74, director gypsum group services, 1980-82, vice president marketing, 1982-84, group vice president consumer products, 1984-85; with Masonite Corp., Chicago, 1985—, president, chief executive officer, 1986-88. Office: USG Corp 101 S Wacker Dr Chicago Illinois 60606

FARLEY, JAMES BERNARD, financial services company executive; born Pittsburgh, November 1, 1930; son of James and Marie (Wallace) F.; married Mary W. Williams, February 14, 1951; children—James J., Michele M., Constance M., J. Scott. Bachelor of Business Administration, Duquesne University, 1953; Master of Business Administration, Case Western Reserve University, 1961. Industrial engineer United States Steel Company, Pittsburgh, 1952-60; superintendent Newburgh & Southern Shore Railway Company, Cleveland, 1960-63; vice president Booz, Allen & Hamilton, New York City, 1963-73, president, chief executive officer, 1973-76, chairman board, chief executive officer, 1976-85, senior chairman board, 1985-88; president, chief op. officer, trustee Mutual of New York, New York City, 1988-89, chairman, president, chief executive officer, trustee, 1989-91, chairman, chief executive officer, trustee, 1991—; director Promus Companies, Incorporated, Memphis,

Ashland Oil Incorporated, Kentucky, Conference Board, New York City; trustee Committee for Economic Devel., New York City. Clubs: Links, Sky (New York City); Gulf Stream Golf (Delray Beach, Florida); Baltusrol Golf (Springfield, New Jersey) (board governors 1978-84). Office: Mutual of N Y 1740 Broadway New York New York 10019

FARLEY, WILLIAM F., corporation executive; born Pawtucket, Rhode Island, October 10, 1942. Bachelor of Arts, Bowdoin College, 1964; Juris Doctor, Boston College, 1969; postgraduate, New York University Graduate School Business, 1969-72. Bar: Massachusetts 1969. Sales manager Crowell Collier and MacMillan, 1966; director mergers and acquisitions NL Industries, New York City; head corp. fin. department Chicago office Lehman Brothers, Incorporated, 1973-78; chairman, owner Farley Industries, Chicago, 1976—; owner Magnus Tool & Engineering Company, Fruit of the Loom, Acme Boot Company, West Point-Pepperell; co-owner, director Chicago White Sox Baseball Club. Board of directors U.S.-USSR Trade and Economic Council, Lyric Opera, Chicago, Goodman Theatre; trustee Bowdoin College; member Illinois Governor's Sci. and High Tech. Commission; presidential aide Boston College. Member Massachusetts Bar Association, American Bar Association, Young Pres.'s Organization, Am. Business Conference, Mid-Am. Committee, Council on Foreign Relations, Illinois Ambassadors (chairman), Urban League (business adv. council). Clubs: Saddle and Cycle, Chicago. Office: Farley Industries Sears Tower 233 S Wacker Dr Suite 6300 Chicago Illinois 60606

FARRELL, DAVID COAKLEY, department store executive; born Chicago, June 14, 1933; son of Daniel A. and Anne D. (O'Malley) F.; married Betty J. Ross, July 9, 1955; children: Mark, Lisa, David. Bachelor of Arts, Antioch College, Yellow Springs, Ohio, 1956. Assistant buyer, buyer, branch store general manager, merchandise manager Kaufmann's, Pittsburgh, 1956-66, vice president, general merchandise manager, 1966-69, president, 1969-74; vice president May Department Stores Company, St. Louis, 1969-75, director, 1974—, chief operating officer, 1975-79, president, 1975-85, chief executive officer, 1979—, chairman, 1985—; director 1st National Bank, St. Louis. Board of directors St. Louis Symphony Society, St. Louis Area council Boy Scouts Am., Arts and Education Fund Greater St. Louis; trustee Committee for Economic Devel., St. Louis Children's Hospital, Washington U., St. Louis; active Salvation Army; member Business Committee for Arts, Civic Progress. Member National Retail Mchts. Association (director). Roman Catholic. Clubs: University (New York City); Duquesne (Pittsburgh); Bogey (St. Louis), Missouri Athletic (St. Louis), Noonday (St. Louis), St. Louis (St. Louis), St. Louis Country (St. Louis). Office: May Department Stores Company 611 Olive St Saint Louis Missouri 63101

FARRINGTON, JERRY S., utility holding company executive; born Burkburnett, Texas, 1934. Bachelor of Business Administration, North Texas State University, 1955, Master of Business Administration, 1958. With Texas Electric Service Company, 1957-60; vice president Texas Utilities Company (parent company), Dallas, 1970-76, president, 1983-87, chairman, chief executive officer, 1987—; president Dallas Power & Light Company, 1976-83; chairman, chief executive officer Texas Utilities Fuel Company, Dallas. Office: Tex Utilities Company 2001 Bryan Tower Dallas Texas 75201

FELDBERG, MEYER, business school dean; born Johannesburg, South Africa, March 17, 1942; son of Leon and Sarah (Kretzmer) F.; married Barbara Erlick, August 9, 1965; children: Lewis Robert, Ilana. Bachelor of Arts, Witwatersrand University, Johannesburg, 1962; Master of Business Administration, Columbia University, 1965; Doctor of Philosophy, Cape Town (South Africa) University, 1969. Product manager B.F. Goodrich Company, Akron, Ohio, 1965-67; dean Grad. School Business, University Cape Town, 1968-79; associate dean J.L. Kellogg School Management, Northwestern University, Evanston, Illinois, 1979-81; professor, dean School Business, Tulane University, New Orleans, 1981-86; president Illinois Institute Tech., Chicago, 1986-89, chairman board governors Research Institute; dean Grad. School Business Columbia University, New York City, 1989—; board of directors Am. National Bank, Chicago, ICL, South Africa, Hotel Properties Am.; visiting professor Massachusetts Institute of Technology, 1974, Cranfield Institute Tech., 1970-76; consultant in field. Author: Organizational Behaviour: Text and Cases, 1975; contributor articles to professional journals. Board of directors Council on Competitiveness, Washington, Isadore Newman School, Touro Hospital. Named Jaycee Young Man of Year, 1972. Clubs: International House (New Orleans); University (New York City); Chicago. Home: 145 Central Park W New York New York 10023 Office: Columbia U Grad School Business New York New York 10027

FELDBERG, SUMNER LEE, retail company executive; born Boston, June 19, 1924; son of Morris and Anna (Marnoy) F.; married; children: Michael S., Ellen R.; stepchildren: Mollye S., Beth, James. Bachelor of Arts, Harvard, 1947, Master of Business Administration, 1949. With New England Trading Corp., 1949-56; treasurer Zayre Corp., 1956-73, senior vice president, 1965-68, executive vice president, 1969-73, chairman board, 1973-87; chairman executive committee Zayre Corp. (name now TJX Companies, Incorporated), 1987—; chairman board Waban Corp., 1989—, TJX Companies, Incorporated, Framingham, Massachusetts, 1989—; trustee Massachusetts Mutual Corp. Investors, Massachusetts Mutual Participation Investors. Trustee Beth Israel Hospital, Combined Jewish Philanthropies of Greater Boston. Served to 1st lieutenant United States Army Air Force, 1943-46. Office: TJX Cos Incorporated 770 Cochituate Road Post Office Box 9175 Framingham Massachusetts 01701 also: Waban Corp 1 Mercer Road Natick Massachusetts 01760

FELDSTEIN, MARTIN STUART, economist, educator; born New York City, November 25, 1939; son of Meyer and Esther (Gevarter) F.; married Kathleen Foley, June 19, 1965; children—Margaret, Janet. Bachelor of Arts summa cum laude, Harvard University, 1961; Master of

Arts, Oxford University, 1964, Doctor of Philosophy, 1967; Doctor.Laws (honorary), Rochester University, 1984, Marquette University, 1985, Bentley College, 1988. Research fellow Nuffield College, Oxford University, 1964-65, ofcl. fellow, 1965-67, lecturer pub. fin., 1965-67; assistant professor economics Harvard University, 1967-68, associate professor, 1968-69, professor, 1969—; George F. Baker professor Harvard University, 1984—; president National Bureau Economic Research, 1977-82, 84—; chairman Council Economic Advisers, 1982-84; chairman Council Economic Advisers, 1982-84; governor Am. Stock Exchange; director TRW, Am. International Group, Great Western Fin.; member international adv. council Morgan Guaranty Bank; trustee Met-Vest Funds. Columnist Wall Street Journal. Fellow Am. Acad. Arts and Sciences, Econometric Society (council 1977-82), National Association Business Economists, Am. Philosophical Society; member Am. Econ. Association (John Bates Clark medal 1977, executive committee 1980-82, vice president 1988), Institute Medicine National Acad. Sciences, Council on Foreign Relations, Trilateral Commission (executive committee 1987—), Phi Beta Kappa. Home: 147 Clifton St Belmont Massachusetts 02178 Office: National Bur Econ Research Incorporated 1050 Massachusetts Avenue Cambridge Massachusetts 02138

FENOGLIO, WILLIAM RONALD, manufacturing company executive; born Clinton, Indiana, May 25, 1939; son of William and Melba (Scaggiari) F.; married Becky S. Williams, July 8, 1961; children—Denise, Todd, William D. Bachelor of Science in Mechanical Engineering, Rose Hulman Institute Tech., 1961. Various management positions General Electric Company, 1961-80; vice president, general manager refrigeration div. General Electric Company, Louisville, 1981; vice president, general manager motor div. General Electric Company, Fort Wayne, Ind., 1981-84; president, chief operating officer Barnes Group Incorporated, Bristol, Connecticut, 1985—. Office: Barnes Group Incorporated 123 Main St Bristol Connecticut 06010

FERGUSON, RONALD EUGENE, reinsurance company executive; born Chicago, January 16, 1942; son of William Eugene and Elizabeth (Hahnneman) F.; married Carol Jean Chapp, December 27, 1964; children: Brian, Kristin. Bachelor of Arts, Blackburn College, 1963; Master of Arts, University Michigan, 1965. Statistician Lumbermans Mutual Casualty Company, Long Grove, Illinois, 1965-69; actuary General Reins. Corp., Greenwich, Connecticut, 1969-70, assistant v.p, 1972-74, vice president, 1974-77, senior vice president, 1977-82, executive vice president, 1982, director, 1983, chairman, 1985—; vice president, group executive General Re Corp., Stamford, 1981, president, chief operating officer, 1983-87, chairman, president, chief executive officer, 1987—; board of directors Finevest Food Services, Incorporated, General Signal Corp., Colgate-Palmolive Company, SEI Center for Advanced Studies in Management Wharton Business School University Pennsylvania, Philadelphia; trustee Underwriters Laboratories Incorporated, Insurance Institute Am. Contributor articles to professional journals.

Served with United States Public Health Service, 1966-68. Fellow Casualty Actuarial Society (board directors 1978-81); member Am. Acad. Actuaries (director 1981—). Congregationalist. Clubs: Patterson. Office: General Reins Corp 695 E Main St Post Office Box 10351 Stamford Connecticut 06904

FERGUSON, WILLIAM CHARLES, telecommunications executive; born Detroit, October 26, 1930; son of William and Bessie F. (Barr) F.; married Joyce G. Soby, June 14, 1952; children: Laura, Ellen, Joanne. Bachelor of Arts, Albion College, 1952. With Michigan Bell Telephone Company, 1952-77, 78-83, district manager, 1961-63, div. manager, 1963-68, general traffic manager, 1968-72, vice president operations staff and engineering, 1972-73, vice president metro, 1973-76, vice president personnel, 1976-77, executive vice president, chief operating officer, 1978-82; vice president New York City region New York Telephone Company, 1977, president, chief executive officer, 1983-86; vice chairman NYNEX Corp., White Plains, New York, 1986-89, June 89, president, chief executive officer, October 1989, chairman, chief executive officer, 1989—; board of directors Marine Midland Bank, General Re Corp, CPC International Corp. Board of directors United Ways of Tri-State, 1988-89; member Governor's Adv. Board; member Conference Board; chairman board trustees Albion College, 1980; board of directors New York State Business Council, New York City Partnership; member New York Governor's Council on Fiscal and Economic Priorities; member Greater New York Blood Donor Program, 1988-89, chairman elect, 1990-91. Served with United States Army, 1952-54. Home: 1113 Westchester Avenue White Plains New York 10604 Office: NYNEX Corp 1113 Westchester Avenue White Plains New York 10604

FERLAND, E. JAMES, electric utility executive; born Boston, March 19, 1942; son of Ernest James and Muriel (Cassell) F.; married Eileen Kay Patridge, March 9, 1964; children: E. James, Elizabeth Denise. Bachelor of Science in Mechanical Engineering, University Maine, 1964; Master of Business Administration, University New Haven, 1979; postgraduate in program management devel., Harvard University Graduate School Business Administration. Electric utility engineer HELCO, New London, Connecticut, 1964-67; superintendent nuclear operations NNECO, Waterford, Connecticut, 1967-78; director rate regulation Northeast Utilities, Berlin, Connecticut, 1978-79, vice president, chief fin. officer, 1980-83, president, chief operating officer, 1983-86; chairman, president, chief executive officer Pub. Service Enterprise Group Incorporated, Newark, 1986—, Pub. Service Electric and Gas Company, 1986—; also board of directors all Pub. Service Enterprise Group subsidiary; board of directors Hartford Steam Boiler Inspection and Insurance Company, First Fidelity Bancorp, Newark, First Fidelity Bank, N.A., New Jersey, Mutual Benefit Life Insurance Company. Office: Pub Service Enterprise Group 80 Park Plaza Newark New Jersey 07101

FERRARA, ARTHUR VINCENT, insurance company executive; born New York City, August 12, 1930; son of Thomas Joseph and Camille

Virginia (Crescenzi) F.; married Isabel D. Flynn, December 26, 1953; children: Thomas G., Margaret Mary, James X. Bachelor of Science, Holy Cross College, 1952. Chartered Life Underwriter. Group sales representative Connecticut General Life Insurance Company, New York City, 1955-56; group sales representative Guardian Life Insurance Company, New York City, 1957-60, agency vice president, 1972-77, senior vice president, 1977-80, executive vice president, 1981-84, president, 1985-88; president, chief executive officer Guardian Life Insurance Company of Am., New York City, 1988—; vice president sales Guardian Insurance & Annuity Company, 1972-78, president, 1985—, director, 1972—; director Guardian Investor Services Corp., 1981; trustee Guardian Life Welfare Trust, Guardian Life Trust; chairman board Guardian Asset Management Corp., Guardian Baillie Gifford, Limited. Board of directors Life Ins. Council New York, Incorporated, 14th St. Union Square Local Devel. Corp.; member cardinals committee of the laity and president council Holy Cross College. Member Am. Society CLUs, National Life Underwriters Association, New York Life Suprs. Association, New York Life Underwriters Association, Am. Society Pension Actuaries, Golden Key Society of CLUs, Life Insurance Council New York (board directors), Am. Council Life Insurance (committee field relations), Health Insurance Association Am. (board directors). Home: 70 Baldwin Farms S Greenwich Connecticut 06831 Office: Guardian Life Ins Company 201 Park Avenue S New York New York 10003

FERRERO, LOUIS PETER, computer services company executive; born New York City, November 1, 1942; son of Raymond Peter and Ethel Gertrude (Cannerelli) F.; married Judith I. Coon, October 19, 1969; children—Juliette, Justin. Bachelor of Science, University Florida, 1966. Sales representative Radio Corporation of America Corp., Tallahassee, Florida, 1966-69; vice president marketing Datagraphix, San Diego, 1969-75; president General Micrographics, Atlanta, 1975-79; senior vice president Computer Micrographics, Atlanta, 1979; senior vice president Anacomp, Incorporated, Indianapolis, 1979-84, chairman, chief executive officer, 1984—. Roman Catholic. Home: 8 W Andrews Dr Atlanta Georgia 30305 Office: Anacomp Incorporated 11550 N Meridian Suite 600 Carmel Indiana 46032 also: 5302 Betsy Ross Dr Santa Clara California 95954

FERY, JOHN BRUCE, forest products company executive; born Bellingham, Washington, February 16, 1930; son of Carl Salvatore and Margaret Emily (Hauck) F.; married Delores Lorraine Carlo, August 22, 1953; children: John Brent, Bruce Todd, Michael Nicholas. Bachelor of Arts, University Washington, 1953; Master of Business Administration, Stanford University, 1955; Doctor of Law (honorary), Gonzaga University, 1982; Doctor of National Resources (honorary), University Idaho, 1983. Assistant to president Western Kraft Corp., 1955-56; production manager 1956-57; with Boise Cascade Corp., Idaho, 1957—, president, chief executive officer, 1972-78, chairman board, chief executive officer, 1978—; board of directors Albertsons, Incorporated, Hewlett-Packard

Company, West One Bancorp, The Boeing Company; active member Business Council; member executive committee, board of directors Am. Paper Institute. Chairman board Idaho Community Foundation; member policy committee Business Roundtable. With United States Navy, 1950-51; member executive committee, board governors NCASI. Named Most Outstanding Chief Executive Officer Fin. World, 1977, 78, 79, 80. Member NCASI (executive committee, board govs.), Arid Club, Hillcrest Country Club, Arlington Club, Links. Office: Boise Cascade Corp 1 Jefferson Square Boise Idaho 83728

FETTEROLF, CHARLES FREDERICK, aluminum company executive; born Franklin, Pennsylvania, July 18, 1928; son of Harry B. and Beryl (Linsey) F.; married Frances Spang, April 11, 1953; children: Regan J., Scott F. Bachelor of Science in Chemistry, Grove City College, 1952. Sales trainee Alcoa Aluminum Company, Pittsburgh, 1952, chemist, general salesman, 1953; chemist, general salesman Alcoa Aluminum Company, Louisville, 1959; chemist, general salesman Alcoa Aluminum Company, San Francisco, 1961, industry assistant flexible packaging, 1965, div. sales manager, 1965-69; assistant district sales manager Alcoa Aluminum Company, Los Angeles, 1969; district sales manager Alcoa Aluminum Company, Philadelphia, 1971, industry manager defense, 1974, general manager marketing, 1975, general manager operations, 1977, vice president, 1977, vice president Alcoa smelting process project, 1979, vice president operations, 1979, vice president sci. and tech., 1981, executive vice president mill products, 1981; president Aluminum Company Am., Pittsburgh, 1983—, chief operating officer, 1985—, also board of directors; board of directors Mellon National Bank, North America, Union Carbide Corp., Allegheny Ludlum, Aluminum Company Am. Board of directors Grove City College, Pittsburgh Ballet Theatre, WQED Pub. Broadcasting; trustee Shadyside Hospital, U. Pittsburgh; member adv. board Coalition for Addictive Disease of Southwest Pennsylvania, 1982—. With United States Navy, 1946-48. Recipient Alumni Achievementaward Grove City College, 1978. Clubs: Duquesne, Laurel Valley, Internat, Allegheny Country. Office: Aluminum Company Am 1501 Alcoa Building Pittsburgh Pennsylvania 15219

FICKLING, WILLIAM ARTHUR, JR., health care administrator; born Macon, Georgia, July 23, 1932; son of William Arthur and Claudia Darden (Foster) F.; married Neva Jane Langley, December 30, 1954; children: William Arthur III, Jane Dru, Julia Claudia, Roy Hampton. Bachelor of Science cum laude, Auburn University, 1954. Executive vice president Fickling & Walker, Incorporated, Macon, 1954-74; chairman board of directors, chief executive officer Charter Medical Corp., Macon, 1969-85, president, chairman board of directors, 1985—; board of directors Georgia Power Company, Riverside Ford, Southlake Ford. Trustee Wesleyan College, Macon. Member Macon Board Realtors, Kappa Alpha, Delta Sigma Phi, Phi Kappa Phi. Methodist. Home: 4918 Wesleyan Woods Dr Macon Georgia 31210 Office: Charter Med Corp 577 Mulberry St Macon Georgia 31298

FIGGIE, HARRY E., JR., corporate executive; born 1923; married; 3 children. Bachelor of Science, Case Institute Tech., 1947, Master of Science in Industrial Engineering, 1951; Master of Business Administration, Harvard University, 1949; Bachelor of Laws, Cleveland Marshall Law School, 1953. Formerly with Western Automatic Screw Machine Company, Parker-Hannifin Corp. and, Booz, Allen & Hamiliton; group vice president industrial products A. O. Smith Corp., 1962-64; with Figgie International (formerly A-T-O Incorporated), 1964—, chairman board, chief executive officer, 1960—; also director; chairman Clark Reliance Corp. Member World Business Council. Office: Figgie International Incorporated 4420 Sherwin Road Willoughby Ohio 44094

FINKELSTEIN, EDWARD SYDNEY, department store executive; born New Rochelle, New York, March 30, 1925; son of Maurice and Eva (Levine) F.; married Myra Schuss, August 13, 1950; children: Mitchell, Daniel, Robert. Bachelor of Arts, Harvard University, 1946, Master of Business Administration, 1948; Doctor of Commercial Science (honorary), New York University, 1988. Successively trainee, buyer merchandise administrator Macy's, New York City, 1948-62; senior vice president, director merchandising Macy's, New Jersey, 1962-67, executive vice president, merchandising and sales promotion, 1967-69; president Macy's, California, 1969-74; president, chairman, chief executive officer Macy's, New York, 1974-80; chairman, chief executive officer R.H. Macy & Company Incorporated, 1980—; director R.H. Macy, Incorporated, 1971—; director Chase Manhattan Bank, Chase Manhattan Corp., Time Warner, Incorporated. Member national adv. council Cystic Fibrosis, 1975-80; trustee Cystic Fibrosis Foundation, 1977-80, hon. trustee, 1980—; board of directors adv. board Harvard Business School, 1983—. Served with United States Navy, 1943-46. Member Harvard Club. Jewish. Office: R H Macy & Company Incorporated 151 W 34th St New York New York 10001

FIREMAN, PAUL, apparel executive; born Cambridge, Massachusetts, February 14, 1944. Student, Boston University. President, chief executive officer Reebok International Limited, Stoughton, Massachusetts, 1979—; chairman Reebok International Limited, 1986—. Office: Reebok International Limited 100 Technology Center Dr Stoughton Massachusetts 02072

FISH, LAWRENCE KINGSBAKER, banker; born Chicago, October 9, 1944; son of Alvin Kingsbaker and Beatrice (Brown) F.; married Atsuko Toko, June 29, 1980; children: Leah Okajima, Edward Takezo, Emily Takako. Bachelor of Arts, Drake University, Des Moines, Iowa, 1966; Master of Business Administration, Harvard Business School, Cambridge, 1968. United States aid officer United States Agency International Capital Devel., 1970-72; internal officer Bank of Boston, Brazil, 1972, director international operations, 1972-74, assistant vice president, general manager, 1974-75, vice president, deputy general manager, 1975, vice president, 1975; vice president, general manager Bank of Boston, Tokyo, 1978-79, 1st vice president, 1979-80; 1st vice president, head Pacific Asia div., Bank of Boston, Hong Kong, 1980-81, senior vice president, 1981-82, executive vice president, 1982-83; executive vice president, head of trust function Asia div., Bank of Boston, Boston, 1983-84, executive v.p, head New England Group, 1984-88; president, chief operating officer Columbia Savings & Loan Association, Beverly Hills, California, 1988-90; chairman, chief executive officer Bank of New England, Boston, 1990—; board of directors Mastercard International. Member executive committee Children's Museum, Boston, 1984-85; president Boston/Kyoto Sister City Foundation, 1984-85; board of directors Japan Society of Boston, 1984-85, Institute Contemporary Art of Boston; member executive board USAID Private Enterprise, Washington, 1984-88; overseer New England Conservatory Music. Woodrow Wilson Foundation fellow, 1984. Club: Longwood (Brookline, Massachusetts). Office: Bank of New England 28 State St Boston Massachusetts 02109

FISHER, CHARLES THOMAS, III, banker; born Detroit, November 22, 1929; son of Charles Thomas Jr. and Elizabeth Jane (Briggs) F.; married Margaret Elizabeth Keegin, June 18, 1952; children: Margaret Elizabeth Jones, Curtis William, Charles Thomas IV (deceased), Lawrence Peter II, Mary Florence Hickey. Bachelor of Arts in Econs, Georgetown University, 1951; Master of Business Administration, Harvard University, 1953. C.P.A., Michigan. With Touche, Ross, Bailey & Smart, Detroit, 1953-58; assistant vice president National Bank Detroit, 1958-61, vice president, 1961-66, senior vice president, 1966-69, executive vice president, 1969-72, president, chief administrative officer, 1972-82, chairman, president, chief executive officer, 1982—, board director; president, board director NBD Bancorp, Incorporated, 1973-82, chairman, president, chief executive officer, 1982—; board of directors General Motors, Am. Airlines. Civilian aide to secretary army State of Michigan, 1974-77; chairman Mackinac Bridge Authority; past chairman Detroit Renaissance, Incorporated, United Way Southeastern Michigan. Named Detroit Young Man of Year Detroit Junior Board Commerce, 1961. Member Association Reserve City Bankers, Am. Institute Certified Public Accountants, Michigan Association Certified Public Accountants, Bloomfield Hills Country Club (Michigan), Country Club of Detroit (Grosse Pointe), Grosse Pointe Club, Detroit Athletic Club (Detroit), Detroit Club, Yondotega Club, Links Club (New York City), Metropolitan Club (Washington). Office: NBD Bank NA 611 Woodward Avenue Detroit Michigan 48226

FISHER, FRANKLIN MARVIN, economist; born New York City, December 13, 1934; son of Mitchell Salem and Esther (Oshiver) F.; married Ellen Jo Paradise, June 22, 1958; children—Abraham Samuel, Abigail Sarah, Naomi Leah. Bachelor of Arts summa cum laude, Harvard University, 1956, Master of Arts, 1957, Doctor of Philosophy, 1960. Assistant professor economics University Chicago, 1959-60; assistant professor economics Massachusetts Institute of Technology, 1960-62, associate professor, 1962-65, professor, 1965—; consultant various law firms; director consultant Charles River Associates, Incorporated; board member National Bureau Economic Research. Editor: Econometrica, 1968-77. Trustee

Combined Jewish Philanthropies, Boston, 1975—, board mgr., 1979—; trustee Beth Israel Hospital, Boston, 1979—; chairman faculty adv. cabinet United Jewish Appeal, 1975-77; board governors Tel Aviv U., 1976—; board of directors New Israel Fund, 1983—, treasurer, 1984—; president Boston Friends of Peace Now, 1984-86; chairman steering committee North America Friends of Peace Now, 1985-88, treasurer 1988—. National Science Foundation fellow, 1962-63; Ford Foundation Faculty Research fellow, 1966-67; Guggenheim fellow, 1981-82; Erksine fellow University Canterbury, New Zealand, 1983. Fellow Econometric Society (council 1972-76, vice president 1977-78, president 1979), Am. Acad. Arts and Sciences; member Am. Econ. Association (John Bates Clark medal 1973). Home: 130 Mt Auburn St Cambridge Massachusetts 02138 Office: Massachusetts Institute of Technology E52-359 50 Memorial Dr Cambridge Massachusetts 02139

FISHER, GEORGE MYLES CORDELL, electronics equipment company executive, mathematician, engineer; born Anna, Illinois, November 30, 1940; son of Ralph Myles and Catherine (Herbert) F.; married Patricia Ann Wallace, June 18, 1965; children: Jennifer, Barcy, William. Bachelor of Science in Engineering, University Illinois, 1962; Master of Science in Engineering, Brown University, 1964, Doctor of Philosophy in Applied Maths., 1964-66. Member tech. staff Bell Telephone Laboratories, Murray Hill, New Jersey, 1965-67; supervisor Bell Telephone Laboratories, Holmdel, New Jersey, 1967-71; department head Bell Telephone Laboratories, Indianapolis, 1971-76; director manufacturing systems. Motorola Incorporated, Schaumberg, Illinois, 1976-77; assistant director mobile operations Motorola Incorporated, Fort Worth, Texas, 1977-78; vice president portable operations Motorola Incorporated, Fort Lauderdale, Florida, 1978-81, vice president paging div., 1981-84; assistant general manager communications sector Motorola Incorporated, Schaumberg, 1984-86, senior executive vice president, 1986-88, president, chief executive officer, 1988-90, chairman, chief executive officer, 1990—. Contributor articles on continuum physics; 3 patents in optical wave guides and digital communications. Trustee Brown U.; board of directors U. Illinois Foundation, National Merit Scholarship Board, Chicago, 1986—. Member Institute of Electrical and Electronics Engineers. Office: Motorola Incorporated 1303 E Algonquin Road Schaumburg Illinois 60196

FISHER, JOHN EDWIN, insurance company executive; born Portsmouth, Ohio, October 26, 1929; son of Charles Hall and Bess (Swearingin) F.; married Eloise Lyon, April 25, 1949. Student, University Colorado, 1947-48, Ohio University, 1948-49, Franklin University, Columbus, Ohio, 1950-51. With Nationwide Mutual Insurance Company, Columbus, 1951—, vice president, office general chairman, 1970-72, president, general manager, director, 1972-81, general chairman, chief executive officer, 1981—, also director; general chairman, chief executive officer, board of directors Nationwide General Insurance Company, Nationwide Mutual Fire Insurance Company, Nationwide Property & Casualty Insurance Company, Nationwide Life Insurance Company, Fin. Horizons Life Insurance Company; board of directors Neckura Versicherungs A.G., Oberursel, Federal Republic Germany; general chairman, board of directors Employers Insurance Wausau, 1985—, Farmland Insurance Companies, 1983—. Chmn. board Nationwide Foundation, 1972—; trustee Franklin County Convention Facilities Authority. Trustee Children's Hospital, president, 1984-87. Member Chartered Property and Casualty Underwriters Association, CLU Society, Association Ohio Life Insurance Companies (president 1972-74), Ohio Insurance Institute (president 1975-77), National Association Ind. Insurers, Am. Risk and Insurance Association, Griffith Insurance Foundation (president 1978-80), Property-Casualty Insurance Council (chairman 1981-82), Property and Liability Underwriters, Insurance Institute Am., Am. Institute Propert-Liability Insurers (chairman 1985-87), Am. Institute Property and Liability Underwriters, Institute Am., International Cooperative Insurance Federation (chairman 1984-90), Am. Council Life Insurance (chairman 1990-91). Office: Nationwide Mut Ins Company 1 Nationwide Plaza Columbus Ohio 43216 also: Employers Ins of Wausau 2000 Westwood Dr Wausau Wisconsin 54401

FISHER, RICHARD B., investment banker; born Philadelphia, July 21, 1936; son of Ernest W. and Doris Virginia (Rans) F.; married Emily Hargroves, September 7, 1957; children: R. Britton, Catherine Curtis, Alexander Dylan. Bachelor of Arts, Princeton University, 1957; Master of Business Administration, Harvard University, 1962. Managing director Morgan Stanley & Company, Incorporated, New York City, 1970—, president, 1984—. Trustee Princeton U., Carnegie Corp. of New York, Urban Institute, Historic Hudson Valley; board of directors Ministers and Missionaries Benefit Board of Am. Baptist Chs. Club: Links, National Golf Links, Blind Brook, Rockaway Hunting. Office: Morgan Stanley Group Incorporated 1251 Avenue of the Americas New York New York 10020

FITES, DONALD VESTER, tractor company executive; born Tippecanoe, Indiana, January 20, 1934; son of Rex E. and Mary Irene (Sackville) F.; married Sylvia Dempsey, June 25, 1960; children: Linda Marie. Bachelor of Science in Civil Engineering, Valparaiso University, 1956; Master of Science, Master.I.T, 1971. With Caterpillar Overseas S.A., Peoria, Illinois, 1956-66; director international customer div. Caterpillar Overseas S.A., Geneva, 1966-67; assistant manager market devel. Caterpillar Tractor Company, Peoria, 1967-70; director Caterpillar Mitsubishi Limited, Tokyo, 1971-75; director engine capacity expansion program Caterpillar Tractor Company, Peoria, 1975-76, manager products control department, 1976-79; president Caterpillar Brasil S.A., 1979-81; vice president products Caterpillar Tractor Company, Peoria, 1981-85, executive vice president, 1985-89; president, chief opd. officer Caterpillar Incorporated, Peoria, 1989-90, chairman, chief executive officer, 1990—, also board of directors; board of directors Mobil

Corp., Equip. Manufacturing Institute, First National Bank of Peoria. Trustee Farm Foundation, 1985—, Methodist Medical Center, 1985—, Knox College, 1986—; member adv. board Salvation Army, 1985—, admintrv. board First United Methodist Church, 1986—; board of directors Keep Am. Beautiful. Member Agricultural Roundtable (chairman 1985-87), SAE. Republican. Clubs: Mt. Hawley Country, Creve Coeur. Home: 7614 N Edgewild Dr Peoria Illinois 61614 Office: Caterpillar Incorporated 100 NE Adams St Peoria Illinois 61629

FITZGERALD, WILLIAM ALLINGHAM, savings and loan association executive; born Omaha, November 18, 1937; son of William Frances and Mary (Allingham) F.; married Barbara Ann Miskell, August 20, 1960; children—Mary Colleen, Katherine Kara, William Tate. Bachelor of Science in Business Administration in Fin., Creighton University, 1959; graduate Savs. and Loan League exec. training program, University Georgia, 1962, University Ind., 1969. With Commercial Federal Savings & Loan Association, Omaha, 1959—, vice president, assistant secretary, 1963-68, executive vice president, 1968-73, president, 1974—. Trustee Ind. College Foundation; vice chairman board of directors Creighton U.; board of directors College of St. Mary, United Way of Midlands; trustee Archbishop's committee for educational devel. Roman Catholic Church Served to lieutenant Fin. Corps, United States Army. Clubs: Omaha Country, Kiewit Plaza. Lodge: Knights of Ak-Sar-Ben (gov.). Office: Commercial Federal Savings & Loan Association 2120 S 72nd St Omaha NE 68124

FITZGERALD, WILLIAM THOMAS, manufacturing company executive; born Akron, Ohio, September 1, 1926. Branch sales supervisor Cooper Tire & Rubber Company, Findlay, Ohio, 1953-59, west coast sales manager, 1959-61, sales manager Cooper brand, 1961-66, assistant vice president sales, 1966-68, vice president marketing, 1968-71, president tire div., 1971-89, executive vice president, 1982-89, president, 1989—, also board of directors. Executive committee, board of directors Community Devel. Foundation, Findlay, 1984—. Served in United States Navy, 1944-46. Member Am. Management Association. Roman Catholic. Clubs: Findlay Country, Palmetto Pine Country. Avocations: golf, skeet shooting, boating. Office: Cooper Tire & Rubber Company Lima & Western Aves Findlay Ohio 45840

FITZGIBBONS, JAMES M., diversified company executive. married. Bachelor of Arts, Harvard University, 1956, PMD, 1963. With Howes Leather Company, 1968—, president, 1986, chairman board of directors; with Boston Company Fund, Trust, 1981—; chairman executive committee, chief executive officer Bangor & Aroostook Railroad Company, 1986—; president, chief operating officer Amoskeag Company, Boston, also board of directors; board of directors Fiduciary Tire Trust Company, Fieldcrest Cannon Incorporated, Lumber Mutual Insurance Company. Office: Amoskeag Company 4500 Prudential Center Boston Massachusetts 02199

FITZSIMONDS, ROGER LEON, bank holding company executive; born Milwaukee, May 21, 1938; son of Stephen Henry and Wilhelmine Josephine (Rhine) F.; married Leona I. Schwegler, July 11, 1958; children: Susan Fitzsimonds Hedrick, Stephen. Bachelor of Business Administration in Fin., University Wis.-Milw., 1960, Master of Business Administration in Fin., 1971, Doctor in Commercial Science (honorary), 1989. Management trainee 1st Wisconsin National Bank, Milwaukee, 1964-66, 1st level officer, 1966-69; president 1st Wisconsin Bank of Green Bay 1970-73, 1st Wisconsin Mortgage Company, 1974-78; executive vice president retail banking and real estate fin. 1st Wisconsin National Bank, Milwaukee, 1978-84, executive vice president commercial fin. group, 1984-86, president, 1986-87; president 1st Wisconsin Corp., 1987-88; president Firstar Corp., 1989—, vice chairman, 1990, chairman, chief executive officer, 1991—, also board of directors; board of directors 1st Wisconsin National Bank, Miw., 1st Wisconsin Trust Company. Board of directors Milwaukee Boys and Girls Club, 1984—, Competitive Wisconsin, Incorporated; chairman board of directors Columbia Health System, Milwaukee, 1986—, Greater Milwaukee Committee, Governor Tommy Thompson's Business Roundtable; member adv. council School Business U. Wisconsin; past president, director executive committee U. Wisconsin, Milwaukee, Milwaukee Foundation, Milwaukee Boys and Girls Club. Captain United States Army, 1960-64. Recipient Alumni of Year award University Wis.-Milw., 1983. Member Wisconsin Association Manufacturers and Commerce (past chairman, board directors 1988—), Association Recording City Bankers, Am. Bankers Association (committee member 1987—). Republican. Lutheran. Club: Milwaukee (board dirs., trustee), Milwaukee Country. Avocations: tennis, golf, skiing, fishing. Home: 9155 N Upper River Road Milwaukee Wisconsin 53217 Office: Firstar Corp 777 E Wisconsin Avenue Milwaukee Wisconsin 53202

FLAMSON, RICHARD JOSEPH, III, banker; born Los Angeles, February 2, 1929; son of Richard J. and Mildred (Jones) F.; married Arden Black, October 5, 1951; children: Richard Joseph IV, Scott Arthur, Michael Jon, Leslie Arden. Bachelor of Arts, Claremont Men's College, 1951; certificate Pacific Coast Banking School, University Washington, 1962. With Security Pacific Corp., Los Angeles, 1955—; vice president Security Pacific National Bank, Los Angeles, 1962-69, senior vice president, 1969-70, executive vice president corp. banking department, 1970-73, vice-chairman, 1973-78, president, chief executive officer, 1978-81, chairman, chief executive officer, 1981-87, director, 1973—; vice-chairman Security Pacific Corp., 1973-78, president, 1978-81, chief executive officer, 1978-90, chairman, 1981—; board of directors Northrop Corp., Allergan Incorporated. Trustee Claremont Men's College 1st lieutenant Army of the United States, 1951-53. Member World Affairs Council, Town Hall, California , Balboa Bay (Newport Beach, California) Club, Balboa Yacht (Newport Beach) Club, Big Canyon Country Club (Newport Beach). Office: Security Pacific Corp 333 S Hope St Los Angeles California 90071

FLETCHER, PHILIP B., food products company executive. President, chief operating officer ConAgra Prepared Food Company subsidiary ConAgra Incorporated, Omaha, until 1990—; president ConAgra Incorporated, Omaha, 1990—. Office: ConAgra Incorporated 1 Central Park Plaza Omaha NE 68102

FLOTO, RONALD JOHN, supermarket executive; born Spangler, Pennsylvania, November 12, 1942; son of John Lester and Frances (McCormick) F.; married Sara Jean Albert, January 6, 1968; children: Lisa, John, Mary, Patricia. Bachelor of Science, United States Military Academy, 1965; Master of Business Administration, Harvard University, 1971. Vice president Masa Feeding Corp., Elk Grove, Illinois, 1977-78, Jewel Food Stores, Melrose Park, Illinois, 1978-81, Jewel Companies Incorporated, Chicago, Il, 1981-83; president Buttrey Food Stores, Great Falls, Montana, 1983-85, Kash n' Karry, Tampa, Florida, 1985—. Board of directors Junior Achievement of Chicago, 1978-81; board of directors Vietnam Vets. Leadership Program, Chicago, 1981-82. Served to captain United States Army, 1965-73. Republican. Roman Catholic. Home: 2116 Magdalene Manor Dr Tampa Florida Office: 6422 Hurney Road Tampa Florida 33610

FLYNN, WILLIAM JOSEPH, insurance executive; born New York City, September 6, 1926; son of William and Anne (Connors) F.; married Margaret M. Collins, March 21, 1952; children: William, Maureen, James, Robert. Master of Arts in Economics, Fordham University, 1951. Vice president group operations Equitable, New York City, 1953-71; president Mutual Am., New York City, 1971-72, president, chief executive officer, 1972-82, chairman board, chief executive officer, 1982—; board of directors Richmond Hill Savings Bank, Floral Park, New York. President board of directors New York Foundling Hospital, New York; board of directors United States Catholic Historical Society, Staten Island, New York, United Student Aid Funds, Indianapolis, College Constrn. Loan Ins. Association, Washington, Elie Wiesel Foundation for Humanity, New York City, Williamsburg Charter Foundation, Washington, United Student Aid Fund, New York City, United Way International, Alexandria, Va; past chairman adv. committee United States Holocaust Memorial Council, Board Life Ins. Council New York, St. Vincent's Svcs. Served with United States Air Force, 1951-53, Korea. Recipient Distinguished Community Service award Brandeis University 1980, Ubi Cantas Deus Ibi award Catholic Charities 1983, National Professional Leadership award United Way Am. 1984, Brotherhood award National Conference of Christians and Jews, 1984, Distinguished Service award United Way Bergen County, 1985. Member Am. Council Life Insurance. Clubs: University (New York City); Garden City (New York) Country. Avocations: golf, reading. Home: 69 2d St Garden City New York Office: Mutual of Am Life 666 Fifth Avenue New York New York 10103

FORD, WILLIAM CLAY, automotive company executive; born Detroit, March 14, 1925; son of Edsel Bryant and Eleanor (Clay) F.; married Martha Firestone, June 21, 1947; children: Martha, Sheila, William Clay, Elizabeth. Bachelor of Science, Yale

University, 1949. Sales and advertising staff Ford Motor Company, 1949; industrial relations, labor negotiations with United Auto Workers, 1949; quality control manager gas turbine engines Lincoln-Mercury Div., Dearborn, Michigan, 1951, manager special product operations, 1952, vice president, 1953, general manager Continental Div., 1954, group vice president Lincoln and Continental Divs, 1955, vice president product design, 1956-80; director 1948—, chairman executive committee, 1978—, vice chairman board, 1980-89; chairman fin. committee Ford Motor Company, 1987—; president, owner Detroit Lions Professional Football Club. Chairman emeritus Edison Institute; trustee Eisenhower Medical Center, Thomas A. Edison Foundation; board of directors National Tennis Hall of Fame, Boy Scouts Am. Member Society Automotive Engineers (associate), Automobile Old Timers, Econ. Club Detroit (director), Masons, Knight Templar, Phelps Association, Psi Upsilon. Office: Ford Motor Company Design Center Post Office Box 6012 Dearborn Michigan 48123 also: Detroit Lions 1200 Featherstone Road Pontiac Michigan 48342

FOX, DAVID WAYNE, banker; born Aurora, Illinois, August 29, 1931; son of Wayne Stauffer and Helen Katherine (Lynch) F.; married Mary Ann Evans, September 22, 1956; children: Susan E., David Wayne, Katherine A., Thomas E. Bachelor of Science in Fin., University Notre Dame, 1953; Master of Business Administration, University Chicago, 1958. With Northern Trust Company, Chicago, 1955—, senior vice president, 1974-78; executive vice president Northern Trust Corp. and Company, Chicago, 1978-81, vice chairman, director, 1981-87, president, chief operating officer, 1987-90, chairman, president, chief executive officer, 1990—; chairman, president, chief executive officer Northern Trust Corp. and Company, Chicago, 1990—; board of directors USG Corp., Chicago, Federal Reserve Bank Chicago; board governors Midwest Stock Exchange, 1991—. Chairman board governors Hinsdale (Illinois) Community House, 1983; trustee Adler Planetarium, Chicago, 1983—, Northwestern Memorial Hospital, Chicago, 1983—, Chicago Symphony Orchestra, 1988—; board of directors United Way Chicago, 1988—, Lyric Opera Chicago, 1990—; member business adv. council U. Notre Dame, Incorporated, 1981-87, Kellogg Grad. School Business, Northwestern U., Evanston, Illinois, 1988—; trustee De Paul U., Chicago, 1988—, member business adv. council, 1982-91. Member Association Reserve City Bankers, Robert Morris Assocs., Marine Corps Reserve Officers Association. Republican. Roman Catholic. Clubs: Chicago, University, Commonwealth, Economic, Commercial, Mid-Day (Chgo), Hinsdale (Illinois) Golf. Avocations: tennis, skiing, fishing. Office: No Trust Corp 50 S LaSalle St Chicago Illinois 60675

FOX, EDWARD A., dean; born New York City, July 17, 1936; son of Herman and Ruth F.; divorced; children: Brian, Laura, Jacqueline. Bachelor of Arts, Cornell University, 1958; Master of Business Administration, New York University, 1963. President, chief executive officer Student Loan Marketing Association,

Washington, 1973—; dean, Amos Tuck School Dartmouth College, Hanover, New Hampshire, 1990—; board of directors Perpetual Savings Bank, F.S.B. Past trustee Talladega College; past president D.C. chapter American Red Cross; board of directors, past president Washington Performing Arts Society; past president board of directors Washington Ballet; vice chairman, board of directors Reading is Fundamental; member board overseers GBA New York University; member adv. board National Center Fin. Services; board visitors School Foreign Service Georgetown U.; board of directors Federal City Council. Office: Student Loan Mktg Association 1050 Thomas Jefferson St Northwest Washington District of Columbia 20007 also: Dartmouth College Amos Tuck School Business Hanover New Hampshire 03755

FOX, JOSEPH CARTER, pulp and paper manufacturing company executive; born Petersburg, Virginia, September 8, 1939; son of William Tarrant and Virginia (Newell) F.; married Carol Spaulding Fox, June 16, 1962; children: Carol Faulkner, Lucy Carter, Baylor Tarrant. Bachelor of Science, Washington and Lee University, 1961; Master of Business Administration, University Virginia, 1963. With Chesapeake Corp., West Point, Virginia, 1963—, controller, 1969-71, controller, assistant treasurer, 1971-74, vice president corp. planning and devel., assistant treasurer, 1974-79, senior vice president, assistant treasurer, 1979-80, president, chief executive officer, 1980—, director affiliate companies; director Robertshaw Controls Company, Crestar Fin. Corp.; trustee North Carolina State Pulp and Paper Foundation. Chairman annual fund Washington and Lee U., 1973-75; member, board of directors Young Men's Christian Association, Richmond, 1988—. Member Am. Paper Institute (board directors 1985—), University Virginia Alumni (board directors 1982—), National Council for Air and Stream Improvement (board govs. 1986—). Episcopalian. Clubs: West Point Country (past president), Commonwealth. Home: 1449 Floyd Avenue Richmond Virginia 23220 Office: Chesapeake Corp 1021 E Cary St Richmond Virginia 23218

FRAHM, DONALD ROBERT, insurance company executive; born Kansas City, Missouri, January 25, 1932; married Jean Phyllis Appleton; children: Heather, Timothy, Mark. Bachelor of Science in Business Administration, Washington University, St. Louis, 1953. Senior vice president CNA Insurance, Chicago, 1955-74; vice president Hartford Insurance Group, Connecticut, 1974-76, senior vice president, 1976-79, executive vice president, 1979-83; president and chief operating officer Hartford Insurance, Connecticut, 1983—. Served to lieutenant United States Army, 1953-55. Home: 29 Cheltenham Way Avon Connecticut 06001 Office: Hartford Ins Group Post Office Box 2999a Hartford Connecticut 06104

FRALEY, JOHN L., transportation company executive; born 1920; married. Assistant superintendent Rhyne Houser Manufacturing Company, 1939-40; secretary, treasurer, general manager, director Bucknit Processing Company, 1945; with Carolina Freight Corp., Cherryville, North Carolina, 1949—, assistant general sales manager, 1951-53, executive vice president, 1953-70, president, 1970-76, chief executive officer, 1976-84, vice chairman, 1976-87, chairman, 1987—. Office: Carolina Freight Corp North Carolina Highway 150 E Post Office Box 697 Cherryville North Carolina 28021 also: Carolina Freight Corp Post Office Box 545 Cherryville North Carolina 28021

FRANK, ANTHONY MELCHIOR, federal official, former financial executive; born Berlin, Germany, May 21, 1931; came to United States, 1937, naturalized, 1943; son of Lothar and Elisabeth (Roth) F.; married Gay Palmer, October 16, 1954; children: Tracy, Randall. Bachelor of Arts, Dartmouth College, 1953, Master of Business Administration, 1954; postgraduate in finance, University Vienna, 1956. Assistant to president, bond portfolio manager Glendale (California) Federal Savings Association, 1958-61; vice president, treasurer Far West Fin. Corp., Los Angeles, 1962; administrative vice president, vice president savings First Charter Fin. Corp., Beverly Hills, California, 1962-66; president State Mutual Savings and Loan Association, Los Angeles, 1966-68, Titan Group, Incorporated, New York City and Los Angeles, 1968-70, INA Properties, Incorporated, 1970-71; president Citizens Savings & Loan, San Francisco, 1971-73, vice chairman, chief executive officer, 1973-74; chairman board, president, chief executive officer FN Fin. Corp., from 1974; Postmaster General US Postal Service, 1988—; also president, vice chairman, industry director Federal Home Loan Bank San Francisco, 1972-77; trustee, treasurer Blue Shield of California, from 1976; director Allianz Insurance Company Am., Federal Home Loan Bank of San Francisco. Chairman, director California Housing Fin. Agency, Sacramento, 1978—; trustee Am. Conservatory Theater; chairman board visitors School Architecture and Planning University of California at Los Angeles, 1971—; board overseers Tuck School; del. California Democratic Convention, 1968. Served with Army of the United States, 1954-56. Member Chief Executives Organization, World Business Forum, Dartmouth Club Northern California, University Club (Los Angeles), Bohemian Club. Office: United States Postal Service Office of Postmaster General 475 L'Enfant Plaza W Southwest Washington District of Columbia 20260

FREEMAN, ROBERT MALLORY, banker; born Richmond, Virginia, May 10, 1941; son of G. Mallory and Mary (Mills) F.; married Margaret Rogers, July 2, 1960; children: Elizabeth C., Margaret M., Robert M. III, Cameron M. Graduate, University Virginia, 1963, Stonier Graduate School Banking, 1971. With Wachovia Bank & Trust Company, Raleigh, NC, 1963-71; vice president Signet Bank, Richmond, 1971-74, senior vice president, 1974-77, senior executive vice president, 1977-78, president, 1978; vice-chairman Signet Banking Corp., Richmond, 1978-89, chief executive officer, president, 1989, chief executive officer, chairman, 1990—; member, past chairman adv. board University Virginia McIntire School Commerce; board of directors Mast Card International. Trustee, past chairman United Way Greater Richmond; member adv. board Robert E. Lee council Boy Scouts Am.; board of directors Richmond Renaissance, Richmond Area Young

Men's Christian Association, U. Richmond; trustee Virginia Commonwealth U. Fund, Colgate Darden Grad. Business School Sponsors; member Capital Area Assembly. Member Virginia Bankers Association (president 1986-87), Association Reserve City Bankers, Association Bank Holding Companies (board directors), Am. Bankers Association (government relations council), Young Pres.'s Organization, University Virginia Alumni Association (board directors), Richmond Metropolitan Chamber of Commerce (past board directors), Bull and Bear Club, Commonwealth Club (board govs.), Country Club Virginia, Sigma Phi Epsilon. Office: Signet Banking Corp Post Office Box 25970 Richmond Virginia 23260

FRENCH, PHILIP FRANKS, agricultural cooperative corporate executive; born Albion, Indiana, June 16, 1932; son of Charles E. and Helene Alwilda (Franks) F.; married Jo Ann Pyle, November 21, 1951 (deceased July 1979); children: Douglas G., Randall B., Deborah A. French Farmer, Rebecca L. French Meidema; married Kathleen Louise DeBaun, March 22, 1980. Bachelor of Science in Commerce, International Business College, 1952. Assistant manager Clay County Farm Bureau Cooperative, Brazil, Ind., 1957-62; general manager Allen County Farm Bureau Cooperative, New Haven, Ind., 1962-66; manager member services Ind. Farm Bureau Cooperative, Indianapolis, 1966-70, assistant executive vice president, 1970-80, president, 1980—; member executive committee CF Industries, Long Grove, Illinois, 1975—; observer on board A.C. Toepfer, International, Hamburg, W. Germany, 1980—; president Countrymark, Incorporated, 1990. Member United States National Alcohol Fuels Commission, Washington, 1980-81; board of directors Ind. Institute Agriculture Food and Nutrition, Grad. Institute Cooperative Leadership, U. Missouri. Member National Council of Farmer Coops. (director), Farm Credit Leasing (director). Republican. Methodist. Club: Columbia (Indianapolis). Office: Indiana Farm Bur Coop Association 950 N Meridian St Indianapolis Indiana 46204

FRENZEL, OTTO N., III, banker; born 1930. Bachelor of Science, University Pennsylvania, 1954. With Merchants National Bank, Indianapolis, 1956—, executive vice president, 1965-70, president, 1970-73, chmn board of directors, 1973—, chief executive officer, 1979—. Served to 1st lieutenant United States Air Force, 1954-56. Office: Mchts National Corp 1 Merchants Plaza Suite 415E Indianapolis Indiana 46255

FRIEDMAN, MILTON, economist, educator emeritus, author; born Brooklyn, July 31, 1912; son of Jeno Saul and Sarah Ethel (Landau) F.; married Rose Director, June 25, 1938; children: Janet, David. Bachelor of Arts, Rutgers University, 1932, Doctor of Laws (honorary), 1968; Master of Arts, University Chicago, 1933; Doctor of Philosophy, Columbia University, 1946; Doctor of Laws (honorary), St. Paul's (Rikkyo) University, 1963, Loyola University, 1971, University New Hampshire, 1975, Harvard University, 1979, Brigham Young University, 1980, Dartmouth College, 1980, Gonzaga University, 1981; Doctor of Science (honorary), Rochester University, 1971; Doctor of Humane Letters (honorary), Rockford College, 1969, Roosevelt University, 1975, Hebrew Union College, Los Angeles, 1981; Doctor of Letters (honorary), Bethany College, 1971; Doctor of Philosophy (honorary), Hebrew University, Jerusalem, 1977; Doctor of Commercial Science (honorary), Francisco Marroquín University, Guatemala, 1978. Associate economist National Resources Committee, Washington, 1935-37; member research staff National Bureau Economic Research, New York City, 1937-45, 1948-81; visiting professor economics University Wisconsin, Madison, 1940-41; principal economist, tax research div. United States Treasury Department, Washington, 1941-43; associate director research, statistical research group, War Research div. Columbia University, New York City, 1943-45; associate professor economics and statistics University Minnesota, Minneapolis, 1945-46; associate professor economics University Chicago, 1946-48, professor economics, 1948-62, Paul Snowden Russell distinguished service professor economics, 1962-82, professor emeritus, 1983—; Fulbright lecturer Cambridge University, 1953-54; visiting Wesley Clair Mitchell research professor economics Columbia University, New York City, 1964-65; fellow Center for Advanced Study in Behavioral Sci., 1957-58; senior research fellow Stanford University, 1977—; member President's Commission All-Vol. Army, 1969-70, President's Commission on White House Fellows, 1971-74, President's Economic Policy Adv. Board, 1981-88; visiting scholar Federal Reserve Bank, San Francisco, 1977. Author: (with Carl Shoup and Ruth P. Mack) Taxing to Prevent Inflation, 1943, (with Simon S. Kuznets) Income from Independent Professional Practice, 1946, (with Harold A. Freeman, Frederic Mosteller, W. Allen Wallis) Sampling Inspection, 1948, Essays in Positive Economics, 1953, A Theory of the Consumption Function, 1957, A Program for Monetary Stability, 1960, Price Theory: A Provisional Text, 1962, (with Rose D. Friedman) Capitalism and Freedom, 1962, (with R.D. Friedman) Free To Choose, 1980, (with Rose D. Friedman) Tyranny of the Status Quo, 1984, (with Anna J. Schwartz) A Monetary History of the United States, 1867-1960, 1963, (with Schwartz) Monetary Statistics of the United States, 1970, (with Schwartz) Monetary Trends in the United States and the United Kingdom, 1982, Inflation: Causes and Consequences, 1963, (with Robert Roosa) The Balance of Payments: Free versus Fixed Exchange Rates, 1967, Dollars and Deficits, 1968, The Optimum Quantity of Money and Other Essays, 1969, (with Walter W. Heller) Monetary versus Fiscal Policy, 1969, A Theoretical Framework for Monetary Analysis, 1972, (with Wilbur J. Cohen) Social Security, 1972, An Economist's Protest, 1972, There's No Such Thing As A Free Lunch, 1975, Price Theory, 1976, (with Robert J. Gordon et al.) Milton Friedman's Monetary Framework, 1974, Tax Limitation, Inflation and the Role of Government, 1978, Bright Promises, Dismal Performance, 1983; editor: Studies in the Quantity Theory of Money, 1956; board editors Am. Econ. Rev, 1951-53, Econometrica, 1957-69; adv. board Journal Money, Credit and Banking, 1968—; columnist Newsweek mag, 1966-84, contributing editor, 1971-84;

contributor articles to professional journals. Decorated Grand Cordon of the 1st Class Order of the Sacred Treasure (Japan), 1986; recipient Nobelprize in econs., 1976; Pvt. Enterprise Exemplar medal Freedoms Foundation, 1978, Presidential medal of Freedom, 1988, National Medal of Sci., 1988; named Chicagoan of Year, Chicago Press Club, 1972, Educator of Year, Chicago United Jewish Fund, 1973. Fellow Institute Math. Statistics, Am. Statistical Association, Econometric Society; member National Acad. Sciences, Am. Econ. Association (member executive committee 1955-57, president 1967; John Bates Clark medal 1951), Am. Enterprise Institute (adv. board 1956-79), Western Econ. Association (president 1984-85), Royal Economic Society, Am. Philosophical Society, Mont Pelerin Society (board directors 1958-61, president 1970-72). Club: Quadrangle. Office: Stanford U Hoover Instn Stanford California 94305-6010

FRIERSON, DANIEL K., textile company executive; born 1942; married. Bachelor of Arts, University Virginia, 1964, Master of Business Administration, 1966. With Ti Caro Incorporated, 1963—, now chairman, chief executive officer; with Dixie Yarns Incorporated, Chattanooga, 1973—, vice president Candlewick div., 1975-77, executive vice president, then president Candlewick div., 1977-79, chairman, chief executive officer, director, 1979—. Office: Dixie Yarns Incorporated 1100 Watkins St Post Office Box 751 Chattanooga Tennessee 37401

FRISBEE, DON CALVIN, retired utilities executive; born San Francisco, December 13, 1923; son of Ira Nobles and Helen (Sheets) F.; married Emilie Ford, February 5, 1947; children: Ann, Robert, Peter, Dean. Bachelor of Arts, Pomona College, 1947; Master of Business Administration, Harvard University, 1949. Senior investment analyst, assistant cashier investment analysis department 1st Interstate Bank Oregon, N.A., Portland, 1949-52, now chairman board of directors; with PacifiCorp, Portland, 1953—, treasurer, 1958-60, then vice president, executive vice president, president, 1966-73, chief executive officer, 1973-89, chairman, 1973—; board of directors First Interstate Bancorp, Weyerhaeuser Company, Standard Insurance Company, Portland., Precision Castparts Corp., Portland, First Interstate Bank of Oregon, Portland. Chairman board trustees Reed College; trustee Safari Game Search Foundation, High Desert Mus., Greater Portland Trust for Higher Education; board of directors Oregon Community Foundation, Oregon Ind. College Foundation; member cabinet Columbia Pacific council Boy Scouts Am.; founder Oregon chapter Am. Leadership Forum; member executive committee Age of Pacific Project, Oregon Partnership for International Education 1st lieutenant Army of the United States, 1943-46. Member Japan-Western United States Association (executive council), Arlington Club, University Club, Multnomah Athletic Club. Office: PacifiCorp 825 NE Multnomah St Suite 1055 Portland Oregon 97232

FRIST, THOMAS FEARN, JR., hospital management company executive; born Nashville, August 12, 1938; son of Thomas Fearn and Dorothy (Cate) F.; married Patricia Champion, December 22, 1961; children: Trisha,

Thomas III, Bill. Bachelor of Science, Vanderbilt University, 1961; Doctor of Medicine, Washington University, 1966. Chairman, chief executive officer Hospital Corp. of Am., Nashville; executive vice president Hospital Corp. Am., Nashville, 1969-77, president, chief operating officer, 1977-82, president, chief executive officer, 1982-85, chairman, chief executive officer, 1985—, also board of directors; board of directors International Business Machines Corporation, Armonk, New York. Trustee Vanderbilt U., Nashville, 1987, United Way of Am., Alexandria, Virginia, 1987. Fellow Am. College Healthcare Executives (hon.); member Business Roundtable, Business Council. Presbyterian. Clubs: Belle Meade Country (Nashville); Links (New York City). Avocations: marathon running, tennis, skiing, flying. Office: Hosp Corp Am 1 Park Plaza Post Office Box 550 Nashville Tennessee 37202

FRONTIERE, GEORGIA, professional football team executive. married Carroll Rosenblum, July 7, 1966 (deceased); children: Dale Carroll, Lucia; married Dominic Frontiere. President, owner Los Angeles Rams, National Football League, 1979—. Board of directors Los Angeles Boys and Girls Club, Los Angeles Orphanage Guild, Los Angeles Blind Youth Foundation. Named Headliner of Year, Los Angeles Press Club, 1981. Office: Los Angeles Rams 2327 W Lincoln Avenue Anaheim California 92801

FTHENAKIS, EMANUEL JOHN, diversified aerospace company executive; born Greece, January 30, 1928; came to United States, 1952, naturalized, 1956; son of John and Evanthia (Magoulakis) F.; married Hermione Jane Coates, 1972; children: John, Basil. Diploma mechanical and electrical engineering, Tech. University Athens, 1951; Master of Science in Electrical Engineering, Columbia University, 1954; postgraduate, University Pennsylvania, 1961-62. Member tech. staff Bell Tel. Laboratories, 1952-57; director engineering missile and space div. G.East, Philadelphia, 1957-61; vice president, general manager space and re-entry div. Philco-Ford Company, Palo Alto, California, 1961-69; president International Telephone & Telegraph Corporation Aerospace Company, Los Angeles, 1969-70, Am. Satellite Corp., Germantown, Maryland, 1971-85; vice president Fairchild Industries, Germantown, 1971-80, senior vice president, 1980-84, executive vice president, 1984; president, chief executive officer Fairchild Industries, Chantilly, Virginia, 1985-86, chairman, chief executive officer, 1986-91; president, chief operating officer The Fairchild Corp., Chantilly, 1990-91; also board of directors Fairchild Corp., Chantilly; adj. professor University Maryland, 1981-84; member President's National Security Telecommunications Adv. Council, 1982-91. Author: A Manual of Satellite Communications, 1984; patentee in field. Member board visitors coll. engring. U. Maryland, 1980—; board of directors Challenger Center for Space Sci. and Education, 1988—, U. Maryland Foundation, 1989—; trustee Univs. Research Association, Incorporated, 1990—. Named Man of Year, Electronic & Aerospace Systems Conference, 1982. Fellow Institute of Electrical and Electronics Engineers; member American Institute of Aeronautics and Astronautics (associate), City Club of Washington, The

George Town Club. Greek Orthodox. Office: CEF Corp Post Office Box 59708 Potomac Maryland 20859-9708

FUCHS, VICTOR ROBERT, economics educator; born New York City, January 31, 1924; son of Alfred and Frances Sarah (Scheiber) F.; married Beverly Beck, August 29, 1948; children: Nancy, Fredric, Paula, Kenneth. Bachelor of Science, New York University, 1947; Master of Arts, Columbia University, 1951, Doctor of Philosophy, 1955. International fur broker 1946-50; lecturer Columbia University, New York City, 1953-54, instructor, 1954-55, assistant professor economics, 1955-59; associate professor economics New York University, 1959-60; program associate Ford Foundation Program in Economic Devel. and Administration, 1960-62; professor economics Grad. Center, City University of New York, 1968-74; professor community medicine Mount Sinai School Medicine, 1968-74; professor economics Stanford University and Stanford Medical School, 1974—, Henry J. Kaiser Junior professor, 1988—; vice president research National Bureau Economic Research, 1968-78, member senior research staff, 1962—; board of directors Principal Fin. Group. Author: The Economics of the Fur Industry, 1957; (with Aaron Warner) Concepts and Cases in Economic Analysis, 1958, Changes in the Location of Manufacturing in the United States Since 1929, 1962, The Service Economy, 1968, Production and Productivity in the Service Industries, 1969, Policy Issues and Research Opportunities in Industrial Organization, 1972, Essays in the Economics of Health and Medical Care, 1972, Who Shall Live? Health, Economics and Social Choice, 1975; (with Joseph Newhouse) The Economics of Physician and Patient Behavior, 1978, Economic Aspects of Health, 1982, How We Live, 1983, The Health Economy, 1986, Women's Quest for Economic Equality, 1988; contributor articles to professional journals. Served with United States Army Air Force, 1943-46. Fellow Am. Acad. of Arts and Sciences; member Am. Econ. Association, Institute of Medicine, National Acad. of Sciences, Am. Statistical Association, Sigma Xi, Beta Gamma Sigma. Home: 796 Cedro Way Stanford California 94305 Office: 204 Junipero Serra Boulevard Stanford California 94305

FULLER, HARRY LAURANCE, oil company executive; born Moline, Illinois, November 8, 1938; son of Marlin and Mary Helen (Ilsley) F.; married Nancy Lawrence, December 27, 1961; children: Kathleen, Laura, Randall. Bachelor of Science in Chemical Engineering, Cornell University, 1961; Juris Doctor, DePaul University, 1965. Bar: Illinois 1965. With Standard Oil Company (and affiliates), 1961—, sales manager, 1972-74, general manager supply, 1974-77; executive vice president Standard Oil Company (Amoco Oil Company div.), Chicago, 1977-78; president Amoco Oil Company, Chicago, 1978-81; executive vice president Standard Oil Company of Ind. (now Amoco Corp.), Chicago, 1981-83; president Amoco Corp., Chicago, 1983-91, chairman, president, chief executive officer, 1991—; board of directors Chase Manhattan Corp., Chase Manhattan Bank N.A., Abbott Laboratories. Board of directors Chicago

Rehabilitation Institute; trustee Northwestern U., Orchestral Association; board of directors Chicago United. Member Illinois Bar Association, Am. Petroleum Institute (board directors). Republican. Presbyterian. Clubs: Mid-Am, Chicago Golf, Chicago. Office: Amoco Corp 200 E Randolph Dr Chicago Illinois 60601

FULTON, PAUL, food products company executive, manufacturing company executive; born 1934; married. Bachelor of Science, University North Carolina, 1957. Vice president marketing services Hanes Corp., 1959-81; vice president, general manager L'eggs Products, 1969-72, president, 1972-76; executive vice president Hanes Corp., 1976-81; with Sara Lee Corp., 1981—, senior vice president, 1986—, then senior vice president, group executive, then executive vice president, to 1988, president, 1988—. With United States Navy, 1957-59. Office: Sara Lee Corp 3 First National Plaza Chicago Illinois 60602

FURLAUD, RICHARD MORTIMER, pharmaceutical company executive; born New York City, April 15, 1923; son of Maxime Hubert and Eleanor (Mortimer) F.; children: Richard Mortimer, Eleanor Jay, Elizabeth Tamsin; married Isabel Phelps Furlaud. Student, Institut Sillig, Villars, Switzerland; Bachelor of Arts, Princeton University, 1944; Bachelor of Laws, Harvard University, 1947. Bar: New York 1949. Associate Root, Ballantine, Harlan, Bushby & Palmer, 1947-51; with legal department Olin Mathieson Chemical Corp., 1955-56, assistant to executive vice president for finance, 1956-57, assistant president, 1957-59, vice president, 1959-64, general counsel, 1957-60, general manager, vice president international div., 1960-64, executive vice president, 1964-66; now director; president, director East R. Squibb & Sons, Incorporated, 1966-68; president, chief executive, director Squibb Beech-Nut, Incorporated (renamed Squibb Corp. 1971), Princeton, New Jersey, 1968-74; chairman, chief executive, director Squibb Corp. (merged with Bristol-Myers Company), New York City, 1974-89; president Bristol-Myers Company (renamed Bristol-Myers Squibb Company), New York City, 1989—, also board of directors; board of directors Mutual Benefit Life Insurance Company, Am. Express Company, Shearson Lehman Brothers Holdings, Incorporated, International Flavors & Fragrances, Incorporated. Member professional staff House of Representatives Committee Ways and Means, 1954; chairman board trustees Rockefeller U.; board mgrs. Memorial Sloan-Kettering Cancer Center 1st lieutenant, Judge Advocate General Corps United States Army, 1951-53. Member Association of Bar of City of New York, Pharmaceutical Manufacturers Association (director 1965-89), Council on Foreign Relations, Links Club, River Club. Home: 745 High Mount Road Palm Beach Florida 33480 Office: Bristol-Myers Squibb Company 345 Park Avenue New York New York 10154

GAGE, EDWIN C., III (SKIP GAGE), travel, hospitality, sales company executive; born Evanston, Illinois, November 1, 1940; son of Edwin Cutting and Margaret (Stackhouse) G.; married Barbara Ann Carlson, June 26, 1965; children—Geoff, Scott, Christine, Richard. Bachelor of Science in Business Administration, Northwestern University, 1963,

Master of Science in Journalism, 1965. Account executive Foote, Cone and Belding, 1965-68, director marketing devel. & research, 1968-70; Vice president direct marketing Carlson Marketing Group of Carlson Companies, Minneapolis, 1970-75, executive vice president, 1975-77, president, 1977-83, also board of directors; executive vice president Carlson Companies Incorporated, Minneapolis, 1983, president, chief operating officer, 1984-89, president, chief executive officer, 1989—; board of directors Marquette Bank Minneapolis, Super Value Stores, Incorporated. Lieutenant United States Navy. Member Young President Organization. Avocations: music folk and popular; tennis. Office: Carlson Cos Incorporated Carlson Parkway Post Office Box 59159 Minneapolis Minnesota 55459

GALBRAITH, JOHN KENNETH, retired economist; born Iona Station, Ontario, Canada, October 15, 1908; son of William Archibald and Catherine (Kendall) G.; married Catherine Atwater, September 17, 1937; children: Alan, Peter, James. Bachelor of Science, University Guelph, 1931, Doctor of Laws (honorary); Master of Science, University California, 1933, Doctor of Philosophy, 1934; postgraduate, Cambridge (England) University, 1937-38; Doctor of Laws (honorary), Bard College, University California, Miami University, University Massachusetts, University Mysore, Brandeis University, University Toronto, University Saskatchewan, University Michigan, University Durham, Rhode Island College, Boston College, Hobart and William Smith Colls., Albion College, Tufts University, Adelphi Suffolk College, Michigan State University, Louvain University, Cambridge University, University Paris, Carleton College, University Vermont, Queens University, Moscow State University, Harvard University, Smith College, others. Research fellow University California, 1931-34; instructor and tutor Harvard University, 1934-39; assistant professor economics Princeton University, 1939-42; economic adviser National Defense Adv. Commission, 1940-41; assistant administrator in charge price div. OPA, 1941-42, deputy administrator, 1942-43; member board of editors Fortune Magazine, 1943-48; lecturer Harvard University, 1948-49, professor economics, 1949-75, Paul M. Warburg professor economics, 1959-75, retired, 1975; hon. fellow Trinity College, Cambridge University; hon. professor University Geneva; United States ambassador to India, 1961-63. Author: numerous books including American Capitalism, 1952, A Theory of Price Control, 1952, The Great Crash, 1955, The Affluent Society, 1958, The Liberal Hour, 1960, Economic Development, 1963, The Scotch, 1964, The New Industrial State, 1967, Indian Painting, 1968, The Triumph, 1968, Ambassador's Journal, 1969, Economics, Peace and Laughter, 1971, A China Passage, 1973, Economics and the Public Purpose, 1973, Money: Whence It Came, Where It Went, 1975, The Age of Uncertainty, 1977, (with Nicole Salinger) Almost Everyone's Guide to Economics, 1978, Annals of an Abiding Liberal, 1979, The Nature of Mass Poverty, 1979, A Life in Our Times, 1981, The Anatomy of Power, 1983, The Voice of the Poor: Essays in Economic and Political Persuasion, 1983, A View From the Stands, 1986, Economics in Perspective: A Critical History, 1987, (with Stanislav Menshikov) Capitalism, Communism and Coexistence, 1988, (novel) A Tenured Professor, 1990; contributor to econ. and sci. journals. Director United States Strategic Bombing Survey, 1945; director Office of Economic Security Policy, State Department, 1946. Fellow Social Sci. Research Council, 1937-38; Recipient Medal Freedom, 1946. Fellow Am. Acad. Arts and Letters (president 1984-87); member American Association for the Advancement of Science, Am. Econ. Association (president 1972), Am. Agricultural Econ. Association, Ams. for Dem. Action (chairman 1967-68). Clubs: Century, Saturday. Home: 30 Francis Avenue Cambridge Massachusetts 02138 Office: Harvard U 207 Littaues Center 633 W 155th St Cambridge Massachusetts 02138

GALEF, ANDREW GEOFFREY, investment and manufacturing companies executive; born Yonkers, New York, November 3, 1932; son of Gabriel and Anne (Fruchter) G.; married Suzanne Jane Cohen, June 26, 1954 (divorced February 1963); children: Stephanie Anne Galef Streeter, Marjorie Lynn Galef England, Michael Lewis; married Billie Ruth Medlin, November 7, 1964 (divorced May 1988); children: Phyllis Anne Galef Bulmer, Catherine Marie; married Bronya Kester, December 18, 1988. Bachelor of Arts, Amherst College, 1954; Master of Business Administration, Harvard University, 1958. Vice president Kamkap, Incorporated, New York City, 1958-60; president Kemline California, San Jose, 1960-61, Zeigler Harris Corp., San Fernando, California, 1961-63; vice president Fullview Industries, Glendale, California, 1963-65; consultant Mordy & Company, Los Angeles, 1965-68; principal Grisanti & Galef, Incorporated, Los Angeles, 1968-84; president Spectrum Group, Incorporated, Los Angeles, 1978—; chairman, chief executive officer MagneTek, Incorporated, Los Angeles, 1984—; chairman board of directors Warnaco Incorporated, Los Angeles, Grantree Corp., Portland; board of directors Post Group, Incorporated, Hollywood, California; chief executive officer Petco Incorporated, San Diego. Member national adv. board Woodland Hills, California, 1984—. Served to captain United States Air Force, 1956-58. Office: Warnaco Incorporated 11150 Santa Monica Boulevard Los Angeles California 90025

GALLAS, DANIEL O., oil pipeline company executive. Bachelor of Science, University Oklahoma, 1954. With Atlantic Richfield Company, 1954—; senior vice president operations Arco Pipe Line Company, Independence, Kansas, 1985-86, president, 1986—, also board of directors. Served to 1st lieutenant Army of the United States. Office: ARCO Pipe Line Company 200 Arco Building Independence Kansas 67301

GALLO, ERNEST, vintner. Co-owner E & J Gallo Winery, Modesto, California. Office: E & J Gallo Winery Post Office Box 1130 Modesto California 95353

GALLO, JULIO, vintner. married Aileen Gallo; 1 child, Bob. Co-owner E & J Gallo Winery, Modesto, California. Office: E & J Gallo Winery 600 Yosemite Boulevard Modesto California 95354

GAMBILL, MALCOLM W., metal products company executive. married. Bachelor of Science, Yale University. With Harsco Corp., 1955—; vice president Heckett div., 1967-69, div. vice president international operations, 1969-73, div. senior vice president operations, 1973-85, div. president, 1975—, corp. executive vice president, 1984-85, corp. president, chief executive officer, 1987—, also director. Served to 1st lieutenant United States Marine Corps. Office: Harsco Corp Post Office Box 8888 Camp Hill Pennsylvania 17011

GAMMIE, ANTHONY PETRIE, pulp and paper manufacturing company executive; born London, December 17, 1934; married. With Bowater United Kingdom, from 1955, manager, 1970-75, chairman board, managing director, from 1975; with Bowater, Incorporated, Darien, Connecticut, 1978—, now chairman, president, chief executive officer, director. Office: Bowater Incorporated 1 Parklands Dr Box 4012 Darien Connecticut 06820

GANTZ, WILBUR HENRY, III, health care company executive; born York, Pennsylvania, December 5, 1937; son of Wilbur Henry and Flora Shaw (Kashner) G.; married Linda Theis, March 22, 1962; children: Matthew John, Leslie Shaw, Caroline Ruhl. Bachelor of Arts, Princeton University, 1959; Master of Business Administration, Harvard University, 1964. With Aetna Life Insurance Company, Hartford, Connecticut, 1959-62, 64-66; assistant to president Baxter International, Incorporated, Deerfield, Illinois, 1967-69; assistant general manager Baxter International, Incorporated, Mexico City, 1967-69; vice president Europe Baxter International, Incorporated, Brussels, 1969-75; president International div. Baxter International, Incorporated, Deerfield, Illinois, 1976-79; group vice president Baxter International, Incorporated, Deerfield, 1979, executive vice president, 1979-83, chief operating officer, 1983-87, president, 1987—; director Harris Bankcorp, Harris Trust and Savings Bank, W.W. Grainger, Incorporated. Trustee National College Education, Evanston, Illinois, Chicago Council on Foreign Relations, Episcopal Charities, Princeton U.; director Mus. Sci. and Industry, Chicago, Ravinia Foundation. Member Chicago Club, Commonwealth Club (secretary), Econ. Club, Commercial Club (Chicago), Sunset Ridge Country Club, Indian Hill Country Club. Office: Baxter International Incorporated 1 Baxter Parkway Deerfield Illinois 60015

GARRISON, U. EDWIN, space and defense products manufacturing company executive. Chairman, president, chief executive officer Thiokol Corp., Ogden, Utah. Office: Thiokol Corp 2475 Washington Boulevard Ogden Utah 84401

GARTENBERG, SEYMOUR LEE, recording company executive; born New York City, May 27, 1931; son of Morris and Anna (Banner) G.; married Anna Stassi, February 18, 1956; children: Leslie, Karen, Mark. Bachelor of Business Administration cum laude, City College of New York, 1952. Assistant controller Finlay Straus, Incorporated, New York City, 1950-56; controller Tappin's Incorporated, Newark, 1956; executive vice president Columbia House div. CBS, New York City, 1956-73; president CBS Toys Div., Cranbury, New Jersey, 1973-78; vice president CBS/

Columbia Group, New York City, 1978—; senior group vice president CBS Records Group, 1979—; executive vice president CBS Records Incorporated, 1987—. Vice president, board of directors City College Fund; treasurer, board of directors T.J. Martell Foundation Leukemia, Cancer and Acquired Immune Deficiency Syndrome Research. Member National Association Accts., Am. Management Association, Recording Industry Association Am. (board directors), Mill Island Civic Association. Office: 51 W 52nd St New York New York 10019

GATES, CHARLES CASSIUS, rubber company executive; born Morrison, Colorado, May 27, 1921; son of Charles Cassius and Hazel LaDora (Rhoads) G.; married June Scowcroft Swaner, November 26, 1943; children: Diane, John Swaner. Student, Massachusetts Institute of Technology, 1939-41; Bachelor of Science, Stanford University, 1943; Doctor of Engineering (honorary), Michigan Tech. University, 1975, Colorado School of Mines, 1985. With Copolymer Corp., Baton Rouge, 1943-46; with Gates Rubber Company, Denver, 1946—, vice president, 1951-58, executive vice president, 1958-61, chairman board, 1961—, now also chief executive officer; chairman board The Gates Corp., Denver, 1982—, chief executive officer, from 1982, also board of directors; board of directors Hamilton Brothers Petroleum Corp., Denver. President, trustee Gates Foundation; trustee Denver Mus. Natural History, California Institute Tech., Pasadena, Colorado chapter The Nature Conservancy; board of directors Colorado Wildlife Heritage Foundation. Recipient Community Leadership and Service award National Jewish Hospital, 1974; Mgmt. Man of Year award National Mgmt. Association, 1965; named March of Dimes Citizen of the West, 1987. Member Conference Board (director), Conquistadores del Cielo. Clubs: Denver Country, Cherry Hills Country, Denver, Outrigger Canoe, Waialae Country, Boone and Crockett, Club Ltd, Country Club of Colo, Roundup Riders of Rockies, Shikar-Safari International, Augusta National Golf, Castle Pines Golf, Old Baldy. Office: Gates Corp 900 S Broadway Denver Colorado 80209

GATES, WILLIAM HENRY, software company executive; born Seattle, October 28, 1955; son of William H. and Mary M. (Maxwell) G. Graduate high school, Seattle, 1973; student, Harvard University, 1975. With MITS, from 1975; chairman board Microsoft Corp., Redmond, Washington, 1976—, now chief executive officer. Recipient Howard Vollum award, Reed College, Portland, Oregon, 1984. Office: Microsoft Corp 16011 NE 36th Way Redmond Washington 98073-9717

GEIER, JAMES AYLWARD DEVELIN, manufacturing company executive; born Cincinnati, December 29, 1925; son of Frederick V. and Amey (Develin) G.; children: Deborah Anne, James Develin, Aylward Whittier. Student, Williams College, 1947-50; honorary doctorate, University Cincinnati, Wilmington College, Cincinnati Tech. College. With Cincinnati Milacron Incorporated, 1951—, vice president, 1964, director, 1966, executive vice president, 1969, president, chief executive officer, 1970-90, chairman executive committee, 1991—; board of directors Clark Equipment Company,

USX Corp., Unison Telecommunications Service, BDM Holdings, Incorporated. Def. policy adv. committee on trade Labor-Industry Coalition for International Trade; commissioner Hamilton County Park District; trustee Cincinnati Mus. Natural History, Rensselaer Polytechnical Institute, 1987—; adv. board Cincinnati Council World Affairs; member Kenton County Airport Board; president Children's Home Cincinnati, 1990—; board of directors Cincinnati chapter American Red Cross; adv. council Cincinnati Zoo. With United States Army Air Force, 1944-46. Member Association Manufacturing Tech. (chairman 1988-89), Conference Board, Mfrs.' Alliance Productivity and Innovation (executive committee), Management Executives Society (executive committee, chairman 1991—), United States Chamber of Commerce (board directors), Commercial Club, Commonwealth Club, Queen City Club, Camargo Club. Republican. Office: Cincinnati Milacron Incorporated River Center Suite 800 50 E River Center Boulevard Covington Kentucky 41011

GEIER, PHILIP HENRY, JR., advertising executive; born Pontiac, Michigan, February 22, 1935; son of Philip Henry and Jane (Gillen) G.; married Faith Power, children—Hope, Johanna Geier. Bachelor of Arts, Colgate University, 1957; Master of Science, Columbia University, 1958. With McCann-Erickson, Incorporated, Cleveland, 1958-60, New York City, 1960-68; chairman McCann-Erickson International United Kingdom Company, London, 1969-73; executive vice president McCann-Erickson Europe, 1973-75; vice chairman international operations McCann Worldwide, London, 1973-75; vice chairman international Interpublic Group of Companies, Incorporated, New York City, 1975-77; president, chief operating officer Interpublic Group of Companies, Incorporated, 1977-80, chairman, chief executive officer, 1980—, president, 1985—; director EAC Industries, Incorporated. Board of directors School Am. Ballet; trustee New York Foundling Hospital, Boy's Club New York, MU of Delta Kappa Epsilon Foundation; dean's adv. council Columbia Business School; president's council Marymount Manhattan College. Member Am. Association Advertising Agys. (committee agy. management), Advertising Council (vice chairman fin. committee), Coalition Service Industries. Clubs: Doubles (New York City); River (New York City); Sloane (London); Hurlingham (London). Office: Interpub Group Cos Incorporated 1271 Avenue of the Americas New York New York 10020

GEISEL, MARTIN SIMON, college dean, educator; born Grand Rapids, Michigan, November 27, 1941; son of Bernard and Jeanette (Rozema) G.; married Susan Amendola, September 28, 1963 (divorced 1974); children: Sandra L., Matthew B.; married Kathy E. Bell, Jul. 25, 1987. Bachelor of Science in Management Science, Case Institute Tech., 1963; Master of Business Administration in Business Economics, University Chicago, 1965, Doctor of Philosophy in Business Economics, 1970. Process engineer E.I. DuPont de Nemours, East Chicago, Ind., 1963-65; assistant then associate professor Carnegie-Mellon University, Pittsburgh, 1968-75; associate professor grad. school management University Rochester,

New York, 1975-79, associate dean for acad. affairs, 1979-85; dean school management University Texas at Dallas, Richardson, 1985-87; dean, professor Owen grad. school management Vanderbilt University, Nashville, 1987—. Contributor articles to professional journals. Board of directors National Coalition for Advanced Mfg., Washington, 1990—, acad. adv. board Grad. Business Foundation, Farifield, Connecticut, 1991; board visitors Edwin L. Cox School Business Southern Methodist U., Dallas, 1988-90; member migratory waterfowl stamp adv. committee, State of New York, 1984-85; board of directors Am. Assembly Collegiate Schools Business, St. Louis, 1987-88. Member Am. Statistical Association, Econometric Society, Society International Business Fellows, Fin. Executives Institute, University Club, Beta Gamma Sigma (board govs. 1990). Avocations: fishing, hunting. Home: 453 Beech Creek N Brentwood Tennessee 37027 Office: Vanderbilt U Owen Grad School of Management 401 21st Avenue S Nashville Tennessee 37203

GEITHNER, PAUL HERMAN, JR., banker; born Philadelphia, June 7, 1930; son of Paul Herman and Henriette Antonine (Schuck) G.; married Irmgard Hagedorn, September 6, 1956; children: Christina, Amy, Paul. Bachelor of Arts cum laude, Amherst College, 1952; Master of Business Administration with distinction, University Pennsylvania, 1957. Sec.-treas. Ellicott Machine Company, Baltimore, 1957-68; successively vice president, senior vice president, executive asst.to the chairman, First Virginia Banks, Incorporated, Falls Church, 1968-85, president, chief administrative officer, 1985—, also board of directors, vice chairman, 1986—; president First Virginia Life Insurance Company, 1974—, First Virginia Bank; board of directors First Virginia Mortgage Company. Executive vice president, board of directors Fairfax (Virginia) Symphony Orchestra, 1988—; board of directors Virginia College Fund, 1987—; trustee Virginia Banker School Bank Mgmt., 1988—, Bridgewater College, 1989—. Lieutenant United States Naval Reserve, 1952-55. Home: 5406 Colchester Meadow Lane Fairfax Virginia 22030 Office: 1st Va Banks Incorporated 6400 Arlington Boulevard Falls Church Virginia 22046

GELB, RICHARD LEE, pharmaceutical corporation executive; born New York City, June 8, 1924; son of Lawrence M. and Joan F. (Bove) G.; married Phyllis L. Nason, May 5, 1951; children: Lawrence N., Lucy G., Jane E., James M. Student, Phillips Academy, 1938-41; Bachelor of Arts, Yale, 1945; Master of Business Administration with Distinction, Harvard University, 1950. Joined Clairol, Incorporated, New York City, 1950, president, 1959-64; executive vice president Bristol-Myers Company, 1965-67, president, 1967-76, chief executive officer, 1972—, chairman board, 1976—; board of directors New York Times Company, New York Life Insurance Company, Federal Reserve Bank New York; member policy committee Business Roundtable; active member Business Council; trustee Committee for Economic Devel.; member Conference Board; partner New York City Partnerships, Incorporated. Charter trustee Phillips Acad., Andover; director Lincoln Center for Performing Arts; member, former director Council Foreign Rels.; vice chairman board overseers, board mgrs. Memorial Sloan-Kettering Cancer Center; chairman board mgrs. Sloan Kettering Institute Cancer Research; chairman New York State Crime Control Planning Board; vice chairman, trustee New York City Police Foundation; trustee New York Racing Association. Home: 1060 Fifth Avenue New York New York 10128 Office: Bristol-Myers Squibb Company 345 Park Avenue New York New York 10154

GEORGES, JOHN A., paper company executive; born El Paso, February 24, 1931; son of John A. and Opal (Biffle) G.; married Zephera M. Givas, June 15, 1952; children: Mark, Andrew, Elizabeth. Bachelor of Science, University Illinois, 1951; Master of Science in Business Adminstrn, Drexel University, 1957. Executive vice president international and wood products and resources International Paper Company, New York City, 1979, vice chairman, 1980, president, chief operating officer, 1981-85, chairman, chief executive officer, 1985—, also director; board of directors Warner Lambert Company, New York Stock Exchange, Federal Reserve Bank New York. Director Business Council New York State. Served with United States Army, 1953-55. Club: New York Yacht. Office: International Paper Realty Corp 2 Manhattanville Road Purchase New York 10577

GERSTNER, LOUIS VINCENT, JR., diversified company executive; born New York City, March 1, 1942; son of Louis Vincent and Marjorie (Rutan) G.; married Elizabeth Robins Link, November 30, 1968; children—Louis, Elizabeth. Bachelor of Arts, Dartmouth College, 1963; Master of Business Administration, Harvard University, 1965. Director McKinsey & Company, New York City, 1965-78; executive vice president Am. Express Company, New York City, 1978-81; vice chairman board Am. Express Company, 1981-83, chairman executive committee, 1983-85, president, 1985-89, also board of directors; chairman, chief executive officer RJR Nabisco Incorporated, New York City, 1989—; board of directors Caterpillar Incorporated, The New York Times Company, American Telephone and Telegraph Company, Bristol-Myers Squibb Company. Board of directors Memorial Sloan Kettering Hospital, 1978-89; trustee Joint Council on Economic Education, 1975-87, chairman 1983-85; board of directors Business Roundtable, Lincoln Center for Performing Arts; board of directors Am-China Society. Member Council Foreign Relations, Grocery Mfs. Am., Next Century Schs. Foundation, New York City Partnership. Office: RJR Nabisco Incorporated 1301 Avenue of the Americas New York New York 10019

GIBSON, VERNA KAYE, retail company executive; born Charleston, West Virginia, June 22, 1942; daughter of Carl W. and Virginia E. (Meyers) LeMasters; married James E. Gibson, April 28, 1962; children: Kelly, Elizabeth. Graduate with honors in fashion marketing and retailing, Marshall University, Huntington, West Virginia, 1962. Buyer, merchandise manager Smart Shops, Huntington, West Virginia, 1965-71; trainee to assistant buyer Limited Stores, Incorporated, Columbus, Ohio, 1971-72, associate buyer to buyer, 1972-77, div. merchandise manager, 1977-79, vice president sportswear, 1979-82, executive vice president general, merchandise manager, 1982-85; president Limited Stores, Incorporated, Columbus, 1985—; director Federal Reserve Board, Cleveland. Board of directors Society of Yeager Scholars, Marshall U. Recipient Harry L. Wexner award Limited Stores, Incorporated, 1983, Distinguished Alumni award Marshall University Alumni Association, 1986; named Merchandiser of Year, Apparel Merchandising, 1986. Member Am. Marketing Association (Marketer of Year Columbus chapter 1990). Office: Limited Stores Incorporated Post Office Box 16528 Columbus Ohio 43216

GIDWITZ, GERALD, cosmetics company executive; born Memphis, 1906; married; 5 children. Bachelor of Arts, University Chicago, 1927. Chairman board, chairman executive committee Helene Curtis Industries, Incorporated, Chicago. Trustee Roosevelt U., Auditorium Theatre Council; board of directors Chicago Crime Commission; board of directors Jamestown Foundation. Member Illinois Manufacturing Association (past board directors). Office: Helene Curtis Industries Incorporated 325 N Wells St Chicago Illinois 60610

GIDWITZ, RONALD J., personal care products company executive; born Chicago, 1945. Graduate, Brown University, 1967. With Helene Curtis Industries, Incorporated, Chicago, 1968—, president, 1979—, chief executive officer, 1985—, also board of directors; board of directors Continental Materials Corp., Am. National Can Company. Board of directors Field Mus. National History, Lyric Opera Chicago; chairman Economic Devel. Commission City of Chicago; member executive board library council Northwestern U.; member national board of directors, trustee Boys Club Am.; trustee Lincoln Acad. Illinois; Republican committeeman 43d Ward Chicago. Member Chicago Association Commerce and Industry (board directors), Chicago Council Foreign Relations. Office: Helene Curtis Industries Incorporated 325 N Wells St Chicago Illinois 60610

GILBERT, ROY W., JR., banker; born 1937; married. Bachelor of Arts, Davidson College, 1959; Master of Business Administration, Samford University, 1968. With SouthTrust Bank of Alabama, Birmingham, 1959—, former chairman, chief executive officer, director; now president, chief operating officer, director SouthTrust Corp., Birmingham. Served with United States Army, 1960-62. Office: SouthTrust Corp 420 N 20th St Post Office Box 2554 Birmingham Alabama 35290

GILL, DANIEL E., optical manufacturing company executive; born Ziegler, Illinois, June 24, 1936; son of Herron E. Gill; married Dorothy Ann McBride, May 28, 1960. Bachelor of Science in Fin., Northwestern University, 1958. With Abbott Laboratories, Chicago, 1965-78, corp. vice president, president hospital products div., 1976-78; group vice president Soflens Products div. Bausch & Lomb, Rochester, New York, 1978-80, president, chief operating officer, 1980-81; president, chief executive officer Bausch & Lomb, Rochester, 1981-82, president, 1982-86, chairman, 1982—, chief executive officer, 1986—, also board of directors. Office: Bausch & Lomb Incorporated 1 Lincoln First Square Box 54 Rochester New York 14601

GILLESPIE, ROBERT WAYNE, banker; born Cleveland, March 26, 1944; son of Robert Walton and Eleanore (Parsons) G.; married Ann. L. Wible, June 17, 1967; children: Laura, Gwen. Bachelor of Arts, Ohio Wesleyan University, 1966; Master of Business Administration, Case Western Reserve University, 1968; postgraduate, Harvard University, 1979. Credit analyst Society National Bank, Cleveland, 1968-70, vice president, 1970-76, senior vice president, 1976-79; executive vice president Society Nat Bank, Cleveland, 1979-81; vice-chairman, chief operating officer Society National Bank, Cleveland, 1981-83, president, chief operating officer, 1983-85, chief executive officer, 1985—, president, 1987—, chairman, 1988—; chairman North Coast Devel. Corp. Trustee Case Western Reserves U., Ohio Wesleyan U., University Hosps. of Cleveland, Greater Cleveland Roundtable, Cleveland Tomorrow. Office: Society Corp 800 Superior Avenue Cleveland Ohio 44114

GILMARTIN, JOHN A., medical products company executive; born 1942. Bachelor of Science, Penn. State University, 1965; Master of Business Administration, Havard University, 1967. With Pfizer Incorporated, 1966-79, vice president, group controller 1967-79; with Millipore Corp., 1979—, controller, senior vice president, president, chief executive officer, then also chairman board, chief operating officer, 1989—. Office: Millipore Corp 80 Ashby Road Post Office Box 255 Bedford Massachusetts 01730

GILMARTIN, RAYMOND V., health care products company executive; born Washington, March 6, 1941; married Gladys Higham; 3 children. Bachelor of Science in Elect. Engineering, Union College, 1963; Master of Business Administration, Harvard University, 1968. Senior consultant Arthur D. Little Incorporated, 1968-76; vice president corp. planning Becton Dickinson & Company, Paramus, New Jersey, 1976-79, president Becton Dickinson div., 1979-87, group president, 1982-83, senior vice president, 1983-86, executive vice president, 1986-87; president Becton Dickinson & Company, Franklin Lakes, New Jersey, 1987—, chief executive officer, 1989—, also board of directors. Trustee Valley Hospital, Ridgewood, New Jersey; executive board, vice president Bergen council Boy Scouts Am., New Jersey; board of directors United Way Bergen County, New Jersey. Member Health Industry Manufacturers Association (board directors). Office: Becton Dickinson & Company 1 Becton Dr Franklin Lakes New Jersey 07417

GINN, SAM L., telephone company executive; born St. Clair, Alabama, April 3, 1937; son of James Harold and Myra Ruby (Smith) G.; married Meriann Lanford Vance, February 2, 1963; children: Matthew, Michael, Samantha. Bachelor of Science, Auburn University, 1959; postgraduate, Stanford University Graduate School Business, 1968. Various positions American Telephone and Telegraph Company, 1960-78; with Pacific Telephone & Telegraph Company, 1978—; executive vice president network Pacific Telephone

& Telegraph Company, San Francisco, 1979-81, executive vice president services, 1981-82, executive vice president network services, 1982, executive vice president, strategic planning and administration, 1983, vice chairman board, strategic planning and administration, 1983-84; vice chairman board, group vice president PacTel Companies Pacific Telesis Group, San Francisco, 1984-86; vice chairman board, president, chief executive officer PacTel Corp. Pacific Telesis Group, San Francisco, 1986; president, chief operating officer Pacific Telesis Group, San Francisco, 1987-88, chairman, chief executive officer, 1988—; member adv. board Sloan program Stanford University Grad. School Business, 1978-85, member international adv. council Institute International Studies; board director 1st Interstate Bank. Trustee Mills College, 1982—. Served to captain United States Army, 1959-60. Sloan fellow, 1968. Republican. Clubs: Blackhawk Country (Danville, California); World Trade, Pacific-Union; Rams Hill Country (Borrego Springs, California), Bankers. Office: Pacific Telesis Group 130 Kearny St San Francisco California 94108

GIVENS, DAVID W., banker; born Gary, Indiana, March 18, 1932; son of James M. Givens; married Betty J. Davis, July 3, 1955; children: Kathryn D., David W. Jr. Bachelor of Arts, Wabash College, 1956; Juris Doctor, Ind. University, 1960. Partner Krieg, DeVault, Alexander & Capehart, Indianapolis, 1960-74; vice president, general counsel Ind. National Bank, Indianapolis, 1974-76, senior vice president, general counsel, 1976-79, executive vice president, 1979—; vice chairman Ind. National Corp., Indianapolis, 1979-85; president Ind. National Corp. (name now INB Fin. Corp.), Indianapolis, 1985—; board of directors, member executive committee VISA/U.S.A.; board of directors VISA International. Board advisers, board visitors Ind. U. School Law; vice chairman adv. council Conner Prairie Settlement; board of directors, chairman Greater Indianapolis Progress Committee; trustee, chairman executive committee Wabash College With United States Army, 1953-54. Member American Bar Association, Ind. Bar Association, Indianapolis Bar Association, Indianapolis Bar Foundation, Ind. Legal Foundation (board directors), Association Bank Holding Companies, Association Reserve City Bankers, State Ind. Board Law Examiners, Am. Bankers Association. Office: INB Fin Corp 1 Indiana Square # 501 Indianapolis Indiana 46266

GLASS, DAVID D., department store company executive; born Liberty, Missouri, 1935; married. General manager Crank Drug Company, 1957-67; vice president Consumers Markets Incorporated, 1967-76; executive vice president fin. Wal-Mart Stores Incorporated, Bentonville, Arkansas, to 1976, vice chairman, chief fin. officer, 1976-84, president, 1984—, chief operating officer, 1984-88, chief executive officer, 1988—, also board of directors. Office: Wal-Mart Stores Incorporated 702 Southwest 8th St Bentonville Arkansas 72716

GLASSER, JAMES J., leasing company executive; born Chicago, June 5, 1934; son of Daniel D. and Sylvia G.; married Louise D. Rosenthal, April 19, 1964; children: Mary, Emily, Daniel. Bachelor of Arts, Yale

University, 1955; Juris Doctor, Harvard University, 1958. Bar: Illinois 1958. Assistant states attorney Cook County, Illinois, 1958-61; member executive staff GATX Corp., Chicago, 1961-69; president GATX Corp., 1974—, chairman board, chief executive officer, 1978—, also director; general manager Infilco Products Company, 1969-70; vice president GATX Leasing Corp., San Francisco, 1970-71, president, 1971-74; director Harris Bankcorp, Incorporated, Harris Trust & Savings Bank, Mutual Trust Life Insurance Company, Oak Brook, Illinois, B.F. Goodrich Company, Stone Container Corp. Board of directors Northwestern Memorial Hospital, Chicago, Michael Reese Hospital and Medical Center.; trustee Chicago Zool. Society. Member Econ. Club Chicago, Chi Psi. Clubs: Casino (Chicago), Chicago (Chicago), Racquet (Chicago), Tavern (Chicago), Commercial (Chicago); Onwentsia (Lake Forest, Illinois), Winter (Lake Forest, Illinois); Lake Shore Country (Glencoe, Illinois). Home: 644 E Spruce Avenue Lake Forest Illinois 60045 Office: GATX Corp 120 S Riverside Plaza Chicago Illinois 60606

GLEASON, A. M., business executive; born 1930; married. Student, University Oregon. With Pacific Power & Light Company Incorporated, Portland, Oregon, from 1949, assistant to vice president, 1952-65, manager pub. accounts, 1965-68, vice president, 1968-73; president Pacific Telecom, Incorporated (formerly Telephone Utilities, Incorporated), Vancouver, Washington, 1973-82, chairman, from 1982, chief executive officer, 1973-82, also board of directors; president, chief executive officer parent company, PacifiCorp, Portland; board of directors Comdial Corp., Blount Incorporated, Tektronix, Legacy Health Can. Office: Pacificorp 700 NE Multnomah Portland Oregon 97232

GOESSEL, WILLIAM W., heavy equipment manufacturing company executive; born 1927; married. Bachelor of Science, Carthage College, 1950. Executive vice president Beloit Corp., 1950-52; president, chief operating officer Harnischfeger Corp. now Harnischfeger Industries Incorporated, Milwaukee, 1982-86, chief executive officer, 1982—, chairman, 1986—. Office: Harnischfeger Industries Incorporated Post Office Box 554 Milwaukee Wisconsin 53201 also: 13400 Bishops Lane Brookfield Wisconsin 53005

GOIZUETA, ROBERTO CRISPULO, food and beverage company executive; born Havana, Cuba, November 18, 1931; came to United States, 1964; son of Crispulo D. and Aida (Cantera) G.; married Olga T. Casteleiro, June 14, 1953; children: Roberto S., Olga M., Javier C. Bachelor of Science, BChemE, Yale University, 1953. Process engineer Industrial Corp. Tropics, Havana, 1953-54; tech. director Coca-Cola Company, Havana, 1954-60; assistant to senior vice president Coca-Cola Company, Nassau, Bahamas, 1960-64; assistant to vice president research and devel. Coca-Cola Company, Atlanta, 1964-66, vice president engineering, 1966-74, senior vice president, 1974-75, executive vice president, 1975-79, vice chairman, 1979-80, president, chief operating officer, 1980-81, chairman board, chief executive officer, 1981—; board of directors SunTrust Banks, Incorporated, Ford Motor

Company, Sonat, Incorporated, Eastman Kodak; trustee Emory University, 1980—, The Am. Assembly, 1979—, Boys Clubs Am., Robert W. Woodruff Arts Center, 1990—. Member Business Council. Member Business Roundtable Policy Committee, Points of Light Initiative Foundation (founding director). Office: Coca-Cola Company Post Office Drawer 1734 Atlanta Georgia 30301

GOLD, STANLEY P., chemical company executive, manufacturing company executive; born 1942. Bachelor of Arts, University California, 1964; Juris Doctor, University Southern California, 1967. Partner Gary Tyre and Brown, 1967—, Shamrock Holdings Incorporated, 1985—; also chairman, chief executive officer Enterra Corp., director; president, chief executive officer Shamrock Holdings. Office: Shamrock Holdings 4444 Lakeside Dr Burbank California 91510 also: Enterra Corp Post Office Box 1535 Houston Texas 77251

GOLDRESS, JERRY E., diversified business executive. Chairman, chief executive officer Best Products Company, Richmond, Virginia, 1988—; also chairman Wherehouse Entertainment Incorporated, Torrance, California, Cardis Corp., Buena Park, California; chairman L.B. Foster Company, Pittsburgh.

GOLDSMITH, BRAM, banker; born Chicago, February 22, 1923; son of Max L. and Bertha (Gittelsohn) G.; married Elaine Maltz; children: Bruce, Russell. Student, Herzl Junior College, 1940, University Illinois, 1941-42. Assistant vice president Pioneer-Atlas Liquor Company, Chicago, 1945-47; president Winston Lumber and Supply Company, East Chicago, Ind., 1947-50; vice president Medal Distilled Products, Incorporated, Beverly Hills, California, 1950-75; president Buckeye Realty and Management Corp., Beverly Hills, 1952-75; executive vice president Buckeye Construction Company, Incorporated, Beverly Hills, 1952-75; chairman board, chief executive officer City National Corp., Beverly Hills, 1975—; chairman, chief executive officer City National Bank, 1975—; director City National Bank, Beverly Hills, 1964—, chairman board, chief executive officer, 1975—; board of directors Cedars/Sinai Medical Center; past director Los Angeles branch San Francisco Federal Reserve Bank. President Jewish Federation Council of Greater Los Angeles, 1969-70; national chairman United Jewish Appeal, 1970-74; regional chairman United Crusade, 1976; co-chairman board of directors National Conference of Christians and Jews; chairman Am. committee for Weizman Institute Sci. Served with Signal Corps United States Army, 1942-45. Member Los Angeles Philharmonic Association (vice president, board directors). Jewish. Clubs: Hillcrest Country, Masons (Los Angeles), Balboa Bay. Office: City National Corp 400 N Roxbury Dr Beverly Hills California 90210

GOLDSMITH, ROBERT HOLLOWAY, manufacturing company executive; born Buffalo, May 15, 1930; son of Henry Stanhope and Frances Edmere (Shickluna) G.; married Diane Cecilia Kramer, June 27, 1957 (divorced September 1981); children: Janeen, Daena, Maria, Lisa, Joseph; married Catherine Helen Draper, October 3, 1981; stepchildren: Deborah, Lori.

BME, University Buffalo, 1951; Master of Business Administration, Xavier University, 1960. Engineer Allied Chemical and Dye Corp., Buffalo, 1951-54; successively engineer, manager, general manager, vice president and general manager aircraft engine projects, vice president strategic planning, vice president and general manager gas turbine div. General Electric Company, various, 1956-81; senior vice president aerospace and industrial Pneumo Corp., Boston, 1981-82; consultant Robert H. Goldsmith Associates, Gloucester, Massachusetts, 1982-83; vice chairman, chief operations officer Precision Forge Company, Oxnard, California, 1983-84; senior vice president operations Rohr Industries, Incorporated, Chula Vista, California, 1984-88, senior vice president business operations, 1988—, also board of directors. Contributor articles to professional journals. Member president's council San Diego State U., 1987—; board of directors United Way, San Diego, California, 1987—. With United States Army, 1954-56. Republican. Roman Catholic. Avocations: golf, reading, do-it-yourself house projects. Office: Rohr Industries Incorporated Foot of H St Post Office Box 878 Chula Vista California 92012

GOLDSTEIN, STANLEY P., retail company executive; born 1934; married. Graduate, Wharton School, University Pennsylvania, 1955. Vice president Mark Seven, Incorporated, 1955-61, Francis I. DuPont, 1961-63; executive vice president Consumer Value Stores, 1963-69; president CVS div. Melville Corp., Harrison, New York, 1969-71, corp. vice president, president CVS div., 1971-85, then corp. executive vice president, 1985-87, president, 1986—, chairman, chief executive officer, 1987—, also board of directors. Office: Melville Corp 3000 Westchester Avenue Harrison New York 10528

GOLUB, HARVEY, financial services company executive; born New York City, April 16, 1939; son of Irving and Pearl (Fader) G.; married Roberta Elizabeth Glunts, August 16, 1980; 1 child, Joshua; children from previous marriage: Matthew, Amy, Jeremy. Bachelor of Science, New York University, 1961. Junior partner McKinsey & Company Incorporated, New York City, 1967-74, senior partner, 1977-83; president Shulman Air Freight, New York City, 1974-77; senior officer Am. Express Company, New York City, 1983-84; chairman, chief executive officer IDS Fin. Corp., Minneapolis, 1984—; vice chairman Am. Express Company, New York City, 1990—. Office: IDS Fin Corp 2900 IDS Tower 10 Minneapolis Minnesota 55440

GOODALE, ROBERT SELDON, food retailing executive; born Marshalltown, Iowa, December 12, 1933; son of Ralph Selson and Clara Marie (Zuercher) G.; married Donna Jane Nelson, August 20, 1956 (divorced July 1972); children: Rob Donald, Elizabeth Anne, Susan Marie; married Janet Marie Nunn, September 30, 1973; children: Rebecca Marie, Jennifer Mae, Amy Joyce. Bachelor of Science, Iowa State University, 1955; Master of Business Administration, University Kansas, 1980. Marketing manager Fairmont Foods Company, Omaha, 1968-70, national accounts manager, 1970-71, sales manager, 1971-72, marketing manager snack div., 1972-76, sales manager dairy group, 1976-77; director of dairy Fleming Foods,

Topeka, 1977-80; senior vice president Harris-Teeter Super Markets, Charlotte, North Carolina, 1980-82, executive vice president, 1982-85, president, chief executive officer, 1985—, also board of directors; board of directors Harris-Teeter Properties, Charlotte. President Florence Crittenton Services, Charlotte, 1985-87; chairman Charlotte/Mecklenburg Pub. Broadcasting Authority, Charlotte, 1986-87; pres.-elect Charlotte Junior Achivement, 1987; board mgrs. Charlotte Young Men's Christian Association, treasurer, 1985-87; chairman Amethyst Foundation, Charlotte, 1987. Recipient Cardinal Key award Iowa State University, Ames, 1955, Circle of Excellence award Leadership Charlotte, 1984, Old Master award Purdue University, West Lafayette, Ind., 1985. Member Charlotte Chamber of Commerce (executive committee 1987). Republican. Episcopalian. Avocations: backpacking, skiing, physical fitness. Office: Harris/Teeter Supermarkets Incorporated 7500 E Independence Boulevard Post Office Box 33129 Charlotte North Carolina 28212

GOODES, MELVIN RUSSELL, manufacturing company executive; born Hamilton, Ontario, Canada, April 11, 1935; son of Cedric Percy and Mary Melba (Lewis) G.; married Arlene Marie Bourne, February 23, 1963; children: Melanie, Michelle, David. Bachelor in Commerce, Queen's University, Kingston, Ontario, Can., 1957; Master of Business Administration, University Chicago, 1960. Research associate Can. Economic Research Associates, Toronto, Ontario, 1957-58; market planning coordinator Ford Motor Company Can., Oakville, Ontario, 1960-64; assistant to vice president O'Keefe Breweries, Toronto, 1964-65; manager new product devel. Adams Brands div. Warner-Lambert Can., Scarborough, Ontario, 1965-68; area manager Warner-Lambert International, Toronto, 1968-69; regional director confectionary operations Warner-Lambert Europe, Brussels, 1969-70; president Warner-Lambert Mexico, 1970-76; president Pan-Am. zone Warner-Lambert International, Morris Plains, New Jersey, 1976-77, president Pan-Am. and Asian zone, 1977-79; president consumer products div. Warner-Lambert Company, Morris Plains, New Jersey, 1979-81, senior vice president, president consumer products group, 1981-83, executive vice president, president United States operations, 1984-85, president, chief operating officer, 1985—, also board of directors; board of directors Chemical Banking Corp., Chemical Bank, Unisys; member executive adv. council National Center Ind. Retail Pharmacy, 1984-85. Board of directors Council on Family Health, New York City, 1981-86, Advt. Education Foundation, New York City, 1989—; member fin. committee Joint Council on Economic Education, 1984—, member executive committee, 1986—; member International Executive Service Corps., 1989—; member adv. council School of Business Queen's U., Kingston, Ontario, Can., 1980-84; trustee Drew U., Madison, New Jersey, 1985-88, Queen's U., 1988—. Fellow Ford Foundation, 1958, Sears, Roebuck Foundation, 1959. Member National Wholesale Druggists Association (associate adv. committee), National Association Retail Druggists (executive adv. council 1983-85),

Pharmaceutical Manufacturers Association (board directors 1989—), Proprietary Association (vice president 1983-88, board directors, member executive committee 1981-88), National Alliance Business (board directors 1984-86). Unitarian. Clubs: Plainfield Country (New Jersey); Econ. (New York City). Avocations: golf; tennis. Office: Warner-Lambert Company 201 Tabor Road Morris Plains New Jersey 07950

GORDON, ROGER L., savings and loan association executive. Formerly senior executive vice president, chief operating officer San Francisco Federal Savings & Loan Association, president, chief executive officer, 1990—. Office: San Francisco Federal Savings & Loan Association 88 Kearny St San Francisco California 94108

GORMAN, JOSEPH TOLLE, corporate executive; born Rising Sun, Indiana, 1937. Bachelor of Arts, Kent State University, 1959; Bachelor of Laws, Yale University, 1962. Associate Baker, Hostetler & Patterson, Cleveland, 1962-67; with legal department TRW Incorporated, Cleveland, 1968-69, assistant secretary, 1969-70, secretary, 1970-72, vice president senior counsel automotive worldwide operations, 1972-73, vice president, assistant general counsel, 1973-76, vice president, general counsel, 1976-80, acting head communications function, 1978, executive vice president industrial and energy sector, 1980-84, executive vice president, assistant president, 1984-85, chief operating officer, 1985-89, chairman, president, chief executive officer, 1988—, chairman board, chief executive officer, 1991—, also board of directors, 1984—; director Aluminum Company of am.; member adv. board BP Am., Incorporated; vice chairman U.S.-Can. Free Trade Panel; board of directors Cleveland Tonorrow, Cleveland Council World Affairs, University Circuit, Incorporated, Cleveland Play House, Town Hall of Cleveland, Mus. Arts Association, Cleveland Institute of Arts.; member United States Automotive Sect Panel. Trustee United Way Svcs., Cleveland Clinic Foundation, Greater Cleveland Roundtable, Committee for Economic Devel., Bus.-Higher Education Forum; member Governor's Education Mgmt. Council. Member Yale Law School Association (executive committee), United States Chamber of Commerce (past chairman corp. governance and policy committee), U.S.-Japan Business Council (trustee, executive committee), Greater Cleveland Growth Association (trustee, executive committee), Japan Import Board, The Business Roundtable (Ohio education reform initiative), Council on Foreign Relations, The Conference Board, The Business Council, Trilateral Commission, Council on Competitiveness, Industry Policy Adv. Committee. Office: TRW Incorporated 1900 Richmond Road Cleveland Ohio 44124

GORMLEY, DENNIS JAMES, manufacturing company executive; born 1939. Graduate, Rensselaer Polytechnic Institute, 1963. With Fed.-Mogul Corp., Southfield, Michigan, 1963—, director corp. planning, 1978-79, group manager general products group, 1979-82, vice president, from 1980, executive vice president, president, chief operating officer, 1988-89, president, chief executive officer, 1989—, also board of directors. Office: Fed-Mogul

Corp Post Office Box 1966 Detroit Michigan 48235 also: Fed-Mogul Corp 26555 Northwestern Highway Southfield Michigan 48034

GORR, IVAN WILLIAM, rubber company executive; born Toledo; son of Paul Robert and Edna Louise (Wandt) G.; married Dorothy J. Brandt, June 21, 1951; children: Louise (Mrs. Gary Stephenson), Jean (Mrs. Donald Jones), Robert C., Amy S., Sally M. Bachelor of Science in Business Administration, University Toledo, 1951. C.P.A., Ohio. Principal Arthur Young & Company, Toledo, Ohio, 1953-72; corp. controller Cooper Tire & Rubber Company, Findlay, Ohio, 1972-75, chief fin. officer, 1975-82, treasurer, 1976-77, executive vice president, treasurer, 1977-82, president, chief operating officer, 1982-89, chairman board, chief executive officer, 1989—; director Fifth Third Bank of Toledo, Amcast Industrial Corp., Cooper Tire & Rubber Company. Chairman, president Blanchard Valley Health Association, Findlay, 1982-85, board of directors, 1974-88; chairman business adv. council U. Toledo, 1986-88, chairman community adv. council for education, 1990—, trustee community devel. foundation, 1991—, ; advisor Findlay Area Arts Council, trustee U. Toledo Foundation, 1990—. With United States Army, 1951-53, Korea. Member National Association Accts. (president Northwestern Ohio chapter 1977), Ohio Society Certified Public Accountants (board directors 1972), United States Chamber of Commerce (board directors 1989—), Rotary, Findlay Country Club. Republican. Lutheran. Avocations: golf, sailing, bowling. Home: 1705 Windsor Place Findlay Ohio 45840 Office: Cooper Tire & Rubber Company Lima & Western Aves Findlay Ohio 45840

GOSSAGE, THOMAS LAYTON, chemical company executive; born Nashville, May 7, 1934; son of Walker E. and Mildred (Davis) G.; married Virginia Eastman, July 27, 1957; children: Laura Eastman, Virginia Lowry. Bachelor of Science, Georgia Institute Tech., 1956, Master of Science, 1957. Process engineer Humble Oil Company, 1957; assistant director government relations Monsanto Research Corp., Dayton, Ohio, 1961-66; director research and devel. marketing Monsanto Research Corp., Dayton, 1966-68; group marketing director Monsanto Company New Enterprises div., St. Louis, 1968-70; marketing director Monsanto Company Specialty Products, St. Louis, 1970-75; director results management Monsanto Industrial Chemicals Company, St. Louis, 1975-77; assistant general manager plasticizers div. Monsanto Industrial Chemicals Company, 1977, general manager plasticizers div., 1977-79, general manager detergents and phosphates, 1979-80, assistant managing director, 1980-81, vice president, managing director, 1981-83; group vice president, managing director Monsanto International, St. Louis, 1983-86; group vice president, senior vice president Monsanto Chemical Company div. Monsanto Company, St. Louis, 1986-88; president Hercules Specialty Chemicals Company, a unit of Hercules, Incorporated, 1988-89; president, chief executive officer The Aqualon Group, a unit of Hercules, 1989—; senior vice president Hercules, Incorporated, 1989—, also board of directors; member adv. council Law Engineering Company, Atlanta.

Member U.S.-China Business Council; trustee United States Council International Business, New York City Served to 1st lieutenant United States Air Force, 1957-60. Home: 8 Wood Road Wilmington Delaware 19806 Office: Aqualon Company Little Falls Center 1, Post Office Box 15417 2711 Centerville Road Wilmington Delaware 19850-5417

GOTTWALD, BRUCE COBB, SR., chemical company executive; born Richmond, Virginia, September 28, 1933; son of Floyd Dewey and Anne Ruth (Cobb) G.; married Nancy Hays, December 22, 1956; children: Bruce Cobb, Mark Hays, Thomas Edward. Bachelor of Science, Virginia Military Institute, 1954; postgraduate, University Virginia, Institute Paper Chemistry, Appleton, Wisconsin. With Albemarle Paper Manufacturing Company, from 1956; vice president Ethyl Corp. (parent), Richmond, Virginia, 1962-64, secretary, 1962-69, executive vice president, 1964-69, president, chief operating officer, 1969—; also board of directors Ethyl Corp. (parent); board of directors James River Corp., Dominion Resources Incorporated, CSX Corp., Tredegar Industries. Former president Virginia Mus.; board trustees Virginia Mil. Institute Foundation; board governors Virginia Council Economic Education. Member National Association Mfgrs. (board directors), Chemical Mfgr. Association. Home: 4203 Sulgrave Road Richmond Virginia 23221 Office: Ethyl Corp 330 S 4th St Richmond Virginia 23219

GOTTWALD, FLOYD DEWEY, JR., chemical company executive; born Richmond, Virginia, July 29, 1922; son of Floyd Dewey and Anne (Cobb) G.; married Elisabeth Morris Shelton, March 22, 1947; children: William M., James T., John D. Bachelor of Science, Virginia Military Institute, 1943; Master of Science, University Richmond, 1951. With Albemarle Paper Company, Richmond, 1943-62, secretary, 1956-57, vice president, secretary, 1957-62, president, 1962; executive vice president Ethyl Corp., Richmond, 1962-64, vice chairman, 1964-68, chairman, 1968—, chief executive officer, chairman executive committee, 1970—; board of directors Tredegar Industries, Incorporated. Board of directors National Petroleum Council; trustee V.Military Intelligence Foundation, Incorporated, U. Richmond; member River Rd. Baptist Church 1st lieutenant United States Army Reserve, 1943-46. Decorated Bronze Star, Purple Heart. Member National Association of Manufacturers (past board directors), Am. Petroleum Institute (board directors), Chemical Mfgr. Association (past board directors). Clubs: Alfalfa, Country of Virginia, Commonwealth. Home: 330 S 4th St 300 Herndon Road Richmond Virginia 23219 Office: Ethyl Corp 330 S 4th St Post Office Box 2189 Richmond Virginia 23219

GOZON, RICHARD C., paper distribution executive; born Pittsburgh, October 9, 1938; son of Frank J. and Helen (Franklin) G.; married Fran A. Burmeister, June 21, 1940; children: Cheryl, Michael, Diana. Bachelor of Science in Business, Valparaiso University, 1960; advanced management program, Harvard University, 1978. With sales department Champion International, Hamilton, Ohio, 1959-61; director sales Nationwide Papers, Chicago, 1961-72; president Rourke Eno

Paper Company, Hartford, Connecticut, 1972-78; executive vice president Unisource Corp., Philadelphia, 1978-79, president, 1979-85; vice president Alco Standard Corp., Philadelphia, 1982, director, 1983, executive vice president, chief operating officer, 1987, president, chief operating officer, 1988—; president Alco Paper & Office Products, Philadelphia, 1983, Paper Corp. of Am., Philadelphia, 1985-87; executive vice president, chief executive officer Alco Standard Corp., Valley Forge, Pennsylvania, 1988—; board of directors Alco Standard Corp., Philadelphia; trustee Richard Roberts Real estate Growth Trus I, Avon, Connecticut; director U.G.I. Corp. Director, World Affaris Council of Philadelphia. Member Sales & Marketing Executives Club. Republican. Lutheran. Clubs: Merion Golf (Ardmore, Pennsylvania); Pine Valley golf (Clementon, New Jersey); Harvard Business Sch. Avocations: golf, tennis, skiing. Home: 533 Waterloo Road Devon Pennsylvania 19333 Office: Alco Standard Corp Post Office Box 834 Valley Forge Pennsylvania 19482

GRACE, J. PETER, business executive; born Manhasset, New York, May 25, 1913; son of Joseph and Janet (Macdonald) G.; married Margaret Fennelly, May 24, 1941. Student, St. Paul's School, Concord, New Hampshire, 1927-32; Bachelor of Arts, Yale University, 1936; Doctor of Laws (honorary), Mount St. Mary's College, Manhattan College, Fordham University, Boston College, University Notre Dame, Belmont Abbey, Stonehill College, Christian Bros. College, Adelphi University, Furman University, Rider College, Mount St. Vincent College; Doctor Latin Am. Relations, St. Joseph's College; Doctor of Science, Clarkson College; Doctor of Commercial Science (honorary), St. John's University; Doctor of Humane Letters (honorary), Fairleigh Dickinson University, Canisius College; Doctor of Laws (honorary), Assumption College, The Citadel, Stevens Institute of Tech. With W.R. Grace & Company, New York City, 1936—, secretary, 1942, director, 1943—, vice president, 1945, president, chief executive officer, 1945-81, chairman, president and chief executive officer, 1986-89, chairman and chief executive officer, 1981-86, 89—; chairman board of directors Chemed Corp., Del Taco Restaurants, Incorporated; board of directors Canonie Environmental Services Corp., Creative Restaurant Management Incorporated, DuBois Chemicals, Milliken & Company, Office Warehouse, Incorporated, Omnicare, Incorporated, Restaurant Enterprises Group, Incorporated, Roto-Rooter, Incorporated, Stone & Webster Incorporated, National Sanitary Supply Company, Grace Energy Corp.; director emeritus Ingersoll-Rand Company; hon. director Brascan Limited; trustee emeritus Atlantic Mutual Insurance Company, Atlantic Reinsurance Company; board of directors, trustee Centennial Insurance Company. Board of directors, president Catholic Youth Organization of Archdiocese of New York; board of directors Boys Clubs Am.; president, trustee Grace Institute; member president's committee Greater New York, corp. grants committee, trustee emeritus, Notre Dame U.; chairman council national trustees National Jewish Center for Immunology and Respiratory Medicine, Denver; chairman

President's Private Sector Survey on Cost Control in Federal Government, 1982-84; co-chairman Citizens Against Government Waste; trustee United States Council for International Business; board governors Thomas Aquinas College; chairman, director Amerishares Foundation, Incorporated; board of directors Americares Foundation. Decorated Knight Grand Cross, Equestrian Order Holy Sepulchre of Jerusalem; decorated by govts. of Colombia, Chile, Ecuador, Panama, Peru. Member Newcomen Society, Council on Foreign Relations, Knights of Malta (president, board councillors), Madison Square Garden Club (governor), Links, Meadow Brook Club, Pacific Union Club, Everglades Club, Lotus Club, River Club. Office: W R Grace & Company Grace Plaza 1114 Avenue of Americas New York New York 10036-7794

GRADE, JEFFERY T., manufacturing company executive; born 1943. Bachelor of Science, Illinois Institute Tech., 1966; Master of Business Administration, DePaul University, 1972. With Plasto Manufacturing Corp., 1965-66, Motorola Incorporated, 1966-67, Bell and Howell, 1967-68, Illinois Central Gulf Railroad, 1968-73; vice president fin. IC Industries, 1973-83; with Harnischfeger Corp., Milwaukee, 1983—, president, chief operating officer, board of directors, 1986—. Served with United States Navy, 1865-66. Office: Harnischfeger Industries Incorporated Post Office Box 554 Milwaukee Wisconsin 53201

GRAHAM, DONALD EDWARD, publisher; born Baltimore, April 22, 1945; son of Philip L. and Katharine (Meyer) G.; married Mary L. Wissler, January 7, 1967; children: Liza, Laura, William, Molly. Bachelor of Arts, Harvard University, 1966. Formerly with Newsweek magazine; with The Washington Post, 1971—, assistant managing editor sports, 1974-75, assistant general manager, 1975-76, executive vice president, general manager, 1976-79, pub., 1979—; president, c.e.o. The Washington Post Company, 1991—; director Washington Post Company, Bowaters Mersey Paper Company Limited. Trustee Federal City Council, 1976. Served with United States Army, 1966-68. Member Am. Antiquarian Society. Office: Washington Post Company 1150 15th St Northwest Washington District of Columbia 20071

GRAHAM, KATHARINE, newspaper executive; born New York City, June 16, 1917; daughter of Eugene and Agnes (Ernst) Meyer; married Philip L. Graham, June 5, 1940 (deceased 1963); children: Elizabeth Morris Graham Weymouth, Donald Edward, William Welsh, Stephen Meyer. Student, Vassar College, 1934-36; Bachelor of Arts, University Chicago, 1938. Reporter San Francisco News, 1938-39; member editorial staff Washington Post, 1939-45, member Sunday, circulation and editorial departments, pub., 1969-79; president Washington Post Company, 1963-73, 77, chairman board, chief executive officer, 1973—; co-chairman International Herald Tribune; board of directors Bowater Mersey Paper Company, Limited, Reuters Founders Share Company Limited, Urban Institute, Federal City Council, Council for Aid to Education. Life trustee, U. Chicago; hon. trustee George Washington U.; member senior adv. board of the Joan Shorenstein Barone Center on the

Press, Politics and Pub. Policy, Harvard U. Fellow Am. Acad. Arts and Sciences; member Am. Society Newspaper Editors, National Press Club, Council Foreign Relations, Overseas Devel. Council, Metropolitan Club, Cosmopolitan Club, 1925 F Street Club. Home: 2920 R St Northwest Washington District of Columbia 20007 Office: Washington Post Company 1150 15th St Northwest Washington District of Columbia 20071

GRAINGER, DAVID WILLIAM, distribution company executive; born Chicago, October 23, 1927; son of William Wallace and Hally (Ward) G. Bachelor of Science in Electrical Engineering, University Wisconsin, 1950. With W.W. Grainger, Incorporated, Chicago, 1952—; chairman board W.W. Grainger, Incorporated, 1968—. Office: W W Grainger Incorporated 5500 W Howard St Skokie Illinois 60077

GRAMM, WENDY LEE, government official. daughter of Joshua and Angeline (AnChin) Lee; married Phil Gramm, November 2, 1970; children: Marshall Kenneth, Jefferson Philip. Bachelor of Arts in Economics, Wellesley College, 1966; Doctor of Philosophy in Economics, Northwestern University, 1971. Staff department quantitive methods University Illinois, 1969; assistant professor Texas A&M University, 1970-74, associate professor department economics, 1975-79; research staff Institute Defense Analyses, 1979-82; assistant director Bureau Economics Federal Trade Commission, 1982-83, director, 1983-85; administrator Office Information and Regulatory Affairs, OMB, 1985-87; chairman Commodity Futures Trading Commision, 1988—. Contributor articles to professional journals. Office: Commodity Futures Trading Commission 2033 K St Northwest Washington District of Columbia 20581

GRANZOW, PAUL H., printing company executive; born 1927. Student, University Dayton; Bachelor of Laws, University Cin, 1950. Partner Turner, Granzow & Hollenkamp; with Standard Register Company, Dayton, Ohio, 1966—, chairman board of directors, 1984—. Served with Army of the United States, 1945-46. Office: Standard Register Company 600 Albany St Dayton Ohio 45408

GRASS, ALEXANDER, retail company executive; born Scranton, Pennsylvania, August 3, 1927; son of Louis and Rose (Breman) G.; married Lois Lehrman, July 30, 1950; children: Linda Jane, Martin L., Roger L., Elizabeth Ann; married Louise B. Gurkoff, April 26, 1974. Bachelor of Laws, University Florida, 1949. Bar: Florida 1949, Pennsylvania 1953. Private practice Miami Beach, Florida, 1949-51; vice president Rite Aid Corp., Shiremanstown, Pennsylvania, 1952-66; president Rite Aid Corp., 1966-69, 77-89, chairman, chief executive officer, 1969—; chairman Super Rite Foods, Incorporated, 1983—; board of directors Hasbro Industries. Member national executive committee United Jewish Appeal, 1968-79, national vice chairman, 1970-79, general chairman, 1984-86, chairman board trustees, 1986-88; president Harrisburg (Pennsylvania) Jewish Federation, 1970-72; chairman Israel Education Fund, 1975-78; board of directors Pennsylvania Right to Work Foundation, 1972-74, Harrisburg Hospital, 1977-81; vice chairman Harrisburg Hospital, 1988—; member Pennsylvania Council Arts, 1982;

board of directors Keystone State Games, 1982—, Israel Center Social and Economic Studies, 1983; trustee Jerusalem Institute Mgmt., 1983; member executive committee Jewish Agency for Israel, 1984-88, board governors 1984—; treasurer United Israel Appeal, 1986-90. With United States Naval Reserve, 1945-46. Member National Am. Wholesale Grocers Association (board directors 1971-73), National Association Chain Drug Stores (board directors 1972—, chairman 1985-86). Jewish (director temple). Home: 4025 Crooked Hill Road Harrisburg Pennsylvania 17110 Office: Rite Aid Corp Post Office Box 3165 Harrisburg Pennsylvania 17110

GRASS, MARTIN LEHRMAN, business executive; born Harrisburg, Pennsylvania, February 17, 1954; son of Alex and Lois (Lehrman) G.; married Jody Harrison, March 24, 1959; 1 child, Leila Rose. Bachelor of Arts, University Pennsylvania, 1976; Master of Business Administration, Cornell University, 1978. Vice president real estate Rite Aid Corp., Shiremanstown, Pennsylvania, 1978-81, vice president corp. planning and devel., 1981-84, senior vice president corp. planning and devel., 1984-87, executive vice president, 1987-89, president, chief operating officer, 1989—, also board of directors; vice chairman super Rite Foods Incorporated. Office: Rite Aid Corp Post Office Box 3165 Shiremanstown Pennsylvania 17015

GRASSO, RICHARD A., stock exchange executive. Bachelor of Science in Accounting, Pace University; postgraduate certificate advanced management, Harvard University, 1985. Member staff New York Stock Exchange, 1968-73, director listing and marketing, 1973-77, vice president corp. services, 1977-81, senior vice president corp. services, 1981-83, executive vice president marketing group, 1983-86, executive vice president capital markets, 1986-88; president, chief operating officer New York Stock Exchange, 1988—; overseer operations New York Future Exchange; coordinator Depository Trust Company, National Securities Clearing Corp.; board of directors Securities Industry Automation Corp. Office: New York Stock Exch 11 Wall St New York New York 10005

GRAY, HARRY JACK, medical products executive, equity fund executive, retired aircraft manufacturing executive; born Milledgeville Crossroads, Georgia, November 18, 1919; married Helen Buckley; children: Pam, Vicky Lynn. Bachelor of Science with honors, University Illinois, 1941, Master of Science, 1947; Doctor of Laws (honorary), Trinity College, Connecticut, 1976, University Hartford, 1978, University Connecticut, 1982; Doctor of Science (honorary), Florida Institute Tech., 1980; Doctor of Engineering (honorary), Worcester Polytechnic Institute, 1983. Instructor University Illinois, 1946-47; sales manager truck div. Esserman Motor Sales, Chicago, 1947-50; executive salesman Platt, Incorporated, Chicago, 1950-51; executive vice president, general manager Greyvan Lines, div. Greyhound Corp., Chicago, 1951-54; president United States Engineering div. Litton Industries, Van Nuys, California, 1956; vice president Litton Industries, Beverly Hills, California, 1958-61; group vice president, director Litton Industries, Beverly Hills, 1961-64, senior vice president components, 1964-65, senior vice president for finance and administration, 1965-67, executive vice president, 1967-69, senior executive vice president, 1969-71; president United Techs. Corp. (formerly United Aircraft), Hartford, Connecticut, from 1971, chief executive officer, 1972-86, chairman, 1974-86, chief operating officer, 1981-84, also board of directors, chairman fin. committee; now chairman, chief executive officer Am. Medical International Incorporated; also principal Harry Gray Associates, Farmington, Connecticut; board of directors Union Carbide. Corporator Hartford Hospital, Institute of Living, Hartford, Good Samaritan Hospital, West Palm Beach, Florida; board of directors Old State House Association, Hartford.; chairman board of directors National Sci. Center Foundation, Washington; member Def. Policy Adv. Committee on Trade. Captain Army of the United States, 1941-46. Decorated Silver Star, Bronze Star with V device. Member Institute of Electrical and Electronics Engineers, Business Council Washington (board directors), Navy League United States. Home: Lost Tree Village 11094 Beach Club Point North Palm Beach Florida 33408 Office: 30 Stanford Dr Farmington Connecticut 06032

GREEHEY, WILLIAM EUGENE, energy company executive; born Forest Dodge, Iowa, 1936; married. Bachelor of Business Administration, St. Mary's University, 1960. Auditor Price Waterhouse & Company, 1960-61; senior auditor Humble Oil and Refining Company, 1961-63; senior vice president fin. Coastal Corp. (and predecessor), 1963-74; with Valero Energy Corp. (formerly Coastal States Gas Producing Company), San Antonio, 1974—, president, chief executive officer, 1979-83, chairman board, 1983—, now also chief executive officer, director, also chairman, chief executive officer numerous subsidiaries; president, chief executive officer LoVaca Gathering Company subsidiary, San Antonio, 1974-79. Office: Valero Energy Corp 530 McCullough San Antonio Texas 78215

GREENBERG, ALAN COURTNEY, stockbroker; born Wichita, Kansas, September 3, 1927; son of Theodore H. and Esther (Zeligson) G.; divorced, August 1976; children: Lynne, Theodore. Student, University Missouri, 1949. With Bear Stearns & Company, New York City, 1949—, general partner, 1958—, chairman board, chief executive officer, 1978—, also chairman executive committee, managing director. Recipient Lehman award Am. Jewish Committee; named Man of Year National Conference of Christians and Jews; winner National Bridge Championship, 1977. Member Am. Stock Exch. (governor), Securities Industry Association (governing council), Society Am. Magicians. Jewish. Clubs: Harmonie, Bond (New York City); Sunningdale Country (Scarsdale, New York). Office: Bear Stearns Cos Incorporated 245 Park Avenue New York New York 01067

GREENBERG, FRANK S., textile company executive; born Chicago, September 11, 1929. Bachelor of Philosophy, University Chicago, 1949. Assistant to president Charm Tred Mills, 1949, vice president, 1953, president, 1953-59; vice president Charm Tred Mills div. Burlington Industries, Incorporated, 1959-61, president, 1961-62; president Monticello Carpet Mill div. Burlington Industries, Incorporated, New York City, 1962-70, group vice president, member management committee, 1970-72, executive vice president, 1972-78; president Burlington Industries, Incorporated, New York City, now Greensboro, North Carolina, 1978-86, chairman, chief executive officer, 1986—, also board of directors. Served with Army of the United States, 1951-53. Office: Burlington Industries Incorporated 3330 W Friendly Avenue Greensboro North Carolina 27410

GREENBERG, MAURICE RAYMOND, insurance company executive; born New York City, May 4, 1925; son of Jacob and Ada (Rheingold) G.; married Corinne Phyllis Zuckerman, November 12, 1950; children: Jeffrey W., Evan G., L. Scott, Cathleen J. Pre-law certificate, University Miami, Florida, 1948; Juris Doctor, New York Law School, 1950; Juris Doctor (honorary), New England School Law, 1970. Bar: New York 1953. With Continental Casualty Company, 1952-60; vice president C.V. Starr & Company, Incorporated, New York City, 1961-66, executive vice president, 1966-68, president, also board of directors, 1968—; president, chief executive officer Am. International Group Incorporated, New York City, 1968-89, chairman board, 1989—; board of directors Federal Reserve Bank New York, international capital markets adv. committee. Chairman board governors New York Hospital; member President's adv. committee on trade negotiations Center for Strategic and International Studies. Served to captain United States Army, World War II, Korea. Decorated Bronze Star. Member New York Bar Association, Foreign Policy Association, Council Foreign Relations, , Hoover Institute, ASEAN-US Business Adv. Council, N.Y.C Partnership, US-USSR Trade and Econ. Council, Coalition Service Industries, Police Athletic League, Sigma Alpha Mu. Clubs: City Athletic, Sky, India House, Lotus, Harmonie (New York City); Georgetown (Washington). Office: Am International Group Incorporated 70 Pine St New York New York 10270

GREENBLATT, MAURICE THEODORE, transportation executive; born Vineland, New Jersey, October 2, 1928; son of Benjamin and Emma (Pollock) G.; married Joan Tobye Bailinger, April 8, 1951; children: David, Daniel. Student, Bucknell University, 1945-48. President Ware's Van and Storage Company, Incorporated, Vineland, 1958—; chairman, chief executive officer United Van Lines, Incorporated, Fenton, Missouri, 1984—; vice chairman Security Savings and Loan, Vineland, 1977—, also board of directors; board of directors United Van Lines Limited, Toronto, Can., Am. Movers Conference, Household Goods Carriers Bureau. Republican. Jewish. Home: Ocean Plaza #417 Longport New Jersey 08403 Office: Ware's Van & Storage Company Post Office Box W Vineland New Jersey 08360 also: Unigroup Incorporated 1 United Dr Fenton Missouri 63026

GREENSPAN, ALAN, economist; born New York City, March 6, 1926; son of Herman Herbert and Rose (Goldsmith) G. Bachelor of Science summa cum laude, New York University, 1948, Master of Arts, 1950, Doctor of Philosophy, 1977. President, chief executive officer Townsend-Greenspan and Company,

Incorporated, New York City, 1954-74, 77-87; consultant Council Economic Advisers, 1970-74, chairman, 1974-77; consultant Congressional Budget Office, 1977-87; member Pres.'s Economic Policy Adv. Board, 1981-87; chairman National Commission on Social Security Reform, 1981-83; member Task Force on Economic Growth, 1969, Pres.'s Foreign Intelligence Adv. Board, 1983-85; Commission on an All-Vol. Armed Force, 1969-70; Commission on Fin. Structure and Regulation, 1970-71; consultant United States Treasury, 1971-74, Federal Reserve Board, 1971-74; member economic adv. board Secretary of Commerce, 1971-72; member central market system committee Securities and Exchange Commission, 1972; member GNP rev. committee Office Management and Budget; senior adviser panel on economic activity Brookings Institution, 1970-74, 77-87; chairman board governors Federal Reserve System, 1987—; member board economists Time magazine, 1971-74, 77-87; adj. professor Grad. School Business Administration, New York University, 1977-87. Member Nixon for President Committee, 1968-69, director domestic policy research; personal representative of Pres.-elect to Bureau Budget for transition period, chairman task force on foreign trade policy.; Board overseers Hoover Institution on War, Revolution and Peace, 1973-74, 77-87. Recipient John P. Madden medal, 1975; joint recipient Pub. Service Achievement award, 1976, William Butler Memorial award, 1977. Fellow National Association Business Economists (past president). Clubs: Hillcrest Country (Los Angeles); Metropolitan (Washington); Century Country, Harmonie. Office: FRS 20th & Constitution Avenue Northwest Washington District of Columbia 20551

GREGORY, MARION F., JR., tool manufacturing executive; born Denison, Texas, October 26, 1933; son of Marion F. and Nannie (Huseman) G.; married Fay, December 27, 1975; children: Mark, Gary, Vivian, Nicole, Colette. With Snap-on Tools Corp., 1955—; general sales manager Snap-on Tools Corp., Kenosha, Wisconsin, 1976-81, vice president, 1977-81, senior vice president manufacturing and product research and devel., 1981-83, executive vice president, director, 1983-85, chief operating officer, director, 1985—, president, 1986—, chairman, 1988—; director Hand Tools Institute, Tarrytown, New York. Served with United States Navy, 1951-55. Member Wisconsin Manufacturing and Commerce Association (board directors 1985—). Office: Snap-on Tools Corp 2801 80th St Kenosha Wisconsin 53140

GREGORY, ROBERT EARLE, JR., apparel company executive, lawyer; born Greenville, South Carolina, May 8, 1942; son of Robert E. and Ellen (Robinson) G.; married Karen Marie Howard, April 24, 1982; children: Scott, Kelly. Bachelor of Arts, Wofford College, 1964; Juris Doctor, University South Carolina, 1968; Advanced management program, Harvard Graduate Business School, Cambridge, Massachusetts, 1978-79. Bar: South Carolina 1968, Fed. 1968, United States Supreme Court 1974. Legal assistant to chief justice South Carolina Supreme Court, Columbia, 1968-70; div. counsel Akzona, Incorporated, Ashevill, North Carolina, 1970-72; general counsel Spartan Mills, Spartanburg, South Carolina,

1972-79, group vice president, general counsel, 1977-79; executive vice president, president Lee Company div. VF Corp., Wyomissing, Pennsylvania, 1980-83; president, chief operating officer VF Corp., Wyomissing, Pennsylvania, 1983—, board of directors; board of directors United Missouri Bank Kansas City, N.A., Missouri, USF&G Corp. Alumni director Wofford College, Spartanburg, 1976-81, secretary, 1979-80, president elect, 1981; trustee Wofford College, Spartanburg. Member South Carolina Bar Association, Young President Organization, Harvard Club (New York City), Harvard Business School Club (Philadelphia). Episcopalian. Home: 320 Wyomissing Boulevard Wyomissing Pennsylvania 19610 Office: VF Corp 1047 N Park Road Wyomissing Pennsylvania 19610

GREHAN, HAROLD SIMON, JR., shipping company executive; born December 16, 1927; son of Harold Simon and Dorothy Hughes (Cone) G.; married Julia Brooke Potts, August 3, 1963; children—Harold Hughes, Brooke Yates. Bachelor of Business Administration, Tulane University. Shipping manager Lykes Brothers, New Orleans, 1948-50; shipping manager Lykes Brothers, New Orleans and Washington, 1953-57; vice president traffic Central Gulf Lines, New York City, 1958-65; senior vice president, executive vice president, director Central Gulf Lines, New Orleans, 1965—; director New Orleans Commodity Exchange. Board of directors International House, New Orleans, 1979-80. Served to lieutenant United States Navy, 1951-52. Republican. Roman Catholic. Clubs: Boston, Stratford (New Orleans). Avocations: tennis; golf; soaring. Home: 1444 State St New Orleans Louisiana 70118 Office: Central Gulf Lines Incorporated 650 Poydras St Suite 1700 New Orleans Louisiana 70130

GREY, RICHARD, toy company executive. President Tyco Toys Incorporated, Mount Laurel, New Jersey, 1973—, chief executive officer, 1986—, chairman, 1991—. Office: Tyco Toys Incorporated 540 Glen Avenue Moorestown New Jersey 08057

GRIEVE, PIERSON MACDONALD, specialty chemicals and services company executive; born Flint, Michigan, December 5, 1927; son of P.M. and Margaret (Leamy) G.; married Florence R. Brogan, July 29, 1950; children: Margaret, Scott, Bruce. Bachelor of Science in Business Administration, Northwestern University, 1950; postgraduate, University Minnesota, 1955-56. With Caterpillar Tractor Company, Peoria, Illinois, 1950-52; staff engineer A.T. Kearney & Company (management consultants), Chicago, 1952-55; president Rap-in-Wax, Minneapolis, 1955-62; executive Associated Press Parts Corp., 1962-67; president, chief executive officer Questor Corp., Toledo, 1967-82; chairman board, chief executive officer (NYSE) Ecolab Incorporated, St. Paul, 1983—, now also president; board of directors St. Paul Companies Incorporated, Norwest Corp., Meredith Corp., US West Incorporated. Adv. council J.L. Kellogg Grad. School Mgmt., Northwestern U.; board overseers School Mgmt., U. Minnesota; board of directors Guthrie Theatre. Served with United States Naval Reserve, 1945-46. Member Minnesota Business Partnership, Chevaliers du Tastevin, Beta Gamma Sigma (directors table). Episcopalian. Clubs: Minnesota (St. Paul); Minneapolis. Office: Ecolab Incorporated Ecolab Center Saint Paul Minnesota 55102

GRILICHES, ZVI, educator, economist; born Kaunas, Lithuania, September 12, 1930; came to United States, 1951, naturalized, 1960; married Diane Asseo, April 26, 1953; children—Eve, Marc. Student, Hebrew University, Jerusalem, 1950-51; Bachelor of Science, University California at Berkeley, 1953, Master of Science, 1954; Master of Arts, University Chicago, 1955, Doctor of Philosophy, 1957. Assistant professor economics University Chicago, 1956-59, associate professor, 1960-64, professor, 1964-69; professor Harvard University, 1969-78, Nathaniel Ropes professor political economy, 1979-87, chairman department economics, 1980-83, Paul M. Warburg professor of economics, 1987—; research associate National Bureau Economic Research, 1959-60, 78—; visiting professor Econometric Institute, Netherlands School Economics, Rotterdam, 1963-64, Hebrew University, 1964, 72, 77, 84, 87; consultant Rand Corp., Brookings Institution; board governors Federal Reserve System, Ford Foundation, National Science Foundation; member President Sci. Adv. Council Panel on Youth, 1970-73. Author: Price Indexes and Quality Change, 1971; Economies of Scale and the Form of the Production Function, 1971; R&D Patents and Productivity, 1984; Handbook of Econometrics, 1986, Technology, Education, and Productivity, 1988; contributor articles to professional journals. Served with Israeli Army, 1948-49. Fellow Am. Acad. Arts and Sciences, Econometric Society (president 1975), Am. Statistical Association, American Association for the Advancement of Science.; member National Acad. Sciences (committee on ability testing 1979-81, committee on national statistics 1980-82, committee on sci., engineering, and pub. policy 1983-88), Am. Econ. Association (member executive committee 1979-81, vice president 1984, J.B. Clark medal 1965), Am. Farm Econ. Association (award of merit 1958, 59, 60, 65), Royal Econ. Society. Home: 62 Shepard Cambridge Massachusetts 02138 Office: Harvard U Department Econ Cambridge Massachusetts 02138

GRISANTI, EUGENE PHILIP, flavors and fragrances company executive; born Buffalo, October 24, 1929; son of Nicholas D. and Victoria (Pantera) G.; married Anne Couming, June 29, 1953; children: Marylee, Christopher, Eugene Paul. Bachelor of Arts magna cum laude, Holy Cross College, 1951; Bachelor of Laws, Boston University, 1953; Master of Laws, Harvard University, 1954. Bar: Massachusetts 1953, New York 1954. Member firm Fulton, Walter & Halley, New York City, 1954-60; general attorney International Flavors & Fragrances Incorporated, New York City, 1960-64, secretary, general attorney; 1964-70, vice president, secretary, general attorney, 1970-74; president International Flavors & Fragrances, New York City, 1974-79; senior vice president, director International Flavors & Fragrances Incorporated, New York City, 1979-85, chairman, president, chief executive officer, 1985—. Member Fragrance Foundation (board directors), Cosmetic Toiletry and Fragrance Association (board directors). Clubs:

Larchmont Yacht, Winged Foot Golf; University (New York City). Office: International Flavor & Fragrances Incorporated 521 W 57th St New York New York 10019

GROSS, RONALD MARTIN, forest products executive. Bachelor of Arts, Ohio State University, 1955; Master of Business Administration, Harvard University, 1960. With Battelle Memorial Institute, Columbus, Ohio, 1957-58, United States Plywood-Champion Papers, Incorporated, 1960-68; with Can. Cellulose Company Limited, Vancouver, British Columbia, 1968-78; president, chief executive officer, director Can. Cellulose Company Limited, 1973-78; president, chief operating officer, director International Telephone & Telegraph Corporation Rayonier, Incorporated, Stamford, Connecticut, 1978-81; president, chief executive officer, director International Telephone & Telegraph Corporation Rayonier, Incorporated, 1981-84, chairman board, 1984—. Office: International Telephone and Telegraph Corporation Rayonier Incorporated 1177 Summer St Stamford Connecticut 06904

GROSSMAN, SANFORD JAY, economics educator; born Brooklyn, July 21, 1953; son of Sloane and Florence G.; married Naava; children: Shulamite and Aviva. Bachelor of Arts in Economics with honors, University Chicago, 1973, Master of Arts in Economics, 1974, Doctor of Philosophy in Economics, 1975. Assistant professor economics Stanford University, California, 1975-77; economist Board Governors Federal Reserve, 1977-78; associate professor economics University Pennsylvania, Philadelphia, 1978-79, professor economics, 1979-81; professor economics University Chicago, 1981-85; John L. Weinberg professor economics Princeton University, New Jersey, 1985-89; Steinberg trustee professor fin. University Pennsylvania, Philadelphia, 1989—. Contributor articles to professional journals. Recipient Irving Fisher grad. monograph award; award for best article Graham and Dodd Scroll, Fin. Analyst Journal, Q Group, Roger F. Murray 1st Prize award; Guggenheim Memorial fellow, Sloan Foundation fellow. Fellow Econometric Society, American Association for the Advancement of Science; member Am. Fin. Association (board directors), Am. Econ. Association (John Bates Clark medal), Econometric Society. Office: U Pennsylvania Department Fin 3251 Steinberg-Dietrich Hall 3620 Locust Walk Philadelphia Pennsylvania 19104-6367

GROVE, ANDREW S., electronics company executive; born Budapest, Hungary, 1936; married; 2 children. Bachelor of Science, City College of New York, 1960, Doctor of Science, 1985; Doctor of Philosophy, University Calif.-Berkeley, 1963; Doctor of Engineering (honorary), Worcester Polytechnic Institute, 1989. With Fairchild Camera and Instrument Company, 1963-67; president, chief operating officer Intel Corp., Santa Clara, California, 1967-87, president, chief executive officer, 1987—, also director. Recipient Medal award, Am. Institute Chemists, 1960; cert. merit, Franklin Institute, 1975; Townsend Harris medal, City College of New York, 1980; Enterprise award Professional Advertising Association, 1987; George Washington award Am. Hungarian Foundation, 1990. Fellow Institute of Electrical and Electronics

Engineers (achievement award 1969, J. J. Ebers award 1974, Engineering Leadership Recognition award 1987); member National Acad. Engineering. Office: Intel Corp 3065 Bowers Avenue Santa Clara California 95051

GROVES, RAY JOHN, accountant; born Cleveland, September 7, 1935; married Anne Keating, August 18, 1962; children: David, Philip, Matthew. Bachelor of Science summa cum laude, Ohio State University, 1957. Certified Public Accountant, Ohio. With Ernst & Whinney, Cleveland and New York City, 1957—; partner Ernst & Whinney, 1966-71, national partner, 1971-77; chairman, chief executive officer Ernst & Whinney, New York City, 1977-89; co-chief executive officer Spenser & Young, 1989—; president adv. council College Business Ohio State University, 1979-80; member adv. council University Chicago Grad. School Business. Councilman City of Lyndhurst, Ohio, 1969-72; chairman board trustees Leadership Cleveland, 1977-79; trustee Hawken School, 1976-86; member board overseers Wharton School U. Pennsylvania; member executive committee U. California Securities Regulation Institute; vice chairman board trustees Ursuline College, Cleveland, 1970-86; managing director, treasurer Metropolitan Opera Association. Member Am. Institute Certified Public Accountants (chairman board directors 1984-85), National Association Securities Dealers (board govs. 1981-84), National Association Accts., Am. Stock Exchange (board govs.). Republican. Clubs: Union; Pepper Pike (Ohio); Mayfield Country (South Euclid, Ohio); Opera, Board Room, Links (New York City); Metropolitan (Washington); Blind Brook (Purchase, New York); Laurel Valley Country. Home: 1566 Ponus Ridge New Canaan Connecticut 06840 also: 15 W 53rd St Apartment 19D New York New York 10019 Office: Ernst & Young 787 7th Avenue New York New York 10019

GRUM, CLIFFORD J., publishing executive; born Davenport, Iowa, December 12, 1934; son of Allen F. and Nathalie (Cate) G.; married Janelle Lewis, May 1, 1965; 1 son, Christopher J. Bachelor of Arts, Austin College, 1956; Master of Business Administration, University Pennsylvania, 1958. Formerly with Republic National Bank, Dallas; former vice president fin. Temple Industries, Diboll, Texas; with Time, Incorporated, New York City, treasurer, 1973-75, vice president, 1975-80, executive vice president, 1980-84, also board of directors; pub. Fortune, 1975-79; president, chief executive officer Temple-Inland, Incorporated, Diboll, 1984—; director Cooper Industries, Incorporated, Premark International, Incorporated. Trustee Austin College. Office: Temple Inland Incorporated 303 S Temple Dr Post Office Drawer N Diboll Texas 75941

GRUNE, GEORGE VINCENT, publishing company executive; born White Plains, New York, July 18, 1929; married Betty Lu Albert, August 9, 1952; children: George, Robert, Steven. Bachelor of Arts, Duke University, 1952; postgraduate, University Florida, 1955-56. Director executive recruitment Continental Group, New York City, 1957-60; sales representative Reader's Digest Association, Incorporated, New York City, 1960-63; advertising sales manager Reader's Digest Association, Incorporated, Pittsburgh, 1963-66; advertising sales manager Reader's Digest Association, Incorporated, New York City, 1966-69, marketing director, 1969-71, vice president, director international sales, director advertising marketing, 1971-74, director international operations, 1974-76, deputy director books and records div., 1975-76, vice president, 1976-83, vice president, director, pub., 1984, chairman, chief executive officer, 1984—; chief executive officer Source Telecomputing Corp., McLean, Virginia, 1982-83; board of directors CPC International, Chemical New York Corp., Chemical Bank. Director Boys Clubs of Am., New York City; board trustees Outward Bound U.S.A.; trustee Metropolitan Mus. Art, New York City, New York Zool. Society, Duke U., Durham, North Carolina, Roy E. Crummer Grad. School Business, Rollins College; chairman Reader's Digest Foundation, Wallace-Reader's Digest Funds; board overseers, board mgrs. Memorial Sloan-Kettering Cancer Center; member Council Foreign Rels., Council Conservators New York Pub. Libr., Institute France, Council for Fin. Aid to Education; member policy committee The Business Roundtable, member President's Committee on the Arts and Humanities. Recipient Henry Johnson Fisher award, 1987; National Leaders' fellow Young Men's Christian Association. Member Conference Board Metropolitan Opera Association (board directors), Fairfield Beach Club, Patterson Golf Club (Connecticut), Blind Brook Club (Purchase, New York), Ponte Vedra Club (Florida), Sawgrass Club (Ponte Vedra Beach, Florida), Union League, Sky Club New York City, Country Club of North Carolina, Burning Tree Club, Augusta National Golf Club. Republican. Home: 36 Hyde Lane Westport Connecticut 06880 Office: Reader's Digest Association Incorporated Pleasantville New York 10570

GUMMERE, JOHN, insurance company executive; born Mount Holly, New Jersey, February 12, 1928; son of John Westcott and Ruth (Clark) G.; married Eleanor Frances Greene, October 9, 1954; children: Cynthia Clark, John Greene. Bachelor of Arts, Yale University, 1948. With Phoenix Mutual Life Insurance Company, Hartford, Connecticut, 1949—; secretary charge underwriting department Phoenix Mutual Life Insurance Company, 1961-64, 2d vice president, 1964-65, vice president, 1965-72, senior vice president, 1972-78, executive vice president, 1978-81, president, chief executive officer, 1981-87, also director, chairman board, chief executive officer, 1987—; director Phoenix Equity Planning Corp., New York Casualty Insurance Company, Phoenix Am. Life Insurance Company, Connecticut National Bank, Phoenix General Insurance Company, PM Mortgage Funding Corp., PM Holdings Incorporated, PML International Insurance Limited. Member executive committee Medical Information, 1972-77, chairman, 1977; board of directors Hartford Grad. Center, Institute of Living, Old State House, Junior Achievement. Fellow Society Actuaries; member Medical Information Bureau (board directors), Greater Hartford Chamber of Commerce (director), Sigma Xi. Office: Phoenix Mut Life Ins Company 1 American Row Hartford Connecticut 06115

GUTFREUND, JOHN H., investment banker; born New York City,

September 14, 1929. Bachelor of Arts, Oberlin College, 1951. With municipal desk Salomon Brothers, Incorporated, New York City, 1953-62, manager syndicate, 1962-63, partner, 1963-66, member executive committee, 1966-78, managing partner, 1978-81, chairman board, chief executive officer, 1981—; co-chair Phibro Corp., New York City, 1981-83; co-chief executive officer Phibro-Salomon Incorporated (formerly Phibro Corp.), New York City, 1983-84, chief executive officer, 1984-86; vice chairman New York Stock Exchange, 1985-87; chairman, chief executive officer, president Salomon Incorporated (formerly Phibro-Salomon Incorporated), New York City, 1986—; chairman, chief executive officer Salomon Brothers, Incorporated, New York City; past vice chairman New York Stock Exchange; past board of directors Securities Industry Association. Trustee Center for Strategic and International Studies, Committee for Economic Devel., Joint Council on Economic Education; chairman Downtown-Lower Manhattan Association, Incorporated; hon. trustee Oberlin (Ohio) College; chairman Wall St. committee Lincoln Ctr.'s Corp. Fund Campaign, 1986-87; treasurer board trustees, chairman fin. committee New York Pub. Libr.; board of directors Montefiore Medical Center Corp.; member executive committee Bretton Woods Committee; member adv. committee The European Bank of Reconstrn. and Devel.; senior member The Conference Board; member Joint Council Economic Education. Member Downtown-Lower Manhattan Association (past chairman), Bond of New York (past president, past board govs.). Office: Salomon Bros Incorporated 1 New York Plaza New York New York 10004

GUYTON, ROBERT POOL, bank executive; born Blue Mountain, Mississippi, March 31, 1937; son of Albert J. and Birma Elizabeth (Pool) G.; married Katherine Cole Taylor, June 1960; children: Robert Pool, Randall Taylor. Bachelor of Business Administration, University Mississippi, 1958; Master of Business Administration, Harvard University, 1966. With Deposit Guaranty National Bank, Jackson, Mississippi, 1960-71; president, director National Bank Georgia, Atlanta, 1971-74, 77-79, 1st Mississippi National Bank, Jackson, 1974-77; chairman, president, chief executive officer, director Bank South Corp., Atlanta, 1980—; board of directors 1st Mississippi Corp., Jackson, Haverty Furniture Company Incorporated, Atlanta Gas Light Company. Board of directors Central Atlanta Progress Incorporated, High Mus. Art, Atlanta Arts Alliance; director, treasurer Central Atlanta Progress; trustee The Westminster Schools; member International Adv. Board Up with People; chairman United Way of Metro Atlanta Campaing, 1989; class agt. Harvard Business School Fund; former senior warden Cathedral of St. Phillip. 1st lieutenant, Army of the United States, 1958-60. Recipient University Mississippi Distinguished Alumni award, 1987; named to University Mississippi Alumni Hall of Fame, 1987. Member Georgia Bankers Association (president 1989-90), Association Reserve City Bankers, Chief Executives Organization, World Business Council, Atlanta Chamber of Commerce (past president), Omicron Delta Kappa, Sigma Chi. Episcopalian. Clubs: Peachtree Golf, Piedmont Driving,

Commerce. Office: Bank S Corp 55 Marietta St Atlanta Georgia 30303

GWALTNEY, EUGENE C., sportswear company executive; born Rock Hill, South Carolina, 1918. Bachelor of Science in Mechanical Engineering, Georgia Institute Tech., 1940; student, Massachusetts Institute of Technology. With Russell Corp., Alexander City, Alabama, 1952—, general superintendent, 1956-59, vice president, general superintendent, 1959-68, chief operating officer, 1968-72, president, 1968-82, chief executive officer, 1972—, chairman, 1982—; vice chairman, board of directors 1st National Bank Alexander City. Office: Russell Corp Lee St Post Office Box 272 Alexander City Alabama 35010

HAAB, LARRY DAVID, utility company executive; born Fairbury, Illinois, September 28, 1937; son of Samuel Frances and Sarah Louise (Steidinger) H.; married Ann Geddes, August 2, 1958; children: Sheryl, David, Julie. Bachelor of Science, Millikin University, 1959. C.P.A., Illinois. Senior accountant Price Waterhouse, St. Louis, 1959-65; with Illinois Power Company, Decatur, 1965—, now chairman, president, chief executive officer; board of directors 1st National Bank of Decatur, Decatur Memorial Hospital, Associated College in Illinois. President Millikin U. Alumni Board, 1981; president Macon County Mental Health Board, Decatur, 1983-86; member adv. council Kellog Grad. School; board of directors Decatur Memorial Hospital, Associated Colleges in Illinois. Member American Institute of Certified Public Accountants, Metro Decatur Chamber of Commerce (chairman board directors 1988-89), Illinois State Chamber of Commerce (board directors), Kellog Grad. School Adv. Council, Country Club of Decatur (president board directors 1988-89). Office: Illinois Power Company 500 S 27th St Decatur Illinois 62525

HAAS, ROBERT DOUGLAS, apparel manufacturing company executive; born San Francisco, April 3, 1942; son of Walter A. Jr. and Evelyn (Danzig) H.; married Colleen Gershon, January 27, 1974; 1 child, Elise Kimberly. Bachelor of Arts, University California, Berkeley, 1964; Master of Business Administration, Harvard University, 1968. With Peace Corps, Ivory Coast, 1964-66; with Levi Strauss & Company, San Francisco, 1973—, senior vice president corp. planning and policy, 1978-80, president new business group, 1980, president operating groups, 1980-81, executive vice president, chief operating officer, 1981-84, president, chief executive officer, 1984—, chairman board, 1989—, also board of directors; board of directors Levi Strauss Foundation. Hon. dir San Francisco Acquired Immune Deficiency Syndrome Foundation; board of directors Bay Area Council. White House fellow, 1968-69. Member Am. Apparel Manufacturers Association (board directors), Brookings Institute (trustee), Bay Area Committee, Conference Board, Council Foreign Relations, Trilateral Commission, Meyer Friedman Institute (board directors), Phi Beta Kappa. Office: Levi Strauss & Company Post Office Box 7215 San Francisco California 94120

HAAVELMO, TRYGVE, economics educator; born Skedsmo, Norway, December 13, 1911. Graduate, University Oslo, 1933; Doctor of Philosophy, Harvard University, 1941.

Research assistant Cowles Commission, University Chicago, 1945-46; with Norwegian Trade Commission, Oslo; professor economics University Oslo, 1948—. Recipient Nobel prize in econs., 1989. Member Am. Econ. Association, Am. Acad. Arts and Letters. Office: U Oslo, POB 1072, Blindern, 0316 Oslo 3, Norway

HABIG, DOUGLAS ARNOLD, manufacturing company executive; born Louisville, 1946; son of Arnold F. and Mary Ann (Jahn) H. Bachelor of Science, St. Louis University, 1968; Master of Business Administration, Ind. University, 1972. Commercial loan officer Ind. National Bank, Indianapolis, 1972-75; executive vice president, treasurer, chief fin. officer Kimball International Incorporated, Jasper, Ind., 1975-81, president, director, 1981—. Office: Kimball International Incorporated 1600 Royal St Jasper Indiana 47546

HABIG, THOMAS LOUIS, manufacturing executive; born Jasper, Indiana, June 18, 1928; son of Arnold Frank and Mary Ann (Jahn) H.; married C. Roberta Snyder, January 31, 1953; children: Randall, Julia, Brian, Sandra, Paul. Bachelor of Business Administration, Tulane University, 1950. With Kimball International, Incorporated (predecessor firm), Jasper, Ind., 1952—; executive vice president Kimball International, Incorporated (predecessor firm), Jasper, 1960-63, president, 1963—, chairman, chief executive officer, 1981—, also board of directors; board of directors Springs Valley Bank & Trust Company. With Army of the United States, 1950-52. Member Am. Legion, Sigma Chi. Roman Catholic. Club: Knights of Columbus. Office: Kimball International Incorporated 1600 Royal St Post Office Box 460 Jasper Indiana 47549

HADDOCK, RONALD WAYNE, oil company executive; born St. Elmo, Illinois, July 29, 1940; son of Clarence and Marie (Price) H.; married Sandra Sue Thomas, September 1957; children: Roni Sue Haddock Campey, Mark Tayler, Rick Wayne. BMechE, Purdue University, 1963. With Exxon Corp., 1963-86; various tech. staff, management positions Baton Rouge Refinery, 1963-71; specialties economics coordinator, administrative manager, planning manager Refining Department Houston headquarters, 1971-75; operations manager, refinery manager Baytown Refinery, 1975-78; corp. planning manager then vice president for refining Houston headquarters, 1978-81; executive assistant to chairman Exxon Corp. Headquarters New York City, 1981-82; vice president, director Esso Eastern Houston headquarters, 1982-85; executive vice president, chief operating officer Fina, Incorporated, Dallas, 1986-88, president, chief executive officer, 1988—; also board of directors Am. Petrofina, Incorporated, Dallas. Member Long Range Strategy Task Force, Pub. Communications Task Force, Dallas Citizens Council, Dallas Morning News Energy Board, Dallas United Board; chief executives Round Table; national chairman Paralysis Foundation; member board, executive committee Dallas Opera. Member Am. Petroleum Institute (pub. policy committee, budget committee, chairman strategic planning oversight grouop), National Petroleum Refiners Association (board directors), Ind. Producers Association Am., Petrochem. Industry Founders

Club, North Dallas Chamber, Dallas Chamber of Commerce (board directors, compensation and benefits committee), Am. Petrofina Foundation, 25 Year Club Petroleum Industry, Energy Club, Petroleum Club. Methodist. Clubs: Energy, Petroleum (Dallas). Avocations: golf, jogging, music. Office: Fina Incorporated Post Office Box 2159 Dallas Texas 75221

HAGEN, JAMES ALFRED, marketing executive; born Forest City, Iowa, March 27, 1932; son of Archie M. and Catherine E. (McGuire) H.; married Mary King, August 16, 1958; children: Joseph Patrick, Margaret Mary. Bachelor of Arts, St. Ambrose College, 1956; Master of Arts, Iowa State University, 1958. Assistant general freight agent Missouri Pacific Railroad, St. Louis, 1958-62; director marketing research, vice president corp. devel. Southern Rwy., Washington, 1963-71, 76-77; associate administrator economics Federal Railroad Administration, Washington, 1971-74; president United States Rwy. Association, Washington, 1974-76; senior vice president marketing and sales Consolidated Rail Corp., Philadelphia, 1977-85, chairman board, president, chief executive officer, 1989—; executive vice president sales and marketing distribution services group CSX Transportation, 1985-88; president distribution services group CSX Transportation, Baltimore, 1988-89; member business adv. committee Northwestern University Transportation Center. Member National Freight Transportation Association, Am. Society Transportation and Logistics. Roman Catholic. Home: 6605 Walnutwood Circuit Baltimore Maryland 21212 Office: Consol Rail Corp 6 Penn Center Philadelphia Pennsylvania 19103

HAGIWARA, KOKICHI, steel company executive; born Tokyo, 1924. Graduate, Tokyo University, 1947. President, chief operating officer National Steel Corp., Pittsburgh, also board of directors. Office: National Steel Corp National Steel Center 20 Stanwix St Pittsburgh Pennsylvania 15222

HAHN, THOMAS MARSHALL, JR., forest products corporation executive; born Lexington, Kentucky, December 2, 1926; son of Thomas Marshall and Mary Elizabeth (Boston) H.; married Margaret Louise Lee, December 27, 1948; children: Elizabeth Hahn McKelvy, Anne Hahn Clarke. Bachelor of Science in Physics, University Kentucky, 1945; Doctor of Philosophy, Massachusetts Institute of Technology, 1950; Doctor of Laws (honorary), Seton Hall University, 1976, Florida Southern College, 1986; Doctor of Philosophy (honorary), Virginia Polytechnic Institute, 1987. Physicist United States Naval Ordinance Laboratory, 1946-47; research assistant Massachusetts Institute of Technology, Cambridge, 1947-50; associate professor physics University Kentucky, Lexington, 1950-52, professor, 1952-54; professor, head department physics Virginia Polytechnic Institute and State University, Blacksburg, 1954-59, president, 1962-75; dean arts and sciences Kansas State University, Manhattan, 1959-62; executive vice president Ga.-Pacific Corp., Atlanta, 1975-76; dean arts and sciences Kansas State University, Manhattan, 1959-62; president, chief operating officer Ga.-Pacific Corp., Atlanta, 1982-83, president, chief executive officer, 1983-84, chairman board, president, chief executive officer, 1984-85, chairman board, chief executive officer, 1985—, 1985—; board of directors Norfolk Southern Corp., Coca-Cola Enterprises, Am. Paper Institute, chairman 1982-83, Sun Trust Banks; Trust Company Bank of Georgia, former chairman New York Stock Exchange Listed Company Adv. Committee. President Southern Association Land Grant Colleges And State Univs., 1965-66; chairman Virginia Metropolitan Area Study Commission, 1966-68, Virginia Cancer Crusade, 1972, United States Savs. Bond Program, Georgia, 1985-87; board visitors Air U., 1966-69, Ferrum Junior College; board of directors Atlanta Arts Alliance, Bus, Council Georgia, Central Atlanta Progress, Keep Am. Beautiful Incorporated; member adv. board Atlanta chapter Boy Scouts Am.; former chairman capital funds campaign Atlanta Area Svcs. for Blind, 1984; board visitors Callaway Gardens; member Atlanta Action Forum, national adv. board and campaign team greater Atlanta Salvation Army; former campaign chairman Georgia chapter Am. Diabetes Association, 1985-86, United Way of Metropolitan Atlanta Incorporated, 1987; Georgia chairman United States Savs. Bond Program, 1985-87; trustee Emory U., Institute Paper Chemistry, Robert W. Woodruff Arts Center, Emory U. (adv. council). With United States Navy, 1945-46. Named Chief Executive Officer of Year for forest products and lumber industry Wall Street Transcript, 1984-86, 88-89, Papermaker of Year, Paper Trade Journal, 1984, Chief Executive Officer of Year, Forest Products and Paper Industry, 1986; recipient Outstanding Citizen Virginia award Toastmasters International, 1966, Outstanding Professional Contbns. award Virginia Citizens Planning Association, 1970, Corp. Leadership award Massachusetts Institute of Technology, 1976. Fellow Am. Physical Society; member The Conference Board, Atlanta Chamber of Commerce, Phi Beta Kappa, Sigma Xi, Omicron Delta Kappa. Republican. Methodist. Clubs: Piedmont Driving, The Links, Shenandoah, Capital City, Ocean Reef, Commerce. Office: Ga-Pacific Corp 133 Peachtree St NE Atlanta Georgia 30303

HALL, DONALD JOYCE, greeting card company executive; born Kansas City, Missouri, July 9, 1928; son of Joyce Clyde and Elizabeth Ann (Dilday) H.; married Adele Coryell, November 28, 1953; children: Donald Joyce, Margaret Elizabeth, David Earl. Bachelor of Arts, Dartmouth, 1950; Doctor of Laws, William Jewell College, Denver University, 1977. With Hallmark Cards, Incorporated, Kansas City, Missouri, 1953—, administrative vice president, 1958-66, president, chief executive officer, 1966-83, chairman board, 1983—, chief executive officer, 1983-85, also director; director United Telecommunications, Incorporated, Dayton-Hudson Corp., William East Coutts Company, Limited; past director Federal Reserve Bank Kansas City, Mutual Benefit Life Insurance Company, Business Men's Assurance Company, Commerce Bank Kansas City, 1st National Bank Lawrence. President Civic Council Greater Kansas City; past chairman board Kansas City Association Trusts and Founds.; Board of directors Am. Royal Association, Friends of Art, Eisenhower

Foundation; board of directors Kansas City Minority Suppliers Devel. Council, Kansas City Minority Suppliers Devel. Council, Harry S. Truman Library Institute, Kansas City Symphony; past president Pembroke Country Day School, Civic Council of Greater Kansas City; trustee, past chairman executive committee Midwest Research Institute; trustee Nelson-Atkins Museum of Art. Served to 1st lieutenant Army of the United States, 1950-53. Recipient Eisenhower Medallion award, 1973; Parsons School Design award, 1977; 3d Annual Civic Service award Hebrew Acad. Kansas City, 1976; Chancellor's medal University Missouri, Kansas City, 1977; Distinguished Service citation University Kansas, 1980. Member Kansas City Chamber of Commerce (named Mr. Kansas City 1972, director), American Institute of Architects (hon.). Home: 6320 Aberdeen Road Shawnee Mission Kansas 66208 Office: Hallmark Cards Incorporated 2501 McGee Trafficway Post Office Box 580 Kansas City Missouri 64141

HALL, JOHN RICHARD, oil company executive; born Dallas, November 30, 1932; son of John W. and Agnes (Sanders) H.; married Donna S. Stauffer, May 10, 1980. Bachelor of Chemical Engineering, Vanderbilt University, 1955. Chemical engineer Esso Standard Oil Company, Baltimore, 1956-58, Ashland Oil Company, Kentucky, 1959-63; coordinator carbon black div. Ashland Oil Company, Houston, 1963-65; executive assistant vice president Ashland Oil Company, 1965-66, vice president, 1966-68, senior vice president, 1970-71; also director; president Ashland Chemical Company, 1971-74; executive vice president Ashland Oil, Incorporated, 1974—, group operating officer, 1976—, chief executive officer petroleum and chemicals, 1978—, vice chairman, chief operating officer, 1979-81, chairman, chief executive officer, 1981—; board of directors Banc One Corp., Columbus, Reynolds Metals Company, Richmond, Virginia. Trustee Vanderbilt U., Nashville, member committee visitors Engring. School; board curators Transylvania U., Lexington, Kentucky Served as 2d lieutenant, Chem. Corps Army of the United States, 1955-56. Member Chemical Manufacturers Association, National Petroleum Refiners Association, Am. Petroleum Institute, National Petroleum Council, Business Roundtable, Tau Delta Pi, Sigma Chi, Delta Kappa. Republican. Home: 99 Stoneybrook Dr Ashland Kentucky 41101 Office: Ashland Oil Incorporated Post Office Box 391 Ashland Kentucky 41114 also: Ashland Oil Incorporated 1000 Ashland Dr Russell Kentucky 41169

HALL, NEWELL J., chain drug store company executive; born Clinton, Indiana, 1932; married. Pharmacist Hook Drugs, Incorporated, Indianapolis, 1961-66, prescription drug buyer, 1966-69, assistant vice president, director professional services, 1969-79, vice president, director professional services, 1972-80, executive vice president, 1980-88; pres, chief executive officer Hook Drugs div. Hook SuperX Incorporated, Indianapolis, 1988—, also president, corp. vice president, chief operating officer. Office: Hook Drugs Div SuperX Incorporated 2800 Enterprise St Post Office Box 26285 Indianapolis Indiana 46226

HAMMETT, WILLIAM M. H., foundation executive; born Oldtown,

Maine, June 21, 1944; son of Walter Mitchel Howard and Lillian Joyce (Morin) H.; divorced; 1 child, Kelly Morin. Bachelor of Arts in Economics, Southern Illinois University, 1970; Master of Arts, University Chicago, 1976. President, trustee Manhattan Institute for Policy Research, New York City, 1980—; pub. New York: The City Journal, 1989—; board of directors Delphi Fin. Group, Incorporated, Reliance Standard Life Insurance Company. With United States Army, 1968-70. Member New York Athletic Club. Office: Manhattan Institute for Policy Research 42 E 71st St New York New York 10021

HAND, ELBERT O., clothing manufacturing and retailing company executive; born 1939. Bachelor of Science, Hamilton College, 1961. With Hart Schaffner and Marx, 1964-83; president, chief executive officer men's apparel group Hartmarx Corp., 1983-85, president, 1985—, now president, chief operating officer. Office: Hartmarx Corp 101 N Wacker Dr Chicago Illinois 60606

HANDLER, MARK S., retail executive; born 1933; married. Student, University Illinois; Bachelor of Science, Roosevelt University, 1957; Master of Science, New York University, 1958. With R.H. Macy & Company Incorporated, New York City, 1958—; merchandise administrator Bamberger's (subsidiary R. H. Macy & Company Incorporated), Newark, 1962-65, vice president, merchandise administrator, 1965-67, senior vice president merchandising, 1967-71, president, 1979, chairman, chief executive officer, 1979-80, also board of directors; president, director R. H. Macy & Company Incorporated, New York City, 1980—. Served with United States Army, 1953-55. Office: R H Macy & Company Incorporated 151 W 34th St New York New York 10001

HANLIN, RUSSELL L., citrus products company executive; born Sioux Falls, South Dakota, 1932; married. Student, University Washington, Los Angeles City College. With Sunkist Growers, Incorporated, Van Nuys, California, 1951—, advertising manager, 1964-72, vice president manufacturing, mkt. research and devel., products group, 1972-78, former chief executive and chief operating officer, president, 1978—, also director. Served with United States Army, 1953-55. Office: Sunkist Growers Incorporated 14130 Riverside Dr Box 7888 Van Nuys California 91409

HANSON, ALLEN DENNIS, grain marketing and processing cooperative executive; born 1936; married. With Harvest States Cooperatives, St. Paul, 1958—; President, chief executive officer Harvest States Cooperative, St. Paul, from 1982, now president, chief executive officer. Office: Harvest States Coops Post Office Box 64594 Saint Paul Minnesota 55164

HARBIN, JOHN PICKENS, oil well company executive; born Waxahachie, Texas, July 17, 1917; son of Elijah Pickens and Mary Joy (Beale) H.; married Dorothy Lee Middleton, December 13, 1920; children: Linda Ann Harbin Robuck. Student, Trinity University, San Antonio, 1935-37; Bachelor of Business Administration, University Texas, 1939. Accountant Carter Oil Company, Tulsa, 1939-40, Creole Petroleum, Venezuela, 1940-42, 45-48; controller Halliburton Company, Duncan, Oklahoma, 1948-

59; vice president fin. Halliburton Company, Duncan and Dallas, 1959-62; vice president fin. and director Halliburton Company, Dallas, 1962-67; senior vice president fin., director Halliburton Company, 1967-72, chairman board, chief executive officer, 1972-83; retired; board of directors Petrolite Corp., St Louis, Circle K. Corp., Phoenix, Penrod Drilling, Dallas, Am. Federal Bank, Dallas, Lone Star Technologies, Dallas. President, trustee Boy Scout Cir. Ten Council Foundation, Dallas, 1967—; board of directors U. Medical Center, Dallas, 1984—; trustee Southwestern Medical Foundation, Dallas, 1975—; elder Highland Park Presbyterian Church. Member Am. Petroleum Institute (hon. director 1983—), Petroleum Equip. Suppliers Association (board directors 1965—, president 1974), Texas Research League (board directors, past chairman 1978-79), Southwestern Medical Foundation (trustee 1975—), Navy League of United States, Dallas Petroleum Club (past president and director), Brook Hollow Golf Club, Dallas Country Club (past director), Chaparral Club (past director) The Brook Club, Beta Alha Psi. Repubican. Avocation: tennis. Home: 4816 Lakeside Dr Dallas Texas 75205 Office: Lone Star Techs Incorporated 2200 W Mockingbird Lane Dallas Texas 75235 also: 2104 Skyway Tower 400 N Olive LB21 Dallas Texas 75201

HARBISON, EARLE HARRISON, JR., chemical company executive; born St. Louis, August 10, 1928; son of Earle Harrison and Rose W. (Hensberg) H.; married Suzanne Groves Siegel, November 18, 1952; children: Earle Douglas, Keith Siegel. Student, Harvard University, 1960; Bachelor of Arts in Political Science, Washington University, St. Louis, 1948; Bachelor of Laws, George Washington University, 1957. Various positions Central Intelligence Agency, Washington, 1949-66, deputy director central reference, 1966-67; director management information systems department Monsanto Company, St. Louis, 1967-73, director corp. organization and management devel. department, 1973-75, general manager specialty chemical div., 1975, general manager plasticizers div., detergents and phosphates div., 1976-77; vice president, managing director Monsanto Commercial Products Company subsidiary Monsanto Company, St. Louis, 1977-79; member corp. administrative committee Monsanto Company, 1977; group vice president, managing director Monsanto Chemical Company (formerly Monsanto Industrial Chemicals Company), St. Louis, 1979-81; executive vice president Monsanto Company, 1981-86, president, chief operating officer, 1986—, also board of directors, 1986—; board of directors Merrill Lynch & Company, Incorporated, National Life Insurance Company, Angelica Corp., G.D. Searle and Company & The NutraSweet Company subsidiary Monsanto Company, Automobile Club of Missouri, St. Louis, Fisher Controls International, Incorporated subsidiary Monsanto Company, St. Louis. Board governors United Way Am., 1985—; board of directors United Way International, Barnes Hospital, St. Louis, 1990—; vice chairman Municipal Theatre Association, 1990—; vice chairman Regional Commerce and Growth Association, 1989—; chairman Arts and Scis. National Council Washington

U., St. Louis, 1991—, president William Greenleaf Eliot Society, 1989—. Captain United States Army Reserve, 1949—. Recipient William A. Jump award United States Government, 1964, Distinguished Alumni award Washington University, 1987, George Washington University, 1991. Member Certified Medical Assistant (board directors 1991—), Federal Bar and National Law Center (board directors 1991—), Am. Chemical Society (corp. liaison board 1986—), Brit.-Am. Chamber of Commerce (adv. director 1989—), U.S.-Japan Business Council (director 1990—), United States Trade Rep. (member investment policy adv. committee 1989-), Product Liability Coordinator Committee, Eldorado Country Club (Indian Wells, California), Ponte Vedra Club (Florida), Bellerive Country Club, Log Cabin Club. Office: Monsanto Company 800 N Lindbergh Boulevard Saint Louis Missouri 63167

HARDYMON, JAMES F., electronics company executive; born Maysville, Kentucky, November 11, 1934; son of Kenneth Thomas and Pauline (Strode) H.; married Rebecca Gay Garred, June 25, 1960; children: Jennifer, Frank. Bachelor of Science in Civil Engineering, University Kentucky, 1956, Master of Science in Civil Engineering, 1958. Vice president planning and devel. Browning div. Emerson Electric Company, 1970-73, executive vice president, 1973-76; president Skil div., vice president special products div. Emerson Electric Company, St. Louis, 1976-79, vice president corp. group, 1979-83, executive vice president, 1983-86, vice chairman, chief operating officer, 1986-88, president, chief operating officer, 1988-89; president, chief operating officer Textron, Incorporated, Providence, 1989—. With United States Army, 1958-59, 61-62. Recipient Corp. Devel. award American Society of Mechanical Engineers, 1976. Republican. Member Christian Church. Office: Textron Incorporated 40 Westminster St Providence Rhode Island 02903

HARLING, CARLOS GENE, savings and loan executive; born Gainesville, Florida, May 11, 1946; son of Hugh Whitman and Hester Elaine (Bonnette) H.; married Ewa Babara-Maria Hadrych, December 27, 1968; children: Nicole Lara, Audrey Anne. Bachelor of Business Administration in Accounting, University Florida, 1968; Master of Business Administration in Fin., Wayne State University, 1969. Certified Public Accountant, Michigan. Mgr.-audit Peat, Marwick, Mitchell & Company, Detroit, 1970-79; chief fin. officer First Federal of Michigan, Detroit, 1979-85, president, chief operating officer, 1985—, chief executive officer, 1989—, also board of directors. Served to 1st lieutenant, United States Army, 1969-70. Office: First Federal of Michigan 1001 Woodward Avenue Detroit Michigan 48226

HARMON, JAMES ALLEN, investment banker; born New York City, October 12, 1935; son of Bert and Belle (Kirschner) H.; married Jane Elizabeth Theaman, August 11, 1957; children—Deborah Lynn, Douglas Lee, Jennifer Ann. Bachelor of Arts, Brown University, 1957; Master of Business Administration, Wharton Graduate School, University Pennsylvania, 1959. With New York Hanseatic Corp., New York City, 1959-74, senior vice president, 1969-74; general partner Wertheim &

Company, Incorporated, New York City, 1975—, vice chairman, 1980-86, chairman, 1987—, chief executive officer, 1988—; board of directors Schroders plc, London, Questar Corp., Salt Lake City, Securities Industry Association; member adv. committee on international capital markets New York Stock Exchange. Trustee Brown U. Home: 43 Kettle Creek Road Weston Connecticut 06883 Office: Wertheim Schroder & Company Incorporated 787 7th Avenue New York New York 10019

HARPER, CHARLES MICHEL, food company executive; born Lansing, Michigan, September 26, 1927; son of Charles Frost and Alma (Michel) H.; married Joan Frances Bruggema, June 24, 1950; children: Kathleen Harper Wenngatz, Carolyn Harper Haney, Charles Michel, Elizabeth Harper Murphy. Bachelor of Science in Mechanical Engineering, Purdue University, 1949; Master of Business Administration, University Chicago, 1950. Supervisor methods engineering Oldsmobile div. General Motors Corp., Detroit, 1950-54; industrial engineer Pillsbury Company, Minneapolis, 1954-55; director industrial engineering Pillsbury Company, 1955-60, director engineering, 1961-66, vice president research, devel. and new products, 1965-70, group v.p.-poultry, food service and venture businesses, 1970-74; executive vice president, chief operating officer, director ConAgra Incorporated, Omaha, 1974-76; president, chief executive officer ConAgra Incorporated, 1976-81, chairman board, chief executive officer, 1981—; board of directors Norwest Corp., Valmont Industries, Incorporated, Peter Kiewit Sons', Incorporated, Burlington Northern, Incorporated; executive committee National Commission on Agricultural Trade and Export Policy, 1984-86. Member council Village of Excelsior (Minnesota), 1965-70, mayor, 1974; trustee Bishop Clarkson Memorial Hospital; hon. chairman Urban League Nebraska Membership Campaign, 1987; board of directors Creighton U., Joslyn Mus.; trustee Committee for Economic Devel., Washington; president Mid Am. Council Boy Scouts Am., 1983-84. Served with Army of the United States, 1946-48. Member United States Chamber of Commerce (board directors, chairman Food and Agriculture committee), Omaha Chamber of Commerce (chairman 1979), Grocery Manufacturers Am. (board directors 1985—), Business Roundtable, Ak-Sar-Ben (governor), University Nebr.-Lincoln College Business Admin. Alumni Association (hon. life), Beta Theta Pi. Office: ConAgra Incorporated 1 ConAgra Dr Omaha NE 68102

HARRELL, HENRY HOWZE, tobacco company executive; born Richmond, Virginia, September 18, 1939; son of Theron Rice and Susan Howze (Haskell) H.; married Jean Covington Camp, February 7, 1970; children—Susan Hampton, Shelby Madison. Bachelor of Arts, Washington and Lee University. Vice president Universal Leaf Tobacco Company, Incorporated, Richmond, 1974-81, senior vice president, 1981-82, executive vice president, 1982-86, president, 1986-88, president, chief executive officer, 1988—; director Jefferson Bankshares Incorporated, Charlottesville, Virginia, Lawyers Title Insurance Company, Richmond. Member Forum Club, Commonwealth Club, Phi Beta

Kappa, Omicron Delta Kappa. Republican. Episcopalian. Clubs: Country of Virginia, Deep Run Hunt (board dirs. 1981-83). Avocations: fishing; gardening.

HARRIS, KING WILLIAM, manufacturing company executive; born 1943. Bachelor of Arts, Harvard University, 1964, Master of Business Administration, 1965. With Pittway Corp., Northbrook, Illinois, 1971—, vice president alarm div., 1971-75, executive vice president electronics div., 1975-80, chairman board of directors, chief executive officer electronics div., 1980-84, now president, chief executive officer, board of directors. Office: Pittway Corp 333 Skokie Boulevard Northbrook Illinois 60065

HARRIS, NEISON, corporate executive; born St. Paul, January 24, 1915; son of William and Mildred (Brooks) H.; married Bette Deutsch, January 25, 1939; children: Katherine, King, Toni. Bachelor of Arts, Yale University, 1936. Founder Toni Company; president Toni div. Gillette Company, president Paper Mate div.; president, board of directors Pittway Corp., Northbrook, Illinois, 1959-84, chairman board, 1984-89; chairman board, director Standard Shares, Incorporated. Named One of Ten Outstanding Young Men United States, Junior Chamber of Commerce, 1948. Clubs: Standard, Lake Shore Country (Chicago); Boca Rio Country (Boca Raton, Florida). Office: Pittway Corp 333 Skokie Boulevard Northbrook Illinois 60065

HART, N. BERNE, banker; born Denver, January 6, 1930; son of Horace H. and Eva (Saville) H.; married Wilma Jean Shadley, September 17, 1952; children: Linda Lea Hart Frederick, Patricia Sue Hart Sweeney, David Bruce. Bachelor of Arts, Colorado College, 1951; postgraduate, Colorado School Banking, 1958-60. Sales trainee United States Rubber Company, 1953; executive trainee United Bank of Denver N.A., 1954-56, assistant operations manager, 1956-58, assistant cashier, 1958-61, assistant vice president, 1961, cashier, 1961-65, vice president operations, 1965-69, senior vice president personal banking div., 1969, senior vice president, trust officer, 1969-73; vice president United Banks Colorado Incorporated, 1974, executive vice president, 1975-77, president, 1977-78, chairman, 1979—; member federal adv. council Federal Reserve Board, 1983-85. Past chairman board of directors St. Joseph Hospital, Denver; past chairman board trustees Colorado School Banking. Served to captain United States Marine Corps Reserve, 1951-53. Named Denver Met. Executive of Year Denver chapter National Secs. Association, 1968; recipient Torch of Liberty award Anti-Defamation League, 1986, Colorado Business Leader of 1988 award, 1988. Member Colorado Bankers Association (past president), Adminstrv. Management Society (past president Denver chapter), Colorado Association Commerce and Industry (chairman 1985-86), Bank Administration Institute (chairman 1980-81), Beta Theta Pi. Republican. Clubs: Rotary (Denver) (president 1982-83), University (Denver); Denver Country, Lakewood Country. Home: 2552 E Alameda Avenue #99 Denver Colorado 80209 Office: United Banks Colorado Incorporated 1 United Bank Center 1700 Lincoln Suite 3200 Denver Colorado 80274-0010

HARTLEY, JOHN T., JR., electronic systems, communications executive; born 1930; married. Bachelor of Science in Chemical Engineering and Bachelor of Science in Electrical Engineering, Auburn University, 1955. With Harris Corp., Melbourne, Florida, 1956-60, vice president, 1960-63, vice president, general manager, 1963-73, corp. vice president, group executive, 1973-76, executive vice president, 1976-78, president, principal operating officer, 1978-82, chief operating officer, 1982-86, president, chief executive officer, 1986—, chairman, 1987—. Office: Harris Corp 1025 W Nasa Boulevard Melbourne Florida 32919

HARVEY, GEORGE BURTON, office equipment company executive; born New Haven, April 7, 1931; married Elizabeth Mary Viola, June 30, 1962; children: Paul, George, David. Bachelor of Science, University Pennsylvania, 1954. Vice president fin. Pitney Bowes, Incorporated, Stamford, Connecticut, 1973-76, group vice president business equipment, 1976-78, president business systems, 1978-81, president, 1981—; chief operating officer Pitney Bowes, Stamford, Connecticut, 1981-83, chairman, president, chief executive officer, 1983—; director Norton Company, Worcester, Massachusetts, Hartford, Connecticut, Business Equipment Manufacturers Association, Washington, Bank of New England; trustee Northeast Utilities, Hartford, Connecticut. Board dirs St. Joseph Hospital, Stamford; board dirs New Neighborhoods Incorporated; trustee King School, Connecticut College, New London. Served with United States Army, 1954-56. Member Southwestern Area Commerce and Industry Association (director), Connecticut Business Industry Association (director). Home: 663 Ponus Ridge Road New Canaan Connecticut 06840 Office: Pitney Bowes Incorporated World Hdqrs Stamford Connecticut 06926

HARVEY, JAMES ROSS, finance company executive; born Los Angeles, August 20, 1934; son of James Ernest and Loretta Berniece (Ross) H.; married Charlene Coakley, July 22, 1971; children: Kjersten Ann, Kristina Ross. Bachelor of Science in Engineering, Princeton University, 1956; Master of Business Administration, University California, Berkeley, 1963. Engineer Chevron Corp., San Francisco, 1956-61; accountant Touche, Ross, San Francisco, 1963-64; chairman board Transamerica Corp., San Francisco, 1965—; board of directors Sedgwick Group, Pacific Telesis Group, McKesson Corp., SRI International, Charles Schwab Corp. Trustee St. Mary's College; board of directors Walter A. Haas School Business, U. California, California State Parks Foundation, Bay Area Council, Mount Land Reliance, National Park Foundation; member Presidion Council With Army of the United States, 1958-59. Member California Nature Conservancy. Office: Transam Corp 600 Montgomery St San Francisco California 94111

HASSENFELD, ALAN GEOFFREY, toy company executive; born Providence, November 16, 1948; son of Merrill Lloyd and Sylvia (Kay) H. Bachelor of Arts, University Pennsylvania, 1970. Assistant to president Hasbro Industries, Incorporated, Pawtucket, Rhode Island, 1969-72, vice president international operations, 1972-78, vice president marketing and sales, 1978-80, executive vice president operations, 1980-84, president, 1984-89, chairman, chief executive officer, 1989—; chairman board Hasbro Can., 1980—. Board of directors International House Rhode Island, Providence, 1974—, Hasbro Incorporated, Hasbro United Kingdom Ltd, Foster Parents Plan, 1989—, Parents Anonymous, 1989—; member Rhode Island Air Adv. Task Force, The Tomorrow Fund Adv. Board, 1985; trustee Miriam Hospital, 1984—; member executive committee Deerfield Acad. Alumni Association, 1985; chairman Governor's Adv. Council on Refugee Resettlement, 1986; board overseers U. Pennsylvania School Arts and Scis., 1986—; board of directors Rhode Island Housing Partnership, 1987; trustee Rhode Island and Southeastern New England region, National Conference of Christians and Jews, 1988; board of directors Jewish Community Center, 1989—, Jewish Federation Rhode Island, 1989—. Served with Air Force National Guard, 1967-73. Member Toy Manufacturers Association (board directors 1978—, chairman 1985—). Office: Hasbro Industries Incorporated 1027 Newport Avenue Pawtucket Rhode Island 02861

HATSOPOULOS, GEORGE NICHOLAS, mechanical engineer, thermodynamicist, educator; born Athens, Greece, January 7, 1927; came to United States, 1948, naturalized, 1954; son of Nicholas and Maria (Platsis) Hatzopoulos; married Daphne Phylactopoulos, June 14, 1959; children: Nicholas, Marina. Student, National Tech. University, Athens, 1945-47; Bachelor of Science, Master of Science, Massachusetts Institute of Technology, 1950, Mechanical Engineer, 1954, Doctor of Science, 1956; Doctor of Science (honorary), New Jersey Institute Tech., 1982. Instructor Massachusetts Institute of Technology, 1954-56, assistant professor mechanical engineering, 1956-58, associate professor, 1959-62, senior lecturer in mechanical engineering, 1962-90; founder, president, chief executive officer, chairman board Thermo Elecron Corp.; developer, manufacturer and marketer products based on thermodynamic technologies of heat transfer and energy conversion, Waltham, Massachusetts, 1956—; member adv. board program tech. and economic policy Kennedy School Government, Harvard University; member Massachusetts Institute of Technology adv. board Center for Tech., Policy/Indsl. Devel.; director Institute for Research on Economics of Taxation., council board on sci., tech. and economic Policy, National Research Council. Author: Principles of General Thermodynamics, 1965, Thermionic Energy Conversion, volume 1, 1973, volume 2, 1979; contributor numerous articles to professional journals. Trustee Maliotis Foundation, Center for Policy Research, Am. Council for Capital Foundation, Congl. Economic Leadership Institute, Boston Mus. Sci.; vice chairman Am. Business Conference; chairman Federal Reserves Bank Boston, 1988-89, College Year in Athens, Incorporated; corp. member The Conference Board; tech. witness numerous Senate and Congl. Hearings. Recipient Am. Achievement Golden Plate award, 1961, Corp. Leadership award Massachusetts Institute of Technology, 1980. Fellow Institute of Electrical and Electronics

Engineers, American Institute of Aeronautics and Astronautics, American Society of Mechanical Engineers (chairman executive committee division energetics 1968-69), National Acad. Engineering, Am. Acad. Arts and Sciences; member Sigma Xi, Pi Tau Sigma (Gold medal award 1960). Greek Orthodox. Home: Tower Road Lincoln Massachusetts 01773 Office: Thermo Electron Corp 101 1st Avenue Post Office Box 9046 Waltham Massachusetts 02254-9046

HAUPTFUHRER, ROBERT PAUL, oil company executive; born Philadelphia, December 31, 1931; son of George J. and Emilie M. (Schoenhut) H.; married Barbara Ellen Dunlop, May 11, 1963; children—Brenda Lynn, Bruce Andrew, Bryan Dunlop. Bachelor of Arts, Princeton University, 1953; Master of Business Administration, Harvard University, 1957. With Sun Company, Incorporated, Radnor, Pennsylvania, 1957-88; senior vice president Sun Company, Incorporated, 1979-83; president Sun Exploration and Production Company, 1984-86; president, chief operating officer Sun Company, Incorporated, 1987-88; chairman, chief executive officer Oryx Energy Company, Dallas, 1988—; board of directors Quaker Chemical Corp., National Association Mfgs., National Gas Supply Association. Trustee Princeton U., 1987—; associate trustee U. Pennsylvania, 1987—; board governors Dallas Symphony Association Lieutenant (junior grade) United States Navy, 1953-55. Member Am. Petroleum Institute (board directors), Ind. Petroleum Association Am. (board directors), National Petroleum Council, The Conference Board, Union League Club, Philadelphia Country Club, Pine Valley Golf Club, Merion Cricket Club. Republican. Presbyterian. Home: 602 Old Eagle School Road Wayne Pennsylvania 19087 Office: Oryx Energy Company 5656 Blackwell Dallas Texas 75221-2880

HAUSMAN, JERRY ALLEN, economics educator, consultant; born Weirton, West Virginia, May 5, 1946; son of Harold H. and Rose (Hausman); married Margaretta Stone, December 21, 1968; children: Nicholas, Claire. Bachelor of Arts, Brown University, 1968; Bachelor of Philosophy., Oxford University, 1972, Doctor of Philosophy, 1973. Member faculty Massachusetts Institute of Technology, Cambridge, 1973—, professor economics, 1979—. Contributor articles to professional journals. Marshall scholar, 1970-72; recipient Frisch medal Econometrics Society, 1980; John Bates Clark award Am. Econs. Association, 1985. Office: Massachusetts Institute of Technology Department Econs Cambridge Massachusetts 02139

HAVERTY, HAROLD V., forms and check printing company executive; born 1930. With Deluxe Check Printers, Incorporated, St. Paul, 1954—, former vice president, now president, chief operating officer, also chief executive officer, 1986—, board of directors. Office: De Luxe Check Printers Incorporated 1080 W County Road F Post Office Box 64399 Saint Paul Minnesota 55112

HAWKINS, ARTHUR MICHAEL, automotive executive; born St. Catharines, Ontario, Canada, September 22, 1942; son of William Thomas and Mary Ann (Deneka) H.; children—William Robert, Tracey Michelle, Michael John, Samantha

Jane. Bachelor of Science in Industrial Engineering, Windsor College of Engineering, 1965; Master of Business Administration, Michigan State University, 1982. Vice president manufacturing Monroe Auto Equipment Company, Monroe, Michigan, 1979-80, vice president operations, 1980-82; senior vice president operations Tenneco Automotive, Bannockburn, Illinois, 1982-83; senior vice president, general manager Walker Manufacturing Company, Racine, Wisconsin, group executive I.T.T. Automotive Products Worldwide, Bloomfield Hills, Michigan, 1984-85; president, chief executive officer Exide Corp., Reading, Pennsylvania, 1985—. Member Am. Management Association, Society Automotive Engineers, Beta Gamma Sigma. Republican. Presbyterian. Home: 1530 Surria Court Bloomfield Hills Michigan 48013 Office: Exide Corp 111 W Long Lake Road Troy Michigan 48098

HAWLEY, PHILIP METSCHAN, retail executive; born Portland, Oregon, July 29, 1925; son of Willard P. and Dorothy (Metschan) H.; married Mary Catherine Follen, May 31, 1947; children: Diane (Mrs. Robert Bruce Johnson), Willard, Philip M. Jr., John, Victor, Edward, Erin, George. Bachelor of Science, University California, Berkeley, 1946; graduate advanced management program, Harvard University, 1967. With Carter Hawley Hale Stores, Incorporated, Los Angeles, 1958—, president, 1972-83, chief executive officer, 1977—, chairman, 1983—, board director; board of directors Atlantic Richfield Company, BankAm. Corp., American Telephone and Telegraph Company, Johnson & Johnson, Weyerhaeuser Company. Trustee California Institute Tech., U. Notre Dame, Huntington Libr. and Art Gallery; board of directors Associates Harvard U. Grad School Business Administration; adv. council Grad. School Business Stanford U.; visiting committee University of California at Los Angeles Grad. School Mgmt., Business Council, Business Roundtable, Conference Board; chairman Los Angeles Energy Conservation Committee 1973-74. Decorated hon. commander Order Brit. Empire, knight commander Star Solidarity Republic Italy; recipient award of merit Los Angeles Junior Chamber of Commerce, 1974, Coro Pub. Affairs award, 1978, Medallion award College William and Mary, 1983; named California Industrialist of Year California Mus. Sci. and Industry, 1975; recipient Alumni award of excellence School Business Administration University Southern California, 1987, Business Statesman of Year award Harvard Business School, 1989, 15th annual Whitney M. Young, Junior award L.S. Urban League, 1988. Member Phi Beta Kappa, Beta Alpha Psi, Beta Gamma Sigma. Clubs: California, Los Angeles Country; Bohemian Pacific-Union (San Francisco); Newport Harbor Yacht (Newport Beach, California); Multnomah (Portland); Links (New York City). Office: Carter Hawley Hale Stores Incorporated 444 S Flower St Los Angeles California 90071

HAY, JESS THOMAS, finance company executive; born Forney, Texas, January 22, 1931; son of George and Myrtle Hay; married Betty Jo Peacock, l95l; children: Deborah Hay Spradley, Patricia Hay Daibert. Bachelor of Business Administration,

Southern Methodist University, 1953, Juris Doctor magna cum laude, 1955. Bar: Texas. Associate firm Locke, Purnell, Boren, Laney & Neely, 1955-61, partner firm, 1961-65; president, chief executive officer Lomas Fin. Corp., Dallas, 1965-69, chairman board, chief executive officer, 1969—; chairman board, chief executive officer, trustee Lomas & Nettleton Mortgage Investors, 1969—; director, chairman board chief executive officer Capstead Mortgage Corp., L & N Housing Corp., Lomas Mortgage Securities Fund, Incorporated; board of directors Trinity Industries, Incorporated, MCorp., Republican Fin. Services, Incorporated, Exxon Corp., Greyhound Corp., Southwestern Bell Corp. Former member Dem. National Committee, also former national fin. chairman; former chairman board regents U. Texas System; former member Dallas Citizens Council, Dallas Assembly; member Greater Dallas Planning Council; board of directors Texas Research League, North Texas Food Bank, Child Car Partnership Dallas, Dallas County Historical Foundation, Texas Foundation for Higher Education, Higher Education Legis. Political Action Committee; trustee Southwestern Medical Foundation. Recipient Distinguished Service award Association Governing Bds. of Universities and Colleges, 1987. Member Dallas Bar Association, Texas Bar Association, Am. Bar Association, Am. Judicature Society, Newcomen Society North America. Methodist. Home: 7236 Lupton Circle Dallas Texas 75225 Office: Lomas Fin Corp 200l Bryan Tower Post Office Box 655644 Dallas Texas 75201

HAYEK, FRIEDRICH AUGUST (VON), economist, educator; born Vienna, Austria, May 8, 1899; son of August and Felicitas (von Juraschek) von H.; children—Christine M. F., Lorenz J. H.; married 2d, Helen Bitterlich, 1950. Dr.jur., University Vienna, 1921, Dr.re.pol., 1923; Doctor of Science in Economics, University London, 1941; Doctor (honorary), University Rikkyo, Tokyo, 1964, University Salzburg, 1974, University Dallas, 1975, Marroquin University, Guatemala, 1977, University Santa Maria, Valparaiso, 1977, University Buenos Aires, 1977, University Giessen, 1982. With Austrian Civil Service, 1921-26; director Austrian Institute for Business Cycle Research, 1927-31; lecturer economics and statistics University Vienna, 1929-31; Tooke professor economic sci. and statistics University London, London School Economics, 1931-50; professor social and moral sci. University Chicago, 1950-62; professor economics University Freiburg (Germany), 1962—; visiting professor University Salzburg (Austria), 1970-74. Author: Prices and Production, 1931; Monetary Theory and the Trade Cycle, 1933; Monetary Nationalism and International Stability, 1937; Profits, Interest and Investment, 1939; The Pure Theory of Capital, 1941; The Road to Serfdom, 1944; Individualism and Economic Order, 1949; John Stuart Mill and Harriet Taylor, 1951; The Sensory Order, 1952; The Counter-Revolution of Science, 1952; The Constitution of Liberty, 1960; Studies in Philosophy, Politics and Economics, 1967; Freiburger Studien, 1969; Law, Legislation and Liberty, Volume I, 1973, Volume II, 1975, Volume III, 1979; Denationalization of Money, 1976; Further

Studies in Politics, 1978; also numerous articles; acting editor Economica, 1940-50. Decorated Companion of Honor (Great Britain), Order Pour le Merite (Germany); Austrian Distinction for Arts and Sci.; recipient Nobel Prize for Econs., 1974. Fellow Brit. Acad.; hon. fellow Austrian Acad. Sci. Research on evolution of civilization. Home: Urachstrasse 27, D7800 Freiburg im Breisgau Federal Republic of Germany

HAYES, CHARLES A., mill company executive; born Gloversville, Kentucky, 1935; married. With Lee Dyeing Company, Incorporated, to 1961; with Guilford Mills, Incorporated, Greensboro, North Carolina, 1961—, executive vice president, 1961-68, president, chief executive officer, 1968-76, chairman board, 1976—, chief executive officer, also director. Office: Guilford Mills Incorporated 4925 W Market St Box U-4 Greensboro North Carolina 27401

HAYES, JAMES B., magazine executive. Pub. Fortune magazine, New York City. Office: Fortune Time & Life Building Rockefeller Center New York New York 10020

HAYES, JOHN PATRICK, manufacturing company executive; born Manistee, Michigan, May 9, 1921; son of John David and Daisy (Davis) H.; married Margaret Barbara Butler, April 12, 1947; children—John Patrick, Timothy Michael. Student, University Detroit, 1939-42, 46-47. With National Gypsum Company, 1947—, group vice president, 1970-75, president, 1975—, chairman board, chief executive officer, 1983—, also director; board of directors Lafarge Coppee, Paris. Served to 1st lieutenant Army of the United States, 1942-45. Clubs: Brook Hollow Golf (Dallas), Petroleum (Dallas). Office: National Gypsum Company 4500 Lincoln Plaza Dallas Texas 75201

HAYS, THOMAS CHANDLER, holding company executive; born Chicago, April 21, 1935; son of Marion C. and Carolyn (Reid) H.; married Mary Ann Jergens, June 8, 1958; children—Thomas, Michael, Paul, Jennifer. Bachelor of Science, California Institute Tech., 1957, Master of Science, 1958; Master of Business Administration with high distinction (Baker scholar), Harvard University, 1963. Operations research analyst Lockheed Corp., Los Angeles, 1963-64; product manager Andrew Jergens Company (formerly subsidiary Am. Brands), Cincinnati, 1964-70; vice president marketing Andrew Jergens Company (formerly subsidiary Am. Brands), 1970-78, executive vice president, 1978, president, chief executive officer, 1979-80; vice president marketing Am. Tobacco Company (subsidiary Am. Brands), 1980-81, executive vice president, 1981-85, president, 1985-87, president, chief operating officer, 1985-86, chief executive officer, 1986-87, chairman, 1987-88; president, chief operating officer Am. Brands, Incorporated, 1988—, also board of directors; board of directors Am. Tobacco, Acushnet Company, Gallaher Limited, Golden Belt Manufacturing Company, MasterBrand Industries, Incorporated, MCM Products, Incorporated, ACCO World Corp., Am. Brands International Corp., Am. Tob. International Corp., Am. Franklin Company, Jim Beam Brands Company, Franklin Life Insurance Company. Trustee, treasurer Cincinnati Country Day School, 1978-80; trustee The Andrew Jergens Foundation, trustee Five-Town Foundation; board of directors, treasurer Memorial Community Center, 1965-75. 1st lieutenant United States Air Force, 1958-61. Republican. Presbyterian. Clubs: Cincinnati Country, Darien Country, Bel Air Bay, Tokeneke.

HAZELRIGG, CHARLES RICHARD, banker; born Cadiz, Ohio, 1933; married. Bachelor of Science, Miami University, Ohio, 1955. Security analyst United Bank of Denver, 1958-61, portfolio manager, 1961-65, manager business devel., 1965-68, vice president, 1968-70, group vice president, 1970-74, senior vice president, 1974-77, executive vice president, 1977-81, senior executive vice president, 1981-82, president, 1982-87; with United Banks of Colorado, Incorporated, 1986—, president, 1986-87, president, chief operating officer, 1987—, also director. Served to captain United States Air Force, 1956-58. Office: United Banks Colorado Incorporated 1700 Lincoln St Suite 3200 Denver Colorado 80274

HAZEN, PAUL MANDEVILLE, banker; born Lansing, Michigan, 1941; married. Bachelor of Arts, University Arizona, 1963; Master of Business Administration, University California, Berkeley, 1964. Assistant mgr Security Pacific Bank, 1964-66; vice president Union Bank, 1966-70; chairman Wells Fargo Realty Advisors, 1970-76; with Wells Fargo Realty Advisors, San Francisco, 1979—, executive vice president, manager Real Estate Industries Group, 1979-80, member executive office Real Estate Industry Group, 1980, vice-chairman Real Estate Industries Group, 1980-84, president, chief operating officer Real Estate Industries Group, 1984—, also director Real Estate Industries Group, 1984—; president, treasurer Wells Fargo Mortgage & Equity Trust, San Francisco, 1977-84, with Wells Fargo & Company (parent), 1978—, executive vice president, then vice-chairman, now president, chief operating officer, director, 1978—; trustee Wells Fargo Mortgage & Equity Trust; board of directors Pacific Telesis Group. Office: Wells Fargo & Company 420 Montgomery St San Francisco California 94163

HEARST, RANDOLPH APPERSON, publishing executive; born New York City, December 2, 1915; son of William Randolph and Millicent (Willson) H.; married Catherine Campbell, January 12, 1938 (divorced April 1982); children: Catherine, Virginia, Patricia, Anne, Victoria; married Maria C. Scruggs, May 2, 1982 (divorced October 1986); married Veronica de Uribe, July, 1987. Student, Harvard University, 1933-34. Assistant to editor Atlanta Georgian, 1934-38; assistant to pub. San Francisco Call-Bull., 1940-44, executive editor, 1947-49, pub., 1950-53; associate pub. Oakland Post-Enquirer, 1946-47; president, director, chief executive officer Hearst Consolidated Publs., Incorporated and Hearst Pub. Company, Incorporated, 1961-64; president San Francisco Examiner, 1972—; director The Hearst Corp., 1965—, chairman executive committee, 1965-73, chairman, 1973—; Director Hearst Foundation, 1945—, president, 1972—; director Wm. Randolph Hearst Foundation, 1950—. Served as captain, Air Transport Command United States Army Air Force, 1942-

45. Roman Catholic. Clubs: Piedmont Driving (Atlanta); Burlingame Country, Pacific Union. Office: Hearst Corp 959 8th Avenue New York New York 10019

HECKEL, JOHN LOUIS (JACK HECKEL), aerospace company executive; born Columbus, Ohio, July 12, 1931; son of Russel Criblez and Ruth Selma (Heid) H.; married Jacqueline Ann Alexander, November 21, 1959; children: Heidi, Holly, John. Bachelor of Science, University Illinois, 1954. Div. manager Aerojet Divs., Azusa, California, 1956-70, Seattle and Washington, 1956-70; president Aerojet-Space General Company, El Monte, California, 1970-72, Aerojet Liquid Rocket Company, Sacramento, 1972-77; group vice president Aerojet Sacramento Companies, 1977-81; president Aerojet General, La Jolla, California, 1981-85; chairman, chief executive officer Aerojet General, 1985-87; president, chief operating officer GenCorp., Akron, 1987—, also board of directors; board of directors WD-40 Corp., Marrow-Tech., San Diego. Board of directors San Diego Economic Devel. Corp., 1983-86, Akron Regional Devel. Board, Akron General Hospital, Summit County United Way. Recipient Distinguished Alumni award University Illinois Annual Alumni Convention, 1979. Fellow American Institute of Aeronautics and Astronautics (associate); member Aerospace Industries Association Am. (governor 1981), Navy League United States, Am. Defense Preparedness Association, San Diego Chamber of Commerce (board directors). Office: GenCorp 175 Ghent Road Fairlawn Ohio 44313-3300

HECKMAN, JAMES JOSEPH, economist, econometrician; born Chicago, April 19, 1944; son of John Jacob and Bernice Irene (Medley) H.; married Lynne Pettler, 1979; children: Jonathan Jacob, Alma Rachel. Bachelor of Arts in Math. summa cum laude (Woodrow Wilson fellow), Colorado College, 1965; Master of Arts in Econs, Princeton University, 1968; Master of Arts, Yale University, 1989; Doctor of Philosophy in Economics (Harold Willis Dodds fellow), Princeton University, 1971. Lecturer Columbia University, 1970-71, assistant professor economics, 1971-73, associate professor, 1973-74; associate professor economics University Chicago, 1973-76, professor, 1976—, Henry Schultz professor economics, 1985—, Henry Schultz professor Harris School Pub. Policy Economics, 1990; research associate National Bureau Economics Research, 1970-77, senior research associate, 1977-85, 87—; A. Whitney Griswold professor economics 1988-90; professor, department statistics Yale University, New Haven, 1990, director evaluation center Harris School Pub. Policy, 1991—; Irving Fisher professor economics Yale University, 1984; treasurer Chicago Economic Research Associates; research associate Economics Research Ctr.-NORC, 1985—; consultant in field; fellow Center for Advanced Study in Behavioral Sciences, Palo Alto, California, 1978-79; consultant Chicago Urban League, 1978-86; member status black Ams. committee National Research Council; research affiliate Am. Bar Foundation, 1989-91. Author: Impact of the Economy and the State on the Status of Blacks; associate editor Journal Econometrics, 1977-83,

Journal Econ. Perspectives, 1989—, Econ. Revs., 1987—; editor: (with B. Singer) Longitudinal Analysis of Labor Market Data, 1985, Journal Labor Econs.; Am. editor Rev. Econ. Studies, 1982-85; editor Journal Political Economy, 1981-87; contributor articles to professional journals. Founding faculty and curriculum committee U. Chicago Harris School of Pub. Policy. Recipient L. Benezet Alumni Prize, Colorado College, 1985; J.S. Guggenheim fellow, 1978-79; Social Sci. Rsch. Council fellow, 1977-78. Fellow Am. Bar Foundation, Econometric Society, Am. Acad. Arts and Sciences; member Am. Econ. Association (John Bates Clark medal 1983), Am. Statistical Association, Industrial Relations Research Association, Econ. Sci. Association (founder), Phi Beta Kappa. Home: 230 Three Corners Road Guilford Connecticut 06437 Office: U Chicago Department Econs 1126 E 59th St Chicago Illinois 60637

HEDIEN, WAYNE EVANS, insurance company executive; born Evanston, Illinois, February 15, 1934; son of George L. and Edith P. (Chalstrom) H.; married Colette Johnston, August 24, 1963; children: Mark, Jason, Georgiana. Bachelor of Science in Mechanical Engineering, Northwestern University, 1956, Master of Business Administration, 1957. Engineer Cook Electric Company, Skokie, Illinois, 1957-64; business manager Preston Sci., Incorporated, Anaheim, California, 1964-66; security analyst Allstate Insurance Company, Northbrook, Illinois, 1966-70, portfolio manager, 1970-73, assistant treasurer, 1973-78, vice president, treasurer, 1978-80, senior vice president, treasurer, 1980-83, executive vice president, chief fin. officer, 1983-85, vice chairman, chief fin. officer, 1986, president, 1986-89, chairman, chief executive officer, 1989—, also board of directors. Member adv. council Kellogg Grad. School of Mgmt. Northwestern U. Member Institute Chartered Fin. Analysts (chartered fin. analyst), Newcomen Society, Econ. Club. Office: Allstate Ins Company Allstate Plaza Northbrook Illinois 60062

HEINER, ROBERT T., banker; born 1925. Student, Weber State College. With First Security Bank of Utah NA, Salt Lake City, 1946—, chairman board, chief executive officer, director; president, chief administrative officer 1st Security Corp., Salt Lake City, 1986—. Office: 1st Security Corp 79 S Main St Post Office Box 30006 Salt Lake City Utah 84130

HEIST, LEWIS CLARK, forest products company executive; born Bridgeport, Connecticut, June 6, 1931; son of Floyd L. and Gladys M. (Hall) H.; married Mary E. Lyman, February 5, 1954; children: Jane, William Peter, Matthew. Bachelor of Arts in Economics, Yale University, 1953, Master of Forestry, 1957. With United States Plywood, Hartford, Connecticut, 1957-61; sales Manager United States Plywood, Pittsburgh, 1961-64; vice president business planning United States Plywood-Champion Paper, New York City, 1970-75; executive vice president Timberlands div. Champion International Corp., Stamford, Connecticut, 1976-82, executive vice president pulp, paper and paperbd. manufacturing, 1982-87, president, chief operating officer, director, from 1987; vice president, director Lyman Farm

Incorporated, Middlefield, Connecticut, 1975—; pres, chief operating officer Gateway Homes, Incorporated, Stanford, Connecticut; board of directors Forest Industries Committee on Timber Valuation and Taxation, National Council Paper Industry Air and Stream Improvement. Board of directors United Way, Greenwich, Connecticut, 1977—, Old Greenwich Community Center, 1973-77. 1st lieutenant United States Marine Corps, 1953-55. Member Society Am. Foresters, Am. Forestry Association, National Forest Products Association. Presbyterian. Club: Rocky Point. Home: 187 Shore Road Old Greenwich Connecticut 16870 Office: Champion International Corp 1 Champion Plaza Stamford Connecticut 06921

HELMSLEY, HARRY B., real estate company executive; born New York City, 1909; married Leona M. President, chief executive officer Helmsley-Spear, Incorporated, New York City; chairman, president, chief executive officer Helmsley Enterprises, Incorporated (parent company), New York City. Office: Helmsley Hotels Helmsley Palace 455 Madison Avenue New York New York 10165

HEMMINGHAUS, ROGER ROY, energy company executive, chemical engineer; born St. Louis, August 27, 1936; son of Roy Geroge and Henrietta E.M. (Knacht) H.; children: Sheryl Ann, Susan Lynn, Sally Ann; married Dorotyh O'Kelly, August 18, 1979; children: R. Patrick, Kelley Elizabeth, Roger Christian. Student, Purdue University, 1954-56; Bachelor of Science in Chemical Engineering, Auburn University, 1958; graduate certificate, Bettis Reactor Engineering, Pittsburgh, 1959; postgraduate, Louisiana State University, 1963-66. Various tech. and management positions Exxon Company United States of America, Baton Rouge, 1962-66, Benicia, California, 1967-70, Houston, 1970-76; refinery general manager C.F. Industries, East Chicago, Ind., 1976-77; president Petro United Incorporated, Houston, 1977-80; vice president planning United Gas Pipe Line, Houston, 1980-82, United Energy Resources, Houston, 1982-84; vice president corp. planning and devel. Diamond Shamrock Corp. (name changed to Maxus Energy Corp., 1987), Dallas, 1984-85, past executive vice president; president Diamond Shamrock Refining & Marketing, San Antonio, 1985—; now also chairman, chief executive officer Diamond Shamrock Refining & Marketing; director InterFirst Bank, San Antonio. Adviser Junior Achievement, Baton Rouge, 1956-66; president congregation Lutheran Church, Baton Rouge, 1965, Moraga, California, 1969; chairman industrial div. United Crusade, Solano County, California, 1970; associate general chairman United Way, Texas Gulf Coast, 1983-84. Served to lieutenant United States Navy, 1958-62. Member Am. Chemical Society, Am. Institute Chemical Engineers, Naval Architects and Marine Engineers, Am. Petroleum Institute, San Antonio Chamber of Commerce (director), Tau Beta Pi, Phi Lambda Upsilon, Phi Kappa Phi, Kappa Alpha. Clubs: Fair Oaks Country; Plaza, Petroleum (San Antonio). Office: Diamond Shamrock R&M Incorporated Post Office Box 696000 San Antonio Texas 78269

HENDEE, JOHN HOLLISTER, JR., banker; born 1926; married. Bachelor of Arts, Williams College, 1949; Master of Business Administration,

University Wisconsin, 1956. With 1st Wisconsin National Bank of Milwaukee, 1949—, senior vice president, 1970-72, executive vice president, 1972-76, president, 1976-86, chairman, chief executive officer, 1986-88, director; chairman Firstar Corp., Milwaukee, 1988—. Office: Firstar Corp 777 E Wisconsin Avenue Milwaukee Wisconsin 53202

HENDERSON, JAMES ALAN, engine company executive; born South Bend, Indiana, July 26, 1934; son of John William and Norma (Wilson) H.; married Mary Evelyn Kriner, June 20, 1959; children: James Alan, John Stuart, Jeffrey Todd, Amy Brenton. Bachelor of Arts, Princeton University, 1956; Baker scholar, Harvard University, 1961-63. With Scott Foresman & Company, Chicago, 1962; staff member Am. Research & Devel. Corp., Boston, 1963; faculty Harvard Business School, 1963; assistant to chairman Cummins Engine Company, Incorporated, Columbus, Ind., 1964-65; vice president management devel. Cummins Engine Company, Incorporated, Columbus, 1965-69, vice president personnel, 1969-70, vice president operations, 1970-71, executive vice president, 1971-75, executive vice president, chief operating officer, 1975-77, president, 1977—; also director Cummins Engine Company, Incorporated; board of directors Cummins Engine Foundation, Inland Steel Ind., Chicago, Ameritech, Chicago, Rohm and Haas Company, Philadelphia, Landmark Communications, Norfolk. Author: Creative Collective Bargaining, 1965. Chairman executive committee, trustee Princeton U.; trustee, president Culver Educational Foundation Lieutenant United States Naval Reserve, 1956-61. Presbyterian (elder). Home: 4228 Riverside Dr Columbus Indiana 47203 Office: Cummins Engine Company Incorporated # 60912 Box 3005 Columbus Indiana 47202-3005

HENNESSY, EDWARD LAWRENCE, JR., diversified aerospace/automotive products and engineered materials executive; born Boston, March 22, 1928; son of Edward Lawrence and Celina Mary (Doucette) H.; married Ruth Frances Schilling, August 18, 1951; children: Michael E., Elizabeth R. Bachelor of Science, Fairleigh Dickinson University, 1955; student, New York University. With Heublein, Incorporated, Hartford, Connecticut, 1965-72, vice president fin., 1965-68, senior vice president administration, fin., 1969-72; senior vice president fin. and administration United Techs. Corp., Hartford, 1972-77; chief fin. officer, group vice president United Techs. Corp. (Systems and Equipment Group), 1977, executive vice president, 1978-79; chairman, president, chief executive officer Allied Corp., Morris Township, New Jersey, from 1979, chairman, chief executive officer, 1985—; board of directors Nova Pharmaceutical Corp., Martin Marietta Corp., Bank of New York, Union Texas Petroleum Holdings, Incorporated. Trustee Catholic U. Am.; trustee Fairleigh Dickinson U., United States Coast Guard Foundation Served with United States Naval Reserve, 1949-55. Member Fin. Executives Institute, Econ. Club New York. Roman Catholic. Clubs: Cat Cay (Bahamas); New York Yacht; Ocean Reef, Anglers (Key Largo, Florida). Office: Allied-Signal Incorporated 496 La Grandia Place Suite 305 New York New York 10012 Office: Allied Signal

Incorporated Post Office Box 2245R Morristown New Jersey 07960-2245

HENNIG, FREDERICK E., retail company executive. married Margaret Jones; 4 children. With F.W. Woolworth Company, New York City, 1949—, senior vice president worldwide merchandise operations, 1984-86, president, chief operating officer, 1987—. Office: F W Woolworth Company 233 Broadway New York New York 10279

HENSLER, WILIAM A., building materials company executive. Chief executive officer Wickes Lumber, Vernon Hills, Illinois. Office: Wickes Lumber Company 706 Deerpath Dr Vernon Hills Illinois 60061

HENSON, PAUL HARRY, communications executive; born Bennet, Nebraska, July 22, 1925; son of Harry H. and Mae (Schoenthal) H.; married Betty L. Roeder, August 2, 1946; children: Susan Irene Flury, Lizbeth Henson Barelli. Bachelor of Science in Electrical Engineering, University Nebraska, 1948, Master of Science, 1950; honorary doctorates, University Nebraska, Ottawa University, Bethany College, University Missouri, University Kansas. Registered professional engineer, Nebraska. Engineer Lincoln (Nebraska) Telephone & Telegraph Company, 1941-42, 45-48, div. manager, 1948-54, chief engineer, 1954-59; vice president United Telecommunications, Incorporated, Kansas City, Missouri, 1959-60, executive vice president, 1960-64, president, 1964-73, chairman, 1966-90, also director, 1964—; chairman board Kansas City Southern Industries, Incorporated, 1990—; board of directors Armco, Duke Power, Hallmark Cards, Ameribanc, Incorporated, Kansas City South Industries, Incorporated, United Telecommunications, Incorporated. Trustee Midwest Research Institute, Tax Foundation, U. Nebraska Foundation, U. Missouri at Kansas City, Children's Mercy Hospital With United States Army Air Force, 1942-45. Member National Society Professional Engineers, Institute of Electrical and Electronics Engineers, Armed Forces Communications Electronics Association, United States Telephone Association (director 1960-76, president 1964-65), Kansas City Country Club, Mission Hills Country Club, River Club, Kansas City Club, Eldorado Country Club, Old Baldy Club, Masons, Shriners, Sigma Xi, Eta Kappa Nu, Sigma Tau, Kappa Sigma (Man of Year 1987). Office: Kansas City Southern Industries Incorporated 114 W 11th St Kansas City Missouri 64105

HERBERT, GAVIN SHEARER, JR., health care products company executive; born Los Angeles, March 26, 1932; son of Gavin and Josephine (D'Vitha) H.; children by previous marriage Cynthia, Lauri, Gavin, Pam; 2d. married Ninetta Flanagan, September 6, 1986. Bachelor of Science, University Southern California, 1954. With Allergan, Incorporated, Irvine, California, 1950—; vice president Allergan, Incorporated, 1956-61, executive vice president, president, 1961-77, chairman board, chief executive officer, 1977—; president Eye and Skin Care Products Group Smith Cline Beckman Corp., 1981-89; executive vice president Smith Kline Beckman Corp., 1986-89; board of directors Beckman Instruments, Incorporated. Trustee U. Southern California; board of directors Richard Nixon Presidential Foundation, Estelle Doheny Eye Foundation With United States Navy, 1954-56. Member Pharmaceutical Manufacturers Association (board directors), Research to Prevent Blindness (board directors), Big Canyon Country Club, Balboa Bay Club, Newport Harbor Yacht Club, Pacific Club, Beta Theta Pi. Republican. Office: Allergan Incorporated 2525 DuPont Dr Irvine California 92715

HERLONG, D. C., agribusiness executive. Chairman Gold Kist Incorporated, Atlanta. Office: Gold Kist Incorporated 244 Perimeter Center Parkway NE Atlanta Georgia 30346

HERMAN, THEODORE LEE, insurance company executive; born Boston, December 21, 1936; son of Harry and Celia H.; married Brenda Herman, May 20, 1962; children—Lynda, Carole. Bachelor of Science, Boston University, 1958; Master of Arts, George Washington University, 1960. With Am. Life Insurance Company of New York, New York City, 1962—; manager Am. Life Insurance Company of New York, 1970-75, president, 1975—, chief executive officer, also director. Served with United States Marine Corps, 1958-60. Office: Am Life Ins Company of New York Office of President 810 7th Avenue New York New York 10019

HERRICK, KENNETH GILBERT, manufacturing company executive; born Jackson, Michigan, April 2, 1921; son of Ray Wesley and Hazel Marie (Forney) H.; married Shirley J. Todd, March 2, 1942; children: Todd Wesley, Toni Lynn. Student public and private schools, Howe, Ind.; Doctor of Humane Letters (honorary), Siena Heights College, 1974; Doctor of Humanities (honorary), Adrian College, 1975, Detroit Institute Tech., 1980; Doctor of Laws, Judson College, 1975; Doctor Engineering (honorary), Albion College, 1981. With Tecumseh Products Company, Michigan, 1940-42, 45—; vice president Tecumseh Products Company, 1961-66, vice chairman board, 1964-70, president, 1966-70, chairman board, chief executive officer, 1970-86, chairman board, 1986—; board of directors Manufacturers National Bank Detroit. Board of directors Howe Mil. School, 1970-81, from Herrick Foundation, 1970; member executive adv. board St. Jude Children's Hospital, from 1978. Served with USAAC, 1942-45. Recipient Hon. Alumni award Michigan State University, 1975; Distinguished Service award Albion College, 1975. Member Lenawee Country Club, Elks, Tecumseh Country Club, Masons. Presbyterian. Office: Tecumseh Products Company 100 E Patterson Tecumseh Michigan 49286

HERRICK, TODD W., manufacturing company executive; born Tecumseh, Michigan, 1942. Graduate, University Notre Dame, 1967. President, chief executive officer Tecumseh (Michigan) Products Company. Office: Tecumseh Products Company 100 E Patterson St Tecumseh Michigan 49286

HERRING, LEONARD GRAY, marketing company executive; born near Snow Hill, North Carolina, June 18, 1927; son of Albert Lee and Josie (Sugg) H.; married Rozelia Sullivan, June 18, 1950; children: Sandra Grey, Albert Lee II. Bachelor of Science, University North Carolina, 1948. With Dun & Bradstreet, Incorporated, Raleigh, North Carolina,

1948-49, H. Weil & Company, Goldsboro, North Carolina, 1949-55; president, chief executive officer Lowe's Companies, Incorporated, North Wilkesboro, North Carolina, 1955—; board of directors First Brands Corp. Danbury, Connecticut, First Union National Bank, Charlotte, North Carolina; member Lowe's Companies Incorporated Employee Stock Ownership Plan management committee; member board visiting University North Carolina. Trustee Pfeiffer College, Misenheimer, North Carolina. Member Chi Psi. Democrat. Methodist. Home: 310 Coffey St North Wilkesboro North Carolina 28659 Office: Lowe's Cos Incorporated Highway 268 E Post Office Box 1111 North Wilkesboro North Carolina 28656

HERRINGTON, JOHN STEWART, lawyer; born Los Angeles, May 31, 1939; son of Alan D. and Jean (Stewart) H.; married Lois Haight, April 10, 1965; children—Lisa Marie, Victoria Jean. Bachelor of Arts in Economics, Stanford University, 1961; Juris Doctor, University California, San Francisco, 1964. Bar: California 1964. Deputy district attorney Ventura County District Attorney's Office, California, 1965-66; partner Herrington & Herrington, Walnut Creek, California, 1966-81; deputy assistant to President White House, Washington, 1981, assistant to President, 1983-85; assistant secretary Department Navy, Washington, 1981-83; secretary Department Energy, Washington, 1985-89; chairman Harcourt Brace Jovanovich, Orlando, 1990—; member Reserve Forces Policy Board, Washington, 1981-83; chairman Def. Department Per Fiem Committee, Washington, 1982-83; chairman United States Del. IEA Ministerial Conference; United States Republican annual general conference International Atomic Energy Agency (rank ambassador), special session on Chernobyl. Trustee, treasurer Ronald Reagan Presidential Foundation, 1985—. Served to 1st lieutenant United States Marine Corps, 1962. Recipient Distinguished Service medal United States Department Defense, 1983, Presidential Citizens medal, 1989. Member United States Naval Institute, California Bar Association, Hastings Alumni Association, Stanford University Alumni Association. Republican. Office: Harcourt Brace Jovanovich Incorporated Orlando Florida 32887

HESS, LEON, oil company executive; born Asbury Park, New Jersey, March 13, 1914; (married). With Hess Oil & Chemical Corp. (and predecessor), 1946-69, president, 1962-65, chairman board, chief executive officer, 1965-69; also director Hess Oil & Chemical Corp.; chairman board Amerada Hess Corp. (merger Hess Oil & Chemical Corp. and Amerada Petroleum Corp.), New York City, 1971—, chief executive officer, 1971-82, 86—, also director; co-owner, now sole owner, chairman board New York Jets Football Team, New York City, 1963—; director ABC, Mutual Benefit Life Insurance Company, Monmouth Park Jockey Club. Served with Army of the United States, 1942-45. Office: Amerada Hess Corp 1185 Avenue of the Americas New York New York 10036 other: New York Jets 598 Madison Avenue New York New York 10022

HEYMAN, SAMUEL J., chemicals and building materials manufacturing company executive; born New York

City, March 1, 1939; son of Lazarus S. and Annette (Silverman) H.; married Ronnie Feuerstein, November 1970; children: Lazarus, Eleanor, Jennifer, Elizabeth. Bachelor of Science magna cum laude, Yale College, 1960; Bachelor of Laws, Harvard University, 1963. Bar: Connecticut 1963. Attorney United States Department Justice, Washington, 1963-64; assistant United States attorney District of Connecticut, New Haven, 1964-67; chief assistant United States attorney New Haven div., 1967-68; president Heyman Properties, Westport, Connecticut, 1968—; chairman, chief executive officer GAF Corp., Wayne, New Jersey, 1983—. Office: GAF Corp 1361 Alps Road Wayne New Jersey 07470

HICKEY, FRANK G., electronic components and equipment manufacturing company executive; born 1927. Bachelor of Science in Business Administration, University Dayton, 1950. Vice president Tait Manufacturing Company, 1953-63; president Fairbanks-Morse Pump div. Colt. Industries Incorporated, 1963-65; with General Instrument Corp., New York City, 1965—, corp. vice president capacitor group, 1966-70, executive vice president components group, 1970-72, president, 1972-87, chief operating officer, 1972-74, chairman, chief executive officer, 1975—, also director. Served with United States Navy, 1945-46. Office: General Instrument Corp 767 Fifth Avenue New York New York 10153

HILLAS, ROGER S., banker; born 1927; married. Bachelor of Arts, Dartmouth College; postgraduate, Wharton School Fin., University Pennsylvania. With Provident National Bank, Philadelphia, 1951—, vice president, 1960-64, executive vice president coml. div., 1964-69, president, chief administrative officer, 1969-75, chairman board, chief executive officer, 1975—, president, from 1980; director Provident National Bank (now PNC Fin. Corp.), Pittsburgh, from 1973; president parent company Provident National Corp., 1969-75, chief executive officer, 1973—, chairman board, 1975—, director; chairman, chief executive officer Meritor Fin. Corp., Philadelphia, 1988—; director Federal Reserve Bank Philadelphia, Lease Financing Corp., P.H. Glatfelter Company, Goodall Company, Philadelphia Facilties Management Corp., Consolidated Rail Corp., Provident Mutual Life Insurance Company. Treasurer, board overseers William Penn Charter School; trustee Temple U. Office: Meritor Fin Group 1212 Market St Philadelphia Pennsylvania 19107 also: Provident National Bank Broad & Chestnut Sts Philadelphia Pennsylvania 19101

HILLENBRAND, DANIEL A., manufacturing company executive; born 1923; married. Student, Purdue University. With Hillenbrand Industries, Incorporated, Batesville, Ind., 1946—, director purchasing, 1946-64, vice president, director marketing, 1964-69, president subsidiary Batesville Casket Company, 1969-72, chairman board, president, chief executive officer parent company, 1972-81, chairman board, chief executive officer, 1981—, also director. Office: Hillenbrand Industries Incorporated Highway 46 E Batesville Indiana 47006

HILLENBRAND, W. AUGUST, manufacturing company executive; born 1940; married. Bachelor of

Science in Management, St. Joseph's College, 1965. With Hillenbrand Industries, Batesville, Ind., 1958—, assistant to president, 1965-70, vice president operations, 1970-79, executive vice president, 1979-81, president, 1981—, chief executive officer, 1989—, also board of directors. Office: Hillenbrand Industries Incorporated Highway 46 E Batesville Indiana 47006

HILLER, WILLIAM ARLINGTON, agriculture executive; born East Stroudsburg, Pennsylvania, January 15, 1928; son of John Jacob and Marguerite Laura H.; married Joan Drake, June 2, 1947; children: William A., Joel, Jay S. Bachelor of Science cum laude, Upper Iowa University, 1950; Master of Science, Pennsylvania State University, 1952. Management trainee Agway Incorporated, Lakewood, New Jersey, 1951-53, retail store manager, 1953-71; vice president corp. marketing Agway Incorporated, Syracuse, New York, 1971-73, group vice president, 1973-79, assistant general manager, 1979-81, president, chief executive officer, 1981—; chairman Texas City (Texas) Refining Incorporated, also board of directors; chairman board Agway Insurance Company; vice chairman, board of directors National Council Farmer Coops; board of directors Syracuse Research Corp., Chase-Lincoln First Bank, Rochester; corp. adv. council Syracuse University School Management. Chairman board Crouse-Irving Memorial Hospital, Syracuse; trustee Upper Iowa U., Fayette; board of directors Hiawatha council Boy Scouts Am., also national vice president administration. Recipient Silver Beaver award Boy Scouts Am., 1981, Silver Antelope award, Distinguished Citizen award. Member Alpha Zeta.

HILTON, BARRON, hotel executive; born 1927; son of Conrad Hilton. Founder, president San Diego Chargers, Am. Football League, until 1966; vice president Hilton Hotels Corp., Beverly Hills, California, 1954; president, chief executive officer Hilton Hotels Corp., Beverly Hills, 1966—, chairman, 1979—, also director; member general administrative board Manufacturers Hanover Trust Company, New York City. Office: Hilton Hotels Corp 9336 Civic Center Dr Beverly Hills California 90210

HINSON, DAVID R., airline company executive. Fighter pilot United States Navy, 1956-60; airline and engineering pilot 1960-72; founder, director Midway Airlines Incorporated, Chicago, Illinois, 1979—, chairman, chief executive officer, 1985—. Office: Midway Airlines Incorporated 5959 S Cicero Avenue Chicago Illinois 60638

HOAG, DAVID H., steel company executive; born 1939; married. Bachelor of Arts, Allegheny College, 1960. With LTV Steel Company, Cleveland, 1960—, sales trainee, 1960-61, salesman Cincinnati and Chicago district sales offices, 1961-68, assistant production manager standard pipe, 1968-69, production manager standard pipe, then assistant district sales manager Pittsburgh district sales offices, 1968-75, then production manager hot rolled sheet, then manager tubular production sales, then general sales specialty steels, 1968-75, general manager marketing, 1975-77, vice president marketing services, 1977-79, president basic steel Eastern div., 1979-

82, executive vice president, from 1982, now president, chief operating officer, also board of directors; former group vice president parent company LTV Corp., Dallas, now executive vice president, board of directors. Office: LTV Steel Company Incorporated 25 W Prospect Avenue Cleveland Ohio 44115 also: LTV Corp 2001 Ross Avenue Dallas Texas 75265

HOBLITZELL, ALAN PENNIMAN, JR., banker; born St. Louis, June 13, 1931; son of Alan Penniman and Dorothy (May) H.; married Louise Perkins; children: Jean, Priscilla S., Marjorie. Bachelor of Science, Princeton University, 1953; postgraduate, Rutgers University Graduate School Banking, 1956, Harvard University Business School, 1966. With Maryland National Bank (now Maryland National Corp.), Baltimore, 1956—; senior vice president Maryland National Bank (now Maryland National Corp.), 1969-72, executive vice president, 1972-76, president, 1976-84, chief executive officer, 1979—, chairman, 1984—; chairman, president, chief executive officer, director MNC Fin. Incorporated (parent), Baltimore, from 1984, now chairman, chief executive officer, director; director Ryland Group, Fidelity & Deposit Company of Maryland, PHH Group, Incorporated. Treasurer Municipal Arts Society; trustee Maryland Institute Served with United States Army, 1953-56. Member Reserve City Bankers, Robert Morris Association. Clubs: Green Spring Valley Hunt, Center, Merchants. Office: MNC Fin Incorporated 10 Light St Post Office Box 987 Baltimore Maryland 21203

HOCH, ORION LINDEL, corporate executive; born Canonsburg, Pennsylvania, December 21, 1928; son of Orion L.F. and Ann Marie (McNulty) H.; married Jane Lee Ogan, June 12, 1952 (deceased 1978); children: Andrea, Brenda, John; married Catherine Nan Richardson, September 12, 1980; 1 child, Joe. Bachelor of Science, Carnegie Mellon University, 1952; Master of Science, University of California at Los Angeles, 1954; Doctor of Philosophy, Stanford University, 1957. With Hughes Aircraft Company, Culver City, California, 1952-54; with Stanford Electronics Laboratories, 1954-57; senior engineer, department manager, div. vice president, div. president Litton Electron Devices div., San Carlos, California, 1957-68; group executive Litton Components div., 1968-70; vice president Litton Industries, Incorporated, Beverly Hills, California, 1970, senior vice president, 1971-74, president, 1982-88, chief executive officer, 1986—, chairman, 1988—, also director; president Intersil, Incorporated, Cupertino, California, 1974-82; board of directors Measurex Corp., Council International Advisers Swiss Bank Corp. Trustee Carnegie-Mellon U. Served with Army of the United States, 1946-48. Member Institute of Electrical and Electronics Engineers, Sigma Xi, Tau Beta Pi, Phi Kappa Phi. Office: Litton Industries Incorporated 360 N Crescent Dr Beverly Hills California 90210

HOCKADAY, IRVINE O., JR., greeting card company executive; born Ludington, Michigan, August 12, 1936; son of Irvine Oty and Helen (McCune) H.; married Mary Ellen Jurden, July 8, 1961; children: Wendy Helen, Laura DuVal. Bachelor of Arts, Princeton University, 1958; Bachelor of Laws, University Michigan, 1961, Juris Doctor, 1961. Bar: Missouri 1961. Attorney firm Lathrop, Koontz, Righter, Claggett and Norquist, Kansas City, 1961-67; attorney, assistant general counsel, assistant to president, vice president Kansas City Southern Industries, Incorporated, 1968-71, president, chief operations officer, 1971-80, president, chief executive officer, 1981-83; executive vice president Hallmark Cards, Incorporated, 1983-85, president, chief executive officer, 1986—, also board of directors, 1978—; Board directors Ford Motor Company, Continental Corp., Dow Jones and Company; trustee Hall Family Foundation, Aspen Institute; past chairman board of directors 10th district Federal Reserve Bank; past chairman Civic Council Kansas City, 1987-89. Club: Kansas City Country. Office: Hallmark Cards Incorporated 2501 McGee Trafficway Post Office Box 419580 Kansas City Missouri 64141

HODGSON, THOMAS RICHARD, health care company executive; born Lakewood, Ohio, December 17, 1941; son of Thomas Julian and Dallas Louise (Livesay) H.; married Susan Jane Cawrse, August 10, 1963; children: Michael, Laura, Anne. Bachelor of Science in Chemical Engineering, Purdue University, 1963; MSE, University Michigan, 1964; Master of Business Administration, Harvard University, 1969. Devel. engineer E.I. Dupont, 1964; associate Booz-Allen & Hamilton, 1969-72; with Abbott Laboratories, North Chicago, Illinois, 1972—, general manager Faultless div., 1976-78, vice president general manager hospital div., 1978-80, president hospital div., 1980-83, group vice president, president Abbott International Limited, 1983-84, executive vice president parent committee, 1985-90; president, chief operating officer Abbott Laboratories, Abbott Park, 1990—. Member Lake Forest (Illinois) Board Education, 1986-90. Baker scholar; National Science Foundation fellow; recipient Distinguished Engineering Alumni award Purdue University, 1985. Member Chicago Council Foreign Relations, Econ. Club, Knollwood Club, Chicago Club, Phi Eta Sigma, Tau Beta Pi. Home: 1015 Ashley Road Lake Forest Illinois 60045 Office: Abbott Labs 1 Abbott Park Road Abbott Park Illinois 60064

HOFFMAN, EDWIN PHILIP, banker; born Allentown, Pennsylvania, September 13, 1942; son of Donald Brooks and Margaret Jane (Gruber) H.; married Marie Rose Ann Smuldis, August 14, 1965 (divorced March 1973); married Sandra Fay Norsworthy, March 31, 1973; children: Lara, Edwin Alexander, Jamie. Bachelor of Science, Muhlenberg College, 1964; Master of Science, Yale University, 1966, Doctor of Philosophy, 1968. Executive trainee Citicorp, New York City, 1969-70, assistant vice president computer services, 1970-72, vice president, head Colombia, 1972-74, senior vice president, div. head Middle East and North Africa, 1974-80, executive vice president individual bank, 1980-84, group executive Latin Am., 1984-87; president, chief op. officer Household International, Prospect Heights, Illinois, 1988—; board of directors Eljer Industries, Scotsman Industries, Schwitzer Incorporated, International Multifoods, Mastercard International, Housch International, Household International. Trustee Presbyterian Church, Mount Kisco, New York,

1984-87, Muhlenberg College, Allentown, Pennsylvania; board overseers Rassias Foundation, Hanover, New Hampshire; board of directors Manhattan Institute, Chicago Symphony Orchestra, 1988—. Member Executive Club Chicago (board directors 1989—), Economics Club Chicago. Republican. Avocations: gardening, hiking. Home: 1580 Kathryn Lane Lake Forest Illinois 60045 Office: Household International Incorporated 2700 Sanders Road Prospect Heights Illinois 60070

HOGAN, JOHN DONALD, college dean, finance educator; born Binghamton, New York, July 16, 1927; son of John D. and Edith J. (Hennessy) H.; married Anna Craig, November 26, 1976; children—Thomas P., James E. Bachelor of Arts, Syracuse University, 1949, Master of Arts, 1950, Doctor of Philosophy, 1952. Registered prin. Nat. Assn. Securities Dealers. Professor economics, chairman department Bates College, Lewiston, Maine, 1953-58; director education fin. research State of New York, 1959, chief municipal fin., 1960; staff economist, director research Northwestern Mutual Life Insurance Company, Milwaukee, 1960-68; vice president Nationwide Insurance Companies, Columbus, Ohio, 1968-76; dean School Business Administration Central Michigan University, Mount Pleasant, 1976-79; vice president Am. Productivity Center, Houston, 1979-80; president, chairman, chief executive officer Variable Annuity Life Insurance Company, Houston, 1980-83; senior vice president Am. General Corp., Houston, 1983-86; dean, professor fin. College Commerce University Illinois, Champaign, 1986—; board of directors First Busey Corp., Urbana, Illinois, Covenant Medical Court, Champaign, Sinfonia da Camera, Champaign, Illinois Council on Economic Education. Author: American Social Legislation, 1965, United States Balance of Payments and Capital Flows, 1967, School Revenue Studies, 1959, Fiscal Capacity of the State of Maine, 1958, American Social Legislation, 1973; editor: Dimensions of Productivity Research (2 volumes), 1981; contributor articles to journals, abstracts to professional meetings. Board of directors Goodwill Industries, Columbus, 1972-76, chairman capital fund drive, 1974-75; member Houston Committee on Foreign Rels., 1980—, Chicago Council on Foreign Rels., 1986—, Chicago committee, 1987—. Served with United States Army, 1944-46, European Theatre of Operations; captain (retired) United States Army Reserve. Maxwell fellow Syracuse University, 1950-52; recipient Best Article award Jur. Risk and Ins., 1964; Maxwell Centennial lecturer Maxwell Graduate School, Syracuse University, 1970. Member Acad. Management, Am. Econ. Association, Institute Management Sciences, National Association Business Economists, National Tax Association (director 1981-85, treasurer, executive committee 1988—), Institute Research in Economics of Taxation (director 1984—), Columbus Chamber of Commerce (chairman econ. policy committee 1972-76), Phi Kappa Phi, Beta Gamma Sigma. Clubs: Columbus Athletic; Heritage (Houston); University (Chicago), Lincolnshire Fields Country (Champaign). Home: 3301 Stoneybrook Dr Champaign Illinois

61821 Office: U Illinois College Commerce Business Adminstrn 1206 S 6th Champaign Illinois 61820

HOGAN, RONALD P., forest products company executive; born 1940. Bachelor of Science, University Houston. Sales representative Houston distribution div. Georgia-Pacific Corp., Atlanta, 1965-68, manager Wichita, Kansas branch, 1968-70, manager Houston branch, 1970-73, manager western region, 1973-76, manager northeast region, 1976-78, vice president distribution div. northeast region, 1978-82, vice president distribution div., 1982-83, group vice president distribution div., 1983-85, senior vice president distribution div., 1985-87, executive vice president operations, 1987-88, executive vice president building products, 1988-89; president, chief operating officer Georgia-Pacific Corp., 1989—, also board of directors. Office: Ga-Pacific Corp 133 Peachtree St NE Atlanta Georgia 30303

HOHN, HARRY GEORGE, insurance company executive, lawyer; born New York City, March 1, 1932; son of Harry George and Violia (Meehan) H.; married Janet Jean LaRosa, June 19, 1954; children: Cynthia, Jennifer, Nancy, Patricia. Bachelor of Science, New York University, 1953, Master of Laws, 1959; Juris Doctor, Fordham University, 1956. Bar: New York 1956, United States Supreme Court 1976. With New York Life Insurance Company, New York City, 1974—, senior vice president, general counsel, 1977-82, executive vice president, general counsel, 1982-83, executive vice president, 1983-86, vice chairman board of directors, 1986-90, chief executive officer, 1990—, chairman board of directors. Editor: Fordham Law Rev, 1955-56. Trustee Foundation Ind. Higher Education, The Am. College. Member Association Life Insurance Counsel (board govs.). Republican. Roman Catholic. Office: New York Life Ins Company 51 Madison Avenue New York New York 10010

HOLDER, RICHARD G., metal products executive. Bachelor of Arts, Vanderbilt University, 1953. With Reynolds Metals Company, Richmond, Virginia, 1953—; various management positions Reynolds Metal Company, Richmond, Virginia, 1953-78, vice president, general manager flexible packaging div., 1978-80, vice president, general manager flexible packaging div. and consumer products div., 1980-83, vice president mill products div., 1983-84, executive vice president, 1984-86, executive vice president, chief operating officer, 1986-88, president, chief operating officer, 1988—, also board of directors. Office: Reynolds Metals Company 6601 W Broad St Richmond Virginia 23230

HOLLIS, MARK C., supermarket company executive. Graduate, Stetson University and Michigan State University. Former vice president, president Publix Supermarkets, Incorporated, Lakeland, Florida, from 1984, now president, chief operating officer, also board of directors. Served with United States Army. Office: Publix Supermarkets Incorporated 1936 George Jenkins Boulevard Box 407 Lakeland Florida 33802

HOLMES, DAVID RICHARD, computer and business forms company executive; born Salt Lake City, August 10, 1940; son of John Rulon and Evelyn Nadine (Schettler) H.;

married Nancy Alice Lewis, September 11, 1965; children: David Matthew, Stephen Michael, Jeffrey Alan. Bachelor of Arts, Stanford University, 1963; Master of Business Administration, Northwestern University, 1965. Category manager, strategic planning manager General Foods Corp., White Plains, New York, 1965-77; director marketing Standard Brands Incorporated, New York City, 1977-78; marketing manager General Electric, Fairfield, Connecticut, 1978-81; vice president, general manager Nabisco Brands Incorporated, New York City, 1981-84; president computer systems div. Reynolds & Reynolds Company, Dayton, Ohio, 1984-87, president, chief operating officer, 1987—, president, chief executive officer, 1989, chairman, president, chief executive officer, 1990, also board of directors. Board of directors Dayton Pub. Radio, 1986, Wright State U. Board, 1989. Served with United States Naval Reserve, 1966-74. Member Am. Management Association, Dayton Phil. Orchestra Association (trustee 1988-91), Dayton C. of c. (board directors 1988). Republican. Presbyterian. Clubs: Am. Yacht (Rye, New York); Dayton Country. Avocations: building furniture, skiing, tennis, sailing. Office: Reynolds & Reynolds Company 115 S Ludlow St Dayton Ohio 45402

HOLTON, EARL D., retail company executive; born 1934. With Meijer, Incorporated, Grand Rapids, Michigan, 1952—, vice president, 1967-76, then executive vice president, now president, director; vice president Meijer Super Markets Incorporated subsidiary Meijer Incorporated, 1967, now executive vice president. Office: Topco Associates Incorporated 7711 Gross Point Road Skokie Illinois 60076

HOOK, HAROLD SWANSON, insurance company executive; born Kansas City, Missouri, October 10, 1931; son of Ralph C. and Ruby (Swanson) H.; married Joanne T. Hunt, February 19, 1955; children: Karen Anne, Thomas W., Randall T. Bachelor of Science in Business Administration, University Missouri, 1953, Master of Arts, 1954; graduate, Southern Methodist University Institute Insurance Mktng., 1957; postgraduate, New York University, 1967-70; Doctor of Laws (honorary), University Missouri, 1983, Westminster College, 1983. Chartered Life Underwriter. Member faculty University Missouri School Business, 1953-54; assistant to president National Fidelity Life Insurance Company, Kansas City, Missouri, 1957-60, director, 1959-66, administrative vice president, 1960-61, executive vice president, investment committee, 1961-62, president, executive committee, 1962-66; senior vice president United States Life Insurance Company, New York City, 1966-67, director, 1967-70, executive vice president, member executive committee, 1967-68, president, 1968-70; president Calif.-Western States Life Insurance Company, Sacramento, 1970-75, chairman, 1975-79, senior chairman, 1979—, also board of directors; member executive committee Am. General Corp., Houston, 1975—, president, 1975-81, chairman, chief, executive officer, 1978—, also board of directors; founder, president Main Event Management Corp., Sacramento, 1971—; board of directors Panhandle Eastern Corp., Houston, Texas Commerce Bancshares,

Incorporated, Houston, United Telecommunications, Incorporated, Kansas City, Mo, Cooper Industries, Incorporated, Houston, Chemical Banking Corp., New York City. Founder, member Naval War College Foundation; trustee, chairman fin. committee Baylor College Medicine, Houston; vice chairman council overseers Jesse H. Hones Grad. School Administration, Rice U., Houston; president national executive board Boy Scouts Am., 1988-90, now member, member adv. board Sam Houston Area council; board of directors Texas Research League, Society for Performing Arts, Houston, Texas Medical Center, Greater Houston Partnership (formerly Houston Chamber of Commerce). Recipient citation of merit University Missouri Alumni Association, 1965, Faculty-Alumni award University Missouri, 1978; Silver Beaver award Boy Scouts Am., 1974, Distinguished Eagle Scout award, 1976, Silver Antelope award, 1989, Silver Buffalo award, 1990; Chief Executive officer award Fin. World magazine, 1979, 82, 84, 86; named Man of Year, Delta Sigma Pi, 1969, Outstanding Chief Executive Officer in Multiline Ins. Industry, Wall Street Transcript, 1981-87. Fellow Life Management Institute; member Philosophical Society Texas, United States Chamber of Commerce (board directors), Texas Association Taxpayers (board directors), National Association Life Underwriters, Houston Association Life Underwriters, Beta Gamma Sigma Directors Table (member 1976, National honoree 1984), Forum Club (board govs.), University Club, River Oaks Country Club, Petroleum Club, Ramada Club, Heritage Club of Houston, Economic Club of New York City, Eldorado Country Club, Rotary. Presbyterian. Home: 2204 Troon Road Houston Texas 77019 Office: Am General Corp 2929 Allen Parkway Houston Texas 77019 also: Post Office Box 3247 Houston Texas 77253

HOOVER, WILLIAM R(AY), computer service company executive; born Bingham, Utah, January 2, 1930; son of Edwin Daniel and Myrtle Tennessee (McConnell) H.; married Sara Elaine Anderson, October 4; children—Scott, Robert, Michael, James, Charles. Bachelor of Science, Master of Science, University Utah. Section chief Jet Propulsion Laboratory, Pasadena, California, 1954-64; vice president Computer Sciences Corp., El Segundo, California, 1964-69, president, 1969—, chairman board, 1972—, now also chief executive officer, also board of directors. Office: Computer Scis Corp 2100 E Grand Avenue El Segundo California 90245

HOSIE, WILLIAM CARLTON, walnut growers company executive; born Stockton, California, June 25, 1936; son of Fred A. and Janet (Russell) H.; married Sherryl Rasmussen, January 12, 1963; children: Shaen Case, Erin Frick. Bachelor of Science, University Calif.-Davis, 1960. Field representative Flotill Incorporated, Stockton, 1960-61; orchardist Hosie Ranch Incorporated, Linden, California, 1961-83; chairman board of directors Diamond Walnut Growers Incorporated, Stockton, 1981—; now also vice chairman; director Sun-Diamond Growers California, Pleasanton; advisor University California Extension-Stockton, 1975—, California Farm Bureau, Sacramento, 1976—, Farmer and Merchants Bank, Linden, 1979;

director Walnut Marketing Board, San Mateo, California, 1981—. President Stockton East Water District, 1969-79. Served with Army of the United States, 1958-59. Member Stockton Chamber of Commerce. Republican. Club: Rotary International. Home: Post Office Box 226 Linden California 95236 Office: Diamond Walnut Growers Incorporated 1050 S Diamond St Stockton California 95205

HOUGH, LAWRENCE A., financial organization executive. In engineering, Stanford University; graduate, Sloan School of Management, Massachusetts Institute of Technology. Fin. analyst Stanford University; with Student Loan Marketing Association, Washington, District of Columbia, 1973-77, 79—; executive vice president, marketing services and systems Student Loan Marketing Association; now, president, chief executive officer Student Loan Marketing Association, Washington, District of Columbia, 1990—. Office: Student Loan Mktg Association 1050 Thomas Jefferson St Northwest Washington District of Columbia 20007

HOUGHTON, JAMES RICHARDSON, glass manufacturing company executive; born Corning, New York, April 6, 1936; son of Amory and Laura (Richardson) H.; married May Tuckerman Kinnicutt, June 30, 1962; children: James DeKay, Nina Bayard. Bachelor of Arts, Harvard University, 1958, Master of Business Administration, 1962. With Goldman, Sachs & Company, New York City, 1959-61; vice president, European area manager Corning Glass International, Zurich, Switzerland, Brussels, Belgium, 1964-68; with Corning Glass Works (name changed to Corning Incorporated 1989), 1962—, vice president, general manager consumer products div., 1968-71, vice chairman board, director, chairman executive committee, 1971-83, chairman board, chief executive officer, 1983—; board of directors Metropolitan Life Insurance Company, J. P. Morgan Company Incorporated, Dow Corning Corp., CBS, Incorporated, Owens-Corning Fiberglas Corp., US-USSR Trade and Economic Council. Trustee Corning Incorporated Foundation, Corning Mus. Glass, Piermont Morgan Library, New York City, Business Council of New York State, Metropolitan Mus. Art; member Business Committee for Arts, New York City, Council on Foreign Rels., Trilateral Commission Business Council With Army of the United States, 1959-60. Member Business Roundtable. Episcopalian. Clubs: Corning Country; River, Harvard, University, Links (New York City); Brookline (Massachusetts) Country; Tarratine (Dark Harbor, Maine); Augusta (Georgia) National Golf; Rolling Rock, Laurel Valley Golf (Ligonier, Pennsylvania). Home: The Field 36 Spencer Hill Road Corning New York 14830 Office: Corning Incorporated Houghton Park Corning New York 14831

HOWARD, JAMES JOSEPH, III, utility company executive; born Pittsburgh, July 1, 1935; son of James Joseph Jr. and Flossie (Wenzel) H.; married Donna Joan Fowler, August 31, 1955; children: James J. IV, Catherine A., Christine A., William F. Bachelor of Business Administration, University Pittsburgh, 1957; Master of Science, Massachusetts Institute of Technology, 1970. With Bell Telephone of Pennsylvania, Pittsburgh, 1957-78, vice president, general manager, 1976-78; vice president operations Wisconsin Telephone Company, Milwaukee, 1978-79, executive vice president, chief operating officer, 1979-81, president, chief executive officer, 1981-83, chairman, chief executive officer, 1983; president, chief operating officer Ameritech, Chicago, 1983-87, director; president, chief executive officer Northern States Power Company, Minneapolis, 1987—, chairman, 1988—; board of directors Equitable Life Assurance Society, New York Board Overseers, Carlson School Management University Minnesota, Walgreen Company, Deerfield, Illinois, Northern States Power Company, Minneapolis, Honeywell, Minneapolis, Am. Nuclear Energy Council, Ecolab, St. Paul. Board trustees College of St. Thomas, St. Paul; board overseers Carlson School Mgmt., GReater Minneapolis Metropolitan Housing Corp., Am. Committee on Radwaste Disposal. Sloan fellow Massachusetts Institute of Technology, 1969. Member Conference Board New York, Greater Minneapolis Chamber of Commerce, Am. Nuclear Energy Council (board directors).

HOWE, STANLEY MERRILL, manufacturing company executive; born Muscatine, Iowa, February 5, 1924; son of Merrill Y. and Thelma F. (Corriel) H.; married Helen Jensen, March 29, 1953; children: Thomas, Janet, Steven, James. Bachelor of Science, Iowa State University, 1946; Master of Business Administration, Harvard University, 1948. Production engineer HON Industries, Muscatine, Iowa, 1948-54; vice president production HON Industries, 1954-61, executive vice president, 1961-64, president, 1964—, chairman, 1984—, now chief executive officer, also director; chairman board Corry Heibert Corp., Heatilator Incorporated, Budget Panels, Incorporated, Gunlocke Company, XLM Company, Holga, Incorporated. Trustee Iowa Wesleyan College. Gerard Swope fellow Harvard University, 1948. Member National Association of Manufacturers, Iowa Manufacturers Association, Am. Management Association. Methodist. Clubs: Rotary, Elks, 33. Office: Hon Industries Incorporated 414 E 3rd St Muscatine Iowa 52761

HOWE, WESLEY JACKSON, medical supplies company executive; born Jersey City, June 7, 1921; son of Wesley Veith and Phyllis (Jackson) H.; married Suzanne Rodrock, July 20, 1946; children: Marc Edward, Richard Douglas, Suzanne. Mechanical Engineer, Stevens Institute Tech., Hoboken, New Jersey, 1943, Master of Science, 1953; Doctor of Engineering (honorary), Stevens Institute Tech., 1981; Doctor of Humane Letters, University New Jersey Medicine & Dentistry (honorary), 1988. With Becton, Dickinson and Company, Rutherford, New Jersey, 1949—, group vice president, then executive vice president, 1970-72, president, chief executive officer, director, 1972-80, chairman board, 1980—, chief executive officer, director, 1980-89, president, 1983-87; director Ecolab Incorporated, Lukens Incorporated; chairman New Jersey Manufacturers Insurance Company, New Jersey Re-Ins. Company, New Jersey Business and Industry. Chairman board trustees Stevens Institute Tech.; trustee Foundation of University Medicine and Dentistry New Jersey Served to 1st lieutenant Army of the United

States, 1944-46, 51-52. Member New Jersey Chamber of Commerce (director). Clubs: Arcola (New Jersey) Country, Upper Montclair (New Jersey) Country; University (New York City). Office: Becton Dickinson & Company 1 Becton Dr Franklin Lakes New Jersey 07417

HOWELL, WILLIAM ROBERT, retail company executive; born Claremore, Oklahoma, January 3, 1936; William Roosevelt and Opal Theo (Swan) H.; married Donna Lee Hatch, June 7, 1956; children: Ann Elizabeth, Teresa Lynn. Bachelor of Business Administration, University Oklahoma, 1958. With J.C. Penney Company, Incorporated, 1958—; store manager J.C. Penney Company, Incorporated, Tulsa, 1968-69; district manager, director Treasury Stores subsidiary, Dallas, 1969-71; div. vice president, director domestic devel. Treasury Stores subsidiary, New York City, 1973-76, regional vice president, western regional manager, 1976-79, senior vice president, director merchandising, marketing and catalog, 1979-81, executive vice president, 1981-82, vice chairman board dirs, 11982-83, chairman, chief executive officer, 1983—; also board of directors Treasury Stores subsidiary; board of directors Exxon Corp., Warner-Lambert Corp., Bankers Trust Company, Halliburton Company. Trustee National Urban League. Member Am. Management Association, Business Council, Business Roundtable, National Retail Federation (board directors), Retail Tax Committee of Common Interest, Am. Society of Corp. Executives, Dirs.' Table, Delta Sigma Pi, Beta Gamma Sigma. Baptist.

HOWSON, ROBERT E., construction company executive; born 1932. Bachelor of Science in Civil Engineering, Louisiana Tech. University, 1953; Master of Science in Civil Engineering, Tulane University, 1961. Chief engineer offshore div. McDermott Incorporated, 1957-63, vice president control and South America, 1972-74, general vice president North sea, 1974-80, senior vice president and general executive McDermott engineering, 1980-81, general president, 1981-88, chairman board, chief executive officer, 1988—; director, also president, chief official officer Babcock & Wilcox & McDermott International Incorporated; senior vice president Ingram Contractors Incorporated, 1963-72. 1st lieutenant United States Marine Corps, 1963-72. Office: McDermott Incorporated Post Office Box 60035 New Orleans Louisiana 70161

HOYT, HENRY HAMILTON, JR., pharmaceutical and toiletry company executive; born Orange, New Jersey, August 10, 1927; son of Henry Hamilton and Anna Clark (Orcutt) H.; married Muriel Virginia Christie, February 5, 1960. Bachelor of Arts cum laude, Princeton University, 1949. With Carter-Wallace Incorporated, New York City, 1950—; chairman board, chief executive officer Carter-Wallace Incorporated, 1975—, also board of directors. Trustee Princeton Elm Club, 1959—, Overlook Hospital, Summit, New Jersey, 1976—; board of directors Deafness Research Foundation, 1977—; trustee Pingry School, Hillside, New Jersey, 1970-78, president board, 1972—. Served with Transportation Corps United States Army, 1946-47. Member Cosmetic, Toiletry and Fragrance Association (director 1965—, treasurer 1966-76),

Pharmaceutical Manufacturers Association (director 1971-75), Proprietary Association (director 1970—). Episcopalian. Clubs: Univ, Met, Princeton of N.Y; Baltusrol Golf (Springfield, New Jersey); Oyster Harbors (Osterville, Massachusetts). Office: Carter-Wallace Incorporated 767 Fifth Avenue New York New York 10153

HUDSON, JAMES T., food company executive; born 1924. Regional director operations Ralston Purina Company, 1946-72; president, chief executive officer Hudson Foods Incorporated, Rogers, Arkansas, 1972-85, chairman, chief executive officer, 1985—, also board of directors; board of directors First National Bank, Rogers. Office: Hudson Foods Incorporated Hudson Road & 13th St Box 777 Rogers Arkansas 72756

HUDSON, MICHAEL T., food company executive; born 1947; son of James T. H. Graduate, University Alabama, 1969. With Ralston-Purina Company, 1969-72; with Hudson Foods Incorporated, Rogers, Arkansas, 1972—, formerly vice president product operations, president, 1985—, also board of directors. Office: Hudson Foods Incorporated Hudson Road & 13th St Box 777 Rogers Arkansas 72756

HUGHES, ROGER K., dairy and grocery store company executive. Chief executive officer Hughes Markets, Los Angeles. Office: Certified Grocers California 2601 S Eastern Avenue Los Angeles California 90040

HUIZENGA, H. WAYNE, entertainment corporation executive; born Evergreen Park, Illinois, December 29, 1937; son of G. Harry and Jean (Riddering) H.; married Martha Jean Pike, April 17, 1972; children: H. Wayne Jr., H. Scott, Ray Goldsby, Pamela Ann. Student, Calvin College, 1957-58. Vice chairman, president, chief operating officer Waste Management Incorporated, Oak Brook, Illinois, 1968-84; principal Huizenga Holdings, Incorporated, Fort Lauderdale, Florida, 1984—; chairman, chief executive officer Blockbuster Entertainment Corp., Fort Lauderdale, 1987—; co-owner Miami Dolphins, Joe Robbie Stadium. Member Florida Victory Committee, 1988-89, Team Repub. National Committee, Washington, 1988-90; organizer Broward Victory 90 PAC, Fort Lauderdale, 1989-90. Recipient Entrepreneur of Year award Wharton School University Pennsylvania, 1989, Excalibur Award Business Leader of Year News/Sun Sentinel, 1990, Silver Medallion Brotherhood award Broward Region National Conference Christians and Jews, 1990, Laureates award Junior Achievement Broward and Palm Beach Counties, 1990, Jim Murphy Humanitarian Award The Emerald Society, 1990, Entrepreneur of Year award Distinguished Panel Judges Florida, 1990, Man of Year Billboard/Time Magazine, 1990, Man of Year Juvenile Diabetes Foundation, 1990, Florida Free Enterpriser of Year award Florida Council on Economic Education, 1990, commendation for youth restricted video State of Florida Office of Gov., 1989, Hon. Member Appreciation award Bond Club Fort Lauderdale, 1989; honored with endowed teaching chair Broward Community College, 1990. Member Lauderdale Yacht Club, Tournament Players Club, Fisher Island Club, Ocean Reef Club, Cat Cay Yacht Club, Coral ridge Country Club, Linville Ridge Country Club. Avocations: golf, collecting antique cars. Office: Blockbuster Entertainment Corp 901 E Las Olas Boulevard Fort Lauderdale Florida 33301-2320

HUNT, JOHNNIE B., trucking company executive; born 1924; married. With Superior Forwarding Company, 1945-61; chairman J B Hunt Transport Incorporated, Towell, Arkansas. Office: J B Hunt Transport Services Incorporated Post Office Box 130 Lowell Arkansas 72745

HUNT, LAMAR, professional football team executive; born 1932; son of H.L. and Lyda (Bunker) H.; married Norma Hunt; children: Lamar, Sharon, Clark. Graduate, Southern Methodist University. Founder, owner Kansas City Chiefs, National Football League, 1959—, president, 1959-76, chairman, 1977-78; founder, president AFL, 1959; (became Am. Football Conf.-NFL 1970); president Am. Football Conference, 1970—; director Great Midwest Corp., Interstate Securities, Traders' National Bank. Board of directors Professional Football Hall of Fame, Canton, Ohio. Named Salesman of Year Kansas City Advertising and Sales Executives Club, 1963; Southwesterner of Year Texas Sportswriters Association, 1969. Office: Kansas City Chiefs 1 Arrowhead Dr Kansas City Missouri 64129 Office: NFL 410 Park Avenue New York New York 10022

HURD, G. DAVID, insurance company executive; born Chicago, December 14, 1929; son of Gerald Walton and Hilldur Ingabore (Hallgren) H.; married Patricia Ann Lamb, February 12, 1955; children—Janet Susan, Sally Jane, Michael David. Bachelor of Arts, Michigan State University, 1951. With The Principal Fin. Group (formerly Bankers Life Company), Des Moines, 1954—, officer, 1960-71, vice president, 1971-83, senior vice president, 1983-85, executive vice president, 1985-87; president The Principal Fin. Group, 1987-88, president, chief executive officer, 1989—; board of directors Principal Mutual Life Insurance Company, Des Moines ; member Pension Research Council, University Pennsylvania Wharton School Business, 1979-85. Member Adv. Council on Employee Welfare and Pension Benefit Plans, Department Labor, Washington, 1977-80; board of directors Drake U., 1986—, Nature Conservancy; chairman Group Assurance International Network, 1987-89; member steering committee Business for Peace. Served to 2d lieutenant Corps of Engineers, United States Army, 1951-53, Korea. Member Employee Benefit Research Institute (board directors 1979-86), Association Private Pension and Welfare Plans (chairman board 1985-87), Des Moines Chamber of Commerce (board directors 1985—). Clubs: Prairie, Des Moines. Avocations: running; birding; writing; bicycling. Home: 3930 Grand St Apartment 406 Des Moines Iowa 50312 Office: Principal Mut Life Ins Company 711 High St Des Moines Iowa 50309

HURWITZ, CHARLES EDWIN, oil company executive; born Kilgore, Texas, May 3, 1940; son of Hyman and Eva (Engler) H.; married Barbara Raye Gollub, February 24, 1963; children: Shawn Michael, David Alan. Bachelor of Arts, University Oklahoma, Norman, 1962. Chairman board, president Investam. Group, Incorporated, Houston, 1965-67, Summitt Management & Research Corp., Houston, 1967-70; chairman board Summit Insurance Company of New York, Houston, 1970-75; with MCO Holdings, Incorporated (and predecessor), Los Angeles, from 1978, chairman board, chief executive officer, from 1980, director, from 1978; chairman board, chief executive officer, director Maxxam Incorporated, Los Angeles; chairman board Federated Reins. Corp.; chairman board, president Federated Devel. Company; director MCO Resources, Incorporated. Co-chairman Committee to Establish George Kozmetsky Centennial Chair in Grad. School Business, U. Texas, Austin, from 1980. Jewish.

HUTCHINSON, PEMBERTON, coal company executive; born Charlotte, North Carolina, 1931. Graduate, University Virginia. Executive vice president Westmoreland Coal Company, Philadelphia; also president subsidiary General Coal Company, 1979-81; president, chief executive officer, director Westmoreland Coal Company, Incorporated, 1981—; board of directors Teleflex, Incorporated, Mellon Bank Corp., Mellon Bank (East), Pep Boys-Manny, Moe & Jack, Philadelphia. Office: Westmoreland Coal Company 700 The Bellevue 200 S Broad St Philadelphia Pennsylvania 19102

HUTTON, EDWARD LUKE, chemical company executive; born Bedford, Indiana, May 5, 1919; son of Fred and Margaret (Drehobl) H.; married Kathryn Jane Alexander; children—Edward Alexander, Thomas Charles, Jane Clarke. Bachelor of Science with distinction, Ind. University, 1940, Master of Science with distinction, 1941. Deputy director Joint Export Import Agency (USUK), Berlin, 1946-48; vice president World Commerce Corp., 1948-51; assistant vice president W.R. Grace & Company, 1951-53, consultant, 1960-65, executive vice president, general manager Dubois Chemicals div., 1965-66, group executive Specialty Products Group and vice president, 1966-68, executive vice president, 1968-71; consultant international trade and fin. 1953-58; fin. vice president, executive vice president Ward Industries, 1958-59; president, chief executive officer Chemed Corp., Cincinnati, 1971—, director; chairman Omnicare, Incorporated, Cincinnati, 1981—; director Omnicare, Incorporated; chairman, director Roto-Rooter, Incorporated, 1984—; board of directors National Sanitary Supply Company, Grace Energy Corp., Sonic Corp. Co-chairman President's Private Sector Survey on Cost Control, executive committee, subcom.; board advisors U. Cincinnati College Business Administration. Recipient Distinguished Alumni Service award Ind. University, 1987. Member International Platform Association, University Cincinnati (CBA board advisors), Dirs.' Table, American Association of University Professors (governing board directors 1958—), Downtown Association, Economics Club, Princeton Club, University Club, Queen City Club, Bankers Club. Home: 6680 Miralake Dr Cincinnati Ohio 45243 Office: Chemed Corp 2600 Chemed Center 255 E 5th St Cincinnati Ohio 45202

HYMAN, MORTON PETER, shipping company executive; born New York City, January 9, 1936; son of Irving S. and Dora (Pfeffer) H.; married Chris Oliphant Stern, March 18, 1979; children: Sarah Anne, David Jacob. Bachelor of Arts, Cornell University, 1956, Doctor of Laws with distinction, 1959; Doctor of Hebrew Literature h.c., New York Medical College. Bar: New York 1960. Associate Proskauer Rose Goetz & Mendelsohn, New York City, 1959-63; officer, director Overseas Discount Corp., New York City, 1963—, president, 1983—; officer, director Overseas Shipholding Group, Incorporated, New York City, 1969—; president Overseas Shipholding Group, Incorporated, 1971—. Board editors Cornell Law Rev. Vice chairman New York State Health Planning Commission, 1977-78; member Pub. Health Council New York, 1971—, vice-chmn., 1977-85, chairman, 1985—; co-chairman New York State Health Issues Forum; chairman New York State Health Care Capital Policy Adv. Committee, 1982—; chairman board trustees Beth Israel Medical Center; trustee Mount Sinai Medical Center; chairman New York State Joint Executive and Legis. Task Force on Delivery of Health Care, 1977-80; chairman New York State Joint Executive and Legis. Task Force on Residential Health Care Facilities, 1977-80; board of directors United Jewish Appeal Federation 2d lieutenant Army of the United States, 1956-57. Fellow New York Acad. Medicine; member New York Bar Association, Harmonie Club, Order of Coif, Phi Kappa Phi. Republican. Home: 998 Fifth Avenue New York New York 10028 Office: Overseas Shipholding Group Incorporated 1114 Avenue of Americas New York New York 10036

IACOCCA, LEE See IACOCCA, LIDO ANTHONY

IACOCCA, LIDO ANTHONY (LEE IACOCCA), automotive manufacturing executive; born Allentown, Pennsylvania, October 15, 1924; son of Nicola and Antoinette (Perrotto) I.; married Mary McCleary, September 29, 1956 (deceased);married Darrien Earle, March 30, 1991; children—Kathryn Lisa Hentz, Lia AntoinetteNagy. Bachelor of Science, Lehigh University, 1945; Mechanical Engineer, Princeton University, 1946. With Ford Motor Company, Dearborn, Michigan, 1946-78; successively member field sales staff, various merchandising and training activities, assistant directors sales manager Ford Motor Company, Philadelphia; district sales manager Ford Motor Company, Washington, 1946-56; truck marketing manager div. office Ford Motor Company, 1956-57, car marketing manager, 1957-60, vehicle market manager, 1960, vice president; general manager Ford Motor Company (Ford div.), 1960-65, vice president car and truck group, 1965-69, executive vice president of company, 1967-69, president of company, 1970-78; also president Ford Motor Company (Ford North America automobile operations); president, chief operating officer Chrysler Corp., Highland Park, Michigan, 1978-79, chairman board, chief executive officer, 1979—. Author: Iacocca: An Autobiography, 1984, Talking Straight, 1988. Past chairman Statue of Liberty-Ellis Island Centennial Commission. Wallace Memorial fellow Princeton University. Member Tau Beta Pi. Club: Detroit Athletic. Office: Chrysler Corp 12000 Chrysler Dr Highland Park Michigan 48288

ICAHN, CARL C., arbitrator and options specialist, corporation executive; born Queens, New York, 1936; married Liba Icahn; 2 children. Bachelor of Arts, Princeton University, 1957; postgraduate, New York University School Medicine. Apprentice broker Dreyfus Corp., New York City, 1960-63; options manager Tessel, Patrick & Company, New York City, 1963-64, Gruntal & Company, 1964-68; chairman, president Icahn & Company, New York City, 1968—; chairman, chief executive officer ACF Industries Incorporated, Earth City, Missouri, 1984—, also board of directors; chairman, board of directors, president, chief executive officer Trans World Airlines Incorporated, New York City, 1986—, also president, chief executive officer, board of directors. Office: Icahn & Company Incorporated 100 S Bedford Road Mount Kisco New York 10549 also: ACF Industries Incorporated 3301 Rider Trail S Earth City Missouri 63045 also: Trans World Airlines Incorporated 605 3rd Avenue New York New York 01058

INCAUDO, CLAUDE J., food products company executive; born 1936; married. With ABC Markets, Los Angeles, 1957-77; with P&C Food Markets Incorporated, Syracuse, New York, 1977—, vice president, 1978-79, senior vice president, 1979, now president, board of directors. Office: P & C Food Markets Incorporated Post Office Box 4965 Syracuse New York 13221

IRANI, RAY R., chemical company executive; born Beirut, Lebanon, January 15, 1935; came to United States, 1953, naturalized, 1956; son of Rida and Naz I.; children: Glenn R., Lillian M., Martin R. Bachelor of Science in Chemistry, Am. University Beirut, 1953; Doctor of Philosophy in Physical Chemistry, University Southern California, 1957. Senior research group leader Monsanto Company, 1957-67; associate director new products, then director research Diamond Shamrock Corp., 1967-73; with Olin Corp., 1973-83, president chemicals group, 1978-80; corp. president, director Olin Corp., Stamford, Connecticut, 1980-83; executive vice president Occidental Petroleum Corp., Los Angeles, 1983-84, president, chief operating officer, 1984—, also director; chairman, chief executive officer Occidental Chemical Corp. subsidiary Occidental Petroleum Corp., Dallas, 1983—; board of directors Am. Petroleum Institute. Author: Particle Size; also author papers in field; numerous patents in field. Trustee St. John's Hospital and Health Center Foundation, Natural History Mus. Los Angeles County. Member Soap and Detergent Association, Chemical Manufacturers Association (board directors), Am. Institute Chemists (hon. fellow award 1983), Am. Chemical Society, Scientific Research Society Am., Industrial Research Institute, Los Angeles Chamber of Commerce (board directors). Office: Can Occidental Petroleum, 1500 635 8th Avenue Southwest, Calgary, Alberta Canada T2P 3Z1 also: Can Occidental Petroleum Limited, 500 635 8th Avenue S W, Calgary, Alberta Canada T2P 3Z1

IRSAY, ROBERT, professional football club executive, construction company executive; born Chicago, March 5, 1923; son of Charles J. and Elaine (Nyrtia) I.; married Harriet Pogorzelski, July 12, 1946; children: Thomas, James. Bachelor of Science in Mechanical Engineering, University Illinois, 1941. President Robert Irsay Company, Skokie, Illinois, 1952-78, Colt Construction and Devel. Company, Skokie, 1978—, Baltimore Football Club, Incorporated, 1972-84; president Indianapolis Colts, 1984—, also treasurer; director Michigan Avenue National Bank, Chicago, 1970-76. Board of directors Clearbrook Center for Handicapped, Rolling Meadows, Illinois, 1982-83; board of directors Troubled Children's Foundation, Hialeah, Florida, 1982-83. Served to lieutenant United States Marine Corps, 1941-46, PTO.

IRVIN, TINSLEY HOYT, insurance broker; born Cornelia, Georgia, May 30, 1933; son of Henry Hoyt and Annie Ruth (Ray) I.; married Gail Lee Wood, June 4, 1955; children: Cynthia Gaye, Diane Gail. Bachelor of Business Administration, Georgia State University, 1955. With Alexander & Alexander Incorporated, New York City, 1953—, vice president, manager Atlanta office, 1965-70, senior vice president Southeast region, 1970-78, chairman, chief executive officer, 1982—, president, chief operating officer, 1982-87, chief executive officer, 1987—, chairman, 1988—. Served with United States Army, 1956-58. Republican. Congregationalist. Home: 8 Deer Park Court Greenwich Connecticut 06830 Office: Alexander & Alexander Services Incorporated 1211 Avenue of the Americas New York New York 10036

ISHIZAKA, JIRO, banker; born Shanghai, China, December 22, 1927; son of Rokuro and Ayako I.; married Masako Hirayama, April 11, 1954. Graduate, Faculty of Law, University Tokyo, 1951. With Bank of Tokyo, 1951—, director, 1977, managing director, 1980; chairman board Bank of Tokyo Trust Company, 1980-84; director California First Bank, 1982-84; resident managing director New York Regional Executive Americas, 1980-84; adv. to president Nippon Life Insurance Company, 1984-89, Bank of Tokyo, 1989; chairman board Union Bank, Los Angeles, 1989—. Trustee California Institute Arts, Junior Achievement, Los Angeles, Japanese Am. National Mus.; board governors Music Center, Los Angeles; board of directors Japan Am. Society, Los Angeles World Affairs Council, Los Angeles Chamber Orchestra, Japan Am. Cultural and Committee Center; board overseers Huntington Libr. and Botanical Gardens; board of directors international Sta. KCET. Member Los Angeles Chamber of Commerce (board directors), Nippon Kogyo Club (Tokyo), Metropolitan Club (New York City), Jonathan Club (Los Angeles), Sagami Country Club (Tokyo). Clubs: Nippon (director New York City); Canyon (Armonk, New York); Morefar (Brewster, New York); City Midday (New York City). Office: Union Bank 445 S Figueroa St Post Office Box 3100 Los Angeles California 90071-1602

ITOH, SEISHICHI, bank executive; born Amagasaki, Japan, March 17, 1935. Osaka University, Japan, 1957. Assistant vice president Bank Tokyo California, 1972-73, vice president, 1973; with Bank Tokyo Limited, 1957-72, 76-83, deputy general manager, 1976-83; vice president California 1st Bank (now Union Bank), San Francisco, 1983—, now president, chief executive officer, board of directors. Office: Union Bank Post Office Box 7104 San Francisco California 94120-1476 also: 350 California St San Francisco California 94104

IVERSON, FRANCIS KENNETH, metals company executive; born Downers Grove, Illinois, September 18, 1925; son of Norris Byron and Pearl Irene (Kelsey) I.; married

Martha Virginia Miller, October 24, 1945; children: Claudia (Mrs. Wesley Watts Sturges), Marc Miller. Student, Northwestern University, 1943-44; Bachelor of Science, Cornell University, 1946; Master of Science, Purdue University, 1947. Research physicist International Harvester, Chicago, 1947-52; tech. director Illium Corp., Freeport, Illinois, 1952-54; director marketing Cannon-Muskegon Corp., Michigan, 1954-61; executive vice president Coast Metals, Little Ferry, New Jersey, 1961-62; vice president Nucor Corp. (formerly Nuclear Corp. Am.), Charlotte, North Carolina, 1962-65, president, chief executive officer, director, 1965-85, chairman, chief executive officer, 1985—, also board of directors; board of directors Ist Wachovia Corp., Wal-Mart Stores Incorporated, Wikoff Color Corp. Contributor articles to professional journals. Served to lieutenant (junior grade) United States Naval Reserve, 1943-46. Named Best Chief Executive Officer in Steel Industry, Wall Street Transcript, 1989. Member American Institute of Mining, Metallurgy and Petroleum Engineers, National Association of Manufacturers, Am. Society Metals, Quail Hollow Country Club. Office: Nucor Corp 4425 Randolph Road Charlotte North Carolina 28211

JACOBS, DONALD P., banking and finance educator; born Chicago, June 22, 1927; son of David and Bertha (Nevod) J.; children: Elizabeth, Ann, David; married Dinah Nemeroff, May 28, 1978. Bachelor of Arts, Roosevelt College, 1949; Master of Arts, Columbia University, 1951, Doctor of Philosophy, 1956. Member research staff National Bureau Economic Research, 1952-57; instructor College City New York, 1955-57; member faculty to Morrison professor fin. Northwestern University Grad. School Management, 1970-78, chairman department, 1969-75, dean, 1975—, Gaylord Freeman Distinguished professor banking, 1978—; participant Institute International Management, Burgenstock, Switzerland, 1965—; formerly chairman board of directors Amtrak; director Commonwealth Edison, Hartmarx Corp., Pet Incorporated, Union Oil Company, 1st Chicago UDC-Universal Devel., L.P., Whitman Corp., Incorporated; co-director fin. studies Presdl. Commission Fin. Structure and Regulation, 1970-71; senior economist banking and currency committee United States House of Representatives, 1963-64; director Conference Savings and Residential Financing, 1967—. Editor proceedings: Conf. Savs. and Residential Financing, 1967, 68, 69; contributor articles to professional journals. Served with United States Naval Reserve, 1945-46. Ford Foundation fellow, 1959-60, 63-64. Member Am. Econ. Association, Am. Statistical Association, Am. Fin. Association, Econometrics Society, Institute Management Sci. Home: 617 Milburn St Evanston Illinois 60201 Office: Northwestern U Grad Sh Management 633 Clark St Evanston Illinois 60208

JACOBS, MELVIN, department store executive; born 1926, 1926. Graduate, Pennsylvania State University, 1947. Merchandise manager Bloomingdales, 1947-71; president then chairman, chief executive officer federated Miami based div. Burdines, 1972-77; vice chairman, board of directors Federated Department Stores Incorporated, 1977-82; former chairman, chief executive officer

Saks and Company, Louisville, from 1982; now chairman, chief executive officer Saks Fifth Avenue. Office: Saks Fifth Avenue Company 12 E 49th St 19th Floor New York New York 10017

JACOBSEN, THOMAS HERBERT, banker; born Chicago, October 15, 1939; son of Herbert Rogde and Catharine (Ball) J.; married Diane Leisa DeMell. Bachelor of Science, Lake Forest (Illinois) University, 1963; Master of Business Administration, University Chicago, 1968; graduate, Advanced Management Program, Harvard University, 1979. From assistant cashier to vice president computer operations First National Bank Chicago, 1966-76; vice president, then senior vice president Barnett Banks Florida, Jacksonville, 1976-79, executive vice president, chief fin. officer, 1979-82, senior executive vice president, 1982-84, vice-chairman, director, 1984-89; chairman, president, chief executive officer Mercantile Bancorp. Incorporated, St. Louis, 1989—; lecturer Grad. School Business, University North Florida. Chairman board trustees North Florida Multiple Sclerosis Society. Member Am. Bankers Association, Student Loan Marketing Association (board directors). Republican. Presbyterian. Clubs: Union League (Chicago); Bob O'Link Golf (Highland Park, Illinois); Players (Ponte Vedra Beach, Florida); N Men's (Northwestern University). Office: Barnett Banks Incorporated 100 Laura St Post Office Box 40789 Jacksonville Florida 32203-0789 also: Mercantile Bancorp Incorporated Mercantile Tower Box 524 Saint Louis Missouri 63166

JACOBSON, ALLEN FRANK, manufacturing company executive; born Omaha, October 7, 1926; son of Alma Frank and Ruth Alice (Saalfeld) J.; married Barbara Jean Benidt, April 18, 1964; children: Allen F., Holly Anne, Paul Andrew. Bachelor of Science in Chemical Engineering, Iowa State University, 1947. Product engineer tape laboratory 3M Company (Minnesota Mining & Manufacturing Company), St. Paul, 1947-50, tech. assistant to plant manager, Hutchinson, Minnesota and Bristol, Pennsylvania, 1950-55, tape production superintendent, Bristol, Pennsylvania, 1955-59, plant manager tape, 1959-61; plant manager tape and AC&S Bristol, 1961-63; tape production manager Tape & Allied Products Group St. Paul, 1963; manufacturing manager tape and allied products 3M Company (Minnesota Mining & Manufacturing Company), St. Paul, 1963-68, general manager industrial tape div., 1968-70, div. vice president industrial tape div., 1970-72; executive vice president, general manager 3M Can., Limited, 1973-75; vice president European operations 1975; vice president tape and allied products group 3M Company (Minnesota Mining & Manufacturing Company), St. Paul, 1975-81, executive vice president industrial and consumer sector, 1981-84, president United States operations, 1984-86, chairman, chief executive officer, 1986—, director, 1983—; board of directors Valmont Industries Incorporated, Valley, Nebraska, United States West Incorporated, Englewood, Colorado, Northern States Power Company, Minneapolis, Mobil Corp., New York City, Potlatch Corp., San Francisco, Sara Lee Corp., Chicago, Minnesota Business Partnership, Minneapolis. Recipient Professional Achievement citation in engineering Iowa State

University, 1983, Marston medal Iowa State University, 1986. Avocations: photography; shooting; gardening; golf; reading. Office: Minnesota Mining & Mfg Company 3M Center 220-14W-04 Saint Paul Minnesota 55144-1000

JARRETT, JERRY VERNON, banker; born Abilene, Texas, October 31, 1931; son of Walter Elwood and Myrtle Elizabeth (Allen) J.; married Martha Ann McCabe, June 13, 1953; children: Cynthia Ann, Charles Elwood, Christopher Allen, John Carlton. Bachelor of Business Administration, University Oklahoma, 1957; Master of Business Administration, Harvard University, 1963. General sales manager Texas Coca-Cola Bottling Company, Abilene, 1957-61; executive vice president Marine Midland Bank, New York City, 1963-73; executive vice president Ameritrust Company, 1973-76, vice chairman, 1976-78, chairman, chief executive officer, 1978—; chairman, chief executive officer Ameritrust Corp. Co-author: Creative Collective Bargaining, 1964. Served with United States Army Air Force, 1950-54. Member Phi Gamma Delta. Home: 2751 Chesterton Road Shaker Heights Ohio 44122 Office: AmeriTrust Corp 900 Euclid Avenue Post Office Box 5937 Cleveland Ohio 44101

JEELOFF, GERRIT, electronics executive; born May 13, 1927; married Jantje Aleida Plinsinga, 1951; two daughter. Graduate, Dutch Training Institute Foreign Trade, Nijerode. With Philips Industries, Eindhoven, Holland, 1950-53, 65-70, Spain, South Am., 1953-65, Varese, Italy, 1970-76; chairman board of directors North America Phillips Corp. (subsidiary N.V. Philips GloeilamfabrieKen, Einhoven, The Netherlands). Commdr. of the Order of the Brit. Emprie. Recipient Commendatore nel Ordine al Merito della Repubblica Italiana, 1974. Member Order of Oranje-Nassau (officer), Royal Thames Yacht Club, Royal Ocean Racing Club, Royal Yacht Squadron. Avocations: sailing, golf. Office: N Am Philips Corp 100 E 42nd St New York New York 10017

JENRETTE, RICHARD HAMPTON, investment and insurance company executive; born Raleigh, North Carolina, April 5, 1929; son of Joseph M. and Emma V. (Love) J. Bachelor of Arts, University North Carolina, 1951; Master of Business Administration, Harvard University, 1957; Doctor of Letters (honorary), University North Carolina. With Brown Brothers Harriman & Company, New York City, 1957-59; with Donaldson, Lufkin & Jenrette, Incorporated, New York City, 1959—, now chairman board, 1986—; chairman, director Equitable Life Assurance Society United States, New York City, 1987—; chairman, chief executive officer Equitable Life Insurance, 1986-90; board director Business Foundation North Carolina, Rockefeller Foundation, Historical Hudson Valley. Trustee New York Historical Society; member Governor's Council on Hudson Valley Greenway; board of directors White House Endowment Fund. 2d lieutenant United States Army Reserve, 1953-55. Member Securities Industry Association (board director, executive committee), Institute Chartered Fin. Analysts, New York Society Security Analysts, Phi Beta Kappa. Democrat. Episcopalian. Clubs: University, Brook, Harvard, Harvard Business Sch., Links (New York City);

Carolina Yacht (Charleston, South Carolina). Office: Equitable Life Assurance Society United States 787 7th Avenue New York New York 10019

JENSEN, EDMUND PAUL, bank holding company executive; born Oakland, California, April 13, 1937; son of Edmund and Olive E. (Kessell) J.; married Marilyn Norris, November 14, 1959; children: Juliana L., Annika M. Bachelor of Arts, University Washington, 1959; postgraduate, University Santa Clara, Stanford University, 1981. Lic. real estate broker, Oregon, California. Manager fin. plan and evaluation Technicolor, Incorporated, Los Angeles, 1967-69; group vice president National Industries & Subs, Louisville, 1969-72; vice president fin. Wedgewood Homes, Portland, 1972-74; various management positions United States Bancorp, Portland, 1974-83; president United States Bancorp, Incorporated, Portland, 1983—; director United States Bancorp, United States National Bank of Oregon, United States Bank Washington. Chairman United Way, 1986, Northwest Business Coalition, 1987; board of directors Saturday Acad., Portland, 1984—, Visa, U.S.A., Marylhurst College, Oregon Business Council, Oregon Downtown Devel. Association, Oregon Ind. College Foundation, 1983—, treasurer, 1986—, chairman 1988—; ; board of directors Oregon Art Institute, 1983—, vice chairman, 1989—. Member Portland Chamber of Commerce (board directors 1981—, chairman 1987), Association Reserve City Bankers, Association for Portland Progress (president 1988), Waverly Country Club, Multnomah Athletic Club, Arlington Club, Rotary. Office: United States Bancorp Post Office Box 8837 Portland Oregon 97208

JEPSEN, ROGER WILLIAM, former senator, credit union administration executive; born Cedar Falls, Iowa, December 23, 1928; son of Ernest and Esther (Sorensen) J.; married Dee Ann Delaney, September 26, 1958; children: Jeffrey, Ann, Craig, Linda, Deborah, Coy. Bachelor of Science, Arizona State University, 1950, Master of Arts, 1953. Branch manager Connecticut General Life Insurance Company, Davenport, Iowa, 1956-72; executive vice president Agridustrial Electronics Company, Bettendorf, Iowa, 1973-76; president H.E.P. Marketing Company, Davenport, 1976-78; member Iowa Senate, 1967-69; lieutenant governor State of Iowa, 1969-73; member United States Senate from Iowa, 1979-85; chairman National Credit Union Administration, 1985—, National Organization Lieutenant Governors, 1971-72; instructor marketing University Northern Iowa, 1955; Supervisor Scott County, Iowa, 1962-66. Served with United States Army, 1946-47. Member National Association Life Underwriters, General Agts. and Mgrs. Association, Association Mentally Retarded, Scott County Y (director), Reserve Officers Association. Republican. Clubs: Shriners, Moose, Jesters. Office: National Credit Union Adminstrn 1776 G St Northwest Washington District of Columbia 20456

JESSUP, STEWART E., agricultural products executive; born 1924; married. Vice chairman, director Arkansas Rice Growers Cooperative Association, Stuttgart; chairman, director Riceland Foods, Incorporated, Stuttgart. Office: Riceland Foods Incorporated 2120 Park Avenue Stuttgart Arkansas 72160

JOBS, STEVEN PAUL, computer corporation executive; born 1955; adopted son of Paul J. and Clara J. (Jobs); married Laurene Powell, March 18, 1991. Student, Reed College. With Hewlett-Packard, Palo Alto, California; designer video games Atari Incorporated, 1974; co-founder Apple Computer Incorporated, Cupertino, California, chairman board, 1975-85, former director; president NeXT, Incorporated, Palo Alto, California, 1985—. Co-designer: (with Stephan Wozniak) Apple I Computer, 1976. Office: NeXT Incorporated 3475 Deer Creek Road Palo Alto California 94304

JOHNSEN, ERIK FRITHJOF, transportation executive; born New Orleans, August 17, 1925; son of Niels Frithjof and Julia Anita (Winchester) J.; married Dorothy Edna Lee, May 3, 1953 (deceased January 1977); children: Karen Klara Johnsen Baldwin, Erik Lee, Anne Elisabet, R. Christian; married Dolly Ann Souchon, March 22, 1978. Bachelor of Science, United States Mcht. Marine Academy, 1945; Bachelor of Business Administration, Tulane University, 1948. Vice president Central Gulf Steamship Corp. (now Central Gulf Lines Incorporated), New Orleans, 1952-66; president Central Gulf Lines Incorporated, New Orleans, 1966—, also board of directors; president International Shipholding Corp., New Orleans, 1979—, also board of directors; board of directors World Trade Center, First Commerce Corp., New Orleans, Canal Barge Company Incorporated, New Orleans; senior United States director Baltic and International Maritime Conference, Copenhagen, 1986—. Hon. consul Government of Norway, 1985—; board of directors Business Council New Orleans, 1987—, Tulane U. Board Adminstrs., 1974—. With Merchant Marine, 1942-46; lieutenant United States Navy, 1950-52. Member World Trade Club of New Orleans (hon. life), Pickwick Club, New Orleans Country Club. Avocations: boating, golf, jogging. Office: Central Gulf Lines 650 Poydras St Suite 1700 New Orleans Louisiana 70130

JOHNSEN, NIELS WINCHESTER, ocean shipping company executive; born New Orleans, May 9, 1922; son of Niels Frithjof and Julia Anita (Winchester) J.; married Millicent Alva Mercer, September 9, 1944; children—Niels Mercer, Ingrid Christina Johnsen Barrett, Gretchen Anita Johnsen Bryant. Student, Tulane University, 1939-42. Vice president States Marine Lines, New York City, 1946-56; vice president Central Gulf Lines, Incorporated, New York City, 1947-65, vice chairman, 1965-71, chairman, 1971—; president, chairman Northwest Johnsen & Company Incorporated, New York City, 1957-67, 1967—; chairman International Shipholding Corp., New York City, 1979—; director Centennial Insurance Company, New York City, Reserve Fund, Incorporated, New York City; trustee Atlantic Mutual Insurance Company, New York City. Board mgrs. Seamens Church Institute, New York City, 1974—. Served to lieutenant (junior grade) United States Maritime Service, 1942-45. Member National Cargo Bureau (board directors 1983-86), Am. Bureau Shipping (board mgrs. 1967—). Republican.

Presbyterian. Clubs: India House (board dirs. 1962—), Whitehall (board dirs. 1964—) (New York City); Rumson Country (president 1985), Seabright Beach. Avocations: golf; skiing. Office: International Shipholding Corp 650 Poydras St New Orleans Louisiana 70130

JOHNSON, ASHMORE CLARK, JR., oil company executive; born Philadelphia, December 7, 1930; son of Ashmore Clark and Elsie (Carstens) J.; married Myra Lee Wheeler, December 2, 1967; 1 daughter, Elyse Charlotte. Bachelor of Arts, Haverford College, 1952; Master of Business Administration, University Pennsylvania, 1954. Vice president marketing Union Texas Petroleum div. Allied Chemical Corp., Houston, 1972-76, executive vice president div., 1976-77; president specialty chemicals div. Allied Chemical Corp., Houston, 1977-79; executive vice president Allied Chemical Company div. Allied Chemical Corp., Morristown, New Jersey, 1979-82, president, 1982-83; president, chief operating officer Union Texas Petroleum Corp. div. Allied Chemical Corp., Houston, 1983-84; chairman, chief executive officer Union Texas Petroleum Corp., Houston, 1985—. Republican. Episcopalian. Office: Union Tex Petroleum Holdings Corp 1330 Post Oak Boulevard Houston Texas 77252

JOHNSON, DALE A., manufacturing company executive; born 1937; married. Bachelor of Science, Mankato State University, 1959; Master of Arts, University Minnesota, 1966, Doctor of Philosophy, 1968. With Owatonna Tool Company, 1974-85; with SPX Corp., 1985—, president, chief executive officer, 1990-91, chairman, president, chief executive officer, 1991—, also director; board of directors Douglas and Lormason Company, First of Am.-West Michigan. Member Michigan Manufacturing Association (board directors), Motor and Equipment Manufacturing Association (board directors). Office: SPX Corp 700 Terrace Point Dr Muskegon Michigan 49443

JOHNSON, DAVID WILLIS, food products executive; born Tumut, New South Wales, Australia, August 7, 1932; came to United States, 1976; son of Alfred Ernest and Eileen Melba (Burt) J.; married Sylvia Raymonde Wells, March 12, 1966; children: David Ashley Lawrence, Justin Christopher Kendall, Harley Alistair Kent. Bachelor of Science in Economics, University Sydney, Australia, 1954, diploma in Education, 1955; Master of Business Administration, University Chicago, 1958. Management trainee Colgate-Palmolive, Sydney, 1959-60, product manager, 1961, assistant to managing director, 1962, brands manager, 1963, general products manager, 1964-65; assistant general manager, marketing director Colgate-Palmolive, Johannesburg, Republic of South Africa, 1966, chairman, managing director, 1967-72; president Warner-Lambert/Parke Davis Asia, Hong Kong, 1973-76; president personal products div. Warner-Lambert Company, Morris Plains, New Jersey, 1977, president Am. Chicle Div., 1978; executive vice president, gen manager Entenmann's div. Warner-Lambert Company, Bay Shore, New York, 1979; president specialty foods group Warner-Lambert Company, Morris Plains, 1980-81, vice president, 1980-82; president, chief executive officer Entenmann's div. Warner-Lambert

Company, Bay Shore, 1982; vice president General Foods Corp., White Plains, New York, 1982-87; president, chief executive officer Entemann's, Incorporated, Bay Shore, 1982-87; chairman, president, chief executive officer Gerber Products Company, Fremont, Michigan, 1987-89, chairman, chief executive officer, 1989-90; president, chief executive officer Campbell Soup Company, Camden, New Jersey, 1990—; board of directors CIGNA Corp., Philadelphia. Member Am. Bakers Association (past board directors), Am. Management Association. Office: Campbell Soup Company Campbell Place Camden New Jersey 08103-1799

JOHNSON, JAMES A., financial organization executive; born Benson, Minnesota, December 24, 1943; son of Alfred I. and Adeline (Rasmussen) J.; married Katherine Marshall, February 15, 1969 (divorced 1973); married Maxine Isaacs, January 12, 1985; 1 child, Alfred Isaacs. Bachelor of Arts, University Minnesota, 1965; Master of Arts, Princeton University, 1968. Special assistant to Sen. Walter Mondale United States Senate, Washington, 1972; director pub. affairs Dayton Hudson Corp., Minneapolis, 1973-76; executive assistant to vice president Walter Mondale The White House, Washington, 1977-81; president Pub. Strategies, Washington, 1981-85; managing director Lehman Brothers, Washington, 1985-89; vice chairman Fannie Mae, Washington, 1990-91, chief executive officer, 1991—, also chairman board of directors. Democrat. Avocations: tennis, golf, travel. Office: Fannie Mae 3900 Wisconsin Avenue Northwest Washington District of Columbia 20016

JOHNSON, JAMES LAWRENCE, telephone company executive; born Vernon, Texas, April 12, 1927; son of Samuel Lonzo and Adeline Mary (Donges) J.; married Ruth Helen Zweig, August 5, 1949; children: James Lawrence, Helayne, Barry, Todd. Bachelor of Business Administration in Accounting, Texas Tech College, 1949. Accountant Whiteside Laundry, Lubbock, Texas, 1949; with General Telephone Company SW, San Angelo, Texas, 1949-59; assistant controller General Telephone Company SW, 1953-59, vice president, controller, treasurer, 1966-69; controller General Telephone Company Michigan, Muskegon, 1959-63; assistant controller telephone operations, then chief accountant consolidated operations General Telephone and Telegraph Service Corp., New York City, 1963-66; vice president, controller telephone operations General Telephone and Telegraph Service Corp., 1969-74; vice president revenue requirements General Telephone & Electronics Corp., Stamford, Connecticut, 1974-76; president General Telephone Company Illinois, Bloomington, 1976-81; also director, also group vice president General Telephone Company Illinois (Northern region); president General Telephone and Telegraph telephone operating group General Telephone & Electronics Corp., from 1981; senior vice president General Telephone and Telegraph Corp., until 1986; president, chief operating officer, director General Telephone and Telegraph Corp., Stamford, Connecticut, 1986-88, chairman, chief executive officer, 1988—; director First Federal Savings & Loan Association, Bloomington.; Member adv. council

College Business, Illinois State University, Normal. Trustee, adv. council Mennonite Hospital, Bloomington; board of directors Bloomington Unlimited; member Wesleyan Assos., Illinois Wesleyan U., Bloomington. Served with United States Naval Reserve, 1945-47. Member National Accts. Association, Fin. Executives Institute, Illinois Telephone Association (director), McLean County Association Commerce and Industry (director). Republican. Methodist. Clubs: Bloomington Country, Crestwicke Country (Bloomington); Woodway Country (Darien, Connecticut). Lodge: Rotary. Office: General Telephone and Electric Company Corp 1 Stamford Forum Stamford Connecticut 06904

JOHNSON, LLOYD PETER, banker; born Minneapolis, May 1, 1930; son of Lloyd Percy and Edna (Schlampp) J.; married Rosalind Gesner, July 3, 1954; children: Marcia, Russell, Paul. Bachelor of Arts, Carleton College, Northfield, Minnesota, 1952; Master of Business Administration, Stanford University, 1954. With Security Trust & Savings Bank, San Diego, 1954-57; vice chairman charge corp. banking, fiduciary services, international banking Security Pacific National Bank, Los Angeles, 1957-84; chairman, chief executive officer Norwest Corp., Minneapolis, 1985—; member faculty Pacific Coast Banking School, 1969-72, chairman, 1979-80; board of directors Minnesota Business Partnership; trustee Minnesota Mutual Life Insurance Company; board of directors Valmont Industries, Incorporated. Chairman board trustees Carleton College, Minneapolis Institute Arts, vice chmn; board of directors United Way Minneapolis, Minnesota Orchestral Association; member U. Minnesota Board Overseers; adv. council Federal Reserve System. Member Association Reserve City Bankers (board directors), California Bankers Association (president 1977-78), Association Bank Holding Companies. Office: Norwest Corp Northwest Center 6th & Marquette Minneapolis Minnesota 55479-1060

JOHNSON, SAMUEL CURTIS, wax company executive; born Racine, Wisconsin, March 2, 1928; son of Herbert Fisk and Gertrude (Brauner) J.; married Imogene Powers, May 8, 1954; children: Samuel Curtis III, Helen Johnson-Leipold, Herbert Fisk III, Winifred Johnson Marquart. Bachelor of Arts, Cornell University, 1950; Master of Business Administration, Harvard University, 1952; Doctor of Laws (honorary), Carthage College, 1974, Northland College, 1974, Ripon College, 1980, Carroll College, 1981, University Surrey, 1985, Marquette University, 1986. With South Carolina Johnson & Son, Incorporated, Racine, 1954—, international vice president, 1962-63, executive vice president, 1963-66, president, 1966-67, chairman, president, chief executive officer, 1967-72, chairman, chief executive officer, 1972-88, chairman, 1988—; board of directors Johnson Wax Companies, England, Switzerland, Can., Deere & Company, Moline, Illinois, Mobil Corp., New York City; chairman board of directors Johnson Heritage Bancorp, Limited, Racine, Wisconsin, Johnson Worldwide Associates, Incorporated, H.J. Heinz Company, Pittsburgh, Johnson International Bancorp, Limited. Trustee emeritus The Mayo Foundation; chairman Johnson's Wax Fund, Incorporated, Johnson Foundation, Incorporated;

trustee emeritus, presidential councillor Cornell U.; founding chairman emeritus Prairie School, Racine; member adv. council Cornell U. Grad. School Mgmt.; board regents Smithsonian Institution; member Business Council, International Council of J.P. Morgan; member national board governors The Nature Conservancy. Member Chi Psi. Clubs: Cornell (New York City, Milwaukee); University (Milwaukee); Racine Country; Am. (London). Home: 4815 Lighthouse Dr Racine Wisconsin 53402 Office: S C Johnson & Son Incorporated 1525 Howe St Racine Wisconsin 53403

JOHNSON, THOMAS STEPHEN, banker; born Racine, Wisconsin, November 19, 1940; son of H. Norman and Jane Agnes (McAvoy) J.; married Margaret Ann Werner, April 18, 1970; children: Thomas Philip, Scott Michael, Margaret Ann. Bachelor of Arts in Economics, Trinity College, 1962; Master of Business Administration, Harvard University, 1964. Instructor Grad. Business School Ateneo de Manila University, Philippines, 1964-66; special assistant to controller United States Department Defense, Washington, 1966-69; with Chemical Bank, New York City, 1969-89, president, director, 1983-89; president, director Manufacturers Hanover Trust Company, Manufacturers Hanover Corp., New York City, 1989—; director Pan Atlantic Incorporated, Railroad Donnelly & Sons, Incorporated. Board of directors Union Theol. Sem., Institute International Education; trustee Trinity College, Asia Society; vice president, board of directors Cancer Research Institute, Sta. WNET-TV. Member Association Reserve City Bankers, The Group of 30, Council Foreign Relations, Bond Club New York, Economics Club New York, Montclair Golf Club, Palm Beach Polo & Country Club, Harvard Business Club (New York City), River Club (New York City) The Links (New York City), Chicago Club. Democrat. Roman Catholic. Office: Mfrs Hanover Trust Company 270 Park Avenue New York New York 10017

JOHNSTON, GERALD ANDREW, aerospace company executive; born Chicago, July 17, 1931; son of Gerald Ervan and Mary Henrietta (Dowell) J.; married Jacquelyn Egan, March 6, 1954; children: Jan, Colleen, Jeffrey, Gregory, Steven. Student, San Bernardino Junior College, 1950-51; Bachelor of Science in Engineering, University California, Los Angeles, 1956, Cert. of Business Management, 1968, Master of Science in Engineering, 1972. Junior engineer Shell Oil Company, 1952-54; test engineer Robinson Aviation, 1955-56; stress analyst North Am. Aviation, 1955; associate engineer, tech. director Douglas Aircraft Company, Santa Monica, California, 1956-68; director, vice president general manager McDonnell Douglas Astronautics, Huntington Beach, California, 1968-87; president McDonnell Douglas Corp., St. Louis, 1988—, also board of directors. Trustee St. Louis U., 1988—. Roman Catholic. Office: McDonnell Douglas Corp Post Office Box 516 Saint Louis Missouri 63166

JOHNSTONE, JOHN WILLIAM, JR., chemical company executive; born Brooklyn, November 19, 1932; son of John William and Sarah J. (Singleton) J.; married Claire Lundberg, April 14, 1956; children: Thomas Edward, James Robert, Robert Andrew. Bachelor of Arts, Hartwick College,

Oneonta, New York, 1954; Doctor of Science (honorary), Hartwick College, 1990; graduate, Advanced Management Program, Harvard University, 1970. With Hooker Chemical Corp., 1954-75, group vice president, 1973-75; president Airco Alloys div. Airco, Incorporated, 1976-79; vice president, general manager industrial products, then senior vice president chemicals group Olin Corp., 1979-80; corp. vice president, president chemicals group Olin Corp., Stamford, Connecticut, 1980-85; president Olin Corp., 1985-87, chief operating officer, 1986-87, president, chief executive officer, chairman, 1988—, also chairman board; board of directors Home Life Insurance Company, Research Corp., Am. Brands, Incorporated. Board of directors Am. Productivity and Quality Center; member defense policy adv. committee on trade; trustee Hartwick College, 1983-91, The Conference Board. Member Am. Management Association, Society Chemical Industry, Soap and Detergent Association (former chairman board directors), Chemical Manufacturers Association (chairman board 1991). Episcopalian. Clubs: Landmark; Duquesne (Pittsburgh); Woodway Country, Blind Brook; Links (New York City). Office: Olin Corp 120 Long Ridge Road Stamford Connecticut 06904

JONES, DALE P., oil field service company executive; born Gillham, Arkansas, October 19, 1936; son of Ray Elgin and Alma Lee (Wheeler) J.; married Anita Ruth Collier, December 28, 1963; children: Lee Anna, Leisa. Bachelor of Science, University Arkansas, 1958; postgraduate, Southern Methodist University, 1966, University Oklahoma, 1970. Certified Public Accountant, Arkansas, Texas, Oklahoma. Senior auditor Arthur Andersen & Company, 1958-59, 62-65; corp. auditor Halliburton Company, Dallas, 1965-66; fin. coordinator Halliburton Services, London, 1967-69; assistant to controller Halliburton Services, Duncan, Oklahoma, 1970-84; president Welex Div., Houston, 1985-87; senior vice president Halliburton Company, Dallas, 1987, executive vice president oil field services, 1987—. Chairman board, president Duncan Regional Hospital Incorporated, 1977-80. Served to captain United States Air Force, 1959-62. Member Am. Petroleum Institute, Fin. Executives Institute, Texas Society Certified Public Accountants, University Arkansas College Business Administration Assocs. Republican. Baptist. Clubs: Petroleum, Plaza Athletic (Dallas); Westlake (Houston). Office: Halliburton Company 500 N Akard St 3600 Lincoln Plaza Dallas Texas 75201

JONES, DAVID ALLEN, health facility executive, electronics executive; born Louisville, August 7, 1931; son of Evan L. and Elsie F. (Thurman) J.; married Betty L. Ashbury, July 24, 1954; children: David, Susan, Daniel, Matthew, Carol. Bachelor of Science, University Louisville, 1954; Juris Doctor, Yale University, 1960. Bar: Kentucky 1960. Founder, chief executive officer Humana Incorporated (formerly Extendicare Incorporated), Louisville, 1961—, also chairman, director; partner Greenebaum, Doll and McDonald and predecessor, Louisville, 1965-69, of counsel, 1969-74; with Department Computing & Telecommunications, University Louisville, 1974—; director Royal

Crown Companies, Incorporated; director, executive committee 1st Kentucky National Corp. and affiliates, 1st Kentucky Trust Company, First National Bank Louisville. Served as lieutenant (junior grade) United States Navy, 1954-57. Member Louisville Area Chamber of Commerce. Home: 35 Poplar Hill Road Louisville Kentucky 40207 Office: U Louisville Department Computing & Telecommunications Louisville Kentucky 40292 also: Humana Incorporated 500 W Main St Box 1438 Louisville Kentucky 40201

JONES, JOHN EARL, construction company executive; born June 24, 1934. Bachelor of Arts, Carleton College, 1956; postgraduate, University Chicago, 1958-60, Northwestern University, 1960-61. Senior vice president Continental Illinois National Bank and Trust Company, Chicago, 1957-80; with China, Burma, India Theatre of Operations Industries, Incorporated, Oak Brook, Illinois, 1980—, executive vice president, treasurer, 1982—; vice chairman board China, Burma, India Theatre of Operations Industries, Incorporated, 1985-88, president, chief operating officer, 1988—, also director; chairman board, president, chief executive officer 1989—; board of directors Allied Products Corp.; director The InterLake Corp. Trustee Glenwood School; member business adv. council U. Illinois. Office: CBI Industries Incorporated 800 Jorie Boulevard Oak Brook Illinois 60521-7001

JONES, NORMAN M., finance executive; born Fargo, North Dakota, August 28, 1930; son of Maurice H. Jones and Minnie (Dustrud) Bohlig; married Eunice Skurdahl, December 20, 1950; children: Janet, Marrietta, Mark, Steven Jones. Student, Concordia College, 1949-50. With Metropolitan Federal Bank, Fargo, 1952-83; chairman, chief executive officer Metropolitan Fin. Corp., Fargo, 1983—; past vice chair Federal Home Loan Bank Board, Des Moines, Iowa; board trustees, executive committee S&L Computer Trust, Des Moines. Member thrift adv. council Federal Reserve; board trustees Lutheran Hosps. and Homes, Fargo; past president First Lutheran Church, Fargo; past chairman Am. Lutheran Church Ea. North Dakota District Council; national steering committee Commitment to Mission Am. Lutheran Church; past. board of directors, vice president, Fargo Junior Chamber of Commerce; founding member Fargo Housing Authority; board of directors Red River Valley Council Boy Scouts Am.; board regents Concordia College, Moorhead, Minnesota Served with United States Army, 1949-51. Recipient President's award Concordia College, Moorhead, Minnesota, 1973, 74, Regent's award, 1977, Sole Dio Gloria award, 1977, Martin Luther award, 1989; named Outstanding Business Leader North Dakota Business Foundation, 1978. Member Fargo Chamber of Commerce (past board directors). Republican. Clubs: Fargo Country; Gainey Ranch Golf (Scottsdale, Arizona). Avocations: golf, hunting, tennis, travel. Office: Met Fin Corp 1600 Radisson Tower Fargo North Dakota 58108

JORDAN, DON D., electric company executive; born Corpus Christi, Texas, 1932; married. University Texas, 1954; Juris Doctor, Southern Texas College Law, 1969. With Houston Lighting & Power Company subsidiary Houston Industries, Incorporated, 1956—P02mgr. commercial sales, 1967-69, manager personnel relations, 1969-71, vice president, assistant to president, 1969-71, 1971-73, group vice president, 1973-74, president, 1974-82, chief executive officer, also board of directors, 1977—, chairman, 1977—, also chairman, chief executive officer Houston Industries, Incorporated, 919982—, also board of directors, 919982—; board of directors Texas Commerce Bancshares, Texas Medical Center, Texas Heart Institute. Office: Houston Industries Incorporated Post Office Box 4567 Houston Texas 77210

JORGENSON, DALE WELDEAU, economist, educator; born Bozeman, Montana, May 7, 1933; son of Emmett B. and Jewell (Torkelson) J.; married Linda Ann Mabus, July 27, 1971; children: Eric Mabus, Kari Ann. Bachelor of Arts, Reed College, 1955; Master of Arts, Harvard University, 1957, Doctor of Philosophy, 1959; Doctor of Philosophy (honorary), Uppsala University, 1991, Oslo University, 1991. Member faculty University California, Berkeley, 1959-69; professor economics University California, 1963-69; professor economics Harvard University, 1969-80, Frederic Eaton Abbe professor economics, 1980—; Ford research professor economics University Chicago, 1962-63. Author: (with J.J. McCall and R. Radner) Optimal Replacement Policy, 1967, Econometric Studies of United States Energy Policy, 1975, (with R. Landau) Technology and Economic Policy, 1986 (with F.M. Gollop and B.M. Fraumeni) Productivity and United States Economic Growth, 1987, (with R. Landau), Technology and Capital Formation, 1989, (with Lars Bergman, Erno Zalai) General Equilibrium Modeling and Economic Policy Analysis, 1990, (with Kun-Young Yun) Tax Return and the Cost of Capital, 1991; contributor articles to professional journals. Fellow Econometric Society (president 1987), Am. Statistical Association, Am. Acad. Arts and Sciences, American Association for the Advancement of Science; member Am. Econ. Association (John Bates Clark medal 1971), National Acad. Sciences, Royal Swedish Acad. Sciences. Home: 1010 Memorial Dr Cambridge Massachusetts 02138 Office: Harvard U Littauer 122 Cambridge Massachusetts 02138

JORNDT, LOUIS DANIEL, drug store chain executive; born Chicago, August 24, 1941; son of Louis Carl and Margaret Estelle (Teel) J.; married Patricia McDonnell, August 1, 1964; children—Kristine, Michael, Kara. Bachelor of Science in Pharmacy, Drake University, 1963; Master of Business Administration, University New Mexico, 1974. Various management positions Walgreen Company, Chicago, 1963-68, district manager, 1968-75; regional director Walgreen Company, Deerfield, Illinois, 1975-79; regional vice president Walgreen Company, Deerfield, 1979-82, vice president, treasurer, 1982-85, senior vice president, treasurer, 1985-89, president, chief operating officer, 1989—. Board of directors Better Business Bureau Chicago, 1982—, Chicago Association Commerce and Industry; national chairman Drake U. Pharmacy Alumni Fund. Member National Association Corp. Treasurer, Fin. Executives Institute. Clubs: Economic (Chicago);

Glen View (Illinois) Golf. Avocations: golf; swimming; reading. Office: Walgreen Company 200 Wilmot Road Deerfield Illinois 60015

JOVANOVICH, PETER WILLIAM, publishing executive; born New York City, February 4, 1949; son of William Illya and Martha Evelyn (Davis) J.; married Robin Adair Thrush, February 14, 1976; children—Nicholas, William. Bachelor of Arts, Princeton University, 1972. Director trade department Macmillan Pub. Company, New York City, 1977-78; director trade department Harcourt Brace Jovanovich, Incorporated, New York City, 1980-83; executive vice president Harcourt Brace Jovanovich, Incorporated, San Diego, 1985-89; president, chief executive officer Orlando, Florida, 1989—, chairman executive committee, 1990—; managing director Acad. Press, London, England, 1983-84, president Associated Press Journals, 1984-85.

JUNKINS, JERRY RAY, electronics company executive; born Fort Madison, Iowa, December 9, 1937; son of Ralph Renaud and Selma Jennie (Kudebeh) J.; married Marilyn Jo Schevers, June 13, 1959; children—Kirsten Dianne, Karen Leigh. Bachelor of Electrical Engineering, Iowa State University, 1959; Master of Science in Engineering Administration, Southern Methodist University, 1968. Engineer, manager Manufacturing group Texas Instruments, Incorporated, Dallas, 1959-73, assistant vice president, manager radar div., 1973-75, vice president, manager equipment group, 1975-81, executive vice president, manager data systems and industrial systems, 1981-85, president, chief executive officer, 1985-88, chmn, president, chief executive officer, board of directors, 1988—; board of directors Proctor and Gamble Company, Caterpillar Incorporated. Board of directors Dallas Citizens Council. Member National Acad. Engineering. Methodist. Office: Tex Instruments Incorporated 13510 N Central Expressway Post Office 655474 MS236 Dallas Texas 75243

JUREN, DENNIS FRANKLIN, petroleum company executive; born Ellinger, Texas, April 4, 1935; son of Daniel Arthur and Ellen Emily J.; married Ruth Birmingham, October 7, 1961; children—Patrick Edward, Ellen Emily, Anne Elizabeth. Bachelor of Arts in economics, University Texas, 1966; Master of Business Administration in fin., University Houston, 1969. Manager supply Eastern States Petroleum Company, Houston, 1956-60; owner Bonded Petroleum Company, Houston, 1960-62; vice president marketing and supply Coastal States Petrochem. Company, Houston, 1962-70; president Tesoro Petroleum Corp., San Antonio, 1970—, chief operating officer, 1987—, also director. Board of directors Young Men's Christian Association, San Antonio, 1979. Served with United States Army, 1954-55. Member San Antonio Chamber of Commerce (director 1982), National Petroleum Refiners Association (director), Am. Petroleum Institute. Methodist. Clubs: Oakhills Country, University Lodge: Masons. Office: Tesoro Petroleum Corp 8700 Tesoro Dr San Antonio Texas 78286

KAHANA, ARON, bank executive; born Egypt, April 25, 1921; married Tirza Farkash; 2 children. Graduate, Oxford International School Banking, 1948. With Ottoman Bank, Israel, 1941-48, Mercantile Bank of Israel,

1948-68; with Israel Discount Bank, Limited, Tel Aviv, 1968—, managing department general manager; executive vice president Israel Discount Bank, New York City, 1967-78, executive president, 1967-78, president, 1987—, also board of directors. Served with Israeli Army. Office: Israel Discount Bank New York 511 Fifth Avenue New York New York 10017

KAMAN, CHARLES HURON, diversified technologies corporation executive; born Washington, June 15, 1919; son of Charles W. and Mabel (Davis) K.; married Helen Sylvander, October 20, 1945 (divorced); children: Charles William II, Cathleen, Steven Wardner; married Roberta C. Hallock, September 1, 1971. Bachelor of Science in Aeronautical Engineering magna cum laude, Catholic University Am., 1940; Doctor of Science (honorary), University Colorado, 1984, University Hartford, 1985; Doctor of Laws (honorary), University Connecticut, 1985. With Hamilton Standard Propellers div. United Aircraft Corp., East Hartford, Connecticut, 1940-45; president Kaman Corp., Bloomfield, Connecticut, 1945-90, chairman board, 1945—, chief executive officer, 1986—; chairman Vertical Lift Aircraft council of Aerospace Industries Association, 1964, Helicopter council, 1954; former member The World Affairs Center Honors adv. board. Board governors Catholic U. Am.; board of directors Institute of Living; founder, president, board of directors Fidelco Guide Dog Foundation, Incorporated; founder, Am. Leadership Forum, U. Hartford; former trustee Western New England College; former member Catholic U. board governors; past corporator Health Care Facilities Planning Council of Greater Hartford; past industrial committee member Greater Hartford Young Men's Christian Association. Recipient Distinguished Service award Connecticut Junior Chamber of Commerce, 1953, Engineer of Year award Connecticut Society of Professional Engineers inc., 1961, Alumni Achievement award Catholic University Am., 1961, Outstanding Young Man of Year award Hartford Junior Chamber of Commerce, 1948, Assoc. award Navy Helicopter Association, 1975, National Human Relations award National Conference of Christian and Jews, 1987, The Fleet Admiral Chester W. Nimitz award Navy League of the United States, 1986. Fellow Am. Helicopter Society (president 1958, director 1959-61, Dr. Alexander Klemin award 1981), American Institute of Aeronautics and Astronautics; member Connecticut Business and Industry Association (director, executive committee), National Acad. Engineering, Connecticut Society Professional Engineers, Aviation Hall of Fame (charter), Navy Helicopter Association (hon.), Newcomen Society Am. 1983, Navy League of United States (national adv. council), Pi Tau Sigma (hon.), Beta Gamma Sigma, Am. Helicopter Society, Connecticut Acad. Sci. and Engineering, Connecticut Aeronautical Historical Association. Office: Kaman Corp 322 Blue Hills Avenue Bloomfield Connecticut 06002

KAMINS, PHILIP E., plastics company executive. Chief executive officer PMC, California. Office: PMC Incorporated 12243 Branford St Sun Valley California 91352

KAMPEN, EMERSON, chemical company executive; born Kalamazoo,

March 12, 1928; son of Gerry and Gertrude (Gerlofs) K.; married Barbara Frances Spitters, February 2, 1951; children—Douglas S., Joanie L. Kampen Dunham, Laura L. Kampen Shiver, Emerson II, Deborah L. Kampen Smith, Cynthia S., Pamela E. Bachelor of Science in Chemical Engineering, University Michigan, 1951. Chemical engr Great Lakes Chemical Corp., West Lafayette, Ind., 1951-57, plant manager, 1957-62, vice president, 1962-67, senior vice president, 1968, executive vice president, 1969-71, president, 1972—, chief executive officer, 1977—; president, chief executive officer, chairman board GLCD, Incorporated, Arkansas, 1988, also board of directors; board of directors GLCD, Incorporated, Bio-Lab, Incorporated, Decatur, Georgia; president, director GLI, Incorporated, Newport, Tennessee, GHC (Properties) Incorporated; board of directors WIL Research Laboratories, Incorporated, Oilfield Service Corp. Am., Lafayette Life Insurance Company, Ind. National Bank, Inland Specialty Chemical Corp., Huntsman Chemical Corp., Salt Lake City, Pub. Service Ind., Plainfield, QO Chemicals, Incorporated, Chicago, Pentech Chemicals, Incorporated, Chicago; chairman board subsidiary consultant E/M Corp., Hydrotech Chemical Corp., Great Lakes Chemical (Europe) Limited; president Arkansas Chemicals; member listed company adv. committee Am. Stock Exchange. Member corp. advising group Huntington's Disease Society Am., New York City; commissioner Ind. United Way Centennial Commission; trustee Ind. U., Bloomington, Purdue U., West Lafayette; board of directors Junior Achievement Greater Lafayette Incorporated, Lafayette Art Association Foundation Incorporated, Purdue Research Foundation, West Lafayette, Lafayette Symphony Foundation; director, vice president Hoosier Alliance Against Drugs, Indianapolis Captain United States Air Force, 1953. Recipient Bronze medal Wall Street Transcript, 1980, 86, Gold medal, 1983, 85, 88, 90, Silver medal, 1989, Man of Year award National Huntington's Disease Association, 1984; co-recipient Gold medal Wall Street Transcript, 1984; named 5th Most InvolvedChief Executive Officer Chief Executive Magazine, 1986, Sagamore of the Wabash, 1988. Fellow Am. Institute Chemists; member Society Chemical Industry, National Association Manufacturers (board directors), Chemical Manufacturers Association, Ind. Chamber of Commerce (board directors), Greater Lafayette Chamber of Commerce. Clubs: Lafayette Country, Skyline (Indianapolis). Lodges: Elks, Rotary. Avocations: golf; family events. Home: 168 Creighton West Lafayette Indiana 47906 Office: Great Lake Chem Corp United States Highway 52 Northwest Post Office Box 2200 West Lafayette Indiana 47906

KAMPOURIS, EMMANUEL ANDREW, corporate executive; born Alexandria, Egypt, December 14, 1934; came to United States, 1979; son of Andrew George and Euridice Anne (Caralli) K.; married Myrto Stellatos, July 4, 1959 (deceased); children: Andrew, Alexander. Student, King's School, Bruton, Somerset, United Kingdom, 1953; Master of Arts in Law, Oxford University, 1957; certificate in ceramic tech., North Staffordshire College of Tech., United Kingdom, 1962. Plant manager, director "KEREM", Athens,

Greece, 1962-64; director "HELLENIT", Athens, Greece, 1962-65; managing director Ideal Standard, Athens, 1966-79; vice president, group executive international and export Am. Standard Incorporated, New Brunswick, New Jersey, 1979-84; senior vice president building products Am. Standard Incorporated, New Brunswick, 1984-89; president, chief executive officer Am. Standard Incorporated, New York City, 1989—; board of directors Ideal Refractories SAI, Athens, Ideal Standard Mexico, Am. Standard Sanitaryware (Thailand) Limited, INCESA, San Jose, Costa Rica, Hoxan Corp., Sapporo, Japan. Board of directors Greek Mgmt. Association, Athens, 1975-77, Federation of Greek Industries, Athens. Member Young President Organization, Chief Executives Organization, Econ. Club of New York, Oxford Union, Oxford Law Society, Am. Hellenic Chamber of Commerce (general secretary 1975-79), Chemists Club, Laurel Valley Golf Club. Greek Orthodox. Clubs: Spring Brook Country (Morristown, New Jersey); Quogue Field, Quogue Beach (Long Island, New York). Avocations: golf; tennis; classical music. Office: Am Standard Incorporated 1114 Avenue of the Americas New York New York 10036-7701 also: Am Standard Incorporated 1 Centennial Plaza Piscataway New Jersey 08855-6820

KANE, EDWARD L., supermarket chain stores executive; born 1938. Bachelor of Journalism, University Connecticut, 1960; Doctor of Laws, New York University, 1963. Formerly partner Haskins Nugent Newnham Kane & Zvetina; with Craig Corp., Los Angeles, 1985—, president, 1988—, also board of directors; chairman board Citadel Holding Corp., Glendale, California. Office: Craig Corp 116 N Robertson Boulevard Los Angeles California 90048 also: Citadel Holding Corp 600 N Brand Boulevard Glendale California 91203

KANN, PETER ROBERT, journalist, business reporting and services company executive; born New York City, December 13, 1942; son of Robert A. and Marie (Breuer) K.; married Francesca Mayer, April 12, 1969 (deceased 1983); married Karen Elliott House, 1984; children: Hillary Francesca, Petra Elliott, Jason Elliott. Bachelor of Arts, Harvard University, 1964. With The Wall St. Journal, 1964—; journalist New York City, 1964-67, Vietnam, 1967-68, Hong Kong, 1968-75; pub., editor Asian edition 1976-79, associate pub., 1979-88; formerly assistant to chairman and member executive committee Dow Jones & Company, 1986-89, president international and magazine groups, 1986-89, also chairman board of directors; pub. Wall St. Journal, 1989—; president Dow Jones & Company, New York City, 1989-91, chairman, chief executive officer, 1991—; director Group Expansion, Paris, 1987—; chairman board Far Eastern Economic Rev., 1987-89; elected member Pulitzer Prize Board, 1987—. Trustee Asia Society, 1989—, Institute for Advanced Study, Princeton, 1990—. Recipient Pulitzer prize for international reporting, 1972. Club: Spee (Cambridge, Massachusetts). Office: Wall Street Jour 200 Liberty St New York New York 10281

KATES, HENRY E., life insurance company executive; born Denver, February 18, 1939; son of I. Allen and Dorothy K.; children: Dorianne,

Bradley. Bachelor of Science in Fin., University Colorado, 1960. Agent Mutual Benefit Life, Newark, 1960-67, general agent, 1967-81; president Mutual Benefit Fin. Service Company (subsidiary Mutual Benefit Life), Providence, 1981-85, executive vice president, 1985-87, president, 1987-89, chief executive officer, 1989—; board of directors Promus Corp., Continental Insurance, Pub. Service Enterprise Group. Author: Body Language in Sales, 1980. Board of directors Boys' and Girls' Clubs of Newark, New Jersey Center for the Performing Arts, Carnegie Hall, U. of Colorado Foundation, Lincoln Center Theaters, Newark Mus., Tri-State United Way, New Jersey Symphony, Newark Performing Arts Center. Member Newark Chamber of Commerce (chairman). Home: 5 Prospect Hill Avenue Summit New Jersey 07901 Office: Mut Benefit Life Ins Company 520 Broad St Newark New Jersey 07102

KAUFFMAN, JOHN THOMAS, utility executive; born Weehawken, New Jersey, August 17, 1926; son of William Carl and Frances E. K.; married Julia A. Crouch, August 19, 1949; children: Anne E. Kauffman Zayaitz, Janet L. Bachelor of Science in Marine Engineering, United States Mcht. Marine Academy, 1946; Bachelor of Science in Mechanical Engineering, Purdue University, 1950. With Pennsylvania Power & Light Company, 1950—; assistant vice president, then vice president System Power & Engineering, 1973-78; executive vice president operations System Power & Engineering, Allentown, 1978—; also director System Power & Engineering; chairman board of directors Pennsylvania Mines Corp., Interstate Energy Company; director affiliates and subsidiary companies. Member Electric Power Research Institute (research adv. committee), American Society of Mechanical Engineers, Am. Nuclear Society, Edison Electric Institute (nuclear power executive adv. committee), Pennsylvania Electric Association (executive committee, chairman), Pennsylvania Industrial and Professional Council, Engineers Club Lehigh Valley, Utility Nuclear Waster Management Group (chairman). Clubs: N.E. River Yacht; Brookside Country (Allentown). Home: 664 Spruce St Emmaus Pennsylvania 18049 Office: Pennsylvania Power & Light Company 2 N 9th St Allentown Pennsylvania 18101

KEESEE, ROGER N., family entertainment company executive; born 1937; married. Bachelor of Science in Electrical Engineering, Virginia Polytechnic and State University, 1960. With General Electric Company, 1960-83, general manager department manufacturing div. video products business, 1981-83; executive vice president sales and marketing engineering Bally Manufacturing Corp., Chicago, 1983-88, formerly chief operating officer, president, 1988—; now president, chief executive officer Six Flags Corp. subsidiary S.F. Acquisition Incorporated, Chicago, also board of directors. Office: Bally Mfg Corp 8700 W Bryn Mawr Chicago Illinois 60631

KEHAYA, ERY W., tobacco holding company executive; born 1923; married. With Standard Commercial Corp., Wilson, North Carolina, 1944—, president, 1954—, now chairman board, chief executive officer, also board of directors. Office: Standard Commercial Corp Post Office Box 450 Wilson North Carolina 27894

KEIFFER, EDWIN GENE, electronics industry company executive; born Dallas, August 25, 1929; son of Edwin L. and Eunice Alpha (Foster) K.; married Carole Ann Porter; children: Edwin Paul, Cheri Ann, Judith Susan, Amy Lynn. Bachelor of Electrical Engineering, Southern Methodist University, 1955, Master of Electrical Engineering, 1962. Lead systems design engineer Chance Vought Company, Grand Prairie, Texas, 1955-58, engineering specialist, 1958, senior engineering specialist, 1958-59, section chief antenna systems, 1959-60, chief antenna and microwave design, 1960-62; branch manager communications and tracking systems Chance Vought Company, Garland, Texas, 1962-63, deputy manager Radiation Laboratory, 1963-66; product line director special projects LTV Electrosystems (name changed to E-Systems, Incorporated), Garland, 1966-70; successively vice president electronic systems, vice president, general manager, Garland div. E-Systems, Incorporated, 1970-83; senior vice president group executive E-Systems, Incorporated, Dallas, 1983-87, president, chief operating officer, 1987-89, chairman, chief executive officer, 1989—, also board of directors. Member chancellor's century council Texas A&M U., College Station, 1988, Dallas Citizens Council, 1989—, Def. Policy Adv. Committee on Trade, 1989; board of directors Dallas Council on World Affairs, 1989—, Dallas County Community College District Foundation, 1990—, United Way of Dallas, 1990—. With United States Marine Corps, 1948-50. Recipient Distinguished Alumni award Southern Methodist University, 1989. Member Institute of Electrical and Electronics Engineers (senior), Am. Defense Preparedness Association, Armed Forces Communications and Electronics Association, Army Aviation Association Am., Aerospace Industries Association (board govs. 1989—), Association United States Army, Navy League United States (life). Republican. Avocation: golf. Office: E-Systems Incorporated 6250 LBJ Freeway Dallas Texas 75240

KEIL, JEFFREY C., banker; born West Orange, New Jersey, 1943. Graduate, University Pennsylvania, 1965; Master of Business Administration, Harvard University, 1968. President Republic National Bank holding company Republic National Bank and Manhattan Savings Bank, New York City; president, board of directors Republic New York Corp. Office: Republic New York Corp 452 Fifth Avenue New York New York 10018

KELLEHER, HERBERT DAVID, lawyer, airline executive; born Camden, New Jersey, March 12, 1931; son of Harry and Ruth (Moore) K.; married Joan Negley, September 9, 1955; children: Julie, Michael, Ruth, David. Bachelor of Arts cum laude (Olin scholar), Wesleyan University, 1953; Bachelor of Laws cum laude (Root Tilden scholar), New York University, 1956. Bar: New Jersey 1957, Texas 1962. Clerk New Jersey Supreme Court, 1956-59; associate Lum, Biunno & Tompkins, Newark, 1959-61; partner Matthews, Nowlin, Macfarlane & Barrett, San Antonio, 1961-69; senior partner Oppenheimer, Rosenberg, Kelleher & Wheatley, Incorporated, San Antonio, 1969-81; founder, general counsel, president, chairman, director Southwest Airlines Company, Dallas, 1967—, now also chief executive officer; board of directors M Corp., Dallas. Past chairman adv. business council Business School U. Texas; president board trustees St. Mary's Hall, San Antonio; president Travelers Aid Society, San Antonio. Named Chief Executive Officer of Year, The Fin. World, 1982, 90, Best Chief Executive Regional Airline Industry Wall St. Transcript, 1982—, Airline Industry Service award, 1988, Texas Business Hall Fame, 1988; recipient Fin. Mgmt. award Air Transport World, 1982. Fellow Texas Bar Foundation (life); member American Bar Association, San Antonio, New Jersey bar associations, State Bar Texas, San Antonio Chamber of Commerce (director), Order of Alamo, Texas Cavaliers. Home: 144 Thelma Dr San Antonio Texas 78212 Office: Southwest Airlines Company Post Office Box 36611 Love Field Dallas Texas 75235

KELLER, THOMAS FRANKLIN, dean, management science educator; born Greenwood, South Carolina, September 22, 1931; son of Cleaveland Alonzo and Helen (Seago) K.; married Margaret Neel Query, June 15, 1956; children: Thomas Crafton (deceased), Neel McKay, John Caldwell. Bachelor of Arts, Duke University, 1953; Master of Business Administration, University Michigan, 1957, Doctor of Philosophy, 1960; Doctor of Humanities (honorary), Clemson University, 1987. Certified Public Accountant, North Carolina. Member faculty Fuqua School Business Duke University, Durham, North Carolina, 1959—, associate professor, 1962-67, professor, 1967-74, R.J. Reynolds Industries professor, 1974—, chairman department management sciences, 1974—, vice provost, 1971-72, dean Fuqua School Business, 1974—; editorial board Duke University Press, 1970-87; visiting associate professor Carnegie Mellon University, 1966-67, University Washington, Seattle, 1963-64; consultant government, industry; Fullbright-Hays lecturer, Australia, 1975; director LADD Furniture, High Point, North Carolina, Southeast Growth Fund, Incorporated, Richmond, Virginia, Hatteras Income Securities, Incorporated, Charlotte, North Carolina, Mebane (North Carolina) Packaging Corp. Author: Accounting for Corporate Income Taxes, 1961, Intermediate Accounting, 1963, 68, 74, Advanced Accounting, 1966, Financial Accounting Theory volume 1, 1965, 73, 85, volume 2, 1970, Earnings or Cash Flows: An Experiment on Functional Fixation and the Valuation of the Firm, 1979; editor: monographs Financial Information Needs of Security Analysts, 1977, The Impact of Accounting Research on Practice and Disclosure, 1978; Contributor articles to professional journals. Served with Army of the United States, 1953-55. Haskins and Sells Foundation fellow University Michigan, 1959, Ford Foundation fellow Duke University, 1960, 61. Member American Institute of Certified Public Accountants, Am. Accounting Association (vice president 1967-68, editor journal 1972-75), North Carolina Association Certified Public Accountants, Fin. Executives Institute, University Club, Treyburn Country Club, Phi Beta Kappa, Phi Kappa Sigma, Beta Gamma Sigma, Alpha Kappa Psi. Presbyterian (elder). Avocations: hiking, fishing, reading, sailing. Office: Duke U Fuqua School Business Towerview Road Durham North Carolina 27706

KELLEY, GAYNOR NATHANIEL, instrumentation manufacturing company executive; born New Canaan, Connecticut, May 12, 1931; son of James Thomas and Mabel Virginia (Seaf) K.; married Diane Curio, March 16, 1974; children: Gaynor Jr., Russell, Theodore, Ronald, Victoria. Bachelor of Science in Mechanical Engineering, Delehanty Institute, 1951; graduate advanced management program, Northeastern University, Boston, 1965. Various management positions Perkin-Elmer Corp., Norwalk, Connecticut, 1951—, president, chief operating officer, 1985—; chairman Concurrent Computer Corp., Tinton Falls, New Jersey, 1986-88; board of directors Clark Equipment Corp., Gateway Bank, Hercules, Incorporated. Chairman Waveny Health Care, New Canaan, 1983-86. Roman Catholic. Avocations: golf, tennis. Home: 1801 Ponus Ridge New Canaan Connecticut 06840 Office: Perkin Elmer Corp 50 Danbury Road Wilton Connecticut 06897

KELLEY, WENDELL J., utilities executive; born Champaign, Illinois, May 2, 1926; son of Victor W. and Erma (Dalrymple) K.; married Evelyn Kimpel, June 12, 1947; children: Jeffrey, David, Alan, Stephen, John. Bachelor of Science in Electrical Engineering, University Illinois, 1949. Registered professional engineer, Illinois. With Illinois Power Company, Decatur, 1949—, operating eng., 1954, manager personnel, 1959-61, vice president, 1961-66, president, 1966-76, chairman and president, 1976-89, chief executive officer, chairman, 1989—, also board of directors; board of directors Am. Brands, Incorporated, Old Greenwich, Connecticut, Edison Electrical Institute, Washington, Magna Millikin Bank of Decatur, NA, Electric Energy, Incorporated, Joppa, Magna Group Incorporated, Belleville, Illinois, Franklin Life Insurance Company, Springfield, Illinois; vice chairman Illinois Business Roundtable, 1989. Chairman Mid-Am. Interpool Network, 1969-71, vice chairman, 1975-77, past member executive committee; board of directors Edison Electric Institute, Washington, 1974-77, 80-83, Association Edison Illuminating Cos., New York City, 1985-87; trustee Millikin U., Decatur; past trustee Northern Am. Reliability Council, vice chairman, 1975-77, chairman, 1978-80; past member Illinois Council on Economic Education, citizens committee U. Illinois, U. Illinois Foundation; past member adv. council St. Mary's Hospital, Decatur, president, 1972-73; past member Shults-Lewis Children's Home, Valparaiso, Ind. Served with United States Army Air Force, 1944-45. Recipient Distinguished Alumnus award, 1973, Alumni Honor award College Engineering, University Illinois, 1974, Alex Van Praag, Junior Distinguished engineering award, 1983. Fellow Institute of Electrical and Electronics Engineers (past chairman central Illinois section, Centennial medal and cert. 1984); member National Society Professional Engineers, Electrical Engineering Alumni Association University Illinois (past president, Distinguished Alumnus award 1973), Illinois State Chamber of Commerce (chairman 1973-74, past director), University Illinois Alumni Association (past director), National, Illinois socs. professional engrs., Eta Kappa Nu.

Member Church of Christ (elder). Home: 65 Dellwood Dr Decatur Illinois 62521 Office: Illinois Power Company 500 S 27th St Decatur Illinois 62525

KELLY, WILLIAM R., employment agency executive; born 1905; married. Graduate, University Pittsburgh, 1925. With Kelly Services, Incorporated, 1946—; chairman Kelly Services, Incorporated, Troy, Michigan, 1965—, also board of directors. Office: Kelly Services Incorporated 999 W Big Beaver Road Troy Michigan 48084

KEMP, JACK FRENCH, secretary of housing and urban development of U.S., former congressman; born Los Angeles, July 13, 1935; married Joanne Main; children: Jeffrey, Jennifer, Judith, James. Bachelor of Arts, Occidental College, 1957; postgraduate, Long Beach State University, California Western University. Special assistant to governor California, 1967; special assistant to chairman Republican National Committee, 1969; member 92d-100th congresses from 31st New York District, 1971-89; secretary Department of Housing and Urban Development, 1989—; professional football player for 13 years; pub. relations officer Marine Midland Bank, Buffalo; candidate for Republican Presdl. nomination, 1987-88. Member President's Council on Physical Fitness and Sports; member executive committee player pension board NFL. Recipient Distinguished Service award New York State Jaycees; Outstanding Citizen award Buffalo Evening News, 1965, 74. Member National Association Broadcasters, Engineers and Technicians, Buffalo Area Chamber of Commerce, Sierra Club, Am. Football League Players Association (co-founder, president 1965-70). Republican. Office: Department of Housing and Urban Development Office of the Secretary 451 7th St Southwest Washington District of Columbia 20410

KEMPER, DAVID WOODS, II, banker; born Kansas City, Missouri, November 20, 1950; son of James Madison and Mildred (Lane) K.; married Dorothy Ann Jannarone, September 6, 1975; children: John W., Elizabeth C., Catherine B., William L. Bachelor of Arts cum laude, Harvard University, 1972; Master of Arts in English Literature, Oxford, Worcester College, 1974; Master of Business Administration, Stanford University, 1976. With Morgan Guaranty Trust Company, New York City, 1975-78; vice president Commerce Bank of Kansas City, Missouri, 1978-79; senior vice president Commerce Bank of Kansas City, 1980-81; president Commerce Bancshares, Inc, 1982-86, president and chief executive officer, 1986—, also director; chairman Commerce Bank of St. Louis, 1985—; bd directors BMA, Kansas City, Missouri, Venture Stores, Incorporated, Tower Properties, Kansas City. Contributor articles on banking to professional journals. Board of directors Missouri Botanical Garden, St. Louis Symphony Orchestra. Member Association Reserve City Bankers, Kansas City Country Club, University Club, River Club (Kansas City), St. Louis Country Club, Racquet Club, Old Warson Country Club (St. Louis). Office: Commerce Bancshares Incorporated 1000 Walnut St Post Office Box 13686 Kansas City Missouri 64199 also: Commerce Bancshares Incorporated Commerce Bank Building 8000 Forsyth Clayton Missouri 63105 also: Commerce Bank of St Louis NA 8000 Forsyth Saint Louis Missouri 63105

KEMPER, JAMES MADISON, JR., banker; born Kansas City, Missouri, October 10, 1921; son of James M. and Gladys (Grissom) K.; married Mildred Lane, March 30, 1948 (deceased December 1986); children: Laura Lane, David Woods, Jonathan McBride, Julie Ann; married Susanne Shutz Curry, August 1, 1987. Bachelor of Arts, Yale University, 1943. With Commerce Trust Company (now Commerce Bank of Kansas City), Kansas City, 1946—; assistant cashier Commerce Trust Company (now Commerce Bank of Kansas City), 1946-49, vice president, director, 1949-55, executive vice president, 1955, president, 1955-64, chairman, 1964; chairman board, president Commerce Bank of Kansas City, 1964-66, chairman board, 1966-83, director, 1983—; chairman, president Commerce Bancshares, Incorporated, Kansas City, Missouri, 1966-86, chairman, chief executive officer, 1986—, chairman board, 1986—; president, chairman Tower Properties, Incorporated; director Commerce Bank, St. Joseph, 1987—, Springfield, 1987—, Columbia, 1988—. Office: Commerce Bancshares Incorporated 1000 Walnut St Post Office Box 13686 Kansas City Missouri 64199-3686

KEMPER, ROBERT LOUIS, data communications company executive; born Sacramento, December 1, 1928; son of Paul L. Kemper and Vivienne (E.) Dutro; married Dorothy I. Shanks, May 2, 1954; 1 child, Catherine. Graduate advanced management program, Harvard Business School, 1974; Bachelor.Science and Commerce, University Santa Clara, 1950. C.P.A., California. Staff accountant Arthur Anderson & Company, San Francisco, 1950-56; vice chairman Wells Fargo Bank, San Francisco, 1956-83; president, chief executive officer BankWire, New York City, 1984—, also director; chairman Bank Administration Institute, Chicago, 1973-74. Vice chairman Golden Gate U., San Francisco, 1983. Office: BankWire 225 Broadway New York New York 10007

KEMPNER, ISAAC HERBERT, III, sugar company executive; born Houston, August 28, 1932; son of Isaac Herbert and Mary (Carroll) K.; married Helen Hill, July 1, 1967. Graduate, Choate School, 1951; Bachelor of Arts, Stanford University, 1955, Master of Business Administration, 1959. Assistant vice president Texas National Bank, Houston, 1959-64; vice president, secretary-treasurer, manager raw sugar Imperial Holly Corp (formerly Imperial Sugar Company), Sugarland, Texas, 1964-71, chairman board, 1971—; chairman board SLT Communication Incorporated; president Foster Farms Incorporated. Trustee H. Kempner Trust Association, Methodist Hospital, Houston, Houston Municipal Arts Commission Served to 1st lieutenant United States Marine Corps Reserve, 1955-57. Member United States Cane Sugar Refiners Association (trustee), Tejas Club, Bayou Club, Camden Ale and Quail Club. Office: Imperial Holly Corp 1 Imperial Square Post Office Box 9 Sugar Land Texas 77478

KENDALL, DONALD MCINTOSH, food products company executive; born Sequim, Washington, March 16, 1921; son of Carroll C. and Charlotte

(McIntosh) K.; married Sigrid Ruedt von Collenberg, December 22, 1965; children—Donna Lee Kendall Warren, Edward McDonnell, Donald McIntosh, Kent Collenberg. Student, Western Kentucky State College, 1941-42; Doctor of Laws, Stetson University, 1971. Special field representative Pepsi-Cola Company, 1947-48, manager fountain sales, 1948-49, branch plant manager fountain sales, 1949-50, special representative, 1950-52, vice president national accounts fountain sales, 1952-57; president Pepsi Cola International, 1953-63, Pepsi-Cola Company (merger with Frito-Lay 1965), 1963-65; president, chief executive officer PepsiCo, Incorporated, 1965—, chairman board, chief executive officer, 1971-86, chairman executive committee, 1986—, also board of directors; board of directors Pan Am. Airways, Atlantic Richfield, Investors Diversified Services Mutual Fund Group; chairman NOVA Pharmaceutical, Lorimar-Telepictures, National Alliance Businessmen, 1969-70, director, 1970-78. Chairman National Center for Resource Recovery, Incorporated 1970-76, board of directors, 1976—; chairman Emergency Committee for Am. Trade, 1969-76, member, 1976—; board of directors U.S.-USSR Trade and Economic Council; chairman Am. Ballet Theatre Foundation, 1973-77, chairman executive committee, 1977-83. Served to lieutenant Air Corps, United States Naval Reserve, 1942-47. Member International Chamber of Commerce (trustee council), Chamber of Commerce United States (director, vice-chmn. 1980-81, chairman 1981-82), Blind Brook Club, Lyford Cay Club, River Club, Round Hill Club, Links. Office: Pepsico Incorporated Office of President Purchase New York 10577

KENNA, EDGAR DOUGLAS, manufacturing company executive; born Summit, Mississippi, June 11, 1924; son of Edgar Douglas and Norma Catchings (Carruth) K.; married Jean Cruise, June 12, 1945; children: Edgar Douglas III, Marilyn, Susan, Michael. Student, University Mississippi, 1941-42; Bachelor of Science, United States Military Academy, 1945. President Fuqua Industries, Atlanta, 1968-70, Robert B. Anderson, Limited, New York City, 1970-73, National Association Manufacturers, Washington, 1973-77, Carrier Corp., Syracuse, 1978-81; partner G.L. Ohrstrom Company, New York City, 1981—; chairman Ropex Corp., Carlisle Company, Incorporated, 1989—, Bertrex, Incorporated, 1989—, Vinnell, Incorporated, 1989—; board of directors Phillips Petroleum Company, Heritage Media, Incorporated, Carlisle Corp., Fleet Fin. Group, Vinnell Corp., Harrow Corp., Vistan Corp., Leach Corp. Trustee United States Mil. Acad. With Army of the United States, 1942-49. Recipient Freedom Foundation award, 1976. Republican. Congregationalist. Clubs: Lost Tree (Palm Beach); Metropolitan (New York City), University (New York City). Developed reentry systems for Apollo, Atlas, Titan, and Minuteman missile systems and Apollo spacecraft. Home: 11340 Old Harbour Road North Palm Beach Florida 33408 Office: Carlisle Cos Incorporated 11340 Old Harbour Road North Palm Beach Florida 33408

KENNEDY, GEORGE D., chemical company executive; born Pittsburgh, May 30, 1926; son of Thomas Reed and Lois (Smith) K.; married Valerie Putis; children: Charles Reed, Jamey Kathleen, Susan Patton, Timothy Christian. Bachelor of Arts, Williams College, 1948. With Scott Paper Company, 1947-52, Champion Paper Company, 1952-65; president Brown Company, 1965-71; executive vice president International Minerals & Chemical Corp., Northbrook, Illinois, 1971-78, president, 1978-86; chairman IMCERA (formerly International Minerals & Chemical Corp.), Northbrook, Illinois, 1986—, chief executive officer, 1983—, also board of directors; committee member, board of directors and chairman audit committee Brunswick Corp.; board of directors, member executive committee Kemper Corp.; board of directors, chairman, comp. committee IMC Fertilizer Group, Incorporated; board of directors, chairman, comp. committee Scotsman Industries, Incorporated, Am. National Can Company; board of directors Illinois Tool Works, Stone Container Corp. Chairman Children's Memorial Hospital and Children's Memorial Medical Center; board of directors McGaw Medical Center Northwestern U.; trustee Chicago Symphony; governor member Chicago Orchestra Association; director Lyric Opera Chicago; national board trustees Boys Club of Am.; trustee Committee for Economic Devel.; member Mid-Am. Chicago Committee; member business adv. council Carnegie Mellon U. Grad. School Industrial Administration; trustee National Committee Against Drunk Driving; chairman Junior Achievement Chicago, 1988-89. Member Board Room Club, New York Athletic Club, Larchmont Yacht Club, Sleepy Hollow Country Club, Skokie Country Club, Commercial Club. Office: IMCERA Group Incorporated 2315 Sanders Road Northbrook Illinois 60062

KENNEDY, JAMES COX, publishing and media executive; born 1947; married. Bachelor of Business Administration, University Denver, 1970. With Atlanta Newspapers, 1972-79, production assistant, 1972-76, executive vice president, general manager, 1976-79; president Grand Junction Newspapers, 1979-80; pub. Grand Junction Daily Sentinel, 1980-85; vice president Cox newspapers div. Cox Enterprises Incorporated, Atlanta, 1985-86; president, chief operating officer Cox Enterprises Incorporated, 1986-87, also board of directors, 1987—, now chairman, chief executive officer, 1988—; also president Cox Communications Incorporated, Atlanta. Office: Cox Enterprises Incorporated 1400 Lake Hearn Dr NE Post Office Box 105357 Atlanta Georgia 30348 also: 1601 W Peachtree St Northwest Atlanta Georgia 30309

KENNEDY, ROBERT DELMONT, petrochemical company executive; born Pittsburgh, November 8, 1932; son of Thomas Reed and Lois (Smith) K.; married Sally Duff, January 28, 1956; children: Robert Boyd, Kathleen Tyson, Thomas Alexander, Melissa Kristine. BSMechE, Cornell University, 1955. With Union Carbide Corp., 1955—; various positions with National Carbon div., 1957-77, president Linde Div., New York City, 1977-82, senior vice president corp., 1981, executive vice president, 1982, president, chief operating officer chemicals and plastics, 1985-86, president, chief executive officer Union Carbide Corp., Apr., 1986—, chairman, chief executive officer, December, 1986—. Past member board governors International School Geneva; chairman board trustees, New Hampton School; moderator program humanistic studies Aspen, 1979—, board trustees; chairman Inroads, Incorporated. Fellow Am. Institute Chemists (hon.); member Chemical Manufacturers Association (chairman board 1989-90, former chairman executive committee). Avocations: golfing, fishing, boating, tennis. Office: Union Carbide Corp 39 Old Ridgebury Road Danbury Connecticut 06817

KEOUGH, DONALD RAYMOND, beverage company executive; born Maurice, Iowa, September 4, 1926; son of Leo H. and Veronica (Henkels) K.; married Marilyn Mulhall, September 10, 1949; children: Kathleen Anne, Mary Shayla, Michael Leo, Patrick John, Eileen Tracy, Clarke Robert. Bachelor of Science, Creighton University, 1949, Doctor of Laws (honorary), 1982; Doctor of Laws (honorary), University Notre Dame, 1985. With Butter-Nut Foods Company, Omaha, 1950-61; with Duncan Foods Company, Houston, 1961-67; vice president, director marketing foods div. The Coca-Cola Company, Atlanta, 1967-71, president div., 1971-73; executive vice president Coca-Cola USA, Atlanta, 1973-74; president Coca-Cola USA, 1974-76; executive vice president The Coca-Cola Company, Atlanta, 1976-79, senior executive vice president, 1980-81, president, chief operating officer, director, 1981—; chairman board of directors Coca-Cola Enterprises Incorporated, 1986—; board of directors National Service Industries, Incorporated, Washington Post Company, H.J. Heinz Company. Member president's council Creighton U.; trustee Spelman College, The Lovett School, Agnes Scott College; chairman board trustees U. Notre Dame. Served with United States Naval Reserve, 1944-46. Clubs: Capital City, Piedmont Driving, Commerce. Office: Coca-Cola Company 1 Coca-Cola Plaza Northwest Atlanta Georgia 30313

KERR, DONALD MACLEAN, JR., physicist; born Philadelphia, April 8, 1939; son of Donald MacLean and Harriet (Fell) K.; married Alison Richards Kyle, June 10, 1961; 1 daughter, Margot Kyle. Bachelor of Electrical Engineering (National Merit scholar), Cornell University, 1963, Master of Science, 1964, Doctor of Philosophy (Ford Foundation fellow, 1964-65, James Clerk Maxwell fellow 1965-66), 1966. Staff Los Alamos National Laboratory, 1966-76, group leader, 1971-72, assistant div. leader, 1972-73, assistant to director, 1973-75, alternate div. leader, 1975-76; deputy manager Nevada operations office Department Energy, Las Vegas, 1976-77; acting assistant secretary defense programs Department Energy, Washington, 1978; deputy assistant secretary defense programs Department Energy, 1977-79, deputy assistant secretary energy tech., 1979; dir Los Alamos National Laboratory, 1979-85; senior vice president EG&G, Incorporated, Wellesley, Massachusetts, 1985-88, executive vice president, 1988-89, president, 1989—; member Navajo Sci. Committee, 1974-77; member sci. adv. panel United States Army, 1975-78; member engineering adv. board University Nevada, Las Vegas, 1976-78, Cornell University, 1985—; chairman committee Research & Development International Energy

Agency, 1979-85; member national security adv. council SRI International, 1980-89; member adv. board University Alaska Geophysical Institute, 1980-85; member sci. adv. group Joint Strategic Planning Staff, 1981-91; member adv. committee Naval Research, 1982-85; member corp. Draper Laboratory, 1982—; member adv. board Georgetown University Center Strategic International Studies, 1981-87; board of directors Mirage Systems, Sunnyvale, California, Resources for the Future, Washington. Published research on plasma physics, microwave electronics, ionospheric physics, energy and national security. Trustee New England Aquarium, 1989—. Fellow American Association for the Advancement of Science; member Am. Physical Society, Am. Geophysical Union, National Association Manufacturers (board directors 1986—), Southwestern Association Indian Affairs, World Affairs Council Boston (board directors 1988—), Sigma Xi, Tau Beta Pi, Eta Kappa Nu. Club: Cosmos (Washington). Office: EG&G Incorporated 45 William St Wellesley Massachusetts 02181

KESEL, GEORGE F., bank executive; born Pittsburgh, June 20, 1932; son of George Logan K.; married Laura Comfort; children: George L. III, David Wistar, Peter Friesell. Student, Williams College; student graduate div., University Pennsylvania. Executive vice president Union National Bank, Pittsburgh, 1973-77, president, chief executive officer, 1977-83, chairman, chief executive officer, 1983-84; president, chief executive officer Union National Corp., Pittsburgh, 1981—. Office: Union National Bank Wood St & 4th Avenue Pittsburgh Pennsylvania 15278 also: 1st National Bank & Trust Company 200 W Beau St Washington Pennsylvania 15301 also: Union National Corp 620 Washington Road Mount Lebanon Pennsylvania 15228

KETCHUM, EZEKIEL SARGENT, banker; born Louisville, April 28, 1935; son of Paul A. and Elizabeth (Sargent) K.; married Barbara J. Frank, June 13, 1959; children: Allison, Randolph, Sarah, Clayton. Bachelor of Arts in Econs, Harvard University, 1957; postgraduate, University Pittsburgh, 1959-60. With Mellon Bank N.A., Pittsburgh, 1958-78; vice president credit policy management Mellon Bank N.A., 1976-78; executive vice president banking group Am. Bank & Trust Company Pennsylvania, Reading, 1978-81; president Am. Bank, 1981-85, Meridian Bank, 1985—; vice chairman, director Meridian Bancorp, Incorporated, 1983-88, president, chief operating officer, 1988—. Board of directors Reading Hospital and Medical Center, 1978—, Reading Area Community College Foundation; council sustaining membership chairman Hawk Mountain council Boy Scouts Am., 1979—, vice president administration; board of directors United Way Berks County, 1980, president, 1986-87. Served with United States Army Reserve, 1957. Member Am. Bankers Association, Robert Morris Association. Office: Meridian Bancorp Incorporated 35 N 6th St Post Office Box 1102 Reading Pennsylvania 19603

KETELSEN, JAMES LEE, diversified industry executive; born Davenport, Ia., November 14, 1930; son of Ernest Henry and Helen (Schumann) K.; children: James V., Lee. Bachelor of Science, Northwestern University,

1952. C.P.A., Texas, Illinois. Accountant Price Waterhouse & Company (C.P.A.s), Chicago, 1955-59; vice president finance, treasurer J.I. Case Company, Racine, Wisconsin, 1962-68; president, chief executive officer J.I. Case Company, 1968-72; executive vice president Tenneco Incorporated, Houston, 1972—; chairman board, chief executive officer Tenneco Incorporated, 1978—, also director; director J.P. Morgan & Company, Sara Lee Corp., General Telephone and Telegraph Corp., Alliance for Free Enterprise, Houston Chamber of Commerce, Executive Council on Foreign Diplomats. Member President's Board of Advisors on Private Sector Initiatives, Committee for Economic Devel.; board of directors Am. Petroleum Institute; trustee Northwestern U., Conference Board Served to lieutenant United States Naval Reserve, 1952-55. Member National Petroleum Council, Business Roundtable, Chi Psi. Clubs: River Oaks Country (Houston), Petroleum (Houston). Office: Tenneco Incorporated Post Office Box 2511 Houston Texas 77252 also: Monroe Auto Equipment Company 1 International Dr Monroe Michigan 48161

KEYES, JAMES HENRY, manufacturing company executive; born LaCrosse, Wisconsin, September 2, 1940; son of Donald M. and Mary M. (Nodolf) K.; married Judith Ann Carney, November 21, 1964; children: James Patrick, Kevin, Timothy. Bachelor of Science, Marquette University, 1962; Master of Business Administration, Northwestern University, 1963. Instructor Marquette University, Milwaukee, 1963-65; Certified Public Accountant Peat. Marwick & Mitchell, Milwaukee, 1965-66; with Johnson Controls, Incorporated, Milwaukee, 1967—, manager systems department, 1967-71, div. controller, 1971-73, corp. controller, treasurer, 1973-77, vice president, chief fin. officer, 1977-85, executive vice president, 1985-86, president, 1986—, chief operating officer, 1986-88, chief executive officer, 1988—. Active Milwaukee Symphony Orchestra, 1980—. Member Fin. Executives Institute, Am. Institute Certified Public Accountants, Wisconsin Institute Certified Public Accountants. Office: Johnson Controls Incorporated 5757 N Green Bay Avenue Box 591 Milwaukee Wisconsin 53201

KIAM, VICTOR KERMIT, II, consumer products company executive; born New Orleans, December 7, 1926; son of Victor Kermit and Nanon (Newman) K.; married Ellen Lipscher; children: Lisa, Victor III, Robin. Bachelor of Arts, Yale University, 1948; certificate langs., University Paris, 1949; Master of Business Administration, Harvard University, 1951; DL, New Hampshire College, 1984, George Washington University, 1985; Doctor in Science and Business Administration (honorary), Bryant College, 1989. Market director Lever Brothers, New York City, 1951-55; executive vice president International Latex Corp., New York City, 1955-68; president Benrus Corp., Ridgefield, Connecticut, 1968-71, chairman, chief executive officer, 1971-77; chairman Friendship Collection, New York City, 1977—; president, chief executive officer Remington Products, Incorporated, Bridgeport, Connecticut, 1979—; chairman board of directors First Teacher, Remington Trading Company, Japan and Hong Kong, Pace

Equities, Remington Apparel, Lady Remington, 1980—; owner New England Patriots (National Football League), 1988—; lecturer Oxford University, 1988. Author: Going For It!, 1986, Live to Win, 1989; contributing editor numerous magazines. Chairman United States Savs. Bonds., U. B. Colgate, United Way. Recipient Wharton Golden Plate award Am. Acad. Achievement, 1984, Northwood Institute Outstanding Business Leader award, 1986, Kate Smith/U.S. Savs. Bonds award, 1988; named National Business and Commerce Father of Year National Father's Day Council, 1982, Outstanding Entrepreneur of Year University Southern California School Business, 1987, Man of Year State Police Junior Olympics, Boston, 1989, Entrepreneur of Year, Connecticut and Western Massachusetts, 1989. Clubs: Century (White Plains, New York); Palm Beach (Florida) Polo; Regency Whist (New York City). Office: Remington Products Incorporated 60 Main St Bridgeport Connecticut 06602 also: New England Patriots Sullivan Stadium Route 1 Foxboro Massachusetts 02035

KIEFER, RAYMOND H., insurance company executive; born Toledo, April 16, 1927; married Eleanor M. Harrison, June 28, 1947; 1 daughter, Deborah Johnson. Bachelor of Business Administration, University Toledo, 1950, Juris Doctor, 1954. Mutual fund director Allstate Insurance Company, Northbook, Illinois, 1969-71, assistant to president, 1971-72, zone sales manager, 1972-73; regional vice president Allstate Insurance Company, Rochester, New York, 1973-74; pres./Can. Allstate Insurance Company, Ontario, 1974-76; regional vice president Illinois region Allstate Insurance Company, 1976-77; vice president eastern zone Allstate Insurance Company, New York, 1977-80; president Allstate Life Insurance Company, Northbrook, 1980-83; president property & casualty Allstate Insurance Company, Northbrook, 1983-89, president, 1989—. Chairperson, board governors Lutheran Social Svcs., 1986-89. Lieutenant United States Marine Corps, 1945-46, PTO, 1950-52, Korea. Named Outstanding Alumnus University Toledo, 1988. Republican. Lutheran. Avocation: golf. Office: Allstate Ins Company Allstate Plaza Northbrook Illinois 60062

KILLINGER, KERRY K., bank executive; born Des Moines, June 6, 1949; married Debbie Killinger. Bachelor of Business Administration, University Iowa, 1970, Master of Business Administration, 1971. Executive vice president Murphey Favre, Incorporated, Spokane, 1976-82; executive vice president Washington Mutual Savings Bank, Seattle, 1982-88, president, 1988—, chief executive officer, 1990—. Board of directors Seattle Repertory Theatre, 1990; co-chairman Acquired Immune Deficiency Syndrome Walk-a-thon, Seattle, 1990. Member Society Fin. Analysts, Life Management Institute, Rotary. Office: Wash Mutual Savings Bank 1201 3d Avenue Suite 1500 Seattle Washington 98101

KING, CAROLYN, insurance executive; born Anderson, South Carolina, August 28, 1950; daughter of Wilburn Lyneer and Lavinia Joan (McFall) K. Bachelor of Science, University Georgia, 1972; postgraduate, Dartmouth College, 1986. Actuarial consultant Booke & Company, Winston-Salem,

North Carolina, 1974-75; with Provident National Assurance Company, Chattanooga, 1975-86, vice president actuary, 1983-86, president, 1987—; vice president portfolio manager Provident Life & Accident, Chattanooga, 1986-87; chairman Provident National Board, Chattanooga, 1987—. Board of directors Young Men's Christian Association, Chattanooga, 1989—, Indls. Devel. Board, Chattanooga, 1989—. Fellow Society Actuaries; member Am. Acad. Actuaries, Phi Beta Kappa. Avocations: canoeing, Kayaking, reading, hiking, skiing. Office: Provident National One Fountain Square Chattanooga Tennessee 37402

KING, OLIN B., electronics systems company executive; born Sandersville, Georgia, 1934; married. Bachelor of Science, N. Georgia College, 1953. With Radio Corporation of America Corp., 1956-57, Army Ballistic Missile Agency, 1957-60, Marshall Space Flight Center, 1960-61; president SCI Systems, Incorporated, Huntsville, Alabama, 1966-81, chief executive officer, from 1973, chairman, 1973—, also board of directors. Served to captain United States Army, 1954-56. Office: SCI Systems Incorporated 5000 Technology Dr Huntsville Alabama 35805

KINNEAR, JAMES WESLEY, III, petroleum company executive; born Pittsburgh, March 21, 1928; son of James Wesley and Susan (Jenkins) K.; married Mary Tullis, June 17, 1950; children: Robin Wood (Mrs. David Bruce Anderson), Susan, James Wesley IV, William M. Bachelor of Science with distinction, United States Naval Academy, 1950. With Texaco, Incorporated, 1954—; sales manager Texaco, Incorporated, Hawaii, 1959-63; div. sales manager Texaco, Incorporated, Los Angeles, 1963-64; assistant to vice chairman board of directors Texaco, Incorporated, New York City, 1964-65, assistant to chairman board of directors, general manager marine department, 1965, vice president supply and distribution, 1966-70, senior vice president strategic planning, 1970-71, senior vice president worldwide refining, petrochems., supply and distribution, 1971-72, senior vice president world wide marketing, also in charge international marine operations and petrochems., 1972-76, senior vice president international marine and aviation sales petrochem. department, marine department, marketing and refining in Europe, 1976-78, director, 1977—, executive vice president, 1978-83; president Texaco USA Texaco, Incorporated, 1982-84; vice chairman board of directors Texaco, Incorporated, White Plains, 1983-86, president, chief executive officer, 1987—; board of directors Corning Glass Works. President board trustees St. Paul's School, Concord, New Hampshire Served to lieutenant commander United States Naval Reserve, 1950-54. Member Am. Petroleum Institute (board directors), National Petroleum Council (board directors), Business Council of New York (board directors), Business Round Table, Business Council, United States Naval Institute, Round Hill Club (Greenwich, Connecticut), Verbank Hunting Club, Brook Club (N.Y.C), Iron City Fishing (Parry Sound, Ontario), Augusta Club (Georgia), National Golf Club. Episcopalian. Home: 149 Taconic Road Greenwich Connecticut 06830 Office: Texaco Incorporated 2000

Westchester Avenue White Plains New York 10650

KIRBY, FRED MORGAN, II, corporation executive; born Wilkes Barre, Pennsylvania, November 23, 1919; son of Allan P. and Marian G. (Sutherl) K.; married A. Walker Dillard, April 30, 1949; children: Alice Kirby Horton, Fred Morgan III, Dillard, Jefferson. Graduate, Lawrenceville School, 1938; Bachelor of Arts, Lafayette College, Easton, Pennsylvania, 1942; postgraduate, Harvard Graduate School Business Administration, 1947. From vice president to president, board of directors Allan Corp., 1953-75; president, chairman board of directors Filtration Engineers, Incorporated, 1951-56; director Alleghany Corp., 1958-61, 63—, vice president, 1961, executive vice president, 1963-67, chairman board, 1967—, president, 1968-77, member executive committee, 1968—; board of directors, chairman executive committee Cyclops Industries; board of directors, member executive committee Pittston Company, F.W. Woolworth Company; board of directors Am. Express Company, Chicago Title and Trust Company, Chicago Title Insurance Company. President, director F.M. Kirby Foundation, Incorporated Served to lieutenant (senior grade) United States Naval Reserve, 1942-46. Member Zeta Psi, Westmoreland Club, Racquet and Tennis Club, Spring Valley Hounds Club, The Club at the World Trade Center, Treyburn Country Club. Office: 17 DeHart St Post Office Box 151 Morristown New Jersey 07963-0151

KIRSCHNER, SIDNEY, diversified services company executive; born Ottawa, Ontario, Canada, 1934; married. Bachelor of Science in Mechanical Engineering, New Mexico Institute Mining and Tech., 1956. Engineer Aerojet-Gen. Corp., 1956-60; director engineering Aerospace Corp., 1960-63; assistant to president Curtiss-Wright Corp., 1963-67; president General Dynamics div. Electro Dynamic, 1967-73; group vice president National Service Industries, Incorporated, Atlanta, 1973-77, executive vice president, 1977-79, chief operating officer, 1977—, president, 1979—, chief executive officer, 1987—, also board of directors. Office: National Service Industries Incorporated 1420 Peachtree St NE Atlanta Georgia 30309

KLATSKY, BRUCE J., apparel company executive; born New York City, July 14, 1948; son of Herbert W. and Pearl (Starkman) K.; married Iris Ann Gussow, August 15, 1970; 1 child, Peter. Bachelor of Science, Western Reserve University, 1970; postgraduate, Georgetown University, 1970-71. Chairman board, chief executive officer Van Heusen Group, Phillips-Van Heusen Corp., New York City, 1971—; president, chief operating officer Phillips-Van Heusen Corp. (parent), New York City, 1987—. Office: Phillips-Van Heusen Corp 1290 Avenue of the Americas New York New York 10104

KLEIN, LAWRENCE ROBERT, economist, educator; born Omaha, September 14, 1920; son of Leo Byron and Blanche (Monheit) K.; married Sonia Adelson, February 15, 1947; children: Hannah, Rebecca, Rachel, Jonathan. Bachelor of Arts, University Calif.-Berkeley, 1942; Doctor of Philosophy, Massachusetts Institute of Technology, 1944; Master of Arts, Lincoln College, Oxford University, 1957; Doctor of Laws (honorary), University Michigan,

1977, Dickinson College, 1981; Doctor of Science (honorary), Widener College, 1977, Elizabethtown College, 1981, Ball State University, 1982, Technion, 1982, University Nebraska, 1983; Doctor honoris causa, University Vienna, 1977; Dr.Educated, Villanova University, 1978; Doctor (h.c.), Bonn University, 1974, Free University Brussels, 1979, University Paris, 1979, University Madrid, 1980. Faculty University Chicago, 1944-47; research associate National Bureau Economic Research, 1948-50; faculty University Michigan, 1949-54; research associate Survey Research Center, 1949-54, Oxford Institute Statistics, 1954-58; faculty University Pennsylvania, Philadelphia, 1958—, professor, 1958—, University professor, 1964—, Benjamin Franklin professor, 1968—; visiting professor Osaka University, Japan, 1960, University Colorado, 1962, City University of New York, 1962-63, 82, Hebrew University, 1964, Princeton University, 1966, Stanford University, summer 1968, University Copenhagen, 1974; Ford visiting professor University California at Berkeley, 1968, Institute for Advanced Studies, Vienna, 1970, 74; consultant Canadian Government, 1947, UNCTAD, 1966, 67, 75, 77, 80, McMillan Company, 1965-74, E.I. du Pont de Nemours, 1966-68, State of New York, 1969, American Telephone and Telegraph Company, 1969, Federal Reserve Board, 1973, UNIDO, 1973-75, Congressional Budget Office, 1977—, Council Economic Advisers, 1977-80; chairman board trustees Wharton Econometric Forecasting Associates, Incorporated, 1969-80, chairman professional board, 1980—; trustee Maurice Falk Institute for Economic Research, Israel, 1969-75; adv. council Institute Advanced Studies, Vienna, 1977—; chairman economic adv. committee Governor of Pennsylvania, 1976-78; member committee on prices Federal Reserve Board, 1968-70; principal investigator econometric model project Brookings Institution, 1963-72, Project LINK, 1968—; senior adviser Brookings Panel on Economic Activity, 1970—; member adv. committee Institute International Economics, 1983; coordinator Jimmy Carter's Economic Task Force, 1976; member adv. board Strategic Studies Center, Stanford Research Institute, 1974-76. Author: The Keynesian Revolution, 1947, Textbook of Econometrics, 1953, An Econometric Model of the United States, 1929-1952, 1955, Wharton Econometric Forecasting Model, 1967, Essay on the Theory of Economic Prediction, 1968, An Introduction to Econometric Forecasting and Forecasting Models, 1980; Author-editor: Brookings Quar. Econometric Model of United States; Ecometric Model Performance, 1976, Lectures in Econometrics, 1983; Editor: International Econ. Rev, 1959-65; asso. editor, 1965—; Editorial board: Empirical Econs, 1976—. Recipient William F. Butler award New York Association Business Economists, 1975; Golden Slipper Club award, 1977; President's medal University Pennsylvania, 1980; Alfred Nobel Memorial prize in econs., 1980. Fellow Econometric Society (past president), Am. Acad. Arts and Sciences, National Association Business Economists; member Am. Philosophical Society, National Acad. Sciences, Social Sci. Research Council (fellow 1945-46, 47-48, committee econ. stability, director 1971-76), Am. Econ. Association

(John Bates Clark medalist 1959, executive committee 1966-68, president 1977), Eastern Econ. Association (president 1974-76). Office: U Pennsylvania School of Arts & Scis Department Econs 3718 Locust Walk Philadelphia Pennsylvania 19104-6297

KLUGE, JOHN WERNER, broadcasting and advertising executive; born Chemnitz, Germany, September 21, 1914; son of Fritz and Gertrude (Donj) K.; children—Samantha, Joseph B. Student, Wayne University; Bachelor of Arts (4 year honor scholar), Columbia, 1937. Vice president, sales manager Otten Brothers, Incorporated, Detroit, 1937-41; president, director radio station WGAY, Silver Spring, Maryland, 1946-59, St. Louis Broadcasting Corp., Brentwood, Missouri, 1953-58, Pittsburgh Broadcasting Company, 1954-59; president, treasurer, director Capitol Broadcasting Company, Nashville, 1954-59, Associate Broadcasters, Incorporated, Fort Worth-Dallas, 1957-59; partner Western New York Broadcasting Company, Buffalo, 1957-60; president, director Washington Planagraph Company, 1956-60, Mid.-Fla. Radio Corp., Orlando, 1952-59; treasurer, director Mid-Fla. Television Corp., 1957-60; owner Kluge Investment Company, Washington, 1956-60; partner Nashton Properties, Nashville, 1954-60, Texworth Investment Company, Fort Worth, 1957-60; chairman board Seaboard Service System, Incorporated, 1957-58; president New England Fritos, Boston, 1947-55, New York Institute Dietetics, New York City, 1953-60; chairman board, president, director Metromedia, Incorporated, New York City, Metromedia, Incorporated (including metropolitan broadcasting div., world wide broadcasting div. and Foster & Kleiser div., outdoor advertising); chairman board, treasurer, director Kluge, Finkelstein & Company (food brokers), Baltimore; chairman board, treasurer Tri-Suburban Broadcasting Corp., Washington, Kluge & Company; chairman board, president, treasurer Washington, Silver City Sales Company, Washington; director Marriott-Hot Shoppes, Incorporated, Chock Full O' Nuts Corp., National Bank Maryland, Waldorf Astoria Corp., Just One Break, Incorporated, Belding Heminway Company, Incorporated; member adv. council Manufacturers Hanover Trust Company; Member Washington Board Trade. Board of directors Brand Names Foundation, Incorporated, Shubert Foundation; vice president, board of directors United Cerebral Palsy Research and Educational Foundation, 1972—; trustee Strang Clinic Miliken U.; board governors New York College Osteo. Medicine. Served to captain United States Army, 1941-45. Member National Food Brokers Association, Washington Food Brokers Association (president 1958), Grocery Wheels Washington, Grocery Manufacturers Reps. Washington, Advertising Club Washington, National Association Radio and Television Broadcasters, Advertising Council New York City, National Sugar Brokers Association. Clubs: Army and Navy (Washington), University (Washington), Figure Skating (Washington), National Capital Skeet and Trap (Washington), Broadcasters (Washington); Metropolitan (New York City), Columbia Associates (New York City), University (New York City); Olympic (San Francisco); Marco Polo (New Hampshire gov.). Office: Metromedia Incorporated 1 Harmon Plaza Secaucus New Jersey 07094

KNABUSCH, CHARLES THAIR, manufacturing company executive; born Detroit, November 25, 1939; son of Edward M. and Henrietta (Muelhisen) K.; married June Ellen Heck, June 30, 1962; children: Charles Jr., Debora, Michael, Christopher. Bachelor of Arts, Cleary College, Ypsilanti, Michigan, 1962. President, chief executive officer La-Z-Boy Chair Company, Monroe, Michigan, 1961—. Member National Association Furniture Manufacturers (president 1981). Office: La-Z-Boy Chair Company 1284 N Telegraph Road Monroe Michigan 48161

KNIGHT, CHARLES FIELD, electrical equipment manufacturing company executive; born Lake Forest, Illinois, January 20, 1936; son of Lester Benjamin and Elizabeth Anne (Field) K.; married Joanne Parrish, June 22, 1957; children: Lester Benjamin III, Anne Field Knight Davidson, Steven P., Jennifer Lee. Bachelor of Science in Mechanical Engineering, Cornell University, 1958, Master of Business Administration, 1959. Management trainee Goetzewerke A.G., Burscheid, W. Germany, 1959-61; president Lester B. Knight International Corp., 1961-63; executive vice president Lester B. Knight & Associates, Incorporated, Chicago, 1963-67; president Lester B. Knight & Associates, Incorporated, 1967-69, president, chief executive officer, 1969-73; vice chairman board Emerson Electric Company, St. Louis, 1973, senior vice chairman board, corp. executive officer, 1973, chairman board, 1974—, chief executive officer, 1973—; board of directors Southwestern Bell Corp., Caterpillar Incorporated, Baxter International Incorporated, Anheuser Busch Companies, Incorporated, The Brit. Petroleum Company p.l.c. Member Civic Progress, 1973; board of directors Arts and Education Council; board of directors, trustee Washington U., St. Louis, Olin Foundation. Member St. Louis Country Club, Log Cabin Club (St. Louis), Cristal Downs Club (Traverse City, Michigan), Glen View Golf Club (Illinois), Chicago Club, Sigma Phi. Office: Emerson Electric Company 8000 W Florissant Avenue Saint Louis Missouri 63136

KNIGHT, PHILIP H(AMPSON), shoe manufacturing company executive; born Portland, Oregon, February 24, 1938; son of William W. and Lota (Hatfield) K.; married Penelope Parks, September 13, 1968; children: Matthew, Travis. Bachelor of Business Administration, University Oregon; Master of Business Administration, Stanford University. C.P.A., Oregon. Chairman, chief executive officer, past president Nike, Incorporated, Beaverton, Oregon, 1967—. Member adv. council Stanford U. Grad School; board of directors U.S.-Asian Business Council, Washington, 1st lieutenant Army of the United States, 1959-60. Named Oregon Businessman of Year, 1982. Member Am. Institute C.P.A.s. Republican. Episcopalian. Office: Nike Incorporated One Bowerman Dr Beaverton Oregon 97005

KNOWLTON, RICHARD L., food and meat processing company executive; born 1932; married. Bachelor of Arts, University Colorado, 1954. With George A. Hormel & Company, Austin, MInn., 1948—; manager meat products div. and route car sales

George A. Hormel & Company, Austin, Minnesota, 1967-69; assistant manager George A. Hormel & Company (Austin plant), 1969; general manager George A. Hormel & Company, Austin, 1974, vice president operations, 1974, group vice president operations, 1975-79; president, chief operating officer George A Hormel & Company, Austin, 1979; chairman, president, chief executive officer George A. Hormel & Company, Austin, 1981—, director; board of directors Hormel Foundation Board, First National Bank of Austin, Northwestern National Life Insurance Company. Board of directors Mayo Foundation, U. Colorado Foundation. Member Am. Meat Institute (director), Minnesota Business Partnership (director). Office: George A Hormel & Company 501 16th Avenue NE Austin Minnesota 55912

KNOX, NORTHRUP RAND, banker; born Buffalo, December 24, 1928; son of Seymour and Helen (Northrup) K.; married Lucetta Crisp, June 21, 1950; children—Linda Gilbert Knox McLean, Northrup Rand Jr. Bachelor of Arts, Yale University, 1950; student, Cornell University, 1952. Director, chairman board Marine Midland Bank, N.A., Marine Midland Banks, Incorporated; director Niagara Share Corp.; board of directors Niagara Share Corp., Hongkong and Shanghai Banking Corp., Hongkong Bank Can. Treasurer, trustee Aiken Preparatory School; vice president Hitchcock Foundation, Buffalo Fine Arts Acad.; board of directors U. Buffalo Foundation, Greater Buffalo Devel. Foundation, Buffalo Philharmonic Orchestra; vice president, board of directors Seymour H. Knox Foundation. World ct. tennis champion, 1959-69. Home: Buffalo Road East Aurora New York 14052 Office: 3750 Marine Midland Center Buffalo New York 14203

KOCH, CHARLES DE GANAHL, corporation executive; born Wichita, Kansas, November 1, 1935; son of Fred Chase and Mary Clementine (Robinson) K. Bachelor of Science in General Engineering, Massachusetts Institute of Technology, 1957, Master of Science in Mechanical Engineering, 1958, Master of Science in Chemical Engineering, 1959. Engineer Arthur D. Little, Incorporated, Cambridge, Massachusetts, 1959-61; vice president Koch Engineering Company, Incorporated, Wichita, 1961-63, president, 63-71, chairman, 1967-78; president Koch Industries, Incorporated, Wichita, 1966-74, chairman, 1967—; board of directors First National Bank. Chairman Institute for Humane Studies George Mason U.; board of directors Cato Institute, Citizens for a Sound Economy, Wesley Foundation, Wichita Collegiate School. Member National Petroleum Council, Mount Pelerin Society. Clubs: Wichita Country, New York Athletic. Office: Koch Industries Post Office Box 2256 Wichita Kansas 67201

KOGAN, RICHARD JAY, pharmaceutical company executive; born New York City, June 6, 1941; son of Benjamin and Ida K.; married Susan Linda Scher, August 29, 1965. Bachelor of Arts, City College of New York, 1963; Master of Business Administration, New York University, 1968. Director planning and administration Ciba Corp., Summit, New Jersey, 1968-69; vice president planning, pharmaceutical div. Ciba-Geigy Corp., Summit, 1970-76; president Can. pharmaceutical div. Ciba-

Geigy Corp., Can., 1976-79; president United States pharmaceutical div. Ciba-Geigy Corp., Summit, 1979-82; executive vice president pharmaceutical operations Schering-Plough Corp., Madison, New Jersey, 1982-86; president, chief operating officer Schering-Plough Corp., Kenilworth, New Jersey, 1986—; board director Schering-Plough Corp., Kenilworth; board of directors National Westminster Bancorp, Rite Aid Corp.; board overseers school business New York University. Office: Schering-Plough Corp 1 Giralda Farms Madison New Jersey 07940

KOHL, HERBERT, senator, professional sports team owner; born Milwaukee, February 7, 1935. Bachelor of Arts, University Wisconsin, 1956; Master of Business Administration, Harvard University, 1956. Owner Milwaukee Bucks (National Basketball Association); United States senator from Wisconsin 1989—; president Herbert Kohl Investments; state chairman Dem. Party, Wisconsin, 1975-77; member judiciary committee, committee on aging. With United States Army Reserve, 1958-64. Office: United States Senate Office Senate Members Washington District of Columbia 20510 also: Milwaukee Bucks Bradley Center 1001 N 4th St Milwaukee Wisconsin 53203-1312

KOHLBERG, JEROME, JR., lawyer, business executive; born New York City, 1925. Graduate, Swarthmore College, 1946; Juris Doctor, Columbia University, 1950. Bar: New York. Formerly with Bear Stearns & Company, Incorporated; senior partner Kohlberg, Kravis, Roberts & Company, New York City, 1976-87; chairman Houdaille Industries, Incorporated, Fort Lauderdale, Florida, chairman executive committee; now chairman Kohlberg and Company, New York City; board of directors Sterndent Corp. Office: Kohlberg and Company care Jennifer Magnone 20 W 55th St New York New York 10019

KOHLER, HERBERT VOLLRATH, JR., diversified manufacturing company executive; born Sheboygan, Wisconsin, February 20, 1939; son of Herbert Vollrath and Ruth Miriam (DeYoung) K.; married Linda Elizabeth Karger, September 23, 1961; children: Laura Elizabeth, Rachel DeYoung, Karger David. Graduate, The Choate School, 1957; Bachelor of Science, Yale University, 1965. With Kohler Company, Wisconsin, 1965—; general supervisor warehouse div. Kohler Company, 1965-67, factory systems manager, 1967-68, vice president operations, 1968-71, executive vice president, 1971-72, chairman board, chief executive officer, 1972—, president, 1974—, director, 1967—; director Harnishchfeger Corp. Member adv. board John Michael Kohler Arts Center, from 1972; board of directors, vice president Friendship House, from 1959; board of directors Kiddies Camp Corp., from 1972; trustee Lawrence U., from 1973; president board of directors Kohler Foundation, from 1968. Served with United States Army, 1957-58. Member National Association of Manufacturers (director 1973—), Sheboygan Chamber of Commerce, Am. Horse Show Association, Am. Morgan Horse Association. Republican. Episcopalian. Club: Sheboygan Economic (president 1973-74). Home: Kohler Wisconsin 53044 Office: Kohler Company 444 Highland Dr Kohler Wisconsin 53044

KONTNY, VINCENT LAWRENCE, engineering and construction company executive; born Chappell, Nebraska, July 19, 1937; son of Edward James and Ruth Regina (Schumann) K.; married Joan Dashwood FitzGibbon, February 20, 1970; children: Natascha Marie, Michael Christian, Amber Brooke. Bachelor of Science in Civil Engineering, University Colorado, 1958. Operator heavy equipment, grade foreman Peter Kiewit Son's Company, Denver, 1958-59; project manager Utah Construction and Mining Company, Western Australia, 1965-69, Fluor Australia, Queensland, Australia, 1969-72; senior project manager Fluor Utah, San Mateo, California, 1972-73; senior vice president Holmes & Narver, Incorporated, Orange, California, 1973-79; managing director Fluor Australia, Melbourne, 1979-82; group vice president Fluor Engineers, Incorporated, Irvine, California, 1982-85, president, chief executive officer, 1985-87; group president Fluor Daniel, Irvine, California, 1987-88, president, chief executive officer, 1988—; also president Fluor Corp., Irvine. Contributor articles to professional journals. Member engring. devel. council, U. Colorado; member engring. adv. committee, Stanford U. Lieutenant United States Navy, 1959-65. Member American Institute of Mining, Metallurgy and Petroleum Engineers (society mining engrs.), Am. Association Cost Engineers, Australian Association Engineers, Am. Petroleum Institute. Republican. Roman Catholic. Club: Cet. (Costa Mesa, California). Avocation: snow skiing. Home: 10255 Overhill Dr Santa Ana California 92705 Office: Fluor Daniel Incorporated 3333 Michelson Dr Irvine California 92730

KOVACEVICH, RICHARD M., banker. Bachelor of Arts, Stanford University, 1965, Master of Business Administration, 1967. executive vice president Kenner div. General Mills, Incorporated, Minneapolis, 1967-72; principal Venture Capital, 1972-75; vice president consumer services Norwest Corp., Minneapolis, from 1975, then senior vice president New York City banking group, then executive vice president, manager New York City bank div., then executive vice president. member policy committee, vice-chairman, chief operating officer banking group, 1986—, also director. Address: Norwest Corp 6th & Marquette Minneapolis Minnesota 55479

KRAL, RICHARD F., apparel executive. Chairman, chief executive officer Crystal Brands Incorporated, Southport, Connecticut. Office: Crystal Brands Incorporated Crystal Brands Road Southport Connecticut 06490§

KRASNOFF, ABRAHAM, business executive; born Newark. Graduate magna cum laude, New York University, post graduate; Doctor of Humane Letters (honorary), Long Island University, 1985. Certified Public Accountant, New York. From controller to treasurer to vice president to executive vice president Pall Corp., Glen Cove, New York, 1951-69, president, vice chairman, chief executive officer, 1969—. Past. board overseers school business New York University, past chairman executive council conference board; past chairman Glen Cove Planning Board; trustee, past chairman board of directors Long Island U.; board of directors Glen Cove Community Hospital, Neighborhood Association. Recipient Madden award New York University, 1982. Member Am. Business Conference (founding). Office: Pall Corp 30 Sea Cliff Avenue Glen Cove New York 11542

KRAVIS, HENRY R., venture financier. married Carolyne Roehm. Partner Kohlberg Kravis Roberts; board of directors Marley Company, Walter Industries, Incorporated, Beatrice Company, L.B. Foster Company, Hondaille Industries Incorporated, Malone and Hyde, Incorporated, Union Texas Petroleum Holdings, Incorporated. Office: Kohlberg Kravis Roberts & Company 9 W 57th New York New York 10019

KREBS, ROBERT DUNCAN, transportation company executive; born Sacramento, May 2, 1942; son of Ward Carl and Eleanor Blauth (Duncan) K.; married Anne Lindstrom, September 11, 1971; children: Robert Ward, Elisabeth Lindstrom, Duncan Lindstrom. Bachelor of Arts, Stanford University, 1964; Master of Business Administration, Harvard University, 1966. Assistant general manager Southern Pacific Transportation Company, Houston, 1974-75; assistant regional operations manager Southern Pacific Transportation Company, 1975-76; assistant vice president Southern Pacific Transportation Company, San Francisco, 1976-77; assistant to president Southern Pacific Transportation Company, 1977-79, general manager, 1979, vice president transportation, 1979-80, vice president operations, 1980-82, president, 1982-83, also director; president, chief operating officer Santa Fe Southern Pacific Corp., 1983-88, president, chief executive officer, chairman board, 1988—, also board of directors. Trustee John G. Shedd Aquarium, Northwestern Memorial Hospital, Chicago, Lake Forest College; member Northwestern U. Associates, board of directors Phelps Dodge Corp., Northern Trust Company, Catellus Devel. Corp., Santa Fe Energy Resources, Incorporated. Member Stanford University Alumni Association, Phi Beta Kappa, Kappa Sigma. Republican. Episcopalian. Clubs: Onwentsia (Lake Forest, Illinois); Pacific Union, World Trade, Bohemian, Chicago. Office: Santa Fe Pacific Corp 1700 E Golf Road Avenue Schaumburg Illinois 60173

KREHBIEL, JOHN H., electronics company executive; born 1906. With Molex, Incorporated, Lisle, Illinois, chairman board of directors, 1957—. Office: Molex Incorporated 2222 Wellington Court Lisle Illinois 60532

KREPS, DAVID MARC, economist, educator; born New York City, October 18, 1950; son of Saul Ian and Sarah (Kaskin) Kreps; married Anat Ruth Admati, January 4, 1984; 1 child, Tamar. Bachelor of Arts, Dartmouth College, 1972; Master of Arts, Doctor of Philosophy, Stanford University, 1975. Assistant professor Stanford University, 1975-78, associate professor, 1978-80, professor, 1980-84, Holden professor, 1984—; research officer University Cambridge, England, 1978-79, fellow commoner Churchill College, Cambridge, 1978-79; visiting professor Yale University, New Haven, 1982, Harvard University, Cambridge, Massachusetts, 1983, University Paris, 1985, University Tel Aviv, 1989-90. Author: Notes on the Theory of Choice, 1988, A Course in Microeconomic Theory, 1990, Game Theory and Economic Modelling,

1990; co-editor Econometrica, 1984-88. Alfred P. Sloan Foundation fellow, 1983, John S. Guggenheim fellow, 1988.; recipient: John Bates Clark medal, 1989. Fellow Econometric Society (council 1987—); member Am. Econ. Association (J.B. Clark medal 1989). Office: Stanford U Grad School of Business Stanford California 94305

KRESA, KENT, aerospace executive; born New York City, March 24, 1938; son of Helmy and Marjorie (Boutelle) K.; married Joyce Anne McBride, November 4, 1961; 1 child, Kiren. Bachelor.S.Associate of Arts, Massachusetts Institute of Technology, 1959, Master.S.Associate of Arts, 1961, E.Associate of Arts, 1966. Senior scientist research and advanced devel. div. AVCO, Wilmington, Massachusetts, 1959-61; staff member Massachusetts Institute of Technology Lincoln Laboratory, Lexington, Massachusetts, 1961-68; deputy director strategic tech. office Defense Advanced Research Projects Agency, Washington, 1968-73; director tactical tech. office Defense Advanced Research Project Agency, Washington, 1973-75; vice president, manager Research & Tech. Center Northrop Corp., Hawthorne, California, 1975-76; vice president, general manager Ventura div. Northrop Corp., Newbury Park, California, 1976-82; group vice president Aircraft Group Northrop Corp., Los Angeles, 1982-86, senior vice president tech. devel. and planning, 1986-87, president, chief operating officer, 1987—; board of directors John Tracy Clinic.; member Chief of Naval Operations executive panel Washington, Def. Sci. Board, Washington, DNA New Alternatives Working Group, Los Angeles, Department Aeronautics and Astronautics Corp. Visiting Committee Massachusetts Institute of Technology. Recipient Henry Webb Salsbury award Massachusetts Institute of Technology, 1959, Arthur D. Flemming award, 1975; Sec. of Defense Meritorious Civilian Service medal, 1975, USN Meritorious Pub. Service citation, 1975, Exceptional Civilian Service award USAF, 1987. Fellow American Institute of Aeronautics and Astronautics; member Naval Aviation Mus. Foundation, Navy League United States, Society Flight Test Engineers, Association of United States Army, National Space Club, Am. Defense Preparedness Association. Club: Mountaingate Country. Office: Northrop Corp 1840 Century Park E Los Angeles California 90067

KRUMM, DANIEL JOHN, manufacturing company executive; born Sioux City, Iowa, October 15, 1926; son of Walter A. and Anna K. (Helmke) K.; married Ann L. Klingner, February 28, 1953; children: David Jonathan, Timothy John. Bachelor of Arts in Commerce, University Iowa, 1950; postgraduate, University Michigan, 1955; Doctor.Bachelor of Arts (honorary), Westmar College, Le Mars, Iowa, 1981; Doctor Commercial Science (honorary), Luther College, Decorah, Iowa, 1983. With Globe Office Furniture Company, Minneapolis, 1950-52; with Maytag Company, Newton, Iowa, 1952-86, vice president, 1970-71, executive vice president, 1971-72, president, treasurer, 1972-74, chief executive officer, 1974-86; president, chief executive officer Maytag Company Limited, Toronto, Ontario, Can., 1970—; chairman, chief executive officer Maytag Corp., Newton,

1986—; board of directors Centel Corp., Chicago, Snap-On-Tools Corp., Kenosha, Principal Fin. Group, Des Moines. Member board of visitors U. Iowa College Business Administration; member steering committee for Iowa Endowment 2000 campaign; past chairman Iowa Natural Heritage Foundation; board governors Iowa College Foundation; chairman board of directors Grand View College, Des Moines; board of directors Des Moines Symphony Association, U. Iowa Foundation, Vocational Rehabilitation Workshop for Handicapped Citizens of Jasper County, Iowa, NAM; vice chairman Iowa Venture Capital Fund, Iowa Business Council; member committee for economic devel. Iowa Peace Institute; trustee FINE Education Research Foundation, 1987—. Served with United States Naval Reserve, 1944-46. Recipient Oscar C. Schmidt Iowa Business Leadership award, 1983; Distinguished Achievement award University Iowa Alumni Assn; named Iowa Business Leader of the Year, 1986. Member Am. Marketing Association (past president Iowa), Electrical Manufacturers Club, Newton Chamber of Commerce (community service award 1980), Maytag Management Club. Republican. Lutheran. Club: Newton Country. Office: Maytag Corp 403 W 4th St N Newton Iowa 50208

KUCHARSKI, JOHN MICHAEL, scientific instruments manufacturing company executive; born Milwaukee, February 10, 1936; son of Harry Raymond and Hedwig (Kopecki) K.; married Marilyn Kay Chovanec, November 28, 1957; children: Mary, Janet, Michalanne, Norah. Bachelor of Science in Electrical Engineering, Marquette University, 1958; Bachelor of Laws, George Washington University, 1965. Bar: District of Columbia 1966. Engineer Air Corps Electronics, Milwaukee, 1958-61; director engineering Howard Research Company, Arlington, Virginia, 1961-65; president Challenger Research, Rockville, Maryland, 1965-72; with EG&G Incorporated, Wellesley, Massachusetts, 1972—, vice president, 1979-81, group vice president, 1981-82, senior vice president, 1982-85, executive vice president, 1985-86, president, director, 1986-89, chief operating officer, 1987, chief executive officer, 1987—, chairman; president, general manager Washington Analytical Services Center (subsidiary), 1972-81; board of directors Bank of New England, N.A. Member National Industrial Security Association (trustee 1980—), Marine Engineering Society. Office: EG&G Incorporated 45 William St Wellesley Massachusetts 02181

KUEHLER, JACK DWYER, computer company executive; born Grand Island, Nebraska, August 29, 1932; son of August C. and Theresa (Dwyer) K.; married Carmen Ann Kubas, July 16, 1955; children—Cynthia Marie, Daniel Scott, Christina L., David D., Michael P. Bachelor of Science in Mechanical Engineering, University Santa Clara. Design engineer jet engines department General Electric Company, Evandale, Ohio, 1954-55; with International Business Machines Corporation, 1958—; director International Business Machines Corporation Raleigh Comunications Laboratory, 1967-70, International Business Machines Corporation San Jose and Menlo Park Laboratories, 1970-72; vice president devel.

general products div. International Business Machines Corporation, 1972-77, assistant group executive data processing product group, 1977-78, president system products div., 1978-80, corp. vice president, from 1980; president general tech. div. International Business Machines Corporation, White Plains, New York, 1980-81, information systems and tech. group executive, 1981-82, senior vice president, 1982-88, vice chairman, 1982-88, president, 1988—. Patentee in field. Trustee U. Santa Clara (California). Served as 1st lieutenant United States Army, 1955-57. Member Institute of Electrical and Electronics Engineers (senior), National Acad. Engineering, Am. Electronics Association. Office: International Business Machines Corporation Old Orchard Road Armonk New York 10504 also: International Business Machines Corporation Info Systems & Tech Group 1000 Westchester Avenue White Plains New York 10604

KUESTER, DENNIS J., banker. With M & I Marshall & Ilsley Bank, Milwaukee, formerly vice president, president, director; president Marshall & Ilsley Corp., Milwaukee. Office: Marshall & Ilsley Corp 770 N Water St Milwaukee Wisconsin 53201

KUFELDT, JAMES, retail grocery store executive; born 1938; married. Bachelor of Arts, Anderson College, 1960. Store manager Winn-Dixie Stores Incorporated, Jacksonville, Florida, 1961-71, produce merchandising, then retail operations superintendent, 1971-79, vice president, 1979-83, senior vice president, 1983—, now president, director. Office: Winn-Dixie Stores Incorporated 5050 Edgewood Court Jacksonville Florida 32205

KUMMER, GLENN F., mobile home company executive; born Park City, Utah, 1933. Bachelor of Science, University Utah, 1961. Senior accountant Ernst & Ernst, 1961-65; trainee Fleetwood Enterprises Incorporated, Riverside, California, 1965-67, purchasing manager, 1967-68, plant manager, 1968-70, general manager recreational vehicle div., 1970-71, assistant vice president operations to vice president operations, 1971-72, senior vice president operations, 1972-77, executive vice president operations, 1977-82, president, 1982—, director. Office: Fleetwood Enterprises Incorporated 3125 Myers St Box 7638 Riverside California 92523

KUNISCH, ROBERT DIETRICH, business services company executive; born Norwalk, Connecticut, July 7, 1941; son of Irving William and Margaret (Diedrich) K.; married Alicia Stephenson, August 22, 1964; children: Alicia Mary, Robert D. Bachelor of Science, New York University, 1964. Regional manager residential sales Homequity, Wilton, Connecticut, 1966-68, director, 1968-69, director corp. marketing, 1969-71, senior vice president marketing and services, 1971-76, president, 1976-84; executive vice president PHH Corp., Incorporated, Hunt Valley, Maryland, 1981-84, president, chief operating officer, 1984-88, president chief executive officer, director, 1988—; chairman board of directors 1989—; board director Corp., Mercantile Bankshares Corp., Baltimore, Alex Brown & Sons Incorporated, Preston Corp.; Distinguished executive lecturer New York University. Trustee Johns Hopkins U., Johns

Hopkins Hospital, Johns Hopkins Health Systems; board director Greater Baltimore Company, Dome Corp.; member United Way Central Maryland; past trustee Am. Shakespearean Theatre; past member devel. committee John F. Kennedy Institute, Baltimore, 1984. Democrat. Roman Catholic. Office: PHH Corp 11333 McCormick Road Hunt Valley Maryland 21031

KUNZ, LARRY P., lumber and building materials company executive. President, chief executive officer Leewards, 1977-83, Ben Franklin Stores, 1985-86; president, chief operating officer Fred Meyer, Incorporated, 1983-85; president, chief operating officer Payless Cashways, Incorporated, Kansas City, Missouri, 1986—, also board of directors. Office: Payless Cashways Incorporated 2301 Main St Box 466 Kansas City Missouri 64141

KUSE, JAMES RUSSELL, chemical company executive; born Lincoln, Nebraska, August 20, 1930; son of Walter Herman and Gladys Katherine (Graham) K.; married Shirley Rae Ernst, September 27, 1953; children: Lynn Kuse Ehret, Carol Kuse Ehlen, Michael. Bachelor.S.Ch.E., Oregon State University, 1955. Industrial chemicals salesman Ga.-Pacific Corp., Atlanta, 1967-68, manager specialty chemical div., 1968-70, manager chemical sales, 1970-74, manager commercial chemicals, 1974-76, vice president chemical div., 1976-78, senior vice president chemical div., 1978-84; chairman Georgia Gulf Corp., 1985—. Board of directors Clark College, Atlanta, 1983. Served to corporal United States Army, 1953-55. Member National Petroleum Refiners Association (director), Am. Institute Chemical Engineers, Chemical Manufacturers Association, Am. Chemical Society. Republican. Lutheran. Club: Capital City (Atlanta). Office: Georgia Gulf Corp 400 Perimeter Center Terrace Suite 595 Atlanta Georgia 30346

KYMAN, ALEXANDER LEON, banker; born New York City, November 8, 1929; son of Jack H. and Fannie (Senauke) K.; married Jean Poffenberger, April 13, 1951; children: Lynn, David, Miriam, Rebecca. Bachelor of Arts, Southern Methodist University, 1950; Bachelor of Laws, Harvard, 1953. Assistant treasurer Chase National Bank., New York City, 1953-62; assistant vice president Sterling National Bank, New York City, 1962-64; vice president Union Bank, Los Angeles, 1964-66; senior vice president City National Bank, Los Angeles, 1966-77; executive vice president City National Bank, 1977-83, president, 1984—, also board of directors; board of directors CNB Mortgage Corp., City Ventures, Incorporated, City National Fin. Services Corp.; president, board of directors City National Corp.; director California Bankers Association. Member Los Angeles Jewish Federation Council, 1967—, National Commission Anti-Defamation League, Anti-Defamation League; board of directors United Way Greater Los Angeles. Member Harvard Law School Association, Am. Bankers Association. Clubs: Harvard Southern Calif, El Caballero Country. Office: City National Bank 400 N Roxbury Dr Beverly Hills California 90210

LABRECQUE, THOMAS G., banker; born Long Branch, New Jersey, September 17, 1938; son of Theodore Joseph and Marjorie (Uprichard) L.; married Sheila English

Cardone, June 16, 1962; children: Thomas, Douglas, Karen, Barbara. Bachelor of Arts, Villanova University, 1960; postgraduate, Am. University, 1962-64, New York University, 1965. With Chase Manhattan Corp., New York City, 1964—, associate secretary to corp. executive office, 1970-71, senior vice president bank portfolio group, 1971-74, executive vice president treasury department, 1974-76, member executive committee responsible for commercial banking, retail banking, trust and fiduciary investment, operations and corp. systems functions; member executive committee Chase Manhattan Corp., 1976-80; vice chairman board, director, chief operating officer Chase Manhattan Corp., New York City, 1980-81, president, 1981-90, chairman, 1990—; director AMAX, Incorporated, Am. Bankers Association. Trustee Brookings Institution, Central Park Conservancy; board of directors Fund for New York City Pub. Education, United Way Tri-State, United Way New York City; board visitors Duke U. Fuqua School Business; member Council Foreign Rels., Trilateral Commission, Bus.-Higher Education Forum, Cystic Fibrosis Research Devel. Council; member executive committee Partnerships for Quality Education. Member Business Council, Business Roundtable. Office: Chase Manhattan Corp 1 Chase Manhattan Plaza New York New York 10081

LAMOTHE, WILLIAM EDWARD, food company executive; born Brooklyn, October 23, 1926; son of William John and Gertrude (Ryan) LaM.; married Patricia Alexander, June 24, 1950; 6 children. Bachelor of Arts, Fordham University, 1950. With Kellogg Sales Company, 1950-60, product devel. coordinator, 1958-60; assistant to president Kellogg Company, Battle Creek, Michigan, 1960-65, vice president, 1962-70, vice president, corporate devel., 1965-70, senior vice president corporate devel., 1970-72, executive vice president, 1972, president, chief operating officer, 1973-80, president, chief executive officer, 1979-80, chairman board, chief executive officer, 1980—, also director; board of directors Burroughs Corp., Kimberly-Clark Corp., Upjohn Company; board of directors Grocery Manufacturers Am., chairman, 1986—; chairman council Better Business Bureaus Incorporated, 1990—. Office: Kellogg Company 1 Kellogg Square Post Office Box 3599 Battle Creek Michigan 49016-3599

LANGENBERG, FREDERICK CHARLES, business executive; born New York City, July 1, 1927; son of Frederick C. and Margaret (McLaughlin) L.; married Jane Anderson Bartholomew, May 16, 1953; children: Frederick C., Susan Jane. Bachelor of Science, Lehigh University, 1950, Master of Science, 1951; Doctor of Philosophy, Pennsylvania State University, 1955; postgraduate execs. program, Carnegie-Mellon University, 1962. With United States Steel Corp., 1951-53; visiting fellow Massachusetts Institute of Technology, 1955-56; with Crucible Steel Corp., Pittsburgh, 1956-68, vice president research and engineering, 1966-68; president Trent Tube div. Colt Industries, Milwaukee, 1968-70; executive vice president Jessop Steel Company, Washington, Pennsylvania, 1970, president, 1970-75, also board of directors; president, board of directors Am. Iron and Steel

Institute, Washington, 1975-78; president Interlake Corp., Oak Brook, Illinois, 1979-81, president, chmn, chief executive officer, 1981—, also board of directors; board of directors Carpenter Tech., Reading, Pennsylvania, Peoples Energy Corp. Contributor articles to tech. journals; patentee in field. Served with United States Naval Reserve, 1944-45. Named Oak Brook Business Leader of the Year, 1986, Distinguished Business Leader, DuPage County, 1988; Alumni fellow Pennsylvania State University, 1977; recipient Distinguished Alumni award, Pennsylvania State University, 1989, Lehigh University, 1990. Fellow Am. Society Metals (distinguished life member 1982, trustee, Pittsburgh Nite lecturer 1970, Andrew Carnegie lecturer 1976; David Ford McFarland award Penn State chapter 1973); member American Institute of Mining, Metallurgy and Petroleum Engineers, Association Iron and Steel Engineers, Metals Powder Industry Federation, Phi Beta Kappa, Sigma Xi, Tau Beta Pi. Clubs: Duquesne, St. Clair Country (Pittsburgh); Congl., Burning Tree, Carlton (Washington); Chicago Golf, Chicago, Butler National Golf, Commercial (Chicago); Laurel Valley, Rolling Rock (Ligonier, Pennsylvania).

LANIER, JOHN HICKS, apparel company executive; born Nashville, April 12, 1940; son of Sartain and Claudia Gwynn (Whitson) L.; married Jane M. Darden, October 15, 1966; children: Jay, Liza, Stephen. Bachelor of Arts, Vanderbilt University, 1962; Master of Business Administration, Harvard University, 1964. President, chairman, chief executive officer Oxford Industries, Incorporated, Atlanta; board of directors Shaw Industries, Incorporated, Dalton, Georgia, Crawford & Company, Trust Company of Georgia Associates. Trustee, Henrietta Egleston Hospital for Children, The Westminster Schools, Atlanta; board of directors Piedmont Hospital, Atlanta. Served with United States Air Force Reserve, 1964-65. Member Am. Apparel Manufacturers Association (past board directors). Republican. Office: Oxford Industries Incorporated 222 Piedmont Avenue NE Atlanta Georgia 30308

LANIGAN, ROBERT J., packaging company executive; born Brooklyn, April 26, 1928; son of John F. and Katherine (Sheehy) L.; married Mary Elizabeth McCormick, December 30, 1950; children—J. Kenneth, Betty Jane Lanigan Snavely, Kathryn Ann Lanigan Pilewskie, Jeanne Marie Lanigan Schafer, Suzanne Marie Lanigan Georgetti. Bachelor of Arts in Economics, St. Francis College, New York City, 1950; Bachelor of Arts (honorary), Nathaniel Hawthorne College, Antrim, New Hampshire, 1979. President domestic operations Owens-Ill., Incorporated, Toledo, 1976-79, president international operations, 1979-82, president, 1982-86, chief operating officer, 1982-84, chief executive officer, 1984-90, chairman board, 1984—; board of directors Chrysler Corp., Detroit, Sonat, Incorporated, Birmingham, Alabama, Dun & Bradstreet Corp., New York City. President Toledo Symphony Orchestra; trustee Toledo Mus. Art. Recipient achievement award St. Francis College Alumni Association, 1980. Member Beer Institute (associate director). Roman Catholic. Club: Burning Tree (Bethesda, Maryland). Avocations: fishing; hunting; golf; tennis. Home:

6206 Valley Park Dr Toledo Ohio 43623 Office: Owens-Ill Incorporated 1 Seagate Toledo Ohio 43666

LANZA, FRANK C., electronics executive; born 1931. Bachelor of Science, Heralds Engineering College, 1956. Project engineer Philco Western Devel. Laboratories, 1957-59; vice president Textron Corp., Providence, 1960-72; with Loral Corp., New York City, 1972—, vice president, 1973-79, executive vice president, 1979-81, corp. president, chief operating officer, 1981—, also board of directors. Served with United States Coast Guard, 1953-55. Office: Loral Corp 600 Third Avenue 36th Floor New York New York 10016

LARGE, JAMES MIFFLIN, JR., banker; born Philadelphia, March 15, 1932; son of James Mifflin and Sarah Morris (Ellison) L.; married Carol E. Large, September 30, 1978; children: James Mifflin III, Richard C., Ginny, Dudly, Jon. Bachelor of Science in Engineering, Princeton University; postgraduate, Stonier Graduate School Banking. Chairman board, president First National Bank Allentown, Pennsylvania, 1982-85; vice chairman Meridian Bancorp, Reading, Pennsylvania, 1984-85; executive vice president, assistant to president 1st Interstate Bancorp, Los Angeles, 1986—; executive vice president, chairman credit policy Centran Corp., 1975-82. Author: Planning Secondary Defenses Against Loan Losses; contributor articles to trade journals. Served with United States Navy, 1955-59. Episcopalian. Clubs: Union (Cleveland); Union League, Corinthian Yacht (Philadelphia); Princeton (New York City); Kirtland Country, Hunt, Saucon Valley. Home: 1050 S Ei Molino Avenue Pasadena California 91106-4416 Office: First Interstate Bancorp 707 Wilshire Boulevard Los Angeles California 90017 also: Anchor Savings Bank FSB 225 Main St Northport New York 11768

LARSEN, RALPH STANLEY, health care company executive; born Brooklyn, New York, November 19, 1938; son of Andrew and Gurine (Henningsen) L.; married Dorothy M. Zeitfuss, August 19, 1961; children: Karen, Kristen, Garret. Bachelor of Business Administration, Hofstra University, 1962. Manufacturing trainee, then supervisor production and director manufacturing Johnson & Johnson, New Brunswick, New Jersey, 1962-77; vice president operations, vice president marketing McNeil Consumer Products Company div. Johnson & Johnson, Fort Washington, Pennsylvania, 1977-81; president Becton Dickenson Consumer Products, Paramus, New Jersey, 1981-83; president Chicopee div. Johnson & Johnson, New Brunswick, 1983-85; company group chairman Johnson & Johnson, New Brunswick, New Jersey, 1985-86, vice chairman, executive committee, board of directors, 1986—, chairman board, chief executive officer, 1989—, also board of directors, member executive committee; Board directors Xerox Corp. Board of directors Ethics Resource Center, United Negro College Fund; member board visitors U. North Carolina Grad. School Business; trustee, Educational Broadcasting Corp.; member Foundation Ind. Higher Education, Foundation for Malcolm Baldrige National Quality award, United States Council International Business. Member Business Council, Business Roundtable (policy committee). Republican.

Avocations: skiing, boating, art. Office: Johnson & Johnson 1 Johnson & Johnson Plaza New Brunswick New Jersey 08933

LARSEN, TERRANCE A., bank holding company executive. Bachelor of Arts, University Dallas, 1968; Doctor of Philosophy, Texas Agricultural and Mechanical University, 1971. With Philadelphia National Bank, from 1977, senior vice president, 1980-83, executive vice president, from 1983; executive vice president Corestates Fin. Corp. (parent), Philadelphia, 1983-86, president, 1986—, chief operating officer, 1986-87, chairman, chief executive officer, 1988—, also board of directors. Office: Core States Fin Corp NE Corner Broad & Chestnut Sts Post Office Box 76 Philadelphia Pennsylvania 19107

LAUBACH, GERALD DAVID, pharmaceutical company executive; born Bethlehem, Pennsylvania, January 21, 1926; son of Steward Lovine and Bertha (Rader) L.; married Winifred Isabel Taylor, October 3, 1953 (deceased October 1979); children: Stephen, Andrea, Hilary. Student, Mount St. Mary's College, 1944-45; Bachelor of Arts in Chemistry, University Pennsylvania, 1947; Doctor of Philosophy, Massachusetts Institute of Technology, 1950; Doctor of Science (honorary), Hofstra University, 1979; Doctor of Humane Letters (honorary), Connecticut College, 1986, Mount Sinai School Medicine City University of New York, 1988. With Pfizer, Incorporated, New York City, 1950—, manager medicinal products research, 1958-61, director department medicinal chemistry, 1961-63, group director medicinal research, 1963-64, vice president medicinal products research and devel., 1964-68, director, 1968—, member executive committee, 1969—, president pharmaceutical operations, 1969-71; executive vice president Pfizer Incorporated, New York City, 1971-72, president, 1972—; director CIGNA Corp. of Philadelphia, Millipore Corp., Bedford, Massachusetts; member National Sci. Board Committee on Precoll. Education in Math., Sci. and Tech., 1982-83, National Committee for Quality Health Care; member visiting committee department biochem. and molecular biology Harvard University; member adv. board Medical Center, New York Hosp.-Cornell Center; member corp. committee for sponsored research Massachusetts Institute of Technology. Patentee in field; contributor articles to tech journals. Member President's Commission on Industrial Competitiveness, 1983-85; member executive committee Council on Competitiveness, 1986—, Institute Medicine, 1987; member Rockefeller U. Council; trustee Connecticut College, 1973-84, chairman, 1978-83, Polytechnical U., 1981-86, Carnegie Institute Washington; member adv. board New York Hosp.-Cornell Center; member corp. committee for sponsored research of Massachusetts Institute of Technology.; member visiting committee department biochemistry and molecular biology Harvard U., 1988—. Recipient International Palladium medal Am. sect. Society de Chemie Industrielle, 1985, Mayor's award for Sci. and Tech., New York City, 1985, Lillian D. Wald award Vis. Nurse Svcs. New York, 1983. Member National Academy of Engineering, American College of Surgeons, American Association for the Advancement of Science, Am.

Institute Chemists (hon. fellow), Am. Acad. Arts Sciences, Society Chemical Industry, Pharmaceutical Manufacturers Association (board directors 1973-89, chairman 1977-78), Am. Management Association, New York Acad. Sciences (board govs.), Chemists Club New York (director 1968—, executive committee 1969—), Food and Drug Law Institute (board directors), Connecticut Acad. Sci. & Engineering. Home: Lyme Connecticut 06371 Office: Pfizer Incorporated 235 E 42nd St New York New York 10017

LAUDER, ESTEE, cosmetics company executive; born New York City; married Joseph Lauder; children: Leonard, Ronald. Doctor of Laws (honorary), University Pennsylvania, 1986. Chairman board Estee Lauder Incorporated, 1946—. Author: Estee: A Success Story, 1985. Named One of 100 Women of Achievement Harpers Bazaar, 1967, Top Ten Outstanding Women in Business, 1970; recipient Neiman-Marcus Fashion award, 1962; Spirit of Achievement award Albert Einstein College Medicine, 1968; Kaufmann's Fashion Fortnight award, 1969; Bamberger's Designer's award, 1969; Gimbel's Fashion Forum award, 1969; International Achievement award Frost Bros., 1971; Pogue's Annual Fashion award, 1975, Golda Meir 90th Anniversary Tribute award, 1988; decorated chevalier Legion of Honor France, 1978; medaille de Vermeil de la Ville de Paris, 9, 1979; 4th Annual award for Humanitarian Service Girls' Club New York, 1979; 25th Anniversary award Greater New York council Boy Scouts Am., 1979; L.S. Ayres award, 1981; Achievement award Girl Scouts U.S.A., 1983; Outstanding Mother award, 1984; Athena award, 1985; honored Lincoln Center, World of Style, 1986; 1988 Laureate National Business Hall of Fame. Office: 767 Fifth Avenue New York New York 10153

LAUDER, LEONARD ALAN, cosmetic and fragrance company executive; born New York City, March 19, 1933; son of Joseph H. and Estee (Mentzer) L.; married Evelyn Hausner, July 5, 1959; children: William Phillip, Gary Mark. Bachelor of Science, Wharton School, University Pennsylvania, 1954. With Estee Lauder, Incorporated, New York City, 1958—, executive vice president, 1962-72, president, 1972-82, president, chief executive officer, 1982—; vice chairman board CFTA, New York City, 1976-79. Trustee Aspen Institute for Humanistic Studies, 1978—, U. Pennsylvania, Philadelphia, 1977—, Whitney Mus. Am. Art, 1977—; board of directors Adv. Commission on Trade Negotiations, Washington, 1983-87; board governors Joseph H. Lauder Institute Mgmt. and International Studies, 1983—. Lieutenant United States Naval Reserve, 1955-58. Member Chief Executives Organization, French-Am. Chamber of Commerce in United States (council frn. relations). Office: Estee Lauder Incorporated 767 Fifth Avenue New York New York 10153

LAUREN, RALPH, designer; born Bronx, New York, October 14, 1939; son of Frank and Frieda Lifshitz; married Ricky Low Beer, December 30, 1964; children: Andrew, David, Dylan. Student, City College of New York; Doctor of Fine Arts (honorary), Pratt University, 1988. Salesperson Bloomingdale's, New York City, Brooks Brothers, New York City;

assistant buyer Allied Stores, New York City; representative Rivetz Necktie Manufacturers, New York City; neckwear designer Polo div. Beau Brummel, New York City, 1967-69; founder Polo Fashions, Incorporated, New York City, 1968—; established Polo Men's Wear Company, New York City, 1968—, Ralph Lauren Womenswear, New York City, 1971—, Polo Leathergoods, 1978—, Polo/Ralph Lauren for Boys, 1978—, Polo/Ralph Lauren Luggage, 1982—, Ralph Lauren Home Collection, 1983—; launched fragrances Polo for Men, Lauren for Women 1979—; chairman Polo Ralph Lauren Corp. (flagship store New York City, 68 other stores in United States and 145 stores worldwide); launched Safari fragrance for women, 1990. Served in United States Army. Recipient Coty Am. Fashion awards, 1970, 73, 74, 76, 77, 81, 84, also Coty Hall of Fame award for Menswear and Womenswear, Tommy award Am. Printed Fabrics Council, 1971, Neiman Marcus Distinguished Service award, 1973, Am. Fashion award, 1975, award Council of Fashion Designers of Am., 1981. Office: Polo Ralph Lauren Corp 40 W 55th St New York New York 10019

LAVENTHOL, DAVID ABRAM, newspaper editor; born Philadelphia, July 15, 1933; son of Jesse and Clare (Horwald) L.; married Esther Coons, March 8, 1958; children: Peter, Sarah. Bachelor of Arts, Yale University, 1957; Master of Arts, University Minnesota, 1960; Doctor of Letters (honorary), Dowling College, 1979; Doctor of Laws (honorary), Hofstra University, 1986. Reporter, news editor St. Petersburg (Florida) Times, 1957-62; assistant editor, city editor New York Herald-Tribune, 1963-66; assistant managing editor Washington Post, 1966-69; associate editor Newsday, Long Island, New York, 1969, executive editor, 1969, editor, 1970-78, pub., chief executive officer, 1978-86, chairman, 1986-87; group vice president newspapers Times Mirror Company, Los Angeles, 1981-86, senior vice president, 1986-87, president, 1987—; pub., chief executive officer Los Angeles Times, 1989—; member Pulitzer Prize Board, 1982—, chairman, 1988—; board of directors Los Angeles Times Post News Service, Washington, 1988—, Newspaper Advertising Bureau, 1989—; vice chairman International Press Institute, 1985—; member Am. Press Institute, 1988—. Board of directors New York Partnership, 1985-87, United Negro College Fund, 1988, Times Mirror Foundation, 1987, Mus. Contemporary Art, Los Angeles, 1989—; member California Mus. Foundation, 1989—. With Signal Corps Army of the United States, 1953-55. Member Am. Society Newspaper Editors (chairman writing awards board 1980-83), Council Foreign Relations. Club: Century. Home: 800 W 1st St Apartment 3202 Los Angeles California 90012 Office: Times Mirror Company Times Mirror Square Los Angeles California 90053

LAVIN, LEONARD H., personal care products company executive; born Chicago, 1919; married. Bachelor of Arts, University Washington, 1940. With Lucien Lelong, 1940-46; vice president sales, general manager Halgar, Incorporated, 1946-51; with Leonard H. Lavin Company, 1951-55; with Alberto-Culver Company, Melrose Park, Illinois, 1955—, now. chairman, president, chief executive officer, also board of directors.

Served to lieutenant commdr. United States Naval Reserve, 1941-45. Office: Alberto-Culver Company 2525 Armitage Avenue Melrose Park Illinois 60160

LAWSON, ANDREW LOWELL, JR., defense industry company executive; born Macon, Georgia, January 16, 1938; son of Andrew Lowell and Valerie Ula (Brazzeal) L.; married Carol Belle Few, December 31, 1961; children: Andrew L. III, Steven Brian. Student, Mercer University, 1955; certificate, Middle Georgia College, 1956-58; Bachelor of Science in Math, University Georgia, 1960. Contract price analyst WRAMA, Robins Air Force Base, Georgia, 1960-64; with E-Systems, Incorporated, Greenville, Texas, various fin. positions, 1964-70; vice president fin., div. controller Huntington, Ind., 1970-73; corp. vice president, controller Dallas, 1973; corp. vice president, div. vice president fin. & administration Greenville, 1973-78, corp. vice president, general manager Greenville div., 1978-83; senior vice president, group executive aircraft systems group Dallas, 1983-87, executive vice president, 1987—, also board of directors. Deacon Ridgecrest Baptist Church, Greenville. Served with United States Naval Reserve, 1955-63. Member Aerospace Industries Association, Am. Defense Preparedness Association, Armed Force Communnications and Electronic Association, Association United States Army, Air Force Association, Navy League, Old Crows. Office: E-Systems Incorporated Post Office Box 660248 Dallas Texas 75266

LAY, KENNETH LEE, diversified energy company executive; born Tyrone, Missouri, April 15, 1942; son of Omer and Ruth E. (Reese) L.; married Linda Ann Phillips, July 10, 1982; children: Robyn Anne, Mark Kenneth, Todd David, Elizabeth Ayers, Robert Ray. Bachelor of Arts, University Missouri, 1964, Master of Arts, 1965; Doctor of Philosophy, University Houston, 1970. Corp. economist Exxon Corp., Houston, 1965-68; associate professor and lecturer in economics George Washington University, 1969-73; tech. assistant to commissioner Federal Power Commission, 1971-72; deputy undersecretary for energy Department Interior, 1972-74; vice president Florida Gas Company (now Continental Resources Company), Winter Park, Florida, 1974-76, president, 1976-79; executive vice president The Continental Group, 1979-81; president, chief operating officer, director Transco Energy Company, Houston, 1981-84; chairman, president, chief exec officer Houston Natural Gas Corp., 1984-85; president, chief executive officer, chief operating officer, director HNG/InterNorth (now Enron Corp.), Omaha, 1985—, also chairman board of directors, Houston; board of directors Baker Hughes Incorporated, Compaq Computer Corp. Board of directors Houston Metropolitan Young Men's Christian Association; chairman board regents U. Houston. Served with United States Navy, 1968-71. Decorated Navy Commendation award; N.A.M. fellow; State Farm fellow; Guggenheim fellow. Member Interstate Natural Gas Association Am. (chairman, director), River Oaks Country Club. Republican. Methodist. Office: Enron Corp Post Office Box 1188 Houston Texas 77251

LAZARUS, CHARLES, retail toy company executive; born 1923; married. With Lash Distributors Incorporated, 1958-67; with Interstate Stores Incorporated (acquired by Toys "R" Us Incorporated, 1978), from 1967, senior vice president, 1971-76, president, chief executive officer, from 1976; with Toys "R" Us Incorporated, Rochelle Park, New Jersey, 1970—, now chairman, president, chief executive officer, also board of directors. Office: Toys R Us Incorporated 461 From Paramus New Jersey 07652

LEACH, JOHN FRANK, trucking executive; born New Ross, Ireland, March 11, 1921; came to United States, 1921; son of John Reginald and Evelyn Muriel (Ard) L.; married Lee Marie Serre, December 1, 1945; children: John Michael, Suzanne Lee Leach, Earnest. Bachelor of Arts in Industrial Management, Wayne State University. Tool and diemaker apprentice Ford Motor Company, Dearborn, Michigan, 1934-38; various manufacturing positions to manager Ford Engine Plant, Cleveland, 1938-54; director manufacturing Studebaker-Packard Corp., Detroit, 1954-56; various positions from vice president manufacturing and president Amphenol Electronics Corp.; executive vice president, chief operating officer Bunker Ramo Corp., Chicago, 1956-72; president, chief executive officer Arcata Corp., Menlo Park, California, 1972-82, chairman board, 1982-85; president, chief operating officer Consolidated Freightways Incorporated, Menlo Park, 1985—; partner Sequoia Associates, Menlo Park, 1990—; chairman board Acme Fixture Company, Oakland, California; board of directors Consolidated Freightways, Palo Alto, National Safe Depository, San Jose, California, Basic Am. Foods Incorporated, San Francisco, Newell Industries, Lowell, Michigan, Champion Road Machinery Company, Limited, Goderich, Ontario, Can., Pacific Fruit Growers & Packers, Incorporated, Wenatchee, Washington, Snow Mountain Pine Lumber Company, Hines, Oregon. Chairman steering committee Friends of Radiology, Stanford U. Medical Center; board of directors Business School, U. California, Berkeley. 2d lieutenant United States Army Air Force. Recipient Medal of Honor Electronic Industries Association, 1972. Member Electrical Industries Association (chairman, chief executive officer Washington chapter 1971-72, EIA medal of honor 1973), Desert Horizons Country Club, Menlo Country Club, Palo Alto Club, Lincoln Club of Northern California (past chairman). Office: Consol Freightways Incorporated 3240 Hillview Avenue Palo Alto California 94303

LEATHERDALE, DOUGLAS WEST, insurance company executive; born Morden, Manitoba, Canada, December 6, 1936; came to United States, 1968; son of Walter West and Lena Elizabeth (Gilligan) L.; children—Mary Jo, Christopher. Bachelor of Arts, United College, Winnipeg, Manitoba, 1957. Investment analyst, officer Great West Life Assurance Company, Winnipeg, 1957-68; associate executive secretary Board Pensions, Lutheran Church, Minneapolis, 1968-72; executive vice president, then vice president St. Paul Investment Management Company, subsidiary St. Paul Companies, Incorporated, 1972-77; v.p.-fin. St. Paul Companies, Incorporated, 1974-81, senior v.p.-fin., 1981-82, executive vice president, 1982-89, also director, president, chief operating officer, 1989—; board of directors St. Paul Fire and Marine Insurance Company, St. Paul Land Resources, Incorporated, St. Paul Real Estate of Illinois, Incorporated, John Nuveen & Company Incorporated, St. Paul Properties, Incorporated, St. Paul Oil and Gas Corp., St. Paul Fire & Marine Insurance Company (United Kingdom) Limited, St. Paul Mercury Insurance Company, St. Paul Guardian Insurance Company, St. Paul Surplus Lines Insurance Company, National Insurance Wholesalers, Atwater McMillian, 77 Water St., Incorporated, Ramsey Insurance Company, St. Paul Risk Services, Incorporated, St. Paul Plymouth Center, Incorporated Athena Assurance Company, St. Paul Fin. Group, Incorporated, Graham Resources, Incorporated, Carlyle Capital, L.P., United HealthCare Corp. Member Twin Cities Society Security Analysts, Fin. Executives Institute. Club: Minnesota (St. Paul). Avocation: horses. Office: St Paul Cos Incorporated 385 Washington St Saint Paul Minnesota 55102

LEAVITT, JULIAN, wholesale food company executive. Office: Sweetlife Foods Incorporated 1120 Harvey Lane Suffield Connecticut 06078

LEBENSFELD, HARRY, manufacturing company executive; born New York City, August 25, 1904; son of Samuel and Bertha (Wolfshaut) L.; married Edith Goldman, September 15, 1937; 1 daughter, Lynne Pasculano. With UIS, Incorporated (formerly United Industrial Syndicate, Incorporated), New York City, 1945—, now chief executive officer, chairman board. Member Harmony Club. Home: 980 Fifth Avenue New York New York 10021 Office: UIS Incorporated 600 Fifth Avenue New York New York 10020

LEE, CHARLES ROBERT, telecommunications company executive; born 1939; married. Bachelor of Science in Metallurgical Engineering, Cornell University, 1962; Master of Business Administration, Harvard University, 1964. Manager business research United States Steel Company, 1964-70; vice president, director Victor Palmiere Company, 1970-79; senior vice president fin. Columbia Pictures Industries, 1979-83; senior vice president fin. and planning General Telephone and Telegraph Corp., Stamford, Connecticut, 1983-88; president, chief operating officer General Telephone and Telegraph Corp., 1989—, also board of directors; board of directors Travelers Corp., MGIC Investment Company. Member Fin. Executives Institute, National Planning Association (committee on new realtities), Stanwich Club. Office: General Telephone and Electric Company Corp 1 Stamford Forum Stamford Connecticut 06904 also: Anglo-Can Tel Company, 8750 Cote de Liesse Road, Montreal, Province of Quebec Canada H41 1H3

LEE, STAN, publisher, writer; born New York City, December 28, 1922; son of Jack and Celia (Solomon) Lieber; married Joan Clayton Boocock, December 5, 1947; 1 daughter, Joan C. Student public schools, New York City. Copy writer, then assistant editor, editor Timely Comics (became Atlas Comics), New York City, 1939-42; editor, creative director Atlas (became Marvel Comics) Comics, until 1961; creative director, editor-in-chief Marvel Comics, 1961-70, pub., 1970—;

creative director Marvel Productions, 1980—; adj. professor popular culture Bowling Green (Kentucky) State University; college lecturer, TV script editor. Creator, former writer and editor Fantastic Four, Incredible Hulk, Amazing Spiderman, numerous others; author: Origins of Marvel Comics, 1974, Son of Origins, 1975, Bring On The Bad Guys, 1976, The Superhero Women, 1977, The Silver Surfer, How to Draw Comics the Marvel Way, 1978, Marvel's Greatest Superhero Battles, 1978, Incredible Hulk, 1978, Fantastic Four, 1979, Doctor Strange, 1979, Complete Adventures of Spiderman, 1979, Captain America, 1979, The Best of the Worst, 1979, The Best of Spider-Man, 1986, others. Served with Army of the United States, 1942-45. Recipient annual award Popular Culture Association, 1974. Member (founder), Acad. Comic Book Arts (award 1973), National Acad. TV Arts and Sciences, National Cartoonists Society, American Federation of TV and Radio Artists. Club: Friars (New York City). Office: Marvel Comics Group 387 Park Avenue S New York New York 10016 also: Cowles Syndicate Incorporated 235 E 45th St New York New York 10017

LEE, WILLIAM STATES, utility executive; born Charlotte, North Carolina, June 23, 1929; son of William States and Sarah (Everett) L.; married Janet Fleming Rumberger, November 24, 1951; children—Lisa, States, Helen. Bachelor of Science in Engineering magna cum laude, Princeton University, 1951. Registered professional engineer, North Carolina, South Carolina. With Duke Power Company, Charlotte; 1955—, engineering manager Duke Power Company, 1962-65, vice president engineering, 1965-71, senior vice president, 1971-75, executive vice president, 1976-77, president, chief operating officer, 1978-82, chairman, chief executive officer, 1982-89, also director, member management and fin. committees; member United States Committee on Large Dams, 1963—; director Liberty Corp., J.P. Morgan Company, Morgan Guaranty Trust Company. Board of directors United Community Services, Am. Nuclear Energy Council, Edison Electric Institute, Foundation of the Carolinas; member, chairman North Carolina Governor's Business Council, 1985—; chairman trustees Queens College, U. North Carolina Charlotte Foundation, Presbyterian Hospital Foundation Served with Corps of Engineers United States Naval Reserve, 1951-54. Named Outstanding Engineer North Carolina Society Engineers, 1969. Fellow American Society of Mechanical Engineers (George Westinghouse gold medal 1972), American Society of Civil Engineers; member National Acad. Engineering, National Society Professional Engineers (Outstanding Engineer award 1980), Edison Electric Institute (director econs. and fin. policy committee, director), Charlotte Chamber of Commerce (chairman 1979), Am. Nuclear Society, Phi Beta Kappa, Tau Beta Pi. Presbyterian (ruling elder). Office: Duke Power Company 422 S Church St Charlotte North Carolina 28242

LEFRAK, SAMUEL J., housing and building corporation executive, real estate development, finance, oil and gas exploration and communications executive, music publisher; born New York City, February 12, 1918; son of Harry and Sarah (Schwarz) LeF.; married Ethel Stone, May 14, 1941;

children: Denise, Richard, Francine, Jacqueline. Graduate, University Maryland, 1940; postgraduate, Columbia University, Harvard University; Doctor of Laws (honorary), University of Studies, Rome, 1971, New York Law School, 1974, Colgate University, 1979; Doctor of Humanities (honorary), Pratt Institute, 1988, University Maryland, 1990. President Lefrak Organization, 1948—, chairman board, 1975—; creator, sponsor, builder Lefrak City, Battery Park City, Gateway Plaza, Newport Complex; member adv. board Station WHLI, 1955; commissioner Landmarks Preservation Commission, New York City, 1966; commissioner pub. works Borough Manhattan, 1956-58; commissioner Interstate Sanitation Commission, 1958; Saratoga Springs Commission, 1962—; member adv. board Chem Bank.; guest lecturer Harvard Grad. School Business Administration, 1971, Yale, 1975, New York University, 1977; guest speaker Fin. Women's Association, New York, 1975; guest lecturer Princeton University, University Haifa, 1983, Oxford University, 1984, Pratt Institute, 1987, Harvard University, 1987, Columbia School Business, 1988, Wharton School Business, 1989, School Business New York University, 1989; speaker United Nations, 1988; featured speaker Institutional Investment Real Estate Conference, 1975, Federal Home Loan Bank Conference, 1990; guest lecturer Japanese Government, Finnish Government, Switzerland, 1967; United States del. International Conference Housing and Urban Devel., Switzerland, 1967; director New York World's Fair Corp., 1964-65, New York Industrial Devel. Corp., 1975—, chairman board Long Island Post; president New York City Comml. Devel. Corp., 1967-71, chairman, 1971—; founding member World Business Council, Incorporated, 1970; member President's Committee Employment Handicapped; special consultant urban affairs State Department, 1969; member adv. council Real Estate Institute, New York University, 1970—; member governor fin. President's Club University Maryland, 1971, committee New York State Traffic Safety Council, 1966; board visitors School Law, Columbia University, 1983; commissioner Saratoga-Capital district New York State Park and Recreation Commission, 1973; member real estate council executive committee Metropolitan Mus. Art, 1982; member New York City Pub. Devel. Corp., National Energy Council, United States Department Commerce, Mayor's Committee on Housing Devel., New York City, 1974—; member executive committee Citizen's Budget Committee for New York City, Incorporated, 1975—; member Governor Cuomo's Adv. Council, 1983, New York State Gov.'s Task Force on Housing, 1974; establish Lefrak Lecture Series, University Maryland, 1982; creator, developer residential and business property. Vice chmn.-at-large American Red Cross, New York; member United States committee United Nations Organization, 1957; chairman national board Histadrut, 1967—; member Israel Bonds Prime Minister Committee, 1980; director Ronald McDonald House, 1986; chairman bldg. committee Saratoga Performing Arts Center; member Fifth Avenue Association; director, chairman real estate div. Greater New York Fund; hon. committee Amateur Athletic Union; Queens chairman United

Greek Orthodox Charities, 1973; chairman Celebrity Sports Night-Human Resources Center, 1973-74, Sports Association Hebrew U. of Jerusalem, 1979; patron Metropolitan Mus. Art; sponsor Israel Philharmonic Orchestra, Jan Groth Exhibit, Guggenheim Mus.; trustee, director Beth-El Hospital; board of directors United Service Organizations, Citizens Housing and Planning Council, New York, 1957—, Interfaith Movement, Diabetics Foundation, Queens Cultural Association, Consumer Credit Counseling Service Greater New York, Astoria Motion Picture and TV Cention; trustee New York Law School, Queens Art and Cultural Center, Jewish Hospital at Denver, N.Y Civic Budget Committee; trustee, medical adv. board Brookdale Hospital Medical Center, Pace U.; member executive board Greater New York couns. Boy Scouts Am.; founder Albert Einstein School Medicine; member Bretton Woods Committee; board governors Invest-in-Am. National Council; member task force on energy conservation Div. Community Housing, 1981—; member committee New York State Traffic Safety Council, 1966; chairman Scandinavia Today, 1981—; board visitors School Law Columbia U., 1983; member adv. board The Explorer's Club, 1984; member National Committee on U.S.-China Rels. Incorporated; board of directors Institute Nautical Archaeology; trustee Queens College, 1989; adv. director Metropolitan Opera, 1990; conference board Keynote Address-Annual Fin. Seminar, 1987. Decorated officer Order of Lion of Finland, 1980, Medal of Parliament, 1988; officer Order St. John of Jerusalem Knights of Malta, 1982; Order of the North Star of Sweden, 1982; commander Royal Norwegian Order of Merit, 1987; recipient Mayor New York City award outstanding citizenship, 1960; National Boys Club award, 1960; Citizen of Year award B'nai Brith, 1963; Am. Achievement award, 1984; Distinguished Achievement award, 1967; Man of Year award Veterans of Foreign Wars, 1963; Brotherhood award National Conference of Christians and Jews, 1964; Chief Rabbi Herzog gold medal; Torah Fellowship citation Religious Zionist Am., 1966; John F. Kennedy Peace award, 1966; Man of Year award Brooklyn Community Hospital, 1967; Builder of Excellence award Brandeis University, 1968; Master Builder award New York Cardiac Center, 1968; Distinguished Citizen award M Club Foundation University Maryland, 1970; Distinguished Alumnus award University Maryland Alumni Association, 1970; Distinguished Citizen and Outstanding Community Service award United Way, 1986; Am. Achievement award Encyclopaedia Britannica, 1984; Am. Eagle award national council Invest-in Am., 1972; Executive Sportsman award Human Resources Center, 1973; Architectural award Fifth Av. Association, 1974; Excellence in Design award Queens Chamber of Commerce, 1974; Flame Truth award Fund Higher Education, 1986; elected hon. citizen Maryland, 1970; Citizen of Year award Brooklyn Philharmonic Orchestra, 1983; dedication of Samuel J. LeFrak Hall University Maryland, 1982, LeFrak Gymnasium, Amherst College, 1986, LeFrak Moot Court, New York Law School, 1990, LeFrak Meadow, New York City, 1991; LeFrak Lecture Series at University Maryland established, 1982; Commander of the Royal

Norwegian Order of Merit, presented by King Olav V, 1987; Rough Riders award Boy Scouts Am., 1987; Torch of Progress Assoc. Builders and Owners Greater New York; award Society Foreign Consuls, 1988, Gold medal and Man of Year award Israel Bonds Foundation, 1990; award Association Graphics Arts, 1990; named to National Sales Club Hall of Fame, 1990. Member Sales Executives Club New York (director), United Hunts Racing Association, Philharmonic Symphony Society New York, Explorers Club (director), Newcomen Society United States, Phi Kappa Phi, Tau Epsilon Phi (established Samuel J. LeFrak scholarship award 1975). Clubs: University Maryland Pres.'s (mem. Gov. New York fin.), Lotos (board dirs. 1975—, Merit award 1973), Grand Street Boys, Friars (director Found.), Advertising, Economic, Downtown Athletic (New York City); Town, Turf and Field; Cat Cay (Nassau, Bahamas); Xanadu Yacht (Freeport, Grand Bahamas); Palm Bay (Miami Beach, Florida); Seawane; Ocean Reef (Key Largo); Sag Harbor Yacht (Long Island). Lodges: Masons (32d degree), Shriners. Office: LeFrak Orgn Incorporated 97-77 Queens Boulevard Forest Hills New York 11374

LEGO, PAUL EDWARD, corporation executive; born Centre County, Pennsylvania, May 16, 1930; son of Paul Irwin and Sarah Elizabeth (Montgomery) L.; married Ann Sepety, July 7, 1956; children: Paul Gregory, Debra Ann, Douglas Edward, Michael John. Bachelor of Science in Electrical Engineering, University Pittsburgh, 1956, Master of Science, 1958. With Westinghouse Electric Corp., 1956—; business unit manager electronic components divs. Westinghouse Electric Corp., Pittsburgh, 1974-77; general manager, vice president lamp divs. Westinghouse Electric Corp., Bloomfield, New Jersey, 1977-80; executive vice president electronics and control group Westinghouse Electric Corp., Pittsburgh, 1980-83, executive vice president control equipment, 1983-85, senior executive vice president corp. resources, 1985-87, president, chief operating officer, 1988-90, chairman, chief executive officer, 1990—, also board of directors; member board strategic advs. Pyramid Tech. Corp., 1986—; board of directors Pittsburgh National Bank, PNC Fin. Corp., USX Corp., USX Foundation, Incorporated. Author papers in field. Trustee, executive committee U. Pittsburgh; chairman board visitors U. Pittsburgh School Engring.; board of directors Presbyn-Univ. Hospital, Pittsburgh, 1988; director Montefiore Hospital; member citizens' sponsoring committee Allegheny Conference on Community Devel., Pittsburgh; trustee Committee for Economic Devel., New York City; member Business Council, Conference Board, Business Roundtable; vice chairman U.S.-Korea Business Council, Washington; board overseers New Jersey Institute of Tech., Newark, 1978—. With Army of the United States, 1948-52. Recipient Westinghouse Order of Merit 1975. Member Valley Brook Country Club, Duquesne Club (Pittsburgh, board directors 1988—), Laurel Valley Golf Club, Rolling Rock Club (Ligonier, Pennsylvania), Sigma Xi. Democrat. Roman Catholic.

LEIN, DON CURTIS, corporate executive; born Maquoketa, Iowa, 1934; married. Bachelor of Science,

University Iowa, 1956; Master of Business Administration, Harvard University, 1962. Pub. accountant Arthur Andersen & Company, 1956-57, 59-60; assistant treasurer Crosby Plans, 1962-63; assistant controller Jostens Incorporated, Minneapolis, 1963-66, controller, 1966-70, vice president, controller, 1970-72, vice president fin., 1972-75, executive vice president fin. and administration, 1975-88, secretary, 1975—, president, 1988—, also board of directors. Served with United States Army, 1957-59. Member Am. Institute (C.P.A.'s), Fin. Executive Institute. Office: Jostens Incorporated 5501 Norman Center Dr Minneapolis Minnesota 55437

LEMIEUX, JOSEPH HENRY, manufacturing company executive; born Providence, March 2, 1931; son of Mildred L. Lemieux; married Frances Joanne Schmidt, August 11, 1956; children: Gerald Joseph, Craig Joseph, Kimberly Mae Lemieux Wolff, Allison Jo. Student, Stonehill College, 1949-50, University Rhode Island, 1950-51; Bachelor of Business Administration summa cum laude, Bryant College, 1957. With Owens-Ill., Toledo, 1957—, various positions with glass container div. and closure and metal container group; executive vice president Owens-Ill. Owens-Ill., Incorporated, Toledo, 1984, president pkg. operations, 1984, president, chief operating officer, 1986—, also board of directors; president, chief executive officer, chief operating officer Owens-Ill., Incorporated, 1990—; board of directors Ohio Citizens Bank, Toledo, National City Corp. Vice chairman board governors Edison Industrial Systems Center U. Toledo, 1986. Served to staff sergeant United States Air Force, 1951-55. Named one of Outstanding Young Men Am., Jaycees, 1965. Member Glass Packaging Institute (chairman 1984-86), Packaging Education Foundation (board directors). Roman Catholic. Clubs: Toledo, Shadow Valley Tennis, Inverness (Toledo). Avocations: golf, tennis. Office: Owens-Ill Incorporated 1 Seagate Toledo Ohio 43666

LENA, ADOLPH JOHN, specialty steel company executive; born Latrobe, Pennsylvania, October 10, 1925; son of Attilio and Leona (Robb) L.; married Dolores Ruth Cunningham, June 9, 1948 (divorced 1978); married Beverly Ann Prue, September 15, 1979; children: Mario, Carol, Kathleen, Lisa, Lauren, Lydia. Bachelor of Science in Metallurgy, Pennsylvania State University, 1948; Master Metallurgical Engineer, Carnegie Mellon University, 1950, Doctor Metallurgical Engineer, 1952. Associate director research Allegheny Ludlum Steel Corp., Pittsburgh, 1953-56, manager basic research department, 1956-63, director product devel., 1963-68, director research, 1968-69, vice president, tech. director, 1969-71, vice president, general manager bar production, 1971-76; chairman, chief executive officer A1 Tech Specialty Steel Corp., Dunkirk, New York, 1976-84; executive vice president, chief operating officer Carpenter Tech. Corp., Reading, Pennsylvania, 1986-87, president, chief operating officer, 1987—, also board of directors; consultant Carpenter Tech. Corp., Reading, 1985-86. Contributor articles to 20 tech. jours; patentee in field. Trustee Reading (Pennsylvania) Hospital, 1987—. Served to lieutenant (junior grade) United States

Navy, 1944-46, World War II. Recipient McFarland award Pennsylvania State University; named Distinguished Citizen New York State, State University of New York Board Regents; Pennsylvania State University alumni fellow. Fellow Am. Society Metals (past chairman Pittsburgh chapter, past national trustee, past national secretary, Distinguished Life Member award). Republican. Roman Catholic. Club: Berkshire Country (Reading). Avocations: reading, golf. Home: 1743 Reading Boulevard Wyomissing Pennsylvania 19610 Office: Carpenter Tech Corp 101 W Bern St Post Office Box 14662 Reading Pennsylvania 19612-4662

LEONTIEF, WASSILY, economist, educator; born Leningrad, Russia, August 5, 1906; son of Wassily and Eugenia (Bekker) L.; married Estelle Helena Marks, December 25, 1932; 1 child, Svetlana Eugenia Alpers. Student, University Leningrad, 1921-25; graduate Learned Economist; Doctor of Philosophy, University Berlin, 1928; Doctor of Philosophy honoris causa, University Bruxelles, Belgium, 1962, University York, England, 1967, University Louvain, 1971, University Paris, 1972, University Pennsylvania, 1976, University Lancaster, England, 1976; Doctor honoris causa, Adelphi College, 1988; Doctor of Humane Letters (honorary), Rensselaer Polytechnic Institute, 1988; Doctor honoris causa, University Cordoba, 1990. Research economist Institute Weltwirtschaft University Kiel, Germany, 1927-28, 30; economic adviser to Chinese government Nanking, 1929; with National Bureau Economic Research, New York City, 1931; instructor economics Harvard University, Cambridge, Massachusetts, 1932-33; assistant professor Harvard University, Cambridge, 1933-39, associate professor, 1939-46, professor, 1946-75, director economic project, 1948-72, Henry Lee professor economics, 1953-75; professor economics New York University, 1975—, university professor, 1983—, founder Institute Economic Analysis, 1978-85, member research staff, 1986; consultant Department Labor, 1941-47, Office of Strategic Services, 1943-45, United Nations, 1961-62, Department Commerce, 1966-82, Environmental Protection Agency, 1975-80 , United Nations, 1980—. Author: The Structure of the American Economy, 1919-29, 2d edition, 1976, Studies in the Structure of the American Economy, 1953, 2d edition, 1977, Input-Output Economics, 1966, 2d edition, 1986, Collected Essays, 1966, Theories, Facts and Policies, 1977, The Future of the World Economy, 1977, (with Faye Duchin) The Future Impact of Automation on Workers, 1986; Contributor articles to sci. journals and periodicals United States and abroad. Member Commission to Study Organization of Peace, 1978; trustee North Carolina School Sci. and Math., 1978; member issues committee Progressive Alliance, 1979; member Committee for National Security, 1980. Decorated officer Order Cherubim University Pisa, 1953, Legion of Honor (France), 1967, Order of Rising Sun (Japan), 1984, French Order of Arts and Letters, Commdr., 1985; recipient Bernhard-Harms prize econs. Federal Republic Germany, 1970, Nobel prize in econs., 1973; Guggenheim fellow, 1940, 50. Fellow Society Fellows Harvard (senior fellow, chairman 1964-75), Econometric Society, Royal Statistical Association (hon.),

Institute de France (corr.); member National Academy of Sciences, American Association for the Advancement of Science, Am. Philosophical Society, International Statistical Institute, Am. Econ. Association, Am. Statistical Association, Royal Econ. Society, Japan Econ. Research Center (hon.), Brit. Acad. (corr.), French Acad. Sciences (corr.), Royal Irish Acad. (hon.), Brit. Association Advancement Sci. (president Sect. F 1976), Union of Soviet Socialist Republics Acad. Sciences (foreign), Society of the Optimate Italian Cultural Isnt., Century Club. Member Greek Orthodox Church. Office: NYU Institute Econ Analysis 269 Mercer St Room 203 New York New York 10003

LERNER, ALFRED, real estate and financial executive; born New York City, May 8, 1933; son of Abraham and Clara (Abrahmson) L.; married Norma Wokloff, August 7, 1955; children: Nancy Faith, Randolph David. Bachelor of Arts, Columbia University, 1965. Chairman board, chief executive officer Multi-Amp Corp., Dallas, 1970-80, Realty Refund Trust, Cleveland, 1971-90; president, chief executive officer Refund Advisers, Incorporated, 1971—, Town & Country Management Corp., 1979—; partner TC Companies, Baltimore; chairman, director Equitable Bancorp., Baltimore, 1981-90, Progressive Corp., Cleveland, 1988—; board director WNC Corp, Baltimore. Chairman board visitors Columbia College 1st lieutenant United States Marine Corps Reserve, 1955-57. Member Young President Organization. Jewish. Clubs: Beechmont (Cleveland), Commerce (Cleveland); Harmonie (New York City). Home: 19000 S Park Boulevard Shaker Heights Ohio 44122 Office: 1385 Eaton Center Cleveland Ohio 44114

LESER, LAWRENCE A., broadcasting company executive; born Cincinnati, 1935; married. Bachelor of Science, Xavier University, 1957. With Haskins & Sells, 1957-68; with Scripps Howard, Cincinnati, 1968—, former secretary, treasurer, former vice president fin., director corp. devel., now president, chief executive officer, also board of directors; member national adv. board Chemical Bank; board of directors Newspaper Advertising Bureau, Union Central Life Insurance Company, Heekin Can. Incorporated. Office: Scripps Howard 1100 Central Trust Tower Cincinnati Ohio 45202

LEVENSON, HARVEY STUART, manufacturing company executive; born New York City, May 1, 1940; son of Abraham and Lucile (Lichtenstein) L.; married Merrilee Borenstein, August 28, 1960; children: Lee Alan, Gary Scott. Bachelor of Arts, Drake University, 1962, Juris Doctor, 1963; Master of Laws, Georgetown University, 1966. Bar: Iowa 1963, New York 1964, Connecticut 1968. Attorney Internal Revenue Service, Washington, 1964-68; associate Murtha, Cullina, Richter & Pinney, Hartford, Connecticut, 1968-69; partner Murtha, Cullina, Richter & Pinney, Hartford, 1970-82; senior vice president, chief fin. officer Kaman Corp., Bloomfield, Connecticut, 1982-90; president, chief operating officer Kaman Corp., Bloomfield, 1990—, board of directors; lecturer University Connecticut Law School, Hartford, 1972-76; board of directors Natural Gas Corp., Hartford Despatch; adv. board of directors Connecticut National Bank;

corporator St. Francis Hospital, Hartford Hospital, Institute of Living. Co-author: Depreciation & The Investment Tax Credit, 1983; contributor various articles on taxation to professional journals. Clubs: University (Hartford, sec. 1981-83); Hartford Golf (West Hartford).

LEVIT, MILTON, grocery supply company executive; born 1924; married. Graduate, University Texas, 1946. With Grocers Supply Company Incorporated, Houston, 1946—, vice president, 1947-75, president, 1975—, also chairman board, director. Served with United States Navy. Office: Grocers Supply Company Incorporated 3131 E Holcombe Boulevard Houston Texas 77021

LEVY, IRVIN L., diversified company executive; born Dallas, 1929. Bachelor of Business Administration, Southern Methodist University, 1950. With NCH Corp. (formerly National Chemsearch Corp.), Irving, Texas, 1950—, now president, also board of directors. Office: NCH Corp 2727 Chemsearch Boulevard Irving Texas 75062 also: Dallas Mus Art 1717 N Harwood Dallas Texas 75201

LEVY, JOHN FELDBERG, retail executive; born Newton, Massachusetts, January 20, 1947; son of Milton and Shirley (Feldberg) L.; married Gail Rothenberg, June 9, 1974; children—Sara, Scott. Bachelor of Arts, Trinity College, Hartford, Connecticut, 1969; Master of Business Administration, Harvard University, 1973. With Zayre Corp., Natick, Massachusetts, 1973—; div. merchandise manager Zayre Corp., Framingham, Massachusetts, 1973-78, senior vice president, general merchandise manager, 1982-85, executive vice president, general merchandise manager, 1985-86, senior executive vice president, 1986, corp. executive vice president, group executive wholesale divs., 1986-89; president Waban, Incorporated (spin-off wholesale div. Zayre Corp.), 1989—; director sales operations Hit or Miss div. Zayre Stores, Stoughton, Massachusetts, 1978-80, general merchandise manager Hit or Miss, 1980-82. Home: 200 Kent Road Waban Massachusetts 02168 Office: Waban Incorporated 1 Mercer Road Natick Massachusetts 01760

LEVY, LESTER A., sanitation company executive; born Dallas, 1922; married. Graduate in law, University Texas, 1945. With NCH Corp. (formerly National Chemsearch Corp.), Irving, Texas, 1946—, now chairman, also board of directors. Office: NCH Corp 2727 Chemsearch Boulevard Irving Texas 75062

LEWIS, DREW, diversified corporation executive. Bachelor of Science, Haverford College, 1953; Master of Business Administration, Harvard University, 1955; postgraduate, Massachusetts Institute Tech, 1968. With Henkels & McCoy Incorporated, 1955-60; vice president, director sales marketing Am. Olean Tile Incorporated, 1960-69; assistant to chairman board, vice president National Gypsum Company, 1969; chairman board of directors, president, chief executive officer Simplex Wire & Cable Company, 1960-72; president, chief executive officer Snelling & Snelling, 1970-74; federal court appointed trust Reading Company, 1971-81; principal Lewis & Associates, 1974-81; secretary United States Department Transportation, 1981-83; chairman board of directors, chief executive officer Warner Amex Cable Communications

Incorporated, 1983-86; chairman board of directors, chief executive officer, director Union Pacific Railroad Company, 1986; president chief operating officer Union Pacifc Corp., 1986—, chairman board of directors, president, chief executive officer, 1987, chairman executive committee, director, 1988. Office: Union Pacific Corp 8th & Eaton Aves Bethlehem Pennsylvania 18018

LEWIS, JOHN CLARK, JR., manufacturing company executive; born Livingston, Montana, October 15, 1935; son of John Clark and Louise A. (Anderson) L.; married Carolyn Jean Keesling, September 4, 1960; children: Robert, Anne, James. Bachelor of Science, Fresno (California) State University, 1957. With Service Bureau Corp., El Segundo, California, 1960-70, Computer Sciences Corp., 1970; with Xerox Corp., El Segundo, 1970-77, president business systems div., 1977; president Amdahl Corp., Sunnyvale, California, 1983-87, chief executive officer, 1983—, chairman, 1987—. Served with United States Naval Reserve, 1957-60. Roman Catholic. Office: Amdahl Corp 1250 E Arques Avenue Sunnyvale California 94088

LEWIS, PETER BENJAMIN, insurance company executive; born Cleveland, November 11, 1933; son of Joseph M. and Helen (Rosenfeld) L.; married, June 19, 1955; children: Ivy, Jonathan, Adam. Bachelor of Arts, Princeton University, 1955. With Progressive Insurance Companies, 1955—; president chief. executive officer Progressive Casualty Insurance Company, The Progressive Corp., Ohio; president chief. executive officer Mayfield Village, 1965-79, chairman board chief executive officer, 1979—; chairman, chief executive officer Progressive Corp., Ohio, 1979-88. Trustee Greater Cleveland Growth Association, Cleveland Center for Contemporary Art, Hillcrest Hospital, 1977-78. Member Chief Executive Officers Association, Society Chartered Property and Casualty Underwriter (president Cleveland chapter), World Business Council. Clubs: Ceve. Racquet, Oakwood, Union. Office: The Prog Corp 6000 Parkland Boulevard Mayfield Heights Ohio 44124

LICHTENBERGER, HORST WILLIAM, chemical company executive; born Yugoslavia, November 5, 1935; came to United States, 1950, naturalized, 1955; son of Andrew W. and Hella L.; married Patricia Ann Thomas, June 15, 1957; children: Erich, Lisa. Bachelor of Arts, University Iowa, 1957, Bachelor of Science in Chemical Engineering, 1959; Master of Business Administration, State University of New York, Buffalo, 1962. With Union Carbide Corp., 1959—; business manager Union Carbide Corp., New York City, 1972-75; vice president, general manager Linde div. Union Carbide Corp., Geneva, 1975-80; vice president marketing Union Carbide Corp., New York City, 1980-82; vice president, general manager gas products Union Carbide Corp., 1982-85, president Solvents and Coatings div., 1985—, president Chemicals and Plastics group, 1986—, president, chief operating officer, 1990—. Member Iowa National Guard, 1954-62. Member Am. Iron and Steel Institute, Chemical Manufacturing Association, Society of Chemical Industry. Republican. Patentee storage cryogenic fluids. Office: Union Carbide Corp 39 Old

Ridgebury Road Danbury Connecticut 06817

LIEDTKE, JOHN HUGH, petroleum company executive; born Tulsa, February 10, 1922; married Betty Lyn; children: Karen, Kristin, John Hugh, Blake, Kathryn. Bachelor of Arts, Amherst College, 1942; postgraduate, Harvard Graduate School, Business Administration, 1943; Bachelor of Laws, University Texas, 1947. President Zapata Petroleum Corp., 1953-62; president, chief executive officer Pennzoil Company, Houston, 1962-68, chairman, 1968—, also board of directors. Trustee Kinkaid School, Houston, Baylor College Medicine, United States Naval Acad. Foundation; council overseers Jesse H. Jones Grad. School Administration Rice U. Served to lieutenant United States Navy, 1942-45. Member Texas Mid-Continent Oil and Gas Association (director), Am. Petroleum Institute (director), National Petroleum Council (director), National Petroleum Refiners Association (board directors), Ind. Petroleum Association Am. (board directors), Penn Grade Association (board directors), Houston Chamber of Commerce (director), Beta Theta Pi, Phi Alpha Delta. Clubs: Houston Country, Ramada, Petroleum; Rolling Rock (Ligonier, Pennsylvania); Racquet (Midland, Texas); Calgary (Alberta, Can.). Office: Pennzoil Company Post Office Box 2967 Houston Texas 77252

LILLIE, JOHN MITCHELL, transportation company executive; born Chicago, February 2, 1937; son of Walter Theodore and Mary Ann (Hatch) L.; married Daryl Lee Harvey, August 23, 1987; children: Alissa Ann, Theodore Perry. Bachelor of Science, Stanford University, 1959, Master of Science, Master of Business Administration, 1962-64. Various positions including director systems devel., also assistant to president Boise Cascade Corp., 1964-68; vice president, chief financial officer Arcata National Corp., Menlo Park, California, 1968-70; executive vice president, chief operating officer Arcata National Corp., 1970-72; president, chief executive officer Leslie Salt Company, Newark, California, 1972-79; executive vice president Lucky Stores Incorporated, Dublin, California, 1979-81, president, 1981-86, chairman, chief executive officer, 1986-89; general partner Sequoia Associates, Menlo Park, California, 1989-90; president, chief operating officer Am. President Companies, Limited, Oakland, California, 1990—. Trustee Stanford (California) U., 1988—; board of directors Am. President Company. Member Beta Theta Pi, Tau Beta Pi. Office: Am President Cos 1111 Broadway Oakland California 94607

LILLIS, WILLIAM G., banking executive; born Ann Arbor, Michigan, October 13, 1930; son of William J. and Selina M. (Moss) L.; married Nancy Wilcox, June 26, 1954; children—Susan, Deborah, Jennifer. Bachelor Civil Engineering, Rensselaer Polytechnic Institute, 1952. Civil engineer Pennsylvania Railroad, New York City, 1954-56; assistant operating superintendent Bush Terminal Building Company, Brooklyn, 1956-66; appraiser, loan officer Metropolitan Life Insurance Company, New York City, 1966-70; executive vice president Helmsley Enterprises, New York City, 1970-77; executive vice president Empire Savings Bank, New York City, 1977-79, president, chief executive officer, 1979-81; president, chief operating officer Am. Savings Bank, New York City, 1981—, also board of directors, 1981-89, president, chief executive officer, 1989—; trustee, director Retirement System for Savings Institutions; chairman Thrift Industry, Group IV/V Savings Bank Association of New York State. Board of directors Community Preservation Corp., 1981—, March of Dimes Teamwalk, New York City, 1983—. Served with United States Naval Reserve, 1952-54. Fellow National Society Real Estate Education Fin. (cert. real estate financier); member National Institute Real Estate Financing (hon.), National Association Real Estate Appraisers (cert.), National Association Rev. Appraiser and Mortgage Underwriters (senior), Real Estate Board New York, Realty Foundation New York (board directors), Urban Land Institute, National Council Savings Institutions, Savings Bank Association (committee on long range planning, svcs. education committee), Savings Banks Association New York State. Republican. Clubs: New York Athletic (New York City); Leetes Island Assoc. (Guilford, Connecticut). Avocations: running; tennis. Home: Stamford Connecticut Office: Am Savings Bank 99 Church St White Plains New York 10601

LINDIG, BILL M., food distribution company executive; born 1936; married. Attended, University Texas. With Sysco Corp., Houston, 1969—, executive vice president, from 1984, chief operating officer, 1984—, now also president, director. Office: Sysco Corp 1390 Enclave Parkway Houston Texas 77077

LINDLEY, JAMES GUNN, bank executive; born Greensboro, North Carolina, June 13, 1931; son of Paul Cameron and Helen Marie (Gunn) L.; married Jane Kennedy, December 3, 1954; children: James Gunn, Patricia Van, Julia Anne. Bachelor of Science in Business Administration, University North Carolina, 1953; Master of Business Administration in Fin., New York University, 1960. Senior vice president Manufacturers Hanover Trust Company, New York City, 1953-75; president, chief executive officer Bankshares of North Carolina and Bank of North Carolina, N.A., Raleigh, 1975-79; chief executive officer South Carolina National Bank, Columbia, 1979—; president South Carolina National Bank, 1979—, now also chairman; chairman, chief executive officer South Carolina National Bank, Columbia, 1981—; president South Carolina National Corp., from 1979. Served to captain United States Naval Reserve, 1953-57. Office: South Carolina National Corp 1426 Main St Columbia South Carolina 29226

LINDNER, CARL HENRY, financial holding company executive; born Dayton, Ohio, April 22, 1919; son of Carl Henry and Clara (Serrer) L.; married Edith Bailey, December 31, 1953; children: Carl Henry III, Stephen Craig, Keith Edward. Cofounder United Dairy Farmers, 1940; president Am. Fin. Corp., Cincinnati, 1959-84, chairman, 1959—, chief executive officer, 1984—; chairman, chief executive officer, chairman executive committee United Brands Company (now Chiquita Brands International Incorporated), New York City, 1984—; chairman, chief executive officer Penn Central Corp., Cincinnati, 1983—, also board of directors; chairman, chief executive officer Great Am. Communications

Company, Cincinnati, 1987—; board of directors Mission Insurance. board advs. Business Administration College, U. Cincinnati. Republican. Baptist. also: Charter Company 1 Charter Plaza Jacksonville Florida 32202

LINDSAY, JAMES WILEY, agricultural company executive; born Des Moines, September 13, 1934; son of Worthington U. Lindsay and Marsha E. (Wiley) Asher; married Shirley L. Shutt, July 2, 1953 (divorced May 1985); children: Elizabeth Lindsay Foster, James W. II, Jennifer, Lindsay; married Jean M. Baumann, August 2, 1986; 1 child, Amanda Marie. Student, Drake University, 1954-60. Manager operations Archer, Daniels, Midland, Fredonia, Kansas, 1968-70, Lincoln, Nebraska, 1970-72; manager export Archer, Daniels, Midland, Decatur, Illinois, 1972-74; vice president western region Archer, Daniels, Midland, Lincoln, 1974-76; vice president operations Archer, Daniels, Midland, Cedar Rapids, Iowa, 1979-80; operations manager Archer, Daniels, Midland, Decatur, 1980-83; president Brazil operations T.Vice President, Incorporated, Campinas, Brazil, 1976-79; chief executive officer AG Processing Incorporated, Omaha, 1983—; board of directors ABC Insurance, Des Moines, 1983—, National Council Farm Cooperatives, Washington, 1983—. Member National Soybean Processors Association (chairman 1987-91), Jaycees (president Fredonia chapter 1963-64, board directors Des Moines chapter 1960). Republican. Roman Catholic. Lodge: Masons. Avocations: singing, guitar, acting. Office: AG Processing Incorporated 11717 Burt St Omaha NE 68154

LIPPINCOTT, PHILIP EDWARD, paper products company executive; born Camden, New Jersey, November 28, 1935; son of J. Edward and Marjorie Nix (Spooner) L.; married Naomi Catherine Prindle, August 22, 1959; children: Grant, Kevin, Kerry. Bachelor of Arts, Dartmouth College, 1957; Master of Business Administration with distinction, Michigan State University, 1964. With Scott Paper Company, Philadelphia, 1959—, staff vice president corp. planning, 1971, div. vice president, consumer products marketing, 1971-72, corp. vice president, marketing, 1972-75, senior vice president, marketing, 1975-77, vice president, group executive packaged products div., 1977, director, 1978, chief operating officer, 1980-82, president, 1980—, chief executive officer, 1982—, chairman, 1983; board of directors Campbell Soup Company, Exxon Corp., The Business Council; trustee Penn Mutual Life Insurance Company. Board overseers Wharton School U. Pennsylvania, Dartmouth Institute; board of directors Fox Chase Cancer Center, Philadelphia Captain United States Army, 1957-59. Member Am. Paper Institute (director, executive committee), Paper Distbn. Council, Grocery Manufacturers Association (board directors), Social Club, Riverton Country Club, Kappa Kappa Kappa, Pi Sigma Epsilon, Beta Gamma Sigma. Member Society of Friends. Office: Scott Paper Company Scott Plaza Philadelphia Pennsylvania 19113

LIUZZI, ROBERT C., chemical company executive; born Boston, 1944; married. Bachelor of Arts, College of Holy Cross, 1965; Bachelor of Laws, University Virginia, 1968. Vice president, general counsel United States Fin., Incorporated, 1969-74; with CF Industries, Long Grove, Illinois, 1975—; executive vice president, chief fin. officer CF Industries, Lake Zurich, Illinois, 1977-80, executive vice president, operating officer, 1980-84, president, chief executive officer, 1985—; chairman board of directors Agri Trans Corp.; chairman ad hoc committee Domestic Nitrogen Products, Washington; board of directors Can. Fertilizers Limited, The Fertilzer Institute, National Council Farmer Cooperatives, Florida Phosphate Council, Tampa, Florida, Potash and Phosphate Institute; co-chairman Petrochem. Trade Group, Washington. Member Northwestern U. Associates, Evanston. Office: CF Industries Incorporated One Salem Lake Dr Long Grove Illinois 60047

LLEWELLYN, JOHN SCHOFIELD, JR., food company executive; born Amsterdam, New York, January 10, 1935; son of John S. and Dorothea (Breedon) L.; married Mary Martha Pallotta, June 9, 1962; children: Mary M., John S. III, Robert J., James P., Timothy J. Bachelor of Arts, Holy Cross College, 1956; Master of Business Administration, Harvard University, 1961. With marketing General Foods Corp., White Plains, New York, 1961-69, Sunshine Biscuit div. Am. Brands, New York City, 1973-77; executive vice president Morton Frozen Foods div. International Telephone & Telegraph Corporation Continental Baking Company, Charlottesville, Virginia, 1977-79; general manager Continental Kitchens International Telephone & Telegraph Corporation Continental Baking Company, Rye, 1980-81; senior vice president Ocean Spray Cranberries Incorporated, Plymouth, Massachusetts, 1982-86; executive vice president, chief operating officer Ocean Spray Cranberries Incorporated, Plymouth, 1986-87, president, chief executive officer, 1988—. Trustee Derby Acad., Hingham, Massachusetts, 1984—; board of directors Massachusetts Environmental Trust, 1991—. Served to captain United States Marine Corps, 1957-63. Member National Food Processors Association (board directors, executive committee). Roman Catholic. Home: Steamboat Lane Hingham Massachusetts 02043 Office: Ocean Spray Cranberries Incorporated 1 Ocean Spray Dr Lakeville-Middleboro Massachusetts 02349

LOBBIA, JOHN E., utility company executive; born 1941; married. Bachelor of Science in Electrical Engineering, University Detroit, 1964. With Detroit Edison Company, 1964—, assistant primary service engineer sales department, 1964-68, acting assistant district manager, director service planning, 1969-72, project manager construction, 1972-74, director generation construction department, 1974-75, manager Ann Arbor div., 1975-76, assistant manager Detroit div., 1976-78, manager Oakland div., 1978-80, assistant vice chairman, 1980-81, assistant vice president, manager fuel support, 1981-82, vice president fin. services, 1982-87, executive vice president, 1987-88, president, chief operating officer, 1988—, also chairman, chief executive officer, 1990—, also board of directors. Office: Detroit Edison Company 2000 2nd Avenue Detroit Michigan 48226

LOCKE, CHARLES STANLEY, manufacturing company executive, director; born Laurel, Mississippi,

March 5, 1929; son of Richard C. and Florence (Parker) L.; married NoraLou Fulkerson, March 15, 1952; children: Cathy, Stanley, Lauren, Pamela. Bachelor of Business Administration, University Mississippi, 1952, Master of Science in Accounting, 1955. With audit staff Price Waterhouse & Company, New Orleans, 1955-58; with Commercial Analysis for Converting div. Westvaco, Incorporated, 1958-64; controller A.East Staley Manufacturing Company, 1964-69; vice president fin., director, member executive committee Brown Company, Pasadena, California, 1969-73; senior vice president, member executive committee Allen Group Incorporated, Melville, New York, 1973-75; vice president fin., director Morton-Norwich, Chicago, 1975-80, president, chief operating officer, director, March 1980, president, chief executive officer, director, Apr. 1980, president, chief executive officer, chairman board, Aug. 1980; chairman board, chief executive officer, director Morton Thiokol, Incorporated (named changed 1982), Chicago, 1981-83, chairman board, chief executive officer, president, director, 1983-84, chairman board, chief executive officer, director, from 1984, director, 1989; chairman, chief executive officer, director Morton International (spin off Morton Thiokol 1989), 1989—; board of directors Thiokol Corp., Avon Products, Incorporated, First Chicago Corp., First National Bank Chicago, NICOR, Incorporated, Northern Illinois Gas Corp. Vice chairman board trustees Mus. Sci. and Industry, Chicago; member The Chicago Committee; board of directors The Lyric Opera, Chicago With United States Army, 1952-54. Member Conference Board, Mid-Am. Committee, Econ. Club, Chicago Club, Rm. 100 Club, Commercial Club, Exec.'s Club (adv. board), Mid-Am. Club, Tower Club, Sky Club, Sunset Ridge Country Club, Old Elm Country Club, Shoreacres Country Club, Beta Alpha Psi. Home: 1504 N Waukegan Road Lake Forest Illinois 60045 Office: Morton International Incorporated 100 N Riverside Plaza Chicago Illinois 60606-1596

LORCH, ERNEST HENRY, lawyer; born Frankfurt, Germany, October 11, 1932; came to United States, 1940; son of Alexander and Kate (Freundt) L. Bachelor of Arts, Middlebury College, 1954; Juris Doctor, University Virginia, 1957; Juris Doctor (honorary), Fairfield University, 1987. Bar: New York 1958. Associate Olwine, Connelly, Chase, O'Donnell & Weyler, New York City, 1957-65, partner, 1965-84; president, chief operating officer Dyson-Kissner-Moran Corp., New York City, 1984-90, president, chief executive officer, 1990—; board of directors Constar International Incorporated, Chattanooga, Envirosource, Stamford, Connecticut; chairman board of directors Varlen Corp., Chicago; director various corp. affiliates. Director various inner city athletic assns, New York City, 1959—, The DYSM Foundation, New York City, 1985—; trustee, director The Riverside Church, New York City, 1961—. Member American Bar Association, New York State Bar Association. Office: Dyson-Kissner-Moran Corp 230 Park Avenue New York New York 10169

LORENZO, FRANCISCO A., airline companies executive; born New York City, May 19, 1940; son of Olegario and Ana (Mateos) L.; married Sharon

Neill Murray, October 14, 1972. Bachelor of Arts, Columbia University, 1961; Master of Business Administration, Harvard University, 1963. Fin. analyst Trans World Airlines, 1963-65; manager fin. analysis Eastern Airlines, 1965-66; founder, chairman board Lorenzo, Carney & Company (fin. advisers), New York City, from 1966; chairman board Jet Capital Corp. (fin. advisers), Houston, from 1969; president Texas International Airlines, Incorporated, Houston, 1972-80, chairman executive committee, 1980-90; president Texas Air Corp., 1980-85, chairman, chief executive officer, 1986-90; chairman New York Airlines, 1980-87, Continental Airlines Corp., Houston, 1982-88, Eastern Air Lines, Incorporated (subsidiary Texas Air Corp.), Miami, 1987-90; chairman board of directors Eastern Airlines. Served with Army of the United States, 1963.

LOUCKS, VERNON R., JR., health care products and services company executive; born Evanston, Illinois, October 24, 1934; son of Vernon Reece and Sue (Burton) L.; married Linda Kay Olson, May 12, 1972; 6 children. Bachelor of Arts in History, Yale University, 1957; Master of Business Administration, Harvard University, 1963. Senior management consultant George Fry & Associates, Chicago, 1963-65; with Baxter Travenol Laboratories, Incorporated (now Baxter International Incorporated), Deerfield, Illinois, 1966—, executive vice president, 1976, also board of directors, president, chief operating officer, 1980, chief executive officer, chairman, 1987—; director Dun & Bradstreet Corp., Emerson Electric Company, Quaker Oats Company, Anheuser-Busch Companies. Trustee Rush-Presbyn.-St. Lukes Medical Center; associate Northwestern U.; successor trustee Yale Corp.; chairman Yale Devel. Board Served to 1st lieutenant United States Marine Corps, 1957-60. Recipient Citizen Fellowship award Chicago Institute Medicine, 1982, National Health Care award B'nai Brith Youth Services, 1986, William McCormick Blair award Yale University, 1989, Semper Fidelis award USMC, 1989; named 1983's Outstanding Executive Officer in the health-care industry Financial World; elected to Chgo.'s Business Hall of Fame, Junior Achievement, 1987. Member Health Industry Manufacturers Association (chairman 1983), Business Roundtable (conference board, member policy committee), Business Council. Clubs: Chicago Commonwealth, Commercial, Mid-America; Links (New York City). Office: Baxter International Incorporated 1 Baxter Parkway Deerfield Illinois 60015

LOVE, HOWARD MCCLINTIC, metal products executive; born Pittsburgh, April 5, 1930; son of George Hutchinson and Margaret (McClintic) L.; married Jane Vaughn, June 9, 1956; children: Marion Perkins, George Hutchinson II, Howard McClintic Jr., Jane Vaughn, Victoria Elizabeth. Bachelor of Arts, Colgate University, 1952; Master of Business Administration, Harvard University, 1956. Management trainee Great Lakes Steel div. National Steel Corp., Ecorse, Michigan, 1956-58, operating management, 1958-63; assistant general manager sales Midwest Steel div., 1963-64; assistant general manager sales Great Lakes Steel div., 1964-65, assistant to president,

1965-66; president Midwest Steel div., 1966—; president Granite City (Illinois) Steel div., 1972—, chief executive officer, 1980—; also director Granite City (Illinois) Steel div., Michigan, member executive committee; chairman board National Intergroup, Incorporated, National Steel Corp., 1981—; chairman board National Steel Corp., 1974—; director Monsanto Company, St. Louis, Hamilton Oil Corp., Denver, Comsat, Washington, University Pittsburgh. President Allegheny Conference Community Devel.; board of directors United Way Allegheny County. With United States Air Force, 1952-54. Member Am. Iron and Steel Institute (executive committee, director), Business Council, Business Roundtable, National Board Smithsonian Assocs., Masons, Beta Theta Pi. Republican. Episcopalian. Office: National Intergroup Incorporated 20 Stanwix St Pittsburgh Pennsylvania 15222

LOYND, RICHARD BIRKETT, consumer products company executive; born Norristown, Pennsylvania, December 1, 1927; son of James B. and Elizabeth (Geigus) L.; married Jacqueline Ann Seubert, February 3, 1951; children: Constance, John, Cynthia, William, James, Michael. Bachelor of Science in Electrical Engineering, Cornell University, 1950. Sales engineer Lincoln Electric Company, Cleveland, 1950-55; with Emerson Electric Company, St. Louis, 1955-68; president Builder Products div. Emerson Electric Company, 1965-68, vice president Electronics and Space div., 1961-65; vice president operations Gould, Incorporated, Chicago, 1968-71; executive vice president Eltra Corp., New York City, 1971-74; president Eltra Corp., 1974-81; chairman Converse, Incorporated, 1982-88; chairman, chief executive officer Interco Incorporated, St. Louis, 1989—. Home: 19 Randall Dr Short Hills New Jersey 07078 Office: Interco Incorporated 101 S Hanley Road Saint Louis Missouri 63105

LUCIANO, ROBERT PETER, pharmaceutical company executive; born New York City, October 9, 1933; son of Peter and Jennie (Mastro) L.; married Barbara Ann Schiavone, June 21, 1953; children: Susan Ann, Richard Peter. Bachelor of Business Administration, City College of New York, 1954; Juris Doctor, University Michigan, 1958. Senior tax associate Royall Koegel & Rogers (now Rogers & Wells), New York City, 1958-66; attorney CIBA Corp., Summit, New Jersey, 1966-68, assistant secretary, 1968-70; assistant general counsel, director pub. affairs CIBA Pharmaceutical Company, Summit, 1970-71, vice president marketing, 1973-75; vice president planning and administration pharmaceutical div. CIBA-GEIGY Corp., Summit, 1971-73, president pharmaceutical div., 1975-77; president Lederle Laboratories div. Am. Cyanamid Company, Pearl River, New York, 1977-78; senior vice president administration Schering-Plough Corp., Kenilworth, New Jersey, 1978-79, executive vice president pharmaceutical operations, 1979-80, president, chief operating officer, 1980-82, president, chief executive officer, 1982-84, chairman board, president, chief executive officer, 1984-86, chairman board, chief executive officer, 1986—; board of directors C.R. Bard Incorporated, Murray Hill, New Jersey, Bank of New York Company Incorporated,

New York City. Assistant editor: University Michigan Law Rev., 1957-58. Served with United States Army, 1954-56. Member American Bar Association, New York Bar Association, National Association Manufacturers (board directors 1982—), New Jersey State Chamber of Commerce (board directors 1986—). Republican. Clubs: Union League, Sky, Econ. (New York City). Office: Schering-Plough Corp 1 Giralda Farms Madison New Jersey 07940-1000

LUDINGTON, JOHN SAMUEL, manufacturing company executive; born Detroit, May 7, 1928; son of Samuel and Fredda (Holden) L.; married Dorothy Lamson, February 14, 1953; children: Thomas, Laura, Ann. Bachelor of Science in Econs, Albion (Michigan) College, 1951, Doctor of Economics (honorary), 1989; Doctor of Laws (honorary), Saginaw Valley State College; DBA (honorary), South Dakota School Mines and Tech.; Doctor of Humanities (honorary), Northwood Institute; Doctor of Philosophy in Economics (honorary), Albion College. With Dow Corning Corp., Midland, Michigan, chairman; director Comerica Bank-Midland. Trustee Albion College, former chairman board; trustee Midland Community Center, Strosacker Foundation Served with Army of the United States. Methodist. Office: Dow Corning Corp 220 W Salzburg Road Box 994 Midland Michigan 48686

LUECKE, JOSEPH E., insurance company executive; born 1927; married. Bachelor of Arts, La Salle College, 1950. With Lumbermen's Mutual Casualty Company, 1951—, chairman, chief executive officer, director, 1981—; with Kemper Corp., 1951—; chairman, chief executive officer Kemper Corp., Long Grove, Illinois, 1979-83; chairman, president, chief executive officer Kemper Corp., Long Grove, 1983-86, chairman board of directors, president, chief executive officer, 1986—; chairman, chief executive officer Am. Motorists Insurance Company, Long Grove, also board of directors; board of directors Kemper Fin. Services Incorporated, Chicago, Kemper International Corp., Chicago, Kemper Reinsurance Company, Long Grove. Office: Kemper Group Route 22 Long Grove Illinois 60049

LUELLEN, CHARLES J., oil company executive; born Greenville, South Carolina, October 18, 1929; son of John B. and Dorothy C. (Bell) L.; married Jo S. Riddle, July 11, 1953; children: Margaret A., Nancy J. Bachelor of Science, Ind. University, 1952. Sales representative Ashland Oil, Incorporated, Kentucky, 1952-70, vice president sales, 1970-72, group vice president sales, 1972-80, president, chief operating officer, 1986—, also director; president Ashland Petroleum Company, 1980-86; board of directors, budget adv. committee Am. Petroleum Institute, Washington, 1982—, Asphalt Institute, Washington, 1974-76; board of directors Ashland Coal, Incorporated, Huntington, West Virginia, Citizens Fidelity Corp., Louisville. Board of directors Kings Daughters, Hospital, Ashland, 1981—, Ashland area Young Men's Christian Association, 1980—, National Chamber Foundation, Washington, 1987; trustee Centre College, Danville, Kentucky, 1988, Joint Council on Economic Education, New York City. Member Ind. University Fellows, United States Chamber of Commerce (member energy & natural resources committee), Beta Gamma Sigma. Club: Bellefonte Country (Ashland); Pendennis (Louisville), 25 Yr. (Washington). Home: 4400 Oak Hollow Dr Ashland Kentucky 41101 Office: Ashland Oil Incorporated Post Office Box 391 Ashland Kentucky 41114 also: Ashland Oil Incorporated 1000 Ashland Dr Russell Kentucky 41169

LUERSSEN, FRANK WONSON, steel company executive; born Reading, Pennsylvania, August 14, 1927; son of George V. and Mary Ann (Swoyer) L.; married Joan M. Schlosser, June 17, 1950; children: Thomas, Mary Ellen, Catherine, Susan, Ann. Bachelor of Science in Physics, Pennsylvania, State University, 1950; MSMetE, Lehigh University, 1951; Doctor of Laws (honorary), Calumet College. Metallurgist research and devel. div. Inland Steel Company, East Chicago, Ind., 1952-54; manager various positions Inland Steel Company, 1954-64, manager research, 1964-68, vice president research, 1968-77, vice president steel manufacturing, 1977-78, president, 1978-85, chairman, 1983—; board of directors Continental Illinois Corp., Morton International, Incorporated. Contributor articles on steelmaking tech. to various publications. Trustee Calumet College, Whiting, Ind., 1972-80, Northwestern U., 1980—; vice president, board of directors Munster (Indiana) Medical Research Foundation, 1972-84; trustee, secretary, treasurer Munster School Board, 1957-66. Served with United States Naval Reserve, 1945-47. Named distinguished alumnus Pennsylvania State University. Fellow Am. Society Metals, National Acad. Engineering; member American Institute of Mining, Metallurgy and Petroleum Engineers (Distinguished life member, B.F. Fairless award), Am. Iron and Steel Institute. Home: 8226 Parkview Avenue Munster Indiana 46321 Office: Inland Steel Industries Incorporated 30 W Monroe St Chicago Illinois 60603

LUISO, ANTHONY, international food company executive; born Bari, Italy, January 6, 1944; son of John and Antonia (Giustino) L.; married Nancy Louise Bassett, June 26, 1976. Bachelor of Business Administration, Iona College, 1967; Master of Business Administration, University Chicago, 1982. Audit senior Arthur Andersen & Company, Chicago, 1966-71; supervisor auditing Beatrice Foods Company, Chicago, 1971-74, administrator assistant to executive vice president, 1974-75, vice president operations international div., dairy div., 1975-77, executive vice president international div., 1977-82, professor international div., 1982-83, chief operating officer international food group, 1984-86, president United States Food segment, from 1986; group vice president International Multifoods Corp., Minneapolis, until 1988, president, 1988—, chief operating officer, 1988-89, chairman, chief executive officer, 1989—; board of directors Black & Decker Company. Member adv. council U. Chicago Grad. School of Business Served with United States Army Reserve, 1968-74. Member American Institute of Certified Public Accountants. Republican. Roman Catholic. Clubs: University (Chicago), International (Chicago). Office: International Multifoods Corp Multifood Tower Box 2942 Minneapolis Minnesota 55402

LUKE, JOHN ANDERSON, paper company executive; born Tyrone, Pennsylvania, November 30, 1925; son of David Lincoln and Priscilla

Warren (Silver) L.; married Joy Carter, December 21, 1946; children: John Anderson, Hope S., Jane T., William H. Bachelor of Arts, Yale University, 1949. Personnel assistant Westvaco Corp., Charleston, South Carolina, 1949-51; personnel manager Westvaco Corp., 1951-53, assistant manager administration, 1953-55; mill manager Westvaco Corp., Luke, Maryland, 1955-60; manager fine papers div. Westvaco Corp., 1960-74; vice president Westvaco Corp., New York City, 1966-74, senior vice president, 1974-76, executive vice president, 1976-80, president, 1980-88, president, chief executive officer, 1988—; also director Westvaco Corp.; director Arkwright Insurance Company, Discount Corp. of New York, Clupak. Served with United States Army Air Force, 1943-45. Member National Association Manufacturers, New Canaan Country Club, Bedford Golf and Tennis Club, River Club. Office: Westvaco Corp 299 Park Avenue New York New York 10171

LUNDBERG, JOHN KESSANDER, bank executive; born Sterling, Colorado, August 15, 1934; son of Paul J.E. and Gladys (McCrery) L.; married Bonnie Jean Fraser, August 20, 1964; children: John Kessander, Christina. Bachelor of Arts, Harvard University, 1956; Bachelor of Laws, University Colorado, 1959. Bar: Colorado 1959, New York 1960. With firm Donovan, Leisure, Newton & Irvine, New York City, 1959-61; assistant counsel, then deputy superintendent and counsel New York State Banking Department, 1961-66, 1st deputy superintendent banks, 1966-68; executive vice president, trustee Am. Savings Bank, New York City, 1968-72; president, chief executive officer Am. Savings Bank, 1972-73, chairman board, president, chief executive officer, 1973-80, chairman board, 1989—; vice-chairman, chief fin. officer, director Crum & Forster, 1981-84, chairman, chief executive officer, 1984-85; private investor 1985-89. Presbyterian. Office: Harvard U Office of Treas Cambridge Massachusetts 02138 also: Am Savings Bank FSB 99 Church St White Plains New York 10601

LUNDEEN, ROBERT WEST, electronics company executive; born Astoria, Oregon, June 25, 1921; son of Arthur Robert and Margaret Florence (West) L.; married Betty Charles Anderson, December 26, 1942; children: John Walter, Peter Bruce, Nancy Patricia. Bachelor of Science, Oregon State University, 1942; postgraduate, Institute Meteorology, University Chicago, 1942-43. With Dow Chemical Company, 1946-87; director business devel. Dow Chemical International, Midland, Michigan, 1963-66; president Dow Chemical Pacific, Hong Kong, 1966-77, Dow Chemical Latin Am., from 1978; executive vice president Dow Chemical Company, 1978-82, chairman board, 1982-87, director, 1973-87; chairman Tektronix Incorporated, Beaverton, Oregon, 1987—. Chairman City Planning Commission, Concord, California, 1960-61; trustee Kettering Foundation, Dayton, Ohio, Monterey Institute International Studies, California, Oregon State U. Foundation, Corvallis, Orcas Island Library District, 1987—. Served with United States Army, 1942-46. Decorated Bronze Star. Member AICE, Am. Chemical Society. Republican. Clubs: Hong Kong, Royal Hong Kong Yacht;

Orcas Tennis, Orcas Island Yacht, Beach and Tennis Club (Pebble Beach, California). Office: Tektronix Incorporated 14150 Southwest Karl Braun Dr Beaverton Oregon 97077

LUPBERGER, EDWIN ADOLPH, utility executive; born Atlanta, June 5, 1936; son of Adolph and Esma L.; married Mary Jane McAllister Redmon, January 6, 1989; children by previous marriage: David Todd, Edward Townsend. Bachelor of Arts in Econs, Davidson (North Carolina) College, 1958; Master of Business Administration, Emory University, 1963. Assistant vice president Southern Company Services, Incorporated, Atlanta, 1963-69; vice president, treasurer Gulf Power Company, Pensacola, Florida, 1969-77; senior vice president fin. Indianapolis Power & Light Company, 1977-79; senior vice president, chief fin. officer Middle South Utilities, Incorporated, New Orleans, 1979-85; chairman, president Entergy Corp., New Orleans, 1985—. Served as ensign United States Navy, 1960. Member Edison Electric Institute. Presbyterian. Clubs: University, World Trade Ctr., Metropolitan.

LURTON, H. WILLIAM, retail executive; born Greenwich, Connecticut, September 18, 1929; son of William Pearl and Elizabeth (McDow) L.; married Susan Harvey, October 26, 1980; children: Scott, Carrie, Nancy, Jennifer. Bachelor of Arts, Principia College, 1951. Sales representative Jostens Incorporated, Minneapolis, 1955-61; yearbook sales and plant manager Jostens Incorporated, Visalia, California, 1961-66; general sales manager yearbook div. Jostens Incorporated, vice president, general manager yearbook div., 1969-70, corp. executive vice president, 1970-71, member executive committee, 1970-72, president, 1971-75, chief operating officer, 1971-72, chief executive officer, 1972—, chairman board, 1975—, also director; director Deluxe Check Printers, Pentair, Incorporated. Board of directors United States Chamber of Commerce, Minneapolis Young Men's Christian Association. Served with United States Marine Corps, 1951-53. Clubs: Wayzata (Minnesota) Country, Minneapolis. Home: 3135 Jamestown Road Long Lake Minnesota 55356 Office: Jostens Incorporated 5501 Norman Center Dr Minneapolis Minnesota 55437

LUTER, JOSEPH WILLIAMSON, III, meat packing and processing company executive; born Smithfield, Virginia, 1939; married. Bachelor of Business Administration, Wake Forest College, 1962. President Smithfield Packing Company, Arlington, Virginia, 1964-69, Bryce Mountain Resort Incorporated, 1969-75; with Smithfield Foods Incorporated, Arlington, 1975—, president, 1975-86, 89—, chief executive officer, 1975—, chairman, 1977—, also board of directors. Office: Smithfield Foods Incorporated 501 N Church St Highway 10 Box 447 Smithfield Virginia 23430

LUTZ, ROBERT ANTHONY, automotive company executive; born Zurich, Switzerland, February 12, 1932; came to United States, 1939; son of Robert H. and Marguerite (Schmid) L.; married Betty D., December 12, 1956 (divorced 1979); children: Jacqueline, Carolyn, Catherine, Alexandra; married Heide Marie Schmid, March 3, 1980. Bachelor of Science in Prodn. Management, University California, Berkeley, 1961, Master of Business

Administration in Marketing, 1962; Doctor of Laws, Boston University, 1985. Research associate, senior analyst IMEDE, Lausanne, Switzerland, 1962-63; senior analyst forward planning General Motors Corp., New York City, 1963-65; manager vehicle div. Paris, 1966-69; staff assistant, managing director Adam Opel, Russelsheim, Federal Republic of Germany, 1965-66, assistant manager domestic sales, 1969, director sales Vorstand, 1969-70; vice president Vorstand Bavarian Motor Works (Bayerische Motoren Werke), Munich, 1970-74; general manager Ford of Europe, Incorporated, Cologne, Federal Republic of Germany, 1974-76; vice president truck ops Brentwood, England, 1976-77, president, 1977-79, chairman, 1979-82, 84-86, also board of directors; executive vice president Ford International, Dearborn, Michigan, 1982-84; executive vice president Chrysler Motors Corp., Highland Park, Michigan, from 1986, now president; member European Adv. Council, Conference Board; board of directors parent company Chrysler Corp., Ford Motor Company, Dearborn, Ford Motor Company Limited, Brentwood. Adv. board School Business, U. California, Berkeley, 1979—. Served to captain United States Marine Corps, 1954-59, Okinawa, Japan, Korea. Named Alumnus of Year, School Business, University California, 1983; Kaiser Foundation grantee 1962. Member Atlantic Institute for International Affairs, United Nations Association (econ. policy council), Society Automotive Engineers. Republican. Avocations: skiing, motorcycling, bicycling. Office: Chrysler Motors Corp 12000 Chrysler Dr Post Office Box 1919 Highland Park Michigan 48288-1919

LUX, JOHN H., corporate executive; born Logansport, Indiana, February 3, 1918; son of Carl Harrison and Mary Emma (Dunn) L.; married Betty F. Passow, August 27, 1940; children—John Ernst, Courtney Rae; married Bernice Weitzel Brown, 1965; married Linda Merrill Brown, March 2, 1978; children—Julia Elizabeth, Jenifyr Claire. Bachelor of Science, Purdue University, 1939; Doctor of Philosophy, 1942. Assistant director research and devel. The Neville Company, 1943-46; vice president, consultant Atomic Basic Chemicals 1946-47; director research Witco Chemical Company, 1947-50; manager new product devel. General Electric Company, 1950-52; vice president Shea Chemical Company, 1952-55; president, director Haveg Industries, Incorporated, Wilmington, Del., 1955-66, Haveg Corp., Tourlux Management Corp. (Puerto Rico); chairman board Hemisphere Products Corp. (Puerto Rico), Reinhold Engineering & Plastics Company, Norwalk, California, Am. Super-Temperatures Wires Company; president Ametek, Incorporated, 1966-69, chairman board, chief executive officer, 1969-90, chairman board, 1990—. Member Am. Institute Chemical Engineers, Am. Chemical Society, Phi Lambda Upsilon. Club: Metropolitan. Office: Ametek Incorporated Post Office Box 8266 Rancho Santa Fe California 92067 also: 410 Park Avenue 21st Floor New York New York 10022 also: Ametek Incorporated Station Square 2 Paoli Pennsylvania 19301

LYNN, JAMES F., insurance executive. Vice president Liberty Mutual Insurance Company, Boston. Office:

Liberty Mut Ins Company 175 Berkeley St Boston Massachusetts 02117

LYNN, JAMES T., insurance company executive, lawyer; born Cleveland, February 27, 1927. Bachelor of Arts, Western Reserve University, 1948; Bachelor of Laws, Harvard University, 1951. Bar: Ohio 1951, District of Columbia 1977. General counsel United States Department Commerce, 1969-71, under secretary, 1971-73; secretary Department of Housing and Urban Development, 1973-75; director Office Management and Budget, 1975-77; assistant President United States, 1975-77; with Jones Day Reavis & Pogue, Washington, 1951-69, 77-84, partner, 1960-69, managing partner, 1977-84; with Aetna Life & Casualty Company, Hartford, Connecticut, 1984—, vice chairman, 1984—, chairman, chief executive officer, 1984—, also president, 1987-88, also board of directors. Case editor Harvard Law Rev., 1950-51. Served with United States Naval Reserve, 1945-46. Member Phi Beta Kappa. Office: Aetna Life & Casualty 151 Farmington Avenue Hartford Connecticut 06156

LYON, WAYNE BARTON, corporate executive; born Dayton, October 26, 1932; married Maryann L., 1961; children: Karyn, Craig, Blair. Bachelor of Science in Chemical Engineering, University Cincinnati, 1955; Master of Business Administration in Marketing, University Chicago, 1969. Registered professional engineer, Michigan. Tech. representative Union Carbide, Chicago, 1955-62; product devel. manager, vice president business devel. Illinois Tool Works, Chicago, 1962-72; group vice president, executive vice president, president Masco Corp., Taylor, Michigan, 1972—; board of directors Emco Limited, London, Ontario, Can., Mechanical Tech. Incorporated, Latham, New York, 1973, Masco Corp., Taylor, Michigan, Manufacturers National Corp., Payless Cashways Incorporated, Formica Corp.; lecturer American Medical Association. Patentee in field. Board governors, trustees Cranbrook Kingswood Schools, Bloomfield Hills, Michigan, 1984—, Orchard Lake Country Club, Michigan, 1985—. Captain United States Army, 1955-63. Clubs: Fairlane (Dearborn, Michigan); Renaissance (Detroit), Detroit Athletic, Orchard Lake Country; Bloomfield Hills Country. Office: Masco Corp 21001 Van Born Road Taylor Michigan 48180

MAAS, GERALD LEE, railroad company executive; born Indianapolis, January 13, 1937; son of Gerald E. and Helen Louise (Hanson) M.; married Raenota Lee Storm, October 1, 1961; children: Brian, Leanne, Michelle. Bachelor of Arts, Eastern Illinois University, 1960; certificate advanced management program, Harvard University, 1980-81. From agent to superintendent New York Central Railroad, 1955-70, div. superintendent, 1971-76; general manager Central Vermont Railway, St. Albans, 1976-77, president, 1986—, also board of directors; from general manager to vice president Grand Trunk Western Railroad, Detroit, 1977-84, executive vice president, 1984-86, president, 1986—, also board of directors; president Grand Trunk Corp., Detroit, 1986—, also board of directors, 1986—; president, board of directors Duluth, Winnipeg & Pacific Railway, Superior, Wisconsin, 1986—, Central Vermont

Railway, St. Albans, 1986—; board of directors Belt Railway Company Chicago, Chicago and Western Ind. Railroad Company. Member Am. Association Railroad Supts., Association Am. Railroad, Michigan Railroad Association (chairman board), Michigan Chamber of Commerce (board directors 1986—), Detroit Chamber of Commerce. Avocation: golf. Office: Grand Trunk Western Rural Route Company 1333 Brewery Park Boulevard Detroit Michigan 48207

MACALLISTER, JACK ALFRED, telephone company executive; born Humeston, Iowa, July 12, 1927; son of Maxwell A. and Opal E. (Caldwell) MacA.; married Marilyn Anderson, June 12, 1950; children: Steven, James, Sue. Bachelor.Commerce, University Iowa, 1950; student, Iowa State Teachers College, Cedar Rapids, 1947-48. With Northwestern Bell Telephone Company, 1950-65, 67-83; vice president operations Northwestern Bell Telephone Company, Omaha, 1974-75, president, 1965-82, chairman, 1982-83; president, chief executive officer United States West, Incorporated, Englewood, Colorado, 1984-86, chairman board of directors, chief executive officer, 1986—; member staff American Telephone and Telegraph Company, New York City, 1965-67; board of directors 1st Interstate Bank of Los Angeles, The St. Paul Companies; board member National Parks Foundation; member adv. board University Pennsylvania Wharton School Fishman-Davidson Center for study of service sector; member national adv. board University Arizona; member international adv. board Stanford Research; member Business Higher Education Forum. Member Foundation Board Denver Art Mus.; member executive board Denver Area council Boy Scouts Am.; co-chair Business Partnership of Educational Commission of the States. Office: United States West Incorporated 7800 E Orchard Road Englewood Colorado 80111

MACDONALD, GERALD V., banker; born 1938; married. Bachelor of Arts, University Michigan, 1960. Commercial loan officer Manufacturers National Bank, Detroit, 1960—, 2d vice president, 1970-75, vice president, 1975-80, president, 1980—, chief executive officer, from 1980, director; chief executive officer Manufacturers National Bank, Southfield, Michigan, 1980-82, president, from 1980. Office: Mfrs National Bank Mfrs Bank Tower 100 Renaissance Center Detroit Michigan 48243

MACHIZ, LEON, electronic equipment manufacturing executive; born Brooklyn, June 23, 1924; son of Isadore and Fanny (Klonsky) M.; married Lorraine Block, March 31, 1951; children: Marc, Linda, Gary. Graduate, Cooper Union. Salesman Sun Radio Company, 1942-52; founder Time Electro Sales Company (merged with Avnet, Incorporated 1952-68), Electro Air of Georgia (merged with Avnet, Incorporated 1968), 1957-68, Electro Air of Florida, 1960-68; senior vice president, director Avnet Incorporated, New York City, 1968-80, president, director, 1980—, vice chairman, chief executive officer, from 1986, now also chief operating officer, director, chairman, chief executive officer, 1988—. Trustee North Shore University Hospital, Boys' Brotherhood Republic. Office: Avnet

Incorporated 80 Cutter Mill Road Great Neck New York 11021

MACKE, KENNETH A., retail executive; born Templeton, Iowa, December 16, 1938; married Kathleen O'Farrell; children: Michael, Jeffrey. Bachelor of Science, Drake University, 1961. With Dayton Hudson Corp. and affiliates, 1961—, former chairman, chief executive officer Target Stores, senior vice president corp., 1977-79, president corp., 1981-84, chairman, chief executive officer, chairman executive committee, 1984—, also board of directors; board of directors Unisys Corp., Detroit. Member board business and industrial advisers U. Wisconsin, Stout, 1978-80; board of directors Walker Art Center, Urban Coalition Minneapolis; trustee Drake U.; board regents Augsburg College, Minneapolis, 1979-80; div. chairman United Way Minneapolis, 1977, 79-80. Member National Massachusetts Retailing Institute (director 1977-81), National Retail Mchts. Association (director 1982-83), Greater Minneapolis Chamber of Commerce (director 1980-82). Office: Dayton-Hudson Corp 777 Nicollet Mall Minneapolis Minnesota 55402

MACNAUGHTON, DONALD SINCLAIR, health care company executive; born Schenectady, New York, July 14, 1917; son of William and Marion (Colquhoun) MacN.; married Winifred Thomas, April 10, 1941; children: Donald, David. Bachelor of Arts, Syracuse University, 1939, Bachelor of Laws, 1948. Bar: New York 1948. Teacher history Pulaski (New York) Acad. and Central School, 1939-42; private practice Pulaski, 1948-54; deputy superintendent insurance New York State, 1954-55; with Prudential Insurance Company Am., 1955-78, president, chief executive officer, 1969-70, chairman board, chief executive officer, 1970-78, also board of directors; chairman board Hospital Corp. Am., Nashville, 1978-82, 1982-85; chairman executive committee Healthtrust Incorporated, 1987—; chairman executive committee Healthtrust Incorporated, 1987—. Member capital campaign committee Harvard U., l985—, member adv. board Business and Government Center, l983—; trustee Vanderbilt U., Nashville, l979—. lst lieutenant United States Army Air Force, l942-46, PTO. Named Man of Year B'nai B'rith Youth Service, New York, 1985, The Ins. Field, 1969; recipient Gold Medal Founders award International Ins. Seminars, New York, 1978, Exceptional Achievement citation Department Treasury, 1972. Member Hospital Corp. Foundation (chairman 1985—), Business Council (hon.), Augusta National Golf Club, Belle Meade Country Club. Avocations: boating, skiing, golf, reading. Office: Health Trust Incorporated 4525 Harding Road Nashville Tennessee 37203

MACOMBER, JOHN D., industrialist; born Rochester, New York, January 13, 1928; son of William Butts and Elizabeth Currie (Ranlet) M.; married Caroline Morgan, October 21, 1955; children: Janet Morgan, Elizabeth Currie, William Butts II. Bachelor of Arts, Yale University, 1950; Master of Business Administration, Harvard University, 1952. With McKinsey & Company, New York City, France and Switzerland, 1954-73; managing director McKinsey & Company, Geneva, 1961-64; continental coordinator Europe McKinsey & Company, Paris, 1964-68; director McKinsey & Company; president Celanese Corp., New York City, 1973-87, chief executive officer, 1977, chairman, 1980-87; chairman J.D. Macomber & Company, New York City, 1987-89; president, chairman Export-Import Bank of United States, Washington, 1989—. 1st lieutenant United States Air Force, 1952-53. Clubs: Metropolitan; Links (New York City), River (New York City), Union (New York City), New York Yacht. Office: Export-Import Bank of United States 811 Vermont Avenue Northwest Washington District of Columbia 20571

MADDEN, RICHARD BLAINE, forest products executive, educator; born Short Hills, New Jersey, April 27, 1929; son of James L. and Irma (Twining) M.; married Joan Fairbairn, May 24, 1958; children: John Richard, Lynn Marie, Kathryn Ann, Andrew Twining. Bachelor of Science, Princeton University, 1951; Juris Doctor, University Michigan, 1956; Master of Business Administration, New York University, 1959. Bar: Michigan 1956, New York 1958. General assistant treas.'s department Socony Mobil Oil Corp., New York City, 1956-57; special assistant Socony Mobil Oil Corp., 1958-59, fin. representative, 1960; assistant to president Mobil Chemical Company; also director Mobil Chemicals Limited of England, 1960-63; executive vice president, general manager Kordite Corp.; also vice president Mobil Plastics, 1963-66; vice president Mobil Chemical Company, New York City, 1966-68; group vice president Mobil Chemical Company, 1968-70; assistant treasurer Mobil Oil Corp., 1970-71; chairman Mobil Oil Estates Limited, 1970-71; president, chief executive to chairman, chief executive officer Potlatch Corp., San Francisco, 1971—; board of directors Pacific Gas and Electric Company; from lecturer to adj. associate professor fin. New York University, 1960-63. Board of directors Am. Paper Institute, National Park Foundation, Smith-Kettlewell Eye Research Institute, San Francisco Opera Association; trustee, member executive committee Am. Enterprise Institute; board governors, member executive committee San Francisco Symphony; trustee Fine Arts Musuems San Francisco; member executive committee Bay Area Council; member Bus.-Higher Education Forum. Lieutenant (junior grade) United States Naval Reserve, 1951-54. Member New York, Michigan bar associations. Roman Catholic. Clubs: University (New York City); Pacific Union (San Francisco), Bohemian (San Francisco); Lagunitas (Ross, California); Metropolitan (Washington).

MAGOON, JOHN HENRY, JR., airlines executive; born Honolulu, December 2, 1915; son of John H. and Juliet (Carroll) M.; married Adele Whitlock, October 28, 1939 (deceased January 29, 1975); 1 daughter, Sara.; married Cynthia Jeanette Baker, March 19, 1976. Student, University Calif.-Berkeley, 1933-35. President Hawaiian Linen Supply, Limited, 1941-60; president, director Hawaiian Securities & Realty, Limited, Honolulu, from 1955; chairman Hawaiian Airlines, Incorporated, Honolulu, 1964—, chief executive officer, from 1964, now also president, board of directors; director Hawaiian Trust Company, Limited, Castle & Cooke, Incorporated, Magoon Brothers, Limited, Magoon Estate, Limited, First Insurance Company Hawaii, Limited, Cox Broadcasting Corp., Atlanta. Member Chamber of Commerce Hawaii (director), Phi Kappa Psi. Clubs: Outrigger Canoe, Pacific, Oahu Country, Waialae Country, Diamond Head Tennis; Metropolitan (Washington). Office: Hawaiian Airlines Incorporated 1164 Bishop St Post Office Box 30008 Honolulu Hawaii 96820

MAGOWAN, PETER ALDEN, grocery chain executive; born New York City, April 5, 1942; son of Robert Anderson and Doris (Merrill) M.; married Jill Tarlau (divorced July 1982; children—Kimberley, Margot, Hilary; married Deborah Johnston, August 14, 1982. Bachelor of Arts, Stanford University; Master of Arts, Oxford University, England; postgraduate, Johns Hopkins University. Store manager Safeway Stores Incorporated, Washington, 1968-70; district manager Safeway Stores Incorporated, Houston, 1970-71; retail operations manager Safeway Stores Incorporated, Phoenix, 1971-72; div. manager Safeway Stores Incorporated, Tulsa, 1973-76; manager international div. Safeway Stores Incorporated, Toronto, Ontario, Can., 1976-78; manager western region Safeway Stores Incorporated, San Francisco, 1978-79; chairman board, chief executive officer Safeway Stores Incorporated, Oakland, California, 1980—; also president Safeway Stores Incorporated, Oakland, 1988—; board of directors Pacific Gas and Electric, Chrysler Corp., Vons Companies Incorporated. Member Food Marketing Institute (board directors). Office: Safeway Incorporated 201 4th St Oakland California 94660

MAHER, JOHN FRANCIS, financial executive; born Berkeley, California, April 25, 1943; son of Edward John and Emilia A. (Radovan) M.; married Ann Elizabeth Breeden (divorced 1975); children: Edward John II, Elizabeth Ann; married Helen Lee Stillman, March 20, 1976; children: Michael Stillman, Helen Cathline. Bachelor of Science, Menlo College, 1965; Master of Business Administration, University Pennsylvania, 1967. General partner Eastman Dillon, New York, 1971; 1st vice president Blyth Eastman Dillon, New York, 1972; executive vice president Blyth Eastman Dillon, Los Angeles, 1976-79; executive vice president, chief fin. officer Great Western Fin., Beverly Hills, California, 1973-76, also board of directors; managing director Lehman Brothers Kohn Loeb, Los Angeles, 1979-86; president, chief operating officer Great Western Fin. Corp., Beverly Hills, 1986—; board of directors Great Western Fin. Corp., Beverly Hills, Baker Hughes Incorporated, Great Western Bank. Board of directors Los Angeles Big Brothers, Incorporated. Joseph Wharton fellow University Pennsylvania, 1965-67. Member California Business Roundtable Group. Office: Great Western Fin Corp 8484 Wilshire Boulevard 10th Floor Beverly Hills California 90211-3212

MAHONEY, EDWARD P., savings and loan association executive. President, chief executive officer, chief operating officer Am. Savings and Loan Association Florida, Miami, also board of directors. Office: Am Savings & Loan Association of Florida

17801 Northwest 2nd Avenue Miami Florida 33169

MAINES, CLIFFORD BRUCE, insurance company executive; born Tacoma, Washington, August 14, 1926; son of Clifford McLean and Ida Vera (Wardall) M.; married Mary Jean Marshall, September 4, 1948; children—Molly, Janet Lynn. Student, Central College, Fayette, Missouri, 1944-45, University Michigan, 1945-46; Bachelor of Science, University Washington, 1948, Bachelor of Laws, 1949, Juris Doctor, 1949. Bar: Washington 1950. Member legal staff Safeco Corp., Seattle, 1950-62, associate general counsel, 1962-66, general counsel, 1966-68, vice president, general counsel, 1968-74, senior vice president, 1974-81, president, chief operating officer, 1981-86; president, chief executive officer Safeco Corp., 1986-89; director Safeco Corp., Seattle, 1977—, chairman, chief executive officer, 1989—; executive vice president, chief operating officer, director General Insurance Company Am., 1974-77, president, 1977-81; now director; executive vice president 1st National Insurance Company Am., 1974-77, president, 1977-81; now director; executive vice president Safeco Insurance Company, 1974-77, president, 1977-81, now director; board of directors Safeco Life Insurance Company. Served with United States Naval Reserve, 1944-46. Member American Bar Association, Washington Bar Association, Seattle-King County Bar Association (past trustee), Washington Insurance Council (past president), Pacific Insurance and Surety Conference, Washington Athletic Club, Broadmoor Golf Club, Seattle Golf Club, Columbia Tower Club, Beta Theta Pi. Methodist. Office: Safeco Corp Safeco Plaza Seattle Washington 98185

MALENICK, DONAL H., metals manufacturing company executive; born 1939. Steel bander, slitting machine operator, later production manager Worthington Industries, Incorporated, Columbus, Ohio, 1958-67, vice president manufacturing, 1967-72, executive vice president, 1972-76, president, 1976—, chief operating officer, from 1976, also board of directors. Office: Worthington Industries Incorporated 1205 Dearborn Dr Columbus Ohio 43085

MALLOY, JAMES B., packaging company executive; born 1927. Bachelor of Science, Babson College, 1951. With United States Gypsum Company, Chicago, 1951-52, International Paper Company, New York City, 1952-78; with Jefferson-Smurfit Corp., Alton, Illinois, 1978—, senior vice president, 1980-82, president, chief operating officer, 1982—, also board of directors. Office: Jefferson Smurfit Corp Post Office Box 66820 Saint Louis Missouri 63166

MALONE, WALLACE D., JR., bank executive; born Dothan, Alabama, 1936; married. Bachelor of Science, University Alabama, 1957; Master of Business Administration, University Pennsylvania, 1960. With First National Bank, 1959-71; with SouthTrust Corp., Birmingham, Alabama, 1972—, now chairman, chief executive officer, director. Office: Southtrust Corp 420 N 20th St Post Office Box 2554 Birmingham Alabama 35203

MAMMEL, RUSSELL NORMAN, food distribution company executive; born Hutchinson, Kansas, April 28,

1926; son of Vyvian E. and Mabel Edwina (Hursh) M.; married Betty Crawford, October 29, 1949; children: Mark, Christopher, Elizabeth, Nancy. Bachelor of Science, University Kansas, 1949. With Mammel's Incorporated, Hutchinson, 1949-57, president, 1957-59; retail general manager Kansas div. Nash Finch Company, Hutchinson, 1959-61; retail general manager Iowa div. Nash Finch Company, Cedar Rapids, 1961-66; director store devel. Nash Finch Company, Minneapolis, 1966-75, vice president, 1975-83, executive vice president, 1983-85, president, chief operating officer, 1985—; also board of directors Nash Finch Company. Served with Army of the United States, 1944-46. Home: 6808 Cornelia Dr Edina Minnesota 55435 Office: Nash Finch Company 3381 Gorham Avenue Saint Louis Park Minnesota 55426

MANCHESKI, FREDERICK JOHN, automotive company executive; born Stevens Point, Wisconsin, July 21, 1926; son of John Stanley and Luella (Zwaska) M.; married Judith Knox; children: Mary Lou, Laura, Marcia, Bruce, Amy Fredericka. Bachelor of Science in Mechanical Engineering, University Wisconsin, 1948. With Timken Roller Bearing Company, Canton, Ohio, 1948-57, McKinsey & Company (management consultant), New York City, 1957-63, Echlin Incorporated, Branford, Connecticut, 1963—; chairman board, chief executive officer Echlin Incorporated, 1969—; director RB&W Corp., The Connecticut National Bank, Portec, Incorporated. Contributing author: Turnaround Management, 1974. Former Member New Haven Devel. Commission; former Member United States Industrial Council Commission; former board of directors Quinnipiac council Boy Scouts Am.; trustee Hospital of St. Raphael, Connecticut Hospice, Quinnipiac College; board of directors Junior Achievement; former trustee Connecticut Pub. Expenditure Council. Recipient Gold award Wall Street Transcript, 1985; named Automotive Man of Year, Automotive Warehouse Distbrs. Association, 1973, Chief Executive of Decade (Bronze award), Fin. World, 1989; named to Automotive Hall of Fame, 1985. Member National Acad. Engineering, World Business Council, Young Pres.'s Organization, National Society Professional Engineers, National Association of Manufacturers (former director), Connecticut Business Industry Association (former director), Greater New Haven Company of C. (former director), Sigma Alpha Epsilon. Clubs: Pine Orchard Country (New Haven), Quinnipiack (New Haven), New Haven Country (New Haven). Home: 10 Old Farm Road North Haven Connecticut 06473 Office: Echlin Incorporated 100 Double Beach Road Post Office Box 451 Branford Connecticut 06405

MANN, GEORGE STANLEY, real estate and financial services corporation executive; born Toronto, Ontario, Canada, December 23, 1932; son of David Philip and Elizabeth (Green) M.; married Saundra Sair, January 2, 1955; children: Michael, Tracy. Attended, North Toronto Collegiate School. Partner Mann & Martel Company Limited, 1959-68, chief executive officer, 1968-70; chief executive officer United Trust Company, 1970-76; president Unicorp Canada Corp., Toronto, 1972-76, chairman board, 1976-90; chairman board, director

Unicorp American Corp., New York City, Union Gas Limited, Chatham, Ontario, 1990—; chairman board of directors Union Gas Limited, Chatham, Ontario, Unicorp Am. Corp., N.Y.C, Union Energy Incorporated, Toronto, Ontario, Lincoln Savings Bank, New York City. Board governors Mount Sinai Hospital, Toronto. Clubs: Oakdale Golf & Country (Toronto); High Ridge Country (Palm Beach, Florida). Avocation: golf. Home: 18 Old Forest Hill Road, Toronto, Ontario Canada M5P 2P7 also: Palm Beach Florida 33480 Office: 21 St Clair Avenue PH, Toronto, Ontario Canada M4T 2T7

MANOOGIAN, RICHARD ALEXANDER, manufacturing company executive; born Long Branch, New Jersey, July 30, 1936; son of Alex and Marie (Tatian) M.; children: James, Richard, Bridget. Bachelor of Arts in Econs, Yale University, 1958. Assistant to president Masco Corp., Taylor, Michigan, 1958-62, executive vice president, 1962-68, president, 1968-85, chairman, 1985—, chief executive officer, from 1985, also director; chairman, director Masco Industries, Incorporated; director Emco Limited, London, Ontario, Can., National Bank of Detroit, Flint & Walling, Kendallville, Ind., R.P. Scherer Corp., Do It Yourself Institute. Trustee U. Liggett School, Associates of Am. Wing, Detroit Institute Arts, Founder's Society, Detroit Institute Arts, Center for Creative Studies. Member Young Presidents Organization, Am. Business Conference. Clubs: Grosse Pointe Yacht, Grosse Pointe Hunt, Country of Detroit, Detroit Athletic. Office: Masco Corp 21001 Van Born Road Taylor Michigan 48180

MARA, WELLINGTON T., professional football team executive; born August 8, 1916. President New York Giants, East Rutherford, New Jersey. Office: New York Giants Giants Stadium East Rutherford New Jersey 07073 Office: National Football League 410 Park Avenue New York New York 10022

MARAKAS, JOHN LAMBROS, retired insurance company executive; born Connellsville, Pennsylvania, July 16, 1926; son of Gust John and Elizabeth Hamilton (Cutler) M.; married Alice Dixon, December 26, 1948; children: Andy, Nancy, Donna. Bachelor of Arts, University Michigan, 1949. Actuarial assistant Acacia Mutual, Washington, 1949-50, Continental Assurance, Chicago, 1950-53; vice president, actuary, executive vice president, president Reserve Life Insurance Company, Dallas, 1953-70; vice president Nationwide Corp., Columbus, Ohio, 1971-72; 1981-91; president Nationwide Corp., Columbus, Ohio, 1972-90, also board of directors; president, director Nationwide Life Insurance Company, Columbus, 1981—, general manager; president, director Nationwide Property Management, Incorporated; chairman, trustee Fin. Horizons Life Insurance Company; vice-chairman Nationwide (PEBSCO Incorporated); director Farmland Life Insurance Company, Nationwide Agribus. Insurance Company, Farmland Mutual Insurance Company, Gulf Atlantic Life Insurance Company, National Casualty Company, Nationwide Investors Services, Incorporated, Nationwide Community Urban Redevelopment Corp., Hickey-Mitchell Insurance Agency, Incorporated, Nationwide Fin. Services Incorporated, Nationwest Insurance

Services, West Coast Life Insurance Company, Nationwide Cash Management Company, California Cash Management Company, National Casualty Company of Am., Limited, National Premium and Benefit Administration Company, Wausau Service Corp.; trustee, president Nationwide Foundation; trustee, chairman Nationwide Investing Foundation, Nationwide Separate Account; chairman, trustee Northwest Tax Free Fund, Northwest Separate Account; board of directors, senior vice president Employers Insurance of Wausau A Mutual Company; director, chairman board Nationwide Health Care Corp. Board of directors, pres.-elect Ohio affiliate National Society to Prevent Blindness. Served with United States Army, 1946-47. Member Am. Acad. Actuaries, Health Insurance Association Am. (chairman 1988-89), Association Ohio Life Insurance Companies.

MARCEAU, RICHARD E., engine manufacturing company executive; born 1926. Bachelor of Business Administration, University Minnesota, 1949. With Honeywell Incorporated, 1956-66; vice president personnel and administration Sola Basic Industries, 1966-78; director human resources Briggs & Stratton Corp., Mllw., 1978, vice president human resources, 1979-81, vice president administration, data processing and personnel, from 1981, chief operating officer, 1988, president, chief operating officer, 1988—. With United States Naval Reserve, 1944-46. Office: Briggs & Stratton Corp Post Office Box 702 Milwaukee Wisconsin 53201 also: 12301 W Wirth St Wauwatosa Wisconsin 53222

MARCUM, JOSEPH LARUE, insurance company executive; born Hamilton, Ohio, July 2, 1923; son of Glen F. and Helen A. (Stout) M.; married Sarah Jane Sloneker, March 7, 1944; children: Catharine Ann Marcum Lowe, Joseph Timothy (deceased), Mary Christina Marcum Manchester, Sarah Jennifer Marcum Shuffield, Stephen Sloneker. Bachelor of Arts, Antioch College, 1947; Master of Business Administration in Fin, Miami University, 1965. With Ohio Casualty Insurance Company and affiliates, 1947—, now chairman board, chief executive officer, also board of directors; board of directors First National Bank Southwest Ohio; board of directors, chairman executive committee First Fin. Bancorp., Monroe, Ohio. Chairman board trustees Miami U., Oxford, Ohio. Captain, infantry United States Army. Member Society Chartered Property and Casualty Underwriter (national director), Am. Institute Property and Liability Underwriters (trustee), Queen City Club, Bankers Club, Can. Club, Metropolitan Club, Princeton Club New York, Eldorado Country Club, Little Harbor Club, Walloon Lake Country Club, Mill Reef Club. Presbyterian. Home: 475 Oakwood Dr Hamilton Ohio 45013 Office: Ohio Casualty Corp 136 N 3rd St Hamilton Ohio 45025

MARCUS, BERNARD, retail executive; born 1929; married. Bachelor of Science, Rutgers University, 1954. Vice president Vornado Incorporated, 1952-68; president Odell Incorporated, 1968-70; vice president Daylin Incorporated, 1970-73; with Handy Don Home Improvement, Los Angeles, 1972-78; with Home Depot Incorporated, Atlanta, 1978—, now chairman, secretary, also board of directors. Office: Home Depot Incorporated 2727 Paces Ferry Road Atlanta Georgia 30339

MARGOLIS, DAVID I(SRAEL), corporate executive; born New York City, January 24, 1930; son of Benjamin and Celia (Kosofsky) M.; married Barbara Schneider, September 7, 1958; children: Brian, Robert, Peter, Nancy. Bachelor of Arts, City College of New York, 1950, Master of Business Administration, 1952; postgraduate, New York University, 1952-55. Security analyst Josephthal Company, 1952-56; assistant treasurer Raytheon Company, 1956-59; treasurer IT&T, New York City, 1959-62; with Coltec Industries Incorporated (formerly Fairbanks Whitney Corp. and Colt Industries Incorporated), New York City, 1962—, now chairman, chief executive officer. member board trustees Presbyterian Hospital City New York; board overseers New York U. Stern School Business; board of directors Offitbank, Council Foreign Relations. Office: Coltec Industries Incorporated 430 Park Avenue New York New York 10022

MARK, REUBEN, consumer products company executive; born Jersey City, New Jersey, January 21, 1939; son of Edward and Libbie (Berman) M.; married Arlene Slobzian, January 10, 1964; children: Lisa, Peter, Stephen. Bachelor of Arts, Middlebury College, 1960; Master of Business Administration, Harvard University, 1963. With Colgate-Palmolive Company, New York City, 1963—; president, general manager Venezuela, 1972-73, Can., 1973-74; vice president, general manager Far East div. 1974-75, vice president, general manager household products div., 1975-79, group vice president domestic operations, 1979-81, executive vice president, 1981-83, chief operating officer, 1983-84, president, 1983—, chief executive officer, 1984—, chairman board, 1986—; lecturer School Business Administration, University Connecticut, 1977. Served with United States Army, 1961. Member Soap and Detergent Association (board directors), Grocery Manufacturers Am. (director), National Executive Service Corp. Office: Colgate-Palmolive Company 300 Park Avenue New York New York 10022

MARKIN, DAVID ROBERT, motor company executive; born New York City, February 16, 1931; son of Morris and Bessie (Markham) M.; children: Sara, John, Christopher, Meredith. Bachelor of Science, Bradley University, 1953. Foreman Checker Motors Corp., Kalamazoo, 1955-57, factory manager, 1957-62, vice president sales, 1962-70, president, 1970—, director; board of directors Jackpot Incorporated. Trustee Kalamazoo College Served to 1st lieutenant United States Air Force, 1953-55. Member Alpha Epsilon Pi. Clubs: Standard (Chicago); Park (Kalamazoo). Home: 2121 Winchell Road Kalamazoo Michigan 49008 Office: International Controls Corp 2016 N Pitcher St Kalamazoo Michigan 49007

MARLEY, JAMES EARL, manufacturing company executive; born Marietta, Pennsylvania, March 18, 1935; son of Earl W. and Elsie H. (Fahringer) M.; married Kathleen Y. Robinson, November 22, 1974; children—Kathy L., Robert B., Kimberly J., Lora B. Bachelor of Science in Aeronautical Engineering,

Pennsylvania State, 1957; Master of Science in Mechanical Engineering, Drexel Institute, 1963. Group director automachine AMP Incorporated, Harrisburg, Pennsylvania, 1969-70, vice president automachine group, 1970-79, vice president manufacturing resources, 1979-80, vice president manufacturing, 1980-81, corp. vice president manufacturing, 1981-83, corp. vice president operations, 1983-86, president, 1986—, also board of directors, 1986—. Inventor and patentee in field. Member Institute of Electrical and Electronics Engineers, Am. Society Mechanical Engineers, Am. Management Association, Manufacturing Council of the Machinery and Allied Products Institute, Harrisburg Chamber of Commerce. Republican. Club: Harrisburg Country (Pennsylvania) (board governors 1983—). Home: 1230 Mountain View Boulevard Dauphin Pennsylvania 17018 Office: AMP Incorporated 470 Friendship Road Post Office Box 3608 Harrisburg Pennsylvania 17105

MARQUARD, WILLIAM ALBERT, diversified manufacturing company executive; born Pittsburgh, March 6, 1920; son of William Albert and Anne (Wild) M.; married Margaret Thoben, August 13, 1942; children: Pamela, Suzanne, Stephen. Bachelor of Science, University Pennsylvania, 1940; Doctor of Humanities (honorary), University Puebla (Mexico). With Westinghouse Electric Corp., Pittsburgh and Mexico City, 1940-52; with Mosler Safe Company, Hamilton, Ohio, 1952-67, senior vice president, 1961-67, president, 1967-70; with Am. Standard, Incorporated, New York City, 1967—, senior executive vice president, 1970, president, chief executive officer, 1971-85, also chairman, 1971-86, chairman executive committee, from 1985; now chairman Am. Standard, Incorporated subsidiary ASI Holding Corp., New York City; board of directors Chemical New York Corp., Chemical Bank, New York Life Insurance Company, Shell Oil Company, N.L. Industries, Incorporated, Allied Stores; chairman, board of directors Arkansas Best Corp. Trustee U. Pennsylvania, New York City Citizens Budget Commission, New York Infirmary-Beekman Downtown Hospital, Washington Opera, Foundation of U. Ams., Committee Economic Devel.; board overseers Wharton School Business, Business Committee for Arts, Brit.-N. Am. Committee; member Committee Corp. Support Private Univs.; board of directors National Minority Purchasing Council. Member Conference Board (senior).

MARRIOTT, JOHN W., JR., hotel and food service chain executive; born Washington, March 25, 1932; son of John Willard and Alice (Sheets) M.; married Donna Garff, June 29, 1955; children: Deborah, Stephen Garff, John Willard, David Sheets. Bachelor of Science in Banking and Fin, University Utah, 1954. Vice president Marriott Hot Shoppes Incorporated, 1959-64, executive vice president, board of directors, 1964; president Marriott Corp., 1964—, chief executive officer, 1972—, chairman board, 1985—; board of directors Outboard Marine Corp., Waukegan, Illinois, General Motors Corporation. Trustee Mayo Foundation, National Geog. Society, Eisenhower Medical Center; member national adv. board Boy Scouts Am.; member conference board Business Council, Business

Roundtable. Lieutenant United States Naval Reserve, l954-56. Recipient Business Leader of Year award, Georgetown University School Business Administration, 1984, Service Above Self award, Rotary Club at JFK International Airport, 1985, Am. Manager of Year award, National Mgmt. Association, 1985, Golden Chain award, Nations's Restaurant News, 1985, Hall of Fame award, Consumer Digest Magazine, 1985, Citizen of Year award, Boy Scouts of Am., 1986, Restaurant Business Leadership award, Restaurant Business Magazine, 1986, Gold Plate award, Am. Acad. Achievement, 1986, Hall of Fame, Am. Hotel and Motel Association, 1986, Hall of Fame award, Culinary Institute of Am., 1987, Hospitality Executive of Year award, Pennsylvania State University, 1987, Bronze winner in Fin. World's Chief Executive Officers award, 1988, Silver Plate award Lodging Hospitality Magazine, 1988, Chief Executive Officer of Year Chief Executive Officer Magazine, 1988, Signature award CA chapter National Multiple Scelerosis, 1988; named Outstanding Marketing Executive Gallagher Report, 1988. Member Conference Board, United States Chamber of Commerce, Sigma Chi. Member Church of Jesus Christ of Latter Day Saints Clubs: Burning Tree (Washington), Metropolitan (Washington). Office: Marriott Corp Marriott Dr Washington District of Columbia 20058

MARRIOTT, RICHARD EDWIN, hotel and contract services executive; born Washington, January 9, 1939; son of John Willard and Alice Taylor (Sheets) M.; married Nancy Peery, March 20, 1962; children: Julie Ann, Sandra, Karen, Mary Alice. Bachelor of Science, University Utah, 1963; Master of Business Administration, Harvard University, 1965. With Marriott Corp., Washington, 1965—, group vice president restaurant operations, 1976-78, corp. group vice president restaurant and theme park operations, 1979-84, executive vice president, 1984, vice chairman, 1986—, also board of directors; chairman board of directors Media Corp., 1973—; board of directors Riggs National Bank of Washington. Member National Commission Against Drunk Driving; trustee Boys Clubs Am., Dole Foundation for Employemnt of Persons with Disabilities. Member National Restaurant Association, Sigma Chi. Member Church of Jesus Christ of Latter Day Saints. Office: Marriott Corp Marriott Dr Washington District of Columbia 20058

MARRON, DONALD BAIRD, investment banker; born Goshen, New York, July 21, 1934; married Catherine D. Calligar. Student, Baruch School Business, 1949-51, 55-57. Investment analyst New York Trust Company, New York City, 1951-56, Lionel D. Edie Company, New York City, 1956-58; manager research department George O'Neill & Company, 1958-59; president D.B. Marron & Company Incorporated, New York City, 1959-65; president Mitchell Hutchins & Company Incorporated (merger with D.B. Marron & Company Incorporated 1965), New York City, 1965-69, president, chief executive officer, 1969-77; president PaineWebber Incorporated (merger with Mitchell Hutchins & Company Incorporated 1977), New York City, 1977-88, chief executive officer,

1980—, chairman board, 1981—, also board of directors; co-founder, former chairman Data Resources, Incorporated; former director New York Stock Exchange. Trustee Dana Foundation. Office: PaineWebber Incorporated 1285 Avenue of the Americas New York New York 10019

MARS, FORREST, JR., candy company executive. son of Forrest Mars Sr.; married. Graduate, Yale University, 1953. Co-pres. Mars Incorporated, 1973—. Office: Mars Incorporated 6885 Elm St McLean Virginia 22101

MARS, FORREST E., SR., candy company executive. son of Frank and Ethel Mars; children: Forrest Jr., John, Jacqueline. Chairman Mars Incorporated, McLean, Virginia. Office: Mars Incorporated 6885 Elm St McLean Virginia 22101

MARSH, MILES L., holding company executive. President Kraft General Foods div. General Foods USA, Glenview, Illinois, until 1989; president, chief operating officer Whitman Corp., Chicago, 1989—. Office: Whitman Corp 111 E Wacker Dr Chicago Illinois 60601

MARTIN, J. LANDIS, lawyer, manufacturing company executive; born Grand Island, Nebraska, November 5, 1945; son of John Charles and Lucile (Cooley) M.; married Sharon Penn Smith, September 23, 1978; children: Mary Frances, Sarah Landis, Emily Penn. Bachelor of Science in Business Administration, Northwestern University, 1968, Juris Doctor cum laude, 1973. Bar: Illinois 1974, District of Columbia 1978, Colorado 1982. Associate Kirkland & Ellis, Chicago, 1973-77; partner Kirkland & Ellis, Washington, 1978-81; managing partner Kirkland & Ellis, Denver, from 1981, firm committee member, Chicago, 1983-87; president, chief executive officer NL Industries Incorporated, Houston, 1987—; chairman, chief executive officer Baroid Corp., Houston, 1987—. Editor-in-chief: Exchange Act Guide to SEC Rule 144, 1973; articles editor Northwestern University Law Rev., 1972-73. President Central City Opera House Association, Denver, 1986-88, chairman, 1987—. Served with United States Army, 1969-71. Member American Bar Association, Illinois Bar Association, Colorado Bar Association, District of Columbia Bar Association. Clubs: Chevy Chase (Maryland), John Evans (Evanston, Illinois), Denver, Denver Country, Castle Pines Golf. Office: NL Industries Incorporated 3000 N Belt E Box 60087 Houston Texas 77205

MARTIN, LYNN MORLEY, secretary of labor; born Evanston, Illinois, December 26, 1939; daughter of Lawrence William and Helen Catherine (Hall) Morley; children from a previous marriage: Julia Catherine, Caroline; married Harry D. Leinenweber, January 1987. Bachelor of Arts, University Illinois, 1960. Former teacher pub. schools; member Illinois House of Representatives, 1977-79, Illinois Senate, 1979-81; member 97th-101st Congresses from 16th Illinois District, 1981-91; secretary Department of Labor, Washington, 1991—. National co-chairman Bush-Quayle Presidential campaign, 1988. Named one of Outstanding Young Women in Am., United States Jaycees; named Rep. Woman of the Year, 1989. Member American Association of University Women, Junior League, Phi Beta Kappa (hon. doctorate). Republican.

Office: Department of Labor Office of Secretary 200 Constitution Avenue Northwest Washington District of Columbia 20210

MARTINI, ROBERT E., wholesale pharmaceutical and electronic products company executive; born Hackensack, New Jersey, 1932. Bachelor of Science, Ohio State University, 1954. With Bergen Brunswig Corp., Orange, California, 1956—, vice president, 1962-69, executive vice president, 1969-81, president, chief operating officer, director, 1981-90, president, chief executive officer, 1990—, now chairman executive committee, president, chief executive office, director; also chairman, director Bergen Brunswig Drug Company, Orange, California; vice chairman, president Commtron Corp., Des Moines. Served to captain United States Air Force, 1954. Office: Bergen Brunswig Corp 4000 Metropolitan Dr Orange California 92668

MASCOTTE, JOHN PIERRE, insurance executive; born Fort Wayne, Indiana, May 19, 1939; son of Leo Cyril and Mary Harriet (Rowen) M.; married Sarah Ann Foret, April 23, 1966; children: Leo Rowen, Mark Foret and Matthew Foret (twins), Mary Marcella. Bachelor of Arts in Philosophy, St. Joseph's College, Rensselaer, Ind., 1961, Bachelor of Science in Accounting, 1961; Bachelor of Laws, University Virginia, 1964. Bar: Ind. 1964. Clerk Tax Court United States, Washington, 964-66; tax specialist Coopers & Lybrand, Fort Wayne, 1966-67; executive vice president Peoples Trust Bank, Fort Wayne, 1967-69; senior vice president Lincoln National Corp., Fort Wayne, 1969-74; executive vice president Mutual Benefit Life Insurance Company, Kansas City, Missouri, 1974-81; president Continental Corp., Kansas City, Missouri, from 1981, also chairman, chief executive officer, 1982—; board of directors Continental Corp., Hallmark Cards, Incorporated. Author: Finding Commission Dollars in Your Clients Financial Statements, 1979. Chairman Kansas City Corp. Industrial Devel., 1980; executive committee Civic Council Greater Kansas City, 1977-81; board of directors Kansas City Neighborhood Alliance, 1980-81; trustee Midwest Research Institute, 1978—. Democrat. Roman Catholic.

MASILLA, THOMAS ANTHONY, JR., banker; born New Orleans, October 18, 1946; son of Thomas A. and Santina (Scorsone) M.; married Kathleen Verdi, April 28, 1973. Bachelor of Business Administration, Loyola University, New Orleans, 1967, Master of Business Administration, 1972. C.P.A., Louisiana. Credit analyst First National Bank Commerce, New Orleans, 1964-67; auditor Peat, Marwick, Mitchell & Company, New Orleans, 1970-73; chief internal auditor Hibernia National Bank, New Orleans, 1973, vice president, controller, 1973-80, senior vice president, administrator, 1980-82, executive vice president administration, 1982—, vice chairman board, 1983-85, chairman, 1985; treasurer Hibernia Corp. Member Fin. Executives Institute, Am. Institute C.P.A.s, Louisiana Society C.P.A.s, Bank Administration Institute, Beta Gamma Sigma, Alpha Sigma Nu, Beta Alpha Psi. Club: City. Home: 969 Porteous St New Orleans Louisiana 70124 Office: Hibernia Corp 313 Carondelet St

Post Office Box 61540 New Orleans Louisiana 70161

MASON, STEVEN CHARLES, forest products company executive; born Sarnia, Ontario, Canada, February 22, 1936. Bachelor of Science, Massachusetts Institute of Technology, 1957. President div. Mead Corp., Dayton, Ohio, 1978-79, group vice president, 1979-82, senior vice president operations, 1982, president, 1982-90, vice chairman board, 1990—. Office: Mead Corp Courthouse Plaza NE Dayton Ohio 45463

MASSEY, JAMES D., bank holding company executive. Student, Butler University, University Wisconsin, Harvard University. With Merchants National Bank & Trust Company, Indianapolis, 1957—, management trainee, 1957-60, manager auto loan department, 1960-63, branch manager, 1963-66, vice president, 1966-70, vice president, branch administration officer, 1970-77, senior vice president, 1977-79, executive vice president, 1979-83, president, chief executive officer, 1983-86, chairman, chief executive officer, 1986—; also president, chief operating officer Merchants National Corp., Indianapolis. Office: Mchts National Corp 1 Merchants Plaza Suite 415E Indianapolis Indiana 46255

MATSUSHITA, MASAHARU, electronics company executive; born Tokyo, September 17, 1912; son of Eiji and Shizuko Hirata; married Sachiko Matsushita; 3 children. Educated, Tokyo Imperial University. With Mitsui Bank, 1935-40; with Matsushita Electric Industrial Company, Limited, 1940—, auditor, 1944-47, director, member board, 1947-49, executive vice president, 1949-61, president, 1961-77, chairman board, 1977—; director Matsushita Electronics Corp., chairman, 1972-85, director 1985—; auditor Matsushita Real Estate Company, Limited, 1952-67, director, 1968—; director Matsushita Communication Industrial Company, Limited, 1958-70, chairman, 1970-86, director 1986-87; director Matsushita Seiko Company Limited, 1956-87, Kyushu Matsushita Electric Company Limited, 1955-87, Matsushita Electric Corp. Am., 1959-74, Matsushita Refrigeration Company, 1961-87; president Electronics Industries Association of Japan, 1968-70; representative director Kansai Committee for Economic Devel., 1962—, director, 1975—. Recipient Blue Ribbon Medal, 1972; Ordem de Rio Branco, 1984, Ordem de Mérito Industrial na classe Ofl. (Brazil), 1984; First Class Order of the Sacred Treasure, 1984; decorated Commander Order of Orange-Nassau (Netherlands), 1975; Commander Order De La Cournne (Belgium), 1981; Comdr's. Cross Order of Merit (Federal Republic Germany), 1986. Member Osaka Chamber of Commerce (member standing committee), Kansai Econ. Federation (standing director). Office: Matsushita Electric Corp-Am 1 Panasonic Way Secaucus New Jersey 07094

MATTSON, WALTER EDWARD, publishing company executive; born Erie, Pennsylvania, June 6, 1932; son of Walter Edward and Florence Evelyn (Anderson) M.; married Geraldine Anne Horsman, October 10, 1953; children: Stephen, William, Carol. Bachelor of Science, University Maine, 1955; Associate of Science, Northeastern University,

1959, honorary doctorate, 1980; postgraduate, Harvard University Advanced Management Program, 1973. Printer various companies 1948-53; advertising manager Anderson Newspapers Company, Oakmont, Pennsylvania, 1954; assistant production manager Boston Herald Traveler, 1955-58; consultant Chas. T. Main Company, Boston, 1959; with New York Times Company, New York City, 1960—, senior vice president, 1972-74, executive vice president, 1974-79, president, 1979—, chief operating officer. Board of directors national council Northeastern U. Served with United States Marine Corps, 1951. Named Distinguished Alumni Northeastern University, 1974. Member ANPA (vice chairman prodn. management committee, chairman), Advertising Council (chairman 1987-88). Office: New York Times Company 229 W 43rd St New York New York 10036

MAXWELL, IAN ROBERT CHARLES, publisher; born Maisons-Laffitte, France, June 15, 1956; son of Ian Robert and Elizabeth Jennie Jeanne (Meynard) M. Master of Arts in History and Modern Languages, Balliol College, Oxford (England) University, 1978. Marketing director Pergamon Press, Incorporated, New York City, 1979-80; managing director Pergamon Press, France and Germany, 1980-83; sales devel. director PBCC plc, London, 1985-86, marketing director, 1986-89; joint managing director Maxwell Communication Corp. plc, London, 1988—; board of directors Hollis plc, Mirror Group Newspapers Limited; chairman board Agence Centrale de Presse, France, 1986-89. Secondment to Prince's Charitable Trust, London, 1983-84; chairman Derby (England) County Football Club, 1984-87; member devel. council Royal National Theatre, 1987-90. Member Club D'Investissement Media (1st president 1989-90). Member Labour Party. Avocation: snow and water skiing. Home: Private Wing, Headington Hill Hall, Oxford England OX3 0BW

MAXWELL, (IAN) ROBERT, publisher, film producer; born Selo Slatina, Czechoslovakia, June 10, 1923; naturalized, 1945; son of Michael and Ann Hoch; married Elisabeth Meynard, March 15, 1945; children: Anne, Philip, Christine, Isabel, Ian, Kevin, Ghislaine. Doctor of Science (honorary), Moscow State University, 1983, Polytechnic Institute New York, 1985; Doctor of Laws (honorary), University Aberdeen, 1988, Temple University, 1989, Washington University, St. Louis, 1990; Doctor honoris causa, University Adama Mickiewicza, Poland, 1989, De l'Univ. du Quebec a Trois-Rivieres, 1989; honorary doctorate, Bar-Ilan University, Israel, 1989. Head press and publs. div. German section British Foreign Office, 1945-47; founder, chairman, pub., director Pergamon Press Limited, Oxford, England, New York City and Paris, 1949—; chairman board, president Pergamon Press Incorporated, New York City, 1950—; chairman, chief executive officer Maxwell Communication Corp. plc (formerly British Printing & Communications Corp. Limited), 1981—, Central TV plc., 1983—; chairman Mirror Group Newspapers Limited, pub. Daily Mirror, Daily Record, Sunday Mail, Sunday Mirror, The People, Sporting Life, Sporting Life Weekender, 1984—, Brit. Cable Services Limited (Rediffusion Cablevision), 1984—; chairman, chief executive officer The Solicitors' Law Stationery Society plc, 1985—; chairman Mirrorvision, 1985—, Robert Maxwell and Company Limited, 1948-86; chairman, chief executive officer Clyde Cablevision Limited, 1985—, Premier, 1986—, Maxwell Pergamon Pub. Corp. plc. (formerly Pergamon BPCC Pub. Corp. plc.), 1986-89, BPCC plc (formerly BPCC Printing Corp. plc.), 1986—, Music Television Europe, 1987—, Maxwell Communication Corp. Incorporated, New York, 1987—, Macmillan Incorporated, New York City, 1988—; pub. China Daily in Europe, 1986—, The London Daily News, 1987; pub. English edition Moscow News, 1988—; pub., editor-in-chief The European, 1988—; pub., owner The Daily News, New York City, 1991—; board of directors Pergamon AGB plc (formerly Hollis plc), 1983—, chairman, 1988—; board of directors SelecTV plc, 1982—, Central TV plc, 1983—, Reuters Holdings plc, 1986—, TF1, 1987—, Agence Centrale de Presse, 1987—, Maxwell Media, Paris, 1987—, Solicitors' Law Stationery Society plc, 1985—, Philip Hill Investment Trust, 1986—; president European Satellite TV Broadcasting Consortium, 1986—; chairman Great Britain-Sasakawa Foundation, 1985—; member international council United States Information Agency, 1987—. Co-producer films: Mozart's Don Giovanni, Salzburg Festival, Bolshoi Ballet, 1957, Swan Lake, 1968; producer children's TV series DODO the Kid from Outer Space, 1968; author: Public Sector Purchasing, 1968; editor: Progress in Nuclear Energy: The Economics of Nuclear Power, 1963; General editor: Leaders of the World series, 1980—, The Econs. of Nuclear Power, 1965, Pub. Sector Purchasing, 1968; co-author: Man Alive, 1968. Labour member Parliament for Buckingham, 1964-70; chairman Labour Fund Raising Foundation, 1960-69; chairman labour working party on sci., government and industry, 1963-64; member Council of Europe, vice-chmn. committee on sci. and tech., 1968; treasurer Round House Trust Limited, 1965-83; chairman Commonwealth Games (Scotland 1986), Limited, 1966; chairman National Aids Trust fundraising group, 1987—; trustee International Centre for Child Studies; member senate U. Leeds, 1986—; trustee Polytechnical University New York, 1987—; president State of Israel Bonds, United Kingdom, 1988—; director Bishopsgate Trust Limited, 1984; chairman media committee NSPCC Centenary Appeal, 1984; chairman United Oxford Football Club plc, 1982-87; chairman Derby County Football Club, 1987—. Decorated Military Cross United Kingdom, 1945, Officer 1st class Order Stara Planina, Bulgaria, 1983, Office 1st cl. Swedish Royal Order of Polar Star, 1984, Commander Order of Merit with Star, Poland, 1986, Commander 1st class Order of the White Rose, Finlare des Arts et des Lettres, France, 1989; recipient Prism award New York University Centre for Graphic Arts Mmgt. and Tech., 1989, World of Difference award Anti-Defamation League, New York, 1989. Fellow Imperial College of London; member Newspaper Pubs. Association (council 1984—), Human Factors Society, Fabian Society Great Brit., International Acad. Astronautics (hon.), Club of Rome (executive director Brit. Group). Avocations: chess, football. Address: Holburn Circus, London EC1A 1DQ, England

Office: Macmillan Incorporated 866 3rd Avenue New York New York 10022 Office: Maxwell Macmillan 55 Railroad Avenue Greenwich Connecticut 06830

MAYHEW, KENNETH EDWIN, JR., transportation company executive; born Shelby, North Carolina, September 27, 1934; son of Kenneth Edwin and Evelyn Lee (Dellinger) M.; married Frances Elaine Craft, April 7, 1957; 1 daughter, Catherine Lynn Prince. Bachelor of Arts, Duke University, 1956. Certified Public Accountant, North Carolina. Senior auditor Arthur Andersen & Company, Atlanta, 1956-58, 60-63; controller Trendline, Incorporated, Hickory, North Carolina, 1963-66; with Carolina Freight Corp., Cherryville, 1966—; treasurer Carolina Freight Carriers Corp., Cherryville, 1969-74, vice president, 1971-72, executive vice president, 1972-85, president, chief operating officer, 1985-89, also director, president, chief executive officer, 1989—; president, director Robo Auto Wash Shelby Incorporated, 1967-73, Robo Auto Wash Cherryville, Incorporated, 1968-73; director Cherryville National Bank. Member North Carolina business adv. board, Fuqua School Business, Duke U.; board of directors, vice-chmn. Gaston Memorial Hospital; trustee Pfeiffer College With Army of the United States, 1958-60. Member American Institute of Certified Public Accountants, Am. Trucking Association (director, vice chairman Regular Common Carrier Conference), North Carolina Trucking Association (director, chairman), Gaston County Chamber of Commerce (vice president pub. affairs), Lions (president Cherryville 1972-73), Phi Beta Kappa, Omicron Delta Kappa, Phi Eta Sigma. Methodist. Home: 507 Spring St Cherryville North Carolina 28021 Office: Carolina Freight Carriers Corp Post Office Box 697 Cherryville North Carolina 28021 also: Carolina Freight Corp Post Office Box 545 Cherryville North Carolina 28021

MCALISTER, MAURICE L., savings and loan association executive; born 1925; married. President, director Downey Savings and Loan, Newport Beach, California, 1957—. Office: Downey Savings & Loan Association 3501 Jamboree Road Post Office Box 6000 Newport Beach California 92660

MCARTHUR, JOHN HECTOR, college dean; born Vancouver, C., Canada, March 31, 1934; came to United States, 1957; son of Hector and Elizabeth Lee (Whyte) McA.; married Netilia Ewasiuk, September 15, 1956; children: Jocelyn Natasha, Susan Patricia. Bachelor in Commerce, University British Columbia, 1957; Master of Business Administration, Harvard University, 1959, DBA, 1962; Doctor of Laws (honorary), Simon Fraser University, 1982, Queens University, 1985, Middlebury College, 1988; honorary degree, University Navarra, 1989. Dean, professor School Business Administration, Harvard University, Boston; board of directors Chase Manhattan Corp., Rohm and Haas Company, Teradyne Incorporated, Data General Corp., Springs Industries, Incorporated, Cabot Corp.; consultant numerous companies and government agys. in Can., Europe and United States. Chairman board trustees Brigham and Women's Hospital; member International Executive Service Corps. Home: 140 Old Connecticut Path Wayland Massachusetts 01778 Office: Harvard U Grad School Business Adminstrn Cambridge Massachusetts 02138

MCCAFFREY, ROBERT HENRY, JR., manufacturing company executive; born Syracuse, New York, January 20, 1927; son of Robert Henry and May Ann (McGuire) McC.; married Dorothy Anne Evers, September 22, 1956; children: Michael Robert, Kathleen Mary. Bachelor of Science, Syracuse University, 1949. Sales assistant Sealright Corp., Fulton, New York, 1949-50; with TEK Hughes div. Johnson & Johnson, Metuchen, New Jersey, 1950-67, general sales manager, 1958-59, vice president sales, 1959-62, president, 1962-67; general manager medical div. Howmet Corp., New York City, 1967-70; group vice president Howmedica, Incorporated, 1970-73, senior vice president, 1973-74, executive vice president, also board of directors, 1974-76; president, chief executive officer C.R. Bard, Incorporated, Murray Hill, New Jersey, 1976-78, chairman board of directors, chief executive officer, 1978-89, chairman board, chief executive officer, 1989—, also board of directors; board of directors Summit and Elizabeth Trust, Summit Bancorp. Trustee Foundation for University Medicine and Dentistry New Jersey, 1987-90; chairman corp. adv. council Syracuse U., 1974-75, trustee, 1979—. With Army of the United States, 1945-46. Member Orthopedic Surgical Manufacturers Association, Health Industry Manufacturers Association (board director, chairman 1982-83), New York Sales Executives Club, Sigma Chi, Pinnacle Club (New York City), Baltusrol Golf Club (Springfield, New Jersey). Office: C R Bard Incorporated 1200 Technology Park Dr Billerica Massachusetts 01821

MCCAIG, JOSEPH J., retail food chain executive; born Brooklyn, 1944. Bachelor of Science, Seton Hall University, 1967. With The Grand Union Company, Elmwood Park, New Jersey, 1965—, general store manager, 1967-68, resident trainer suburban div., 1968-69, supervisor personnel, 1969-70, district manager, 1970-72, superintendent stores, 1972-73, assistant to senior vice president store operations, 1973-74, vice president empire div. and vice president northern region, 1974-78, vice president northern region, 1978-80, senior vice president, 1980-81; president, chief operating officer The Grand Union Co, Wayne, New Jersey, 1981-89, 1989—. Office: Grand Union Company 201 Willowbrook Boulevard Wayne New Jersey 07470

MCCAIN, WARREN EARL, supermarket company executive; born Logan, Kansas, December 17, 1925. Associate of Arts, Oregon State University, 1948; postgraduate, University Illinois. Supervisor sales Mountain States Wholesale Company, 1951-59; with Albertson's Incorporated, Boise, Idaho, owner, operator supermarkets, 1959—, became manager non-foods, 1959, manager store, 1962-65, supervisor merchandise, 1965-67, director intermountain region, 1967-68, vice president operations, 1968-72, executive vice president, 1972-74, president, 1974-84, chairman board, chief executive officer, 1976—, also director; director Idaho 1st National Bank. Office: Albertson's Incorporated 250 Parkcenter Boulevard Boise Idaho 83726

MCCASKEY, MICHAEL, professional sports team executive; born Lancaster, Pennsylvania, December 11, 1943; son of Edward B. and Virginia (Halas) McCaskey; married Nancy McCaskey; children: John, Kathryn. Graduate, Yale University, 1965; Doctor of Philosophy, Case Western Reserve University. Teacher University of California at Los Angeles, 1972-75, Harvard University School Business, Cambridge, Massachusetts, 1975-82; president, chief executive officer Chicago Bears (National Football League), 1983—. Author: The Executive Challenge: Managing Change and Ambiguity. Named Executive of Year Sporting News, 1985. Office: Chicago Bears 250 N Washington Road Lake Forest Illinois 60045

MCCAUGHAN, JOHN F., chemical company executive; born Montreal, Canada, June 24, 1935. Bachelor of Arts, Sir George Williams University, 1957. Chairman, chief executive officer Betz Laboratories Incorporated, Trevose, Pennsylvania. Office: Betz Labs Incorporated 4636 Somerton Road Trevose Pennsylvania 19047

MCCLELLAND, WILLIAM CRAIG, paper company executive; born Orange, New Jersey, April 21, 1934; son of William N. and Pauline (Lee) McC.; married Alice Garrett, December 28, 1956; children: Suzanne, Alice Elizabeth, Heather. Bachelor of Science in Economics, Princeton University, 1956; Master of Business Administration, Harvard University, 1965. Salesman, branch manager PPG Industries, Cleveland and Erie, Pennsylvania, 1960-63; president Watervliet Paper Company div. Hammermill Paper Company, Michigan, 1969-73; product, marketing manager Hammermill Paper Company, Erie, Pennsylvania, 1965-69, vice president, 1973-80, senior vice president, 1980-83, executive vice president, director, 1983-85, president, chief executive officer, 1985-88, also board of directors; senior vice president International Paper Company, 1986-87, executive vice president, 1987-88, also board of directors; executive vice president Union Camp Corp., Wayne, New Jersey, 1988-89, president chief operating officer, 1989—; board of directors Quaker State Corp., PNC Fin. Corp., Allegheny Ludlum Corp. Member Council Fellows, Behrend College of Pennsylvania State U., 1980-88; director Pittsburgh Theol. Seminary, 1988—. Lieutenant (junior grade) United States Navy, 1956-59. Home: 7 Ridge Crest Road Saddle River New Jersey 07458

MCCOLL, HUGH LEON, JR., banker; born Bennettsville, South Carolina, June 18, 1935; son of Hugh Leon and Frances Pratt (Carroll) McC.; married Jane Bratton Spratt, October 3, 1959; children: Hugh Leon III, John Spratt, Jane Bratton. Bachelor of Science in Business Adminstrn, University North Carolina, 1957. Trainee NCNB National Bank, Charlotte, 1959-61, officer, 1961-65, vice president, 1965-68, senior vice president, 1968, div. executive, 1969, executive vice president, 1970-73, vice chairman board, 1973-74, president, 1974-83, also director; president NCNB Corp., 1981-85, chairman board 1983—; board of directors Sonoco Products Incorporated, Hartsville, South Carolina, Ruddick Corp., Charlotte. Trustee Heineman Foundation, Charlotte, 1976—, U. South Carolina Business School, Columbia, Queens College, Charlotte, U. North Carolina at Charlotte; board visitors Grad. School Business U. North Carolina at Chapel Hill; chairman Charlotte Uptown Devel. Corp., 1978-81, 85. 1st lieutenant United States Marine Corps Reserve, 1957-59. Member Association Reserve City Bankers, Am. Bankers Association, North Carolina Bankers Association (president 1974). Democrat. Presbyterian. Office: NCNB Corp 1 NCNB Plaza Charlotte North Carolina 28255

MCCONNELL, JOHN HENDERSON, metal and plastic products manufacturing executive; born New Manchester, West Virginia, May 10, 1923; son of Paul Alexander and Mary Louise (Mayhew) McC.; married Margaret Jane Rardin, February 8, 1946; children—Margaret Louise, John Porter. Bachelor of Arts in Business, Michigan State University, 1949; Doctor Law (honorary), Ohio University, 1981. Sales trainee Weirton Steel Company, West Virginia, 1950-52; sales management Shenango-Steel Company, Farrell, Pennsylvania, 1952-54; founder, chief executive officer Worthington Industries, Incorporated, Columbus, Ohio, 1955—, also chairman; director Alltel Corp., Hudson, Ohio, Anchor Hocking, Lancaster, Ohio, National City Corp., Cleveland. Board of directors Children's Hospital, Columbus; trustee Ashland College, Ohio. Served with United States Navy, 1943-46. Recipient Ohio Governor's award Gov. State of Ohio, 1980; Horatio Alger award Horatio Alger Association, 1983; named Outstanding Chief Executive Officer, Fin. World Magazine, 1981. Member Columbus Area Chamber of Commerce (chairman 1978). Republican. Presbyterian. Clubs: Golf (New Albany, Ohio) (president 1983—); Brookside Country (Columbus) (president 1964-65). Lodge: Masons. Avocations: flying; golf. Office: Worthington Industries Incorporated 1205 Dearborn Dr Columbus Ohio 43085

MCCORD, WILLIAM CHARLES, diversified energy company executive; born San Antonio, April 1, 1928; son of Sam Byard and Helen (Schoepfer) McC.; divorced; children: Kathleen McCord Burnett, Martha McCord Pennington, Billy, Helen McCord Curry, Elizabeth McCord Paschal, Richard Douglas, James, Quannah, Korrin Li, Minta Ann. Bachelor of Science in Mechanical Engineering, Texas Agricultural and Mechanical University, 1949. With Enserch Corp. (formerly Lone Star Gas Company), 1949—, director building management, 1965-67; vice president Enserch Corp. (Dallas div.), 1967, senior vice president operations, 1968-70, president, principal executive officer, 1970-77, chairman, president, 1977—; senior vice president Nipak, Incorporated, chemical subsidiary, Dallas, 1967—; board of directors Employers Casualty Company, Enserch Exploration, Incorporated; managing general partner Enserch Exploration Ptnrs., Limited; with Pool Energy Services Company. Past president, member executive board Circle Ten council Boy Scouts Am.; member national executive board Boy Scouts Am.; board of directors, former chairman Texas Research League, Dallas Citizens Council, State Fair Texas, Children's Medical Center Dallas; trustee Southwestern Medical Foundation. Member Am. Petroleum Institute (director), National Petrolium Council, Tau Beta Pi. Baptist. Office:

Enserch Corp 300 S St Paul St Dallas Texas 75201

MCCORMICK, CHARLES PERRY, JR., food products company executive; born Baltimore, May 29, 1928; son of Charles P. and Marion (Hinds) McM.; married Marlene Darby Hicks, July 29, 1950 (divorced 1980); children: Charles P. III, William C., Linda M., Gail P.; married Jimi Helen Faulk, July 1, 1980. Student, Johns Hopkins University, 1946-47, Duke University, 1948-49. Vice president new products McCormick Company, Incorporated, Hunt Valley, Maryland, 1962-70, vice president corp. devel., 1970-81, vice president packaging group, 1986-87, president, chief executive officer, 1987-88, chairman, chief executive officer, 1988—; chairman, president Setco, Incorporated, Anaheim, California, 1981-87, Tubed Products Incorporated, Easthampton, Massachusetts, 1985-87. Republican. Club: Annapolis Yacht, Hunt Valley Golf Club. Avocations: sailing, racing, golf, tennis. Office: McCormick & Company Incorporated 11350 McCormick Road Hunt Valley Maryland 21031

MCCORMICK, JAMES EDWARD, oil company executive; born Providence, November 5, 1927; son of James Edward and Edna Josephine (Smith) McC.; married Catherine Sullivan, August 30, 1952. Bachelor of Arts in Geology, Boston University, 1952. Engineer trainee Sun Oil Company, Beaumont, Texas, 1953-54; junior geologist Sun Oil Company, Houston, 1954-67, exploration manager, 1967-70; regional manager geology Sun Oil Company, Dallas, 1970-71, exploration program manager, 1971-74, div. manager strategy planning, 1974-77, vice president international exploration and production, 1977-86, president exploration and production, 1986—; board of directors Texas Research League, Austin, Am. Petroleum Institute, Texas Commerce Bank, B.J. Services Company, Houston, University Texas Devel. Board. Board of directors United Way Metropolitan Dallas, 1986—; member Dallas Citizens Council, 1986—. Served as sergeant United States Air Force, 1945-48. Member Am. Association Petroleum Geologists, New York Acad. Sciences, National Ocean Industries Association (board directors 1986—), Northwood Country Club, Las Colinas Country Club, Energy Club, Dallas Petroleum Club. Roman Catholic. Clubs: Northwood Country, Las Colinas Country. Office: Oryx Energy Company 13155 Noel Road Dallas Texas 75240-5067

MCCORMICK, WILLIAM THOMAS, JR., electric and gas company executive; born Washington, September 12, 1944; son of William Thomas and Lucy Valentine (Offutt) McC.; married Ann Loretta du Mais, June 13, 1969; children: Christopher, Patrick. Bachelor of Science, Cornell University, 1966; Doctor of Philosophy, Massachusetts Institute of Technology, 1969. Member staff Institute for Defense Analysis, Arlington, Virginia, 1969-72; member staff Office of Sci. and Tech., Executive office of the President, Washington, 1972-73; senior staff member Energy Policy Office, The White House, 1973-74; chief sci. and energy tech. branch Office Management and Budget, Executive Office of the President, 1974-75; director commercialization United States Energy Research and Devel. Administration, 1975-76; vice president policy and government relations Am. Gas Association, 1976-78; vice president, assistant to chairman Am. Natural Resources Company, Detroit, 1978-80; executive vice president Michigan Wisconsin Pipeline Company, Am. Natural Resources System, Detroit, 1980-82; president Am. Natural Resources Company, Detroit, 1982-85; chairman, chief executive officer Consumers Power Company, Jackson, Michigan, 1985—; board of directors Bancorp. Principal author, editor: Commercialization of Synthetic Fuels in the U.S, 1975. Board of directors Detroit Symphony, St. John Hospital. Alfred P. Sloan scholar, 1962-66. Member Econ. Club Detroit (board directors), Greater Detroit Chamber of Commerce (board directors), Econ. Alliance Michigan (board directors). Roman Catholic. Clubs: Cosmos (Washington); Detroit Athletic, Country of Detroit, Detroit. Office: Consumers Power Company 212 W Michigan Avenue Jackson Michigan 49201

MC COY, JOHN BONNET, banker; born Columbus, Ohio, June 11, 1943; son of John Gardner and Jeanne Newlove (Bonnet) McC.; married Jane Deborah Taylor, April 21, 1968; children: Tracy Bonnet, Paige Taylor, John Taylor. Bachelor of Arts, Williams College, 1965; Master of Business Administration, Stanford University, 1967. With Banc One Corp., Columbus NA, Columbus, Ohio, 1970—, banking officer, 1970-73, vice president, 1973-77, president, 1977-83; president, chief operating officer Banc One Corp., Columbus, Ohio, 1983-84, president, chief executive officer, 1984-87, chairman, chief executive officer, 1987—; president Bank One Trust Company, 1979-81, board of directors Cardinal Distribution Incorporated, Banc One Corp., Federal National Mortgage Association, Ameritech, federal adv. council Federal Reserve System, 1991. Active Boy Scouts Am.; trustee, vice chairman Kenyon College, 1989—, Stanford University, Children's Hospital, United Way of Franklin County, Columbus Acad.; president Columbus Area Growth Foundation; chairman Capitol South Urban Redevel. Corp. Served to captain United States Air Force, 1967-70. Member Columbus Chamber of Commerce (past chairman, trustee), Am. Bankers Association, Association Reserve City Bankers (board directors 1989—), Association Bank Holding Companies, Young Pres.' Organization (chairman Columbus chapter 1982-83). Episcopalian. Clubs: Columbus, Links (New York City). Office: Banc One Corp 100 E Broad St Columbus Ohio 43271-0261

MCCOY, ROBERT S., JR., bank executive; born Traverse City, Michigan, 1938. Bachelor of Business Administration, Western Michigan University, 1961. With Price Waterhouse, until 1984; executive vice president South Carolina National Bank, Columbia, 1984—; president South Carolina National Corp., Columbia, 1984—. Home: 6346 Westshore Road Columbia South Carolina 29206 Office: South Carolina National Corp 1426 Main St Columbia South Carolina 29226

MC CULLOUGH, SAMUEL ALEXANDER, banker; born Pittsburgh, November 10, 1938; son of Alexander and Mary Ruth (Brady) McC.; married Katharine Graham, September 23, 1967; children:

Bonnie McCullough Wideman, Elizabeth McCullough White, Rebecca D., Anne D., Mary D. Bachelor of Business Administration, University Pittsburgh, 1960; Doctor of Laws (honorary), Albright College, Reading, Pennsylvania, 1990. With Mellon Bank, N.A., Pittsburgh, 1956-75, assistant cashier, 1964-68, assistant vice president, 1968-71, vice president, 1971-75; senior vice president corp. banking group Am. Bank and Trust Company of Pennsylvania, Reading, 1975, executive vice president, 1977, president, chief executive officer, 1978-82, chairman, chief executive officer, 1982—; president, chief executive officer Meridian Bancorp., Incorporated, Reading, 1983-88, chairman, chief executive officer, 1988—, also board of directors; and board of directors to all principal subsidiary companies; former representative 3d Federal Reserve District, board member; vice chairman, board of directors Greater Philadelphia 1st Corp.; executive committee Pennsylvania Chamber Business and Industry; board of directors, member audit and pub. relations committees Federal Reserve Bank Philadelphia. Board of directors Philadelphia Orchestra Association; trustee Albright College, chairman executive committee; member executive board Valley Forge council Boy Scouts Am., also board of directors, member executive committee N.E. region, member national executive board, member audit and nominating committees; board governors, chairman Pennsylvanians for Effective Government; member steering committee Business Leaders Organized for Catholic Schools; board member Commonwealth Foundation, U. Pittsburgh Joseph M. Katz Grad. School Business. Recipient Distinguished Pennsylvanian award, 1982, Pagoda award for outstanding contributions to community Berks County Junior Achievement, 1985, William H. Doran Memorial award, 1987, Bicentennial medal University Pitts., 1988, Annual Enterprise award Pennsylvania Council on Economic Education, 1989, Outstanding Vol. Fund Raiser award Greater Northeastern Pennsylvania chapter National Society Fund Raising Executives, Good Scout award Philadelphia Council Boy Scouts Am., 1990, Silver Antelope award, 1991; named Business Person of Year Berks County Chamber of Commerce, 1985. Member Am. Institute Banking, Am. Bankers Association, Pennsylvania Bankers Association, Berks County Bankers Association, Asns. Reserve City Bankers, Association Bank Holding Companies (board directors, legis. policy committee, chairman elect), International Fin. Conference (board directors, past chairman), Fin. Svcs. Council, Greater Philadelphia Chamber of Commerce (executive committee), Allegheny Country Club, Berkshire Country Club. Republican. Presbyterian. Office: Meridian Bancorp Incorporated 35 N 6th St Post Office Box 1102 Reading Pennsylvania 19603

MC CUNE, WILLIAM JAMES, JR., manufacturing company executive; born Glens Falls, New York, June 2, 1915; son of William James and Brunnhilde (Decker) McC.; married Janet Waters, April 19, 1940; 1 daughter, Constance (Mrs. Leslie Sheppard); married Elisabeth Johnson, August 8, 1946; children: William Joseph, Heather H.D. Bachelor of Science, Massachusetts Institute of Technology, 1937. With

Polaroid Corp., Cambridge, Massachusetts, 1939—, vice president engineering, 1954-63, vice president, assistant general manager, 1963-69, executive vice president, after 1969, president, chief executive officer, director, 1980-82, chairman board, president, chief exec officer, 1982-86, chairman board, 1986—. Chairman board, trustee Mitre Corp.; Trustee Boston Mus. Sci., Massachusetts General Hospital. Fellow Am. Acad. Arts and Sciences; member National Acad. Engineering. Office: Polaroid Corp 549 Technology Square Cambridge Massachusetts 02139

MCDERMOTT, THOMAS CURTIS, health care and consumer products company executive; born Somerville, Massachusetts, June 25, 1936; son of Thomas Curtis and Kathryn (Vinicomb) McD.; married Gloria Newmark, June 7, 1958; children—Thomas, Mark, James, Andrew. Bachelor of Science, Providence College. Manager corp. security Bristol Myers, New York City, 1965-70; director personnel, industrial relations E.R. Squibb & Son, Princeton, New Jersey, 1971-78; vice president human resources Bausch & Lomb, Rochester, New York, 1978-80, senior vice president human resources, 1981-82, group president, 1982-85, executive vice president, president United States operations, 1985—, president, chief operating officer, 1986—; vice president human resources General Cinema, Chestnut Hill, Massachusetts, 1980-81; board of directors Bausch & Lomb, Rochester, Chase Lincoln First Regional Bank. Trustee Rochester Institute Tech. Served to 1st lieutenant United States Army, 1958-62. Member Society Former Federal Bureau of Investigation Agts., Rochester Chamber of Commerce (board directors). Roman Catholic. Clubs: Genessee Valley (Rochester), Oak Hill Country. Avocations: tennis; golf; skiing. Home: 3465 East Avenue Rochester New York 14618

MCGEE, WILLIAM G., air transportation company executive. Chairman, chief executive officer, chief operating officer Braniff, Incorporated, Orlando, Florida. Office: Braniff Incorporated 8500 Parkline Boulevard Orlando Florida 32812

MC GILLICUDDY, JOHN FRANCIS, banker; born Harrison, New York, December 30, 1930; son of Michael J. and Anna (Munro) McG.; married Constance Burtis, September 9, 1954; children: Michael Sean, Faith Burtis Benoit, Constance Erin Mc Gillicuddy Mills, Brian Munro, John Walsh. Bachelor of Arts, Princeton, 1952; Bachelor of Laws, Harvard, 1955. With Manufacturers Hanover Trust Company subsidiary Manufacturers Hanover Corp., New York City, 1958—, vice president, 1962-66, senior vice president, 1966-69, executive vice president, assistant to chairman, 1969-70, vice chairman, director, 1970, president, 1971—, chairman, chief executive officer, 1979—; chairman, chief executive officer Manufacturers Hanover Corp., New York City; board of directors USX Corp., Continental Corp., UAL Corp., Federal Reserve Bank of New York. Board of directors National Multiple Sclerosis Society; trustee New York Hospital, Princeton U., New York Pub. Library. Served to lieutenant (junior grade) United States Naval Reserve, 1955-58. Member Association Reserve City Bankers, Business Council, Business Roundtable. Roman Catholic. Clubs:

Westchester Country (Rye, New York); Blind Brook (Port Chester, New York); Princeton (New York City). Office: Mfrs Hanover Corp 270 Park Avenue New York New York 10017

MCGOWAN, GEORGE VINCENT, public utility executive; born Baltimore, January 30, 1928; son of Joseph H. and Ethna M. (Prahl) McG.; married Carol Murray, August 6, 1977; children by a previous marriage: Gregg Blair, Bradford Kirby. Bachelor of Science in Mechanical Engineer, University Maryland, 1951. Registered professional engineer, Maryland. Project engineer nuclear power plant Baltimore Gas & Electric Company, 1967-72, chief nuclear engineer, 1972-74, president, chief operating officer, 1980-87, chairman board dirs, 1988—, manager corp. staff services, 1974-78, vice president management and staff services, 1978-79; board of directors Baltimore Life Insurance Company, McCormick & Company, Life of Maryland Incorporated, Am. Gas Association, UNC Incorporated, Organization Resources Counselors, Incorporated, MNC Fin., Incorporated. Board of directors Am. Nuclear Energy Council, Washington, 1982—; chairman board regents U. Maryland System; board of directors U. Maryland Medical System; chairman Governor's Volunteer Council State of Maryland; trustee Walters Art Gallery, Baltimore, 1982—; board of directors Baltimore chapter American Red Cross, Baltimore Symphony Orchestra, Greater Baltimore Committee; chairman of board United Way Central Maryland. Recipient Distinguished Alumnus award University Maryland College Engineering, 1980, 87. Member American Society of Mechanical Engineers, Am. Nuclear Society, United States Energy Association of the World Energy Conference, Engineering Society Baltimore (Founders Day award 1988), Maryland Chamber of Commerce(board directors). Presbyterian. Clubs: The Center (Baltimore); University Maryland M (College Park, Maryland); Chartwell Golf & Country (Severna Park, Maryland); Annapolis Yacht (Maryland); Maryland (Baltimore). Office: Baltimore Gas & Electric Company Post Office Box 1475 Baltimore Maryland 21203

MC GOWAN, WILLIAM GEORGE, telecommunications company executive; born Ashley, Pennsylvania, 1927; married. Bachelor of Arts, King's College, 1952; Master of Business Administration, Harvard University, 1954. Business consultant 1954-68; with MCI Communications Corp., Washington, DC, 1968—; founder, chairman, chief executive officer MCI Communications Corp., Washington, 1968—, also director. Board of directors Georgetown U. Office: MCI Communications Corp 1133 19th St Northwest Washington District of Columbia 20036

MC GRAW, HAROLD WHITTLESEY, JR., publisher; born Brooklyn, January 10, 1918; son of Harold Whittlesey and Louise (Higgins) McG.; married Anne PerLee, November 30, 1940; children: Suzanne, Harold Whittlesey III, Thomas Per-Lee, Robert Pearse. Graduate, Lawrenceville (New Jersey) School, 1936; Bachelor of Arts, Princeton University, 1940. With G.M. Basford (advertising agency), New York City, 1940-41, Brentano's Bookstores, Incorporated, 1946; with McGraw-Hill Book Company,

Incorporated, New York City, 1947—, successively promotion manager, director company advertising and trade sales, 1947-55, director, vice president charge trade book, industrial and business book departments, company advertising, 1955-61, senior vice president, 1961-68, president, chief executive officer, 1968-74; president, chief executive officer McGraw-Hill, Incorporated, 1974-83, chairman, 1976-88; chairman emeritus 1988—; board of directors McGraw Hill, Incorporated, 1954-88. Founder, president, board of directors Business Council Effective Literacy and Business Press Educational Foundation Served as captain United States Army Air Force, 1941-45. Clubs: University (New York City); Blind Brook (Purchase, New York); Wee Burn (Darien, Connecticut). Home: Watch Tower Road Darien Connecticut 06820 Office: McGraw-Hill Incorporated 1221 Avenue of the Americas New York New York 10020

MCINNES, HAROLD A., manufacturing company executive; born Groton, Connecticut, 1927. Bachelor of Science in Mechanical Engineering, Massachusetts Institute of Technology, 1949. With Delco Appliance div. General Motors Corp., 1949-55, Tracerlab, Incorporated, 1955-60, Reed Rolled Thread Die Company, 1960-62, Dresser Industries, Incorporated, 1962-65, AMP, Incorporated, Harrisburg, Pennsylvania, 1965—; manufacturing manager packaging components AMP, Incorporated, 1966-70, manager automach div., 1970-73, group director general products, 1973-78, vice president manufacturing resources planning, 1978-79, corp. vice president engineering and tech. resources, 1979-81, president, 1981-86, vice chairman, board of directors, 1986-90, chairman, chief executive officer, 1990—; board of directors PPG Industries, Pittsburgh. Office: AMP Incorporated 470 Friendship Road Harrisburg Pennsylvania 17111

MCKENNA, QUENTIN CARNEGIE, tool company executive; born Claremont, California, September 2, 1926; son of George Alexander and Lillian Frances (Street) McK.; married Barbara Louise Williamson, September 12, 1948 (divorced 1984); children: Candace, Megan, Carl, Erin; married Barbara K. Somogye, March 18, 1989. Bachelor of Arts cum laude, Pomona College, 1948; postgraduate, Stanford University (Hewlett Packard fellow), 1948-50, University Southern California, 1951-53, University of California at Los Angeles, 1968-69. Member tech. staff guided missile div. Hughes Aircraft Company, 1950-52; with Industrial Electronics, 1952-55; with Hughes Aircraft Company, 1955-78, assistant group executive missile systems group, 1977-78; with Kennametal, Incorporated, Latrobe, Pennsylvania, 1978—, chairman board, chief executive officer, 1989—; board of directors Interlake Corp., Pittsburgh National Bank, PNC Fin. Corp.; adj. professor industrial administration Grad. School Industrial Administration, Carnegie-Mellon University, 1990—. Patentee in field. Trustee St. Vincent College, 1981-89; member committee board trustees Buhl Sci. Center, Carnegie Institute, 1989. Recipient Eli Whitney Memorial award, Society Mfg. Engineers, 1983. Member Phi Beta Kappa, Sigma Xi. Episcopalian.

MCKENNA, WILLIAM JOHN, textile products executive; born New York

City, October 11, 1926; son of William T. and Florence (Valis) McK.; married Jean T. McNulty, August 27, 1949 (deceased November 1984); children: Kevin, Marybeth, Peter, Dawn; married Karen Lynne Hilgert, August 6, 1988; 1 child, Katherine Lynne. Bachelor of Business Administration, Iona College, 1949; Master of Science (University Store Service scholar), New York University, 1950. Vice president Hat Corp. Am., New York City, 1961-63, vice president marketing, 1961-63, executive vice president, 1963-67; president Manhattan Shirt Company, New York City, 1967-74, Lee Company, Incorporated, Shawnee Mission, Kansas, 1974-82, also director; president, director Kellwood Company, St. Louis, 1982—, chief executive officer, 1984-91, also board of directors, chairman, president, chief executive officer, 1991—; director Genovese Drug Stores, Melville, New York, United Missouri Bancshares, Kansas City, Missouri. Trustee St. Louis U.; chairman Boys Hope. Served with United States Navy, 1944-46, PTO. Roman Catholic. Clubs: St. Louis, Bellerive Country. Office: Kellwood Company 600 Kellwood Parkway Saint Louis Missouri 63017

MCKENNY, JERE WESLEY, energy firm executive; born Okmulgee, Oklahoma, February 14, 1929; son of Jere Claus and Juanita (Hunter) McK.; married Anne Ross Stewart, May 4, 1957; children: Jere James, Robert Stewart. Bachelor of Science in Geological Engineering, University Oklahoma, 1951, Master of Science in Geological Engineering, 1952. With Kerr-McGee Corp., Oklahoma City, 1953—, manager oil and gas exploration, 1968-69, vice president oil and gas, 1969-74, vice president exploration, 1974-77, vice chairman, 1977—, president, 1983—, chief operating officer, 1988—; Member alumni adv. council School Geology and Geophysics University Oklahoma. Served with United States Army, 1953-55. Member Am. Association Petroleum Geologists, Am. Petroleum Institute (board directors), Ind. Petroleum Association Am. (board directors), Houston Geological Society, Oklahoma City Geological Society, Sigma Xi, Sigma Gamma Epsilon, Oklahoma City Golf and Country Club. Episcopalian. Office: Kerr-McGee Corp Post Office Box 25861 Oklahoma City Oklahoma 73125

MCKERNAN, LEO JOSEPH, manufacturing company executive; born Philadelphia, February 17, 1938; son of Leo Joseph and Mary (Dever) McK.; married Gail Marie Ryan, February 3, 1962; children: Kim, Jennifer. Student, Iona College, 1956-59, New York University, 1961-62, University Bridgeport, 1962-64. With Eaton Corp., Carol Stream, Illinois, 1959-74; manager manufacturing Controls div. Eaton Corp., Carol Stream, 1974; vice president general manager Axle div. Clark Equipment Company, Buchanan, Michigan, 1974-77, group vice president, 1977-83, senior vice president, then executive vice president, then chief operating officer, 1983-86; president, chief executive officer Clark Equipment Company, South Bend, Ind., 1986—, chairman, 1988—, also board of directors; member supervisory board VME Group N.V.; board of directors 1st Source Corp., Lincoln National Corp. Board of directors South Bend Civic Center Foundation, Ind., 1978-83;

member U. Notre Dame Engring. Adv. Council, 1985—, corp. grants committee, 1988—. Member Constrn. Ind. Manufacturers Association, Society Automotive Engineers, U.S.-Korea Business Council, Brazil-U.S. Business Council. Office: Clark Equipment Company 100 N Michigan St Box 7008 South Bend Indiana 46634

MCKINNON, ARNOLD BORDEN, transportation company executive; born Goldsboro, North Carolina, August 13, 1927; son of Henry Alexander and Margaret (Borden) McK.; married Oriana McArthur, July 19, 1950; children: Arnold Borden Jr., Colin McArthur, Henry Alexander. Bachelor of Arts, Duke University, 1950, Bachelor of Laws, 1951; graduate Advanced Management Program, Harvard University, 1972. Bar: District of Columbia 1951, North Carolina 1966. With Norfolk Southern Corp. (formerly Southern Railway System), Norfolk, Virginia, 1951—, vice president law, 1971-75, senior vice president law and accounting, 1975-77, executive vice president law and accounting, 1977-81, executive vice president law and fin., 1981-82, executive vice president marketing, 1982-86, vice chairman, 1986-87, chairman, president, chief executive officer, 1987—; board of directors C&S/Sovran Corp., Avantor Fin. Corp., National Maritime Center Foundation, Atmospheric Fluidized Bed Devel. Corp., Knoxville. Board visitors Old Dominion U., Norfolk, Fuqua School Business, Duke U., Durham; member Coal Industry adv. board; member business adv. committee Northwestern U. Transportation Center; member Mil. Civilian Liaison Group, National Coal Council, North Carolina Citizens Business and Industry, Virginia Business Council; board trustees Boys and Girls Clubs Am., Virginia Foundation for Ind. Colleges, Medical College Hampton Roads Foundation; vice chairman gov.'s adv. council Revenue Estimates; elder 1st Presbyterian Church, Norfolk. Served with United States Army, 1946-47. Member American Bar Association, North Carolina Bar Association, District of Columbia Bar Association, Am. Society Corp. Executives, The Conference Board, The House Wednesday Group, National Freight Traffic Association, Association Am. R.R.s (board directors), Am. Society Transportation Logistics, Business Roundtable, Norfolk Chamber of Commerce, Norfolk Yacht and Country Club, Town Point Club, The Harbor Club, Chevy Chase Club, Metropolitan Club (Washington), The Links Club, The Broad Street Club (New York City), Laurel Valley Golf Club (Ligonier, Pennsylvania), The Business Roundtable. Home: 552 Mowbray Arch Norfolk Virginia 23507 Office: Norfolk Southern Corp 3 Commercial Place Norfolk Virginia 23510-2191

MC KONE, DON T., manufacturing company executive; born Jackson, Michigan, 1921. Graduate, University Michigan, 1947. With Aeroquip Corp. (subsidiary TRINOVA Corp.), Jackson, Michigan, 1949-68; with Libbey-Owens-Ford Company (name changed to TRINOVA Corp. in 1986) Aeroquip Corp. (subsidiary TRINOVA Corp.), Toledo, Ohio, 1968—, executive vice president, 1970-75, president, chief operating officer, 1975-79, president, chief executive officer, 1979-80; chairman board, director TRINOVA Corp. (formerly Libbey-Owens-Ford Company), Maumee,

Ohio, 1980—, chief executive officer, 1980-86; board of directors NBD Bancorp., Incorporated, Consumers Power Company, Ashland Oil Company. Office: TRINOVA Corp 3000 Strayer St Maumee Ohio 43537

MCLARTY, THOMAS F., III (MACK MCLARTY), gas company executive; born Hope, Arkansas, June 14, 1946; son of Thomas Franklin and Helen (Hesterly) McL.; married Donna Kay Cochran, June 14, 1969; children—Mark Cochran, Franklin Hesterly. Bachelor of Arts, University Arkansas, 1968. Founder McLarty Leasing System, Little Rock, 1969-79; president McLarty Company, 1979-83, Arkansas Louisiana Gas Company, 1983, Arkla, Incorporated, Little Rock, 1984-88; chairman, chief executive officer Arkla, Incorporated, Little Rock and Shreveport (Louisiana), 1985—; now also chairman, chief executive officer, director Arkla Exploration Company subsidiary Arkla, Incorporated, Shreveport; chairman Arkla Energy Marketing Company, Shreveport, Louisiana, Arkla Chemical Corp., Chreveport, AER-Ark. Gas Transit Company, Shreveport; chairman, chief executive officer, Mississippi River Transmission Corp., St. Louis, MRT Energy Marketing Company, St. Louis, Arkansas Louisiana Fin. Corp., Shreveport. Member Arkansas House of Representatives, 1970-72; chairman Arkansas Democratic Committee; member Dem. National Committee, 1974-76; treasurer David Pryor Gubernatorial Campaign, 1974, Governor Bill Clinton campaign, 1978; board of directors Hendrix College, Conway, Arkansas; board visitors U. Arkansas, Little Rock; former chairman United Negro College Fund Campaign, fund-raising campaign Arkansas Symphony. Member Greater Little Rock Chamber of Commerce (president 1983). Office: Arkla Exploration Company Post Office Box 21734 Shreveport Louisiana 71151

MCMILLAN, HOWARD LAMAR, JR., banker; born Jackson, Mississippi, August 29, 1938; son of Howard Lamar and Mary Frances (Byars) McM.; married Mary Eliza Love, July 5, 1964; children: Eliza Love McMillan Garraway, Howard Lamar III. Bachelor of Arts in Banking & Finance, University Mississippi, Oxford, 1960; postgraduate, Louisiana State University, 1966, Harvard University, 1979. With Deposit Guaranty National Bank, Jackson, 1960, vice president, 1972-73, senior vice president, 1973-77, executive vice president corp. div., 1977-81, executive vice president state bank div., 1981-84, president, director, 1987—; president, director Deposit Guaranty Corp., Jackson, 1984—. General chairman United Way, Jackson, 1989—. Member Am. Bankers Association (board directors 1988—), Mississippi Bankers Association (chairman federal legis. committee), Jackson Chamber of Commerce (board directors 1989—), University Mississippi Alumni Association (president 1988), 100 Club (Jackson). Avocations: golfing, snow skiing, reading. Office: Deposit Guaranty National Bank Post Office Box 1200 Jackson Mississippi 39215-1200

MC MULLIAN, AMOS RYALS, food company executive; born Jackson County, Florida, August 28, 1937; son of Andrew Jackson and Willie Ross (Ryals) McM.; married Jackie Williams, August 27, 1960; children: Amos Ryals, Britton Jackelyn.

Bachelor of Science, Florida State University, 1962. Successively assistant controller, data processing coordinator, administrative assistant to general manager, assistant plant manager, plant manager Flowers Baking Company, Thomasville, Georgia, 1963-70, president Atlanta Baking Company div., 1970-72, regional vice president parent company, 1972-74, president, chief operating officer bakery div., 1974-76, chief operating officer industry, 1976-81, president, 1976-83, director, 1981—, chief executive officer, 1983—, co-chairman executive committee, 1983—, vice chairman industry and chairman executive committee, 1984-85, chairman board, 1985—. Member adv. board, president's club Florida State U.; member gridiron society U. Georgia; past Thomasville Chamber of Commerce With United States Marine Corps, 1958-61; trustee Southeastern Legal Foundation. Named Outstanding Business Alumnus Florida State University. Member National Association Manufacturers (board directors), Atlanta Bakers Club (past president), Atlanta Commerce Club, Thomasville Landmarks Society. Episcopalian (vestry, sr. warden). Office: Flowers Industries Incorporated United States Highway 19 S Post Office Drawer 1338 Thomasville Georgia 31799

MCNAMARA, JOHN F., health services company executive; born 1935. Vice president, general manager McKesson Drug Company, Los Angeles, 1974-78, president Value Rite div., 1978-81; with Alco Health Services Corp. Incorporated, Valley Forge, Pennsylvania, 1981—, president Kauffman-Lettimer div., 1981-83, vice president, 1983-84, executive vice president, 1984-85, chief operating officer, executive vice president, 1985-87, president, chief operating officer, 1987-88, chairman, president, chief executive officer, 1988—, also board of directors. Office: Alco Health Services Corp 300 Chester Field Parkway Malvern Pennsylvania 19335

MC NEALY, SCOTT, computer company executive. Chairman, president, chief executive officer Sun Microsystems Incorporated, Mountain View, California. Office: Sun Microsystems Incorporated 2550 Garcia Avenue Mountain View California 94043

MCNEIL, JOHN D., insurance company executive; born Southampton, England, February 17, 1934; came to Canada, 1956; son of Spencer Ewart and Janet McNeil; married Isobel Esther Spence, December 24, 1956; children: Spencer, Claire, John, Alison, David. Master of Arts with honors, University Edinburgh, 1956. With Sun Life Assurance Company of Can., Montreal, Quebec, 1955-56, with investment department, 1956, assistant treasurer, 1962-66, vice president securities and investments, 1979, senior vice president, general manager United States div., 1982-85, executive vice president, 1985-87, deputy chairman, director, 1987—; with Mutual Funds Management Corp., Limited, 1966-73, Morrison, Krembil, Limited, 1974-75; administrator Morrison, Krembil Limited, 1974-75; board of directors, chairman, president, trustee numerous affiliated Sun Life companies. Member Institute Chartered Fin. Analysts, Toronto Society Fin. Analysts. Club: Canadian (board dirs.). Home: 10 McKenzie Avenue, Toronto, Ontario Canada M4W 1J9

Office: Sun Life Assurance Company Can, POB 4150 Station A, Toronto, Ontario Canada M5W 2C9

MCNUTT, JACK WRAY, oil company executive; born Norphlet, Arkansas, September 7, 1934; son of Fay D. and Mattie E. (Garner) McN.; married Jordine Chesshir, August 19, 1955; 1 child, Marsha. Bachelor of Science, Harding College, 1956; Master of Science, Columbia University, 1957. Accountant Murphy Oil Corp., El Dorado, Arkansas, 1957-68, executive management assistant, 1968-69, executive vice president, 1981-88, chief operating officer, 1986-88, president, chief executive officer, 1988—, also board of directors; vice president planning Murphy Eastern Oil Company, London, 1969-72, president, 1972-81; board of directors Ocean Drilling & Exploration Company, New Orleans, First National Bank El Dorado, Arkansas, Murphy Oil Company Limited, Calgary, Alberta, Can. Member Am. Petroleum Institute, Am. Econ. Association, National Association Business Economists, 25 Year Club of Petroleum Industry, National Petroleum Council. Home: 1705 W Cedar El Dorado Arkansas 71730 Office: Murphy Oil Corp 200 Peach St El Dorado Arkansas 71730

MC PHERSON, FRANK ALFRED, corporation executive; born Stilwell, Oklahoma, April 29, 1933; son of Younce B. and Maurine Francis (Strauss) McP.; married Nadine Wall, September 10, 1955; 4 children. Bachelor of Science, Oklahoma State University, 1957. With Kerr-McGee, 1957—; general manager Gulf Coast Oil and gas operations, Morgan City, Louisiana, 1969-73; president Kerr-McGee Coal, 1973-76, Kerr-McGee Nuclear, 1976-77; vice chairman Kerr-McGee Corp., 1977-80, president, 1980-83, chairman, chief executive officer, 1983—; board of directors Kimberly-Clark Corp., Federal Reserve Bank Kansas City. Patentee in field. Board of directors Oklahoma chapter Nature Conservancy, United States Olympic Committee for Oklahoma, Baptist Medical Center Oklahoma, Oklahoma Medical Research Foundation, Baptist Medical Center Oklahoma, Oklahoma State U. Foundation, United Way Greater Oklahoma City; board of directors State Fair Oklahoma, member Task Force 2000, Education Business Council; trustee Oklahoma City Community Foundation; member board governors Kirkpatrick Center; member appeals rev. board Greater Oklahoma City, Oklahoma Foundation Excellence, Oklahoma Acad. for State Goals, Business Roundtable; member adv. committee U. Oklahoma College Medicine; co-chair Oklahoma City Pub. School Education Task Force. Captain United States Air Force, 1957-60. Member Conference Board, Society Mining Engineers Am. , Am. Petroleum Institute (director), National Petroleum Council, 25-Yr. Club of Petroleum Industry Oklahoma City Chamber of Commerce (director), Oklahoma State Chamber of Commerce. Republican. Baptist. Office: Kerr-McGee Corp Post Office Box 25861 Oklahoma City Oklahoma 73125

MCQUARRIE, GERALD H., savings and loan association executive; born Minersville, Utah, June 28, 1921; son of Herrick and Lucy Irene (Hall) McQ.; married Oneida B. Martin, February 22, 1946; children: Sandra Irene, Gerald Brent, Roger Scott. Graduate, Compton College, 1941.

President McQuarrie Realty Company; co-founder, now chief executive officer, secretary Downey Savings and Loan Association, Newport Beach, California, also board of directors. With United States Naval Reserve, 1945-46, United States Air Force, 1950-52. Member Church of Jesus Christ of Latter Day Saints. Office: Downey Savings & Loan Association 3501 Jamboree Road Newport Beach California 92660

MCWHORTER, RALPH CLAYTON, health care company executive; born Chattanooga, 1933. Bachelor of Science, Samford University, 1955; postgraduate, University Tennessee. Assistant administrator Phoebe Putney Memorial Hospital, 1956-65; administrator Americus-Sumter Regional Hospital, 1965-67, West Georgia Medical Center, 1967-70; administrator Palmyra Park Hospital Hospital Corp. Am., Nashville, 1970-73, div. vice president, 1973-76, senior vice president hospital operations United States, 1976-80, executive vice president domestic operations, 1980-85, president, chief operating officer, 1985-87, also board of directors; chairman, chief executive officer HealthTrust, Incorporated, Nashville, 1988—. Office: HealthTrust Incorporated 4525 Harding Road Nashville Tennessee 37203

MEAD, GEORGE WILSON, II, paper company executive; born Milwaukee, October 11, 1927; son of Stanton W. and Dorothy (Williams) M.; married Helen Patricia Anderson, September 3, 1949 (divorced February 1990); children: Deborah, David, Leslie; married Susan A. Feith, August 25, 1990. Bachelor of Science, Yale University, 1950; Master of Science, Institute Paper Chemistry, Wisconsin, 1952. With Consolidated Papers, Incorporated, Wisconsin Rapids, Wisconsin, 1952—, vice president operations, 1962-66, president, chief executive officer, 1966-71, chairman board, chief executive officer, 1971—, also director; president, director Consolidated Water Power Company; chairman board 1st Wisconsin National Bank; board of directors Snap-On Tools Corp., Firstar Corp. Co-chairman bldg. fund drive Riverview Hospital, Wisconsin Rapids, 1963-64, member board, 1961-77; board of directors Consol.'s Civic Foundation; board of directors National Council for Air and Stream Improvement; trustee Lawrence U.; chairman board trustees Institute Paper Sci. and Tech., 1988-90. Member Technical Association of the Pulp and Paper Industry (director 1969-72), Am. Paper Institute (director 1967-69, 80—), Milwaukee Athletic Club, Chicago Club, Elks (exalted ruler 1958), Rotary. Office: Consol Papers Incorporated Post Office Box 8050 Wisconsin Rapids Wisconsin 54495-8050

MEADE, JAMES EDWARD, economist; born Dorset, England, June 23, 1907; son of Charles Hippisley and Kathleen (Cotton-Stapleton) M.; married Elizabeth Margaret Wilson, March 14, 1933; children—Thomas Wilson, Charlotte Elizabeth Meade Lewis, Bridget Ariane Meade Dommen, Carol Margaret Meade Dasgupta. Student, Oriel College, Oxford University, 1926-30, Trinity College, Cambridge University, 1930-31; Master of Arts, Oxford University, Cambridge University; Doctor (honorary), University Basel, University Hull, University Bath, University Oxford. Fellow, lecturer economics Hertford College, Oxford University,

1930-37; hon. fellow London School Economics; editor World Economic Survey, League of Nations, Geneva, 1937-40; member economic section Cabinet Secretariat, London, 1940-45, director, 1945-47; professor commerce London School Economics, 1947-57; professor political economy Cambridge University, 1957-69, senior research fellow Christ's College, 1969-74; visiting professor Australian National University, 1956; chairman Economic Survey Mission to Mauritius, 1960; chairman Committee on Structure and Reform of Direct Taxation, 1974-77; governor National Institute Economic and Social Research, 1947—, LSE, 1960-74, Malvern College, 1972—. Author: The Rate of Interest in a Progressive State, 1933; Economic Analysis and Policy, 1936; Consumers Credits and Unemployment, 1937; League of Nations World Economic Surveys, 1938 and 1939; Economic Basis of a Durable Peace, 1940; Planning and the Price Mechanism, 1948; The Balance of Payments, 1951; Trade and Welfare, 1955; A Geometry of International Trade, 1952; Problems of Economic Union, 1953; The Theory of Customs Unions, 1955; Control of Inflation, 1958; Neo-Classical Theory of Economic Growth, 1960; Efficiency, Equality and the Ownership of Property, 1964; The Sationary Economy, 1965; The Theory of Indicative Planning, 1967; The Growing Economy, 1968; The Controlled Economy, 1971; The Theory of Economic Externalities, 1973; The Intelligent Radical's Guide to Economic Policy, 1975; The Just Economy, 1976; Stagflation, Volume I: Wage-Fixing, 1982, Volume II, Demand Management, 1983, Alternate Systems of Business Organization and of Workers' Renumeration, 1986; Collected Papers: Volumes 1, 2, and 3, 1988, Volume 4, 1989; Macroeconomic Policy: Inflation, Wealth and the Exchange Rate (jointly), 1989; Agathotopia: The Economics of Partnership, 1989. Decorated companion Order of Bath; recipient Nobel prize in econs., 1977. Fellow Brit. Acad.; member Royal Econ. Society (past president), Brit. Association (past section president), National Acad. Sciences (United States) (foreign associate), Eugenics Society (past member council), Am. Acad. Arts and Sciences (foreign hon.). Office: Christ's College, Cambridge England

MEADLOCK, JAMES W., computer graphics company executive; born 1933; married. Bachelor of Science in Electrical Engineering, North Carolina State University, 1956. Department manager International Business Machines Corporation, 1956-69; president Intergraph Corp., Huntsville, Alabama, 1969—; also chairman board of directors Intergraph Corp., Huntsville; chief executive officer Intergraph Corp., 1989—. Office: Intergraph Corp 1 Madison Industrial Park Huntsville Alabama 35807

MEDLIN, JOHN GRIMES, JR., banker; born Benson, North Carolina, November 23, 1933; son of John Grimes and Mabel (Stephenson) M. Bachelor of Science in Business Administration, University North Carolina, 1956; graduate, The Exec. Program, University Virginia, 1965. With Wachovia Bank & Trust Company, Winston-Salem, North Carolina, 1959—, president, 1974; president, chief executive officer Wachovia Bank and Wachovia Corp., Winston-

Salem, North Carolina, 1977, chairman, chief executive officer, 1985; president, chief executive officer Wachovia Corp. (formerly First Wachovia Corp.), Winston-Salem, North Carolina, 1985—, also board of directors, chairman; board of directors USAir Group, Incorporated, RJR Nabisco, Incorporated, First Wachovia Corp., BellSouth Corp., National Service Industries, Incorporated. Trustee National Humanities Center, The Conference Board, Wake Forest U.; board of directors Kenan Institute Private Enterprise; active numerous civic and service organizations, North Carolina Business Council Mgmt. and Devel. With United States Naval Reserve, 1956-59. Member Association Reserve City Bankers (past president), Am. Bankers Association, Order Holy Grail, Order Old Well, Phi Delta Theta. Club: Old Town (Winston-Salem). Lodge: Rotary (president Winston-Salem 1973—). Office: Wachovia Corp 301 N Main St Post Office Box 3099 Winston-Salem North Carolina 27150

MEEK, PAUL DERALD, oil and chemical company executive; born McAllen, Texas, August 15, 1930; son of William Van and Martha Mary (Sharp) M.; married Betty Catherine Robertson, April 18, 1954; children: Paula Marie Meek Burford, Kathy Diane Meek Hasemann, Carol Ann Meek Miller, Linda Rae Meek. Bachelor of Science in Chemical Engineering, University Texas, Austin, 1953. Member tech. department Humble Oil & Refining Company, Baytown, Texas, 1953-55; with Cosden Oil & Chemical Company, 1955-76, president, 1968-76; director Fina, Incorporated (formerly Am. Petrofina, Incorporated), Dallas, 1968—; vice president parent company Am. Petrofina, Incorporated, Dallas, 1968-76, president, chief operating officer, 1976-83, president, chief executive officer, 1983-86, chairman board, president, chief executive officer, 1984-86, chairman board, 1986—; appointed by Governor Wm. P. Clements, Junior chairman Pub. Uitilites Commission of Texas, 1989—. Contributing author: Advances in Petroleum Chemistry and Refining, 1957. Chairman chem. engring. visiting committee U. Texas, 1975-76; member adv. council College Engring. Foundation, U. Texas, Austin, 1979—, Young Women's Christian Association of Dallas, 1983-87, U. Texas Longhorn Foundation, 1989—, College of Natural Scis. Foundation 1989—; co-chairman industrial div. United Way of Metropolitan Dallas, 1981-82; associate board visitors U. Texas M.D. Anderson Cancer Center, 1985—, member prof. excellence committee, 1989—. Named Distinguished Engineering Graduate University Texas, Austin, 1969. Member Am. Petroleum Institute, 25 Year Club of the Petroleum Industry, Founders Club of the Petrochem. Industry, Dallas Wildcat Committee (chairman executive committee 1987-88). Office: Fina Incorporated 8350 N Central Expressway Post Office Box 2159 Dallas Texas 75221

MELLOR, JAMES ROBB, defense company executive; born Detroit, May 3, 1930; son of Clifford and Gladys (Robb) M.; married Suzanne Stykos, June 8, 1953; children: James Robb, Diane Elyse, Deborah Lynn. Bachelor of Science in Electrical Engineering and Math, University Michigan, 1952, Master of Science, 1953. Member tech. staff Hughes Aircraft Company, Fullerton,

California, 1955-58; president Data Systems div. Litton Industries, Van Nuys, California, after 1958; executive vice president Litton Industries, Incorporated, Beverly Hills, California; president, chief operating officer AM International, Incorporated, Los Angeles, to 1981; executive vice president, director General Dynamics Corp., 1981-90, president, chief operating officer, 1990—; director Bergen Brunswig Corp., Kerr. Patentee in fields of storage tubes and display systems; contributor articles to professional publications. 1st lieutenant, Signal Corps, Army of the United States, 1953-55. Member Institute of Electrical and Electronics Engineers, Am. Management Association, Armed Forces Communications and Electronics Association (director), Computer and Business Equipment Manufacturers Association (director), Sigma Xi, Tau Beta Pi, Eta Kappa Nu, Phi Kappa Phi. Clubs: Los Angeles Country, Old Warson Country, St. Louis, California, Eldorado. Home: 7759 Kingsbury Boulevard Saint Louis Missouri 63105 Office: General Dynamics Corp Pierre Laclede Center Saint Louis Missouri 63105

MELONE, JOSEPH JAMES, insurance company executive; born Pittston, Pennsylvania, July 27, 1931; son of Dominick William and Beatrice Marie (Pignone) M.; married Marie Jane DeGeorge, January 23, 1960; children—Lisa, Carol. Bachelor of Science, University Pennsylvania, 1953, Master of Business Administration, 1954, Doctor of Philosophy in Econs, 1961. C.L.U., 1963 C.P.C.U., 1964. Associate professor insurance University Pennsylvania, 1959-66, member pension research council, 1961-66; research director Am. College Life Underwriters, 1966-68; vice president Prudential Insurance Company, Boston, 1969-76; senior vice president Prudential Insurance Company, Newark, 1976-81, executive vice president, 1981-84, president, 1984-90; president, chief operating officer, board of directors The Equitable Life Assurance Society United States, New York City, 1990—; chairman, trustee Equitable Funds; board of directors Foster Wheeler Corp., Alliance Capital Management, Donaldson, Lufkin & Jenrette. Author: Collectively Bargained Multi-Employer Pension Plans, 1961; co-author: Risk and Insurance, 1963, Pension Planning, 1966. Trustee Newark Mus.; member Archbishop's Committee of Laity of Newark Archdiocese, Archdiocesan Board Administration, Newark; board overseers Wharton School U. Pennsylvania. Member Am. Risk and Insurance Association, Am. Society CLUs, Am. College (trustee), Am. Institute Property and Liability Underwriters (trustee), Pennsylvania State University International Insurance Society, International Acad. Management, Health Insurance Association Am. (chairman), U.S.-Korea Business Council, Morris County Country Club, Alpha Tau Omega. Home: 281 Hartshorn Dr Short Hills New Jersey 07078 Office: Equitable Life Assurance 787 7th Avenue New York New York 10019

MELROSE, KENDRICK BASCOM, manufacturing company executive; born Orlando, Florida, July 31, 1940; son of Henry Bascom and Dorothy (Lumley) M.; children: Robert, Vella, Kendra. Bachelor of Science cum laude, Princeton University, 1962; Master of Science, Massachusetts Institute of Technology, 1965; Master of Business Administration, University Chicago, 1967. Marketing manager Pillsbury Company, Minneapolis, 1967-69; director corp. planning Bayfield Techs., Incorporated, Minneapolis, 1969-70; with Toro Company (manufacturers outdoor power equipment), Minneapolis, 1970—, executive vice president outdoor power equipment div., 1980-81, president, 1981-88, chief executive officer, 1988, also chairman. Congregationalist. Office: Toro Company 8111 Lyndale Avenue S Minneapolis Minnesota 55420

MENDOZA, ROBERTO G., JR., banker; born Cuba, 1945. Bachelor of Arts, Yale University, 1967; Master of Business Administration, Harvard University, 1974. With Morgan Guaranty Trust Company, New York City, 1967—, formerly managing director; v. chairman J.P. Morgan & Company, New York City, 1990—, also director for global mergers and acquisitions. Office: J P Morgan & Company 23 Wall St New York New York 10015

MERCER, RONALD L., food company executive; born Camargo, Oklahoma, October 19, 1934; son of Joseph William and Lura (Dewald) M.; married D. Yvonne Edwards, July 23, 1954; children: Gary D., Marla K., Lisa R., Michael D. Bachelor of Business Administration, Southern Nazarene University, Bethany, Oklahoma, 1970; Doctor of Humanities, Southern Nazarene University, 1989; PMD, Harvard University, 1973. Branch sales manager Xerox Corp., Dallas, 1961-65; branch manager Xerox Corp., Oklahoma City, 1965-70; manager sales planning Xerox Corp., Rochester, New York, 1970-71; regional sales manager Xerox Corp., Chicago, 1971-74; regional vice president, general manager Xerox Corp., Greenwich, Connecticut, 1975-79; senior vice president Xerox Corp., Rochester, 1982-87; president, chief executive officer Xerox Can., Incorporated, Toronto, Ontario, 1979-82; chairman, chief executive officer Wilson Foods Corp. wholly owned subsidiary Doskocil Companies, Incorporated, Oklahoma City, 1988-89; president, chief operating officer Doskocil Companies, Incorporated, 1989—; board of directors 1st National Bank, Bethany, Oklahoma, Intertechnica, Oklahoma City, Doskocil Companies, Incorporated, Hutchinson, Kansas, Southern Nazarene University, International Church Nazarene, Kansas City, Kansas. Chairman international Layman's Conference, Nashville, 1991. Republican. Member Church of Nazarene. Avocation: golf. Home: 7917 Northwest 38th St Bethany Oklahoma 73008 Office: Doskocil Cos Incorporated Post Office Box 1570 Hutchinson Kansas 67504-1570

MERLO, HARRY ANGELO, forest products executive; born Stirling City, California, March 5, 1925; son of Joseph Angelo and Clotilde (Camussa) M.; 1 son, Harry A. Bachelor of Science, University Calif.-Berkeley, 1949, postgraduate, 1949. Vice president Rockport Redwood Company, Cloverdale, California, 1967; vice president Northern California div. Ga.-Pacific Corp., Samoa, California, 1967-69; vice president Western lumber div. Ga.-Pacific Corp., Portland, Oregon, 1969-71, executive vice president Western timber, plywood and lumber operations, 1971-73; president, chairman board La.-Pacific Corp., Portland, 1973—; adv. board School

Business Administration University California, Berkeley; board of directors World Forestry Center, Whitman Industries. Member President's Council, Columbia Pacific council Boy Scouts Am.; former member national adv. council Salvation Army; trustee Hugh O'Brian Youth Foundation, Oregon Mus. Sci. and Industry, Goodwill Industries; past chairman board Am. Acad. Achievement; former western fin. chairman United States Olympic commission; chairman, adv. board Salvation Army, Oregon; board of directors Marshall U. Society Yaeger Scholars. Lieutenant United States Marine Corps Reserve. Named Man of Year Ga.-Pacific Corp., 1969; recipient Golden Plate award Am. Acad. Achievement, 1974; Horatio Alger award, 1980, Gold award for forest products industry The Wall St. Transcript, 1982, 83, Distinguished Service award Louisiana Tech. University, 1984, Aubrey Watzek award Lewis and Clark College, 1984, Citizen of Merit award Assoc. Builders and Contractors, 1986, Piemontese Del Munde award, 1986, Merit award California Parks & Recreation Society, 1988, John J. Mulrooney award N.Am. Wholesale Lumber Association, 1989. Member California Redwood Association (past president, board directors), Am. Paper Institute (board directors), Horatio Alger Association (president), National Forest Products Association (board directors), Founders Club (board dirs), Waverly County Club, Arlington Club, Multnomah Athletic Club, Ingomar Club, Knights of the Vine. Office: La-Pacific Corp 111 Southwest 5th Avenue Portland Oregon 97204

MERRILL, RICHARD THOMAS, publishing executive; born Chicago, June 26, 1928; son of Thomas William and Mary Ann (Colvin) M.; married Lisi Y. Snyder, June 7, 1952; children: T. William II, James R., Stephen J. Bachelor of Arts, University Missouri, 1950, Bachelor of Journalism, 1951. With Commerce Clearing House, Chicago, 1953—, vice president, 1962-76, executive vice president, 1976-79, president, chief executive officer, 1980—, also director; board of directors CCH Australia, CCH Can. Limited, National Quotation Bureau, CT Corp. System, Computax, State Capitol Information Service, Facts on File, Blvd. Bank, Chicago, Blvd. Bancorp. Incorporated, Washington Service Bureau, McDougall, Littell and Company, Fiscal y Laboral (S.A. de C.V.). Captain United States Air Force, 1951-53. Home: 5 Astor Court Lake Forest Illinois 60045 Office: Commerce Clearing House Incorporated 2700 Lake Cook Road Riverwoods Illinois 60015 also: Commerce Clearing House Incorporated 4025 W Peterson Avenue Chicago Illinois 60646

MERTEN, ALAN GILBERT, university dean; born Milwaukee, December 27, 1941; son of Gilbert Ervin and Ruth Anna (Ristow) M.; married Sally Louise Otto; children: Eric, Melissa. Bachelor of Science, University Wisconsin, 1963; Master of Science, Stanford University, 1964; Doctor of Philosophy, University Wisconsin, 1970. Assistant professor University Michigan, Ann Arbor, 1970-74, associate professor, 1974-81, professor, 1981-86, associate dean, 1983-86; dean University Florida, Gainesville, 1986-89; dean Johnson Grad. School of

Management Cornell University, Ithaca, New York, 1989—; board of directors Comshare, Incorporated, Ann Arbor, Tompkins County Trust Company, Ithaca, Am. Assembly of Collegiate Schools Business; member information system adv. council Whirlpool Corp., Benton Harbor, Michigan, 1987—; member Gov.'s Select Committee on Workforce 2000, Florida, 1988-89. Author: Internal Control in United States Corporations, 1980, Senior Management Control of Computer-Based Information Systems, 1983. Board of directors University Musical Society, Ann Arbor, 1985-86; member Airport Authority, Gainesville, Florida, 1986-89; member Speakers Adv. Committee on the Future, Tallahassee, Florida, 1987-88. Served to captain United States Air Force, 1963-67. Lutheran. Home: 532 Cayuga Heights Road Ithaca New York 14850 Office: Cornell U Johnson Grad School Management Ithaca New York 14853

MEYER, DANIEL JOSEPH, machinery company executive; born Flint, Michigan, May 31, 1936; son of John Michael and Margaret (Meehan) M.; married Bonnie Harrison, June 22, 1963; children—Daniel P., Jennifer. Bachelor of Science, Purdue University, 1958; Master of Business Administration, Ind. University, 1963. C.P.A., New York. Manager Touche, Ross & Company, Detroit, 1964-69; controller Cincinnati Milacron, Incorporated, 1969-77, vice president fin., treasurer, 1977-83, executive vice president fin. and administration, 1983-86, president, chief operating officer, 1987-99, president, chief executive officer, 1990-91, chairman, president, chief executive officer, 1991—, also board of directors; board of directors E.W. Scripps Incorporated, Hubbell Incorporated, Star Bank Corp. Served with United States Army, 1959. Member Am. Institute C.P.A.'s. Club: Kenwood Country (Cincinnati). Home: 8010 Peregrine Lane Cincinnati Ohio 45243 Office: Cincinnati Milacron Incorporated 4701 Marburg Avenue Cincinnati Ohio 45209

MEYER, JEROME J., diversified technology company executive; born Caledonia, Minnesota, February 18, 1938; son of Herbert J. and Edna (Staggemeyer) M.; married Sandra Ann Beaudoin, June 18, 1960; children—Randall Lee, Lisa Ann, Michelle Lynn. Student, Hamline University, 1956-58; Bachelor of Arts, University Minnesota, 1960. Devel. engineer Firestone Tire & Rubber Company, Akron, Ohio, 1960-61; vice president, general manager Sperry Univac, St. Paul, 1961-79; group vice president Honeywell, Incorporated, Minneapolis, 1979-84; president, chief operating officer Varian Associates, Palo Alto, California, 1984-86, also board of directors; president, chief executive officer Honeywell Incorporated, 1986—; director Magnetic Data Incorporated, Minneapolis, Keycom Electronic Pub. Company, Chicago, Honeywell Erickson Devel. Company, Anaheim, California. Board of directors Young Men's Christian Association, West St. Paul, Minnesota, 1977. Clubs: Southview Country (West St. Paul) Palo Alto Hills Country, Mission Viejo Country. Avocation: golf. Office: Honeywell Incorporated Honeywell Plaza Minneapolis Minnesota 55408

MILER, MARTIN C., bank holding company executive. With Hibernia Corp., New Orleans, 1972—, formerly president, chief executive officer, now also chairman. Office: Hibernia Corp 313 Carondelet St Post Office Box 61540 New Orleans Louisiana 70161

MILGRIM, HALE A., recording industry executive; born California, August 22, 1948; son of David A. Milgrim and Miriam (Glickman) Milgrim Wolfe; married Anne Mewhirter, January 24. Graduate high school, Lubbock, Texas, 1955. Writer, producer Acuff-Rose, Nashville, 1959-62; manager label head United Artist Record, Nashville, 1966-69; owner House of Golf Music, Nashville, 1969-82; director creative service Tree Publication, Nashville, 1986-88; vice president artistic and repretoir Epic Records div. CBS Records, Nashville, 1989—. Writer songs including Misty Blue, 1966, Back in Babys Arms, 1972; publisher song Behing Closed Doors, 1972; producer records including Some Memories Just Want, 1983, Chiseled in Stone, 1989. Recipient Robert Burton award BMI, 1975. also: 810 7th Avenue New York New York 10019

MILLER, ALAN B., hospital management executive; born New York City, August 17, 1937; son of Daniel and Mary (Blumenthal) M.; married Jill K. Stein, October 5, 1968; children: Marc Daniel, Marni Elizabeth, Abby Danielle. Bachelor of Arts, College William and Mary, 1958; Master of Business Administration, University Pennsylvania, 1960. Vice president Young & Rubicam, Incorporated, New York City, 1964-69; senior vice president Am. Medicorp., Incorporated, Los Angeles, 1970; president, chief executive officer Am. Medicorp., Incorporated, Philadelphia, 1973-77, chairman board, 1977; chairman board Hospital Underwriting Group, 1977-78; founder, president, chairman board Universal Health Services, King of Prussia, Pennsylvania, 1978—; chairman, founder UHT-Real Estate Trust, King of Prussia, 1986—; health care adviser Federal Mediation and Conciliation Service; board member Lenoard David Institute University Pennsylvania; member adv. board Temple University School Business; chairman, president Universal Health Services Real Estate Investment Trust, New York Stock Exchange, 1986—; board of directors General Motors Corporation Information Services, Incorporated. Trustee College of William and Mary; board of directors Penjerdel Council, Opera Company of Philadelphia. Member Philadelphia Chamber of Commerce (board director). Home: 57 Crosby Brown Road Gladwyne Pennsylvania 19035 Office: Universal Health Services Incorporated 367 S Gulph Road King of Prussia Pennsylvania 19406

MILLER, CHARLES DALY, business executive; born Hartford, Connecticut, 1928; married. Graduate, Johns Hopkins University. Sales manager Yale & Towne Manufacturing Company, 1955-59; associate Booz, Allen & Hamilton, 1959-64; with Avery International Corp., Pasadena, California, 1964—, group vice president, 1969-72, executive vice president operations, 1972-75, president, 1975-77, chief executive officer, 1977—, now also chairman, director. Office: Avery International Corp 150 N Orange Grove Boulevard Pasadena California 91103

MILLER, DONALD E., rubber company executive; born Denver, December 17, 1930; son of Alex H.

and Nina A. (Schlatter) M.; married Barbara J. Rehm, June 15, 1952; children: Steven, David. Graduate, Colorado School Mines, 1953. With Gates Rubber Company, Denver, 1963—; field sales manager industrial sales Gates Rubber Company, 1963-66, vice president manufacturing, 1966-69, vice president autohardware sales, 1969-73, vice president marketing, 1973-81, group vice president automotive, 1981-82, president, 1982—. 1st lieutenant United States Army, 1954-56. Presbyterian. Home: 5965 E Princeton Circle Englewood Colorado 80111 Office: Gates Rubber Company 900 S Broadway Post Office Box 5887 Denver Colorado 80209

MILLER, EUGENE ALBERT, banker. married. Bachelor of Business Administration, Detroit Institute Tech., 1964; graduate, School Bank Administration, Wisconsin, 1968. With Comerica Bank-Detroit (formerly The Detroit Bank, then Detroit Bank & Trust Company), 1955—, vice president, 1970-74, controller, 1971-74, senior vice president, 1974-78, executive vice president, 1978-81, president, 1981-89, chief executive officer, 1989—, chairman, 1990—; with parent company Comerica Incorporated (formerly DETROITBANK Corp.), 1973—, treasurer, 1973-80, president, 1981—, chief executive officer, 1989—, chairman board, 1990—, also board of directors. Office: Comerica Incorporated 211 W Fort St Detroit Michigan 48275-1049

MILLER, LEWIS N., JR., banker; born 1944. Bachelor of Arts, Washington and Lee University, 1966; postgraduate, University Virginia, 1972. With 1st & Merchants National Bank, 1969-70; planning manager Central Fidelity Bank N.A., Richmond, Virginia, 1972-73, planning officer, then assistant vice president, 1973-75, vice president, 1975-76, senior vice president, manager fin. group, 1976-78, chief fin. officer, 1978-79, executive vice president, 1979-82, executive vice president, chief administrative officer, from 1982; with Central Fidelity Banks Incorporated, Richmond, 1972—, senior vice president, 1980-82, corp. executive officer, 1982-83; executive vice president Central Fidelity Banks Incorporated, Richmond, Virginia, 1983-84; president, later also treasurer Central Fidelity Banks Incorporated, Richmond, from 1984, now president. Lieutenant United States Navy, 1966-69. Office: Central Fidelity Banks Incorporated Broad at 3d St Post Office Box 27602 Richmond Virginia 23261

MILLER, MERTON HOWARD, finance educator; born Boston, May 16, 1923; son of Joel L. and Sylvia F. (Starr) M. Bachelor of Arts, Harvard University, 1943; Doctor of Philosophy, Johns Hopkins University, 1952. With Treasury Department 1944-47, Federal Reserve Board, 1947-49; assistant lecturer London School Economics, 1952; assistant professor, then associate professor Grad. School Industrial Administration, Carnegie Institute Tech., Pittsburgh, 1958-61; professor banking and fin. Grad. School Business University Chicago, 1961—. Coauthor: Theory of Finance, 1972, Macroeconomics, 1974. Recipient Nobel prize in econs., 1990. Fellow Econometric Society; member Am. Fin. Association (president 1976), Am. Econ. Association, Am. Statistical Association. Office: U Chicago

Grad School Business 1101 E 58th St Chicago Illinois 60637

MILLER, RICHARD ARTHUR, utility company executive; born 1927. Bachelor of Business Administration, Case Western Reserve University, 1950; Bachelor of Laws, Harvard University, 1953. With Cleveland Electric Illuminating Company, 1960—, senior tax accountant, 1960-61, principal tax consultant, 1961-62, controller, 1962-69, vice president fin., 1969-75, vice president fin. and general counsel, 1975-77, executive vice president, 1977-83, president, director, 1983-86; president Centerior Energy Corp., Independence, Ohio, 1986-88, chairman, chief executive officer, 1988—. Served with United States Army, 1945-47. Office: Centerior Energy Corp 6200 Oak Tree Boulevard Cleveland Ohio 44101

MILLER, THOMAS MILTON, banker; born Corydon, Indiana, March 2, 1930; son of R. Earl and Catherine (Hudson) M.; married Kathryn Janet Owens, August 28, 1954; children: Kimberleigh Kathryn, Thomas Milton, Jennifer Allen. Bachelor of Science in Bus, Ind. University, 1952; postgraduate, University Wisconsin Graduate School Banking, 1961. With Ind. National Bank, Indianapolis, 1954—; head Ind. div. Ind. National Bank, 1964-68, senior vice president, head metropolitan, 1968-71, executive vice president, head commercial banking div., 1971-76, president, from 1976, chairman, chief executive officer, 1979—; chairman INB National Bank, INB Fin. Corp.; director State Life Insurance Company, Indianapolis Water Company, Boehringer Mannheim United States Holdings, Incorporated. Member executive committee Indianapolis Convention and Visitors Association, chairman board; member adv. board Ind. U.-Purdue U., Indianapolis; director, member executive committee Ind. U. Foundation Served to 1st lieutenant Army of the United States, 1952-54. Member Am. Bankers Association, Reserve and City Bankers, Association Bank Holdings Companies (director), Ind. Chamber of Commerce (director, member executive committee), Indianapolis Chamber of Commerce, Ind. University Alumni Association, Ind. Society Chicago, Ind. University Varsity Club, Meridian Hills Country Club (Indianapolis), Economic Club (Indianapolis, past president), Masons, Sigma Chi. Republican. Methodist. Home: 410 Somerset Dr Indianapolis Indiana 46260 Office: INB Fin Corp 1 Indiana Square Suite 501 Indianapolis Indiana 46266

MILLIKEN, ROGER, textile company executive; born New York City, October 24, 1915; son of Gerrish and Agnes (Gayley) M.; married Justine V. R. Hooper, June 5, 1948; children: Justine, Nancy, Roger, David, Weston. Student, Groton School, 1929-33; Bachelor of Arts, Yale University, 1937; Doctor of Laws (honorary), Wofford College, Rose-Hulman Institute Tech., Philadelphia College Textiles and Science, Brenau College, The Citadel; Doctor Textile Industry (honorary), Clemson University; Doctor of Hebrew Literature (honorary), Converse College. President Milliken & Company, New York City, 1947-83, chairman, chief executive officer, 1983—; board of directors Mercantile Stores Company, W.R. Grace & Company; chairman board Institute Textile Tech., 1948—; board of directors Am. Textile Manufacturers Institute, South Carolina Textile Manufacturers Association. Chairman Greenville-Spartanburg Airport Commission; trustee Wofford College, South Carolina Foundation Ind. College. Member Business Council, Textile Institute (England) (companion member). Clubs: Union League, Links, Augusta National Golf, Yeamans Hall. Office: Milliken & Company Post Office Box 3167 Spartanburg South Carolina 29304

MINCER, JACOB, economics educator; born Tomaszow, Poland, July 15, 1922; came to United States, 1948; son of Isaac and Dora (Eisen) M.; married Flora Kaplan, 1951; children—Deborah, Carolyn. Bachelor of Arts, Emory University, 1950; Doctor of Philosophy, Columbia University, 1957. Assistant professor City University of New York, 1954-59; associate professor Columbia University, New York City, 1960-62; professor economics Columbia University, 1962—; Member research staff National Bureau Economic Research, New York City, 1960—. Author: Schooling, Experience and Earnings, 1974; author, editor: Economic Forecasts and Expectations, 1969. Contributor numerous articles to professional publications. Postdoctoral fellow University Chicago, 1957-58; Guggenheim fellow, New York City, 1971. Fellow Am. Statistical Association, Econometric Society, Am. Econ. Association (Distinguished); member Am. Acad. Arts and Sciences, National Acad. Education. Home: 448 Riverside Dr New York New York 10027 Office: Department Econs Columbia University 118th St at Amsterdam Avenue New York New York 10027

MITCHELL, DAVID T., electronic computing equipment company executive; born 1942. Production control manager Honeywell Incorporated, Minneapolis, 1966-69; director manufacturing planning Memorex Corp., Santa Clara, California, 1969-72; director materials Fairchild Camera and Instrument Corp., Mountain View, California, 1972-75; president Castell Incorporated, Santa Ana, California, 1975-77; director materials Bendix Corp., San Francisco, 1977-78; general manager Commodore Business Machines Incorporated, Santa Clara, 1978-80; president, chief operating officer Seagate Tech., Scotts Valley, California, 1980—, also board of directors. Captain United States Marine Corps, 1963-66. Office: Seagate Tech 920 Disc Dr Scotts Valley California 95066

MITCHELL, EDWARD FRANKLIN, utility company executive; born Harrisonburg, Virginia, December 23, 1931; son of Charlotte Elaine M. married Suzanne S. Sublette, August 20, 1955; children: Karen Mitchell Holland, Brian. Bachelor of Electrical Engineering, University Virginia, 1956; Master.E.A., George Washington University, 1960. Registered professional engineer, District of Columbia. With Potomac Electric Power Company, Washington, 1956—, vice president electrical engineering, 1971-76, senior vice president system engineering and operations, 1976-80, executive vice president, chief operating officer, 1980-83, president, chief operating officer, 1983—, also director; member adv. council University Maryland Engineering College; director Suburban Bank. Member Vienna (Virginia) Town Council, 1963-66; member Vienna Planning and Zoning Commission, 1963-66; elder

Vienna Presbyterian Church; board of directors D.C. chapter American Red Cross., National Rehabilitation Hospital Served with United States Navy, 1950-52. Member Maryland Chamber of Commerce (board directors). Home: 9409 Duxford Court Potomac Maryland 20854 Office: Potomac Electric Power Company 1900 Pennsylvania Avenue Northwest Washington District of Columbia 20068

MITCHELL, GEORGE P., gas and petroleum company executive; born Galveston, Texas, 1919; married. Bachelor of Science, Texas Agricultural and Mechanical University, 1940. Exploration engineer, geologist Amoco Production Company, 1940-41, consultant geologist, engineer, 1946-51; with Mitchell Energy & Devel. Corp., The Woodlands, Texas, 1947—, chairman, president, 1972—, chief executive officer, from 1972, also board of directors; president George Mitchell & Associates. Served to major United States Army, 1942-46. Office: Mitchell Energy & Devel Corp 2001 Timberloch Place The Woodlands Texas 77387

MITCHELL, JAMES AUSTIN, insurance company executive; born Cincinnati, December 16, 1941; son of James Austin and Jeannette Louise (Stiles) M.; married Patricia Ann McNulty, August 12, 1967; 1 child, J. David. Bachelor of Arts, Princeton University, 1963. Chartered Life Underwriter; chartered fin. consultant; FSA. Various positions Connecticut General Life Insurance Company, Hartford, 1963-73, vice president, controller, 1973-77; vice president, chief fin. officer Aetna Insurance Company, Hartford, 1977-82; president Cigna RE Corp., Hartford, 1982-84; president, chief executive officer IDS Life Insurance Company, Minneapolis, 1984—; director IDS Fin. Services and Affiliated Companies, Minneapolis. Member executive committee Minneapolis Institute Arts, 1987—; president Princeton Alumni Society, 1986—. With United States Army, 1964-70. Fellow Society Actuaries; member Society C.L.U.s. Republican. Presbyterian. Club: Minneapolis. Avocations: tennis; skiing; reading. Home: 2685 N Shore Dr Wayzata Minnesota 55391 Office: IDS Life Ins Company 2900 IDS Tower Minneapolis Minnesota 55474

MODELL, ARTHUR B., professional football team executive; born Brooklyn, June 23, 1925; married Patricia Breslin, July 25, 1969; stepchildren: John, David. Owner, president Cleveland Browns football team, 1961—; president National Football League, 1967-70. Office: Cleveland Browns Cleveland Stadium Cleveland Ohio 44114

MODIGLIANI, FRANCO, economics and finance educator; born Rome, June 18, 1918; came to United States, 1939, naturalized, 1946; son of Enrico and Olga (Flaschel) M.; married Serena Calabi, May 22, 1939; children: Andre, Segio. Doctor Jurisprudence, University Rome, 1939; Doctor Social Science, New School Social Research, 1944; Doctor of Laws (honorary), University Chicago, 1967; Doctor honoris causa, University Louvain, Belgium, 1974, Istituto Universitario di Bergamo, 1979, Hartford University; Doctor of Humane Letters (honorary), Bard College, 1989; HLD (honorary), Brandeis University, 1986, New School Social Research, 1989, Michigan State University, 1989; Doctor (honorary), University Illinois,

1990. Instructor economics and statistics New Jersey College Women, New Brunswick, 1942; instructor, then associate economics and statistics Bard College, Columbia, 1942-44; lecturer, assistant professor math. economics and econometrics New School Social Research, 1943-44, 46-48; research associate, chief statistician Institute World Affairs, New York City, 1945-48; research consultant Cowles Commission Research in Economics University Chicago, 1949-54; associate professor, then professor economics University Illinois, 1949-52; professor economics and industrial administration Carnegie Institute Tech., 1952-60; visiting professor economics Harvard University, 1957-58; professor economics Northwestern University, 1960-62; visiting professor economics Massachusetts Institute of Technology, 1960-61, professor economics and finance, 1962—, Institute professor, 1970-88, Institute professor emeritus, 1988—; Fellow political economy University Chicago, 1948; Fulbright lecturer University Rome, also, Palermo, Italy, 1955. Author: The Debate Over Stabilization Policy, 1986, Il Caso Italia, 1986, The Collected Papers of Franco Modigliani, 3 volumes, 1980, 4th and 5th volumes, 1989; co-author: National Incomes and International Trade, 1953, Planning Production, Inventories and Work Forces, 1960, The Role of Anticipations and Plans in Economic Behavior and Their Use in Economic Analysis and Forecasting, 1961, New Mortgage Designs for Stable Housing in an Inflationary Environment, 1975. Member macro econs. policy group Center for European Policy Studies, 1985—. Recipient Nobel prize in econ. sci., 1985; Cavaliere Di Gran Groce Repubblica Italiana, 1985, Premio Coltura for Econs., Repubblica Italiana, 1988, Premio APE award, 1988, Graham and Dodd award, 1975, 80, James R. Killian Junior Faculty Achievement award, 1985, Lord Foundation prize, 1989, Italy Premio Columbus, 1989, Italy Premio Guido Dorso, 1989, Itlay Pemio Stivale D'oro, 1991. Fellow Econometric Society (council 1960, vice president 1961, president 1962), Am. Econ. Association (vice president 1975, president 1976), International Econ. Association (vice president 1977-83, hon. president 1983—), Am. Acad. Arts and Sciences; member National Acad. Sciences, Am. Fin. Association (president 1981). Home: 25 Clark St Belmont Massachusetts 02178 Office: Massachusetts Institute of Technology Sloan School Management Cambridge Massachusetts 02139

MOE, PALMER L., gas company executive; born Billings, Montana, 1944. Bachelor of Science in Business Administration, University Denver, 1966. Member audit staff to managing partner Arthur Anderson Company, 1965-83; president, chief operating officer Valero Energy Corp., San Antonio, 1983—; vice chairman, board of directors Valero Transmission Company, Valero Refining and Marketing Company, Valero Natural Gas Company; board of directors Valero Storage, Valero Offshore Incorporated, Valero Offshore Properties Incorporated, Valero Producing Company. Served with United States Army Reserve, 1963-69. Office: Valero Energy Corp 530 McCullough St San Antonio Texas 78215

MOFFETT, JAMES ROBERT, oil and gas company executive; born Houma, Louisiana, August 16, 1938; son of Robert E. and Mary G. (Pollack) M.; married Louise C. Hohmann, June 5, 1960; children: Crystal Louise, James R. Bachelor of Science, University Texas, 1961; Master of Science, Tulane University, 1963. Cons. geologist oil and gas industry New Orleans, 1964-69; vice president founding partner McMoRan Exploration Company, New Orleans, 1969-74; president, chief executive officer McMoRan Oil & Gas Company, New Orleans, 1974-81, 81-85; chairman, chief executive officer McMoRan Oil & Gas Company, from 1985; director McMoRan Oil & Gas Company, New Orleans, from 1974; vice-chairman Freeport McMoRan Incorporated, New Orleans, 1981-85, chairman, chief executive officer, 1985—, director, 1981—; board of directors Hibernia Bank, New Orleans, McMoRan Oil & Gas Company. Member National Petroleum Council, Washington, 1979, Commission on the Future of South, 1986; board of directors Louisiana Energy National PAC, Metairie, Louisiana, 1979, World Trade Center, New Orleans, Am. Cancer Society Greater New Orleans, Business Task Force Education, Incorporated; chairman board Louisiana Council Fiscal Reform; chairman business council New Orleans and River Region, 1985-87. 2nd lieutenant United States Army, 1961-68, captain Reserves retired. Recipient T award Ex Students Association University Texas, 1960, Hornblower Year award Pub. Relations Society Am., 1986, Vol. Year award Urban League Greater New Orleans, 1987; Minnie Stevens Piper Foundation scholar University Texas, 1960, Jacques E. Yenni, S.J. award Loyola University of New Orleans for Outstanding Community Service, Junior Achievement Business Hall of Fame award, 1987, Loyola University of New Orleans' Integritas Vitae award, 1988; named One of Ten Outstanding Persons of 1985 Institute for Human Understanding, New Orleans. Member All Am. Wildcatters, New Orleans Geological Society, Petroleum Club New Orleans, Greater New Orleans Marketing Committee (executive committee 1987), Geology Found University Texas (adv. council 1972-85), Devel. board University Texas, Louisiana Ind. producers Royalty Owners Association. South Louisiana Mid-Contintent Oil Gas Association (vice president), Dinner Steering Committee (Disting, Citizen award 1983, 85 Boy Scouts Am. New Orleans division), Green Wave Club. Republican. Office: Freeport-McMoRan Incorporated 1615 Poydras St New Orleans Louisiana 70112-1217

MONAGHAN, THOMAS STEPHEN, restaurant chain executive; born Ann Arbor, Michigan, March 25, 1937; married Marjorie Zybach, August 25, 1962; children—Mary, Susan, Margaret, Barbara. Student, Ferris State College, University Michigan; Doctor of Philosophy (honorary), Cleary College, 1982, Madonna College, 1983, Eastern Michigan University, 1984, Southern Florida University, 1985. Partner Dominick's Pizza, Ypsilanti, Michigan, 1960-65; president, chairman board founder Domino's Pizza, Incorporated, Ann Arbor, Michigan, 1960—; owner Detroit Tigers, 1983—. Author: (autobiography) Pizza Tiger. Board of directors Cleary College, Ypsilanti, Henry Ford Hospital, Detroit, Detroit

Renaissance, U. Steubinville, Ohio, St. Joseph's Hospital Devel. Board, Ann Arbor. Served with United States Marine Corps, 1956-59. Named Entrepreneur of Year Harvard University Business School, 1984, Pizzaman of Year National Association Pizza Owners, 1984; recipient Golden Plate award Am. Acad. Achievement, 1984, Golden Chain award Multi Unit Franchise Service Organization, 1986, Horatio Alger award, 1986, Restaurant Business Leadership award, 1986, Pope John Paul II Family Fidelity award 1988, Pine Mission's Knights of Charity award, 1990, Semper Fidelis award USMC, 1990. Member International Franchise Association (Entrepreneur of Year 1986), National Restaurant Association (Silver Plate award 1985), Michigan Restaurant Association, Ypsilanti Chamber of Commerce, University Michigan Pres.'s Club, Ann Arbor Pres.'s Association, Missionary Vehicle Association (board directors), American Institute of Architects (hon.), Michigan Society Architects (hon.). Club: Barton Hills Country (Ann Arbor). Lodge: Knights of Columbus. Avocations: collecting Frank Lloyd Wright furniture and memorabilia, classic cars. Office: Domino's Pizza Incorporated Post Office Box 997 Ann Arbor Michigan 48106

MONTGOMERY, JAMES FISCHER, savings and loan association executive; born Topeka, November 30, 1934; son of James Maurice and Frieda Ellen (Fischer) M.; married Linda Jane Hicks, August 25, 1956; children: Michael James, Jeffrey Allen, Andrew Steven, John Gregory. Bachelor of Arts in Accounting, University of California at Los Angeles, 1957. With Price, Waterhouse & Company, C.P.A.'s, Los Angeles, 1957-60; controller Conejo Valley Devel. Company, Thousand Oaks, California, 1960; assistant to president Great Western Fin. Corp., Beverly Hills, California, 1960-64; fin. vice president, treasurer United Fin. Corp., Los Angeles, 1964-69, executive vice president, 1969-74, president, 1975; president Citizens Savings & Loan Association, Los Angeles, 1970-75; chairman, chief executive officer, director Great Western Fin. Corp., also Great Western Bank, Beverly Hills, 1975—. Served with Army of the United States, 1958-60. Office: Great Western Fin Corp 8484 Wilshire Boulevard Beverly Hills California 90211

MOONEY, EDWARD JOSEPH, JR., chemical company executive; born Omar, West Virginia, May 19, 1941; son of Edward Joseph Sr. and Johnny Mae (Kidd) M.; married Mary Martha May, August 22, 1964; children—Elizabeth Anne, Edward Joseph III. Bachelor of Science in Chemical Engineering, University Texas, 1964, Juris Doctor, 1967; Senior Exec. Program, Massachusetts Institute of Technology, 1979. Bar: Texas 1967, Illinois 1973. Corp. counsel Howe-Baker Corp., Tyler, Texas, 1969-70; general counsel Nalco Chemical Company, Oak Brook, Illinois, 1970-80, group general manager, 1980-82, vice president, 1982-84, senior vice president, 1985; group vice president Nalco Chemical Company, Sugarland, Texas, 1985—. Member Illinois Bar Association, State Bar Texas, Am. Patent Law Association. also: One Nalco Center Naperville Illinois 60566

MOORE, GORDON E., electronics company executive; born San Francisco, January 3, 1929; son of Walter Harold and Florence Almira (Williamson) M.; married Betty I. Whittaker, September 9, 1950; children: Kenneth, Steven. Bachelor of Science in Chemistry, University California, 1950; Doctor of Philosophy in Chemistry and Physics, California Institute Tech., 1954. Member tech. staff Shockley Semicondr. Laboratory, 1956-57; manager engineering Fairchild Camera & Instrument Corp., 1957-59, director research and devel., 1959-68; executive vice president Intel Corp., Santa Clara, California, 1968-75; president, chief executive officer Intel Corp., 1975-79, chairman, chief executive officer, 1979-87, chairman, 1987—; board of directors Varian Associates Incorporated, Transamerica Corp. Fellow Institute of Electrical and Electronics Engineers; member National Acad. Engineering, Am. Physical Society. Office: Intel Corp 3065 Bowers Avenue Santa Clara California 95051

MORAN, JAMES MICHAEL, lawyer; born New Haven, February 20, 1957; son of Francis Richard and Anne (Dugan) M.; married Kathy Hildebrandt, September 22, 1984 (divorced 1987). Bachelor of Arts, Loyola University, New Orleans, 1979; Juris Doctor, University Florida, 1982. Bar: Florida 1982. Associate Barton, Cox & Davis, Gainesville, Florida, 1982-85, Patterson, Turk & Hudson Professional Association, Cape Coral, Florida, 1985-86; vice president legal affairs Sun Bank of Lee County N.A., Fort Myers, Florida, 1986—. Member Acad. Trial Lawyers Am., Acad. Florida Trial Lawyers, Phi Sigma Alpha, Beta Alpha Phi. Avocations: windsurfing, scuba diving. Office: Sun Bank Lee County 12730 New Brittany Boulevard Fort Myers Florida 33919

MORAN, JOHN A., investment company executive; born Los Angeles, March 22, 1932; son of Benjamin Edward and Louise (Chisholm) M.; married Mary Darlene Whittaker, August 14, 1954 (divorced October 1984); children—Kelli, Marisa, Elizabeth. Bachelor of Science, University Utah, 1954; postgraduate, New York University, 1958-59, University Southern California, 1959-60. Associate Blyth & Company, Inc, New York City and Los Angeles, 1958-64; vice president Blyth & Company, Inc, Los Angeles, 1964-67; vice president Dyson-Kissner Corp., New York City, 1967-74, executive vice president, 1974-75, president, 1975-84, chairman, 1984—; chairman Dyson-Kissner-Moran, New York City, 1984—; chairman EnviroSource, Incorporated; board of directors Conquest Exploration Company; chairman Fortune Fin. Group. Lieutenant United States Naval Reserve, 1955-58. Member Chief Executives Organization. Republican. Roman Catholic. Clubs: Metropolitan, Racquet and Tennis (New York City); Larchmont Yacht (New York); Winged Foot Golf, (Mamaroneck, New York).

MORGAN, ROBERT B., insurance company executive; born 1934. Bachelor of Arts, Eastern Kentucky University, 1954. Teacher Ind. School System, 1954-56; casualty underwriter Insurance Company of North America, Philadelphia, 1960-66; assistant casualty manager Cincinnati Insurance Company, Incorporated, 1966-69, assistant vice president, 1969-71, vice president, general manager, 1972-75, executive vice president, general manager, 1975, president, 1976, president, chief executive officer, 1986—; president Cincinnati Fin. Corp., 1981, president, chief executive officer, 1991—. Captain Army of the United States, 1956-68. Office: Cincinnati Fin Corp 6200 S Gilmore Road Fairfield Ohio 45014

MORITA, AKIO, electronics company executive; born Nagoya, Japan, January 26, 1921; son of Kyuzaemon and Shuko (Toda) M.; married Yoshiko Kamei, May 13, 1950; children: Hideo, Masao, Naoko. Graduate in physics, Osaka Imperial University, 1944. Co-founder Tokyo Telecommunications Engineering Corp. (now Sony Corp.), Tokyo, 1946, executive vice president, 1959-71, president, 1971-76, chairman, 1976—, chief executive officer, 1976-89; president Sony Corp. Am., 1960-66, chairman board, 1966-72, chairman fin. committee, 1972-74, 77-81, chairman executive committee, 1974-77, from 1981; member international council Morgan Guaranty Trust Company; vice chairman Keidanren, chairman Committee on International Industrial Cooperative. Recipient Medal of Honor with Blue Ribbon, Royal Society Arts Albert medal. Home: 5-6 Aobadai 2-Chome, Meguro-Ku Tokyo 153, Japan Office: Sony Corp, Tokyo Int Box 5100, Tokyo Japan 100-31 also: Sony Corp of America 9 W 57th St New York New York 10019

MORITZ, CHARLES WORTHINGTON, business information and services company executive; born Washington, August 22, 1936; son of Sidney Jr. and Ruth Whitman (Smith) M.; married Susan Prescott Tracy, June 14, 1958; children: Peter W., Tracy W., Margaret Anne. Bachelor of Arts, Yale University, 1958. With R.H. Donnelley Corp., 1960-76, vice president, general manager marketing div., 1972-74, senior vice president, 1974-76, director, 1975-85; executive vice president Dun & Bradstreet Corp., New York City, 1976-78; vice chairman Dun & Bradstreet Corp., 1979-81, director, 1979—, president, chief operating officer, 1981-84, chairman, chief executive officer, 1985—. Served to lieutenant (junior grade) United States Naval Reserve, 1958-60. Member Direct Marketing Association (director 1973-76), Am. Management Association, Sales Executives Club, Econ. Club New York, Pine Valley (New Jersey) Club, Wee Burn Country Club, National Golf Links Am. Club, John's Island Club, Blind Brook Club, Links Club, Zeta Psi. Republican. Episcopalian.

MORLEY, JOHN C., electronic equipment company executive; born 1931. Bachelor of Arts, Yale University, 1954; Master of Business Administration, University Michigan, 1958. Managing director Esso Pappas Chemical Ae., Greece, 1969-70; president Esso Eastern Chemicals Incorporated, New York, 1970-71; executive vice president Enjay Chemical Company, 1971-74; president Exxon Chemical Company United States of America, Houston, 1974-78, senior vice president, 1978-80; president, chief executive officer Reliance Electric Company Incorporated, Cleveland, 1980—, also board of directors. Served to lieutenant (junior grade) United States Naval Reserve, 1954-56. Office: Reliance Electric Company Incorporated

Post Office Box 248020 Cleveland Ohio 44124-8020

MORTON, EDWARD JAMES, insurance company executive; born Fort Wayne, Indiana, November 8, 1926; son of Clifford Leroy and Clara Marie (Merklein) M.; married Jean Ann McClernon, April 30, 1949; children: Marcia Lynn, Anne; married Matthild Schneider, September 19, 1986; 1 child, Katharine. Bachelor of Arts, Yale University, 1949. With John Hancock Mutual Life Insurance Company, Boston, 1949—, vice president, then senior vice president, 1967-74, executive vice president, 1974-82, president, chief operating officer, 1982-86, chairman, chief executive officer, 1987-91; director, M/A-COM, Incorporated; Boston geographic chairman, United States Savings Bonds. Trustee Boston Plan for Excellence in the Pub. Schools, Gettysburg College, Mus. Fine Arts, chairman Egyptian and Ancient Nr. Ea. Art; member corp. adv. committee; board overseers Boston Symphony Orchestra, Children's Hospital, Member Corp., Center for Blood Research, Northeastern U.; active Board Jobs for Massachusetts; director New England Council; member Boston Pub. Libr. Partnership; hon. director National Scoliosis Foundation; director Boston Private Ind. Council, Life Ins. Association of Massachusetts, Massachusetts Business Roundtable, The Freedom Trail Foundation, Greater Boston Arts Fund, John F. Kennedy Center for Performing Arts, Washington; chairman 1991 Boston Geographic Savs. Bonds Campaign. Fellow Society Actuaries; member Am. Council Life Insurance (board directors), National Association Security Dealers (principal), Health Insurance Association of Am. (board directors), Am. Life Insurance Association of Am., Actuaries Club Boston, City Club of Washington, Commercial Club of Boston, Algonquin Club of Boston, Phi Beta Kappa. Office: John Hancock Mut Life Ins Company Post Office Box 111 Boston Massachusetts 02117

MOSBACHER, ROBERT ADAM, secretary of commerce of U.S.; born Mount Vernon, New York, March 11, 1927; son of Emil and Gertrude (Schwartz) M.; married Georgette Paulsin; children—Diane, Robert, Kathryn, Lisa Mosbacher Mears. Bachelor of Science, Washington and Lee University, 1947, Doctor of Laws (honorary), 1984. Independent oil and gas producer 1948-89; secretary Department of Commerce, Washington, 1989—; former chairman, chief executive officer Mosbacher Energy Company, Houston; director Texas Commerce Bancshares, Houston, New York Life Insurance Company. Board of directors Choate School, Wallingford, Connecticut; director Aspen Institute, Center for Strategic and International Studies; chairman board visitors M.D. Anderson Hospital; national fin. chairman George Bush for President; chairman President Ford Fin. Committee; co-chairman Republican National Fin. Committee; director Texas Heart Institute. Member Am. Petroleum Institute (director, executive committee), National Petroleum Council (past chairman), All Am. Wildcatters Association (past chairman), Am. Association Petroleum Landmen (past president). Presbyterian. Office: Commerce Department 14th & Constitution Avenue Northwest Washington District of Columbia 20230

MULLANE, DENIS FRANCIS, insurance executive; born Astoria, New York, August 28, 1930; son of Patrick F. and Margaret (O'Neill) M.; married Kathryn Mullman, June 28, 1952; children: Gerard, Kevin, Denise. Bachelor of Science in Military Engineering, United States Military Academy, 1952; Doctor of Humane Letters (honorary), University Connecticut, 1988, St. Joseph's College, 1990. C.L.U. With Connecticut Mutual Life Insurance Company, Hartford, 1956—, vice president, 1969-72, senior vice president, 1972-74, executive vice president, 1974-76, president, 1977—, chief executive officer, 1983-85, chairman, chief executive officer, 1985-90; chief executive officer, president Connecticut Mutual Life Insurance Company, 1990—; board of directors Connecticut Natural Gas Company. 1st lieutenant Corps of Engineers, United States Army, 1952-56. Recipient John Newton Russell award, 1987, Knight of St. Gregory award. Member Am. Council Life Insurance, Am. Society Corp. Executives, National Association Life Underwriters, Association Grads. United States Military Acad. (president). Republican. Roman Catholic. Office: Connecticut Mut Life Ins Company 140 Garden St Hartford Connecticut 06154

MULLANE, ROBERT E., manufacturing company executive; born Cincinnati, May 27, 1932; son of Robert E. and Marie M.; children: Katherine, Constance, Margaret, Sarah. Graduate, Georgetown University, 1954; Master of Business Administration, Harvard University, 1956. With Automatic Vending Company, 1953-73, Carousel Time, Incorporated, 1973-74; vice president Bally Manufacturing Corp., Chicago, 1974-79, president, 1979-89, chairman board of directors, chief executive officer, 1979—; chairman, chief executive officer Bally's Grand Incorporated, Las Vegas, Nevada; board of directors Bally's Park Place, Incorporated. Office: Bally Mfg Corp 8700 W Bryn Mawr Avenue Chicago Illinois 60631

MULRONEY, JOHN PATRICK, chemical company executive; born Philadelphia, 1935; married. Bachelor of Science, University Pennsylvania, 1957, Master of Science, 1959. With Rohm & Haas Company, Philadelphia, 1958—, group leader engineering department, 1962-64, department head, 1964-67, assistant director research, 1967-71, president, chief operating officer, 1986—; assistant general manager Filital, Milan, 1971-73, general manager, 1973-75; business manager AG Chemical, Europe, 1975-77, regional director Europe, 1977-78; vice president polymers, resins, monomers Industrial Chemical, 1978-80, vice president tech., 1980-82, vice president corp. business, from 1982, also board of directors, 1982—; board of directors Aluminum Corp. Am., Teradyne Incorporated. Member Am. Institute Chemical Engineers, Am. Chemical Society. Office: Rohm & Haas Company Independence Mall W Philadelphia Pennsylvania 19105

MUNGER, CHARLES T., diversified company executive; born 1924; married. Partner Wheeler Munger & Company, 1961-76; chairman, chief executive officer Blue Chip Stamps, 1976-78; vice chairman Berkshire Hathaway, Incorporated, Omaha, Nebraska, 1978—. Office: Berkshire Hathaway Incorporated 1440 Kiewit Plaza Omaha NE 68131

MUNN, STEPHEN P., manufacturing company executive. President, chief executive officer Carlisle Companies Incorporated, Cincinnati, also board of directors; board of directors Carrier Corp. New York. Office: Carlisle Cos Incorporated 250 E 5th St Cincinnati Ohio 45202

MURCHIE, EDWARD MICHAEL, accountant; born New York City, April 21, 1947; son of Edward Thomas and Dorothy (Busk) M.; married Karen M. Raftery, August 26, 1967; children: David, Maureen, Carolyn. Bachelor of Science, Fordham University, Bronx, New York, 1968. C.P.A., New York. Staff accountant Price Waterhouse, New York City, 1968-71, senior auditor, 1971-74, audit manager, 1974-75; director internal audit Eltra Corp., New York City, 1975-78, assistant controller, 1978-79; vice president fin. Eltra Corp., Morristown, New Jersey, 1981-82, Converse Rubber, Wilmington, Massachusetts, 1979-81, Allied Corp: Components Company, Morristown, 1982-84; vice president fin. and control Emery Air Freight Corp., Wilton, Connecticut, 1984-85, senior vice president, chief fin. officer, 1985-87; senior vice president, chief fin. officer Fairchild Industries, Incorporated, Chantilly, Virginia, 1987—. Chairman, South Brunswick Rank Levelling Board, New Jersey, 1977-78; board of directors Norwalk/Wilton chapter American Red Cross, 1985. Member Am. Institute C.P.A.s, Fin. Executives Institute. Republican. Roman Catholic. Avocations: photography; hiking. Office: Fairchild Industries Incorporated 300 W Service Road Box 10803 Chantilly Virginia 22021

MURCHISON, DAVID RODERICK, lawyer; born Washington, May 28, 1948; son of David Claudius and June Margaret (Guilfoyle) M.; married Kathy Ann Kohn, March 15, 1981; children: David Christopher, Benjamin Michael. Bachelor of Arts cum laude, Princeton University, 1970; Juris Doctor, Georgetown University, 1975. Bar: District of Columbia 1975. Legal assistant to vice chairman Civil Aeronautics Board, Washington, 1975-76, enforcement attorney, 1976-77; senior attorney Air Transport Association, Washington, 1977-80, assistant vice president, secretary, 1981-85; senior associate Zuckert, Scoutt and Rasenberger, Washington, 1980-81; vice president, assistant general counsel Piedmont Aviation, Incorporated, Winston-Salem, North Carolina, 1985-88; vice president, general counsel, secretary Braniff, Incorporated, Dallas, 1988-89; chief executive officer Braniff, Incorporated, Orlando, 1990—; lecturer continuing legal education program Wake Forest University, Winston-Salem, 1988. Contributor articles to legal journals. Lieutenant United States Naval Reserve, 1970-72. Member American Bar Association, Metropolitan Club Washington. Republican. Roman Catholic. Home: 4227 Pecan Lane Orlando Florida 32812 Office: Braniff Incorporated 9955 Benford Road Orlando Florida 32855

MURDOCH, ROBERT W., cement and construction materials company executive. President LaFarge Corp., Reston, Virginia, chief operating officer, until 1989, chief executive officer, 1989—. Office: Lafarge Corp, 606 Cathcart, Montreal, Province of Quebec Canada H3B 1L7

MURDOCH, (KEITH) RUPERT, publisher; born Melbourne, Australia,

March 11, 1931; came to United States, 1974, naturalized, 1985; son of Keith and Elisabeth Joy (Greene) M.; married Anna Maria Torv, April 28, 1967; children: Prudence, Elisabeth, Lachlan, James. Master of Arts, Worcester College, Oxford, England, 1953. Chairman News Am. Pub. Incorporated (pubs. Boston Herald, London Times), 1974—, News International, Limited Group, London; chief executive officer, managing director News Limited Group & Associated Companies, Australia; chairman 20th Century Fox Productions, 1985—, William Collins PLC, Glasgow, 1989—; owner, pub. numerous newspapers, magazines and TV stations in United States of America, Australia, United Kingdom 1983—. Office: News Am Pub Incorporated 1211 Avenue of the Americas 3rd Floor New York New York 10036 also: 1 Virginia St, London E1 9XN, England also: New Group Boston Incorporated 1 Herald Square Boston Massachusetts 02106

MURDOCK, DAVID H., diversified company executive; born Los Angeles, April 10, 1923. Doctor of Laws (honorary), Pepperdine University, 1978; Doctor of Humane Letters (honorary), University Nebraska, 1984, Hawaii Loa University, 1989. Now sole proprietor, chairman, chief executive officer Pacific Holding Corp., Los Angeles, California; chairman, chief executive officer Castle & Cooke, Incorporated, Los Angeles, 1985—, also board of directors. Co-chairman Joffrey Ballet, Los Angeles,; trustee Asia Society, New York City, Los Angeles; founder, board of directors Foundation for Advanced Brain Studies, Los Angeles; board visitors University of California at Los Angeles Grad. School Mgmt.; board governors Performing Arts Council of Music Center, Los Angeles; board governors East-West Center, Los Angeles; patron of opera Metropolitan Opera, New York City With USAAC, 1943-45. Member Regency Club (founder, president), Bel-Air Bay Club, Sherwood Country Club (founder, president), Bel-Air Country, Metropolitan Club (New York City). Office: Castle & Cooke Incorporated 10900 Wilshire Boulevard Los Angeles California 90024 also: Pacific Holding Company 10900 Wilshire Boulevard Suite 1600 Los Angeles California 90024

MURPHY, CHARLES HAYWOOD, JR., petroleum company executive; born El Dorado, Arkansas, March 6, 1920; son of Charles Haywood and Bertie (Wilson) M.; married Johnie Walker, October 14, 1939; children: Michael Walker, Martha, Charles Haywood, III, Robert Madison. Educated public schools, Arkansas; Doctor of Laws (honorary), University Arkansas, 1966. Ind. oil producer 1939-50; chairman Murphy Oil Corp., El Dorado, Arkansas, 1972—, also board of directors; chairman executive committee 1st Comml. Corp., Little Rock. Board governors Oschner Medical Foundation; board adminstrs. Tulane U.; member national adv. board Smithsonian Institution; past member Arkansas Board Higher Education Served as infantryman World War II. Recipient citation for outstanding individual service in natural resource mgmt. National Wildlife Federation. Member Am. Petroleum Institute (past executive committee, hon. board directors), National Petroleum Council (past chairman), 25 Year Club Petroleum Industry (past president). Office:

Murphy Oil Corp 200 Peach St El Dorado Arkansas 71730

MURPHY, JOHN ARTHUR, tobacco, food and brewing company executive; born New York City, December 15, 1929; son of John A. and Mary J. (Touhey) M.; married Carole Ann Paul, June 28, 1952; children: John A., Kevin P., Timothy M., Kellyann, Robert B., Kathleen. Bachelor of Science, Villanova University, 1951; Juris Doctor, Columbia University, 1954. Bar: New York 1954. Since practiced in New York City; partner firm Conboy Hewitt O'Brien & Boardman, 1954-62; assistant general counsel Philip Morris Company Incorporated, New York City, 1962-66, vice president, 1967-76, executive vice president, 1976-78, group executive vice president, 1978-84, president, 1984—, also board of directors; assistant to president Philip Morris International, 1966-67, executive vice president, 1967-71; president, chief executive officer Miller Brewing Company, Milwaukee, 1971-78, chairman board, chief executive officer, 1978-84; director National Westminster Bank USA. Trustee North Shore University Hospital, Marquette U.; member executive committee Keep Am. Beautiful, Incorporated; member board consultors School Law Villanova U.; member business committee Metropolitan Mus. Art. Decorated Knight of Malta. Member American Bar Association, New York State Bar Association. Office: Philip Morris Cos Incorporated 120 Park Avenue New York New York 10017

MURRAY, PAUL BRADY, lawyer, banker; born Brooklyn, October 2, 1923; son of Thomas Edward and Marie (Brady) M.; married Anne McVoy, November 27, 1946; children—Paul, Joseph, Anne, John, Marie, Margot, Patricia, Marcia, Catherine, Elizabeth, Angelia. Bachelor of Science, Georgetown University, 1943; Doctor of Laws, Fordham University, 1949. Bar: New York State bar 1949. Member firm Schmidt, Eagan, Murray, New York City, 1949-52; vice president, treasurer Murray Manufacturing Corp. (electrical products), Brooklyn, 1946-50; president Murray Manufacturing Corp. (electrical products), 1950-69; executive vice president Arrow-Hart Incorporated, Hartford, Connecticut, from 1969; now chief executive officer East New York Sav. Bank, Brooklyn; chairman board First Empire State Corp.; board of directors First National Bank of Highland, M & T Bank. Lieutenant (junior grade) United States Naval Reserve, 1943-45. Office: East New York Sav Bank 41 W 42rd St New York New York 10036 also: 1st Empire State Corp 1 M&T Plaza Buffalo New York 14240

MURRAY, TERRENCE, banker; born Woonsocket, Rhode Island, July 11, 1939; son of Joseph W. and Florence (Blackburn) M.; married Suzanne Young, January 24, 1960; children: Colleen, Paula, Terrence, Christopher, Megan. Bachelor of Arts, Harvard University, 1962. With Fleet National Bank, Providence, 1962—, president, 1978-86; with Fleet Fin. Group Incorporated (now Fleet/Norstar Fin. Group), Providence, 1969—, president, 1978—, chairman, president, chief executive officer, 1982-88, president, 1988, chairman, president, chief executive officer, 1988—, also board of directors; board of directors Fleet National Bank, A.T. Cross Company, Federal Reserve Bank of Boston; chairman board of directors Fleet

National Bank. Trustee Rhode Island Charities Trust, Rhode Island School of Design. Recipient Outstanding Business Leader award Northwood Institute, 1986, Humanitarian award National Jewish Center for Immunology and Respiratory Medicine, 1988, Never Again award Jewish Federation, 1989, New Englander of Year award New England Council, 1990. Member Association of Reserve City Bankers (board directors), Harvard Alumni Association (board directors). Office: Fleet/ Norstar Fin Group Incorporated 50 Kennedy Plaza Providence Rhode Island 02903

MYLOD, ROBERT JOSEPH, banker; born Brooklyn, November 21, 1939; son of Charles Joseph and Katherine (Normile) M.; married Monica Manieri, July 11, 1964; children: Rosemary, Robert, Kevin, Paul, Monica, Megan. Bachelor of Arts, St. John's University, 1961. Vice president Citibank (N.A.), New York City, 1965-70; Vice president Citicorp., New York City, 1970-73; executive vice president residential loan div. Advance Mortgage Corp., Detroit, 1973-75; president Advance Mortgage Corp., 1975-83; president, chief operating officer, director Federal National Mortgage, 1983-85; chairman, president, chief executive officer, director Michigan National Corp., 1985—; chairman, president, chief executive officer, director Michigan National Bank, 1987—, chairman, director, 1985—. Served to lieutenant (junior grade) United States Navy, 1961-65. Office: Michigan National Corp Post Office Box 9065 Farmington Hills Michigan 48333-9065

NEDERLANDER, ROBERT E., film and television executive, lawyer, sports team executive; born Detroit, April 10, 1933; son of David T. and Sarah (Applebaum) N.; married Caren Berman (divorced); children: Robert E. Jr., Eric; Gladys Rackmil, January 1, 1988. Bachelor of Arts in Economics, University Michigan, 1955, Juris Doctor, 1958, Doctor of Laws (honorary), 1991. Partner Nederlander, Dodge & Rollins, Detroit, 1960-90; president Nederlander Organization, Incorporated, New York City, 1981—, Nederlander TV & Film Productions, New York City, 1985—; managing general partner New York Yankees. Regent U. Michigan, Ann Arbor, 1969-84; trustee Am. Health Foundation, 1989—; chairman Gateway Am., 1991—. Recipient Distinguished Alumni Service award University Michigan, 1985, Presidential Society Service citation, 1988; named Man of Year by Gov's. Committee on Scholastic Achievement, New York City, 1991. Fellow American Bar Association, Michigan Bar Association. Democrat. Avocations: tennis, baseball. Office: Nederlander Orgn 810 7th Avenue New York New York 10019

NEFF, PETER JOHN, chemicals, mining and metal processing executive; born New Brunswick, New Jersey, October 31, 1938; son of Peter and Carrie (Colasurdo) N.; married Joan Ruth Knapp, June 18, 1960; children: Lisa, Kristopher, Greg. Bachelor of Science in Chemistry, Rutgers University, 1969; Master of Business Administration, Rider College, Lawrenceville, New Jersey, 1978. Research chemist Exxon Chemicals, Linden, New Jersey; product manager Standard Brands Chemical Industries, Edison, New Jersey, 1970-73; sales manager St. Joe Minerals Corp., New York

City, 1973-77; director planning St. Joe Zinc Company, Pittsburgh, 1977-80; vice president St. Joe International Corp., New York City, 1980-83, president, 1983-85; president, chief executive officer St. Joe Minerals Corp., St. Louis, 1985-89; president, chief operating officer Rhone-Poulenc Incorporated, Princeton, New Jersey, 1987—. With United States Navy, 1956-59. Member Chemical Manufacturing Association (board directors), French. Am. Chamber of Commerce. Avocations: furniture design and construction. Home: 47 Dogwood Lane Skillman New Jersey 08558 Office: Rhone-Poulenc Incorporated CN 5266 Princeton New Jersey 08543

NEUBAUER, JOSEPH, business executive; born October 19, 1941; son of Max and Herta (Kahn) N.; married Antonia R. Brody, May 21, 1965; children: Lawrence, Melissa. Bachelor of Science in Chemical Engineering, Tufts University, 1963; Master of Business Administration in Fin, University Chicago, 1965. Assistant treasurer Chase Manhattan Bank, 1965-68, assistant vice president, 1968-70, vice president, 1970-71; assistant treasurer Pepsico Incorporated, Purchase, New York, 1971-72; treasurer Pepsico Incorporated, 1972-73, vice president, 1973-76; vice president fin. and control Wilson Sporting Goods Company, River Grove, Illinois, 1976-77, senior vice president, general manager team sports div., 1977-79; executive vice president fin. and devel., chief fin. officer, director ARA Services, Incorporated, Philadelphia, 1979-81; president, chief operating officer, director ARA Services, Incorporated, Philadelphia, 1981-83, president, chief executive officer, 1983-84, chairman, president, 1984—; board of directors First Fidelity Bancorp, VS Services, Limited, Bell of Pennsylvania; trustee Penn Mutual Life Insurance Company. Board of directors Philadelphia Orchestra Association, Mann Music Center; chairman Inroads/Phila., Incorporated; trustee Hahnemann U., Tufts U., Mus. Am. Jewish History, Greater Philadelphia First Corp., Committee for Economic Devel.; board governors Joseph H. Lauder Institute Mgmt. and International Studies, U. Pennsylvania. Member Philadelphia Chamber of Commerce (board directors). Clubs: Union League, Locust, Philadelphia. Office: ARA Services Incorporated ARA Tower 1101 Market St Philadelphia Pennsylvania 19107

NEWHOUSE, SAMUEL I., JR., publishing executive; born 1928; married Victoria Newhouse. Chairman Condé Nast Publs. Incorporated New York City. Recipient Henry Johnson Fisher award Magazine Pubs. Association, 1985. Office: care Condé Nast Publs Incorporated 350 Madison Avenue New York New York 10017 also: Advance Pubs Incorporated 950 Fingerboard Road Staten Island New York 10305

NICHOLS, JOHN D., diversified manufacturing corporation executive; born Shanghai, China, 1930; married Alexandra M. Curran, December 4, 1971; children: Kendra E., John D. III. Bachelor of Arts, Harvard University, 1953, Master of Business Administration, 1955. Various operating positions Ford Motor Corp., 1958-68; director fin. controls International Telephone & Telegraph Corporation Corp., 1968-69; executive vice president, chief operating officer Aerojet-Gen. Corp., 1969-79; executive vice president Illinois Tool Works Incorporated, Chicago, 1980-81; president Illinois Tool Works Incorporated, 1981—, chief operating officer, 1981-82, chief executive officer, director, 1982—, chairman, 1986—; board of directors Household International, Rockwell International, NICOR, Stone Container Corp. Trustee U. Chicago, Argonne National Lab., Chicago Symphony Orchestra, Lyric Opera Chicago, Mus. Sci. and Industry, Junior Achievement Chicago, Chicago Commerce Civic Committee, Business Roundtable, Art Institute Chicago Served to lieutenant Army of the United States, 1955-58. Clubs: Harvard (New York); Indian Hill (Winnetka, Illinois); Olympic (San Francisco), Chicago, Comml., Econ. Club Chicago. Office: Illinois Tool Works Incorporated 3600 W Lake Avenue Glenview Illinois 60025-5811

NOHA, EDWARD J., insurance company executive; born New York City, August 25, 1927; married. Bachelor of Business Administration, Pace College. With Department Justice, 1944-52, Metropolitan Life Insurance Company, 1952-55; executive vice president Allstate Insurance Company, 1955-74; chairman board, president, chief executive officer Continental Casualty Company, 1955-74, Continental Assurance Company, Chicago, 1955-74; chairman board National Fire Insurance Company of Hartford, Incorporated, Transcontinental Insurance Company. Office: Continental Casualty Company CNA Plaza Chicago Illinois 60685

NORDSTROM, BRUCE A., department store executive; born 1933; married. Bachelor of Arts, University Washington, 1956. With Nordstrom, Incorporated, Seattle, 1956—, vice president, 1964-70, president, 1970-75, chairman, 1975-77, co-chairman, 1977—, director. Office: Nordstrom Incorporated 1501 5th Avenue Seattle Washington 98101

NORDSTROM, JAMES F., apparel company executive; born 1940; married. Bachelor of Business Administration, University Washington, 1962. Various positions Nordstrom, Incorporated, Seattle, 1960—, executive vice president, 1975-78, president, 1975-78; president Nordstrom, Incorporated, Seattle, 1978—; also board of directors Nordstrom, Incorporated. Office: Nordstrom Incorporated 1501 5th Avenue Seattle Washington 98101

NORDSTROM, JOHN N., department store executive; born 1937; married. Bachelor of Arts, University Washington, 1958. With Nordstrom, Incorporated, Seattle, 1958—, vice president, 1965-70, executive vice president, 1970-75, president, 1975-77, co-chairman, 1977—, director; board of directors Federal Reserve Bank San Francisco. Office: Nordstrom Incorporated 1501 Fifth Avenue Seattle Washington 98101

NORRIS, JOHN WINDSOR, JR., manufacturing company executive; born Marshalltown, Iowa, February 10, 1936; son of John Windsor Norris and Mary Merrill Margerin; married Terry Reibsamen, December 26, 1956; children: John Windsor III, Julie, Jeffrey. Bachelor of Science in Business Adminstrn, Massachusetts Institute of Technology, 1960. With Lennox Industries Incorporated, Dallas, 1960—, senior vice president, 1975-77; president Lennox Industries Incorporated, 1977-80, president, chief executive officer, 1980—, also director; also president, chief executive officer Lennox International, Dallas; director Central Life Assurance Company, Des Moines. Chairman parents div., member annual gifts council Texas Christian U. Member ARI (director at large, vice chairman cert. programs and policy committee, vice chairman communications committee), GAMA (chairman furnace division 1978-79, chairman board 1980). Club: Bent Tree Country (Dallas). Office: Lennox Industries Incorporated Post Office Box 799900 Dallas Texas 75379

NORRIS, THOMAS CLAYTON, paper company executive; born York, Pennsylvania, May 9, 1938; married Joan G. Wachob, March 24, 1962; children: Robert, Richard, Mary Catherine. Bachelor of Arts, Gettysburg College, 1960. Chairman, president, chief executive officer P.H. Glatfelter Company, Spring Grove, Pennsylvania, 1980—. Home: 330 Rhonda Dr York Pennsylvania 17404 Office: P H Glatfelter Company 228 S Main St Spring Grove Pennsylvania 17362

NUGENT, DANIEL EUGENE, business executive; born Chicago, December 18, 1927; son of Daniel Edward and Pearl A. (Trieger) N.; married Bonnie Lynn Weidman, July 1, 1950; children: Cynthia Lynn, Mark Alan, Dale Alan. Bachelor of Science in Mechanical Engineering, Northwestern University, 1951. With United States Gypsum Company, Chicago, 1951-71, director corp. devel., to 1971; president Am. Louver Company, Chicago, 1971-72; vice president operations International Telephone & Telegraph Corporation Corp., Cleveland, 1972-74; executive vice president International Telephone & Telegraph Corporation Corp., St. Paul, 1974-75, president, chief operating officer, 1974-75; president, chief operating officer Pentair, Incorporated, St. Paul, 1975-86, chairman, chief executive officer, 1986—; also board of directors Pentair, Incorporated; board dirs.Apogee Enterprises, Incorporated, Niagara of Wisconsin Paper Corp., Cross Point Paper Corp., Porter-Cable Corp., Delta International Machinery Corp., McNeil Ohio Corp., Fed.-Hoffman, Incorporated. Vice chairman local planning commission, 1968-72; co-chairman Wellspring Corp., 1989—; trustee Harper College, Palatine, 1970-73; member executive committee Indianhead council Boy Scouts Am. With Army of the United States, 1946-47. Member North Oaks Golf Club, Minneapolis Club. Republican. Presbyterian. Office: Pentair Incorporated 1700 W Highway 36 Suite 700 Saint Paul Minnesota 55113

NYE, ERLE ALLEN, utilities executive, lawyer; born Fort Worth, June 23, 1937; son of Ira Benjamen N.; married Alice Ann Grove, June 5, 1959; children: Elizabeth Nye Kirkham, Pamela Nye Schneider, Erle Allen Jr., Edward Kyle, Johnson Scott. Bachelor of Electrical Engineering, Texas Agricultural and Mechanical University, 1959; Juris Doctor, Southern Methodist University, 1965. With Dallas Power & Light Company, 1960-75, vice president, 1975-80; executive vice president Texas Utilities Company, Dallas, 1980-87, president, 1987—. Board of directors Dallas Bar Foundation, 1980-83, Dallas Central Business Plan Committee, 1980-83, Inroads/Dallas-Ft. Worth, Incorporated, 1984—; trustee Baylor Dental College, Dallas, 1985—. Served to 2d lieutenant United States Army, 1959-60. Member American Bar Association, Dallas Bar Association, Texas State Bar Association. Methodist. Clubs: Engineers (president 1982-83), Northwood (Dallas). Home: 6924 Desco Dallas Texas 75225 Office: Tex Utilities Company 2001 Bryan Tower Dallas Texas 75201

O'BRIEN, JOHN, aerospace company executive. Graduate, State University of New York, 1951; Master of Business Administration, Massachusetts Institute of Technology, 1966. With Grumman Corp., Bethpage, New York, 1954—, president, chief operating officer, 1986-88, chairman, chief executive officer, 1988—; from flight test engineer to president Grumman Data Systems, 1958-86. Served to 1st lieutenant United States Army, 1951-54. Office: Grumman Corp 1111 Stewart Avenue Bethpage New York 11714

O'BRIEN, KENNETH ROBERT, life insurance company executive; born Brooklyn, June 18, 1937; son of Emmett Robert and Anna (Kelly) O'B.; married Eileen M. Halligan, July 1, 1961; children: Joan Marie, Margaret Mary, Kathy Ann. Bachelor of Science in Business Adminstrn, College Holy Cross, Worcester, Massachusetts, 1959. With New York Life Insurance Company, New York City, 1962—; 2d vice president New York Life Insurance Company, 1973-77, vice president investments, 1977-82, senior vice president pensions, 1982-87, senior vice president individual products, 1987-89, executive vice president, 1989—. Active Catholic Youth Organization Served to 1st lieutenant United States Air Force, 1959-62. Member National Consumer Fin. Association, Fin. Forum, New York Society Security Analysts. Home: 165 E Loines Avenue Merrick New York 11566 Office: New York Life Ins Company 51 Madison Avenue New York New York 10010

O'BRIEN, RAYMOND FRANCIS, transportation executive; born Atchison, Kansas, May 31, 1922; son of James C. and Anna M. (Wagner) O'B.; married Mary Ann Baugher, September 3, 1947; children: James B., William T., Kathleen A., Christopher R. Bachelor of Science in Business Administration, University Missouri, 1948; graduate, Advanced Management Program, Harvard, 1966. Accountant-auditor Peat, Marwick, Mitchell & Company, Kansas City, Missouri, 1948-52; controller, treasurer Riss & Company, Kansas City, Missouri, 1952-58; regional controller Consolidated Freightways Corp. of Del., Indianapolis, also, Akron, Ohio, 1958-61; controller Consolidated Freightways, Incorporated, San Francisco, 1961—; vice president, treasurer Consolidated Freightways, Incorporated, 1962-63, board of directors, 1966, vice president fin., 1967-69, executive vice president, 1969-75, president, 1975—, chief executive officer, 1977-88 90-91, chairman, 1988—; president CF Motor Freight subsidiary Consolidated Freightways, Incorporated, 1973; director Transam. Corp., Watkins-Johnson, Incorporated; past chairman WesternHwy. Institute, Champion Road Machinery, Limited. Former member business adv. board Northwestern U., U. California, Berkeley; board of directors, regent, former chairman board trustees St. Mary's College; board of directors Charles Armstrong School, 1991—; member President's Adv. Council,

Herbert Hoover Boys and Girls Club; director Boy Scouts Am. Bay Area Council; board of directors National Legal Center for Pub. Interest; chairman National Commission Agaisnt Drunk Driving; president adv. council National Legal center for Pub. Interest. Served to 1st lieutenant United States Army Air Force, 1942-45. Recipient Distinguished Service Citation Automotive Hall Fame, 1991; named Outstanding Chief Executive five times Financial World Magazine. Member Am. Trucking Association (board directors Foundation, executive committee), Pacific Union Club, Palo Alto Club, World Trade Club, Commonwealth Club (San Francisco), Burning Tree Country Club, Menlo Country Club, Firestone Country Club. Home: 26347 Esperanza Dr Los Altos Hills California 94022 Office: Consol Freightways Incorporated 3000 Sand Hill Road Building 2 Suite 130 Menlo Park California 94025

O'BRIEN, THOMAS HENRY, bank holding company executive; born Pittsburgh, January 16, 1937; son of J. Vick and Georgia (Bower) O'B.; married Maureen Sheedy; children—Thomas Henry, Lauren C., Timothy B. Bachelor of Science in Commerce, University Notre Dame, 1958; Master of Business Administration, Harvard University, 1962. With Pittsburgh National Bank, 1962—, vice president, 1967-73, senior vice president, 1973-80, executive vice president, 1980-83, vice chairman, 1983-84; president, board of directors, chief executive officer PNC Fin. Corp., 1984—; also chairman PNC Fin. Corp., Pittsburgh, 1988—; board of directors Hilb, Rogal & Hamilton Company, Aristech Chemical Corp., Bell Atlantic Corp., Private Export Funding Corp., Federal Adv. Council, International Monetary Conference. Board of directors United Way Southwest Pennsylvania, Pittsburgh Symphony Society, Children's Hospital, Pittsburgh, Allegheny Trails council Boy Scouts Am., Pittsburgh Allegheny Conference Community Devel., U. Pittsburgh, World Affairs Council Pittsburgh, Carnegie Institute Reserves City Bankers. Named Man of Year in fin. Vectors, Pitts., 1985. Member Association Reserve City Bankers, Pennsylvania Bankers Association. Roman Catholic. Clubs: Duquesne, Allegheny (board dirs.), Pittsburgh Field, Rolling Rock, Laurel Valley Golf. Avocation: golf. Office: PNC Fin Corp 5th Avenue & Wood St Pittsburgh Pennsylvania 15265

O'BRIEN, WILLIAM JOHN, insurance company executive; born Yonkers, New York, November 18, 1932; son of Vincent J. and Margaret L. (Schaefer) O'B.; married Catherine Kelaher, July 27, 1963; children: Kathleen, William V., Christopher. Bachelor of Science, Fordham University, 1954; graduate student, Seton Hall University, 1957-59. Underwriter, then special agent Safeco Insurance Company, New York City, 1956-60; with Security Insurance Group, New Haven, 1960-67; vice president agency department Security Insurance Group, 1960-67; vice president, zone executive Glens Falls Insurance Company, New York, 1967-71; vice president marketing Hanover Insurance Company, Worcester, Massachusetts, 1971-79, president, 1979—; board of directors, executive committee Citizens Insurance Company Am., Howell, Michigan, Beacon Insurance Company Am., Columbus, Ohio, Am.

Select Insurance Company, Columbus; trustee Am. Institute Property adn Liability Institute, Incorporated. Served with infantry United States Army, 1954-56. Clubs: Fayville Athletic Assn, Worcester Econ. (past president). Home: 22 Red Gate Lane Southboro Massachusetts 01772 Office: Hanover Ins Company 100 N Parkway St Worcester Massachusetts 01605

O'CONNOR, JAMES JOHN, utility company executive; born Chicago, March 15, 1937; son of Fred James and Helen Elizabeth O'Connor; married Ellen Louise Lawlor, November 24, 1960; children: Fred, John (deceased), James, Helen Elizabeth. Bachelor of Science, Holy Cross College, 1958; Master of Business Administration, Harvard University, 1960; Juris Doctor, Georgetown University, 1963. Bar: Illinois 1963. With Commonwealth Edison Company, Chicago, 1963—, assistant to chairman executive committee, 1964-65, commercial manager, 1966, assistant vice president, 1967-70, vice president, 1970-73, executive vice president, 1973-77, president, 1977-87, chairman, 1980—, chief executive officer, also board of directors; board of directors Corning, Incorporated, Midwest Stock Exchange, Tribune Company, United Air Lines, Scotsman Industries, Am. National Can., First Chicago Corp., The First National Bank of Chicago; past chairman Nuclear Power Oversight Committee, Advanced Reactor Corp.; board director, past chairman Edison Electric Institute; board of directors Am. Nuclear Energy Council, Electric Power Research Institute, United States Council for Energy Awareness. Member Christopher Columbus Quincentary Jubilee Commission; board of directors Associates Harvard U. Grad. School Business Administration, Leadership Council for Metropolitan Open Communities, Lyric Opera, Mus. Sci. and Industry, St. Xavier College, Reading is Fundamental, Helen Brach Foundation, Leadership Greater Chicago; board of directors United Way Crusade of Mercy, Chicago; chairman Citzenship Council of Metropolitan Chicago, 1986—; past chairman Metropolitan Savs. Bond Campaign; trustee Adler Planetarium, Michael Reese Medical Center, Northwestern U., College Holy Cross; board of directors, past chairman Chicago Urban League; board advisors Mercy Hospital and Medical Center; past chairman board trustees Field Mus. Natural History; trustee Mus. Sci. and Industry; member citizens board; executive board Chicago area council Boy Scouts Am.; chairman Cardinal Bernardin's Big SHoulders FUnd; executive vice president The Hundred Club Cook County. With United States Air Force, 1960-63. Member American Bar Association, Illinois Bar Association, Chicago Bar Association, Chicago Association Commerce and Industry (board director, chairman), Illinois Business Roundtable. Home: 9549 Monticello Avenue Evanston Illinois 60203 Office: Commonwealth Edison Company 1 First National Plaza Post Office Box 767 Chicago Illinois 60690

O'HARE, DON R., corporate executive; born Joliet, Illinois, 1922; married. Bachelor of Science, University Minnesota, 1943. Plant engineer Western Electric Company, 1946-47; sales engineer Wallace & Tiernan Company, 1947-50; sales trainee Falk Corp., Milwaukee, 1950-51, sales engineer, 1951-55, district office manager, 1955-72, vice president, sales manager, 1972-74, president, 1974-76; with Sundstrand Corp., Rockford, Illinois, 1976—, vice president, 1976-77, group vice president, 1977-79, vice chairman, 1980-88, chairman, 1989—, also board of directors; director M & I Corp., Modine Manufacturing Corp. Served with United States Navy, 1943-46. Office: Sundstrand Corp 4949 Harrison Avenue Box 7003 Rockford Illinois 61125-7003

OHGA, NORIO, electronics executive; born Numazu, Japan, January 29, 1930; married Midori Ohga. Graduate, Tokyo National University Fine Arts and Music, 1953, Kunst University, Berlin, 1957. Cons., advisor Tokyo Tsushin Kogyo (later Sony Corp.), 1953-59; general manager tape recorder div., product planning div., industrial design div. Sony Corp., Tokyo, 1959, board of directors, 1964-72, managing director, 1972-74, senior managing director, 1974-76, deputy president, 1976-82, president, chief operating officer, 1982—, chief executive officer, 1989—; representative director, chairman board CBS/Sony Incorporated. Member Electric Home Appliance Fair Trade Association (president), Association Devel. Broadcasting Tech. (president), Association Electric Home Applicances (president). Office: Sony Corp, 6-7-35 Kita-Shinagawa, Shinagawa-Ku Tokyo Japan 141

O'LEARY, THOMAS HOWARD, resources executive; born New York City, March 19, 1934; son of Arthur J. and Eleanor (Howard) O'L.; married Barbara A. Mc Donough, 1977 (deceased); children: Mark, Timothy, Thomas, Denis, Daniel, Mary Frances. Bachelor of Arts, Holy Cross College, 1954; postgraduate, University Pennsylvania, 1959-61. Assistant cashier First National City Bank, New York City, 1961-65; assistant to chairman finance committee Missouri Pacific Railroad Company, 1966-70, vice president finance, 1971-76, director, 1972-82, chairman finance committee, 1976-82; treasurer Missouri Pacific Corp., St. Louis, 1968-71; vice president finance Missouri Pacific Corp., 1971-72, executive vice president, 1972-74, director, 1972-82, president, 1974-82; chairman board, chief executive officer Mississippi River Transmission Corp., 1974-82; vice chairman, also director Burlington Northern, Incorporated, Seattle, 1982-89; president, chief executive officer Burlington Resources Incorporated, Seattle, 1989—; board of directors BF Goodrich, Kroger Company. Served to captain United States Marine Corps, 1954-58. Clubs: Blind Brook (New York City), Chicago. Office: Burlington Resources Incorporated 999 3rd Avenue Suite 4500 Seattle Washington 98104

OLSON, EUGENE RUDOLPH, printing company executive; born St. Paul, April 9, 1926; son of Rudolph and Martha E. (Karlson) O.; married Leona F. Solie, June 28, 1952; children: Kathleen, Wayne, Brian. With Deluxe Check Printers Incorporated, St. Paul, 1944—, manager related products div., 1964-70, national director market research, 1970-72, vice president, 1972-76, president, 1976—, chief executive officer, 1977-86, chairman, 1981—, also director; director Minnesota Mutual Insurance Company, 1st Trust Company, St. Paul. Board of directors Minnesota Private College Fund; member World Trade Center Adv. Council. Member

Vineyards Country Club (Naples). Baptist. Home: 2024 Evergreen Court Saint Paul Minnesota 55113 Office: De Luxe Check Printers Incorporated 1080 W County Road F Saint Paul Minnesota 55112

OLSON, FRANK ALBERT, car rental company executive; born San Francisco, July 19, 1932; son of Alfred and Edith Mary (Hazeldine) O.; married Sarah Jean Blakely, October 19, 1957; children—Kimberly, Blake, Christopher. Associate of Arts, City College San Francisco, 1961. General manager Barrett Transportation Incorporated, San Francisco, 1950-64; vice president, general manager Valcar Company subsidiary Hertz Corp., San Francisco, 1964-68; manager New York zone Hertz Corp., New York City, 1968-69, vice president, manager eastern region, 1969-70, vice president, general manager rent-a-car div., 1970-73, executive vice president rent-a-car div., general manager, also board of directors, 1973-77, president, chief executive officer, 1977-80, chairman board, 1980, also director, chief executive officer, from 1982; chairman, chief executive officer Allegis Corp., 1987; president, chief executive officer United Airlines, 1987; chairman, chief executive officer Hertz Corp., Park Ridge, New Jersey, 1987—; board of directors UAL. Trustee National Commission Against Drunk Driving; board of directors National Multiple Sclerosis Society; member adv. board for Religion in Am. Life; president San Francisco Junior Chamber of Commerce, 1960-63. Served to 1st lieutenant United States Army, 1957-63. Member Sales Executives Club New York City. Republican. Roman Catholic. Clubs: Arcola Country (Paramus, New Jersey); Prouts Neck Country (Scarburgh, Maine); Metropolitan (New York City). Office: Hertz Corp 225 Brae Boulevard Park Ridge New Jersey 07656

O'MALLEY, SHAUN F., accounting firm executive. married Julie O'Malley; 3 children. Bachelor of Science in Economics, University Pennsylvania. Member staff Price Waterhouse, Philadelphia, 1959, Tokyo, Osaka, 1966; member national office research department Price Waterhouse, New York City, 1968-70, member national office accounting and auditing service department, 1979; partner Price Waterhouse, Philadelphia, 1970-80, partner in charge, 1980-88; elected to World Firm Council of Ptnrs. Price Waterhouse, 1982, elected to Policy Board, 1984; chairman, senior partner Price Waterhouse, New York City, 1988—; chief officer, chief executive officer Price Waterhouse World Firm, New York City, 1990—; member energizing markets adv. committee Securities and Exchange Commission; president board trustees Fin. Accounting Foundation. Contributor articles to professional journals. Member executive committee New York City Mayor's Private Sector Survey, New York City Ptnrship.; co-chair New York City Alliance for International Business, Limited; board of directors Curtis Institute Music; former chairman board Young Audiences of Eastern Pennsylvania; board governors Pennsylvania Economy League; member Wharton President's Council, U. Pennsylvania; board of directors SEI Center Advanced Studies in Mgmt., Wharton School Economic, member adv. board, member alumni Board

Mentors, Benjamin Franklin Associate. Member American Institute of Certified Public Accountants. Office: Price Waterhouse 1251 Avenue of the Americas New York New York 10020

O'MALLEY, THOMAS D., diversified company executive; born New York City, 1941. Graduate, Manhattan College, 1963. Vice chairman, director Salomon, Incorporated (formerly Phibro-Salomon, Incorporated), New York City; former chairman, chief executive officer, president Phibro Energy Incorporated, Greenwich, Connecticut; chairman Argus Investments (formerly Argus Resources), Stamford, Connecticut, from 1987; now chairman, chief executive officer Tosco Corp., Connecticut. Office: Tosco Corp 2401 Colorado Avenue Box 2401 Santa Monica California 90406 also: Argus International Post Office Box 9508 Hato Tejas Bayamon Puerto Rico 00619-8044

ONG, JOHN DOYLE, lawyer; born Uhrichsville, Ohio, September 29, 1933; son of Louis Brosee and Mary Ellen (Liggett) O.; married Mary Lee Schupp, July 20, 1957; children: John Francis Harlan, Richard Penn Blackburn, Mary Katherine Caine. Bachelor of Arts, Ohio State University, 1954, Master of Arts, 1954; Bachelor of Laws, Harvard, 1957; Doctor of Humane Letters, Kent State University, 1982. Bar: Ohio 1958. Assistant counsel B.F. Goodrich Company, Akron, 1961-66, group vice president, 1972-73, executive vice president, 1973-74, vice chairman, 1974-75, president, director, 1975-77, president, chief operating officer, director, 1978-79, chairman board, president, chief executive officer, 1979-84, chairman board, chief executive officer, 1984—; assistant to president International B.F. Goodrich Company, Akron, 1966-69, vice president, 1969-70, president, 1970-72; board of directors Cooper Industries, Am. Information Technologies Corp., The Kroger Company, Asarco, Incorporated. Vice president exploring Great Trail council Boy Scouts Am., 1974-77; board of directors National Alliance for Business; trustee Mus. Arts Association, Cleveland, Bexley Hall Sem., 1974-81, Case Western Reserves U., 1980—, Kenyon College, 1983-85, Hudson (Ohio) Libr. and Historical Society, president, 1971-72, Western Reserves Acad., Hudson, 1975—, president board trustees, 1977—, U. Chicago, 1991—; national trustee National Symphony Orchestra, 1975-83; member business adv. committee Transportation Center, Northwestern U., 1975-78, Carnegie-Mellon U. Grad. School Industrial Administration, 1978-83; member adv. board Blossom Music Center Served with Judge Advocate General Corps Army of the United States, 1957-61. Member Ohio Bar Association (board govs. corp. counsel section 1962-74, chairman 1970), Rubber Manufacturers Association (director 1974-84), Chemical Manufacturers Association (board directors 1988—), Conference Board, Business Roundtable, Business Council, Portage Country Club, Union Club, Links, Union League, Ottawa Shooting Club, Metropolitan Club., Rolling Rock Club, Castalia Trout Club, Phi Beta Kappa, Phi Alpha Theta. Episcopalian. Home: 230 Aurora St Hudson Ohio 44236 Office: The B F Goodrich Company 3925 Embassy Parkway Akron Ohio 44333-1799

ORCUTT, GUY HENDERSON, economist, educator; born Wyandotte, Michigan, July 5, 1917; married; four children. Bachelor of Science with honors in Physics, University Michigan, 1939, Master of Arts in Economics, 1940, Doctor of Philosophy, 1944. Teaching fellow University Michigan, Ann Arbor, 1940-41, Rackham fellow, 1944; laboratory assistant, statistician University Michigan Hospital, 1944; instructor economics Massachusetts Institute of Technology, Cambridge, 1944-46; senior researcher department applied economics Cambridge (England) University, 1946-48; assistant professor to associate professor economics Harvard University, 1949-58, director Littauer Statistical Laboratory, 1952-56, visiting professor, 1965-66; Brittingham professor economics University Wisconsin, Madison, 1958-69, director Social Systems Research Institute, 1959-62, director research, 1962-64, chairman department, 1964-65; Irving Fisher visiting professor Yale University, New Haven, 1969-70, professor economics, A. Whitney Griswold professor urban studies, 1970—, chairman Center for Studies of City and Its Environment, 1970-73; economist International Monetary Fund, 1949, consultant, 1951-53; consultant Federal Reserve Board, 1954, Office Statistical Standards, Bureau of Budget, 1961-62; director poverty and inequality project Urban Institute, 1968-75; senior advisor International Bank for Reconstrn. and Devel. (World Bank), 1967-68; member executive committee div. behavorial sciences, NAS-NRC, 1968-70; board of directors Social Sci. Research Committee, 1975—, treas, 1976—. Contributor articles to professional journals. Nuffield fellow, 1947. Fellow Am. Statistical Association (vice president 1959-61), Am. Econ. Association (executive committee 1972-75), Econometric Society (council member 1961-62, 68-71). Office: Box 127 Grantham New Hampshire 03753

OREFFICE, PAUL FAUSTO, chemical company executive; born Venice, Italy, November 29, 1927; came to United States, 1945, naturalized, 1951; son of Max and Elena (Friedenberg) O.; married Franca Giuseppina Ruffini, May 26, 1956; children: Laura Emma, Andrew T. Bachelor of Science in Chemical Engineering, Purdue University, 1949. With Dow Chemical Company, various international locations, 1953—; assigned to Switzerland, Italy, Brazil and Spain to 1969; president Dow Chemical Latin Am., Coral Gables, Florida, 1966-70; corporate fin. vice president Dow Chemical Company, Midland, Michigan, 1970-75, president Dow Chemical United States of America, 1975-78, president, chief executive officer, 1978-86, chairman, president, chief executive officer, 1986-87, chairman board, 1987—; board of directors Morgan Stanley Group Incorporated, Incorporated, CIGNA Corp., Northern Telecom Limited, Coca Cola Company. Chairman board trustees Am. Enterprise Institute; trustee Morehouse College; board governors National Parkinson Foundation; chairman board overseers Institute Civil Justice; member senior adv. board Arthritis Foundation. Decorated Encomienda del Merito Civil Spain, 1966. Member Chemical Manufacturers Association, Business Council (member adv. committee for trade policy and negotiations). Office: The Dow Chem Company 2030 Willard H Dow Center Midland Michigan 48674

O'ROURKE, J. TRACY, manufacturing company executive; born Columbia, South Carolina, March 14, 1935; son of James Tracy and Georgia Adella (Bridges) O'R.; married Lou Ann Turner, March 19. 1954; 1 son, James Tracy. Bachelor of Science in Mechanical Engineering, Auburn University, 1956. Teflon specialist duPont Company, Wilmington, Del., 1957-62; president, chief executive officer LNP Corp., Malvern, Pennsylvania, 1962-72; vice president Carborundum, Niagara Falls, New York, 1972-76; executive vice president Chemetron, Chicago, 1975-78; senior vice president Allen Bradley Company subsidiary Rockwell International Corp., Milwaukee, 1978-81, president, chief operating officer, 1981-90, also chief executive officer, director, 1986-89; chairman, chief executive officer Varian Associates, Palo Alto, California, 1990—. Served to 1st lieutenant United States Air Force, 1957-59. Office: Varian Associates 3100 Hansen Way Palo Alto California 94304

OSBORN, GUY A., food products company executive; born 1936. Bachelor of Science in Business Administration, Northwestern University, 1958. Group marketing manager Pillsbury Company, Minneapolis, 1958-65; with Universal Foods Corp., Milwaukee, 1971—, director marketing, 1971-73, vice president special products, 1973-78, group vice president, 1978-82, executive vice president, 1982-84, president, 1984—, chief operating officer, 1984-88, chief executive officer, 1988—. Office: Universal Foods Corp 433 E Michigan Avenue Milwaukee Wisconsin 53202

OSBORNE, RICHARD JAY, electric utility company executive; born New York City, February 16, 1951; son of Victor and Evelyn Celia (Sweetbaum) O. Bachelor of Arts, Tufts University, 1973; Master of Business Administration, University North Carolina, 1975. Fin. analyst Duke Power Company, Charlotte, North Carolina, 1975-78, senior fin. analyst, 1978-80, manager fin. relations, 1980-81, manager treasury activities, 1981, treasurer, 1981-88, vice president fin., 1988—; board of directors NCM Capital Management Group Incorporated. Board of directors Mecklenburg County council Boy Scouts Am., 1987; board of directors Planned Parenthood of Greater Charlotte, Charlotte Jewish Federation; board of directors Historical Elizabeth Neighborhood Foundation. Member Fin. Executives Institute, Southeastern Electric Exchange (fin. section), Edison Electric Institute (fin. committee). Democrat. Jewish. Lodge: Rotary. Office: Duke Power Company 422 S Church St Charlotte North Carolina 28242

O'TOOLE, ROBERT JOSEPH, manufacturing company executive; born Chicago, February 22, 1941; son of Francis John O'Toole; children: William, Patricia, Timothy, Kathleen, John. Bachelor of Science in Accounting, Loyola University, Chicago, 1961. Fin. analyst A.O. Smith Corp., Milwaukee, 1963-66, manager corp. fin. analysis and planning, 1966-68; controller electric motor div. A.O. Smith Corp., Tipp City, Ohio, 1968-71; managing director Bull Motors, Ipswich, England, 1971-74; general plant manager electric motor div. A.O.

Smith Corp., Tipp City, 1974-79, vice president, general manager, 1979-83; senior vice president A.O. Smith Corp., Milwaukee, 1984-85, president, chief operating officer, 1986-89, president, chief executive officer, 1989—, also board of directors; board of directors 1st Wisconsin National Bank, Milwaukee; member executive committee TEC XIV, Milwaukee, Wisconsin Manufacturers and Commerce, Madison, Manufacturers Alliance for Productivity and Innovation, The Business Roundtable. Member Greater Milwaukee Committee, Competitive Wisconsin, Incorporated. Member Metropolitan Milwaukee Association Commerce (board directors), Milwaukee County Club, University Club. Office: A O Smith Corp 1 Park Plaza 11270 W Park Place Milwaukee Wisconsin 53224-3690

OVERSTROM, GUNNAR S., JR., banker; born Buffalo, 1942. Bachelor of Science in Business Administration, Babson College; Master of Arts, Trinity College; Bachelor of Laws, Suffolk University, 1968. With Travelers Insurance Company, 1969-73; fin. consultant B.L. McTeague & Company, 1973-75; with Connecticut National Bank, Hartford, 1975—, chief fin. officer, executive vice president, 1979-88, president, chief operating officer, board of directors, 1988—; also chief operating officer Shawmut National Corp. (formerly Hartford National Corp.). Office: Connecticut National Bank 777 Main St Hartford Connecticut 06115

OWEN, CLAUDE BERNARD, JR., tobacco company executive; born Danville, Virginia, June 12, 1945; son of Claude Bernard and Mildred Carter (Fulton) O.; married Mary Lamar Lewis, August 14, 1965; children: Christopher E., Jennifer L. Bachelor of Arts in Economics, Davidson College, 1967; Master of Business Administration in Fin., University Maryland, 1969. Fin. analyst Dibrell Brothers, Incorporated, Danville, 1971-73, assistant vice president, 1973-76, vice president, 1976-81, senior vice president, 1981-84, executive vice president, 1984-86, president, 1986-89, chairman, chief executive officer, 1990—; adv. committee member Atlantic Venture Ptnrs., Richmond, 1982—; board of directors Am. National Bankshares, Danville; chairman board Richfood Holdings Incorporated, Richmond. Board of directors Danville Mus. Fine Arts and History, Danville, 1986; trustee Averett College, Danville, 1985; president Danville-Pittsylvania County United Way, 1989. Served to 1st lieutenant United States Army, 1969-71. Member Danville Golf Club (vice president 1984-86), Commonwealth Club (Richmond), Country Club of Virginia (Richmond), Rotary. Methodist. Avocations: golfing, raquetball, skiing. Office: Dibrell Bros Incorporated 512 Bridge St Danville Virginia 24543

PACKARD, DAVID, manufacturing company executive, electrical engineer; born Pueblo, Colorado, September 7, 1912; son of Sperry Sidney and Ella Lorna (Graber) P.; married Lucile Salter, April 8, 1938 (deceased, 1987); children: David Woodley, Nancy Ann Packard Burnett, Susan Packard Orr, Julie Elizabeth Stephens. Bachelor of Arts, Stanford University, 1934, Electrical Engineer, 1939; Doctor of Laws (honorary), University California, Santa Cruz, 1966, Catholic University, 1970, Pepperdine University, 1972; Doctor of Science (honorary),

Colorado College, 1964; Doctor of Letters (honorary), Southern Colorado State College, 1973; Doctor of Engineering (honorary), University Notre Dame, 1974. With vacuum tube engineering department General Electric Company, Schenectady, 1936-38; co-founder, partner Hewlett-Packard Company, Palo Alto, California, 1939-47, president, 1947-64, chief executive officer, 1964-68, chairman board, 1964-68, 72—; United States deputy secretary defense Washington, 1969-71; director Genetech, Incorporated, 1981—; board of directors Caterpillar Tractor Company, 1972-83, Chevron, 1972-85; chairman Presdl. Commission on Def. Management, 1985-86; member White House Sci. Council, 1982-88. Member President's Commission Pers. Interchange, 1972-74, President's Council Advisors on Sci. and Tech., 1990—, Trilateral Commission, 1973-81, Directors Council Exploratorium, 1987; president board regents Uniformed Svcs. U. of Health Scis., 1975-82; member U.S.-USSR Trade and Economic Council, 1975-82; trustee The Ronald Reagan Presidential Foundation, 1986—; member board overseers Hoover Institution, 1972—; board of directors National Merit Scholarship Corp., 1963-69, Foundation for Study of Presidential and Congl. Terms, 1978-86 , Alliance to Save Energy, 1977-87, Atlantic Council, 1972-83, (vice chairman 1972-80), Am. Enterprise Institute for Public Policy Research, 1978—, National Fish and Wildlife Foundation, 1985-87, Hitachi Foundation Adv. Council, 1986—; trustee Herbert Hoover Foundation, 1974—; vice chairman The California Nature Conservancy, 1983—; trustee Stanford U., 1954-69, (president board trustees 1958-60), Hoover Institution, The Herbert Hoover Foundation. Decorated Grand Cross of Merit Federal Republic of Germany, 1972, Medal Honor Electronic Industries, 1974; numerous other awards including Silver Helmet Defense award American Veterans of World War II, Korea, Vietnam, 1973, Washington award Western Society Engineers, 1975, Hoover medal American Society of Mechanical Engineers, 1975, Gold Medal award National Football Foundation and Hall of Fame, 1975, Good Scout award Boy Scouts Am., 1975, Vermilye medal Franklin Institute, 1976, International Achievement award World Trade Club of San Francisco, 1976, Merit award Am. Cons. Engineers Council Fellows, 1977, Achievement in Life award Encyclopaedia Britannica, 1977, Engineering Award of Distinction San Jose State University, 1980, Thomas D. White National Defense award USAF Acad., 1981, Distinguished Info. Sciences award Data Processing Mgmt. Association, 1981, Sylvanus Thayer award United States Military Acad., 1982, Environmental Leadership award Natural Resources Defense Council, 1983, Dollar award National Foreign Trade Council, 1985, Gandhi Humanitarium Award, 1988, Roback Award National Contract Mgmt. Association, 1988, Pub. Welfare Medal National Academy of Sciences, 1989, Chevron Conservation Award, 1989, Doolittle Award Hudson Institute, 1989, Distinguished Citizens Award Commonwealth Club San Francisco, 1989, William Wildback award, National Conference Standards Labs., Washington, 1990; named to Silicon Valley Engineering Hall of Fame by Silicon Valley Engineering Council, 1991, Pueblo (Colorado) Hall of Fame,

1991. Fellow Institute of Electrical and Electronics Engineers (Founders medal 1973); member National Acad. Engineering (Founders award 1979), Instrument Society Am. (hon. lifetime member), Wilson Council, The Business Roundtable, Business Council, Am. Ordnance Association (Crozier Gold medal 1970, Henry M. Jackson award 1988, National Medal Tech. 1988, Presidential Medal of Freedom 1988), Sigma Xi, Phi Beta Kappa, Tau Beta Pi, Alpha Delta Phi (Distinguished Alumnus of Year 1970). Office: Hewlett-Packard Company 3000 Hanover St Palo Alto California 94304

PAINE, ANDREW J., JR., banker; born Chicago, October 18, 1937; son of Andrew J. and Louise (Kelly) P.; married Jane Medaris, June 25, 1960; children: Linda, Stephanie, Andrew. Bachelor of Arts, DePauw University, 1959; Master of Business Administration, Ind. University, 1967; graduate, Stonier Graduate School Banking, 1969. Assistant cashier Ind. National Bank, Indianapolis, 1964-66; assistant vice president Ind. National Bank, 1966-68, vice president, 1968-72, senior vice president, 1972-76, executive vice president corp. devel., 1976-77, executive vice president corp. banking, 1977-79, president, 1979—, chief operating officer; also vice chairman Ind. National Corp., 1981—; director Indianapolis Life Insurance Company, Hammond Company, Newport Beach, California. Member past president's council Junior Achievement Central Ind.; national board of directors Junior Achievement Incorporated; trustee Children's Mus., DePauw U.; board of directors Community Service Council Metropolitan Indianapolis; board governors United Way, chairman campaign, 1983. Recipient Key Man award Indianapolis Jaycees, 1972; Alumni citation DePauw University, 1978. Member Am. Bankers Association (chairman government relations council), Young Presidents Organization, Ind. University School Business Alumni Association (past president). Methodist. Clubs: Columbia, Meridian Hills Country. Office: Indiana National Bank 1 Indiana Square #501 Indianapolis Indiana 46266

PAINTER, JOHN WILLIAM, diversified company executive; born Herrin, Illinois, July 24, 1929; son of Charles F. and Helen A. (Anderson) P.; married Dorothy E. Woodward, February 1, 1952; children: John W., Thomas A., Andrew W. Bachelor of Science in Business Adminstrn, University Illinois, 1950. General sales manager Hupp Aviation Company, Chicago, 1950-60; marketing manager Lord Manufacturing Company, Erie, Pennsylvania, 1960-64; president Ohio Rubber Company div. Eagle-Picher Industries, Willoughby, Ohio, 1964-73; group vice president parent company Eagle-Picher Industries, Cincinnati, 1974-76; executive vice president Eagle-Picher Industries, 1977, president, 1977—, executive vice president, 1980-89, president, chief operating officer, 1989—, also board director; board of directors Central Trust Bank, Cincinnati. Board of directors Boys' Clubs of Greater Cincinnati, Bethesda Hospital. Member Alpha Chi Rho, Sigma Iota Epsilon. Clubs: Kenwood Country (Cincinnati), Commonwealth (Cincinnati), Queen City (Cincinnati). Home: 5475 Graydon Meadow Lane Cincinnati Ohio 45243 Office: Eagle-Picher Industries Incorporated 580

Walnut St Post Office Box 779 Cincinnati Ohio 45201

PALMER, RUSSELL EUGENE, investment executive; born Jackson, Michigan, August 13, 1934; son of Russell E. and Margarite M. (Briles) P.; married Phyllis Anne Hartung, September 8, 1956; children: Bradley Carl, Stephen Russell, Russell Eugene, III, Karen Jean. Bachelor of Arts with honors, Michigan State University, 1956; Doctor in Commercial Science (honorary), Drexel University, 1980; Master of Arts (honorary), University Pennsylvania, 1984; Doctor of Philosophy (honorary), Chulalongkorn University, 1988, Free University of Brussels, 1989, York College, 1989. With Touche Ross & Company, New York City, 1956-83, managing partner, chief executive officer, 1972-82, also board of directors, executive committees; managing director, chief executive officer Touche Ross International, 1974-83; dean, Reliance professor management and private enterprise Wharton School University Pennsylvania, 1983-90, chief executive officer The Palmer Group, chairman The Huntsman Center, Wharton School, 1990—; board of directors Contel Cellular Incorporated, The Goodyear Tire & Rubber Company, General Telephone and Telegraph Corp., The May Department Stores Company, Bankers Trust Company, Allied-Signal, Incorporated, Imasco Limited; corp. board Alco Standard Corp., Safeguard Scientifics, Incorporated, Federal Home Loan Mortgage Corp. Member pub. bds. Directors & Bds., Mergers & Aquisitions, Directory Corp. Affiliations, Directory Leading Pvt. Cos. President Fin. Acctg. Foundation, 1979-82; trustee Acctg. Hall of Fame; board of directors Joint Council Economic Education, 1978-83, United Fund Greater New York, 1980-83, United Nations Association United States of America; member Business Committee Arts, 1977-83; member President's Mgmt. Improvement Council, 1979-80; member New York adv. board Salvation Army; former member adv. council Columbia U. School International and Pub. Affairs, Stanford U. Grad. School Business, Womens Way; member Associates Council Business School, Oxford U.; former member national adv. board Salvation Army; adv. panel Comptroller General United States; member United States Secretary Labor's Commission on Workforce Quality and Labor Market Efficiency; pub. member Hudson Institute, member adv. board Radnor Venture Partners; board of directors SEI Center for Advanced Studies in Mgmt. Recipient Gavin Memorial award Beta Theta Pi, 1956, Distinguished Community Service award Brandeis University, 1974, Outstanding Alumnus award Michigan State University, 1978, LEAD Business award, 1984, Good Scout award Philadelphia Council Boy Scouts Am., 1987, Distinguished Aux. Service award Salvation Army, Humanitarian award Federation Jewish Philanthropies. Member Directors Table (board govs.), Links Club, Union League Club, The Cts. of Phila Club, Merion Cricket Club, Round Hill Club, Lost Tree Country Club, Beta Gamma Sigma (board govs.), Conference Board (board directors). Presbyterian. Office: The Palmer Group 3600 Market St Suite 530 Philadelphia Pennsylvania 19104

PAPITTO, RALPH RAYMOND, manufacturing company executive;

born Providence, November 1, 1926; son of John and Maria (David) P.; married Norma J. Ewart, June 10, 1943 (divorced); children: Andrea (Mrs. Harry Crump), Aurelia, David John; married Barbara Auger, April 1982. Bachelor of Science in Finance, Bryant College, Providence, 1947, Doctor of Science Business Administration (honorary), 1987; student, Boston University Law School, 1948-49; Doctor of Science Business Administration (honorary), Roger Williams College, 1985; Doctor of Laws (honorary), New England Institute Tech., 1985, Suffolk University, 1986, New England Institute Tech. With Arthur Andersen & Company and Ernst & Ernst, Providence, 1948-51; executive vice president fin. Ritz Products, Incorporated, Providence, 1951-55; founder, president, chairman, director Glass-Tite Industries, Incorporated, Providence, 1956-63, chairman board, 1963—, also board of directors; founder, chief executive officer, president, chairman Nortek Incorporated, Providence, 1967—, board of directors; board of directors Hi-G, Incorporated. Fin. director, Town Johnston, Rhode Island, 1955-59; trustee Roger Williams College, Bristol, Rhode Island, now chairman board trustees, 1972—; board of directors Meeting St. School Retarded; member Governor's Blue Ribbon Commission, Roger Williams Hospital; member Aurora Civic Association. Named Man Year in Rhode Island, Rhode Island Chamber of Commerce, 1961. Member Alpine Country Club (president 1966-68, 90—), Jockey Club, Surf Club, LaGorce Country Club (Florida). Office: Nortek Incorporated 50 Kennedy Plaza Providence Rhode Island 02903

PARKER, GORDON RAE, natural resource company executive; born Cape Town, South Africa, December 2, 1935; came to United States, 1981; son of David Rae and Gwen Elizabeth (Armstrong) P.; married Pamela Margaret Pearce, September 1, 1962; children: Gillian Rae, David Rae. Bachelor of Science, Montana College Mineral Science and Tech., 1958, Master of Science, 1959; Master of Business Administration, University Cape Town, 1966. Managing director Tsumeb Corp., Namibia, South Africa, 1975-81; managing director O'okiep Copper Company, Cape, South Africa, 1975-81; vice president Newmont Mining Corp., New York City, 1981-84, president, 1984-86, chief executive officer, 1985-86, chairman, president and chief executive officer, 1986—, also board of directors; board of directors The Williams Companies, Incorporated, Newmont Gold Company, Newmont Australia Limited, Peabody Holding Company Incorporated; past chairman World Gold Council, 1986—, chairman Western regional council, 1987—. Fellow Institution Mining and Metallurgy (London), South African Institute Mining and Metallurgy; member American Institute of Mining, Metallurgy and Petroleum Engineers, British North Am. Committee. Clubs: Mining, Sky, Union League (New York City); Blind Brook (Purchase, New York); Silver Spring Country (Ridgefield, Connecticut), Mid Ocean, Hamilton, Bermuda. Avocation: golf. Home: 13 Sunset Dr Englewood Colorado 80110

PARKER, PATRICK STREETER, manufacturing executive; born Cleveland, 1929. Bachelor of Arts, Williams College, 1951; Master of

Business Administration, Harvard University, 1953. With Parker-Hannifin Corp. and predecessor, Cleveland, 1953—, sales manager fittings div., 1957-63, manager aerospace products div., 1963-65, president Parker Seal Company div., 1965-67, corp. vice president, 1967-69, president, 1969-71, president and chief executive officer, 1971-77, chairman board and chief executive officer, 1977-84, chairman board, 1984—, president, 1982-84, also board of directors, 1982-84. Board trustees Case Western Reserves U.; trustee Woodruff Foundation With United States Navy, 1954-57. Member Union Club, Country Club, Pepper Pike Club. Office: Parker Hannifin Corp 17325 Euclid Avenue Cleveland Ohio 44112

PARKINSON, JOHN DAVID, electrical and electronic manufacturing company executive; born Philadelphia, November 26, 1929; son of Granville and Dorothy (Crooks) P.; married Sally Ann Brokaw, November 10, 1956; children: David Gregory, Rex Granville, Leanne. Bachelor of Science, Rutgers University, 1951. With Thomas & Betts Corp., Elizabeth, New Jersey, 1954—; various sales management positions Thomas & Betts Corp., Syracuse, 1954-67; vice president marketing Thomas & Betts Corp., 1968, vice president, general manager, 1969, president div., 1969, vice president corp., 1971, executive vice president, 1971-74, president, chief executive officer, 1974-84, chairman board, 1975—, also director, 1968—. Member National Electrical Manufacturers Association (board govs., chairman), Electrical Manufacturers Club. Office: Thomas & Betts Corp 1001 Frontier Road Bridgewater New Jersey 08807

PATE, JAMES LEONARD, economist, oil company executive; born Mount Sterling, Illinois, September 6, 1935; son of Virgil Leonard and Mammie Elizabeth (Taylor) P.; married Donna Charlene Pate, October 23, 1955; children: David Charles, Gary Leonard, Jennifer Elizabeth. Student, University Maryland, 1957-58; Bachelor of Arts, Monmouth College, 1963; Master of Business Administration, University Ind., 1965, Juris Doctor, 1968. Professor economics Monmouth (Illinois) College, 1965-68; senior economist Federal Reserve Bank Cleveland, 1968-72; chief economist B.F. Goodrich Company, Akron, Ohio, 1972-74; assistant secretary Department Commerce, Washington, Ohio, 1974-76, special adviser to White House, 1976, senior vice president fin., 1976; vice president fin. Pennzoil Company, Houston, Ohio, 1976-89, executive vice president, 1989, executive vice president, chief operating officer, 1990, president, chief executive officer, 1990. Contributor articles to professional journals and text books. Board governors Rice U.; member Senate Monmouth College; board of directors Am. Petroleum Institute, National Petroleum Council. Fellow Royal Econ. Society; member Pi Gamma Mu. Republican. Home: 5346 Longmont Dr Houston Texas 77056 Office: Pennzoil Company Post Office Box 2967 Houston Texas 77252

PAULSON, ALLEN EUGENE, aircraft manufacturing executive; born Clinton, Iowa, April 22, 1922; son of Harry Godfrey and Lillian (Rothert) P.; married Irene Eddy Kastner (divorced); children: Robert (deceased), Richard Allen, James Douglas, John Michael; married Mary Lou Paulson (divorced). Student, University West Virginia, 1941, Iowa State Teachers College, 1943; Doctor of Laws, Lynchburg College, 1983; Doctor of Humanities, Winthrop College; Doctor of Business, Bethany College, Doctor of Business Arts; Doctor of Aviation Management, Embry-Riddle Aeronautical University; Doctor of Business Administration, University Charleston. Comml. pilot, FAA. Flight engineer Transworld Airlines, various locations, 1945-53; chairman, chief executive officer, president California Airmotive Corp., Burbank, 1951-70, Am. Jet Industries, Van Nuys, California, 1970-78; chairman, chief executive officer, president Gulfstream Aerospace Corp. (subsidiary Chrysler Corp.), Savannah, Georgia, 1978—, also board of directors; board of directors Sun Trust Bank, Chrysler Corp., Greyhound Corp. Board of directors Savannah Symphony Society, 1981—, Telfair Acad. Arts and Sci., Savannah, 1982—, Air Force Acad. Foundation, 1982—, Memorial Medical Center, Savannah, Georgia, 1985, Eisenhower Medical Center, California, 1986, Embry-Riddle Aeronautical U.; member adv. council Georgia Tech. U.; adv. board Am. U. Served with United States Army Air Force, 1943-45. Recipient Horatio Alger Association award 1984, Am. Acad. Achievements Golden Plate, 1984, Industrialist of Year award Industrial Mgmt. Council, Spirit Georgia award Entrepreneur Year, Wright Bros. Memorial trophy, 1987; as captain of jet airplane Gulfstream IV, set 24 World and City-to-City speed records flying out of Le Bourget, Paris, June 1987. Member General Aircraft Manufacturing Association (board directors 1978—), Society Experimental Test Pilots (Doolittle Trophy 1982), Air Force Association (board directors 1981—), National Aeronautical Association (board directors 1980—).

PEARLMAN, JERRY KENT, electronics company executive; born Des Moines, March 27, 1939; son of Leo R. Pearlman; married; children: Gregory, Neal. Bachelor of Arts, Princeton University, 1960; Master of Business Administration, Harvard University, 1962. With Ford Motor Company, 1962-70; vice president fin. director Behring Corp., 1970-71; controller Zenith Electronics Corp., Glenview, Illinois, 1971-74, vice president, 1972-74, vice president fin., 1974-78, senior vice president fin., 1978-81, senior vice president fin., group executive, 1981-83, president, chief executive officer, 1983—, chairman, 1984—, also director; director Stone Container Corp., First Chicago Corp. Director Evanston (Illinois) Hospital; trustee Mus. Sci. and Industry, Northwestern U. Office: Zenith Electronics Corp 1000 Milwaukee Avenue Glenview Illinois 60025

PEARSON, RONALD DALE, retail food stores corporation executive; born Des Moines, 1940; married. Bachelor of Science in Business Administration, Drake University, 1962. With Hy-Vee Food Stores Incorporated, Chariton, Iowa, 1962—, former executive vice president, now president, chief operating officer; director Beverage Manufacturers, Incorporated, Civic Center Cts., Incorporated. Office: Hy-Vee Food Stores Incorporated 1801 Oceola Avenue Chariton Iowa 50049

PECK, CHARLES EDWARD, construction and mortgage company executive; born Newark, December 1, 1925; son of Hubert Raymond and Helen (White) P.; married Delphine Murphy, October 15, 1949; children: Margaret, Charles Edward, Katherine, Perry Anne. Graduate, Phillips Academy, 1943; Bachelor of Science, University Pennsylvania, 1949; postgraduate, Massachusetts Institute of Technology, 1944. With Owens-Corning Fiberglas Corp., various locations, 1949-61; sales manager home building products Owens-Corning Fiberglas Corp., Toledo, 1961-66; vice president home building products marketing div. Owens-Corning Fiberglas Corp., 1966-68, vice president construction group, 1968-75, vice president building materials group, 1976-78, executive vice president, 1978-81, board director; co-chairman The Ryland Group, Columbia, Maryland, 1981-82; chairman The Ryland Group, Columbia, 1982-90; director The Delaware Group of Funds, 1991—; vice president Producers Council, Washsington, 1974-77; member statutory visiting committee United States national Bureau Standards, 1972-77; member adv. committee Federal National Mortgage Association, 1977-78, 85-86; visiting committee Massachusetts Institute Tech.-Harvard Joint Center for Urban Studies; chairman Producers Adv. Forum, 1977-81. Member visiting committee Harvard U. Grad. School Design, 1981-86; chairman Howard County United Way Campaign, Maryland, 1987; board of directors National Institute for Urban Wildlife, 1986-90, United Way Central Maryland, 1987-91, Howard County General Hospital, 1988—, Columbia Festival, Incorporated, 1988—, NAHB Research Foundation, 1989—, Alliance to End Childhood Lead Poisoning, 1990—; member adv. board U. Maryland Engring. School; adv. board continuing education Johns Hopkins U., 1988—; chairman chancellor's adv. council U. Maryland System, 1988—; chairman University Maryland Foundation, 1990—. 2d lieutenant United States Army Air Force, 1944-46. Member United States Chamber of Commerce (board director 1975-81), Ohio Chamber of Commerce (board director 1975-81), Depression and Related Affective Disorders Association (president 1986-89, board directors 1986—), Belmont Country Club (Perrysburg, Ohio), Capitol Hill Club (Washington), Talbot Country Club (Maryland), City Club (Washington), Center Club (Baltimore), Phi Gamma Delta. Home: 7649 Woodstream Way Laurel Maryland 20723 Office: Box 1102 Columbia Maryland 21044

PEEVEY, MICHAEL ROBERT, electric company executive; born New York City, February 8, 1938; son of Willard Michael Bliss and Miriam Gardiner (Cooke) Bliss Peevey; married Lauretta Ann Peevey, March 17, 1961 (divorced 1976); children: Darcie Ann, Maria Beth; married Carole Jean Liu, May 27, 1978; 1 child, Jared Liu. Bachelor of Arts in Economics, University Calif.-Berkeley, 1959, Master of Arts in Economics, 1961. Economist United States Department Labor, Washington, 1961-65; coordinator community programs Institute Industrial Relations, University Calif.-Berkeley, 1969-70; director research California Labor Federation, American Federation of Labor and Congress of Industrial Organizations, 1971-73, 65-69; president California Council for Environl./Econ. Balance, San Francisco, 1973-84; vice president Southern California Edison Company, Rosemead, 1984-85, senior vice president, 1985-86, executive vice president, 1986-90, president, 1990—; co'hmn. Electric Transportation Coalition, 1991—; chairman electric transportation steering committee Edison Electric Institute, 1991—. Board of directors California Housing Fin. Agency, Sacramento, 1984-86; member Commission to Revise the Master Plan for Higher Education, California, 1985—; trustee California State U. and Colleges, 1977-85, Joint Council on Economic Education, New York, 1969-85; member Governor's Infrastructure Review Task Force, Sacramento, 1983-84; board governors Economic Literacy Council of California, 1982—; board visitors California Maritime Acad., 1980-83; member steering committee State Solid Waste Mgmt. Board, 1980-83; commissioner National Commission on State Workmen's Compensation Laws, Washington, 1971-72; board of directors Consumer Federation California, 1972-78; co-chairman Citizens for Adequate Energy, 1979-82. Member Industrial Relations Research Association, World Trade Club, Sutter Club, California Club. Democrat. Episcopalian. Office: Southern California Edison Company 2244 Walnut Grove Avenue Rosemead California 91770

PEPPER, JOHN ENNIS, JR., consumer products company executive; born Pottsville, Pennsylvania, August 2, 1938; son of John Ennis Sr. and Irma Elizabeth (O'Connor) P.; married Frances Graham Garber, September 9, 1967; children: John, David, Douglas, Susan. Bachelor of Arts, Yale University, 1960. With Procter & Gamble Company, Cincinnati, 1963—, general manager Italian subsidiary, 1974-77; vice president, general manager div. packaged soap and detergent Proctor & Gamble Company, Cincinnati, 1977-80, group vice president, 1980-84, executive vice president, 1984-86, president, 1986—, also director. Trustee Cincinnati Symphony Orchestra, Cincinnati Medical Institute; group chairman Cincinnati United Appeal Campaign, 1980; board trustees Xavier U., 1985—. Served to lieutenant United States Navy, 1960-63. Member National Alliance Businessmen (chairman communication committee), Soap and Detergent Association (board directors). Office: Procter & Gamble Company 1 Procter & Gamble Plaza Cincinnati Ohio 45202

PEPPER, LOUIS HENRY, financial executive, lawyer; born Libertyville, Illinois, July 21, 1924; son of Louis Henry and Dora Anna (Sievers) P.; married Mollie Venables, April 25, 1953; children: Louis S., Margaret E. Pepper Glessner, Elizabeth A., Catherine A. Bachelor of Arts, University Wisconsin, 1950, Juris Doctor, 1951. Bar. Washington 1951. Senior partner Foster Pepper Riviera, Seattle, 1952-81; president, chief executive officer Washington Mutual Savings Bank, Seattle, 1981-82, chairman, chief executive officer, 1982-90, chairman, 1990—; chairman Joint House Fin. Institute Commission, Washington State Legis., Olympia, 1984-85; member thrift institution adv. council Federal, Reserve Board, Washington, 1988-89. Regent Washington State U., Pullman, 1986—; board of directors Downtown Seattle Association,

1985—, Washington Savs. League, 1988—, Federal Home Loan Bank of Seattle, 1988, 89, 90; chairman Seattle School Levy campaign, 1986, 88, Seattle-King County Economic Devel. Council, 1987-88. Served to 1st lieutenant United States Army Air Force, 1943-46, PTO. Named one of top 20 banking attys. in United States National Law Journal, 1983. Member American Bar Association (committee chairman 1977-82), Washington Bar Association, Am. College Real Estate Lawyers, Anglo-Am. Real Property Institute, Association Mutual Savings Banks (general counsel 1954-80), National Council Savings Institutions (board directors 1986—, chairman committee legis., regulatory policy 1982-84), Greater Seattle Chamber of Commerce (board directors 1984-88), Rainier Club, University Club, Seattle Tennis Club (president 1972-74), Rotary. Avocations: skiing, writing. Office: Wash Mut Savings Bank 1201 3d Avenue Post Office Box 834 Seattle Washington 98111

PERDUE, FRANKLIN P., poultry products company executive. married Mitzi Henderson Ayala, July 1988. Chairman board Perdue Farms Incorporated, Salisbury, Maryland; also chairman board Perdue Incorporated subsidiary Perdue Farms Incorporated, Salisbury. Office: Perdue Farms Incorporated Post Office Box 1537 Salisbury Maryland 21801

PERELLA, JOSEPH ROBERT, investment banker; born Newark, September 20, 1941; son of Dominic A. and Agnes P.; married Amy Gralnick, January 20, 1974. Bachelor of Science, Lehigh University, 1964; Master of Business Administration, Harvard University, 1972. C.P.A., New York. Pub. accountant Haskins & Sells, New York City, 1964-70; consultant International Bank for Reconstruction & Devel., Washington, 1971; associate The First Boston Corp., New York City, 1972-74, assistant vice president, 1974-75, vice president, 1975-78, managing director, 1978-88; chairman Wasserstein, Perella & Company, New York City, 1988—. Office: Wasserstein Perella & Company 31 W 52d St New York New York 10019

PERELMAN, RONALD OWEN, diversified holding company executive; born Greensboro, North Carolina, 1943; son of Raymond and Ruth (Caplan) P.; married Claudia Cohen; 4 children. Bachelor of Arts, University Pennsylvania, 1964; Master of Business Administration, Wharton School Fin., 1966. With Belmont Industries Incorporated, 1966-78; chairman, chief executive officer, director MacAndrews & Forbes Holdings Incorporated, Wilmington, Del., 1983—; chairman, chief executive officer MacAndrews & Forbes Group Incorporated (subsidiary), New York City, 1978—; chairman, chief executive officer, director Revlon Group Incorporated (subsidiary MacAndrews & Forbes Group Incorporated), New York City, 1985—, Revlon Incorporated (subsidiary), New York City, 1985—; also chairman National Health Laboratories Incorporated, La Jolla, California, 1985—, Andrews Group Incorporated, New York City, 1985—. Jewish. Office: Revlon Group Incorporated 21 E 63rd St New York New York 10021 also: MacAndrews & Forbes Group Incorporated 36 E 63rd St New York New York 10021

PERINI, DAVID B., construction company executive; born Framingham, Massachusetts, May

19, 1937; son of Louis R. and Florence R. P.; married Eileen Callahan, July 14, 1962; children: Jennifer, David, Kristin, Timothy, Andrea. Bachelor of Science, College of Holy Cross, 1959; Juris Doctor, Boston College, 1962. Assistant to general counsel Perini Corp., Framingham, 1962-65; div. counsel Midwest and Southwest divs. Perini Corp., Evansville, Ind., 1965-67, div. counsel Western div., 1968; assistant general counsel Framingham, Evansville, Ind., 1968-69, vice president, general counsel, 1969-71, vice chairman board, 1971-72, president, chairman, 1972—; board of directors Framingham; chairman Perini Investment Properties, Incorporated, State St. Boston Corp., New England Telephone Company, Dennison Manufacturing Company. Member executive board Boston council Boy Scouts Am., 1976; member President's Council Holy Cross College, trustee, 1977—. Decorated knight Order of Malta, 1979; recipient Merit citation National Conference of Christians and Jews, 1980; named 1 of 10 Outstanding Young Leaders, Boston Junior Chamber of Commerce, 1973; medalist Italian Am. Charitable Society, 1979. Member American Bar Association, Massachusetts Bar Association, World Association Lawyers, Moles (president 1980), Society Am. Military Engineers, Associated General Contractors Am. (chairman international constrn. committee 1980—), Associated General Contractors Massachusetts (director 1973-75). Office: Perini Corp 73 Mt Wayte Avenue Framingham Massachusetts 01701

PERKINS, THOMAS JAMES, venture capital company executive; born Oak Park, Illinois, January 7, 1932; son of Harry H. and Elizabeth P.; married Gerd Thune-Ellefsen, December 9, 1961; children: Tor Kristian, Elizabeth Siri. Bachelor of Science in Electrical Engineering, Massachusetts Institute of Technology, 1953; Master of Business Administration, Harvard University, 1957. General manager computer div. Hewlett Packard Company, Cupertino, California, 1965-70, director corp. devel., 1970-72; general partner Kleiner & Perkins, San Francisco, 1972-80; senior partner Kleiner Perkins Caufield & Byers, San Francisco, from 1980; chairman board Tandem Computers, Genentech; director Spectra Physics., Corning Glass Works, Collagen Corp., LSI Logic Corp., Hybritech Incorporated, Econics Corp., Vitalink Communications Corp. Author: Classic Supercharged Sports Cars, 1984. Trustee San Francisco Ballet, 1980—. Member National Venture Capital Association (chairman 1981-82, president 1980-81). Clubs: New York Yacht, Links, Am. Bugatti (president 1983—). Office: Tandem Computers Incorporated 10435 Tantau Avenue Cupertino California 95014 also: Genentech Incorporated 460 Point San Bruno San Francisco California 94080

PERLMAN, LAWRENCE, business executive; born St. Paul, April 8, 1938; son of Irving and Ruth (Mirsky) P.; married Medora Scoll, June 18, 1961; children: David, Sara. Bachelor of Arts, Carleton College, 1960; Juris Doctor, Harvard University, 1963. Bar: Minnesota 1963. Law. clerk for federal judge 1963; associate, partner Fredrikson & Byron, Minneapolis, 1964-75; general counsel, executive vice president United

States pacing operations Medtronic, Incorporated, Minneapolis, 1975-78; senior partner Oppenheimer, Wolff & Donnelly, Minneapolis, 1978-80; secretary, general counsel, vice president corp. services Control Data Corp., Minneapolis, 1980-82; president, chief operating officer, director Commercial Credit Company, 1983-85; president Data Storage Products Group (Imprimis Tech., Incorporated), 1985-88; president, chief operating officer Control Data Corp., Minneapolis, 1989; president, chief executive officer Control Data Corp., 1990—, also board of directors; board of directors G & K Services, Incorporated, Inter-Regional Fin. Group, Incorporated, Seagate Tech., Incorporated, Computer Network Tech., Incorporated; adj. professor Law School, University Minnesota, 1974-76, 79-80. Vice-chmn. board of directors Walker Art Center; board of directors Minnesota Orchestral Association; trustee Carleton College. Member Phi Beta Kappa. Club: Minneapolis. Home: 2366 W Lake of the Isles Parkway Minneapolis Minnesota 55405 Office: Control Data Corp 8100 34th Avenue S Minneapolis Minnesota 55420

PERNA, FRANK, JR., manufacturing company executive; born Detroit, January 15, 1938; son of Frank and Mary (Cataldo) P.; married Monika Doering, May 10, 1960; children: Laura, Reneé, Christopher. Bachelor of Science in Mechanical Engineering, General Motors Institute, 1960; Master of Science in Electrical Engineering, Wayne State University, 1966; Master of Business Administration in Management (Sloan fellow), Massachusetts Institute of Technology, 1970. Assistant to director reliability General Motors Corp., Detroit, 1955-70; vice president, director engineering Sun Electric Corp., Crystal Lake, Illinois, 1971-77, executive vice president operations, 1977-78, president, chief executive officer, 1978-81; vice president, group executive Whittaker Corp., Los Angeles, 1983-85; president MagneTek, Incorporated, Los Angeles, 1985—; board of directors 1st State Bank and Trust, Hanover Park, Illinois, 1st National Bank of Hoffman Estates, Illinois. Named one of Outstanding Young Man of Am., 1968. Member Board Professional Engineers. Avocations: skiing, golf, tennis, wind surfing. Office: MagneTek Incorporated 11111 Santa Monica Boulevard Los Angeles California 90025

PESKIN, KENNETH, retail executive. Postgraduate, Harvard University. President, chief operating officer Pathmark div. Supermarkets General, New Jersey, 1984-86, president, chief executive officer, 1986-87; chairman, chief executive officer Supermarkets General Holdings Corp., New Jersey, 1987—. Office: Supermarkets General Corp 301 Blair Road Woodbridge New Jersey 07095

PETERSON, ROGER ERIC, hardware wholesale company executive; born Chicago, December 14, 1937; son of Erick Herman and Greta (Moren) P.; married Joyce Marlene Holtz, August 22, 1959; children: Stephen, Cindy, Linda, Kristin, Kathrin, Scott. Bachelor of Business Administration, University Miami, 1960. Industrial engineering supervisor Montgomery Ward, Chicago, 1960-63; area manager J.C. Penney, Wauwatosa, Wisconsin, 1963-67; district devel. manager Ben Franklin div. City Products, Des

Plaines, Illinois, 1967-72; executive vice president C.P. Products Corp., Elkhart, Ind., 1972-76; national distribution manager Ace Hardware Corp., Oak Brook, Illinois, 1976-82, vice president operations, 1982-85, executive vice president, 1985-86, president, 1986—; president, chief executive officer 1990—; member Midwest adv. board Allendale Insurance Company, Providence, 1986-90; board of directors Home Center Institute. Board of directors Center Institute, 1989. Member National Wholesale Association (board directors 1990—), National Association Wholesale Distributors (board directors 1990—), Am. Scandinavian Council (board directors 1989—), Elgin (Illinois) Country Club. Office: Ace Hardware Corp 2200 Kensington Court Oak Brook Illinois 60521

PETERSON, ROLAND OSCAR, electronics company executive; born Brooklyn, January 18, 1932; son of Oscar Gustaf and Klara Ingegerd (Lindau) P.; married Agnes Frances Walsh, September 12, 1953; children: Joan, Lauren, Paul, Michael. Bachelor of Electrical Engineering, Polytechnic Institute New York, 1953, Master of Electrical Engineering, 1954. Registered professional engineer, New York. Research fellow Microwave Research Institute, Brooklyn, 1953-54; senior engineer Sperry Gyroscope Company, Great Neck, New York, 1956-60; with Litton Industries Incorporated, Woodland Hills, California, 1961—; vice president advanced systems engineering Guidance and Control Systems div., Litton Industries Incorporated, Woodland Hills, California, 1973-76, vice president business devel., 1976-77, president, 1977-83; vice president Litton Industries Incorporated, 1979-83; senior vice president, group executive Litton Industries Incorporated, Beverly Hills, California, 1983-88, president, chief operating officer, 1988-90, senior vice president, group executive, chief scientist, 1990—. Regional chairman Los Angeles United Way campaign , 1985-86. Served to 1st lieutenant United States Army, 1954-56. Recipient Distinguished Alumni award Polytechnic Institute New York, 1986. Member Am. Electronics Association, Institute Navigation (western regional vice president 1975-76, Hays award 1982). Roman Catholic. Avocations: skiing, tennis.

PETRY, THOMAS EDWIN, manufacturing company executive; born Cincinnati, November 20, 1939; son of Edwin Nicholas and Leonora Amelia (Zimpelman) P.; married Mary Helen Gardner, August 25, 1962; children: Thomas Richard, Stephen Nicholas, Daniel Gardner, Michael David. Bachelor of Science, University Cincinnati, 1962; Master of Business Administration, Harvard, 1964. Group vice president, treasurer Eagle-Picher Industries, Incorporated, Cincinnati, 1968-81; president Eagle-Picher Industries, Incorporated, 1981-89, chief operating officer, from 1981, chief executive officer, director, 1982—. Republican. Clubs: Queen City, Terrace Park (Ohio) Country, Cincinnati Country. Office: Eagle-Picher Industries Incorporated 580 Walnut St Cincinnati Ohio 45202

PEW, ROBERT CUNNINGHAM, II, office equipment manufacturing company executive; born Syracuse, New York, June 4, 1923; son of Robert Carroll and Bernice (Evans) P.; married Mary Bonnell Idema, August 23, 1947; children: Robert Cunningham, John Evans, Kate

Bonnell. Bachelor of Arts, Wesleyan University, Middletown Connecticut; Doctor of Humanities (honorary), Aquinas College, Doctor of Laws (honorary). Labor relations executive Doehler-Jarvis Corp., Grand Rapids, Michigan, 1948-51; with Steelcase Incorporated, Grand Rapids, 1952—; executive vice president Steelcase Incorporated, 1964-66, president, 1966-75, chairman board, president, from 1975, formerly chairman, chief executive officer, now chairman board; director Old Kent Financial Corp., Foremost Corp. Am. Board control Grand Valley State College; board of directors Economic Devel. Corp. Grand Rapids, Michigan Strategic Fund, National Organization on Disability; member Governor's Commission on Jobs and Economic Devel. Served to 1st lieutenant United States Army Air Force, 1942-45; to captain United States Air Force, 1951-52. Decorated Purple Heart, Air medal with 2 oak leaf clusters. Member Grand Rapids Chamber of Commerce (director), Grand Rapids Employers Association (director), Chi Psi. Episcopalian. Clubs: Lost Tree (North Palm Beach Florida); Peninsular; University, Kent Country (Grand Rapids). Home: 210 Greenwich Road NE Grand Rapids Michigan 49506 Office: Steelcase Incorporated 901 44th St Southeast Post Office Box 1967 Grand Rapids Michigan 49501

PFEIFFER, CARL E., manufacturing company executive; born 1930. Bachelor of Science in Mechanical Engineering, Michigan State University. With Quanex Corp., 1953—, now chairman, chief executive officer; plant manager Gulf States Tube Corp. subsidiary, vice president, 1958-68, executive vice president, 1968-71, president, 1971-72, chairman executive committee, now president, chief executive officer, also board of directors. Office: Quanex Corp 1900 W Loop S Houston Texas 77027

PHILBIN, EDWARD JAMES, federal agency chairman, legal educator, lawyer; born New York City, August 7, 1932; son of Harry B. and Carlotta Isabel (Matthews-Kratz) P. Bachelor of Science in Engineering, San Diego State University, 1957; Juris Doctor summa cum laude, University San Diego, 1965; disting. graduate, Air War College, 1978. Commissioned 2d lieutenant United States Air Force, 1949, advanced through grades to major general, 1986; research director Reserve Forces Policy Board Department Defense, 1980, deputy assistant secretary defense (res. affairs), 1981-84; commissioner Federal Maritime Commission, 1984-90; chairman Interstate Commerce Commission, Washington, 1990—; design research engineer General Dynamics, San Diego, 1957-60, physicist, senior physicist, 1960-66; attorney Hecsh, Hegner & Philbin, San Diego, 1966-70; associate professor, assistant dean Law School University San Diego, 1970-73, professor law, 1973-85; visiting professor international law Air War College, 1978-79. Contributor articles to professional journals. Trustee San Diego Aerospace Mus., 1968-70; president Air Force Association, San Diego, 1968-70. Decorated Legion of Merit, Soverien Military Order of Temple of Jersalem; St. Thomas More Scholar, 1963, 64, 65; Dean's Scholar, 1963, 64, 65; recipient General Orvil A. Anderson Award National Geog. Society, 1978. Member Navy League

United States (director 1974-77), Reserve Officers Association, National Guard Association of United States, California Bar Association, San Diego County Bar Association, RAF Club, Army Navy Club, International Club, Theta Chi. Republican. Roman Catholic. Office: ICC 12th & Constitution Avenue Northwest Washington District of Columbia 20423

PHILLIPS, EDWARD EVERETT, insurance company executive; born Orange, New Jersey, September 14, 1927; son of Edward Everett, Jr. and Margaret (Jaffray) P.; married Margaret Whitney, September 7, 1952; children: John Whitney, Margaret Jaffray, Nancy Osborne. Bachelor of Arts cum laude, Amherst College, 1952; Bachelor of Laws, Harvard University, 1955; Doctor of Pub. Service (honorary), Northeastern University, 1979; Doctor of Humane Letters (honorary), University Massachusetts, 1987, Lesley College, 1990. Bar: Massachusetts 1955. With Mirick, O'Connell, De Mallie & Lougee, Worcester, Massachusetts, 1955-57, John Hancock Mutual Life Insurance Company, Boston, 1957-69; vice president agency department John Hancock Mutual Life Insurance Company, 1965-69; with New England Mutual Life Insurance Company, Boston, 1969—, vice president, secretary, 1969-72, executive vice president, 1972-74, president, 1974-81, chairman, chief executive officer, 1978—, also board director, 1973—; board of directors Affiliated Publs., Incorporated, NYNEX. Trustee emeritus Amherst College; board overseers Boston Mus. of Fine Arts; chairman Greater Boston Arts Fund; past. chairman Massachusetts Business Roundtable, board of directors; past member Massachusetts Cultural Council; chairman board trustees New England Conservatory; board of directors, treasurer United Way of Am. Office: New England Mut Life Ins Company 501 Boylston St Boston Massachusetts 02117

PHILLIPS, LAWRENCE S., apparel company executive; born 1927; son of Seymour J. P.; married. Bachelor of Arts, Princeton University, 1948. With Phillips-Van Heusen Corp., New York City, 1948—, vice president, 1951-59, executive vice president, 1959-68, president, 1968-87, also chief executive officer, director, chairman., 1987—. Member Am. Apparel Manufacturers (director). Office: Phillips-Van Heusen Corp 1290 Avenue of Americas New York New York 10104

PHILLIPS, THOMAS L., corporate executive; born Istanbul, Turkey, May 2, 1924. Bachelor of Science in Electrical Engineering, Virginia Polytechnic Institute, 1947, Master of Science in Electrical Engineering, 1948; honorary doctorates, Stonehill College, 1968, Northeastern University, 1968, Lowell University, 1970, Gordon College, 1970, Boston College, 1974, Babson College, 1981, Suffolk University, 1986, University Massachusetts, Amherst, 1989. With Raytheon Company, Lexington, Massachusetts, 1948-91, executive vice president, 1961-64, chief operating officer, 1964-68, president, 1964-75, chief executive officer, 1968-91, chairman board, 1975-91, retired, 1991; board of directors John Hancock Mutual Life Insurance Company, Knight-Ridder, Incorporated, Raytheon Company, Digital Equipment Corp. Trustee Gordon College, State St. Research and Mgmt. Company, Northeastern U.; member corp. Joslin Diabetes Center, Mus. Sci., Boston, Massachusetts General Hospital. Recipient Meritorious Pub. Service award for work in Sparrow III missile system, United States Navy, 1958. Member National Acad. Engineering, Business Council, Am. Acad. Arts and Sciences. Office: Raytheon Company 141 Spring St Lexington Massachusetts 02173

PICARD, DENNIS J., electronics company executive. Formerly senior vice president Raytheon Company, Lexington, Massachusetts, now president. Office: Raytheon Company Missile Systems Div Hartwell Road Bedford Massachusetts 01730

PICCININI, ROBERT M., grocery store chain executive. Chief executive officer Save Mart Supermarkets, Modesto, California. Office: Save Mart Supermarkets Post Office Box 4278 Modesto California 95352

PICHLER, JOSEPH ANTON, food products executive; born St. Louis, October 3, 1939; son of Anton Dominick and Anita Marie (Hughes) P.; married Susan Ellen Eyerly, December 27, 1962; children: Gretchen, Christopher, Rebecca, Josh. Bachelor of Business Administration, University Notre Dame, 1961; Master of Business Administration, University Chicago, 1963, Doctor of Philosophy; Doctor of Philosophy, 1966. Assistant professor business University Kansas, 1964-68, associate professor, 1968-73, professor, 1973-80; dean University Kansas (School Business), 1974-80; executive vice president Dillon Companies Incorporated, 1980-82, president, 1982-86; executive vice president Kroger Company, 1985-86, president, chief operating officer, 1986—, also board of directors, 1986-90, president, chief executive officer, 1990, chairman, chief executive officer, 1990—; special assistant to assistant secretary for manpower United States Department Labor, 1968-70; chairman Kansas Manpower Services Council, 1974-78; board of directors B.F. Goodrich Company; industrial consultant. Author: (with Joseph McGuire) Inequality: The Poor and the Rich in America, 1969; contributing author: Creativity and Innovation in Manpower Research and Action Programs, 1970, Contemporary Management: Issues and Viewpoints, 1973, Institutional Issues in Public Accounting, 1974, Co-Creation and Capitalism: John Paul II's Laborem Exercens, 1983; Co-editor, contributing author: Ethics, Free Enterprise, and Public Policy, 1978; Contributor articles to professional journals. Board of directors Kansas Charities, 1973-75, Benedictine College, Atchison, Kansas, 1979-83, Cincinnati Opera; national board of directors Boys Hope, 1983—, Tougaloo College, 1986—; member national board National Alliance of Business; board advisors U. Cincinnati College Business Administration. Recipient Performance award United States Department Labor Manpower Administration, 1969; Woodrow Wilson fellow, Ford Foundation fellow, Standard Oil Industrial Relations fellow, 1966, Woodrow Wilson fellow, Adv. Committee, 1990. Member Business Roundtable, Queen City Club, Commercial Club of Cincinnati. Office: Kroger Company 1014 Vine St Cincinnati Ohio 45202

PIERGALLINI, ALFRED A., beverage company executive; born

Easton, Pennsylvania, August 1, 1946. Bachelor of Arts, Lafayette College, 1968; Master of Business Administration, University Chicago, 1970. Regional director Beverage Management Incorporated; sales manager Procter & Gamble Company, then brand manager; president Shasta Beverages Incorporated, Hayward, California, 1985-90; chairman, president, chief executive officer Gerber Prods. Company, Fremont, Michigan, 1985-90. Office: Gerber Products Company 445 State St Fremont Michigan 49412

PIETRINI, ANDREW GABRIEL, automotive aftermarket executive; born Bryn Mawr, Pennsylvania, February 27, 1937; son of Bernard and Irene (Norcini) P.; married Pam Mari, September 29, 1962; children: Darrin, Wayne. Bachelor of Science, Villanova University, 1958. C.P.A., Pennsylvania. Junior accountant Fernald & Company, Philadelphia, 1958-60; senior accountant O & W Audit Company, Narberth, Pennsylvania, 1960-62; assistant secretary James Talcott, Incorporated, New York City, 1962-68; president UIS, Incorporated, New York City, 1968—, director, 1972—. Board of directors Lebensfeld Foundation, New York City, 1979—. Member Am. Institute C.P.A.s, Fin. Executives Institute. Republican. Roman Catholic. Avocations: sailing; golf. Office: UIS Incorporated 600 Fifth Avenue New York New York 10020

PILGRIM, LONNIE (BO), poultry production company executive; born 1928; married. Formerly partner Pilgrim Industries Incorporated, Pittsburg, Texas, chairman board, chief executive officer, 1968—. Served with United States Armed Forces, 1951-53. Office: Pilgrim Industries Incorporated 110 S Texas St Pittsburg Texas 75686

PISTNER, STEPHEN LAWRENCE, retail chain executive; born St. Paul, March 14, 1932; son of Leopold and Prudence Charlette (Selcer) P.; children: Paul David, John Alan, Betsy Ann. Bachelor of Science in Business Administration, University Minnesota, 1953. President, chief executive officer Target Stores, Incorporated, Minneapolis, 1973-76, chairman, chief executive officer, 1976; executive vice president Dayton Hudson Corp., Minneapolis, 1976-77, president, chief operating officer, 1977-81, also director; president, chief executive officer Montgomery Ward & Company, Incorporated, Chicago, 1981-85; chairman board, chief executive officer McCrory Corp., 1985-88; executive vice president Rapid-Am. Corp., New York City, 1985-88; chairman, chief executive officer Ames Dept Stores, Incorporated, Rocky Hill, Connecticut, 1990—. Office: Ames Department Stores Incorporated 2418 Main St Rocky Hill Connecticut 06067-0801

PLASKETT, THOMAS G., transportation company executive; born Raytown, Missouri, December 24, 1943; son of Warren E. and Frances S. (Winegar) P.; married Linda Lee Maxey, June 8, 1968; children—Kimberly, Keith. Bachelor.I.E., General Motors Institute; Master of Business Administration, Harvard University. Supervisor industrial engineering General Motors, Flint, Michigan, 1968, superintendent industrial engineering, 1969-73; senior staff assistant, treas General Motors, New York City, 1973; assistant controller Am. Airlines, New York City, 1974, vice president marketing administration,

1975-76, senior vice president fin., 1976-80; senior vice president marketing Am. Airlines, Dallas, from 1980; president, chief executive officer Continental Airlines Incorporated, Houston, Texas, until 1988; chairman, chief executive officer, president Pan Am Corp., New York City, 1988—; board of directors Tandy Corp., Fort Worth. Member visitors committee Edwin L. Cox School Business; member business adv. committee Northwestern U. Transportation Center; trustee GMI Engring. and Mgmt. Institute, Flint, Michigan. Avocations: golf, skiing, squash. Office: Pan Am Corp 200 Park Avenue New York New York 10166

POLING, HAROLD ARTHUR, automobile company executive; born Troy, Michigan, October 14, 1925; son of Plesant Arthur and Laura Elizabeth (Thompson) P.; married Marian Sarita Lee, 1957; children—Pamela Lee, Kathryn Lynn, Douglas Lee. Bachelor of Arts, Monmouth (Illinois) College, 1949, Doctor of Humane Letters (honorary), 1981; Master of Business Administration, Ind. University, 1951, Doctor of Humane Letters (honorary), 1990; Doctor of Humane Letters (honorary), Hofstra University, 1986, University Detroit, 1990. With Ford Motor Company, Dearborn, Michigan, 1951-59, 60—, assistant controller transmission and chassis div., 1964-66, controller transmission and chassis div., 1966-67, controller engine and foundry div., 1967-68; controller product devel. group Ford Motor Company, 1968-72; vice president finance Ford of Europe, 1972-75; president Ford of Europe, Incorporated, Brentwood, England, 1975-77; chairman board Ford of Europe, Incorporated, 1977-79; executive vice president Ford Motor Company, Dearborn, Michigan, 1979, executive vice president North America automotive operations, 1980-85, member office of chief executive, 1984, president, chief operating officer, 1985-87, vice-chairman, chief operating officer, 1987-90, chairman, chief executive officer, 1990—, also board of directors; member President's Export Council; board of directors NCR Corp., Shell Oil Company. Board of directors The Monmouth (Illinois) College Senate; member dean's adv. council Ind. U. School Business; member National 4-H Council; board visitors School Econs. and Mgmt. Oakland U., Michigan, Grad. School Business U. Pittsburgh; member The Conference Board, vice president Boys and Girls Club Southeast Michigan; member Bus.-Higher Education Forum, United States Korea Business Council, The Brookings Council With United States Naval Reserve, 1943-45. Recipient Distinguished Service Citation award Auto. Hall Fame, 1986, Leadership award Engineering Society Detroit, 1987. Member The Business Roundtable. Office: Ford Motor Company The American Road Dearborn Michigan 48121

POLLARD, CHARLES WILLIAM, diversified services company executive; born Chicago, June 8, 1938; son of Charles W. and Ruth Ann (Humphrey) P.; married Judith Ann, June 8, 1959; children: Julie Ann, Charles W., Brian, Amy. Bachelor of Arts, Wheaton College, 1960; Juris Doctor, Northwestern University, 1963. Bar: Illinois 1963. Member firm Wilson and McIlvaine, 1963-67, Vescelus, Perry & Pollard, Wheaton, Illinois, 1968-72; professor, vice president fin.

Wheaton College, 1972-77; senior vice president ServiceMaster Industries, Downers Grove, Illinois, 1977-80, executive vice president, 1980-81, president, 1981-83; president, chief operating officer ServiceMaster Industries, 1981-83; president, chief executive officer ServiceMaster Company, Downers Grove, Illinois, 1983—; board of directors Gary-Wheaton Bank, Wheaton College, Herman Miller Incorporated. Office: Servicemaster LP 2300 Warrenville Road Downers Grove Illinois 60515

POLLIN, ABE, professional basketball executive, builder; born Philadelphia, December 3, 1923; son of Morris and Jennie (Sack) P.; married Irene S. Kerchek, May 27, 1945; children: Robert Norman, James Edward. Bachelor of Arts, George Washington University, 1945; student, University Maryland, 1941-44. Engaged in home building business 1945—; president Abe Pollin Incorporated, Baltimore, 1962—; president, chairman Baltimore Bullets Basketball Club, Incorporated (now Washington Bullets), 1964—; director County Federal Savings & Loan Association, Rockville, Maryland. Board of directors United Jewish Appeal, National Jewish Hospital, Jewish Community Center; board of directors, adv. committee John F. Kennedy Cultural Center. Member National Association Home Builders, Associate Builders and Contractors Maryland, Washington Board Trade. Jewish. Office: Washington Bullets Capital Center Landover Maryland 20785

POMERANTZ, JOHN J., manufacturing executive; born New York City, July 4, 1933; son of Fred P. and Greta (Grainsky) P.; married Laura H. Herman; children: Andrea, Susan, Marnie. Bachelor of Science in Economics, University Pennsylvania, 1955. With Leslie Fay Companies, Incorporated, New York City, 1955—, executive vice president, 1968-71, president, 1971-87, chairman, chief executive officer, 1987—; board trustees Fashion Institute Tech., president educational foundation F.I.T. Board of directors Am. Committee for Shenkar College Textile Tech. and Fashion in Israel, Incorporated; founder Albert Einstein College Medicine, New York City, National Jewish Hospital and Research Center, Denver, Israel Bonds Century Club; fundraising committee Am. Cancer Society; past chairman Greater New York Council Boy Scouts Am. Receipient award of Merit, Jack Martin Fund, Champion of Youth award International Officers of B'nai B'rith, Humanitarian award Albert Einstein College Medicine. Clubs: Quaker Ridge (Scarsdale, New York); Palm Beach (Florida) Country. Office: Leslie Fay Cos 1400 Broadway New York New York 10018

PONTIKES, KENNETH NICHOLAS, computer leasing company executive; born Chicago, March 15, 1940; married Lynne M. Weston, June 21, 1980. Bachelor of Science, Southern Illinois University, 1962. With International Business Machines, 1961-67; sales department OEI Sales Corp., 1967; sales representative Officer Eletrs Incorporated, Chicago, 1967-68; manager brokerage operations Data Power Incorporated, Chicago, 1968-69; president Comdisco, Incorporated, Des Plaines, Illinois, 1969-76; chairman board, president, chief executive officer Comdisco, Incorporated, 1976—. With United

States Army Reserve, 1963-69. Office: Comdisco Incorporated 6111 N River Road Rosemont Illinois 60018

POPOFF, FRANK PETER, chemical company executive; born Sofia, Bulgaria, October 27, 1935; came to United States, 1940; son of Eftim and Stoyanka (Kossoroff) P.; married Jean Urse; children: John V., Thomas F., Steven M. Bachelor of Science in Chemistry, Ind. University, 1957, Master of Business Administration, 1959. With The Dow Chemical Company, Midland, Michigan, 1959—, executive vice president, 1985-87, director, president, chief executive officer, 1987—, also board of directors; executive vice president, then president Dow Chemical Europe subsidiary, Horgen, Switzerland, 1976-85; board of directors Dow Corning Corp., Am. Express, National Research Council Corp., Chemical Bank & Trust Company, Chemical Fin. Corp., Midland. Member Dean's Adv. Council, Ind. U.; member visiting committee U. Michigan School Business. Member Chemical Manufacturers Association (board directors), United States Council for International Business , Business Roundtable, Conference Board, Am. Chemical Society. Office: Dow Chem Company 2030 Dow Center Midland Michigan 48674

POPPA, RYAL ROBERT, manufacturing company executive; born Wahpeton, North Dakota, November 7, 1933; son of Ray Edward and Annabelle (Phillips) P.; married Ruth Ann Curry, June 21, 1952; children: Sheryl Lynn, Kimberly Marie. Bachelor of Business Administration, Claremont Men's College, 1957. Sales trainee International Business Machines Corporation, Los Angeles, 1957-59, sales representative, 1959-62, product marketing representative, 1963, sales manager, 1964-66; vice president, general manager Commercial Computers Incorporated, Los Angeles, 1966-67; vice president Greyhound Computer Corp., Chicago, 1967-68, president, chief executive officer, board of directors, 1969-70; president, chief executive officer, board of directors, member executive committee Data Processing Fin. & General, Hartsdale, New York, 1970-72; executive vice president, chief fin. officer, board of directors, member executive committee Mohawk Data Sci. Corp., Utica, New York, 1972-73; chairman, president, chief executive officer Pertec Computer Corp., Los Angeles, 1973-81, BMC Industries, Incorporated, St. Paul, 1982-85; president, chairman, chief executive officer Storage Tech. Corp., Louisville, Colorado, 1985—; founder Charles Babbage Institute; past director Spacelabs, Incorporated. Trustee Claremont Men's College, Colorado Music Festival; member Chmn.'s Circle Colorado Reps.; past member President Committee National Medal of Sci. Recipient Executive of Year award University Colorado MBA Alum Association, 1986, Community Service award Institute Human Rels. Am. Jewish Committee, 1980, Colorado Business Leader of Year CACI, 1991. Member World Business Council, Chief Executive Organization, Computer and Communications Industry Association (past board directors, chairman, member executive committee), Am. Electronics Association (past board directors, member executive committee Colorado chapter), Electronic Manufacturers Club, Boulder Country Club. Office: Storage Tech Corp 2270 S 88th St Louisville Colorado 80028-4315

PORTER, IRWIN W., food store chain executive; born 1912; married. Chairman, director Giant Eagle, Incorporated (formerly Giant Eagle Markets Incorporated), Pittsburgh. Office: Giant Eagle Incorporated 101 Kappa Dr Pittsburgh Pennsylvania 15238

POSNICK, ADOLPH, chemical company executive; born Yellow Creek, Saskatchewan, Canada, May 3, 1926; came to United States, 1947; son of Frank and Joanne (Shimko) P.; married Sarah Anne Briggs, May 16, 1947; children—Joann Elizabeth, Barbara Ellen. Bachelor of Science in Ceramic Engineering, University Saskatchewan, 1947. Research engineer Ferro Corp., Cleveland, 1947-50; tech. director Ferro Enamel-Brazil, Sao Paulo, 1950-56; managing director Ferro Enamel-Brazil, 1956-65; vice president international operations Ferro Corp., Cleveland, 1965-74; senior vice president operations Ferro Corp., 1974-75, executive vice president, 1975-76, president, chief executive officer, 1976-88, chairman board of directors, chief executive officer, 1988—; board of directors foreign subsidiaries; member Brazil-Am. Business Council. Member Am., Brazilian ceramic socs., Cleveland World Trade. Clubs: Clevelander, Mid Day, Chagrin Valley Country, Union, Pepper Pike Country. Office: Ferro Corp 1000 Lakeside Avenue Cleveland Ohio 44114

POTTER, WILLIAM BARTLETT, trucking company executive; born Washington, January 4, 1938; son of George Holland and Virginia (Bartlett) P.; married Simone Robert, June 6, 1964; children: Eva Simone, William Bartlett. Bachelor of Arts, Princeton University, 1960; Master of Business Administration, Emory University, 1962. With Merc.-Safe Deposit & Trust Company, Baltimore, 1962—; assistant secretary, assistant treasurer Merc.-Safe Deposit & Trust Company, 1964-66, assistant vice president, 1966-68, vice president, 1968-69, senior vice president, 1969-76, executive vice president, 1976; executive vice president Preston Trucking Company, 1976-77, president, 1977-86; chairman, president Preston Corp., 1986—; chairman Preston Trucking Company, 1986—; board of directors Mercantile Bankshares Corp., Harley Davidson Incorporated. Trustee Aspen Institute. Member Maryland Club, Chesapeake Bay Yacht Club, Depression Related Affective Disorders Association (president). Home: 6611 Peachblossom Point Road Easton Maryland 21601 Office: Preston Corp 151 Easton Boulevard Preston Maryland 21655

POULOS, MICHAEL JAMES, insurance company executive; born Glens Falls, New York, February 13, 1931; son of James A. and Mary Poulos; married Mary Kay Leslie; children: Denise, Peter. Bachelor of Arts, Colgate University, 1953; Master of Business Administration, New York University, 1963. Chartered Life Underwriter, 1970. With sales and management United States Life Insurance Company, New York City, 1958-70, secretary, treasurer director, 1968, v.p administration, 1969, member executive committee, 1970; with Calif.-Western States Life Insurance Company, Sacramento, 1970-79, president, chief executive officer, 1975-79, director, 1975; with Am. General Corp., Houston, 1979—, senior vice president div. head life insurance,

1979-81, president, member of executive and fin. committees, director, 1981—. Member Sam Houston Area council Boy Scouts Am. Member Am. Society CLU's, National Association Life Underwriters, Houston Association Life Underwriters, Am. Management Association, Heritage Club, The Houstonian Club. Greek Orthodox. Office: Am General Corp 2929 Allen Parkway Houston Texas 77019

POWELL, GEORGE EVERETT, JR., motor freight company executive; born Kansas City, Missouri, June 12, 1926; son of George Everett and Hilda (Brown) P.; married Mary Catherine Kuehn, August 26, 1947; children: George Everett III, Nicholas K., Richardson K., Peter E. Student, Northwestern University. With Riss & Company, Incorporated, Kansas City, Missouri, 1947-52, treasurer, 1950-52; with Yellow Freight System, Incorporated, Kansas City, Missouri, 1952—, president, 1957-68, chairman board, 1968—; president Yellow Freight Systems, Incorporated of Del., Overland Park, Kansas, 1987-88; director 1st National Charter Corp., Butler Manufacturing Company. Trustee, member executive committee Mid-West Research Institute, Kansas City, Missouri, from 1961, chairman board trustees, from 1968; board governors Kansas City Art Institute, from 1964, chairman board trustees, 1973-75. Served with United States Naval Reserve, 1944-46. Member Kansas City Chamber of Commerce (board directors 1964-68). Office: Yellow Freight System Incorporated Del Post Office Box 7563 Overland Park Kansas 66207

POWELL, GEORGE EVERETT, III, trucking company executive; born Kansas City, Missouri, October 18, 1948; son of George Everett Jr. and Mary Catherine (Kuehn) P.; married Wendy Jarman, July 29, 1972; children: Jessica Jarman, Ashley Sinclair. Bachelor of Science in Business Administration, Ind. University, 1970. From planning analyst trainee to president, chief executive officer Yellow Freight System Incorporated, Overland Park, Kansas, 1971—, also board of directors. Trustee Midwest Research Institute; member Powell Family Foundation, Kansas City Pub. TV. Member Regular Common Carrier Conference (board govs.), Young Pres.'s Organization. Home: 5801 Ward Parkway Kansas City Missouri 64113 Office: Yellow Freight System Incorporated 10990 Roe Avenue Box 7563 Overland Park Kansas 66207

POWELL, WILLIAM ARNOLD, JR., banker; born Verbena, Alabama, July 7, 1929; son of William Arnold and Sarah Frances (Baxter) P.; married Barbara Ann O'Donnell, June 16, 1956; children: William Arnold III, Barbara Calhoun, Susan Thomas, Patricia Crain. Bachelor of Science in Business Administration, University Alabama, 1953; graduate, Louisiana State University School Banking of South, 1966. With Am. South Bank, N.A., Birmingham, Alabama, 1953—, assistant vice president, 1966, vice president, 1967, vice president, branch supervisor, 1968-72, senior vice president, branch supervisor, 1972-73, executive vice president, 1973-79, president, 1979-83, vice chairman board, 1983—, also board of directors; pres First National Bank Birmingham, 1983—, also board of directors; president AmSouth Bancorp., 1979—; board of directors AmSouth Mortgage Company, Incorporated, AmSouth Bancorp. Board of directors Am. Cancer

Society, Birmingham Better Business Bureau, School Banking of South; trustee Alabama Ind. Colleges; board visitors, U. Alabama; president United Way; member president's council U.A.B.; board of directors, secretary-treasurer Warrior-Tombigbee Devel. Association, Birmingham Mus. Art, School Fine Arts Foundation, Brookwood Medical Ctr.-AMI, Big Bros./Big Sisters oof Greater Birmingham; campaign chairman United Way, 1987. Lieutenant Army of the United States, 1954-56. Member Birmingham Area Chamber of Commerce (chairman executive committee), Birmingham Historical Society (board directors), The Club, Downtown, Summit Club, Mountain Brook, Birmingham Country Club, Green Valley Country Club (Birmingham), Rotary (Birmingham). Home: 3309 Thornton Dr Birmingham Alabama 35226 Office: AmSouth Bank NA Post Office Box 11007 Birmingham Alabama 35288

PRATT, EDMUND T., JR., pharmaceutical company executive; born Savannah, Georgia, February 22, 1927; son of Edmund T. and Rose (Miller) P.; married Jeanette Louise Carneale, February 10, 1951; children: Randolf Ryland, Keith Taylor. Bachelor of Science in Electrical Engineering magna cum laude, Duke University, 1947; Master of Business Administration, University Pennsylvania, 1949; honorary degrees, Long Island University, Marymount Manhattan College, Polytechnic University of New York, St. Francis College. With International Business Machines Corporation Corp., 1949-51, 54-57, assistant to executive vice president, 1956-57; with International Business Machines Corporation World Trade Corp., 1958-62, controller, 1958-62; assistant secretary fin. management Department Army, 1962-64; controller Pfizer, Incorporated, New York City, 1964-67, vice president operations international subsidiary, 1967-69, chairman board, president international subsidiary, 1969-71, executive vice president, 1970-71, president, 1971-72, chairman, chief executive officer, 1972—, also board of directors; board of directors Chase Manhattan Corp., International Paper Company, GMC. Board of directors New York City Partnership; member New York State Business Adv. Council; member Emergency Committee for Am. Trade; member adv. committee for trade policy and negotiations; member National Industrial Adv. Council for Opportunities Industrialization Centers of Am. Lieutenant (junior grade) United States Naval Reserve, 1952-54. Member Business Roundtable (immediate past chairman, member policy committee), New York Chamber of Commerce and Industry (board directors), Rus. Council, Phi Beta Kappa.

PRINCE, LARRY L., automotive parts and supplies company executive. With Genuine Parts Company, Atlanta, 1958—, vice president, then group vice president, 1977-83, executive vice president, 1983-86, president, chief operating officer, 1986-90, also board of directors, chairman board of directors, 1990—, chief executive officer, 1989—. Office: Genuine Parts Company 2999 Circle 75 Parkway Atlanta Georgia 30339

PRITZKER, JAY ARTHUR, lawyer; born Chicago, August 26, 1922; son of Abraham Nicholas and Fanny (Doppelt) P.; married Marian Friend, August 31, 1947; children: Nancy (deceased), Thomas, John, Daniel,

Jean. Bachelor of Science, Northwestern University, 1941, Juris Doctor, 1947. Bar: Illinois 1947. Assistant custodian Alien Property Administration, 1947; private practice law Chicago; partner firm Pritzker & Pritzker, 1948—; chairman board Hyatt Corp., Marmon Group, Incorporated; board of directors Dalfort Corp.; partner Chicago Mill & Lumber Company, Mich.-Calif. Lumber Company. Life trustee U. Chicago Lieutenant United States Navy, WW II. Member American Bar Association, Chicago Bar Association. Clubs: Standard (Chicago), Comml. (Chicago), Lake Shore (Chicago), Mid-Day (Chicago), Arts (Chicago), Vince (Chicago). Office: Pritzker & Pritzker 200 W Madison Chicago Illinois 60606

PRITZKER, ROBERT ALAN, manufacturing company executive; born Chicago, June 30, 1926; son of Abram Nicholas and Fanny (Doppelt) P.; children: Matthew, Liesel, James, Linda, Karen. Bachelor of Science in Industrial Engineering, Illinois Institute Tech., Chicago, 1946; postgraduate in business administration, University Illinois. Engaged in manufacturing 1946—; president, director Union Tank Car Company, Chicago; chief executive officer, president, director The Marmon Group, Incorporated, Chicago, Marmon Corp., Chicago, Marmon Industrial Corp., Chicago; president, director The Colson Group, Incorporated, Marmon Holdings, Incorporated, Marmon Industries, Incorporated, Chicago; board of directors Hyatt Corp., Chicago, Dalfort Corp., Union Tank Car Company, S&W Berifsord P.L.C. Chairman board Pritzker Foundation, Chicago; trustee, chairman Illinois Institute Tech., Chicago Symphony Orchestra; immediate past chairman Field Mus. of Natural History; board of directors Rush-Presbyn.-St. Luke's Medical Center. Member National Acad. of Engineering. Office: Marmon Group Incorporated 225 W Washington St Chicago Illinois 60606

PRITZKER, THOMAS JAY, lawyer, business executive; born Chicago, June 6, 1950; son of Jay Arthur and Marian (Friend) P.; married Margot Lyn Barrow-Sicree, September 4, 1977; children—Jason, Benjamin, David. Bachelor of Arts, Claremont Men's Coll, 1971; Master of Business Administration, University Chicago, 1972, Juris Doctor, 1976. Associate Katten, Muchin, Zavis, Pearl and Galler, Chicago, 1976-77; executive vice president Hyatt Corp., Chicago, 1977-80, president, 1980—; chairman board Hyatt Hotels Corp., Chicago, 1980-86, 1988; chairman executive committee Hyatt Hotels Corp., 1986-88; partner Pritzker & Pritzker, Chicago, 1976—; president Rosemont Shipping, Chicago, 1980-86; chairman Health Care Compare Corp.; board of directors Dalfort, Chicago, Continental Bank Corp. Chicago. Trustee Art. Institute Chicago, 1988—. Member American Bar Association, Illinois Bar Association, Chicago Bar Association. Clubs: Standard (Chicago); Lake Shore Country (Glencoe, Illinois). Office: Hyatt Corp 200 W Madison Avenue Chicago Illinois 60606

PUELICHER, JOHN A., bank holding company executive; born 1920. With Marshall & Ilsley Company, Milwaukee, 1959—, executive vice president, 1959-63, president, 1963-79, chairman board of directors, 1979-81, now chairman board of directors, chief executive officer. Office: Marshall & Ilsley Corp 770 N Water St Milwaukee Wisconsin 53201

PUGH, LAWRENCE R., textile corporation executive; born 1933; (married). Graduate, Colby College, 1956. Div. sales manager Borden Incorporated, 1958-66; product manager, general marketing manager Hamilton Beach Company, 1966-70; director marketing Ampex Corp., 1970-72; group president Beatrice Foods Company, 1972-80; president V.F. Corp., Reading, Pennsylvania, 1980-83; chairman, chief executive officer V.F. Corp., Wyomissing, Pennsylvania, 1983—. Office: VF Corp 1047 N Park Road Box 1022 (19603) Wyomissing Pennsylvania 19610

PURDUM, ROBERT L., manufacturing company executive; born Wilmington, Ohio, 1935; married. Bachelor of Science, Purdue University, 1956. With United States Navy and Ind. Toll Road Commission, 1956-62; with Armco Incorporated, Middletown, Ohio, 1962—, district engineer metal product div., 1962-66, sales staff, 1966-72; district manager Columbus, Ohio, 1972-76; general manager administration Armco Incorporated, Columbus, Ohio, 1976-78; vice president div. subsidiary, president Midwestern Steel, Kansas City, Missouri, 1978-80; area vice president Midwestern Steel, Columbus, Ohio, 1980-82; group vice president, chief executive officer steel services group Middletown, Ohio, 1982-86; executive vice president, chief operating officer Armco Incorporated, Middletown, Ohio; president, chief operating officer Armco Incorporated, Parsippany, New Jersey, 1986-90, president, chief executive officer, 1990—, also. board of directors, chairman. Captain United States Naval Reserve. Recipient Distinguished Engineering Alumnus award Purdue University, 1986. Office: Armco Incorporated 300 Interpace Parkway Parsippany New Jersey 07054

QUESTROM, ALLEN I., retail executive; born Newton, Massachusetts, April 13, 1941; son of Irving Allen and Natalie (Chadbourne) Q.; married Carol Brummer, September 9, 1967. Bachelor of Science, Boston University, 1964. From executive trainee to div. merchandise manager Abraham & Straus, Brooklyn, 1965-73; vice president, general merchandise manager home store Bullock's, Los Angeles, 1973-74, senior vice president, general merchandise manager all stores, 1974-77; executive vice president Bullock's div. Federated Department Stores, Los Angeles, 1977-78; president Rich's div. Federated Department Stores, Atlanta, 1978-80, chairman board, chief executive officer, 1980-84; chairman board, chief executive officer Bullock's/Bullocks Wilshire div. Federated Department Stores, Los Angeles, 1984-88; corp. executive vice president Federated Department Stores, Cincinnati, 1987-88, vice-chairman, 1988; chairman, chief executive officer Federated Department Stores Incorporated, Cincinnati, 1990; also chairman, chief executive officer Allied Stores Corp., Cincinnati, 1990—; president, chief executive officer Neiman Marcus Group Incorporated, Dallas, 1988-90. Avocations: skiing; golf; travel.

QUINLAN, MICHAEL ROBERT, fast food franchise company executive; born Chicago, December 9, 1944; son of Robert Joseph and Kathryn (Koerner) Q.; married Marilyn De-

Lashmutt, April 23, 1966; children: Kevin, Michael. Bachelor of Science, Loyola University, Chicago, 1967, Master of Business Administration, 1970. With McDonald's Corp., Oak Brook, Illinois, 1966—, vice president, 1974-76, senior vice president, 1976-78, executive vice president, 1978-79, chief operations officer, 1979-80, president McDonald's United States of America, 1980-82, president, 1982-89, chief operating officer, 1982-87, chief executive officer, 1987—, chairman, 1989—, also board of directors. Republican. Roman Catholic. Clubs: Butterfield Country, Oakbrook Handball-Racquetball. Office: McDonald's Corp 1 McDonald's Plaza Oak Brook Illinois 60521

RABIN, STANLEY ARTHUR, metal products manufacturer; born New York City, 1938. Bachelor of Arts, Bachelor of Science in Metallurgical Engineering, Columbia University, 1958; Master of Business Administration, University Santa Clara, 1969. With Commercial Metals Company, Incorporated, Dallas, 1970—, president, 1978—, now also chief executive officer, member executive committee, director. Office: Commercial Metals Company Incorporated 7800 Stemmons Freeway Dallas Texas 75247

RADNER, ROY, economist, educator, researcher; born Chicago, June 29, 1927; son of Samuel and Ella (Kulansky) R.; married Virginia L. Honoski, July 26, 1949 (deceased April 1976); children: Hilary A., Erica H. (deceased), Amy E., Ephraim L.; married Charlotte Virginia Kuh, January 22, 1978. Bachelor of Philosophy with honors, University Chgo, 1945, Bachelor of Science in Math., 1950, Master of Science in Math., 1951, Doctor of Philosophy in Math. Statistics, 1956. Research assistant Cowles Commission for Research in Economics University Chicago, 1951, 1951-54, assistant professor, 1954-55; member Cowles Foundation for Research in Economics Yale University, New Haven, 1955-57, assistant professor economics, 1955-57; associate professor economics and statistics University California, Berkeley, 1957-61, professor economics and statistics, 1961-79, chairman department economics, 1966-69; Taussig professor economics Harvard University, Cambridge, Massachusetts, 1977-78, visiting professor Kennedy School Government, 1978-79; member tech. staff American Telephone and Telegraph Company Bell Labs, Murray Hill, New Jersey, 1979-84, distinguished member tech. staff, 1985—; research professor economics New York University, New York City, 1983—; member committee on fundamental research relevant to education NRC-Nat. Acad. Sciences, 1976-77, member commission on human resources, 1976-79; member assembly of behavioral and social sciences National Research Council, 1979-82, member committee on risk and decision making, 1980-81, member working group on basic research in behavioral and social sciences, 1985-86; member Committee on Prevention of Nuclear War, also various other professional committees, boards, panels. Author: (books, monographs) Notes on Theory of Economic Planning, 1963, (with D. Jorgenson and J.J. McCall) Optimal Replacement Policy, 1967, (with J. Marshack) Economic Theory of Teams, 1972, (with L.S. Miller)

Demand and Supply in United States Higher Education, 1975, (with C.V. Kuh) Mathematicians in Academia, 1980; also articles on econ. theory, organization theory, econs. of education; co-editor: Decision and Organization, 1972, Education as an Industry, 1976, Information, Incentives and Economic Mechanisms, 1987, Perspectives on Deterrence, 1989; associate editor Management Science, 1959-70, Econometrica, 1961-68, Journal Econ. Theory, 1968—, Am. Econ. Rev., 1970-82, Games and Economic Behavior. 2d lieutenant United States Army, 1945-48, PTO. William Cook scholar University Chicago, 1944-45; fellow Center Advanced Study in Behavioral Sciences, Stanford, California, 1955-56, Guggenheim Foundation fellow, 1961-62, 65-66, overseas fellow Churchill College, Cambridge University, England, 1969-70, 89. Fellow American Association for the Advancement of Science (distinguished fellow), Econometric Society (vice president 1970-72, president 1972-73), Am. Acad. Arts and Sciences, Am. Econ. Association (distinguished fellow); member Institute Math. Statistics, Am. Statistical Association, National Acad. Sciences, Phi Beta Kappa. Avocations: music, backpacking, cross-country skiing. Home: 1 Park Place Short Hills New Jersey 07078 Office: AT&T Bell Labs 600 Mountain Avenue Murray Hill New Jersey 07974

RALES, STEVEN M., automotive parts company executive; born Pittsburgh, March 31, 1951; married. Bachelor of Arts, DePauw University, 1973; Juris Doctor, America University, 1978. With Equity Group Holdings, Washington, 1979—; chairman, chief executive officer Danaher Corp., Washington, 1984—. Office: Danaher Corp 1250 24th St Northwest Washington District of Columbia 20037

RANKIN, ALFRED MARSHALL, JR., business executive; born Cleveland, October 8, 1941; son of Alfred Marshall and Clara Louise (Taplin) R.; married Victoire Conley Griffin, June 3, 1967; children: Helen P., Clara T. Bachelor of Arts in Economics magna cum laude, Yale University, 1963, Juris Doctor, 1966. Management consultant McKinsey & Company, Incorporated, Cleveland, 1970-73; with Eaton Corp., Cleveland, 1974-81, president materials handling group, 1981-83, president industrial group, 1984-86, executive vice president, 1986, vice chairman, chief operating officer, 1986-89; president, chief operating officer NACCO Industries, Incorporated, Cleveland, 1989—, also board of directors, 1989-91, president, chief executive officer, 1991—; board of directors B.F. Goodrich Company, The Standard Products Company. Former president, trustee Hathaway Brown School; trustee Holden Arboretum, Oberlin College, University Hosps., Mus. Arts Association, University Cir., Incorporated, World Resources Institute, Greater Cleveland Growth Association. Member Ohio Bar Association. Republican. Clubs: Chagrin Valley Hunt, Union, Tavern, Pepper Pike, Kirtland Country (Cleveland); Rolling Rock (Ligonier, Pennsylvania); Metropolitan (Washington). Home: Old Mill Road Gates Mills Ohio 44040 Office: NACCO Industries Incorporated 12800 Shaker Boulevard Cleveland Ohio 44120

RATCLIFFE, GEORGE JACKSON, JR., lawyer, business executive; born Charleston, West Virginia, March 22, 1936; son of George Jackson and Dorothy (Ward) R.; married Nancy Lenhardt, October 5, 1963; children: George Jackson III, Dorothy Margaret. Bachelor of Arts, Duke University, 1958; Juris Doctor, University Virginia, 1961. Bar: New York 1964, Ohio 1962. Associate Taft, Stettinius & Hollister, Cincinnati, 1961-63; lawyer International Business Machines Corporation Corp., 1963-65; associate Perkins, Daniels & McCormack, New York City, 1965-70, partner, 1970; vice president, secretary, general counsel Helme Products Incorporated, New York City, 1970, executive vice president, 1971-74, president, 1974; vice president, secretary, general counsel Hubbell Incorporated, Orange, Connecticut, 1975-80, senior vice president fin. and law, 1980-83, executive vice president administration, 1983-87, chairman board, 1987—, president, chief executive officer, 1987—; board of directors Hydraulic Company, Bridgeport, Connecticut, Handy & Harman, New York City, People's Bank, Bridgeport. Member Connecticut Business and Industry Association (board directors), National Electrical Manufacturers Association (board govs.), Brooklawn Country Club (Fairfield, Connecticut), Aspetuck Fish and Game Club (Bridgeport), Clove Valley Rod and Gun Club (LaGrangeville, New York), Loblolly Pines Club (Hobe Sound, Florida), Merion Golf Club (Ardmore, Pennsylvania), Blind Brook Country Club (Purchase, New York). Home: 278 Sherwood Dr Southport Connecticut 06490 Office: Hubbell Incorporated 584 Derby Milford Road Post Office Box 549 Orange Connecticut 06477-4024

RAU, JOHN EDWARD, banker; born Milwaukee, June 9, 1948; son of Edward J. and Grace Barbara (Kutschenreuter) R.; married Sandra Davis, September 12, 1981; children—Michael James, Caroline Kingsley, Rebecca Lee. Bachelor of Arts, Bachelor of Science, Boston College, 1970; Master of Business Administration, Harvard University, 1972. Director corp. devel. 1st Chicago Corp, 1973-74, corp. officer fin. and treasury, 1975; manager planning and administration 1st National Bank of Chicago, 1976-77, manager central operations group, 1977-78, general manager international trade fin., 1978-79; executive vice president Exchange National Bank of Chicago, 1979-83, president, 1983-89; president, chief executive officer Exchange National Bank of Chicago and La Salle National Bank, 1990—; director adv. council Keller Grad. School Management, Chicago, 1984—; national director at large Bank Administration Institute, Illinois, 1985-88; board of directors Northwestern University Banking Research Center, Evanston, Illinois, 1981—; director Chicago Clearing House Associates, 1983—. Author: (with D. J. Vitale) The Corporate Treasurers Handbook, 1976; also articles on bank strategy and devel., 1982—. Co-chairman NFL Players Association McKay awards dinner Better Boys Foundation, Chicago, annually 1983-87; chief crusader Crusade of Mercy-United Way, Chicago, annually 1985-89; trustee Glenwqwod School for Boys; board of directors Chicago Land Enterprise Center, Rehabilitation Institute, 1990—. Served with United States

Army, 1970-71. Finnegan outstanding grad. grantee Boston College, 1969-70; Goldman-Sachs senior fin. fellow Harvard University, Boston, 1971-72. Member Association Reserve City Bankers, Chicago Association Commerce and Industry (board directors), Bankers Club, Economic Club, Young Pres.' Organization, Chicago Club, Harvard University Business School Club Chicago (board directors, president), Glen View Club. Home: 239 Essex Road Kenilworth Illinois 60043 Office: La Salle National Bank 120 S LaSalle St Chicago Illinois 60603

RAWL, LAWRENCE G., petroleum company executive; born 1928. Graduate, University Oklahoma, 1952. With Exxon Corp., 1952—, assistant manager East Texas production div., 1965-66, executive assistant to chairman, 1967-69; general manager supply Exxon Company USA div. then vice president marketing, 1969-72, vice president then senior vice president, 1972-76; executive vice president Exxon Company USA div., 1976-80; senior vice president Exxon Corp., New York City, 1980-86, president, 1986, chairman, chief executive officer, 1986—; also board dirs Exxon Corp.; board of directors Chemical Banking Corp., Chemical Bank, Warner-Lambert Company, Champion International Corp. Trustee Am. Mus. Natural History; board governors United Way Am. Member Am. Petroleum Institute (board directors), National Petroleum Council, Council on Foreign Relations, Emergency Committee for Am. Trade, The Business Council, The Business Roundtable, National Center for State Cts., Texas Professional Engineers. Office: Exxon Corp 225 E John W Carpenter Freeway Irving Texas 75062-2298

RAYMOND, LEE R., oil company executive; born Watertown, South Dakota, August 13, 1938; married Charlene Raymond. Bachelor of Science in Chemical Engineering, University Wisconsin, 1960; Doctor of Science in Chemical Engineering, University Minnesota, 1963. Various engineering positions Exxon Corp., Tulsa, Houston, New York City and Caracas, Venezuela, 1963-72; manager planning International Company div. Exxon Corp., New York City, 1972-75; president Nuclear Company div. Exxon Corp., 1979-81, executive vice president Exxon Enterprises div., 1981-83; senior vice president, director Exxon Corp., New York City, 1984-86, president, director, 1987—; vice president, director Lago Oil, Netherlands Antilles, 1975-76, president, director, 1976-79; president, director Esso Inter-Am. Incorporated, Coral Gables, Florida, 1983-84, senior vice president, director, 1984—; board of directors J.P. Morgan & Co, Incorporated, New York City, Morgan Guaranty Trust Company of New York, New York City, Business Council of New York State Incorporated, New York Chamber of Commerce and Industry Incorporated, New York City Partnership Incorporated, Am. Petroleum Institute. Board of directors Council Aid. to Education, Incorporated, New York City, 1987—, National Action Council Minorities in Engring. Incorporated, New York City, 1985—, United Way Tri-State, New York City, 1986—; trustee Wisconsin Alumni Research Foundation, 1987—; member Am. Council on Germany, 1986—, Brit.-N.Am.

Committee, 1985—, visiting committee U. Wisconsin Department Chem. Engring., 1987—. Member Am. Petroleum Institute (board directors 1987—), German Am. Chamber of Commerce (board directors 1985—)., Council Foreign Relations. Club: Country of Darien (Connecticut).

RECANATI, RAPHAEL, shipping and banking executive; born Salonique, Greece, February 12, 1924; son of Leon and Mathilde (Saporta) R.; married Diane Hettena, October 8, 1946; children: Yehuda, Michael. Student Israel and Eng. Chairman El-Yam Ships Limited, 1953—; chairman Discount Bank & Trust Company, Geneva, Switzerland, 1970; chairman, managing director IDB Bankholding Limited, 1970—. Home: 944 Fifth Avenue New York New York 10021 Office: 511 Fifth Avenue New York New York 10017 also: Overseas Shipholding Group Incorporated 1114 Avenue of the Americas New York New York 10036

REDSTONE, SUMNER MURRAY, entertainment corporation executive, lawyer; born Boston, May 27, 1923; son of Michael and Belle (Ostrovsky) R.; married Phyllis Gloria Raphael, July 6, 1947; children: Brent Dale, Shari Ellin. Bachelor of Arts, Harvard University, 1944, Bachelor of Laws, 1947. Bar: Massachusetts 1947, United States Court Appeals (1st circuit) 1948, United States Court Appeals (8th circuit) 1950, United States Court Appeals (9th circuit) 1948, District of Columbia 1951, United States Supreme Court 1952. Law secretary United States Court Appeals for 9th Circuit, San Francisco, 1947-48; instructor law and labor management University San Francisco, 1947; special assistant to United States attorney general, Washington, 1948-51; partner firm Ford, Bergson, Adams, Borkland & Redstone, Washington, 1951-54; president, chief executive officer Natl. Amusements Incorporated, Dedham, Massachusetts, 1967—, chairman board, 1986—; chairman board Viacom International Incorporated, Viacom Incorporated, New York City; professor Boston University Law School, 1982, 85-86. Chairman metropolitan div. NE Combined Jewish Philanthropies, Boston, 1963; member corp. New England Medical Center, 1967—, Massachusetts General Hospital; trustee Children's Cancer Research Foundation; chairman Am. Cancer Crusade, State of Massachusetts, 1984-86; Art Lending Library; sponsor Boston Mus. Sci.; chairman Jimmy Fund Foundation, 1960; vice president, member executive committee Will Rogers Memorial Fund; board of directors Boston Arts Festival; board overseers Dana Farber Cancer Center, Boston Mus. Fine Arts; member presidential adv. committee on arts John F. Kennedy Center for Performing Arts; board of directors John F. Kennedy Library Foundation Served to 1st lieutenant Army of the United States, 1943-45. Decorated Army Commendation medal; recipient William J. German Human Relations award Am. Jewish Committee Entertainment and Communication Div., 1977, Silver Shingle award Boston University Law School, 1985; named one of ten outstanding young men Greater Boston Chamber of Commerce, 1958, Communicator of Year B'nai B'rith Communications/Cinema Lodge, 1980, Man of Year Entertainment Industries Div. of UJA Federation, New York, 1988. Member

Theatre Owners Am. (assistant president 1960-63, president 1964-65), National Association Theatre Owners (chairman board directors 1965-66), Motion Picture Pioneers (board directors), American Bar Association, Boston Bar Association, Massachusetts Bar Association, Harvard Law School Association, Am. Judicature Society. Clubs: Mason, University, Variety New England (Humanitarian award 1989), Harvard (Boston). Home: 98 Baldpate Hill Road Newton Center Massachusetts 02159 Office: National Amusements Incorporated 200 Elm St Dedham Massachusetts 02026

REED, JOEL LESTON, diversified manufacturing company executive; born Enid, Oklahoma, January 21, 1951; son of Arrel Leston and Velma Jo (Kesner) R.; married Alicia Kay Biller, November 28, 1970 (deceased); married Ann Denise Timmersman, June 6, 1981; children: Benjamin Joel, Elizabeth Ann, Peter David. Bachelor of Science in Accounting, Oklahoma State University, 1972, Master of Science in Accounting, 1973. Certified Public Accountant, Okla, Colorado. Successively staff accountant, senior accountant, manager Deloitte Haskins & Sells, Denver, 1973-81; controller, treasurer Ensource Incorporated, Englewood, Colorado, 1981-82, vice president, chief fin. officer, 1983-84; chief fin. officer Wagner & Brown, Midland, Texas, 1984-89; president, chief executive officer Insilco Corp., 1989—. Contributor articles to professional journals. Member American Institute of Certified Public Accountants (oil and gas committee, Elijah Watt Sells award 1973), Colorado Society Certified Public Accountants, Am. Petroleum Institute, Ind. Petroleum Association Am., Porsche Car Club Am., Beta Alpha Psi. Home: 2002 Humble Avenue Midland Texas 79705 also: Insilco Corp Post Office Box 1919 Midland Texas 79702

REED, LAURENCE A., chemical company executive; born 1939. Bachelor of Science, University Minnesota, 1961; Master of Science, Northwestern University, 1962; Master of Business Administration, Central Michigan University, 1969. Research assistant University Minnesota, 1960-61; with Dow Corning Corp., Midland, Michigan, 1964—, chemical engineer, 1964-66, staff specialist, 1967-68, economic evaluation engineer, 1968-78, vice president chief fin. officer, controller, 1978-81, executive vice president business, from 1981, president, 1984—, chief operating officer, 1984-88, chief executive officer, 1988—. Served with United States Navy, 1962-64. Office: Dow Corning Corp 2200 W Salzburg Road Midland Michigan 48686-0994

REHM, JACK DANIEL, media executive; born Yonkers, New York, October 10, 1932; son of Jack and Ann (McCarthy) R.; married Cynthia Fenning, October 18, 1958; children: Lisabeth R., Ann M., Cynthia A., Jack D. Jr. Bachelor of Science in Business Administration, College of the Holy Cross, 1954. Advertising sales trainee, assistant account executive Batten, Barton, Durstine & Osborne, New York City, 1954-59; manager Suburbia Today, New York City, 1959-62; with advertising sales department Better Homes and Gardens Meredith Corp., New York City, 1962-66; manager advertising sales Meredith Corp., Philadelphia, 1966-67; manager advertising sales

Meredith Corp., New York City, 1967-69, advertising sales director Better Homes and Garden magazine, 1969-73, vice president, pub. director magazine div., 1973-75, vice president, pub. Better Homes and Gardens, pub. director magazine div., 1975-76, vice president pub. group, general manager, magazine pub., 1976-80; president pub. group Meredith Corp., Des Moines, 1980-86, executive vice president corp. services, 1986-88, president, chief operating officer, 1988—, president, chief executive officer, 1989—, also board of directors; board of directors First Interstate Bank Iowa, Incorporated, Des Moines, Vernon Company, Newton, Iowa, Equitable of Iowa Companies, Am. Council for Capital Formation. Chairman board trustees Des Moines Civic Center, 1988—; board governors Drake U., 1988—; board trustees College of Holy Cross, Worcester, Massachusetts; member business committee Mus. Modern Art, New York City, Greater Des Moines Committee, Incorporated; mag. and print committee United States Information Agency With United States Army, 1956-57. Member Magazine Pubs. Am. (board directors 1981—, chairman 1983-85, Publisher of Year 1988), Pine Valley Golf Club, Scarsdale Golf Club, Wakonda Golf Club. Roman Catholic. Avocation: golf. Home: 2913 Druid Hill Dr Des Moines Iowa 50315 Office: Meredith Corp 1716 Locust St Des Moines Iowa 50336

REICHARDT, CARL E., banker; born 1931. Bachelor of Arts, University Southern California, 1956; student, Stanford University, 1965; student in mortgage banking, Northwestern University, 1965. Program manager operations and lending Citizens National Bank, 1955-59; senior statistics analyst North Am. Aircraft, 1959-60; area executive vice president Union Bank, 1960-70; with Wells Fargo Realty Advisors, 1970—; executive vice president real estate industries group Wells Fargo Bank, N.A., San Francisco, 1975-78, corp. president, from 1981, now chairman, chief executive officer, also board of directors; with parent company Wells Fargo & Company, San Francisco, 1973—, executive vice president real estate industries group, 1975-79, president, 1979-84, chief operating officer, 1979-82, chairman, chief executive officer, 1982—, also board of directors. With United States Navy, 1951-54. Office: Wells Fargo & Company 420 Montgomery St 12th Floor San Francisco California 94163

REICHERT, JACK FRANK, manufacturing company executive; born West Allis, Wisconsin, September 27, 1930; son of Arthur Andrew and Emily Bertha (Wallinger) R.; married Corrine Violet Helf, April 5, 1952; children: Susan Marie, John Arthur. Cert. marketing, University Wis.-Milw., 1957; AMP, Harvard University, 1970. Various marketing positions General Electric Company, 1948-57; with Brunswick Corp., Skokie, Illinois, 1957—; president Mercury Marine div. Brunswick Corp., Skokie, 1972-77, corp. vice president, 1974-77, group vice president Marine Power Group, 1974-77, president, chief operating officer, 1977—; chief executive officer Brunswick Corp., 1982—, chairman board, 1983—, director, 1977—; board of directors The Dial Corp., Phoenix, First Chicago Corp. Trustee Carroll College, Waukesha, Wisconsin, 1972; board of directors INROADS/

Chgo., Incorporated; industrial chairman Fond du Lac United Fund, 1977. Served with Corps of Engineers United States Army, 1951-53. Named Distinguished Alumnus of the Year, University Wisconsin, Milwaukee 1979, Top Chief Executive Officer in Multi-Industry Group, Fin. World Magazine, 1984; recipient Gold award in leisure industry Wall St. Transcript, 1983, 86, Bronze award in multi-industry category Wall St. Transcript, 1985, Leisure Industry Silver award, 1988. Member Am. Management Association (member adv. council), University Wis.-Milw. Alumni Association, Econ. Club of Chicago, Commercial Club of Chicago, Knollwood Club, Harvard Club, Mid-Am. Club, Metropolitan Club, Beta Gamma Sigma (hon.). Presbyterian. Avocations: golf, reading. Home: 580 Douglas Dr Lake Forest Illinois 60045 Office: Brunswick Corp 1 Brunswick Plaza Skokie Illinois 60077

REICHMANN, ALBERT, real estate corporation executive. President Olympia and York Devel., Toronto; board of directors Trizec Corp., Calgary, Abitibi-Price Incorporated, Toronto, Gulf Can. Corp., Toronto, GW Utilities Limited, Toronto, Campeau Corp., Toronto. Office: Olympia & York Devels, 2 First Can Place Suite 2800, Toronto, Ontario Canada M5X 1B4

REICHMANN, PAUL, real estate corporation executive. Executive vice president Olympia and York Devels., Toronto; board of directors Abitibi-Price Incorporated, Toronto, Gulf Can. Corp., Toronto, GW Utilities Limited, Toronto, Trizec Corp., Calgary. Office: Olympia & York Devels, 2 First Can Place Suite 2700, Post Office Box 2700, Toronto, Ontario Canada M5X 1B5

REICHMANN, RALPH, real estate corporation executive. General manager Olympia and York Devels., Toronto; board of directors Abitibi-Price Incorporated, Toronto, Gulf Can. Corp, Toronto. Office: Olympia & York Devels, 2 First Can Place Suite 2800, Post Office Box 20 130 Kings St W, Toronto, Ontario Canada M5X 1B5

REID, JAMES SIMS, JR., automobile parts manufacturer; born Cleveland, January 15, 1926; son of James Sims and Felice (Crowl) R.; married Donna Smith, September 2, 1950; children: Sally, Susan, Anne (deceased), Jeanne. Bachelor of Arts cum laude, Harvard University, 1948, Juris Doctor, 1951. Bar: Michigan, Ohio 1951. Private practice law Detroit, 1951-52, Cleveland, 1953-56; with Standard Products Company, Cleveland, 1956—, director, 1959, president, 1962-89, chairman, chief executive officer, 1989—; board director Society Corp., Cleveland. Trustee John Carroll U., 1967—, chairman, 1987-91, Musical Arts Association of Cleveland Orchestra, 1973—. Office: Standard Products Company 2130 W 110th St Cleveland Ohio 44102

REINSDORF, JERRY MICHAEL, lawyer, professional athletic franchise executive, real estate executive; born Brooklyn, February 25, 1936; son of Max and Marion (Smith) R.; married Martyl F. Rifkin, December 29, 1956; children: David Jason, Susan Janeen, Michael Andrew, Jonathan Milton. Bachelor of Arts, George Washington University, 1957; Juris Doctor, Northwestern University, 1960. Bar: District of Columbia, Illinois 1960; Certified Public Accountant, Illinois; certified specialist real estate securities, rev. appraiser; registered mortgage underwriter. Attorney staff regional counsel Internal Revenue Service, Chicago, 1960-64; associate law firm Chapman & Cutler, 1964-68; partner Altman, Kurlander & Weiss, 1968-74; of counsel firm Katten, Muchin, Gitles, Zavis, Pearl & Galler, 1974-79; general partner Carlyle Real Estate Limited Partnerships, 1971, 72; president Balcor Company, Skokie, Illinois, 1985; chairman board Balcor Company, 1973-88; managing partner TBC Films, 1975-83; chairman Chicago White Sox, 1981—, Chicago Bulls Basketball Team, 1985—; partner Bojer Fin., 1987—; lecturer John Marhsall Law School, 1966-68; former board of directors Shearson Lehman Brothers, Incorporated, Project Academus of DePaul University, Chicago, Sports Immortals Mus., 1987-89, Committee Commemorate United States Constitution, 1987; lecturer in real estate and taxation. Author: (with L. Herbert Schneider) Uses of Life Insurance in Qualified Employee Benefit Plans, 1970. Co-chairman Illinois Professionals for Senator Ralph Smith, 1970; member Chicago Region Board Anti-Defamation League, 1986—. Member American Bar Association, Illinois Bar Association, Chicago Bar Association, Federal Bar Association, National Association Rev. Appraisers and Mortgage Underwriters, Northwestern University Law School Alumni Association (board directors), Order of Coif, Omega Tau Rho. Office: Bojer Fin Limited 980 N Michigan Avenue Suite 1011 Chicago Illinois 60611 also: Chicago Bulls 1 Magnificent Mile 980 N Michigan Avenue #1600 Chicago Illinois 60611

REUM, W. ROBERT, manufacturing executive; born Oak Park, Illinois, July 22, 1942; married Sharon Milliken. Bachelor of Arts, Yale University, 1964; Juris Doctor, University Michigan, 1967; Master of Business Administration, Harvard University, 1969. Director investment analysis City Investing Company, New York City, 1969-72; vice president corp fin. Michigan National Corp., Bloomfield Hills, Michigan, 1972-78; vice president, treasurer White Motor Corp., Cleveland, 1978-79; vice president fin., chief fin. officer Lamson & Sessions, Cleveland, 1980-82; vice president fin., chief fin. officer The Interlake Corp., Oak Brook, Illinois, 1982-88, executive vice president, 1988-90, chairman, president, chief executive officer, 1991—. Contributor articles to Harvard Bus. Rev. Member Chicago Golf Club, Chicago Club. Office: Interlake Corp 550 Warrenville Road Lisle Illinois 60532-4387

REYNOLDS, A. WILLIAM, manufacturing company executive; born Columbus, Ohio, June 21, 1933; son of William Morgan and Helen Hibbard (McCray) R.; married Joanne D. McCormick, June 12, 1953; children: Timothy M., Morgan Reynolds Brigham, Mary Reynolds Miller. Bachelor of Arts in Economics, Harvard University, 1955; Master of Business Administration, Stanford University, 1957. President Crawford Door Company, Detroit, 1959-66; staff assistant to treas TRW Incorporated, Cleveland, 1957-59, assistant to executive vice president automotive group, 1966-67, vice president automotive aftermarket group, 1967-70, executive vice president industrial and replacement sector, 1971-81, executive vice president automotive worldwide sector, 1981-84; president GenCorp, Akron, Ohio, 1984-85, president, chief executive officer, 1985—, chairman, chief executive officer, 1987—, also board of directors; board of directors Eaton Corp., Cleveland, Boise (Idaho) Cascade Corp., Federal Reserve Bank Cleveland; member dean's adv. council Stanford (California) University Grad. School Business, 1981-88. Chairman United Way-Red Cross of Summit County, Ohio, 1987; trustee University Hosps. of Cleveland, 1984—, chairman, 1987—. Member Society Automotive Engineers, Business Roundtable (policy committee), Council on Foreign Relations. Episcopalian. Clubs: Kirtland Country (Willoughby, Ohio); Union (Cleveland); Rolling Rock (Ligonier, Pennsylvania); John's Island (Vero Beach, Florida); Pepper Pike (Cleveland); Harvard (New York). Avocations: hunting, fly fishing, skiing, golf. Office: GenCorp Incorporated 175 Ghent Road Fairlawn Ohio 44313

RICE, CHARLES EDWARD, banker; born Chattanooga, Tennessee, August 4, 1935; son of Charles Edward and Louise (Goodson) R.; married Dianne Tauscher; children: Danny, Celeste, Michelle. Bachelor of Business Administration, University Miami, 1958; Master of Business Administration, Rollins College, Winter Park, Florida, 1964; graduate, Advanced Management Program, Harvard University, 1975. Vice president, then president Barnett Bank, Winter Park, 1965-71; executive vice president Barnett Banks Florida, Incorporated, Jacksonville, 1971-73, president, from 1973, chief executive officer, 1979—, now also chairman director; board of directors Sprint Corp. Board of directors St. Vincent Medical Center, Jacksonville; trustee Rollins College. Club: Jacksonville Country. Office: Barnett Banks Incorporated 100 Laura St Post Office Box 40789 Jacksonville Florida 32203-0789

RICHARDS, REUBEN FRANCIS, natural resource company executive; born August 15, 1929; son of Junius A. and Marie R. (Thayer) R.; married Elizabeth Brady, November 28, 1953; children: Reuben Francis, Timothy T., Andrew H. Bachelor of Arts, Harvard University, 1952. With Citibank, N.A., New York City, 1953-82, executive vice president, 1970-82; chairman Inspiration Resources Corp., New York City, 1982—; board of directors Adobe Resources Corp., New York City, Ecolab, Incorporated, St. Paul, Potlach Corp., San Francisco, Independence MiningCo. Incorporated, Elko, Nevada; chairman, board of directors Engelhard Corp., Menlo Park, New Jersey, Minorco, Luxembourg; chairman Minorco (United States of America) Incorporated. With United States Naval Reserve, 1948-50. Office: Inspiration Resources Corp 250 Park Avenue New York New York 10177

RICHARDSON, DEAN EUGENE, retired banker; born West Branch, Michigan, December 27, 1927; son of Robert F. and Helen (Husted) R.; married Barbara Trytten, June 14, 1952; children: Ann Elizabeth, John Matthew. Bachelor of Arts, Michigan State University, 1950; Juris Doctor, University Michigan, 1953; postgraduate, Stonier Graduate School Banking, 1965. With Industrial National Bank, Detroit, 1953-55; with Manufacturers National Bank, Detroit, 1955-90; vice president administration Manufacturers National Bank, 1964-66, senior vice president, 1966-67, executive vice president, 1967-69, president, 1969-73, chairman board of directors, 1973-89, chairman executive committee, 1989-90; chairman board Mfrs.-Detroit International Corp., 1973-90; chairman executive committee Manufacturers National Bank, 1989-90; board of directors Detroit Edison Company, Tecumseh Products Company, Ford Holdings, Incorporated; chairman AAA of Michigan. Served with United States Naval Reserve, 1945-46. Member Michigan, Detroit bar associations. Episcopalian. Clubs: Masons, KT, Detroit Athletic, Detroit, Country of Detroit. Office: care Mfrs National BankBldg 20180 Mack Avenue Grosse Pointe Woods Michigan 48236

RICHARDSON, FRANK H., oil industry executive; born March 15, 1933. Bachelor of Science, South Dakota School Mines, 1955. With Shell Oil Company, Houston, 1955—, various engineering and management positions, 1955-72, production manager western exploration and production region's west coast div., 1972-74, general manager production, western region, 1975-77, vice president corp. planning, 1978-80, senior vice president, 1980-82, executive vice president, 1983-88, president, chief executive officer, 1988—. Office: Shell Oil Company 1 Shell Plaza Houston Texas 77002

RICHARDSON, JEROME JOHNSON, food service company executive; born 1936; married. Bachelor of Arts, Wofford College, Spartanburg, South Carolina, 1959. Professional football player Baltimore Colts, 1959-61; president, board of directors TW Services Incorporated, Paramus, New Jersey; chairman, chief executive officer Denny's Incorporated (div. TW Services Incorporated), La Mirada, California; with Spartan Food Systems Incorporated (div. TW Services Incorporated), Spartanburg, South Carolina, 1961—; president, chief executive officer Spartan Food Systems, Incorporated, Spartanburg, South Carolina, 1987—, Canteen Company, Paramus, New Jersey, 1990—.

RICKETTS, THOMAS ROLAND, savings bank executive; born Detroit, March 4, 1931; son of Samuel Charles and Lillian May (Schwab) R.; married Priscilla Anne Irving, August 10, 1957; children: Robert T., Karen L. Bachelor of Business Administration, University Michigan, 1953, Juris Doctor, 1956. Bar: Michigan 1956. With Standard Federation Bank, Troy, Michigan, 1956—; branch manager Standard Federal Savings Bank, Troy, Michigan, 1958-62, vice president advertising, pub. relations, personnel, 1962-70, senior vice president, treasurer, 1970-72, executive vice president, chief administrative officer, 1972-73, president, chief administrative officer, 1973-74, president, managing officer, 1974-81, chairman board, president, managing officer, 1981—. Board of directors Detroit Symphony Orchestra, New Detroit, United Foundation, Detroit; trustee Citizens Research Council; former board of directors Detroit-Wayne County Port Authority, Detroit Economic Growth Corp., Detroit Economic Growth Fund; chairman Michigan Infrastructure Coalition. Member Savings Institution Marketing Society (president 1968),

Michigan Savings and Loan League (president 1976), State Bar Michigan, Econ. Club Detroit. Office: Standard Federal Bank 2600 W Big Beaver St Troy Michigan 48084

RIDDER, PAUL ANTHONY, newspaper executive; born Duluth, Minnesota, September 22, 1940; son of Bernard H. and Jane (Delano) R.; married Constance Louise Meach, November 6, 1960; children: Katherine Lee Pennoyer, Linda Jane, Susan Delano Cobb, Paul Anthony, Jr. Bachelor of Arts in Economics, University Michigan, 1962. With Aberdeen (South Dakota) Am. News, 1962-63, Pasadena (California) Star News, 1963-64; with San Jose (California) Mercury News, 1964-86, business manager, 1968-75, general manager, 1975-77, pub., 1977-86, president, 1979-86; president Knight-Ridder Newspaper Div., Miami, Florida, 1986-89, Knight-Ridder, Incorporated, Miami, 1989—; board of directors Seattle Times, Knight-Ridder, Incorporated; pres.' adv. board University Michigan. Board of directors Tech. Center of Silicon Valley, 1983—, Newspaper Advt. Bureau; member adv. board Center for Economic Policy Devel. Stanford U., U. Michigan; member board Coconut Grove Playhouse, Doral Ryder Open. Named California Pub. of Year, 1983. Member Florida Chamber of Commerce (board directors), Young Presidents Organization. Clubs: Cypress Point (Pebble Beach, California); Indian Creek (Miami Beach, Florida). Avocations: golf; skiing, tennis, jogging.

RIKLIS, MESHULAM, manufacturing and retail executive; born Turkey, December 2, 1923; came to United States, 1947, naturalized, 1955; son of Pinhas and Betty (Guberer) R.; children: Simona Riklis Ackerman, Marcia Riklis Hirschfeld, Ira Doron, Kady Zadora Riklis, Kristofer Riklis. Student, University Mexico, 1947; Bachelor of Arts, Ohio State University, 1950, Master of Business Administration, 1968. Co-dir. youth activities and military training Hertzlia High School, Tel-Aviv, 1942; teacher Hebrew Talmud Torah School, Minneapolis, 1951; research department Piper, Jaffray & Hopwood, 1951-53, sales representative, 1953-56; vice chairman McCrory Corp., New York City, 1960-69, vice chairman executive committee, from 1970, chairman, 1975-85, director, former president; with Rapid-Am. Corp., New York City, 1956—, chairman, 1956—, president, chief executive officer, 1957-73, chairman, chief executive officer, 1973-76, chairman, president, chief executive officer, 1976—; E-II Holdins, 1988-90. Served Brit. 8th Army, 1942-46. Member Pi Mu Epsilon. Jewish. Office: McCrory Corp 725 Fifth Avenue New York New York 10022

RINEHART, CHARLES R., savings and loan association executive; born San Francisco, January 31, 1947; son of Robert Eugene and Rita Mary Rinehart; married; children: Joseph B., Kimberly D., Michael P., Scott. Bachelor of Science, University San Francisco, 1968. Executive vice president Fireman's Fund Insurance Companies, Novato, California, 1969-83; president, chief executive officer Avco Fin. Services, Irvine, California, 1983-89; president, chief operating officer, director H.F. Ahmanson & Company, Home Savings of Am., Irwindale, California, 1989—. Served to 2d lieutenant United States Army, 1968-69. Fellow Casualty Actuarial Society; member Am. Management

Association, Am. Acad. Actuaries, Young President Organization (California Coast chapter). Republican. Roman Catholic. Avocations: athletics, gourmet cooking, model trains. Office: Home Savings of Am 4900 Rivergrade Road Irwindale California 91706

ROBERTS, BERT C., JR., telecommunications company executive; born 1942; married. Bachelor of Science, Johns Hopkins University, 1965. Project director, manager Westinghouse Electric Corp., 1960-69; director Leasco Response Incorporated, 1969-72; with MCI Communications Corp., Washington, 1972—, vice president corp. devel., 1974-76, senior vice president planning devel., 1976-79, senior vice president, 1979-85, chief operating officer, president, 1985—, also chief operating officer subsidiary MCI Telecommunications Corp., 1985—. Office: MCI Communications Corp 1133 19th St Northwest Washington District of Columbia 20036

ROBERTS, BURNELL RICHARD, paper company executive; born Wisconsin, May 6, 1927; son of Roy C. and Ann (Jones) R.; married Karen H. Ragatz, August 8, 1953; children: Evan, Kari, Paul, Nancy. Bachelor of Business Administration, University Wisconsin, 1950; Master of Business Administration, Harvard University, 1957. With Bendix Aviation Corp., 1953-58; with General Tire & Rubber Company, 1957-62; treasurer, controller subsidiary A.M. Byers Company, Pittsburgh, 1962-66; assistant to executive vice president Mead Corp., Dayton, Ohio, 1966-68, controller, vice president finance, 1968-71; group vice president, president Merchants group div. Mead Corp., Dayton, Ohio, 1971-74, Mead Paper div. Mead Corp., Dayton, Ohio, from 1974; senior vice president Mead Corp., 1979-81, president, 1981-83, chairman, chief executive officer, 1982—, also director; board of directors National City Bank, Cleveland, Northwood Pulp & Paper, Prince George, British Columbia, Armco Corp., Perkins-Elmer, DPL, Incorporated. Chairman board trustees Kenyon College, Sinclair Community College, Business Roundtable, Aspen Institute Served with United States Naval Reserve, 1944-46. Member Fin. Executives Institute, Am. Paper Institute, Japan Society (chair executive committee). Office: Mead Corp Courthouse Plaza NE Dayton Ohio 45463

ROBERTS, THEODORE HARRIS, banker; born Gillett, Arkansas, May 14, 1929; son of D. Edward and Gertrude (Harris) R.; married Elisabeth Law, July 17, 1953; children: Susan, William, Julia, John. Bachelor of Arts in Government, Northwestern State University, 1949; Master of Arts in Political Science, Oklahoma State University, 1950. With Harris Trust and Savings Bank, Chicago, 1953-83; executive vice president, secretary, treasurer Harris Bank and Harris Bankcorp Incorporated, 1971-83, director, executive committee, 1975-83; president Federal Reserve Bank St. Louis, 1983-85; chairman board, chief executive officer Talman Home Federal Savings & Loan, Chicago, 1985—. Chairman leadership committee Neighborhood Housing Svcs. Chicago, Incorporated; member Chicago committee Chicago Council Foreign Rels.; board of directors Chicago Central Area Committee. Member United States League of Savings Institutions (government affairs council, committee on strategic objectives), Chicagoland Association Savings Institutions (chairman board directors), Chicago Club, Commercial Club Chicago, Econ. Club Chicago, Exmoor Country Club (Highland Park, Illinois). Office: Talman Home Federal Savings & Loan 30 W Monroe St Chicago Illinois 60603

ROBINSON, E. B., JR., bank executive; born Centreville, Mississippi, September 14, 1941; son of Emerson B. and Dolly (McGehee) R.; married Judy M. Treppendahl, September 7, 1963; children: E.B. III, John Green. Bachelor of Science, Davidson College, 1963; Master of Business Administration, Harvard University, 1967. Management trainee Deposit Guaranty National Bank, Jackson, Mississippi, 1967-69, investment officer, 1969-71, assistant vice president, 1971-73, vice president, 1973-75, executive vice president, 1976-79, president, chief operations officer, 1979-84; president, chief operations officer Deposit Guaranty Corp., Jackson, 1982-84; chairman and chief executive officer Deposit Guaranty National Bank and Deposit Guaranty Corp., Jackson, 1984—; board of directors Federal Reserve Bank of Atlanta. Chairman fin. committee Millsaps College, Jackson; treasurer Council for Support of Pub. HIgher Education, Jackson; board of directors Columbia Sem., Atlanta. Served with United States Army, 1963-65. J. Spencer Love fellow Harvard University, 1963. Member Young Pres.'s Organization, Association of Reserve City Bankers (government relations committee), Dealer Bank Association (Glass-Stegall committee), Jackson Chamber of Commerce (president 1987), Phi Beta Kappa. Presbyterian. Clubs: Country of Jackson; Harvard (New York City). Avocation: running. Office: Deposit Guaranty Corp 1 Deposity Guaranty Plaza 210 E Capital St Jackson Mississippi 39205

ROBINSON, JAMES DIXON, III, corporate executive; born Atlanta, November 19, 1935; son of James Dixon Jr. and Josephine (Crawford) R.; married Bettye Bradley (divorced); children: Emily E. Robinson-Cook, James Dixon IV; married Linda Gosden, July 27, 1984. Bachelor of Science, Georgia Institute Tech., 1957; Master of Business Administration, Harvard University, 1961; Doctor of Humane Letters (honorary), Spelman College, 1982; Doctor of Laws (honorary), Adelphi University, 1982. Officer various departments Morgan Guaranty Trust Company of New York, New York City, 1961-66, assistant vice president, staff assistant to chairman board and president, 1967-68; general partner corp. fin. department White, Weld & Company, 1968-70; executive vice president Am. Express Company, New York City, 1970-75, president, 1975-77, chairman board of directors, chief executive officer, 1977—, also board of directors; president, chief executive officer Am. Express International Banking Corp., 1971-73; board of directors Bristol-Myers Squibb Company, Coca Cola Company, Union Pacific Corp.; chairman Adv. Committee Trade Policy and Negotiations; board of directors New York City Partnership. Chairman board mgrs., chairman board overseers Memorial Sloan-Kettering Cancer Center; trustee Alfred P. Sloan Foundation Lieutenant United States Naval Reserve, 1957-59. Member Business Roundtable (co-chmn.), New York City Chamber of Commerce and Industry (board directors), Business Council of New York State, Incorporated (board directors, vice chairman), Council Foreign Relations, Japan Society (board directors), Council on Competitiveness, Econ. Club (New York City), Pilgrims of United States Club. Office: Am Express Company Am Express Tower 200 Vesey St New York New York 10285-5100

ROBINSON, SAMUEL L., wholesale grocery company executive. With Super Food Services, Incorporated, Dayton, 1972—, merchandising manager, then div. manager, senior vice president Ohio operations, now president, chief operating officer. Office: Super Food Services Incorporated 3185 Elbee Road Dayton Ohio 45439 also: 3233 Newmark Dr Miamisburg Ohio 45342

ROBY, DONALD FRANKLIN, savings and loan association executive; born Osceola, Iowa, January 20, 1929; son of William Doyle and Wilma Louise (Hurst) R.; married Margaret Sarah Watters, July 25, 1953; children: George M., Marcia L. Roby Gilmer, Jeanne Ellen (deceased), Alan R. Bachelor.South Carolina, Drake University, Des Moines, 1950. C.P.A., Iowa. Partner Augustine & Company (C.P.A.s), Des Moines, 1953-60; controller Dewey Electric, Incorporated, Ventura, Iowa, 1960-61; senior accountant Meriwether, Wood & Miller (C.P.A.s), Des Moines, 1961-64; executive vice president Federal Home Loan Bank, Des Moines, 1964-77; president, director First Federal Savings and Loan Association, Minneapolis, 1977-83; president Federal Home Loan Bank of Des Moines, 1983-86; consultant Farm & Home Savings Association, Nevada, Missouri, 1986—; board of directors Century Companies of Am., Waverly, Iowa, CUNA Mutual Insurance Group, Madison, Wisconsin. Board of directors National Fund Medical Education. Member American Institute of Certified Public Accountants, Scottish Heritage Society Iowa, Des Moines Golf and Country Club, Shriners. Republican.

RODE, JAMES DEAN, banker; born Cleveland, February 4, 1948; son of Andrew Joseph and Eileen M. (Costello) R.; married Leslie Ann Biles, June 27, 1970. Bachelor of Arts in Econs, Ohio University, Athens, 1969; Master of Business Administration in Fin, Case Western Reserve University, 1974. With AmeriTrust Company, Cleveland, 1969—; senior vice president consumer fin. AmeriTrust Company, 1979-80, executive vice president retail banking, 1980-83, senior executive vice president banking services group, 1983, president, 1984—; director AmeriTrust Corp. & Company, Bearings, Incorporated. Trustee University Hosps. of Cleveland, Case Western Reserves, Hathaway Brown School; board of directors United Way Svcs., Cleveland Served with United States Air Force Reserve, 1969. Member Association Reserve City Bankers. Roman Catholic. Clubs: Skytop (Pennsylvania); Union (Cleveland); Pepper Pike. Office: AmeriTrust Corp 900 Euclid Avenue Post Office Box 5937 Cleveland Ohio 44101

ROE, JOHN H., manufacturing company executive; born 1939. Bachelor of Arts, Williams College, 1962; Master of Business Administration, Harvard University, 1964. With Bemis Company Incorporated, Minneapolis, 1964—, plant superintendent, 1964-67, sales representative, 1967-68, sales manager, 1968-70, plant manager, 1970-73, general manager film div., 1973-76, executive vice president operations, 1976-87, president, chief operating officer, from 1987, chief executive officer, 1990—, also board of directors. Office: Bemis Company Incorporated 800 Northstar Center 625 Marquette Avenue Minneapolis Minnesota 55402

ROEDEL, PAUL ROBERT, steel company executive; born Millville, New Jersey, June 15, 1927; son of Charles Howard and Irene (Voorhees) R.; married June Gilbert Adams, June 25, 1951; children—Beth Anne, Meg Adams. Bachelor of Science in Accounting, Rider College, 1949. With Carpenter Tech. Corp., Reading, Pennsylvania, 1949—; assistant controller Carpenter Tech. Corp., 1957-65, controller, 1965-72, treasurer, 1972-73, vice president fin., treasurer, 1973-75, executive vice president, 1975-79, president, 1979—, chief operating officer, 1979-81, chief executive officer, 1981—, director, 1973—, chairman, chief executive officer, 1987—; director Meridian Bancorp Incorporated, General Public Utilities Corp., 1979—. Board of directors Hawk Mountain council Boy Scouts Am., Children's Home Reading; trustee Gettysburg College, Wyomissing Foundation; board of directors Reading Center City Devel. Fund, I976. With United States Naval Reserve, I945-46. Member Fin. Executives Institute, Stainless Steel Industry United States (chairman adv. board 1984-86), Pennsylvania Business Roundtable, Reading-Berks Chamber of Commerce. Home: 416 Wheatland Avenue Shillington Pennsylvania 19607 Office: Carpenter Tech Corp 101 W Bern St Reading Pennsylvania 19612

ROEMER, WILLIAM FREDERICK, banker; born Youngstown, Ohio, September 21, 1933; son of James Alexander and Helen France (James) R.; married Linda Jo Cooper, June 30, 1956; children: Karen Roemer Seese, James Cooper, Gail Irwin, Sarah. Bachelor of Arts, Princeton University, 1955. Various positions Mellon Bank, Pittsburgh, 1959-69; president Bradford (Pennsylvania) National Bank, 1970-72, First Laurel Bank, St. Marys, Pennsylvania, 1972-75; president Pennbank, Titusville, Pennsylvania, 1975-82, chairman, 1982-85; president, chief executive officer Pennbancorp, 1980-88; president, chief executive officer Integra Fin. Corp., Pittsburgh, 1989-91, chairman, chief executive officer, 1991—; board of directors Pittsburgh branch of Federal Reserve Bank Cleveland. Board of directors Titusville Hospital, 1977-86, president, 1979-81; senior warden, lay reader St. James Episcopal Church, Titusville, 1980-88; various committees Episcopal Diocese Northwetern Pennsylvania, 1979-88, diocesan council, 1982-88, campaign chairman for venture in mission capital fund drive, 1981; vestryman St. Stephens Episcopal Church, Sewickley, 1990—; board of directors Pittsburgh Symphony Orchestra, 1990—, United Way Southwestern Pennsylvania, 1990—; member board Allegheny Trail council Boys Scouts Am., 1990—. Lieutenant United States Navy, 1955-58. Member Am. Bankers Association (government relations council 1982-85, bank political action committee 1989-90), Association Reserve City Bankers, Pennsylvania Bankers Association (director pub. affairs committee 1977-88, government relations policy committee 1987-90, executive committee

1989-90), Harvard-Yale-Princeton Club, Duquesne Club, Allegheny Country Club, Laurel Valley Golf Club. Republican. Home: 900 Academy Place Sewickley Pennsylvania 15143

ROGERS, JUSTIN TOWNER, JR., utility executive; born Sandusky, Ohio, August 4, 1929; son of Justin Towner and Barbara Eloise (Larkin) R. Bachelor of Arts cum laude, Princeton University, 1951; Juris Doctor, University Michigan, 1954. Bar: Ohio 1954. Associate Wright, Harlor, Purpus, Morris & Arnold, Columbus, 1956-58; with Ohio Edison Company, 1958—; vice president, then executive vice president Ohio Edison Company, Akron, 1970-79; president Ohio Edison Company, 1980—, director, 1970—; chairman board, board director Pennsylvania Power Company, New Castle; board director First National Bank Ohio, First Bancorp. of Ohio. Past president, trustee Akron Community Trusts, Akron Child Guidance Center; past chairman Akron Associated Health Agencies, U. Akron Associates; past chairman board trustees Akron General Medical Center; board of directors Akron Devel. Corp.; past board of directors Association Edison Illuminating Cos., Electric Power Research Institute; past board of directors, adv. committee Edison Electric Institute; board of directors Ohio Electric Utility Institute; business adv. council College Business Administration Kent State U.; executive committee, trustee Akron General Medical Center; trustee Health Network Ohio. Member Phi Delta Phi, Beta Gamma Sigma (hon.). Clubs: Akron City, Portage Country, Mayflower (Akron); Rockwell Springs Trout (Castalia, Ohio); Princeton (New York City); Capitol Hill (Washington); Union (Cleveland). Office: Ohio Edison Company 76 S Main St Akron Ohio 44308

ROGERS, RALPH B., business executive; born Boston, 1909; married. Educated, Northeastern University. With Cummins Diesel Engine Corp., Edwards Company, Hill Diesel Engine Company, Ideal Power Lawnmower Company, Indian Motocycle Company, Rogers Diesel & Aircraft Corp., Rogers International Corp., Armstrong Rubber Export Corp.; with Texas Industries Incorporated, Dallas, 1950—, chairman board, president, chief executive officer, 1951-75, chairman board, 1975—; director numerous subsidiaries. Chairman board of directors Texas Industries Foundation; chairman emeritus Pub. Communication Foundation North Texas, Pub. Broadcasting Service, U. Medical Center, Incorporated; past board of directors National Captioning Institute; trustee Northeastern U., St. Mark's School Texas; former chairman board mgrs. Dallas County Hospital District; founding chairman, chairman emeritus Dallas Arboretum and Botanical Society; president Dallas Foundation for Health, Education and Research; co-founder Children's TV Workshop. Lodge: Masons. Office: Tex Industries Incorporated 7610 Stemmons Freeway Dallas Texas 75247

ROGERS, ROBERT D., steel company executive; born 1936. Graduate, Yale University, 1958; Master of Business Administration, Harvard University, 1962. With George A. Fuller Company div. Oklahoma Cement Company, 1962-63; with Texas Industries, Incorporated, Dallas, 1963—, vice president operations,

1968-70, president, chief administrative officer, 1970-74, president, chief executive officer, also board of directors; chairman board of directors Chaparral Steel Company, Midlothian, Texas; chairman board of directors, chief executive officer Brookhollow Corp., Dallas. Served with United States Navy, 1958-60. Office: Tex Industries Incorporated 7610 Stemmons Freeway Dallas Texas 75247

ROLLAND, IAN MCKENZIE, insurance executive; born Fort Wayne, Indiana, June 3, 1933; son of David and Florence (Hunte) R.; married Miriam V. Flickinger, July 3, 1955; children: Cheri L., Lawrence D., Robert A., Carol Ann, Sara K. Bachelor of Arts, DePauw University, 1955; Master of Arts in Actuarial Science, University Michigan, 1956. With Lincoln National Life Insurance Company, Fort Wayne, 1956—, senior vice president, 1973-75, president, 1977-81, chief executive officer, 1977—, chairman, president, 1981—; president Lincoln National Corp., 1975—, chief executive officer, 1977—; board of directors Northern Ind. Public Service, Lincoln National Bank and Trust Company, General Telephone Company Ind., Incorporated, Tokheim Corp., Lincoln National Sales Corp., Am. States Insurance Companies, Security-Conn. Life Insurance Company, Am. States Insurance Companies, Cannon Assurance Limited, First Penn-Pacific Insurance Company, The Richard Leahy Corp., Modern Portfolio Theory Associates, Incorporated.; past chairman Am. Council of Life Insurance Agents; executive committee Associated Ind. Life Insurance Companies. Chairman citizens board St. Francis College, 1978—; S. S. Huebner Foundation; executive committee The American College; member adv. board Ind. U.-Purdue U., 1977; chairman Ind. Fiscal Policy Committee; trustee Hudson Institute; member Indiana Acad. Member Society Actuaries, Acad. Actuaries, Health Insurance Association Am., Am. Council Life Insurance (past chairman board directors), Associate Ind. Life Insurance Companies (executive committee), Ind. Insurance Society (board directors), International Insurance Society (board directors), Ind. Chamber of Commerce (member executive committee). Office: Lincoln National Life Ins Company 1300 S Clinton St Fort Wayne Indiana 46801

ROLLWAGEN, JOHN A., scientific computer company executive; born 1940; married. Bachelor of Science in Electrical Engineering, Massachusetts Institute of Technology, 1962; Master of Business Administration, Harvard University, 1964. Marketing representative Control Data Corp., 1964-66; production manager Monsanto Corp., 1966-68; vice president International Timesharing Corp., 1968-75; vice president fin. Cray Research Incorporated, 1975-76, vice president marketing, 1976-77, president, 1977-80, president, chief executive officer, 1980-88, chairman, chief executive officer, 1981—, also board of directors; board of directors Dayton Hudson Corp., Minnesota; chairman board of directors Federal Reserve Bank Minnesota. Office: Cray Research Incorporated 608 2nd Avenue S Post Office Box 154 Minneapolis Minnesota 55402

ROONEY, PHILLIP BERNARD, waste management company executive; born Chicago, July 8, 1944; son of Christopher Thomas and Rita Ann (Mitchell) R.; married Suzanne Victoria Perillo, January 29, 1966; children: Philip B., Trisha A., Michael P., Sean B. Bachelor of Arts magna cum laude, St. Bernard College, 1966. Assistant to president Waste Management, Incorporated, Oak Brook, Illinois, 1969-71, vice president, 1971-74, senior vice president, 1981-84, president, chief operating officer, 1984—, also board of directors, member executive committee; board of directors First National Bank La Grange, Illinois, Chemical Waste Management, Incorporated, The Brand Companies, Wheelabrator Techs. Active Robert Crown Center, Hinsdale, Illinois; member adv. board Hinsdale Community House, 1984—; board of directors Lyric Opera Chicago, Keep Am. Beautiful, Nazareth Acad., La Grange, 1981—, Hinsdale Hospital Foundation; trustee Denison U. Captain United States Marine Corps Reserve, 1966-69. Decorated Bronze Star, Navy Commendation medal. Member Am. Pub. Works Association, National Solid Wastes Management Association. Roman Catholic. Clubs: Butler National, Butterfield Country (Oak Brook, Illinois); Jupiter Hills (Florida) Golf. Office: Waste Management Incorporated 3003 Butterfield Road Oak Brook Illinois 60521

ROSE, MICHAEL DAVID, hotel corporation executive; born Akron, Ohio, March 2, 1942; son of William H. and Annabel L. (Kennedy) R.; children: Matthew Derek Franco, Gabrielle Elaine Franco, Morgan Douglas. Bachelor of Business Administration, University Cincinnati, 1963; Bachelor of Laws, Harvard University, 1966. Bar: Ohio 1966. Lecturer University Cincinnati, 1966-67; attorney firm Strauss, Troy & Ruehlmann, Cincinnati, 1966-72; executive vice president Winegardner International, Cincinnati, 1972-74; vice president hotel group Holiday Inns, Incorporated, Memphis, 1974-76, president hotel group, 1976-78, corp. executive vice president, 1978-79, president, from 1979, chief executive officer, 1981—, chairman board, director, 1984—; chairman, chief executive officer Holiday Corp.; director First Tennessee National Corp., General Mills, Incorporated, Po Folks Incorporated. Fellow advance mgmt. program Harvard U. Grad. School Business Administration; board of directors Memphis Arts Council, from 1979; member Future Memphis, from 1979; member board advisors U. Cincinnati, from 1979; hon. chairman board trustees Junior Achievement, Memphis. Member Ohio Bar Association, Young Pres.'s Organization, Conference Board, Service Industry Council of United States Chamber of Commerce, Jobs Skills Task Force, Am. Hotel and Motel Association (industry real estate financing adv. council). Club: Econ. Memphis. Office: Holiday Inns Incorporated 3796 Lamar Avenue Memphis Tennessee 38196

ROSE, PAUL EDWARD, publishing company executive; born Spokane, Washington, April 27, 1947; son of Albert Edward and Karen (Murray) R.; married Karen Pearl Rose, August 23, 1971; children: Marcus, David, Julianne. Bachelor of Science, Brigham Young University, 1970, Master in Accounting, 1971. Certified Public Accountant, New York, Illinois. Auditor Ernst & Whinney, New York City, 1971-75; budget manager Dun & Bradstreet, New York City, 1975-

77; controller, director circulation sales Offcl. Airline Guides, Oak Brook, Illinois, 1977-82; fin. controller John Morrell & Company, Northfield, Illinois, 1982-83; vice president fin. Standard Rate and Data Service, Wilmette, Illinois, 1983-85; senior vice president Macmillan Directory Div., Wilmette, 1985-87, executive vice president, 1987-89, president National Register Pub. Company, 1989-91, executive vice president Maxwell Macmillan Information Services Group, 1991—. Recipient Outstanding Pianist award Washington State Music Teachers Association, 1968. Member American Institute of Certified Public Accountants. Office: National Register Pub Company 3004 Glenview Road Wilmette Illinois 60091

ROSEN, BENJAMIN MAURICE, venture capitalist; born New Orleans, March 11, 1933; son of Isidore J. and Anna Vera (Leibof) R.; married Alexandra Ebere, September 29, 1967; children—Jeffrey Mark, Eric Andrew. Bachelor of Science, California Institute Tech., 1954; Master of Science, Stanford University, 1955; Master of Business Administration, Columbia University, 1961. Engineer Raytheon Corp., Oxnard, California, 1955-56; engineer Sperry Corp., Great Neck, New York, 1957-59; vice president Quantum Sci. Corp., New York City, 1961-65; partner Coleman & Company, New York City, 1965-75; vice president Morgan Stanley & Company Incorporated, New York City, 1975-80; president Rosen Research Incorporated, New York City, 1980-83; partner Sevin Rosen Management Company, New York City, 1981—; chairman board Compaq Computer Corp., Houston, Ansa Corp., Belmont, California; director General Parametrics Corp., Berkeley, California, Expertel, Incorporated, Dallas; former founder director Lotus Devel. Corp.; member adv. board School Business, Tulane University, New Orleans. Board of directors Tech. Center Silicon Valley, San Jose, California, member president's council Memorial Sloan-Kettering Cancer Center, New York City; trustee California Institute Tech., Pasadena. Member New York Society Security Analysts. Office: Sevin Rosen Management Company 200 Park Avenue New York New York 10166 also: Compaq Computer Corp 20555 SH 249 Post Office Box 69-2000 Houston Texas 77269

ROSENBERG, HENRY A., JR., petroleum executive; born Pittsburgh, November 7, 1929; son of Henry A. and Ruth (Blaustein) R.; children: Henry A. III, Edward Lee, Frank Blaustein; married Dorothy Lucibello, June 30, 1984. Bachelor of Arts in Economics, Hobart College, 1952. With Crown Central Petroleum Corp., Baltimore, 1952—, president, 1966-75, chairman executive committee, 1966—, chairman board, 1975—, also chief executive officer; director Am. Trading & Prodn. Corp., USF&G Corp., Signet Banking Corp.; member listed company adv. committee Am. Stock Exchange. Board of directors Johns Hopkins Hospital, Goucher College, McDonogh School, National Flag Day Foundation, Young Men's Christian Association Greater Baltimore, United Way Central Maryland; past chairman Greater Baltimore Committee; member national executive board Boy Scouts Am.; chairman adv. board William Donald Schaefer Center for Pub. Policy; trustee Hobart and William Smith Colleges. Member National Petroleum Refiners Association (chairman, director, executive committee), National Petroleum Council, Am. Petroleum Institute, 25 Year Club Petroleum Industry. Office: Crown Central Petroleum Corp 1 N Charles St Post Office Box 1168 Baltimore Maryland 21203

ROSENBERG, RICHARD MORRIS, banker; born Fall River, Massachusetts, April 21, 1930; son of Charles and Betty (Peck) R.; married Barbara K. Cohen, October 21, 1956; children: Michael, Peter. Bachelor of Science, Suffolk University, 1952; Master of Business Administration, Golden Gate College, 1962, Bachelor of Laws, 1966. Publicity assistant Crocker-Anglo Bank, San Francisco, 1959-62; banking services officer Wells Fargo Bank, N.A., San Francisco, 1962-65; assistant vice president Wells Fargo Bank, N.A., 1965-68, vice president marketing department, 1968, vice president, director marketing, 1969, senior vice president marketing and advertising div., 1970-75, executive vice president, from 1975, vice chairman, 1980-83; vice chairman Crocker National Corp., 1983-85; president, chief operating officer Seafirst Corp., 1986-87, also director; president, chief operating officer Seattle First National Bank, 1985-87; vice chairman board BankAmerica Corp., San Francisco, 1987-90, chairman, chief executive officer, 1990—; director Airborne Express, Visa; chairman Mastercard International. Board of directors Marin Ecumenical Housing Association; board regents School Bank Marketing, U. Colorado; trustee Golden Gate U., California Institute Tech. Served from ensign to lieutenant United States Naval Reserve, 1953-59. Member Hillcrest Club. Jewish. Office: BankAm Corp Bank America Center San Francisco California 94104

ROSKENS, RONALD WILLIAM, federal government administrator, association administrator, former academic administrator; born Spencer, Iowa, December 11, 1932; son of William E. and Delores A.L. (Beving) R.; married Lois Grace Lister, August 22, 1954; children: Elizabeth, Barbara, Brenda, William. Bachelor of Arts, University Northern Iowa, 1953, Master of Arts, 1955, Doctor of Humane Letters (honorary), 1985; Doctor of Philosophy, State University Iowa, 1958; Doctor of Laws (honorary), Creighton University, 1978, Huston-Tillotson College, 1981, Midland Lutheran College, 1984, Hastings College, 1981; Doctor of Letters (honorary), Nebraska Wesleyan University, 1981; Doctor of Philosophy (honorary), Ataturk University, Turkey, 1987; Doctor of Humane Letters (honorary), University Akron, 1987. Teacher Minburn (Iowa) High School, 1954, Woodward (Iowa) State Hospital, summer 1954; assistant counselor to men State University Iowa, 1956-59; dean of men, assistant professor special education Kent (Ohio) State University, 1959-63, associate professor, then professor, 1963-72, assistant to president, 1963-66, dean for administration, 1968-71, executive vice president, professor educational admisntrn., 1971-72; chancellor, professor educational administration University Nebraska, Omaha, 1972-77; president University Nebraska System, 1977-89, president emeritus, 1989; hon. professor East China Normal University, Shanghai, 1985; administrator Agency International Devel., Washington, 1990—; director

Enron Corp., Art's Way Manufacturing Company, Guarantee Mutual Life Insurance Company, Am. Charter Federal Savings and Loan Association; member Bus.-Higher Education Forum, 1979-89, executive committee, 1984-84; member governmental relations committee Am. Council Education, 1979-83, board of directors, 1981-86, vice chair, 1983-84, chair, 1984-85; chairman committee on financing higher education National Association State Universities and Land Grant Colleges, 1978-83, vice chairman committee on financing higher education, 1983-84, chairman committee on federal student fin. assistance, 1981-87; member national adv. committee on accreditation and institutional eligibility United States Department Education, 1983-86, chairman, 1986; board of directors Council for Aid to Education, 1985-89; executive board North Central Association, 1979-84, chairman executive board, 1982-84, president, 1989-90. Co-editor: Paradox, Process and Progress, 1968; contributor articles professional journals. Member Kent City Planning Commission, 1962-66; board of directors Metropolitan Young Men's Christian Association, Omaha, 1973-77, Mid-Am. council Boy Scouts Am., 1973-77, Midlands United Community Services, 1972-77, National Conference of Christians and Jews, 1974-77, Foundation Study Presidential and Congl. Terms, 1977-89; trustee Huston Tillotson College, Austin, Texas, 1968-81, chairman, 1976-78; trustee Joslyn Art Mus., 1973-77, Nebraska Methodist Hospital, 1974-77, Brownell-Talbott School, 1974-77, Harry S. Truman Institute, 1977-89, Willa Cather Pioneer Memorial and Educational Foundation, 1979-87; president Kent Area Chamber of Commerce, 1966; board of directors First Plymouth Congl. Church, 1989-90. Decorated comdrs. cross Order of Merit (Federal Republic of Germany); recipient Brotherhood award National Conference of Christians and Jews, 1977, Americanism citation B'nai B'rith, 1978, Gold medal National Interfraternity, 1987, Agri award Triumph Agr. Exposition, Omaha, 1989; numerous others; named National 4-H Alumnus, 1968, Outstanding Alumnus University Northern Iowa, 1974, King AK-Sar-Ben LXXXVI, 1980. Member American Association for the Advancement of Science, American Association of University Professors, Am. College Pers. Association, Association Urban Univs. (president 1976-77),, Am. Educational Research Association, Am. Psychological Association, Chief Executives Organization, Young President Organization, Lincoln Chamber of Commerce (board directors 1989—), Phi Delta Kapp Phi Eta Sigma, Sigma Tau Gamma (president grand council 1968-70, Distinguished Achievement award 1980, Distinguished Scholar award 1981), Omicron Delta Kappa (national president 1986—). Lodge: Masons (32 degree). Home: 2357 S Queen St Arlington Virginia 22202

ROSS, STEVEN J., communications company executive; born New York City, 1927; married. Student, Paul Smith's College, 1948. President, director Kinney Services Incorporated, 1961-72; president Warner Communications Incorporated, New York City, from 1972, chairman board, chief executive officer, 1972—; co-chairman, co-chief executive officer Time-Warner

Incorporated, New York City, 1989-90, chairman, co-chief executive officer, 1990—; board of directors New York Convention and Visitors Bureau, Mus. of TV and Radio; member board sports medicine Lenox Hill Hospital. Office: Time Warner Incorporated 75 Rockefeller Plaza New York New York 10019

ROSSO, LOUIS T., scientific instrument manufacturing company executive; born San Francisco, 1933; married. Bachelor of Arts, San Francisco State College, 1955; Master of Business Administration, University Santa Clara, 1967. Product specialist Spinco div. Beckman Instruments, Incorporated, Fullerton, California, 1959-63; marketing manager Beckman Instruments, Incorporated, 1963-69, manager Spinco div., 1969-70, manager clinical instruments div., 1970-74, corp. vice president, manager analytical instruments group, 1974-80, corp. senior vice president, 1980-83, president, 1983—, now also chairman, chief executive officer, also board of directors; vice president SmithKline Beckman Corp., Philadelphia. Office: Beckman Instruments Incorporated 2500 Harbor Boulevard Fullerton California 92634

ROSTOW, WALT WHITMAN, economist, educator; born New York City, October 7, 1916; son of Victor Aaron and Lillian (Helman) R.; married Elspeth Vaughan Davies, June 26, 1947; children: Peter Vaughan, Ann Larner. Bachelor of Arts, Yale University, 1936, Doctor of Philosophy, 1940. Instructor economics Columbia University, 1940-41; assistant chief German-Austrian economic div. Department State, 1945-46; Harmsworth professor Am. history Oxford (England) University, 1946-47; assistant to executive secretary Economic Commission for Europe, 1947-49; Pitt. professor Am. history Cambridge (England) University, 1949-50; professor economic history Massachusetts Institute of Technology, 1950-60; staff member Center International Studies, 1951-60; deputy special assistant to President for national security affairs 1961; counselor, chairman policy planning council Department State, 1961-66; special assistant to President 1966-69; United States representative, ambassador Inter-Am. committee Alliance for Progress, 1964-66; now Rex G. Baker Junior professor political economy, departments economics and history University Texas, Austin, professor emeritus; member Board Foreign Scholarships, 1969-72. Author: The American Diplomatic Revolution, 1947, Essays on the British Economy of the Nineteenth Century, 1948, The Process of Economic Growth, 1953, 2d edition, 1960, (with A.D. Gayer, A.J. Schwartz) The Growth and Fluctuation of the British Economy, 1790-1850, 1953, 2d edition, 1975, (with A. Levin, others) The Dynamics of Soviet Society, 1953, (with others) The Prospects for Communist China, 1954, (with R.W. Hatch) An American Policy in Asia, 1955, (with M.F. Millikan) A Proposal: Key to an Effective Foreign Policy, 1957, The United States in the World Arena, 1960, The Stages of Economic Growth, 1960, 2d edition, 1971, View from the Seventh Floor, 1964, A Design for Asian Development, 1965, (with William E. Griffith) East-West Relations: Is Detente Possible?, 1969, Politics and the Stages of Growth, 1971, The Diffusion of Power, 1972, How It All Began, 1975, The World Economy:

History and Prospect, 1978, Getting From Here to There, 1978, Why the Poor Get Richer and the Rich Slow Down, 1980, Pre-Invasion Bombing Strategy: General Eisenhower's Decision of March 25, 1944, 1981, British Trade Fluctuations, 1868-1896: A Chronicle and a Commentary, 1981, The Division of Europe After World War II: 1946, 1981, Europe After Stalin: Eisenhower's Three Decisions of March 11, 1953, 1982, Open Skies: Eisenhower's Proposal of July 21, 1955, 1982, The Barbaric Counter-Revolution: Cause and Cure, 1983, Eisenhower, Kennedy, and Foreign Aid, 1985, The United States and the Regional Organization of Asia and the Pacific: 1965-1985, 1986, Rich Countries and Poor Countries, 1987, Essays on a Half Century: Ideas, Policies and Action, 1988, History, Policy, and Economic Theory, 1989, Theorists of Economic Growth From David Hume to the Present with a Perspective on the Next Century, 1990; editor: The Economics of Take-Off Into Sustained Growth, 1963. Major Office of Strategic Services, Army of the United States, 1942-45. Decorated Legion of Merit, Hon. Order Brit. Empire (mil.); recipient Presidential Medal of Freedom with distinction; Rhodes scholar Balliol College, 1936-38. Member Am. Acad. Arts and Sciences, Am. Philos Society, Massachusetts Historical Society. Clubs: Cosmos (Washington); Elizabethan (New Haven). Home: 1 Wildwind Point Austin Texas 78746

ROUBOS, GARY LYNN, diversified manufacturing company executive; born Denver, November 7, 1936; son of Dorr and Lillian Margaret (Coover) R.; married Terie Joan Anderson, February 20, 1960; children: Lyndel, Leslie. Bachelor of Science in Chemical Engineering with high honors, University Colorado, 1959; Master of Business Administration with distinction, Harvard University, 1963. With Boise Cascade Corp., 1963-71, Dieterich Standard Corp., Boulder, Colorado, 1971-76; executive vice president, then president Dieterich Standard Corp. (company acquired by Dover Corp. 1975), 1975-76; executive vice president Dover Corp., New York City, 1976, president, 1977—, chief executive officer, 1981—, chairman, 1989—; board of directors Omnicom Incorporated, New York City, Scott Paper Company, Philadelphia, Gabelli-O'Connor Treasurer Fund, Greenwich, Connecticut; member New York adv. board Liberty Mutual. Board of directors Colorado U. Foundation, 1976-89; board governors Board Rm., 1989—. 1st lieutenant Corps of Engineers, United States Army, 1959-61. Member Tokeneke Club, Board Rm. Club, Winged Foot Golf Club, Econ. Club of New York. Office: Dover Corp 280 Park Avenue New York New York 10017

ROWLAND, LANDON HILL, diversified holding company executive; born Fuquay Springs, North Carolina, May 20, 1937; son of Walter Elton and Elizabeth Carr (Williams) R.; married Sarah Fidler, December 29, 1959; children: Sarah Elizabeth, Matthew Hill, Joshua Carr. Bachelor of Arts, Dartmouth College, 1959; Bachelor of Laws, Harvard University, 1962. Bar: Missouri. Associate Watson, Ess, Marshall & Enggas, Kansas City, Missouri, 1962-70; partner Watson, Ess, Marshall & Enggas, 1970-80; vice president Kansas City Southern

Industries, Incorporated, 1980-83, president, chief operating officer, 1983-86, president chief executive officer, 1987—, also director; professional lecturer antitrust law University Mo.-Kansas City, 1977-79; chairman board of directors DST Systems, Incorporated, Kansas City, 1983—; chairman Kansas City Southern Railway Company, 1990—, also board director; chairman, board director Boatmen's Bank & Trust Company, Kansas City, 1990—; board of directors Am. Royal, Kansas City, Missouri. Co-author: West's Missouri Practice Series. Trustee Midwest Research Institute, Kansas City, Missouri; chairman board of directors Swope Ridge Health Care Center, Kansas City, Lyric Opera of Kansas City; board of directors Jacob L. & Ella C. Loose Foundation; chairman Metropolitan Performing Arts Fund. Member American Bar Association, Missouri Bar Association, Phi Beta Kappa. Clubs: Kansas City Country, Kansas City, River. Home: Ever Glades Farm 12717 Mt Olivet Road Kansas City Missouri 64166 Office: Kansas City Southern Industries Incorporated 114 W 11th St Kansas City Missouri 64105

RUCH, RICHARD HURLEY, manufacturing company executive; born Plymouth, Indiana, April 15, 1930; son of Dallas Claude and Mabel (Hurley) R.; married Patricia Lou Overbeek, June 27, 1931; children: Richard, Michael, Christine, Douglas. Bachelor of Arts, Michigan State University, 1952. Stores accounting supervisor Kroger Incorporated, Grand Rapids, Michigan, 1954-55; chief accountant Herman Miller Incorporated, Zeeland, Michigan, 1955-58, controller, 1958-63, director manufacturing, 1963-67, vice president manufacturing, 1967-77, vice president administration, 1978, vice president corp. resources, 1979-85, chief fin. officer, senior vice president, 1985-87, chief executive officer, 1988-90, pres, chief executive officer, 1990—; board of directors Milcare, Zeeland, Herman Miller Research Corp., Zeeland. Active Hope College, Twentieth Century Club, Holland, Michigan; formerly active Holland Chamber of Commerce, Zeeland Planning Committee. Member Scanlon Plan Assocs. (board directors, past president). Avocations: tennis, running. Office: Herman Miller Incorporated 8500 Byron Road Zeeland Michigan 49464

RUCKELSHAUS, WILLIAM DOYLE, waste disposal services company executive; born Indianapolis, July 24, 1932; son of John K. and Marion (Doyle) R.; married Jill Elizabeth Strickland, May 11, 1962; children: Catherine Kiley, Mary Hughes, Jennifer Lea, William Justice, Robin Elizabeth. Bachelor of Arts cum laude, Princeton University, 1957; Bachelor of Laws, Harvard University, 1960. Bar: Ind. 1960. Attorney Ruckelshaus, Bobbitt & O'Connor, Indianapolis, 1960-68; deputy atty.-gen. Ind. 1960-65, chief counsel office atty.-gen. Ind., 1963-65; minority attorney Ind. Senate, 1965-67; member Ind. House of Representatives, 1967-69, majority leader, 1967-69; assistant atty.-gen. charge civil div. Department Justice, 1969-70; administrator Environmental Protection Agency, Washington, 1970-73; acting director Federal Bureau of Investigation, 1973; deputy attorney general United States, 1973; member firm Ruckelshaus, Beveridge, Fairbanks and Diamond, Washington, 1974-76; senior vice president

Weyerhaeuser Company, Tacoma, 1975-83; administrator Environmental Protection Agency, Washington, 1983-85; member firm Perkins Coie, Seattle, 1985-88; now chairman, chief executive officer Browning-Ferris Industries, Incorporated, Houston, 1988—; board of directors Cummins Engine Company, Monsanto Company, Nordstrom, Incorporated, Texas Commerce Bancshares, Incorporated, Weyerhaeuser Company, Incorporated; chairman, chief executive officer Browning-Ferris Industries, Houston. Nominee for United States Senate, Ind., Republican Party, 1968; trustee Conservation Foundation, World Wildlife Fund. With Army of the United States, 1953-55. Member Federal Bar Association, Ind. Bar Association, District of Columbia Bar Association, Indianapolis Bar Association. Office: Browning-Ferris Indiana Incorporated 757 N Eldridge Houston Texas 77079

RUKEYSER, LOUIS RICHARD, economic commentator; born New York City, January 30, 1933; son of Merryle Stanley and Berenice Helene (Simon) R.; married Alexandra Gill, March 3, 1962; children: Beverley Jane, Susan Athena, Stacy Alexandra. Bachelor of Arts, Princeton University, 1954; Doctor of Letters (honorary), New Hampshire College, 1975; Doctor of Laws (honorary), Moravian College, 1978, Mercy College, 1984; DBA (honorary), Southeastern Massachusetts University, 1979; Doctor of Humane Letters (honorary), Loyola College, 1982, Johns Hopkins University, 1986. Reporter Baltimore Sun newspapers, 1954-65; chief political corr. Evening Sun, 1957-59; chief London bureau The Sun, 1959-63, chief Asian corr., 1963-65; senior corr., commentator ABC News, 1965-73, Paris corr., 1965-66, chief London bureau, 1966-68, economic editor, commentator, 1968-73; host Wall St. Week with Louis Rukeyser PBS-TV, 1970—; nationally syndicated economic columnist McNaught Syndicate, 1976-86, Tribune Media Services, 1986—; frequent lecturer. Author: How to Make Money in Wall Street, 1974, 2d edition, 1976 (Literary Guild selection 1974, 76), What's Ahead for the Economy: The Challenge and the Chance, 1983, 2d edition, 1985 (Literary Guild selection 1984), Louis Rukeyser's Business Almanac, 1988, 2d edition, 1991. Served with Army of the United States, 1954-56. Recipient Overseas Press Club award, 1963, Overseas Press Club citation, 1964, G.M. Loeb award University Connecticut, 1972, Janus award for excellence in fin. news programming, 1975, George Washington Honor medal Freedoms Foundation, 1972, 78, New York Fin. Writers Association award, 1980, Free Enterprise Man of the Year award Texas Agricultural and Mechanical University Center for Education and Research in Free Enterprise, 1987, Women's Economic Round Table award, 1990. Office: 586 Round Hill Road Greenwich Connecticut 06831

RUMSFELD, DONALD H., former government official, corporate executive; born Chicago, July 9, 1932; son of George Donald and Jeannette (Husted) R.; married Joyce Pierson, December 27, 1954; 3 children. Bachelor of Arts, Princeton University, 1954; honorary degree, De Paul University College Commerce, Illinois College, Lake Forest College, Park College, Tuskegee Institute, National

College Education, Bryant College, Claremont (California) Graduate School. Administrative assistant United States House of Representatives, 1958-59; with A.G. Becker & Company, Chicago, 1960-62; member 88th-91st Congresses from 13th Illinois district, Pres.'s Cabinet, 1969-73; director OEO, assistant to president, 1969-70; counselor to President Richard Nixon, director economic stabilization program 1971-72; United States ambassador and permanent representative to North Atlantic Treaty Organization, 1973-74; White House chief of staff for President Gerald Ford Washington, 1974-75; secretary Department Defense, 1975-77; president, chief executive officer, then chairman G.D. Searle & Company, Skokie, Illinois, 1977-85; special envoy of President Reagan to Middle East 1983-84; senior advisor William Blair & Company, Chicago, 1985-90; now chairman, chief executive officer General Instrument Corp., New York City; board of directors Rand Corp., ABB Asea Brown Boveri, Limited, Kellogg Company, Vulcan Materials Company, Sears, Roebeck & Company, Gilead Sciences, Incorporated. Chairman Eisenhower Exch. Fellowships, 1986—; board trustees Institute Contemporary Studies. Naval Aviator United States Navy, 1954-57. Recipient Presidential Medal of Freedom, George Catlett Marshall award, Woodrow Wilson award. Office: 135 S LaSalle St Suite 1740 Chicago Illinois 60603

RUSSELL, KEITH PALMER, JR., financial services executive; born Los Angeles, October 23, 1945; son of Keith Palmer and Betty Jane (Stratton) R.; married Margaret Ann Richards, March 18, 1967; 1 child, Hope Ann. Bachelor of Arts, University Washington, 1967; Master of Arts, Northwestern University, 1970. Vice president Security Pacific Corp., London and Hong Kong, 1979-81; senior vice president Security Pacific Corp., Los Angeles, 1981-83; executive vice president Glendale (Calif) Federal Bank, 1983-84; senior executive vice president Glendale (California) Federal Savings & Loan Association, 1984-85, president and chief operating officer, 1985-88; director, chief operating officer Glenfed, 1988—, president, 1989-91, also board of directors. Member Jonathan Club (Los Angeles), California Club (Los Angeles). Republican. Epsicopalian. Avocations: tennis, biking. Office: GLENFED Incorporated 700 N Brand Boulevard Glendale California 91203

RUSSELL, OSCAR CECIL, JR. (BUD RUSSELL), banker; born Huntsville, Alabama, November 10, 1945; son of Oscar Cecil and Lovena (Moss) R. Bachelor of Science, University Alabama, 968; graduate, Georgia State University, 1977. With Citizens & Southern National Bank, Atlanta, 1973-77; vice chairman administration Hibernia National Bank, New Orleans, 1977—; board of directors, member executive committee Southern Fin. Exchange, 1977-82, 83—. Board of directors, vice president New Orleans Ballet, 1981—; fin. vice president New Orleans City Ballet and joint artistic resource committee Cincinnati and New Orleans Ballet Cos., 1983—. Served to captain United States Army, 1968-73. Member Am. Institute Banking, Bank Administration Institute, National Automated Clearing House Association (chairman 1987—), New Orleans Clearing

House Association (past president), Phi Kappa Psi. Republican. Roman Catholic. Home: 2437 Jefferson Avenue New Orleans Louisiana 70115 Office: Guaranty Bank & Trust Company 934 3rd St Alexandria Louisiana 71301

RYAN, ARTHUR FREDERICK, banker; born Brooklyn, September 14, 1942; son of Arthur Vincent and Gertrude (Wingert) R.; married Patricia Elizabeth Kelly; children: Arthur, Kelly Ann, Kevin, Kathleen. Bachelor of Arts in Math., Providence College, 1963. Area manager Data Corp., Washington, 1965-72; project manager Chase Manhattan Corp. and Bank, New York City, 1972-73, 2d vice president, 1973-74, vice president, 1974-75, from 1978, former operations executive, from 1978, former executive vice president, from 1982, former vice-chairman, now president, 1990—; member policy and planning committee; board of directors, chairman audit committee Depository Trust Company; past member executive committee, Cedel (European Depository); past chairman steering committee, program manager CHIPS Same Day Settlement, New York Clearing House. Past board of directors Urban Acad. New York City Lieutenant United States Army, 1963-65. Member Am. Bankers Association (vice chairman ops. and automation division and government relations council, past chairman international ops. committee). Home: 144 The Helm East Islip New York 11730 Office: Chase Manhattan Corp 1 Chase Manhattan Plaza New York New York 10081

RYAN, PATRICK G., insurance company executive; born Milwaukee, May 15, 1937; married Shirley Welsh, April 16, 1966; children—Patrick III, Robert J., Corbett M. Bachelor of Science, Northwestern University, 1959. Sales agent Penn Mutual, 1959-64; Pat Ryan & Associates Penn Mutual, Chicago, 1964-71; chairman, president Ryan Insurance Group Incorporated, Chicago, 1971-82; president, chief executive officer Combined International Corp., Northbrook, Illinois, 1982—, board of directors, 1982—, now also president chief executive officer, 1982—; president, chief executive officer Aon Corp., Chicago; board of directors Commonwealth Edison, Chicago, First Chicago Corp., First National Bank., Chicago, Gould Incorporated, Rolling Meadows, Illinois. Past president Chicago Boys Clubs; trustee Rush-Presbyterian-St. Luke's Medical Center, Chicago, Northwestern U., Field Mus. Natural History, Chicago. Recipient Distinguished Manager award, Lake Forest College, Illinois, 1983. Roman Catholic. Office: A on Corp 123 N Wacker Dr Chicago Illinois 60606 also: Combined Ins Company of Am 222 N Dearborn Chicago Illinois 60601

SAATCHI, CHARLES, communications and marketing company executive; born June 9, 1943; married Doris Lockart, 1973. Student, Christ's College, Finchley. Associate director Collett Dickenson Pearce, 1966-68; director Cramer Saatchi, 1968-70; owner, director Saatchi & Saatchi, 1970—.

SAATCHI, MAURICE, communications and marketing company executive; born June 21, 1946; son of Nathan and Daisy Saatchi; married Josephine Hart, 1984; 1 son, 1 stepson. Bachelor of Science in Economics, London School Economics and Political

Science, 1967. Co-founder Saatchi & Saatchi Company, 1970, chairman, 1984—. Avocations: gardens, plays. Office: 80 Charlotte St, London W1A 1AQ, England also: Saatchi & Saatchi Company, Berkeley Square, London England W1X 5DH

SAFIOL, GEORGE E., electronics company executive; born Brooklyn, April 23, 1932; son of Charles and Effie (Patika) S.; married Demetra Karambelas, July 12, 1958; children: Olympia Safiol Twomey, Peter, Christina. Bachelor of Science in Engineering, New York University, 1954; postgraduate School Engineering, Columbia University, 1954-55. Vice president, general manager Northern Am. Telecom, International Telephone & Telegraph Corporation, Memphis, 1960-69; executive vice president, chief operating officer Sycor, Incorporated, Ann Arbor, Michigan, 1969-70; vice president investments Heizer Company, Chicago, 1970-71; senior vice president General Instrument Corp., Chicopee, Massachusetts, 1971-77; president, chief executive officer Am. Biltrite, Framingham, Massachusetts, 1977-83; various senior executive positions General Instrument Corp., New York City, 1984-87, chief operating offficer, president, 1987—, also director; private practice management consultant, 1983-84. Served to 1st lieutenant United States Army, 1955-57. Member Alpha Omega. Republican. Greek Orthodox. Club: Metropolitan (New York City). Avocations: racquetball, golf, reading. Home: 64 Juniper Road Weston Massachusetts 02193 Office: General Instrument Corp 767 Fifth Avenue New York New York 10153

SAIKI, PATRICIA (MRS. STANLEY MITSUO SAIKI), federal agency administrator, former congresswoman; born Hilo, Hawaii, May 28, 1930; daughter of Kazuo and Shizue (Inoue) Fukuda; married Stanley Mitsuo Saiki, June 19, 1954; children: Stanley Mitsuo, Sandra Saiki Williams, Margaret C., Stuart K., Laura H. Bachelor of Arts, University Hawaii, 1952. Teacher United States history Punahou School, Kaimuki Intermediate School, Kalani High School, Honolulu, 1952-64; secretary Rep. Party Hawaii, Honolulu, 1964-66, vice chairman, 1966-68, 82-83, chairman, 1983-85; research assistant Hawaii State Senate, 1966-68; member Hawaii House of Representatives, 1968-74, Hawaii State Senate, 1974-82, 100th-101st Congresses from 1st Hawaii district, Washington, 1987-91; admin. Small Business Administration, Washington, 1991—; member President's Adv. Council on Status of Women, 1969-76; member National Commission International Women's Year, 1969-70; commissioner Western Interstate Commission on Higher Education; fellow Eagleton Institute, Rutgers University, 1970. Member Kapiolani Hospital Auxiliary; secretary Hawaii Republican Committee, 1964-66, vice chairman, 1966-68, chairman, 1983-85; del. Hawaii Constitutional Convention, 1968; alternate del. Republican National Convention, 1968, del., 1984; Republican nominee for lieutenant governor Hawaii, 1982; member Federation Republican Women.; trustee Hawaii Pacific College; past board governors Boys and Girls Clubs Hawaii; member adv. council American Red Cross; board of directors National Fund for Improvement of Post-Secondary Education, 1982-85 ; past board of directors Straub Medical Research

Foundation, Honolulu, Hawaii's Visitors Bureau, Honolulu, Education Commission of States, Honolulu, Hawaii Visitors Bureau, 1983-85; trustee U. Hawaii Foundation, 1984-86, Hawaii Pacific College, Honolulu. Episcopalian. Avocation: golf. Home: 784 Elepaio St Honolulu Hawaii 96816 Office: Small Business Administration Office of the Admin 409 Third St Southwest Washington District of Columbia 20416

SAINE, CARROLL LEE, banker; born Lincolnton, North Carolina, September 14, 1934; son of Henry Greer and Velma Prue (Hallman) S.; married Wanda Mauney Boring, June 24, 1956; children: Mark, Martha. Bachelor of Arts, Lenoir-Rhyne College, Hickory, North Carolina, 1954; Master of Science in Business Adminstrn, University Richmond, Virginia, 1965. With Central Fidelity Bank (N.A.), Richmond, 1957—; director Central Fidelity Bank (N.A.), 1975—, executive vice president, 1973-76, president, chief executive officer, 1976, 1976, also director, chairman, chief executive officer, 1981—. With United States Army Reserve, 1954-56. Lutheran. Clubs: Commonwealth (Richmond), Country of Virginia (Richmond). Office: Central Fidelity Banks Incorporated 1021 E Cary St Richmond Virginia 23219

ST. DENNIS, JERRY A., banker; born 1942. Bachelor of Arts, University of California at Los Angeles, 1965, Master of Arts, 1967. Vice president Claremont Economics Institute, 1978-87; chief fin. officer, executive vice president, director CalFed Incorporated, Los Angeles, 1981-89, president, chief operating officer, 1989-90, chairman, president, chief executive officer, 1990—. Office: CalFed Incorporated 5700 Wilshire Boulevard Los Angeles California 90036

ST. JACQUES, ROBERT H., food products executive; born March 3, 1924; son of Emile C. and Marie R. (Messier) St. J.; married Beverly A. Trussel, June 29, 1975; children: Roberta, Elizabeth, Raymond, David. BME, Cornell University, 1948. President Hayden Manufacturing Company, Wareham, Massachusetts, 1948—; chairman Ocean Spray Cranberries Incorporated, Lakeville, Massachusetts, 1984—; member executive committee Plymouth Savings Bank., 1975—. Mgr. community trust funds, Wareham, 1968-89. Sergeant United States Army, 1943-46, European Theatre of Operations. Republican. Roman Catholic. Avocations: golf, sailing. Home: 79 Oak St Wareham Massachusetts 02571 Office: Ocean Spray Cranberries Incorporated 225 Water St Plymouth Massachusetts 02360

SALDICH, ROBERT JOSEPH, chemical company executive; born New York City, June 7, 1933; son of Alexander and Bertha (Kasakove) S.; married Anne Rawley, July 21, 1963 (divorced November 1979); 1 child, Alan; married Virginia Vaughan, September 4, 1983; stepchildren: Tad Thomas, Stan Thomas, Melinda Thomas, Margaret Thomas. Bachelor of Arts, Bachelor of Science in Chemical Engineering, Rice University, 1956; Master of Business Administration, Harvard University, 1961. Manufacturing manager Procter & Gamble Manufacturing Company, Dallas, Kansas City, Kansas, 1956-59; research assistant Harvard Business School, Boston, 1961-62; assistant to president Kaiser Aluminum & Chemical Corp., Oakland, California, 1962-64;

manager fin. and personnel, then general manager various divs. Raychem Corp., Menlo Park, California, 1964-83, with office of president, 1983-87, senior vice president telecommunications and tech., 1988-90, president, chief executive officer, 1990—; president Raynet Corp. subsidiary Raychem Corp., 1987-88. Member California Roundtable, San Francisco Committee on Foreign Relations. Jewish. Avocations: sailing, skiing. Office: Raychem Corp 300 Constitution Dr Mailstop 120/7815 Menlo Park California 94025

SALTZMAN, ROBERT PAUL, insurance company executive; born Chicago, October 25, 1942; daughter of Al and Viola (Grossman) S.; married Diane Maureen Schulman, April 10, 1964; children: Amy, Adam, Suzanne. Bachelor of Arts in Math., Northwestern University, 1964. Manager Continental Casualty Company, Chicago, 1964-69; senior vice president Colonial Penn Group, Philadelphia, 1969-83; president, chief executive officer Sun Life Insurance of Am., Atlanta, 1985—; executive vice president marketing Kaufman & Broad (now Broad, Incorporated), Los Angeles, 1987—; board of directors Sun Life Group, Atlanta, Anchor National Fin. Services and Anchor National Life Insurance Company, Phoenix. Office: Sun Life Group of Am 260 Peachtree St Northwest Atlanta Georgia 30303

SAMPSELL, ROBERT BRUCE, toy company executive; born Evanston, Illinois, July 22, 1941; son of David Sylvester and Harriet Corson (Fenner) S.; married Bonnie Louise McClelland, June 26, 1965. Bachelor of Science, Yale University, 1963; Master of Business Administration, Harvard University, 1965. Plant management Procter & Gamble Company, Chicago, 1965-69; with Quaker Oats Company, Chicago, 1969—; president chemicals div. Quaker Oats Company, 1978-81; vice president United States Grocery Products Research & Development, Barrington, Illinois, 1980-83; president Fisher-Price div., East Aurora, New York, from 1983; director M&T Bank, Buffalo, 1984—; vice chairman, chief operating officer, director First Empire State Corp.; board of directors First Empire State Corp., First Operations Resource, Incorporated. Board of directors Indian Creek Nature Center, Cedar Rapids, Iowa, 1973-76, president, 1975-76; trustee Mercy Hospital, Cedar Rapids, 1973-76, Mount Mercy College, 1975-83; board of directors Cedar Rapids Symphony, 1973-76, Greater Buffalo Devel. Foundation, 1983—, Buffalo State College Foundation, 1985; board of directors Planned Parenthood Chicago Area, 1980-83, Buffalo and Erie County, 1984—. Member Toy Manufacturers Am. (board directors 1984—), Buffalo Chamber of Commerce (1984—). Home: 324 Rivermist Dr Buffalo New York 14202 Office: First Empire State Corp One M & T Plaza Buffalo New York 14240

SAMUELSON, PAUL ANTHONY, economics educator; born Gary, Indiana, May 15, 1915; son of Frank and Ella (Lipton) S.; married Marion E. Crawford, July 2, 1938 (deceased); children: Jane Kendall, Margaret Wray, William Frank, Robert James, John Crawford, Paul Reid.; married Risha Eckaus, 1981. Bachelor of Science, University Chicago, 1935; Master of Arts, Harvard University, 1936, Doctor of Philosophy (David A.

Wells prize 1941), 1941; Doctor of Laws, University Chicago, Oberlin College, 1961, Boston College, 1964, Ind. University, 1966, University Michigan, 1967, Claremont Graduate School, 1970, University New Hampshire, 1971, Keio University, 1971, Widener College, 1982, Catholic University at Riva Aguero University, Lima, Peru, 1980; Doctor of Science, East Anglia University, Norwich, England, 1966; Doctor of Literature (honorary), Ripon College, 1962, Northern Michigan University, 1973; Doctor of Humane Letters, Seton Hall College, 1971, Williams College, 1971; Doctor of Science, University Massachusetts, 1972, University Rhode Island, 1972; Doctor of Laws, Harvard, 1972, Gustavus Adolphus College, 1974, University Southern California, 1975, University Pennsylvania, 1976, University Rochester, 1976, Emmanuel College, 1977, Stonehill College, 1978, Widener College, 1982; Doctorate Honoris Causa, University Catholique de Louvain, Belgium, 1976, City University, London, 1980, New University Lisbon, 1985; Doctor of Literature., Valparaiso University, 1987; Doctor of Literature, Columbia U, 1988; Doctor of Science, Tufts University, 1988; Doctor Honoris Causa, University National de Educacion a Distancia, Madrid, 1989. Professor economics Massachusetts Institute of Technology, 1940—, institute professor, 1966, professor emeritus, Gordon Y. Billard fellow, 1986—; member staff Radiation Laboratory, 1944-45; professor international economic relations Fletcher School Law and Diplomacy, 1945; consultant National Resources Planning Board, 1941-43, WPB, 1945, United States Treasury, 1945-52, 61—, Bureau Budget, 1952, RAND Corp., 1948-75, Federal Reserve Board, 1965—; council Economic Advisers, 1960—; economic adviser to President Kennedy; senior adviser Brookings Panel on Economic Activity; member special commission on social sciences National Science Foundation, 1967—; consultant int Economic Council, Congressional Budget Office; Institute professor, Institute professor emeritus, Gordon Y Billard Fellow Massachusetts Institute of Technology, Boston, 1986—; visiting prof of political economic Center Japan-U.South Business and Economic Studies, New York University, 1987—; Stamp Memorial lecturer, London, 1961, Wicksell lecturer, Stockholm, 1962, Franklin lecturer, Detroit, 1962; Hoyt visiting fellow Calhoun College, Yale, 1962; Carnegie Foundation reflective year, 1965-66; John von Neumann lecturer University Wisconsin, 1971; Gerhard Colm Memorial lecturer New School for Social Research, New York City, 1971; Davidson lecturer University New Hampshire, 1971; Sulzbacher Memorial lecturer Columbia Law School, New York City, 1974; J. Willard Gibbs lecturer Am. Math. Society, San Francisco, 1974; John Diebold lecturer Harvard, 1976; Horowitz lecturer Jerusalem and Tel Aviv, 1984; lecturer Harvard 350 Symposium, Harvard University, 1986; Vernon F. Taylor visiting distinguished professor Trinity University, San Antonio, Texas, 1989; Olin lecturer University Virginia Law School, 1989, many other lectureships; acad. consultant Federal Reserve Board. Author: Foundations of Economic Analysis, 1947, enlarged edition, 1983, Economics, 1948-85, Readings in Economics, 1955, 13th edition, 1989 (with R. Dorfman and R.M.

Solow) Linear Programming and Economic Analysis, 1958, Collected Scientific Papers, 5 volumes, 1966, 72, 78, 86; co-author numerous other books.; Contributor numerous articles to professional journals; Columnist for, Newsweek, 1966-81; associate editor: Journal Pub. Econs., Journal International Econs., Journal Fin. Econs., Journal Nonlinear Analysis; adv. board Challenge Magazine; editorial board Proceedings National Acad. Scis. Chairman President's Task Force Maintaining Am. Prosperity, 1964; member National Task Force on Economic Education, 1960-61; economic adviser to President John F. Kennedy, 1959-63; member adv. board National Commission Money and Credit, 1958-60. Hon. fellow London School Econs. and Political Sci. Guggenheim fellow, 1948-49; Ford Foundation research fellow, 1958-59; recipient John Bates Clark medal Am. Economic Association, 1947, Alfred Nobel Memorial prize in econ. sci., 1970, Medal of Honor University Evansville, Illinois, 1970, Albert Einstein Commemorative award, 1971, Alumni medal University Chicago, 1983, Britannica award, 1989. Fellow Brit. Acad. (corr.), Am. Philosophical Society, Econometric Society (vice president 1950, president 1951), Am. Econ. Association (hon.; president 1961); member Committee Econ. Devel. (commission on national goals, research adv. board 1959-60), Am. Acad. Arts and Sciences, International Econ. Association (president 1966-68, hon. president), National Acad. Sciences, Leibniz-Akademie der Wissenschaften und der Literatur (corr. member 1987—) National Association of Investment Clubs (distinguished Service award in Investment Education 1974), Phi Beta Kappa, Omicron Delta Kappa (trustee), Omicron Delta Epsilon (trustee). Home: 94 Somerset St Belmont Massachusetts 02178 Office: Massachusetts Institute of Technology Department Econs Cambridge Massachusetts 02139

SANDERS, WALTER JEREMIAH, III, electronics company executive; born Chicago, September 12, 1936; son of Walter J. and Kathleen (Finn) S.; married Linda Lee Drobman, November 13, 1965 (divorced 1982); children: Tracy Ellen, Lara Whitney, Alison Ashley. Bachelor of Electrical Engineering, University Illinois, 1958. Design engineer Douglas Aircraft Company, Santa Monica, California, 1958-59; applications engineer Motorola, Incorporated, Phoenix, 1959-60; sales engineer Motorola, Incorporated, 1960-61; with Fairchild Camera & Instrument Company, 1961-69; director marketing Fairchild Camera & Instrument Company, Mountain View, California, 1961-68, group director marketing worldwide, 1968-69; president Advanced Micro Devices Incorporated, Sunnyvale, California, until 1987, chairman board, chief executive officer, 1969—; director Donaldson, Lufkin & Jenrette. Member Semicondr. Industry Association (co-founder, director), Santa Clara County Manufacturing Group (co-founder, director). Office: Advanced Micro Devices Incorporated 901 Thompson Place Sunnyvale California 94086

SANDLER, HERBERT M., savings and loan association executive; born New York City, November 16, 1931; son of William B. and Hilda (Schattan) S.; married Marion Osher, March 26, 1961. BSS, City College of New York, 1951; Juris Doctor, Columbia University, 1954. Bar: New York

1956. Assistant counsel Waterfront Commission New York Harbor, 1956-59; partner firm Sandler & Sandler, New York City, 1960-62; president, director, member executive committee Golden West Savings & Loan Association and Golden West Fin. Corp., Oakland, California, 1963-75; chairman board, chief executive officer, director, member executive committee World Savings & Loan Association and Golden West Fin. Corp., Oakland, 1975—; charter member Thrift Institutions Adv. Council to Federal Reserve Board, Oakland, 1963-75; board of directors Federal Home Loan Bank, San Francisco; former chairman legis. and regulation committee California Savings Loan Leage. President, trustee California Neighborhood Services Foundation; chairman Urban Housing Institute; member policy adv. board Center for Real Estate and Urban Econs. U. California, Berkeley. With United States Army, 1954-56. Office: Golden W Fin Corp 1901 Harrison St Oakland California 94612

SANDLER, MARION OSHER, savings and loan association executive; born Biddeford, Maine, October 17, 1930; daughter of Samuel and Leah (Lowe) Osher; married Herbert M. Sandler, March 26, 1961. Bachelor of Arts, Wellesley College, 1952; postgraduate, Harvard U.-Radcliffe College, 1953; Master of Business Administration, New York University, 1958; Doctor of Laws (honorary), Golden Gate University, 1987. Assistant buyer Bloomingdale's (department store), New York City, 1953-55; security analyst Dominick & Dominick, New York City, 1955-61; senior fin. analyst Oppenheimer & Company, New York City, 1961-63; senior vice president, director Golden West Fin. Corp. and World Savings & Loan Association, Oakland, California, 1963-75, vice chairman board, co-mng. officer, director, member executive committee, 1975-80, president, co- chief executive officer, director, member executive committee, 1980—; member Thrift Institutes Adv. Council to Federal Reserve Board, 1989—, vice president, 1989, president, 1990. Vice-chmn. industry adv. committee Federal Savs. and Loan Ins. Corp., 1987-88; board overseers New York University Schools Business, 1987-89; member capital formation task force White House Conference on Small Business, 1979; member President Carter's Housing Task Force, 1980, President's Mgmt. Improvement Council, 1980; member policy adv. board Center for Real Estate and Urban Econs. U. California, Berkeley, 1981—, member executive committee policy adv. board, 1985—; member ad hoc committee to rev. Schools Business Administration U. California, 1984-85; member adv. council Federal National Mortgage. Association, 1983-84; member Thrift Insts. Adv. Council to Federal Reserves Board, 1989—, vice president, 1989, president 1990. Member Phi Beta Kappa, Beta Gamma Sigma. Office: Golden W Fin Corp 1901 Harrison St Oakland California 94612

SANDNER, JOHN FRANCIS, commodity futures broker, lawyer; born Chicago, November 3, 1941; son of James and Margaret (Elmore) S.; married Carole Ruth Erhardt, February 14, 1970; children: Kathleen Dyan, Christopher John, Angela Marie, Michael John, Nicholas James, Allysann Elizabeth.

Bachelor of Arts, Southern Illinois University, 1965; Juris Doctor, University Notre Dame, 1968. Bar: Illinois 1968, United States District Court 1969, United States Supreme Court 1975. Private practice Chicago, 1968—; member Chicago Mercantile Exchange, 1971-91; senior policy advisor 1989-91; chairman board governors Chicago Mercantile Exchange, 1980-82, 86-89, 91—; member International Monetary Market, 1973—; president John F. Sandner & Associates (commodity futures brokers), Chicago, 1973—, Rufenacht, Bromagen, & Hertz, Incorporated (commodity futures clearing firm), Chicago, 1978—; law adv. council member University Notre Dame, 1988—. Member Commodity Adv. Committee, State of Illinois, 1980—; board of directors Fund for Integrative Bio-med. and Educational Research, 1981, Jones Institute for Reproductive Medicine, Ea. Virginia Medical School, 1984—; member Illinois Volunteer Parole Officer Program, 1976-78; commissioner Prospect Heights (Illinois) Park District, 1977-78; trustee Foundation for Brain Life Research, 1983—. Member American Bar Association, Am. Arbitration Association, Illinois Bar Association, Chicago Bar Association (arbitration committee 1976-77, mental health committee 1976-77), National Futures Association (board directors 1982, chairman central region business conduct committee 1982—), Notre Dame Law Association (board directors 1984—), Notre Dame Club of Chicago (governor), Mid-Am. Club, Metropolitan Club. Office: 30 S Wacker Dr Chicago Illinois 60606

SANDS, DON WILLIAM, agricultural products company executive; born Durant, Oklahoma, August 30, 1926; son of William Henry and Mary (Crutchfield) S.; married Joan Cantrell, March 28, 1947; children: Susan Sands Hendrix, Stan W., Steve J. Bachelor of Science, Southeastern Oklahoma State University, 1949. Office manager Durant Cotton Oil & Peanut Corp., Oklahoma, 1947-53; assistant manager Greenwood Products Company, Graceville, Florida, 1953-57; with Cotton Producers Association (changed name to Gold Kist Incorporated, 1970); executive vice president, member executive committee Gold Kist Incorporated, Atlanta, 1978-84, president, chief operating officer, member executive committee, 1984-88, president, chief executive officer, chairman executive committee, 1989—; chairman Golden Poultry Company, Incorporated subsidiary Gold Kist Incorporated, Atlanta, 1987—; board of directors National Data Corp., Atlanta, Illinois Cooperative Futures Company, Chicago, In-Trade, Incorporated, Curacao, Netherlands Antilles, Georgia World Congress Center, Atlanta, Business Council Georgia, Southern Center for International Studies; board of directors, member executive committee, chairman compensation committee Citizens & Southern Georgia Corp., Atlanta; chairman board Golden Poultry Company, Incorporated, Atlanta; member Atlanta District Export Council; member profit sharing committee Citizens & Southern National Bank, Atlanta; board of directors, audit committee National Data Corp., Atlanta. Adv. board member Institute International Education, Atlanta, 1980; adv. board member Japan-U.S. Southeast Association, 1975; board of directors Georgia Board Industry and Trade,

1979, Business Council Georgia, Southern Center for International Studies, Atlanta; board of directors, member executive committee, chairman compensation committee Citizens and Southern Georgia Corp., Atlanta; chairman board trustees, member fin. committee Georgia Council on Economic Education; active Pleasant Hill Presbyterian Church, Duluth, Georgia Served with United States Navy, 1944-46. Member National Council Farmer Coops., Georgia Chamber of Commerce (director), Japan-Am. Society Georgia (chairman board directors), Southeast U.S./Japan Association (member Georgia adv. board, chairman), Atlanta Athletic Club (general chairman 1990 United States Women's Open). Democrat. Presbyterian (elder). Club: Atlanta Athletic (president). Office: Gold Kist Incorporated 244 Perimeter Center Parkway NE Atlanta Georgia 30346

SANFORD, CHARLES STEADMAN, JR., banker; born Savannah, Georgia, October 8, 1936; son of Charles Steadman and Ann (Lawrence) S.; married Mary McRitchie, June 19, 1959; children: Ann Whitney, Charles Steadman III. Bachelor of Arts, University Georgia, 1958; Master of Business Administration, University Pennsylvania, 1960. Vice president national div., relationship manager Bankers Trust Company, New York City, 1961-68, 1st vice president, assistant to head resources management, 1969-71, senior vice president, 1973, head resources management, from 1972, executive vice president, 1974, president, 1983-86, deputy chairman, from 1986, chairman, chief executive officer, 1987—, member management committee, 1979—; chairman New York Clearing House Committee, 1987-88; board of directors Gen Re Corp., Mobil Corp. Member Business Roundtable; board overseers Wharton School, U. Pennsylvania With artillery United States Army, 1958-59. Member Council Foreign Relations. Office: Bankers Trust New York Corp Church St Post Office Box 318 New York New York 10015

SAPP, A. EUGENE, JR., electronics executive; born Winston-Salem, North Carolina, 1936; married. Bachelor of Electrical Engineering, Georgia Institute Tech., 1959. With Texas Instruments Incorporated, 1959-62, SCI Systems Incorporated, Hunstville, Alabama, 1962—; vice president SCI Systems Incorporated, 1973-80, executive vice president, 1980—, now president, chief operating officer. Office: SCI Systems Incorporated 5000 Technology Dr Huntsville Alabama 35807

SARNI, VINCENT ANTHONY, manufacturing company executive; born Bayonne, New Jersey, July 11, 1928; son of Alfred M. and Louise M. (Zoratti) S.; married Dorothy Bellavance, November 4, 1950; children: Louise Marie, Karen Lee, Vincent Anthony. Bachelor of Science, University Rhode Island, 1949; postgraduate, New York University, 1950-52, Harvard University, 1973; Doctor of Laws (honorary), Juniata College, 1979, University Rhode Island, 1985. Plant accountant Rheem Manufacturing Company, Linden, New Jersey, 1950-53; director manufacturing services Crown Can Company, Baltimore, 1953-57; director marketing services Olin Corp., Stamford, Connecticut, 1957-68; with PPG Industries, Incorporated, Pittsburgh, 1968—; vice president marketing industrial chemical department PPG Industries Incorporated, Pittsburgh, 1968-69, vice president, general manager industrial chemical department, 1969-75, vice president, general manager chem div., 1975-77, group vice president chemicals group, 1977-80; senior vice president PPG Industries Incorporated (parent company), Pittsburgh, 1980-83, vice chairman, 1984, chairman, chief executive officer, 1984—; board of directors PNC Fin. Corp., Pittsburgh Baseball Associates; chairman, chief executive officer Institute for Training of Handicapped in Advanced Tech. Chairman Allegheny Conference on Community Devel.; trustee U. Rhode Island Foundation, Juniata College, Carnegie-Mellon U.; board of directors Pittsburgh Guild for Blind, 1980, Allegheny General Hospital; member business adv. council U. Rhode Island, 1975—; chairman Pittsburgh Opera Society; board of directors River City Brass Band; chairman National Organization on Disability. Member Chemical Manufacturers Association, Society Chemical Industry, Business Higher Education Forum, Business Roundtable, The Business Council, Duquesne Club, Rolling Rock Club, Laurel Valley County Club, Chartiers Country Club, Allegheny Club, Point Judith Country Club. Office: PPG Industries Incorporated 1 PPG Place Pittsburgh Pennsylvania 15272

SCHACHT, HENRY BREWER, diesel engine manufacturing company executive; born Erie, Pennsylvania, October 16, 1934; son of Henry Blass and Virginia (Brewer) S.; married Nancy Godfrey, August 27, 1960; children: James, Laura, Jane, Mary. Bachelor of Science, Yale University, 1956; Master of Business Administration, Harvard University, 1962. Sales trainee Am. Brake Shoe Company, New York City, 1956-57; investment manager Irwin Management Company, Columbus, Ind., 1962-64; vice president finance Cummins Engine Company, Incorporated, Columbus, 1964-66; vice president, central area manager international Cummins Engine Company, Incorporated, London, England, 1966-67; group vice president international and subsidiaries Cummins Engine Company, Incorporated, 1967-69; president Cummins Engine Company, Incorporated, Columbus, 1969-77; chairman, chief executive officer Cummins Engine Company, Incorporated, 1977—; board of directors American Telephone and Telegraph Company, CBS., Chase Manhattan Corp., Chase Manhattan Bank N.A. Member Business Council, Council Foreign Relations; member The Associates, Harvard Business School; trustee Brookings Institution, Committee Economic Devel., Conference Board, The Ford Foundation, Yale Corp. Served with United States Naval Reserve, 1957-60. Member Tau Beta Pi. Republican. Office: Cummins Engine Company Incorporated MC-60910 Box 3005 Columbus Indiana 47202

SCHAEFER, GEORGE ANTHONY, manufacturing company executive; born Covington, Kentucky, June 13, 1928; son of George Joseph and Marie Cecelia (Sandheger) S.; married Barbara Ann Quick, August 11, 1951; children: Mark Christopher, Sharon Marie. Bachelor of Science in Commerce, St. Louis University, 1951. With Caterpillar Incorporated, Peoria, Illinois, 1951—, div. manager, 1968-73; plant manager Caterpillar

Incorporated, Decatur, Illinois, 1973-76, vice president, 1976-81, director, 1981-84; vice chairman, executive vice president Caterpillar Incorporated, Peoria, 1984-85, chairman, chief executive officer, 1985-90; fin. and accounting manager Caterpillar France S.A., Grenoble, 1962-68; db. directors San Diego, 1st Chicago Corp.; member business council Emergency Committee for Am. Trade Negotiations. Member adv. council College Commerce and Business Administration U. Ill, Champaign, 1979; trustee Bradley U.; economic devel. committee Proctor Community Hospital Served with United States Marine Corps, 1946-48. Member Business Council. Republican. Roman Catholic. Club: Peoria Country. Office: Caterpillar Incorporated 100 NE Adams St Peoria Illinois 61629

SCHAPIRO, MARY, federal agency administrator. Commr. Securities and Exchange Commission, Washington, District of Columbia. Office: Securities and Exchange Commission 450 5th St Northwest Stop 6-7 Washington District of Columbia 20549

SCHARFFENBERGER, GEORGE THOMAS, diversified industry executive; born Hollis, New York, May 22, 1919; son of George L. and Martha L. (Watson) S.; married Marion Agnes Nelson, July 17, 1948; children: Ann Marie, George Thomas, John Edward, Thomas James, James Nelson, Joan Ellen. Bachelor of Science, Columbia University, 1940; Doctor of Hebrew Literature (honorary), University Southern California, 1984, Georgetown University, 1987. C.P.A., New York. With Arthur Andersen & Company, 1940-43; with International Telephone & Telegraph Corporation (subs.'s and divs.), 1943-59; vice president Litton Industries, Incorporated, 1959-66; chairman, chief executive officer, director City Investing Company, New York City, 1966-85; chairman AmBase Corp., 1984—; board of directors Northrop Corp., The Earl M. Jorgensen Company, Rockefeller Group, Incorporated. Trustee U. Southern California; board of directors Georgetown U.; active Acad. Political Sci. With Army of the United States, World War II. Member California Club, Regency Club (Los Angeles), Brook Club, River Club, Down Town Association, Rockefeller Centers (New York City). Home: 40 E 94th St New York New York 10128 also: 4 Appaloosa Lane Rolling Hills California 90274 also: Snowmass Village Colorado 81615 Office: AmBase Corp 59 Maiden Lane New York New York 10038

SCHARFFENBERGER, WILLIAM J., steel company executive; born New York City, 1921. Degree, Columbia University, 1942. President Wheeling-Pittsburgh Steel Corp., 1987-98, chief executive officer, 1987—, chairman, 1989—; board of directors Alco Standard Corp., Allegheny International Corp. Office: Wheeling-Pitts Steel Corp 1134 Market St Wheeling West Virginia 26003

SCHICK, THOMAS EDWARD, airline executive; born New York City, July 1, 1941; son of Frederick and Nora (Ahearn) S.; married Collete Olga Salvator; children; Margaret Escobar, Carole, Suzanne. AAS in Management, Farmingdale College; Bachelor of Science in Business Administration, State University of New York, Albany. Various management positions to director material management Pan Am Airlines, New York City, 1961-78; senior consultant

Coopers and Lybrand, New York City, 1978-79; director purchase services USAir Incorporated, Pittsburgh, 1979-81, assistant vice president material services, 1980-81, assistant vice president maintenence services, 1981-82, vice president maintenence operations, 1982-86; vice president maintenence and engineering Piedmont Airlines, Winston-Salem, North Carolina, 1986-87, senior vice president operations, 1987—; elected president, chief operating officer Piedmont Aviation, Incorporated, 1988—, also board of directors; senior vice president tech. operations USAir, Incorporated, 1989-90; president Midway Airlines, Chicago, 1990—. Member aeronautic education adv. commission Board Education New York City, 1984—. Member Air Transport Association (various committees 1984—), Society Aeronautical Engineers. Club: Wings. (New York City). Avocations: fishing, golf, walking, sports, reading.

SCHIFF, JOHN JEFFERSON, JR., insurance company executive; born Cincinnati, April 19, 1916; son of John Jefferson and Marguerite (Cleveland) S.; married Mary Reid, July 26, 1941; children: John Jefferson, Suzanne, Thomas R. Bachelor of Science in Commerce, Ohio State University, 1938. Vice chairman Cincinnati Insurance Company, 1979—; president Cincinnati Fin. Corp., 1979-91, chief executive officer, 1987-91; chairman, executive committee Cin Fin Corp., 1991—; chairman board Inter-Ocean Insurance Company, Cincinnati, 1979; vice president Deaconess Hospital of Cincinnati, Griffith Foundation for Insurance. President Cincinnati Art Mus.; trustee Am. Institute for Property and Liability Underwriters. Served to lieutenant commander Supply Corps, United States Navy, 1942-46. Named Ins. Man of Year in Cincinnati, Cincinnati Ins. Board, 1977. Member Cincinnati Chamber of Commerce (vice president 1972). Republican. Methodist. Clubs: Queen City, Western Hills Country, Cincinnati Country, Royal Poinciana Golf. Home: 1926 Beech Grove Dr Cincinnati Ohio 45233 Office: Cincinnati Fin Corp Post Office Box 145496 Cincinnati Ohio 45250

SCHLOEMER, PAUL GEORGE, diversified manufacturing company executive; born Cincinnati, July 29, 1928; son of Leo Bernard and Mary Loretta (Butler) S.; married Virginia Katherine Grona, August 28, 1954; children: Michael, Elizabeth, Stephen, Jane, Daniel, Thomas. Bachelor of Science in Mechanical Engineering, University Cincinnati, 1951; Master of Business Administration, Ohio State University, 1955. Research and devel. engineer Wright Patterson Air Force Base, Dayton, Ohio, 1951-52; Research & Development officer Wright Patterson Air Force Base, Dayton, 1952; resident engineer Parker Hannifin Corp., Dayton, 1957; also Eastern area manager Parker Hannifin Corp., Huntsville, Alabama, 1957-65; vice president aerospace group Parker Hannifin Corp., Irvine, California, 1965-77; president aerospace group Parker Hannifin Corp., Irvine, 1977, corp. vice president, 1978-81, executive vice president, 1981; president Parker Hannifin Corp., Cleveland, 1982-84, chief executive officer, 1984—; board of directors Ameritrust Corp., Cleveland, Rubbermaid Incorporated, AMP Incorporated, N.A.M. Pakrer Hannifin. Captain United States Air Force, 1952-53. Member Machinery and Allied Products Institute (executive committee), Aerospace Industry Association, Conference Board, Incorporated. Republican. Roman Catholic. Club: The Country, Big Canyon Country, The Pepper Pike. Office: Parker Hannifin Corp 17325 Euclid Avenue Cleveland Ohio 44112

SCHMIEGE, ROBERT, railroad executive; born Madison, Wisconsin, May 24, 1941; married. Bachelor of Arts, University Notre Dame, 1963, Juris Doctor, 1966. Attorney National Railway Labor Conference, Chicago, 1966-68, Chicago & North Western Transportation Company, Chicago, 1968-74, Southern Pacific Transportation Company, Los Angeles, 1974-75; partner Albert & Schmiege, Los Angeles, 1975-76; assistant vice president labor relations Chicago & North Western Transportation Company, Chicago, 1976-79, vice president labor relations, 1979-84, senior vice president administration, 1984-88, chairman, president, chief executive officer, 1988—; chairman, president, chief executive officer Chicago North Western Transportation Company, 1988—; also board of directors CNW Corp. and Chicago & North Western Transportation Company, Chicago. Office: CNW Corp 1 Northwestern Center Chicago Illinois 60606

SCHMITT, WOLFGANG RUDOLPH, consumer products executive; born Koblenz, Germany, March 12, 1944; son of Josef H. and M.H. (Baldus) S.; married Toni A. Yoder, June 30, 1974; children: Christopher, Corey, Clayton. Bachelor of Arts, Otterbein College, 1966; AMP, Harvard University Business School, 1986. With Rubbermaid Incorporated, Wooster, Ohio, 1966—, president, general manager housewares products div., 1984-91, executive vice president, board of directors, 1987-91, president, chief operating officer, 1991—; chairman, chief executive officer Rubbermaid-Allibert Incorporated, 1989—. President board of directors Wooster United Way, 1987. Member National Housewares Manufacturers Association (board directors 1986—). Republican. Avocations: archaeology, tennis, sailing. Office: Rubbermaid Incorporated 1147 Akron Road Wooster Ohio 44691

SCHNUCK, CRAIG, grocery stores company executive; born 1948. Master of Business Administration, Cornell University, 1971. With Schnuck Markets, Incorporated, Hazelwood, Missouri, 1971—, vice president, 1975-76, executive vice president, secretary, 1976-83, president, 1983—, also board of directors. Office: Schnuck Markets Incorporated 12921 Enterprise Way Bridgeton Missouri 63044

SCHOFIELD, GEORGE H., corporate executive; born Newark, November 18, 1929; son of George H. and Louise (Minder) S.; married Barbara Shimmin; children—George, Linda, Lauren, Robert. Bachelor of Science, University Vermont, 1951. Various fin. positions General Electric Company, 1951-72; general manager medium steam turbine generator production department General Electric Company, Lynn, Massachusetts, 1972-75; general manager mechanical drives turbine department General Electric Company, Finchburg, Massachusetts, 1975-78; vice president, general manager industrial and marine turbine div. General Electric Company, Lynn, 1978-85; president, chief executive officer Zurn Industries Incorporated,

Erie, Pennsylvania, 1985-86, chairman, chief executive officer, 1986—; board of directors Autoclave Engineers, Incorporated, National Fuel Gas, Incorporated. Member board corporators St. Vincent Foundation for Health & Human Svcs., adv. committee ACES; trustee Gannon U.; board of directors Erie Conference Community Devel., United Way Erie County, 1988—, member executive committee, 1990—; chairman Leadership Giving; president Northwest Pennsylvania Coalition for Health Cost Containment. Member Pennsylvania Business Roundtable, Pennsylvania Chamber Business and Industry (board directors). Avocations: golf; skiing; reading. Office: Zurn Industries Incorporated 1 Zurn Place Erie Pennsylvania 16505

SCHOTT, MARGE, professional sports team owner; born 1928; daughter of Edward and Charlotte Unnewehr; married Charles J. Schott, 1952 (deceased 1968). Owner Schottco, Cincinnati; limited partner Cincinnati Reds, 1981-84, general partner, 1984-85, owner, president, 1985—, chief executive officer. Office: Cincinnati Reds 100 Riverfront Stadium Cincinnati Ohio 45202

SCHREYER, WILLIAM ALLEN, investment firm executive; born Williamsport, Pennsylvania, January 13, 1928; son of William L. and Elizabeth (Engel) S.; married Joan Legg, October 17, 1953; 1 child, Drue Ann. Bachelor of Arts, Pennsylvania State University, 1948. With Merrill Lynch, Incorporated and predecessors, New York City, 1948—; vice president Merrill Lynch, Pierce, Fenner & Smith, Incorporated, New York City, 1965-78, sales director, 1969-72, metropolitan regional director, 1972-73; chairman Merrill Lynch Government Securities, Incorporated, New York City, 1973-76, executive vice president capital markets activities, 1976-78, president, 1978-85, chairman, 1981-85, president, chief operating officer, 1982-85; chief executive officer Merrill Lynch & Company, New York City, 1984—, chairman, 1985—, also bd directors various subsidiary; board of directors Schering-Plough Corp. Chairman Sigma Phi Epsilon Educational Foundation, 1979—. With United States Air Force, 1955-56. Member Business Roundtable (budget task force committee), Committee of Econ. Devel. (trustee), Foreign Policy Association (governor), Center for Strategic and International Studies (trustee), The Conference Board (senior), Japan Society (board directors), Council on Foreign Relations, New York City Partnership (board directors), New Jersey Business Roundtable, Econ. Club New York, Bond Club (New York City), River Club, Links Club, Saturn Club (Buffalo), Springdale Golf Club (Nassau), Bedens Brook Club (Princeton), Eldorado Country Club, Georgetown Club, Metropolitan Club (Washington), Knights of Malta. Roman Catholic. Office: Merrill Lynch & Company World Fin Center N Tower New York New York 10281-1332

SCHULTZ, THEODORE WILLIAM, retired educator, economist; born Arlington, South Dakota, April 30, 1902; son of Henry Edward and Anna Elizabeth (Weiss) S.; married Esther Florence Werth; children: Elaine, Margaret, T. Paul. Graduate, School Agriculture, Brookings, South Dakota, 1924; Bachelor of Science, South Dakota State College, 1927,

Doctor of Science (honorary), 1959; Master of Science, University Wisconsin, 1928, Doctor of Philosophy, 1930; Doctor of Laws (honorary), Grinnell College, 1949, Michigan State University, in 1962, University Illinois, 1968, University Wisconsin, 1968, Catholic University Chile, 1979, University Dijon, France, 1981; Doctor of Laws, North Carolina State University, 1984. Member faculty Iowa State College, Ames, 1930-43; professor, head department economics and sociology Iowa State College, 1934-43; professor economics University Chicago, 1943-72, chairman department economics, 1946-61, Charles L. Hutchinson Distinguished Service professor, 1952-72, professor emeritus, 1972—; economic adviser, occasional consultant Committee Economic Devel., United States Department Agriculture, Department State, Federal Reserve Board, various congl. committees, United States Department Commerce, Food and Agriculture Organization (of the United Nations), United States Department Def., Germany, 1948, Foreign Economic Administration, United Kingdom and Germany, 1945, International Bank for Reconstruction and Development, Resources for the Future, Twentieth Century Fund, National Farm Institute, others.; director National Bureau Economic Research, 1949-67; research director Studies of Tech. Assistance in Latin Am.; board member National Planning Association; chairman Am. Famine Mission to India, 1946; studies of agricultural developments, central Europe and Russia, 1929, Scandinavian countries and Scotland, 1936, Brazil, Uruguay and Argentina, 1941, Western Europe, 1955. Author: Redirecting Farm Policy, 1943, Food for the World, 1945, Agriculture in an Unstable Economy, 1945, Production and Welfare in Agriculture, 1950, The Economic Organization of Agriculture, 1953, Economic Test in Latin America, 1956, Transforming Traditional Agriculture, 1964, The Economic Value of Education, 1963, Economic Crises in World Agriculture, 1965, Economic Growth and Agriculture, 1968, Investment in Human Capital: The Role of Education And of Research, 1971, Human Resources, 1972, Economics of the Family: Marriage, Children, and Human Capital, 1974, Distortions of Agricultural Incentives, 1978, Investing in People: The Economics of Population Quality, 1981; co-author: Measures for Economic Development of Under-Developed Countries, 1951; editor: Journal Farm Econs., 1939-42; contributor articles to professional journals. research fellow Center Advanced Study in Behavioral Sci., 1956-57; recipient Nobel prize in Econs., 1979. Fellow Am. Acad. Arts and Sciences, Am. Farm Economics Association, National Acad. Sciences; member Am. Farm Association, Am. Econ. Association (president 1960, Walker medal 1972), Royal Econ. Society, Am. Philosophical Society, others. Home: 5620 Kimbark Avenue Chicago Illinois 60637 Office: U Chicago Department Econs 1126 E 59th St Chicago Illinois 60637

SCHWAB, CHARLES R., discount broker; born Woodland, California; married Helen O'Neill; 5 children. Graduate, Stanford Business School, Stanford University. Formerly mutual fund manager Marin County, California; founder brokerage San Francisco, 1971; now chairman Charles Schwab & Company, Incorporated. Author: How to be Your Own Stockbroker, 1984. Republican. Office: Charles Schwab & Company Incorporated 101 Montgomery St 28th Floor San Francisco California 94104

SCHWARTZ, BERNARD L., electronics company executive; born 1925. Bachelor of Business Administration, City College of New York, 1948. Partner Schnee, Hover & Schwartz, 1948-62; senior vice president APL Corp., Florida, 1962-68; with Leasco Corp., 1969-72; chairman board, chief executive officer Leasco Corp., Miami Beach, 1969-72; with Loral Corp., New York City, 1972—, former president, 1973-81, chairman, chief executive officer, 1972—; chairman, chief executive officer, K&F Industries, Incorporated. With United States Army, 1943-45. Office: Loral Corp 600 3rd Avenue New York New York 10016

SCHWARTZ, ROBERT GEORGE, insurance company executive; born Czechoslovakia, March 27, 1928; came to United States, 1929, naturalized, 1935; son of George and Frances (Antoni) S.; married Caroline Bachurski, October 12, 1952; children: Joanne, Tracy, Robert G. Bachelor of Arts, Pennsylvania State University, 1949; Master of Business Administration, New York University, 1956. With Metropolitan Life Insurance Company, New York City, 1949—, vice president securities, 1962-70, vice president, 1970-75, senior vice president, 1975-78, executive vice president, 1979-80, vice chairman board, 1980-83; chairman investment committee 1980—; chairman board Metropolitan Life Insurance Company, New York City, 1983—, president, chief executive officer, 1989; board of directors Potlatch Corp., San Francisco, Lowe's Companies, Incorporated, North Wilkesboro, North Carolina, Communications Satellite Corp., Washington, Mobil Corp., New York City, Reader's Digest Association, Incorporated, Consolidated Edison Company of New York, CS First Boston, Incorporated, Am. Quality Foundation, Am. Council Life Insurance, Business Council New York State. Trustee Committee for Economic Devel., Economic Club of New York, Foundation for Malcolm Baldridge National Quality Award, Incorporated; vice chairman Greater New York council Boy Scouts Am.; member board overseers Leonard Stern School Business New York University. With Army of the United States, 1950-52. Member Business Council, Business Roundtable, New York State Business Roundtable, Alpha Chi Rho. Clubs: Seaview Country (Absecon, New Jersey); Springdale Country (Princeton, New Jersey); Sky (New York City). Office: Met Life Ins Company 1 Madison Avenue New York New York 10010

SCOTT, JONATHAN LAVON, corporate executive; born Nampa, Idaho, February 2, 1930; son of Buell Bonnie and Jewel Pearl (Horn) S.; children: Joseph Buell, Anthony Robert (deceased), Richard Teles, Daniel Ross. Bachelor of Arts magna cum laude, College Idaho, 1951; graduate, Advanced Management Program, Harvard University, 1968, 69. With Albertson's Incorporated, Boise, Idaho, 1955-75; vice chairman board, chief executive officer Albertson's Incorporated, 1972-75; vice chairman board Great Atlantic & Pacific Tea Company, Incorporated, Montvale, New Jersey, 1975; chairman board, chief executive officer Great Atlantic & Pacific Tea Company, Incorporated, 1975-80, J.L. Scott Enterprises Incorporated, Irving, Texas, 1980-86; chairman, chief executive officer Am. Superstores Incorporated, Wilmington, Del., 1987-89; president, chief executive officer Am. Stores Company, Salt Lake City, 1990—; board of directors Morrison-Knudsen Company, Trus Joist Corp. Trustee Committee Economic Devel. Served to 1st lieutenant United States Air Force, 1953-55. Home: 3898 Thousand Oaks Circuit Salt Lake City Utah 84124

SCOTT, WALTER, JR., construction company executive; born 1931. Bachelor of Science, Colorado State University, 1953. With Peter Kiewit Sons, Incorporated, Omaha, 1953—, manager Cleveland district, 1962-64, vice president, 1964, executive vice president, 1965-79, chairman board of directors, president, 1979—; also president Joslyn Art Mus., Omaha. Served with United States Air Force, 1954-56. Office: Peter Kiewit Sons Incorporated 1000 Kiewit Plaza Omaha NE 68131 also: Joslyn Art Mus 2200 Dodge St Omaha NE 68102

SCRIPPS, CHARLES EDWARD, newspaper publisher; born San Diego, January 27, 1920; son of Robert Paine and Margaret Lou (Culbertson) S.; married Louann Copeland, June 28, 1941 (divorced 1947); married Lois Anne MacKay, October 14, 1949 (deceased 1990); children: Charles Edward Jr., Marilyn Joy, Eaton Mackay, Julia Osborne. Student, College William and Mary, 1938-40, Pomona College, 1940-41. Reporter Cleveland Press, 1941; successor-trustee Edward W. Scripps Trust, 1945, chairman board trustees, 1948—; vice president E.W. Scripps Company, 1946—, chairman, 1953—, also board of directors; board of directors various Scripps-Howard newspapers and affiliated enterprises; board of directors Star Bank, Star Banc Corp., Cincinnati. Board of directors Community Improvement Corp. of Cincinnati; member national adv. board Salvation Army; trustee Freedoms Foundation; board governors Webb School Served to lieutenant (junior grade) United States Coast Guard Reserve, 1942-45. Member CAP, Theta Delta Chi. Office: Scripps Howard 1100 Central Trust Tower Cincinnati Ohio 45202

SCULLEY, JOHN, computer company executive; born New York City, April 6, 1939; son of John and Margaret Blackburn (Smith) S.; married Carol Lee Adams, March 7, 1978; children: Margaret Ann, John Blackburn, Laura Lee. Student, Rhode Island School Design, 1960; Bachelor of Architecture, Brown University, 1961; Master of Business Administration, University Pennsylvania, 1963. Assistant account executive Marschalk Company, New York City, 1963-64, account executive, 1964-65, account supervisor, 1965-67; director marketing Pepsi-Cola Company, Purchase, New York, 1967-69, vice president marketing, 1970-71, senior vice president marketing, 1971-74, president, chief executive officer, 1977-83; president PepsiCo Foods, Purchase, 1974-77; president, chief executive officer Apple Computer Incorporated, Cupertino, California, 1983—; also chairman Apple Computer Incorporated, Cupertino, Calif, 1986—; board of directors Comsat Corp. Chairman Wharton Grad. Executive Board, 1980; member art adv. committee Brown U., 1980; board of directors Keep Am. Beautiful.; member board overseers Wharton School, U. Pennsylvania. Member United States Chamber of Commerce. Clubs: Indian Harbor, New York Athletic; Coral Beach (Bermuda); Wharton Business Sch. of New York (board dirs.); Camden (Maine) Yacht. Office: Apple Computer Incorporated 20525 Mariana Avenue Cupertino California 95014

SEATON, W. B. (BRUCE SEATON), container transport and distribution executive; born Philadelphia, April 1, 1925; married. Bachelor of Science, University of California at Los Angeles, 1949. With J.F. Forbes & Company, 1950-53; treasurer, controller Douglas Oil Company, 1953-66; assistant treasurer Occidental Petroleum Company, 1966-70; vice president, secretary, treasurer Natomas Company, 1970-72, vice president fin., treasurer, 1972-74, senior vice president, 1974-78, executive vice president marketing and transportation, 1978-79, executive vice president, director, 1979-83, president, 1983; president, chief operating officer Am. President Lines Limited, Oakland, California, 1977-83, chief executive officer, 1983—; chairman, chief executive officer, board of directors Am. President Companies, Oakland, 1983—, president, 1983-90. Board trustees University of California at Los Angeles Foundation. Recipient Excellence in Tech. award Gartner Group, 1988, International Achievement award World Trade Club of San Francisco, 1988; named Maritime Man of Year United States Propeller Club, 1987. Office: Am President Cos Limited 1111 Broadway Oakland California 94607

SEEGERS, PAUL R., construction company executive; born Hammond, Indiana, January 27, 1930; married. Bachelor of Arts, Valparaiso University, 1952; Master of Business Administration, Northwestern University, 1958. With Centex Corp, Dallas, 1961—, president, 1972-78, vice chairman, co-chief executive officer, 1978-85, chairman, 1985—; chief executive officer Centex Corp, 1985-90; also director, chairman executive committee Centex Corp, Dallas; board of directors RepublicBank Corp., Dallas. Office: Centex Corp 3333 Lee Parkway Box 19000 Dallas Texas 75219

SEELENFREUND, ALAN, distribution company executive; born New York City, October 22, 1936; son of Max and Gertrude (Roth) S.; married Ellyn Bolt; 1 child, Eric. BME, Cornell University, 1959, Master in Industrial Engineering, 1960; Doctor of Philosophy in Management Science, Stanford University, 1967. Assistant professor business administration Grad. School Business Stanford University, Palo Alto, California, 1966-71; management consultant Strong, Wishart and Associates, San Francisco, 1971-75; various management positions McKesson Corp., San Francisco, 1975-84, vice president, chief fin. officer, 1984-86, executive vice president, chief fin. officer, 1986-89, chairman, chief executive officer, 1989—, also board of directors; board of directors Armor All Products Corp. Member World Affairs Council Northern California, San Francsico Chamber of Commerce (board directors), Business Roundtable, California Business Roundtable, Bankers Club, St. Francis Yacht Club, Villa Taverna Club. Avocations: sailing, skiing. Office: McKesson Corp 1 Post St San Francisco California 94104

SEGER, MARTHA ROMAYNE, government official, economist; born Adrian, Michigan, 1932. Bachelor of Business Administration, University Michigan, 1954, Master of Business Administration, 1955, Doctor of Philosophy, 1971. Began career in economics department General Motors Corporation; later with Federal Reserve Bank Chicago, 3 years; chief economist Detroit Bank & Trust Company, 1967-74 ; vice president in charge of economics and investment Bank of Commonwealth, Detroit, 1971-74; associate professor business economics University Michigan, 1976-79; associate professor economics and fins. Oakland University, 1980; commissioner fin institutions State of Michigan, 1981-82; professor fin. Central Michigan University, 1983-84; member board governors Federal Reserve System, 1984—. Office: FRS Bd of Govs 20th & Constitution Avenue Northwest Washington District of Columbia 20551

SEIDMAN, L(EWIS) WILLIAM, federal agency administrator; born Grand Rapids, Michigan, April 29, 1921; son of Frank E. and Esther (Lubetsky) S.; married Sarah Berry, March 3, 1944; children: Thomas, Tracy, Sarah, Carrie, Meg, Robin. Bachelor of Arts, Dartmouth College, 1943; Bachelor of Laws, Harvard University, 1948; Master of Business Administration, University Michigan, 1949. Bar: Michigan 1949, District of Columbia 1977. Special assistant fin. affairs to governor of Michigan 1963-66; national managing partner Seidman & Seidman C.P.A.s, New York City, 1969-74; assistant for economic affairs to President Gerald R. Ford, 1974-77; director Phelps Dodge Corp., New York City, 1977-82; vice chairman Phelps Dodge Corp., 1980-82; dean College Business Administration Arizona State University, Tempe, 1982-85; chairman Federal Deposit Insurance Corporation, Washington, 1985—; chairman Detroit Federal Reserve Bank Chicago, 1970; co-chairman White House Conference on Productivity, 1983-84. Served to lieutenant United States Naval Reserve, 1942-46. Decorated Bronze Star. Member Am. Institution C.P.A.s, Michigan Bar Association, District of Columbia Bar Association. Clubs: Chevy Chase (Maryland); University (New York City and Washington); Crystal Downs (Michigan). Home: 1694 31st St Northwest Washington District of Columbia 20007 Office: FDIC 550 17th St Northwest Washington District of Columbia 20429

SELLS, BOAKE ANTHONY, retail company executive; born Fort Dodge, Iowa, June 24, 1937; son of Lyle M. and Louise (Gadd) S.; married Marian S. Stephenson, June 20, 1959; children: Damian, Brian, Jean Ann. BSC, University Iowa, 1959; Master of Business Administration, Harvard University, 1969. Business office manager Northwestern Bell Tel., Des Moines, 1959-63; salesman Hydraulic Companies, Fort Dodge, 1964-67; president Cole National Corp., Cleveland, 1969-83; vice chairman Dayton Hudson Corp., Minneapolis, 1983-84, president, 1984-87; chairman, president, chief executive officer Revco D.South, Incorporated, Twinsburg, Ohio, 1987—; board of directors Promus Companies. Pub.-sector representative to adv. board United States Olympic

Committee, 1989—; trustee Cleveland Center for Contemporary Art, Cleveland Play House, Cleveland Tomorrow. Member National Retail Federation (board directors), National Association Chain Drug Stores, Incorporated (board directors). Office: Revco DS Incorporated 1925 Enterprise Parkway Twinsburg Ohio 44087

SELLS, HAROLD E., retail company executive; born Ozark, Arkansas, 1928; married. Various operational, marketing positions Kinney Shoe Corp., 1945-65, president real estate div., 1965-74; with Woolworth Corp (formerly F.W. Woolworth Company), New York City, 1974—; vice president real estate F.W. Woolworth Company, New York City, 1974-80, senior vice president corp. devel., 1980-81, senior vice president international operations, property devel., 1982, president, chief operating officer, 1983-87, chairman, chief executive officer, 1987—, also board of directors; board of directors Bank of New York, Centennial Insurance Company, Atlantic Reins. Company; trustee Atlantic Mutual Insurance Company. Office: Woolworth Corp Woolworth Building 233 Broadway New York New York 10279

SEMROD, T. JOSEPH, banker; born Oklahoma City, December 13, 1936; son of L.J. and Theda Jo (Hummel) S.; married Janice Lee Wood, June 1, 1968 (divorced 1988); children: Ronald, Catherine, Christopher, Elizabeth; married Jaye Patricia Hewitt, May 27, 1989; 1 child, Kelsey. Bachelor of Arts in Political Science, University Oklahoma, 1958, Bachelor of Laws, 1963. Bar: Oklahoma 1963. With Liberty National Bank, Oklahoma City, 1963-81; vice president Liberty National Bank, 1967-69, senior vice president, 1969-71, executive vice president, 1971-73, president, 1973-81; president Liberty National Corp., Oklahoma City, 1976-81; chairman board, president, chief executive officer United Jersey Banks (name now UJB Fin. Corp.), Princeton, New Jersey, 1981—; chairman board of directors United Jersey Bank, Hackensack, New Jersey, 1981—. Trustee, member executive committee National Urban League; member board advisors Outward Bound, Ind., 1984—, Ind. College Fund New Jersey, 1986-90; commissioner Citizens Commission on Acquired Immune Deficiency Syndrome, board of directors, international fin. conference; chairman board regents Stonier Grad. School Banking, Rutgers U., 1983; member New Jersey Transportation Trust Fund Authority, 1985-87; chairman The Partnership for New Jersey, 1989-90, chairman education task force committee, 1985-88. 1st lieutenant United States Army, 1958-60. Member Am. Bankers Association, New Jersey Bankers Association (executive committee), New Jersey Bar Association, Oklahoma Bar Association, Association Reserve City Bankers (board directors 1987-89), Regional Plan Association (board directors), Young President Organization, Am. Running and Fitness Association (board directors 1983-86), New Jersey State Chamber of Commerce (board directors). Democrat. Roman Catholic. Clubs: Bedens Brook (Skillman, New Jersey); River (New York City); Metedeconk (Jackson, New Jersey). Office: UJB Fin Corp 301 Carnegie Center Post Office Box 2066 Princeton New Jersey 08543

SHAFTO, ROBERT AUSTIN, insurance company executive; born Council Bluffs, Iowa, September 15, 1935; son of Glen Granville and Blanche (Radigan) S.; married Jeanette DeFino, December 17, 1954; children: Robert, Dennis, Teri, Shari, Michael. Bachelor of Science in Actuarial Science, Drake University, Des Moines, 1959. Manager computer services Guarantee Mutual Life Insurance Company, Omaha, 1959-65; vice president Beta div. Electronic Data Systems, Dallas, 1965-71; from 2d vice president to vice president for computer systems devel. and information services The New England, Boston, 1972-75, senior vice president policy holder and computer services, 1975-81, administrative vice president, 1981-82, executive vice president individual insurance operations, 1982-88, president insurance and personal fin. services, 1988-90, president, chief operating officer, 1990—; also board of directors and chairman board New England Fin. Advisors, Boston; board of directors, president New England Variable Life. Board overseers Children's Hospital, Boston, 1989—; board of directors The Computer Mus., Boston, 1989—; member corp. Dana Farber Cancer Institute; board of directors United Way of Massachusetts. Member Life Insurance Marketing and Research Assns. (member strategic mktgs. issues committee), ACLI , Commission on Fin. Svcs. Integration, International Business Machines Corporation Insurance Industries Customer Adv. Council. Roman Catholic. Avocations: tennis, golf, scuba diving, jogging. Office: New England Mut Life Ins Company 501 Boylston St Boston Massachusetts 02117

SHANK, STEPHEN GEORGE, lawyer, toy manufacturing executive; born Tulsa, December 6, 1943; son of Louis Warren and Lillian Margaret Shank; married Judith Frances Thompson, July 17, 1966; children: Susan, Mary. Bachelor of Arts, University Iowa, 1965; Master of Arts (Woodrow Wilson fellow), Fletchers School, Tufts University, 1966; Juris Doctor, Harvard University, 1972. Bar: Minnesota 1972. Partner Dorsey, Marquart, Windhorst, West & Halladay, Minneapolis, 1972-74, 78-79, Dorsey, Windhorst, Hannaford, Whitney & Halladay, Minneapolis, 1978-79; general counsel Tonka Corp., Hopkins, Minnesota, 1974-78, secretary, 1974-79, president, chief executive officer, 1979-88; chairman, chief executive officer Tonka Corp., Minnetonka, Minnesota, 1988—, also board of directors; assistant professor law William Mitchell College Law, 1974-77; board of directors Nat Computer Systems, Incorporated, Eden Prairie, Minnesota. Associate editor: Harvard Law Rev., 1971-72. Board of directors Loring-Nicollet-Bethlehem Center, Minneapolis, 1977, Walker Art Center, 1989—; board governors Methodist Hospital, 1982-85; trustee Minneapolis Society Fine Arts, 1986-87, Minnesota Medical Foundation, 1986-87; chairman Vanguard A div., Minneapolis United Way Campaign, 1986. With United States Army, 1966-69. Decorated Distinguished Service Medal. Member American Bar Association, Minnesota State Bar Association, National Association Manufacturers (board directors 1985, 87—), Toy Manufacturers Am. (vice-chmn. 1983, adv. committee 1983-84, chairman 1984). Home: 330 Peavey Lane Wayzata Minnesota 55391 Office: Tonka Corp 6000

Clearwater Dr Minnetonka Minnesota 55343

SHAPIRA, DAVID S., food chain executive; born 1942; married. Bachelor of Arts, Oberlin College, 1964; Master of Arts, Stanford University, 1966. Vice president Giant Eagle, Incorporated (formerly Giant Eagle Markets, Incorporated), Pittsburgh, 1974-81, president, from 1981, chief executive officer, also board of directors; chief executive officer Phar-Mor Incorporated, Youngstown. Office: Giant Eagle Incorporated 101 Kappa Dr Pittsburgh Pennsylvania 15238

SHARP, ROBERT GLENN, insurance company executive; born Stockton, California, May 9, 1935; son of David G. and Muriel R. (Burger) S.; married Patricia Ann Fenley, June 6, 1957 (divorced 1974); children: Brenda, Linda, Steven, David. Bachelor of Arts, University California, Sacramento, 1957. Senior vice president California Western Life Insurance Company, 1958-70, Life/Equity Information Company, 1970-75; administrative officer Nationwide Life Insurance Company, Columbus, Ohio, 1975-79; president, chief executive officer Keystone Provident Life Insurance Company, Boston, Ohio, 1979—; board of directors Keystone Provident Life Insurance Company; board of directors Keystone Provident Fin. Services Corp., Boston. Fellow Life Office Management Association; member Association CLUs, National Association Securities Dealers (registered principal). Office: Keystone Provident Life Ins Company 99 High St Boston Massachusetts 02110

SHAYKIN, LEONARD P., investor; born Chicago, November 17, 1943; son of Lawrence L. and Rose (Yaker) S.; married Norah Josephine Kan, June 26, 1966; children: Benjamin, Gabriel, Rebecca. Bachelor of Arts, University Chicago, 1965, Master of Arts, 1966, Master of Business Administration, 1973; postgraduate, University Sussex, Brighton, England, 1970. Investment officer First Capital Corp., Chicago, 1970-74; assistant to chairman Apeco Corp., Chicago, 1975-76; div. president Brown Manufacturing Company, Woodstock, Illinois, 1976-78; vice president Citicorp Venture Capital, New York City, 1978-79; vice president, director Citicorp Capital Investors, New York City, 1979-82; managing partner Adler & Shaykin, New York City, 1983—; board of directors Addiction Recovery Corp. Waltham, Massachusetts, GP Tech. Incorporated, Somerville, New Jersey, Joy Techs., Incorporated, Pittsburgh, Best Products, Incorporated, Richmond, Folger-Adam Incorporated, Illinois, Athena Ptnrs., Israel; chairman, board of directors Peterson Outdoor Advertising, Incorporated, Orlando, 1986-88, Chicago Sun-Times, 1986—; chairman, president New York Venture Capital Forum, New York City, 1983; chairman USIL Investments, Israel. Chairman Hebrew Arts School and Merkin Concert Hall, New York City, 1983-86. Avocations: sailing, skiing. Home: 101 Central Park W Apartment 2F New York New York 10023 Office: Adler & Shaykin 375 Park Avenue New York New York 10152 also: Chicago Sun-Times Incorporated 401 N Wabash Room 110 Chicago Illinois 60611

SHEA, FRANCIS XAVIER, banker; born New York City, February 8,

1941; son of Francis Xavier and Virginia S.; married Joy Allison, May 24, 1980; children—Francis Xavier, Caitlin Allison; children by previous marriage—Deirdre Ellen, Maura Elizabeth. Bachelor of Science cum laude, Lehigh University, 1962. Trainee Chase Manhattan Bank, New York City, 1962-64, assistant treasurer, 1964-68, bank forward planning group manager, 1968-70, staff group manager international department, 1970-75, service products group manager domestic instnl. banking, 1975-80; Asia instnl. manager Chase Manhattan Bank, Hong Kong, 1980-83; country manager Chase Manhattan Bank, Jakarta Selatan, Indonesia, 1983-88; Asia trade fin. executive Chase Manhattan Bank, Jakarta Selatan, 1989—. Contributor articles to professional journals. Member The American Club. Avocations: sports; astronomy; hiking. Home: #4 Red Hill Park, #12 Pak Pat, Shan Road, Tai Tam Hong Kong Office: Chase Manhattan Bank, World Trade Ctr-12, Causeway Bay Hong Kong

SHEINBERG, SIDNEY JAY, recreation and entertainment company executive; born Corpus Christi, Texas, January 14, 1935; son of Harry and Tillie (Grossman) S.; married Lorraine Gottfried, August 19, 1956; children: Jonathan J., William David. Bachelor of Arts, Columbia College, 1955; Bachelor of Laws, Columbia University, 1958. Bar: California 1958. Associate in law University of California at Los Angeles School Law, 1958-59; with MCA, Incorporated, Universal City, California, 1959—, president TV div., 1971-74, corp. executive vice president, 1969-73, corp. president, chief operating officer, 1973—. Member Association Motion Picture and Television Producers (chairman board). Office: MCA Incorporated 100 Universal City Plaza North Hollywood California 91608

SHERMAN, GEORGE M., manufacturing company executive; born New York City, August 6, 1941; son of Joseph B. and Fredericka (Hand) S.; married Betsy Rae Bicknell, November 26, 1966; children: Jonathan, David, Michael, Matthew. Bachelor of Science, Long Island University, 1963; Master of Business Administration, University Louisville, 1971. Product general manager General Electric Company, Bridgeport, Connecticut, 1966-79; president Weed Eater div. Emersen Electric Company, Houston, 1979-80; president Skil Corp. div. Emerson Electric Company, Chicago, 1980-82; group vice president United States power tools group Black & Decker Corp., Baltimore, 1985, senior vice president, president power tools group, from 1986, then executive vice president, president power tools group, until 1990; now chief executive officer Danaher Corp, Washington, District of Columbia, 1990—; member adv. board National Home Center Show, Chicago, 1987; board of directors D.I.Y. Research Institute, Lincolnshire, Illinois, 1988. Board of directors Center Stage, Baltimore, 1988. Served with United States Army, 1964-66. Member Am. Management Association (member general management council 1988). Clubs: Center (Baltimore); Hillendale Country (Phoenix, Maryland). Avocations: flying, skiing, scuba diving, racquetball, golf. Office: Black & Decker Corp 1250 24th St Northwest Washington District of Columbia 20037

SHERMAN, JEFFREY BARRY, retail executive; born Passaic, New Jersey, June 25, 1948; son of Maxwell and Elinor (Richman) S.; married Karin Lynn Swann, May 1, 1971; children—Erik, Brett, Peter, Kristin. Bachelor of Science in Economics, City College of New York, 1971; Master of Business Administration, New York University, 1975. With Bloomingdale's, New York City, 1971—; vice president merchandising Bloomingdale's, 1982-83, senior vice president, 1983-85, executive vice president, from 1985, now president. Avocations: skiing; sailing. Office: Bloomingdale's 59th St & Lexington New York New York 10022

SHERRILL, HUGH VIRGIL, investment banker; born Long Beach, California, 1920. Educated, Yale. Senior director Prudential-Bache Securities, Incorporated, 1977—. Trustee Memorial Hospital, New York City, Boys' Club. Office: Prudential-Bache Securities Incorporated 1 Sea Port Plaza 34th Floor New York New York 10292

SHIPLEY, WALTER VINCENT, banker; born Newark, November 2, 1935; son of L. Parks and Emily (Herzog) S.; married Judith Ann Lyman, September 14, 1957; children: Barbara, Allison, Pamela, Dorothy, John. Student, Williams College, 1954-56; Bachelor of Science, New York University, 1961. With Chemical Bank, New York City, 1956—, executive vice president in charge international div., 1978-79, senior executive vice president, 1979-81, president, 1982-83, chairman board, 1983—; Board directors Champion International Corp., NYNEX Corp., Reader's Digest Association, Incorporated. Board of directors Japan Society, Lincoln Center for Performing Arts Incorporated, New York City Partnership Incorporated, Goodwill Industries Greater New York Incorporated, United Way Tri-State; trustee New York University. Member The Business Council, Business Roundtable, Council Foreign Relations, New York Chamber of Commerce (board directors), Links, Augusta National Golf Club, Baltusrol Golf Club (Springfield, New Jersey), Blind Brook Golf Club. Office: Chem Banking Corp 277 Park Avenue New York New York 10172

SHOEMATE, CHARLES RICHARD, agricultural products executive; born LaHarpe, Illinois, December 10, 1939; son of Richard Osborne and Mary Jane (Gillette) S.; married Nancy Lee Gordon, September 16, 1962; children: Steven, Jeffrey, Scott. Bachelor of Science, Western Illinois University, 1962; Master of Business Administration, University Chicago, 1973. Supervisor Corn Products Company, Summit, Illinois, 1962-72; comptroller Corn Products Unit of CPC International, Englewood Cliffs, New Jersey, 1972-74; plant manager Corn Products Unit of CPC International, Corpus Christi, Texas, 1974-76; vice president operations Corn Products Unit of CPC International, Englewood Cliffs, 1976-81; president Can. Starch Company, Montreal, Quebec, 1981-83; vice president Corn Refining div. CPC International, Englewood Cliffs, 1983-86, president, 1986-88; corp vice president CPC International, Englewood Cliffs, 1983-88, president, 1988—, chairman, chief executive officer, 1990. Office: CPC International Incorporated International Plaza Englewood Cliffs New Jersey 07632

SHUGART, ALAN F., electronic computing equipment company executive; born Los Angeles, September 27, 1930. Bachelor of Science in Engineering and Physics, University Redlands, 1951. Director engineering International Business Machines Corporation, San Jose, California, 1952-69; vice president Memorex Corp., Sunnyvale, California, 1969-73; president Shugart Associates, 1973-78; chairman, chief executive officer Seagate Tech., Scotts Valley, California, 1978—, also board of directors. Office: Seagate Tech 920 Disc Dr Scotts Valley California 95066

SIGLER, ANDREW CLARK, forest products company executive; born Brooklyn, September 25, 1931; son of Andrew J. and Eleanor (Nicholas) S.; married Margaret Romefelt, June 16, 1956; children: Andrew Clark, Patricia, Elizabeth. Bachelor of Arts, Dartmouth, 1953; Master of Business Administration, Amos Tuck School, 1956. With Champion Papers Company, Hamilton, Ohio, 1957—; president Champion Papers div. Champion International Corp., 1972, executive vice president, director parent company, 1972-74, president, chief executive officer, Stamford, Connecticut, 1974-79, chairman board, chief executive officer, 1979—; director Bristol-Myers Squibb Company, Chemical Bank, General Electric Company. Trustee Dartmouth College Served from 2d lieutenant to 1st lieutenant United States Marine Corps Reserve, 1953-55. Office: Champion International Corp 1 Champion Plaza Stamford Connecticut 06921

SILAS, CECIL JESSE, petroleum company executive; born Miami, Florida, April 15, 1932; son of David Edward and Hilda Videll (Carver) S.; married Theodosea Hejda, November 27, 1965; children—Karla, Peter, Michael, James. Bachelor of Science in Chemical Engineering, Georgia Institute Tech., Atlanta, 1953. With Phillips Petroleum Company, Bartlesville, Oklahoma, 1953—; president Europe-Africa, Brussels and London Phillips Petroleum Company, 1968-74; managing director natural resource group Europe/Africa London, 1974-76; vice president gas and gas liquids div. natural resources group Bartlesville, 1976-78, senior vice president natural resources group, 1978-80, executive vice president natural resources group, 1980-82, president, chief operating officer, 1982-85, chairman, chief executive officer, 1985—; also board of directors, member executive committee; director First National Bank, Tulsa. Board of directors Junior Achievement, Stamford, Connecticut, Regional Medical Devel. Foundation, Bartlesville, Business-Industry Political Action Committee, Washington, Okla Research Foundation, Oklahoma City, TARGET-Drug Prevention div. National Federation High Schools, Boys Clubs Am., New York City; trustee U. Tulsa, Georgia Tech. Foundation Incorporated, Atlanta; trustee Frank Phillips Foundation, Bartlesville, Oklahoma; member Am. Council Education, Bus.-Higher Education Forum; partron councillor Atlanic Clun. of the United States; trustee, member projects committee Bluestem Regional Medical Devel. Foundation; member Brit.-N.Am. Committee; board of directors Ethics Resource Center, Incorporated; trustee Frank Phillips Foundation, Incorporated; trustee Nature Conservancy; board of directors Oklahoma Foundation for Excellence; member chmn.'s adv. council Oklahoma Green Country, Incorporated Served to 1st lieutenant Chem. Corps Army of the United States, 1954-56. Decorated commander Order St. Olaf (Norway); inducted into Georgia Institute Tech. Athletic Hall of Fame, 1959, recipient Former Scholar-Athlete Total Person award, 1988; inducted into Oklahoma Business Hall of Fame, 1989; named CEO of Year, International TV Association, 1987. Member Conference Board, Am. Petroleum Institute (board directors, management committee), United States Chamber of Commerce (chairman board directors 1991), Atlantic Council, Council on Foreign Relations, Bartlesville Area Chamber of Commerce, Oklahoma State Chamber of Commerce and Industry (board directors long-range planning committee), Phi Delta Theta. Avocations: fishing, golf, hunting. Office: Phillips Petroleum Company 18 Phillips Building Bartlesville Oklahoma 74004

SIMMONS, HARDWICK, investment banker; born Baltimore, June 8, 1940; son of Edward Ball and Margaret (Hardwick) S.; married Sarah Bradlee Dolan, September 9, 1962; children—Elizabeth, Huntington, Benjamin. Bachelor of Arts, Harvard University, 1962, Master of Business Administration, 1966. With Shearson Lehman Brothers Incorporated, 1966—; regional officer Shearson Lehman Brothers Incorporated, New England, 1972-75; vice chairman, director Shearson Lehman Hutton Incorporated (formerly Shearson Lehman Brothers Incorporated), New York City, 1975-90; chief executive officer Prudential Securities Incorporated, New York City, 1990—; director Chicago Board Options Exchange. Served with United States Marine Corps Reserve, 1959-60. Member Bond Club New York City. Republican.

SIMMONS, JOSEPH JACOB, III, federal commissioner; born Muskogee, Oklahoma, March 26, 1925; son of Jacob, Jr. and Eva (Flowers) S.; married Bernice Elizabeth Miller, January 30, 1947; children: Jacob IV, Mary Agnes, Bernice, Jacolyn, Eva Frances. Student, University Detroit, 1942-44, 46-47; Bachelor of Science in Geological Engineering, St. Louis University, 1949. Registered professional engineer, Oklahoma. Vice president, secretary-treasurer, geologist Simmons Royalty Company, Muskogee, 1949-61; regional oil and gas mobilization specialist United States Department of the Interior, Battle Creek, Michigan, 1961-62; domestic petroleum production specialist Office of Oil and Gas United States Department of the Interior, Washington, 1962-66, assistant director Office of Oil and Gas, 1966-68, deputy administrator Oil Import Administration, 1968-69, administrator Oil Import Administration, 1969-70, Under Secretary, 1983-84; vice president government relations Amerada Hess Corp., New York City, 1970-82; commissioner Interstate Commerce Commission, Washington, 1982-83, 84—; vice chairman Interstate Commerce Commission, 1986, 89; member fuel oil marketing adv. committee Department Energy, 1978-82; commissioner President's Commission on Executive Exchange, 1970-81; commissioner Statue of Liberty Ellis Island Commission, 1983-88, board of directors Foundation, 1984-86 ;

member National Academy of Sciences Board of Earth Sciences and Resources, 1984—; member adv. board Department of Interior Outer Continental Shelf, 1984—. Youth director National Association for the Advancement of Colored People, 1950-55; candidate Oklahoma House of Representatives, 1956, City Council, 1956; trustee Madonna College, Livonia, Michigan, 1969-76. Served with United States Army Air Force, 1944-46. Recipient Alumni Merit award St. Louis University, 1968, Special Act of Service award Department Interior, 1963, Outstanding Performance award, 1968, Distinguished Service award, 1970. Member Am. Association Petroleum Geologists (Pub. Service award 1984), Society Petroleum Engineers, American Institute of Mining, Metallurgy and Petroleum Engineers.

SIMMONS, RICHARD DE LACEY, mass media executive; born Cambridge, Massachusetts, December 30, 1934; son of Ernest J. and Winifred (McNamara) S.; married Mary DeWitt Bleecker, May 20, 1961; children: Christopher DeWitt, Robin Bleecker. Graduate, 1951; Bachelor of Arts, Harvard College, 1955; Bachelor of Laws, Columbia University, 1958. Bar: New York 1959. Vice president, general counsel Dun & Bradstreet Corp., New York City, 1969-73, executive vice president, 1976-79, vice chairman, 1979-81P04pres.; vice chairman Moody's Investors Service, New York City, 1973-75; president Dun & Bradstreet, Incorporated, New York City, 1975; president, chief operating officer Washington Post Company, Washington, 1981—; president International Herald Tribune Washington Post Company, Paris, 1989—; board of directors Fiduciary Trust International New York, Union Pacific Corp.; equity adv. board General Electric Company Investment Corp. Trustee International House, Rockefeller U. Council; member council White Burkett Miller Center Pub. Affairs, U. Virginia. Office: Washington Post Company 1150 15th St Northwest Washington District of Columbia 20071

SIMMONS, RICHARD P., steel company executive; born 1931; married. Graduate, Massachusetts Institute of Technology, 1953. With Titanium Metals Corp. Am., 1957-59, Republic Steel, 1959-68; with Allegheny Ludlum Steel Corp., Pittsburgh, 1960—, chief executive officer, 1980—, chairman, 1986—; also director Allegheny Ludlum Corp. (formerly Allegheny Ludlum Steel Corp.), Pittsburgh, formerly also president. Office: Allegheny Ludlum Steel Corp 1000 6th PPG Place Pittsburgh Pennsylvania 15222

SIMON, HERBERT A(LEXANDER), social scientist; born Milwaukee, June 15, 1916; son of Arthur and Edna (Merkel) S.; married Dorothea Pye, December 25, 1937; children: Katherine S. Frank, Peter Arthur, Barbara. Bachelor of Arts, University Chicago, 1936, Doctor of Philosophy, 1943, Doctor of Laws (honorary), 1964; Doctor of Science (honorary), Case Institute Tech., 1963; Doctor.S.c (honorary), Yale University, 1963, Marquette University, 1981, Columbia University, 1983, Gustavus Adolphus University, 1984, Michigan Tech. University, 1988, Carnegie-Mellon University, 1990; Fil. Doctor (honorary), Lund University, Sweden, 1968; Doctor of Laws (honorary), McGill University, Montreal, Quebec, Can., 1970, University

Michigan, 1978, University Pittsburgh, 1979, University Paul Valery, France, 1984, Harvard University, 1990; Doctor Economic Science (honorary), Erasmus University Rotterdam, Netherlands, 1973, Duquesne University, 1988; Doctor of Science (honorary), Doctor of Humane Letters (honorary), Illinois Institute Tech., 1988; Doctor in Political Science (honorary), University Pavia, Italy, 1988. Research assistant University Chicago, 1936-38; staff member International City Mgrs.' Association; also assistant editor Pub. Management and Municipal Year Book, 1938-39; director administrative measurement studies Bureau Pub. Administration, University California, 1939-42; assistant professor political sci. Illinois Institute Tech., 1942-45, associate professor, 1945-47, professor, 1947-49; also chairman department political and social sci. 1946-49; professor administration and psychology Carnegie-Mellon University, Pittsburgh, 1949-65, Richard King Mellon university professor computer sciences and psychology, 1965—; head department industrial management Carnegie-Mellon University, Pittsburgh, 1949-60; associate dean Grad. School Industrial Administration, 1957-73, trustee, 1972—; consultant to International City Managers Association, 1942-49, United States Bureau Budget, 1946-49, United States Census Bureau, 1947, Cowles Foundation for Research in Economics, 1947-60; consultant and acting director Management Engineering branch Economic Cooperation Administration, 1948; Ford Distinguished lecturer New York University, 1959; Vanuxem lecturer Princeton, 1961; William James lecturer Harvard, 1963, Sigma Xi lecturer, 1964, 76-78, 86; Harris lecturer Northwestern University, 1967; Karl Taylor Compton lecturer Massachusetts Institute of Technology, 1968; Wolfgang Koehler lecturer Dartmouth, 1975; Katz-Newcomb lecturer University Michigan, 1976; Carl Hovland lecturer Yale, 1976; Ueno lecturer, Tokyo, 1977; Gaither lecturer University California, Berkeley, 1980; Camp lecturer Stanford University, 1982; Gannon lecturer Fordham University, 1982; Oates visiting fellow Princeton University, 1982; Marschak lecturer University of California at Los Angeles, 1983; Auguste Comte lecturer London School Economics, 1987; Lee Kuan Yew lecturer University Singapore, 1989, Hitchcock lecturer University California, Berkeley, 1990; hon. professor Tianjin (China) University, 1980, Beijing (China) University, 1986; hon. research scientist Institute Psychology, Chinese Acad. Sciences, 1985; chairman board of directors Social Sci. Research Council, 1961-65; chairman div. behavioral sciences National Research Council, 1968-70; member President's Sci. Adv. Committee, 1968-72; trustee Carnegie Institute, Pittsburgh, 1987—; consultant business and governmental organizations. Author or co-author books relating to field, including Administrative Behavior, 1947, 3d edition, 1976, Public Administration, 1950, Models of Man, 1956, Organizations, 1958, New Science of Management Decision, 1960, rev. edition, 1977, The Shape of Automation, 1965, The Sciences of the Artificial, 1968, 2d edition, 1981, Human Problem Solving, 1972, Skew Distributions and Business Firm Sizes, 1976, Models of Discovery,

1977, Models of Thought, Volume I, 1979, Volume II, 1989, Models of Bounded Rationality, 1982, Reason inHuman Affairs, 1983, Protocol Analysis, 1984, Scientific Discovery, 1987, Models of My Life, 1991. Chairman Pennsylvania Governor's Milk Inquiry Committee, 1964-65. Recipient adminstrs. award Am. College Hospital Administrators, 1957, Frederick Mosher award Am. Society Pub. Administration, 1974, Alfred Nobel Memorial prize in econ. scis., 1978, Dow-Jones award, 1983, scholarly contributions award Acad. Mgmt., 1983, National Medal of Sci., 1986, Pender award University Pennsylvania, 1987, Fiorino d'Oro City of Florence, Italy, 1988, Am. Psychol. Foundation Gold medal, 1988, award for excellence in the scis. Gov. of Pennsylvania, 1990. Fellow American Association for the Advancement of Science, Am. Econ. Association (Ely lecturer 1977, distinguished), Econometric Society, Am. Acad. Arts and Sciences, Am. Psychological Association (Distinguished Sci. Contbn. award 1969), Am. Sociological Society, Institute Management Sciences (life, vice president 1954, Von Neumann Theory award 1988), Brit. Psychological Association (hon.); member Institute of Electrical and Electronics Engineers (hon.), New York Acad. Sciences (hon.), Jewish Acad. Arts Sciences, Am. Political Sci. Association (James Madison award 1984), Association for Computing Machinery (A.M. Turing award 1975), National Academy of Sciences (member committee sci. and pub. policy 1967-69, 82-90, chairman committee air quality control 1974, chairman committee behavioral scis. National Science Foundation 1975-76, council 1978-81, 83-86, chairman committee scholarly communication with PRC, 1983-87 co-chmn. committee behavioral sci. in prevention of nuclear war, 1986-90), Society Experimental Psychologists, Am. Philosophical Society, Royal Society Letters (Lund) (foreign member), Orgnl. Sci. Society (Japan, hon.), Yugoslav Acad. Sciences (foreign), Indonesian Economists Association (hon.), Cosmos Club, University Club Pittsburgh, Phi Beta Kappa, Sigma Xi (Procter prize 1980). Democrat. Unitarian. Office: Carnegie-Mellon U Department Psychology Schenley Park Pittsburgh Pennsylvania 15213

SIMON, LEONARD SAMUEL, banker; born New York City, October 28, 1936; son of Nathaniel and Lena (Pasternack) S.; married Marion Appel, September 1, 1957; children: Andrew, Jonathan. Bachelor of Science, Massachusetts Institute of Technology, 1958; Master of Science, Columbia University, 1959, Doctor of Philosophy, 1963. Member faculty Grad. School Management, University Rochester, 1962-79, professor, 1974-79; vice president Community Savings Bank, Rochester, New York, 1969-74; senior vice president Community Savings Bank, 1974-77, executive vice president, 1977-83; executive vice president Rochester Community Sav. Bank, 1983-84, chairman, chief executive officer, 1984—; chairman Telephone Computing Service Corp., 1974-79; trustee Teachers Insurance Annuity Association; board of directors Federal Home Loan Bank of New York. Editor-in-chief, founding editor: Interfaces, 1970-76; Author books and articles in field. Past chairman Rochester-Monroe County chapter American Red Cross, Rochester Area Educational TV Association, Women's Career Center; life trustee Center for Government Research; member Urban Policy Conference, Brookings Institution, 1972-73, 64th Am. Assembly. Ford Foundation grantee, 1964; recipient Massachusetts Institute of Technology Corp. Leadership award, 1987. Member Savings Bank Association New York State, National Council Savings Institutions, Genesee Valley Club, Beta Gamma Sigma. Office: Rochester Community Savings Bank 235 Main St E Rochester New York 14618

SIMPSON, LOUIS A., insurance company executive; born Chicago, December 23, 1936; son of Irving and Lillian (Rubin) S.; married Margaret Rowley, December 16, 1959; children: Irving, Kenneth, Edward. Student, Northwestern University, 1954-55; Bachelor of Arts, Ohio Wesleyan University, 1958; Master of Arts, Princeton University, 1962. Instructor economics Princeton University, 1961-62; associate, partner Stein Roe & Farnham, Chicago, 1962-69; vice president Shareholders Management, Los Angeles, 1969-70; senior vice president, executive vice president, president Western Asset Management, Los Angeles, 1970-79; vice chairman board Geico Corp., Washington, 1979—; board of directors Potomac Capital Investment. Board of directors Potomac Electric Power, 1990—, Children's Hospital National Medical Center, 1980—; trustee Maryland Health Foundation, Chevy Chase, 1984—. Woodrow Wilson fellow, 1958. Member Washington Society Insurance Analysts (board directors 1981-84), Columbia Country Club, California Club, Los Angeles Country Club, Arts Club Chicago, Princeton Club New York, City Club Washington. Episcopalian. Office: Geico Corp Geico Plaza Washington District of Columbia 20076

SKATES, RONALD LOUIS, computer manufacturing executive; born Kansas City, Missouri, September 25, 1941; son of Raymond and Suzanne (Lispi) S.; married Mary Austin; children: Melissa, Elizabeth. Bachelor of Arts cum laude, Harvard University, 1963, Master of Business Administration, 1965. Accountant Price Waterhouse, Boston, audit partner, 1976-86; senior vice president fin. and administration Data General Corp., Westboro, Massachusetts, 1986-88, executive vice president, chief operating officer, 1988-89; director, president, chief executive officer Data General Corp., 1989—. Trustee Brigham and Women's Hospital, Boston; overseer Mus. Fine Arts, 1989. Member American Institute of Certified Public Accountants, Massachusetts Society Certified Public Accountants. Office: Data General Corp 4400 Computer Dr Westborough Massachusetts 01580

SKINNER, SAMUEL KNOX, secretary of transportation of U.S., lawyer; born Chicago, June 10, 1938; son of Vernon Orlo and Imelda Jane (Curran) S.; married Mary Jacobs, 1989; children: Thomas, Steven, Jane. Bachelor of Science, University Illinois, 1960; Juris Doctor, DePaul University, 1966. Bar: Illinois 1966. Assistant United States attorney Northern District Illinois, Chicago, 1968-74, 1st assistant United States attorney, 1974-75, United States attorney, 1975-77; partner Sidley & Austin, Chicago, 1977-84; chairman Regional Transportation Authority, Chicago, 1984; United States secretary of transportation 1989—. Chairman Illinois Capitol Devel. Bd, 1977-84; member Adv. Commission on confs. on Ocean Shipping, National Space Council, Commission Minority Business Devel., Adv. Committee on Intergovtl. Rels. Served as 1st lieutenant United States Army, 1960-61. Member American Bar Association, Illinois Bar Association, Chicago Bar Association. Republican. Presbyterian. Clubs: Chicago Ontwentsia, Shoreacres. Office: United States Department Transp 400 7th St Southwest Washington District of Columbia 20590

SKLENAR, HERBERT ANTHONY, industrial products manufacturing company executive; born Omaha, June 7, 1931; son of Michael Joseph and Alice Madeline (Spicka) S.; married Eleanor Lydia Vincenz, September 15, 1956; children—Susan A., Patricia I. Bachelor of Science in Business Administration summa cum laude, University Omaha, 1952; Master of Business Administration, Harvard University, 1954. C.P.A., West Virginia. Vice president, comptroller Parkersburg-Aetna Corp., West Virginia, 1956-63; vice president, director Marmac Corp, Parkersburg, 1963-66; manager fin. control Boise-Cascade Corp., Idaho, 1966-67; executive vice president fin. and administration, secretary Cudahy Company, Phoenix, 1967-72; president, chief executive officer Vulcan Materials Company, Birmingham, Alabama, 1972—, also director; board of directors AmSouth Bancorp., Birmingham. Author: (with others) The Automatic Factory: A Critical Examination, 1955. Board of directors Young Men's Christian Association, Birmingham; trustee Birmingham Southern College, Southern Research Institute, Alabama Symphony Association. Recipient Alumni Achievement award University Nebr.-Omaha, 1977, cert. merit West Virginia Society C.P.A.s. Member American Institute of Certified Public Accountants (Elizah Watts Sells award 1965), Shoal Creek Club (Alabama), Birmingham Country Club, The Club (Birmingham), University Club (New York City), Chicago Club, Delta Sigma Pi (leadership award 1952), Omicron Delta Kappa, Phi Kappa Phi, Phi Eta Sigma. Republican. Presbyterian. Home: 2809 Shook Hill Circuit Birmingham Alabama 35223-2618 Office: Vulcan Materials Company 1 Metroplex Dr Birmingham Alabama 35209

SLACK, EDWARD JOSEPH, glass and chemicals manufacturing company executive; born Harwick, Pennsylvania, 1923; married. Bachelor of Science, University Pittsburgh, 1956; graduate, Harvard University Business School, 1965. With PPG Industries Incorporated, Pittsburgh, 1946-88, production manager, Kokomo, Ind., 1958-61, plant manager, Ford City, Pennsylvania, 1961-66, plant manager, Henryetta, Oklahoma, 1961-66, plant manager, Fresno, California, 1961-66, general manager plate float and special glass plants, 1966-70, vice president employee relations, 1970-77, vice president, general manager Auto & Aircraft Glass div., 1977-80, vice president, manager Fiberglass div., 1980-83, group vice president glass and fiberglass, 1983-84, president, chief operating officer, 1984-88. Served with United States Army, 1943-46. Office: PPG Industries Incorporated 1 PPG Place Pittsburgh Pennsylvania 15272

SLOOK, GEORGE FRANCIS, finance company executive; born Philadelphia, August 14, 1946; son of Herbert F. and Eleanor L. (Barth) S.; married Nancy Kathleen Krupsha, September 23, 1972; children—Sally Ann, George Michael. Bachelor of Science in Business Administration, Villanova University, 1968; Master of Business Administration in Fin., Widener University, 1982. Corp. auditor Sears, Roebuck & Company, Chicago, 1971-72; accountant Sears, Roebuck & Company, New York City, 1972-73; mechanization coordinator Sears, Roebuck & Company, Chicago, 1973-75, corp. accountant, 1975-77; assistant treasurer Sears Roebuck Acceptance Corp., Wilmington, Del., 1977-80, vice president, comptr., 1980—. Republican precinct captain, Hoffman Estates, Illinois, 1976; treasurer Longview Farms Civic Association, Wilmington, 1979-81; board of directors Junior Achievement, Delaware, 1985—; treasurer 1986—. Served with United States Army, 1968-70. Member Fin. Executives Institute (director Philadelphia chapter 1985, president Del. chapter 1986), National Association Accts. Roman Catholic. Office: Sears Roebuck Acceptance Corp 3711 Kennett Pike Greenville Delaware 19807

SLOVIN, BRUCE, diversified holding company executive; born New York City, 1935. Bachelor of Arts, Cornell University, 1957; Juris Doctor, Harvard University Law School, 1960. Sole practice New York City, 1960-64; with Kane Miller Corp., 1964-74, Hanson Industries, Incorporated, 1974-80; with MacAndrews & Forbes Group, Incorporated, New York City, 1980—, now president, director; president, director MacAndrews & Forbes Holdings, Incorporated (parent), Wilmington, Del.; president, chief operating officer, director Revlon Group, Incorporated (subsidiary), New York City; chairman executive committee Revlon, Incorporated (subsidiary), New York City; director Oak Hill Sportswear Corp., Gulf Resources & Chemical Corp., Moore Medical Corp., Four Star International Incorporated. Office: Revlon Group 555 Southwest 12th Avenue Pompano Beach Florida 33069 also: Revlon Group Incorporated 21 E 63d St New York New York 10021

SMITH, ALEXANDER JOHN COURT, insurance executive; born Glasgow, Scotland, April 13, 1934; son of John Court and Mary Walker (Anderson) S.; married Margaret Gillespie, October 15, 1968. Student, Scottish schools. Actuarial trainee Scottish Mutual Insurance Company, Glasgow, 1957; assistant actuary Zurich Life Insurance Company, Toronto, Can., 1958-61; from actuary to executive vice president William M. Mercer Limited, Toronto, 1961-74; senior vice president, director Marsh & McLennan Companies, Incorporated, New York City, 1974-78, president, 1974-82, group vice president, 1982-84, president, 1984-85, vice-chairman, 1984-86, president, 1986—; also director Marsh & McLennan Companies, Incorporated, New York City 1977—; trustee Employee Benefit Research Institute, 1979—. Fellow Faculty Actuaries Edinburgh, Can. Institute Actuaries, Conference Actuaries in Public Practice; associate Society Actuaries; member Am. Acad. Actuaries, International Congress Actuaries, International Association Cons. Actuaries. Clubs: Racquet and Tennis

(New York City); Royal Can. Yacht; Apawamis (Rye, New York); Caledonian (London). Home: 630 Park Avenue New York New York 10021 Office: Marsh & McLennan Cos Incorporated 1166 Avenue of the Americas New York New York 10036

SMITH, CRAIG RICHEY, machinery manufacturing company executive; born Cleveland, May 30, 1925; son of Wilbur Thomas and Helen (Stearns) S.; married Mary Wood Glover, December 17, 1945; children: Timothy VanGorder, Craig Richey, Patricia Sodon, Marcia Colby. Bachelor of Science in Master.E, Case Institute Tech., 1945; postgraduate, Harvard Business School, 1974. With Warner & Swasey Company (merger Bendix Corp. 1980, Allied Corp. 1983), 1946—; general manager Wiedemann div. Warner & Swasey Company, King of Prussia, Pennsylvania; vice president Turning Machine Div. Warner & Swasey Company, Cleveland, 1969-73; group vice president machine tools Warner & Swasey Company, 1973-77, president, chief operating officer, 1977-79, chairman chief executive, 1979-80, president industrial group, 1980-82, chairman industrial group, 1982—; director AmeriTrust Corp., Cleveland, Cleveland Electric Illuminating Company, Cleveland, Austin Powder Company, Cleveland. Campaign leader United Way Services, 1977—; trustee Judson Park, 1977—, Greater Cleveland Growth Association, 1979—, Case Western Reserve University, 1979—; trustee Vocational Guidance & Rehabilitation Services, 1972-79, 1st vice president, 1976-79. Served with United States Navy, 1943-46, 1952-53. Member Society Manufacturing Engineers, National Machine Tool Builders Association (director 1971-74, 79—, chairman 1980-81), Machinery and Allied Products Institute (member executive council 1979—), Cleveland Engineering Society. Clubs: Union, Pepper Pike Country, Chagrin Valley Hunt, Cleveland Skating. Home: 13754 County Line Road Chagrin Falls Ohio 44022 Office: 11000 Cedar Avenue Cleveland Ohio 44106

SMITH, DANIEL R., bank holding company executive; born 1934. With First of Am. Bank Corp. Michigan, 1955-82, senior vice president, 1971-77, president, then president, chief executive officer, 1977-82; with First of Am. Bank Corp., Kalamazoo, 1982—, president, 1982-85, chairman board, chief executive officer, 1985—. Captain United States Army Reserve, 1955-64. Office: First Am Bank Corp 108 E Michigan Avenue Kalamazoo Michigan 49007

SMITH, DARWIN EATNA, paper and consumer products manufacturing company executive, lawyer; born Garrett, Indiana, April 16, 1926; son of K. Bryant and Hazel (Sherman) R.; married Lois Claire Archbold, August 19, 1950; children: Steven, Pamela, Valerie, Blair. Bachelor of Science in Business with distinction, Ind. University, 1950; Bachelor of Laws cum laude, Harvard, 1955. Bar: Illinois 1955. Associate attorney Sidley, Austin, Burgess & Smith, Chicago, 1955-58; with Kimberly-Clark Corp., Neenah, Wisconsin, 1958—, general attorney, 1960—, vice president, 1962-67, vice president fin. and law, 1967-70, president, 1970—, chairman, chief executive officer, 1971—. Served with Army of the United States, 1944-46. Office: Kimberly-Clark Corp Post Office Box 619100 Dallas Texas 75261

SMITH, FREDERICK WALLACE, transportation company executive; born Marks, Mississippi, August 11, 1944; son of Frederick Smith; married Diane avis. Graduate, Yale University, 1966. Certified comml. pilot. Owner Ark Aviation, 1969-71; founder, chairman board, chief executive officer Federal Express Corp., Memphis, 1972—, now also president, director. Served with United States Marine Corps, 1966-70. Office: Federal Express Corp Post Office Box 727 Memphis Tennessee 38194

SMITH, JAMES F., oil industry executive; born 1932; married. Student, St. Louis University; graduate, University Tulsa, 1956. Various positions in oil industry 1951-72; with Tesoco Petroleum Corp., Houston, 1972-86; president, chief operations officer Crown Central Petroleum Corp., Baltimore, 1986—. Office: Crown Central Petroleum Corp 1 N Charles St Box 1168 Baltimore Maryland 21203

SMITH, JOHN BURNSIDE, transportation company executive; born Indianapolis, 1931; married Barbara J.; children: John S., Lynn B., Nancy L. Graduate, University Ind., 1957, postgraduate School Business Administration, 1958; Doctor of Laws (honorary), Butler University, 1984. President, chairman, chief executive officer, director Mayflower Group, Indianapolis; director Citizens Gas & Coke Utility, Ind. National Corp. Board governors James Whitcomb Riley Associates; board of directors Wholesale Club. Member Ind. State Chamber of Commerce (board directors). Office: Mayflower Group Incorporated Post Office Box 107 Indianapolis Indiana 46206-0107

SMITH, MICHAEL L., transportation company executive; born 1948. Bachelor of Arts, DePauw University, 1970. Vice president College Marketing & Research Corp., 1968-70; with Arthur Andersen & Company, 1970-75; div. controller Mayflower Group, Carmel, Ind., 1975-77, group vice president, warehouse div., 1977, then executive vice president, now president, chief operating officer, 1989—, also board of directors; with Mayflower Transit Company subsidiary Mayflower Group, Carmel, 1975—, then senior vice president, president, chief executive officer, 1989—, also board of directors. Office: Mayflower Group Incorporated 9998 N Michigan Road Carmel Indiana 46032

SMITH, ORIN ROBERT, chemical company executive; born Newark, August 13, 1935; son of Sydney R. and Gladys Emmett (DeGroff) S.; married Ann Raymond, July 11, 1964; children—Lindsay, Robin. Bachelor of Arts in Econometrics, Brown University, 1957; Master of Business Administration in Management, Seton Hall University, 1964. Various sales and marketing management positions Allied Chemical Corp., Morristown, New Jersey, 1960-70; director sales and marketing Richardson-Merrell Company, Phillipsburg, New Jersey, 1970-72; with M&T Chemicals, Greenwich, Connecticut, 1972-77, president, 1974-77; with Engelhard Minerals & Chemicals Corp., Menlo Park, Edison, New Jersey, 1977-81, corp. senior vice president, 1978-81, president div. minerals and chemicals, 1978-81, also board of directors, 1979-81, president, director various United States subsidiary, 1979-81; executive vice president,

president div. minerals and chemicals Engelhard Corp., Menlo Park, Edison, 1981-84; president, chief executive officer Engelhard Corp., Edison, 1984—, also board of directors; board of directors Summit Trust Company, The Summit Bancorp., Vulcan Materials Company, New Jersey Manufacturers Insurance Company, New Jersey Reins. Company. Member executive committee Mfrs. Alliance for Productivity and Innovation; board overseers New Jersey Institute Tech.; vice chairman Centenary College; member adv. board Watchung Area council Boy Scouts Am.; board of directors Welkind Rehabilitation Hospital; past chairman Ind. College Fund New Jersey; past dir.-at-large U. Maine Pulp and Paper Foundation Lieutenant (junior grade) United States Navy, l957-60. Member Chemical Manufacturers Association (board directors), Am. Management Association (general management council), New Jersey Chamber of Commerce (board directors), New Jersey Business and Industry Association (trustee), Econ. Club (New York City), Union League Club (N.Y.C), Essex Hunt Club (Peapack, New Jersey), Roxiticus Golf Club (Mendham, New Jersey), New York Yacht Club. Home: Fox Chase Farm Gladstone New Jersey 07934 Office: Engelhard Corp Menlo Park CN 40 Edison New Jersey 08818

SMITH, RICHARD ALAN, movie theater and specialty retailing executive; born Boston, 1924; married. Bachelor of Science, Harvard University, 1946; Doctor of Laws (honorary), Boston College, 1988. With Smith Management Company, 1947-61; chairman board, chief executive officer General Cinema Corp., Chestnut Hill, Massachusetts, 1961—, Neiman Marcus Group, Chestnut Hill, Massachusetts, 1987—; director Liberty Mutual Insurance Company, 1st National Bank of Boston Corp. Office: General Cinema Corp 27 Boylston St Chestnut Hill Massachusetts 02167

SMITH, ROBERT HOWARD, banker; born Glendale, California, September 3, 1935; son of James Howard and Marie Viana (Jenkins) S.; married Loretta Marie Gesell, February 8, 1958; children—Gregory (deceased), Jeffrey, Stephen, Sarah Beth. Bachelor of Science in Pub. Administration, University Southern California, 1957; Juris Doctor, Van Norman University, Los Angeles, 1966. Various positions Security Pacific Bank, Los Angeles, 1961-66, manager, 1969-71, regional vice president, 1971-74, senior vice president, 1974-80, executive vice president, 1980-84, vice chairman, from 1984, president, chief executive officer, 1987—; vice chairman Security Pacific Bank & Security Pacific Corp, Los Angeles, 1984—; chief executive officer Security Pacific Corp., Los Angeles, 1990—. Served to lieutenant United States Navy, 1958-61. Clubs: Jonathan (Los Angeles); Annandale Golf (Pasadena, California). Home: 1617 Fairmount Avenue La-Canada California 91011 Office: Security Pacific Corp 333 S Hope St Los Angeles California 90071

SMITH, SHERWOOD HUBBARD, JR., utilities executive; born Jacksonville, Florida, September 1, 1934; son of Sherwood Hubbard and Catherine Gertrude (Milliken) S.; married Eva Hackney Hargrave, July 20, 1957; children: Marlin Hamilton, Cameron Hargrave, Eva Hackney. Bachelor of Arts, University North

Carolina, 1956, Juris Doctor, 1960. Bar: North Carolina 1960. Associate Lassiter, Moore & Van Allen, Charlotte, 1960-62; partner Joyner & Howison, Raleigh, 1963-65; associate general counsel Carolina Power & Light Company, Raleigh, 1965-70, senior vice president, general counsel, 1971-74, executive vice president, 1974-76, president, 1976—, chairman board, 1980—; board of directors Am. Nuclear Energy Council, United States Council Energy Awareness, 1st Wachovia Corp., Southeastern Electric Exchange, Hackney Brothers Body Company, Wilson, North Carolina, Durham Life Insurance Company, Durham Corp.; board of directors, chairman Edison Electric Institute, Southeastern Electric Reliability Council; member New York Stock Exchange Listed Company adv. committee. Chairman Raleigh Civic Center Authority, 1973-77; vice chairman Morehead Scholar Central Selection Committee, U. North Carolina, 1970—; member Governor's Efficiency Study Commission, 1973; North Carolina Council Mgmt. and Devel.; board of directors Business Foundation North Carolina, 1977—, secretary, 1977-81, president, 1981; trustee Z. Smith Reynolds Foundation, 1978—; chairman Idn. College Fund of North Carolina, 1986-88; chairman board of directors North Carolina Heart Association, 1971-74; board of directors United Fund Wake County; board of directors, executive committee North Carolina Citizens for Business and Industry, chairman 1985-86; board of directors Research Triangle Foundation of North Carolina; member committee United States World Energy Conference; board of directors Microelectronics Center of North Carolina, 1980—; chairman board trustees Rex Hospital; member President's Council for International Youth Exch., Kenan Institute Private Enterprise; trustee Committee for Economic Devel. Ensign United States Navy, 1956-57. Member Electric Power Research Institute (board directors 1984-89), Greater Raleigh Chamber of Commerce (president 1979), Am. Nuclear Society, United States Chamber of Commerce (energy committee), Phi Beta Kappa. Home: 408 Drummond Dr Raleigh North Carolina 27609 Office: Carolina Power & Light Company 411 Fayetteville St Raleigh North Carolina 27602

SMITH, TOM EUGENE, food retail executive; born Salisbury, North Carolina, May 2, 1941; son of Ralph Eugene and Cora Belle (Ervin) S.; married Martha Hatley; children: Leigh Ann, Nancy Thompson. Bachelor of Arts in Business Administration, Catawba College, 1964, Doctor of Laws (honorary), 1986. With Del Monte Sales Company, 1964-67; account manager Del Monte Sales Company, Hickory, North Carolina, 1967-68; sales supervisor Del Monte Sales Company, Charlotte, North Carolina, 1969-70; buyer Food Lion Stores, Incorporated, Salisbury, 1970-74, vice president distribution, 1974-77, executive vice president, 1977-81, president, 1981—, chief executive officer, 1986—, also board of directors; chairman board 1990—; chief executive officer Food Lion Incorporated, Salisbury, 1986—; board of directors North Carolina National Bank (chairman board Salisbury chapter), North Carolina Food Dealers (president 1988). Trustee Catawba College, 1986—; board of directors United Way, Salisbury, 1975-77. Recipient Martin Luther King Humanitarian award 1987, bronze and silver Chief Executive Officer of Year awards Fin. World Magazine, 1988. Member National Association Retail Grocers, Sales Executives Club (board directors 1974-79, president 1980), North Carolina Food Dealers Association (board directors 1981—, 3d vice president 1985, 2d vice president 1986—), Am. Legion, Chamber of Commerce (board directors 1975-77). Republican. Lutheran. Club: Salisbury Country. Lodge: Rotary (board dirs. 1975-76). Avocations: traveling, big game hunting. Office: Food Lion Incorporated Harrison Road Post Office Box 1330 Salisbury North Carolina 28144

SMITH, WARD, manufacturing company executive, lawyer; born Buffalo, September 13, 1930; son of Andrew Leslie and Georgia (Ward) S.; married Gretchen Keller Diefendorf, October 29, 1960; children: Jennifer Hood, Meredith Ward, Jonathan Andrew, Sarah Katherine. Student, Georgetown University, 1948-49; Bachelor of Arts, Harvard, 1952; Juris Doctor, University Buffalo, 1955. Bar: New York 1955, Massachusetts 1962, Ohio 1977. Associate Lawler & Rockwood, New York City, 1959-62; secretary, general counsel Whitin Machine Works, Whitinsville, Massachusetts, 1962-66; secretary White Consolidated Industries, Incorporated, Cleveland, 1966-69, vice president, 1967-69, senior vice president, 1969-72, executive vice president, 1972-76, president, chief administrative officer, 1976-84, president, chief operating officer, 1984-86, president, chief executive officer, 1985-86, chairman, 1986; president NACCO Industries, Incorporated, Cleveland, 1986-89, chief executive officer, 1986—, also chairman board; board of directors Society Bank and Society Corp., Sundstrand Corp., Rockford, Illinois. President, trustee The Musical Arts Association; op. trustee The Cleveland Orchestra, Case Western Reserves U., Cleveland, others. Served to lieutenant United States Naval Reserve, 1955-59. Member American Bar Association, New York State Bar Association. Clubs: Pepper Pike Country (Ohio); Union, Tavern (Cleveland). Home: 19701 N Park Boulevard Shaker Heights Ohio 44122 Office: NACCO Industries Incorporated 12500 Shaker Boulevard Cleveland Ohio 44120

SMITHBURG, WILLIAM DEAN, food manufacturing company executive; born Chicago, July 9, 1938; son of Pearl L. and Margaret L. (Savage) S.; married Alberta Hap, May 25, 1963; children: Susan, Thomas. Bachelor of Science, DePaul University, 1960; Master of Business Administration, Northwestern University, 1961. With Leo Burnett Company, Chicago, 1961-63, McCann-Erickson, Incorporated, Chicago, 1963-66; various positions Quaker Oats Company, Chicago, 1966-71, vice president, general manager cereals and mixers div., 1971-75, president food div., 1975-76, vice president United States grocery products, 1976-79, president, 1979-83, chief executive officer, 1979—, chairman, 1983—, also board of directors. Served with United States Army Reserve, 1959-60. Roman Catholic. Office: Quaker Oats Company Quaker Tower 231 N Clark St Chicago Illinois 60610

SMURFIT, MICHAEL W. J., manufacturing company executive; born 1936. With Jefferson Smurfit Group PLC, Dublin, Ireland, 1961—, president, from 1966, now chairman, chief executive officer; president Jefferson Smurfit Corp., Alton, Illinois, 1979-82, now chief executive officer, chairman board, 1982—. Office: Jefferson Smurfit Corp 8182 Maryland St Saint Louis Missouri 63105

SNELL, RICHARD, holding company executive; born Phoenix, November 26, 1930; son of Frank L. and Elizabeth (Berlin) S.; married Alice Cosette Wiley, August 1, 1954. Bachelor of Arts, Stanford University, 1952, Juris Doctor, 1954. Bar: Arizona. Partner firm Snell & Wilmer, Phoenix, 1956-81; president, chairman, chief executive officer Ramada Incorporated, Phoenix, 1981-89; chairman, chief executive officer Aztar Corp., 1989-90, chairman, board of directors, 1990—; chairman, chief executive officer, president Pinnacle West Capital Corp., Phoenix, 1990—, board of directors; board of directors Valley National Corp., Valley National Bank Arizona; board of directors, chairman Arizona Pub. Service Company. Trustee Am. Grad. School International Mgmt., Phoenix; past president Young Men's Christian Association Metropolitan Phoenix and Valley of Sun. Served with United States Army, 1954-56. Member American Bar Association, Arizona Bar Association, Maricopa County Bar Association. Republican. Lutheran. Clubs: Paradise Valley Country, John Gardiner's Tennis Ranch. Office: Pinnacle West Capital Corp Post Office Box 52132 Phoenix Arizona 85072

SNETZER, MICHAEL ALAN, multi-industry executive; born Denver, May 26, 1940; son of Robert Ellis and Kathryn (Wake) S.; married Peggy Ann Sparks, January, 1964 (divorced 1973); children: Michael Ellis, Gregory Alan; married Deborah Kay Gee, March 15, 1975; 1 child, Robert Adam. Bachelor of Science, University Arkansas, 1963; Master of Business Administration, Southern Methodist University, 1969. Industrial engineer Collins Radio Company, Dallas, 1966-69; vice president fin. UCCEL Corp., Dallas, 1969-77; vice president fin. Contran Corp., Dallas, 1977-84, executive vice president, 1984-87; president Valhi, Incorporated, Dallas, 1987—; board of directors NL Industries, Incorporated, Houston, Baroid Corp., Houston, Amalgamated Sugar Company, Ogden, Utah; chairman, director Medford (Oregon) Corp. wholly owned sub. Valhi Incorporated. Served to captain Special Forces, United States Army, 1963-66, Vietnam. Recipient Bronze star. Member University Club, Bent Tree Country Club. Republican. Methodist. Home: 18722 Campbell Road Dallas Texas 75252 Office: Valhi Incorporated 3 Lincoln Center 5430 LBJ Freeway Dallas Texas 75240 also: Medford Corp 1901 N Pacific Highway Medford Oregon 97501

SNOW, JOHN WILLIAM, railroad executive; born Toledo, August 2, 1939; son of William Dean and Catharine (Howard) S.; married Fredrica Wheeler, June 11, 1964 (divorced 1973); children: Bradley, Ian; married Carolyn Kalk, August 31, 1973; 1 child, Christopher. Bachelor of Arts, University Toledo, 1962; Doctor of Philosophy, University Virginia, 1965; Bachelor of Laws,

George Washington University, 1967. Assistant professor economics University Maryland, College Park, 1965-67; associate Wheeler & Wheeler, Washington, 1967-72; assistant general counsel Department Transportation, Washington, 1972-73, deputy assistant secretary for policy, plans and international affairs, 1973-74, assistant secretary for governmental affairs, 1974-75, deputy under secretary, 1975-76; administrator National Highway Traffic Safety Administration, Washington, 1976-77; vice president government affairs Chessie System Incorporated, Washington, 1977-80; senior vice president corp. services CSX Corp., Richmond, Virginia, 1980-84, executive vice president, 1984-85; president, chief executive officer Chessie System R.R.s, Baltimore, 1985-86, CSX Rail Transport, Jacksonville, Florida, 1986-87, CSX Transportation, Jacksonville, Virginia, 1987-88; president, chief operating officer CSX Corp., Richmond, Virginia, 1988-89, president, chief executive officer, 1989-91, chairman, president, chief executive officer, 1991—, also board of directors; adj. professor law George Washington University, 1972-75; visiting professor economics University Virginia, Charlottesville, spring 1977; visiting fellow Am. Enterprises Institute, Washington, spring 1977; board of directors C&S/Sovran Corp., Best Products Company, Bassett Furniture Industries Incorporated, Columbia Gas System Incorporated. Board of directors Virginia Mus. of Fine Arts. Member American Bar Association, District of Columbia Bar Association, Virginia Bar Association. Episcopalian. Clubs: Chevy Chase, Metropolitan (Washington); Commonwealth, Country of Virginia (Richmond). Office: 1 James Center Richmond Virginia 23119

SNYDER, WILLIAM BURTON, insurance executive; born Clarksburg, West Virginia, July 9, 1929; son of William Burton and Mary Catherine (Cornwell) S.; married Georgie Gaye, October 27, 1951; children: William Burton, Melissa Ann. Bachelor of Business Administration in Accounting cum laude, Texas Tech. University, 1955. With Travelers Insurance Company, 1955-77, vice president, 1970-77; with Government Employees Insurance Company, Washington, 1977—, president, 1979-85, director, 1979—, chairman, chief executive officer, 1985—; president GEICO Corp., 1981-89, also board of directors, chairman, chief executive officer, 1985—; board of directors Avemco Corp. Chairman Economic Adv. Council Montgomery County. Decorated Air medal. Member Hwy. Users Federation Safety and Mobility (executive committee), National Association Ind. Insurers (board directors, chairman 1989-90), Federal City Council (trustee), Kenwood Country Club (Bethesda, Maryland). Republican. Baptist. Office: GEICO Corp Geico Plaza Washington District of Columbia 20076

SODERQUIST, DONALD G., retail executive; born Chicago, 1934. Bachelor of Arts, Wheaton College, 1955. President Ben Franklin Stores div. City Products Company, 1963-80; senior vice president Wal-Mart Stores Incorporated, Rogers, Arkansas, 1980, formerly executive vice president operations administration, now vice-chairman, chief operating officer, also board of directors; board of directors First National

Bank, Rogers, International Massachusetts Retail Association.

SOFIA, ZUHEIR, banker; born 1944; married Susan Owen Ryburn; children: Sarah, Joseph, Zachary. Bachelor of Science in Business Administration, Western Kentucky University, 1968; Master of Arts, Washington University, 1970, Rutgers University, 1977. Manager credit, loan administration, international divs. First Union National Bank, Charlotte, North Carolina, 1968-71; with Huntington National Bank, Columbus, Ohio, 1971—, executive vice president, 1981-83, vice chairman, director, 1983—; president Huntington Bancshares, Incorporated, Columbus, 1984-86, president, chief operating officer, treasurer, 1986—, also board of directors. Author: External Debt of Developing Countries: Its Application to Country Risk Analysis, 1978; contributor articles to professional journals. Trustee Columbus Symphony Orchestra, immediate past chairman; trustee United Way, Columbus School for Girls, Franklin U., vice president, president elect of board trustees; trustee Colour Columbus; trustee, founder Columbus Council World Affairs. Recipient Mayor's Award for Voluntary Service to Columbus, 1978; numerous others. Member Association Reserve City Bankers, Association Bank Holding Companies, Young Pres.' Organization, Rotary, Capital Club, University Club, Columbus Country Club. Office: Huntington Bancshares Incorporated 41 S High St Post Office Box 1558 Columbus Ohio 43287

SOLOW, ROBERT MERTON, economist, educator; born Brooklyn, August 23, 1924; son of Milton Henry and Hannah Gertrude (Sarney) S.; married Barbara Lewis, August 19, 1945; children: John Lewis, Andrew Robert, Katherine. Bachelor of Arts, Harvard University, 1947, Master of Arts, 1949, Doctor of Philosophy, 1951; Doctor of Laws, University Chicago, 1967, Brown University, 1972, University Warwick, 1976, Tulane University, 1983; Doctor of Literature, Williams College, 1974, Lehigh University, 1977, Wesleyan University, 1982; Doctor of Science (honorary), University Paris, 1975, University Geneva, 1982; Doctor of Social Science, Yale University, 1986; Doctor of Science, Bryant College, 1988; Doctor Social Science, University Massachusetts, Boston, 1989; Doctor of Laws, Dartmouth College, 1990; Doctor of Literature, Colgate University, 1990; Doctor in Social Science, University Helsinki, 1990. Member faculty Massachusetts Institute of Technology, 1949—, professor economics, 1958—, Institute professor, 1973—; senior economist Council Economic Advisers, 1961-62, consultant, 1962-68; consultant RAND Corp., 1952-64; Marshall lecturer, fellow commononer Peterhouse, Cambridge (England) University, 1963-64; Eastman visiting professor Oxford University, 1968-69; overseas fellow Churchhill College, Cambridge; senior fellow Society Fellows, Harvard University, 1975-89; board of directors Boston Red. Reserve Bank, 1975-80, chairman, 1979-80; member President's Commission on Income Maintenance, 1968-70, President's Committee on Tech., Automation and Economic Progress, 1964-65, Carnegie Commission Sci., Tech. and Governments, 1988—. Author: Linear Programming and Economic Analysis, 1958, Capital

Theory and the Rate of Return, 1963, The Sources of Unemployment in the United States, 1964, Growth Theory, 1970, Price Expectations and the Behavior of the Price Level, 1970, (with M. Dertouzos, R. Lester) Made in America, 1989. Board of directors, member executive committee National Bureau Economic Research; trustee Institute for Advanced Study, Princeton U., 1972-78, Woods Hole Oceanographic Institute, 1988—. Served with Army of the United States, 1942-45. Fellow Center Advanced Study Behavioral Sciences, 1957-58, trustee, 1982—, chairman, 1987—; recipient David A. Wells prize Harvard University, 1951, Seidman award in political economy, 1983, Nobel prize in Econs., 1987. Fellow Am. Acad. Arts and Sciences, Brit Acad. (corr.); member American Association for the Advancement of Science (vice president 1970), Am. Philosophical Society, National Acad. Sciences (council 1977-80), Acad. dei Lincei, Am. Econ. Society (executive committee 1964-66, John Bates Clark medal 1961, vice president 1968, president 1979), Econometric Society (president 1964, member executive committee). Home: 528 Lewis Wharf Boston Massachusetts 02110 Office: Massachusetts Institute of Technology Department Econs Cambridge Massachusetts 02139

SOVEY, WILLIAM PIERRE, manufacturing company executive; born Helen, Georgia, August 26, 1933; son of Louis Terrell and Kathryn Bell (White) S.; married Kathryne Owen Doyle, December 28, 1958; children: Margaret Elizabeth, John Todd. Bachelor.S.I.E., Georgia Institute Tech., 1955; graduate, Advanced Management Program, Harvard University, 1976. General manager automotive div. Atwood Vacuum Machine Company, Rockford, Illinois, 1963-68; vice president international A.G. Spalding & Brothers, Incorporated, Chicopee, Massachusetts, 1968-71; president Ben Hogan Company div. AMF Incorporated, Fort Worth, 1971-77; corp. vice president, group executive industrial products group AMF Incorporated, Stamford, Connecticut, 1977-79; president, chief operating officer, director AMF Incorporated, White Plains, New York, 1982-85; president, chief operating officer Newell Company, Freeport, Illinois, 1986—, also board of directors. Served with United States Navy, 1955-58. Home: 5349 Winding Creek Dr Rockford Illinois 61111 Office: Newell Company Post Office Box 117 Beloit Wisconsin 53511

SPENCE, A. MICHAEL, economist, college dean; born Montclair, New Jersey, 1943; married Ann. Bachelor of Arts, Princeton University, 1966; Doctor of Philosophy, Harvard University, 1972; Master of Arts, Oxford University, 1968. Instructor Harvard University, 1971-72, professor economics, 1976-90, professor business administration, 1979-90, dean faculty arts and sciences, 1984-90; instructor Stanford University, 1973-75, professor economics and business administration, 1990—, dean Grad. School Business, 1990—; member economics adv. panel National Science Foundation, 1977-79. Author: Market Signaling: Information Transfer in Hiring and Related Screening Processes, 1974; (with R.E. Caves and M.E. Porter) Competition in the Open Economy, 1980; member editorial board various journals including Bell Journal Econs., Journal Econ. Theory, Pub. Policy. Rhodes scholar, 1966-68; recipient Galbraith Prize for Teaching Excellence, 1978, John Bates Clark Medal, Am. Economic Association, 1981. Office: Stanford U Grad School Business Stanford California 94305-1684

SPORCK, CHARLES E., electronic products manufacturing company executive; born 1928. Bachelor of Science, Cornell University. With semiconductor div. Fairchild Camera and Instrument Company, 1949-67; president, chief executive officer National Semiconductor Corp., Santa Clara, California, 1967—, also director, 1967—. Office: National Semiconductor Corp 2900 Semiconductor Dr Santa Clara California 95051

SPRAGUE, PETER JULIAN, semiconductor company executive, lecturer; born Detroit, April 29, 1939; son of Julian K. and Helene (Coughlin) S.; married Tjasa Krofta, December 19, 1959; children: Carl, Steven, Kevin, Michael. Student, Yale University, 1961, Massachusetts Institute of Technology, 1961, Columbia University, 1962-66. Chairman board of directors National Semiconductor Corp., Santa Clara, California; board of directors GEO International Corp. Trustee Strang Clinic. Club: Yale. Home: 249 Undermountain Road Lenox Massachusetts 01240 Office: Cryptologics International Incorporated 599 Lexington Avenue 41st Floor New York New York 10022 also: National Semiconductor Corp Post Office Box 58090 Santa Clara California 95052

SPRAGUE, WILLIAM WALLACE, JR., food company executive; born Savannah, Georgia, November 11, 1926; son of William Wallace and Mary (Crowther) S.; married Elizabeth Louise Carr, October 3, 1953; children: Courtney, Lauren Duane, William Wallace III, Elizabeth Louise. Bachelor of Science in Mechanical Engineering, Yale University, 1950. With Savannah Foods & Industries, Incorporated, 1952—, secretary, 1961-62, vice president, 1962-72, president, chief executive officer, 1972—, also board of directors; chairman executive committee, board of directors C&S Corp., Atlanta; board of directors C&S National Bank, Savannah, Everglades Sugar Refinery, Clewiston, Florida, Savannah Food Service of Florida, Miami; chairman board of directors Michigan Sugar Company, Saginaw, Colonial Sugars, Gramercy, Louisiana, Food Carrier, Incorporated, Savannah, Transales Corp., Savannah; board of directors, president Adeline Sugar Factory Company, Limited, Savannah, Coastal Management Corp., Savannah. Chairman Southeastern Legal Foundation; trustee Savannah Business Group, chairman; member steering committee United Way Savannah; trustee Savannah Benevolent Association; chairman Youth Futures Authority, Savannah; adv. council Medical College Georgia, Augusta; vice-chmn. Savannah Chief Executive Officer Council With United States Navy, 1945-46. Named Sugar Man of Year and recipient Dyer Memorial award B.W. Dyer & Company, 1985; named Industrialist of Year International Mgmt. Council, 1988. Member World Sugar Research Organization (chairman 1982-85), Grocery Manufacturers Association (board directors), The Sugar Association (board directors),

National Association of Manufacturers, Business Council Georgia (board govs.), Savannah Chamber of Commerce (board directors), Carolina Plantation Society, St. Andrews Society, Oglethorpe Club, Century Club (Savannah). Office: Savannah Foods & Industries Incorporated Post Office Box 339 Savannah Georgia 31402

SPRINGER, NEIL ALLEN, retired manufacturing company executive; born Fort Wayne, Ind, May 2, 1938; son of Roy V. and Lucille H. (Gerke) S.; married Janet M. Grotrian, September 3, 1960; children: Sheri Lynn, Kelly Jean, Mark Allen. Bachelor of Science, University Ind, 1960; Master of Business Administration, University Dayton, 1966. Staff assistant accounting International Harvester Company (now Navistar International Corp.), Bridgeport, Connecticut, 1966-68; assistant comptroller International Harvester Company (now Navistar International Corp.), Fort Wayne, Ind., 1968-70; staff assistant International Harvester Company (now Navistar International Corp.), Chicago, 1970-75, assistant corp. comptroller, 1975-77, vice president fin., 1977-79, vice president general manager trucks, 1979-81, president truck group, 1981-84, president, chief operating officer, 1984-87; chairman, president, chief executive officer Navistar International Transportation Corp., Chicago, 1987-90; president, chief operating officer Navistar International Corp./Navistar Interant. Transportation Corp., Chicago, 1990; retired 1990; board of directors Century Companies Am., Waverly, Iowa, IDEX Corp., Northbrook, Illinois, Am. Trucking Association Foundation. Active business dean's adv. council Ind. U., 1988—; board of directors Wittenberg U., Springfield, Ohio, 1988—, Ind. School Business, 1988—. Member Motor Vehicle Manufacturing Association (board directors), Illinois Society Certified Public Accountants, Hwy. Users Federation Safety and Mobility (member executive committee). Office: Navistar International Corp 401 N Michigan Avenue Chicago Illinois 60611

STAGER, DONALD K., construction company executive. Chief executive officer Dillingham Construction, California. Office: Dillingham Constrn Corp 5960 Inglewood Dr Pleasanton California 94566

STALEY, DELBERT C., telecommunications executive; born Hammond, Indiana, September 16, 1924; son of Eugene and Nellie (Downer) son of; married Ingrid Andersen, March 16, 1946; children—Crista Staley Ellis, Cynthia, Clifford, Corinn. Student, Rose Polytechnic Institute, Hammond, 1943-44; graduate advanced management program, Harvard University, 1962; Doctor Engineering (honorary), Rose Hulman Institute Tech., 1981; Doctor of Laws (honorary), Skidmore College, 1983. With Illinois Bell Telephone, 1946-76, vice president operations, 1972-76; president Ind. Bell, 1976-78; vice president residence marketing American Telephone and Telegraph Company, 1978-79; president New York Telephone, 1979-83, chairman board, chief executive officer, 1983; chairman board, chief executive officer NYNEX Corp., White Plains, New York, 1983-89; chairman board, also director NYNEX International Management Committee, White Plains, New York, 1989—; board of directors Dean Foods, Franklin Park,

Illinois, Ball Corp., Muncie, Ind., Bank New York, New York City, Allied-Signal Incorporated, John Hancock Mutual Life Insurance Company, Polaroid Corp. Member national board governors American Red Cross, chairman, Greater New York City; vice chairman United Way, New York City With United States Army, 1943-46; European Theatre of Operations. Recipient Puerto Rican Legal Defense and Education Fund award, 1981, Cleveland Dodge award Young Men's Christian Association Greater New York, 1983, New Yorker for New York award Citizens Committee for New York, 1984, Leadership in Mgmt. award Pace University, 1988, Albert Schweitzer Leadership award Hugh O'Brian Youth Foundation, 1988, Hammond Achievement award The Hammond Historical Society, 1988, Gold Medal award USO, 1988. Member Ind. Acad. (hon.), Telephone Pioneers Am. (president 1983-84). Presbyterian. Clubs: Westchester Country, Sky, Blind Brook, Exmoor, Royal Poinciana. Home: 32 Polly Park Road Rye New York 10580 Office: Nynex Corp 335 Madison Avenue New York New York 10017

STANDISH, JOHN SPENCER, textile manufacturing company executive; born Albany, New York, April 17, 1925; son of John Carver and Florence (Spencer) S.; married Elaine Joan Ritchie, October 20, 1962 (divorced 1984); children: John Carver, Christine Louise; married Patricia Hunter, November 9, 1985. Bachelor of Science, Massachusetts Institute of Technology, 1945. Assistant to production manager Forstmann Woolen Company, Passaic, New Jersey, 1945-52; various positions Albany International Corp., 1952-72, vice president, 1972-74, executive vice president, 1974-76, vice chairman, 1976-84, chairman, 1984—; board of directors Berkshire Life Insurance Company, Pittsfield, Massachusetts, Key Bank N.A., Albany. Board of directors Albany chapter American Red Cross, 1966—, chapter chairman, 1971-74; board governors American Red Cross, Washington, 1980-86; board of directors United Way of Northeastern New York, Albany, 1980—, president, 1984-85; trustee Albany Medical College and Center, 1984—; trustee Sienna College, Loudonville, New York, 1987—; chairman U. Albany Fund, 1982-87, 89—. Served to sergeant United States Army, 1945-46. Member Am. Management Association, World Econ. Forum. Republican. Episcopalian. Clubs: Fort Orange, Wolferts Roost Country (Albany); Schuyler Meadows Country (Loudonville). Avocations: bridge, tennis, golf. Home: 1 Schuyler Meadows Road Loudonville New York 12211 Office: Albany International Corp Post Office Box 1907 Albany New York 12201

STANGELAND, ROGER EARL, retail chain store executive; born Chicago, October 4, 1929; son of Earl and Mae E. (Shaw) S.; married Lilah Fisher, December 27, 1951; children: Brett, Cyndi Stangeland Meili, Brad. Student, St. Johns Military Academy, 1943-47, Carleton College, 1947-48; Bachelor of Science, University Illinois, 1949-51. With Coast to Coast Stores, Minneapolis, 1960-78, president, 1972-77; senior vice president, executive vice president Household Merchandising, Chicago, 1978-84; chief executive officer, chairman board Vons Grocery Company, Los Angeles, 1984-85; chairman, chief executive officer The Vons Companies, Incorporated, El Monte, California, 1986—. Chairman Wauconda (Illinois) Board Education, 1957-60, Hopkins (Minnesota) Board Education, 1968-74; board of directors Claremont (California) U. Center & Grad. Sch0, 1986, Hugh O'Brian Youth Foundation, Los Angeles Council Boy Scouts Am., Junior Achievement. Member Food Marketing Institute (board directors), Food Employer Council (board directors), Mchts. & Manufacturers Association (board directors), Los Angeles Area Chamber of Commerce (board directors). Clubs: Jonathan (Los Angeles). Home: 842 Oxford Road San Marino California 91108 Office: Vons Cos Incorporated 10150 Lower Azusa Road El Monte California 91731

STANLEY, DAVID, retail company executive; born Kansas City, Missouri, 1935; married. Graduate, University Wisconsin, 1955; Bachelor of Laws, Columbia University, 1957. Associate Paul, Weiss, Rifkind, Wharton & Garrison, New York City, 1957-60; partner Faegre & Benson, Minneapolis, 1960-71; executive vice president Piper, Jaffray & Hopwood, Minneapolis, 1971-80; president Payless Cashways, Incorporated, Kansas City, 1980-86, chief executive officer, 1982—, chairman, 1985—, also board of directors; board of directors Local Initiaves, Support Corp., National Equity Fund, Incorporated, Piper Jaffray Incorporated. Board of directors Dole Foundation. Office: Payless Cashways Incorporated Post Office Box 419466 Kansas City Missouri 64141

STEAD, JERRE L., electronics company executive; born Maquoketa, Iowa, January 8, 1943; son of H. Victor and Anna Catherine (Grindrod) S.; married Mary Joy Kloppenburg, December 26, 1961; children: Joel A., Jay A. Bachelor of Business Administration, University Iowa, 1965; graduate advanced management program, Harvard University, 1982. Manager regional sales Honeywell Corp., Philadelphia, 1971-73; director production Honeywell Corp., Minneapolis, 1974-75, director distribution, 1975-76, vice president fin. and administration, Brussels, 1979-82; vice president, general manager Honeywell-Phillips Medical Electronics, Brussels, 1981-82; vice president, general manager Honeywell Corp., Minneapolis, 1982-85, vice president, group executive, 1986; president, chief operating officer Square D Company, Palatine, Illinois, 1987-89, also board of directors, president, chief executive officer, chairman board, 1989—, also board of directors; board of directors Eljer Industries, Plano, Texas, Ameritech, Chicago, USG, Chicago. Member President's council Am. Lung Association, New York City, 1986—, The Washington Center National Campaign Committee; business adv. committee North Carolina A&T U.; trustee Coe College, Cedar Rapids, Iowa, 1987; member council on competitiveness Illinois Business Roundtable; board visitors U. Iowa, Iowa City. Member National Electrical Manufacturers Association (board govs. 1984—), National Association Electrical Distbrs. (education committee), Chicago Committee, Electrical Manufacturers Club. Republican. Methodist. Office: Square D Company 1415 S Roselle Road Palatine Illinois 60067

STEERE, WILLIAM CAMPBELL, JR., pharmaceutical company executive; born Ann Arbor, Michigan, June 17, 1936; son of William Campbell and Dorothy (Osborne) S.; married Lynda Gay Powers, January 29, 1957; children: William, Mark, Christopher. Bachelor of Science, Stanford University, 1959. Sales representative Pfizer & Company, Modesto, California, 1959-61; district manager Pfizer & Company, San Jose, California, 1961-63; product manager Pfizer & Company, New York City, California, 1963-68, vice president marketing, 1968-73; vice president marketing Roerig, New York City, California, 1970-72; vice president, director operations Pfizer Labs, New York City, California, 1980-82; senior vice president, director operations Pfizer Pharmaceuticals, New York City, California, 1982-84, executive vice president, 1984-86; president Pifzer Pharmaceuticals, New York City, California, 1986—; also board of directors Pifzer Pharmaceuticals. Chairman Pfizer United Way of Tri State, 1987; member national pub. relations adv. council Connecticut College; member executive committee Ind. College Funds; president council Memorial Sloan-Kettering; trustee New York Botanical Garden. Member Am. Manufacturing Association (steering committee marketing section), Am. Marketing Association, Ad Club of New York, National Association of Retail Druggists (executive adv. committee), United States Council for International Business (trustee executive committee), Pharmaceuticals Manufacturing Association (marketing section steering committee).Clubs: University, New York Yacht. Avocations: sailing, skiing. Office: Pfizer & Company 235 42nd St New York New York 10017

STEIGER, JANET DEMPSEY, government official; born Oshkosh, Wisconsin, June 10, 1939; 1 child, William Raymond. Bachelor of Arts, Lawrence College, 1961; postgraduate, University Reading, England, 1961-62, University Wisconsin, 1962-63. Legis. aide Office of Governor Wisconsin, 1965; vice president The Work Place, Incorporated, 1975-80; commissioner Postal Rate Commission, Washington, 1980-89, acting chairman, 1981-82, chairman, 1982-89; commissioner and chairman Federal Trade Commission, Washington, 1989—. Author: Law Enforcement and Juvenile Justice in Wisconsin, 1965; co-author: To Light One Candle, a Handbook on Organizing, Funding and Maintaining Public Service Projects, 1978, 2d edition, 1980. Chairman Commission on Vets. Education Policy, 1987-90. Woodrow Wilson scholar; Fulbright scholar, 1961. Member Phi Beta Kappa. Office: Federal Trade Commission Office of Chairman 6th and Pennsylvania Avenue Northwest Washington District of Columbia 20580

STEIN, DIETER, chemical company executive; born Koblenz, Federal Republic Germany, 1934. Graduate, University Mainz, Federal Republic Germany, 1955. With BASF Corp., Parsippany, New Jersey, 1961—, now chairman, president, chief executive officer. Office: BASF Corp 8 Campus Dr Parsippany New Jersey 07054

STEINBERG, JOSEPH SAUL, investment company executive; born Chicago, February 5, 1944; son of Paul S. and Sylvia (Neikrug) S.; children from previous marriage, Sarah Aliza, Paul Steven; married Diane L. Heidt, 1987. Bachelor of Arts, New

York University, 1966; Master of Business Administration, Harvard University, 1970. Volunteer Peace Corps, Kingston, Jamaica, 1966-68; vice president Carl Marks & Company, Incorporated (investment bankers), New York City, 1970-78; president Leucadia National Corp., New York City, 1979—, also board of directors; president Phlcorp, Incorporated, 1987—, also board of directors; board of directors Empire Insurance Group, Bolivian Power Company Limited. Clubs: Harvard, National Arts (New York City). Office: Leucadia National Corp 315 Park Avenue S New York New York 10010

STEINBERG, ROBERT M., holding company executive; born Brooklyn, 1942; married. Student, North Carolina State University, 1964. Assistant vice president Ideal Rubber Company, 1964-65; with Reliance Group Incorporated, New York City, 1965—, salesman, 1965-67, assistant director corp. devel., 1967-68, assistant vice president computer services, 1968-69, vice president administration, 1969-74, senior vice president administration, 1974-78, executive vice president, 1978-81, president, chief operating officer, 1981—, also director; also president, chief operating officer, director Reliance Group Holdings Incorporated, New York City; president, chief operating officer Leasco Corp.; chairman, chief executive officer Reliance Insurance Company; director Empire Incorporated, Zenith National Insurance, Days Inn Corp., Frank B. Hall & Company, Telemundo Group, Incorporated. Board of directors Jewish Guild for Blind. Office: Reliance Group Holdings Incorporated 55 E 52nd St New York New York 10055

STEINBERG, SAUL PHILLIP, holding company executive; born New York City, August 13, 1939; son of Julius and Anne (Cohen) S.; married Barbara Herzog, May 28, 1961 (divorced 1977); children—Laura, Jonothan, Nicholas; married Laura Sconocchi, December 21, 1978 (divorced December 1983); 1 child, Julian; married Gayfryd McNabb, January 22, 1984; children—Rayne, Holden. Bachelor of Science, Wharton School, University Pennsylvania, 1959. Founder, chairman, chief executive officer Reliance Group Holdings Incorporated, New York City; chairman board of directors Telemundo Group Incorporated; chairman executive committee Frank B. Hall & C. Incorporated; board of directors Symbol Techs. Incorporated, Zenith National Insurance Corp. Chairman board overseers Wharton School U. Pennsylvania; member board overseers Cornell U. Medical College, New York City; trustee Jewish Medical Center, New York City, U. Pennsylvania, New York Pub. Libr. Jewish. Clubs: Glen Oaks, The Board Room (New York City). Home: 740 Park Avenue New York New York 10021 Office: Reliance Group Holdings Incorporated 55 E 52nd St New York New York 10055

STEPHENS, JAMES M., federal agency administrator; born Rochester, New York, September 16, 1946; married; two children. Bachelor of Arts, Wittenberg University, 1968; Juris Doctor, Case Western Reserve University, 1971. Associate Roetzel and Ambress, Akron, Ohio, 1973-77; assistant minority labor counsel committee education and labor United States House Representatives, 1977-81; majority labor counsel committee labor and human resources United States Senate, 1981-85; chairman National Labor Relations Board, Washington, 1985—. Office: NLRB 1717 Pennsylvania Avenue Northwest Washington District of Columbia 20570

STEPHENS, WILLIAM THOMAS, manufacturing resource company executive. married. Bachelor of Science, University Arkansas, 1965, Master of Science, 1966. Various management positions Manville Forest Products Corp., from 1963; assistant to president, then senior vice president, president forest products group Manville Corp., Denver, executive vice president fin. and administration, from 1984, now president, chief executive officer, chairman. Office: Manville Corp Manville Plaza 717 S 17th Denver Colorado 80202 also: Manville Corp Post Office Box 5108 Denver Colorado 80217

STERN, DAVID JOEL, basketball association executive; born New York City, September 22, 1942; son of William and Anna (Bronstein) S.; married Dianne Bock, November 27, 1963; children—Andrew, Eric. Bachelor of Arts, Rutgers University, 1963; Bachelor of Laws, Columbia University, 1966. Bar: New York 1963. Associate Proskauer Rose Goetz & Mendelsohn, New York City, 1966-74, partner, 1974-78; general counsel National Basketball Association, New York City, 1978-80, executive vice president business and legal affairs, 1980-84, commissioner, 1984—; adj. professor law Cardozo Law School, New York City, 1983—. Trustee Beth Israel Medical Center, New York City, 1985—, Fair Housing Council Bergen County, Hackensack, New Jersey, 1972-82. Member American Bar Association, New York State Bar Association, Association Bar City New York (chairman committee on entertainment and sports 1983—). Office: NBA Olympic Tower 645 Fifth Avenue New York New York 10022

STEVENS, FREDERICK M., retail executive; born 1936; married. Bachelor of Science, Louisiana State University, 1959; postgraduate, Harvard University, 1984. With K Mart Corp., Troy, Michigan, 1959-88, store manager, 1963-64, district manager, 1969-76, assistant manager western region, 1976-78, assistant western region manager real estate, 1978-80, vice president corp. facilities, 1980-82, senior vice president sales general merchandise, 1982-84, executive vice president specialty retailing div., 1984-88; chairman, chief executive officer Fred Meyer Incorporated, Portland, Oregon, 1988—. Office: Fred Meyer Incorporated 3800 S E 22nd Portland Oregon 97202

STEWARD, H. LEIGHTON, oil company executive; born Fairfield, Texas, December 1, 1934; son of Hugh Birt and Lucille (Riley) S.; married Lynda Brady, June 6, 1959; children; Leighton Brady, Blake Worth. Bachelor of Science in Geology, Southern Methodist University, 1958, Master of Science in Geology, 1960. Chief exploration operations Shell Oil Company, Houston, 1977-79; vice president energy and minerals Burlington Northern Incorporated, Billings, Montana, 1979-81; executive vice president, chief operations office Kilroy Company of Texas, Houston, 1981-82; senior vice president, then executive vice president Louisiana Land & Exploration Company, New Orleans, 1982-84, president, chief operating officer, 1985-88, chairman, chief executive officer, 1989; chairman LL&E Petroleum Marketing Incorporated, LL&E Pipeline Corp., LL&E (United Kingdom) Incorporated. Served to captain United States Air Force, 1959-62. Member Am. Association Petroleum Geologists, Am. Petroleum Institute (board directors 1985-86), Mid Continent Oil and Gas Association. Republican. Clubs: Metairie Country (Louisiana); New Orleans Petroleum.

STEWART, CORNELIUS JAMES, II, power systems company executive; born Houston, June 27, 1925; son of Ross and Catherine (Rial) S.; married Gretchen Elizabeth Braun, November 28, 1947; children: Cornelius James, III, Richard Ross, David Rial, Gretchen Elizabeth Stewart Anderson, Catherine Maria Stewart Carrigan. Student, University Texas, 1945-47. With Stewart & Stevenson Services, Incorporated, Houston, 1947—; vice president Stewart & Stevenson Services, Incorporated, 1956-73, president, 1973-75, chairman board, 1975—; chairman board, director C. Jim Stewart & Stevenson, Incorporated, Stewart & Stevenson Realty Corp., Stewart & Stevenson International Corp., Stewart & Stevenson Transportation, Incorporated, Stewart & Stevenson Power Incorporated, Machinery Acceptance; director Reagan Commerce Bank, 1973-76, Southern State Bank, 1973—; adv. director Texas Commerce Bank, 1975-80, now director. Chairman Houston City Planning Commission, 1974-83; board of directors Better Business Bureau Metropolitan Houston, 1976—, vice chairman, 1981-82, chairman, 1983-85; board of directors Holly Hall, 1972-76; board of directors, member fin. devel. committee Houston chapter American Red Cross, 1984—; board of directors Kelsey Seybold Foundation; board of directors Salvation Army, 1989—; chairman Houston/Grampian Region Association, 1978—; international adv. director Up With People, 1979—; co-chairman Houston Fundraising, 1982; member engring. council devel. committee Texas A&M University, 1989—. Served with United States Army Air Force, 1943-45. Member National Association Manufacturing (board directors 1988—), Purchasing Agts. Association Houston (president 1959-60, director 1961-62), United States Chamber of Commerce (international policy committee 1983-85), Houston Chamber of Commerce (director 1969, 76, 78, 80, 82, 84, member aviation steering committee 1976—, chairman business devel. committee 1980-81), National Industrial Conference Board, Newcomen Society. Presbyterian. Clubs: Rotary (Houston) (director 1978—, vice president 1980, president 1981), Breakfast, Houston (president 1973, pension com. 1974—), Houston Country (director 1974-76), Ramada (Houston). Office: Stewart & Stevenson Services Incorporated Post Office Box 1637 Houston Texas 77251-1637

STEWART, S. JAY, chemical company executive; born Pineville, West Virginia, September 18, 1938; son of Virgil Harvey and Lena Rivers (Repair) S.; married Judith Ann Daniels, June 3, 1961; children: Julie Annette, Jennifer Amy, Steven Jay. Bachelor of Science in Chemical Engineering, University Cincinnati, 1961; Master of Business Administration, West Virginia University,

1966. Various positions in engineering, manufacturing, marketing Monsanto Company, St. Louis, 1961-73; director marketing Ventron Corp. subsidiary Morton Thiokol, Incorporated, Beverly, Massachusetts, 1973-77, general manager, 1977-79; president Dynachem Corp. subsidiary Morton Thiokol, Incorporated, Santa Ana, California, 1979-82; group vice president Thiokol Corp., Newtown, Pennsylvania, 1982; group vice president specialty chemicals Morton International, Incorporated (formerly Morton Thiokol, Incorporated), Chicago, 1983-86, president, chief operating officer, 1986—; also board of directors Morton International, Incorporated, Chicago. Member corp. adv. council College Engring. Cincinnati U., 1988,. Anchor Cross Society Rush Presbyn.-St. Luke's Medical Center, 1987—, Charles McMicken Society U. Cincinnati Foundation, Northwestern U. Associates, 1988—; trustee Rush Presbyn.-St. Luke's Medical Center, Chicago, 1987—; member adv. board National Foundation for History of Chemistry, 1991—. Recipient Distinguished Alumnus award University Cincinnati, 1984. Member Am. Chemical Society, Am. Institute Chemical Engineers, Chairman Manufacturers Association (board directors 1984-87), Commercial Devel. Association, Association Governing Bds. Univs. and Colls., Chemical Marketing Association (board directors 1990), Commercial Club Chicago, The Chicago Club. Republican. Methodist. Office: Morton International Incorporated 100 N Riverside Plaza Chicago Illinois 60606

STIGLER, GEORGE JOSEPH, economist, educator; born Renton, Washington, January 17, 1911; son of Joseph and Elizabeth (Hungler) S.; married Margaret Mack, December 26, 1936 (deceased August 1970); children: Stephen, David, Joseph. Bachelor of Business Administration, University Washington, 1931; Master of Business Administration, Northwestern University, 1932; Doctor of Philosophy, University Chicago, 1938; Doctor of Science, Carnegie Mellon University, 1973, University Rochester, 1974, Helsinki School Economics, 1976, Northwestern University, 1979; Doctor of Laws, Brown University, 1980; Doctor of Hebrew Literature, Columbia University, 1990. Assistant professor economics Iowa State College, 1936-38; assistant professor University Minnesota, 1938-41, associate professor, 1941-44, professor, 1944-46; professor Brown University, 1946-47; professor economics Columbia University, 1947-58; Walgreen professor Am. institutions University Chicago, 1958—, director center study economy and the state, 1977—; lecturer London School Economics, 1948; vice chairman, board of directors Securities Investor Protection Corp., 1971-74; board of directors Chicago Board Trade, 1980-83, Lynde and harry Bradley Foundation, 1986-89, Duff-Phelps Selected Utility Fund, 1987-89. Author: Production and Distribution Theories, 1940, The Theory of Price, 1946, Trends in Output and Employment, 1947, Five Lectures on Economic Problems, 1949, (with K. Boulding) Readings in Price Theory, 1952, Trends in Employment in the Service Industries, 1956, (with D. Blank) Supply and Demand for Scientific Personnel, 1957, The Intellectual and the Market Place, 1964, 84, Essays in the History of

Economics, 1965, The Organization of Industry, 1968, (with J.K. Kindahl) The Behavior of Industrial Prices, 1970, The Citizen and the State, 1975, The Economist as Preacher, 1982, The Essence of Stigler, 1986, Memoirs of an Unregulated Economist, 1988; Editor: Chicago Studies in Political Economy, 1988; editor Journal Political Economy, 1972—; contributor articles to professional journals. Member atty. gen.'s. committee for study anti-trust laws, 1954-55; member Blue Ribbon Def. Panel.; trustee Carleton College. Recipient Nobel prize in econs., 1982; Guggenheim fellow, 1955; fellow Center for Advanced Study in Behavioral Sciences, 1957-58; recipient National Medal of Sci., 1987. Fellow Am. Acad. Arts and Sciences, Am. Statistical Society, Econometric Society, National Acad. Sci.; member Am. Econ. Association (president 1964), Royal Econ. Society Am. Philosophical Society, History of Economics Society (president 1977), Mount Pelerin Society (president 1977-78). Office: U Chicago GSB 1101 E 58th St Chicago Illinois 60637

STIGLITZ, JOSEPH EUGENE, economics educator; born Gary, Indiana, February 9, 1943; son of Nathaniel David and Charlotte (Fishman) S.; married Jane Hannaway, December 23, 1978; children—Siobhan, Michael, Edward, Julia. Bachelor of Arts, Amherst College, Mass, 1964; Doctor of Hebrew Literature, Amherst College, 1974; Doctor of Philosophy in Economics, Massachusetts Institute of Technology, 1966; Master of Arts (honorary), Yale University, 1970. Professor economics Cowles Foundation, Yale University, New Haven, 1970-74; visiting fellow St. Catherine's College, Oxford, England, 1973-74; professor economics Stanford University, 1974-76, 88—; Oskar Morgenstern district fellow Institute Advanced Studies Math., Princeton, New Jersey, 1978-79; Drummond professor political economy Oxford University, England, 1976-79; professor economics Princeton University, 1979-88; consultant World Bank, State of Alaska, Seneca Indian Nation, Bell Communications Research. Editor: Journal Econ. Perspectives, 1986—; Am. editor Rev. of Econ. Studies, 1968-76; associate editor Am. Econ. Rev., 1968-76, Energy Econs., Managerial and Decision Econs.; member editorial board World Bank Econ. Rev. Recipient John Bates Clark award Am. Economic Association, 1979, International prize Accademia Lincei, 1988, Union des Assurances de Paris prize, 1989; Guggenheim fellow, 1969-70; Hoover Institution senior fellow, 1988—. Fellow National Academy of Sciences, Agency for International Development (institute policy reform), Econometric Society (council); member Am. Econ. Association (executive committee 1982-84, vice president 1985), Am. Acad. Arts and Sciences.

STIRITZ, WILLIAM P., food company executive; born Jasper, Arkansas, July 1, 1934; son of Paul and Dorothy (Bradley) S.; married Susan Ekberg, December 4, 1972; children—Bradley, Charlotte, Rebecca, Nicholas. Bachelor of Science, Northwestern University, 1959; Master of Arts, St. Louis University, 1968. Member marketing management staff Pillsbury Company, Minneapolis, 1959-62; account management staff Gardner Advertising Company, St. Louis, 1963—; with Ralston Purina Company, St. Louis, 1963—; president, chief executive officer, chairman Ralston Purina Company, 1981—; board of directors Angelica Corp., Ball Corp., Boatmen's Bancshares, Incorporated, General Am. Life Insurance Company, May Department Stores, South Carolina Johnson & Son. With United States Navy, 1954-57. Member Grocery Manufacturers Association (director). Office: Ralston Purina Company Checkerboard Square Saint Louis Missouri 63164

STOKES, BARBARA S., lawyer. Secretary J. P. Morgan & Company Incorporated, New York, Morgan Guaranty Trust Company New York, New York. Office: JP Morgan & Company Incorporated 60 Wall St New York New York 10260

STONE, CHESTER B., JR., mining company executive; born Texarkana, Arkansas, April 28, 1935; son of Chester B. Stone Sr. and Melissa (McCaskill) Wilson; married Camilla Wood Stone, April 21, 1957; children: Tamara, Marian. Bachelor of Business Administration in Accounting, University Houston, 1958. Senior tax specialist Arthur Andersen & Company, Houston, 1958-60; assistant chief accountant Butler, Miller & Lentz, Houston, 1960-64; manager tax department Peat, Marwick, Mitchell & Company, Houston and New Orleans, 1964-69; co-director corp. devel. Lykes Corp., New Orleans, 1968-71; vice president planning Youngstown (Ohio) Sheet & Tube Company, 1971-74; president Lykes Resources, Incorporated, Pittsburgh, 1974-78; executive vice president Amoco Minerals Company, Chicago and Englewood, Colorado, 1978-85; executive vice president, chief fin. officer Cyprus Minerals Company, Englewood, 1985-89; senior vice president, coal and iron ore Cyprus Minerals Company, Denver, 1989-90, president, chief operating officer, 1990-91, president, chief executive officer, 1991—; also board of directors Cyprus Minerals Company, 1985—. Board of directors National Repertory Orchestra, Denver, 1986—. Member Am. Institute Certified Public Accountants, Colorado Society Certified Public Accountants, Phi Kappa Phi. Clubs: Metropolitan (Englewood, Colorado); Denver Petroleum. Home: 29110 Buchanan Evergreen Colorado 80439 Office: Cyprus Mineral Company 9100 E Mineral Circle Box 3299 Englewood Colorado 80195

STONE, IRVING I., greeting card company executive; born Cleveland, April 5, 1909; son of Jacob and Jennie (Canter) Sapirstein; married Helen K. Sill, December 12, 1976; children: Hensha (Mrs. Hirsch Gansbourg), Neil, Myrna (Mrs. Harold Tatar), Judith (Mrs. Morry Weiss). Student, Case-Western Reserve University, Cleveland Institute Art. With Am. Greetings Corp., Cleveland, 1923—, president, 1960-78, chairman board, 1978—, chief executive officer, 1978-87, also chairman executive committee. Chairman board Hebrew Acad. Cleveland; board of directors Cleveland Institute Art, Young Israel of Cleveland, Yeshiva U.; trustee Simon Wiesenthal Center for Holocaust Studies; 1st vice president Telshe Yeshiva; life member board of directors Jewish Community Federation of Cleveland; vice president Am. Association for Jewish Education, Bureau Jewish Education, Cleveland, Am. Friends of Boys Town

Jerusalem; founder Kiryat Telshe Stone, Israel. Office: Am Greetings Corp 10500 American Road Cleveland Ohio 44144

STONE, SIR (JOHN) RICHARD (NICHOLAS), retired finance, accounting educator, economist; born England, August 30, 1913; son of Gilbert Stone; married Winifred Jenkins, 1936 (divorced); married Feodora Leontinoff, 1941 (deceased 1956); 1 daughter; married Mrs. Giovanna Croft-Murray, 1960. Master of Arts, Cambridge (England) University, 1938; Doctor of Science, Cambridge (England) University, England, 1957. With Corps of Engineers Heath and Company, Lloyd's Brokers, England, 1936-39, Ministry Economic Warfare, England, 1939-40, Central Statistical Office, Offices of War Cabinet, England, 1940-45; director department applied economics Cambridge (England) University, 1945-55, P.D. Leake Professor finance, accounting, 1955-80, retired, 1980—. Author: The Role of Measurement in Economics, 1951, Quantity and Price Indexes in National Accounts, 1956, Input-Output and National Accounts, 1961, Mathematics in the Social Sciences and Other Essays, 1966, Mathematical Models of the Economy, and Other Essays, 1970, Demographic Accounting and Model Building, 1971, Aspects of Economic and Social Modelling, 1980, several books with others; editor, author: (with others) A Programme for Growth, 1962-74; contributor articles to professional journals. Named Fellow King's College University Cambridge, 1945—, hon. fellow Gonville and Caius College University Cambridge, 1976; recipient numerous hon. doctorates, Nobel prize for Econs., 1984. Member International Statistical Institute, Econometric. Society (president 1955). Avocation: staying at home. Home: 13 Millington Road, Cambridge 2821TN, England

STONE, ROGER WARREN, container company executive; born Chicago, February 16, 1935; son of Marvin N. and Anita (Masover) S.; married Susan Kesert, December 24, 1955; children: Karen, Lauren, Jennifer. Bachelor of Science in Economics, University Pennsylvania, 1957. With Stone Container Corp., Chicago, 1957—, director, 1968-77, vice president, general manager container div., 1970-75, president, chief operating officer, 1975-79, president, chief executive officer, 1979—, chairman board, chief executive officer, 1983—; board of directors First Chicago, Morton International, Stamford, Connecticut, Am. Appraisal Associates, McDonald's Corp. Past trustee Glenwood (Illinois) School for Boys; trustee Chicago Symphony Orchestra Association; fellow Lake Forest (Illinois) Acad.; board overseers U. Pennsylvania Wharton School, term trustee; member adv. council Economic Devel. Named Best or Top Chief Executive Officer in firm's industry, Wall St. Transcript, 1981-86; recipient Top Chief Executive Officer award in Forest & Paper Specialty Products Industry, Fin. World Magazine, 1984. Member Am. Paper Institute (chairman board 1985-86, board directors), Chief Executives Organization, Corrugated Industry Devel. Corp. (past president), Institute Paper Sci. and Tech. (trustee), The Chicago Committee, Mid-Am. Committee, Chicago Council Foreign Relations, Standard Club, Tavern Club, Commercial Club, Econ. Club, Lake Shore County Club. Republican.

Office: Stone Container Corp 150 N Michigan Avenue Chicago Illinois 60601-7568

STONECIPHER, HARRY C., manufacturing company executive. Bachelor of Science, Tennessee Polytech Institute, 1960. With General Electric Company, 1960-61, 62-86, Martin Aircraft Company, 1961-62; executive vice president Sundstrand Corp., 1987, president, chief operating officer, 1987-88, president, chief executive officer, 1988—, also board of directors. Office: Sundstrand Corp 4751 Harrison Avenue Box 7003 Rockford Illinois 61125

STORHOFF, DONALD C., agricultural products company executive; born 1935; married. Supervisor Meadowland Dairy, 1953-69; assistant plant manager Associated Milk Producers Incorporated, 1969-72; plant manager Wisconsin Dairies Cooperative, Baraboo, 1972-74, product manager, 1974-77, manager, 1977-84, president, 1984—, also board of directors; president Wisconsin Federation Cooperative Dairy Div. & Whey Products Institute; board of directors Am. Dry Milk Institute, National Milk Producers Federation, National Cheese and Butter Institute. Office: Wisconsin Dairies Coop Route 3 Highway 12 W Baraboo Wisconsin 53913

STOVER, WILLIAM RUFFNER, insurance company executive; born Washington, August 31, 1922; son of Daniel I. and Carrie E. (Brubaker) S.; married Carolyn McKean, July 19, 1947; children—Deborah Ann Stover Bowgren, Wendi Lee Stover Mirretti, Sheree Kay. Student, Northwestern University, 1941-45. Sales representative Old Republic Life Insurance Company, 1945-1949, vice president, 1949-60, senior vice president, 1960-68, president, 1968-69, also board of directors; president Old Republic International Corp., 1969-90, chairman board, chief executive officer, 1976-90, chairman board, 1990—; director Old Republic Life New York, Old Republic Insurance Company, International Business and Mercantile Reassurance Company, Home Owners Life Insurance Company and subsidiary, Minnesota Title Fin. Corp., Bitco Corp., Founders Title Group, Incorporated, Republic Mortgage Insurance Company. Republican. Home: 907 N Sheridan Road Waukegan Illinois 60085 Office: Old Republic International Corp 307 N Michigan Avenue Chicago Illinois 60601

STOWE, DAVID HENRY, JR., agricultural and industrial equipment company executive; born Winston-Salem, North Carolina, May 11, 1936; son of David Henry and Mildred (Walker) S.; married Lois Burrows, November 28, 1959; children: Priscilla, David Henry. Bachelor of Arts in Economics, Amherst College, 1958. Vice president First National Bank Boston, 1961-68; manager Deere & Company, Moline, Illinois, 1968-71; director Deere & Company, Moline, 1971-77, vice president, 1977-82, senior vice president, 1982-87, executive vice president, 1987-90, president, chief operating officer, 1990—. Home: 4510 5th Avenue Moline Illinois 61265 Office: Deere & Company John Deere Road Moline Illinois 61265

STRANG, CHARLES DANIEL, marine engine manufacturing company executive; born Brooklyn, April 12, 1921; son of Charles Daniel and Anna Lincoln (Endner) S.

Bachelor.Mechanical Engineer, Polytechnic Institute Brooklyn, 1943. Member mechanical engineering staff Massachusetts Institute of Technology, 1947-51; vice president engineering, executive vice president Kiekhaefer Corp. div. Brunswick Corp., Fond du Lac, Wisconsin, 1951-64; vice president marine engineering Outboard Marine Corp., Waukegan, Illinois, 1966-68; executive vice president Outboard Marine Corp., 1968-74, president, general manager, 1974-80, president, chief executive officer, 1980-82, chairman board, chief executive officer, 1982-90, chairman, 1990—, also director. Patentee engine design and marine propulsion equipment; contributor research papers to sci. publications. Board of directors Polytechnical Institute New York Served with United States Army Air Force, 1944-47. Member Am. Power Boat Association (past president), Society Automotive Engineers, Union International Motorboating (vice president), Sigma Xi. Club: Waukegan Yacht. Home: 25679 W Florence Avenue Antioch Illinois 60002 Office: Outboard Marine Corp 100 Sea Horse Dr Waukegan Illinois 60085

STRATTON, FREDERICK PRESCOTT, JR., manufacturing executive; born Milwaukee, May 25, 1939; married. Bachelor of Science, Yale University; Master of Business Administration, Stanford University, 1963. With Arthur Andersen & Company, 1963-65, Robert W. Baird & Company, Incorporated, 1965-73; with Briggs & Stratton Corp., Wauwatosa, Wisconsin, 1973—, assistant service manager, 1973-75, assistant sales manager, 1975-76, group sales and service administration, 1976-77, vice president administration, 1977; formerly president Briggs & Stratton Corp., Wauwatosa, to 1987; chairman board, chief executive officer Briggs & Stratton Corp., Wauwatosa, Wisconsin, 1987—, chairman board of directors; board of directors Banc One Corp., Columbus, Ohio, Wisconsin Energy Corp., Milwaukee, Weyenberg Shoe Man Company, Milwaukee. Office: Briggs & Stratton Corp 12301 W Wirth St Wauwatosa Wisconsin 53222

STRENGER, CHRISTIAN H., brokerage house executive; born 1943. Student, Cologne University, Federal Republic of Germany. Senior vice president Deutsche Bank, Frankfort, Federal Republic of Germany, 1972-82; general mge. Deutsch Bank A.G., London, 1982-85; president, chief executive officer, managing director Deutsche Bank Capital Corp., New York City, 1985—; board of directors Deutsche Credit Corp., Deerfield, Illinois. Office: Deutsche Bank Capital Corp 31 W 52nd St 3rd Floor New York New York 10005

STRICKLAND, ROBERT LOUIS, business executive; born Florence, South Carolina, March 3, 1931; son of Franz M. and Hazel (Eaddy) S.; married Elizabeth Ann Miller, February 2, 1952; children: Cynthia Anne, Robert Edson. Bachelor of Arts, University North Carolina, 1952; Master of Business Administration with distinction, Harvard University, 1957. With Lowe's Companies, Incorporated, North Wilkesboro, North Carolina, 1957—, senior vice president, 1970-76, executive vice president, 1976-78, chairman board, 1978—, chairman executive committee, 1988—, member office of president, 1970-78, also board of directors; founder Sterling Advertising, Limited, 1966; vice president, member administrative committee Lowe's Profit-Sharing Trust, 1961-87, chairman operations committee, 1972-78; member management committee Lowe's ESOP plan, 1978; board of directors Summit Communications, Atlanta, T. Rowe Price Associates, Baltimore; board of directors, member executive committee Elk River Devel. Corp., 1982—; panelist investor relations field, 1972—; speaker, panelist employee stock ownership field, 1978—; speaker London Instnl. Investor Conference, 1980; speaker on investor relations, London, Edinburgh, Glasgow, Paris, Zurich, Frankfurt, Geneva, Vienna, Amsterdam, Brussels, Tokyo, Singapore and Hongkong, 1980—. Author: Lowe's Cybernetwork, 1969, Lowe's Living Legend, 1970, Ten Years of Growth, 1971, The Growth Continues, 1972, 73, 74, Lowe's Scoreboard, 1978, also articles. Member North Carolina House Reps., 1962-64, Republican Senatorial Inner Circle, 1980—; member executive committee North Carolina Republican Committee, 1963-73; trustee U. North Carolina Chapel Hill, 1987—; director United States Council of Better Business Burs., 1981-85; board of directors, vice president National Home Improvement Council, 1972-76; board of directors North Carolina School Arts Foundation, 1975-79, North Carolina Board Natural and Economic Resources, 1975-76; board of directors, member government affairs committee Home Center Institute; trustee, secretary board Wilkes Community College, 1964-73; chairman, president board of directors Do-It-Yourself Research Institute, 1981-89; president Hardware Home Improvement Council City of Hope National Medical Center, Los Angeles, 1987-89. With United States Navy, 1952-55, lieutenant Reserves 1955-62. Named Wilkes County North Carolina Young Man of Year, Wilkes Junior Chamber of Commerce, 1962; recipient Bronze Oscar of Industry award Fin. World, 1969-74, 76-79, Silver Oscar of Industry award, 1970, 72-74, 76-79, Gold Oscar of Industry award as best of all industry, 1972, 87, Excellence award in corp. reporting Fin. Analysts Federation, 1970, 72, 74, 81-82, cert. of Distinction Brand Names Foundation, 1970, Retailer of Year award, 1971, 73, Distinguished Mcht. award, 1972, Spirit of Life award City of Hope, 1983; named to Home Center Hall of Fame, 1985. Member National Association Over-the-Counter Companies (board advisers 1973-77), Newcomen Society, Employee Stock Ownership Association (president 1983-85, chairman 1985-87), Scabbard and Blade, Phi Beta Kappa, Pi Kappa Alpha. Clubs: Twin City, Forsyth Country, Piedmont City (Winston-Salem, North Carolina); Hound Ears (Blowing Rock, North Carolina); Elk River (Banner Elk, North Carolina); Roaring Gap (North Carolina). Home: 226 N Stratford Road Winston-Salem North Carolina 27104 Office: Lowe's Cos Incorporated Post Office Box 1111 Highway 268 E North Wilkesboro North Carolina 28656

STUZIN, CHARLES BRYAN, savings and loan association executive; born Miami, Florida, 1942. Graduate, University Florida, 1964, postgraduate, 1967. With Stuzin and Camner, Miami, 1973—; president Citizens Savings and Fin. Corp., Miami,

1980—; chairman Citizens Savings and Fin. Corp., 1982—; chairman Citizens Mortgage Corp.; chairman, president Citizens Federal Savings and Loan; chairman, chief executive officer Loan Am. Fin. Corp.; vice president, secretary Moore Insurance Agency; partner Webster Park Associates, Sarasota Properties. Office: Citizens Savings Fin Corp 999 Brickell Avenue Miami Florida 33131

SULZBERGER, ARTHUR OCHS, SR., newspaper executive; born New York City, February 5, 1926; son of Arthur Hays and Iphigene (Ochs) S.; married Barbara Grant, July 2, 1948 (divorced 1956); children—Arthur Ochs, Karen Alden; married Carol Fox, December 19, 1956; 1 daughter, Cynthia Fox; adopted daughter, Cathy. Bachelor of Arts, Columbia, 1951; Doctor of Laws, Dartmouth, 1964, Bard College, 1967; Doctor of Humane Letters, Montclair State College, 1972, Tufts University; Doctor of Laws (honorary), University Scranton. With New York Times, New York City, 1951—; assistant treasurer New York Times, 1958-63, president, pub., 1963—, also director; director Times Printing Company, Chattanooga. Trustee Columbia, Metropolitan Mus. Art (chairman board trustees, 1987—). Served to captain United States Marine Corps Reserve, World War II, Korea. Member Bureau Newspaper Advertising (director), Newspaper Pubs. Association, S.A.R. Clubs: Overseas Press (New York City), Explorers (New York City); Metropolitan (Washington); Century Country ((Purchase, New York). Office: New York Times Company 229 W 43rd St New York New York 10036

SULZBERGER, ARTHUR OCHS, JR., newspaper publisher; born Mount Kisco, New York, September 22, 1951; son of Arthur Ochs Sulzberger and Barbara Winslow Grant; married Gail Gregg, May 24, 1975; children: Arthur Gregg, Ann Alden. Bachelor of Arts, Tufts University, 1974; postgraduate, Harvard University Business School, 1985. Reporter The Raleigh (North Carolina) Times, 1974-76; corr. Associated Press, London, 1976-78; Washington corr. New York Times, 1978-81, city hall reporter, 1981, assistant metro editor, 1981-82, group manager advertising department, 1983-84, senior analyst corp. planning, 1985, production coordinator, 1985-87, assistant pub., 1987-88, deputy pub., 1988—. Board of directors North Carolina Outward Bound School, Morganton, l979, New York City Outward Bound Center, Greenwich, Connecticut, l988, Am. Press Institute, l989; vice chairman Task Force on Minorities in Newspaper Business, l989. Office: The New York Times 229 W 43rd St New York New York 10036

SUTTON, THOMAS CARL, metal products manufacturing corporation executive; born Longmont, Colorado, January 10, 1921; son of Carl and Alice J. (Hunter) S.; married Jayne A. Harrington, June 22, 1946; children: Scott T., Leslie Lynn. Bachelor of Business Administration, University Cincinnati, 1948. With Dover Corp., New York City, 1951—; president OPW div. Dover Corp., 1961-63, executive vice president corp., 1963-64, president, chief executive officer, 1964-71, chairman, chief executive officer, 1971-81, chairman, 1981—, also director; director Dover Elevator Company, Dover Corp. (Canada), Limited, Dover International, Incorporated, Alberta Oil Tool Company, Incorporated, F & M Schaefer Corp. Served to major, pilot, United States Army Air Force, 1942-46. Decorated Distinguished Flying Cross (2), Air medal (7). Clubs: University, Winged Foot Golf; Queen City (Cincinnati). Office: Dover Corp 277 Park Avenue New York New York 10172

SWANSON, DAVID HEATH, agricultural company executive; born Aurora, Illinois, November 3, 1942; son of Neil H. and Helen J. (McKendry) S.; married Cynthia Tripp; children: Benjamin Health, Matthew Banford. Bachelor of Arts, Harvard University, 1964; Master of Arts, University Chicago, 1969. Account executive 1st National Bank Chicago, 1967-69; deputy manager Brown Brothers Harriman & Company, New York City, 1969-72; assistant treasurer Borden, Incorporated, New York City, 1972-75; vice president, treasurer Continental Grain Company, New York City, 1975-77, vice president chief fin. officer, 1977-79, general manager European div., 1979-81, executive vice president and general manager World Grain div., 1981-83, corp. senior vice president, chief fin. and administrative officer, 1983-86, group president, 1985-86; president, chief executive officer Central Soya, Fort Wayne, Ind., 1986—; adv. board United States Export-Import Bank, 1985-86; member Gov.'s Agricultural Board Ind., Ind. State Board Education. Board of directors International Policy Council on Agriculture and Trade; member adv. board Purdue U. Agriculture School; member Governor's Economic Devel. Board; board governors Executive Council on Foreign Diplomats and United States Agriculture Libr.; governor Foundation for United States Constitution. Member Council Foreign Relations (board directors), Ind. Chamber of Commerce (board directors), Fort Wayne Chamber of Commerce (board directors), Fort Wayne Historical Society (board directors), Am. Alpine Club (board directors), Scottish Deerhound of Am. Club, Links Club (New York), Racquet and Tennis Club (New York), Fort Wayne Country Club, Explorers Club (board directors, secretary, vice president). Republican. Congregationalist. Office: Central Soya Company Incorporated Post Office Box 1400 Fort Wayne Indiana 46801

SWINDELLS, WILLIAM, JR., lumber and paper company executive; born 1930; married. Bachelor of Science, Stanford University, 1953. With Willamette Industries, Incorporated, Portland, Oregon, 1953—; senior vice president production, marketing building materials Willamette Industries, Incorporated, until 1978, executive vice president, 1978-80, president forest products div., 1980-82, president, chief executive officer, 1982—, also director, chairman, 1984—; director Oregon Bank, Portland. Office: Willamette Industries Incorporated 3800 1st Interstate Tower Portland Oregon 97201

TAGLIABUE, PAUL JOHN, lawyer, professional football league commissioner; born Jersey City, November 24, 1940; son of Charles and Mary T.; married Chandler M. Minter, August 28, 1965; children: Drew, Emily. Bachelor of Arts, Georgetown University, 1962; Juris Doctor, New York University, 1965. Bar: N.J 1965, District of Columbia 1969. Attorney to secretary defense Department Defense, Washington,

1966-69; associate Covington & Burling, Washington, 1969-74, partner, 1969-89; commissioner National Football League, New York City, 1989—. Contributor articles to professional journals. Member American Bar Association (chair sports and entertainment industry committee antitrust section 1986—), District of Columbia Bar Association. Office: NFL Commr's Office 410 Park Avenue New York New York 10022 also: Covington & Burling 1201 Pennsylvania Avenue Northwest Post Office Box 7566 Washington District of Columbia 20044

TALBOT, JAMES THOMAS, entrepreneur, real estate developer, airline executive; born Los Angeles, December 11, 1935; son of James Thomson and Katherine Kingman (Kingsland) T.; married Linda Williams, September 10, 1959 (divorced 1969); married Karen Millicent Anderson, July 1, 1972; children: Susan, Amy, Thomas S. Bachelor of Arts, Stanford University, 1957; Doctor of Laws, University California, San Francsico, 1963. Bar: California 1963. Associate Walker, Wright, Tyler & Ward, Los Angeles, 1963-65, Gates, Talbot, Morris & Merrill, Los Angeles, 1965-69; vice president Dunn Properties Corp., Santa Ana, California, 1970-71, president, 1971-72, chairman, chief executive officer, 1972-75; partner Shaw and Talbot, Newport Beach, California, 1975—; president, chief executive officer, director Hawaiian Airlines, Honolulu, 1989—, HAL, Incorporated, 1989—; board of directors E.F. Hutton Group, New York City, Hallwood Group, Cleveland, GCA Corp., Andover, Massachusetts, Brock Hotels, Dallas. Served to captain United States Air Force, 1958-60. Member California Bar Association. Clubs: Big Canyon Country (board dirs., president 1974-77), Pacific (president 1981-86 (Newport Beach); Pauma Valley (California) (board dirs. 1979-82). Avocation: golf. Office: Talbot Company Post Office Box 8230 Newport Beach California 92658 Home: 25 Northampton Court Newport Beach California 92660

TARNOW, ROBERT L., manufacturing corporation executive; born Rochester, New York, 1924. Bachelor of Arts in Physics, Oberlin College, 1949. With sales department Goulds Pumps Incorporated, Seneca Falls, New York, 1951-66, vice president administration, 1966-69, vice president manufacturing, 1969-71, president, 1971-78, chairman board, chief executive officer, director, 1978-83, chairman board of directors, 1983—; board of directors Raymond Corp., Utica Mutual Insurance Company, Bausch & Lomb, Norstar Bancorp. Office: Goulds Pumps Incorporated 240 Fall St Seneca Falls New York 13148

TARR, ROBERT JOSEPH, JR., consumer products company executive, retail executive; born Freeport, New York, December 7, 1943; son of Robert Joseph and Janet Christman (Laughton) T.; married Molly Worthington Upton, February 28, 1970; children: William Upton, Robert Joseph, III, David Worthington. Bachelor of Science, United States Naval Academy, 1966; Master of Business Administration, Harvard University, 1973; Master of Arts, Tufts University, 1976. Assistant vice president corp. fin. Paine Webber Jackson Curtis, Boston, 1973-75; director corp. planning, then vice president, treasurer General Cinema Corp., Chestnut Hill, Massachusetts,

1976-78, senior vice president, 1978-83, executive vice president, chief operating officer, 1983-85, president, chief operating officer, 1985—, also director; president, chief operating officer The Neiman Marcus Group Incorporated, 1987—, also board of directors. Chairman board visitors Fletcher School Law and Diplomacy; board of directors Northeastern U. Corp.; trustee Tenacre Country Day School, Belmont Hill School Lieutenant United States Navy, 1966-71. Member National Retail Federation (board directors). Clubs: Newton Squash and Tennis, Quissett Yacht. Home: 40 White Oak Road Wellesley Massachusetts 02181 Office: General Cinema Corp 27 Boylston St Chestnut Hill Massachusetts 02167

TASCO, FRANK JOHN, insurance brokerage company executive; born New York City, August 18, 1927; son of Frank and Jean (Pisapia) T.; married Edwardine Dordoni, October 30, 1954; children—Jill, Lisbeth, Diana. Bachelor of Arts, New York University, 1949. Vice president Guy Carpenter & Company, New York City, 1962-76; director Guy Carpenter & Company, 1971—, president, chief executive officer, 1976-84; president, chief operating officer Marsh & McLennan Companies, New York City, 1984-85, chairman, chief executive officer, 1986—, also board of directors; board of directors New York Insurance Exchange, 1980, 85, Faugere & Jutheau, Paris, Terra Nova Insurance Company, London, Borden, Incorporated, New York Telephone Company, Hudig-Langeveldt Groep bv, Netherlands; member industries adv. committee Advertising Council, publishers' adv. panel Fortune magazine; member Listed Companies adv. committee to New York Stock Exchange. Member Corp. Fund Leadership Committee Lincoln Center, New York City, board Inner-City Scholarship Fund; board of directors St. Francis Hospital, Roslyn, New York, 1981—, Phoenix House Foundation Incorporated, New York City Partnership, National Multiple Sclerosis Society; trustee National Commission Against Drunk Driving; patron Project 100 for Mentally Handicapped of Bermuda; board governors Metropolitan New York United States Olympic Committee Served with United States Navy, 1945-46. Member Foreign Policy Association, Business Council for United Nations, Life Saving Benevolent Association New York. Clubs: City Midday Drug and Chem. (board dirs. 1972-77), Economic, Links (New York City); Hartford (Connecticut); Meadow Brook (Jericho, New York).

TEERLINK, RICHARD FRANCIS, motor company executive; born Chicago, October 12, 1936; son of James and Martha (Vogel) T.; married Ann L. Hofing, April 23, 1960; children—John Robert, Leslie Ann, Victoria Lynn. Bachelor of Science, Bradley University, 1961; Master of Business Administration, University Chicago, 1976. Senior vice president administration Union Special Corp., Chicago, 1971-78; vice president fin. RTE Corp., Waukesha, Wisconsin, 1978-80; senior vice president, chief fin. officer Herman Miller, Incorporated, Zeeland, Michigan, 1980-81; vice president, chief fin. officer Harley Davidson Motor Company, Incorporated, Milwaukee, 1981-88, also board of directors; president, chief executive officer Harley Davidson, Incorporated, Milwaukee, 1987—. Served with United States

Army, 1955-58. Home: 1765 Wedgewood W Elm Grove Wisconsin 53122 Office: Harley-Davidson Incorporated 3700 W Juneau Avenue Milwaukee Wisconsin 53208

TEETS, JOHN WILLIAM, diversifed company executive; born Elgin, Illinois, September 15, 1933; son of John William and Maudie T.; married Nancy Kerchenfaut, June 25, 1965; children: Jerri, Valerie Sue, Heide Jane, Suzanne. Student, University Illinois. President, partner Winter Garden Restaurant, Incorporated, Carpenterville, Illinois, 1957-63; vice president Greyhound Food Management Company; president Post Houses, Incorporated, and Horne's Enterprises, Chicago, 1964-68; president, chief operating officer John R. Thompson Company, Chicago, 1968-71; president, chief operating officer Restaurant div., also corp. v.p Canteen Corp., Chicago, 1971-74; executive vice president, chief operating officer Bonanza International Company, Dallas, 1974-76; chairman, chief executive officer Greyhound Food Management, Incorporated, Phoenix, 1976; group vice president food service Greyhound Corp., Phoenix, 1976-81, group vice president services group, 1980-81, vice chairman, 1980-82, chairman, chief executive officer, 1981—, now also president and director; chairman, president Armour & Company, from 1981; chief executive officer Dial Corp., Phoenix; chairman, chief executive officer Greyhound Food Management Incorporated, Phoenix, 1982—; chairman Greyhound Support Services Incorporated, Phoenix; vice chairman President's Conference on Foodservice Industry; member adv. board Phoenix and Valley of Sun Convention and Visitors Bureau, 1979-82. Recipient Silver Plate award, Golden Plate award International Foodservice Mfrs. Association, 1980. Member National Automatic Mdsg. Association, National Restaurant Association, National Institute Foodservice Industry (trustee), Am. Management Association, Christian Businessmen's Association (chairman steering committee 1977), National Speakers Association. Club: Arizona. Office: The Greyhound Corp Greyhound Tower Station 3103 Phoenix Arizona 85077

TELLEP, DANIEL MICHAEL, aerospace executive, mechanical engineer; born Forest City, Pennsylvania, November 20, 1931. Bachelor of Science in Mechanical Engineering with highest honors, University California, Berkeley, 1954, Master of Science, 1955; graduate Advanced Management Program, Harvard University, 1971. With Lockheed Missiles & Space Company, 1955—, chief engineer missile systems div., 1969-75, vice president, assistant general manager advanced systems div., 1975-83, executive vice president, 1983-84, president, 1984—, 1986—; chairman, chief executive officer Lockheed Corp., 1989—; consultant in field. Contributor article to professional journals. Fellow American Institute of Aeronautics and Astronautics (Lawrence Sperry award 1964, Missile Systems award 1986), Am. Astronautical Society; member National Academy of Engineering, Sigma Xi, Pi Tau Sigma, Tau Beta Pi. Office: Lockheed Corp 4500 Park Granada Boulevard Calabasas California 91399

TELLER, ALVIN NORMAN, record company executive; born New York

City, September 3, 1944; son of Sheldon and Selma (Gofsaof) T.; married Jennifer Rodsjo, August 26, 1979; 1 child, Alexis. Bachelor of Science in Electronics Engineering, Columbia University, 1965, Master of Science in Operations Research, 1967; Master of Business Administration, Harvard University, 1969. Assistant to president CBS Records, CBS, Incorporated, New York City, 1969-70, vice president merchandising, 1971-74; director corp. devel. Playboy Enterprises, Chicago, 1970-71; president United Artists Records, Los Angeles, 1974-76; management consultant Alvin North Teller & Associates, Los Angeles, 1976-79; president Windsong Records, Los Angeles, 1979-81; senior vice president, general manager Columbia Records CBS, Incorporated, New York City, 1981-85, president CBS Records div., 1985-88; president, chief operating officer MCA Records, Incorporated, 1988—; vice president MCA Incorporated, 1988—. Board of directors Rock and Rock Hall of Fame Foundation, 1985—; hon. director T.J. Martell Foundation for Cancer Research, New York City, 1981—. Named Humanitarian of Year T.J. Martell Foundation for Cancer Rsch., 1988. Member Recording Industry Association Am. (board directors 1985—), National Acad. Recording Arts and Sciences (pres.'s adv. council). Office: MCA Records 70 Universal City Plaza North Hollywood California 91608

TEMPLE, ARTHUR, investment company executive; born Texarkana, Arkansas, April 8, 1920; son of Arthur and Katherine (Sage) T.; married Mary MacQuiston (divorced 1963); children: Arthur III, Charlotte; married Charlotte Dean, September 4, 1963. Student, University Tex.-Austin, 1937-38; Doctor of Laws (honorary), Pepperdine University, 1982. Bookkeeper, assistant manager retail yard Temple Lumber Yard, Lufkin, Texas, 1938-48; president, chairman board Temple Associates, Incorporated, Diboll, Texas, 1941-70; executive vice president Temple Industries, Incorporated, Diboll, Texas, 1948-51, president, chief executive officer, 1951-75, chairman board, 1972-73; board of directors Temple-Eastex Incorporated, Diboll, Texas, 1973——, chairman board, 1975-83; chairman planning and devel. committee Time Incorporated, Diboll, Texas, 1973-81, group vice president, 1973-78, board of directors, executive committee, 1973—, vice chairman, 1978-83; Pchmn. board Exeter Investment Company, Lufkin, Texas, 1982-83; chairman board Temple-Inland Incorporated, Lufkin, Texas, 1984—, board of directors, member executive committee, 1979; board of directors Contractor's Supplies, Lufkin, Lufkin Block, Lumberman's Investment Corp., Austin, Sunbelt Insurance Company, Austin, Great Am. Reserve Insurance Company, Dallas, Temple-Inland Fin. Services Incorporated, Temple Inland Properties Incorporated, Austin Crest Hotel Incorporated; chairman board T&T Corp., Lufkin, Pineland State Bank; limited partner Dallas Cowboys. Football Club, 1984—; president, board of directors Texas Southeastern Railroad (board of directors). Pes. Angelina County Chamber of Commerce, 1950; active State Board Education, 1949; board regents Lamar Tech. U., 1957; trustee Duke U., 1983, John E. Gray Institute, T.L.L. Temple Founds.; board of directors St. Michael Hospital Foundation, Texarkana, 1984—, National Park Foundation, 1984—. Recipient 1 0f 5 Outstanding Young Men in Texas award Texas Junior Chamber of Commerce, 1948, Conservationist of Year award, 1977, East Texan of Year award Deep East Texas Council Govts., 1983, Conservationist of Year award Safari Club International, 1983; named to Texas Business Hall of Fame, 1983. Member National Forest Product Assn (past chairman, president, board directors), National Association Mfrs (board directors), Southern Forest Products Association (past chairman, president), Lumbermen's Association Texas (past chairman, president), Am. Forest Products Association (trustee), Crown Colony Club (board directors), Delta Kappa Epsilon. Office: Temple-Inland Incorporated Post Office Drawer N 303 S Temple Diboll Texas 75941

TERRY, HOWARD L., savings and loan association executive. Chairman, director Farm & Home Savings Association, Nevada, Missouri. Office: Farm & Home Savings Association 221 W Cherry Nevada Missouri 64772§

TERRY, RONALD ANDERSON, bank holding company executive; born Memphis, December 5, 1930; son of John Burnett and Vernon (Lucas) T.; married Wynoka W. Evans, May 21, 1989; children by previous marriage: Natalie Carol, Cynthia Leigh. Bachelor of Science, Memphis State University, 1952; postgraduate, Southern Methodist University, 1961, Harvard University, 1970. Management trainee First Tennessee Bank, Memphis, 1957; president First Tennessee National Corp., Memphis, 1971, chairman, chief executive officer, 1973—; chairman, chief executive officer First Tennessee Bank N.A., Memphis, 1979—, also board of directors; board of directors BellSouth Corp., Promus Companies, Incorporated. Past president, board of directors Boys Clubs Memphis, Arts Appreciation Foundation; past chairman Memphis Jobs Conference; board of directors, president Future Memphis; board of directors St. Jude Hospital; chairman adv. council Baptist Memorial Hospital; trustee U. Tennessee, Rhodes College, Memphis; past Tennessee State chairman committee for economic devel.; adv. board Memphis Arts Council Lieutenant United States Navy, 1953-57. Member Am. Bankers Association (treasury adv. committee, board directors, past chairman government relations council), Association Reserve City Bankers (director, past chairman government relations committee and pub. affairs committee), Association Bank Holding Companies (legis. policy committee, past president federal adv. council), Econ. Club of Memphis (past president). Office: 1st Tennessee National Corp Post Office Box 84 Memphis Tennessee 38101

TESSLER, ALLAN ROGER, lawyer; born Philadelphia, September 29, 1936; son of Irving and Rhoda T.; married Frances Goudsmit, June 17, 1958; children: Andrea, Christopher, Karla. Bachelor of Arts, Cornell University, 1958, Bachelor of Laws, 1963. Bar: New York 1963, United States DIst. Court (southern district) New York 1963. Associate Cleary Gotlieb, Steen and Hamilton, New York City, 1963-67; arbitrageur Loeb, Rhoades, New York City, 1967-68; managing partner Devon Securities, New York City, 1969-72; executive vice president Landenburg, Thalman, New York City, 1972; president, chairman Fifth Avenue Coach Lines, New York City, 1972-73; president Slater Walker of Am., New York City, 1973-75; of counsel Spengler, Carlson et al, New York City, 1975-76; senior partner Shea & Gould, New York City, 1976-88, of counsel, 1989—; chairman, board of directors Enhance Fin. Services, New York City; board of directors Checker Motors Corp., New York City, Jackpot Enterprises, Incorporated, Las Vegas, International Fin. Group, Incorporated, New York City, The Limited, Incorporated, Columbus, Ohio, Infotechnology, Incorporated, New York; chairman Service Resources Corp., New York. National chairman Cornell LaW School Fund, 1983-85; member adv. council Cornell Law School, 1987—. Served to lieutenant (junior grade) United States Navy, 1958-61. Member Phi Beta Kappa. Clubs: Harmonie, Sky (New York City). Office: International Controls Corp 2016 N Pitcher St Kalamazoo Michigan 49007

TETI, ALFRED L., bank executive; born Philadelphia, 1935; married Barbara; 3 daughters. Student, Gettysburg College. Vice president, director operations 1st Pennsylvania Bank, Philadelphia, until 1980; chief operating officer Manufacturers Hanover Fin. Services, 1980-83; with Collective Hanover Savings & Loan, 1983-84; chief operating officer, senior executive vice president Centrust Savings Bank, Miami, Florida, 1984-89; president, chief executive officer Amerifirst Bank, Miami. Office: Amerifirst Bank One S E 3rd Avenue Box 026029 Miami Florida 33102

THAYER, ARTEMAS BRONSON, financial services company executive, banker; born Mineola, New York, September 2, 1939; son of Thomas Redmond and Louise (Little) T.; married Stella L. Ferguson, May 3, 1969; 1 daughter, Susannah. Bachelor of Arts, Harvard University, 1961; Master of Business Administration, New York University, 1967. Chartered fin. analyst. Vice president Dominick & Dominick, New York City, 1963-72; senior vice president fin. Lykes Brothers Incorporated, Tampa, Florida, 1972—; chairman board of directors First Florida Banks Incorporated, Tampa, Florida, 1983—; director Bank of Clearwater, Florida, 1971—; chairman board Bank of Clearwater, Florida, 1974—; director LTV Corp., Dallas, 1982—. Member Florida Resource Recovery, Tallahassee, 1976-77; chairman Clearwater Downtown Devel. Authority, 1980. Served in United States Marine Corps Reserve, 1962-66. Fellow Fin. Analysts Federation; member Society Secutiy Analysts Central Florida, New York Society Security Analysts, Greater Tampa Chamber of Commerce (director 1982-83), Harvard Alumni Association (treasurer 1983), Beta Gamma Sigma. Republican. Episcopalian. Clubs: Harvard (New York City), Links (New York City). Home: Fort King Highway Thonotosassa Florida 33592 Office: First Florida Banks Incorporated Post Office Box 31265 Tampa Florida 33631

THIELE, WILLIAM EDWARD, insurance company executive; born New York City, November 12, 1942; son of Elmer William and Ethel Mae (Stein) T.; married Nancy June Watt, May 2, 1964; children: Christina, Jeanette, Amanda. Bachelor of Arts, Queens (New York) College, 1963. Trainee underwiter Phoenix Assurance, New York City, 1963-68; underwriter, assistant secretary, assistant vice president, vice president, senior vice president General Reinsurance Corp., Stamford, Connecticut, 1968-83; executive vice president Continental Corp., New York City, 1983-88, senior executive vice president, 1988-89, president, chief operating officer, 1990—; chairman Lombard Insurance Group, Hong Kong, 1984-88, Associate Aviation Underwriters, Short Hills, New Jersey, Insurance Services Office, New York City, Continental Corp.; trustee College of Insurance, Queens College Foundation. Contributor articles to professional journals. Trustee South St. Seaport Mus. Republican. Methodist. Club: Milford (Connecticut) Yacht. Avocations: sailing, skiing. Office: Continental Corp 180 Maiden Lane New York New York 10038

THOMAS, BIDE LAKIN, utility executive; born Mason City, Iowa, August 14, 1935; son of Brice Lakin and Jane (Duffield) T.; married Mary Nell; children: Brice, Lorraine, Carolyn. Bachelor of Science in Industrial Administration, Yale University, 1957; Master of Business Administration, Harvard University, 1959. With Commonwealth Edison Company, Chicago, 1959—, div. vice president, 1970-73, general div. manager, 1973-75, vice president div. operations, 1975-76, vice president industrial relations, 1976-80, executive vice president, 1980-87, president, 1987—; board of directors Commonwealth Edison Company, Northern Trust Corp., Northern Trust Company, Railroad Donnelley & Sons Company. Trustee Rush-Presbyn.-St. Luke's Medical Center, DePaul U., Illinois Institute Tech.; board mgrs. Young Men's Christian Association Metropolitan Chicago, chairman 1985-86; board of directors Civic Federation, Chicago Crime Commission, Chgo.-Cities in Schools, Rush/Copley Health Care Systems Incorporated, board of directors Robert Crown Center for Health Education, Associate Northwestern U.; board of directors United Way Chicago; board governors Argonne National Lab., IIT Research Institute, Chicago Lighthouse of the Blind; member governing board Illinois Council Economic Education; adv. board J.L. Kellogg Grad. School Mgmt. Member Chicago Club, Econ. Club of Chicago, Commercial Club. Office: Commonwealth Edison Company 1 First National Plaza Post Office Box 767 Chicago Illinois 60690

THOMAS, DEROY C., lawyer, business and insurance company executive; born Utica, New York, February 16, 1926. Bachelor of Arts, Iona College, 1949; Bachelor of Laws, Fordham University, 1952. Bar: New York 1952. Assistant professor law Fordham University, New York City, 1953-58; assistant counsel Association Casualty and Surety Companies, New York City, 1959-64; with firm Watters & Donovan, 1964; with Hartford Fire Insurance Company and subsidiary companies, Connecticut, 1964—; general counsel Hartford Fire Insurance Company and subsidiary companies, 1966-69, vice president, 1968-69, senior vice president, 1969-73; executive vice president Hartford Fire Insurance Company and subs companies, 1973-76; president, chief executive officer Hartford Fire Insurance Company and subsidiary companies, 1976-83, chairman, chief executive officer, 1979—, also board of directors; executive vice president International Telephone & Telegraph Corporation Corp., New York City, 1983-85, vice-chairman, 1985-88; president, chief operating officer International Telephone & Telegraph Corporation Corp., 1988—; president, chief executive officer International Telephone & Telegraph Corporation Diversified Services Corp., 1983—. Member American Bar Association. Office: International Telephone and Telegraph Corporation Corp 320 Park Avenue New York New York 10022 also: Hartford Life Ins Company Hartford Plaza Hartford Connecticut 06115

THOMAS, RICHARD LEE, banker; born Marion, Ohio, January 11, 1931; son of Marvin C. and Irene (Harruff) T.; married Helen Moore, June 17, 1953; children: Richard L., David Paul, Laura Sue. Bachelor of Arts, Kenyon College, 1953; postgraduate (Fulbright scholar), University Copenhagen, Denmark, 1954; Master of Business Administration (George F. Baker scholar), Harvard University, 1958. With First National Bank Chicago, 1958—, assistant vice president, 1962-63, vice president, 1963-65; vice president, general manager First National Bank Chicago (London (England) branch), 1965-66; vice president term loan div. First National Bank Chicago (London branch), 1968, vice-chairman board, 1973-75, president, director, 1975—; senior vice president, general manager First Chicago Corp., 1969-72, executive vice president, 1972-73, vice chairman board, 1973-74, president, 1974—, also director, 1973-74; director CNA Fin. Corp., Sara Lee Corp. Trustee, past chairman board trustees Kenyon College; trustee Rush-Presbyn.-St. Luke's Medical Center; trustee Northwestern U.; chairman board, Orchestral Association With Army of the United States, 1954-56. Member Chicago Council Foreign Relations, Phi Beta Kappa, Beta Theta Pi. Clubs: Sunningdale Golf (London); Economic (past president), Commercial, Chicago, Casino, Mid-America (Chicago); Indian Hill (Winnetka, Illinois); Old Elm (Highland Pk., Illinois). Office: First Chicago Corp 1 First National Plaza Chicago Illinois 60670

THOMPSON, JERE WILLIAM, retail food company executive; born Dallas, January 18, 1932; son of Joe C. and Margaret (Philp) T.; married Peggy Dunlap, June 5, 1954; children: Michael, Jere W., Patrick, Deborah, Kimberly, Christopher, David. Graduate high school, 1950; Bachelor of Business Administration, University Texas, 1954. With Southland Corp., Dallas, 1954—; vice president stores Southland Corp. (merged with Thompson Company 1988), Dallas, 1962-73, executive vice president, 1973-74, president, 1974—, director, 1962—, chief executive officer, 1986-91, co-vice chairman, 1991—; board of directors MCorp, Lamonts Corp. Board of directors St. Paul Hospital Foundation Served to lieutenant (junior grade) United States Naval Reserve, 1954-56. Office: Southland Corp 2711 N Haskell Avenue Dallas Texas 75204

THOMPSON, JOHN P., retail food executive; born Dallas, November 2, 1925; son of Joe E. and Margaret (Philip) T.; married Mary Carol Thomson, June 5, 1948; children: Mary Margaret, Henry Douglas, John P. Bachelor of Business Administration, University Texas, 1948. With

Southland Corp. (merged with Thompson Company 1988), Dallas, 1948—, president, 1961-69, chief executive officer, 1969-86, chairman, 1969—, also board of directors. Office: Southland Corp 2828 N Haskell Avenue Dallas Texas 75204

THOMPSON, W. REID, utility company executive; born Durham, North Carolina, 1924; marride. Bachelor of Science in Commerce, University North Carolina, 1945; Bachelor of Laws, Harvard University, 1949. Member North Carolina General Assembly, 1955-57; judge Superior Court North Carolina, 1958-60; executive vice president, general counsel Carolina Power and Light Company, 1960-71; with Potomac Electric Power Company, Washington, 1971—, chairman board of directors, president chief executive officer, 1971-83, chairman board of directors, chief executive officer, 1983—; board of directors Geico Corp., Riggs National Corp. Office: Potomac Electric Power Company 1900 Pennsylvania Avenue Northwest Washington District of Columbia 20068

THORNE, OAKLEIGH BLAKEMAN, publishing company executive; born Santa Barbara, California, 1932. Bachelor of Arts, Harvard University, 1954. With First National City Bank New York, 1954-62; chairman, director Ct Corp. Systems; with Commerce Clearing House, Incorporated, Deerfield, Illinois, 1959—; chairman Commerce Clearing House, Incorporated, Deerfield, 1975—. Office: Commerce Clearing House Incorporated 2700 Lake Cook Road Riverwoods Illinois 60015

TILGHMAN, RICHARD GRANVILLE, banker; born Norfolk, Virginia, September 18, 1940; son of Henry Granville and Frances (Fulghum) T.; married Alice Creech, June 28, 1969; children—Elizabeth Arrington, Caroline Harrison. Bachelor of Arts, University Virginia, 1963. Assistant cashier United Virginia Bank-Seaboard National, Norfolk, Virginia, 1968-70, assistant vice president, 1970-72; president, chief administrative officer United Virginia Bank, Richmond, 1978-80; assistant vice president United Virginia Mortgage Corp., Norfolk, Virginia, 1972, vice president, 1972-73, president, chief executive officer, 1974-76; president, chief executive officer United Virginia Leasing Corp., Richmond, Virginia, 1973-74; senior vice president bank related United Virginia Bankshares, Incorporated, Richmond, 1976-78, executive vice president corp. banking, 1980-84, vice chairman, 1984-85; president, chief executive officer United Virginia Bankshares, Incorporated, now Crestar Fin. Corp., Richmond, 1985—, chairman, 1986—; board of directors director Chesapeake Corp., Richmond, 1986—; chairman Virginia Public building Authority, Richmond, 1982-87; principal Virginia Business Council, 1987—. Chairman board of directors Richmond Symphony, 1984-85; board of directors, general adv. council Sheltering Arms Hospital, Richmond, 1981-89; board of directors Virginia Free, 1989-90, Richmond Symphony Foundation, 1989—, Virginia Mus. Foundation, 1986—, Virginia Foundation Ind. Colleges, 1988—, St. Catherine's School, 1989—, Virginia Literacy Foundation, 1986-89; trustee Randolph-Macon College, 1985—, Richmond Renaissance, 1986—; co-chairman National Conference of Christians and Jews. 1st lieutenant United States Army, 1963-66. Member Association Reserve City Bankers, Am. Bankers Association, Am. Institute Bankers, Virginia Bankers Association, Robert Morris Assocs. Episcopalian. Clubs: Commonwealth, Country of Virginia. Office: Crestar Fin Corp 919 E Main St Post Office Box 26665 Richmond Virginia 23261-6665

TIMKEN, W. ROBERT, JR., manufacturing company executive; born 1938; married. Bachelor of Arts, Stanford University, 1960; Master of Business Administration, Harvard University, 1962. With Timken Company (formerly The Timken Roller Bearing Company), Canton, Ohio, 1962—, assistant vice president sales, 1964-65, director corp. devel., 1965-68, vice president, 1968-73, vice-chairman board, chairman fin. committee, 1973-75, chairman board, chairman fin. committee, 1975—, chairman executive committee, 1983—, also director. Office: Timken Company 1835 Dueber Avenue Southwest Canton Ohio 44706

TINBERGEN, JAN, economist; born The Hague, The Netherlands, April 12, 1903; son of Dirk Cornelis and Jeannette (Van Eek) T.; married Tine Johanna de Wit, July 19, 1929 (deceased); children: Tine (Mrs. Adriaan M. Van Peski) (deceased), Elsje (Mrs. Maurits J. Barendrecht), Hanneke (Mrs. Steven Hoentjen), Marianne. Doctor Physics, SLeiden University, 1929; honorary degree Doctor.Economics, universities of Helsinki, Durham, Amsterdam, Freiburg, Lisbon, Brussels, Strasbourg, Grenoble, Oslo, 1929, universities of Paris, Bilbao, Ghent, Kiel, Bordeaux, Turin, Cluj, Cambridge, 1929. Statistician Central Bureau Statistics, The Hague, 1929-45; temporarily attached to League of Nations Secretariat, 1936-38; director government Central planning bureau, The Netherlands, 1945-55; professor The Netherlands School Economics (now Erasmus University), Rotterdam, 1933-73; consultant United Nations, World Bank, The Netherlands, Surinam, UAR, Turkey, Venezuela; research director 20th Century Fund, 1960-62. Author: Economic Policy: Principles and Design, 1956; The Design of Development, 1958; Shaping the World Economy, 1962; Lessons from the Past, 1964; Development Planning, 1967; Income Distribution: Analysis and Policies, 1975; World Security and Equity, 1990; co-author: Labor Plan, 1935, Warfare and Welfare, 1987. Recipient Erasmus prize, 1967; Nobel prize econs., 1969. Member National, Royal Dutch, Royal Flemish, Am. Acad. Sci., Brit. Acad. Sci., French Acad. Sci., Econometric Society, Am. Econ. Association, Royal Statistical Society. Member Dutch Labor Party. Home: Haviklaan 31, 2566 XD The Hague The Netherlands

TISCH, ANDREW HERBERT, tobacco company executive; born Asbury Park, New Jersey, August 14, 1949; son of Laurence Alan and Wilma Zelda (Stein) T.; children: Alexander, Lacey. Bachelor of Science, Cornell University, Ithaca, New York, 1971; Master of Business Administration, Harvard University, 1977. Brand manager Lorillard Company, New York City, 1971-75; manager operational analysis Loews Corp., New York City, 1977-79, vice president, 1985—; president Bulova Corp., Woodside, New York, 1985-

89; chairman, chief executive officer Lorillard Tobacco Company, New York City, 1989—; also board of directors Lorillard Tobacco Company, Bulova Corp., Woodside, New York; board of directors Wyndham Foods, Incorporated, Loews Corp., Bulova Systems and Instruments Corp. Contributor articles to professional journals. Member foreign affairs committee Am. Jewish Committee, New York City, 1983—; board of directors Outward Bound, Incorporated, Greenwich, Connecticut, 1983-88; trustee Central Synagogue, New York City, 1984—; general chairman United Jewish Appeal Federation of Jewish Philanthropies New York, vice chairman United Jewish Appeal, chairman Prime Minister's Council, 1987—; board of directors New York Shakespeare Festival, 1987—; chairman Children's Hearing Institute, 1988; board member New York City Sports Commission. Member 24 Karat Club New York, Century Country (Purchase, New York), Harmonie (New York City), Plumb (New York). Avocations: tennis, running. Office: Lorillard Tobacco Company 1 Park Avenue New York New York 10016-5895

TOBIN, JAMES, economics educator; born Champaign, Illinois, March 5, 1918; son of Louis Michael and Margaret (Edgerton) T.; married Elizabeth Fay Ringo, September 14, 1946; children: Margaret Ringo, Louis Michael, Hugh Ringo, Roger Gill. Bachelor of Arts summa cum laude, Harvard University, 1939, Master of Arts, 1940, Doctor of Philosophy, 1947; Doctor of Laws (honorary), Syracuse University, 1967, University Illinois, 1969, Dartmouth College, 1970, Swarthmore College, 1980, New School Social Research, 1982, New York University, 1982, Bates College, 1982, University Hartford, 1984, Colgate University, 1984, Gustavus Adolphus College, 1986, Western Maryland College, 1984, University New Haven, 1986; Doctor in Economics (honorary), New University Lisbon, 1980; Doctor of Humane Letters (honorary), Hofstra University, 1983, Sacred Heart University, 1990; Doctor in Social Sciences honoris causa, University Helsinki, 1986. Associate economist OPA, WPB, Washington, 1941-42; teaching fellow economics Harvard University, Cambridge, Massachusetts, 1946-47, with Society Fellows, 1947-50; associate professor economics Yale University, New Haven, 1950-55, professor, 1955—, Sterling professor economics, 1957-88, professor emeritus, 1988—; member Council Economic Advisers, 1961-62, National Acad. Sciences. Author: National Economic Policy, 1966, Essays in Economics-Macroeconomics, volume 1, 1972, The New Economics One Decade Older, 1974, Consumption and Econometrics, volume 2, 1975, Asset Accumulation and Economic Activity, 1980, Theory and Policy, Volume 3, 1982, Policies for Prosperity, 1987. Served to lieutenant United States Naval Reserve, 1942-46. Recipient Nobel prize in econs., 1981; Social Sci. Research Council faculty fellow, 1951-54; Grand cordon Order of the Sacred Treasure, Japan, 1988; Centennial medal Harvard Graduate School, 1989. Fellow Am. Acad. Arts and Sciences, Econometric Society (president 1958), Am. Statistical Association, Brit. Acad. (corr.); member Am. Philosophical Society, Am. Econ. Association (John Bates Clark medal

1955, vice president 1964, president 1971), Acad. Sciences Portugal (foreign associate), Phi Beta Kappa. Home: 117 Alden Avenue New Haven Connecticut 06515 Office: Yale U Department Econs Post Office Box 2125 New Haven Connecticut 06520

TOLLER, WILLIAM ROBERT, chemical and oil company executive; born Fort Smith, Arkansas, August 10, 1930; son of Audly Sr. and Martha (Anderson) T.; married Jo Ella Perry, June 13, 1959; children: William R. Jr., Michelle D., Gregory A. Bachelor of Business Administration, University Arkansas, 1956; postgraduate, Stamford University, 1971. Various positions Conoco Incorporated, Oklahoma, Texas and Colorado, 1955-77; vice president fin. and administration Continental Carbon Company, Houston, 1977-81, president, chief executive officer, 1981-84; vice president, general manager Concarb div. Witco Corp., Houston, 1984-86; director, chairman board, chief executive officer Witco Corp., New York City, 1990—. Member Republican National Committee, Washington, 1988-91. Member Am. Chemical Society, Am. Petroleum Institute, Fin. Executives, Certified Medical Assistant Board Member. Presbyterian. Avocations: golf, skiing. Home: 102 Windsor Circle Washington Township New Jersey 07675 Office: Witco Corp 520 Madison Avenue New York New York 10022-4236

TOLLETT, LELAND EDWARD, food company executive; born Nashville, Arkansas, January 21, 1937; son of Vergil E. and Gladys V. (Sturgis) T.; married Betty Ruth Blew, June 2, 1961; children—Terri Lynn, Gary Dwayne. Bachelor of Agricultural Science, University Arkansas, 1958, Master.S.A., 1959. Director Research Tyson Foods, Incorporated, Springdale, Arkansas, 1959-64, gen manager production, 1965-66, vice president production, 1966-80, chief operating officer, 1981-83, president, chief operating officer, 1984—, also director; president, chief operating officer Spring Valley Farms Incorporated, Poultry Growers Incorporated, Lane Processing Incorporated, Tyson-Carolina Incorporated, Eagle Distributing Incorporated, Lane Farms Incorporated, Tyson Export Sales Incorporated. Served with United States Air Force, 1961-62. Member National Broiler Council (board directors 1979—). Avocations: hunting; golfing. Home: 2801 S Johnson Road Springdale Arkansas 72764 Office: Tyson Foods Incorporated 2210 W Oaklawn Dr Springdale Arkansas 72764

TOOKER, GARY LAMARR, electronics company executive; born Shelby, Ohio, May 25, 1939; son of William Henry and Frances Ione (Melick) T.; married Diane Rae Kreider, August 4, 1962; children: Lisa, Michael. Bachelor of Science in Electrical Engineering, Arizona State University, 1962. With Motorola Incorporated, Phoenix, 1962—, vice president, general manager international semicondr. div., 1980-81, vice president, general manager semicondr. products sector, 1981-82, senior vice president, general manager semicondr. products sector, 1982-83; executive vice president, general manager semicondr. products sector Motorola Incorporated, 1983-86; senior executive vice president, chief corp. staff officer Motorola Incorporated,

Schaumburg, Illinois, 1986-88, senior executive vice president, chief operating officer, 1988-90, president, chief operating officer, 1990—; also board of directors; member engineering adv. council Arizona State University, Tempe, 1982-86. Board of directors Scottsdale (Arizona) Boys Club, 1980-86, Junior Achievement Chicago, 1988—; chief crusader, major. corp. group United Way, Chicago, 1988-91; member alumni board Arizona State U., 1991—. Named Outstanding Alumni of Year, Arizona State University, 1983. Member Institute of Electrical and Electronics Engineers, Am. Management Association, Semicondr. Industry Association (board directors 1981-86, chairman board 1982-86), Airz. Asns. Industries (board directors 1981-86), Am. Electroics Association (board directors 1988—, chairman board 1991), Econ. Club of Chicago. Republican. Office: Motorola Incorporated 1303 E Algonquin Road Schaumburg Illinois 60196

TOOT, JOSEPH F., JR., bearing manufacturing company executive; born 1935; married. Bachelor of Arts, Princeton University, 1957; postgraduate, Harvard University Graduate School Business Administration, 1961. With Timken Company, Canton, Ohio, 1962—; deputy manager Timken (France) Company, 1965-67; vice president international div. Timken Company, Canton, 1967-68, corp. vice president, then executive vice president, 1968-79, president, 1979—, also board of directors; board of directors Rockwell International. Office: Timken Company 1835 Dueber Avenue Southwest Canton Ohio 44706

TOPOL, SIDNEY, electronics company executive; born Boston, December 28, 1924; son of Morris and Dora (Kalinsky) T.; married Lillian Friedman, December 15, 1951; children: Deborah Jane, Joanne, Martha Grace. Bachelor of Science, University Massachusetts, 1947, Doctor of Science (honorary), 1984; postgraduate, University California, 1948-49. Physicist Naval Research Laboratory, 1947-48; engineer Raytheon Company, Boston, 1949-57, assistant manager engineering div. commercial equipment, 1957-59; director planning and marketing Raytheon Co.-Europe, Rome, 1959-65, general manager communications operations, 1965-71; president Sci.-Atlanta, Incorporated, 1971-83, chief executive officer, from 1975, chairman board, 1978—; director 1st Atlanta Corp., 1st National Bank of Atlanta., Continental Telecom Incorporated; member Conference Board, Pres.' Committee on the National Medal Sci. Member mgmt. adv. council College Mgmt., Georgia Institute Tech.; board visitors Emory U.; trustee Atlanta U., member adv. council, School Business Administration; board of directors Atlanta Chamber of Commerce, Atlanta Symphony Orchestra League; board governors Georgia Business & Industry Association; director Atlanta Partnership of Business and Education; member United States Council for World Communications Year '83, Marconi Fellowship Council. Served with United States Army Air Force, 1943-46. Recipient Corporate Leadership award Massachusetts Institute of Technology; recipient Beisswenger Memorial award National Cable Television Association, Emmy award National Acad. Television Arts and Sciences, Pioneer in Communications award Di Gamma Kappa - University Georgia; named Man of

Year Boston Latin School, 1982. Member Institute of Electrical and Electronics Engineers, Electronic Industries Association (past chairman, board govs.), Beta Gamma Sigma. Club: Rotary. Office: Sci-Atlanta Incorporated 1 Technology Parkway Atlanta Georgia 30092

TOPPEL, HAROLD H., diversified company executive; born Franklin, New Jersey, 1924; married. Bachelor of Arts, University Illinois, 1948. Salesman Lever Brothers Company, 1944, Food Fair Corp. and Penn Fruit Company, Incorporated, 1945-50; president National Grocery Company, Metuchen, New Jersey, 1950-54; chairman board, chief executive officer Pueblo International, Incorporated, formerly Pueblo Supermarkets, Incorporated, 1955—. Office: Pueblo International Incorporated 1300 Northwest 22nd St Pompano Beach Florida 33069

TORELL, JOHN RAYMOND, III, banker; born Hartford, Connecticut, July 10, 1939; son of Raymond John and Gertrude May (Bent) T.; married Anne A. Keller, February 17, 1962; children: John Raymond, Anne Elizabeth, Susan Allgood. Bachelor of Arts, Princeton University, 1961. With Manufacturers Hanover Trust Company, New York City, 1961—, assistant secretary, 1964-67, assistant vice president, 1967-70, vice president national div., 1970, vice president credit department, 1970-71, vice president corp. planning, 1971-72, senior vice president planning, marketing and special products, 1973-75, senior vice president, deputy general manager retail banking, 1975-76, executive vice president metropolitan div., 1976-78, vice chairman, director, 1978-82, president, director, 1982-88; executive vice chairman, director Manufacturers Hanover Corp. (parent), New York City, from 1982, president, until 1988; chairman, chief executive officer Calfed Incorporated, Los Angeles, Ca., 1988-89; chairman California Federal Savings and Loan, Los Angeles, Ca., 1988-89; Board directors Am. Home Products, Volt Information Systems Incorporated, chmn./dir. Fortune Corp., associate Private Capital Ptnrs. Incorporated. With United States Navy, 1962. Republican. Clubs: Blind Brook, Siwanoy Country, Bronxville Field. Home: 33 Northway Bronxville New York 10708 Office: Private Capital Partners 535 Madison Avenue New York New York 10022

TOWER, HORACE LINWOOD, III, consumer products company executive; born New Haven, July 16, 1932; son of Horace Linwood, Jr. and Madeline Elizabeth (Davin) T.; married Elizabeth Wright, December 29, 1956; children: Cynthia, William, John. Bachelor of Arts, Cornell University, 1955, Master of Business Administration, 1960; Doctor of Hebrew Literature (honorary), Westfield (Massachusetts) State College, 1984. Branch manager Procter & Gamble Corp., Cincinnati, 1960-62; management consultant Booz, Allen & Hamilton, New York City, 1962-63; product manager General Foods Corp., White Plains, New York, 1963-67; advertising and merchandising manager General Foods Corp., 1967-69, director corporate devel., 1969-71; executive vice president General Foods Corp. (Maxwell House div.), 1971-73, president div., 1973-78, president div. parent corp., 1978—; chairman board

Stanhome Incorporated; director Tambrands, Incorporated. Member board visitors United States Air Force Air U. Captain United States Air Force, 1956-59. Member Air Force Association, Sabre Pilots Association, Colony Club (Springfield, Massachusetts), Suffield (Connecticut) Country Club, Suffield Paddle Club, Fox Hollow Club (Suffield), Thimble Island Sailing and Lit. Society, Stoney Creek Boating Club, Pi Kappa Phi, Sigma Gamma Epsilon. Office: Stanhome Incorporated 333 Western Avenue Westfield Massachusetts 01085

TOYODA, EIJI, automobile manufacturing company executive; born Kinjo, Nishikasugai, Aichi, Japan, September 12, 1913; son of Heikichi and Nao T.; married Kazuko Takahashi, October 19, 1939; children: Kanshiro, Tetsuro, Shuhei, Sonoko. Bachelor.Mechanical Engineer, Tokyo University, 1936. Director Toyota Motor Corp., Aichi, Japan, 1945—, managing director, 1950-53, senior managing director, 1953-60, executive vice president, 1960-67, president, 1967-82, chairman board, 1982—; chairman Towa Real Estate Company, Limited; chairman board Toyota Central Research and Devel. Laboratory, Incorporated; director Aichi Steel Works Company, Limited, Toyoda Machine Works Limited, Toyoda Automatic Loom Works Limited, Aisin Seiki Company Limited; auditor Toyoda Tsusho Corp. Author: Toyota Fifty Years in Motion, 1988. Member Japan Automobile Manufacturers Association (supreme adv. 1980, president 1972-80), Japan Motor Industrial Federation (adv. 1980), Federation Econ. Orgns. (Keidanren) (vice chairman 1984), Telecommunications Council (chairman 1988—). Office: Toyota Motor Corp, 1 Toyota-cho Toyota-shi, Aichi 471, Japan

TREYBIG, JAMES G., computer company executive; born 1940. Mkgt. manager Hewlett-Packard Company, 1968-72; with Kleiner and Perkins, 1972-74; with Tandem Computer Incorporated, Cupertino, California, 1974—, now president, chief executive officer, director. Office: Tandem Computers Incorporated 19333 Vallco Parkway Cupertino California 95014

TROGDON, DEWEY LEONARD, JR., textile executive; born Summerfield, North Carolina, February 17, 1932; son of Dewey Leonard and Ethel (Miller) T.; married Barbara Jean Ayers, September 10, 1955; children: Mark, Leonard. Bachelor of Arts in Economics, Guillford College, Greensboro, North Carolina, 1958; postgraduate, University North Carolina, 1967-68, University Virginia, 1970, Advanced Management Program, Harvard University, 1978. With Cone Mills Corp., Greensboro, 1958—, staff assistant to chief executive officer, 1970-74, executive vice president, 1978, president, 1979—, chief executive officer, 1980-90, chairman, 1981—; president subsidiary company Otto B. May, 1974-78; vice president Cone Mills Marketing Company, 1977-78; director First Union Corp. Trustee Guilford College Served with United States Naval Reserve, 1949-53. Member Am. Textile Manufacturers Institute (president 1986-87), North Carolina Textile Manufacturers Association (past president, director). Methodist. Office: Cone Mills Corp 1201 Maple St Greensboro North Carolina 27405

TRUSHEIM, H. EDWIN, insurance executive; born Chicago, May 3, 1927; son of H. Edwin and Lucy (Genslein) T.; married Ruth M. Campbell; children—John E., Mark R. Bachelor of Science in Education, Concordia Teachers College, Chicago, 1948; Master of Arts in Political Science, Northwestern University, 1955; postgraduate in political sci. and economics, Washington University, St. Louis, 1951-54. With General Am. Life Insurance Company, St. Louis, vice president, 1966-67, senior vice president, 1974, executive vice president, 1974-79, president, 1979—, also chief executive officer, 1981—, chairman, 1986—; chairman board Federal Reserve Bank of St. Louis; board of directors Am. Council Life Insurance, Washington. Board of directors Angelica Corp., St. Louis, Civic Progress, St. Louis, United Way Greater St. Louis. Office: General Am Life Ins Company 700 Market St Saint Louis Missouri 63101

TUCKER, RICHARD FRANK, petroleum company executive; born New York City, December 25, 1926; son of Frank W. and Marion (Ohm) T.; married Genevieve P. Martinson, October 13, 1951. Bachelor of Chemical Engineering, Cornell University, 1950. With Esso Standard Oil Company, 1950-55; with Caltex Oil Company, 1955-61; with Mobil Corp., 1961—, vice chairman board, 1986—; president, chief operating officer Mobil Oil Corp., 1986—; director Nova Pharmaceutical Corp., Perkin Elmer Corp., United States Trust, Am. Petroleum Institute. Trustee Cornell U.; member board overseers Cornell U. Medical School Served with United States Navy, 1945-46. Member National Acad. Engineering, Council Foreign Relations. Clubs: Cornell, Sky (New York City). Office: Mobil Corp 3225 Gallows Road Fairfax Virginia 22037-0001

TUMMINELLO, STEPHEN CHARLES, electronic parts manufacturing company executive; born Paterson, New Jersey, November 7, 1936. Graduate, Fairleigh Dickinson University, 1958. Former president North America Philips Lighting Corp.; executive vice president, former vice president, group executive North America Philips Corp., 1984-90; president, chief executive officer North America Philips Corp., New York City, 1990—. Office: N Am Philips Corp 100 E 42nd St New York New York 10017

TURLEY, STEWART, retail company executive; born Mount Sterling, Kentucky, July 20, 1934; son of R. Joe and Mavis S. Turley; married Linda A. Mulholland; children: Carol, Karen. Student, Rollins College, 1952-53, University Kentucky, 1953-55. Plant manager Crown Cork & Seal Company, Orlando (Florida), Philadelphia, 1955-66; manager non-drug operations, director corporate employee relations and special services Jack Eckerd Corp., Clearwater, Florida, 1966-68, vice president, 1968-71, senior vice president, 1971-74, director, 1971—, president, chief executive officer, 1974—, chairman board, 1975—; board of directors United Telecommunications, Incorporated, Barnett Banks, Incorporated, Springs Industries, Incorporated, Pinellas County Economic Devel. Corp. Trustee Eckerd College, St. Petersburg, US Ski Educational Federation. Member Florida Council Econ. Education (board directors), National Association Chain Drug Stores (board directors, chairman board 1978-79, 88-89), National Retail Federation (board directors), Florida Council 100 (board directors), Business Roundtable, World Business Council, Incorporated, Chief Executives Organization, Incorporated, Pinellas Eocn. Devel. Corp. (board directors), Carlouel Yacht Club (Clearwater), Belleair Country Club, Bayou Club, Kappa Alpha. Home: Belleair Florida 34616 Office: Jack Eckerd Corp 8333 Bryan Dairy Road Post Office Box 4689 Clearwater Florida 34618

TURNER, FRED L., fast food franchiser executive; born 1933; married. Bachelor of Science, De Paul University, 1952. With McDonald's Corp., Oak Brook, Illinois, 1956—, executive vice president, 1967-68, president, chief administrative officer, 1968-77, chief executive officer, 1977-87, chairman, 1977—, also director; board of directors Baxter International Incorporated. Served as 1st lieutenant United States Army, 1943-45. Office: McDonald's Corp 1 McDonald's Plaza Oak Brook Illinois 60521

TURNER, ROBERT EDWARD, television executive; born Cincinnati, November 19, 1938; son of Robert Edward and Florence (Rooney) T.; married Judy Nye (divorced), married Jane Shirley Smith, June 1965 (divorced 1988); children: Beau, Rhett, Jennie; children by previous marriage: Laura Lee, Robert Edward IV. Graduate in classics, Brown University; Doctor of Science in Commerce (honorary), Drexel University, 1982; Doctor of Laws (honorary), Samford University, 1982, Atlanta University, 1984; Doctor Entrepreneurial Science (honorary), Central New England College Tech., 1983; Doctor in Pub. Administration (honorary), Massachusetts Maritime Academy, 1984; Doctor in Business Administration (honorary), University Charleston, 1985. Account executive Turner Advertising Company, Atlanta, 1961-63, president, chief operating officer, 1963-70; president, chairman board Turner Broadcasting System, Incorporated, Atlanta, 1970—; president Atlanta Braves, 1976—; chairman board Atlanta Hawks, 1977—; Sponsor, creator The Goodwill Games, Moscow, 1986. Chairman board Better World Society, Washington, 1985—; board of directors Martin Luther King Center, Atlanta. Won America's Cup in his yacht Courageous, 1977; named Yachtsman of Year 4 times.Recipient Outstanding Entrepreneur of Year award Sales Marketing and Mgmt. Magazine, 1979, Salesman of Year award Sales and Marketing Executives, 1980, Pvt. Enterprise Exemplar medal, Freedoms Foundation at Valley Forge, 1980, Communicator of Year award Pub. Rels. Society Am., 1981, Communicator of Year award New York Broadcasters, 1981, International Communicator of Year award Sales nad Marketing Executives, 1981, National News Media award Veterans of Foreign Wars, 1981, Distinguished Service in Telecommunications award Ohio University College Communication, 1982, Carr Van Anda award Ohio University School Journalism, 1982, Special award Edinburgh International TV Festival, Scotland, 1982, Media Awareness award United Vietnam Vets. Organization, 1983, Board Govs. award Atlanta chapter National Academy of Television Arts and Sciences, 1982, Special Olympics award Special Olympics Committee,

1983, Dinner of Champions award Georgia chapter, Multiple Sclerosis Society, 1983, Praca Special Merit award New York Puerto Rican Association for Community Affairs, 1983, World Telecommunications Pioneer award, New York State Broadcasters Association, 1984, Golden Plate award Am. Acad. Achievement, 1984, Outstanding Supporter Boy Scouting award National Boy Scout Council, 1984, Silver Satellite award Am. Women in Radio and TV, Lifetime Achievement award New York International Film and TV Festival, 1984, Corp. Star of Year award National Leukemia Society, 1985, Distinguished Achievement award University Georgia, 1985, Tree of Life award Jewish National Fund, 1985, Business Executive of Year award Georgia Security Dealers Association, 1985, Life Achievement award Popular Culture Association, 1986, George Washingtonn Distinguished Patriot award S.R., 1986, Missouri Honor medal School Journalism, University Missouri, 1987, Golden Ace award National Cable TV Acad., 1987 Sol Taishoff award National Press Foundation, 1988, Citizen Diplomat award Center for Soviet-Am. Dialogue, 1988, Chmn.'s award Cable Advertising Bureau, 1988, Directorate award National Academy of Television Arts and Sciences, 1989, Paul White award Radio and TV News Directors Association, 1989 Business Marketer of Year Am. Marketing Association, 1989, Distinguished Service award Simon Wiesenthal Center, 1990, Glasnost award Vols. Am. and Soviet Life magazine, 1990, numerous others; inducted into Hall of Fame, Promotion and Marketing Association, 1980, Dubuque (Iowa) Business Hall of Fame, 1983, National Association for Sport and Physical Education Hall of Fame, 1986. Member National Cable TV Association (Pres.'s award 1979, 89, Ace Special Recognition award 1980), National Association for the Advancement of Colored People (life, board directors Atlanta chapter, Regional Employer oar award 1976), National Audubon Society, Cousteau Society, Bay Area Cable Club (hon.). Avocations: sailing, fishing. Office: Turner Broadcasting System Incorporated 1 CNN Center Box 105366 Atlanta Georgia 30348-5366

TUSHER, THOMAS WILLIAM, apparel company executive; born Oakland, California, April 5, 1941; son of William C. and Betty J. (Brown) T.; married Pauline B. Kensett, January 1, 1967; children: Gregory Malcolm, Michael Scott. Bachelor of Arts, University California, Berkeley, 1963; Master of Business Administration, Stanford University, 1965. Assistant to vice president international Colgate Palmolive Company, New York City, 1965-67; product manager Colgate-Palmolive Puerto Rico, 1967-68; superintendent corp. planning Levi Strauss & Company, San Francisco, 1969; president Levi Strauss International, 1977-84; senior vice president Levi Straus & Company, before 1984, executive vice president, chief operating officer, director, from 1984, now president, chief operating officer; regional general manager, Australia/N.Z., Levi Strauss Australia, 1970-74; area general manager Levi Strauss Northern Europe, London, 1974-75; president European div. Levi Strauss International, San Francisco, 1976; director various subs's. Levi Strauss International; director Great Western Garment Company, Can. Board of directors California Council International Trade, 1977—, U. California Grad. Business School Served with Intelligence Corps. United States Army Reserve, 1966-67. Member San Francisco Chamber of Commerce (director). Republican. Presbyterian. Clubs: World Trade, Bay. Office: Levi Strauss & Company Levi's Plaza Box 7215 San Francisco California 94120

TUTTLE, ROBERT D., manufacturing and distributing company executive; born July 16, 1925; married. Bachelor of Science, Northwestern University, 1951; Master of Business Administration, University Chicago, 1960. Marketing manager The H.M. Harper Company, Morton Grove, Illinois, 1951-60; management consultant Booz Allen & Hamilton, Chicago, 1960-62; vice chairman board, executive vice president operations Illinois Tool Works Incorporated, 1962-80; president, chief operating officer SPX Corp., Muskegon, Michigan, 1980-84, president, chief executive officer, 1984-85, chief executive officer, 1985-89, chairman, 1985-91; board of directors CMS Energy Corp., Woodhead Industries, Walbro Corp., Consumers Power Company, Guardsman Products, Incorporated, FMB Corp., Little Rapids Corp., Batts Corp. Served to 2d lieutenant United States Air Force, 1943-46. Named Industrialist of Year Mich.'s Impression 5 Sci. Mus., Lansing, 1988. Office: 100 Terrace Plaza Muskegon Michigan 49443

TWYMAN, JACK, wholesale grocery company executive, management services company executive; born May 11, 1934; married. Educated, University Cincinnati. Basketball player Cincinnati Royals, 1955-67; announcer ABC, 1967-72; vice-chairman Super Food Services, Incorporated, Dayton, Ohio, from 1972, formerly president, chief operating officer, now chairman, chief executive officer. Office: Super Food Services Incorporated 3185 Elbee Road Dayton Ohio 45439 also: 3233 Newmark Dr Miamisburg Ohio 45342

TYSON, DONALD JOHN, food company executive; born Olathe, Kansas, April 21, 1930; son of John W. and Mildred (Ernst) T.; married Twilla Jean Womochil, August 24, 1952; children: John H., Cheryl J., Carla A. Student, University Arkansas. Plant manager Tyson Foods, Incorporated, Springdale, Arkansas, 1951-55, president, 1955-67, chairman, chief executive officer, 1967—, also director; chief executive officer Eagle Distributing Incorporated, Tyson Export Sales Incorporated, Poultry Growers Incorporated, Tyson Carolina Incorporated, Spring Valley Farms Incorporated, Lane Processing Incorporated, Lane Farms Incorporated. Lodge: Elks. Home: 2210 Oak Lawn Dr Springdale Arkansas 72764 Office: Tyson Foods Incorporated 2210 W Oaklawn Dr Springdale Arkansas 72764

UKROPINA, JAMES ROBERT, energy company executive, lawyer; born Fresno, California, September 10, 1937; son of Robert J. and Persida (Angelich) U.; married Priscilla Lois Brandenburg, June 16, 1962; children—Michael Steven, David Robert, Mark Gregory. Bachelor of Arts, Stanford University, 1959, Master of Business Administration, 1961; Bachelor of Laws, University Southern California, 1965. Bar: California 1966, District of Columbia 1980. Associate firm O'Melveny & Myers, Los Angeles, 1965-72;

partner O'Melveny & Myers, 1972-80; executive vice president, general counsel Santa Fe International Corp., Alhambra, California, 1980-84, director, 1981-86; executive vice president, general counsel Pacific Enterprises, Los Angeles, 1984-86, president and director, 1986-89; chairman board and chief executive officer 1989—; board of directors Security Pacific Corp., Lockheed Corp., Pacific Mutual Life Insurance Company; lecturer in field. Editor-in-chief: Southern California Law Rev, 1964-65. Trustee Occidental College, Stanford U.; member adv. council Stanford Business School; member California Economic Devel. Corp. Board. Member American Bar Association, CAlif. Bar Association, Los Angeles County Bar Association, California Chamber of Commerce (board directors), California Business Roundtable (board directors), California Club, Beta Theta Pi. Office: Pacific Enterprises 801 S Grand Avenue Los Angeles California 90017

UNRUH, JAMES ARLEN, business machines company executive; born Goodrich, North Dakota, March 22, 1941; married Candice Leigh Voight, April 28, 1984; children: Jeffrey A., Julie A. Bachelor of Science in Business Administration, Jamestown College, 1963; Master of Business Administration, University Denver, 1964. Director corp. planning and analysis Fairchild Camera & Instrument, California, 1974-76, vice president treasury and corp. devel., 1976-79, vice president fin., 1979-80; vice president fin. Memorex Corp., Santa Clara, California, 1980-82; vice president fin. Burroughs Corp. (now known as Unisys Corp.), Detroit, 1982-84, senior vice president fin., 1984-86, executive vice president fin., 1986, executive vice president, 1986-89, president, chief operating officer, 1989-90, president, chief executive officer, 1990-91, chairman board of directors, chief executive officer, 1991—. Board of directors Detroit Renaissance Center, U. Michigan visiting Committee, Greater Philadelphia First Corp.; board trustees Jamestown College, North Dakota; board overseers Wharton School Business, U. Pennsylvania. Member Greater Philadelphia Chamber of Commerce (executive committee), Pennsylvania Business Roundtable (executive committee). Home: 208 Rose Lane Haverford Pennsylvania 19041 Office: Unisys Corp Post Office Box 500 A-1 Blue Bell Pennsylvania 19424

VAGELOS, PINDAROS ROY, pharmaceutical company executive; born Westfield, New Jersey, October 8, 1929; son of Roy John and Marianthi (Lambrinides) V.; married Diana Touliatos, July 10, 1955; children: Randall, Cynthia, Andrew, Ellen. Bachelor of Arts, University Pennsylvania, 1950; Doctor of Medicine, Columbia University, 1954; Doctor of Science (honorary), Washington University, 1980, Brown University, 1982, University Medicine and Dentistry of New Jersey, 1984, New York University, 1989, Columbia University, 1990; Doctor of Laws (honorary), Princeton University, 1990. Intern medicine Massachusetts General Hospital, 1954-55, assistant resident medicine, 1955-56; surgeon Laboratory Cellular Physiology, National Institutes of Health, 1956-59; surgeon Laboratory Biochemistry, 1959-64, head section comparative biochemistry, 1964-66; professor biochemistry, chairman department biological chemistry Washington University School Medicine, St. Louis, 1966-75; director div. biology and biomed. sciences Washington University School Medicine, 1973-75; senior vice president research Merck, Sharp & Dohme Research Laboratories, Rahway, New Jersey, 1975-76, president, 1976-84; corp. senior vice president Merck & Company, Incorporated, Rahway, New Jersey, 1982-84, also board of directors, 1984—, executive vice president, 1984-85, president, chief executive officer, 1985-86; chairman, president, chief executive officer Merck & Company, Incorporated, 1986—; member molecular biology study section National Institutes of Health, 1967-71, member physiological chemistry study section, 1973-75; member Commission on Human Resources, National Research Council, 1974-76, Institute Medicine, National Academy of Sciences, 1974—; chairman sci. adv. board Center for Advanced Biotech. and Medicine, 1985—; board of directors TRW, Incorporated, Prudential Insurance Company. Member editorial bds. journals in field. Trustee U. Pennsylvania, 1988—, Rockefeller U., 1976—, Danforth Foundation, 1978—, Partnership for New Jersey, 1989—; member Business Council, 1987—; board managing directors Metropolitan Opera Association, Incorporated, 1989—. Recipient New Jersey Sci./Tech. medal R & D Council New Jersey, 1983. Member Am. Chemical Society (award enzyme chemistry 1967), Am. Society Biological Chemists, National Acad. Sciences, Am. Acad. Arts and Sciences, Business Roundtable (policy committee 1987—). Avocations: jogging, tennis, sculling. Discoverer of acyl-carrier protein. Home: 10 Canterbury Lane Watchung New Jersey 07060 Office: Merck & Company Incorporated 126 E Lincoln Avenue Post Office Box 2000 Rahway New Jersey 07065

VAN ANDEL, JAY, home and personal products company executive; born Grand Rapids, Michigan, June 3, 1924; son of James and Nella (Vanderwoude) Van A.; married Betty J. Hoekstra, August 16, 1952; children: Nan, Stephen, David, Barbara. Student, Pratt Junior College, 1945, Calvin College, 1942, 46, Yale, 1943-44; DBA (honorary), Northern Michigan University, 1976, Western Michigan University, 1979; Doctor of Laws (honorary), Ferris State College, 1977. Formerly engaged in aviation, restaurant and mail order businesses; co-founder, chairman board Amway Corp., Ada, Michigan; United States commissioner for Genoa Expo '92' World's Fair marking 500 Anniversary of Columbus Journey to Am.; chairman board Amway International, Amway Management Company (Amway Hotel Properties), Amway Environmental Foundation, Nutrilite Products, Incorporated; board of directors Michigan National Bank, Grand Rapids Regional Board, Van Andel & Flikkema Motor Sales, Grand Rapids. Member adv. council National 4H Foundation; trustee Ferguson Hospital, Grand Rapids, Hillsdale (Michigan) College, Citizens Research Council Michigan; chairman board of directors Jamestown Foundation, Washington; trustee Hudson Institute, Indianapolis; board of directors National Endowment for Democracy, Washington, Gerald R. Ford Foundation, Washington, Center for International Private Enterprise,

Washington, Heritage Foundation, Washington; president Van Andel Foundation; Served to 1st lieutenant United States Army Air Force, 1943-46. Knighted Grand Officer of Orange-Nassau, The Netherlands; recipient Distinguished Alumni award Calvin College, 1976, Golden Plate award Am. Acad. Achievement, Great Living Am. award and Business and Professional Leader of the Year award Religious Heritage Am., George Washington medal of Honor Freedom Foundation, Gold medals Netherland Society of Philadelphia and New York City, Distinguished Citizen award Northwood Institute, Patron award Michigan Foundation for Arts, 1982, Achievement award United Nations Environment Programme, 1989, United Nations Environment Programme Achievement award Amway, 1989; named Business Person Year Economic Club Grand Rapids, 1990; named to Grand Rapids Business Hall of Fame. Member Sales and Marketing Executives International Acad. Achievement (charter), Direct Selling Association (board directors, named to Hall of Fame), United States Chamber of Commerce (past chairman board), Mensa, Peninsular Club, Cascade Hills Club, Lotus Club, Capitol Hill Club (Washington), Macatawa Bay Yacht Club (Holland, Michigan), Le Mirador Club (Switzerland), Omiicron Delta Kappa. Member Christian Reformed Church (elder). Home: 7186 Windy Hill Road Grand Rapids Michigan 49546 Office: Amway Corp 7575 Fulton St E Ada Michigan 49355

VAN BUREN, ROBERT, banker; born Plainfield, New Jersey, 1925. Graduate, Washington and Lee University, 1950; Master of Business Administration, New York University, 1956. Chairman, chief executive officer Midlantic Banks, Incorporated (name changed to Midatlantic Corp.), Edison, New Jersey; chairman, chief executive officer Midlantic National Bank, West Orange, New Jersey; director Champion Products, Incorporated. Trustee United Hosps. of Newark, Muhlenberg Hospital. Office: Midlantic Corp Metro Park Plaza Post Office Box 600 Edison New Jersey 08818

VAN WACHEM, LODEWIJK CHRISTIAAN, petroleum company executive; born Pangkalan Brandan, The Netherland East Indies, July 31, 1931; married Elisabeth G. Cristofoli, 1958; 3 children. Student, Tech. University, Delft, The Netherlands. With Bataafsche Petroleum Maatschappij, The Hague, The Netherlands, 1953; mechanical engineer Cia Shell de Venezuela, 1954-63; chief engineer Shell-BP Petroleum Devel. Company Nigeria, 1963-66, manager engineer, 1966-67, chairman, managing director, 1972-76; head tech. administration Brunei Shell Petroleum Company Limited, 1967-69, tech. director, 1969-71; head production div. Shell International Petroleum Maatschappij, The Hague, 1971-72, coordinator exploration and production, 1976-79; managing director Royal Dutch Petroleum Company, until 1982, president, 1982—; member presidium board of directors Shell Petroleum N.V.; managing director Shell Petroleum Company Limited, 1977; chairman Shell Oil Company USA; board of directors Shell Can.; chairman joint committee managing directors Royal Dutch/Shell Group, 1985—. Decorated Commander Order of Orange, Nassau; recipient K.B.E.,

1988, Knight Order Netherlands Lion, 1981. Office: Shell Oil Company 1 Shell Plaza Houston Texas 77252 also: Royal Dutch/Shell Group Cos, 16 Carel van Bylandtlaan, 2596 HR Hague The Netherlands

VARNEDOE, HEETH, III, food products company executive; born 1937; married. Graduate, University Georgia, 1959. With Flowers Industries Incorporated, 1959—, president baked foods div., 1976-83, executive vice president operations, from 1983, now president, chief operating officer., also director. Office: Flowers Industries Incorporated United States Highway 19 Post Office Box 1338 Thomasville Georgia 31799

VASTOLA, MICHAEL J., toy and game company executive. Chairman, chief executive officer Lionel Corp., New York City. Office: Lionel Corp 35 W 34th St New York New York 10001

VECCI, RAYMOND JOSEPH, airline executive; born New York City, January 22, 1943; son of Romeo John and Mary (Fabretti) V.; married Helen Cecelia Clampett, September 3, 1967; children: Brian John, Damon Jay. Bachelor of Business Administration, City College of New York, 1965; Master of Business Administration, New York University, 1967. Administrative assistant International Air Transport Association, New York City, 1961-66; economic analyst United Airlines, Chicago, 1967-74; assistant vice president planning and regulatory affairs Alaska Airlines Incorporated, Seattle, 1975-76, staff vice president planning and regulatory affairs, 1976-79, staff vice president planning, 1979, vice president planning, 1979-85, executive vice president, chief operating officer, 1986-90, president, chief executive officer, 1990—. Served with United States Army, 1968-69, Vietnam. Decorated Bronze Star. Roman Catholic. Office: Alaska Airlines Incorporated 19300 Pacific Highway S Seattle Washington 98188

VENTRES, ROMEO JOHN, manufacturing company executive; born Boston, November 2, 1924; son of Christy and Marzia (Giammarco) V.; married Norma Louise Chapman, July 10, 1948; children: Judith, Jane, Mary, Patricia, Katherine, Michael, Peter. Bachelor of Science in Chemical Engineering, Worcester Polytechnic Institute, 1948; Doctor of Science (honorary), Mercy College, 1989. Lic. professional engineer, Massachusetts. Junior engineer Atlantic Refining Company, Philadelphia, 1948-55, group leader, 1955; oil industrial engineer Government Refineries Administration, Baghdad, Iraq, 1955-57; assistant chief engineer Borden Chemical Div. Borden Incorporated, Leominster, Massachusetts, 1957, chief engineer, 1958, operations manager, 1961, general manager, 1966, div. vice president, 1968-72, group vice president, 1972-74; executive vice president Haven Industries, Philadelphia, 1974-79; group vice president Borden Chemical div. Borden Incorporated, Columbus, Ohio, 1979-83, div. president, 1983-85; president Borden Incorporated, New York City, 1985-90, chief executive officer, 1986—, chairman, 1987—; board of directors Banc One Corp., Marsh & McLennan Companies Incorporated, Schering-Plough Corp., Grocery Manufacturers Am. Trustee St. Clare's Hospital, New York City With United States Navy, 1944-46, PTO. Republican. Roman Catholic. Office:

Borden Incorporated 277 Park Avenue New York New York 10172

VILLALPANDO, CATALINA VASQUEZ, treasurer of U.S.. Congressional liaison OEO; business specialist Dallas region United States Department Commerce, 1973-78; vice president Mid-South Oil Company, Dallas; staff assistant White House Office Presidential Personnel, 1981—; senior vice president communications International, Incorporated; special assistant for pub. liaison President Reagan, 1983-85; treasurer Government of United States, 1989—; chairman Republican National Hispanic Assembly, 1987-90. Board of directors Southwest voter registration and education project Southwest Texas State U. Foundation. Member National Council Hispanic Women, National Association Latino Elected and Appointed Ofcls., League United Latin Am. Citizens, Hispanic Chamber of Commerce of Virginia, Am. G.I. Forum. Office: Treas of the United States 15th & Pennsylvania Avenue Northwest Washington District of Columbia 20220

VINCENT, FRANCIS THOMAS, JR., sports executive; born Waterbury, Connecticut, May 29, 1938; son of Francis Thomas and Alice (Lynch) V.; married Valerie McMahon, July 3, 1965; children: Anne, William, Edward. Bachelor of Arts cum laude, Williams College, 1960; Bachelor of Laws, Yale University, 1963. Bar: Connecticut 1963, New York 1964, District of Columbia 1969. Associate Whitman & Ransom, New York City, 1963-68; partner Caplin & Drysdale, Washington, 1968-78; associate director div. corp. fin. Securities and Exchange Commission, Washington, 1978; president, chief executive officer Columbia Pictures Industries, Incorporated, New York City, 1978-83, chairman, chief executive officer, 1983-87; president, chief executive officer entertainment business section The Coca-Cola Company, New York City, 1987; deputy commissioner, chief operating officer Major League Baseball, New York, 1989, commissioner, 1989—. Trustee Williams College, 1970-88, Hotchkiss School, 1975—, Carleton College, 1988—. Member New York Athletic Club, Belle Haven Club, Phi Beta Kappa. Roman Catholic. Clubs: University, Belle Haven.

VON WYSS, MARC ROBERT, cement company executive; born Zurich, Switzerland, February 12, 1931; came to United States, 1971; son of George H. and Mariejenny A. (Burckhardt) von W.; married Marina V. Gygi, September 4, 1963; children—George M., Martin C. Graduate in mechanical engineering and aerodynamics, Federal Institute Tech., Zurich, 1956. Control systems design engineer Svenska Aeroplan AB, Joenkoeping, Sweden, 1957-60; control systems design engineer, assistant department head Contraves AG, Zurich, 1961-65; senior vice president Holderbank Management & Cons. Limited, Holderbank, Switzerland, 1966-71; president, chief executive officer Holnam Incorporated (formerly Dundee Cement Company), Michigan, 1971—. Office: Post Office Box 122 Dundee Michigan 48131

WACHNER, LINDA JOY, apparel marketing and manufacturing executive; born New York City, February 3, 1946; daughter of Herman and Shirley W.; married Seymour Applebaum, December 21, 1973 (deceased, 1983). Bachelor of Science in Economics and Business,

University Buffalo, 1966. Buyer Foley's Federated Department Store, Houston, 1968-69; senior buyer R.H. Macy's, New York City, 1969-74; vice president Warner div. Warnaco, Bridgeport, Connecticut, 1974-77; vice president corp. marketing Caron International, New York City, 1977-79; chief executive officer United States div. Max Factor & Company, Hollywood, California, 1979-82, president, chief executive officer, 1982-83; president, chief executive officer Max Factor & Company Worldwide, 1983-84; managing director Adler & Shaykin, New York City, 1984-86; owner, president, chief executive officer Warnaco Incorporated, New York City, 1986—; chairman, chief executive officer South Acquisition Corp., 1990—; board of directors Standard Brands Paints, Fingerhut Company, Primerica Corp.; member Co-operation Ireland. Presidential appointee Adv. Committee for Trade, Policy, Negotiations, Commission on Workforce Quality and Market Efficiency; trustee Martha Graham Center Contemporary Dance, Incorporated; Business Roundtable; trustee U. Buffalo Foundation. Recipient Silver Achievement award Los Angeles YWCA; named Outstanding Woman in Business Women's Equity Action League, 1980, Woman of Year, MS. Magazine, 1986, one of the Yr.'s Most Fascinating Business People, Fortune Magazine, 1986, one of 10 Most Powerful Women in Corp. Am., Savvy Woman Magazine, 1989, 90. Member Young Pres.'s Organization, Committee of 200, Am. Management Association, Am. Apparel Marketing Association (board directors), Business Roundtable. Republican. Jewish. Office: Warnaco Incorporated 90 Park Avenue New York New York 10016 also: Warnaco Incorporated 11111 Santa Monica Boulevard Los Angeles California 90025

WADDELL, OLIVER W., banker; born Covington, Kentucky, December 27, 1930; son of Frank and Ida Mae Waddell; married Virgilee Casey; children—Jeffrey, Gregory, Michelle. Bachelor of Arts, Duke University, 1954; Juris Doctor, University Kentucky, 1957; graduate, Stonier Graduate School Banking, Rutgers University, 1969. Management trainee First National Bank of Cincinnati, 1957-64, assistant cashier, 1964-65, assistant vice president, 1965-71, vice president, 1971-76, senior vice president, 1976-80, president, director, 1980-82, president, chief executive officer, 1982-83; chairman First National Bank of Cincinnati (became Star Bank N.A., Cincinnati, 1988), 1983—; board of directors Myers Y. Cooper Company, Cincinnati, Ohio National Life Insurance Company, Cincinnati Gas. & Electric Company, Star Banc Corp.; adv. board Greater Cincinnati International Airport; with Cin Business Company. Trustee Christ Hospital. Member Greater Cincinnati Chamber of Commerce, Commercial Club, Cincinnati Country Club, Queen City Club. Republican. Methodist. Office: Star Bank NA Cincinnati 425 Walnut St Cincinnati Ohio 45202

WALGREEN, CHARLES RUDOLPH, III, retail store executive; born Chicago, November 11, 1935; son of Charles Rudolph and Mary Ann (Leslie) W.; married Kathleen Bonsignore Allen, January 23, 1977; children: Charles Richard, Tad Alexander, Kevin Patrick, Leslie Ray, Chris Patrick; stepchildren—Carleton A. Allen Jr., Jorie L. Allen. Bachelor of Science in Pharmacy, University

Michigan, 1958. With Walgreen Company, Chicago, 1952—; administrative assistant to vice president store operations Walgreen Company, 1965-66, district manager, 1967-68, regional director, 1968-69, vice president, 1969, president, 1969-75, chairman, 1976—, also director. Member business adv. council Chicago Urban League.; board of directors Junior Achievement Chicago. Member National Association Chain Drug Stores (board directors), Illinois Retail Mchts. Association (board directors 1966—), Am. Pharmaceutical Association, Illinois Pharm Association, Delta Sigma Phi. Clubs: Economic, Commercial (Chicago); Great Lakes Cruising; Yacht and Country (Stuart, Florida); Exmoor Country (Highland Park, Illinois); Key Largo Anglers (Florida). Office: Walgreen Company 200 Wilmot Road Deerfield Illinois 60015

WALKER, K. GRAHAME, manufacturing company executive; born West Bridgford, Nottinghamshire, England, June 19, 1937; came to United States, 1979; son of John P. and Lilian (Wright) W.; married Robina Mairy Bendell, August 20, 1959 (divorced 1979); children: Belinda Sharon, Victoria Jane; married Shirley Dean Allison, December 6, 1980. Student, Merchant Taylors' School, 1948-55; graduate, Britannia Royal Naval College, 1955-57, Royal Naval Engineering College, 1959-62. Marketing executive Rank Organization, England, 1962-65; managing director Hysol Sterling Limited, England, 1965-74, Dexter GmbH, Federal Republic Germany, 1974-79; president Hysol div. Dexter Corp., Industry, California, 1979-85; president specialty chemicals and services group Dexter Corp., Windsor Locks, Connecticut, 1985-88, president, chief operating officer, 1988-89, president, chief executive officer, director, 1989—; board of directors Life Techs., Incorporated (subsidiary Dexter Corp.). Board of directors Greater Hartford chapter American Red Cross, 1986-89, chairman, 1990—; board of directors Barnes Group Incorporated, Bristol, 1988—, New England Air Mus., Windsor Locks, 1988—; trustee Hartford Grad. Center, 1990—; corporator Institute Living and Hartford Hospital, 1990. Lieutenant Royal Navy, 1955-62. Member Connecticut Business and Industry Association (board directors 1990), Hartfor Club, Golf Club Avon. Avocations: skiing, golf, gardening, literature. Office: Dexter Corp 1 Elm St Windsor Locks Connecticut 06096

WALKER, RONALD F., corporate executive; born Cincinnati, April 9, 1938; married. Bachelor of Business Administration, University Cincinnati, 1961. Vice president Kroger Company, Cincinnati, 1962-72; with Am. Fin. Corp., Cincinnati, 1972—, executive vice president, 1978-84, president, chief operating officer, director, 1984—; executive vice president Great Am. Insurance, Cincinnati, 1972-80, president, 1980-87, vice chairman, 1987—; president Penn Central Corp., 1980-87; chief operating officer 1987—; also board of directors Penn Central Corp., chief operating officer, 1987—; board of directors United Brands, Cincinnati, Am. Fin. Enterprises, Cincinnati, Sprague Techs., Incorporated. Office: Great Am Ins Company Post Office Box 2575 Cincinnati Ohio 45201 also: Am Fin Corp 1 E 4th St Cincinnati Ohio 45202

WALKER, WINSTON WAKEFIELD, JR., insurance company executive; born Traverse City, Michigan, October 19, 1943; son of Winston W. and Ann (Bridges) W.; married Mary Martin, September 11, 1965; children: Alan, Ross. Bachelor of Arts, Tulane University, 1965; Doctor of Philosophy, University Georgia, 1969. Assistant professor Wake Forest University, Winston Salem, North Carolina, 1970-73; assistant actuary Provident Life & Accident Insurance Company, Chattanooga, 1974, executive vice president, 1985-86, executive vice president, chief fin. officer, 1986-87, president, chief operating officer, 1987-88, president, chief executive officer, 1988—, also board of directors; acutary Provident National Assurance Company, Des Moines, 1975-78; vice president administration Provident National Assurance Company, Chattanooga, 1978-80, president, 1980-85; president Provident General Insurance Company, Chattanooga, 1984-85; board of directors Am. National Bank, Chattanooga. Member board of directors executive committee Greater Chattanooga United Way, 1986—. Fellow Am. Society Actuaries; member Southeastern Actuaries Club, Rotary, Mountain City Club, Lookout Mountain Fairyland Club. Office: Provident Life & Accident Ins Company 1 Fountain Square Chattanooga Tennessee 37402

WALLACE, ROBERT FERGUS, banker; born Brooklyn, October 5, 1934; son of Fergus F. and Isabelle (Wilson) W.; married Florence Faminow, December 18, 1959; children: Douglas, Barbara. Bachelor of Arts, Colgate University, 1956. Commercial loan officer Chemical Bank, New York City, 1956-68; chairman First Interstate Bank, Portland, Oregon, 1968-81; president National Westminster Bank United States of America, New York City, 1982—. Board of directors New York City Opera Company, 1986—. Served to lieutenant United States Navy, 1957-60. Member Association Reserve City Banks, Downtown-Lower Manhattan Association (treasurer 1988). Republican. Presbyterian. Club: Econ. of New York. Office: National Westminster Bank USA 175 Water St New York New York 10038

WALLACE, WILLIAM RAY, fabricated steel manufacturing company executive; born Shreveport, Louisiana, March 25, 1923; son of Jason Mohoney and Mattie Evelyn (Adair) W.; married Minyone Milligan Rose, October 5, 1966; children: Jayne Cecile Rose McDearman, Susan Rose O'Brien, H. Robert Rose; children by previous marriage: Patrick Scott, Michael B., Timothy R., Shelly W. Taetz. Bachelor of Science in Engineering, Louisiana Tech., 1944. Field engineer Austin Bridge Company, Dallas, 1944-45; core analyst Core Laboratories, Bakersfield, California, 1945-46; chief engineer, then secretary-treasurer, executive vice president Trinity Industries, Incorporated, Dallas, 1946-58, president, chief executive officer, 1958—, also board of directors; board of directors Lomas Fin. Corp., Trinity Industries, ENSERCH Corp. Trustee Dallas Methodist Hosps. Foundation. Methodist. Office: Trinity Industries Incorporated 2525 Stemmons Freeway Post Office Box 568887 Dallas Texas 75356-8887

WALLIN, WINSTON ROGER, manufacturing company executive;

born Minneapolis, March 6, 1926; son of Carl A. and Theresa (Hegge) W.; married Maxine Houghton, September 10, 1949; children: Rebecca, Brooks, Lance, Bradford. Bachelor of Business Administration, University Minnesota, 1948. With Pillsbury Company, Minneapolis, 1948-85, vice president commodity operations, 1971-76, executive vice president, 1976, president, chief operating officer, 1977-84, vice chairman board, 1984-85; with Medtronic, Incorporated, Minneapolis, 1985-88, chairman board, president, chief executive officer, 1989-91, chairman board, 1991—; board of directors Bemis Company, McGlynn Bakeries, Supervalu. Board of directors Abbott North, Minnesota Zool. Board; chairman board trustees Carleton College, Minneapolis Institute Arts, 1991—. Served with United States Navy, 1944-46. Member Minneapolis Grain Exchange (board directors 1977-82). Clubs: Minneapolis, Minikahda, Interlachen. Home: 7022 Tupa Circle Edina Minnesota 55439 Office: Medtronic Incorporated 7000 Central Avenue NE Minneapolis Minnesota 55432

WALTER, JAMES W., construction materials company executive; born Lewes, Delaware, 1922; married Monica Saraw, 1946; children: James W., Robert. Partner Walter Construction Company, 1948-55; chairman board, director Walter Industries Incorporated (formerly Jim Walter Corp.), Tampa, Florida, 1955—; president Dixie building Supplies Incorporated, Tampa; director Walter East Heller International Corp., General Telephone & Electronics Company, Biejerinvest, Sweden. Served United States Navy, 1942-46. Office: Walter Industries Incorporated Post Office Box 31601 Tampa Florida 33601 also: Hillsborough Holdings Corp 1500 N Dale Mabry Highway Tampa Florida 33607

WANG, CHARLES B., computer company executive; born Shanghai, Rep. China, August 19, 1944. Bachelor of Science, Queens College, 1967. Office: Computer Associates International Incorporated 711 Stewart Avenue Garden City New York 11530

WARD, MILTON HAWKINS, mining company executive; born Bessemer, Alabama, August 1, 1932; son of William Howard and Mae Ivy (Smith) W.; married Sylvia Adele Randle, June 30, 1952; children: Jeffrey Randle, Lisa Adele. Bachelor of Science, University Alabama, 1955, Master of Science, 1981; Master of Business Administration, University New Mexico, 1974. Registered professional engineer, Texas, Alabama. Supervisor, engineer Magma Copper Company, San Manuel, Arizona, 1955-60; general superintendent Kerr-McGee Corp., Grants, New Mexico, 1960-66; general manager Homestake Mining Company, Grants, 1966-70; vice president operations Ranchers Exploration & Devel. Corp., Albuquerque, 1970-74; president, board of directors Freeeport Minerals Company, New York City, 1974-85; president, chief operating officer Freeport-McMoRan, Incorporated, New Orleans, 1985—, also board of directors; board of directors Mineral Information Institute, Incorporated, Am. Foundation for Phosphate Prodn., International Copper Association; board of directors, member executive committee Sulfer Institute. Contributor articles to professional journals. Board trustees New Orleans

Mus. Art, Children's Hospital, New Orleans; board of directors Smithsonian National Mus. Natural History; member corp. adv. committee World Wildlife Fund; member Tulane U. Business Council. Fellow Institute Mining & Metallurgy (London); member Am. Mining Congress (chairman), Am. Institute Mining Engineers (secretary chairman, award), Mining and Metallurgical Society Am. (president 1981-83, executive committee), Society Mining. Engineers (award), National Association Manufacturers (member natural resource committee), New Orleans City Club (board govs.), Mining Club (vice president, governor 1979—), Petroleum Club (New Orleans), Sierra Club. Republican. Presbyterian. Clubs: City, New Orleans Country; University (New York City). Avocations: tennis, enology, flying. Office: Freeport-McMoRan Incorporated Post Office Box 61119 New Orleans Louisiana 70161

WAREHAM, JAMES L., steel company executive; born Clinton, Iowa, October 8, 1939; son of Lyman Hugh and Ulainee Maria (Pitts) W.; married Patricia Josephine Wrubel, June 18, 1966; children: Lisa Jo, Tara Lynn. Bachelor of Science in Electrical Engineering, University Notre Dame, 1961. Various management positions United States Steel-Gary Works, Ind., 1961-69, div. manager, 1976-79; various management positions United States Steel-Tex. Works, Baytown, 1969-72; various management positions United States Steel-South Works, Chicago, 1972-76, general plant manager, 1979-84; vice president engineering United States Steel, Pittsburgh, 1984-86; president, chief executive officer Bliss Salem, Incorporated, Ohio, 1986-89; president, chief operating officer Wheeling-Pitts. Steel Corp., West Virginia, 1989—; also board of directors Wheeling-Pitts. Steel Corp., W.V.; board of directors Pittsburgh Forgins Company, Westbanco. Area coordinator Thompson for Governor, Homewood, Illinois, 1978; div. chairman United Way, Gary, Ind., 1976; general chairman, United Way Wheeling, West Virginia, 1990; board of directors Unied Way of Upper Ohio Valley, Wheeling Jesuit College, 1989—, Wheeling Medical Park Hospital, 1990—. Named Small Businessman of Year Salem Chamber of Commerce, 1988, Entrepreneur of Year Ernst & Young, Pitts., 1989. Member Am. Iron & Steel Institute, Association Iron & Steel Engineers, Association Iron & Metallurgical Engineers, Wheeling Chamber of Commerce. Home: 234 Greenwood Dr Canonsburg Pennsylvania 15317 Office: Wheeling-Pitts Steel Corp 1134 Market St Wheeling West Virginia 26003

WARNER, DARRELL G., petroleum company executive. President Exxon Pipeline Company, Houston. Office: Exxon Pipeline Company Post Office Box 2220 Houston Texas 77252§

WARNER, DOUGLAS ALEXANDER, III, banker; born Cincinnati, June 9, 1946; son of Douglas Alexander Jr. and Eleanor (Wright) W.; married Patricia Grant, May 13, 1977; children: Alexander, Katherine, Michael. Bachelor of Arts, Yale University, 1968. Offficer's assistant Morgan Guaranty Trust Company, New York City, 1968-70, assistant treasurer, 1970-72, assistant vice president, 1972-75, vice president, 1975-85; senior vice president Morgan Guaranty Trust Company, London,

1983-87; executive vice president Morgan Guaranty Trust Company, New York City, 1987-89, managing director, 1989-90, president, 1990—, also board of directors. Trustee Pierpont Morgan Libr., Cold Spring Harbor Lab. Member Association Reserve City Bankers, Foreign Policy Association (governor), Links River Club, Meadowbrook Club (Long Island). Avocations: golf, tennis, shooting. Home: 765 Remsen's Lane Oyster Bay New York 11771 Office: J P Morgan & Company Incorporated 60 Wall St New York New York 10260

WASSERMAN, BERT W., communications and publishing company executive. With office of president Time-Warner Incorporated, New York City. Office: Time-Warner Incorporated 75 Rockefeller Plaza New York New York 10019

WASSERMAN, LEW R., film, recording, publishing company executive; born Cleveland, March 15, 1913; married Edith T. Beckerman, July 5, 1936; 1 daughter, Lynne Kay. Doctor (honorary), Brandeis University, New York University. National director advertising and publicity Music Corp. Am., 1936-38, vice president, 1938-39, became vice president charge motion picture div., 1940; now chairman, chief executive officer, director, member executive committee MCA, Incorporated, also chairman board, chief executive officer, director subsidiary corps.; director Am. Airlines; chairman emeritus Association Motion Picture and TV Producers. Trustee John F. Kennedy Library, John F. Kennedy Center Performing Arts, California Institute Tech., Jules Stein Eye Institute, Carter Presidential Center, Lyndon Baines Johnson Foundation; president president Hollywood Canteen Foundation; chairman Research to Prevent Blindness Foundation; hon. chairman board Center Theatre Group Los Angeles Music Center; board of directors Amateur Athletic Foundation of Los Angeles (chairman fin. committee), Los Angeles Music Center Foundation; board gov.'s Ronald Reagan Presidential Foundation. Recipient Jean Hersholt Humanitarian award Acad. Motion Picture Arts and Sciences, 1973. Democrat. Office: MCA Incorporated 100 Universal City Plaza Universal City California 91608

WASSERSTEIN, BRUCE, investment banker; born New York City, December 25, 1947; son of Morris and Lola Wasserstein; married Christine Parrott; children: Pamela, Ben, Alex. Bachelor of Arts with honors, University Michigan, 1967; Master of Business Administration with high distinction, Harvard University, 1971, Juris Doctor cum laude, 1971; diploma in law, Cambridge University, 1972. Associate Cravath, Swaine & Moore, New York City, 1972-77; managing director The First Boston Corp., New York City, 1977-88; president Wasserstein, Perella and Company, NYC, 1988—. Author: Corporate Finance Law. Trustee Dalton School. Member Council on Foreign Relations. Democrat. Office: Wasserstein Perella & Company 31 W 52d St 27th fl New York New York 10019

WATKINS, HAYS THOMAS, railroad executive, retired; born Fern Creek, Kentucky, January 26, 1926; son of Hays Thomas Sr. and Minnie Catherine (Whiteley) W.; married Betty Jean Wright, April 15, 1950; 1 son, Hays Thomas III. Bachelor of Science in Accounting, Western

Kentucky University, 1947; Master of Business Administration, Northwestern University, 1948; Doctor of Laws (honorary), Baldwin Wallace College, 1975, Alderson Broaddus College, 1980, College of William and Mary, 1982, Virginia Union University, 1987. C.P.A. With C. & O. Railway Cleveland, 1949-80, vice president fin., 1964-67, vice president administrative group, 1967-71, president, chief executive officer, 1971-73, chairman board, chief executive officer, 1973-80; with B. & O. Railroad, 1964-80, vice president finance, 1964-71, president, chief executive officer, 1971-73, vice chairman board, chief executive officer, 1973-80; chairman, chief executive officer Chessie System, Incorporated, 1973-80; president and co-chief executive officer CSX Corp. (merger of Chessie System, Incorporated and Seaboard Coast Line Industries, Incorporated), Richmond, Virginia, 1980-82, chairman board, chief executive officer, 1982-89, chairman board, 1989-91; chairman emeritus 1991—; board of directors Black & Decker Manufacturing Company, Westinghouse Electric Corp., Signet Banking Company, Richmond, Fredericksburg & Potomac Railroad; chairman Center for Innovative Tech., Virginia, 1984-87. Vice rector board visitors College William and Mary, 1984-87, rector, 1987—; trustee Mus. Arts Association (Cleveland Orchestra), Richmond Symphony Orchestra; member Virginia Business Council With Army of the United States, 1945-47. Named Man of Year, Modern R.R. magazine, 1984; recipient Excellence in Mgmt. award Industry Week magazine, 1982. Member National Association Accts., Am. Institute C.P.A.'s. Clubs: Commonwealth (Richmond, Virginia); Country of Virginia (Richmond). Home: 22 Lower Tuckahoe Road W Richmond Virginia 23233 Office: CSX Corp Post Office Box C-32222 Richmond Virginia 23219

WATSON, THOMAS J., JR., former ambassador, retired business executive; born Dayton, Ohio, January 8, 1914; son of Thomas J. and Jeanette Kittredge) W.; married Olive Field Cawley, December 15, 1941; children: Thomas J. III, Jeanette, Olive, Lucinda, Susan, Helen. Bachelor of Arts, Brown University, 1937; honorary degrees from following universities, Columbia University, Harvard University, Brown University, Oxford University, Yale University, Catholic University Am., Lafayette College, University Notre Dame, Pace University, Union College, Rensselaer Polytechnic Institute, Amherst College, Syracuse University, St. Michael's College, Vermont, University Colorado, University Vermont, Trinity College, Wheaton College, Massachusetts, Bard College. With International Business Machines Corporation, 1937-40, 46-79, president, 1952-61, chief executive officer, 1956-71, chairman, 1961-71, chairman executive committee, 1971-79, director, chairman emeritus, 1981—; United States ambassador to Union of Soviet Socialist Republics 1979-81; board of directors Learjet Corp.;member President's Commission National Goals, 1960-61, President's Adv. Committee Labor-Mgmt. Policy, 1961-69, Adv. Committee Troop Information and Education, Department Def., 1962, President's Task Force on War Against Poverty, 1964-68, National Commission on Tech., Government, Automation and Economic Progress,

1965-66, President's Commission on Income Maintenance Programs, 1968-70, Am. Committee on East-West Accord, 1975-78; chairman general adv. committee Arms Control and Disarmament Agency, 1978-79. President Greater New York Councils, Boy Scouts Am., 1953-56, president National Council, 1964-68; trustee Brown U., 1947-85, vice chancellor, 1979-85, member board of fellows, 1985—; trustee Am. Mus. National History, 1955-78, hon. trustee, 1978—; trustee M.I.T., 1957-62; trustee George C. Marshall Research Foundation, 1958-89, trustee emeritus, 1989—; trustee California Institute Tech., 1960-79, 1981-84, life trustee, 1984—; trustee Rockefeller Foundation, 1963-71, John F. Kennedy Library, 1964—, Mystic Seaport, Incorporated, 1967-69, 1981—, Institute Advanced Study, Princeton, 1968-75, World Wildlife Fund, 1974-78; trustee Mayo Foundation, 1975-79, 1981-85, emeritus pub. trustee, 1985—; senior fellow Woodrow Wilson National Fellowship Foundation, 1973-79; board of directors Alliance to Save Energy, New York City Mission Society, 1981-84, National Executive Service Corps, 1982—, Atlantic Council of United States, 1982-86; member Committee of Ams. for the Canal Treaties, 1977-78; citizen regent Smithsonian Institution, 1967-79, regent emeritus, 1981—. Served to lieutenant colonel United States Air Force, 1940-45. Decorated Air medal; Presidential medal of Freedom; commander Order of Merit, Rep. of Italy; officer Legion of Honor France; officer Order of Leopold II Belgium; commander Al Mérito por Servicios Distinguídos Peru; Grand Cross; Equestrian Order of St. Sylvester Vatican; commander Royal Order of Vasa Sweden; officer Order of Southern Cross Brazil; recipient Silver Antelope, Buffalo, Beaver awards Boy Scouts Am., 1958; Rosenberger medal Brown University, 1968; Gold medal National Institute Social Sciences, 1971; Citation of Merit Salvation Army, 1972; Gold medal Electronic Industries Association, 1972; Pub. Service award Advertising Council, 1972; Herbert Hoover Memorial award Boys Clubs Am., 1975; National Business Hall of Fame award for bus. leadership, 1976; Medallion School of Business, College of William and Mary, 1976; Pub. Service award Phoenix House, 1981; International Achievement award World Trade Club of San Francisco, 1981; Service to Democracy award Am. Assembly, 1983; Blue Water medal, 1986, Am. Society French Legion of Honor medal for Distinguished Achievement, 1988, Medal of Achievement Am. Electronic Association, 1989. Member Council on Foreign Relations, Business Council, International Chamber of Commerce (trustee United States Council 1949-64, chairman 19557), Am. Philosophical Society (Benjamin Franklin award 1988), Psi Upsilon. Clubs: Links (New York City), River (New York City), New York Yacht (New York City); Metropolitan (Washington); Round Hill, Hope (Providence); Cruising of Am. Office: care International Business Machines Corporation Old Orchard Road Armonk New York 10504

WEAVER, CHARLES RICHARD, household products company executive; born Kingman, Indiana, September 16, 1928; son of Atha Lavern and Jennie Mildred (Best) W.; married Phyllis Jane Plaster,

September 30, 1950 (divorced 1982); children—Wendy, Cynthia, Daniel; married Donna Lee Lambert, November 21, 1982. Bachelor of Science, Purdue University, 1950. Sales trainee Faultless Caster Company, Evansville, Ind., 1950-51; product manager Westinghouse Corp., Pittsburgh, 1951-53; brand manager Procter & Gamble Corp., Cincinnati, 1953-59; manager special products div. Procter & Gamble Corp., Italy, 1963-66; marketing manager Clorox Company, Oakland, California, 1959-62, advertising manager, 1966-69, vice president, 1969-81, advertising manager, 1969-82, president, chief operating officer, 1982-85, president, chief executive officer, 1985-86, chairman, chief executive officer, 1986—. Served with United States Marine Corps, 1946-47. Office: Clorox Company 1221 Broadway Oakland California 94612

WEBER, MAX O., glass fiber products manufacturing company executive; born 1929. With Owens Corning Fiberglass Corp., Toledo, Ohio, 1955—, vice president, 1975-86, senior vice president, president construction producers group, 1986-88, vice president, 1975-81; senior vice president Owens Corning Fiberglass Corp., Toledo, 1986-88, president, chief operating officer, 1988-90; president and chief executive officer 1990—. Office: Owens-Corning Fiberglas Corp Fiberglas Tower Toledo Ohio 43659

WEBER, ROY EDWIN, savings and loan association executive; born Ann Arbor, Michigan, August 17, 1928; son of Edwin J. and Ruth E. (Nichols) W.; married Carol Warren, October 29, 1948; children—Michael R., Douglas J. Student, Michigan State University, 1946-48; Doctor Business Administration (honorary), Cleary College, 1987. With Great Lakes Bancorp, 1948—, vice president, treasurer, 1959-68, executive vice president, treasurer, 1968-69, president, 1969—, chairman board, 1973—; past director Federal Home Loan Bank, Indianapolis; 6th District representative to adv. council Federal Home Loan Bank Board, 1980-81; trustee Fin. Institutions Retirement Fund, 1984-89. Member city council, Ann Arbor, 1969-71; member regional board Catherine McAuley Health Center; trustee Ann Arbor Foundation; board of directors McKinley Foundation, 1986—; campaign chairman Washtenaw United Way, 1989. Member Michigan Savings and Loan League (director 1970, president 1976), United States Savings and Loan League (legis. committee 1969—), Ann Arbor Chamber of Commerce (past director). Republican. Lutheran. Club: Barton Hills Country. Home: 3340 Riverbend Dr Ann Arbor Michigan 48105 Office: Great Lakes Bancorp-Fed Savings Bank 401 E Liberty St Ann Arbor Michigan 48107

WEBSTER, ELROY, diversified supplies and machinery executive. Former 2d vice president, now chairman Farmers Union Central Exchange, Incorporated. Office: Farmers Union Central Exch Incorporated 5500 Cenex Dr Inver Grove Heights Minnesota 55075 also: Cenex Post Office Box 64089 Saint Paul Minnesota 55164§

WEINBERG, HARVEY A., apparel company executive; born 1937; married. Bachelor of Science, University Wisconsin, 1959. President, chief executive officer James K. Wilson, 1969-81; with Specialty Stores Group, 1980—, chairman, chief executive officer, 1981-84; with Hartmarx Corp., Chicago, Illinois, 1984—, vice chairman, 1986-87, vice chairman, chief executive officer, from 1987, now chairman, chief executive officer; also board of directors Hartmarx Corp. Office: Hartmarx Corp 101 N Wacker Dr Chicago Illinois 60606

WEINER, WALTER HERMAN, banker, lawyer; born Brooklyn, August 29, 1930; son of Harry and Sylvia (Freifeld) W.; married Nina Ester Avidar, October 11, 1966; children: Thomas Field, Jon Michael. Bachelor of Arts, University Michigan, 1952, Juris Doctor (associate editor Law Rev.), 1953. Bar: New York 1953. Senior partner Kronish, Lieb, Weiner & Hellman, New York City, 1965-79; chairman executive committee, chief executive officer Republic New York Corp., 1980-81, president, chief executive officer, 1981-83, chairman board, chief executive officer, 1983—; chairman executive committee, chief executive officer Republic National Bank of New York, 1980-82, president, chief executive officer, 1981-86; chairman board, chief executive officer Republic Bank of New York, 1986—; board of directors Republic Bank Corp., Republic National Bank of New York. Board of directors Bryant Park Restoration Corp., International Sephardic Education Foundation; trustee Guild Hall, East Hampton, New York; member New York Holocaust Memorial Commission; board visitors U. Michigan Law School. Recipient Humanitarian award National Association for the Advancement of Colored People, 1987, Human Relations award Accts., Bankers, Factors and Fin. div. Am. Jewish Committee, 1988, Man of Year award Brooklyn School for Special Children, 1988. Member American Bar Association, New York State Bar Association, Association Bar City New York, Am. Bankers Association. Home: 876 Park Avenue New York New York 10021 Office: Republic New York Corp 452 Fifth Avenue New York New York 10018

WEIS, KONRAD MAX, chemical company executive; born Leipzig, Germany, October 10, 1928; came to United States, 1971, naturalized, 1985; son of Alfred and Margarete (Leipoldt) W.; married Gisela Lueg, August 3, 1956; children—Alfred, Bettina. Doctor of Philosophy, University Bonn, 1955. Joined Bayer AG, Leverkusen, Federal Republic Germany, 1956, mgmt./exec. positions, 1961-74; president, chief executive officer Mobay Corp. subsidiary Bayer AG, Pittsburgh, 1974-81, chairman, president, chief executive officer, 1981-86; president, chief executive officer Bayer USA Incorporated, Pittsburgh, 1986-91, hon. chairman, 1991—; chairman board Agfa Corp., Miles Incorporated, Mobay Corp; board of directors Cyclops Industries, Incorporated, Dravo Corp., PNC Fin. Corp., Pittsburgh National Bank. Trustee Carnegie-Mellon U., 1981—, The Carnegie, Pittsburgh, 1984—; trustee, board of directors Presbyn.-Univ. Hospital, Pittsburgh, 1986—; vice president Allegheny Conference on Community Devel., 1983—; member Policy committee Pennsylvania Business Roundtable, 1983—; board of directors Pittsburgh Symphony Society, 1987—. Member Chemical Manufacturers Association (director, executive committee 1985-88), German Am. Chamber of Commerce (director 1981-88), World Affairs

Council Pittsburgh (director 1983—). Clubs: Links (New York City); Pittsburgh Golf, Duquesne (Pittsburgh); Fox Chapel (Pennsylvania) Golf; Rolling Rock Country (Ligonier, Pennsylvania). Office: Bayer USA Incorporated 1 Mellon Center 500 Grant St Pittsburgh Pennsylvania 15219-2502

WEISS, MORRY, greeting card company executive; born Czechoslovakia, 1940; married Judith Stone. Graduate, Wayne State University. Salesman, field manager Am. Greetings Corp., Cleveland, 1961-66, advertising manager, 1966-68, vice president, 1969-73, group vice president marketing and sales, 1973-78, formerly chief operating officer, from 1978, president, 1978—, also board of directors, chief executive officer, 1987—. Office: Am Greetings Corp 10500 American Road Cleveland Ohio 44144

WEISS, WILLIAM LEE, communications executive; born Big Run, Pennsylvania, May 21, 1929; son of Harry W. and Dorothy Jane (McKee) W.; married Josephine Elizabeth Berry, June 3, 1951; children: Susan Leigh Weiss Miller, David William, Steven Paul. Bachelor of Science in Industrial Engineering, Pennsylvania State University, 1951; Doctor of Management (honorary), Purdue University, 1988; Doctor of Laws (honorary), DePaul University, 1990. With Bell Telephone Company of Pennsylvania, 1951, 1953-76; vice president staff Bell Telephone Company of Pennsylvania, Philadelphia, 1973-74; vice president, general manager Bell Telephone Company of Pennsylvania (western area), 1974-76; vice president operations Wisconsin Telephone Company, Milwaukee, 1976-78; president Ind. Bell Telephone Company, Indianapolis, 1978-81; also director Ind. Bell Telephone Company; president Illinois Bell Telephone Company, Chicago, 1981, chairman, 1982-83; chairman, chief executive officer Ameritech, Chicago, 1983—, also board of directors; board of directors Abbott Laboratories, Chicago, The Quaker Oats Company, Chicago. Board of directors Chicago Council on Foreign Relations, vice chairman corp. service committee, 1988; Lyric Opera Chicago; trustee Mus. Sci. and Industry, 1982, chairman board trustees, 1989—; trustee Northwestern U., 1982, Orchestral Association, Chicago, 1982, Committee for Economic Devel.; member Information Industry Council, Business Roundtable; member adv. council J.L. Kellogg Grad. School Mgmt., member board committee Research Park, Northwestern U.; member Business Committee for the Arts, United Way of Am. Board Govs, member Business Council, member Conference Board Served with United States Air Force, 1951-53. Member Commercial Club (president 1989—), Chicago Club, Econ. Club, Mid-Am. Club (Chicago), Glen View (Illinois) Club, Old Elm (Illinois) Country Club of North Carolina (Pinehurst), Milwaukee Country Club, Tau Beta Pi, Phi Delta Theta. Avocations: civic work, golf, travel, family activities.

WELCH, JOHN FRANCIS, JR., electrical manufacturing company executive; born Peabody, Massachusetts, November 19, 1935; son of John Francis and Grace (Andrews) W.; married Carolyn B. Osburn, November 1959 (divorced 1987); children: Katherine, John, Anne, Mark; married Jane Beasley, April

1989. Bachelor of Science in Chemical Engineering, University Massachusetts, 1957; Master of Science, University Illinois, 1958, Doctor of Philosophy, 1960. With General Electric Company, Fairfield, Connecticut, 1960—, vice president, 1972, vice president, group executive components and materials group, 1973-77, senior vice president, sector executive, consumer products and services sector, 1977-79, vice chairman, executive officer, 1979-81, chairman, chief executive officer, 1981—; also director General Electric Fin. Services. Patentee in field. Member National Academy of Engineering, Federal Reserve Board (board directors), Business Council (chairman), Business Roundtable. Office: General Electric Company 3135 Easton Turnpike Fairfield Connecticut 06431

WELLINGTON, ROBERT HALL, manufacturing company executive; born Atlanta, July 4, 1922; son of Robert H. and Ernestine V. (Vossbrinck) W.; married Marjorie Jarchow, November 15, 1947; children: Charles R., Robert H., Christian J., Jeanne L. Bachelor of Science, Northwestern Tech. Institute, 1943; Master of Science in Business Adminstrn, Master of Business Administration, University Chicago, 1958. With Griffin Wheel Company, 1946-61; vice president parent company AMSTED Industries, Incorporated, Chicago, 1961-74, executive vice president, 1974-80, president, chief executive officer, 1981-88, chairman board, chief executive officer, 1988-90, also director; board of directors L.East Myers Company, Chicago, DeSoto Incorporated, Chicago, Centel, Prudential Money Market Assets, Prudential Rsrch. Fund, Incorporated, Prudential Intermediate Income Fund, Incorporated. Served to lieutenant United States Navy, 1943-46. Member Chicago Club, Chicago Athletic Club, Econ. Club, Tavern Club, Mid-Am. Club, Commercial Club. Office: Amsted Industries Incorporated 205 N Michigan Avenue 44 Floor Chicago Illinois 60601

WELLMAN, W. ARVID, window manufacturing executive; born 1918. With Andersen Corp., Bayport, Minnesota, 1937—, president, from 1975, now chairman board, chief executive officer, director. Office: Andersen Corp 100 4th Avenue N Bayport Minnesota 55003

WELLS, FRANK G., lawyer, film studio executive; born March 4, 1932. Bachelor of Arts summa cum laude, Pomona College, 1953; Master of Arts in Law, Oxford (England) University, 1955; Bachelor of Laws, Stanford University, 1959. Former vice chairman Warner Brothers Incorporated; partner Gang Tyre & Brown, 1962-69; president, chief operating officer Walt Disney Company, Burbank, California, 1984—. Co-author: Seven Summits. Board trustees Pomona College, National History Mus., Sundance Institute; board overseers for RAND/UCLA Center Study of Soviet Behavior; member services policy adv. committee United States Trade Regulation. 1st lieutenant United States Army, 1955-57. Rhodes scholar, 1955. Member American Bar Association, State Bar California, Los Angeles County Bar Association, Explorers Club, Phi Beta Kappa. Office: Walt Disney Company 500 S Buena Vista St Burbank California 91521

WELLS, JOEL REAVES, JR., bank executive; born Troy, Alabama, November 14, 1928; son of Joel Reaves and Julia (Talley) W.; married Betty Stratton, June 27, 1953; children: Linda, Martha, Joel. Bachelor of Science in Business Administration, University Florida, 1950, Juris Doctor, 1951. Bar: Florida. Partner Maguire, Voorhis & Wells, Orlando, Florida, 1956-75; president Major Realty Company, Orlando, 1972-75; executive vice president SunBanks, Incorporated, Orlando, 1975-76, president, 1976-84, chairman, chief executive officer, 1982-89; president SunTrust Banks, Incorporated, Atlanta, 1985-90, chairman, 1990—, also board of directors; board of directors SunBank, N.A., SunBanks, Incorporated, Coca-Cola Enterprises, Incorporated, Atlanta, Columbian Mutual Life Insurance Company, Binghamton, New York. Member Florida Council of 100, from 1975; president Central Florida Devel. Committee, 1965; chairman Municipal Planning Board, Orlando, 1962, 63; president United Appeal Orange County, 1960; trustee Berry College, Rome, Georgia. Recipient Distinguished Service award Orlando Jaycees, 1960. Member Orlando Chamber of Commerce (president 1970), Atlanta Chamber of Commerce (past board directors). Methodist. Clubs: Rotary (president 1966-67), University, Citrus, Country (Orlando). Office: SunTrust Banks Incorporated Post Office Box 4418 Atlanta Georgia 30302 also: Sun Banks Incorporated 200 S Orange Avenue Orlando Florida 32801

WELSH, WILLIAM F., II, manufacturing company executive. President, chief operating officer Valmont Industries Incorporated, Valley, Nebraska. Office: Valmont Industries Incorporated Highway 275 Valley NE 68064§

WENTWORTH, JACK ROBERTS, business educator, consultant; born Elgin, Illinois, June 11, 1928; son of William Franklin and Elizabeth (Roberts) W.; married Rosemary Ann Pawlak, May 30, 1956; children—William, Barbara. Student, Carleton College, 1946-48; Bachelor of Science, Ind. University, 1950, Master of Business Administration, 1954, DBA, 1959. Coordinator displays Cadillac Div., General Motors Corp., Detroit, 1954-56; assistant professor business, associate director research School of Business Ind. University, Bloomington, 1957-60, associate professor, director research, 1960-70, professor, 1970—, chairman MBA program, 1970-76, chairman department, faculty representative National Collegiate Athletic Association, 1978-85, dean School of Business, 1984—; marketing consultant, Bloomington, 1960—; board of directors IPCO, Incorporated, White Plains, New York, Kimball International, Jasper, Ind.; Forum Retirement Ptnrs., L.P., Indianapolis, Bank One, Bloomington, Market Facts Incorporated, Chicago. Editor: (monograph) Marketing Horizons, 1965; executive editor Bus. Horizons, 1960-70. Served to 1st lieutenant United States Air Force, 1950-53. Recipient Teaching award MBA Association, 1973, 78, 81, 84, 85, Service award Association for Business and Economic Rsch., 1983. Member Am. Marketing Association (vice president 1971-73), Grad. Management Admissions Council (chairman board trustees 1977-78), University Club, Masons, Beta Gamma Sigma (president Alpha of

Ind. chapter 1971-72, board govs. 1986—). Republican. Episcopalian. Avocations: athletic events; travel; bicycling; model railroading; magic. Office: Indiana U School Business Bloomington Indiana 47405

WENTZ, HOWARD BECK, JR., manufacturing company executive; born Pittsburgh, January 10, 1930; son of Howard and Emmy Lou W.; married Judith Ann Blough, June, 1958; children: Howard, Roger, Elizabeth. Bachelor of Science in Engineering, Princeton University, 1952; Master of Business Administration, Harvard University, 1957. Manufacturing executive TRW Corp., 1957-60; associate Robert Heller and Associates, Cleveland, 1960-63; executive vice president Paterson-Leitch Company, Cleveland, 1963-69; president Duff-Norton subsidiary Amstar Corp., Charlotte, North Carolina, 1969-72; corp. vice president parent company Duff-Norton subsidiary Amstar Corp., New York City, 1972-79; executive vice president Duff-Norton subsidiary Amstar Corp., 1979-81; chief operating officer Amstar Corp., 1979-81, president, 1981—, chief executive officer, 1982—, chairman, 1983-89, also board of directors; chairman Eastar Incorporated; board of directors Am. European Reins. Company, Skandia Corp., Colgate-Palmolive Company, Tam Brands, Incorporated, Crompton & Knowles Corp. With United States Navy, 1952-55. Office: Long Wharf Maritime Center 555 Long Wharf Dr Suite 12 New Haven Connecticut 06511

WENZEL, FRED WILLIAM, apparel manufacturing executive; born St. Louis, January 14, 1916; son of Frederick H. and Ella M. (Heuerman) W.; married Mary Edna Cruzen; 1 child, Robert F. Graduate, University Wisconsin, 1937. Chairman H. Wenzel Tent & Duck Company St. Louis, 1937-52; president Hawthorn Company, New Haven, Missouri, 1952-64; vice president Kellwood Company, Chicago, 1961-64; chairman board Kellwood Company, St. Louis, 1964, president, chairman, 1965-76, chairman, chief executive officer, 1976-84, chairman, 1984—. Home: 13315 Fairfield Square Dr Chesterfield Missouri 63017 Office: Kellwood Company Post Office Box 14374 Saint Louis Missouri 63178

WERRIES, E. DEAN, food distribution company executive; born Tescott, Kansas, May 8, 1929; son of John William and Sophie E. Werries; married Marjean Sparling, May 18, 1962. Bachelor of Science, University Kansas, 1952. With Fleming Foods Company, Topeka, 1955-89, executive vice president, 1973-76; executive vice president Eastern operations Fleming Foods Company, Philadelphia, 1976-78; president Fleming Foods Company, Oklahoma City, 1978-81; president, chief operating officer Fleming Companies, Incorporated, Oklahoma City, 1981-88, also director; president, chief executive officer Fleming Companies, Incorporated, 1988-89, chairman, chief executive officer, 1989—. Served with United States Army, 1952-54, Korea. Member National Am. Wholesale Grocers Association (board directors 1979—), Food Marketing Institute (board directors 1984—, chairman 1989-90), Ind. Grocers Alliance (board directors 1984—). Republican. Presbyterian. Office: Fleming Cos Incorporated 6301 Waterford Boulevard Oklahoma City Oklahoma 73118

WEST, BYRON KENNETH, banker; born Denver, September 18, 1933; son of Willis Byron and Cecil Bernice (Leathers) W.; married Barbara Huth, June 25, 1955. Bachelor of Arts, University Illinois, 1955; Master of Business Administration, University Chicago, 1960. With Harris Bank, Chicago, 1957—, investment analyst, 1957-62, vice president, 1966-76; group executive Harris Bank International Banking Group, Chicago, 1974-76, head banking department, executive vice president, 1976-80, president, 1980; chairman board, chief executive officer Harris Bankcorp, Incorporated, Chicago, 1984—, also board of directors; chairman, chief executive officer Harris Trust and Savings Bank, Chicago, 1985—; board of directors Motorola, Incorporated, Association Reserve City Bankers. Trustee U. Chicago, Rush-Presbyn.-St. Luke's Med Center; member governing board Chicago Orchestral Association; board of directors U. Illinois Foundation Served with United States Navy, 1955-57. Member Reserve City Bankers Association, Christian Laymen of Chicago, Phi Beta Kappa. Republican. Clubs: Skokie Country (Glencoe, Illinois); Pine Valley (New Jersey); University, Chicago, Commonwealth, Comml., Econ. (Chicago). Home: 200 Forest St Winnetka Illinois 60093 Office: Harris Bankcorp Incorporated 111 W Monroe St Post Office Box 755 Chicago Illinois 60690

WEST, ROBERT H., manufacturing company executive; born 1938. Bachelor of Arts, Princeton University, 1960. Vice president First National Bank of Kansas City, 1962-68; assistant treasurer Butler Manufacturing Company, Incorporated, Kansas City, Missouri, 1968-70, controller building div., 1970-73, corp. vice president, controller buildings div., 1973-74, senior vice president administration, 1974-76, executive vice president, 1976-78, president, chief operating officer, 1978-86, chairman, chief executive officer, 1986—, also director; board of directors Kansas City Power & Light Company, Santa Fe Pacific Corp., Commerce Bancshares, Incorporated. Board of directors St. Lukes Hospital Served to 1st lieutenant United States Army, 1960-62. Office: Butler Mfg Company Incorporated BMA Tower Penn Valley Park Kansas City Missouri 64108

WEST, ROBERT VAN OSDELL, JR., petroleum executive; born Kansas City, Missouri, April 29, 1921; son of Robert Van Osdell and Jacqueline (Quistgaard) W.; divorced; children: Robert Van Osdell, III, Kathryn Anne, Suzanne Small, Patricia Lynn; married Helen L. Boecking, 1978. Bachelor of Science, University Texas, 1942, Master of Science, 1943, Doctor of Philosophy, 1949. Registered profl engineer, Texas. Petroleum engineer Slick Urschel Oil Company, 1949-56; president Slick Secondary Recovery Corp., 1956-59; vice president Texstar Corp., 1959; president Texstar Petroleum Company subsidiary Texstar Corp., 1959-64; founder Tesoro Petroleum Corp., San Antonio, 1964, chairman board of directors, chief executive officer, 1971-88, chairman board, 1988—; chief executive officer Tesoro Petroleum Corp., 1989—; board of directors Continental Telecom Incorporated, Frost National Bank; engineering foundation adv. council University Texas; adv. council, trustee St. Mary's University School

Business. Trustee Texas Research and Tech. Foundation San Antonio; past trustee San Antonio City Public Service Board; trustee Southwest Research Institute; board of directors Ford's Theatre, Washington; past chairman San Antonio Economic Devel. Foundation; director World Affairs Council, San Antonio; chairman board of directors Tiwanaku Archaeol. Foundation, Bolivia.; chairman executive committee Caribbean/Central Am. Action, Washington; chairman general campaign United Way of San Antonio and Bexar County, 1986, vice chairman board trustees, 1988—; chairman pub. sector campaign subcom. United Way of Am., 1988—. Named Distinguished Graduate, University Texas College Engineering, 1973; recipient People of Vision award National Society Prevention of Blindness, 1982, International Citizens award World Affairs Council, 1986, Good Scout award Boy Scouts Am., 1987. Member Am. Petroleum Institute (board directors), Ind. Petroleum Association Am., Texas Ind. Producers and Royalty Owners Association, Mid-Continent Oil and Gas Association (board directors), 25 Year Club Petroleum Industry, Association Private Enterprise Education (Herman W. Lay Memorial award 1986), Am.'s Society, National Petroleum Council, Sigma Chi (Significant Sig award 1979). Episcopalian. Club: All-Am. Wildcatters. Office: Tesoro Petroleum Corp 8700 Tesoro Dr San Antonio Texas 78286

WESTON, JOSH S., data processing company executive; born Brooklyn, December 22, 1928; married. Bachelor of Science, City College of New York, 1950; Master of Arts, University New Zealand, 1951. Executive vice president Popular Services, Incorporated, 1955-70; vice president planning administration Automatic Data Processing, Incorporated, Roseland, New Jersey, 1970-75, executive vice president, 1975-77, president from 1977, chief executive officer, 1982—, former chief operating officer, now also chairman; director Shared Medical Systems, Pub. Service Electric & Gas Company, Mutual Benefit Life Insurance Company. Office: ADP Incorporated 1 Automatic Data Processing Boulevard Roseland New Jersey 07068

WEXNER, LESLIE HERBERT, retail executive; born Dayton, Ohio, 1937. Bachelor of Science with honors, Ohio State University, 1959, Doctor of Humanities (honorary), 1986; Doctor of Laws (honorary), Hofstra University, 1987; Doctor of Humane Letters, Brandeis University, 1990. Founder, president, chairman board The Limited, Incorporated, fashion chain, Columbus, 1963—; director, member executive committee Banc One Corp., Sotheby's Holdings Incorporated; member business administration adv. council Ohio State University. Board of directors Columbus Urban League, 1982-84, Hebrew Immigrant Aid Society, New York City, 1982—; trustee Columbus Symphony Orchestra, Whitney Mus. Am. Art; co-chairman International United Jewish Appeal Committee; national vice chairman United Jewish Appeal; board of directors, member executive committee Am. Jewish Joint Distribution Committee, Incorporated; trustee Columbus Jewish Federation, 1972, Capitol South Community Urban Redevel. Corp., Columbus Mus. Art; founding member, first chair Columbus Capital Corp. for Civic Improvement, Ohio State U. Found; governor committee Columbus Foundation; trustee Ohio State U., Columbus Mus. Art; executive committee Am. Israel Pub. Affairs Committee. Decorated cavaliere Republic of Italy. Named Man of Year Am. Marketing Association, 1974. Member Young Presidents Organization, Sigma Alpha Mu. Club: B'nai B'rith. Office: Limited Incorporated 2 Limited Parkway Box 16000 Columbus Ohio 43216

WEYERHAEUSER, GEORGE HUNT, forest products company executive; born Seattle, July 8, 1926; son of John Philip and Helen (Walker) W.; married Wendy Wagner, July 10, 1948; children: Virginia Lee, George Hunt, Susan W., Phyllis A., David M., Merrill W. Bachelor of Science with honors in Industrial Engineering, Yale University, 1949. With Weyerhaeuser Company, Tacoma, 1949—, successively mill foreman, branch manager, 1949-56, vice president, 1957-66, executive vice president, 1966-88, president, chief executive officer, 1988, chairman board, chief executive officer, 1988—; board of directors Boeing Company, SAFECO Corp., Chevron Corp.; member Business Council, Business Roundtable, Washington State Business Roundtable. Office: Weyerhaeuser Company Office of Chairman Tacoma Washington 98477

WHARTON, CLIFTON REGINALD, JR., insurance company executive, former academic administrator; born Boston, September 13, 1926; married Dolores Duncan, 1950; children: Clifton, Bruce. Bachelor of Arts, Harvard University, 1947; Master of Arts, Johns Hopkins University, 1948, Doctor of Laws (honorary), 1970; Master of Arts, University Chicago, 1956, Doctor of Philosophy in Economics, 1958; Doctor of Laws (honorary), University Michigan, 1970, Wayne State University, 1970, Hahneman Medical School, 1975, Georgetown University, 1976, Virginia State University, 1977, City College of New York, 1978, Wright State University, 1979, Clark Atlanta University, 1990, Howard University, 1991, Lincoln University, 1979, Albany Law School, 1980, Duke University, 1981, Amherst College, 1983, University Illinois, 1984, University Vermont, 1987, Colgate University, 1987, Tuskegee University, 1987, Tufts University, 1988, Michigan State University, 1988, Claremont University Center and Graduate School, 1989, University Notre Dame, 1989, Clark Atlanta University, 1990, Howard University, 1991; DPS (honorary), Central Michigan University, 1970, University Pittsburgh, 1989; Doctor of Letters (honorary), North Carolina Agricultural and Tech. State University, 1988; Doctor of Humane Letters (honorary), Oakland University, 1971, Northern Michigan University, 1975, Columbia University, 1978, Brandeis University, 1981, New York University, 1981, University Connecticut, 1983, University Massachusetts, Boston, 1985, Southern Illinois University, 1987, George Mason University, 1988, Long Island University, 1989, Virginia Commonwealth University, 1990, State University of New York, 1990; Doctor of Science (honorary), Mercy College, 1989, Bryant College, 1990. Executive trainee Am. International Association Economic and Social Devel., 1948-49, program analyst, 1949-51, head reports and analysis, 1951-53; research assistant economics University Chicago, 1953-56, research associate, 1956-57; executive associate Agricultural Devel. Council, 1957-58, associate, 1958-64, director Am. universities research, 1964-67, vice president, 1967-69; president Michigan State University, 1970-78; chancellor State University of New York System, 1978-87; chairman, chief executive officer Teachers Insurance & Annuity Association College Retirement Equities Fund, New York City, 1987—; board of directors New York Stock Exchange; past board of directors Equitable Life Assurance Society, PBS, TIme, Incorporated, Burroughs Corp., Federated Dept Stores, Federal Reserve Bank New York, deputy chairman, 1985-86. Co-author: Patterns for Lifelong Learning, 1973; editor: Subsistence Agriculture and Economic Development, 1969; contributor articles to professional journals. Trustee Rockefeller Foundation, 1970-87, chairman, 1982-87; trustee Asia Society, 1967-77, Overseas Devel. Council, 1969-79, Carnegie Foundation, 1970-79, Agricultural Devel. Council, 1973-80, Aspen Institute, 1980—, Committee Economic Devel., 1980—, Council Fin. Aid to Education, 1983-86, Council Foreign Rels., 1983—, Foreign Policy Association, 1983-87, Massachusetts Institute of Technology Corp., 1984-86, Acad. Educational Devel., 1985-86; member Commission on Intercollegiate Athletics, Knight Foundation, 1990—, New York City Mayor's Council Economic Advisors, 1990—, Adv. Comn. on Trade Policy and Negotiations, 1990—. Member Am. Agricultural Economics Association, Am. Economics Association, Association Asian Studies, National Acad. Education, Bus.-Higher Education Forum, University Club (New York City). Office: TIAA-CREF 730 3rd Avenue New York New York 10017

WHEELER, THOMAS BEARDSLEY, insurance company executive; born Buffalo, August 2, 1936; son of William Henry and Ruth (Matthews) W.; married Anne Tuck Robertson, November 15, 1961; children: Elizabeth Wheeler Soule, Wendy Bennett. Bachelor of Arts, Yale University, 1958. C.L.U. Sales representative International Business Machines Corporation, White Plains, New York, 1961-62; sales representative, assistant general agent Massachusetts Mutual Life Insurance Company, Boston, 1962, general agent, 1972-83; executive vice president Massachusetts Mutual Life Insurance Company, Springfield, 1983-86, president, 1987-88, president, chief executive officer, 1988—; board of directors Bank of Boston Corp., Am. Council Life Insurance. Co-author: Managing Sales Professionals, 1984. Trustee Springfield College, 1985—, Am. College, Bryn Mawr, Pennsylvania, 1987-90, Baystate Health Systems, Incorporated, Springfield, 1983—, Springfield Orchestra Association, Basketball Hall of Fame, Springfield. Lieutenant United States Naval Reserve, 1958-60. Member Yale University Devel. Board, Springfield Life Underswriter's Association, Am. Society C.L.U.s (Pioneer Valley chapter, president Boston chapter 1980-81), Boston Life Underswriter's Association (president 1972-73), Massachusetts Association Life Underwriters (president 1976-77), Health Insurance Association Am. (board directors 1990—), Million Dollar Round Table. Republican.

Clubs: Yale of New York, Colony (Springfield), Longmeadow Country, Boca Grande, Chapoquoit Yacht (sec. 1973-75); The Links (New York City). Avocations: skiing, boating, art, antiques, music. Office: Mass Mut Life Ins Company 1295 State St Springfield Massachusetts 01111

WHITACRE, EDWARD E., JR., telecommunications executive; born Ennis, Texas, November 4, 1941. Bachelor of Science in Industrial Engineering, Texas Tech University, 1964. With Southwestern Bell Telephone Company, 1963-85; various positions in operations departments Texas, Arkansas, Kansas; president Kansas div. Topeka, 1982-85; group president Southwestern Bell Corp., St. Louis, 1985-86, vice president revenues and pub. affairs, vice-chairman, chief fin. officer, 1986-88, president, chief operating officer, 1988-89, chairman, chief executive officer, 1990—, also board of directors; board of directors Mercantile Bancorp., Incorporated, St. Louis, Anheuser-Busch Companies, Incorporated, 1988—, May Department Stores Company. Board of directors St. Louis Area council Boy Scouts Am., 1986—, Texas Tech U. and Health Scis. Research Foundation, Lubbock, 1986-88, St. Louis Art Mus. Presbyterian. Office: Southwestern Bell Corp 1 Bell Center Suite 4200 Saint Louis Missouri 63101

WHITE, SIR (VINCENT) GORDON LINDSAY, textile company executive; born May 11, 1923; son of Charles and Lily May (Wilson) W.; married Virginia Anne White, 1974; 3 children. Graduate, De Aston School, Lincolnshire, England. Chairman Welbecson Limited, 1947-65; department chairman Hanson Trust Limited, 1965-73; chairman Hanson Industries North America, Iselin, New Jersey, 1983—; member special commission Hanson's Trust's opportunities overseas, 1979-83. Member Council for Police Rehabilitation Appeal, 1985—; board of directors Shakespeare Theatre, Golger Library, Washington, 1985—; board of directors, chairman international committee Congl. Award, 1984—; governor BFI, 1982-84. Served with British military, 1940-46. Named Knight Comd. Order of the Briit. Empire; St. Peter's College hon. fellow, 1984; recipient National Vol. Leadership award, Congl. award, 1984, Aims of Industry Free Enterprise award, 1985. Clubs: Spl. Forces; Brook, Explorer's (New York City); Mid-Ocean (Bermuda). Avocations: fying helicopters, horseback riding, skiing, tennis. Office: Hanson Industries Incorporated 410 Park Avenue New York New York 10022

WHITE, JEFF V., information services company executive; born Mobjack, Virginia, January 8, 1925; son of Leonard S. and Gracie F. (Drisgill) W.; married Rosalyn White, December 29, 1946; children: Robert, Lynne. With Equifax, Incorporated, Atlanta, 1942—; successively assistant vice president, vice president, vice president and operations manager, executive vice president, president Credit Bureau Incorporated affiliate Equifax, Incorporated, Atlanta, 1962-74; vice president Equifax, Incorporated, Atlanta, 1976-77, group vice president, 1977-79, executive vice president, 1979-81, president, 1981-87, chief executive officer, 1983-89, vice chairman, 1987-88, chairman, chief executive officer, 1988-89, chairman, 1988, also board of directors; board of directors affiliated companies 1st National Bank Atlanta, 1st Atlanta Corp., Central Atlanta Progress; member adv. council College Business Administration Georgia State University, INROADS/Atlanta. Board of directors adv. council Georgia State U. College Business Asminstrn.; member adv. council United Way of Metro Atlanta; board visitors Emory U.; board trustees Fernbank Sci. Center; member The Conference Board, 1988. Served to lieutenant United States Army, 1943-46. Member Can. Am. Society Southeast United States. Office: Equifax Incorporated 1600 Peachtree St Northwest Atlanta Georgia 30302

WHITE, WILLIAM JAMES, information management and services company executive;; born Kenosha, Wisconsin, May 30, 1938; son of William H. and Dorothy Caroline White; married Jane Schulte, August 13, 1960; children: James N., Thomas G., Maria J., Gretchen S. Bachelor of Science, Northwestern University, 1961; Master of Business Administration, Harvard University, 1963. Mechanical planning engineer Procter & Gamble Corp., 1961-62; corp. vice president Hartmarx Corp., Chicago, 1963-74; group vice president Mead Corp., Dayton, Ohio, 1974-81; president, chief operating officer, director Masonite Corp., Chicago, 1981-88; executive vice president and director USG Corp., 1985-88, president, chief executive officer Whitestar Enterprises, Incorporated, 1989-90; chairman, president, chief executive officer Bell & Howell Company, 1990—. Author: (with Henderson et al) Creative Collective Bargaining, 1965. Member The Chicago Committee, adv. council The McCormick School of Engring. & Applied Scis., Northwestern U.; member business adv. council U. Illinois, Chicago, 1981—; board director Material Scis. Corp., Elk Grove Village, Illinois, Midwest Stock Exchange, Chicago, Evanston (Illinois) Hospital, Evanston Maths. and Sci. Acad., Aurora; former board of directors Harris Bankcorp, Harris Trust & Savs. Bank. Chairman Am. Cancer Society, Illinois div. Clubs: Economic, Chicago. Office: Bell & Howell Company 5215 Old Orchard Road Skokie Illinois 60077-1076

WHITE, WILLIS SHERIDAN, JR., utilities company executive; born near Portsmouth, Virginia, December 17, 1926; son of Willis Sheridan and Carrie (Culpepper) W.; married LaVerne Behrends, October 8, 1949; children: Willis Sheridan III, Marguerite Louise White Spangler, Cynthia D.W. Haight. Bachelor of Science, Virginia Polytechnic Institute, 1948; Master of Science, Massachusetts Institute Tech., 1958. With Am. Electric Power Company System, 1948—; assistant engineer Am. Electric Power Service Corp., New York City, 1948-52, assistant to president, 1952-54, office manager, 1954-57, administrative assistant to operating vice president, 1958-61; div. manager Appalachian Power Company, Lynchburg, Virginia, 1962-66; assistant general manager Appalachian Power Company, Roanoke, Virginia, 1966-67, assistant vice president, 1967-69; vice president Am. Electric Power Service Corp. (Appalachian Power Company), Roanoke, Virginia, 1969, executive vice president, director, 1969-73; senior executive vice president operations, director Am. Electric Power Service Corp., New York City, 1973-75, vice chairman operations, director,

1976—, chairman, chief executive officer; chairman, chief executive officer Central Ohio Coal Company, 1988-90; director Am. Electric Power Company, New York City, 1972—, chairman board, 1976—, chief executive officer, 1976-90; chairman, director AEP Energy Services, Incorporated, AEP Generating Company, Appalachian Power Company, Roanoke, Virginia, Columbus Southern Power Company, Ind. Michigan Power Company, Kentucky Power Company, Kingsport Power Company, Michigan Power Company, Ohio Power Company, Wheeling Power Company; president, director, chairman Ohio Valley Electric Corp., Ind.-KTY Electric Corp., 1977—, Cardinal Operating Company; president, director Cedar Coal Company, Castlegate Coal Company, Central Appalachian Coal Company, Central Coal Company, Central Ohio Coal Company, Central Operating Company, Franklin Real Estate Company, Ind. Franklin Realty Company, Colomet, Incorporated, Kanawha Valley Power Company, Michigan Gas Exploration Company, Ind. Franklin Realty, Price River Coal Company, Simco, Incorporated, Southern Appalachian Coal Company, Southern Ohio Coal Company, Twin Branch Railroad Company, West Virginia Power Company, Wheeling Electric Company, Windsor Power House Coal Company. Trustee, Battelle Memorial Institute Served with United States Naval Reserve, 1945-46. Sloan fellow, 1957-58. Member Institute of Electrical and Electronics Engineers, National Coal Association (director), National Coal Council (board directors), Association Edison Illuminating Companies (executive committee), National Association of Manufacturers (director), National Acad. Engineering, Eta Kappa Nu. Methodist.

WHITMORE, KAY REX, photographic company executive; born Salt Lake City, July 24, 1932; son of Rex Grange and Ferrol Terry (Smith) W.; married Yvonne Schofield, June 6, 1956; children: Richard, Kimberly, Michele, Cynthia, Suzanne, Scott. Student, University Utah, 1950-53, Bachelor of Science, 1957; Master of Science, Massachusetts Institute of Technology, 1975. With Eastman Kodak Company, Rochester, New York, 1957—, engineer film manufacturing, 1957-67; with factory start-up Eastman Kodak Company, Guadalajara, Mexico, 1967-71; various management positions film manufacturing Eastman Kodak Company, Rochester, 1971-74, assistant vice president, general manager Latin Am. Region, 1975-79, vice president, assistant general manager United States and Can. Photog. Div., 1979-80, executive vice president and general manager, 1981-83, president, 1983-90, chairman board, president, chief executive officer, 1990—, also board of directors; board of directors The Chase Manhattan Corp. Trustee U. Rochester. With United States Army, 1953-55. Member Am. Society for Quality Control, Business Roundtable, Business Council. Member Church of Jesus Christ of Latter Day Saints. Office: Eastman Kodak Company 343 State St Rochester New York 14650-0229

WHITWAM, DAVID RAY, appliance manufacturing company executive; born Stanley, Wisconsin, January 30, 1942; son of Donald R. and Lorraine (Stoye) W.; married Barbara Lynne Peterson, April 13, 1963; children:

Mark, Laura, Thomas. Bachelor of Science, University Wisconsin, 1967. General manager sales Southern California div. Whirlpool Corp., Los Angeles, 1975-77; merchandise manager ranges Benton Harbor, Michigan, 1977-79, director builder marketing, 1979-80, vice president builder marketing, 1980-83, vice president whirlpool sales, 1983-85, vice chairman, chief marketing officer, 1985-87, chairman, president, chief executive officer, 1987—, also board of directors; board of directors Combustion Engineering Incorporated, Stamford, Connecticut. President board of directors The Soup Kitchen, Benton Harbor, 1980—; member National Council Housing Industry, Washington. Served to captain United States Army, 1968-68. Fellow Aspen Institute. Republican. Lutheran. Club: Point O'Woods (Benton Harbor). Office: Whirlpool Corp 2000 M-63 North Benton Harbor Michigan 49022

WIBORG, JAMES HOOKER, chemicals distribution company executive; born Seattle, August 26, 1924; son of John R. and Hazel (Hooker) W.; married Ann Rogers, July 1948; children: Katherine Ann, Mary Ellen, Caroline Joan, John Stewart. Bachelor of Arts, University Washington, 1946. Owner, Wiborg Manufacturing Company, Tacoma, 1946-50; securities analyst Pacific Northwest Company, Seattle, 1950-53; founder Western Plastics Corp., Tacoma, 1953; president Western Plastics Corp., 1953-55, chairman board, director, retired; executive vice president Washington Steel Products Company, Tacoma, 1955-58; management consultant Tacoma, 1958-60; vice president United Pacific Corp., Seattle, 1960; president Pacific Small Business Investment Corp., Seattle, 1961-63; senior vice president industrial div. United Pacific Corp., Seattle, 1963-65; president, chief executive officer, director United Pacific Corp., 1965; past president, chief executive officer, director Univar Corp. (formerly VWR United Corp.), Seattle, from 1966; chairman, chief executive officer Univar Corp. (formerly VWR United Corp.), 1983-86, chairman, chief strategist, 1986—; director, chairman, chief strategist VWR Corp., 1986—; director Seattle, Seafirst Corp., PACCAR Incorporated, Seattle-First National Bank, Gensco Incorporated, Tacoma, Penwest Limited. Trustee U. Puget Sound. Clubs: Tacoma Country and Golf, Tacoma, Tacoma Yacht; Rainier (Seattle), Harbor (Seattle). Office: Univar Corp 801 2nd Avenue Seattle Washington 98104

WILL, JAMES FREDRICK, steel company executive; born Pittsburgh, October 12, 1938; son of Fred F. and Mary Agnes (Ganter) W.; married Mary Ellen Bowser, December 19, 1964; children: Mary Beth, Kerry Ann. Bachelor of Science in Electrical Engineering, Pennsylvania State University, 1961; Master of Business Administration, Duquesne University, 1972. Works manager Kaiser Steel Corp., Fontana, California, 1976-78, vice president operations, 1978-80, vice president planning, 1980-81, executive vice president, 1981, president, 1981-82; executive vice president, president industrial group Cyclops Corp., Pitts, 1982-86; president, chief operating officer Cyclops Corp., Pittsburgh, 1986-88, president, chief executive officer, 1989—. Home: 1521 Candlewood Dr Pittsburgh Pennsylvania 15241 Office: Cyclops Corp 650 Washington Road Pittsburgh Pennsylvania 15228

WILLES, MARK HINCKLEY, food industry executive; born Salt Lake City, July 16, 1941; son of Joseph Simmons and Ruth (Hinckley) W.; married Laura Fayone, June 7, 1961; children: Wendy Anne, Susan Kay, Keith Mark, Stephen Joseph, Matthew Bryant. Bachelor of Arts, Columbia University, 1963, Doctor of Philosophy, 1967. Member staff banking and currency committee House of Representatives, Washington, 1966-67; assistant professor fin. University Pennsylvania, Pittsburgh, 1967-69; economist Federal Reserve Bank, Philadelphia, 1967, senior economist, 1969-70, director research, 1970-71, vice president, director research, 1971, 1st vice president, 1971-77; president Federal Reserve Bank of Minneapolis, 1977-80; executive vice president, chief fin. officer General Mills, Incorporated, Minneapolis, 1980-85, president, chief operating officer, 1985—. Office: General Mills Incorporated 1 General Mills Boulevard Minneapolis Minnesota 55426

WILLIAMS, JAMES BRYAN, banker; born Sewanee, Tennessee, March 21, 1933; son of Eugene G. and Ellen (Bryan) W.; married Betty G. Williams, July 11, 1980; children: Ellen, Elizabeth, Bryan. Bachelor of Arts, Emory University, 1955. Chairman, chief executive officer SunTrust Banks, Incorporated, Atlanta, 1991—; board of directors The Coca-Cola Company, Genuine Parts Company, Rollins Incorporated, Ga.-Pacific Corp., RPC Energy Services, Incorporated (all Atlanta), Sonat Incorporated, Birmingham, Alabama. Trustee Emory U.; chairman board trustees Robert W. Woodruff Health Scis. Center Lieutenant United States Air Force, 1955-57. Member Am. Bankers Association (board directors), Reserve City Bankers Association. Presbyterian. Clubs: Piedmont Driving (Atlanta), Capital City (Atlanta), Commerce (Atlanta), Augusta Country. Office: SunTrust Banks Incorporated 25 Park Place Atlanta Georgia 30303

WILLIAMS, JAMES E., food products manufacturing company executive. married. With Golden State foods Corp., 1961—; president, chief executive officer Golden State foods Corp., Pasadena, California, 1978—. Office: Golden State Foods Corp 234 E Colorado Boulevard Pasadena California 91101

WILLIAMS, JOSEPH DALTON, pharmaceutical company executive; born Washington, Pennsylvania, August 15, 1926; son of Joseph Dalton and Jane (Day) W.; married Mildred E. Bellaire, June 28, 1973; children: Terri, Daniel. Bachelor of Science in Pharmacy, University Nebraska, 1950, Doctor of Pharmacy (honorary), 1978, Doctor of Science (honorary), 1989; Doctor of Humane Letters (honorary), Albany College Pharmacy, Union University, 1980, Rutgers University, 1987, Long Island University, 1988; Doctor of Science (honorary), Philadelphia College Pharmacy and Science, 1988, Long Island University, 1988; Doctor Human Svcs. (honorary), Caldwell College, 1989; Doctor of Laws (honorary), Bethune-Cookman College, 1990, College St. Elizabeth, 1990, Seton Hall University, 1990. President Parke-Davis Company, Detroit, 1973-76; president pharmaceutical group Warner-Lambert Company, Morris Plains,

New Jersey, 1976-77; president International Group, 1977-79; president, director Warner-Lambert Corp., 1979-80, president, chief operating officer, 1980-84, chairman, 1985—; board of directors American Telephone and Telegraph Company, J.C. Penney & Company, Exxon Corp. Board of directors People to People Health Foundation; trustee Columbia U. Served with United States Naval Reserve, 1943-46. Member Am. Pharmaceutical Association, New Jersey Pharmaceutical Association, Somerset Hills Country Club, Links Club, Pine Valley Golf Club, Baltusrol Golf Club, Mid Ocean Club. Office: Warner-Lambert Company 201 Tabor Road Morris Plains New Jersey 07950

WILLIAMS, LARRY EMMETT, oil company executive; born Chickasha, Oklahoma, July 11, 1936; son of J. Emmett and Zella M. (Venrick) W.; married Xan Z. Hart, September 7, 1957; children—Jesslyn, Jon. Bachelor of Science in Mechanical Engineering, University New Mexico, 1958, Master of Science in Mechanical Engineering, 1959. Various positions Cities Service Company, 1959-74; vice president Cities Service Company, Tulsa, 1974-83; president, chief executive officer National Cooperative Refinery Association, McPherson, Kansas, 1983—; board of directors Bank IV McPherson, Jayhawk Pipeline Company, Wichita, Kansas, Osage Pipeline Company, Denver, Kaw Pipeline Company, Denver, Petroleum Resources Company, Cushing, Oklahoma, Farmers Alliance Mutual Insurance Company, McPherson; president, board of directors Clear Creek, Incorporated, McPherson, 1983—. Member National Petroleum Refiners Association (board directors), Am. Ind. Refiners Association, Am. Petroleum Institute, National Council Farmer Coops. (board directors, energy policy committee), National Cooperative Business Association, McPherson Healthcare Foundation, Country Club of McPherson, Petroleum Club (Wichita). Clubs: Country (McPherson), Petroleum (Wichita). Office: National Coop Refinery Association 2000 S Main St Post Office Box 1404 McPherson Kansas 67460

WILLIAMS, ROBERT C., paper company executive; born 1930. Bachelor of Science in Mechanical Engineering, University Cincinnati; Master of Business Administration, Xavier University; postgraduate, Institute Paper Chemistry, Rochester Institute Tech. Various tech. and supervisory positions Gardner div. Diamond International Corp., 1947-59; with research and devel. department Albermarle Paper Company, 1963-68; co-founder James River Corp. of Virginia, Richmond, 1969—, now president, chief operating officer; board of directors Sovran Fin. Corp. Office: James River Corp Va Box 2218 Richmond Virginia 23217 also: James River Corp Nevada 1 Bush St San Francisco California 94104

WILLIAMS, WALTER FRED, steel company executive; born Upland, Pennsylvania, February 7, 1929; son of Walter James and Florence (Stott) W.; married Joan B. Carey, August 26, 1950; children: Jeffrey F., Richard C., Douglas E. Bachelor in Civil Engineering summa cum laude, University Delaware, 1951; postgraduate, Harvard, 1969; Doctor (honorary), Allentown College, 1983, Leigh University, 1990. With

Bethlehem Steel Corp., Pennsylvania, 1951—, assistant chief engineer on staff vice president operations, 1965-66, chief engineer construction, 1966-67, chief engineer projects group engineering department, then manager engineering in charge projects, design and construction, 1967-68, assistant to vice president engineering, 1968, assistant vice president shipbldg., 1968-70, vice president shipbldg., 1970-75, vice president steel operations, 1975-77, senior vice president steel operations, 1978-80, president, chief operating officer, 1980-85, chairman, chief executive officer, 1986—, also director; board of directors General Re Corp. 1st lieutenant United States Army, 1951-53. Member National Association of Manufacturers (board directors), Am. Iron and Steel Institute (board directors), Business Roundtable, International Iron and Steel Institute (board directors), Conference Board, Business Council, Saucon Valley Country Club, Hobe Sound Golf Club. Methodist. Home: Saucon Valley Road 4 Bethlehem Pennsylvania 18015 Office: Bethlehem Steel Corp 8th & Eaton Aves Bethlehem Pennsylvania 18016

WILLIAMS, WALTER W., molded rubber and plastic products manufacturing executive. With General Electric Company, 1956-87, vice president, general manager housewares and audio products div., 1979-83; chairman, president General Electric Information Services Company, 1983-86; senior vice president marketing and sales General Electric Company, 1986-87; now president, chief operating officer Rubbermaid Incorporated, 1987—, also board of directors. Office: Rubbermaid Incorporated 1147 Akron Road Wooster Ohio 44691

WILLIAMSON, GILBERT PEMBERTON, computer company executive; born Danville, California, April 26, 1937; married Joyce Caroline (Schaefer), August 28, 1960; children: Jennifer Mary, Heidi Elizabeth. AAEE, Diablo Valley College, 1957; Bachelor of Science in Industrial Management, San Jose State University, 1960. Vice president NCR Corp., Dayton, Ohio, 1974-86, executive vice president, 1987-88, president, 1988—; member Krannert School Dean's Adv. Council, Swissair Adv. Board North America. Chairman Student Employment Encourages Kids, 1990. Recipient Distinguished Alumnus award San Jose State University School Business, 1990. Member Dayton Council on World Affairs (chairman board directors), Moraine County Club, Delta Sigma Phi (Career Achievement award 1989). Avocations: tennis, jogging, photography, golf.

WILLIS, GEORGE EDMUND, chemical processing and electrical manufacturing executive; born Newmarket, Ontario, Canada, July 16, 1920; came to United States, 1925; son of George Clarence and Marion Romer (Gillespie) W.; married Dorothy Anne Rice, June 7, 1943; children: Dorothy Anne, Jacqueline Pamela, Marion Jean, George Patterson Rice, James Edmund, Lorna Isabel; married Rolande Germaine deLipowski Hastings, July 23, 1983; stepchildren: Julian Martin, Marianne Frances. Bachelor of Science in Chemical Engineering cum laude, Michigan State University, 1942; Master of Business Administration, Harvard University, 1947; Doctor of Hebrew Literature (honorary), Lake

Erie College, 1984. Engineer Lincoln Electric Company, Cleveland, 1947-51, superintendent, 1951-59, vice president, 1959-69, executive vice president, 1969-72, president, 1972-87, chief executive officer, 1987—, also chairman board; board of directors Lincoln Big Three, Incorporated, Baton Rouge, Big Three Lincoln Alaska, Incorporated, Anchorage, Big Three Lincoln (United Kingdom) Limited, Ross-Shire Scotland, Lincoln Electric Company (Europe) S.A., Grand-Quevilly, France, Lincoln Electric Company Can., Limited, Toronto, Ontario, Lincoln Electric Company (Australia) Pty., Limited. Chairman board trustees, treasurer Camp Ho Mita Koda; board governors Geauga County Young Men's Christian Association; board trustees Lake Erie College; trustee, executive committee Cleveland Council World Affairs, active Cleveland Committee Foreign Relations. Served to major Army of the United States, 1942-46, European Theatre of Operations. Decorated Bronze Star with oak leaf cluster. Member Am. Welding Society, Wire Association, Greater Cleveland Growth Association, Cleveland Engineering Society, Electrical Manufacturers Club, Alpha Chi Sigma, Tau Beta Pi, Phi Kappa Phi. Clubs: Fifty, Harvard Business Sch. (Cleveland); Chagrin Valley Hunt, St. Christopher's-by-the-River, The Hangar. Avocations: fencing, riding, tennis, canoeing. Home: 11661 Sperry Road Chesterland Ohio 44026 Office: Lincoln Electric Company 22801 St Clair Avenue Cleveland Ohio 44117

WILMERS, ROBERT GEORGE, banker; born New York City, April 20, 1934; son of Charles K. and Cecilia (Eitingon) W.; married Gertrude de Gersdorff, January 5, 1963; children—Robert G. Jr., Christopher C. Bachelor of Arts, Harvard University, 1956; postgraduate, Harvard Business School, 1958-59. Deputy fin. administrator City of New York, 1966-70; vice president Morgan Guaranty Trust Company, New York City and Belgium, 1970-80; owner Robert G. Wilmers Associates, New York City, 1980—; president, chief executive officer, director First Empire State Corp., Buffalo, 1982—; chairman board, president, chief executive officer, director Manufacturers & Traders Trust Company, Buffalo, 1983—; president, chief executive officer ENY Savings Bank, New York City; board of directors Buffalo branch, Federal Reserve Bank New York, 1st National Bank of Highland, Niagara Share Corp., Buffalo. Chairman WNY Health Scis. Consortium, Greater Buffalo Devel. Foundation; board of directors Buffalo Foundation, Artpark, Buffalo, SUNY-Buffalo Foundation, l986, Buffalo Philharmonic Orchestra, l987—. Decorated officier de l'Ordre de la Couronne (Belgium). Member Greater Buffalo Chamber of Commerce. Home: 800 W Ferry St Buffalo New York 14222 also: 15 W 81st St New York New York 10024 Office: Mfrs & Traders Trust Company 1 M&T Plaza Buffalo New York 14240

WILMOUTH, ROBERT K., commodities executive; born Worcester, Massachusetts, November 9, 1928; son of Alfred F. and Aileen E. (Kearney) W.; married Ellen M. Boyle, September 10, 1955; children: Robert J., John J., James P., Thomas G., Anne Marie. Bachelor of Arts, Holy Cross College, 1949; Master of Arts, University Notre Dame, 1950,

Doctor of Laws, 1984. Executive vice president, director 1st National Bank Chicago, 1972-75; president, chief administrative officer Crocker National Bank, San Francisco, 1975-77; president, chief executive officer Chicago Board Trade, 1977-82; chairman LaSalle National Bank, 1982—; president, chief executive officer National Futures Association, 1982—; director Private Export Funding Corp. Trustee U. Notre Dame, chairman investment committee; member adv. council Kellogg Grad. School Mgmt., Northwestern U. 2d lieutenant United States Air Force, 1951-53. Member Chicago Club, Barrington Hill Country Club, Economic Club (director). Home: Rural Route 2 429 Caesar Dr Barrington Illinois 60010 Office: 200 W Madison St Chicago Illinois 60606

WILSON, JAMES LAWRENCE, chemical company executive; born Rosedale, Mississippi, March 2, 1936; son of James Lawrence and Mary Margaret (Klingman) W.; married Barbara Louise Burroughs, August 30, 1958; children: Lawrence Burroughs, Alexander Elliott. Bachelor.Mechanical Engineering, Vanderbilt University, 1958; Master of Business Administration, Harvard, 1963. Vice president Nyala Properties, Incorporated, Philadelphia, 1963-65; staff associate Rohm & Haas Company, Philadelphia, 1965-67; executive assistant to president Rohm & Haas Company, 1971-72, treasurer, 1972-74; regional director Rohm & Haas Company, Europe, 1974-77; group vice president Rohm & Haas Company, 1977-86, vice-chairman, 1986-88, chairman, 1988—; treasurer Warren-Teed Pharms., Incorporated, Columbus, Ohio, 1967-68, vice president, 1969; president Consolidated Biomed. Laboratories, Incorporated, Dublin, Ohio, 1970-71; board of directors Rohm and Haas Company, Shipley Company, Incorporated, Vanguard Group Investment Companies, Cummins Engine Company, Incorporated. Co-author: Creative Collective Bargaining, 1964. Trustee Vanderbilt U., 1987—, Culver Educational Foundation, 1988—; chairman Philadelphia High School Acads., 1989—. Office: Rohm & Haas Company Independence Mall W Philadelphia Pennsylvania 19105

WOBST, FRANK GEORG, banker; born Dresden, Germany, November 14, 1933; came to United States, 1958, naturalized, 1963; son of Robert Georg and Marianne (Salewsky) W.; married Joan Shuey Firkins, August 24, 1957; children: Franck Georg, Ingrid, Andrea. Student, University Erlangen, 1952-54, University Goettingen, 1954-58, Rutgers University, 1964. With Fidelity American Bankshares, Incorporated, Lynchburg, Virginia, 1958-74, executive vice president, director, 1974-85; chairman, chief executive officer, director Huntington National Bank, 1974-85, chairman executive committee, 1986—; chief executive officer director Huntington Bancshares, Incorporated, 1974—. Member Greater Columbus Chamber of Commerce, Am. Institute Banking, Association Reserve City Bankers, Robert Morris Assos., Newcomen Society. Club: Scioto Country. Home: 129 N Columbia Avenue Columbus Ohio 43209 Office: Huntington Bancshares Incorporated 41 S High St Post Office Box 1558 Columbus Ohio 43287

WOLF, STEPHEN M., airline executive; born Oakland, California, August

7, 1941. Bachelor of Arts, San Francisco State University, 1965. Various positions Am. Airlines, Los Angeles, 1965-79, vice president western div., 1979-81; senior vice president marketing Pan Am. World Airlines, New York City, 1981-82; president, chief operating officer Continental Airlines, Houston, 1982-83; president Republic Airlines, Minneapolis, 1984-85, president, chief executive officer, 1985-86; chairman, president, chief executive officer Tiger International, Los Angeles, 1986-87, UAL Corp. and United Airlines, Chicago, 1987—. Board of directors Rush Presbyterian St. Lukes Medical Center, Chicago, 1988—, Alzheimers Disaease and Related Disorders Association, Chicago, 1988—, ConAgra, Incorporated, 1991—, Chicago Symphony Orchestra, 1989—, The Conference Board, New York, 1989—, J.L. Kellogg Grad. School Business, Northwestern U., 1991—. Member Business Roundtable. Office: United Airlines Incorporated Post Office Box 66100 Chicago Illinois 60666 also: JAL Corp 1200 E Algonguin Road Elk Grove Village Illinois 60006

WOLFE, KENNETH L., food products manufacturing company executive; born 1939; married. Bachelor of Arts, Yale University, 1961; Master of Business Administration, University Pennsylvania, 1967. With Bankers Trust Corp., 1961-62; with Hershey Foods Corp., Pennsylvania, 1968—, assistant treasurer, 1968-70, budget director, 1970-76, treasurer, 1976-80, vice president fin. administration Hershey Chocolate Company, from 1980, vice president, chief fin. officer, 1981-84, senior vice president, chief fin. officer, 1984-85, president, chief operating officer, 1985—, also director. Office: Hershey Foods Corp Post Office Box 814 Hershey Pennsylvania 17033

WOLLENBERG, RICHARD PETER, paper manufacturing company executive; born Juneau, Alaska, August 1, 1915; son of Harry L. and Gertrude (Arnstein) W.; married Leone Bonney, December 22, 1940; children: Kenneth Roger, David Arthur, Keith Kermit, Richard Harry, Carol Lynne. Bachelor of Science in Mechanical Engineering, University California, Berkeley, 1936; Master of Business Administration, Harvard University, 1938; graduate, Army Industrial College, 1941; Doctor in Pub. Affairs (honorary), University Puget Sound, 1977. Production control Bethlehem Ship, Quincy, Massachusetts, 1938-39; with Longview (Washington) Fibre Company, 1939—, safety engineer, assistant chief engineer, chief engineer, manager container operations, 1951-57, vice president, 1953-57, vice president operations, 1957-60, executive vice president, 1960-69, president, 1969-78, president, chief executive officer, 1978-85, president, chief executive officer, chairman board, 1985—, also board of directors; member Washington State Council for Postsecondary Education, 1969-79, chairman, 1970-73; member western adv. board Allendale Insurance. Bassoonist SW Washington Symphony. Trustee Reed College, Portland, 1962—, chairman board 1982-90. Served to lieutenant colonel United States Army Air Force, 1941-45. Member National Association of Manufacturers (board directors 1981-86), Pacific Association Pulp and Paper

Manufacturers (president 1982—), Institute Paper Sci. and Tech. (trustee), Washington State Roundtable, Crabbe Huson (board directors). Home: 1632 Kessler Boulevard Longview Washington 98632 Office: Longview Fibre Company Post Office Box 606 Longview Washington 98632

WOOD, JAMES, supermarket executive; born Newcastle-upon-Tyne, England, January 19, 1930; came to United States, 1974; son of Edward and Catherine Wilhelmina (Parker) W.; married Colleen Margaret Taylor, August 14, 1954; children: Julie, Sarah. Graduate, Loughborough College, Leicestershire, England; honorary Doctor of Humane Letters, St. Peter's College, New Jersey. Chief food chain Newport Cooperative Society, South Wales, United Kingdom, 1959-62, Grays Food Cooperative Society, England, 1962-66; director, joint deputy managing director charge retailing Cavenham, Ttd., Hayes, England, 1966-80; president Grand Union Company, Elmwood Park, New Jersey, 1973-79; chief executive officer, director Grand Union Company, from 1973, chairman board, 1979-80; chairman board, chief executive officer, president Great Atlantic & Pacific Tea Company, Incorporated, 1980—; board of directors United Jersey Bank and Asarco, Incorporated, Irma Fabrikerne A/S, Denmark, Schering-Plough Corp. Active World United Service Organizations, United Nations International Children's Emergency Fund, United Jersey Bank. With Brit. Army, 1948-50. Member Food Marketing Institute (board directors). Roman Catholic. Office: Great Atlantic & Pacific Tea Company 2 Paragon Dr Montvale New Jersey 07645

WOOD, QUENTIN EUGENE, oil company executive; born Mechanicsburg, Pennsylvania, March 5, 1923; son of Lloyd Paul and Greta (Myers) W.; married Louise Lowe, April 14, 1958. Bachelor of Science, Pennsylvania State University, 1948. Petroleum engineer Quaker State Oil Refining Corp., Parkersburg, West Virginia, 1948-52; chief engineer Quaker State Oil Refining Corp., Bradford, Pennsylvania, 1952-55; manager production Quaker State Oil Refining Corp., 1955-68; vice president production Quaker State Oil Refining Corp., Oil City, Pennsylvania, 1968-70; executive vice president Quaker State Oil Refining Corp., Oil City, 1970-73, president, chief operations officer, 1973-75; president, chief executive officer Quaker State Oil Refining Corp., 1975-82, chairman, chief executive officer, 1982-88, chairman board, 1988—; director Mellon Bank Corp., Pennsylvania Manufacturers Insurance Company; chairman industry tech. adv. committee United States Bureau Mines, 1960-70, Penn Grade Tech. Advisory Committee, 1955-69, Pennsylvania Oil and Gas Conservation Commission, 1961-71. President board trustees Pennsylvania State U. Served to 1st lieutenant United States Army Air Force, 1943-46. Member Am. Institute Metallurgical Engineers, Pennsylvania Grade Crude Oil Association (director), Pennsylvania Oil Producers Association (past president, director Bradford district), Am. Petroleum Institute (director), National Petroleum Refiners Association. Home: 160 Seahammock Way Ponte Vedra Beach Florida 32082

Office: Quaker State Corp 255 Elm St Oil City Pennsylvania 16301

WOOD, RICHARD DONALD, pharmaceutical company executive; born Brazil, Indiana, October 22, 1926; son of Howard T. and Dorothy F. (Norfolk) W.; married Billie Lou Carpenter, December 29, 1951; children: Catherine Ann Wood Lawson, Marjorie Elizabeth Wood Brentlinger. Bachelor of Science, Purdue University, 1948; Master of Business Administration, University Pennsylvania, 1950, LLDS03Purdue University, 1973; LLDS03Purdue University, De Pauw University, 1972S05Phila. College Pharmacy and Science, De Pauw University, 1975, Ind. State University, 1978S07Ind. University, Ind. State University, 1989; Doctor of Science, Butler U, 1974. General manager operations in Argentina Eli Lilly & Company, 1961; director operations, Mexico and Central Am., 1962-70, president Eli Lilly International Corp., 1970-72, Eli Lilly & Company, Indianapolis, 1972-73, president, chairman board, chief executive officer, director, 1973—; director Chemical Banking Corp. (formerly Chemical New York Corp.), Amoco Corp., Dow Jones & Company, The Chubb Corp. Board of directors Lilly Endowment, Incorporated; trustee Indianapolis Mus. of Art, De Pauw U., Am. Enterprise Institute for Pub. Policy Research, Committee Economic Devel.; board of directors U.S.-USSR Trade and Economic Council. Member Council Foreign Relations, Business Roundtable, The Conference Board, Meridian Hills Country Club, Woodstock Club. Presbyterian. Office: Eli Lilly & Company Lilly Corporate Center Indianapolis Indiana 46285

WOODALL, WILLIAM LEON, insurance executive; born Kirby, Arkansas, July 29, 1923; son of Ocie Doan and Hazel Cornelia (Paslay) W.; married Patricia Ann Reese, September 30, 1950; children: Michael Reese, David William, Stacy Ann. Bachelor of Science, Miami University, Oxford, Ohio, 1947. CPCU. Home office underwriter Ohio Casualty Group Insurance Companies, Hamilton, 1947-52, underwriter Minneapolis branch office, 1952-53, field representative, Des Moines, 1953-54, underwriter Detroit branch office, 1962-64, manager Indianapolis branch office, 1964-68, company vice president, Hamilton, 1968-77, senior vice president, 1977-84, executive vice president, secretary, 1984-88, president, chief operating officer, 1988—, also board of directors; partner Cady Insurance Agency, Burlington, Iowa, 1954-62. Republican. Methodist. Lodge: Elks. Home: 116 Craig Dr Hamilton Ohio 45013 Office: Ohio Casualty Corp 136 N 3rd St Hamilton Ohio 45201

WOODHOUSE, JOHN FREDERICK, food distribution company executive; born Wilmington, Delaware, November 30, 1930; son of John Crawford and Anna (Houth) W.; married Marilyn Ruth Morrow, June 18, 1955; children: John Crawford II, Marjorie Ann Woodhouse Purdy. Bachelor of Arts, Wesleyan University, 1953; Master of Business Administration, Harvard University, 1955. Business devel. officer Can. Imperial Bank of Commerce, Toronto, Ontario, 1955-59; various fin. positions Ford Motor Company, Dearborn, Michigan, 1959-64, Cooper Industries, Incorporated, Mount Vernon, Ohio, 1964-67; treasurer, Houston, 1967-69;

treasurer Crescent-Niagara Corp., Buffalo, 1968-69; executive vice president, chief fin. officer Sysco Corp., Houston, 1969-71, president, chief operating officer, 1972-83, president, chief executive officer, 1983-85, chief executive officer, chairman board, 1985—, member executive and fin. committees, also board of directors; board of directors NCNB, Texas, NCR Corp. Chairman Michigan 16th district Republican Club, 1962-64; treasurer Cooper Industries Foundation, 1967-69; trustee Wesleyan U., 1976—, vice-chmn., trustee, 1986—; board of directors International Foodservice Distbrs. Association, 1988—; ruling elder Presbyterian church. Member National Am. Wholesale Grocer's Association (board directors 1990), Houston Society Fin. Analysts, Fin. Executives Institute, Harvard Business School Club (board directors), Sigma Chi. Avocations: backpacking, canoeing, tennis. Office: Sysco Corp 1390 Enclave Parkway Houston Texas 77077-2027

WOODS, JAMES DUDLEY, manufacturing company executive; born Falmouth, Kentucky, July 24, 1931; son of Alva L. and Mabel L. (Miller) W.; married Darlene Mae Petersen, November 8, 1962; children: Linda, Debbie, Jeffrey, Jamie. Associate of Arts, Long Beach City College, 1958; Bachelor of Arts, California State U.-Fullerton, 1967, postgraduate, 1968-70. Manager planning and control Baker International Corp., Los Angeles, 1965-68, vice president fin. and administration Baker div., 1968-73, corp. vice president, group fin. officer, 1973-76, corp. vice president, 1977, past executive vice president; president, chief executive officer Baker International Corp., Houston; also director Baker International Corp.; president Baker Packers, Houston, 1976-77, Baker Oil Tools, Orange, California, 1977-87; now chairman, president, chief executive officer Baker Hughes Incorporated, Houston. Served with United States Air Force, 1951-55. Republican. Lutheran. Office: Baker Hughes Incorporated 3900 Essex Lane Houston Texas 77027

WOODS, JOHN WITHERSPOON, banker; born Evanston, Illinois, August 18, 1931; son of J. Albert and Cornelia (Witherspoon) W.; married Loti Moultrie Chisolm, September 5, 1953; children: Loti, Cindy, Corrie. Bachelor of Arts, University of South, 1954. With Chemical Bank, New York City, 1954-69; vice president, head Chemical Bank (Southern div.), 1965-69; chairman, chief executive officer Am South Bancorp., 1972—, Am South Bank N.A., 1983—; director Protective Life Insurance Company, Birmingham, Alabama, Power Company Birmingham. Trustee Southern Research Institute, Birmingham, Tuskegee University; board of directors Community Chest-United Way Jefferson County, past president; past chairman working committee of 35 Governor's Educational Reform Commission; trustee Alabama Institute for Deaf and Blind Foundation; board of directors Alabama High School Math. and Sci.; co-chairman, board of directors Alabama Mgmt. Improvement Program,, Incorporated 1st lieutenant United States Air Force, 1955-57. Named to Alabama Acad. Honor. Member Birmingham Area Chamber of Commerce (president 1978, director, executive committee), Association Bank Holding Companies (board directors). Office: AmSouth

Bancorp 1900 5th Avenue N Suite 1400 Post Office Box 11007 Birmingham Alabama 35203

WOOLARD, EDGAR S., JR., chemical company executive; born Washington, North Carolina, April 14, 1934; son of Edgar Smith and Mamie (Boone) W.; married Peggy Harrell, June 9, 1956; children: Annette, Lynda. Bachelor of Science, North Carolina State University, 1956. With Du Pont, 1957—; industrial engineer Kinston, North Carolina, 1957-59; group supervisor industrial engineering Du Pont, Kinston, North Carolina, 1959-62, supervisor manufacturing section, 1962-64, planning supervisor, 1964-65; staff assistant to production manager Wilmington, Del., 1965-66; product supervisor Hickory, Tennessee, 1966-69; engineering superintendent Du Pont, Hickory, Tennessee, 1969-70; assistant plant manager Camden, South Carolina, 1970-71; plant manager Camden, 1972-73; director products marketing div. Wilmington, Del., 1973-75; managing director textile marketing div. Du Pont, Wilmington, Del., 1975-76, manager corp. plans department, 1976-77, general director products and planning div., 1977-78, general manager textile fibers, 1978-81, vice president textile fibers, 1981-83, executive vice president, 1983-85, vice chairman, 1985-87, president, chief operating officer, 1987-89, chairman, 1989—; also board of directors; Du Pont; board of directors Wilmington (North Carolina) Textile Foundation, Raleigh, Citicorp., International Business Machines Corporation Corp, Council for Aid to Education, Joint Council on Economic Education Seagrams Company Limited. Trustee Medical Center Del., 1985—, North Carolina State U., Winterthur Mus. Lieutenant United States Army. Office: Du Pont 1007 Market St Wilmington Delaware 19898

WRAY, MARC FREDERICK, minerals company executive; born Evanston, Illinois; son of George M. and Anabelle (Moriarity) W.; married Suzanne Elliott, June 16, 1965; children—Marc Thomas, Andrew Elliott. Bachelor.South Carolina, Loyola University, Chicago, 1955; Master of Business Administration, Harvard University, Chicago, 1964. Senior commercial credit analyst Am. National Bank, Chicago, 1956-57; 0cons. Stoddard Quirk Manufacturing, Cudahy, Wisconsin, 1958-60; consultant Jacksonville Paper, Florida, 1960-63; executive vice president Nicolas Salgo & Company, New York City, 1964-68; vice president corp. devel. Bangor Punta Corp., New York City, 1968-70; executive vice president Manati Industries, New York City, 1970-72; director corp. diversification International Paper Company, New York City, 1972-75, vice president, group executive, 1979—; president GCO Minerals Company, Houston, 1975—; director Union Bank, Houston. Served with United States Army, 1955-56. Member Houston Chamber of Commerce. Roman Catholic. Clubs: Petroleum, Forest, Harvard Business Sch. (Houston); Harvard (New York City). Home: Post Office Box 4258 Houston Texas 77210-4258 also: Joy Techs Incorporated 301 Grant St Pittsburgh Pennsylvania 15219

WREN, THOMAS WAYNE, banker; born Springtown, Texas, June 28, 1922; . William A. and Nannie Mae (Thomas) W.; married Jane Dunlap, April 7, 1944; children: Wayne, W.

Casey, Rebecca Wren Kelly. Bachelor of Science, University N. Texas, 1942. Vice president Republic Bank, Dallas, 1944-66; executive vice president InterFirst Bank Houston, N.A., 1966-76; president University State Bank, Houston, 1976-81, vice chairman board, 1981-83, 85-90, president, 1983-85, 86—; director Riggs National Corp., Washington, 1981-89, vice chairman board, 1983-89, director, vice chairman board Riggs National Bank Maryland, 1990—, director Riggs National Bank Virginia, 1990, chairman board, 1990—. Board of directors, member executive committee D.C. chapter American Red Cross, 1983-86. Office: Riggs National Corp 800 17th St Northwest Washington District of Columbia 20006

WRIGHT, FELIX E., manufacturing company executive; born 1935; married. Student, East Texas State University, 1958. With Leggett & Platt, Incorporated, Carthage, Missouri, 1959—, senior vice president, from 1976, chief operating officer, executive vice president, 1979, now president, chief operating officer, 1985—. Office: Leggett & Platt Incorporated 1 Leggett Road Carthage Missouri 64836

WRIGHT, MICHAEL WILLIAM, wholesale food company executive; born Minneapolis, June 13, 1938; son of Thomas W. and Winifred M. Wright; married Susan M. Guzy. Bachelor of Arts, University Minnesota, 1961, Juris Doctor with honors, 1963. Partner Dorsey & Whitney, Minneapolis, 1966-77; senior vice president Super Valu Stores, Incorporated, Minneapolis, 1977-78, president, chief operating officer, 1978—, chief executive officer, 1981—, chairman, 1982—; board of directors, immediate past chairman Federal Reserve Bank, Minneapolis; board of directors Norwest Corp., Deluxe Corp., Honeywell, Incorporated, The Musicland Group, International Association Chain Stores, Food Marketing Institute, National Am. Wholesale Grocers Association, Incorporated; chairman Food Marketing Institute. 1st lieutenant United States Army, 1964-66. Office: Super Valu Stores Incorporated 11840 Valley View Road Post Office Box 990 Minneapolis Minnesota 55440

WRIGHT, ROBERT F., petroleum products company executive. Previously executive vice president Amerada Hess Corp., New York City, president, chief operating officer, 1986—, also board of directors. Office: Amerada Hess Corp 1185 Avenue of the Americas New York New York 10036

WRIGLEY, WILLIAM, corporation executive; born Chicago, January 21, 1933; son of Philip Knight and Helen Blanche (Atwater) W.; married Alison Hunter, June 1, 1957 (divorced 1969); children: Alison Elizabeth, Philip Knight, William; married Julie Burns, November 28, 1981. Graduate, Deerfield Academy, 1950; Bachelor of Arts, Yale, 1954. With Wm. Wrigley Junior Company, Chicago, 1956—, vice president, 1960-61, president, chief executive officer, 1961—, director, 1960—; director Wrigley Philippines, Incorporated, Wrigley Company, Limited (United Kingdom), Wrigley Company (New Zealand), Limited, Wrigley Company Pty., Limited (Australia), The Wrigley Company (H.K.) Limited (Hong Kong), Wrigley Company (East Africa) Limited (Kenya), Wrigley Company (P.N.G.) Pty. Limited,

Wrigley & Company Limited, Japan; chairman William Wrigley Junior Company Foundation; member audit committee Grocery Manufacturers Am., Incorporated; director, member committee non-mgmt. directors, member nominating committee Texaco Incorporated; director, member compensation committee National Blvd. Bank of Chicago; board of directors, member executive committee, chairman, chief executive officer Santa Catalina Island Company; board of directors Am. Home Products Corp. Board of directors Wrigley Memorial Garden Foundation; board of directors, member personnel committee Northwestern Memorial Hospital; benefactor, member Santa Catalina Island Conservancy; member adv. board Center for Sports Medicine, Northwestern U. Medical School, 1976—; trustee Chicago Latin School Foundation, 1975—; director Geneva Lake Water Safety Committee, 1966—, member executive committee, 1968—. Served from ensign to lieutenant (junior grade) United States Naval Reserve, 1954-56; now lieutenant commander Reserves. Member Navy League United States, Chicago Historical Society, Field Mus., Wolf's Head Society, University Southern California Oceanographic Assocs., Catalina Island Museum Society, 410 Club, Delta Kappa Epsilon. Clubs: Saddle and Cycle, Racquet, Chicago Yacht, Tavern (Chicago), Commercial (Chicago); Catalina Island Yacht, California, Catalina Island Gun; Los Angeles Yacht, Lake Geneva (Wisconsin) Country, Lake Geneva Yacht; The Brook (New York City). Office: Wm Wrigley Jr Company 410 N Michigan Avenue Chicago Illinois 60611

WULBERN, JOHN CUMMINS, retired banker; born Rye, New York, January 11, 1936; son of Edward B. Wulbern; married Catherine Brantly; married 2d. Nancy C. Daly, May 13, 1967; children: Walter J. Daly, John C., Robert C., Allan E. Student, Rollins College, 1954-55, University Florida, 1957; graduate, Stonier Banking School, 1966; graduate advanced management program, Harvard University, 1981. From assistant cashier to vice president Barnett 1st National Bank, Jacksonville, Florida, 1958-64; chairman board Barnett Bank East Ocala, Florida, 1968-77; from executive v.p to president Barnett Bank Ocala, Florida, 1969-77; executive vice president Mid-State Federal Savings and Loan, Ocala, 1977-78; from senior vice president to president 1st Florida Banks, Incorporated, Tampa, 1978-91; board of directors 1st. Florida Banks, Incorporated, 1st Florida Bank, N.A. Named one of Outstanding Young Men Am., 1970. Member Florida Bankers Association (president 1976-77), Tampa Chamber of Commerce (board directors), Florida Chamber of Commerce (board directors). Democrat. Episcopalian. Avocations: golf, reading, jogging, skiing. Office: First Florida Banks Incorporated Post Office Box 31265 Tampa Florida 33631

WUNDERLICH, HERMANN, diversified corporation executive. Vice chairman board management Bayer AG, Leverkusen, Federal Republic Germany; chairman board Bayer USA, Incorporated (subsidiary Bayer AG), Pittsburgh. Office: Bayer USA Incorporated 500 Grant St Pittsburgh Pennsylvania 15219

WURTELE, CHRISTOPHER ANGUS, paint and coatings company

executive; born Minneapolis, August 25, 1934; Valentine and Charlotte (Lindley) W.; married Heather Campbell (divorced February 1977); children: Christopher, Andrew, Heidi; married Margaret Von Blon, August 21, 1977. Yale University, 1956; Master of Business Administration, Stanford University, 1961. V.p. Minn. Paints, Incorporated (merged with Valspar Corp 1970) Minneapolis, 1962-65; executive vice president, 1965, president, chief executive officer, 1965-70; president, chief executive officer The Valspar Corp., Minneapolis, 1970-73, chairman, chief executive officer, 1973—; director General Mills Incorporated, Donaldson Company, Northwestern National Life Insurance Company. Member adv. council Stanford U. Grad. School Bus' board dirs.Walker Art Center With United States Navy, 1956-59. Member Am. Business Conference, Minneapolis Club, National Paint & Coatings Association (board directors). Episcopalian. Home: 2409 E Lake of the Isles Parkway Minneapolis Minnesota 55405 Office: Valspar Corp 1101 3rd St S Minneapolis Minnesota 55415

WYATT, OSCAR SHERMAN, JR., energy company executive; born Beaumont, Texas, July 11, 1924; son of Oscar Sherman Sr. and Eva (Coday) W.; married Lynn Wyatt; children: Carl, Steven, Douglas, Oscar Sherman III, Brad. Bachelor of Science in Mechanical Engineering, Texas Agricultural and Mechanical College, 1949. With Kerr-McGee Company, 1949, Reed Roller Bit Company, 1949-51; partner Wymore Oil Company, 1951-55; founder Coastal Corp., Corpus Christi, Texas, 1955; now chairman Coastal Corp., Houston. Served with United States Army Air Force, World War II. Home: 1620 River Oaks Boulevard Houston Texas 77019 Office: Coastal Corp 9 Greenway Place Houston Texas 77046

YAMADA, OSAMU, banker. Chairman board, president, chief executive officer Bank of California, San Francisco. Office: Bancal Tri-State Corp Office of the President 400 California St San Francisco California 94104

YAMAMOTO, KENICHI, automotive executive; born Hiroshima, Japan, September 16, 1922; married; 2 children. Bachelor of Science in Mechanical Engineering, Tokyo University, 1944. Registered professional engineer, Tokyo. Manager designing department tech. div. Mazda Motor Corp., Aki-gun, Japan, 1956-63, manager rotary engine research and devel. div., 1963-78, managing director, general manager research and devel., 1978-80, managing director, general manager advanced tech., 1980-82, senior managing director, 1982-84, president, 1984-87, chairman, 1987—. Recipient Man of Year award Automotive Industries magazine 1986. Member Society Mechanical Engineers (award 1970). Avocations: painting, music. Office: Mazda Motor Corp, Fuchu-cho, 3-1 Shinchi, Aki-gun, Hiroshima 750-91 Japan

YAWKEY, JEAN R., baseball club executive; born Brooklyn, 1909; married Tom Yawkey, 1944 (deceased 1976). Fashion model New York City, 1934-44; former president Boston Red Sox, Am. League, from 1976, now majority owner, chairwoman board of directors. Trustee Yawkey Foundation; past chairman board and trustee Jimmy Fund Sidney Farber Cancer Institute. Office: Boston Red Sox 24 Yawkey Way Boston Massachusetts 02215

YEARLEY, DOUGLAS CAIN, mining and manufacturing company executive; born Oak Park, Illinois, January 7, 1936; son of Bernard Cain and Mary Kenny (Howard) Y.; married Elizabeth Anne Dunbar, February 8, 1958; children: Sandra, Douglas Jr., Peter, Andrew. BMetE, Cornell University, 1958; postgraduate, Harvard University, 1968. Engineer welding General Dynamics, Groton, Connecticut, 1958-60; director research, project engineer Phelps Dodge Copper Products, Elizabeth, New Jersey, 1960-68; manager operations Phelps Dodge International Company, New York City, 1968-71; vice president operations Phelps Dodge Tube Company, Los Angeles, 1971-73; executive vice president Phelps Dodge Cable and Wire Company, Yonkers, New York, 1973-75; president Phelps Dodge Brass Company, Lyndhurst, New Jersey, 1975-79, Phelps Dodge Sales Company, New York City, 1979-82; vice president marketing Phelps Dodge Corp., New York City, 1979-82, senior vice president, 1982-87, executive vice president, 1987-89, chairman, chief executive officer, 1989—, also board of directors; board of directors Valley National Bank, Valley National Corp., Phoenix, Lockheed Corp., Calabasas, California, INROADS, Incorporated. Member Arizona Economic Council, 1989—, Conference Board, 1989—; board of directors Am. Grad. School International Mgmt., 1990—, Phoenix Symphony, 1988—; chairman Arts Coalition, 1989—. Member National Electrical Manufacturers Association (board directors 1983—), International Cooper Association (board directors 1987—, chairman 1990—), Copper Devel. Association (chairman 1989—), National Association Manufacturers (board directors 1988—), Business Roundtable, Sky Club, Echo Lake Country Club, Paradise Valley Country Club, The Links, Mansion Club, Blind Brook Country Club. Republican. Congregationalist. Avocations: tennis, golf, classical music. Home: 8201 Viaduct del Lago Scottsdale Arizona 85258 Office: Phelps Dodge Corp 2600 N Central Avenue Phoenix Arizona 85004-3014

YOUNG, A. THOMAS, defense, aerospace, energy company executive; born Wachapreague, Virginia, April 19, 1938; son of William Thomas and Margaret (Colonna) Y.; married Page Carter Hayden, June 24, 1961; children: Anne Blair, Thomas Carter. BMechE, Bachelor in Aeronautical Engineering, University Virginia, 1961; Master in Management, Massachusetts Institute of Technology, 1972. Designer Newport News (Virginia) Shipbldg. & Drycock Company, 1961; with National Aeronautics and Space Administration, 1961-82; various positions Langley Research Center, Hampton, Virginia, 1961-69; staff member and mission director Viking Project Hampton, 1969-76; director Headquarters Planetary Program Washington, 1976-79; deputy director Ames Research Center, Moffett Field, California, 1979-80; director Goddard Space Flight Center, Greenbelt, Maryland, 1980-82; with Martin Marietta Corp., 1982—; vice president aerospace research and engineering Bethesda, Maryland, 1982-83; vice president, general manager

Baltimore Aerospace, 1983-84, president, 1984-85; executive vice president, then. president Orlando (Florida) Aerospace, 1985-87; president Electronics & Missiles Group, Orlando, 1987-89; senior executive vice president Martin Marietta Corp., 1989-90, president, chief operating officer, 1990—; board of directors Sun Bank, Orlando, 1986-89; chairman Gov.'s Space Commission, Tallahassee, Florida, 1987-88. Prin. Center for Excellence in Government, Washington, 1987; trustee U. Central Florida, 1987-89; member Orange County (Florida) School Board Foundation, 1987-89. Sloan fellow Massachusetts Institute of Technology, 1971-72; decorated Distinguished Service Medal Viking Project National Aeronautics and Space Administration, 1977; recipient Outstanding Leadership medal Voyager Program National Aeronautics and Space Administration, 1980, Meritorious Executive Presidential Rank award President Jimmy Carter, 1980, Distinguished Executive award President Ronald Reagan, 1981. Fellow American Institute of Aeronautics and Astronautics, Am. Astronautical Society. Republican. Methodist. Avocations: boating, fishing. Office: Martin Marietta Corp 6801 Rockledge Dr Bethesda Maryland 20817

YOUNG, ROBERT A., III, freight systems executive; born Fort Smith, Arkansas, September 23, 1940; son of Robert A. and Vivian (Curtis) Y.; married Mary Carleton McRae; children—Tracy, Christy, Robert A. IV, Stephen. Bachelor of Arts in Economics, Washington and Lee University, 1963. Supervisor terminal operations Arkansas Best Freight, Fort Smith, 1964-65; president Data-Tronics Inc, Fort Smith, 1965-67; senior vice president National Bank of Commerce, Dallas, 1967-70; vice president fin. Arkansas Best Corp., Fort Smith, 1970-73, executive vice president, 1973, president, chief operating officer, 1973-88, chief executive officer, 1988—; president ABF Freight Systems, Incorporated, Fort Smith, 1979—; board of directors First National Bank, Fort Smith, Mosler Corp., Hamilton, Ohio. President United Way, Fort Smith, 1981; vice chairman board of directors Sparks Regional Medical Center, Fort Smith, 1985; chairman board trustees Arkansas College; board of directors ATA Foundation, Incorporated, Fort Smith Boys Club. Served with United States Air Force, 1963. Recipient Silver Beaver award Boy Scouts Am. Member Am. Trucking Association (vice chairman), Arkansas State Chamber of Commerce (vice president, board directors), Phi Delta Theta. Presbyterian. Home: Post Office Box 48 Fort Smith Arkansas 72902 Office: ABF Freight Systems Incorporated 301 S 11th St Fort Smith Arkansas 72901 also: Arkansas Best Corp 1000 S 21st St Fort Smith Arkansas 72901

ZABAN, ERWIN, diversified manufacturing company executive; born Atlanta, August 17, 1921; son of Mandle and Sara Unis (Feidelson) Z.; married Judy Zaban; children: Carol Zaban Cooper, Laura Zaban Dinerman, Sara Kay Franco. Officer Zep Manufacturing Company, 1942-62; executive vice president National Service Industries, Atlanta, 1962-66, president, 1966-79, chief executive officer, 1972-87, chairman, 1975, also director; board director Engraph, Incorporated, Wachovia Corp.;

elected member board visitors Berry College. Board of directors Atlanta Symphony Orchestra, 1982, Jewish Home for the Aged, 1985; trustee Atlanta Historical Society, 1985. Named Man of Year B'nai B'rith, 1977, Father of Year Father's Day Council; recipient Distinguished Service award Atlanta Urban League, 1979, National Conference of Christians and Jews, 1988, Human Rels. award Anti-Defamation League, 1981, Board Govs. award 11-Alive Community Service Awards, 1990; named to Georgia State University College Business Administration Hall of Fame, 1989. Member Standard Club, Commerce Club (board directors). Office: National Svs Industries Incorporated 1420 Peachtree St NE Atlanta Georgia 30309

ZALOKAR, ROBERT H., bank executive; born 1927. Bachelor of Science, University Kansas, 1950. Examiner Federal Deposit Insurance Corporation, Washington, 1950-55; assistant vice president Old Dominion Bank, 1955-58; executive vice president Bank of Annadale, 1958-65; president Falls Church Bank, 1965-69; executive vice president First Virginia Bank, 1969-74, president, chief administrative officer, 1974-78, president, chief executive officer, 1978—, also chairman board, director, 1984—. With United States Navy, 1945-46. Office: 1st Va Banks Incorporated 1 1st Virginia Plaza 6400 Arlington Boulevard Falls Church Virginia 22046

ZEHFUSS, LAWRENCE THOMAS, hardware supply company executive; born Pittsburgh, February 2, 1938. Bachelor of Science in Business Administration, Duquesne University, 1960. C.P.A., Pennsylvania. Accountant, analyst H.J. Heinz Company, Pittsburgh, 1960-61; public accountant Professional Association Love & Company, Pittsburgh, 1961-65; fin. manager Am. Hardware Supply Company (now Servistar Corp.), Butler, Pennsylvania, 1965-70, vice president fin., treasurer, 1970-79, chief executive officer, from 1979, president, 1979—; director corp., bank; speaker for industry associations. Vice chairman Butler Memorial Hospital. Member Pres.'s Association. Office: Servistar Corp Post Office Box 1510 Butler Pennsylvania 16001

ZEIEN, ALFRED M., consumer products company executive; born New York City, February 25, 1930; son of Alphonse and Betty (Barthelemy) Z.; married Joyce Valerie Lawrence, December 26, 1952; children—Scott, Grey, Claudia. Bachelor of Science, Webb Institute; Master of Business Administration postgraduate, Harvard University. Group vice president Gillette Company, Boston, 1973-74, senior vice president, 1978-81, vice chairman, 1981-90, president, 1990-91, chairman, chief executive officer, 1991—; div. general manager Braun AG, Frankfurt, Federal Republic of Germany, 1974-76, chairman board, 1976-78; board of directors Polaroid Corp., Cambridge, Massachusetts, Repligen Corp., Cambridge, Square D Company, Palatine, Illinois. trustee University Hospital, Boston, 1983—. Avocations: sailing; tennis. Home: 185 Old Pickard Road Concord Massachusetts 01742 Office: Gillette Company Prudential Tower Building Boston Massachusetts 02199

ZELL, SAMUEL, transportation leasing company executive; born Chicago, September 28, 1941; married. Bachelor of Arts, University

Michigan, 1963, Juris Doctor, 1966. With Yates Holleb and Michelson, 1966-68; president Equity Fin. and Management Company, 1968—; chairman, president Great Am. Management and Investment Incorporated, 1981—; chairman, chief executive officer Itel Corp., 1985—, also board of directors. Office: Great Am Management & Investment Incorporated 2 N Riverside Plaza 6th Floor Chicago Illinois 60606

ZEMKE, (E.) JOSEPH, computer company executive. Chief operating officer Auto-Trol Tech., Denver, 1981-84; chief operating officer Amdahl Corp., Sunnyvale, California, 1985—, president, 1987—. Office: Amdahl Corp 1250 E Arques Avenue Sunnyvale California 94086

ZILKHA, EZRA KHEDOURI, banker; born Baghdad, Iraq, July 31, 1925; came to United States, 1941, naturalized, 1950; son of Khedouri A. and Louise (Bashi) Z.; married Cecile Iny, February 6, 1950; children: Elias Donald, Donna Zilkha Krisel, Bettina Louise. Graduate, Hill School, Pottstown, Pennsylvania, 1943; Bachelor of Arts, Wesleyan University, Middletown, Connecticut, 1947; Doctor of Laws (honorary), Wesleyan University, 1987. President Zilkha & Sons, Incorporated, New York City, 1956—; board of directors Chicago Milwaukee Corp., Chicago, Newhall Land & Farming, California, CIGNA Corp., Philadelphia, Cambridge Associates, Boston, Fortune Fin. Group, Incorporated, Florida; chairman Union Holdings, Incorporated, Kansas. Chairman International Center for Disabled, New York City; trustee French Institute, New York City, Brookings Institute, Washington, Lycée Français, New York City; trustee emeritus Wesleyan U.; former trustee Spence School, New York City. Decorated chevalier Legion d'Honneur, officier Ordre National du Merite (France); recipient Freedom of Human Spirit award International Center for Disabled, 1989. Member Council Foreign Relations. Clubs: Racquet and Tennis (New York City), Knickerbocker (New York City); Meadow (Southampton, New York); Travellers (Paris), Polo (Paris). Office: Zilkha & Sons 30 Rockefeller Plaza New York New York 10112

ZIMMERMAN, RAYMOND, retail chain executive; born 1923; married. Vice president Service Merchandise Company, Incorporated, Nashville, from 1959, president, 1973—, chairman, 1981—, now chief executive officer, also board of directors. Office: Service Mdse Company Incorporated 1283 Murfreesboro Road Nashville Tennessee 37217

ZIMMERMAN, RICHARD ANSON, food company executive; born Lebanon, Pennsylvania, April 5, 1932; son of Richard Paul and Kathryn Clare (Wilhelm) Z.; married Nancy J. Cramer, December 27, 1952; children: Linda Joan, Janet Lee. Bachelor of Arts in Commerce, Pennsylvania State University, 1953. Assistant secretary Harrisburg (Pennsylvania) National Bank, 1956-58; with Hershey (Pennsylvania) Foods Corp., 1958—, assistant to president, 1965-71, vice president, 1971-76, president, chief operating officer, 1976-84, president, 1984-85, chief executive officer, 1984—, chairman, 1985—; board of directors Hershey Trust Company, Westvaco Corp., Eastman Kodak Company, Pennsylvania Business Roundtable. Lieutenant United States Navy, 1953-56. Recipient Alumni fellow award Pennsylvania State University, 1978,

Distinguished Alumni award Pennsylvania State University, 1987, N.C.C.J. National Brotherhood award, 1988. Member Grocery Manufacturers Am. (board directors), Pennsylvania Chamber of Commerce (board director), Alumni Association Pennsylvania State University (president 1982-83), Carlton Club, Masons, Rotary (president Hershey club 1973-74), Hershey Country Club, Phi Kappa Psi. Methodist. Office: Hershey Foods Corp Post Office Box 814 Hershey Pennsylvania 17033

ZYLSTRA, STANLEY JAMES, farmer, food company executive; born Hull, Iowa, December 18, 1943; son of Jerald S. and Dora (Te Slaa) Z.; married Ruth Eileen Van Batavia, January 3, 1964; children: Rachel Ann, Carl Dean. Bachelor of Arts, Northwestern College, 1965; Master of Arts, University South Dakota, 1969. Math teacher, counselor Boyden-Hull School, 1965-73; farmer Hull, 1970—; director Land O'Lakes, Minneapolis, 1985—, chairman board of directors, 1988—. Member Kiwanis (president 1974-75). Republican. Member Reformed Church in America. Home: Rural Route 1 Box 200 Hull Iowa 51239 Office: Land O'Lakes Incorporated 4001 Lexington Avenue N Arden Hills Minnesota 55112